SOCIAL

SCIENCE

SOCIAL 4th edition

SCIENCE An

Introduction

to the Study of

Society

ELGIN F. HUNT   Formerly Chairman of the Social Science
Department, Wilson Junior College, and Lecturer, Northwestern University

The Macmillan Company, New York
Collier-Macmillan Limited, London

The Macmillan Company
866 Third Avenue, New York,
New York 10022

Collier-Macmillan Canada, Ltd.,
Toronto, Ontario

Library of Congress
catalog card number: 71-161428

PRINTING   3456789   YEAR   456789

Preface

the six years since publication of the third edition of *Social Science* have seen more social unrest and social change than any similar period in the memories of men now living, not only in the United States but in many other areas of the world. Because of this it has been necessary to introduce important changes into the present volume. For example, in the chapter on the natural environment, an extensive section dealing with pollution has been added because of our recent recognition of the urgency of this problem. Also, an entirely new chapter on religion has been included, not only to give students an understanding of the major role that religion has played in the development of human societies and cultures but also to present some of the difficult problems facing our modern religious institutions. Because of the importance of the black Americans in our society, the discussion of their history, progress, and problems has been expanded into a second new chapter. Later in the book more attention than formerly is given to the problem of poverty and to the possibilities of eliminating it. Other significant changes could be mentioned, such as the revision in Chapter 1 of much of the material dealing with the evolution of man, in order to present this subject more clearly, in the light of recent additions to our knowledge. In almost every chapter an important amount of revising has been done to update or clarify the text and to make desirable changes in viewpoint or emphasis.

Textbooks, as any experienced instructor knows, have their limitations. Nevertheless, they can be extremely valuable learning and teaching aids, especially in introductory courses. A good one can present to students in an organized and understandable fashion the major aspects of a broad field of knowledge and thus can leave the instructor free to supplement, modify, and discuss material with which his students are already familiar.

In preparing the present edition of *Social Science,* the author made every effort to retain certain qualities that contributed to the wide adoption and use of the earlier editions. The basic purpose is the same, namely, to give the student, in language he can understand, a clear concept of our society and its major problems. An important characteristic retained from earlier editions is a wide and balanced coverage of the social science field, with a more adequate treatment of economics, government, and international relations than is found in most introductory texts. *Social Science* is intended to meet the needs of a basic introductory course, one that should give the "terminal" student a useful understanding of society and at the same time provide a foundation for the student who plans to do advanced work in the field.

Because in the final analysis man's social life is a unity, this book attempts to present an integrated picture of human society. However, the social life of modern man is a very complex unity, and the author believes that nothing is to be gained by disregarding the traditional division of social science into such special disciplines as anthropology, sociology, economics, and political science. Instead, he has sought to emphasize their many interrelationships and to draw upon all of them for integrating concepts, as we have tried to show in the illustration on the cover of this book. Special emphasis is placed on the culture concept in recognition of the fact that all phases of social life are a part of the human cultures from which they have developed.

Like its predecessors, this edition is organized so as to permit a considerable degree of flexibility in use. Though in a very general way it proceeds from the earlier and simpler aspects of social organization to those that are later and more complex, in most cases there is no close interdependence between individual chapters. Insofar as possible, each chapter is a complete unit. This means that an instructor can often make omissions or changes in sequence without destroying the unity of his course. Though the book can be adapted to shorter courses, it is designed for use as a text in a year course that is divided into two semesters. Parts One and Two, comprising the first sixteen of the thirty-two chapters, are for use in the first semester; and Parts Three, Four, and Five are for use in the second semester. Many instructors will desire, in addition, to use some supplementary readings.

A number of teaching aids have been provided. At the end of each chapter will be found (1) a list of terms to be understood, (2) questions for review and discussion, and (3) a list of books for further study, including a number of useful and relatively inexpensive paperbacks. In addition to the teaching aids included in *Social Science,* a special manual has been prepared for instructors. In large part this consists of true-false, multiple-choice, and completion questions for use in objective tests. It also lists a number of sixteen-millimeter films for possible use with each chapter and tells where these films can be obtained.

Of those who aided the author directly or indirectly in preparing the present volume, special mention should be made of several. Dr. S. C. Gilfillan provided detailed suggestions concerning the chapter on technology and made useful comments on several other chapters. Charles E. Smith, the Macmillan editor directly concerned with the preparation of this edition, was extremely helpful. Besides obtaining from others some critical appraisals of the preceding edition and the manuscript of the present edition, he himself made innumerable useful criticisms and suggestions. Finally, the author's greatest debt is, once again, to his wife, whose services as typist, secretary, research assistant, and critic were indispensable.

E. F. H.

Contents

ix

CONTENTS

Figures,

Tables,

and Photos

Tables

Photos

Part One

Basic

Factors

in

Social

Life

Chapter 1

Man

and Society

Our ancestors in the not so distant past believed that the globe we live on was the major part of the universe and that all the heavenly bodies revolved around it. Today we know that it is only an infinitesimal part of the cosmic universe of space and matter. To human beings, however, this tiny part is more important than all the rest; for man's greatest concern is with himself, with the planet on which he lives, with his origin, his destiny, and his relationships to other men. Even if he hopes for a future life in some far-off heaven, he still longs to make his life on earth happier, more meaningful, and more satisfying.

1. City Crowds. (Courtesy *U.S. News & World Report.*)

Man is first of all a social creature. He normally spends his entire life in association with other human beings and as a member of various organized social groups. In some cases, as within the family, his association with others is constant and close. In some, as with the majority of the citizens of his village or town, his association is occasional and often impersonal. In the case of the larger social groups to which he belongs, he may have no direct contact at all with many of the other members. To cite an extreme example, most citizens of the United States never even see one another. Nevertheless, they are all members of the same larger society, for they are all bound together to some degree by a common language, common interests and ways of living, common loyalties, and reliance on a common national government for their defense and for much of their general welfare. To a great extent the ability of people to live happy and satisfying lives depends on the nature of the society they live in.

The study of the group life of man is called *social science*. The social scientist is interested in all human relationships and especially in those that take place in organized groups. He is concerned with the influence of the individual on the group and with the impact of the group on the individual. He studies and tries to explain group attitudes, beliefs, and customs, and likewise such complex and variable social institutions as government, the business corporation, the family, and the church. He seeks also to predict group behavior and to provide the knowledge that may help to guide it in directions that will benefit the group.

UNIQUE CHARACTERISTICS OF MAN

Man is unique among living creatures. He possesses in a high degree three great abilities that in animals other than man are either rudimentary or nonexistent.

First, man can think and reason. Experiments have indicated that animals can think to some degree. For example, chimpanzees can solve certain types of simple problems to obtain food that is out of reach. But the power of human beings to think and to solve complex problems is so much greater than that of chimpanzees that for practical purposes human thought is something different in kind.

Second, man can communicate with others by means of language; and his ability to think depends, at least in part, on his power to use language. Language is a system of arbitrary vocal symbols, combined in special ways to transmit knowledge and ideas. The symbols (words) and the methods of combination (grammar) vary from language to language, but all human groups do have a language by means of which they communicate. Animals do not have languages, and they cannot, in a literal sense, talk. They do, it is true, use sounds to communicate; but there is no evidence that any animal uses sounds, as human beings use words, to stand for abstract concepts like house, man, or tree. Animal sounds are instinctive and very limited in range. Animals can express warnings, or feelings of friendliness, hostility, or fear; but no animal can communicate to another even such

"Now that we've learned to talk, let's not speak in vague generalities." (Courtesy Herbert Goldberg. Copyright 1969 *Saturday Review, Inc.*)

a simple idea as is contained in the sentence "There is a house just beyond the top of the hill."

Because men can communicate by means of language, the knowledge of one person can be passed on to another. Similarly, the sum total of the knowledge of a social group can be handed down from generation to generation and can gradually increase as individuals make new contributions. This ability of human societies to accumulate knowledge was greatly increased by the invention of writing and, later, of printing. Over long periods of time, writing and printing are far more dependable as methods of transmitting knowledge than is word of mouth.

The *third* ability that distinguishes man from animals is the use of tools. Man's ability to devise tools and use them skillfully depends to a great extent on his possession of a prehensile hand, which can grasp objects firmly between thumb and fingers. These hands are really his forefeet, but because in the evolutionary process he learned to stand erect, he does not have to employ them for walking. As a result, they are always free for other uses. Man's ability to use tools also rests on his ability to think and to invent and on his power to transmit knowledge of tools and their uses from one generation to another. There is evidence that wild animals, especially apes and monkeys, sometimes use tools, but only rudimentary ones such as sticks picked up from the ground.[1] Even some birds have been seen to hold grass stems in their beaks to push insects out of crevices in logs.

Because of his ability to think, to transmit knowledge by means of language, and to use tools, man controls his natural environment to a far greater degree than any other creature. He has been able to control or eliminate most other creatures when they have stood in his way,[2] and, except for the coldest arctic regions, he has spread his habitations over most of the land surface of the earth.

THE ORIGIN OF MAN

Where man originated, no one knows for sure. Modern scientists believe that somewhere in the dim past the processes of evolution produced our first human ancestors, creatures very much like modern man in their basic physical characteristics. Though theories as to where this happened are still speculative, recent findings of L. S. B. Leakey and others have led most anthropologists to believe that the first manlike creatures, the distant and primitive ancestors of all modern men, probably developed in a

[1] See Jane Goodall, "My Life Among Wild Chimpanzees," *National Geographic*, August 1963, pp. 307–308. Also Baroness Jane Van Lawick-Goodall, "New Discoveries Among Africa's Chimpanzees," *National Geographic*, December 1965, pp. 802–831.

[2] He has not, however, been too successful in controlling insects or such vermin as rats and mice; and in attempting to control his environment for his own benefit, he has sometimes severely damaged it.

savannah region similar to the one in South Africa in which the fossils of *Australopithecus* were found in the 1920's. We shall say more about *Australopithecus* later in this chapter.

Darwin and the Theory of Evolution. *Evolution* in its broadest sense refers to any process of progressive change. Thus, one may speak of the evolution of the novel, of art, or of religion. But when used without qualification, *evolution ordinarily means organic evolution, or the theory that all the complex life forms of today have descended from simpler ones that existed long ago.* Up to the time of Charles Darwin, it was not generally believed, even by scientists, that man and other complex species of life had developed slowly from earlier and simpler forms. Rather, it was thought that each species represented a separate act of creation. It was the studies of Darwin, more than anything else, that brought about a general acceptance by scientists of the principle of evolution.

Darwin, in the capacity of a naturalist, made a five-year voyage with a British surveying expedition on the steamer *Beagle* (1831–1836). During this time he had unusual opportunities to study a great variety of plant and animal life. He was puzzled by the similarities and differences he found and by the progressive steps that often seemed evident in going from the simpler to the more complex forms of life. Ultimately he developed his theory of evolution to explain these relationships. The first major work in which he presented his conclusions was *The Origin of Species* (1859). Later, in another famous book, *The Descent of Man,* he dealt specifically with the evolution of the human race.

Though Darwin was largely responsible for the widespread acceptance by scientists of the theory of evolution, he was neither the first to suggest the idea nor the first to be impressed by the remarkable physical similarity of man to certain animals. As far back as the fourth century before Christ, Aristotle believed in the gradual development of complex organisms from simpler ones, and a generation before Darwin, the French zoologist Chevalier de Lamarck had published a theory of evolution. Also, a hundred years before Darwin, the great Swedish naturalist Carolus Linnaeus realized that the resemblances of man to the apes and monkeys could not be overlooked in classifying animals into types. As a result, he grouped man, the great apes, and the monkeys into a single order which he called *Primates.*

According to Darwin's version of the theory of evolution, variations are constantly found among the individuals of every species; those with variations more favorable for meeting the conditions of life are more likely to survive, and their characteristics are then passed on to future generations by heredity. Thus the direction that evolution takes is largely determined by "the survival of the fittest," or *natural selection.*

Darwin was handicapped by the fact that he knew nothing of the modern science of *genetics,* the science that attempts to explain how the hereditary characteristics of species and individuals are transmitted biologically to their offspring and why new hereditary characteristics sometimes appear. Though the work of one of the great pioneers in this field, the Austrian monk Gregor Mendel, was done during Darwin's lifetime, and the most important report on its results was published in 1866, Mendel was ignored by the scientific community. Not until 1900 were his findings on heredity rediscovered, including his now famous experiment in interbreeding tall and short varieties of peas.

Darwin was convinced of the correctness of the theory of evolution he had developed, but, lacking a knowledge of genetics, was troubled by his inability to explain why variations that could be inherited should arise in the first place. In an attempt to meet this problem, he presented in the 1872 edition of the *Origin of Species* and in other writings the hypothesis of *pangenesis,* which was an effort to show that acquired characteristics might be inherited. He realized that he had no supporting evidence for this idea, but he was unwilling to give it up as a possible explanation of the origin of inheritable variations. His distinguished cousin, Francis Galton, carried on carefully controlled experiments with rabbits in the hope of proving or disproving the pangenesis hypothesis. The results were negative, but Darwin would not accept them as conclusive.[3]

Since Darwin's time great advances have been made in genetics. In very recent years scientists have extended their knowledge of the chromosomes that plants and animals carry in their germ cells and that are now known to contain the *genes,* the hereditary units that determine the development and the biological characteristics of each newly formed individual. We have also learned a great deal about the roles played by the nucleic acids (RNA and DNA) and the enzymes in the reproduction and growth processes.[4] Indeed, our knowledge of genetics has expanded so greatly that some scientists believe that in time we may be able to control effectively some aspects of human heredity. Such control would have its dangers, but it might conceivably mean that we could eliminate a number of inherited diseases, including diabetes, hemophilia, and sickle-cell anemia. In 1970 a group of scientists at the University of Wisconsin, headed by a Nobel prize winner, H. Gobind Khorana, announced that they had created a man-made gene.[5] Modern geneticists are very sure of one thing, namely, that Darwin was wrong in his idea that characteristics acquired by individuals during their lifetime might possibly be inherited by their progeny. But his basic theory of evolution, somewhat modified and clarified by the findings of modern genetics, has been universally accepted by scientists.

In spite of the great progress in genetics, even today the process by which evolution takes place is not fully understood. However, most students would probably agree with the following statement: In every living species individuals occasionally show new characteristics. These are now believed to result from unpredictable changes, or *mutations,* in the genes

---

[3] For an explanation of pangenesis and a quotation from Galton describing the rabbit experiment, see Haig P. Papazian, *Modern Genetics,* paperback, New York, The New American Library, Inc., 1968, pp. 29–31.

[4] For a survey of the findings of modern genetics, see Papazian, ibid.

[5] *The Chicago Tribune,* June 3, 1970, Section 1, p. 6.

of a parent plant or animal. Just how or why these mutations occur we do not really know, but we do know that, if the resulting offspring survive, their new characteristics can be passed on to future generations. Mutations are random. They seem to be accidents, partial failures of the process by which a species is able to reproduce its kind. We also know that mutations are increased by exposure to certain chemicals or certain types of radiation. Most mutations are harmful or even fatal to the offspring; but some are neutral or beneficial, and it is presumably the latter that make evolution possible. Over long periods of time, evolution can bring about very great changes in the character of a plant or animal species, and in the process the structure and biological functioning of the species often become much more complex.

Examples of changes in a species that seem to be the result of gene mutations and the operation of natural selection (survival of the fittest) are not difficult to find. The peppered moth in Great Britain is a case that has been studied in detail. This moth spends much of its time clinging to trees and is a favorite food of some birds. Until the middle of the nineteenth century all peppered moths found by naturalists who collected specimens seem to have been light in color. Since the bark of the trees was usually light and often lichen-covered, this served as protection by making it difficult for the birds to see them. But after the Industrial Revolution had been under way for some time, so much soot fell in some areas of central Britain that the tree trunks and branches became darker. This made dark moths harder to see than the light ones, and therefore the dark moths lived longer on the average and produced more progeny. Because moths go through a great many generations in a relatively short period of time, in some of the more highly industrialized areas of Britain natural selection has now almost completely replaced the light peppered moths with the dark ones.[6]

The peppered moths are a relatively simple example of the operation of natural selection. The color of these moths is known to result from a dominant gene for dark color or a pair of recessive genes for light color. In sexually reproducing organisms, genes affecting particular characteristics are transmitted to offspring in pairs called *alleles,* one from each parent. Sometimes one of these alleles is *dominant* and the other *recessive.* If two dominant genes are paired or if one such is paired with a recessive gene, the dominant gene will determine the characteristic affected; but if two recessive genes are paired, they will determine it. Thus, in peppered moths, individuals receiving two genes for dark color will be dark; also those receiving one gene for dark color and one for light; but those receiving two (recessive) genes for light color will be light.

Some human characteristics are also known to result from a single dominant gene in a pair of alleles, or else from two recessive genes. Eye color is an example. In this case, genes for brown eyes are dominant, those for

[6] Papazian, op. cit., pp. 206–208.

blue recessive. But skin color in human beings is believed to be determined by a number of genes, or pairs of genes, each making a minor contribution to the coloring of the individual. The first men or their manlike ancestors probably evolved in tropical regions where survival was possible without clothing. It is not unlikely that they had very dark skin, because light skin would have given little protection against the burning rays of the sun. But in time human groups migrated farther and farther north, eventually reaching areas where, in order to survive, they had to learn to clothe themselves. In the most northern of these areas the sun was very weak, especially in the long winters, and was often hidden by clouds or fog. Dark skin became not an advantage, but a disadvantage, because the sun's rays, by penetrating human skin, help produce vitamin D, which is an essential element in nutrition. Populations that remained in these colder regions for very long periods of time—perhaps 100,000 years or more—seem gradually, through gene mutations and the process of natural selection, to have developed much lighter shades of skin.

Natural selection does not completely account for all evolutionary changes. In small groups some such changes may result from gene mutations that are harmless but do not create characteristics that contribute to survival. But other characteristics developed by such groups may increase their chances of survival, and so they grow in numbers and spread over wider areas. Natural selection may explain the dark skins of black Africans and the lighter skins of northern Europeans, but it is not an obvious explanation of some other racial characteristics, such as the seemingly slanted eyes of some Mongoloid peoples, especially the Chinese and Japanese.

Man's Subhuman Ancestors and His Animal Relatives. To modern scientists it is quite clear that man is closely related to the other higher primates, and today virtually all anthropologists are convinced that man's nearest living animal relatives are the great apes rather than the Old World monkeys, as a few anthropologists had earlier maintained.[7] But it should be emphasized that man is not a descendant of apes as we know them, because these are modern creatures. Rather, it appears that *both* men and apes are descended from some early common ancestral species.

The anthropoid apes and men are remarkably similar in their body posture and the structure of the skeleton, teeth, muscles, and sexual organs. They are also similar in their bodily chemistry, including their blood—so much so that one scientist, George Gaylord Simpson, has stated that biochemical evidence "proves definitely" that apes are man's closest living relatives.[8] Today there are four kinds of anthropoid apes: the gibbon (including the siamang), of which a number of species are found in India and Indonesia; the orangutan, found only in Borneo and Sumatra; and the chimpanzee and the gorilla, both of which are African. The chimpanzee

[7] Fred T. Adams, *The Way to Modern Man,* New York, Teachers College Press, Columbia University, 1968, p. 159.
[8] Ibid.

is perhaps the most manlike of the apes, followed by the gorilla, the orangutan, and the gibbon, in that order.

Though man is closely related to the other primates, we are not certain of the exact nature of this relationship. However, with allowance for oversimplification, Figure 1 probably represents the views of the majority of anthropologists regarding the descent of monkeys, apes, and men from their common primate ancestral type.

It seems certain that all the primates once lived in trees and that during this period they developed limbs of great strength, with prehensile fingers and toes for grasping branches. Most primates, including the gibbon and the orangutan, still live in trees, but the gorilla, like man, lives on the ground. The chimpanzee sleeps in tree nests but spends much of the daytime on the ground. Apparently one reason for this return to the ground was increase in size. The gorilla typically weighs from 400 to 600 pounds and is far too heavy for a life in the trees, and even the chimpanzee is too heavy to swing about through the branches unless he chooses them with care. The great apes can, like man, walk on two legs, but they have not achieved man's erect posture, and normally they walk on all fours.

Figure 1. *Possible Lines of Descent of Man and Other Higher Primates from Their Common Ancestral Type.*

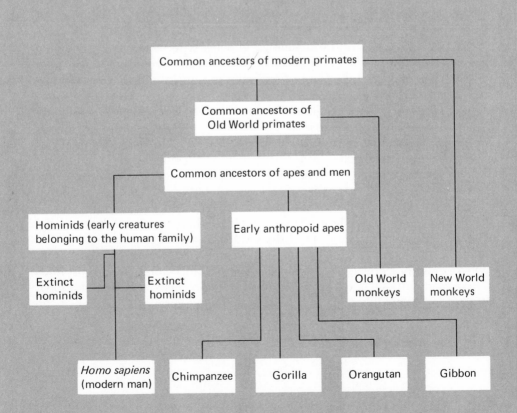

Perhaps the most important physical difference between man and apes is in the size and complexity of the brain. Between various animal species there seems as a rule to be some relationship between intelligence and the weight of the brain, especially its weight in relation to the body. But the most important factor is the organization of the brain. The chief advantage of large size seems to be that it provides space for additional cells and for more complex mechanisms. On the average, chimpanzees are smaller than men, but some weigh as much as 120 or 130 pounds. The brain of a small man typically weighs about three times that of a chimpanzee of the same body weight; and a normal human cerebral cortex, the part of the brain most concerned with memory and thought, may have ten times as many cells as the cerebral cortex of a typical ape. Today there seems little doubt that this complex human brain is an essential basis of man's power to acquire a vast store of memories, to use word symbols, and to carry on abstract thought.[9]

With respect to behavior, there are both striking similarities and striking differences between apes and human beings. Like men, apes have family life and care for their young. They have emotional responses, can express gratitude and shame, and are often sociable and cooperative. On occasion they compete with one another, and sometimes they engage in play. Certain chimpanzees have responded well to training in various types of behavior such as smoking, riding a bicycle, eating with knife and fork, and drinking from a bottle. They have also shown ability to solve problems requiring reasoned judgment. But to all these accomplishments there are limits that argue unmistakably for the superior intellectual qualities of human beings.

Some years ago Winthrop Kellogg and his wife, a team of American psychologists, performed an experiment in which they attempted to rear their own child, Donald, under precisely the same conditions as a young chimpanzee they named Gua. They tested both subjects as they went along. The tests, increasingly difficult, continued until the boy was nineteen months old and the ape sixteen months old. Up to the age of about a year, Gua was consistently ahead of the child. But shortly after that Donald began advancing at a rate that left Gua hopelessly behind, and soon the experiment had to be discontinued as no longer useful. In terms of mental capacity, man is far ahead of his nearest relatives in the animal world.

Predecessors of Modern Man. Enough of their fossilized bones have been found in different parts of the world to provide evidence that hundreds of thousands and even millions of years ago, creatures existed that were midway between man and his animal ancestors. Important finds were made in Java and China. The fossil remains discovered there appear to belong to manlike creatures with brains much larger than those of the

[9] Bernard G. Campbell, *Human Evolution,* Chicago, Aldine Publishing Co., 1966, pp. 50–52, 230–234.

2. Meshie. (By permission from Harry L. Shapiro, *Man, Culture, and Society,* New York, Oxford University Press, Inc., 1956; and courtesy of The American Museum of Natural History.)

3. Human Hands. Man's hand is a primitive but essential bit of equipment basically like the hand of his primate relatives. With it he can manipulate objects as monkeys and apes do. But, guided by superior intelligence, he can also fashion with it marvelous tools and can create the materials of civilization. (By permission from Harry L. Shapiro, *Man, Culture, and Society,* New York, Oxford University Press, Inc., 1956; and courtesy of The American Museum of Natural History.)

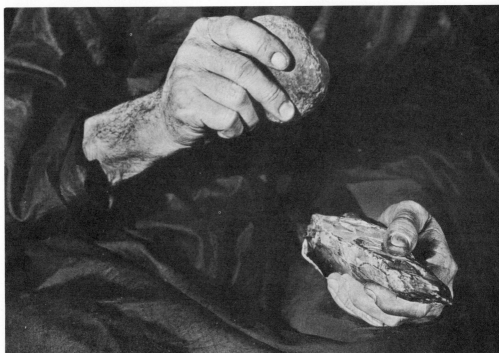

great apes but only about two thirds as large as those of living men. The first of these fossil discoveries in the Far East was made in Java in 1891 by a Dutch surgeon named Eugene Dubois. It was called *Pithecanthropus erectus,* the "erect ape-man," and was referred to by many as the "missing link" between man and his apelike prehuman ancestors. *Pithecanthropus* was thought to have lived about 600,000 years ago, and though he was not quite a man of our species, *Homo sapiens,* he seems to have been well on the way to becoming fully human.

Until rather recent years very few fossils had been discovered that would throw light upon earlier stages in man's evolution, but in the last few decades the search for such remains has been intensified. As a result a number of discoveries have been made of the fossilized remains of *hominids,* that is, of early creatures that can be regarded as members of the human family because they had developed definitely human as opposed to apelike characteristics. Unfortunately, most of these finds are fragmentary. Instead of a complete skeleton, one or a few bones are found, perhaps a portion of a skull, or a jawbone, or a few teeth. Frequently the bones are broken into small pieces, which must be fitted together. Such finds are very difficult to classify and interpret, and hence anthropologists often disagree as to their nature and significance. Even on the rare occasions when more adequate skeletal remains are discovered, it is impossible to determine with certainty whether they represent direct ancestors of modern men or only near-human types that eventually became extinct.

One of the first discoveries of what most anthropologists now recognize as an early hominid and a probable ancestor of modern man was found in 1924 by Raymond Dart of the Witwatersrand University in South Africa. He succeeded in separating from some limestone blocks a brain cast, parts of the skull itself, and most of the face bones of a creature that, he believed, showed hominid characteristics. At the time, however, it was classified as an ape and became known as *Australopithecus africanus* ("the southern ape of Africa"). Later finds of the remains of similar creatures helped to convince anthropologists that *Australopithecus* was a hominid and that he walked erect; also there seems now to be archeological evidence that he used primitive tools. However, he had a relatively small brain, one that, on the average, was no larger than the brains of some modern large apes.[10] John E. Pfeiffer suggests that Australopithecines may have first appeared as long ago as four or five million years.

In 1934 Edward Lewis described a new species of fossil primate, *Ramapithecus* (Rama is a hero of Hindu mythology), a portion of whose upper jaw along with some teeth had been found in the Suvalik Hills of India. Though Lewis noted hominid characteristics, he classified it as an ape. But in the 1960's, partly as a result of arguments advanced by Elwyn L. Simons of Yale, *Ramapithecus* gained increasing acceptance among an-

[10] Adams, op. cit., Chap. 11.

thropologists as a probable hominid. Since the age of the fossilized bones is estimated at ten to twelve million years, *Ramapithecus* is a possible ancestor not only of man but also of *Australopithecus*. [11]

In very recent years one of the most dedicated and successful searchers for the fossil remains of early hominids has been Louis S. B. Leakey. He has found materials at various East African sites that, according to Pfeiffer, have "identified earlier hominids, ancestors of *Ramapithecus,* which may be more than twenty million years old." [12]

In 1959 Leakey reported finding in Olduvai Gorge (in what is now northern Tanzania) teeth and skull fragments that, fitted together, provided an almost complete skull except for the lower jaw. He called this creature *Zinjanthropus,* and radioactive dating put its age at nearly two million years. Its age and its close resemblance to fossils found by Dart and others in South Africa caused many anthropologists to classify it as *Australopithecus*. There were indications that Leakey's new find had used primitive stone tools, for these were found close to its remains.

In 1961 Leakey found in Kenya parts of the upper jaw and teeth of a creature he named *Kenyapithecus wickeri,* which radioactive dating showed to be about fourteen million years old. But after comparing this specimen with *Ramapithecus,* Simons and other scientists concluded that they were very similar, and later classified both into a single genus, *Ramapithecus*.

The most publicized discoveries of Leakey were made a little later in the 1960's when he found in Olduvai Gorge a number of specimens of what he and his associates considered a new species of hominid. They christened it *Homo habilis* ("man with ability"). Leakey maintained that it was more human in its characteristics than *Zinjanthropus* (*Australopithecus?*) and that it was probably a direct ancestor of modern man. Leakey deduced that *Homo habilis* was about four feet tall, stood erect, and had a jawbone large enough to hold a tongue capable of forming words. The creature apparently used tools because crude ones were found near his remains. Radioactive dating showed his bones to be not far from two million years old. Leakey believes that *Homo habilis* was contemporary with *Zinjanthropus*. He also thinks that only *Homo habilis* was ancestral to man and that the less-human *Zinjanthropus* was headed for extinction and hence has left no descendants.

But many anthropologists are not willing to accept Leakey's conclusions. Some think that *Homo habilis* was only a geographical variation of *Australopithecus;* others that he was a more advanced type of the latter; and some doubt that he was a direct ancestor of man.

Despite substantial progress, our knowledge of man's early hominid ancestors and the stages in his evolution is still very sketchy and incomplete. Today most scientists appear to regard *Ramapithecus* as probably

[11] Ibid. See therein pp. 167–169.
[12] John E. Pfeiffer, *The Emergence of Man,* New York, Harper & Row, Publishers, 1969, p. 53.

ancestral to *Australopithecus* and *Homo habilis* and regard one or both of the latter as ancestral to man. In time we may have a much more adequate record of man's descent from his prehuman ancestors.[13] But as one anthropologist reminds us, the earth is not a well-stocked museum. Rather, it is a very poor one, and only as a result of a rare combination of circumstances are the fossils of fairly large animals preserved, in good condition, over periods that may greatly exceed a million years; and at best, as Leakey once remarked, "We shall never be able to point to a specific creature and say, Here man began."

Neanderthal man was the first type of prehistoric creature to bear a rather close resemblance to modern man. According to Pfeiffer, "He was one of the subspecies of *Homo sapiens* which lived in the Old World from about 70,000 to 35,000 years ago, and it should be no surprise that he walked fully erect. After all, his ancestors had been walking that way for at least a million years before him."[14] Some scientists, including Kenneth Oakley, believe that Neanderthals first appeared much earlier than 70,000 years ago.

Neanderthal man was powerfully built but somewhat shorter than modern man. He had a sloping forehead, heavy ridges over his eyes, a large wide nose, and protruding jaws, but his brain was at least as large as that of the average modern European. Remains of Neanderthal men have been found in many parts of Europe.

The first human beings whose skeletal remains are like those of living men belonged to the group called *Cro-Magnon* man, after the name of the French village near which the first specimens were found. According to Pfeiffer there is evidence that Cro-Magnon man developed in the Near East 40,000 to 50,000 years ago. He began to appear in Europe about 35,000 years ago and his remains have been found in many localities. He was tall, well built, and had a skull capacity comparable to that of both Neanderthal man and present-day Europeans. Judging him on the basis of his skeletal structure he can be regarded as the first modern man.

HUMAN NATURE AND MAN'S ORIGINAL NATURE

Human nature is a broad and, for many people, rather vague concept. But if we mean by human nature *the attitudes and behavior characteristic of human beings living in association with others,* then it is quite clear that human nature is not something with which man is endowed at birth. At that time he is completely helpless and wholly lacking in understanding of either himself or the world around him. As a newborn baby, he cannot walk, he cannot talk, he cannot even sit up or turn himself over. If he can be said to be "conscious," his consciousness is so vague and diffused

[13] Adams, op. cit., pp. 167–171, 189–191.
[14] Pfeiffer, op. cit., pp. 164–165.

that in later years he can recall nothing of his early babyhood. What, then, is the original nature of man? And by what process does he eventually acquire what we may call human nature?

The Original Nature of Man. The human organism at birth is equipped with a characteristic framework. This consists of muscles and bones; a lymphatic system and a blood system, carrying their respective streams of substances throughout the organism; an endocrine system, dependent on glands that secrete specific chemical substances and discharge them into the blood stream; a nervous system, consisting of a brain and a network of appendages and extensions reaching into every living part of the organism; a respiratory apparatus; a sex and reproductive system; and a system for ingesting and digesting food and excreting waste products. These structures are inherited, and, except for the reproductive system, they are ready to perform at birth. Indeed, some of them function before birth.

The original nature of man reveals itself through the functioning of the organism of the newborn baby. It includes, first of all, a large variety of relatively simple responses, such as winking, blinking, sneezing, sucking, and jerking. These are known as *reflexes*. It includes, furthermore, such *drives* as those for food, sleep, temperature change, and elimination. When these drives are satisfied, the infant is contented, and emotion is at a minimum. When drives are thwarted, the infant is unhappy and often becomes angry. When unfamiliar or threatening situations present themselves, the individual experiences anxiety or fear.

The newborn baby has no understanding of what is going on around him, no power to make conscious adjustments. Yet within his organism, if he is normal, is a potentiality for growth and development; for acquiring not only a great variety of skills but also knowledge and understanding of the world around him. Gradually he acquires *human nature* and develops behavior patterns that enable him to adjust to a world in which he is almost constantly coming into contact with other people.

Let us now ask the question, How does this development of human nature, of human personality, come about? Is it the spontaneous unfolding of something already latent in the individual? Or is it the result of a learning process—that is, of the adjustments the human organism makes as the result of contacts with its external environment? Actually, it is both. No other creature has the capability of developing human nature, but even man cannot acquire it without coming into contact with other people, learning from them, and reacting to them.

Instinct as an Explanation of Behavior. At one time psychologists attributed much of human behavior to *instinct* rather than to learning, but today they generally maintain that man possesses no true instincts. This difference in point of view arises largely from a change in definition. Formerly, psychologists generally used the term *instinct* broadly. They included in it not only inherited behavior patterns but also inherited emotional reactions like fear of loud noises, and basic biological drives like hunger and sex. Today, however, they define *instinct* more narrowly. In modern usage *an instinct is a complex, inherited behavior pattern*. It does not have to be learned but comes into play automatically in response to an appropriate situation. Nest building by birds is a good example of instinctive behavior.

If we define instincts as complex, inherited patterns of behavior, it is clear that human beings do not have them. Except for a number of reflexes, like crying, sucking, and swallowing, all human behavior must be learned. On the other hand, instinctive behavior plays a very important role in the lower forms of life. Most insects and animals are born with nervous systems so constructed that they can carry on more or less complicated types of activity when certain situations arise, and they can do so without any previous learning experience.

This is not to say that all instinctive behavior patterns are equally strong. At a certain stage in its development a kitten, if it sees a mouse, is likely to stalk it and spring upon it even though it has had no previous experience with mice. However, some cats never catch mice unless they have seen other cats do so. On the other hand, in birds certain instincts are highly developed. We have mentioned nest building. Birds of a certain species will always build nests of a certain type when the mating season arrives, even though they have never seen such a nest built. When we come to the insect world, the complexity of instinctive behavior patterns is almost unbelievable, especially in the case of social insects such as bees and ants.

Since man cannot meet life situations by following instinctive patterns of behavior, he must meet them in other ways. Let us see how this problem is solved for human beings.

Human Nature and the Learning Process. Today psychologists generally agree that the development of human nature is largely a learning process. Gradually an individual matures physically, and as he matures, his ability to learn increases. Man starts with little more than a biological organism, but one with great potentialities for development and with certain basic needs that demand fulfillment. What is called the *learning process* consists in discovering ways in which these needs can be met. Once a need is satisfied, there is usually established a learned pattern of response. This later becomes the basis for mastering still newer patterns of action. Thus, the individual adds new knowledge to old knowledge and enlarges the range of his reactions to his environment. Starting with simple reflexes as the first responses to basic organic needs, he goes on to develop motor habits as complex as eating, walking, and writing. From simple guttural sounds, he develops through association with other people the complex and symbolic verbal responses we call language, and as his activities and contacts expand his emotional reactions become more varied. Thus the human organism, starting with relatively simple reactions and an exceedingly plastic nervous system, gradually acquires the habits, skills, knowledge, attitudes, and emotional responses that constitute the human personality.

Human Nature and the Process of Socialization. To appreciate what a human being is like if he fails to acquire human nature by associating with others, let us look at what becomes of a human organism that grows up in isolation. There have been rare cases of children who were kept in attics or cellars from babyhood, with no human contacts except when food was passed to them through a door or window. Such children did not develop human nature. They behaved more like animals than human beings. They showed no signs of human intelligence; they had no skills; they lacked our basic habits of sanitation and hygiene; they had no hopes, no ideals, no conscience; they could not even talk. Only a child reared in contact and interaction with other human beings can become truly human.

The character and personality of every human being is in great part a reflection of the society in which he lives. It is from his social environment that the individual acquires his knowledge, skills, customs, ideals, religion, and morals. The process that brings this about, that shapes the personality of the individual so that he can adjust to and become a member of his society, is called *socialization*. In the United States most of us feel, think, and act like Americans because we have spent all our lives among Americans and in the American social environment. If, from earliest childhood, we had associated only with a group of Eskimos who had never had any contacts with the outside world, we would not understand and could not take part in the American way of life because we would feel, think, and act like those Eskimos.

This does not mean that all Americans, or even all Eskimos, are alike in their personalities. There are significant differences in our family backgrounds and in many other aspects of our personal social environment. Moreover, though to develop human nature we must be human beings and inherit human potentialities, no two people will ever react to the same environment in just the same way. There are biologically inherited differences that affect the intelligence and temperament of every person and that therefore affect his thinking and his behavior. In any given individual, social inheritance and biological inheritance are so closely bound together that we can never be sure of the relative influence of each. However, for nearly all of us the general pattern of life is largely determined by social environment. Almost everything that we believe or know or do we learn from observing other people, from listening to other people, or from reading and thinking about what other people have written.

THE NATURE OF SOCIETY

Even though the personality of each individual is in great part molded by society, it is clear that society can have no existence apart from the people who comprise it. A society consists of people, and the characteristics of every society are gradually shaped and changed, over succeeding generations, by innovations introduced by the people who belong to it. The influence of any one individual may be small, but the contributions of many individuals, over long periods of time, can be very great.

Society and Social Organization. A group of people do not necessarily constitute a society. A number of people who come together temporarily, and perhaps accidentally, are merely a crowd, or an unorganized aggregate. To constitute a society a group must be bound together by established relationships. It must, in other words, be organized. *A society is a group of people who have lived together long enough to get themselves organized and to think of themselves as a social unit.* [15]

Though the basis of any society is a group of individuals, equally important to its establishment is the continued existence of this group over a period of time. As Ralph Linton once pointed out, a crowd brought together for a football game is an *aggregate,* but it is not a society. Its members are close together in space and for the moment are united by a common interest. However, any sense of unity they may have is superficial and temporary. When the game is over, they disperse. They are not together long enough to organize into a society. But if the same people were marooned for a year on an uninhabited island, they would be forced to organize themselves into a society. They would develop common ideas and interests, and techniques for living and working together. [16]

Culture and Its Role in Human Societies. A society is an organized group of people who follow a given way of life. *The culture of a society is the way of life that its people follow.* In even simpler terms, as the late Melville J. Herskovits once put it, "a society is composed of people; the way they behave is their culture." The culture of a society includes everything in the lives of its members that is of human origin—that is, everything they learn through their direct or indirect contacts with other people. It includes the customary ways of behaving in everyday life; religious beliefs; moral standards; the way family life is organized; the methods used to provide food and shelter; language; government; and forms of artistic expression. It is the total social heredity of mankind, or, to quote Herskovits again, "the man-made part of the environment."

Culture develops only through the association of human beings, and thus presupposes society; at the same time, culture is what makes a human society possible. Only when people develop in some degree a common culture can they function as an organized group, for only then do they know what to expect of one another and how to behave to meet the requirements of the group. A society can exist because nature, in ways not wholly understood, has endowed men with the capacity for creating culture and transmitting it to succeeding generations. Thus culture creates societies, and societies are dependent on culture.

[15] See Ralph Linton, *The Study of Man,* New York, Appleton-Century-Crofts, Inc., 1936, p. 91.
[16] Ibid., p. 92.

Primary and Secondary Groups. Some social groups are very large, some very small. Our American society, consisting of all the people who live in the United States, today numbers well over 200 million persons. On the other hand, primitive or preliterate tribal groups often have only a few hundred members and sometimes only a few score. But any group large enough to be thought of as a society always contains within it various subgroups.

When a relatively few people are closely associated, as in a family, a neighborhood, or a small rural community, they constitute what sociologists call a *primary group. Primary groups are those characterized by intimate face-to-face relationships among their members.* In a primary group everyone knows everyone else, and social controls over the behavior of individuals are largely informal. People tend to behave as the group expects for several reasons. First, most individuals in such groups are likely to share essentially the same beliefs and attitudes. Second, the behavior of each individual is likely to be known to the whole group. Third, because people know personally those with whom they come into daily contact, they value their good opinion, and they fear disapproval, gossip, and possible ostracism from the group.

In a very large social group the situation is quite different. Here we have what sociologists call a *secondary group.* A good example is the residents of a larger urban community. *Most of the members of a secondary group seldom or never meet face-to-face, and their contacts with one another are largely indirect.* Such indirect contacts occur through organizations of one kind or another and through such media of communication as newspapers, radio, and television. The contact of the television viewer with the newscaster on the screen may seem to be primary but it really is not in the sense in which we use the term. It does not represent direct communication between people who know one another. The viewer may know the newscaster but the latter does not know that the former even exists. There is no interchange or "feedback." Even direct contacts with other people may be rather impersonal in a secondary group, because often they are contacts between strangers. One seldom knows the clerk in the store, the driver of the bus, or the people at the lunch counter.

In secondary groups social controls tend to be formal. Cultural differences between people are likely to be greater, partly because there are wide differences in social class and a wide variety of subgroups with different ethnic and national backgrounds, and partly because there are groupings on the basis of occupation or special interests. Aside from the members of certain small subgroups, people seldom know one another personally, and gossip and public opinion are less effective in restraining them from antisocial behavior. To a much greater degree than in primary groups, social control in secondary groups must be exercised through such formal agencies as the police and the courts; but often these *formal controls* are not as effective as the *informal controls* exercised by a primary group.

At the beginning of this chapter we defined *social science* as *the study of the group life of man.* In Chapter 2 we shall discuss at some length the nature of social science, its methods, and certain of its limitations.

Terms to Be Understood

social science	*Pithecanthropus erectus*	drives
evolution	*Homo sapiens*	instincts
primates	hominids	learning process
natural selection	*Australopithecus*	socialization
genetics	*Ramapithecus*	society
pangenesis	*Zinjanthropus*	aggregate (of people)
genes	*Kenyapithecus*	culture
mutations	*Homo habilis*	primary group
alleles	Neanderthal man	secondary group
dominant gene	Cro-Magnon man	informal controls
recessive gene	human nature	formal controls
anthropoid apes	reflexes	

Questions for Review and Discussion

1. Why do we say that man is a social creature?
2. What is social science?
3. What three unique abilities gave man advantages over all other creatures?
4. Why are men, apes, and monkeys all placed in the biological order of primates?
5. Explain Darwin's theory of evolution.
6. What is the nature of the scientific evidence supporting the theory of evolution?
7. How have modern geneticists modified Darwin's theory?
8. How do men resemble and how do they differ from apes?
9. Have men descended from apes? Explain the scientific theory of the origin of man.
10. Who is Louis S. B. Leakey? Why do he and other anthropologists believe that man probably evolved from his subhuman ancestors in South and East Africa?
11. What are the possible relationships of *Ramapithecus, Australopithecus,* and *Homo habilis* to one another and to modern man?
12. Why is it believed that Cro-Magnon man, rather than Neanderthal man, was the immediate ancestor of living man?
13. What is man's "original nature"? How does he acquire "human nature"?
14. Explain why instincts play a very small role in human behavior.
15. Explain the relationship between culture and society.
16. Is a family a primary social group? Why or why not?
17. Why are formal social controls more necessary in a secondary group than in a primary group?

For Further Study

Adams, Fred T., *The Way to Modern Man,* New York, Teachers College Press, Columbia University, 1969. An excellent brief introduction to human evolution.

Beals, Ralph Leon, and Harry Hoijer, *Introduction to Anthropology,* 4th ed., New York, The Macmillan Company, 1971.

Campbell, Bernard J., *Human Evolution,* Chicago, Aldine Publishing Co., 1966.

Clarke, Grahame, and Stuart Piggott, *Prehistoric Societies,* paperback, Baltimore, Penguin Books, Inc., 1970.

Darlington, C. D., *The Evolution of Man and Society,* New York, Simon & Schuster, Inc., 1969.

Darwin, Charles, *Origin of Species,* edited by J. W. Burrow, paperback, Baltimore, Penguin Books, Inc., 1969.

Downs, James F., and Hermann K. Bleibtreu, *Human Variation,* New York, The Free Press, 1969.

Dubos, René, *So Human an Animal,* paperback, New York, Charles Scribner's Sons, 1968.

Hammond, Peter B., *Introduction to Social and Cultural Anthropology,* New York, The Macmillan Company, 1971.

Hunt, Elgin F., and Jules Karlin, eds., *Society Today and Tomorrow,* 2d ed., paperback, New York, The Macmillan Company, 1967. See therein "Talk with a Stranger" by Robert Redfield.

Jolly, Alison, *The Evolution of Primate Behavior,* paperback, New York, The Macmillan Company, 1972.

Kohler, Wolfgang, *The Mentality of Apes,* Vintage paperback, New York, Alfred A. Knopf, Inc., 1959.

Leakey, L. S. B., *Adam or Ape,* paperback, Cambridge, Mass., Schenkman Publishing Company, 1970.

Mercier, Paul, *History of Anthropology,* paperback, New York, Frederick A. Praeger, Inc., 1969.

Papazian, Haig P., *Modern Genetics,* paperback, New York, New American Library, Inc., 1968. Especially Chap. 20.

Pfeiffer, John E., *The Emergence of Men,* New York, Harper & Row, Publishers, 1969.

Pilbeam, David R., *The Ascent of Man,* paperback, New York, The Macmillan Company, 1972.

————, *The Evolution of Man,* London, Thames and Hudson, Ltd., 1970.

Tax, Sol, *Horizons of Anthropology,* paperback, Chicago, Aldine Publishing Co., 1964.

Chapter 2

Social

Science

and Its

Methods

the scientific study of organized human groups is a relatively recent development, but already a vast amount of information has been accumulated concerning the social life of man, and on the basis of this information there has been built an extensive body of theory about the nature, growth, and functioning of human societies.

THE MAJOR FIELDS OF KNOWLEDGE

All human knowledge is (1) knowledge of man himself, including his culture and his products, and (2) knowledge of his natural environment. Human culture and human knowledge have been gradually changing and accumulating ever since that far-distant time when man first acquired his distinctively human character. But until rather recent times this knowledge was not scientific in the modern sense. *Scientific knowledge* is knowledge that has been systematically gathered, classified, related, and interpreted. In earlier times men seldom gathered, learned, and interpreted facts systematically. Most of their knowledge they acquired unconsciously, as we today still acquire our native language and many of the basic elements in our culture. For the most part they accepted the world as they found it, and if any explanations seemed called for, they invented supernatural ones. Some primitive peoples believed that every stream, tree, or rock contained a spirit that controlled its behavior.

In modern times our emphasis is on the search for scientific knowledge. We have divided the sum total of human knowledge into a number of areas or fields, and every science represents the systematic collection and study of data in some one of these areas.

All systematic human knowledge can be classified roughly into three major fields, *social science, natural science,* and the *humanities.* Each of these fields is subdivided into a number of specialized sciences or disciplines to facilitate more intensive study and deeper understanding. Social science, as we already know, is the field of human knowledge that deals with all the aspects of the group life of man. Natural science deals with the natural environment in which man is placed. It includes such sciences as physics and chemistry, which deal with the laws of matter, motion, space, mass, and energy; it also includes the biological sciences, which deal with living things. The humanities are closely related to social science in that both treat man and his culture. Social science, however, is most concerned with those basic elements of culture that determine the general patterns of human behavior. The humanities deal with certain special aspects of human culture; they are primarily concerned with man's attempts to express spiritual and esthetic values through literature, music, and art and to discover the meaning of life through religion and philosophy.

THE SOCIAL SCIENCES

No field of study is more important to man than the social sciences. To understand society is to learn not only the conditions that limit our lives but also the opportunities open to us for improving what some writers call "the human condition." In the long run, increasing our knowledge of human society may be far more important than learning more about mathematics, physics, chemistry, or engineering; for unless we can develop societies in which human beings can live happy, meaningful, and satisfying lives, there is not much use in learning how to make better automobiles and skyscrapers, how to travel to the moon, or how to construct better hydrogen bombs.

Because all phases of human culture are related and interdependent, to gain a real understanding of human society we must have some knowledge of all its major aspects. If we concentrate on some phases and completely neglect others, we are sure to have a distorted picture. But, unfortunately, social science is today such a vast and complex field that no one student can hope to master all of it. However, it is important that he should very early gain a useful concept of modern society as a whole. Hence, one of the major purposes of this book is to give him a broad and integrated picture of the general nature of human society, along with some understanding of the major forces operating within it. To be sure, if he is to acquire any great depth of knowledge, the student must ultimately concentrate most of his attention on one or a few of the many different phases of social life. For this reason, the specialized social sciences have developed, each dealing with some limited aspect of human behavior. This breaking up of the study of social science into specialized fields has disadvantages, but it represents a necessary division of labor. Without it we would have difficulty in continuing to expand our knowledge of society and of the laws or principles that govern it. Let us consider briefly the nature of each of the major social sciences.

History. History is the study of the past development of human societies, especially during the period for which written records have been available. It is a social science in the sense that it represents a systematic attempt to learn about and to verify past events, to relate them to one another, and to discover their influence in shaping our civilization.

To understand any social situation we must know what brought it about. We cannot understand the present unless we know the past. History, however, cannot give us a complete explanation of how or why the present developed from the past; nor can it, with any certainty, predict the future. There are no general principles or "laws" of historical development that make such prediction possible.

We often say that history repeats itself, but literally this is not true. All that we mean is that the events of one period often show resemblances to those of an earlier period. Frank Knight, of the University of Chicago, once defined history as "the nonrepetitive aspects of human experience." If history repeated itself, it would not be history. That the sun rises each morning is not history, for it occurs with regularity and according to a pattern that can be forecast with precision.

Though history does not enable us to predict the future with any certainty, it does enable us to discover certain trends in the development of human societies. For example, a trend that has been operating for two hundred years with increasing intensity is the spread of industrialism. When such a trend has continued without diminution up to the present, we may reasonably expect it to continue for some time into the future. However, we should always remember that historical trends sometimes change with unexpected rapidity.

Anthropology. Anthropology is sometimes called the *science of man,* and in a sense it is the broadest of all the social sciences. It is concerned, first, with all aspects of human group behavior and also with comparing human behavior with that of man's primate relatives, the apes and monkeys. Second, it is concerned with such matters as the fossil evidence for the evolution of man and the other primates; the influence of natural environment on the physical characteristics of man; racial differences; the inheritance of physical traits; and population genetics. Anthropology can therefore be divided into two broad fields, *cultural anthropology* and *biological anthropology*. The two, however, are very closely related because one of the tasks of anthropology is to study relationships between man's biological traits and his socially acquired characteristics.

Cultural anthropology, in practice, has been mainly concerned with relatively simple, nonliterate tribal cultures; but increasing attention is now being given to modern cultural patterns. Here, too, there is a relationship because we can increase our understanding of today's societies by comparing them with those of earlier times or with the tribal societies that still survive in some parts of the world. The study of other societies helps us to look at our own society more impersonally, to become aware of its special characteristics, and to see its problems in perspective.

Economics. Economics is the study of the ways in which man makes a living. More precisely, it is "the study of the social organization by means of which men satisfy their wants for scarce goods and services."[1] As used here, "scarce goods and services" refer to all those things that, in the modern world, we commonly buy for money.

Human beings have many wants, but not all these wants can be satisfied. Neither the goods we want nor the resources required to produce them exist in sufficient quantities to satisfy all our desires. The result is that we must economize. Economizing is the great economic problem. It means making the most of what we have by employing scarce resources to satisfy as fully as possible our more or less unlimited wants.[2]

The importance of economics as a social science arises from the fact that satisfying their economic wants is the most pressing problem most human beings face. The vast majority of the people of the world spend most of their waking hours in activities concerned with earning a living.

Political Science. Political science deals with government. In the broadest sense government includes all the social arrangements to maintain peace and order within a given society, to put pressure on individuals to conform to social patterns, and to provide for collective action for the common good, for example, in organizing a military force, in building roads, or in conserving natural resources. In a modern society, political authority is centered in an institution called the *state*, or sometimes the *nation-state*. The state is the special phase of the social order that political scientists single out for investigation.

[1] Myron H. Umbreit, Elgin F. Hunt, and Charles V. Kinter, *Economics*, New York, McGraw-Hill, Inc., 1957, p. 4.
[2] *Ibid.*, p. 11.

The major interests of political scientists are as follows: (1) politics, or the struggle for power among those who seek to control the state; (2) laws, and the ways in which they are created and interpreted; (3) administration, or the organization provided for enforcing laws and carrying out public policies; (4) political theories of the nature and functions of the state; (5) international relations, or the ways in which independent sovereign powers deal with one another in the world community of nations.

Sociology. The field of sociology is not easy to define. As one textbook puts it, sociology undertakes "in its more expansive moods to exercise an oversight over the social science rancho as a whole." In any case, sociology appears to cover a somewhat broader field and to be less clearly delimited than either economics or political science. In general, sociologists avoid centering their attention on relationships that are primarily economic or political. There is, however, a considerable amount of overlapping between sociology and cultural anthropology, but the sociologist puts more emphasis on present-day social relationships than do most anthropologists. Sociologists study social institutions and they attempt to discover the factors that determine social organization and behavior. They are very much concerned with the study of the social interaction (1) of individuals with one another, (2) of individuals with groups, and (3) of groups with one another. Among their special interests are such topics as personality development, social classes, race relations, community organization, marriage and the family, crime, and the structure and functioning of various types of small social groups.

Psychology and Social Psychology. *Psychology* is not usually regarded as a social science, because it deals chiefly with the mind and personality of the individual. Because, however, man is a social creature, his personality is largely shaped by his social environment and his reactions largely relate to that environment. In other words, psychology is necessarily very closely associated with the social sciences. *Social psychology* is a specialized field in which the interests of psychologists, sociologists, and anthropologists meet. It is the study of the social development of the individual and the interaction between the individual and the group. Social psychologists center their attention on the individual's behavior as it influences and is influenced by the behavior of others.

THE SCIENTIFIC METHOD AND ITS APPLICATION

In modern times, as compared with the past, the rate at which human knowledge has accumulated has been phenomenal. Perhaps the most important single reason for this has been the development of modern science and the *scientific method* of searching for truth.

Conditions Favorable to Scientific Inquiry. Before we attempt to list formally the fundamental steps in scientific inquiry, we should note that such inquiry is possible only in a society in which certain attitudes are developed or tolerated. Scientific investigation, to be successful, requires on the part of the investigator not only intelligence but also certain mental attitudes. One of these is curiosity. Another is skepticism of explanations based only on tradition or ancient authorities. Still another is objectivity. The objective investigator seeks impartially for the truth. He makes every effort not to allow his personal preconceptions, prejudices, or desires to color the facts he observes or to influence his interpretation of these facts.

In preliterate tribal societies the obstacles to the development of scientific methods of inquiry are very great. Such societies are much more bound by custom and tradition than are modern societies. The traditional way of doing things is regarded as the only right way. Moreover, any serious deviation from established procedures is likely to be regarded as a danger to the group and, as such, to be punished very severely.

We cannot classify Europe in the Middle Ages as either preliterate or tribal. Nevertheless, respect for tradition, for ancient authorities, and for religious dictates was so strong that there was little chance for the growth of a scientific spirit. The development of modern science had to wait until the Crusades, the Renaissance, the great voyages of discovery, the Reformation, and other historical developments had loosened the hold of tradition. Even as late as the early seventeenth century the great astronomer Galileo was sentenced to prison because he maintained, contrary to the dictates of the Church, that the earth revolved around the sun.[3]

Nature of the Scientific Method. Modern science is based on the assumption that this is an orderly universe, ruled by the law of cause and effect. Any given set of circumstances always produces the same result. If seemingly identical situations have different results, they were not really alike; some significant difference existed and was overlooked. Further investigation should disclose what this difference was.

To make the nature of the scientific method as clear as possible, let us attempt to list the major steps in scientific inquiry. Such a listing is useful but to some degree arbitrary because the steps named do not always follow one another in the rigid time sequence that a list suggests. A scientific investigator will frequently have to return from later stages of his inquiry to earlier ones to find additional facts or rectify errors.

For present purposes let us assume that the following six steps are required to develop and establish a new scientific theory:

1. *Observation.* All scientific knowledge relates to the natural or the social environment, and all knowledge begins with facts gathered through careful observation. However, the facts that start the process of scientific investigation may not have been gathered systematically or with any special end in view.

---

[3] We might add that even as late as 1925 John Scopes, a Tennessee school teacher, was brought to trial on the charge of teaching his pupils the theory of evolution.

2. *Formulation of a problem.* The acute observer becomes curious as to what causes some of the phenomena he discovers in the world about him. Perhaps he notices that some of the facts he has gathered seem to be related in peculiar ways that cannot be wholly accidental. His problem then becomes to discover the pattern of relationship between certain facts and the reason for this pattern.

3. *Collection and classification of more facts.*

4. *Generalization.* The investigator who has collected and classified a large amount of factual material related to his problem will seek to discover uniform relationships among his facts, relationships that he can state in the form of scientific laws. For example, suppose he has experimented with a number of different gases by applying increased pressure while holding the temperature constant. If in all cases doubling the pressure on a gas halves its volume, he is in a position to state, as a scientific law, that the volume of a gas is inversely proportional to the pressure. This is the principle now known as Boyle's law.

5. *Formulation of a hypothesis.* The fifth step in the scientific process is to seek a theory that will explain the law that has been discovered. A *tentative theory* is called a *hypothesis.*

6. *Testing and verification.* The sixth and final step is to test the hypothesis through seeking further facts, by experiment or otherwise, that it should fit. If the hypothesis seems to fit all possible situations to which it is intended to apply, it then becomes an accepted *scientific theory.*

Boyle's law, for example, is explained by the molecular theory of gases. According to this theory, a gas consists of great numbers of minute particles, called molecules, that move at high speeds in all directions. If this is the case, when a certain amount of gas is forced into a tight container, its molecules will put outward pressure on surrounding surfaces by continually striking against them. If now the volume of the gas is reduced by one-half through forcing it into a container only half as large, its molecules will be crowded together, so that in a given period of time twice as many will hit a given area of surface. Hence, if the average speed of the molecules is the same —and it will be if the temperature has been held constant—the pressure exerted by the gas will be twice as great.

Science offers no final explanations of the universe and its phenomena. Time, space, matter, energy—existence itself—are mysteries the ultimate nature of which are probably forever beyond the grasp of the human mind. But an accepted scientific theory may be regarded as an explanation, up to a certain point, of a scientific law.

The scientific method as outlined above can be employed most simply in posing and solving certain problems of the natural sciences, and for this reason we have used an illustration from physics. However, scientific investigation is seldom as simple as might be inferred from our description of the scientific method. Each field of knowledge has its special problems, and the investigator must always adjust his methods to the peculiarities of the situation with which he deals. A method of investigation of great importance in many fields, but of very little use in others, is the setting up and carrying out of controlled experiments.

The Experimental Method and Its Limitations. In chemistry, physics, and biology, controlled experiments play a very important role in discovering facts and testing hypotheses. In these sciences an investigator can often create a situation in which he controls all the significant factors that bear on a problem. He then changes one of these factors and watches to see what happens. If further changes result, he knows that such changes must have been caused by the factor he modified, because everything else remained constant.

But there are limits to the use of the *experimental method* even in such sciences as chemistry and physics. In other physical sciences, like astronomy, geology, and meteorology, it can be used little or not at all, principally because the scientist cannot control the situations that are significant for the solution of his problems.

In the social sciences very little use can be made of the method of controlled experiment except in dealing with certain relationships that involve rather small groups. Again the reason is that the investigator cannot control the situations in which he must seek answers to his problems. For example, many people once believed that high tariffs would bring prosperity. One way to prove or disprove this would be to apply very heavy duties to all goods entering the United States for a considerable period of time, meanwhile holding constant all other factors affecting business activity. If a sustained increase in prosperity followed, we would then have substantial evidence to support the thesis that high tariffs are a cause of prosperity. Though this might seem a simple method of proving the point at issue, it is obviously an impossible one. First, no investigator, in this case let us say an economist, can control the country's tariff policy. Even if he could, while the high tariff was in effect many other social changes would be taking place, such as strikes, the establishment of new industries, and perhaps even wars. Some of these other changes would doubtless have much more influence on the state of national prosperity than would the high tariff.

Most of the significant problems of interest to social scientists involve very large groups of people, often society as a whole. Obviously, the method of controlled experiment cannot be used in solving such problems. When, however, a social scientist can solve a problem by dealing with small groups, he may be able to make a limited use of the experimental method if the people involved will cooperate with him.

Many people, when they talk about social experiments, do not mean controlled experiments carried on under the direction of scientific investigators. All they mean is the introduction and "trying out" of new social policies. For example, the nationalization of basic British industries by the British Labour Party is often called a "social experiment." But from a scientific point of view an uncontrolled experiment has little value. Furthermore, large-scale social "experiments," such as nationalizing British industry, often present a special problem. Whether the results are good or bad, it soon becomes almost impossible to abandon the new system and return to the old. A system of competitive private industry develops through a slow process of growth. It can be destroyed rather easily, but it is very difficult to recreate.[4] This is not an argument against social change. Rather, it emphasizes the importance of gaining as full an understanding as possible of the effects of proposed major changes, and of seeking to implement them only if there is good reason to believe that they will improve rather than injure the quality of human life.

Degrees of Precision in Scientific Knowledge. In some fields of scientific investigation, laws have been discovered that can be stated in rather precise, measurable terms. This is true of chemistry, physics, astronomy, and mathematics. In other fields, as for example in geology and meteorology, anything approaching precision is difficult to attain.

The whole field of social science is one in which it is peculiarly difficult to discover and formulate laws that are exact. For this reason some people have insisted that social science is not science. Except for the prestige carried by the word, whether we call the study of society a science is not too important. It is merely a question of definition. If we mean by *science* the natural sciences only, then social science is not true science; or if we mean by *science* only the so-called exact sciences, then again social science is not included. If, however, we use *science* broadly, to include all systematic attempts to expand human knowledge by applying the scientific method, then social science must definitely be included in the scientific family. What is really important is that social scientists have discovered many significant relationships that are sufficiently dependable to add greatly to our understanding of social behavior and to serve as useful guides in dealing with some social problems.

THE METHODS OF SOCIAL SCIENCE

The basic procedures of the scientific method are as important in social science as in physical science. The social scientist, like the physical scientist, must observe carefully, classify and analyze his facts, make generalizations, and attempt to develop and test hypotheses to explain his generalizations. His problem, however, is often more difficult than that of

---

[4] It is true that the British returned the steel industry to private owners after it was taken over by the government the first time. However, the industry had been under government ownership for a very short time. The Labour government of Prime Minister Wilson nationalized it again in 1965, and a return to private ownership would now present greater problems.

the physical scientist. The facts gathered by the social scientist—for example, those concerning the cultures of different peoples—have similarities, but each fact may also be unique in significant respects. Facts of this kind are difficult to classify and interpret. Further, as we have already noted, the generalizations or laws that the social scientist can make are likely to be less definite and certain than those of the physical scientist.

The difficulty of discovering relatively exact laws that govern social life results from several circumstances. First, the things of greatest importance in our social life—satisfactions, welfare, social progress, democracy, and what you will—are not really measurable. Second, society is extremely complex. It is difficult and usually impossible to find and evaluate all the many causes of a given situation, though often we can discover the factors that were most important in bringing it about. Third, in every social situation there is the human element. Frequently the course of social events depends on the reactions of a few individuals who are leaders, and, except in routine situations, we can seldom predict individual behavior with complete certainty.

If the social scientist finally does succeed in finding uniformities or "laws" of social behavior and in setting up hypotheses to explain them, he faces still another difficulty—namely, that he can seldom employ controlled experiments to test his hypotheses. To a considerable extent the social scientist must substitute careful observation and the mental process

"There's an ethnic group waiting to see you about quick solutions to mounting problems."

of abstraction for experiments. He abstracts from a given situation some one factor in order to consider what effect it would have if acting alone. In order to do this, he imagines that any other factors present remain constant or inert. He asks, for example, such a question as, If other factors affecting economic life remained constant, what would be the economic effect of raising tariff rates on imports?

A social scientist who has a thorough knowledge of a situation may correctly calculate the effect of a given causal factor by assuming that all other things remain equal. However, to reach correct conclusions by this method, he must be both competent and painstaking. Even then the dangers of error are very great. If anything, there is more need for competence in the social scientist than in the physical scientist. The theories of a physical scientist can often be proved right or wrong by experiments, but this is seldom true of those of the social scientist. An unfortunate result is that it is easier in social science than in physical science to be needlessly vague, to perpetuate errors, and to cover up incompetence.

The social scientist also has more difficulty than the physical scientist in being objective. Because he deals with human beings, of whom he himself is one, he finds it hard to put aside his own likes and dislikes, his sympathies, prejudices, and frustrations. As a result he sometimes falls into the trap of trying to justify his own hopes, beliefs, or prejudices instead of really seeking to discover the truth. We should always be on guard against those who pose as social scientists but in fact substitute propaganda and charisma for objectivity and competence.

The Historical Method. Because most social developments—such as the government of the United States—have unique characteristics, in order to understand them as fully as possible the social scientist must rely heavily on a study of their historical background. We can never understand completely how any historical situation came to exist, because there are limits to our historical knowledge and because causes become increasingly complex and uncertain as we trace them further into the past. We can, however, make both historic events and present social situations much more intelligible by tracing the principal past developments that seem to have been directly significant in bringing them about.

We have noted that history never really repeats itself. Nevertheless, present and past situations often have such striking similarities that a knowledge of the past can give us insights into present situations and sometimes into future trends.

The Case Method. Writers on the methodology of social research have devoted a great deal of attention to the case method, its characteristics, its variations, the uses it can serve, its advantages and its limitations. Here we shall only attempt to state its basic nature. A *case study* involves making a detailed examination and analysis of a particular problem situation. This might be a ghetto, a criminal gang, a disorganized family, or the social structure of a particular community. A case study can be intended to discover how to bring about desirable changes in a particular problem situation, for example, to find the most effective ways of upgrading or rehabilitating a given slum area. But more often, as the name implies, the chief purpose of a case study is to throw light on many similar situations that exist in a society. The hope is that an understanding of one or a few cases will throw light on the others and thus aid in meeting the various social problems they present. Naturally, the case or cases selected should be typical of the group they purport to represent.

But such a requirement can be a limiting factor in the usefulness of the case study method. Suppose one wanted to make a study of the class structure of American society as a whole. Obviously, it would be easier to select as cases for study several relatively small and isolated cities in various sections of the country. But it is questionable whether these would give us a true picture for the country as a whole, because today a great proportion of our people live in large metropolitan areas where the class structure is likely to be much more complex than in smaller and more isolated communities. However, to study and describe in detail the class structure of such an area may be prohibitively difficult and expensive, and therefore impractical.

The Comparative and the Cross-cultural Methods. The *comparative* method has been employed by many social scientists in their attempts to gain a better understanding of the nature of human societies. Formerly they often compared one society with another in the hope of discovering evolutionary sequences in the development of human institutions, that is, patterns of social development or progress that would be universal. For example, it was sometimes assumed that there were definite stages in the development of governmental institutions, and it was thought that these stages could be discovered by studying societies that differed in the level of their development. Today this attempt to find patterns of social evolution that can be applied to all societies has been largely abandoned.

However, comparison of different societies still plays an important role in anthropological studies through what is called the *cross-cultural method.* This consists in making detailed studies of the culture patterns of a number of societies for the purpose of comparing the different ways in which their people meet similar needs. George P. Murdock and his associates have been especially active in developing such studies, and at present they are available for several hundred primitive societies. They sometimes show surprising similarities in the cultural traits of widely separated peoples who appear to have had no direct or indirect contacts with one another.

Comparison of the characteristics of different societies involves problems. At times, it is difficult to decide whether two or more societies are independent or should be treated as one. Another problem involves definitions. If we are comparing the family institution in different societies we must define "family" broadly enough to cover cultural variations, yet specifically enough to make comparisons meaningful. Sociologists do not always agree on just what a family is. Again, if we are comparing unemployment in urban-industrial societies we must agree on what we mean by "unemployment." Different countries define the concept differently for the purpose of counting or estimating the number of workers unemployed.[5]

The Use of Statistics. Though the use of *statistics* can scarcely be called a method of studying society and its problems, statistics are of special importance to the social scientist because they provide him with certain types of information that he needs when he attempts to understand many social relationships and processes. Statistics do not enable us to measure directly such basic social values as good citizenship, happiness, or welfare. However, statistics are useful in measuring numerous factors that underlie social life; for example, the size of the population of a country, or the number of families whose incomes fall below some level that we set as the minimum for decent and healthful living. Statistical relationships also give us many insights into social problems. If we find that the proportion of boys in reformatories who come from broken homes is substantially greater than the proportion of boys in the population at large who come from such homes, this suggests that broken homes may be an important factor contributing to juvenile delinquency. But statistics must always be interpreted with care, for it is often easy to read into them conclusions they do not justify. Also, it is sometimes possible to manipulate them so that they appear to show what we want them to.

Over the years increasing use has been made of statistics to measure the results of social activity and to discover trends. For example, national income and product statistics, issued regularly by the Department of Commerce since 1929, give us a great deal of information about the level of economic activity in the United States and the directions in which changes are taking place. Another important use of statistics is to test theories and discover relationships. This is illustrated by the new science of *econometrics,* which attempts to employ mathematical-statistical research for testing and developing economic theories. The use of statistics has been greatly facilitated by the introduction of computers, which make it possible to process statistics quickly into the arrangements most useful to the research scientist.

For some time the use of *surveys* has been taking on greater importance as a means of gathering special types of statistical information. Workers are sent out to question the people in a certain group on such matters as their incomes, their beliefs on certain issues, or the political candidate for whom they intend to vote; or perhaps questionnaires are mailed with

[5] Gideon Sjoberg and Roger Nett, *A Methodology for Social Research,* New York, Harper & Row, Publishers, 1968, pp. 134–136.

a request to fill them in and return them. If the group being surveyed is large, questioning is likely to be limited to a representative sample, as is the case with the Gallup or Harris public opinion polls.

The Interdisciplinary Approach. Modern industrial societies and their problems are becoming increasingly complex; and since no one person today can master all the social sciences (or even one of them completely), increasing emphasis is being placed on the need for an interdisciplinary approach to many social problems. This sometimes means that a group of social scientists with different specialties will work together on a certain problem not all of whose aspects any one of the group fully understands. For some problems, such as those concerned with pollution, it may even be necessary to call in a physical scientist, a biological scientist, a geologist, and an engineer.

In concluding this discussion of the methods of social science, it is worth noting that, though few social relationships can be reduced to exact and invariable "laws," human beings in large groups everywhere show great likenesses of behavior under conditions which are really similar. Thus there is reason to believe that we can, through systematic study and research, greatly increase our understanding of the nature and development of human societies; and, hopefully, this may ultimately lead to greater tolerance and cooperation between diverse groups and between nations.

SOCIAL SCIENCE AND SOCIAL CONTROL

There are many people who believe that the social sciences are lagging far behind the natural sciences. They point out not only that social science has no exact laws but also that it has failed to eliminate many of our great social evils, including such conditions as racial discrimination, crime, poverty, and war. They imply that social scientists have failed to accomplish what might reasonably have been expected of them. However, such critics are usually unaware of the real nature of social science, of its special problems and basic limitations. For example, they forget that the solution of a social problem requires not only knowledge but also the ability to influence people. Even if the social scientist knows the procedures that should be followed to achieve social betterment, he is seldom in a position to control social action. For that matter, even a dictator finds that there are limits on his power to change society.

In modern times three elements, among others, compound the problems we face: (1) the population explosion, (2) the rapidity of technological change, and (3) instant communication. Today sheer numbers of people create almost insuperable problems; and these are increased by the desire of people for all the comforts and luxuries that modern technology offers and by the rapidity with which developments in one part of the world become known in others through radio, TV, and the movies. People in the poorer countries, who formerly knew little about life in the richer ones, become envious and frustrated. At the same time, we in the more fortunate countries learn quickly of the misery in other parts of the world, as well as that of some people in our own countries, and we feel guilty and conscience stricken. All this presents a great challenge to social scientists because the only hope of solving social problems is through study, competent research, and effective communication of findings to the public and especially to the people who have the greatest influence on public opinion and public policy.

As commonly used by sociologists, the term *social control* has an impersonal connotation. It refers to all the social processes that cause individuals and groups to adjust to one another and to behave in ways that are socially acceptable. But if we mean by social control *conscious* attempts to *improve* society, we raise the difficult questions of who is to decide what constitutes improvement and who is to do the controlling. If everyone tries to control everyone else, the result is futility and anarchy. On the other hand, to put control in the hands of a small, self-perpetuating, elite group or of a dictator, is contrary to the basic ideals of a free and democratic society such as our own. True, majority decisions made at

(Drawing by Lorenz; © 1969 *The New Yorker Magazine, Inc.*)

free elections will not please everyone, but the alternatives are likely to be much less attractive.

If democracy is to succeed, most people, including major minority groups, must have an interest in its success. They must also have some tolerance of the opinions of others; some recognition of the problems of others; and a desire to treat all citizens justly. If such a situation can be created and maintained in a society, democracy is likely to prove workable. There will still be differences of opinion and different political parties, but if good will prevails, compromises can be made and respected; and needed social action can be carried on cooperatively and by mutual agreement.

One of the great problems in a democracy is to get the majority of people to reach substantial agreement on the major policies that should be followed to create a better society. Social scientists can aid in bringing about this agreement by helping people to understand the issues, the difficulties involved, and the possible steps to a solution. If we express social objectives in sufficiently general terms, agreement is not so hard to obtain. Most people would like to have a heaven-on-earth characterized by peace and good will toward men, with freedom, justice, security, health, and happiness for all. But when it comes to drawing up a blueprint for reaching these objectives, disagreements and obstacles become apparent. Social scientists themselves, even the ablest, are not always in complete agreement on either what our specific social goals should be or on how we can best work toward them.

In any case, the function of social science and of those who practice it is not primarily to determine social objectives. Its major function is to discover how our objectives can be achieved. The determination of the goals themselves—our social values—is not a scientific problem but one having to do with our likes and dislikes, our esthetic concepts, our moral standards, and our philosophical and religious beliefs. We shall have more to say about social values in the following chapter.

Terms to Be Understood

scientific knowledge
natural science
the humanities
history
anthropology
cultural anthropology
biological
   anthropology
economics
political science

sociology
psychology
social psychology
scientific method
scientific law
hypothesis
scientific theory
Boyle's law
experimental
   method

historical method
case method
comparative method
cross-cultural method
statistics
econometrics
survey
interdisciplinary
   approach
social control

Questions for Review and Discussion

1. What is scientific knowledge?
2. Distinguish between the three major fields of human knowledge.
3. Name the principal social sciences and define the field with which each deals.
4. Why would it have been difficult to carry on scientific investigations in primitive societies or even in the Middle Ages?
5. State the six steps in the scientific method as they are listed in this chapter.
6. What basic assumption underlies the use of the scientific method?
7. What is the experimental method?
8. Why is it difficult to formulate precise laws in the field of social science?
9. In what sense is social science scientific?
10. Why is it often impossible to study social problems by means of the experimental method?
11. Explain the ways in which the problems of social science differ from those of the exact natural sciences.
12. What are the advantages of the interdisciplinary approach to the study of many social problems?
13. Explain the nature of the problem of social control, and the relation of social science and the social scientist to this problem.

For Further Study

Berelson, Bernard, ed., *The Behavioral Sciences Today,* New York, Basic Books, Inc., 1963. Chap. 6: "Methods of Research Used by American Social Scientists" by Samuel A. Stouffer.

Blalock, Hubert M., Jr., *Introduction to Social Research,* paperback, Englewood Cliffs, N.J., Prentice-Hall, Inc., 1970.

Bronowski, Jacob, *Science and Human Values,* rev. ed., Torchbook paperback, New York, Harper & Row, Publishers, 1965.

Chase, Stuart, *The Proper Study of Mankind,* rev. ed., Colophon paperback, New York, Harper & Row, Publishers, 1963.

Chinoy, Ely S., *Sociological Perspective: Basic Concepts and Their Application,* rev. ed., New York, Random House, Inc., 1968.

Ford, Clellan Stearns, ed., *Cross-Cultural Approaches: Readings in Comparative Research,* New Haven, Conn., HRAF Press, 1967.

Foster, George M., *Applied Anthropology,* paperback, Boston, Little, Brown & Company, 1969.

Kardiner, Abram, and Edward Preble, *They Studied Man,* Mentor paperback, New York, New American Library, Inc., 1963. Brief accounts of the contributions of ten important scientists to our understanding of man.

MacKenzie, Norman, ed., *A Guide to the Social Sciences,* paperback, New York, New American Library, Inc., 1968.

Myrdal, Gunnar, *Objectivity in Social Research,* New York, Pantheon Books, Inc., 1969.

Nadge, John, *The Tools of Social Science,* Anchor paperback, New York, Doubleday & Company, Inc., 1965.

Pelto, Pertti J., *Anthropological Research: The Structure of Inquiry,* New York, Harper & Row, Publishers, 1970.

Phillips, Bernard, *Social Research: Strategy and Tactics,* 2d ed., New York, The Macmillan Company, 1971.

Prince-Williams, D. R., ed., *Cross-Cultural Studies,* paperback, Baltimore, Penguin Books, Inc., 1970.

Senn, Peter, *Social Science and Its Methods,* paperback, Boston, The Holbrook Press, Inc., 1970.

Simon, Julian Lincoln, *Basic Research Methods in Social Science,* New York, Random House, Inc., 1969.

Sjoberg, Gideon, *A Methodology for Social Research,* New York, Harper & Row, Publishers, 1968.

Smelser, Neil J., and James Davis, eds., *Sociology,* paperback, Englewood Cliffs, N.J., Prentice-Hall, Inc., 1970. Eight authorities report on the present status and future needs of sociology.

Chapter 3

The Role

of Culture

a s we noted in Chapter 1, man is not endowed at birth with complex instincts.
Practically all human behavior must be
learned from other human beings, and the
behavior that an individual learns in any
given group is part of the culture of that
group. Culture includes not only patterns
of behavior as such but also the attitudes
and beliefs that motivate behavior. Culture creates human beings and human
societies as we know them. At the same
time, by slow accumulation over many
generations, culture is the product of
human societies and of the individuals
who compose them.

THE UNIQUENESS OF HUMAN CULTURE

Only man can create true culture. The social insects have developed highly complex societies, but these are based purely on instinct. Many animals live in social groups that have a leader and some rudimentary organization, but animals cannot transmit abstract ideas to one another, nor can they transmit experience and knowledge from generation to generation, constantly adding to its quantity and complexity.

Faint Suggestions of Culture Among Animals. Anticipations of culture can be found in the animal world. Chimpanzees can solve some simple problems and one chimpanzee can learn by watching another. Many animals have some power to learn from others of their kind. Some birds, it seems, can modify their instinctive song patterns by imitating a recorded bird song, provided they are exposed to it long enough while young. Further, once the new type of song has been learned, older birds will influence younger ones so that a kind of cultural tradition is carried on. However, such learning is purely imitative and has little relation to the transmission of ideas and complex modes of behavior by human beings.

The Role of Language. We have already pointed out that the ability to use language is one of the basic factors that set man apart from other living creatures. This ability seems to explain, more than any other single human characteristic, the development and transmission of culture. Man's use of language is essential, not only for transmitting ideas but also for carrying on abstract reasoning. Modern psychologists question whether our typically human reasoning processes would be possible if we did not have word symbols to stand for abstract concepts. Individuals who know two languages well are keenly aware that they can carry on a chain of thought in either of these languages, but not without the use of a language. However, language is not the sole explanation of culture, for some cultural elements, like the use of simple tools and the construction of rude huts or other primitive shelters, could probably be transmitted without it.

The Organic Basis of Man's Capacity for Culture. We noted earlier that the specific physical or organic basis of man's capacity to create culture is unknown and that the human brain appears to differ from that of a chimpanzee or gorilla only by being larger and presumably more complex. Yet it seems probable that somewhere in this larger brain lie the secrets of man's power to invent and use a variety of tools, to solve relatively difficult problems, and to transmit ideas by means of speech. Chimpanzees have vocal organs similar to those of men, but they will not even attempt to imitate human speech. We may suppose that when certain areas of the brain had developed sufficiently in the process of evolution, human beings gradually acquired the capacity to develop, learn, and transmit not only language but also the other elements of culture. We do have some evidence that seems to support such an assumption; for example, injury to a certain area of the brain destroys the power of speech.

THE CONTENT OF CULTURE

The character of any culture may be found in such elements as its folkways and mores, its institutions and the concepts that motivate them, its technology, its material products, its beliefs, and its values. Let us consider briefly some of these elements of culture.

Folkways and Mores. *Folkways* are the simple, everyday customs of a group that represent the usual ways of behaving. Folkways change slowly, and many of them are very persistent. In our society it is customary to sleep on a bed, to eat at a table, to handle our food with knives, forks, and spoons rather than chopsticks or our fingers, and to greet an acquaintance on the street. All these are folkways. Folkways are established customs to which we attach little moral significance. We may think that people who violate them are odd or uncouth, but we do not completely ostracize such persons or send them to prison. That not everyone treats folkways with respect is illustrated by the following verse of unknown origin:

> *I eat my peas with honey;*
> *I've done it all my life.*
> *It makes the peas taste funny*
> *But keeps them on the knife.*

The *mores* are types of behavior considered essential to the welfare of the group. They involve moral judgments by society as to what is right and wrong. They relate to such important aspects of life as honesty and fairness in dealing with others, relationships between the sexes, safety of life and property, and loyalty to the nation. Not all violations of the mores are regarded as equally serious, but for the most extreme violations very severe legal penalties have been provided. In modern societies, for example, a common punishment for premeditated murder is death.

The following is a simple example of the difference between folkways and mores. If a businessman wore a tuxedo every day to his office, he would be violating the folkways, and he would doubtless be considered odd or eccentric. On the other hand, if he went to his office without any clothes at all, he would be violating the mores and would soon find himself in trouble, perhaps even in jail or a mental hospital.

Social Institutions. *A social institution is an established, complex pattern of behavior in which a number of persons participate in order to further important group interests.* Institutions are usually organized around some central interest or need. The church is the institution that enables people to express their religious beliefs by joining others in worshipping God in customary ways. The school provides for formal education of the young. The family, one of the most basic of all social institutions, provides for stable, socially approved unions between persons of the opposite sex and thus assures the care and training of children. The family also helps meet many of the needs of daily life, such as those for shelter, food, close companionship, and affection.

We have defined the term *social institution* broadly to include any complex pattern of behavior that furthers an important group interest. If we accept such a broad definition, we can fit almost every cultural trait of a society into some institutional pattern, so that the sum total of the culture of a group is much the same thing as the sum total of its social institutions.

Following the definition we have given, an excellent example of a social institution is *language*. A language is a complex pattern of behavior common to all the people of a certain group and serving their need for communication. The people who speak a language use their lips, tongues, and vocal cords in certain ways to produce a great number of special sounds, or words. These have arbitrary but well-established meanings and are combined in customary ways to enable the members of the group to transmit to one another a great variety of information and ideas.

Often, however, when we think of social institutions, we are not thinking just of a generalized pattern of behavior, such as is involved in using a language. Rather, we are thinking of organized groups of people in which different individuals perform different functions and occupy positions that differ in the power and prestige they confer.

If we have in mind social institutions of this type, we can, following the eminent sociologist William Graham Sumner, analyze their structure into four closely related elements. These are (1) personnel, (2) equipment,

4. Mask of Tutankhamen. This funerary mask is believed to be a likeness of the boy-king who ruled Egypt 3,300 years ago. The mask is life-size and made of beaten gold inlaid with semi-precious stones. (Photo taken by author in National Museum, Cairo.)

(3) organization, and (4) ritual. By *personnel* Sumner meant the members of the group especially qualified and duly selected to perform certain services. Teachers in educational institutions and the officers of business corporations will serve as examples. By *equipment* he meant the material and nonmaterial possessions of the group, with the aid of which the purposes of the institution are carried out. Taking the church as an illustration, the material equipment includes buildings, pews, pulpits, and Bibles or other religious books. The nonmaterial possessions include the history of the church and its basic beliefs, or creed. The *organization* of an institution consists of the various special relationships of the members to one another and of the ways in which they arrange and use the equipment. Organization usually requires some concentration of authority. Certain individuals hold positions of authority, others of subordination, and the positions people hold greatly influence their relations with one another and with the group. The *ritual* of an institution consists of the customs and regulations that determine the behavior of members when they perform their various prescribed roles.

Status and Role. Insofar as institutions offer the individual clearly defined channels for his social activities, they simplify his life. From birth, he is identified with such institutions as the family, the church, and the state. Later on he becomes identified with schools, business or professional organizations, clubs, and political parties. Because he plays a part in various institutions throughout his lifetime, much of his social behavior is prescribed for him. Within each institution the individual's rights and duties are usually clearly defined. However, they vary as his social position or *status* changes. For instance, the child is supported and protected by the family, but when he grows to adulthood, he is expected to support himself and protect the interests of others. Likewise, the child gets special protection and schooling from the state, but when he grows up, he may be required to serve in the armed forces. As an adult he also has the responsibility of voting, paying taxes, and helping to guide the policies of the state. And so the individual at each stage in his life accepts different *roles*. That is, he regulates his behavior along given lines, according to what is expected of him, because of his status in each of the various institutions in which he participates.

Thus we see that the statuses and roles of an individual may vary widely during a lifetime. He is a child, a student, a husband, a father, a factory worker, a business executive, a judge, or the President of the United States; and in each of these statuses he is expected to play a certain role—that is, to follow a certain customary and expected pattern of behavior.

The Material Products of Culture. Strictly speaking, culture is never material. It is in the minds and personalities of people. It is what they have learned from their social environment—attitudes, beliefs, knowledge, and ways of behaving. However, important in every culture is knowledge of how to produce and use a variety of material products, including food, clothing, houses, tools, machines, and works of art. Such

"A thing of beauty—and a joy until planned obsolescence does its work."
(Courtesy Ed Fisher. Copyright 1969 *Saturday Review, Inc.*)

products of human skill and effort are sometimes called *culture objects,* or *artifacts.* However, they are more than mere expressions of the culture that produces them; they become essential to its functioning, because without them people could not carry on the necessary activities of daily life. This is strikingly true in a modern industrial society. Such a society would be paralyzed if it could not use railroads, automobiles, telephone systems, power plants, and factories with their machines.

Common Needs Met by All Cultures. Certain basic needs and desires are common to people in all societies and are in some degree provided for by every culture. The particular ways in which different cultures satisfy these needs may vary greatly. Yet sometimes behavior patterns developed by widely separated groups show marked similarities. Such similarities are probably the result not only of the common biological nature of all human beings but also of common elements in the natural environments of people living in different parts of the world. But whether or not the ways of meeting needs are similar, certain needs are found in all societies, and they may be classified as follows:

1. The care and rearing of children. In every society this need is met by some type of organized family group, though for some children an orphanage or a *kibbutz*[1] may be substituted.

[1]A kibbutz is an Israeli farm community in which the community as a whole provides care centers for all children. Parents see their children at certain specified hours each day.

5. Paintings in Hall of the Bulls in a Cave at Lascaux, France. A fine example of the art of the prehistoric cave-dwellers of Europe. Above some of the paintings, the smudges from the artists' lamps can still be seen. The paintings are now preserved by climate-control measures, which include triple air-lock doors and a limit on visitors. (Courtesy the French Government Tourist Office.)

2. The need of each individual to have a recognized place, or status, in his society so that he feels secure and can behave in such ways as to meet the expectations of the group.
3. Needs and desires for essentials such as food, shelter, and clothing.
4. The regulation and safeguarding of property.
5. Group action to maintain order and serve the common welfare. When arrangements for group action are sufficiently formalized, they are called *government*.
6. Explanations of man, the universe, and the meaning of life. These explanations usually resort to the supernatural: magic, mythology, religion.
7. Esthetic expression through such media as poetry, songs, instrumental music, dancing, painting, sculpture, and architecture.
8. Communication. All social groups have a language, without which human cultures as we know them could not exist.
9. Possibly defense and aggression. Some more or less isolated non-literate peoples do not engage in warfare, but the cultures of most societies include patterns of behavior for carrying on war.

Contrasts Between Cultures. In our culture, children are brought up in families in which one man is married to one woman; in certain other cultures a man may have a number of wives and a group of children by each of them. In primitive societies food and clothing are produced with the aid of simple hand weapons and tools, but in modern America we produce them with the aid of complex power-operated machines. In some primitive societies—for example, in that of the Camaiura Indians, pictured in Photo 6—little or no clothing is worn. Archaic tribal societies often differ from one another greatly, but unless they are brought into contact with powerful outside influences, they tend to be relatively stable. On the other hand, industrial societies are much more subject to change. In them people's wants tend to multiply rapidly, and likewise do the products with which to satisfy them. As we go from one culture to another, family relations, economic activities, government, religion, and art take on an endless variety of forms.

Culture and the Individual. As we noted in Chapter 1, though we are all in large part products of our cultural environment, no two persons will

6. Meeting of Old and New. Primitive Camaiura Indians of the Amazon region running from bush to watch Brazilian Air Force Beechcraft land on a wilderness strip, one of many hacked from the jungle in recent years to help open up the back country. The shirt on the native was traded for bow and arrows by a *Time* correspondent who had hiked to the Camaiura village. (Courtesy *Time* Magazine. Photo by Anthony Linck.)

have exactly the same personal experiences. Furthermore, they will not inherit biologically the same physical and nervous constitutions, and these inherited differences will cause them to react differently to many of the elements in their cultural environment. As E. Adamson Hoebel points out, the personality of the individual is a blend resulting from (1) the patterns of his culture, (2) his unique experiences in contact with the physical world and other people, and (3) his unique physical and nervous constitution. [2]

Cultural Evolution. Cultures as we know them have evolved through a long process of progressive change, a process that is sometimes called *cultural evolution*. Any modern culture is largely the product of the originality and initiative of great numbers of individuals in times past, though in most cases the contribution of any one person has been so small that it cannot even be identified. Sometimes the introduction of new culture traits has resulted in the displacement or modification of old ones, but often the new are merely added on to the old, and thus over the ages cultures have tended to become increasingly complex.

Sometimes changes take place that are not made consciously and are so gradual that the members of a society are scarcely aware of them. But more often change results from the conscious application of new discoveries, and the adoption of new inventions; or perhaps from the copying of the customs, techniques, and institutions of other social groups, a process which is known as *culture diffusion*.

We shall have more to say about discovery, invention, and culture diffusion when we come to the chapter that deals with social change and social problems.

SOCIAL VALUES

Social values are the things that a given society considers desirable because they are believed to contribute to the good life and the general welfare. In our cultural environment honesty, courage, justice, and respect for law and for the rights of others are highly regarded social values. So also, on a somewhat different level, are financial success, health, and education.

The desires of individuals tend to reflect the values stressed in the societies to which they belong. Our society is often said to be materialistic. This may not be a wholly correct characterization, yet it contains an element of truth. In modern America we have great respect for success in business, and we also lay great stress on the importance of raising standards of living and abolishing poverty. Because we put such a high rating on material welfare, many of our people have come to regard the earning of

[2] E. Adamson Hoebel, "The Nature of Culture," in *Man, Culture, and Society*, edited by Harry L. Shapiro, New York, Oxford University Press, 1956, p. 181.

more and more money as their major life objective. Others, of course, look on money merely as a means to the achievement of more important objectives. These more important objectives may involve such "higher" social values as the education of one's children; charity; the appreciation and encouragement of art, science, and religion; and the rendering of public service.

Social values are the motive power that make institutions function effectively. The church, for example, will be a dynamic force in society only so long as a large portion of its members firmly believe in God and have faith that the church is an essential instrument for personal salvation and the creation of a good society. Where religion has a strong hold on a society, it is usually a conservative force tending to preserve established moral values.

Social values are relative rather than absolute. They often vary widely from one culture to another, and each individual acquires from his own culture his ideas of what is desirable or undesirable, good or bad, right or wrong. In some societies sex relations before marriage are regarded as a cardinal sin; in others they are permitted or even expected. In some societies women must be very plump to be regarded as beautiful; in others they must be rather slim. In most if not all modern societies, the killing of infants is regarded with horror, but some nonliterate tribal societies regard it as commendable under certain circumstances—for instance, if the infants are physically defective.

In every society, the great majority of people tend to take for granted the firmly established social values of their own culture. When they come into contact with other cultures having other values, they judge these foreign values as good or bad, right or wrong, according to whether such values agree with or differ from their own value system. Missionaries to certain South Sea Islands were shocked to find that the native women wore no clothing above the waist. When they converted the natives to Christianity, they also converted the women to wearing Mother Hubbards, a shapeless type of house dress that kept their bodies well covered. To the missionaries this increase in modesty seemed a great gain. From a health standpoint it may have been very unfortunate. In a tropical rainy climate, these Mother Hubbards were wet much of the time, and today some medical authorities believe that this contributed to a rapid rise in the death rate from tuberculosis.

Cultural Relativism and Ethnocentrism. The doctrine of *cultural relativism* was accepted by most anthropologists many years ago. It asserts, as Ruth Benedict once said, that all cultures are "equally valid." Today few students of society would question that any culture that has enabled a group to meet its basic needs and to survive over a long period of time is worthy of respect, as are the individuals who practice its customs and follow its moral precepts. To understand other cultures, we must try to look at them through the eyes of those who have been brought up under

7. Ruins of Machu Picchu, the "Lost City of the Incas." Hiram Bingham, a Yale anthropologist, discovered it in 1911 in a remote area of the Andes in Peru. (Photo by author.)

their influence rather than through our own eyes. If we do this we may find that they meet needs that we have failed to recognize. For example, we may discover that to someone raised in a polygamous society this form of marriage has merits we were not aware of. But if we extend the doctrine of cultural relativism by asserting that every established culture pattern serves the needs of the group that has developed it as well or better than any other would, we raise troublesome questions. Does a culture in which ritual human sacrifices have a prominent role serve the welfare of its people as well as one without this practice? Or does a culture in which slavery is an established and accepted institution serve as well as one in which all men are free? The late Robert Redfield, who was Distinguished Service Professor and head of the Department of Anthropology at the University of Chicago, wrote an interesting article on cultural relativism in which he suggested that if our concern is human welfare, there may sometimes be good reasons for preferring one way of thinking or acting to another way.[3]

[3] Elgin F. Hunt and Jules Karlin, eds., *Society Today and Tomorrow,* 2d ed., paperback, New York, The Macmillan Company, 1967. See therein "Cultural Relativism and Social Values" by Robert Redfield.

The tendency to judge other cultures by one's own culture and its standards is called *ethnocentrism*. It is the belief of a group that its people and its way of life are superior to all others. An extreme example in modern times was the Nazi doctrine that the Germans are a super race. A high degree of ethnocentrism seems to have prevailed in most nonliterate tribal societies, and it is obvious that the attitudes represented have by no means completely disappeared in modern times. Even social scientists often have difficulty when they try to escape from them in order to study other cultures from an objective point of view.

When the whole human race consisted of a great number of relatively small nonliterate tribal societies, ethnocentrism might have had survival value for some by giving them confidence in the superiority of their own people and their own way of life. But in the modern world, survival, in the long run, is likely to depend upon achieving understanding and cooperation among races, peoples, and nations. This leaves no room for the cultivation of ethnocentrism, which can only result in misunderstanding, prejudice, ill feeling, and conflict.

Our Approach to the Study of Society.   In this book we are primarily concerned with the nature of modern American society. Most of the discussion is therefore centered on our own culture and its basic values and on the problems that arise in connection with efforts to achieve these values. However, we can understand our own society better if we see it in perspective. Hence, from time to time attention is called to other societies and cultures, to the characteristics common to all cultures, and to the differences that distinguish them.

Since it is not the function of science to determine social values, we shall for the most part assume the validity of the basic ideals of our own democratic society; and, as occasion demands, we shall attempt to clarify these ideals. But our principal efforts will be concerned with giving a picture of the general character of American society. We shall attempt to explain its values and its social institutions. We shall also discuss its failures to achieve its goals and the frustration and conflict that are sometimes the result; and we shall consider the nature of its major problems and explore the possibilities of solving them through social action.

Terms to Be Understood

folkways	ritual	cultural evolution
mores	status	culture diffusion
social institution	role	social values
language	culture object	cultural relativism
personnel	artifact	ethnocentrism
equipment	kibbutz	
organization	government	

Questions for Review and Discussion

1. Does culture determine the behavior and personality of individuals, or do individuals determine the nature of culture? Explain.
2. Why does culture develop in human societies but not in animal groups?
3. Distinguish carefully between folkways and mores.
4. Explain the nature and functions of social institutions.
5. Explain what is meant by each of the following as aspects of a social institution: personnel, equipment, organization, ritual.
6. What is the relationship between culture and the material products of human effort?
7. What are the basic human needs that must be provided for by every culture?
8. What three factors influence the personality of every individual?
9. How does cultural evolution take place?
10. What are social values? Why do they differ from one society to another?
11. Explain the theory that supports the doctrine of cultural relativism.
12. What are the disadvantages of ethnocentrism?
13. Why are modern industrial societies more likely to lose faith in many of their traditional social values than were earlier societies?
14. Have young people today lost faith in most of the traditional values of Western societies? Defend your answer.
15. From what point of view does this book approach the study of social science?

For Further Study

Beck, Philip K., ed., *Culture Shock: A Reader in Modern Cultural Anthropology,* paperback, New York, Alfred A. Knopf, Inc., 1970.

Benedict, Ruth, *Patterns of Culture,* Mentor paperback, New York, New American Library, Inc., 1964.

Hammond, Peter B., ed., *Cultural and Social Anthropology: Selected Readings,* paperback, New York, The Macmillan Company, 1964.

Kluckhohn, Clyde, *Mirror for Man,* Premier paperback, New York, Fawcett World Library, 1959.

Linton, Ralph, *The Tree of Culture,* Vintage paperback, New York, Alfred A. Knopf, Inc., 1959.

Mead, Margaret, *Growing Up in New Guinea,* paperback, New York, Apollo Editions, Inc., 1962.

Montagu, M. F. Ashley, ed., *Culture: Man's Adaptive Dimension,* paperback, New York, Oxford University Press, 1968.

Murdock, George Peter, *Culture and Society: Twenty-four Essays,* paperback, New York, Pitman Publishing Corporation, 1969.

———, *Outline of World Cultures,* 3d ed., paperback, New York, Taplinger Publishing Company, Inc., 1964.

Chapter 4

Culture,

the Natural

Environment,

and the

Pollution

Problem

though cultures are created by human beings through association with one another, it is clear that the culture of any group of people must in some degree be adjusted to their natural environment. Whether clothing is worn (or how much is worn) and what type of shelter is developed will depend in part on the climate. Furthermore, the materials used in making clothing and constructing shelters must be chosen from those found in the environment of the group or from materials that can be produced in that environment, unless transportation has been developed to the point of making it practical to bring goods in from outside areas. All the material aspects of culture are influenced and limited by the character of the natural environment. On the other hand, man's efforts to satisfy his material wants can also change his natural environment, sometimes in ways that greatly damage it. But it is not only his material culture that is influenced by his natural surroundings. These also exert an influence on his attitudes, beliefs, and modes of artistic expression. For example, the religion and art of any people are likely to be profoundly influenced by whether their habitat is in the mountains, on the desert, or by the sea. However, religion and art are less dependent on the natural environment than are the technological and economic aspects of culture.

The Meaning of Environment. The *environment* of man consists of all the external influences that impinge upon the human organism. These influences exert their effects through physical stimuli that produce sights, sounds, tastes, smells, and other bodily sensations. It is these sensations that make man aware of his environment, and it is through them that he is able to interpret this environment and react to it.

We can better understand man's total environment if we separate the human elements in it from those that are nonhuman. The elements in our surroundings that are human or of human origin we call the *social environment*. The nonhuman elements constitute the *natural environment*. The general character of our social environment depends chiefly on the culture of the group to which we belong. The character of our natural environment depends primarily on the climate, water resources, soil, topography, plant and animal life, and the mineral resources of the part of the world we live in. However, once man, especially civilized man, has lived in an area for a long period of time, he is certain to have made changes, for better or worse, in his environment. It then becomes difficult to draw a sharp line between the man-made physical environment and some aspects of the natural environment.

The Ecological Balance. *Ecology,* a term in popular use today, is the science concerned with the interactions between living things and their environment. The environment of each species of organism includes not only the inanimate world but also all other living species that affect it directly or indirectly. It includes the population density of its own members and the character of their behavior.

Human ecology deals with the way in which human societies adjust to their environments. It treats the processes by which populations adapt to their surroundings, taking into account the technology and the types of social organization by which adjustment is achieved. Human ecology applies some of the findings of the biological sciences to problems dealt with by the social sciences.

In the world of nature there is normally an *ecological balance*. Each plant or animal species, with its own characteristics and needs, has found ways of adjusting to its environment and surviving. But other species, which have, likewise, adjusted to the environment, prevent it from expanding in numbers indefinitely and from crowding them out. Most species depend on other species for food and/or for meeting other needs. Though the natural ecological balance is not absolutely static, normally it changes slowly over very long periods of time. New species that can make superior adjustments evolve and may destroy or crowd out old species and render the latter extinct; or changes in climate may occur that some species cannot survive. Dinosaurs disappeared from the face of the earth ages ago and we are not quite sure why.

But in modern times man has brought rapid changes in the ecological balance in many parts of the world. Sometimes the results have been good from his point of view, but sometimes they have been almost disastrous. He introduced rabbits into Australia where, since they had no natural enemies, they multiplied by the millions and became a national problem. By building the St. Lawrence Seaway, man allowed lampreys to enter the Great Lakes, where they almost completely destroyed the whitefish. Unintentionally, he has brought insect pests from one part of the world to another; and since World War II, by using DDT to control insect pests, he has also destroyed or damaged desirable forms of life and has endangered human health. Today the possibility of bringing on truly disastrous ecological changes has been multiplied by the rising rate at which man is polluting his natural environment.

THE CULTURAL ENVIRONMENT

In earlier chapters we have emphasized that the personality of every human being is largely the product of his cultural environment. More accurately, his personality is the product of the interaction of his cultural environment with his original, biologically inherited nature. This is not to say that the natural environment or habitat plays no part whatever in shaping the personality of the individual. Its role, however, is a secondary one. As was said in substance earlier in this book, the reason that we think and behave like twentieth-century Americans, and not like Turks, Chinese, or Eskimos is that we have been brought up in constant contact with American culture rather than with the cultures of the Turks, Chinese, or Eskimos. Undoubtedly, the natural environment has had a strong influence on the cultures of all these groups, including our own, but natural environment is not an adequate explanation of the differences between these cultures.

Cultures change over the years in ways that we can never fully trace or completely understand. But whatever the reasons for cultural change, at any given time the extent to which a human group is able to utilize its natural environment depends largely on its culture. A primitive stone-age tribe may be surrounded by a wealth of mineral resources and be completely unaware of their existence. To such a group, coal, iron ore, petroleum, and other minerals are really not resources at all, for even if mineral outcroppings are readily visible, no one knows how to use them.

Even when the people of a society do know how to use certain resources, they are sometimes prevented from doing so by cultural beliefs or attitudes. Grazing may be prohibited on the slopes of a mountain that is regarded as sacred because it is the home of a god; or the killing of a certain animal for food may be forbidden because the people believe that it is their ancestor and inhabited by a sacred spirit. Again, it is said that for centuries the ancient Chinese knew of the existence of coal and that it would burn; yet they made no attempt to use it because they feared that mining would disturb the earth and thus displease the spirits of their ancestors. Even in modern America most people refuse to eat horse meat, not because horse meat is tough or unpleasant in flavor, but because our culture teaches us that it is not a proper food for human beings.

Importance of the Material Aspects of Culture. When we attempt to assess the importance of the cultural environment in shaping the character and behavior of individuals, we must remember that a large part of man's physical environment is actually cultural and not natural in its origins. This is especially true of modern industrial civilizations. The clothes that we wear, the houses we live in, the vehicles in which we travel, the factories and offices in which we work—all are man-made. The resident of a large modern city scarcely comes in contact with nature in its original state. The entire area of an urban center is likely to be covered by buildings, pavements, sidewalks, and carefully landscaped parks. True, the city dweller, if he chooses, can look for the stars at night; but usually he forgets about them, and often he cannot see them anyway because of smoke and dust in the air.

Man-Made Geographic Patterns. Even outside the cities man has greatly changed the surface of the earth in order to make better use of his natural environment. Everywhere in settled regions we can find man-made geographic patterns. In agricultural districts man has cut down forests, cleared lands, drained swamps, irrigated deserts, and constructed buildings and fences. Some of his projects have changed his physical environment over very wide areas. This is especially true of projects that have involved the construction of transportation, communication, and power facilities. Every country with an advanced technical culture is today covered by a complex network of roads, railroads, telephone and telegraph lines, and power lines. In some regions canals and dredged river channels are also found, or great dams that have created large lakes behind them.

THE NATURAL ENVIRONMENT

We have emphasized the importance of man's social environment and the wide range of cultural differences that are possible in any given type of natural environment. However, in the long run nature greatly influences the development of culture, and in some directions it sets rather rigid limits to the kinds of cultural adjustment that are possible. Whatever else the culture of a society may or may not do, it must enable people to adjust reasonably well to the physical conditions of the world around them. This means, as a minimum, that it must enable them to obtain sufficient food, clothing, and shelter for survival. Let us therefore examine briefly man's natural environment and its variations.

The natural environment of plants, animals, or men is sometimes called their *habitat*. By the habitat of a group of people we mean both the area in which they live and the natural conditions that prevail in that area. Differences in natural conditions from one area to another can be broadly classified as differences in climate, topography, and resources.

Climate. No aspect of the natural environment is more important than climate, and the most essential elements of climate are temperature and rainfall. Half the land area of the world has very little population, and some regions none at all, because the climate is either too dry, too wet, or too cold.

On the basis of temperature the earth is divided into three zones—the arctic, the temperate, and the tropical. Some arctic regions are sparsely populated by scattered primitive tribes; others have no population at all. In the areas where people can live, the short summers and long winters permit little or no agriculture, and hence existence must be maintained by hunting and fishing or by herding reindeer. In the temperate zones dense populations are often found. Here people depend for a livelihood principally on meat and grain products and on industry. It is in the temperate zones that we find the peoples who have made the greatest material progress. Some writers, such as Ellsworth Huntington, explain this by maintaining that temperate climates make people more energetic and increase their willingness to work. Sometimes dense populations are also found in the tropics. There they depend largely on raising products like rice, sugar, tea, cocoa, rubber, and bananas.

Rainfall is essential for the support of human populations because rain is the source of all fresh water, and water is necessary not only for the growing of crops but also for industry. Enterprises such as steel mills, paper mills, chemical plants, and mines require huge quantities of water. Rainfall varies greatly in different regions. Areas where it is less than eight or ten inches per year can support very few people because they do not have sufficient water for industry, agriculture, or even grazing. Occasionally, however, rivers or canals bring in water from a distance. Egypt, for example, has a very dry climate, but the Nile River supplies both agriculture and industry with water from regions far to the south, and with the aid of the Aswan Dam it will now supply water to a larger area of the country.

Areas where the annual rainfall is less than ten inches are found in central Australia, parts of Tibet and Mongolia, the Sahara, Arabia, the west coast of South America, and our own Southwest. By contrast, the average yearly rainfall in Java and parts of India is 100 or more inches, and in tropical seacoast Brazil it reaches 133 inches. Most temperate regions that are suitable for agriculture have an annual rainfall of from 20 to 90 inches per year, but cattle can sometimes be raised where the rainfall is only 8 or 10 inches.

Mountains, Plains, Rivers, and Oceans. The number of people an area can support depends not only on temperature and rainfall but also on the *topography* of the area, or its physical characteristics. Mountains are not favorable to either agriculture or industry. People tend to concentrate on lowlands—on the great fertile plains of the world and along river valleys. Rivers provide water for industries, and often they provide transportation routes. Even if rivers are not navigable, railroads and highways are easier to build along their valleys than through surrounding hills or mountains. Most of the great cities of the world—London, New York, Paris, Buenos Aires—are found along rivers, frequently on harbors formed at their mouths. Few large cities are built at high altitudes. Mexico City, at 8,000 feet, and La Paz, Bolivia, at 12,500 feet, are notable exceptions.

In earlier times the oceans were great mysteries. They were the end of the world, and no one knew what lay beyond them. Today they are still barriers, especially to invasion by massed armies, but even more they are routes for migration, communication, travel, and trade. In the last four hundred years whole continents have been settled by European emigrants travelling over the oceans. Today the oceans are regularly crossed by thousands of ships and planes following regular routes between the major centers of world commerce and travel. Ocean-borne commerce has become so important that it has caused large cities to develop around many of the good harbors of the world.

Natural Resources. *Natural resources consist of those gifts of nature that man can use for his own benefit,* but different regions vary greatly in the resources with which they are endowed. The known petroleum reserves of the world are largely concentrated in certain parts of North America, the Caribbean region, North Africa, and the Near East. Tin deposits are found chiefly in Malaya and Bolivia, nickel in Canada. Iron ore and coal are much more widely distributed, and yet countries like Ireland and Italy have practically none. Since iron, coal, and oil are resources important to the development of modern industry, any country that lacks them is definitely limited in its possibilities for economic growth.

Perhaps the most important of all natural resources is land suitable for the growth of forests and crops. Fertile farm land is especially essential to human welfare because it is on such land that the world depends for the great part of its food supply. The earliest of our great civilizations developed in areas well provided with fertile land—the flood plain of the Nile, the irrigated lowlands of Mesopotamia along the Tigris and Euphrates rivers, and the plains of China.

In a discussion of man's natural resources, we must not overlook the importance of wild life in the form of trees, plants, animals, fish, and insects. Not all this wild life falls into the category of natural resources. Many insects are pests from the human point of view. They annoy man, they spread human diseases, or they destroy crops. On the other hand, wild trees, plants, animals, and fish, and sometimes even insects, provided early man with his entire food supply. Later, man domesticated many wild trees and plants and cultivated them to obtain a more dependable and abundant supply of food. He also domesticated certain wild animals, not only for food but also for use as beasts of burden.

RELATION OF THE NATURAL ENVIRONMENT TO CULTURE

We have already noted that, although the natural environment or habitat unquestionably has a great influence on culture, it is by no means an adequate explanation of all cultural differences.

Extent of Influence of the Natural Environment. Though it is apparent that the culture of any people must in some degree be adjusted to their habitat, there are different ways in which the necessary adjustments can be made. Some ways of making adjustment may be superior to others, but frequently two alternative types of adjustment to the same kind of habitat are equally successful. Just why one culture makes one type of adjustment while another culture in a similar habitat makes a very different type is often impossible to explain. Clearly, however, natural environment is not the sole determinant of culture, not even of the aspects of culture most closely related to it.

Many important phases of culture have little obvious relationship to the natural environment and appear to be largely independent of it. They may be influenced by it, but in indirect ways that are frequently difficult to trace. Religion, family organization, kinship systems, art, music, and moral concepts may differ widely between cultures, and often these differences seem to correspond very little to differences in habitat.

The natural environment is, then, only one of the factors that determine the culture of a people. As we pointed out earlier, culture is cumulative, and new elements are constantly being added. The direction in which any culture develops is influenced not only by the habitat but also by institutional patterns already established, by invention, by borrowing from other cultures, and perhaps by additional factors that are more subtle and not easy to identify.

An Example of Different Adjustments to Similar Habitats. Melville J. Herskovits gives an interesting and vivid example of two quite different types of adjustment to habitats that are very similar.

We have already commented on the effectiveness of the adaptation made by the Eskimo, especially the eastern Eskimo, to their habitat. It has been pointed out with what efficiency they use the materials at hand, building igloos out of snow blocks, using walrus ivory for eyeshields, preserving the precious wooden handles of their harpoons by devising haftings that permit the handle to be recovered when the prey has been struck. The efficient use they make of their dogs, their only domesticated animal, in pulling their sleds, the waterproof boats called kayaks in which they can turn over completely and still survive, and other skills of adaptation that have for years intrigued students might also have been mentioned. It is accepted as a truism that anyone who would live in this harsh habitat must follow the ways of life of the Eskimo, adapting himself to the Arctic winter as they do if he would survive.

Yet when we turn to the Siberian Arctic, inhabited by such tribes as the Chuckchi and Koryak and Yukaghir, though the rigors of the climate are the same as in northernmost North America, we find quite a different type of culture. The igloo is unknown, and shelters are made of skins that are attached to a framework of wood, even though wood is as scarce here as elsewhere above the Arctic circle. The Siberians are herders rather than hunters, their economic mainstay being reindeer rather than walrus, and this, again, despite the fact that many of them are not too far removed from the sea coast to be hunters like the Eskimo.

The picture that is drawn of how, early in a wintry Arctic day, when the reindeer have exhausted the tundra on which they feed, the encampment must be changed, is impressive in teaching how varied are the ways in which man adapts himself to his habitat, how tenaciously he follows the dictates of his tradition, struggling against conditions that render this difficult. With the thermometer thirty degrees or more below zero, the men drive off the herd to its new feeding ground, leaving behind the women and children. It is the women's task to break camp. They get to work at once, dismantling the tents and loading skins, tent-poles, utensils, and the young children on the pack-reindeer that must transport them. The men and the herd reach the new feeding-ground long before the women. They do not put up a snow shelter as the Eskimo would, however, and they have no wood to make a fire to warm themselves. So they sit about in the cold, waiting until the pack animals arrive and the skin tents can be erected by the women, for the men would demean themselves by doing this kind of work.

Here, in the difficult circumpolar habitat, then, we have two quite different ways of life, one based on hunting, the other on herding. The adaptation of both peoples is equally successful, inasmuch as the only test of success of adaptation is survival, and Siberians no less than the Eskimo have managed to cope with their Arctic setting for untold generations. The efficiency of Eskimo adaptation over that of the Siberians strikes us as greater, but this does not mean that the Siberians would concur in this evaluation. It is clear, therefore, that factors other than habitat enter in this varied adaptation. Once we perceive this, the all-powerful influence of the environment in shaping culture, as is required by the hypothesis of environmental determinism, is to be seen as calling for qualification.[1]

In further support of the thesis that the adjustments of a group to their natural environment are often determined by cultural factors rather than

[1]Melville J. Herskovits, *Man and His Works,* New York, Alfred A. Knopf, Inc., 1948, 157–158. Copyright 1947, 1948 by Melville J. Herskovits.

by habitat, Herskovits gives a number of examples to show that where the same natural resources are available to different social groups, some groups will use them to advantage, whereas others will disregard them. This is not difficult to understand when two groups are widely separated in space or in the stages of their technological progress. However, Herskovits cites cases where one primitive people will make good use of a certain resource, whereas an adjacent tribe, to whom it is equally available and who have every opportunity to learn its use, will refuse to have anything to do with it. He gives examples from southeastern Africa:

> *In this same region, the BaTswa, the BaTsonga, and the BaRonga tribes have every reason to know and to use the bark of the special tree from which the neighboring BaChopi make their useful bark cloth; but none of them do. The raw materials out of which the Chopi make marimbas are found everywhere, and all these tribes like to hear, and many people like to play, the instrument. However, they obtain them by purchase or trade with the BaChopi. The makwakwe fruit is accessible to all, with its strychnine-laden meat; the Chopi and a few BaTsonga eat its sweet food and are immunized against its poison, but the others pass it by. The ocean is free for all who live near the coast; yet only the BaTonga fish and ply the waters with boats. In the same territory it is the Hlengwe group of the Batwa tribes that weave milala, found everywhere, into baskets and mats which people of other tribes, to whom the raw materials are equally accessible, buy or obtain by trade; while it is a Moccodoene group which make and sell or trade earthenware pots to others in the same country for corn, peanuts, or other foodstuffs, following a definite ritual in their trade practices.* [2]

Identical Culture Traits in Unlike Habitats. Not only can different culture traits be found in similar habitats, but culture traits that are almost identical can often be found in habitats that are entirely unlike. The polyandrous family, which still exists in Tibet, was at one time found in other parts of Asia, where the natural environment was very different. The monogamous family prevails today throughout much of the world and in every conceivable type of habitat. Modern industrialism had its birth in England and has developed most vigorously in countries in the temperate zone, but it is gradually spreading into countries that, like India, provide a very different type of habitat.

Natural Barriers and Human Differences. In the million years more or less during which man has lived on earth, it is not surprising that human groups in different regions have acquired markedly different physical and cultural characteristics. This would scarcely have been possible if these groups had been in constant contact, and if travel and communication between them had been easy. But in times long past, natural barriers like oceans, mountains, and deserts were usually insuperable obstacles to contact between the peoples whom they separated. Long distances were

[2] Ibid., p. 159.

8. An Example of Adjustment to the Natural Environment. A view of the Ifugao rice terraces of the Philippines. Driven from the lowlands and hemmed in by warring neighbors, the forefathers of the present generation terraced the steep mountain slopes to obtain land on which to cultivate rice. The mountains were cut into broad slopes or terraces and faced with retaining walls of stone so expertly piled together, without the use of cement, that they have withstood the ravages of time and the elements for more than 1,500 years. (Courtesy Wide World Photos.)

almost equally effective as a barrier. At best, travel was extremely slow and difficult, and travel over great distances was ordinarily impossible, for it meant crossing the territories of many strange and hostile peoples.

The greatest of all natural barriers were the oceans. The Indians of the New World are believed to have come originally from northeastern Asia, probably on a land bridge across what is now the Bering Strait. However, once they were established in America, the oceans closed over the land bridge and effectively separated them from contact with the peoples and cultures of the Old World. The oceans also isolated various other groups, including the aborigines of Australia and the inhabitants of many islands. The Sahara desert was for tens of thousands of years almost as formidable a barrier as the oceans. It kept most of the Negro peoples to the south of

9. A Similar Adjustment to the Natural Environment on the Other Side of the World. These agricultural terraces were built by the Indians of the Inca Empire at Machu Picchu, Peru. (Photo by author.)

it almost completely isolated from the Caucasian groups to the north and east. Likewise, the Himalayas and the swamps and forests of Southeastern Asia rather effectively separated the peoples of India from the Mongoloid peoples to the north and east.

In former times, because of the almost complete lack of contact between distant peoples, many unique and distinctive cultures developed in different parts of the world. Today, with travel, trade, and communication relatively easy, culture diffusion takes place much more quickly. Nonliterate or nonindustrial cultures have difficulty in holding their own when they come into contact with our literate and technically advanced European, or Western, culture. Western civilization seems to be spreading rapidly to even the most distant regions, but this is more markedly true of Western science and technology than of other aspects of Western culture.

Culture as a Buffer Against the Environment. From the standpoint of man every habitat has its disadvantages. At times it is either too wet, too dry, too hot, or too cold; it may contain troublesome insects or dangerous beasts of prey; and frequently it breeds terrible diseases. Through discoveries and inventions called forth by the need for making adjustments to his environment, man has succeeded in modifying his culture in ways that protect him in part from many of the disagreeable and dangerous aspects of his habitat. He has developed weapons to protect him from the attacks of wild animals and to enable him to hunt them for food; clothing to keep him warm; shelters to protect him from sun, wind, rain, and cold; and methods of making fire, not only for cooking food but also for warmth. More recently he has developed refrigeration, both to preserve his food and to keep his dwellings and places of work cool in hot weather.

We must, however, be careful not to assume that every human need necessarily calls forth an invention and a cultural adjustment that adequately meets it. From time immemorial, human beings have lived in shelters that, during much of the year, were too hot or too cold, and most of the world's people still live in such shelters. Likewise, from earliest times, people have been subject to attack by deadly infections and contagious diseases, but until rather recent times no great progress was made in meeting this danger. Man's adjustment to his habitat has always been good enough to permit the species to survive,[3] but it has never been good enough to prevent hardship, suffering, and early death for great numbers of people.

Perhaps the most striking single example of modern man's ability to improve his adjustment to his environment lies in the fields of medicine and sanitation. Although there are today many diseases—cancer, some heart and circulatory conditions, arthritis, the common cold—for which man and his culture still have found no dependable cures, great advances have been made during the last hundred years. Today a number of diseases

[3] There are, however, cases where tribal groups have dwindled and finally disappeared.

that were once widely prevalent have all but disappeared from many areas of the world. Some, such as smallpox, that today give us relatively little concern, at one time took tens of thousands of lives annually. Furthermore, there has been great progress in finding more effective treatments for many diseases still prevalent.

Modern Transportation and the Natural Environment. Modern transportation has done a great deal to free man from the restrictions imposed upon him by the particular locality in which he lives. The natural resources of any given area are limited. Also, each region has its own peculiar climate, and, as a result, there are many products its people cannot produce. But because with modern transportation most of these products can easily be brought in from elsewhere, the people of each locality can now enjoy a much greater variety of goods than was formerly possible.

Cheap and rapid transportation makes possible *regional specialization.* Each area tends to concentrate on producing the kinds of goods for which its climate and natural resources are especially suited, or in the making of which its people have developed special skills. These products are then shipped to distant markets, and other goods that the people of the locality need are brought in from the outside. As a result, not only do the people of each locality enjoy a greater variety of goods than would be possible without this interregional trade, but they also obtain these goods at lower prices from the places where they can be produced most efficiently. For example, California and Florida specialize in raising oranges, Brazil in producing coffee, the city of Akron in making tires, and the Detroit area in making automobiles.

Transportation also enables man to produce goods requiring various raw materials that are not found together in the same place. Thus the mills of South Chicago and Gary produce steel with coal brought from southern Illinois, iron ore from the Mesabi Range in Minnesota, and limestone from various localities along the shores of the Great Lakes.

One result of rapid transportation and regional specialization is that the nations of the world are becoming increasingly interdependent for many goods. The ordinary American in his everyday life comes into contact with products containing materials from all over the globe. These include coffee, tea, bananas, cocoa and chocolate, silk, rubber products, furniture made from tropical woods, English woolens, oriental rugs, tin cans, German and Japanese cameras, and French perfumes.

Modern transportation also makes it easy for many people to travel from country to country, and it thereby facilitates the diffusion of culture traits. But it creates various special problems, such as overcrowded airports, traffic jams on the highways leading to them, safety hazards, and sonic booms and other noises over residential areas.

Relation of Natural Resources to Economic Activity and Technology. *Economic activities are those activities of man that are concerned with making a living,* and they necessarily play a major role in every culture. Their character is largely determined by three factors. First, all human beings have *wants* for many kinds of *scarce goods. By scarce goods we mean those that exist in limited quantities and that we can obtain only if we produce them or if we offer something valuable in exchange for them.* The desire to satisfy specific wants is the motive power behind all economic activity. The second factor that guides economic activity is available *resources.* Desirable goods such as food, clothing, houses, or weapons cannot be created out of nothing. If man is to have them, he must find materials in nature—*natural resources*—from which they can in some way be produced. Unless he can find such materials, his wants will remain unsatisfied no matter how great his efforts. With ingenuity, however, he may discover that he can turn to his advantage materials that at first seemed quite useless. The third factor controlling man's economic activity is *technology,* meaning *knowledge of how to use resources to produce desirable goods, including services.*

Both the technology of a society and the economic activities in which its people engage are greatly influenced, though by no means wholly determined, by the extent to which various natural resources are available. For example, power is a basic essential in a modern industrial economy, but even a modern economy cannot make extensive use of power unless substantial amounts of power-producing resources are available. Furthermore, the methods used to generate power tend to depend on the relative availability and cost of water power, coal, natural gas, petroleum, and fissionable materials such as uranium. In the future the methods employed are also likely to be greatly influenced by the success with which we can eliminate their contributions to polluting or otherwise damaging our environment.

Our Natural Resources and the Problem and Limits of Economic Growth. With regard to natural resources, the United States is in a relatively fortunate position, for it is probably better supplied with them than is any other similar area in the world. This endowment of natural resources has provided the material basis for our phenomenal economic development and our present political and military strength. We have great areas of fertile farm lands and also of forests. We are relatively well provided with such sources of power as petroleum, natural gas, coal, and sites for hydroelectric plants. We also have large reserves of iron ore and of other important minerals. True, we lack certain metals, such as nickel, chromium, and tin, but ordinarily we have no difficulty in importing these from abroad.

But though our position is still strong with respect to most basic resources, the outlook for the future is not clear. We have enough coal to last for hundreds or thousands of years, but our supply of some other important resources is less satisfactory. Meanwhile, population, and output and consumption per capita, continue to rise. Much of our farm land is being injured by erosion, and some of it is no longer worth cultivating. Our forests are being destroyed by lumbering, diseases, insects, and fire, faster than they are being replaced. We still have vast reserves of low-grade iron ore, but our best deposits are rapidly becoming exhausted. Already we are importing substantial amounts of high-grade ores from abroad. Furthermore, until recent discoveries in northern Alaska, it seemed likely that our reserves of petroleum available by drilling wells would soon begin to diminish. No one knows how much oil is in Alaska; some guesses put it at two or three times our previous proved reserves. But here the problem is to drill wells and transport the oil to market at reasonable costs and without great damage to the environment through destruction of much of the Alaskan tundra and the wild life dependent on it. Whether we can obtain the oil without such damage remains to be seen. However, the possibility of a long-run critical shortage of petroleum is still far in the future, because there are vast reserves in the oil sands of the Athabasca River in Canada and in the oil shales of the western United States. The immediate problem is that with our present technology it would be relatively expensive to obtain oil from these sources on a large scale. The long-run outlook for the supply of metals like copper, zinc, lead, and nickel is not too good. It has been estimated that if their per capita use in the rest of the world equalled that in the United States, known reserves would be exhausted in less than ten years.

A very essential natural resource that, until the last two or three decades, most people had taken for granted is fresh water. True, it has long been scarce in some of the dry areas of the Southwest, but now we are experiencing shortages in regions where we had assumed the supply to be inexhaustible. Contributing to the shortage of usable fresh water has been the extensive *pollution* of rivers and lakes by sewage and industrial wastes. Even in such a large body of water as Lake Erie, pollution has reached a level that has destroyed commercial fishing and made most beaches unusable; and it has now become a critical problem in Lake Michigan. Pure air also has become scarce in many of our urban centers, where much of the time the inhabitants must breathe a mixture of air combined with auto fumes, dust, and various waste products from trash fires, incinerators, and the smoke stacks and flares of industrial plants.

With our population still growing at a rapid rate, there is great need for protecting our basic resources from waste and pollution. Yet even if we develop an effective program of *conservation,* we will face an increasing scarcity of some resources in the not-distant future.

For many years the United States has had the highest total output of goods of any country in the world, the highest output per capita, and the highest average standard of living. Moreover, our people have become accustomed to expecting ever higher standards of living, that is to say, more and more of the things that money can buy. But even if we only maintained present standards of living, we would still need to increase total output, because as population grows we must provide goods and employment for millions of new citizens. There are also other pressures that tend to expand output. Many of our citizens are still in poverty, with unreasonably low standards of living; much of our housing is inadequate and badly needs replacement; also there is still a great need for upgrading our educational system and other public services, and this will require more equipment made by our factories as well as more personnel.

All this creates a dilemma. As a result of our philosophy of maximizing material welfare and of our failure to put adequate checks on population growth, we are using up scarce resources at an ever-increasing rate, and we are more and more polluting the environment with man-made wastes. Unless the process can be reversed, the quality of human life will soon deteriorate and man's very existence will be threatened.

A suggestion that is made by many today is that we should become more concerned with the quality of life and less with the quantity of goods we have thought we must have. From the economist's point of view this would involve greater economy in the use of goods. We would not buy things that really add little to our happiness or welfare, we would not eat more than is good for us, and if we were concerned with preserving resources and avoiding pollution of the environment, we would also make a greater effort to avoid all forms of waste. We would repair and maintain goods whenever possible, including automobiles, houses, and other buildings, instead of discarding them. All this would help. But even if people generally can be induced to consume less and waste less, the closely related problems of conservation and pollution will not be completely solved without further measures.

THE PROBLEMS OF POLLUTION

The control of pollution is one phase of the problem of conservation, because used in a broad sense *conservation* is concerned with preserving all the aspects of the natural world essential to the continuing survival and welfare of mankind. It includes not only preserving forests, mineral resources, and wild areas where the beauties of nature are unspoiled but also protecting from contamination our rivers and lakes, the places where we live and work, and the air that we breathe.

The early conservation movement in this country, which had its origins in the nineteenth century, was not at the beginning primarily concerned with problems of pollution. Instead, its emphasis was on such goals as preserving and renewing our forests, saving scenic or wilderness areas by making them into national or state parks, reducing waste of mineral resources, and protecting farm lands against destruction by erosion. The anti-pollution movement, on the other hand, is first of all concerned with such matters as pollution of the landscape by used containers, automobile graveyards, and other debris; pollution of the air by smoke, various kinds of dust, and poisonous gases from auto exhausts and industrial plants; pollution of lakes, rivers, and ocean waters by sewage, oil from

"I struck oil." (Courtesy Joseph G. Farris. Copyright 1970 *Saturday Review, Inc.*)

tankers and offshore oil wells, and dangerous or objectionable industrial wastes; pollution of farm lands and forests by poisonous insecticides that destroy desirable kinds of wild life; and radioactive pollution of the environment from bomb tests and atomic power plants. All these are problems that increase in intensity as population grows and standards of living rise.

Efforts against pollution are not new. For example, successful attempts to provide towns and cities with running water that was safe to drink go back more than a hundred years. But only in the 1960's did the pollution problem become a matter of intense public concern. Basically this was because only then had the rapid growth of population, plus rising standards of living and a great expansion of industry, brought so rapid a rise in the rate of pollution that it reached frightening proportions.

Even scientific studies in the fields of pollution and ecological damage did not begin to assume major proportions until the 1950's. Rachel Carson's book *Silent Spring,* published in 1962, helped to stir public concern about one aspect of the problem: the use of pesticides. Other books soon followed. Increasingly, writers and speakers, among them scientists, journalists, and politicians, called attention to the devastating effects of pollution on all life forms, to its possibly disastrous effects in upsetting the ecological balance, and to the urgency of the problem. Protests against pollution quickly gained momentum, and in a very short time the anti-pollution movement had achieved wide backing.

In order to coordinate local groups into a nation-wide popularly supported crusade, a group called Environmental Action organized "Earth Day" on April 22, 1970, a peaceful demonstration involving millions of people in colleges and universities, high schools, and communities. Speakers all over the country called attention to various phases of the problem from their own standpoints, and urged both a change in attitudes and concerted action to implement reform.[4]

Major Aspects of the Pollution Problem. We can for convenience think of pollution in terms of five major areas or aspects, namely, (1) air pollution, (2) water pollution, (3) land pollution by solid wastes, (4) land pollution by pesticides, and (5) noise pollution.

Air Pollution. Air pollution is perhaps our most serious problem because it is so pervasive, so hard to escape from. Many of our early attempts to control it were concerned with the reduction of dust, smoke, and soot, mostly from the chimneys of factories, power plants, and homes. Here and there some progress was made in reducing air pollution from dust and soot, but we discovered that chimneys released other products injurious to health, among them carbon monoxide and sulfur dioxide. Still later the Los Angeles smog problem drew attention to nitrogen oxides and other contaminants in the gases from the exhausts of internal-combustion engines in automobiles and trucks. Gradually this type of pollution became a major problem in other cities. Meanwhile we had begun to pay more attention to pollution from the burning of solid wastes, especially in incinerators. We are making increasing efforts to reduce pollution from all these sources, but there is urgent need for more effective action. Many industrial plants are now using fuels that burn cleanly, like natural gas or types of oil and coal with a low sulfur content, but such fuels are relatively scarce. Other plants have installed expensive devices that catch certain contaminants before they reach the air.

Perhaps the greatest effort today is to control contamination from automotive exhausts. California was a leader in requiring that automobiles be provided with devices for reducing the emission of air contaminants. Ralph Nader has led an unremitting crusade to force automobile manufacturers, especially General Motors, to develop an engine that would not contaminate the air. We do not yet have such a motor that would be satisfactory in most automotive vehicles. Present efforts are largely directed toward reducing pollution from internal-combustion engines. One move in this direction is a plan to eliminate as soon as possible the sale of gasoline to which a lead compound has been added. Lead is a poison that autos release into the air and that accumulates in the human body. It also causes deterioration of devices for reducing pollution from automobile exhausts. But elimination of lead from motor fuel requires both changes in the distillation of gasoline and changes in the design of most automotive engines. Lead-free gasolines that can be used in some engines are now being sold by the oil companies.

Water Pollution. Water pollution, like air pollution, is a complex problem, but the matters of most urgent concern are (1) to prevent raw sewage or inadequately treated sewage water from being discharged into rivers,

[4] See National Staff of Environmental Action, eds., *Earth Day—The Beginning,* paperback, New York, Arno Press, Inc., 1970.

lakes, or coastal waters and (2) to stop industrial wastes from being dumped into them. The first is largely the responsibility of local governments, and the chief obstacle is usually money and lack of sufficient public concern. The second is the responsibility of corporations, and here, too, the pressure of public opinion is essential. Government must enforce laws, and often new legislation must be passed. It is sometimes said, correctly, that corporations do not have consciences. As such they do not. Their actions are only a reflection of the consciences—and the intelligence—of the men who control them. The same is true of governments. The degree to which they serve the public interest depends on the quality of the men we elect to office and the pressures we put upon them.

Land Pollution by Solid Wastes. The disposal of solid wastes becomes more difficult each year. According to one estimate they now pile up at the rate of 3.5 billion tons annually; and according to another the American public pays $6 billion per year for waste collection and disposal. Some solid waste is burned in open fires or incinerators, but this means pollution of the air. More of it is put into dumps or old quarries and eventually buried; but locations where it can be deposited become harder and harder to find. Meanwhile, waste grows faster than population because people buy more products and have more to dispose of. Compounding the problem in a small but annoying way is the trend toward selling soft drinks and beer in cans or nonreturnable bottles. "Litterbug" ads notwith-

"Hey! Who do you think is going to clean up after you—some archeologist?" (Courtesy Ed Fisher. Copyright 1970 *Saturday Review, Inc.*)

standing, quantities of these then get scattered by motorists along the highways and in our public parks. Likewise, paper litter tossed by people into streets and alleys has markedly increased over the last decade. Such behavior is disturbing because it shows that great numbers of people still have little respect for their environment and little sense of personal responsibility for maintaining it.

Insofar as it is feasible, the ideal way to dispose of many solid wastes, especially paper, paperboard, and metals, is to *recycle* them, that is, to use them over in the manufacture of new products. Some companies are making efforts to collect and reuse such waste, but the obstacle is that the cost of sorting, collecting, and transporting waste materials is usually too high to make it profitable or even to cover its cost. Nevertheless, recycling of products is receiving more and more attention. One development that should help in the disposal of solid wastes is the invention of compactors that compress them with great force into cubes of relatively small volume. These take up much less space than uncompressed wastes and are better suited for land-fill projects. Some cities are experimenting with the use of large compactors.

Land Pollution by Pesticides. Reducing land pollution by such products as insecticides and fungicides has become a great problem. Some maintain that if we stopped their use completely, an ecological balance would be established that would keep down pest populations and render the use of pesticides unnecessary. But many are skeptical about that, and meanwhile American farmers feel very dependent on such products for maintaining production. It would be very difficult to suddenly forbid the use of all of them. If we forbid the employment of some that prove to be destructive of desirable wild life or dangerous to man, we must have substitutes, or find other methods of pest control. One pest, a species of fly, was brought under control in the Southwest by breeding millions of sterile males and releasing them at the proper time in infested areas to mate with females. Most of the latter then laid eggs that would not hatch larvae. A method that has been successful in a few cases is to introduce another insect that preys upon and destroys the pest. But the introduction to an area of a new insect always involves risk. It may upset some aspect of the ecological balance and cause new damage.

The great objection to using DDT as a spray is not only its short-run destructive effect on wild life but also the fact that it does not break down readily. Once applied to an area, it stays there until some of it is later spread by rains and then carried into lakes and rivers. On the other hand, DDT has saved countless lives by controlling diseases carried by insects in tropical countries, and for some purposes no adequate substitute has been found. In Ceylon it brought cases of malaria down to seventeen in 1963. Its use was stopped in 1964, and by 1968 there were a million cases of malaria. As a result, the use of DDT house spray was reintroduced. In the United States it was announced in 1970 that a government-sponsored research grant had resulted in a type of DDT containing a catalytic agent that in time breaks it down into a substance much less toxic. But early in 1971 the sale and use of DDT was stopped by government order pending further research.

Noise Pollution. Whether loud and incessant noises in cities and factories are "pollution" is debatable, but many people are calling them that. Possibly, doing so is pollution of the English language, but, in any case, loud noises are often an undesirable feature of the environment. Very loud sounds, if persistent or if repeated over a long period, can cause serious and permanent impairment of hearing. If loud enough, even a single sound, like that of a forty-five caliber pistol fired close to the ear, can destroy the ability to hear.

Among the people likely to suffer most from loud noises are those who work in certain types of mills and factories, or around airplanes, or in the construction industry, or who fire artillery weapons in battle or in military training. However, the noise level from traffic and other activities is high in some areas of cities, and, in the opinion of some observers, it has increased substantially in recent years. Sound intensity is measured in *decibels.* On what is called the *A scale,* greater weight is given to high-pitched tones because these most distress the ear. Persistent exposure to a noise level above 85 decibels on this scale will, in many people, eventually reduce hearing acuity for sounds in the range that must be heard to understand human speech. Heavy city traffic in streets lined solidly by buildings often registers 90 decibels; and some rock music bands, heard close up, register as much as 120 decibels.[5] Besides their possible effect on hearing acuity, persistent or repeated noises also jangle the nerves, make concentration difficult, interrupt sleep, and prevent deep sleep.

What can be done to reduce noise in the environment? A good deal, say students of the problem. It is even possible to make quieter factory and construction machines, but they cost more. A group in New York City, Citizens for a Quieter City, has received a $300,000 grant from the Ford Foundation for an experimental project to reduce the noise in a sixty-block area of Manhattan. In Chicago, the city council early in 1971 passed an antinoise ordinance said to be the first of its kind in the country. Among other things, the law requires the use of quieter machinery on projects carried out under city contracts.

Meeting the Pollution Problem. There are at least four lines of action, all of which are important if we hope to bring a sharp reversal in the deterioration of our environment: (1) changing our attitudes toward goods and reordering our priorities; (2) putting pressure on governments and on corporations to eliminate as soon and completely as possible all significant sources of pollution that we know how to control; (3) shifting our emphasis in the use of science and technology from how to increase the output of goods to finding ways to prevent or reduce pollution; and (4), the most

[5]"The Next Sound You Hear May Be Just Too Much," *Changing Times,* March, 1971, pp. 33–35.

crucial issue in the long run, slowing and as soon as possible stopping population growth.

The problem of population growth will be discussed more fully in the chapter on population, but it is clear that we can never solve the pollution problem if population increases indefinitely. It is also obvious that at best it will take time in most countries to stop population growth. In the short run, such growth will continue, though we should be able to slow it. In the meantime, the majority of workers still look forward to higher wages, higher pensions, and the purchase of more goods.

This brings us back to point number one: changing the public's attitudes and priorities. William D. Ruckelshaus, Environmental Protection Agency administrator, put it this way in speaking to the National Press Club: "A new *environmental ethic,* one that views the world with affection and care, is necessary if this country is to battle pollution successfully."[6] This means, among other things, that businessmen must develop an increased sense of social responsibility; that government must increasingly press for and enforce standards, laws, and regulations; and that consumers as consumers must also become environmentalists. When they become concerned enough as environmentalists, they not only will join in demanding strong controls on all industrial pollution and a reordering of priorities in the government's budget and planning but they also will be willing to control their own habits and desires in order to preserve the environment.

One of the hopeful signs of today is the fact that both science and technology are turning increased attention to the problems of pollution. Another is that through publicity of all kinds, as well as through bombardment of the senses, the general public is becoming more and more environment conscious. Programs for action are appearing in all areas of society. For instance, at Stanford University, student workshops on political and social issues have had the dual result (1) of giving student activists an opportunity to study and research specific social issues and (2) of producing, as a result of students' reports, action in the form of laws restricting various forms of the pollution and waste of natural resources.

The Need for More Knowledge. One of our handicaps in dealing with pollution is that we know little about many of the potentially dangerous contaminants in the environment. René Dubos, a distinguished microbiologist and pathologist at Rockefeller University, remarks that statesmen, social planners, and technologists often say the financial cost is the great obstacle to air-pollution control. But he doubts if even with unlimited resources we could formulate fully effective programs because at present we know so little about the origin, nature, and effects of many air contaminants.[7]

According to Dubos, some 70 per cent of the minute particles that contaminate urban air are still unidentified. He further notes that recent

[6] *Chicago Tribune,* January 14, 1971, Section 1A, p. 8.
[7] René Dubos, "We Can't Buy Our Way Out," *Psychology Today,* March 1970, p. 20.

experiments indicate that newborn animals exposed to these contaminants sometimes show disastrous effects when they mature. Stopping the emissions of internal-combustion engines is certainly essential; but he doubts whether it would go as far as some people hope toward solving our problems of air pollution, because there are so many other contaminants; and he calls attention to the fact that asbestos particles from the brake linings of motor cars or from insulation materials have been detected in significant amounts in the lungs of city dwellers and that there is no doubt that asbestos is a great health hazard. Polychlorinated biphenyls (PCB's), released into the air in great amounts by rubber tires as they wear out, are also a health hazard. Dubos believes that the study of ecological problems in technological societies will bring "new, exciting knowledge of man and his environment," and he urges able students who are really concerned about reducing pollution to engage in serious research in this field.

As we learn more about pollution, the problem becomes increasingly complex, and the need for research becomes more and more evident. A few years ago we thought that the chief objection to flushing detergents into our sewers and ultimately into rivers or lakes was their permanence. Bacteria could not readily break them down, and so they remained to produce suds or foam on water surfaces. Soon detergents were developed that bacteria could break down. But then we found that the soluble phosphates in these detergents encouraged the growth of algae in lakes and sluggish streams. The algae form scum on the surface, and when they die they use up the oxygen in the water and thus kill fish. Enzymes were also found to be undesirable in detergents; but efforts were made to meet this problem, and now we have some detergents that clean effectively and that contain neither phosphates nor enzymes. Again, we discovered not so long ago that a number of lakes and streams are polluted by mercury, which tends to become concentrated in fish and makes them unsafe for human consumption. This seems to be an even more serious problem in Japan than in this country.

One of the more recent areas of controversy concerns the environmental effects of electric generating plants. In order to supply enough electricity to satisfy essential needs for the present and future, many who have studied our power requirements contend that the building of nuclear power plants will be necessary. These will reduce air pollution from the smoke and sulfur dioxide produced by fossil fuels, but they will increase the level of radioactivity in the environment. Though the release of radioactivity can be greatly reduced by controls, some scientists are not convinced that it can be reduced adequately. They fear that in the long run an accumulation of radioactivity will endanger not only the health of human beings but even the continued existence of our species and of other forms of life.

One problem in the operation of nuclear power plants is whether the radioactive wastes they produce can be disposed of by deep burial or otherwise in such a way as to permanently protect the public and the environment from their effects. Lamont Cole, a biologist and ecologist, pointed out in a speech on Earth Day,[8] that in the three locations where such wastes already are being stored, they are so hot that they will boil spontaneously for a very long time. One estimate places this period at three hundred years or more, and the Atomic Energy Commission has itself asserted that they must be kept from polluting the environment for at least six hundred years. In the meantime, the tanks in which some of them were stored have had to be replaced after only twenty years.

Cole also points out that tritium, or radioactive hydrogen, is released into the air by nuclear installations and that this gets built into water. It emits a very feeble beta ray, but its effects may be serious, as it accumulates in the environment and enters the human body.

A much less critical problem that atomic power plants create is the discharge of large quantities of hot water into lakes and rivers. Biologists maintain that the resulting increase in temperature stimulates the growth of undesirable forms of aquatic life such as algae. Such effects can be avoided by erecting devices to cool the water before it is discharged, but these are very expensive.

The fact that competent nuclear scientists are in sharp disagreement as to whether radiation from power plants can be adeqautely reduced, suggests that we need more knowledge before we plan and build more such plants. However, this faces us with a dilemma. With our present population and the industrial organization necessary to support it, we cannot provide essential material goods and essential services without power; and in the next few years, unless we take Spartan measures, we are likely to require more power, not only to avoid blackouts but also to provide jobs and goods for young people who will be entering the labor force. If we do not build atomic plants, we will have to continue to use and build fossil fuel plants, reducing the air pollution from them as much as we can. The possibility of building more hydroelectric plants is very limited if we wish to avoid damaging the beauty and the wild life in our remaining wilderness areas.

An entirely different but important field where further research is needed is soil fertility. Conservationists point out that one of the most important requirements for the continued existence of mankind is soil fertility; and, as David Stenhouse puts it, "Fertility can be lost even when something that looks like soil still remains. An infertile soil is useless."[9] He argues for greatly expanded research in "soil science," especially in the exploration of its self-renewing properties.

We have indicated only a few of the many areas in the general field of conservation and pollution where more knowledge is needed; but perhaps they will suffice to bring home to the reader the size and complexity of the problem. The opportunities for significant research are almost un-

[8] See National Staff of Environmental Action, op. cit., pp. 32–33.
[9] David Stenhouse, Crisis in Abundance, London, Heinemann Educational Books Ltd., 1966, pp. 74–75.

limited, with the whole world and the atmosphere around it as the area to be investigated.

The Cost of Pollution Control. Though pollution cannot be controlled just by spending money, any attempt to stop and reverse the present deterioration in our environment will require large expenditures. There is not much point in trying to estimate the total money cost. Over a period of years it will certainly add up to many billions of dollars. Who will pay it? You and I, the general public. Initially most of it will be paid by governments and business corporations, but the government share will mean higher taxes unless expenditures can be cut elsewhere, and the corporation share is likely to mean, at least in the short run, higher business costs and hence higher prices.

There will, however, be offsetting savings. For example, purer air in cities will mean a great reduction in cleaning and decorating bills and also a reduction in medical and hospital bills. Other gains will include greater use and enjoyment of parks, beaches, and water sports, cleaner and pleasanter city streets, a pleasanter countryside, and a longer life expectancy.

Activities of the Federal Government and the United Nations. Government at various levels has passed a good deal of legislation dealing with the pollution problem. One development requires special mention because it may increase appreciably the effectiveness of efforts by the federal government to improve the environment. In the summer of 1970 a new and independent *Environmental Protection Agency* (EPA) was established. It was created to carry out policies determined by the federal Council on Environmental Quality, and it took over powers and functions that had previously been scattered among a number of different federal departments and agencies.

The United Nations World Health Organization (WHO) is also active in this field. In January, 1971, it was announced that a world-wide air-pollution–monitoring network had been set up, with Washington and London serving as hubs, with Moscow, Nagpur (India), and Tokyo as regional centers, and with twenty laboratories throughout the world. The network will also initiate an international study of the six major air pollutants, with the aim of setting up standards for air quality. In addition, WHO is working on a program and code of environmental health. Taken into account will be effects of water, soil, food, and air pollution, noise, and other environmental factors harmful to well-being.

The Need for All-Out Public Support. Some who are appalled by the extent and rapid rise of pollution predict that, unless drastic action is taken immediately, man cannot survive. Varying "periods of grace" such as five or twenty years have been mentioned. No one really knows how much pollution the human race can adjust to, after a fashion, but one thing is certain. If we allow the rate of pollution to increase as it has been doing in recent decades, and do nothing about it for five to twenty years more, a good many people will die earlier and life will not be very pleasant for the remainder. Though some of the things that must be done will be difficult, if we wait a while before undertaking them they will be much more so. Nevertheless, problems involving the whole range of ecology—human, plant, and animal—are not all going to be solved in a hurry, no matter how hard we try.

The degree to which we shall be able to improve our environment, either in the short or the long run, will in the last analysis depend on the attitudes of the public. The great majority of the American people must be determined to seek improvement year after year and be willing to pay the cost. They must put pressure on both government and business to reduce and eliminate pollution as completely as possible. They must be willing to make personal efforts and sacrifices to preserve and improve the quality of the environment. If the present concern over pollution spreads rapidly to enough people and becomes permanent, the chances of a bright future for the human species will be immeasurably enhanced.

Terms to Be Understood

environment	topography	pollution
social environment	natural resources	conservation
natural environment	regional specialization	recycling waste
ecology	economic activities	environmental ethic
ecological balance	scarce goods	EPA
habitat	technology	

Questions for Review and Discussion

1. To what extent must the culture of a group be adjusted to the natural environment?
2. Distinguish between the social or cultural environment and the natural environment.
3. What are some possible unfortunate results of disturbing the ecological balance?
4. How may culture limit man's use of his natural environment?
5. State the most important ways in which the culture of a group is influenced by (a) climate, (b) topography, and (c) natural resources.
6. Is the United States likely to face serious shortages of important natural resources in the future? Why or why not? If shortages should develop, how can we attempt to meet them?
7. To what extent is the cultural environment of a group independent of the natural environment? Explain.
8. Explain the social importance of the material aspects of culture.
9. Show by means of examples that the natural environment of a people has only a limited influence on their culture.
10. In what sense is culture a buffer against man's natural environment?

11. To what extent are the economic activities of a people determined by the natural resources available to them?
12. Which of our potential shortages of natural resources are likely to be most serious in the decades just ahead? Defend your answer.
13. How has modern transportation freed man from some of the restrictions of his natural environment?
14. Explain the influence of natural barriers upon cultural differences (a) in the past; and (b) today.
15. Which is the more dynamic element in social change, the cultural or the natural environment? Explain.
16. What are the limitations on economic growth, that is, on producing more and more goods to provide more and more people with ever higher standards of living?
17. How did the early conservation movement differ from the present antipollution movement?
18. Explain why most Americans did not become intensely concerned about pollution until the 1960's.
19. What are the underlying causes of the increasing seriousness of the pollution problem?
20. Explain why the problem of air pollution is complex and difficult to deal with.
21. List the various ways in which attempts are being made to reduce or eliminate air pollution from automobile exhausts.
22. What are the chief sources of (a) water pollution? (b) land pollution? (c) noise pollution? In each case suggest remedies.
23. List the four lines of action suggested in the text as essential if we are to deal adequately with the problem of pollution. Explain why each is necessary.
24. Why does René Dubos believe that an adequate solution of the pollution problem will require a good deal more than just spending money?
25. Point out the problems we are likely to face if we do not expand our output of electric power; also point out the pollution problems we must solve if we do expand it (a) by employing fossil fuels or (b) by constructing nuclear power plants.
26. Why will the general public bear most of the costs of pollution controls? List as many ways as you can think of in which the public will save money because of such controls.
27. Give examples of the ways in which our federal government and the United Nations are helping in the attack on pollution.
28. What one thing is absolutely essential if we are to deal successfully with all phases of the pollution problem?

For Further Study

Allen, Shirley W., and J. W. Leonard, *Conserving Natural Resources,* 3d ed., New York, McGraw-Hill, Inc., 1966.
Anderson, Walt, ed., *Politics and Environment,* paperback, Pacific Palisades, Calif., Goodyear Publishing Company, 1970.
Bernard, H. Russell, and Pertti Pelto, eds., *Technological Innovation and Culture Change,* New York, The Macmillan Company, 1971.

Blau, Sheridan, and John von Rodenbeck, *The World We Live In: An Environment Reader,* paperback, New York, The Macmillan Company, 1971.

Borgstrom, Georg, *The Hungry Planet: The Modern World at the Edge of Famine,* paperback, New York, The Macmillan Company, 1967.

Cailliet, Greg, et al., *Everyman's Guide to Ecological Living,* New York, The Macmillan Company, 1971.

Dogan, Mattei, ed., *Quantitative Ecological Analysis in the Social Sciences,* Cambridge, Mass., M.I.T. Press, 1969.

Dubos, René, *Reason Awake,* paperback, New York, Columbia University Press, 1970.

Ehrlich, Paul R., and A. H. Ehrlich, *Population, Resources, Environment,* San Francisco, Freeman, Cooper & Co., 1970.

Ewald, William R., Jr., ed., *Environment and Change: The Next Fifty Years,* paperback, Bloomington, Indiana University Press, 1968.

———, ed., *Environment for Man,* paperback, Bloomington, Indiana University Press, 1967.

Helfrich, Harold W., Jr., *The Environmental Crisis,* paperback, New Haven, Conn., Yale University Press, 1970.

Hoyt, Joseph B., *Man and the Earth,* 2d ed., Englewood Cliffs, N.J., Prentice-Hall, Inc., 1967.

National Staff of Environmental Action, eds., *Earth Day—The Beginning: A Guide for Survival,* Bantam paperback, New York, Arno Press, Inc., 1970.

Revelle, Roger, and Hans H. Landsberg, eds., *America's Changing Environment,* paperback, Boston, Houghton Mifflin Company, 1970.

Rockefeller, Nelson A., *The Environment Can Be Saved,* paperback, New York, Doubleday & Company, Inc., 1970.

Roosevelt, Nicholas, *Conservation, Now or Never,* New York, Dodd, Mead & Company, Inc., 1970.

Stenhouse, David, *Crisis in Abundance,* London, Heinemann Educational Books Ltd., 1966.

Wagner, Philip L., *The Human Use of the Earth,* paperback, New York, The Free Press, 1960.

———, and Marvin W. Mikesell, eds., *Readings in Cultural Geography,* Chicago, University of Chicago Press, 1962.

Chapter 5

Social

Change

and Social

Problems

Ah Love! could you and I with Him conspire
To grasp this sorry Scheme of Things entire,
Would not we shatter it to bits—and then
Re-mold it nearer to the Heart's Desire![1]

ntil modern times, the lot of human beings, with the exception of a small minority, has been a hard one. To provide shelter and enough to eat was a constant struggle, as it still is for the people of many countries. Famine struck each group time after time, as did marauding enemies, who themselves were seeking food and greater security; and there was little or no protection against natural disasters and recurring epidemics of deadly diseases. But in modern times much has changed in the more "advanced" nations of the world. Science has given man some con-

[1] From the *Rubaiyat of Omar Khayyam* as translated by Edward Fitzgerald.

trol over nature, including many diseases; advances in technology have given him the power to produce more food, to clothe and house himself more adequately, and to have many things that add to his comfort and pleasure and that were never known before. All these changes and others, all this progress, has brought visions of an even brighter future: of the elimination of war and poverty, of the continuing reduction of disease and physical infirmity, of greater security and a widening of human freedoms, and of greater opportunities for all men to live fuller and more satisfying lives.

Though all societies are subject to change, during most of human experience social change must have been a very slow process. Man may have lived on earth in much his present physical form for a half-million years or more, but up to about five thousand or six thousand years ago all human beings belonged to rather small primitive or preliterate groups. Though the groups varied greatly in the nature and complexity of their cultures, as a rule the customs and traditions of each were so firmly established that its members tended to follow much the same way of life over a great many generations.

For the most part, our human predecessors of six thousand years ago lived in caves or built rude shelters, used stone tools, and obtained their food by hunting or by gathering such nuts, herbs, roots, and berries as could be found in nature. Only in a few favored regions, such as Mesopotamia and the Nile Valley, were they beginning to plant crops, domesticate animals, and build small cities; and it was in these areas that the first complex human civilizations developed. At about the same time, similar developments took place in parts of China and northern India.

THE RISING RATE OF SOCIAL CHANGE

From the days of early Egypt and Mesopotamia, social change has gradually gained momentum, until in our modern urban and industrial societies it is very rapid indeed as compared with the past.

Certain factors have been especially important in contributing to this increasing rate of change. Outstanding among these was the development of agriculture and, about five thousand years ago, the invention of writing. Writing made it possible to record human knowledge and to transmit it to future generations more adequately than ever before; and as the sum total of human knowledge increased, the rate of its accumulation accelerated. Agriculture or the growing of crops forced people to live in permanent dwellings. Also, by increasing the food supply, it brought about an increase in population and, gradually, the growth of towns and cities.

Later developments that did much to speed up the rate of social change include the invention of printing, the rise of modern science, and the

10. Camels Hauling Rubber-Tired, Two-Wheel Freight Carts in Aden. (Photo by author.)

shift in methods of production that we call the Industrial Revolution. A more recent factor of great importance in accelerating change has been the annihilation of distance through the development of rapid transportation and communication. Today we can even send men to the moon, and carry on telephone conversations with them as President Nixon did in 1969 with the first astronauts to land there. Differences in language are still a barrier to free communication between people on earth, but not an insuperable one. Because today all the major cultural groups of the world are in constant contact with one another, we see great changes taking place, especially in the societies that are technologically retarded. Western science and technology are now spreading throughout the world at an accelerating pace.

One result of increasingly close contacts between distant lands is that the peoples of the world are becoming more and more alike in their dress, their customs, the products they use, and the ways they earn a living. This has been strongly impressed upon the author by his journeys to other parts of the world. Though wide cultural differences between peoples can still be found and may never completely disappear, such differences are diminishing at a more rapid rate than ever before. In the most faraway places one now finds automobiles, gas stations, electric household utilities, familiar brands of cosmetics and soft drinks, and Western dress. Conversely, styles of dress, food specialties, art forms, and modes of thought in other continents and societies are bringing changes to our own culture.

SOCIAL CHANGE AND THE FACTORS THAT CONTROL IT

Change in itself is not necessarily good or bad. It means only that old situations are being replaced by new ones. *Evolution* has more definite implications than change. In its basic scientific meaning it refers to the biological process by which plant and animal species evolve from earlier (and usually simpler) types. Used more loosely, *evolution* implies a gradual development from simpler forms of life, art, technology, or social organization to more complex, and perhaps more desirable, forms. That is to say, in common usage, *evolution* implies not only development but progress. Often we use the expression *social evolution* to refer to the long and complex processes of change and interaction by which earlier and simpler cultures gradually evolved into our modern industrial civilization. *Progress* means improvement, or change toward a condition believed to be somehow better than what preceded it. Stated even more simply, progress is change toward a desired goal. Progress has meaning only in relation to personal or social values. Any given social change represents progress if it contributes to a fuller realization of our basic social values.

Some Popular Theories of Social Change. Human beings often have a tendency to glorify the past. Some, when they reach middle age, become firmly convinced that the "good old days" of their youth and childhood were far superior to the prosaic and decadent present. One of the earliest theories of social change was that of certain Greek philosophers who held that man once lived in an ideal golden age. From this he gradually descended to a silver, then a bronze, and finally an iron age. This concept is similar to that found in the biblical story of the Garden of Eden. It will be recalled that this "garden" was a paradise in which man lived an ideal existence until he was expelled from it because he fell into sin.

A quite opposite theory of social change has been popular in Europe and America in the last century or two. This is the doctrine of inevitable progress, the belief that "the world is always getting better and better." Not even two world wars or the hydrogen bomb have been able to shake the faith of those who hold firmly to this doctrine. They believe that a comparison of modern civilization with past times shows that continuing improvement must be part of the divine plan for the human race. This point of view was stated with force some years ago in a special issue of *The Kiplinger Washington Letter:*

30 years hence, 1983. *Of course we do not know, and no one does, but out of our experience as observers comes a conviction, which is this:* The world will be better. *Improvement is the basic law of life. Things have improved in the past, the long pull past. Still continuing, even though at certain periods things look dark, and problems insoluble, and the way out seems totally blocked. But the way out opens, somehow. It's a marvel, a miracle. It suggests the inevitable progress of life.*

Another theory of social change, popularized by certain historians, is that such change runs in cycles. A generation or two ago the best-known advocate of the cycle theory was Oswald Spengler.[2] Later, until his recent death, Arnold Toynbee was its outstanding exponent. According to this theory institutions, societies, and civilizations pass through cycles of growth, climax, and decline. Modern civilization is no exception and is bound ultimately to disintegrate. This cycle theory of social change is based on the idea that "history repeats itself." Some cycle theorists maintain that modern civilization is now on the verge of a decline, and to support this contention they point to the fate of certain past civilizations, including ancient Greece and the Roman Empire. Cycle theories vary considerably, but they all tend to support the thesis that civilizations first advance, ultimately reach a peak, and finally decline.

Other attempts to explain social change have relied on the supernatural, on racial characteristics, on economic conditions, on culture diffusion, or on invention. Any given culture, however, is the result of too many factors to be explained adequately by any simple formula. Yet one thing is sure: Change is inevitable. Man's relationship to his environment is dynamic no matter where he lives, and this dynamic relationship produces change.

Sometimes social change takes place gradually, without being thought of or planned by anyone. It occurs because members of a social group yield to various pressures without awareness of what the result will be. But most social changes are first conceived in the minds of men; in other words, they begin as ideas. However, once a new culture element is well established in one society, it may spread to others, a process that is called *culture diffusion*.

Let us now consider some of the specific factors that contribute to social change. We shall discuss briefly discovery and invention, culture diffusion, wars, idea systems that are called ideologies, planned group action, and, finally, geography and climate.

Change Through Discovery and Invention. The anthropologist Ralph Linton gave us short definitions of *discovery* and *invention* that are frequently quoted. In his *Study of Man* he said: *"We may define a discovery as any addition to knowledge, and an invention as a new application of knowledge."* However, the weakness of this distinction is that inventions as well as discoveries add to our knowledge.

A *discovery* consists of learning something about the physical or social environment that was not known before. In the past, explorers have discovered new islands and continents, astronomers have discovered the laws that regulate the motions of the heavenly bodies, and anthropologists have discovered many interesting differences between the cultures of primitive peoples. Discoveries about the natural world often furnish the

[2] See Oswald Spengler, *The Decline of the West,* New York, Alfred A. Knopf, Inc., 1926.

basis for inventions. For example, it was the discoveries of some of the great scientists about electricity that made it possible for Edison to invent the incandescent electric light bulb and various other useful devices.

An *invention* is a cultural innovation devised by one or several individual members of a social group. It is a new way of doing something or a new object or mechanical device developed to serve some specific purpose. Inventions may be either material or nonmaterial. Such familiar machines as the lawn mower, the steam engine, and the airplane are material inventions. Old-age insurance, the city-manager plan, and crop rotation are examples of nonmaterial inventions. One of the greatest of all nonmaterial inventions was the alphabet, which made possible our present system of writing and printing.

An invention is really a special kind of discovery, and hence no sharp line can be drawn between the two. We can call the making of fire by striking together flint stones either a discovery or an invention. All mechanical inventions involve the discovery that materials combined and used in certain ways will give certain desired results. Inventions bring about changes in technology, and in modern societies technological change has been a powerful force behind social change.

Effects of Culture Diffusion. Most of the important elements in any culture are the result of past inventions, either material or nonmaterial. However, not all the elements found in the culture of a given group were invented or developed within that group. In most cases the greater part of the content of any culture has been borrowed from other cultures. We have

11. Damman Coast Group Performing for TV in Saudi Arabia. The only television station in the country brings local talent to a wide audience. Here, this instrumental quartet is appearing on the "New Faces" program. (Courtesy Arabian American Oil Company.)

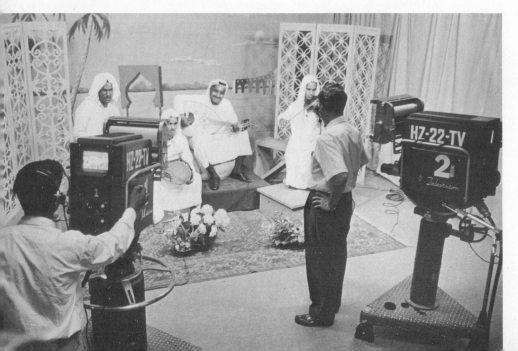

already identified as *culture diffusion* this tendency of culture to be transmitted from one society to another. In most societies culture diffusion is an extremely important factor in social change. Societies that are isolated from outside contacts tend to be static, whereas those that can readily communicate with other groups constantly acquire new culture elements.

Culture diffusion, more than any other factor, has been responsible for the development of Western civilization. The cradle of Western civilization was Europe, and its center is still there. Yet most of the basic elements of this civilization did not originate in Europe but were borrowed from other peoples in other parts of the world. Let us note several outstanding examples. Our modern number system, so superior to that of the Romans, was borrowed from the Arabs, who in turn borrowed it from the Hindus. Without this number system or a good substitute, it would be almost impossible for us to carry on the mathematical calculations now required by both business and science. Again, our alphabet, which with modifications is used for writing and printing all European languages, was borrowed originally from the Phoenicians; and it seems probable that they, or a neighboring people speaking a similar Semitic language, were the original inventors.[3] Lastly, the Christian religion, which has had such a powerful influence on Western culture for nearly 2,000 years, had its origin in ancient Palestine.

War and Social Change. Wars also bring about social change in various ways. First, they contribute to culture diffusion. Invading armies carry their culture with them, and when they return home they bring back some of the culture characteristics of the people in the invaded territories. Major wars also force governments to raise taxes and to place various controls over individuals and industry; and after the war some of these controls are likely to be retained. Wars may be social disasters, especially if foreign invasion takes place or there is destruction of property on a great scale. At best they are brutal and take lives; and if a major war drags on without much success or much prospect of ending, it creates hardship, fear, and frustration, and it can create a situation ripe for revolution. In Russia the Kerensky revolution in World War I and seizure of power soon afterward by the communists were made possible by the discouragement of the Russian people and the weakness and disorganization of the czarist government after a series of major defeats by the Germans.

Influence of Ideas and Ideologies. We have pointed out that social change may be initiated by new ideas conceived in the minds of men. Relatively simple, "practical" ideas may result in inventions that soon are accepted and that become a recognized part of the culture pattern—a new type of dance, a new kind of business corporation, or a new mechanical

---

[3] The Phoenician alphabet contained only consonants. The Greeks, who were the first Europeans to take it over, added vowels.

gadget. However, not all new ideas are of this type. Some represent important changes in social attitudes and basic social values. Such ideas may in time—as did the "liberty, equality, and fraternity" of the French Revolution—gain a powerful hold on the minds of men. Often they come to represent hopes and aspirations that, though they can never be fully realized, can be approached in a great variety of ways. Once ideas of this kind become well established in any society, they become a powerful force for continuing social change in directions that are thought to lead toward their realization.

Even in the modern world it usually takes considerable time for major new ideas to gain a firm foothold. Various writers have maintained that social change is always dominated by the discoveries or theories of great thinkers of a past generation. Karl Marx, for example, had little effect on society during his lifetime; and the "new economics," outlined by John Maynard Keynes in the 1930's, did not have any great impact on the public and on government policies until the 1960's. Except perhaps in the field of the natural sciences, important new ideas seldom become widely known and accepted during the lifetime of their originator.

An *ideology* is an organized system of ideas for remodeling society so as to bring it "nearer to the heart's desire." We may regard it as a composite of ideas, values, and emotions. Those who believe in it often support it with religious fervor. Fascism, communism, socialism, and democracy are all ideologies. Each has its system of values and each would organize society, supposedly to further the common good, according to a somewhat different pattern. No ideology ever achieves the ideal society that its adherents envision. We regard our American society as democratic, but we are often keenly aware that we fall short of the democratic ideal in many ways. We think of modern Russia as a communist society, but the Russians seem to be even further from achieving the ideals of communism than we are from achieving those of democracy.[4]

Change Through Collective Action. Most social change takes place gradually and is not planned and carried out by some central agency. At times, however, social changes of importance are brought about more or less rapidly by planned group action. Group action by an entire society, such as a modern nation, usually means government action, because the government is the only agency that can make and enforce rules that in theory apply to the whole social group. Japan is a nation that, within the last century, has experienced a great social transformation. It has changed from a feudal society to a modern, highly industrialized democracy. Much of this change has been brought about by government policies that were definitely designed to bring Japan into the modern world.

The outstanding twentieth-century examples of drastic and far-reaching social changes carried out by government on a vast scale are to be found in modern Russia and China. There, in two of the largest and most popu-

[4]Certain social ideologies will be discussed more fully in Chaps. 17 and 25.

lous countries of the world, when the communist leaders came into power they completely changed in a relatively short time many basic aspects of the political, social, and economic structure. In an attempt to create societies based on the communist ideology of Karl Marx, the state seized vast amounts of property and often "liquidated" the middle- and upper-class owners; uprooted millions of peasants from their small holdings and put them to work on collective farms or communes; and took over the operation and expansion of practically all productive enterprises. But the achievement of such broad and rapid changes was possible only through the establishment of powerful dictatorships that had small regard for the rights and freedoms of individuals and that probably had the willing support of only a small minority of the people.

Important social changes can also be brought about in democratic countries through planned government action, but only if they have popular support. However, such changes are implemented more slowly and are much less drastic than those that can be made by a communist dictatorship. In democracies, social changes planned by government are usually embodied in legislation that is designed to meet certain social problems. For example, in the United States acts of Congress and of state legislatures have almost eliminated the employment of child labor; at the same time they have helped increase school attendance, both by providing free public schools and by making school attendance compulsory. Legislation under the New Deal established in their original forms our farm income-support program and our Social Security system. It also stimulated the growth of labor unions by strengthening their legal position and their bargaining power.

Legislation, however, has its limitations. To be effective in promoting social change in a democracy, it must reflect the established beliefs of the people and, as we said, have wide popular support. If legislation violates what the majority of citizens believe to be their just rights and privileges, it has little chance of success. The Prohibition Amendment to the United States Constitution, legally in force from 1919 to 1932, failed and was finally repealed because the majority of Americans felt that outlawing the sale of liquor was an unreasonable violation of their personal liberties.

Influence of Geography and Climate. When people live in a given region over a long period of time, they become adjusted to local conditions of geography and climate. However, changes in the natural environment can and do occur. In extreme cases droughts, earthquakes, the exhaustion of important natural resources, or changes in climate may require radical cultural adjustments.

Geography and climate are also important factors in social change when people migrate from one region to another. The European settlers who emigrated to the Americas, South Africa, Australia, and New Zealand found many differences of climate, topography, and natural resources. These new conditions brought about numerous cultural changes, especially in food, clothing, houses, and ways of earning a living.

Resistance to Social Change. Though social change is always taking place, it encounters strong resistance. As a result, most social change is gradual, and most cultures have a considerable degree of stability. In modern industrial societies social change is more rapid than in the past. It is sometimes identified with progress, and under this name it is given a high rating in our list of social values. Yet even in present-day America, underlying the many changes that are constantly taking place in our culture there is a great body of stabilizing elements that give continuity to our way of life.

Stability of Folkways, Mores, and Social Institutions. In spite of the high value that some industrial societies place on "progress," human beings appear to be basically conservative. The human mind and personality are so constituted that once people acquire certain beliefs, attitudes, and patterns of behavior, they find difficulty in changing them. This is especially true of the basic elements in our culture, which we acquire unconsciously in the impressionable years of early childhood. Our beliefs and attitudes may include some approval of change—for example, changes in styles—but only within limits. The mores, the principal institutions of our society, and even many of its folkways are so firmly impressed upon us that they become an essential part of our own personalities.

A chief reason for the persistence of folkways, mores, and social institutions is that they become largely habitual for all members of the social group. Habits are ways of behaving that have been learned so well that they can be carried on without conscious attention. Once acquired, however, they are difficult to change, because they become a part of the personality of the individual, perhaps by forming definite channels in the nerve cells of the brain.

A second reason for the persistence of folkways, mores, and institutions is that we and our group attach values to them. In the case of folkways these values may be small, but in the case of the mores and certain basic institutions they are great. When we believe that established patterns of behavior have high moral value and when, in addition, they arouse in us strong feelings of emotion, these patterns become resistant to change.

Vested Interests. Social changes of any importance, even though favored by the majority, are likely to meet opposition from many individuals and groups who have vested interests. A *vested interest* is a privilege or advantage that one enjoys because of the *status quo.* If a workman is a skilled plasterer, he has a vested interest in the plastering trade, and he is not likely to look with favor on substituting wallboard for plaster. Various unions in the building industry, in order to protect the jobs of their members, have fought against prefabricated housing and have insisted on retention of the slower, more expensive, "on-the-spot" building methods. Likewise, manufacturers of established products have sometimes tried to prevent their replacement by new products.

Industry and labor are not alone in opposing, for selfish reasons, the introduction of new elements into our culture. Many people stand to lose by changes in the *status quo,* not only materially but in power or prestige. Theologians, philosophers, and even scientists have again and again opposed new ideas and new knowledge for fear that their own established beliefs and theories would be discredited.

Social Change Versus Social Stability. Many of the things we value in our modern society—for example, our relatively high standards of living— could not have been brought about without a receptive attitude toward social change. Most people probably believe that, on balance, the changes of the last several centuries have contributed to human welfare. Many, however, fear that population growth, pollution, and invention of the nuclear bomb may prove to be the fatal exceptions. In any case, every major social change requires other changes, and we can never foresee just what the end result will be. Few could have guessed, when the first power machines were substituted for hand labor in eighteenth-century England, that one result of machine industry would be to concentrate most people in huge urban areas with all their complex problems.

Since all change brings new situations, if it occurs very rapidly it may create new problems for which we are unprepared. Instead of bringing about a better world, it can bring on periodic crises and give people a constant sense of uncertainty and insecurity. Every social group feels the need for some degree of stability. If this stability is to be maintained, change in our basic institutions must be rather gradual. It must take place by evolution rather than by revolution. For any large modern society to meet the needs of its people as well as it does requires a remarkably complex organization; and the organization can be challenged, it can be adapted, it can be changed, but any belief that it can be destroyed and quickly replaced with something better is totally unrealistic. Social revolutions are never complete and they bring few of the results that are envisioned. The communist revolution in Russia, after years of struggle and confusion, produced Stalin; and the National Socialist revolution in Germany produced Hilter. Neither produced the benefits that were promised.

SOCIAL CHANGE AND SOCIAL PROBLEMS

In a small, stable, well-integrated society, social problems are likely to be at a minimum. By a *well-integrated society* we mean one in which there is general agreement on basic beliefs, one in which nearly all persons follow the same general patterns of life, subject only to accepted differences of status and role, and one in which the various aspects of the culture have become well adjusted to one another. Small primitive societies were often highly integrated; large modern societies are much less so. They contain important subgroups with differing culture patterns, and they are likely to be subject to inconsistencies, strains, and conflicts that speed up social change and that often are intensified by it.

What Is a Social Problem? Although not all social scientists would agree as to the exact nature of a *social problem,* for our purposes the following definition will suffice. For a social problem to exist, two conditions must be fulfilled. First, there must be wide recognition of some condition that affects adversely the welfare of large numbers of people. Second, there must be a belief that this condition can and should be changed. To admit the existence of a social problem clearly implies the possibility of change, for no matter how undesirable a situation may be, it is not a problem unless we believe that there is a way to change it. In primitive societies drought, famine, and pestilence may not be regarded as problems because there is nothing that can be done about them. They must simply be accepted. However, they become problems if it is believed that there are ways of averting them—for instance, by making adequate sacrifices to the gods.

In a sense, social problems are always individual problems, for it is individuals who experience their adverse effects. We call them *social problems* for two reasons: first, because they affect such large numbers of people as to constitute a threat to the welfare or safety of the whole group; second, because they cannot be adequately met by individuals. If they are to be solved at all, it must be by some kind of group action. This becomes clear when we consider such major social problems as widespread poverty, disease, recurrent periods of mass unemployment, crime, family disorganization, and war.

The fact that social problems affect individuals does not mean that all individual problems are social problems. If a person wishes to climb a difficult mountain, that is his personal problem, one with which society

(Courtesy VAL. Copyright 1969 *Saturday Review, Inc.*)

has little concern. However, if enough people tried to climb mountains and if the casualty rate became very high, there is no doubt that even mountain climbing would soon be regarded as a social problem.

When we attempt to define and study any particular social problem, we encounter certain difficulties. For one thing, every social problem is closely related to a number of other social problems, and to understand one of them we must know something about the others. Thus, to understand fully the problem of family disorganization and divorce we may, for example, need to know something about bad housing, unemployment, and social classes. A second difficulty is that every major social problem is highly complex. Often it is only a part of some still larger problem, and usually it can be divided into various smaller problems. The problem of mass unemployment is a good illustration On the one hand, recurring periods of mass unemployment are only one aspect of that larger problem, business recessions. On the other hand, the general problem of unemployment can be divided up into a number of more specific problems. Unemployment may be a severe problem in the steel industry, a very minor one in the food-processing industries. Again, it may be a minor problem for workers in their thirties, but a very serious one for teenagers or for workers over forty-five.

There is seldom any simple or complete solution for a major social problem. The causes are always complex, and practical remedies are difficult to find. Moreover, the action necessary to solve or mitigate a social problem may be effectively blocked by public indifference and ignorance and by the opposition of vested interests. This does not mean that all attempts at social improvement are useless. It does mean, however, that a number of our major social problems are likely to remain with us in some form or degree for the indefinite future.

Culture Lag and Social Problems. There is no reason to suppose that all aspects of a culture will change at the same rate at the same time. For example, religious beliefs and rituals may undergo marked changes while technology remains rather constant; or it may be the other way around, with religious beliefs remaining stable while important changes are taking place in technology.

We have already defined *technology* as knowledge of the methods used in producing goods and services to satisfy human wants. Sometimes we mean the methods themselves. Technology, however, like other aspects of culture, is really something that exists inside of people. Today technology is often associated with the invention and use of machines, but, strictly speaking, any improvement in methods of production represents technological progress. A good example of a nonmechanical advance in technology was the discovery that the output of farm lands could be increased by rotating crops.

Though some elements in culture may change while others remain relatively constant, the various aspects of a given culture are by no means entirely independent of one another. To illustrate, religion may have a substantial influence on technological change. On the one hand, it may encourage technological change by teaching that material progress is in accord with the divine will; on the other hand, it may discourage such change by teaching that mechanical innovations are works of the devil.

The late eminent sociologist William F. Ogburn assigned great importance, as a source of social disorganization, to what he called *cultural lag*.[5] According to his theory, the culture of any society constitutes a pattern of interrelated elements. Once integration and stability have been achieved, a change in any one part of the pattern may create strains and disturbances in the closely related parts. Eventually adjustments will be made to restore harmony, but meanwhile there may be a considerable time lag during which tension persists. In modern industrial societies it is technological change that sets the pace. According to Ogburn's theory, *technological progress produces rapid changes in the material aspects of our culture, but the nonmaterial aspects fail to adjust, or they do so only after an excessive time lag.* As a result, many troublesome social problems are created.

A frequently cited type of cultural lag is the failure of political organization to adjust to advances in transportation. To illustrate, the system of counties and county governments that we now have in the United States was established when the only way to travel to the county seat was by horse and buggy. Twenty miles or so was the practical limit of a day's travel. Because of this, larger units of local government would have been difficult to administer. Today there is no such restriction on travel, for by automobile we can travel more than a hundred miles in two hours. Students of government now maintain that most of our rural counties are far too small to be efficient units of local government. However, our governmental institutions are so resistant to change that any substantial modification of existing county lines is almost impossible.

Limitations of the Cultural Lag Theory. The cultural lag theory is useful provided we have clearly in mind its meaning and its limitations.

In the first place, we must not assume that changes in the material aspects of culture always precede changes in the nonmaterial aspects. There is a constant interaction between the two, and in the long run, technological progress itself is largely dependent on certain nonmaterial factors, such as social attitudes and forms of social organization. Most if not all of the material products of culture originate in the minds of men, and new material devices will not be invented and put to use unless the nonmaterial cultural atmosphere is favorable. The rapid material progress characteristic of present-day society is itself the result of earlier changes in our nonmaterial culture, changes that made possible the development of modern machine technology. We have already called attention to some of these earlier developments. One was the increased receptivity to change

[5] William F. Ogburn, *Social Change,* New York, The Viking Press, Inc., 1950, pp. 200–213.

that was brought about by such historical movements as the Renaissance, the Reformation, and the great voyages of discovery. Another and closely related factor was the development of mental attitudes that made it possible to apply the scientific method to the search for truth.

In the second place, when changes occur in the material culture we may sometimes have difficulty in agreeing on the kinds of adjustment that are needed in the nonmaterial culture. Consider, for example, the invention of the automobile and its widespread adoption as a means of transportation. The automobile brought about many social changes, including changes in the customs of courtship and dating. One of its effects was to enable dating couples to escape, in some degree, the close supervision of their elders. Did this represent an unsatisfactory adjustment of our nonmaterial culture to the automobile? Some observers maintained that it did. They considered it an example of cultural lag and argued that new ways of supervising dating couples had to be devised to maintain moral standards. Others, however, regarded greater freedom in the relations between the sexes, not as a problem, but as a development that represented social progress.

But even if there is general agreement that the nonmaterial culture has not made satisfactory adjustments to changes in the material culture, to bring about the desired adjustments may be difficult or conceivably impossible. The world "lag" *implies* optimistically that the satisfactory solution of social problems resulting from technological change is merely a matter of time, but in some cases that may be doubtful. To take an extreme example, let us consider the development and production of nuclear bombs and nuclear missiles. Can our society and world society, after a certain lag, adjust to the existence of such inventions so that we and our children can continue to survive and live as satisfying lives as would be possible if such missiles had never been developed? No one knows the answer for certain. It depends on future social developments that we cannot forecast with complete assurance.

Social Values and Social Problems. Social problems exist only in relation to social values. If in a given society people set a high value on personal freedom, then arbitrary and needless restrictions on freedom are regarded as political oppression and constitute a social problem. The solution, if one is possible, may be through peaceful political change or through violent revolution. However, in a society in which rather rigid restrictions on personal liberty were regarded as natural and proper, restrictions on freedom would not constitute a problem at all. It would occur to scarcely anyone that an effort should be made to remove them. In the past there have been societies that regarded slavery as the natural and proper state for great numbers of people. It therefore constituted no social problem. Such societies have included not only ancient civilizations like those of the Greeks and Romans but also many preliterate tribal societies. Even in our own South, when black slaves began to be imported, many slave owners actually believed that blacks were better off in captivity, on

"This voice of conscience—what channel is it?" (Courtesy George Borg —*Chicago Tribune Magazine*.)

the assumption that they had too little intelligence to be able to look after themselves.

Many of our modern social problems would not have been regarded as problems in the past. Such matters as widespread poverty, unequal educational opportunities, unequal legal privileges between different social classes, and racial discrimination would once, like slavery, have been regarded in many societies as natural and normal social conditions. But today they are widely recognized as social problems for which remedies should be sought.

Our changed viewpoints are a result of the strong hold that democratic and humanitarian ideals have gained on Western civilization during the last several centuries. This hold is so strong that it is sometimes said we have developed a *social conscience* that expresses the dominant values of Western society.[6] We do not always follow the dictates of this "conscience," but we are troubled when we fail to do so. Our social conscience tells us that we should put a high value on human life and human welfare; that we should seek to eliminate poverty; that we should revere justice and respect the rights of every individual; and that we should, so far as possible, provide all citizens with equal opportunities; and that each of us should, in his capacity as a citizen, make positive contributions to the welfare of his community and nation.

The present is a period of widespread social unrest, not only in the United States but also throughout the world. It is a time when many people, especially those of the younger generation, are questioning traditional

[6] Undoubtedly other societies have also developed a "social conscience" based on their own major social values.

social values. But the encouraging aspect of today's unrest is that, though some values are being questioned or rejected, there appears to be no trend toward rejecting the basic humanitarian values of our society. Thus, if we can avoid mistakenly destroying gains already made, there is hope that today's uncertainties and conflicts can be resolved and that we may in the future be able to create a society much more firmly based on humanitarian ideals than any society now to be found in the world.

Terms to Be Understood

social evolution
progress
cycle theory of
   change
culture diffusion
discovery

invention
ideology
vested interest
well-integrated
   society
social problem

cultural lag
technology
social values
social conscience

Questions for Review and Discussion

1. What important cultural changes that have contributed to the development of modern civilization began in Mesopotamia and the Nile Valley five thousand or six thousand years ago?
2. What developments of the last five or six centuries have been of greatest importance in speeding up the rate of social change? Tell why in each case.
3. Why are the peoples of the world gradually becoming more alike in their ways of living?
4. Distinguish carefully between change, evolution, and progress.
5. Comment on the statement "Not all discoveries are inventions, but all inventions are discoveries."
6. State several popular theories of social change.
7. Explain the relation to social change of the following: discovery and invention; culture diffusion; ideas and ideologies; collective action; geography and climate.
8. Why does social change usually encounter strong resistance? Is this fortunate or unfortunate? Explain.
9. Why does rapid change always create social problems?
10. What is a social problem? Why is a particular social problem often difficult to define or isolate?
11. State the theory of cultural lag and discuss its limitations.
12. Explain the relation of social problems to social values.
13. What is meant when it is said that our Western civilization has developed a social conscience?
14. Of today's major social problems, which three seem to you most critical? Defend your choice.
15. Most of us are dissatisfied with many aspects of our social system. Should we then dismantle it completely and start over? Why or why not?

For Further Reading

Allen, Francis R., *Socio-Cultural Dynamics,* New York, The Macmillan Company, 1971.

Appelbaum, Richard P., *Theories of Social Change,* paperback, Chicago, Markham Publishing Company, 1970.

Bernard, Russell, and Pertti Pelto, eds., *Technological Innovation and Culture Change,* New York, The Macmillan Company, 1971.

Bibby, Geoffrey, *Four Thousand Years Ago,* paperback, Baltimore, Penguin Books, Inc., 1969. Account of life in Crete, Egypt, and the Near East between 2000 B.C. and 1000 B.C.

Chase, Stuart, *Most Probable World,* paperback, Baltimore, Penguin Books, Inc., 1969. An attempt to look into the future.

Congressional Quarterly Service, *Challenges for the 1970's: An Editorial Research Report,* paperback, Washington, D.C., Congressional Quarterly, Inc., 1970.

Editors of National Observer, *The Seventies: A Look at the New Decade,* paperback, Princeton, N.J., Dow Jones & Company, 1970.

Etzioni, Amitai, and Eva Etzioni, *Social Change: Sources, Patterns, and Consequences,* New York, Basic Books, Inc., 1964.

Hacker, Andrew, *The End of the American Era,* New York, Atheneum Publishers, 1970.

Hoffer, Eric, *The Ordeal of Change,* paperback, New York, Harper & Row, Publishers, 1967.

Hunt, Elgin F., and Jules Karlin, eds., *Society Today and Tomorrow,* 2d ed., paperback, New York, The Macmillan Company, 1967. See "The Meaning of Social Change" by Kingsley Davis; "The Hypothesis of Cultural Lag" by William F. Ogburn.

Mead, Margaret, *Continuities in Cultural Evolution,* New Haven, Conn., Yale University Press, 1964.

Michael, Donald M., *Future Society,* paperback, Chicago, Aldine Publishing Co., 1970.

Ogburn, William F., *On Culture and Social Change: Selected Papers,* edited by Otis Dudley Duncan, Phoenix paperback, Chicago, University of Chicago Press, 1964.

Redfield, Robert, *The Primitive World and Its Transformations,* Great Seal paperback, Ithaca, N.Y., Cornell University Press, 1957.

Warner, Aaron W., and D. Morse, eds., *Technological Innovation and Society,* New York, Columbia University Press, 1966.

Chapter 6

Religion as a Social Force

I never saw a moor,
I never saw the sea;
Yet know I how the heather looks,
And what a wave must be.

I never spoke with God,
Nor visited in heaven;
Yet certain am I of the spot
As if the chart were given.[1]

If we think of *religion* as including all beliefs in supernatural powers, conceived of as controlling the lives of men and including various types of spirits and gods, religion probably had its beginnings in some of the earliest human societies. The findings of archeologists and anthropologists suggest that from time immemorial men have sought for explanations of human existence and of natural phenomena that would go beyond the range of what can be learned from the ordinary experiences of life or from observation of the natural world. An aspect of life

[1] "Chartless" by Emily Dickinson.

that very early troubled men was the seeming inevitability of death, and religion often promised them a life beyond. Also, as cultures and civilizations developed, people longed to find purposes and satisfactions in life that would transcend the needs and desires of everyday living and thus give human existence greater dignity and meaning; and to satisfy this longing they turned to the supernatural.

That religious beliefs, institutions, and rituals have been a major element in the culture patterns of most societies can scarcely be questioned. Even in modern industrial societies many of our oldest values and traditions are rooted in religion. In our own country numerous evidences of religious influence are obvious. They include the millions of people who attend churches, the thousands of church buildings, the celebration of such holidays (holy days) as those associated with Christmas and Easter, and the practice of having witnesses in court swear on the Bible to tell the truth.

In this chapter our purpose is not to show the truth or falsehood of the doctrines of any particular church or faith. Rather, it is (1) to describe the nature of religion and the general character of certain major religions of the past and present; (2) to give some attention to the role that religion has played in the development of human societies, not only to integrate and stabilize them but also, at times, to create conflicts; and (3) to consider the present-day influence of social change on religion and, conversely, the influence of religion on social change.

The Nature of Religion. Today when we say that a man is religious we usually mean that he believes in the existence of God and that this belief to an important degree determines his moral precepts and his behavior. He regards some things as of great value, or sacred, and he probably belongs to a religious institution called a church, where he worships more or less regularly with others whose beliefs are similar to his own.

However, religions vary greatly. Most include a belief in God or gods, some concept of an afterlife, and some theory of salvation, either by earning the right of entry into heaven or the privilege of reincarnation in a higher form of life or a higher social status. But there are religions that seem to have no God in any sense in which we ordinarily use that term. One of these is *original Buddhism,* which, unlike some later forms of this faith, is a religion without a deity, without a personal concept of God, and without any theory of salvation except the bliss of escaping perpetual rounds of reincarnation and suffering by achieving the state of *Nirvana,* in which all desire and even all consciousness is lost.[2]

It is not easy to give a formal definition of religion that is wholly satisfactory, but the one suggested by Hans-Joachim Schoeps is perhaps useful. According to him "religion may be defined, in its broadest sense, as the relationship between man and the superhuman power he believes in and

---

[2] See Hans-Joachim Schoeps, *The Religions of Mankind,* Anchor paperback, New York, Doubleday & Company, Inc., 1968, pp. 176–184.

feels himself to be dependent upon." Such a relationship is expressed in various ways, including feelings of trust or fear, legends, myths, prayer, rituals, and the application of religious precepts to the conduct of life.

The Religion of Primitives. Much of the religion of primitive societies was and is based on *animism,* which is the belief that all natural objects have a soul or spirit. These spirits can do harm, and so it may be necessary to propitiate them or find ways of controlling them. In primitive societies, religion and magic are likely to be so intertwined that it is difficult to separate them. *Magic* consists of formulas by which man (the magician) can "control" supernatural powers to achieve his own purposes. For example, he may believe that he can injure an enemy by making a small image of him and sticking pins in it. But in religion, man recognizes a supernatural power or powers greater than himself. He may believe he can gain the favor of such powers by doing their will, by praise, by prayer, by ritual, or by gifts (sacrifices), but he cannot control them. The supernatural beliefs of some early primitive groups probably went beyond their faith in magic and in the existence of innumerable spirits in nature. Some may even have believed in a great spirit whose power overshadowed that of all other supernatural beings.

Most primitive peoples appear to have had some concept of a life after death, though often their ideas about this were rather vague. Frequently they believed that every human being had a *spiritual double,* or soul. This spiritual double might wander away from the body at times, as during illness or sleep, and might then have its own adventures (dreams). It might also linger, or return after death and possibly be a danger to the living.

One of the best ways to approach the study of religion and its role in human societies is to compare different religions, with their different theological beliefs, rituals, and forms of institutional organization. We shall therefore attempt to describe, so far as limited space permits, the character, first, of some ancient polytheistic religions, and, second, the nature and origin of certain of the great religions of today.

SOME ANCIENT POLYTHEISTIC RELIGIONS

As cultures and early civilizations developed, religion tended more and more to take the form of belief in a hierarchy of gods each of whom had control of special aspects of nature and human fortunes. In the earliest periods for which we have historical records, almost every people had its own gods to whom it turned for aid in times of war, famine, or other disasters. These gods, however, were usually regarded as local or tribal deities, because the existence of the gods of other peoples was also recognized, and sometimes when one tribe or city defeated another, it also took over the gods of its conquered rival. Some of these might later be recognized as identical with its own gods except in name.

The religions of early civilizations were closely related to nature. Usually the sun, moon, stars, high mountains, thunder and lightning, and water-falls were among the gods propitiated by offerings and worship to protect man from harm. For example, in the Inca empire on the high Peruvian and Bolivian plain in the Andes (the altiplano), the sun was the chief god and the greatest object of worship because it not only made the growing of food possible but also gave warmth to the people in the daytime to offset the sharp chill of the night. As the sun moved farther north in the month of June, the Indians feared it might continue its flight and leave them to starve and freeze. But, fortunately, their priests, on the twenty-first or twenty-second of June, were able to tie it to the stone post of a sundial in the Temple of the Sun and start pulling it back again. When it was once more overhead, there would be great rejoicing.

Before the birth of Christ, with the exception of Judaism and, later, Zoroastrianism in Persia, all the major religions of the Near East and Europe were *polytheistic*. Included in this group are the early religions of the Egyptians, Babylonians, Phoenicians, Greeks, and Romans. Perhaps we should also mention those of the Celtic and Teutonic tribes of western

12. Sun Dial, or "The Hitching Post of the Sun," in the Temple of the Sun at Machu Picchu. It is believed that the temples of the Incas did not have roofs because it was im-portant not to ob-struct the entrance of the sun, moon, and other deities. Notice the terraces on the higher moun-tain above. (Photo by author.)

and northern Europe. All had *one thing in common:* They recognized a whole family or *pantheon* of gods. Otherwise they varied from one another in many ways, and they also went through many changes with the passage of time.

Religion in Ancient Egypt. One of the most interesting of these extinct religions is that of the Egyptians. In Egypt, as in most ancient civilizations, religion and the state were closely bound together. During the long period of greatness of Egyptian civilization, religion went through many changes as dynasties and capitals changed or as foreign conquerors gained temporary control. Some gods vanished, or changed in importance, and others appeared. Nevertheless, certain unique characteristics of the old Egyptian religion were retained throughout the whole period, some of them long after the country became a Roman province in 30 B.C. One of these was the preservation of early *animal cults* along with personalized deities. Many of the gods are represented by human bodies with animal heads. On the other hand, the great Sphinx at Gîzeh, which symbolizes the divine power of the pharaoh, has a human head with a lion's body. The great god of Egyptian mythology was Re, the sun god, sometimes known as Aten and later as Amon-Re. Other major gods were Osiris and his wife Isis. Osiris, earlier the ruler of the underworld, gradually expanded his role and importance in Egyptian mythology.

The whole Egyptian state religion was based on the divinity of the kings or pharaohs. They were regarded as sons of the sun god, and in order to preserve their divinity and that of their descendants, they were required to marry their sisters. Powerful priesthoods developed to serve the various gods at their respective temples and to carry out the highly detailed rituals that were required. However, since the pharaoh was himself divine, the priests carried on only as his representatives.

The Egyptians believed in life after death, and the greatest structures that have survived from ancient times, the Pyramids, were built as funeral monuments to the pharaohs and were designed to protect their mummified corpses. Apparently it was thought important that the body should be preserved if an individual were to enjoy the future life. When the soul returned to the grave, it would desire food and other comforts. Food was therefore stored in the tomb and later offered to the deceased at regular intervals. Egyptian beliefs in immortality also included a final judgment to which everyone was subject. The *Book of the Dead*[3] tells how the deceased must behave on his long journey to the throne of Osiris, where he must be judged before he can enter the land of the blessed. There he faces the scales of justice, with a feather symbolizing righteousness in one pan and his heart in the other. But before a final verdict is given he must justify himself, not by confessing and repenting his sins but by reciting a list of evil deeds he has *not* committed.

---

[3] Copies of this on papyrus were placed in coffins for the benefit of the dead.

13. The great Sphinx and the Pyramid of Khafra. (Photo by author.)

Religion of the Early Greeks. Perhaps the ancient religion that has most influenced Western art, thought, and literature is that of the Greeks. To the Greeks their gods were not only far-off powers, dwelling in the sky and controlling the cosmos; they were also the supreme embodiments of the human characteristics that the Greeks most admired. In early Greek times the gods were believed to live on the cloud-hidden peak of Mount Olympus, where they constituted a kind of family, related to one another much as human beings might be. The greatest of them all was Zeus, the father of men and gods, the quintessence of divinity and power. He was the god from whom the kings of earth were descended and who controlled the whole natural order. It was in his honor that the famous Olympic games were held every four years. Begun in 776 B.C., they were attended for more than a thousand years by Greeks from all cities and tribes.

But other gods shared the power of Zeus and were also worshipped with devotion. Outstanding among these was Apollo, the god of light, healing, music, manly youth, and prophecy. His most famous shrine was the *Oracle at Delphi*. There the faithful would flock for advice about the future, and Apollo's priestess, in a trance and seated over a fissure in the rocks, would utter prophesies that would then be interpreted by the priests. It is said that the Delphic oracle became a means of spreading among the people concepts of right and justice, and the fundamental commandments of morality. Another important Greek god was Athena, the special goddess of Athens, but also worshipped elsewhere in Greece as the protector of cities and the patron of arts and crafts. The famous Parthenon at Athens, one of the world's most beautiful works of art, was erected as a temple to Athena. Other members of the Greek pantheon include Poseiden, god of the sea; Hermes, the messenger of the gods, who guided human souls to Hades; Ares, the god of war; Aphrodite, the goddess of beauty and love; and Eros, the god of love.

Greek religion was centered on life in this world rather than on that in the world to come. The picture that it presented of life after death was a shadowy and gloomy one. Homer, the great epic poet, has Achilles say in the Odyssey: "I would rather be above ground, the servant of some man of meager means, than ruler over all those dead and gone."

It is interesting to note that the classical period in Greek history (about 500 B.C. to 323 B.C.) had its own "enlightment" some two thousand years before the age of modern science. Philosophical criticism and rationalism began to undermine the traditional faith in gods, at least among the intellectuals in the cities. Heroditus, the historian, declared that the poets Homer and Hesiod had given the Greeks their gods; and the philosopher Euhemerus tried to demonstrate rationally that the gods had been merely men of distinction. Others maintained that they had never existed except as lifeless statues.[4]

Roman and Teuton Polytheism. Roman religion had similarities to that of the Greeks, but its gods were not strongly personified and it had no geneologies of the gods and few real myths. However, when Greek influence became powerful during the period of the Republic, the Greek myths had a strong appeal for the Romans, and the personified Greek gods were equated with their native gods. For example, the greatest of the Roman gods, Jupiter, was identified with Zeus, Mercury with Hermes, Neptune with Poseiden, and Venus with Aphrodite. Family and hearth gods seem to have had an especially important place in Roman worship. Outstanding among these was two-faced Janus, god of the door. Later he became the god of all things in their beginnings; and therefore January, the first month of the year, was named after him.

The religion of the Teutons was somewhat similar to that of the Greeks in that it personified its gods and had a fairly extensive mythology. But it was a much more somber and pessimistic religion. Not only was life after death a rather dreary state, even in Valhalla where the fallen war heroes gathered, but also the gods themselves were not regarded as immortal.

[4] Schoeps, op. cit., p. 141.

THE GREAT RELIGIONS OF TODAY

In the world of today there are innumerable religions and sects, including the primitive religions of many people who still live in tribal groups and who cling to ancient animistic beliefs and the practice of magic. But if we are to list the great religions of the world, each of which is still a vital force in the lives of many millions of human beings, we should include at least four, namely, Hinduism, Buddhism, Mohammedanism (Islam), and Christianity. Probably we should also include Judaism, for though the number professing this faith is relatively small, its historical importance is great. It provided much of the background out of which both Christianity and Islam developed.

Whether *Confucianism* and Taoism in China and *Shintoism* in Japan should be included in the great religions of today is questionable. Under communism the status and future of China's ancient religions is uncertain. Furthermore, Confucianism is often said to be more a philosophy than a religion. Shintoism is the ancient religion of Japan but has had strong competition from Buddhism. In 1868 reformed Shintoism was made the official religion, but after World War II religious freedom was declared. However, it is said that millions of Japanese still retain their faith in Shintoism. It is a mixture of nature, ancestor, and emperor worship and is closely associated with Japanese nationalism.

Hinduism. Hinduism is the religion that, since ancient times, has had a strong hold on India and even today dominates the lives of the majority of the people. A minority of Indians have been converted to such foreign faiths as Christianity or Islam, or to religions like Buddhism, Jainism, or Sikhism, all three of which developed out of Hinduism itself.

To Westerners Hinduism is a strange religion. It has no founder, no distinct creeds like those of Christianity, no clearly laid-out path to final salvation. At the same time, it has a number and variety of gods that suggests the ancient pantheons of the Egyptians, Greeks, and Romans. Over the centuries it has gradually added new gods, new concepts, and new rituals. Among different groups and in different parts of India it takes on somewhat different forms. It includes the most varied types of religious belief: fetishism, animal cults (sacred cows), and polytheism. Along with the subtle and sublime, it includes many crude and primitive views and customs. In addition to sacred cows, which must not be killed, sacred monkeys roam the country and cause much damage. They are regarded as holy because the mythological monkey god Hanuman once aided the god Rama; and it is said that Sadhus (supposed to be holy men) still kidnap babies to sacrifice them to Durga or black Kali.[5]

The original doctrines of Hinduism are expressed in the *Veda,* a collection of classical religious texts written in *Sanskrit* from about 1500 B.C. to 800 B.C. Sanskrit was the language of the Indo-European, or Aryan,

[5] Ibid., p. 171.

conquerors who began moving into India from the north about 1500 B.C. It is closely related to Greek and Latin and to the Celtic, Germanic, and Slavic languages, because other Aryan tribes migrated westward in successive waves and ultimately occupied most of Europe, including the British Isles.

What has made it possible for a religion containing such diverse elements as Hinduism to survive for some three thousand years? Longer, if we carry its origin back to the earliest writings in the Veda. According to Schoeps the "ultimate reality" of Hinduism, which explains much of its hold on its believers and their society, is the doctrine of *Karma*.[6] This holds that there is no beginning or end. All beings have immortal souls thoughout eternity but these go through an endless series of reincarnations. If one's acts are good in this life, one becomes something better in the next, and vice versa. Karma, regarded as a major element in eternal cosmic law, supports the Hindu caste system and justifies differences in social status. Any privileges or wealth that higher caste Indians enjoy become the deserved recompense for good behavior in past incarnations, and the miseries of the outcastes become just punishments for past sins. One may be reborn into a higher caste but only if he scrupulously observes the ritual, the many detailed rules of conduct that his caste status imposes on him in this life. If his conduct is wholly unworthy, he may be reborn as a dog or pig or something still lower.

The nature of the caste system and its relation to Karma will be discussed further in Chapter 12, "Social Stratification." If the caste system should break down, as it tends to do in industrialized cities, this might pose a threat to the survival of Hinduism.

Buddhism. Buddhism is another great religion of the Eastern world. It developed out of early Hinduism, and one of its chief objectives is to free men from the endless cycle of reincarnations that is part of the doctrine of Karma. Buddhism was founded more than five hundred years before Christ by a young Nepalese prince, Siddharta Gautama, who later became known as Buddha ("the enlightened one"). After observing the troubles of his father's subjects the prince became convinced that all life results in suffering and that the only escape for man is to overcome his desire for life and its pleasures, because it is these that lead to suffering. So he left his parents and his princely existence and became a wandering ascetic monk in order to seek the path by which man could escape from suffering.

After practicing yoga and asceticism for seven years, with five other monks he wandered on again until, somewhere in north central India, he allowed himself to fall into the lowest stage of absorbed concentration. In this state of joyless and painless equanimity he received the Enlightenment and thus became a Buddha. His sense of bliss was so great that he recognized the insignificance of all his former life experiences. He

[6] Ibid., p. 163.

had now accomplished his greatest task by achieving an earthly foretaste of Nirvana. For him the cycle of rebirth and suffering was ended. But should he use this new knowledge solely for his own benefit or should he share it with the world? After a struggle with himself he decided to communicate to others the truth he had discovered. So for the next forty-five years, until his death at the age of eighty, he lived the simple life of a wandering preacher, often accompanied by many of his disciples.

To the enlightened ones who had followed the "Eightfold Path" of concentration in order to subdue the self and curb desires, and who had thus obtained a foretaste of Nirvana, death would bring entrance into final Nirvana. Nirvana seems to be the end of the ego, the end of consciousness. But Buddha would only say that it was the end of painful becoming; the final peace; an eternal state of being; a condition of happiness and bliss. However, entrance into Nirvana was possible only for those who had voluntarily accepted poverty and become monks. The Buddhist monastic community was founded by the Buddha himself, and its organization and character is said to be the one element in Buddhism that has changed relatively little over the centuries. Even to this day Buddhist monks shave their heads and wear the traditional yellow robes.

Original Buddhism was more a philosophy than a religion, although it included such supernatural beliefs as Karma with its doctrine of reincarnation. Buddha himself made no claim to divine origin, and he had little or nothing to say about gods. But over the centuries, as Buddhism gained converts and spread to other countries it underwent many changes, some of which greatly increased its popular appeal. Also, a variety of sects developed. Some began to recognize the Buddha as a divine being and even developed a doctrine of his immaculate conception. (He descended from heaven in the form of an elephant and entered his mother's womb while she lay sleeping in a palace.) Then other heavenly Buddhas were discovered, and also *Bodhisattvas*. The latter are beings who, out of pity for men, have renounced their Buddha nature and given up entrance into Nirvana in order to help others find salvation. Salvation was made a little easier by introducing the concept of a paradise that might be attained even by those who were not monks and who therefore could not hope to enter into Nirvana. Some sects also introduced the worship of gods (whom Buddha had not actually rejected) instead of concentrating on the Search for Enlightenment by following the Eightfold Path. As early as the first century B.C., under Greek influence, statues of the Buddha had become common in northwestern India and they began to serve as centers of worship; and gradually elaborate rituals were developed. In early Buddhism there was little or no ritual and the Buddha was not represented at all.

Buddhism gradually declined in India and today has relatively few supporters there. But it spread to Tibet, China, Korea, Japan, Southeast Asia, and Ceylon, taking on markedly different forms in different areas. Its future in Tibet and China under communism is uncertain. In the

South, in such countries as Ceylon, Burma, and Thailand, Buddhism is firmly established and is said to have retained more of its original character than in other regions. In Burma and Thailand it is now the state religion.

Judaism. Despite the fact that Judaism has played a very important historical role, the total number of its adherents is relatively small. By early 1971 the entire Jewish population of the world was probably not much over 14 million, and this included some who no longer believed in or practiced Judaism.

Judaism developed out of the religion of the ancient Hebrew tribe. According to the Bible story a great leader of this tribe, Abraham, put his trust in a single God to guide him and his people in their migrations. Even today most Jews are likely to think of themselves as lineal descendants of Abraham, though it is true that in later times Judaism became willing to accept converts from among the gentiles. Whether Abraham regarded his God as the maker of the universe and the all-powerful ruler of heaven and earth, or just as the great god of the Hebrews, is not certain. The latter seems more probable. Much later the Hebrews, or Israelites as they came to be called,[7] moved into the fertile Nile Delta to escape famine, and there they were eventually enslaved by the Egyptians.

It was during the period of their slavery, probably sometime between 1450 B.C. and 1400 B.C., that there arose a great leader, Moses. He not only led them to freedom, as God had directed him to do, but he came to be commonly regarded as the real founder of Judaism. After the escape of the Israelites from Egypt, Moses ascended Mt. Sinai, where God appeared to him and through him made a sacred covenant with what were by then the twelve tribes of Israel. "The people acknowledged 'the God of Israel' as ruler of the world and creator of heaven and earth, while God recognized the people of Israel as his [chosen] followers among the nations of the earth."[8] Moses had been instructed by God to call him *Yahveh*, or as it is sometimes translated, "Jehovah." When Moses came down from the mountain, he brought with him two stone tablets on which were inscribed Yahveh's Ten Commandments. These were later amplified into the many commandments and prohibitions set forth in the *Torah* (the Pentateuch, or the Five Books of Moses) which is part of both Jewish scriptures and the Christian Old Testament.

Judaism has several unique characteristics. First, though it makes claims to universality, it was and still is primarily the religion of a group of people who can, with qualifications, regard themselves as descendants of the ancient Israelites, who believed that they were God's chosen people. Second, it has preserved much of its essential character for more than three thousand years. This in spite of the fact that for more than eighteen hundred years, ever since their last major rebellion against Rome was

[7] After Jacob (or Israel), the grandson of Abraham.
[8] Schoeps, op. cit., p. 221.

crushed by the Emperor Hadrian in A.D. 135, the Jews have been a widely scattered and often persecuted minority among alien peoples. Finally, and most important, Judaism was the first great religion to develop a clear and unequivocal concept of a single God as the creator and ruler of the universe.

Judaism believes in the resurrection of the dead and that a person must account beyond the grave for his good and evil deeds. It looks for the coming of the Messiah and for a *Messianic age* in which the kingdom of eternal peace will prevail and in which all evil impulses will be removed from men's hearts. But it rejects the Christian belief that the Messiah has already come with his message of salvation.

During the Middle Ages and early modern times the rights of Jews in Europe were greatly restricted and they were forced to live in special sections of the cities called *ghettos*. The French Revolution and Napoleon did much to free Jews from the ghettos. But later there was a reaction, and it was not until after the social upheavals of 1848 that in most countries the Jews received full rights of citizenship on a more or less permanent basis. But this did not end their troubles, for the very success that many of them soon enjoyed in the professions stirred up new waves of anti-Semitism that reached a climax in Hitler's concentration camps and gas chambers.

However, the freeing of the Jews in the nineteenth century from their former restrictions brought about great changes in Judaism itself. Gradually the Jews, not only in Europe but also in America, became divided into three major groups: the orthodox, who resist all change in beliefs and ritual; the reform group that rejects the idea of a Jewish state and much of Jewish traditionalism and believes that Judaism should be regarded as a changing and developing religion; and the conservatives, who cannot accept orthodoxy but who object to an extreme break with traditions, and who therefore seek a middle way.

A most remarkable achievement of the more orthodox elements in Judaism was the establishment after World War II of the state of Israel. Unfortunately, however, the establishment of this state created a prime source of international friction because of the intense antagonism of the Arabs toward it. Much of this antagonism resulted from the fact that when Israel was created large numbers of Palestinian Arabs were displaced from their homes and became refugees.

The Religion of Islam. Islam, like Judaism, is a religion based on divine revelation, and its founder, Mohammed, like Moses, made no claims to divinity for himself. He believed only that he had been chosen by God, or Allah, to receive from the angel Gabriel revelations of Allah's will. These revelations, which became frequent, he repeated in full to those who would listen, and shortly after his death they were assembled by his friend Abu Bakr to form the Koran, the scriptures of the Moslems. Abu became the first successor, or *caliph,* to carry on Mohammed's work.

Mohammed was born about A.D. 570 at *Mecca,* in the western part of what is now Saudi Arabia. According to tradition he was orphaned when he was six years old and then became a ward of his grandfather and, later, of an uncle, both of whom were prominent members of the Koreish tribe. Later he was a merchant, and at about the age of twenty-five he became the business adviser to a rich widow, fifteen years his senior, whom he eventually married. Meanwhile he had come into contact with the Arabian religion of his time, which was a mixture of animism and polytheism. He had also learned something about Judaism and Christianity, because among Mohammed's acquaintances in Mecca were followers of both religions. His contacts with Jews and Christians probably contributed to his dissatisfaction with the beliefs and practices of his fellow Arab tribesmen.

Though Mohammed himself created the religion of Islam, or Mohammedanism, he was greatly influenced by Christianity and Judaism, and somewhat by the native beliefs and practices of the Arabs. He considered that he was completing and perfecting the work of Moses, Jesus, and other heavenly messengers whom he recognized as his forerunners. Similarities of Islam to Judaism or Christianity or both include (1) prohibitions against consuming various kinds of food, to which Mohammed added a requirement to abstain from alcohol; (2) the idea of a Sabbath, which Islam celebrates on Friday; and (3) very similar eschatological notions, that is, ideas about the last or final things.[9] Much of the Koran is concerned with the resurrection of the dead, the last judgment, retribution, paradise, and hell. But Mohammed denied the Christian doctrine of the Trinity and the divinity of Christ. According to the Koran, God is one and God is eternal. He neither begets nor is begotten. One of the chief borrowings of Islam from earlier Arab religious concepts was veneration of the Kaaba stone, which became the chief objective of the pilgrimage to Mecca, a journey every believer was required to undertake at least once in his life. Another pagan element he adopted was the Arab belief in jinns, demons who dwelt in the desert but who sometimes could be controlled by magic and ordered to perform magical services for human beings.

The Arabic *Islam* means "submission," and *Moslems* are submitters to the will of God. The devout Moslem's problem is fairly simple. He has only to perform his duties as outlined in the Koran and as exemplified by the acts of Mohammed in his lifetime. The Koran is infallible. He does have the privilege, denied to Christians and Jews, of having four wives at the same time.

The *Five Pillars of Islam* state the indispensable religious duties of a believer. They are (1) acceptance and frequent repetition of the creed "There is no God but Allah and Mohammed is His prophet"; (2) the per-

---

[9] John B. Noss, *Man's Religions,* 3rd ed., New York, The Macmillan Company, 1963, p. 734. Also see 4th ed., 1969, pp. 522–523, 530–531.

formance five times a day of prescribed rituals of prayer and devotion; (3) the giving of alms to the needy; (4) the fast during Ramadan, the month when the Koran was revealed to Mohammed by the angel Gabriel; and (5) the pilgrimage to the Kaaba stone at Mecca.

The great success of Islam from almost the beginning was a result not only of the appeal that its simple doctrines and rituals had for the pagan Arab tribesmen but also of the political and organizational ability of Mohammed and his early successors (caliphs). Mohammed's first attempts to convert the inhabitants of Mecca were not very successful, and even created enemies who became a danger to him. But he succeeded in getting himself invited to the neighboring city of Medina by some of its citizens who felt that they needed a strong ruler to control the blood feuds that had been troubling them. Some of his enemies in Mecca tried to prevent him from leaving, but he successfully made the Hegira ("flight" or "departure") to Medina in 622, the year that Moslems consider the beginning of the Islamic age. There he organized a religious community that, as the transmitter of Allah's commandments to the people, he ruled with a firm hand. Soon war broke out with Mecca, but in 630, after experiencing

14. The Citadel Mosque in Cairo. (Photo by author.)

varying fortunes, Mohammed was able to march back into Medina with a victorious army.

Even before Mohammed's death in 632 great progress had been made, by persuasion or force, in converting and unifying the Arab tribes and thus laying the foundations, not only for the later Mohammedan empire but also for ultimately making Islam one of the world's great religions. Within a hundred years of Mohammed's death the Moslem empire stretched from Saragossa, Spain, to the Caucasus. Later the central power of the caliphs declined and vanished, but Islam continued to gain as the Turks and other Moslem groups made new conquests. In time Moslem political and military power began to fade, but not the Islamic faith. It now dominates North Africa, the Middle East, Iran, Pakistan, Indonesia, and even some areas of the southern Philippines. In recent times it has been gaining many converts, especially in some of the new nations of central Africa.

But Islam, like other great world religions, has had its internal conflicts, some of them rather bitter. Today it is divided into a number of sects that do not see eye to eye on all questions. It is also being subjected to pressures by Western culture with its modern science and technology. So questions can be raised about the future of Islam just as about the future of other world religions. Some believe that the establishment of the state of Israel may tend to unify Moslems, especially in the Arab countries, and at least for a time strengthen the resistance of Islam to the forces of change.

The Christian Religion. Christianity, the principal religion of the Western world, developed from Judaism, and the greater part of the Christian Bible (the Old Testament) still consists of Jewish sacred writings. The ancient Jews believed that at his chosen time God would confound their enemies and set up a new Jewish kingdom under a *Messiah* (deliverer) descended from King David. Later some came to believe that the Messiah would come down from heaven at the end of the world, at the time of the resurrection of the dead, and would carry out the last judgment.

Jesus of Nazareth, the founder of Christianity, was born at Bethlehem in Judea at the beginning of our era, and at some point in his life he became convinced that he was the Messiah or Christ, and the divine son of God. Often he is called *Jesus Christ,* which simply means "Jesus, the Messiah." Soon after he started his ministry, at about the age of thirty, he converted and gathered around him twelve close associates, the *Apostles,* who were to be his chief aids and who were to carry on his ministry after his death.

Our knowledge of the life of Jesus is actually very limited. Our knowledge of his teachings is greater, but it comes to us indirectly. He did not write them down but depended on his disciples to preach from memory what he had taught. Our chief sources of knowledge about him are, first, the Gospels of the New Testament and, second, the Epistles. But these were prepared long after his death. The four Gospels are thought by historians to have been written between A.D. 65 and about A.D. 100. Presumably, they were based on documents in which some of his followers had recorded his sayings as they remembered them and also certain of the circumstances of his life. But how accurately his sayings and the events of his life were recorded or how much was changed or added by successive copiers or revisers of the Gospels, historical scholarship cannot tell us with any certainty.

If we follow the account in the Gospel According to Luke, when Jesus was about thirty years old he was baptized in the Jordan River by the ascetic preacher from the desert, John the Baptist; and as he came out of the water he had a vision in which the heavens opened and a voice said to him, "You are my beloved Son." He then went into the wilderness beyond the Jordan where for forty days he meditated, resisting various suggestions with which the devil tempted him. After that he recrossed the Jordan into Galilee and began his ministry, proclaiming the good news of salvation and amazing people by curing the sick and performing other miracles.

Jesus never doubted the reality of God or of his own special relationship to him. But he knew he had not been sent, as some of his hearers hoped, to deliver the Jews from Rome by re-establishing the earthly kingdom of David. Rather, he had been sent by his Father to show all men, Jews and Gentiles alike, the way to heavenly salvation. Like many Jews of his day, he believed that the long-foretold Messianic Kingdom of God would come rather soon, but for him it was a kingdom in heaven and it was only for those who would believe in him, who would truly repent of their sins, and who would surrender to the will of God before it was too late.

Jesus taught that the most important thing is to believe in God and do his will, and to believe in Jesus as the son of God. God is utterly good: supremely righteous and just but also forgiving and merciful. Therefore, men should trust him completely and should regularly seek spiritual aid through prayer. Jesus also taught that God demands that men should love one another, friend and foe alike, and this has been one of the most difficult teachings for devout Christians to interpret and to apply as a practical guide to daily conduct. Jesus also taught his disciples that they should obey the Ten Commandments, which God transmitted to Moses on Mount Sinai, and should follow the golden rule. The latter helps to interpret the doctrine of universal love of mankind. We usually state it in the form "Do unto others as you would that they should do unto you."

Jesus' success in drawing crowds in Galilee soon attracted the attention of the leaders of the two principal Jewish sects or parties in Jerusalem, the Sadducees and the Pharisees. They had their own differences but both became enemies of Jesus because his teaching and his actions did not always follow the dictates of either Judaic law or tradition. After he had been preaching for three or four years, Jesus decided to go to Jerusalem at the time of the Passover, when Jews from a wide area would be assembled for the great annual festival. This gave the enemies of Jesus an opportunity to stir up ill feeling against him among the people. Finally they seized him, made false accusations against him, and denounced him to the Roman governor, Pilate, on the ground that he claimed to be king of the Jews. Pilate doubted his guilt, but when the crowd demanded death, the governor acquiesced and ordered his Crucifixion at Golgotha.

Three events reported in the Gospels and the Epistles are of crucial significance for Christianity: (1) the Last Supper of Jesus with his disciples on the evening before the Crucifixion; (2) his Crucifixion; and (3) his Resurrection on the third day after his death. Even before coming to Jerusalem, Jesus had foretold his death and resurrection to the twelve apostles. The great central mystery of the Christian religion is the belief that in some sense Jesus died to redeem the sins of men and thus opened for them the way to salvation. In the sacrament of *Communion,* or the Eucharist, which was first celebrated by Jesus with the twelve disciples at the Last Supper, devout communicants believe that they enter into a special relationship with Christ. The wine they drink and the bread they eat symbolize, or else as in Catholic doctrine in some mystic way become, the blood and body of Christ. As Schoeps expresses it, "Christ himself must thus be conceived as present in the bread and wine."[10] The communicant is thus strengthened in his attempts to achieve salvation by the redemptive power that Christ achieved through his death and Resurrection.

The Early Christians. The spread of Christianity after Jesus' death was relatively rapid, but the early Christian groups, or churches, were only loosely linked. However, by the end of the first century, administrative organization had begun to develop in Rome and elsewhere, and bishops began to assume authority not only to appoint priests to oversee local churches but also to settle disputes over doctrine. Gradually the primacy of the bishop of Rome became recognized throughout the Empire, and by the end of the third century he had taken the title of pope.

But throughout this entire early period the Christians, as a troublesome though growing minority, had been subjected sporadically to terrible persecutions. All this changed when Constantine, after defeating his rivals, became emperor of the Roman Empire near the beginning of the fourth century A.D. He not only placed the sign of Christ in Greek letters (**XP**) on the standards of his legions, but when he built a second capital at Byzantium, renamed Constantinople, he built a magnificent church. By the end of the fourth century Christianity had become the sole religion in the Roman Empire because, after the Emperor Theodosius had declared paganism a crime, the open practice of pagan cults disappeared rapidly.

During the early centuries of the Church, many developments occurred. *Monasticism* became established, and later the monks became important in preserving and transmitting to future generations the literature and learning of ancient Greece and Rome. A canonical (approved) version

[10] Schoeps, op. cit., p. 276.

15. The Cathedral of Notre Dame in Paris. (Photo by author.)

of Christian scriptures was established, and many doctrinal disputes were settled officially, though not necessarily to the satisfaction of all parties involved. One of the most troublesome problems of Christian doctrine has been to reconcile the divinity of Christ as the son of God with the basic Christian concept of a single good and all-powerful God who created the universe. The answer of most Christian bodies, Catholic, Orthodox, or Protestant, has been the *Trinity*—"God in three persons" or three manifestations: Father, Son, and Holy Spirit. But the problem is still troublesome, and some groups, like the modern Unitarians, reject the concept of the Trinity.

The Middle Ages and After. Before the final collapse of the Roman Empire in the West in A.D. 476, the Catholic Church had become strong enough to prevent the complete breakdown of order and civilization that might otherwise have resulted from the successive invasions of the Empire by Germanic tribes. During the Middle Ages the Church dominated the religious and intellectual life of Europe and to a great extent its politics. Meanwhile the Eastern Roman Empire with its capital at Constantinople still survived, and the Eastern Church, later known as the Orthodox Church, became increasingly independent of Rome. The final break or schism between the two parts of the Church occurred in 1054 and it remains to this day.

The next great defection from the Church of Rome did not occur for several hundred years. In the fifteenth century, perhaps even earlier, many Christians felt that the Church was undergoing moral decay. Great preachers like Savonarola began calling for reforms. The *Renaissance,* which brought a renewal of interest in art, literature, and the works of classical antiquity undoubtedly contributed to a general stir and unrest. Reformers began to urge that religion revert to its sources. One particular cause for complaint was the sale of indulgences, which in some places had reduced the sacrament of penance into a money-gathering device. The result was the *Reformation* (Protestant Revolt), which began in 1517 when Martin Luther posted his famous ninety-five theses on the door of the church in Wittenberg in Germany. Other important leaders of the Reformation included Ulrich Zwingli and John Calvin in Switzerland and John Knox in Scotland.

The Reformation led to a considerable period of religious and political turmoil, including religious wars and repression of dissident groups in various countries; and though it did not win over the majority of Catholics to Protestantism, it did result in very substantial defections from the Roman Church. But the Protestants who succeeded in gaining freedom from control by Rome did not succeed in joining together to form a major independent church body. Instead they became divided into a number of *sects* or denominations. Several of these, including the Puritans and Quakers, played an important role in the settlement of the English colonies in America.

European migration to the Americas during and after the age of the great discoveries, and to such areas as South Africa, Australia, and New Zealand, carried Christianity with it. In some areas, as in the United States and in Canada except Quebec, Protestant settlers from northwest Europe were in the majority. In other areas, as in practically all of Latin America, settlers came largely from overwhelmingly Catholic countries like Spain, Portugal, and Italy. Christianity was also carried to other parts of the world by the strong missionary movement that developed in the nineteenth century, but in most non-Christian countries missionaries succeeded in converting only a very small fraction of the people.

THE ROLE OF RELIGION IN SOCIETY

There can be little doubt that in primitive societies and in the earliest civilizations religious beliefs and practices were a strong integrative factor in most societies. Because of these beliefs and practices, people knew how they must behave individually and as a group to avoid the ill will of the gods and to win their favor. They knew that certain things were sacred and that if the group was to avoid famine or other misfortunes no one must be allowed to treat them with disrespect. Religious beliefs were tied to rules of behavior and usually gave strong support to custom and tradition. As has already been mentioned, in early historical times almost every "nation" had its own gods and sometimes, as in ancient Egypt, the king himself was regarded as divine. (Even in modern Japan, up to 1945, Shinto doctrine held that the emperor was a descendant of the sun goddess.) The result was that the people were drawn together, not only by their common beliefs but also by their participation in common rituals of prayer, praise, and sacrifice.

Not infrequently, however, in the more highly developed civilizations of the world differences in religious beliefs have been a source of social conflict, especially when groups with different religious beliefs have lived within the same national borders. We have mentioned the persecution and frequent martyrdom to which the early Christians were subjected in the Roman Empire and have also mentioned the religious wars that accompanied the Reformation in Europe. A much more recent example can be found in modern India. After the British withdrew and the predominantly Moslem state of Pakistan was created and separated from India in 1947, large numbers of Hindus and Moslems were killed or injured in riots and massacres resulting from enmity between the two groups. Even more recently there has been open, if less bloody, conflict between Protestants and Catholics in Northern Ireland.

Religion as a Source of Moral Values. Religion, then, can be a socially disruptive force, but it seems rather clear that over the years its major influence has been in the direction of integrating and stabilizing nations and cultures. In the Western world, where Christianity in its various forms is by a wide margin the predominant faith, our ethical and moral values have, over the centuries, been modified and given greater vitality by the teachings of the Christian religion. This is true in spite of the many crimes committed in the name of Christianity in the past, including the torture or burning at the stake of heretics in the Middle Ages, and in spite of such reversions to mass brutality as those master-minded by non-Christians like Hitler and Stalin. Christian ideals have had a great influence not only on those who profess the faith but also on many persons of good will who cannot accept its supernatural doctrines. As a result, humanitarianism has progressed far since the days of ancient Rome, with its gladitorial games and the general acquiescence in ruthless treatment of enemies, prisoners, slaves, and troublesome minorities.

For the believer, religion gives divine authority to ethical and moral principles. This raises the question, How important is religion in the glue that holds a society together? Certainly there is no sure and simple answer. But some who have studied this question believe that if too many people should lose their religious faith it would be very difficult to maintain an orderly society with free elections and a wide range of personal freedoms; to produce goods with enough efficiency to hope to eliminate poverty; and in general to maintain the level of civilization we have already achieved. If so, there would be little chance of enabling people to live more meaningful and more satisfying lives. Some suggest that communism may be a substitute for religion as a doctrine for motivating human beings to action for the social good. But so far communists have succeeded only in setting up totalitarian societies ruled by dictators who, with the aid of secret police, have greatly restricted human rights and liberties.

Such societies have not even been able to produce goods with enough efficiency to provide their people with what we would consider adequate standards of living.

Through its influence on individuals, religion has an impact on economic and political institutions. The ethical level of business and politics depends not only on the morality of business men and politicians but also on the morality of the general public and the ethical standards that it adheres to and demands.

The Protestant Ethic and Capitalism. The great German sociologist, Max Weber (1864–1920), developed an interesting thesis in his book *The Protestant Ethic and the Spirit of Capitalism.* According to his theory, the new Protestant sects that developed out of the Reformation, especially those that were influenced by the doctrines of Calvin, made a major contribution to the economic prosperity of England and western Europe and to the development of modern industrial capitalism. They did so because they believed in the *Protestant ethic,* that is, they believed that God expects good Christians to work hard, to save, to invest their savings, and to show business initiative. They also believed that material success is one indication of divine approval and election to salvation. Though it would be naive to assume that the Protestant ethic—sometimes called the *Puritan ethic*—was the sole explanation of the rapid growth of industrial capitalism, it may well have been an important contributing factor.

In recent years the Protestant ethic has been under attack, on the ground that we are too materialistic, that money making is not the most important thing in life. Certainly it is not. But money, or, rather, the goods it represents, is an essential means to many good ends; and if too many Americans lose their incentive to work, to save, to invest, to organize productive enterprises and to operate them efficiently, idealistic plans for abolishing poverty and providing many of the social services we need will not make much progress.

True, our problems are not as simple as this suggests. In the future, efficient operation of industry must be interpreted to include minimizing social costs as well as those of private business. As mentioned earlier, if we are to achieve a better society, we must make great efforts to conserve natural resources and to fight pollution. This means, among other things, economizing in our use of both natural resources and consumer goods. A certain amount of material goods is essential to the "quality" of life, however we define it, but we cannot and need not expand their output indefinitely.

Putting a high value on work and on the kinds of behavior necessary for material progress was never a monopoly of Puritans or Protestants. It is a characteristic found everywhere among people who are determined to improve their condition. Today the Israelis, the Japanese, and the West Germans all have it in good measure, though the first two are neither Protestant nor Christian and the West Germans are predominantly Roman Catholic.

Impact of Religion on Education, the Arts, and Literature. The influence of religion on education, the arts, music, and literature is rather obvious. During the Middle Ages it was the Church and especially the monasteries that preserved ancient literature and kept learning alive. In the United States, from colonial times until well into the nineteenth century most of our colleges and universities were started and controlled by religious organizations. Many of them are still church controlled, and some religious bodies, most notably the Roman Catholic Church, operate extensive systems of secondary and primary schools. A large portion of the great works of art of ancient Greece and the European Renaissance are representations of personalities or events with religious significance. In the field of religious music we find such outstanding composers as Bach and Handel, and in literature we have great poems such as Dante's *Inferno* and Milton's *Paradise Lost*.

RELIGION IN THE UNITED STATES

From early colonial times religion has played an important part in the history of what is now the United States. Several colonies were settled by religious groups chiefly or partly for religious reasons. Massachusetts and Connecticut were settled by Puritans who not only wanted to escape persecution in England but also desired to establish communities based on their own religious beliefs. Rhode Island was settled by dissidents who were exiled from Massachusetts, and Maryland was originally settled by Catholics. The Quakers, though not the first colonizers in what is now Pennsylvania, became an important factor in its settlement when King Charles II made a land grant to one of their leaders, William Penn.

Long before the Revolutionary War most colonies had established religious freedom; and in the first amendment to the Constitution of the United States, which was ratified and in force by the end of 1791, Congress was forbidden to make any law concerning the establishment of religion or prohibiting freedom of religious belief.

Some Developments Since 1800. According to some estimates church membership was at a low level in this country in the year 1800. In any case, it expanded tremendously during the nineteenth century. Much of this expansion was simply a result of the great growth of population, but there was also a renewal of interest in religion, one evidence of which was the appearance of new sects and denominations. Among the new sects, one, the Mormons, or the Church of Jesus Christ of Latter Day Saints, is of special interest, not only because of the uniqueness of its creed and organization but also because of the prominent role that it played in the early settlement of what is now the state of Utah. Joseph Smith, the founder of the Latter Day Saints, is believed by his followers to have received a special divine revelation, namely the Book of Mormon. In their early days at Nauvoo, Illinois, the Mormons suffered severe persecution partly because, at that time, they permitted a man to marry a number of wives. Today in their relationship to our larger society they are not very different from any Protestant Christian sect. Another indication of increased interest in religion during the early nineteenth century was the popularity of camp meetings and revivalists. These were most successful in winning converts to Christianity in the new communities of the West and along the advancing frontier.

Up to the mid–nineteenth century, American Christians were overwhelmingly Protestant, but after the Irish potato famine of 1845 and 1846, large numbers of Irish Roman Catholic immigrants began arriving, and most of them settled in the growing cities. After the social disturbances of 1848 in Europe, German immigrants started to enter this country in large numbers, and many of them were also Catholics. But the greatest influx of Catholic immigrants began in the late 1890's with the arrival annually of hundreds of thousands of Italians, Poles, and the nationals of various other central European countries. Even today, American Christians remain predominantly Protestant, but Roman Catholics constitute a minority of about 37 per cent of the total of some 133 million reported members of all Christian sects, including 3 million or 4 million members of various Orthodox Church organizations. Besides Christians there are in this country some 5.8 million members of Jewish congregations.[11] Religions other than Christianity or Judaism have relatively few adherents in this country.

Secularism and the Decline of Faith. We have noted that in ancient times and in the Middle Ages, religion and the political state were tied together very closely. Persons who refused to accept the official faith or to participate in traditional rituals were often subjected to severe penalties, including death by burning or by other forms of torture. But in modern industrial countries the direct ties between church and state have been very much loosened and in many cases completely broken. In communist countries, governments even oppose and discourage religion, though to some extent they tolerate it. Over the years, in the technologically advanced countries, more and more activities have been *secularized* or removed from the direct control and influence of religious bodies. In the United States this trend has gone further than in some other countries. Our government supports no church organization and sets no religious requirements for holding either elective or appointive public offices. It does permit churches to operate schools and colleges at their own expense, but education in this country is becoming more and more secular, or nonreligious, as the public schools and colleges keep expanding at the expense of church-controlled school systems. Increasingly the lives of people are being secularized, that is, filled by occupational, social, and recreational activities that have no direct relationship to religious institutions

[11] These approximate figures for various religious groups are derived from statistics in *The 1971 World Almanac,* New York, Newspaper Enterprise Association, Inc., 1970, pp. 323–324.

"And I would like to remind you good people that the cost of salvation has gone up, too." (Courtesy *Wall Street Journal*.)

and rituals. Moreover, there is a large minority of the population that belongs to no church and professes no religious faith.

The Impact of Science and Materialistic Philosophies. Modern science assumes that we live in an orderly universe ruled by definite laws, or sequences of cause and effect that can be predicted and sometimes controlled if we sufficiently understand them. Science deals with the natural world, religion with the supernatural. We cannot see, feel, weigh, or measure God. There is no satisfactory scientific evidence of the transmigration of souls, or of any kind of life after death, or of the existence of heaven, or even of the existence of God; and because science has proved so dependable in the field of natural phenomena and has so greatly increased our control over our physical environment, we tend to be more than skeptical of religious teachings that seem to contradict well-tested scientific laws. Hence, great numbers of people are unable to accept as anything more than myths or allegories the miraculous and supernatural events that are an important part of almost all of the long-established religious creeds.

However, this does not mean that religion and science must necessarily be in conflict. Actually it is possible to find outstanding scientists who are deeply religious men. Science may conflict with religion if religious doctrines include pronouncements about the natural world that contradict scientific knowledge. If one's religion requires him to believe that the world is flat, it denies the findings of the science of astronomy and also the visual evidence provided for us by the astronauts. Likewise, if it requires him to believe that man was created by God in a moment or a day, interpreted literally, it is in conflict with the accepted scientific theory of evolution. But even scientists can accept as symbolic, biblical accounts that, taken literally, disagree with scientific findings; and to those who believe firmly in both science and an all-powerful God, the findings of science merely reveal to man the great complexity and orderliness of the universe God has created, and the marvelous way in which he carries out his will through the processes of nature.

In the final analysis, religious beliefs are a matter of faith. They concern a world of the spirit that is not material and that is assumed to be beyond the scope of scientific investigation. Religious beliefs may be supported by certain philosophical concepts. For example, many people find it difficult to conceive of a universe without a creator or planner. To them, the very existence of an orderly cosmos seems to prove that there must be a God. But this is not proof in a scientific sense. Science deals with the phenomena of the natural world, and presumably it can neither prove nor disprove the existence of a supernatural realm of the spirit, nor the existence of a good and omnipotent God, nor the existence of a life after death. To the devout believer, these are eternal truths, truths whose validity rests on faith. But even a belief in God does not solve the most basic of mysteries, namely, that anything at all exists, because it does not explain the origin of God. To be sure, we can assume that God, or the universe, or both, have always existed and will never end, but that is accepting existence rather than explaining it.

Though science and religion are not necessarily in conflict, there is little doubt that science and the *materialistic philosophies* sometimes associated with it have tended over the years to weaken the influence of religion. Materialistic philosophies tend to deny ultimate reality to anything but matter, the energy associated with it, and the movements, variations, and combinations of matter and energy. They even view such phenomena as consciousness and "will" as manifestations of tremendously complex combinations or relationships of matter and energy. In most

"Wrong number. 'Dial-a-prayer' is nine-seven-five-eight." (© PUNCH, LONDON.)

modern societies the proportion of the people who are professed and convinced atheists and agnostics is probably small, but observation, discussion, and a few studies based on questionnaires seem to indicate that there are many more who profess a belief in God but are not very certain about it, and for whom God is some vague, impersonal force or power that may somehow pervade and control the universe. Many hope for a future life but are not at all sure there is one. Whether this kind of faith can give support and solace in time of trouble or can induce people to meet their moral obligations is a question. Persons who hold such tentative beliefs are found not only outside the churches but also among church members, especially in the more liberal Protestant denominations.

The conservative Protestant groups who insist that, since the Bible is the word of God, everything in it must be literally true, including all accounts of miraculous happenings, are called *fundamentalists*. The modernist or liberal groups include those who tend to adjust their interpretation of the Bible to the findings of science, including historical research. But they vary greatly in the extent to which they are willing to concede, for example, that certain miraculous events that the Bible records could not literally have taken place. Sometimes it is hard to draw the line between the more extreme types of *religious liberalism* and *agnosticism* (the belief that we have no way of knowing whether there is a God). Furthermore, in all church bodies some persons can be found who have not broken their nominal church affiliation but who have completely lost their religious faith. Throughout the ages there have been unbelievers, even among primitive peoples, though presumably in the distant past they were relatively few. But there seems to be increasing evidence that doubts about religious doctrines are today more widespread than in the past.

SOME PROBLEMS OF OUR MODERN CHURCHES

Population Shifts and Racial Problems. Population shifts have long been a problem for churches. The constant shrinkage of our farm population since early in this century has forced the closing and abandonment of more and more rural churches; and at least since the Civil War, churches in our larger cities have faced problems because business centers have expanded into residential areas and good residential sections have gradually changed into slums, usually with a change in the ethnic character and the religious affiliations of the population. But for the last three decades, and to a lesser degree ever since our entry into World War I, the major population shifts in our cities have been the replacement of whites by blacks from the South, and the exodus of the whites to the suburbs.

The result has been the closing of many city churches; the moving of some to new locations while the old church buildings were sold to black congregations; and the integration of others. All these changes resulted in turmoil and problems. Before a church was disbanded, moved, or integrated, it usually had shrunk greatly in membership and had experienced financial problems because of reduced contributions. Moreover, integration has seldom been successful over a long period, because whites continue to move out of districts into which blacks are moving. This is usually attributed to prejudice against the blacks, which in part is correct; but it must be remembered that the Southern Negroes who move in have cultural backgrounds very different from those of the old residents. They come largely from rural areas where educational opportunities have been lacking for blacks and where incomes have been very low. A similar outward movement of old residents would occur, perhaps more slowly, if these areas were being invaded by Mexican Americans, Puerto Ricans, poor whites from Appalachia, or alien (immigrant) whites. When such population shifts take place, the old residents gradually discover that more and more of their friends are leaving, that the area is deteriorating physically, that the schools are deteriorating, and that the streets are becoming less safe.

Today many old, established inner-city churches are striving desperately to survive, to integrate, and to offer a meaningful ministry to the blacks by whom they are surrounded. Often these efforts are a failure, but here and there they meet with some success. At the same time, new Afro-American churches are springing up because many and probably most of the blacks prefer to organize their own congregations.

Denominationalism and the Ecumenical Movement. According to the *Yearbook of American Churches for 1969*, 238 religious bodies reported membership figures, mainly for 1967, which in total represented more than 63 per cent of our population. However, several comments should be made. First, many churches are slow in pruning from their lists of members those who have moved away or become completely inactive, and this tends to exaggerate membership figures. On the other hand, most Protestant churches do not count as members infants and children who have merely been baptized. Only persons who "join" the church are included. The Roman Catholic Church and a few Protestant bodies count everyone who has been baptized. If all churches followed this practice, total church membership would be appreciably higher. Finally, the figures undoubtedly fail to include many small religious groups who do not report their membership. However, the total membership of such groups, mostly fundamentalist, is probably rather small.

The fact that 90 per cent or more of the 238 religious bodies that reported their membership are Protestant groups indicates the extent to which Protestantism is divided. A few of these groups are large, like the Methodist Church and the Southern Baptist Convention, each of which has over eleven million members; but others are very small. In the last several decades both the clergy and the laity of many church bodies have begun to recognize that in the modern world the differences in creed between Protestant denominations are frequently of very little importance. Often church members are not aware of these differences or do not understand

FIRST MINISTERIAL CHURCH

DAILY SERVICE 7:45 SUN. 10:00

RT. REV. WM. R. BATES PASTOR

DR. J. DUDLEY HALE ORGANIST

MISS MARY SPRAGUE VOCALIST

MR. MIKE JAGG ELECTRIC HARP

MR. ZONK COLE LEAD GUITAR

MR. SPECS WAYNE UKELELE

MR. PILLS RUDD RHYTHM BASS

MR. HOP WATTS BONGOS

(Courtesy Ed Fisher
and *LOOK* Magazine.)

them. This, combined with the old Christian ideal of a single unified Church of Christ, led to the development of the modern *ecumenical* or church-union movement. As a result a number of mergers of Protestant bodies with similar creeds have already taken place, and others are under discussion. But differences in creed and organization, and especially differences between liberal and fundamentalist groups, are still sufficient to create obstacles that make it highly unlikely that the majority of Protestants will be brought together in a single church organization in the foreseeable future. However, a significant step in the direction of greater cooperation was made by the establishment of the World Council of Churches in Amsterdam in 1948. This group includes more than 230 Protestant, Anglican, Orthodox, and Old Catholic church bodies that represent a total of about 400 million members from some ninety different countries. The Council holds a meeting every six or seven years.

The Roman Catholic Church does not belong to the World Council, but it has sent observers to its meetings and invited Protestant observers to Vatican Council II (1962–1965). It has felt the influence of modernism and the ecumenical movement in various ways. Under the impetus provided by Pope John XXIII, who was pontiff from 1958 to 1963, the Church has liberalized its attitude toward other Christian groups, and even toward other religions, and has become more willing to work with them in efforts to further the welfare of mankind, including cooperating with the World Council of Churches in areas of relief, development, justice, and peace. But Roman Catholic doctrines appear to make merger with other Christian bodies possible only on the condition that the latter would accept Catholic beliefs and submit to the authority of the Roman Catholic Church.

The Social Gospel. Devout Christians have always followed to some degree the dictates of what we now call the *social gospel,* because Christ admonished his followers to love their neighbors and even their enemies; to give to the poor; and to do to others as they would have others do to them. Traditionally, churches have emphasized the responsibility of members to follow Christian precepts in their daily lives, and as organizations they have carried on missionary enterprises, dispensed charity, built hospitals, and operated schools and colleges.

But today's advocates of the social gospel feel that most modern churches have tended to lose touch with the world and its problems and to be chiefly concerned with maintaining their organization and ministering to the comfort and spiritual welfare of their own members, rather than with activating Christ's teachings in the world outside the churches. They point out that Christ himself preached a gospel of social and moral revolution and that those who profess to be his followers can do no less than emulate his great concern for the poor, the downtrodden, the sick, and the weary by becoming directly involved in social action designed to give them help. Christians, they say, have a duty to fight actively against hypocrisy, indifference, prejudice, misuse of funds, injustice, and all the other sins found in public life as well as in private life. Many advocates of the social gospel believe that major changes are needed in our social organization in order to achieve their aims; and they are impatient with a church that seems to them to isolate itself from the great problems of mankind. From their point of view such a church has become irrelevant as a factor in social progress.

There are probably no sincere Christians who would argue against the philosophy behind the social gospel, and its followers have carried on many activities of which all Christians approve. Nevertheless, proposals and activities of some of its advocates have brought conflict and division in many congregations, along with a decline in church attendance and financial support. The explanation is that there are many controversial social and political issues and that Christians do not always agree on the type of action that is wise, just, and truly helpful to the unfortunate. Also, many members object when clergymen take sides on controversial issues in the name of the church and, presumably, the church membership. But in spite of the problems it has created within the churches, the social gospel is an attempt to strengthen their influence in creating a better society.

Attracting and Holding Clergymen. In recent years most Protestant denominations and also the Roman Catholic Church have had difficulty in attracting enough dedicated and able men to their seminaries to provide adequately for the staffing of their parishes. One problem has been that many clergymen and seminary students become so involved in social projects that they are not much interested in the parish ministry and in performing the services necessary for maintaining the religious life—the vitality—of the individual churches. The Catholic Church has suffered not only from a shortage of priests but also from a decline in the number of candidates available to enter religious orders. This creates difficulties for Catholic schools, which have depended heavily on teaching sisters. It has required the employment of more lay teachers at substantially higher cost. Most Protestant denominations are not affected by this problem, since they do not maintain either religious orders or extensive school systems.

But loss of clergymen to other occupations has been an increasing problem for all churches. For the Catholic Church it became a serious matter in the late 1960's, when the loss of priests reached several hundred annually and when, in addition, the yearly loss of nuns reached several thousand. Some of these defections appear to have resulted from dissension over Pope Paul VI's 1968 encyclical upholding the traditional ban on "artifical" birth control; some from a desire of priests to marry; and some from dissatisfaction with the traditional authoritarianism of the Church.

The problems of the Roman Catholic Church in operating its school system have not been entirely a result of the loss of nuns. Costs other than those of instruction have also risen, with the result that financial problems have brought about the closing of a number of schools.

In addition to the specific reasons mentioned, the shortage of ministers and priests seems to be related to the increasing secularization of society; the difficulty of finding dedicated men with a firm and sure faith in the doctrines of the established churches; and finally, the great opportunities available in other fields, not only for making substantially more money but also for doing interesting kinds of work and providing useful social services.

Problems in the Mission Field. Missionaries have played a major role in the propagation of all great religions. A religion's founder, when there was a founder, was the first to expound his doctrines and to win converts. But later his work had to be carried on by loyal disciples, and their success in spreading the faith depended on their numbers, their dedication, their courage, and the strength of their own faith.

During the first three or four centuries of Christianity, when it was spreading throughout the Roman Empire and even beyond, there must have been hundreds or thousands of Christian missionaries. One of the earliest and perhaps the greatest was St. Paul. Another early missionary, who lived some four hundred years later, was St. Patrick, credited with converting the Irish. But when a religion becomes firmly established and there are no more heathen to be converted except in distant and inaccessible lands, missionary fervor is likely to wane, as it did in Europe during much of the Middle Ages.

The great voyages of discovery of the fifteenth and sixteenth centuries gave a new impetus to the missionary movement. When Spain and Portugal were developing their empires in the Americas, they sent over not only soldiers and settlers but also missionary priests to convert the Indians; and later, in North America, French Jesuit priests undertook missionary work among the Indians. In the nineteenth century the churches of Christian countries undertook a great expansion of missionary activities in non-Christian lands including Africa, parts of Asia, and the islands of the Pacific. Undoubtedly, the expansion of foreign missions in this period was related to colonialism, because the acquisition of new colonies by European countries, especially in Africa, opened up to trade, to travel, and to missionary endeavors many areas that were previously almost or wholly unknown to the Christian world. The missionary movement resulted not only in the winning of many converts but also in the establishment of hospitals and schools. By carrying Western culture and knowledge to many relatively primitive colonial areas, the missionaries played a major role in bringing them into the modern world and thus in preparing them for later nationhood and independence.

But today the situation is greatly changed. For many years, missionaries, perhaps under the influence of the social gospel, have been putting more and more emphasis on projects for social and economic improvement and less emphasis on evangelism; and since World War II, increasing resistance has been encountered in many lands to all types of missionary work. Red China and some other communist countries have expelled Christian missionaries and forbidden Christian services. Burma, the Sudan, and Guinea have excluded foreign clergymen or have limited their activities. In other areas nationalism and the association of Christianity with colonialism have made the position of missionaries increasingly difficult. For example, some African countries have closed church-operated schools.

To meet these problems, the mission-established Christian churches are more and more "going national." That is, they are turning over to local churches and clergymen the work of evangelizing and of administering church projects. Even in the absence of opposition to foreign evangelism this would be a normal development in countries where churches have become well established. Liturgy and hymns are being translated into local dialects, and other efforts are being made to adjust worship to local culture patterns. But in some areas denominational rivalries still handicap missionary efforts.

In spite of the difficulties, which are likely to grow, the churches of Christian countries are still supporting extensive missionary activities, and in some areas these are meeting with a fair degree of success. *U.S. News & World Report* recently cited estimates that 80,000 to 100,000 Christian missionaries are working full time in foreign lands and that Americans account for about a third of the total. Nevertheless, it is clear that no great progress is being made toward converting the whole world to Christianity. Gains elsewhere in the present century have probably been more than offset by heavy losses in some communist countries.

The Future of Religion. All the great religions of today were established when human knowledge of the natural world was very limited and when only a select few among the people could even read or write. These religions were also established before the age of printing, before the age of science, and before the age of modern technology with its seemingly miraculous achievements. In other words, they were established at a time when it was easier for people to believe in supernatural events than it is today.

But as we have already said, if a supernatural realm does exist, it is something with which science cannot deal. It must be accepted on faith. Many people believe that God *must* exist because the very nature of the universe indicates that it must have been created by a supreme intelligence. Probably more believe in God because they are convinced that he has revealed himself and his will to chosen human messengers like Moses or Mohammed, or through a divine representative on earth like Jesus Christ.

Whatever the basis of belief may be, the fact is that the great religions have existed for many centuries, and that in the modern world they can count hundreds of millions of more or less devout believers. On the basis of history and what we know of the nature of man, there is no good reason to assume that these great religions will soon die out. To the true believer such an outcome is inconceivable, for, to him, the basic tenets of his faith represent eternal and immutable truth.

Nevertheless, it is clear that religion does not dominate the lives of most human beings as much as it did in the Middle Ages or in some ancient and primitive societies. Furthermore, many students of religion believe that people are increasingly unwilling to accept as literal truth the supernatural revelations and events on which religious creeds are usually based. Pope Paul VI, in a speech marking his sixth anniversary as head of the Roman Catholic Church, mentioned as one of its major problems "a lessened sense of doctrinal orthodoxy toward . . . the deposit of faith that the Church has inherited from its apostolic origin." If people are increasingly questioning traditional church creeds and if the trend continues, can the majority of men still retain a meaningful faith in God? And can the churches in the long run continue to be an important stabilizing force in society and become, hopefully, an active force for social betterment?

Some students of religion, including some theologians, think that the problem is not so much one of faith; they believe that the churches have become too institutionalized, too formalized, and too rigid to meet the needs of man in the changing modern world. They maintain that the churches need to be revitalized by putting renewed emphasis on the fundamental teachings of Christianity; by developing a new spirit of evangelism; and by putting increased emphasis on meeting human needs in the world of today.

One attempt to make religion more meaningful in people's lives is the *religious underground movement*. Small, intimate groups get together more or less regularly in homes or other convenient meeting places, perhaps in an attempt to emulate the early Christians. They seek to establish a close fellowship with one another, exchange views and share the experiences of worship; they try new rituals and seek to feel the power and goodness of God and to communicate with him through music, prayer, and meditation. A recent estimate placed the number of such underground groups at 2,000 or more, but by their very nature it is difficult to estimate their number very accurately. Usually they do not have the approval of church authorities, but sometimes they include ministers or priests. Some are Catholic, some Protestant, some interfaith, and they often include persons with no regular church affiliation. How much such groups will contribute to a general revival of religious faith and a quickening of the life of the churches is, of course, not known, because the movement is relatively new. But, to many, it represents the essence of Christianity; and, for some, it gives religion a vital, emotional, personal quality that carries its influence over into all the activities of daily life.

Whatever problems the churches may face in this modern age, they still exert tremendous influence on millions of individuals, and, through them, on society. For great numbers of people there is no substitute for religion, for a faith that sustains them in the struggles of life and gives them comfort and hope. Today the churches are going through a difficult period of adjustment, and no purely objective observer can be certain of the outcome. But many faithful churchmen are confident that the final result will be more meaningful forms of worship, and a deeper faith that will make the church and religion more relevant to the problems of our present-day society.

Terms to Be Understood

religion	Karma	Renaissance
original Buddhism	Bodhisattvas	Reformation
Nirvana	Yahveh	Protestant ethic
animism	Torah	sect
magic	Messianic age	secularism
spiritual double	caliph	materialistic philosophies
polytheism	Mecca	fundamentalists
pantheon of gods	Five Pillars of Islam	religious liberalism
Delphic oracle	Moslem	agnosticism
Confucianism	Messiah	ecumenical movement
Shintoism	Apostles	social gospel
animal cults	Communion	religious underground
Veda	monasticism	movement
Sanskrit	Trinity	

Questions for Review and Discussion

1. Why has religion had a strong appeal to human beings from earliest times?
2. In primitive (archaic) societies, religion and magic are often intertwined. Explain.
3. What was the relation of the Egyptian religion to the state?
4. What was the purpose of the Book of the Dead?
5. How did the religion of the Greeks differ in spirit and emphasis from that of the Egyptians?
6. Identify the following Greek gods or goddesses: Zeus, Apollo, Athena, Poseidon, Hermes, Ares, Aphrodite, and Eros.
7. When the classical period in Greek history had its "enlightenment" what was the attitude of intellectuals toward the gods?
8. Compare first Roman, and then Teuton polytheism with that of the Greeks.
9. To Westerners, Hinduism seems a strange faith. Why?
10. How did Prince Gautama Siddharta found Buddhism?
11. Why is original Buddhism sometimes said to have been more a philosophy than a religion?
12. What changes occurred in Buddhism over the centuries?
13. What are the unique characteristics of Judaism?
14. What are the three major Jewish groups today and how do they differ?
15. What was the origin of the Koran?
16. State some of the similarities of Islam to Judaism or Christianity; also state some of the more important differences.
17. What are the Five Pillars of Islam?
18. Why did the Islamic faith spread so rapidly?
19. Why is our knowledge of the life of Jesus very limited, and our knowledge of his teachings indirect?
20. List as many as you can of the more important teachings of Jesus.
21. Why are the Last Supper of Jesus with his disciples, his crucifixion, and his resurrection of crucial significance for Christianity?
22. Explain the significance to Christianity of (a) the Roman emperor Constantine; (b) the schism in the Church in 1054; and (c) the Reformation in the sixteenth century.
23. Tell how Christianity spread from Europe to other parts of the world after the great discoveries of the fifteenth and sixteenth centuries.
24. On balance, has religion been an integrative or divisive factor in our American society? Defend your answer.
25. Why are religious beliefs likely to strengthen the moral and ethical principles of a society?
26. Why did Max Weber believe that the Protestant ethic made an important contribution to the economic development of the Western world?
27. In the early nineteenth century most Christians in this country were Protestants. Explain the growth of our present large minority of Roman Catholics.
28. What does it mean to say that life in the United States is becoming more secular?
29. Does science conflict with religion? Explain.
30. How do Protestant liberals differ from fundamentalists in their beliefs?
31. How do the problems of rural churches and those in large central cities differ?

32. Do you believe that the ecumenical movement will soon succeed in uniting all Christian church bodies? Why or why not?
33. What is the significance of the "social gospel"?
34. Do you believe that emphasis on the social gospel will bring churches new vigor and influence? Defend your answer.
35. Why are the churches having difficulty in recruiting and holding clergymen and members of religious orders?
36. What are the people who participate in the "underground" movement seeking?
37. Is religion likely to continue as a strong moral and social force, or will it wither away because people increasingly lose their faith? Defend your opinion.

For Further Reading

Borg, Marcus, *Conflict and Social Change,* Minneapolis, Augsburg Publishing House, 1971. A presentation of the social gospel and its importance.

Budge, E. Wallis, *Gods of the Egyptians, or Studies in Egyptian Mythology,* paperback, New York, Dover Publications, Inc., 1969.

Fuchs, Stephen, *The Origin of Man and His Culture,* New York, Asia Publishing House, 1963. Chaps. 17–21 deal with the origin of religions, especially that of the Hindu religion. The book was written for students in India.

Goode, William J., *Religion Among the Primitives,* New York, The Free Press, 1951.

Leith, John H., ed., *Creeds of the Churches,* Chicago, Aldine Publishing Co., 1967.

Lewis, H. D., and Robert Lawson Slater, *Study of Religions,* paperback, Baltimore, Penguin Books, Inc., 1969.

Lowie, Robert H., *Primitive Religion,* rev. ed., paperback, New York, Liveright Publishing Corporation, 1970.

Noss, John B., *Man's Religions,* 4th ed., New York, The Macmillan Company, 1969.

Ross, Floyd H., and Tynette Hills, *Great Religions by Which Men Live,* paperback, New York, Fawcett World Library, 1969.

Schoeps, Hans-Joachim, *The Religions of Mankind,* Anchor paperback, New York, Doubleday & Company, Inc., 1968.

Smith, Huston, *The Religions of Man,* Colophon paperback, New York, Harper & Row, Publishers, 1965.

Wach, Joachim, edited by J. M. Kitagawa, *Comparative Study of Religions,* paperback, New York, Columbia University Press, 1958.

———, edited by J. M. Kitagawa, *Understanding and Believing,* Torchbook paperback, New York, Harper & Row, Publishers, 1968.

Watt, W. Montgomery, *Islamic Philosophy and Theology,* Chicago, Aldine Publishing Co., 1962.

Weber, Max, *The Sociology of Religion,* paperback, Boston, The Beacon Press, 1964.

Yinger, J. Milton, *The Scientific Study of Religion,* New York, The Macmillan Company, 1970.

Chapter 7

Technology

and

Social Change

We have noted that economic activities have a place of major importance in the culture of every social group. Aside from the time spent in eating and sleeping, most people devote the greater part of their lives to earning a living. As a result, the patterns of their daily activities are greatly influenced by their *technology*—that is to say, by the kinds of goods, including services, that they know how to produce and by the methods they employ to produce them. In primitive societies, production is carried on with the aid of simple hand tools, and people spend most of their time hunting, fishing, tilling the soil, preparing food, making clothing, and constructing rude shelters. On the other hand, in modern industrial societies such as ours, millions of men and women spend most of each day in offices, factories, or laboratories; and often they travel long distances by automobile, bus, or train to reach their places of work.

TECHNOLOGY AS THE BASIS OF THE MATERIAL ASPECTS OF CULTURE

The material products of every society are the result of its technology. In primitive or nonliterate societies, technology is relatively simple. By contrast, the technology of a modern industrial society is highly complex. Such a society produces a tremendous variety of goods, and has available a vast accumulation of knowledge concerning scientific and technical methods of production.

The great efficiency of modern production depends to a high degree on *machine technology,* or *knowledge of how to make and use power machines.* By the use of modern machines man can produce vastly more, with a given amount of time and effort, than he could in the past with hand tools. He can also produce great numbers of new products, many of which could not be made at all without the aid of machines. For example, it is clear that a man could not conceivably make a modern automobile by hand directly from the resources provided by nature. No matter how skillful, if he tried to make a car with only hand tools, he would fail completely unless at many steps he used materials and parts produced by others with the aid of machines.

The Self-expanding Character of Machine Technology. As we have noted in an earlier chapter, technological change does not occur independently of changes in other aspects of culture. Nevertheless, in modern industrial societies technological change appears to be the most dynamic element in the process of cultural change. Often it seems to disrupt and throw out of balance the whole cultural pattern. This is the phenomenon that Ogburn was observing when he developed his theory of cultural lag.

One explanation of the dynamic character of technology can be found in the ever-increasing use of machines. The invention of power machines and their employment in fabricating goods represents a technique that, once applied, is capable of almost indefinite expansion. Machine technology is a self-expanding phenomenon in the sense that, once introduced, its further spread and development are almost inevitable. As soon as machines were successfully applied in an industry, those familiar with them began to think of improvements and of new applications and new machines. Their use spread from industry to industry. One invention led to another, and the end of this process of expansion seems no closer now than it was when power machines were first installed in factories in eighteenth-century England.

All technological change arises from discovery and invention. We learned in Chapter 5 that discovery means acquiring new knowledge—finding facts and relationships in the world around us of which we were previously ignorant. Invention, as has been said, is a special type of discovery. It means finding new ways to combine materials, or devising new procedures, in order to achieve some desired end. Inventions, it is important to remember, may be nonmaterial as well as material.

The Origin of Inventions. Some early inventions may have been wholly the result of the ingenuity of one man, but as technology advances and inventions accumulate, new ones are usually based on earlier ones. Also, they are often made possible only by earlier scientific discoveries. Even though an invention is associated with the name of a particular person, it nearly always represents the labor and accumulated knowledge of many people over a long period.

Sometimes a particular person has made a unique and important contribution to the final result and deserves great credit, but frequently the man who receives the credit for an invention has little claim to it. For example, the invention of the steamboat is often attributed to Robert Fulton, and yet some thirty-five steamboats had been tried in both this country or Europe before Fulton built his famous *Clermont.* He was the first man to make a commercial success of the steamboat, but he was not its originator.[1] The claim of the Wright brothers to the invention of the airplane rests on somewhat firmer ground. It seems to be generally agreed that they built the first plane that really flew. Yet other planes had been built that would almost fly, and there seems little doubt that if the Wright brothers had not built a practical airplane, someone else would very soon have done so. One of the most important factors that made possible the invention of the airplane was the previous development of a light, efficient, internal-combustion engine.

Inventions grow out of human curiosity and ingenuity plus the desire to satisfy wants more adequately or with less effort. Our earliest human ancestors found the struggle for survival very difficult. Often they died for lack of the means of subsistence. The desire to escape cold, hunger, and death should have provided them with a strong incentive to seek more effective ways of obtaining the essentials for comfort and survival, but in primitive societies technological progress was generally slow and uncertain. Custom and tradition had so strong a hold on men's minds that only rarely did it occur to them to seek for something new or different. Moreover, unfamiliar devices and procedures were generally looked on with suspicion and fear. Very slowly culture developed, including techniques for hunting animals, catching fish, gathering other kinds of food, making clothing, and providing shelter. Gradually, better tools and more efficient techniques were invented, but much more than a million years may have elapsed from the time men or their hominid ancestors first learned to kill

[1] S. C. Gilfillan, *Inventing the Ship,* Chicago, The Follett Publishing Co., 1935, pp. 91ff. (The M.I.T. Press has taken over the remaining copies of this book.)

animals with stones or heavy sticks, to the time they learned to make an arrow with a chipped flint head and shoot it from a bow.

One could make a very long list of the inventions that, over the ages, have helped man to solve his problems of subsistence and to provide himself with some comforts and luxuries. The more outstanding inventions include the making of fire, the bow and arrow, the wheel, the domesticating of animals, the growing of crops, the smelting and working of metals, and the construction and use of various types of power-operated machines.

Though there is no doubt that a need or strong desire for something is often a stimulus to invention, the old saying that "necessity is the mother of invention" can be very misleading. Much more than need must be present to bring forth an invention. For example, many inventions are impossible until other inventions have preceded them, or until the general development of science and technology has reached a certain stage. Also, the social situation must be such that people will accept new devices or techniques. For thousands of years the Australian aborigines "needed" the bow and arrow, yet they never invented it. They survived without it, but it would have eased their problem of obtaining food by hunting. Again, for a very long time the human race has needed a cure for cancer, but so far the best efforts of modern scientists have not succeeded in discovering or inventing a dependable one. This may be a case in which success will soon be achieved, but only time can answer that question,

The Diffusion of Inventions. Inventions of a technological nature tend to spread from one group of people to another, just as do other elements of culture. In earlier times, when communication was slow and transportation difficult, it sometimes took centuries for knowledge and use of an important invention to spread a few thousand miles. The Indians of the Inca empire in South America, in spite of their relatively high level of culture, knew nothing of the wheel or writing, although both had been in use in other parts of the world for several thousand years. Though today the process of diffusion is more rapid, even now there are obstacles that prevent some countries from quickly adopting inventions whose use is well established in other countries. For example, technologically backward countries may find that they do not have the trained personnel, the capital, and the industrial organization to use some of the devices and techniques that have been invented and employed to great advantage in more technically advanced countries.

However, in modern times there are many factors that tend to carry the technology of the more advanced nations to all parts of the earth. Many large corporations maintain sales agencies throughout much of the free world, so that it is not unusual to find such products as Ford cars, Kodak film, or bottles of Coca-Cola in some of the most out-of-the-way places. Also many corporations build and operate plants in foreign countries. Students in considerable numbers go from one country to be educated in another, often on an exchange basis. Then there are systematic efforts on the part of governments to spread knowledge and use of the most efficient production techniques. An example of this is the Point Four Program of the United States, under which our government sends specialists in various fields to backward countries to teach their people methods of production that will increase their output and raise their standards of living. Finally, there are the organized attempts of the communist countries through "five-year plans" and other means to expand their industry and to raise production by employing the most efficient techniques available.

Though many countries cling tenaciously to tradition and are slow to adopt the inventions of others, modern industrialism seems to be spreading at a faster rate than ever before. In fifty or a hundred years there will probably be few parts of the world where it has not, in some degree, become established.

The Interdependence of Inventions. We have called attention to the self-expanding nature of machine technology. This characteristic is largely explained by the fact that one invention leads to another. Moreover, almost every complex machine is made possible by combining a number of inventions, and can be improved by adding still others. As a result, inventions become increasingly interdependent.

The modern automobile is a good example of a complex mechanism that represents the combination of many inventions. Not to mention such ancient inventions as the wheel and the wagon, it was made possible by the prior invention of a gasoline motor, of vulcanized rubber for making pneumatic tires, and of methods of obtaining petroleum from the ground and of extracting gasoline from petroleum. Actually, gasoline was originally a by-product of the distillation method developed for obtaining kerosene. The first automobiles were little more than carriages with motors installed, but even this required invention of devices for controlling the motor and for transferring power to the wheels. Among the more important inventions that have increased the efficiency, comfort, safety, or convenience of the automobile may be included shock absorbers, hydraulic brakes, the self-starter, safety glass, the all-steel body, the automatic gearshift, smooth hard-surfaced roads, traffic lights, and the motel.

Conditions That Encourage Invention. Though some of the greatest inventions in human history occurred ages ago, we have noted that social attitudes in primitive societies were seldom such as to encourage invention. Even in Europe in the Middle Ages the hold of tradition was so strong that it discouraged innovations. But as the Middle Ages were giving way to the Renaissance, one very significant invention was made, namely, printing. This indirectly prepared the way for more inventions and was of crucial importance in stimulating the development of modern science and technology and the whole complex of modern civilization. It seems probable that Johann Gutenberg invented movable type for use in a printing press, and the date usually given is about A.D. 1440. In any case, the first large book produced by this method was the Gutenberg Bible, published in 1456.

"You see, Dad, Professor McLuhan says the environment that man creates becomes his medium for defining his role in it. The invention of type created linear, or sequential, thought, separating thought from action. Now, with TV and folk singing, thought and action are closer and social involvement is greater. We again live in a village. Get it?" (Drawing by Alan Dunn; © 1966 *The New Yorker Magazine, Inc.*)

Printing resulted both in better preserving the knowledge accumulated by society in the past and in spreading it much more rapidly and widely. Once printing came into common use important books could be produced in quantity so that university students and other literate persons could own them or have relatively easy access to them instead of having to depend on lectures or on the uncertain chance of being able to locate and read rare and costly manuscripts. This spread of knowledge and of already-developed techniques led to a quickening of further advances. Possibly, if printing had been invented and widely employed in Greek and Roman times, the good start the Greeks had made in such fields as mathematics, physics, and astronomy would have continued, and the present stage of scientific and technical knowledge might have been reached centuries ago. That is speculation, but it is certain that a much earlier use of printing would have changed the course of history in various ways.

Marshall McLuhan, the English teacher from the University of Toronto who has become a social philosopher, is a controversial figure in academic and intellectual circles. But most agree that he has performed a useful service in emphasizing the crucial role played by media of communication in shaping the personalities of individuals and the character of societies. His most famous saying is the cryptic sentence "The medium is the message." McLuhan contends that our present society is being remolded by electricity as a result of the invention of the telegraph, telephone, radio, and, finally, television. It is, he says, bringing us back to the "tribal village" by unifying all mankind into a contemporaneous, world-encompassing whole. But the distinguished economist and social scientist Kenneth E. Boulding insists that we are not going back to the tribal village but rather "into something quite new and strange"; and he adds, "It is perhaps typical of very creative minds that they hit very large nails not quite on the head."[2]

Improved methods of communication undoubtedly have stimulated invention in many fields. Other factors, some of them related to methods of communication, have also encouraged invention. We have mentioned human curiosity and ingenuity, and the desire to satisfy needs more easily. To these we should add rapid advances in science; the great extension of educational opportunities over the last century or more, especially of opportunities to receive technical and scientific training; and, in some countries, the availability of raw materials, such as iron for making machines and sources of power for operating them. Finally, an important incentive for invention has been the issue of patents.

The Patent System. Today every society that puts a high value on technological progress is likely to recognize the desirability of stimulating invention. One way of doing this is to grant patents to inventors to enable them to obtain at least part of any profits that may result. *A patent is a legal right to the exclusive use of an invention for a given period of years.* The patent system was invented in Venice, and the first patent legislation was contained in a statute enacted by that city in 1474. However, it was a long time before patent laws were widely adopted. Meanwhile it was not uncommon for a king or a legislative body to give an inventor special recognition, either by a grant of monopoly rights to his invention or by a cash award.

When the Constitution of the United States was drawn up in 1787, the Founding Fathers recognized that both invention and publishing ought to be encouraged. They therefore included in the Constitution a provision giving Congress the right to pass legislation establishing copyrights and patents. Under our patent laws any inventor who creates a really new device or compound can obtain complete control of his invention for a period of seventeen years. He may manufacture it and employ it himself for profit, may sell to others his rights in it, or may keep it unused.

Beyond question our patent system has been an important stimulus to

---

[2] See Kenneth E. Boulding in *McLuhan Hot and Cold,* edited by Gerald E. Stearn, Signet paperback, New York, The New American Library, Inc., 1969, pp. 68–75.

invention. Thousands of patents are granted in the United States every year, and on June 5, 1970, the United States patent office announced that the 3.5 millionth patent had just been issued to a Bell Laboratories inventor and the widow of his co-inventor. Because of patents, American inventors have sometimes become wealthy. A few, such as Eli Whitney and Thomas Edison, have also become national heroes and have been acclaimed throughout the world for their great achievements.

Patents as an Indicator of the Number of Inventions. The number of patents the United States Patent Office has issued suggests the importance of the role that invention has played in the economic development of this country. Table 1 presents these figures for each tenth year, beginning with 1790, and also for 1932, when the number of patents issued reached a pre–World War II high, and for 1966 and 1968. The first year in which patents were granted was 1790. Note that for more than a hundred years the number of patents granted annually rose rapidly, though irregularly, until 1932. After that it declined somewhat and later resumed its rise at a slower pace. Then in the 1960's it spurted upward again to reach an all-time high in 1966.

Some students of patents believe that there are far more inventions than the number of patents would indicate and that this is truer today than in the past. S. C. Gilfillan points out that many inventions now result from government-sponsored research and are not patented. Also, many inventions are of such a nature that they do not fit the legal rules that govern the issue of patents. Even when patents are issued, their value is often

Table 1. *United States Patents Issued in Certain Years from 1790 to 1969*

Source: *Historical Statistics of the United States, Colonial Times to 1957; and Statistical Abstract of the United States, 1970.*

Year	Number of Patents
1790	3
1800	41
1810	223
1820	155
1830	544
1840	458
1850	883
1860	4,357
1870	12,137
1880	12,903
1890	25,313
1900	24,644
1910	35,141
1920	37,060
1930	45,226
1932	53,458
1940	42,238
1950	43,040
1960	49,986
1966	71,887
1969	71,229

questionable because a very large proportion of all patents that are tested in the courts are invalidated. Usually, minor inventions are put to use with no attempt to patent them.[3]

Organized Research and Invention. Today in our country a great part of the support of invention, and of the scientific research projects designed to feed it, comes from the federal government. Military power is its chief aim, but military inventions in aviation, rocketry, atomic energy, metallurgy, navigation, and medicine in time find uses in everyday life. Several years ago Gilfillan estimated that government, principally the federal government, provided about 60 per cent of the funds spent on research, business less than 40 per cent, and private philanthropy only 1 or 2 per cent.[4]

Perhaps the best known of all research organizations is the Atomic Energy Commission of the federal government. The AEC has spent billions of dollars, employs thousands of workers, and operates some very large plants. Its chief functions are to produce and stockpile atomic and hydrogen bombs and to carry on nuclear research for military purposes. However, it also carries on research concerning possible applications of nuclear energy in fields such as medicine and industry, and it furnishes nuclear materials by means of which others can carry on such research.

In addition, a tremendous amount of research is carried on by industry both for itself and for the government. Corporations making very large expenditures for this purpose include producers of chemicals, drugs, oil, glass, foods, metals, electrical machinery, electronic devices, office equipment, and aircraft. Universities also carry on a great deal of research, largely with funds provided by business or government. In the *Statistical Abstract of the United States* for 1970, it was estimated that our total expenditures in that year on research and the development of new products and processes would exceed 27 billion dollars. Research on this scale can hardly fail to bring about technological advances that will provide us with more and better goods and in many ways change the conditions under which we live. We can hope that most of the changes will be for the better, but sometimes technological advances have very undesirable side effects such as sonic booms, higher accident rates in traffic, and pollution of our air and water.

The Control of Inventions. During the depression of the 1930's a few writers suggested that the government ought to control the introduction of labor-saving inventions such as the cotton picker, so that workers would not be displaced too fast. But the great weight of informed opinion holds that such controls would be most unwise. It is labor-saving inventions, more than anything else, that make possible economic progress with higher standards of living for everyone, including more dependable and more nearly adequate provision for the elderly, the unemployed, and the handi-

[3]S. C. Gilfillan, *Invention and the Patent System,* prepared for Joint Economic Committee of Congress, Washington, D.C., U.S. Government Printing Office, 1964, Chap. 3.
[4]Ibid.

capped; and even though technological progress in our industrial society is far faster than in earlier societies, the introduction into use of important new inventions still requires considerable time. It almost always takes many years, say twenty to thirty, to advance a major invention from its first working model to commercial success. Interference with this process by some governmental agency would be likely to slow it still more. George Stigler of the University of Chicago once remarked facetiously that if there had been an Interstate Commerce Commission 150 years ago, Casey Jones, the locomotive engineer in the famous ballad, would still be driving a horse and buggy.

There are, however, situations in which the government must control the introduction of inventions in order to make possible their effective use. For instance, in the field of radio and television the number of wave bands is limited, and to avoid complete confusion someone must decide who is to have the privilege of broadcasting on those that are available.

THE INDUSTRIAL REVOLUTION

When primitive man learned to use crude tools, he took a tremendous step forward on the path of human progress. However, his power to produce was still limited by the strength of his own muscles. When, a million or so years later, modern man first learned to apply natural power to machines, he took another great step forward, because he could then turn to his own uses the mighty forces represented by wind, falling water, and the burning of coal or other combustible materials. Because this shift from production with hand tools to production with power machines represented a very radical change in man's methods of getting a living, we call it the *Industrial Revolution.*

The Industrial Revolution in England. Although some use of water and wind power for irrigation, drainage, milling grain, and sawing wood goes back to much earlier times, the Industrial Revolution had its real beginning in England about 1750. There for the first time people began to employ power machines for industrial production and to build factories to house them. By 1800 this movement had made very substantial progress.

The English Industrial Revolution was brought about by a cumulation of inventions. A new invention in one industry was followed by improvements and by inventions in related industries. This is well illustrated by the textile inventions of the eighteenth century. These inventions were first employed in the cotton-goods industry, which was relatively small and new, and the machinery was operated by water power. When Watt devised a greatly improved steam engine, further impetus was given invention. Machinery for producing cotton textiles was modified and applied to the production of woolen cloth, the output of which expanded by leaps and bounds. Costs and prices were so reduced that a great new demand developed both for finished textiles and for raw wool and cotton.

The developments just described gave England an advantage over her competitors. Because she was able to mechanize her industries so much sooner than other countries, she was for many years the workshop of the world. Her production, trade, and wealth rose to what were then regarded as high levels. But in time industrialism began to spread to other nations.

The Development of Industrialism in America. In the early nineteenth century, machine industry and the factory system began to develop in the United States. The Napoleonic Wars and the War of 1812 gave American industrialization a strong push, because they made it difficult for us to import English textiles. To make up for the resulting shortage, many new textile factories were established in this country. They had to pay higher wages than the English factories, but as long as English textiles were not available, they could operate profitably. When peace came to Europe and normal trade was re-established, many of these new factories were forced to close down. Others, however, survived, and from that time on, the United States gradually became more and more industrialized.

In some respects conditions in the United States favored industrialization. First, our domestic market was rapidly growing. Second, raw materials were plentiful. Third, labor was relatively scarce and wages higher than in Europe, partly because workers kept leaving their jobs to settle on free or cheap land along the frontier; and although this raised costs of production, it also put a premium on the introduction of labor-saving machines. To reduce costs, as many operations as possible were shifted to power machines. As a result, production increased much faster than the number of workers, standards of living gradually rose, and wealth began to accumulate.

Standardization and Mass Production. Early machines were crude by our standards. Since their parts did not fit together perfectly, they ran with a great deal of noise and clatter and frequently broke down. Often their products were very imperfect, so that further work had to be done on them by hand to make them acceptable. One of the great advances in industrial technology was the gradual development of precision machines that would run smoothly and that could also turn out *standardized,* accurately made parts for more or less complex finished products such as watches, guns, washing machines, and automobiles. This development made it physically possible for a machine to produce thousands of units of a given part, all so nearly alike that they could be freely substituted for one another. Meanwhile other machines could be making other parts, and great quantities of the finished product could be turned out by merely assembling the proper parts.

Naturally, it does not pay to make large amounts of a product if they cannot be sold. But when the market is large enough, the use of standard interchangeable parts makes *mass production* possible and substantially reduces costs. To construct an expensive machine to make a standardized part would not pay if the machine could be used to produce only a few units of output, because the original cost of the machine would have to be allocated to these few units. But if mass production is possible and a machine can be employed to produce thousands or hundreds of thousands of units, the portion of the cost that must be charged to each unit becomes small or even negligible. It then pays to use a machine in place of manpower whenever one can be devised to perform a necessary operation. When standardized parts made by machines are combined into a finished product on a modern assembly line, as in the automobile industry, mass production reaches a very high level of efficiency. It is this type of highly mechanized production that accounts in large degree for the present leadership of the United States in manufacturing.

THE SOCIAL EFFECTS OF TECHNOLOGY

That technology has played a dominant role in shaping our modern world is beyond question. Culture, to be sure, is much more than technology. But modern civilization as we know it could not have developed without its technological base. Technology largely determines the way in which man utilizes his habitat and the extent to which he can benefit from the potential resources which it may contain. When Columbus discovered America, the territory that is now the United States could probably support, by the methods of production known to the Indians, fewer than half a million people. Today the same territory supports four hundred times as many and provides them with a much more adequate and dependable supply of material goods. This difference cannot be explained in terms of the natural environment. It is explained mainly by the fact that our modern industrial technology is vastly superior in productive efficiency to the primitive technology of the American Indians.

Though technological progress has conferred great benefits on man, it also has created many problems for him. This was true even when machines were first used in factories, two hundred years before the invention of the atom bomb. The first factories took men away from their homes all day and disrupted the established pattern of domestic life. They also forced large numbers of people to live close to their new places of work, which in turn resulted in crowded industrial towns and cities. On the other hand, there is evidence that even the early factories gave the masses more opportunities to earn and a better chance of survival. One indication of this was a fall in the death rate and an increase in the rate of population growth.

Now the nuclear bomb threatens to bring about social changes even more drastic than those we have already experienced. Atomic fission and fusion open up almost unlimited possibilities of technological progress, but at the same time they bring us face to face with the possibility that man may ultimately destroy the whole fabric of civilization and perhaps even the human species. More recently, technological advances have brought us into the space age with its dramatic achievements. This may have important social repercussions—for example, through military uses of space—but, as yet, prediction is difficult except for the writers of science fiction.

Technology and the Tempo of Human Life. That inventions have in many ways accelerated the tempo of human life seems beyond question. This tendency was described vividly some years ago in one of the monthly letters of The Royal Bank of Canada:

Earlier civilizations had, relative to their stage of development, just as onerous conditions, just as exciting and worrisome experiences, but they were forced, by the lack of modern inventions, to have periods of inactivity.

As illustrations, consider the following:

The absence of adequate artificial light forced many projects to be confined to daylight hours; now they are carried on into the night.

The slowness of transportation gave much more leisure in traveling, though there was less comfort.

The slow rate of communication forced transactions to be spread over a longer period of time.

The dearth of professional entertainment—stage, screen, radio, and others—left time for meditation and thought.

The dispersal of a smaller population over rural districts provided fewer social contacts than are necessitated by today's urban crowding.

As a prominent physician said to us when discussing this subject: "Not so very many years ago the words 'meditation' and 'contemplation' commanded a good deal of respect. Some people published their 'Meditations,' and 'The Contemplative Life' was considered to be quite respectable and not without value to the community. Since then, in our Western civilization, the fashion has grown of putting more emphasis on 'doing' rather than 'thinking.' Many people have formed the habit of filling every waking hour with 'doing something,' so that they are incapable of spending an hour alone with their thoughts without being bored and unhappy."[5]

Technology and Standards of Living. For as long as we continue to make advances in technology, we are likely to enjoy rising standards of living.[6] Technological progress not only has provided us with new kinds of goods and greater quantities of goods but also has improved conditions of life for the average man in various other ways. It has given him more leisure, because as the productivity of labor has increased, he has not taken all the gain in the form of more goods; instead, he has taken part of it by reducing his working hours per day or week. Again, it has greatly improved the quality and usefulness of many of the material goods he buys, including such things as washing machines, refrigerators, and automobiles. It has also permitted him to travel quickly and comfortably, to communicate almost instantly with people who are far away, and to receive information

[5] *Monthly Letter,* The Royal Bank of Canada, November 1947.

[6] Provided we can check population growth, avoid exhaustion of essential resources, and employ science and technology to meet many of the problems of pollution.

and entertainment by radio and television while sitting in his living room. These are only a few of the ways in which technology has added to human comforts, conveniences, and interests.

The Increasing Productivity of Labor. One way to explain why technology raised standards of living is to point out that the expanding use and constant improvement of machines, along with other advances in technology, has tremendously increased the *productivity of labor,* or *average output per man-hour.* The late Sumner Slichter of Harvard University estimated that in the hundred years from 1840 to 1940 the hourly output of the average American worker increased roughly about six times. Since 1940 there has been a further increase, for the economy as a whole, of over 100 per cent; but in agriculture for the same period the increase has been about 400 per cent. Much of this increase was the result of employing more and better machines. Since 1940 increases of several hundred per cent have occurred in the use of tractors, combines, corn pickers, cotton pickers, and milking machines. But an important part of the increased productivity of farm workers must be attributed to the introduction of improved varieties of livestock and plants, better fertilizers, more effective pest controls, and better farm management.

If we take the long view by going back 140 years, we find that for certain farm products increases in the productivity of labor have been truly phenomenal. On a large, level wheat farm it is probable that one man, with a combine and other modern equipment, can now accomplish about as much as a hundred men in the days before any use was made of machinery.

Machines and the Need for Skilled Workers. A belief that was once widely held is that machines reduce the need for human skills. It was said that before the machine age the individual worker was a craftsman who performed by hand all the operations on the product he made. He was a weaver, a shoemaker, a candlemaker, or a tailor. Standards of workmanship were high, and because a worker made an entire product himself, he had to be highly skilled. After the advent of machines his skills became useless. Machines performed the principal operations required to make a product, and the worker became an automaton whose function was to operate or feed the machine. He perhaps did nothing but move a lever up and down; or he placed a piece of metal in a machine, removed it when the machine had operated, and repeated this task all day long. Such work required no skill, and so the typical worker became a common laborer instead of a craftsman.

The reasoning presented above is plausible but highly misleading. Before the age of the machine, skilled craftsmen represented a very tiny portion of the working population in most countries. The great majority of the people lived and worked on the land. The work was heavy, the hours long, and the returns small. It is true that the introduction of machines put certain skilled artisans out of work or forced them to work in factories as unskilled labor. For example, after the introduction of the power loom in England in the eighteenth century, the price of cloth dropped so sharply that skilled handweavers could no longer make a living at their trade. This does not mean, however, that the introduction of machinery reduced the total demand for workers with special skill or training. Quite to the contrary. The skills required became different, but in the long run machine industry made it necessary for a much larger portion of the population than ever before to acquire specialized skill, training, or knowledge. Furthermore, in modern factories such purely routine and mechanical jobs as feeding materials into a machine are continually disappearing, because machines can be devised to perform these operations automatically. An outstanding characteristic of modern automation is the constant shifting of routine activities from men to machines.

To compensate for this loss of routine jobs, modern machine technology has created great numbers of jobs that require specialized skill or knowledge. There are engineers who plan and design machines and factories, skilled construction workers, plumbers, electricians, and a great variety of machinists and mechanics who aid in making, operating, and repairing machines. There are people who are especially trained in the organization and administration of industrial enterprises, in advertising and selling, and in various phases of transportation. There are accountants who keep records, and a great many skilled clerical workers, including stenographers and typists. More recently the use of electronic computers has brought great increases in the scientists who work to improve them, the technicians who assemble and repair them, the systems men who devise plans for using them to solve business problems, and the programmers who put these plans into operation. Another important source of increased demand for highly trained workers is industrial research, the total amount of which has greatly increased in recent years. Census statistics of the number of workers in various occupations indicate that since 1910 professional, skilled, and semiskilled workers have increased rapidly, while the number of unskilled workers has been almost static.

Machines and Unemployment. In addition to the belief that machines reduce the demand for skilled workers, there is an even more persistent notion that has little foundation in past experience. This is the idea that advances in machine technology, by replacing labor, progressively decrease total job opportunities and total employment. This belief had a strong appeal in the 1930's when millions of men were out of work. At that time many writers argued that our economy had become "mature" and that in order to provide enough jobs in the future, it would be necessary either to "spread the work" by progressively shortening the work week or else to have the government keep creating more jobs through an expanding program of public works. In addition to shortening the work week, it was often proposed that young people should be kept in school longer and that older workers should be retired at earlier ages.

No one questions that machines from time to time displace men from certain jobs and that in the short run this often creates difficult problems. For example, the use of diesel engines by railroads has made firemen unnecessary, and sooner or later, in spite of union opposition, jobs for firemen on railroads are likely to disappear. However, such problems are temporary. Ultimately, advances in machine technology tend to reduce costs and prices (assuming a constant value of the dollar), or to hold them down; and by enabling people to buy more goods, they create new employment opportunities. If some industries employ fewer workers, others employ more. At the same time, new products are introduced and new industries come into existence. In periods of high prosperity the necessary adjustments in employment take place rather easily, with a minimum of hardship to all concerned; but in periods of economic recession, adjustments are likely to be delayed, so that workers who lose their jobs have great difficulty in finding others.

For total employment to expand in spite of rapid advances in machine technology, two things must happen concurrently. First, consumer purchasing power must keep rising so that more and more goods can be taken off the market as they become available. Second, conditions in the economy must be such that it is possible to produce more of the things that people want, including not only material goods like houses and automobiles but also services such as hospital care, travel, and education. Production must increase fast enough not only to provide new jobs for men replaced by machines but also to provide jobs for a larger working force as the young workers who enter it exceed the old workers who retire.

But we should never forget that more spending by consumers (or government) is not in itself a sure cure for unemployment. If there are serious obstacles to an adequate expansion of production, goods will merely become scarce as spending rises, and the result will be higher prices rather than more output and more jobs. If expansion of employment is the objective, all policies that tend to restrict production should be resisted except in cases where increased output would necessarily cause pollution, or would put a strain on scarce and essential natural resources.

So far, the historical record seems to refute completely the theory that there is any long-run tendency for machines to bring about a progressive decrease in employment. Ever since the Industrial Revolution began, machines have been increasing the productivity of labor. Yet the ultimate result has not been to reduce employment but, rather, to increase incomes and standards of living. In the period since World War II, employment, output per worker, and consumption of goods per capita have reached the highest levels on record. True, unemployment has at times been a problem, but considering the rapid growth of our population and labor force, it has usually remained at very moderate levels. However, an unfortunate fact is that the impact of even moderate unemployment falls chiefly on certain groups of "marginal" or disadvantaged workers.

Other Social Effects of Technology. The influence of modern technology has permeated our entire social life. For one thing, it has brought about a great expansion of government controls over business. For example, if left to themselves, large industrial enterprises may become monopolies, and to prevent this antitrust laws became necessary. Our public utilities, including radio and television, are products of technological progress, and they, too, require various controls to protect the public interest. Technology has also brought important changes in the family, in our educational system, and in the problems we face in dealing with crime and delinquency. Modern technology has not only stimulated the growth of cities but has also greatly changed the way of life of both city and country people. Finally, through the development of nuclear bombs and guided missiles since World War II, it has had a major impact on international relations. However, these and certain other social effects of technology will be dealt with later, and so we will not discuss them at this point.

TECHNOLOGICAL PROGRESS IN RECENT DECADES

In a report published in 1937 by the National Resources Committee, Gilfillan listed certain inventions as most likely to be of social importance in the future. Later events demonstrated that his predictions were largely correct. Included among the inventions mentioned were the mechanical cotton picker, air-conditioning equipment, facsimile transmission, artificial textile fibers, plastics, synthetic rubber, the house trailer, the helicopter, prefabricated houses, television, gasoline produced from coal, and the photoelectric cell.[7] All of the inventions mentioned have since been put to important uses. Meanwhile, many other inventions have been made, and some have already brought significant changes in our culture.

Automation. Ever since World War II there has been a strong tendency in a number of industries toward *automation,* or *the use of automatic devices for controlling complex productive processes with little or no human intervention.* These automatic devices are themselves inventions and are in some cases inventions of considerable importance.

Automation is not something wholly new. Rather, it is a continuation at a more complex level of the long process of mechanization through which machines have gradually taken over more and more of the activities once carried on by men. But the development of electronic devices brought a new dimension to the process of mechanization. *Electronics* not only made possible radio and television but it also resulted in the invention of much more complex and efficient automatic controls than had been possible before. Electronic devices respond very quickly to signals, can take measurements and detect faults accurately, and can operate from a distance so that large areas of a plant can be controlled automatically.

[7] National Resources Committee, *Technological Trends and National Policy,* Washington, D.C., Government Printing Office, 1937, Section 3. Gilfillan, who has done much work in investigating the social significance of inventions, is the author of Sections 2 and 3.

16. Examining Steel by Electron Microscope. (Courtesy *Steelways* Magazine, published by American Iron and Steel Institute.)

In their earlier stages, electronic devices were based on the vacuum tube, but after the *transistor* was invented at Bell Telephone Laboratories more than twenty years ago, the vacuum tube became obsolete for many purposes, especially where not much power is required. Transistors introduced the age of miniaturization and of what engineers call "solid state" electronics. Each one can be made from a bit of crystal smaller than the letter *o* on this page. Transistors are very important where it is necessary to save space and weight, as in military aviation, space exploration, or pocket radios. But another great advance in electronics was the integrated circuit, pioneered at Texas Instruments not much more than a decade ago. In this new device for miniaturization, an entire electronic circuit, consisting of transistors, diodes, resistors, and other components, can be put into a chip of silicon crystal small enough to go through the eye of a needle. Such integrated circuits are relatively unaffected by

17. Man on the Moon. Astronaut Edwin E. Aldrin, Jr., lunar-module pilot, walks on the surface of the moon near a leg of the lunar module of Apollo 11. Astronaut Neil A. Armstrong, commander, took this photograph. (Courtesy National Aeronautics and Space Administration, Houston, Texas.)

moisture, aging, or vibration, and make it possible for us to do many things we could not do before. They were essential for constructing the lightweight, accurate, and dependable controls that made it possible for the United States to land Neil Armstrong and Edwin Aldrin on the moon in 1969, and later others, including David Scott and James Irwin in 1971.[8]

Although electronic controls have played the major role in the development of automation, other types of controls have advantages in some situations. Within the last decade, *fluidics* (a contraction of *fluids* and *logic*) has made an important addition to the science of control. Fluidics

[8] See Kenneth F. Weaver, "Crystals, Magical Servants of the Space Age," *National Geographic,* August 1968.

amplifies power and passes on "orders" by using tiny jets of fluid in tubes to control larger streams. Fluidic controls are not quite as fast as electronic controls, but they are safe and practical in many cases where a spark would be dangerous.

A very significant technological development of recent years is the invention, construction, and widespread use of electronic *computers,* sometimes called "thinking machines." Actually, computers do very limited kinds of "thinking," because all their operations must be directed by a program that is fed into them. They are really data-processing machines capable of analyzing statistics, making complex mathematical calculations, keeping records, and checking results. They represent a type of automation sometimes called *cybernetics.* In fact, the rapid rise in the use of computers for processing information and making it readily avail-

"Still the same answer. To increase the margin of profit, put more bread crumbs in the hamburger." (Drawing by J. Mirachi; © 1966 *The New Yorker Magazine, Inc.*)

able has made such an impression on some writers that they call our times "the age of cybernetics."

For many business enterprises and government agencies, computers have revolutionized office work. They can perform very rapidly many tasks that formerly required hundreds or thousands of man-hours. But in spite of the expanding use of computers the total number of office workers continues to rise sharply. One reason is that the use of computers encourages the gathering and analyzing of more kinds of information. Another is the constant increase in the number and complexity of reports demanded from business enterprises by government agencies.

We are as yet far from the goal, foreseen by some writers, when whole factories will be able to operate without human intervention. But in industries such as oil refining, the production of certain chemicals, and the making of some automobile parts, automation has been carried to a high point.

This raises again the old question of whether the supply of new jobs can keep up with the rate at which men are displaced by machines. Unless it does, there will be little social gain from automation. However, most economists believe that jobs will continue to increase, and past experience lends them support.[9] Some predictions that mass unemployment would result from the computer have already proved wrong. In 1948, when computers were just emerging from the laboratory stage, one of those who helped develop them, M.I.T. mathematics professor Norbert Wiener, made a dire prophecy. He predicted in his book *Cybernetics* that factory workers would largely disappear by 1970 and that unemployment would exceed that of the depressed 1930's.

Automation does have limitations. There are many kinds of work where the possibilities of employing it are small. But where automation can be applied, it often greatly reduces the need for manpower; usually, however, not as much as appears on the surface. This is not only because automation makes it possible to undertake new tasks but also because the production, programming, servicing, and repairing of automated systems require substantial amounts of human labor. The difficulty is that the jobs eliminated by automation are often unskilled, while those created usually require either skill or technical knowledge. This faces us with the social problem of providing a larger and larger portion of our workers with a fairly high level of education and training.

Other Recent Technological Developments. Since World War II many new inventions have appeared, and older ones have for the first time found significant uses. Among such inventions are the microfilm, the helicopter, radar, radar telescopes, and electronic microscopes. *Radar telescopes* magnify objects in space much more than the best conventional tele-

---

[9] See Yale Brozen, "Automation: A New Look at an Old Problem," *Society Today and Tomorrow,* 2d. ed., edited by Elgin F. Hunt and Jules Karlin, New York, The Macmillan Company, 1967, pp. 116–121.

18. Laser Light Ray Striking a Diamond. The diamond is on the pedestal at the right and the laser ray, if turned on repeatedly, will make a hole through it. The ray itself is not visible. It comes through the lens at the left from a source outside the picture. The "smoke" is vaporized diamond particles. Larger particles, blasted loose by the ray, make the continuous streaks that are slanting downward toward the left. (Courtesy General Electric Company.)

scopes, and *electron microscopes* make it possible to see viruses so small that they cannot be detected by other microscopes. Another development on which a good start has been made is the conversion of brackish water or sea water to fresh water. Rather recent developments include the *fuel cell* and the *laser.* The former is a small electric generator with no moving parts; to produce current it requires only to be heated. Fuel cells are placed on the outside coating of satellites to generate power from sunlight for the operation of radios and other instruments. The laser is a beam of light in which the light waves, instead of spreading out, are highly concentrated and move straight forward on a very narrow front. Lasers can generate intense heat in a very small area at some distance from the origin of the light. Their uses include measuring distances very accurately and operating surgically within the human eye without making an incision; and in the future it may be possible to employ them for sending great numbers of messages for long distances. It has even been suggested that the laser may prove to be the long-imagined death ray of science fiction. A serious limitation is that, like any form of light, the laser cannot pass through rain or fog.

Nuclear fission, which led to the atom bomb and later led to the hydrogen bomb, was a scientific achievement of World War II that had far-reaching effects. On the other hand, *jet propulsion* is a principle that has long been known but that has come into its own only since World War II. Jet propulsion is what causes a rocket to soar. Rockets were used in the War of 1812, and they were invented centuries earlier by the Chinese, but before they could be sent to great heights or distances, it was necessary to develop an adequate source of power.

No technical development of recent times, unless it be the nuclear bomb, has had more impact on our society than the expanding uses of jet propulsion. It is jet propulsion that can send missiles, armed with hydrogen bombs, for thousands of miles; it is jet propulsion that is sending satellites around the world, to the moon, and into outer space; and it is jet propulsion that enables us to travel in airplanes at speeds never before dreamed of. Now planes are being constructed to fly between 1,300 and 2,000 miles per hour.

During the past decade technological progress has continued at a high level, not only as a result of basically new discoveries and inventions but also through finding new uses for them and refining the methods or devices used to apply them. An interesting and recently reported development is the discovery that soft woods and some fibrous materials can be made almost wear proof by impregnating them with the basic chemicals of plastics and then irradiating them. Another recent discovery, credited to the Agricultural Research Service of the United States Department of Agriculture, is that a certain compound, fed to sheep, interrupts growth of their wool at the root. A week later the wool can be rolled off with no waste and no pain to the animals. This will be less wasteful and much cheaper than shearing, provided it is found that the sheep suffer no serious side effects. Another technological advance worth mentioning is the production of a submarine lifeboat for the navy, which can operate at depths up to five thousand feet and which attaches itself to the submarine's escape hatch much as a lunar landing module joins the command satellite before they start back to earth.[10] A very interesting development of great possible future significance is successful experiments in building plastic houses.[11] Finally, a really astonishing achievement has been the development of extremely sensitive photographic and electronic equipment for so-called spy-satellites. Thus equipped, these satellites can obtain detailed information about installations on the ground from a distance of 150 miles. They can, for example, even pick up radio and telephone messages from inside Russia and China.[12]

One of the most remarkable of all modern technological advances is our modern telephone system with its present high level of convenience, speed, and efficiency. Perhaps the greatest single improvement in this system, at least since World War II, has been the establishment of nationwide dialing. Dialing is now being changed by the American Telephone and Telegraph Company from an electromechanical system to an electronic system. This will provide even more convenience to the telephone user in making and receiving calls and, with other advances that reduce costs, will make personal conversations over great distances more and more common.

[10] See "A Submarine Lifeboat," *Technology Review*, June 1969.
[11] See *Petroleum Today*, Fall 1968, pp. 1–5.
[12] See "Spies in Space," *U.S. News & World Report*, September 9, 1968.

THE FUTURE OF TECHNOLOGICAL PROGRESS

Technological progress is likely to continue at a rapid rate for some time to come, partly because so many processes and devices are still in their early stages of development and partly because of recent advances in science. But whether it will continue at anything like its present rate for fifty or a hundred years is far from certain. We have already discovered that some technological innovations have undesirable side effects that tend to outweigh their benefits.

Revolutionary Possibilities in the Future. Whatever the long-run outlook for technological progress may be, for the foreseeable future its prospects seem bright. In the next quarter century we are likely to see some extraordinary developments, though possibly nothing quite so dramatic as the first landing of men on the moon.

First of all it now seems possible that in time men will be landed on Mars. The difficulties are great. It would mean a space journey, not of a few days, but of many months. Perhaps no nation will consider that such an attempt would be worth the risk and the cost. But there are other advances in technology that might be more revolutionary in their social effects, and some of them could conceivably be realized in the not-too-

"He never used to howl at it, but now that Harry's there . . . ." (Courtesy Rowland B. Wilson and *LOOK* Magazine.)

distant future. On balance they might or might not be beneficial to mankind. Let us consider several interesting possibilities.

Power is cheaper than ever before in history, but it is still not cheap enough to be used for some purposes, such as desalting great quantities of sea water for irrigation. If we could succeed in unlocking at extremely low cost the power in the atom, and at the same time prevent pollution of the environment by nuclear radiation, we could bring about some dramatic changes in human life on this planet by transforming many dry and barren areas into prosperous farming and industrial communities.

We already have nuclear power plants, but they produce power at costs similar to those of plants using coal, oil, or gas. However, the noted scientist Glenn T. Seaborg, until recently head of the Atomic Energy Commission, predicts that by the 1980's we will have multimillion-kilowatt breeder reactors; and by the 1990's he thinks that such reactors will have reduced the cost of electric power to two or three mills per kilowatt-hour or to even less. *Breeder reactors* can reduce power costs greatly because they produce more fuel than they burn.[13]

With very cheap electric power it would be economically feasible not only to desalt sea water for irrigating some of the arid regions of the earth like the west coast deserts of South America, and parts of North Africa, the Near East, and Australia, but also to manufacture quantities of low-cost fertilizer from air, water, and chemicals. That would give us what Seaborg calls a "food factory." It would also be possible in these same regions, depending on their location and mineral resources, to produce many industrial products at reduced costs and thus to create economic complexes that could support great numbers of people.

But would such a development be desirable? What would be its climatic and ecological effects and its contribution to world-wide pollution? Do we want to keep filling the wild and relatively empty spaces in the world with more and more people?

If what we want is to increase the world's food supply, there is an even more revolutionary approach to the problem that some day we might conceivably be able to apply. We might develop methods for synthesizing foods *directly from inorganic materials found in nature* and thus free ourselves from dependence on farm land and on the cultivation of crops and the raising of meat animals. We have not yet progressed very far toward producing *synthetic foods* for human beings, though we have been able to make synthetically some drugs and vitamins that were formerly derived from products grown on farms. However, already we can supply cattle with a part of the protein they require by feeding them with urea mixed with corn, molasses, and vegetable compounds. Urea is a nitrogen compound synthesized from the air. To most animals it is poisonous, but cattle, sheep, goats, and other ruminants are able to digest it. It has been

[13] See interview with Glenn T. Seaborg: "Ahead: More Atomic Marvels," *U.S. News & World Report,* September 2, 1968.

used regularly as cattle feed by, among others, Roswell Garst, the Iowa farmer who entertained former Russian Premier Khrushchev on his visit to the United States in 1959.

The Social Basis for Technological Progress. Technological progress may be inevitable as long as social conditions encourage it and make it possible, but it is quite conceivable that some day conditions could change in such a way as to stop it. There have been times and places in the history of the world when people have lost ground instead of making progress. At present, aside from the mere momentum of technological progress, basic conditions in the United States seem favorable for its continuation. We expect and we welcome changes for the better in our material environment; and today we especially need to employ science and technology to help us in meeting some of the problems of pollution. Both government and industry make large contributions to scientific and technical research; and though vested interests sometimes oppose change, on the whole our private enterprise economic system encourages it.

There are, however, offsetting factors that might in the long run greatly retard our technological progress. The costs of the research and equipment necessary for meeting certain problems of pollution are likely to be resisted by many corporations and also, where government is directly involved, by many taxpayers. Technological progress also tends to be slowed by organized pressure groups that have an interest in limiting the output of certain products and in opposing the introduction of new methods or products in order to maintain the demand and the prices for the things that they sell. For example, labor unions often oppose the introduction of methods or materials that might reduce the jobs available to their members, and producers of building materials sometimes seek to discourage the introduction of substitutes for their products, even though these may be better and cheaper and may use materials that are more plentiful. Again, many farmers demand that the government should take measures to reduce farm output in order to raise farm prices and incomes. Pressure groups tend to multiply, and if the government should increasingly cooperate with them to limit the production and raise the prices of more and more products, this might ultimately become an effective obstacle, not only to expansion of employment and to higher standards of living but also to many innovations that might economize on the use of both labor and scarce natural resources. It would certainly discourage technological progress, because the chief purposes of technical innovation, aside from the introduction of new products, are to reduce costs, improve quality, and increase output.

A more subtle influence that might slow up technological progress would be the growth among our people of a less receptive attitude toward change. This might result not only from a lack of interest in consuming more goods but also from a feeling of indifference toward improving both the quality of goods and the quality of the environment; or it might result from a gradual dilution of the spirit of adventure and from an increasing emphasis on security. Change and progress often seem dangerous and disturbing. They put some people out of jobs and force them to seek types of employment that are not to their liking. They cause some business enterprises to contract or fail, even though others may be expanding rapidly. A society that puts its whole emphasis on stability and security is not likely to look with favor on radical technological innovations.

In the long run, our ability to maintain a high rate of technological progress will depend on our ability to maintain the kind of social environment that encourages men to invent and apply new and more effective methods, not only to meet man's needs for material goods but also to meet his desires for such things as better education, better government, better health, and a more attractive, pollution-free environment.

Terms to Be Understood

technology	automation	fuel cell
machine technology	electronics	laser
invention	transistor	nuclear fission
patent	fluidics	jet propulsion
Industrial Revolution	computer	breeder reactor
standardization	cybernetics	synthetic foods
mass production	radar telescope	
productivity of labor	electron microscope	

Questions for Review and Discussion

1. Why is machine technology sometimes said to be "self-expanding?"
2. What is a nonmaterial invention? Give examples.
3. How do inventions originate? Why is it that the entire credit for a major invention can never be given to any one man?
4. It is often said that "necessity is the mother of invention." Criticize this statement.
5. What factors cause inventions to spread, or fail to spread, from one group to another?
6. What was the social significance of Gutenberg's invention of movable type for printing?
7. How does Marshall McLuhan explain most of the changes taking place in modern society?
8. List as many factors as you can that tend to stimulate invention.
9. Why are many inventions put to use without being patented?
10. List several technological developments that some scientists believe possible in the next several decades and that might have revolutionary social effects. In each case do you think the results would be desirable? Defend your answers.
11. Why are inventions said to be cumulative?

12. Describe the Industrial Revolution (a) in England and (b) in the United States.
13. To what extent should we attempt to control or regulate inventions? Explain your point of view.
14. Explain the relation of standardization of parts to mass production.
15. Describe the effects of advances in technology on (a) the tempo of human life; (b) standards of living; (c) the productivity of labor; (d) the need for skilled workers; (e) unemployment; (f) government.
16. Will automation increase the rate of unemployment within the next twenty years? Defend your answer.
17. Make as long a list as you can of inventions or technological developments that have been applied to important uses only during the last twenty-five or thirty years, and indicate the social importance of each.
18. What future developments might discourage invention and slow up technological progress? Explain why in each case.
19. What are the principal characteristics of a social environment that encourages technological progress?

For Further Reading

Bernard, H. Russell, and Pertti Pelto, eds., *Technology and Culture Change*, New York, The Macmillan Company, 1972.

Gilfillan, S. C., *Invention and the Patent System*, prepared for the Joint Economic Committee of Congress, Washington, D.C., Government Printing Office, 1964. A report on a study made by Gilfillan for the committee.

———, *The Sociology of Invention*, Chicago, Follet Publishing Co., 1935. Remaining copies now held by M.I.T. Press, Cambridge, Mass.

Hetzler, Stanley, *Technological Growth and Social Change*, New York, Frederick A. Praeger, Inc., 1969.

Hunt, Elgin F., and Jules Karlin, eds., *Society Today and Tomorrow*, 2d ed., paperback, New York, The Macmillan Company, 1967. See "A New Look at an Old Problem" by Yale Brozen.

Jaffe, A. J., and Joseph Froomkin, *Technology and Jobs: Automation in Perspective*, New York, Frederick A. Praeger, Inc., 1968.

Kranzberg, Melvin, and Carroll W. Purcell, Jr., eds., *Technology in Western Civilization*, 2 vols., New York, Oxford University Press, 1967. Vol. 1: *Emergence of Modern Industrial Society: Earliest Times to 1900*. Vol. 2: *Technology in the Twentieth Century*.

McLuhan, Marshall, *Understanding Man*, Signet paperback, New York, New American Library, Inc., 1969.

Mantoux, P., *Industrial Revolution in the Eighteenth Century*, Torchbook paperback, New York, Harper & Row, Publishers, 1961.

Mead, Margaret, ed., *Cultural Patterns and Technical Change*, Mentor paperback, New York, New American Library, Inc., 1956.

Moore, A. D., *Invention, Discovery, and Creativity*, Anchor paperback, New York, Doubleday & Company, Inc., 1969.

Nelson, Richard R., et al., *Technology, Economic Growth, and Public Policy*, Washington, D.C., Brookings Institute, 1967.

Oakley, Kenneth P., *Man the Tool-Maker,* 3d ed., Phoenix paperback, Chicago, University of Chicago Press, n.d.

Rezler, Julius, *Automation and Industrial Labor,* paperback, New York, Random House, Inc., 1969.

Schon, Donald A., *Invention and Evolution of Ideas,* Social Science paperback, New York, Barnes & Noble, Inc., 1967.

Stearn, Gerald Emanuel, ed., *McLuhan: Hot and Cold,* paperback, New York, New American Library, Inc., 1967. See especially comments of Kenneth E. Boulding, pp. 68–75.

Warner, Aaron W., and D. Morse, eds., *Technological Innovation and Society,* New York, Columbia University Press, 1966.

Wiener, Norbert, *Cybernetics, or Control and Communication in the Animal and the Machine,* 2d ed., Cambridge, Mass., M.I.T. Press, 1961.

———, *Human Use of Human Beings: Cybernetics and Society,* paperback, New York, Avon Books, 1969.

Chapter 8

Population

f we wish to learn as much as possible about any large group of human beings, a good way to begin is to study its characteristics as a population. *Population* refers to the number of people who live in a given area. However, the student of population is concerned not only with the number of people in an area but also with the factors that may be causing their number to increase or decrease. These include such matters as the state of medicine and sanitation, the extent to which birth control is practiced, and the availability to food and other resources. Further, he is concerned with the distribution of people among countries and among regions, and between rural and urban areas. He is also interested in the different kinds of people who make up any given population and in their physical, mental, and cultural characteristics. In this connection, he finds it useful to classify and count people on the basis of such characteristics as age, sex, marital status, occupation, income, nationality, and race.

HISTORY OF POPULATION GROWTH

We have little definite information about the size of populations before 1800, and even less before 1750. There is reason to believe that in the past the populations of various regions of the earth have gone through periods both of expansion and contraction. However, until relatively recent times we have practically no population figures based on an actual census. A *census is an official, systematic count of the number of people who live in a given area.* Usually when the people are counted, other kinds of information about them, such as age and sex, are also gathered. Lacking any census figures, we can make only rough guesses about populations and population changes before the latter part of the eighteenth century.

The first reliable census of a European country was taken by Sweden in 1749. In the United States the first census was taken in 1790. About this time or not long after, several European countries began to take censuses, and by 1850 reasonably accurate figures were available for western Europe, for the United States, and for some countries in other parts of the world. Today we have fairly dependable population statistics for most countries; yet there are still areas for which our population estimates are not much better than guesses.

Changes in World Population. Changes in world population obviously depend on the relation between births and deaths. If births exceed deaths, population will grow. If deaths exceed births, it will shrink. There is little doubt that through most of human history the death rate has been high. Disease, malnutrition, starvation, and sometimes war have taken a very heavy toll. The birth rate must also have been high, for otherwise the human race could not have survived. *The birth rate is commonly expressed as the number of births per thousand of the population per year. The death rate is the number of deaths per thousand.*[1]

In past times the critical factor limiting population was usually means of subsistence, especially food. In spite of the ravages of disease, populations were likely to grow where food was relatively plentiful. Where food was scarce, periodic famines killed people in great numbers, and chronic malnutrition raised the death rate from disease. Until modern times, most of the people of the world have suffered from chronic or periodic short-

---

[1] These definitions apply to what are sometimes called the *crude* rates. Other ways of expressing birth and death rates are more significant for certain purposes.

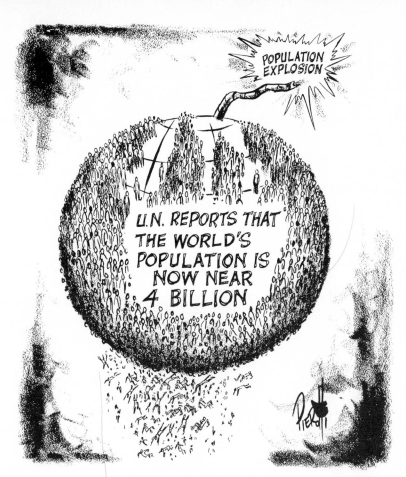

The Biggest Bomb of All. (*New York Post* Cartoon by Pierotti, © 1969. Reprinted by permission of New York Post Corporation.)

ages of food. Even today it is said that half the people of the world go to bed hungry every night, and this seems to be borne out by a survey of the Food and Agricultural Organization of the United Nations. This survey indicated that more than half the people of the world have a diet inadequate to maintain health.

There are now more than 3.6 billion people in the world. As indicated by Table 2, world population appears to have grown rapidly ever since 1650. It has increased more than six times in about 320 years. Though this growth has been uneven for different parts of the world, we can be certain that the total population is greater today than ever before, because by past methods of production it would have been impossible to provide subsistence for the number of people now living. The *rate* of growth is also greater than ever before—in fact, so rapid that many writers call it a *population explosion.*

Year	Population (in millions)
1650	545
1750	728
1800	906
1850	1,171
1900	1,608
1940	2,171
1950	2,495
1960	2,930
1969	3,552

Table 2. *Estimated Growth of World Population Since 1650*

Source: Adapted from A. M. Carr-Saunders, *World Population,* New York, Oxford University Press, 1936, p. 42. The figures for 1940, 1950, 1960, and 1969 are from the Statistical Office of the United Nations, June, 1970.

Growth of Population in Europe. During the period from 1650 to World War II the population of Europe increased more rapidly than that of the world as a whole. Despite the lack of dependable data for the years before 1800, it seems certain that there was a very considerable increase in the eighteenth century. In the nineteenth century and the early part of the twentieth century, the population of Europe increased nearly three times.

However, by the end of the nineteenth century there had already been a marked decline in the *rate* of increase, a decline that continued into the twentieth century. In France the decline in the rate was especially noticeable, so much so that even before World War I the population had become almost stationary. After the war it became increasingly apparent that the same trend, though less advanced, was operating in all the nations of western Europe. Some writers predicted that the population of western Europe as a whole would soon become stationary, after which it might begin to decline. Meanwhile, the rate of population growth had begun to rise in some of the more backward countries of the world.

Since World War II the trend toward a stationary or declining population has been reversed, even in France, but there seems no likelihood that the rate of growth in Europe will return to the high levels of the nineteenth century. Today the highest rates of growth are found in some of the less-developed countries of Asia, Africa, and Latin America.

Population Growth in the United States. The growth of population in the United States has been spectacular. Though the population of Europe increased considerably more than three times from 1800 to 1970, during the same period that of the United States increased about thirty-seven times. From a nation of 5.3 million in 1800 we have expanded to about 205 million in 1970. When the first census was taken in 1790, we had fewer than 4 million people; today the births in a single year are not far below that number. The increase in population in the United States can be partly explained by immigration, but the greater portion of it has resulted from a rapid rate of natural increase.

Table 3 shows the population of the United States for each census year from 1790 through 1970, and the percentage of increase for each decade.

Table 3. *Growth of Population in the United States, 1790–1970*

Census Year	Population	Increase over Preceding Census	
		Number	Per Cent
1790	3,929,214		
1800	5,308,483	1,379,269	35.1
1810	7,239,881	1,931,398	36.4
1820	9,638,453	2,398,572	33.1
1830	12,866,020	3,227,567	33.5
1840	17,069,453	4,203,433	32.7
1850	23,191,876	6,122,423	35.9
1860	31,443,321	8,251,445	35.6
1870	39,818,449	8,375,128	26.6
1880	50,155,783	10,337,334	26.0
1890	62,947,714	12,791,931	25.5
1900	75,994,575	13,046,861	20.7
1910	91,972,266	15,977,691	21.0
1920	105,710,620	13,738,354	14.9
1930	122,775,046	17,064,426	16.1
1940	131,669,275	8,894,229	7.2
1950*	151,325,798	19,656,523	14.5
1960	179,323,175	27,997,377	18.5
1970	204,765,770	25,442,595	13.4

*Alaska and Hawaii included beginning in 1950.
Source: U.S. Bureau of the Census

Growth of the Black Population in the United States. According to Warren S. Thompson and David T. Lewis, not until about 1700 was the value of the black man as a laborer in the tobacco fields fully realized.[2] At that time slaves began to be imported in large numbers. When the first census was taken in 1790, there were more than 750,000 blacks in the country, and they constituted 19.3 per cent of our population. After 1808 it became illegal to import slaves, but many were smuggled in up to the time of the Civil War. However, the rise in the black population after 1808 was principally the result of natural increase. By 1970 our black population had multiplied some thirty-one times to a total of about 23.2 million.

In spite of the rapid rate at which blacks increased, the white population increased still faster, so that the percentage of blacks in the total population fell from 19 in 1810 to 9.7 in 1930. The more rapid increase of the whites was probably accounted for by their substantially lower death rate plus the fact that their numbers were reinforced by a large immigration from Europe. However, since 1930 the black population has grown somewhat faster than the white, so that it now constitutes about 11.3 per cent of the total. This change in trend can be explained by three factors. First, the birth rate of blacks is higher than that of whites. Second, even though

[2] Warren S. Thompson and David T. Lewis, *Population Problems*, New York, McGraw-Hill, Inc., 1965, p. 210.

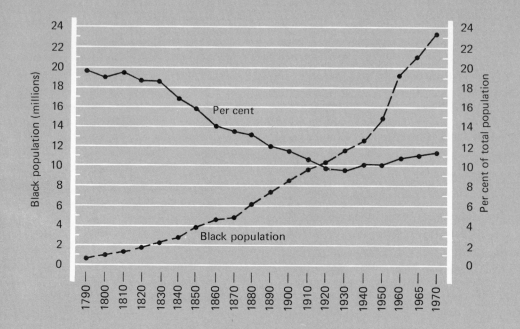

Figure 2. Growth of the Black Population in the United States. (Source of data: U.S. Bureau of the Census.)

their death rate also remains higher, it has in recent years been dropping more rapidly. Third, since 1930 there has been relatively little addition to the white population by immigration. Figure 2 shows graphically changes in our black population since 1790, both in numbers and as a percentage of the total population.

Immigration and Population Growth. It has been estimated that about 42 million persons, mainly from Europe, came to settle in the United States from 1780 to 1930.[3] Since these immigrants were largely young adults of the right ages to have children, their contribution to our total population has been considerably larger than this number would indicate.

After 1930, immigration was so greatly reduced that it became a very minor factor in adding to population. This reduction in immigration was influenced by the depression, but it was chiefly the result of restrictive legislation. In 1921 an act had been passed limiting immigration to certain annual *quotas* for each national group. Later the quotas were reduced, until finally the maximum total number of immigrants to be admitted annually was cut down to only 150,000. From time to time some changes

[3] However, official records of immigration go back only to 1820.

have been made in our immigration laws, but since 1921, immigration has been a minor factor in the growth of our population.

There has been disagreement among students of population as to the net effect of immigration on population in earlier periods. From about 1845 through 1914 immigration was relatively large, and the trend was upward. It reached a peak in the ten years preceding World War I. In six of these years more than a million aliens were admitted annually. Yet in spite of this rising tide of immigration, for the whole period 1845 to 1914 the *rate* of population increase declined sharply. This decline in the rate of growth led some writers to conclude that immigration has made no net contribution to our population. They maintain that its principal effect was to cause the birth rate of our native population to fall much more rapidly than would otherwise have been the case. Without immigration, they say, our native population would have increased faster and our total numbers would now be just as great.

Though there is no way of proving that this assumption is wrong, it seems highly improbable. It may, on the other hand, contain an element of truth. The immigrants usually took the low-paid jobs. Most of them were handicapped by lack of education, and nearly all of them by unfamiliarity with our language and customs. Their presence made it possible for the native population to rise more rapidly in the social and economic scale; and because people in the higher income brackets have on an average fewer children than those in the lower brackets, this rise in social status may have somewhat accelerated the decline in the birth rate of the native population.

Why World Population Has Grown Rapidly Since 1800. The great increase in world population since 1800 has resulted directly from a continuing decline of the death rate. Two factors were responsible for this: first, great advances in sanitation and medicine; second, a relatively rapid increase in the per capita output of both food and manufactured goods, so that for large numbers of people, standards of living rose substantially above a subsistence level. In part, the increase in per capita output was made possible by the opening up for trade and settlement of some of the undeveloped areas of the world. Principally, however, it can be regarded as a result of the Industrial Revolution. It is the great advances of science and technology in the nineteenth and twentieth centuries that have made it possible for the world to support a rapidly rising population. Furthermore, in Western industrial countries not only has it been possible to support larger populations, but it has been possible to support them on higher standards of living than were ever known in the past.

In the latter part of the nineteenth century certain of the more backward parts of the world began to experience some of the benefits of modern science, industry, and transportation. Even in parts of India and China, where most of the population of Asia lives, sanitation and medicine began to reduce the death rate and to increase the rate of population growth. Figure 3 compares the distribution of the world's population by regions in

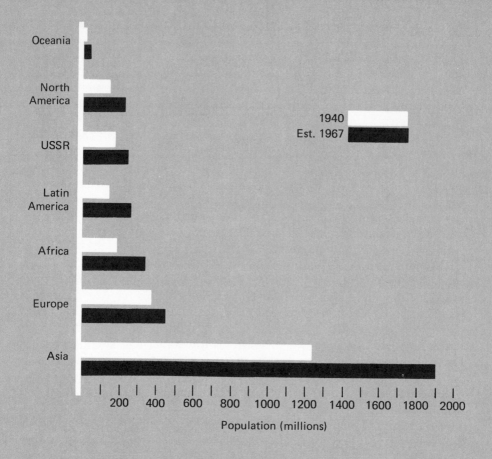

Figure 3. Distribution of the World's Population by Regions, 1940 and Estimated 1967. (Source: *United Nations Statistical Yearbook 1968.*)

1940 and 1967; and shows that, in the period between, some of the less-developed regions of the world, such as Asia and Latin America, made substantially greater gains in population than did Europe, the United States, and Canada.

However, increases in population in the less-developed areas of the world tended to be at the expense of standards of living. Birth rates remained high, and production expanded slowly.

If an increase in the food supply temporarily put off famine or relieved malnutrition, it was soon matched by a further increase in population. Since 1900 the population of Asia has more than doubled; today more than half the people of the world are found there, but for the most part they are living at a bare subsistence level. Early in 1969 the population of India was officially reported to be about 531 million. The country is only about one third the size of the United States, and a large part of it cannot be cultivated. Extreme poverty is the lot of the majority, and in many areas homelessness and starvation are common. At night the pavements of the cities are lined with sleepers. In Calcutta alone, the common estimate for the homeless is from one to two million.[4] The population of China is the greatest for any country in the world and it appears to be growing rapidly in spite of extreme poverty and frequent food shortages. According to the *United Nations Yearbook* for 1969, it had reached about 720 million in 1967. The possibility that this great mass of Chinese may become a powerful force for aggression against surrounding countries disturbs both the Russians and many people in the democracies; but such great numbers of largely poverty-stricken people are probably a burden rather than a source of either economic or military strength.

CHANGING TRENDS OF POPULATION GROWTH

In the past two hundred years or more, the population of the world has increased greatly because during most of this period the death rate has fallen markedly faster than the birth rate. But in many of the more advanced countries the decline of death rates slowed up in the early decades of the twentieth century as the average age of their populations rose. This, combined with a continuing substantial fall in birth rates, led many writers to predict for the near future stable or declining populations. However, during and after World War II, birth rates made an unexpected recovery in most of these countries, though not to the high levels of the nineteenth century.

In the world as a whole, population is now increasing at a faster rate than ever before. This is because in recent years there has been a notable decline of the death rate in many of the less developed countries, with no equivalent decline of the birth rate. Rapid growth of population in crowded countries with limited resources makes it almost impossible to raise or even maintain standards of living. In several of these countries, notably India, the government is making efforts to encourage birth control practices, but how much success these efforts will have remains to be seen. In India they have not been carried on long enough for us to judge whether they will succeed in reducing the pressure of population on means of subsistence.

Since the future of population growth will depend on the relation of the birth rate to the death rate, let us consider the factors that have af-

[4] Edward Rice, "The Cities of India—Classic Studies in Urban Collapse," *Vista*, January–February, 1970.

fected these in the past and are likely to influence them in the future, with special attention to the trends of population growth in the United States.

The Declining Death Rate. The death rate is the number of people who die, in a given year, per thousand of the population. The current death rate in the United States is somewhat less than 10, as compared with 17 in 1900, but for twenty-five years or more the rate has been almost static. As long ago as 1941 it had fallen to 10.5.

Whether the death rate will drop further in coming years will depend both on changes in the age composition of our population and on the rate of advance in medical science. Other things being equal, a higher average age for our people will mean a higher death rate. With respect to advances in medical science, we have already progressed a long way in controlling the infectious and contagious diseases that killed so many people in the past. The latest major advance was the development of vaccines for preventing infantile paralysis, commonly called polio. Although there is still room for progress in controlling some of these diseases, the chief problem today is to control the maladies that largely attack older people. These include cancer, arthritis, and various degenerative diseases that affect such organs as the heart, blood vessels, liver, and kidneys. Though it is possible that great discoveries lie just ahead, as yet our progress in dealing with these diseases has been slow. Meanwhile, our success in controlling infectious and contagious diseases is increasing life expectancy and contributing to a gradual rise in the proportion of our population over sixty-five. Because of this increase in the proportion of old people, the crude death rate may actually rise a little in coming decades. In any case, unless we make great advances in controlling degenerative diseases and the aging process itself, the future of population growth will depend largely on the trend of the birth rate.

The decline of the death rate over the years has been reflected in the increased *life expectancy,* or *probable length of life of the average person.* In Massachusetts in 1789 the average boy baby could be expected to live about thirty-five years from birth. In 1850 this figure had risen only to thirty-eight years, but by 1950 it was about sixty-six for the male population of the United States as a whole. For the female population it was over seventy-one. Today for the entire population, life expectancy at birth is at an all-time high of over seventy years. But this represents an increase of only two or three years since 1950. Women have a life expectancy about seven years greater than men. The life expectancy of blacks is still several years less than that of whites.

Reasons for the Long Decline of the Birth Rate. Any decline in the birth rate that narrows its margin over the death rate will slow down population growth. A definite downward trend in birth rates in the Western world was first observed early in the nineteenth century in France among the prosperous people living in cities. Later it spread to the remainder of western Europe and to various countries that had been settled by Europeans. Even in the United States a long decline of the birth rate began about 1800 and continued almost without interruption until it was definitely reversed in the 1940's.

It is not possible to give either a simple or a completely satisfactory explanation of this protracted decline. A few writers believe that the greatest influence was exerted by biological factors such as a decline in *fecundity*[5] and a rise in the proportion of miscarriages and stillbirths. There is not much evidence, however, of any significant decline of fecundity in Western countries. The bulk of the evidence seems to indicate that the decline of the birth rate was brought about primarily by social and economic forces that made people less willing to accept the trouble, expense, and responsibility involved in raising large families.

There are several ways in which a reduced willingness to accept the responsibilities of family life may reduce the birth rate. One is by causing many people to defer marriage until a relatively late age or even to avoid it entirely. Late marriage sharply reduces the number of children in a family, not only because it shortens the childbearing period of the wife but also because the average woman is less fertile in her thirties than in her late teens and early twenties. In a few countries both late marriage and failure to marry have been significant factors in reducing the birth rate. Ireland provides a notable example. In Ireland opposition to birth control has been strong on religious grounds. Nevertheless, the birth rate has fallen greatly since early in the nineteenth century. One reason for this is apparent when we note that in 1949 only 26 per cent of the men fifteen to forty-four years of age were married and only 39 per cent of the women. The corresponding figures for England and Wales were 58 per cent and 63 per cent, and in the United States they were even higher. As a result of their attitudes toward marriage, the birth rate of the Irish has for many years remained at a moderate level. This, combined with emigration, caused the population of Ireland to fall by one half in a little more than a century. But since World War II the Irish birth rate has risen somewhat.

In most countries the long decline of the birth rate cannot be explained by late marriages or failure to marry. Certainly these factors did not account for it in the United States in the fifty years before World War II. During that period not only did the average age at first marriage fall, but there was also a sharp rise in the proportion of married people in the total population. In 1890 about 53 per cent of all Americans fourteen years old and over were married. By 1940, shortly before we entered the war, the proportion had risen to nearly 60 per cent, and today it is about 65 per cent. Undoubtedly, one of the factors that caused the birth rate to begin rising after 1940 was the continuing increase in the popularity of marriage.

In most Western countries before 1940 the principal direct cause of

[5] *Fecundity* refers especially to the reproductive powers of the females of a species. The fecundity of a population is the number of children it is biologically capable of producing. This can only be estimated or guessed. The *fertility* of a population is measured by the number of children it actually produces.

declining birth rates seems to have been the voluntary limitation of family size by married couples. There are several ways in which such limitation could conceivably be brought about. They include voluntary sterilization, sexual restraint in marriage, abortions, and the practice of birth control. Of these it is probably safe to rule out the first two as relatively unimportant. The third, abortion, is widely practiced, and probably more so today than in the past. But in many places it is still illegal except when necessary to protect the life or health of an expectant mother. In addition, it involves costs, risks, and discomforts most women would rather avoid. We must therefore conclude that the principal method employed by married couples to limit their families has been birth control. By *birth control* we refer to various devices and practices that prevent conception, or make it less likely, as the result of sexual relations.

Let us now consider briefly the social and economic factors that, in Western industrial countries, over a long period kept reducing the willingness of people to have children, or at least their willingness to have large families.

The Influence of Social and Economic Factors on the Birth Rate. Most students of population believe that the growth of intellectual and social freedom in modern times has been an important factor in contributing to the limitation of births. Some years ago Warren S. Thompson, then a leading writer on population, expressed this as follows: "In an atmosphere in which people were comparatively free to consider the consequences to themselves of a high birth rate accompanied by a declining death rate, it is not in the least surprising that fertility began to decline as soon as means were found to reduce the rate of conception, means which did not too much offend against the established moral values."[6] Besides, as Thompson pointed out, moral values themselves were undergoing rapid change. Thus, in spite of much opposition, in a few decades the knowledge and practice of birth control had spread very widely.

The Birth Rate and Standards of Living. In modern times low birth rates have been associated, not with extreme poverty and a struggle for bare subsistence, but with industrial progress, rising incomes, and higher standards of living. One might suppose that higher incomes would make people more willing to have children. Paradoxically, this seems not to be the case. In general the lowest birth rates are found in the more advanced countries, where living standards are relatively high. Furthermore, in such countries people whose incomes are well above the average usually have fewer children than people whose incomes are low.

Many students of society have had difficulty in explaining to their own satisfaction the inverse relation that is found in the modern world between income and the willingness to have children. The general explanation seems to be that when people achieve a level of income that enables them

[6] By permission from Warren S. Thompson, *Population Problems,* New York, McGraw-Hill Book Company, Inc., p. 216. Copyright 1930, 1935, 1942, 1953, by the McGraw-Hill Book Company, Inc.

to enjoy a satisfying kind of life, they become very unwilling to give up the advantages they have gained. Rather, they wish to rise still higher in the social and economic scale, and they want their children to enjoy a status at least equal to their own. In order to achieve these ambitions, they seek to limit their offspring to the number they can adequately support and educate without too much financial strain. On the other hand, the poor are willing to have large families because they have little to lose. They may even regard children as a compensation for other satisfactions that they lack. They do not expect to give their children much education. In the past they counted on the children, as they grew up, to help support the family. The parents do not expect to grow rich or even to save very much. They know that if adversity strikes, they will always be able to fall back on charity, relief, or, possibly, social security.

The Birth Rate and Urbanization. One development that has made an important contribution to the decline of the birth rate in industrial countries is the increasing proportion of people who live in cities. For a number of reasons, city people have far fewer children than country people. In the first place, children are more trouble in the city and are more in the way because there is less space for them to play in. Again, in the country, farm chores keep parents at home most of the time anyway, so that children do not much reduce their freedom of movement. In the city it is quite otherwise. People have limited working hours, so that couples without children are rather free to come and go as they please. On the other hand, couples with children are pretty much tied down, and to make this bondage especially distasteful, city parents are more likely than country parents to have a variety of interests outside the home and the family. Then, too, country people have an advantage as parents in that children on a farm are a relatively light economic burden. Much of their food can be raised at home; also, the children can do a great deal of the farm work and thus help support themselves and the family. In the city, on the contrary, children are very expensive. They must be housed, fed, and clothed for many years, and they can seldom earn much until they are nearly grown and about ready to leave home.

The Birth Rate and the Social Position of Women. Another factor contributing to the decline of the birth rate in modern times is the freeing of women from some of the economic and social limitations to which they were once subject. In former times it was assumed that a woman's place was in the home, and she had little opportunity for outside activities. Employment opportunities through which she could earn her own living were almost nonexistent. The expression "old maid" was an epithet that carried with it a degree of contempt, for in most cases the situation of a woman who was unable to snare a husband was far from pleasant. A very few women might find employment as teachers or governesses, but the majority of those who lacked husbands were obliged to take work as domestic servants or else to live with some relative, perhaps a married sister, and help with the housework and the children.

When women had few outside activities and all their interests were centered in their homes and children, most of them were willing to have large families. If they were not always entirely willing, they knew no way to avoid it, and they looked upon the birth of children as an expression of the divine will. In recent times all this has changed. Children can now be put off indefinitely or limited to one, two, or three. Also, numerous employment opportunities have become available to women, and as a result they are economically much more independent. Large numbers of them, both married and single, hold regular jobs. Many of these jobs are well paid, so that sometimes a married woman actually earns more than her husband. But a woman who has a job that she is unwilling to give up is in no position to raise a large family. She is likely to feel that she is doing very well in this respect if she can arrange to stop work long enough to have one or two children.

Even women who do not help earn the family income are likely today to have a variety of interests outside the home. They take an active part in church work, clubs, social organizations, charities, and other enterprises that affect their own welfare or that of their communities. Clearly these outside interests and activities are not compatible with large families, especially in an age when the cost of servants is prohibitive except for the very well-to-do.

The Birth Rate and Education. Still another factor that seems to have reduced the birth rate is the increasing amount of education that the masses of our people have been receiving. As people acquire more knowledge, education, and foresight, they are more likely to plan for the future. At the same time they become more keenly aware of their responsibilities toward their children and of the sacrifices that raising a large family would require. Furthermore, people who go to college, and especially those who do graduate work or enter a professional school, still tend to delay marriage, or to delay having children. That there is an inverse relation between the education of parents and the number of their children has been shown by various statistical studies.[7]

Rise of the Birth Rate After the 1930's. We have already discussed the long decline of the birth rate in the United States. Before the trend was reversed there occurred, in the 1920's and the early 1930's, a final rather sharp drop. In 1921 the birth rate was 28.1 per 1,000 of the population. By 1933 it had fallen to a low point of only 18.4, a figure from which it made very little recovery until after the outbreak of World War II. Then it began to rise sharply, until by 1947 it had reached 26.6, the highest level in several decades. By 1950 it had declined moderately to 24.1, but throughout most of the 1950's it remained rather stable at about 25. In 1958 it began to drop again, and by 1968 it had fallen to 17.4. That the birth rate should have held at a high level as long as it did is somewhat surprising, because the

[7] *Current Population Reports,* Series P-23, No. 38, Bureau of the Census, April 16, 1971, p. 31.

marriage rate began a slow decline after 1950. Decline of the marriage rate is explained by the fact that most people who reached marriageable age in the 1950's were born in the depression years, when births were relatively few.

Ordinarily a decline in the number of marriages reduces the birth rate rather quickly, because most children are born in the first few years of a marriage. Maintenance of the birth rate in face of a declining marriage rate was evidence that more couples were having second, third, and fourth children.

The rise of the birth rate during and after World War II took most students of population by surprise, so much so that even their estimates of the population of the United States for the ensuing several years proved to be greatly in error. For example, in a special report issued in 1943 by the Bureau of the Census, Warren Thompson and P. K. Whelpton predicted that the population of the United States in 1950 would attain a level of

Figure 4. Annual Rates of Net Population Growth, Births, Deaths, and Net Immigration, 1935–1968. (From U.S. Bureau of the Census, *Current Population Reports,* Series P-25, No. 418, March 14, 1969.)

143 to 145 million; but when the census was taken, the count showed over 150 million. Principally as a result of the increase of the birth rate, but partly too because of a decline in the death rate, our population in the decade 1940–1950 increased more than 19 million as against an increase of about 9 million in the preceding decade. In the following decade, 1950–1960, population increased about 28 million, a rise that twenty-five years ago hardly anyone would have believed possible.

Figure 4 shows annual rates of net population growth, births, deaths, and net immigration, 1935 to 1968. The rise in births that occurred in the 1940's was by no means limited to the United States. According to W. S. and E. S. Woytinsky, in the area comprising Western Europe, the United States, Canada, Australia, and New Zealand, some 50 million more babies were born from 1940 to 1949 than would have been anticipated from the trend of births in the 1913–1929 period.[8] In the following decade the addition to the baby crop was even greater.

Reasons for Higher Birth Rates in the Forties and Fifties. What was the significance of the higher birth rate that prevailed in many Western countries in the years following World War II? When the birth rate of the United States began to rise markedly during the war, most of our American population experts regarded this as a temporary phenomenon that would soon be reversed. But when the higher rate persisted into the 1950's, many accepted it as something that might be with us for years to come. Actually, the birth rate of the United States did not begin another marked decline until the late 1950's. Let us consider briefly the reasons for the war and postwar increase of births in this country, and the factors that are likely to determine the future trend of the birth rate and population growth.

During the 1930's the birth rate of the United States dropped to the lowest level in history. Whether this was wholly a result of the depression is doubtful, because even during the prosperous 1920's the birth rate had been falling. But economic conditions were probably in part responsible for the low level finally reached, and even without a war there would probably have been some recovery from this level. However, there is reason to believe that World War II stimulated the birth rate in several ways. In the first place, it caused many marriages to take place sooner than they otherwise would have. Many young men wished to marry before they went overseas. Others married in the hope that as husbands and fathers they would be deferred from the draft. But the most important effects of the war on the birth rate were indirect. The war stimulated economic activity and raised the level of employment and wages. Good jobs at high wages induced many people to marry who would otherwise not have done so and induced couples already married to add to their families. In the two years following the war, the birth rate was further raised by the return

[8] W. S. and E. S. Woytinsky, *World Population and Production,* New York, The Twentieth Century Fund, 1953, p. 161.

of servicemen to their wives and by marriages taking place that had been deferred. As noted earlier, the high point was reached in 1947.

But the sharp decline of the birth rate that many expected in the following years did not materialize. One factor in maintaining the birth rate in the postwar years was probably the continuing high level of economic prosperity; but in the prosperous 1920's the birth rate, as already mentioned, had declined, and rather substantially. It is therefore quite possible that other and less tangible factors played a greater part than prosperity in maintaining the postwar birth rate. Even before the war important changes seem to have been taking place in the attitudes of young people toward marriage and sex. The war brought further changes, and one result was a greater willingness to marry and have children. The new generation of youth seemed to put a higher valuation on marriage and family life than did the preceding one.

Ever since World War II people have been marrying at younger ages than in earlier times. Partly this may result from a more matter-of-fact, if not more casual, attitude toward sex; but largely it is because the social and economic obstacles to youthful marriage have diminished. Once most colleges would have expelled an undergraduate who married while attending school; but not long after the end of the war many schools had whole colonies of married students. Once, before a man could marry, he had to be able to support a wife. Now for wives to work is socially acceptable, and since many jobs are available to women, there is no need to put off marriage until the prospective husband can support at least two people.

Though the war was not entirely responsible for the changes that brought earlier marriages and larger families, it was surely a contributing factor. When millions of young men were taken away for long periods of time from their homes and the normal activities of everyday life and when all established values and life itself seemed in imminent danger, many of them—and likewise the young women they left behind—appear to have realized as never before the extent to which human happiness and welfare depend on wives, husbands, children, and normal family life.

New Decline of the Birth Rate. As has been said, in 1958 the birth rate began to fall again. This can be partly explained by the relatively low marriage rate that prevailed in the late 1950's and early 1960's. In 1963 the marriage rate started a slow rise as the larger number of children born in the 1940's began to reach marriageable age. But the birth rate continued to fall into the late 1960's, and the decline was sufficient to indicate that people were somewhat less willing to have large families than they had been in the early postwar years. Just why this was so is difficult to say, but in part the number of children desired is a matter of what might be called fashion. That is, it is influenced by ideas, beliefs, and attitudes that become popular at a given time but change from period to period for reasons difficult to discover. In the 1960's the large family seems to have become a little less popular than it was a few years earlier. Another factor that probably had some influence on the birth rate in the 1960's was the contraceptive pill, approved for use in 1961 by the Food and Drug Administration. Some writers doubt that its effect has been important. The question is whether most women who use the pill would not employ some other reasonably reliable method of contraception if the pill were not available.

The Future Population of the United States. Largely because of the fall of the birth rate, instead of our population increasing in the 1960's by almost 28 million as it did in the preceding decade, it rose by less than 25 million. Since 1957 not only has the birth rate been falling but also the fertility rate, or the number of children born annually per thousand women fifteen to forty-four years of age. In 1957 the fertility rate was 123. By 1968 it had dropped to 85.8

But in spite of the decline of the fertility rate, the fall in the birth rate may be reversed in the 1970's. This is because millions of the babies born in the 1950's, when birth rates were high, will then be marrying and having

19. Population Explosion. (Courtesy Wide World Photos.)

children. The Census Bureau forecasts that the number of women of child-bearing ages will rise from 40.8 million in 1968 to 51.9 million in 1980. Assuming the same fertility rate as in 1968, this would mean an increase of births from 3.5 million in 1968 to 4.4 million in 1980, and as a result the rate of population growth would rise substantially. A further sharp decline in the fertility rate could prevent this, but it seems unlikely that it will decline sufficiently to do so.

If the rate of population growth that prevailed in this country toward the end of the 1960's (about 1 per cent annually) should continue, we will have over 275 million people by the year 2000, and in the neighborhood of 450 million by 2050. But though estimates of future population may be interesting, if they cover any long period of time they are not to be taken too seriously. Abraham Lincoln once tried his hand at population prediction. He estimated that by 1960 his 30 million fellow citizens would be represented by 500 million descendants. "He could not," says Robert Cook, "have been more wrong had he been an expert."[9]

The Trend of World Population. Today the population of the world is growing at a faster rate than ever before in history. According to a recent study by the Department of Social and Economic Affairs of the United Nations, current growth rates will double population in less than forty years. If this rate of increase continued for six hundred years, a simple arithmetic calculation shows that there would be only about one square yard of land surface for each person in the world, even if we include the arctic regions and all the deserts and mountain tops. Obviously this cannot happen, because anything even approaching such a density of human beings would presumably be impossible. Sooner or later something will occur to slow population growth and eventually to stop it.

THE MALTHUSIAN DOCTRINE

For more than a century most discussions of the population problem have started from the theory of Thomas Robert Malthus concerning the relationship of population to the means of human subsistence. Malthus was an early English economist who published in 1798 a short treatise called "An Essay on the Principle of Population as It Affects the Future Improvement of Society, with Remarks on the Speculations of Mr. Godwin, M. Condorcet, and Other Writers." During the next thirty years or more he revised this treatise six times. The seventh and final edition was not published until 1834, after the author's death. Throughout all these editions the basic argument remained the same, but in the second and later editions Malthus brought together a very considerable amount of data to support his population doctrines.

Population and Means of Subsistence. Reduced to its simplest terms,

[9] Robert C. Cook, *Human Fertility*, New York, William Sloane Associates, 1951, p. 73.

Malthus' theory can be summed up in the statement that *population tends to outrun the means of subsistence*. This was not a new idea, but Malthus developed it with such clarity and force that his treatise attracted wide attention. He contended that man is impelled to increase his numbers by a powerful natural urge, the attraction between the sexes. As a result, if there are no obstacles, population will increase rapidly and without any limit. Furthermore, it will increase in geometric ratio—that is, by multiplication. By this Malthus meant that if a population could double in, say, twenty-five years, it would double again in the next twenty-five years, and so on indefinitely. He believed, however, that the means of subsistence could be increased only in arithmetic ratio—in other words, slowly and to a limited extent. Consequently, population would always tend to press against the food supply. When the food supply became inadequate to support more people, any further increase in population would be prevented by the *"positive" checks* of malnutrition, famine, disease, and war.

Malthus' belief that population growth would necessarily tend to out-run means of subsistence was based on *the law of diminishing returns*. In terms of the relationships between land, labor, and food output, the law of diminishing returns may be stated somewhat as follows: *If more and more men are employed on a given area of land, beyond a certain point, even though total output may continue to expand, average output per worker will shrink.*

The amount of good farm land to be found in the world is limited. Once all the undeveloped regions of the earth have been settled and cultivated more or less intensively, further attempts to increase food production will become less and less effective because they will bring into operation the law of diminishing returns. It will still be possible to increase output by employing more workers on the land already cultivated or by cultivating less fertile land. However, assuming no advances in agricultural technology, this will bring about a decrease in the average output per worker, a decrease that will become greater and greater as attempts are made to raise production to higher and higher levels. It is possible that advances in agricultural technology might, for a long time, more than offset this tendency toward diminishing returns; but they could not do so indefinitely if population continued to grow. Sooner or later the amount of land per person would become impossibly small.

Malthus recognized that conceivably certain *preventive checks* might slow population growth by reducing the birth rate. These preventive checks he summarized under the general heading of "moral restraint." By this term he apparently referred to premarital chastity and late marriage. However, he did not believe that these preventive checks were likely to be practiced sufficiently to have much effect in keeping down births. Malthus apparently opposed both postmarital abstinence and contraception. He thought that marriage and its sexual satisfactions should carry with them the risk of bringing children into the world with the responsibility to support them. Otherwise, man would "get something for nothing" and be deprived of his main incentive for economic improvement.

Since Malthus had little hope that the preventive checks would be effective in keeping population from exerting pressure on the means of subsistence, he was pessimistic about the chances of greatly improving the economic condition of the masses of mankind. However, in the final edition of his essay he recognized that conditions in Europe were slowly improving in spite of the growth of population, and he expressed the hope that some way might yet be found to make possible the "gradual and progressive improvement" of human society.

Developments Since the Time of Malthus. Though more than 170 years have passed since Malthus first presented his population theories, in countries of Western European civilization his pessimistic predictions have not yet been realized. This can be explained by two major developments that he failed to foresee. First, he did not realize the speed with which production would increase, not only as a result of the development of new regions of the earth but even more through very rapid advances in the techniques of production. Second, he did not realize that the preventive checks to population growth, especially the practice of birth control, would become increasingly effective in industrial countries as standards of living rose. In nearly all industrial countries the long-run trend of the birth rate was downward from Malthus' time up to World War II. Furthermore, in all important industrial countries—certainly in all those outside the Iron Curtain—standards of living, including nutrition, are now higher than ever before in history.

Until recent years, however, declining birth rates were evident principally in countries of Western European civilization, and not in such lands as India and China. In these latter countries the situation was much as Malthus would have predicted. Any increase of production seemed to be fully matched by a prompt increase of population, so that the masses of the people remained in a constant state of extreme poverty. In the future, of course, social forces may develop that will very much reduce the birth rate. In India a decline, but not a sufficient one, has already taken place. Unless their birth rates fall to lower levels, there is little possibility of permanently raising standards of living in poor and overcrowded countries.

POPULATION AND NATURAL RESOURCES

In the final analysis, the size of the population that the earth can support is limited by the supply of natural resources and the methods or technology by which they are exploited. Our most important single natural resource is good farm land. The limited supply of such land was in part what led Malthus to believe that production of food could scarcely be expected to keep up with growth of population. But advances in technology have made it possible to utilize farm land as well as other resources with increasing

(Courtesy Joseph G. Farris.)

efficiency; and, as a result, the more advanced nations have for many decades been able to raise standards of living by increasing "means of subsistence" at a faster rate than the growth of population. But at any given level of technological development there will be a limit to the number of people for which the earth can provide even a minimum level of subsistence, and the number for which it can provide comfortable standards of living will be considerably smaller.

To support the population of the entire world at standards of living anywhere near equal to those most Americans already enjoy would mean overcoming enormous obstacles. At present many resources are not available in sufficient amounts to make this possible. For example, it has been estimated that if people everywhere used copper, lead, and zinc at the same rate as the United States, all the known reserves of the world would be exhausted in not much more than five years. Even with the standards of living now prevailing in the world, we will ultimately experience shortages of important resources.

The Concept of an Optimum Population. In any country, *given the level of technological development,* growth of population beyond a certain point would mean lower standards of living. Relative shortages would develop of farm lands, fuels, timber, metals, and other resources. On the other hand, a very small population would also have disadvantages. In very thinly populated areas it is often difficult to maintain law and order, to provide medical and hospital services, or to provide schools. Also, there are not enough people to build adequate roads or to make it worthwhile to operate public transportation services. What then is the *optimum,* or best, size of population from the standpoint of maximizing material welfare?

Actually there is no way of determining with even approximate accuracy what the optimum population of a country would be at any given stage in its development. Yet for any country there is certainly a point beyond which an increase in population would strain its resources, reduce average output per worker, and hence reduce standards of living.

The late P. K. Whelpton, who was then one of our best-known students of population, wrote in the *Eugenical News* of September, 1939:

A population of 100,000,000, as compared with 150,000,000 in the United States, should have a higher output per worker in agriculture, forestry, and mining, about the same output in manufacturing and trade, and a lower output in communication and transportation. . . . The United States is now overpopulated from the standpoint of per capita economic welfare, but fortunately not as seriously overpopulated as most nations.

If Whelpton was right in 1939, one might suppose that the United States is now, with over 200 million people, greatly overpopulated from the standpoint of achieving maximum per capita economic welfare. However, he was expressing a judgment or opinion not really susceptible to proof or disproof. Since he wrote the above statement, we have not only increased our population by more than 70 per cent, but we have also greatly improved our technology of production, and as a result have about doubled per capita output and consumption of goods. However, we now realize that these developments have raised the level of pollution of the environment to a critical point and that in many ways we would be better off with far fewer people.

Status of the Population Problem in the United States. It is now widely recognized that population growth has become a very serious problem for the United States. Not all would agree that it is the most critical one that we face, but increasingly we are coming to recognize that rapid population growth has made various other social problems much more difficult to deal with. Not only does the size of our population create problems, but the rapid rate at which it has increased makes needed social adjustments more difficult. Another factor that has intensified our population problem is the great increase in the per capita consumption of goods. Our use of natural resources and the extent to which we pollute the environment have increased about twice as fast as population.

A generation or so ago, a few writers, including Robert Cook and Julian Huxley, were already convinced that the rapid growth of world population had become man's greatest single social problem. Huxley said, "Human population is probably the gravest problem of our time—certainly more serious in the long perspective than war or peace. . . . The urgency is indeed tremendous."[10] Today more and more writers are calling attention to the critical nature of the population problem. They point out, among other things, that half the people of the world are already undernourished, and these writers predict that food shortages will become more and more acute.

But we have noted that the desirable size of a population is not determined solely by the adequacy of the food supply or the overall quantity of economic goods produced and consumed. High production and consumption by great numbers of people can itself create problems. Too many people can make life less attractive in many ways. They fill highways with dense traffic; they overcrowd vacation resorts and public parks; they force us to operate huge mass-production schools and universities; they create cities and metropolitan areas so vast that it is almost impossible to govern them adequately and to provide all the public services needed; they make it necessary to restrict personal freedoms by more rules and regulations; and they make it more difficult to maintain a close relationship between the people and their government. It seems probable that if our population had grown more slowly, cities would have been more successful in preventing or eliminating slums, racial tensions and conflicts would have been less, and satisfactory solutions for various social problems easier to achieve.

For a number of reasons it would be highly desirable to slow or stop population growth in this country, but, as we have indicated, the rate of increase may actually rise in the 1970's. This result can be avoided only if more people decide to have smaller families and if knowledge and use of contraceptives spreads more widely and thus becomes more effective in preventing the birth of unwanted children. One obstacle to the latter development is that many people still object to contraceptives on religious grounds. Some have suggested that legislation might be required to discourage people from having more than two or three children. But at present there would be great opposition to any attempt by government to put positive pressure on people to discourage them from having children. For example, removal of income tax exemptions based on child dependents would not be at all popular. Though direct controls over the birth rate are probably not now politically acceptable, voluntary restriction of births, encouraged by social and economic pressures, may in time stop population increases. The recent decline in the fertility rate suggests this possibility.

OTHER ASPECTS OF POPULATION

A thorough knowledge of the population of a country, of its history, size, composition, and rate of growth, throws much light on the processes

[10] Ibid., "Introduction" by Julian Huxley, p. vii.

of social change. We have already dealt briefly with the history of population in this country and in the world, and with death rates, birth rates, and marriages as they affect rates of growth. Also, we have pointed out some of the social and economic implications of population growth, especially as it affects the human environment and the availability of natural resources. At this point it seems desirable to discuss briefly two other significant aspects of population, with special reference to the United States. These are (1) its composition in terms of age groups and sex and (2) the effects of migration on its geographical distribution.

Composition of Population by Age and Sex. For much more than a hundred years the average age of our population has been rising, and so also has the proportion of people who are sixty-five and over. Two factors have contributed to this rise. One was the falling birth rate that prevailed until the mid-1930's and that kept reducing the proportion of young children. The other was advances in medicine and sanitation, which up to the present time have kept lengthening the average span of life. From 1900 to 1950 the number of children under fifteen increased only about 50 per cent, and the number of people between the ages of fifteen and forty-four only about 85 per cent. Meanwhile the 45–64 group increased 200 per cent, and the group "sixty-five and over" 300 per cent. In 1900 the sixty-five-and-over group was only three million. By 1950 it had risen to more than twelve million, and by 1968 to over nineteen million. The marked recovery in the birth rate after 1940 slowed the rise in the *proportion* of older people to total population, but even so the sixty-five–and–over group increased from 8.1 per cent in 1950 to 9.6 per cent in 1969.

While the *percentage* of individuals in the sixty-five–and–over group may not rise much, if at all, in the years just ahead, their total numbers will. By 1980 we are likely to have about 25 million of them. This should not create any very serious problems, but the support of these people will impose on the economy a heavier burden than in the past. A great part of this burden has already been taken over by the Social Security system, which is supported by taxes on almost all active workers and their employers. In a later chapter this system will be discussed in some detail.

Figures 5 and 6 are population "Christmas tree" charts that show graphically the distribution of our population by age and sex. They indicate the steady increase in the proportion of older people in the hundred-year span from 1870 to 1969. They also show the increase in the proportion of women, especially in the age group above seventy. This resulted from the greater rise in their life expectancy in comparison with men. The hollows in the trees in Figure 6 reflect the low birth rates of the 1930's. The hollow in the 1969 tree has naturally moved up, but the possible beginning of a new one is just discernible at the bottom, reflecting the lower birth rates in the mid-sixties.

To the author's knowledge, no one really knows just why women now live longer than men. Possible contributing factors may be that men as a

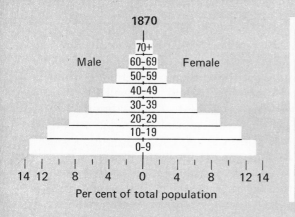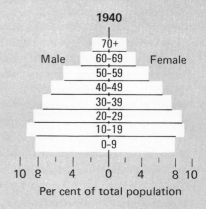

Figure 5. Age and Sex Distribution in the United States by Per Cent of Total Population, 1870 and 1940. (U.S. Bureau of the Census, *Current Population Reports,* Series P-25, No. 441, March 19, 1970.)

group are more active, less regular in their habits, and take greater risks of various kinds. The smoking of cigarettes may also be a factor. A number of statistical studies indicate that people who have smoked cigarettes heavily over a period of years have appreciably higher death rates in each

Figure 6. Age and Sex Distribution in the United States by Per Cent of Total Population, 1960 and 1969. (U.S. Bureau of the Census, *Current Population Reports,* Series P-25, No. 441, March 19, 1970.)

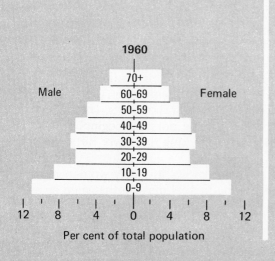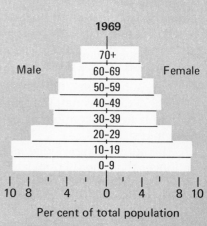

age group than nonsmokers; and statistical sampling shows that a far larger proportion of men than of women smoke and that the men as a group smoke more heavily. Thirty or forty years ago relatively few women smoked, and this too may contribute to their lower death rate and greater longevity.

Migration and the Distribution of Population. *Migration* of people from one region to another has been taking place for as long as the human species has been in existence, and growth of population has been one of the major factors behind migrations. Early peoples often found their numbers becoming too great for the territory in which they lived. Sooner or later some of them would migrate into other regions in the search for more game or for new farms and grazing lands. There is reason to believe that many of the ancestors of the peoples of modern Europe settled there in prehistoric times after a series of step-by-step migrations from central Asia. In modern times one of the principal causes of the immigration of millions of Europeans into the United States and other parts of the Americas has been the relatively crowded condition of Europe. To many Europeans the prosperous and uncrowded New World offered vastly greater economic opportunities than were available at home. Recently, however, advancing technology and productivity have enabled Europe to raise the standards of living of its people substantially, even though population is greater than ever before.

Within the United States, ever since the earliest settlements were made along the Atlantic coast, the major trend of migration has been from the older and more thickly populated East to the newer regions of the West. According to the Bureau of the Census this trend continued in the 1960's but at a lower rate than in the past. The map in Figure 7, showing relative changes in population by states from 1960 to 1969, suggests the westward movement, but not as clearly as similar maps made for earlier periods. By far the greatest total and percentage gain in population was made by an area in the far Southwest that includes California, Arizona, and Nevada. On the other hand, the population of the western prairie states was relatively static, while some states in the Northeast and South, most notably Florida and Texas, made substantial gains.

Every decade, the center of population of the United States has moved west, and in the 1960's it also moved somewhat south. During the 1920's the inhabitants of the Pacific Coast states increased by almost 50 per cent, and even in the depression decade of the 1930's they increased about 20 per cent. During and after World War II the westward movement gained new strength. From 1940 to 1960 the total population of the three Pacific Coast states rose more than 85 per cent, from less than ten million to over eighteen million. Most of this increase was in California, which had already become, in the census of 1950, the second most populous state in the Union. In the 1960's the rate of migration to the far West and Southwest slowed somewhat but still remained high. In that period the largest gain in residents was made by California, which passed New York by more

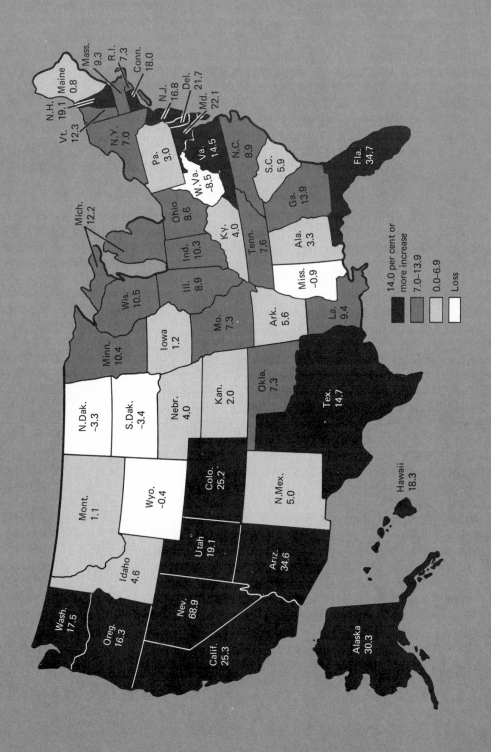

Figure 7. Population Changes by States, 1960–1970. (Based on preliminary figures from the U.S. Census of 1970.)

Wash. 17.5
Oreg. 16.3
Calif. 25.3
Nev. 68.9
Idaho 4.6
Mont. 1.1
Wyo. −0.4
Utah 19.1
Ariz. 34.6
Colo. 25.2
N.Mex. 5.0
N.Dak. −3.3
S.Dak. −3.4
Nebr. 4.0
Kan. 2.0
Okla. 7.3
Tex. 14.7
Minn. 10.4
Iowa 1.2
Mo. 7.3
Ark. 5.6
La. 9.4
Wis. 10.5
Ill. 8.9
Mich. 12.2
Ind. 10.3
Ky. 4.0
Tenn. 7.6
Miss. −0.9
Ala. 3.3
Ohio 8.6
W. Va. −8.5
Va. 14.5
N.C. 8.9
S.C. 5.9
Ga. 13.9
Fla. 34.7
Pa. 3.0
N.Y. 7.0
N.H. 19.1
Vt. 12.3
Maine 0.8
Mass. 9.3
R.I. 7.3
Conn. 18.0
N.J. 16.8
Del. 21.7
Md. 22.1
Hawaii 18.3
Alaska 30.3

14.0 per cent or more increase
7.0–13.9
0.0–6.9
Loss

than 1.7 million to become the most populous of all the states. But by far the greatest relative increase of the 1960's was in Nevada, where the population rose over 70 per cent as compared with 27 per cent for California.

A different type of migration, but one of great importance, has been the shift of population from the farms to the cities. This shift has been brought about by economic forces and will be discussed in the chapter dealing with the urbanization of America.

THE PROBLEM OF POPULATION QUALITY

In modern times many students of human society have been concerned over the possibility that forces are now operating that in time will bring about a serious deterioration of the biological quality of human populations. They fear that the danger is greatest in the countries that have made the most social and economic progress. This deterioration may take two forms: (1) a decline of the physical quality and stamina of individuals, with an increasing incidence of physical defects, and (2) a decline of native intelligence—that is to say, of the capacity for mental development.

Will Our Population Suffer Biological Deterioration? Those who fear physical deterioration of the race argue that the advances we have made in medicine and science are more and more making it possible for the weaklings and the physical defectives among our children to survive, grow to maturity, and propagate their kind. The process of deterioration may be relatively rapid, or it may be very slow; but increasingly, according to this line of reasoning, we will become a race of physical weaklings. The principle of the survival of the fittest will no longer operate, or it will be greatly weakened. In short, humanitarianism and science, instead of saving the human race, will ultimately destroy it.

To what extent such fears are justified is difficult to say. We do know that the physical type of an animal species can be changed by selective breeding—that is, by allowing only those members of the species to breed that possess certain desired physical qualities. Though selective breeding of human beings has never been attempted for a long enough period to demonstrate its possible results, there is reason to believe that *natural selection* has done something to maintain desirable physical qualities in our race. By natural selection is meant the tendency of the strong and well-adapted to survive, while the weak and poorly adapted die out. If natural selection has helped to maintain the quality of the race, it is quite conceivable that successful attempts to bring to maturity a greater proportion of weak and defective children will ultimately cause racial deterioration.

However, the danger of serious physical deterioration may prove to be less than some suppose. Our greatest progress in saving human life has come through learning to control infectious and contagious diseases. Can we be sure that those who were formerly struck down by such diseases were generally the weak or defective? It may be that all that they lacked was natural resistance or immunity to these diseases. In the future this immunity may not be important, for we will be able to protect people against such diseases by sanitation, inoculation, and other methods of control. We are already able to do this to a great extent. Moreover, even if we do bring to maturity some weaklings and defectives who formerly would have perished, will they marry and have children to the same extent as the more vigorous members of the community? Probably not. Finally, the physical vigor of our population is not wholly determined by biological inheritance. We can increase it markedly by providing people with better food and living conditions.

Those who fear a decline of native intelligence and ability in our population usually point to the difference in the birth rate between the upper and middle classes on the one hand and the lower classes on the other. They assume that success in life is correlated to a significant degree with desirable qualities that are biologically inherited, and they point out that in modern industrial countries people with good income, education, and social position usually have fewer children than the poor, ignorant, or shiftless.

To what extent economic and social success result from inborn qualities that the upper classes possess in greater measure than the lower classes, no one can be certain. We know that individual success depends on both social environment and biological inheritance. There is always an interplay between the two. "It cannot," says Thompson, "be emphasized too strongly that the individual personality as we know it at any moment is the resultant of the hereditary qualities a person possesses as developed by the particular environment in which he has lived." Is it not, then, reasonable to suppose that among the successful groups in the population there is a larger proportion of people with desirable inherited qualities than among the unsuccessful groups? Many writers are convinced of the truth of this proposition, and to them the differential birth rate is a matter of profound concern.[11]

Some writers, on the other hand, take a more optimistic view. They believe that though heredity is often a major factor in determining the success of individuals, we have no clear evidence that inferior heredity characterizes any large social group. Neither is it certain that the lower income groups have a higher survival rate than the middle and upper classes. Their birth rate is higher, but their death rate as shown by insurance statistics is also higher. Moreover, some recent evidence indicates that the fertility differential between higher- and lower-income groups has been declining and in a few places has been reversed.

Eugenics and Its Limitations. A study of socially acceptable measures

[11] See, for example, Cook, ibid., Chap. 13.

for improving the biological quality of the human race was first proposed by Francis Galton, a cousin of Charles Darwin and himself a distinguished scientist. He called this study *eugenics*. He maintained that newly married couples could be divided into three classes with respect to the probable worth of their children—a small class of "desirables," a large class of "passables," and a small class of "undesirables." He believed that it was very important to find acceptable ways of checking the birth rate of the undesirables and of increasing the birth rate of the desirables by enabling the latter to marry early and raise large families under healthful conditions.[12]

Thompson points out that the practices of various peoples in the past resulted in some degree of eugenic selection. Infanticide, for example, probably tended to eliminate the weaker and the deformed babies. Also, crippled and malformed children were often neglected, so that their death rate was high. In modern times direct elimination of children visibly weak at birth has been less rigorous, but Thompson questions whether this has very much increased their rate of reproduction.

Any systematic plan for improving the quality of the human race by increasing the children of the fit and reducing those of the unfit would have to overcome two serious difficulties. First, standards would have to be agreed on to determine those who are fit and those who are unfit. Second, we would have to find some way of preventing or discouraging the unfit from marrying or having children and find some way of inducing the fit to marry and raise large families.

Selecting the fit would not be easy. We could probably agree in a general way that future generations should be healthy and intelligent. Beyond that, we would have a good deal of difficulty in agreeing on just what qualities would be desirable. Furthermore, our knowledge of the extent to which personal characteristics are inherited is limited. We know that some physical and mental traits, including certain defects, are passed on from one generation to another, but in the case of most characteristics we are not certain about the role played by inheritance. In any case, it would often be very difficult to determine the extent to which particular individuals possessed the characteristics considered most desirable.

Even more difficult than selecting the right people for propagating the race would be the problem of controlling their mating. The Nazis actually initiated experiments in bringing together selected individuals of opposite sex for the avowed purpose of producing superior children. However, in a free, democratic society such a procedure would be vigorously resisted and would be regarded by many as immoral and abhorrent. The right to select a mate and to control in large measure the raising of one's children is one of the most cherished of all personal freedoms.

[12] See Francis Galton, *Memories of My Life*, 2d ed., New York, E. P. Dutton & Co., Inc., 1908.

Very limited efforts have been made in the direction of *negative eugenics,* or preventing the unfit from propagating their kind. In this country, for instance, a few states provide by law for the sterilization of persons with serious mental defects that are believed to be inheritable. A more widespread method of rendering such people infertile is to segregate them in institutions. This, however, is so costly that it is applied to only a small portion of the mentally defective and unstable persons who might transmit their defects to posterity.

Taking all factors into consideration, the possibilities of improving the human race by a program of eugenics appear to be very limited, especially in a free and democratic society like our own. On the whole that may be fortunate, though most would probably agree that it would be desirable, if possible, to eliminate such inheritable diseases as diabetes and hemophilia.

Terms to Be Understood

population	fecundity	preventive checks
census	fertility	optimum population
birth rate	birth control	migration
death rate	Malthusian doctrine	natural selection
population explosion	law of diminishing	eugenics
immigration quota	returns	negative eugenics
life expectancy	positive checks	

Questions for Review and Discussion

1. What characteristics of a group of people are of special interest to the student of population?
2. What are the principal factors that determine the rate of growth of a population?
3. Tell briefly what is known about the growth of population since 1650 (1) in the world as a whole and (2) in Europe.
4. Describe and explain the growth of population in the United States from 1790 to the present time.
5. How has the growth of our black population differed from that of the white population in the period since 1790? Explain.
6. Explain why some writers argue that immigration has made no net contribution to our population. Do you agree? Why or why not?
7. How can the rapid growth of world population since 1800 be explained?
8. Discuss the effect of prosperity on the birth rate.
9. How can the higher birth rates following World War II be explained?
10. Even if the fertility rate of American women declines further, the (crude) birth rate may remain near present levels or even rise somewhat. Why?

11. State the Malthusian doctrine. Why have Malthus' predictions not yet been realized? Do you think they will be realized eventually? Why or why not?
12. With the known natural resources of the world and our present technology, could we raise the living standards of all countries to a par with those of the United States? Discuss.
13. Explain the concept of an optimum population in the economic sense. In relation to the optimum, is the population of the United States too small, too large, or just right? Defend your answer.
14. What are the prospects for a further decline of the death rate? Explain.
15. In most Western countries, up to World War II, the trend of the birth rate had been downward for over a hundred years. How do you account for this?
16. How much is the population of the United States likely to increase in the next ten years? The next twenty years? The next hundred years? Point out the difficulties of making population forecasts.
17. Julian Huxley once said: "Human population is probably the gravest problem of our time." Do you agree? Why or why not?
18. Explain why population growth might raise standards of living in some countries whereas in others it would lower them.
19. Explain why the proportion of older people in our population has risen sharply since 1900.
20. State the two principal ways in which migration has changed the distribution of population in the United States since 1790.
21. State and criticize the arguments of those who believe that our population is undergoing biological deterioration.
22. Point out the possibilities and the difficulties of improving the human race through a program of eugenics.

For Further Reading

Borgstrom, Georg, *The Hungry Planet: The Modern World at the Edge of Famine,* paperback, New York, The Macmillan Company, 1967.

Brown, Lester R., *Seeds of Change: The Green Revolution and Development in the 1970's,* paperback, New York, Frederick A. Praeger, Inc., 1970.

Bureau of the Census, *Current Population Reports,* Washington, D.C. Population estimates for the United States issued monthly; special reports from time to time.

Day, Lincoln H., and Alice Day, *Too Many Americans,* Delta paperback, New York, Dell Publishing Company, n.d.

Erlich, Paul R., *The Population Bomb,* New York, Ballantine Books, Inc., 1968.

Freedman, Ronald, ed., *Population, the Vital Revolution,* Anchor paperback, New York, Doubleday & Company, Inc., n.d.

Hauser, Philip, ed., *The Population Dilemma,* 2d ed., Spectrum paperback, Englewood Cliffs, N.J., Prentice-Hall, Inc., 1970.

Hutchinson, E. P., *Population Dilemma,* Boston, Houghton Mifflin Company, 1967.

Malthus, Thomas, Julian Huxley, and Frederick Osborn, *On Population: Three Essays,* Mentor paperback, New York, New American Library, Inc., n.d.

Nam, Charles B., ed., *Population and Society: A Textbook of Readings,* Boston, Houghton Mifflin Company, 1968.

Notestein, Frank W., et al., *Overcoming World Hunger,* paperback, Englewood Cliffs, N.J., Prentice-Hall, Inc., 1969.

Ohlin, Goran, *Population Control and Economic Development,* Washington, D.C., Organization for Economic Cooperation and Development, 1967.

Petersen, William, *Population,* 2d ed., New York, The Macmillan Company, 1969.

Thomlinson, Ralph, *Population Dynamics: Causes and Consequences of World Demographic Change,* New York, Random House, Inc., 1965.

Thompson, Warren S., *Population and Progress in the Far East,* Chicago, University of Chicago Press, 1959.

————, and David T. Lewis, *Population Problems,* 5th ed., New York, McGraw-Hill, Inc., 1965.

Wrong, Dennis H., *Population and Society,* rev. ed., paperback, New York, Random House, Inc., 1967.

Part Two

Social

Adjustment

and

Social

Problems

Chapter 9

Personal

Adjustment

a s we begin our discussion of personal adjustment, let us recall certain characteristics of human society that were emphasized earlier. Though a society is merely an established and organized group of individuals, every society is nevertheless somewhat unique because it has its characteristic culture patterns that represent the special ways in which its members behave in their relations with one another. These culture patterns are not biologically inherited but must be learned. For any society to survive and to function for the benefit of its members, it must pass on to each new generation the basic elements of its culture. Furthermore, in order to live the life of a normal human being, every child born into a society must learn patterns of behavior that are accepted and expected by the group. The process by which an individual gradually acquires culture and adjusts himself to the group we have called *socialization*.

CULTURE, SOCIETY, AND THE INDIVIDUAL

Although every person is to a large extent shaped and molded by his culture, his own influence upon it is usually slight. He must accept it much as he finds it, and if he hopes to lead a satisfactory life as a human being, he must adjust himself to it. This dependence of the individual on culture sometimes makes culture appear to be an independent entity, something that has an existence and continuity irrespective of the people who are its carriers. This impression is strengthened when we view culture historically and note that many of its basic elements persist generation after generation. Two hundred years ago the English language was in its essential characteristics not very different from what it is today. Yet of all those who spoke English two hundred years ago not a single person is now alive.

For some purposes it is convenient to think of culture as if it had an independent, objective existence. In the final analysis, however, this is untrue. All cultures have been created by people. As Melville J. Herskovits points out, when we analyze culture closely, we find only a series of patterned reactions that are characteristic of the *individuals* who belong to a given group.[1] It is *people* who hold beliefs, have attitudes, practice customs, and behave in conformity with patterns accepted by the group. Cultures are built up very slowly, so slowly and gradually that it is seldom possible to isolate the contributions made by particular individuals. In a large society the individual is only one among millions. Furthermore, most individuals accept the social situation in which they find themselves and make little attempt to change it. Yet cultures develop and cultures change, and the changes that take place in culture can come about only through changes in the attitudes and ways of life of the individual members of a society.

It is only in the case of outstanding leaders that we become clearly aware of individual contributions to our culture patterns. We know that such men as Shakespeare, Napoleon, Karl Marx, Einstein, the Wright brothers, and Henry Ford have had some impact on the course of history and on the development of Western culture. In the case of such leaders it is probable that we often overestimate the extent of their influence. We do not know how much different the culture of the Western world would now be if Napoleon or Marx had died in childhood, but we can be rather sure that we would have had airplanes without the efforts of the

[1]Melville J. Herskovits, *Man and His Works,* New York, Alfred A. Knopf, Inc., 1948, pp. 28–29.

Wright brothers, and mass production of automobiles without the efforts of Henry Ford. However, both developments would probably have been somewhat delayed.

The fact that every individual is to a large degree shaped by his culture does not mean that he is deprived of all freedom to control his behavior and to choose his mode of life. Any general cultural pattern is flexible to a degree and permits some variations from the norms. In simple, primitive societies the permissible variations may be rather limited, but in modern complex societies they are great. However, in any society the average individual is seldom aware of the extent to which culture restricts his freedom. His culture becomes so "internalized"—so much a basic part of his own *personality*—that most of the time he does not wish to behave in ways other than those that are culturally approved. Only in special situations does he become keenly aware of conflicts between his own desires and the kind of conduct that is socially permissible.

PERSONALITY AND ITS DEVELOPMENT

To have a full understanding of the relationship between individuals and society, it is helpful to have a clear concept of the meaning of *personality*. It has been said that *every man is in some respects like all other men, in some respects like some other men, and in some respects like no other man*. This statement applies to man's biological characteristics and perhaps even more to his personality.

Personality may be defined as *the total organization of the inherited and acquired characteristics of an individual as evidenced by his behavior*. It is the product of the interaction between his original biological nature and his social and natural environment. It therefore bears the imprint of four things: (1) the inherited potentialities of the individual, (2) his natural environment, (3) the culture of his society, and (4) his unique personal experiences. However, once personality has begun to form, it becomes an independent force that may play a dominant part in its own future development and in the adjustment of the individual to his total environment.

The Biological Basis of Personality, and the Learning Process. In Chapter 1 we pointed out that the human baby is a very helpless creature at birth. It cannot walk; it cannot talk; it cannot even sit up, turn itself over, or grasp an object that is offered to it. It is not equipped, as are most animals, with hereditary instincts. Such *instincts*, as the term is used here, are inherited complex patterns of behavior that do not have to be learned and that enable animals to satisfy needs that arise at various stages of their development. A good example is the nest-building instinct of birds.

All that a baby has at birth is the basic structures of the human organism, certain reflexes and *drives*, and the innate capacity for growth and development. Gradually, however, it begins to learn to adjust to its environment, and in the process it slowly becomes conscious of itself as a person, separate from its environment. As it develops physically, its power to learn keeps increasing, but all the patterns of behavior that will later characterize it as a normal human being must be learned, and the learning process is not always easy.

The drives that a baby inherits are urges toward satisfying basic needs, such as those for sleep, elimination, or food. When not satisfied, they are felt as tension or discomfort. It is these drives that provide the stimulus for learning. One of the most powerful of human drives is hunger. To satisfy hunger, a baby depends on its mother's breast or perhaps on a bottle. But when it becomes hungry, the bottle is not always present, and as its discomfort increases, it cries. This may bring the bottle and with it the pleasure that is felt as hunger is satisfied. Before long the baby associates crying with the appearance of the bottle, and so it cries as soon as hunger begins in order to bring the bottle. This illustrates the beginning of the learning process and perhaps also the beginning of the development of personality.

The Freudian Concept of Personality. Perhaps no single individual, certainly no psychologist or psychiatrist, has had a greater impact on modern life and thought than Sigmund Freud. Freud's life covered the period from 1856 to 1939, and most of it was spent in Vienna. He was trained as a physician, but he specialized in neurology, and in those days this meant that most of his patients were people with emotional problems.

Freud became famous as the originator of the system of psychotherapy known as *psychoanalysis*. Essentially, the method of psychoanalysis is that of free association. A patient is induced to express anything that comes to his mind in the hope of uncovering memories or ideas of which he is unaware but which may be causing mental and emotional conflicts. For example, perhaps he had a terrifying experience in early childhood that has been repressed below the level of consciousness. The psychoanalyst believes that if he can be helped to recall such an experience, he will be able to deal with it realistically, so that the mental disturbances it has been causing will disappear. But to bring unconscious mental processes to the level of consciousness may take time and persistence on the part of both the psychoanalyst and his patient.

In time Freud became recognized as one of the great original thinkers in the field of psychology; and today most psychologists believe that he made important contributions to our understanding of the human personality. But his theories have been the center of much controversy.[2] This can be explained in part by their novelty; in part by the difficulty of subjecting them to conclusive scientific proofs; and in part by the great emphasis they place upon sex. In some degree this emphasis grows out of the fact

[2] There are today a number of psychologists and psychiatrists who believe that psychoanalysis has contributed very little to our ability to deal successfully with people who are mentally and emotionally disturbed. See Hans J. Eysenck, with seventeen contributors, *The Effects of Psychotherapy*, New York, International Science Press, 1966. Eysenck is a professor of psychology at the University of London.

that Freud regarded as sexual some elements in human experience that are not usually thought of as such. In any case, he believed that sex plays a chief role in the development of the human personality, not only in the adolescent and adult years but also in the earliest years of childhood.

However, at present we are more concerned with the general nature of Freud's theories concerning personality. Freud developed a theory that attempts to take into account the nature of the original biological organism of man and the mental and emotional changes that occur in it as a result of both biological maturation and the impingement of environmental forces. He also tried to explain the various personality traits, difficulties, and abnormalities that may come into existence as the personality of an individual develops.

To Freud personality consisted of three major systems or "structures," which he called the *id,* the *ego,* and the *superego.* In the normal person these three systems in personality cooperate to enable the individual to satisfy his basic needs and desires within the environmental setting; but when they are in serious conflict with one another, the person is said to be maladjusted.

The id, according to Freud, consists of the innate drives[3] of the human organism. The id is dominated by the *pleasure principle,* that is, it is always striving to obtain pleasure or avoid pain. It is also the original source of *psychic energy,* which Freud conceived as being analogous to physical energy. He regarded psychic energy as the capacity for doing psychic or mental work just as physical energy is the capacity for doing physical work. If reflex or impulsive actions could relieve all the tensions and discomforts to which the organism is subject, there would be no need for the development of any psychic system beyond the id. But this is not the case; for example, no reflex action will provide food when food is not present. So frustrations occur, and the organism becomes dimly aware of the conflicts between its desires and reality. As a result, there develops gradually within it a new psychological structure, the ego.

The ego is the conscious self and is dominated by the *reality principle.* As it develops, it is able to perceive situations in the outside world and to store up experiences in memory. Then, with the aid of thinking and action it attempts to create situations in which the desires of the id can be satisfied. It delays attempts at satisfaction until conditions exist that make this possible.

But as the ego develops, another psychological structure, the superego, also comes into being. This is the moral or judicial aspect of personality, the primitive conscience. It opposes satisfaction of some of the desires that arise in the id, and if the ego overrides its opposition, it gives the lat-

---

[3] Psychoanalysts generally refer to drives as *instincts;* but in doing so they are giving the word *instinct* a different meaning from that assigned it by modern psychologists. Hence we employ the word *drive.* This confusion of terms grew out of the fact that when Freud's works began to be translated into English, the German word *trieb* ("drive") was translated as *instinct.*

ter feelings of guilt and shame. The ego must mediate between the id and the superego, satisfy both as far as possible, and attempt to maintain harmony within the personality. Freud believed that the superego largely reflects the child's conception of what its parents conceive to be morally good or bad, as evidenced by rewards and punishments.

The id, ego, and superego are, of course, not independent entities—"little men," as one writer put it, living in the same individual. Rather, they are convenient terms to designate different groups of forces that interact within the human personality. They may or may not represent the best possible concepts for giving us insight into the nature of personality. However, the great majority of psychologists and psychiatrists believe that Freud's theories have been very useful in studying the origins and the development of personality.

The Dynamics of Personality. By the *dynamics* of personality is meant the forces that operate within it to form, change, and control it. Freud believed that all the psychic energy used for activating the personality is obtained from the drives that reside in the id. In his final formulation of his theories, he divided these drives into two principal groups, the life drives and the death drives. Of the first, the most important and all-pervasive is sex; the second expresses itself chiefly in various forms of aggression. It was to the life drives that Freud devoted most attention, and the form of psychic energy that activates these he called *libido*.

Freud believed that the amount of psychic energy available to an individual is limited. The dynamics of personality is the flow of this energy to different parts of the personality and its employment in different uses. What a person is and does depends on how it is distributed. For example, if most of the psychic energy is retained by the id, his actions will be impulsive. If it is largely controlled by the ego, they will be realistic. But if most of it is monopolized by the superego, his behavior will be moralistic. In Freud's theories concerning the development of personality, frustrations, anxiety, unconscious mental processes, and the sex instinct all play important roles.

The Oedipus Complex. One of the most controversial of Freud's theories is the *Oedipus complex*. He gave it this name because of its analogy to the Greek myth about Oedipus, the man who unknowingly killed his father and married his mother. Freud's formulation of the Oedipus complex grew out of the fact that rather early in his career he believed he had uncovered, in the unconscious mental processes of his neurotic patients, fantasies of sex relations with the parent of the opposite sex, combined with jealous anger against the parent of the same sex. Later he came to believe that a strong sexual attraction to the parent of the opposite sex, along with jealousy of the other parent, is a universal experience of childhood in the years before the age of five. After this period the Oedipus complex is repressed and disappears from the conscious mind because of recognition of the impossibility of fulfilling the sexual wishes; also, in the case of a boy, because of fear of retaliation from the father. At this stage the child

"First of all, Mr. Hawley, I would say you have a strong mother complex." (Courtesy Ralston Jones and *The Saturday Evening Post*.)

begins to identify itself with the parent of the same sex. Freud believed that the Oedipus complex was an essential factor in the development of every child's personality and hence in determining the nature of all human societies.

The Oedipus complex received much publicity and aroused widespread opposition. To many people, especially of a past generation, it seemed not only fantastic but also shocking. Others, less shocked, still found it difficult to accept, in the form in which Freud presented it. He made it clear that the Oedipus complex referred to a definite desire of the child for sex relations with the parent of the opposite sex, and to jealousy of the other parent because of the sex relationship; but in our society it seems doubtful that most very young children have even a vague concept of the existence or nature of sex relations. Certainly many do not, and in that case it is hard to see how they can desire them or be jealous on account of them. Even among psychoanalysts who subscribe to most of Freud's theories there are those who question or reject the Oedipus complex. They believe that the psychoanalytical data upon which it is based can be interpreted in other ways. Also, some anthropologists have questioned this complex, or at least its universality.[4]

SOCIALIZATION OF THE INDIVIDUAL

Today psychologists and sociologists, whether Freudians or not, agree that socialization plays a major role in the development of human personality. This does not mean that a child's personality may not be greatly influenced by its biological inheritance and by contacts with the physical

[4] See Melville J. Herskovits, *Man and His Works,* New York, Alfred A. Knopf, Inc., 1948, Chap. 4, for a discussion of the difficulty of finding Freud's version of the Oedipus complex in some primitive societies.

environment. For the most part, however, it is from people that the child learns its patterns of behavior and also the attitudes, beliefs, and expectations that motivate behavior. All these learnings are largely cultural in origin, and therefore, as the child grows and develops, its behavior reflects to an ever greater degree the culture of the society into which it has been born.

Significance of the Early Years of Childhood. The experiences of the young child within the family group seem to have the greatest influence on the development of human personality. Very early a normal baby begins to recognize familiar faces, sense approval and disapproval, seek attention, and in other ways react to the social environment. By the age of two years, the child has made a very good start in becoming socialized and in acquiring culture. He has begun to use words and to refer to himself by name. He can imitate actions of others and play with other children and with toys. He can wash his hands, help dress himself, use a spoon, obey commands, and in various ways meet many of the requirements of the cultural setting.

As the child gradually matures, his capacity for learning increases, and he reaches more advanced stages of socialization. However, whether he develops a stable and well-adjusted personality continues to depend largely on his immediate social environment. Recent studies of parent-child relations agree that a child must be accepted and receive affection if he is to develop emotional stability; but overprotection and overaffection are not desirable, for they tend to lead to dependency and immaturity. At the other extreme, parental rejection and lack of affection create feelings of insecurity and inferiority, and often bring on compensatory reactions such as aggressive, rebellious, or domineering behavior.

As the young child grows, he comes into contact not only with parents, brothers and sisters, and perhaps other members of the household, but also with outsiders such as relatives, neighbors, and playmates. He acquires greater physical competence and greater skill in the use of language and continually makes adjustments to new people and new situations. These early experiences leave an indelible impression on him and influence the "set" of his personality. Recent studies such as those of Benjamin S. Bloom of the University of Chicago provide convincing evidence of the crucial importance of the preschool years.

Early childhood experiences, however, are not the whole of life, and there are cases where, after a delayed development in certain respects, children seem to have gone through a period of rapid catching up. The personality of a normal person is dynamic. It is never exactly the same from day to day, and to some degree it continues to develop and change throughout life. However, some people seem to possess greater elasticity and power to make adjustments than others. They succeed in overcoming the effects of an unfortunate childhood when others fail, or they continue to develop in adult life when others seem to stagnate. In terms of Freud's

20. Personal Problem.
(Courtesy Wide World Photos.)

theory of personality, stagnation might result from a weak ego and domination of the personality by either the id or the superego.

All socialization is education in the broad sense that it is a learning process. A child imitates the actions and words of others, senses their approval or disapproval, and responds to their expectations. Without being really aware of what is happening, he acquires speech, modes of behavior, and attitudes. Much of this takes place even if no effort is made to teach him. But very early in the life of a child, adults do make conscious efforts to teach him, and before long the child on his part is making conscious efforts to learn. When efforts are made to teach a child, and the child responds with efforts to learn, the educative process is well under way on a conscious level.

Significance of Differences in Individual Environment. It is questionable whether any two persons have precisely the same hereditary characteristics, though in the case of identical twins there is a close approach to this situation. It is certain that no two individuals have exactly the same social environment. Some of the differences in the environments of individuals are obvious to the most casual observer, but other differences are not so easy to see.

We are all aware that in a country like the United States people often grow up in social environments that differ widely. To begin with, there are noticeable differences in the language, attitudes, and customs of the people in different regions. Also, even in the same region, there are differences between rural life and city life; and in a city of even moderate size there can be found a great variety of more or less distinct social groups. Among the more important of these groups are those set off from one another by differences in income and social prestige, religion, nationality, or race. But differences in individual social environment go further than this. In any given social group, particular families are likely to differ significantly from one another in their modes of life, so that a child brought up in one family may have a quite different environment from that of a child reared in another.

All these differences are fairly obvious. It is not quite so obvious, but nonetheless true, that two children brought up in the same family at the same time may have quite unlike environments. This is because one's social environment depends, not only on the people with whom he comes in contact, but also on the nature of his personal relations with them. One child in a family may be loved by the parents, given every advantage, perhaps may be overindulged, whereas another child may be disliked, neglected, even mistreated. Clearly such children do not have at all the same social environment, and the differences are sure to have deep and lasting effects on their mental and emotional development, on their personalities, and on their relations with other people in later years.

Effects on Children of Extreme Isolation. The study of children who have been largely isolated from social contacts is significant, because it demonstrates the importance of socialization by showing what happens in its absence. It also gives us some knowledge of the possibility of compensating in later years for development that failed to take place earlier at the normal time.

It is impossible to find children who have been *completely* isolated from other human beings from the time of birth. The reason is simple. The human infant is so helpless that it cannot possibly survive without receiving some care from older people who understand its needs. However, cases have been reported of children who, in early life, have been partially or completely isolated from human contacts over considerable periods. These reports are of two types: (1) cases of *feral* or "wild" children who have lived with animals and (2) cases of children kept isolated in a room, basement, or attic and given little attention except for being provided with food and drink.

Feral Children. Stories of feral children appeal to the imagination. They have been told in all ages about children believed to have been cared for when very young by boars, wolves, bears, or other animals. These stories have nearly always been spread by hearsay, and it is doubtful whether any of them are based on fact. Perhaps the oldest of such tales is that about the legendary founders of Rome, the twins Romulus and Remus, who are said to have been abandoned as infants and suckled by a wolf. However, a modern report of the discovery of two feral children seems to have been accepted by some social scientists. It concerns two children, Amala and Kamala, who are said to have been found some years ago in a wolf den in India. They could not talk, and they are reported to have run on all fours and in all other respects to have exhibited animal-like behavior. Under human care they responded very little to the attempts that were made to socialize and educate them. Both died at an early age.[5] However, Bruno Bettelheim, head of the Orthogenic School at the University of Chicago, says that the reported behavior of Amala and Kamala resembles closely that of children suffering from *infantile autism,* a condition resulting from extreme rejection by parents in infancy and very early childhood. He doubts that young children could survive very long in the jungle without human care and thinks that Amala and Kamala were probably abandoned not very long before they were found.[6]

Children Kept in Isolation. Though stories of feral children should be regarded with skepticism, there appear to be well-authenticated cases of children who for considerable periods of time have been locked in basements, attics, or upstairs rooms and have been isolated from almost all normal human contacts. Kingsley Davis, the well-known sociologist, has reported two such cases.[7] One was that of a girl named Isabelle, who, because she was illegitimate, was kept secluded in a dark room with her deaf-mute mother until she was six-and-a-half years old. The other was that of a girl named Anna, who was kept in a room alone until she was about six. In each of these cases, when the girl was discovered, her behavior in many respects resembled that of an infant or a wild animal. But Isabelle, when placed in a normal social environment and given special training, "caught up" very rapidly. In a few years she was making good progress in school and gave the impression of a bright, cheerful, energetic little girl. However, when Anna was placed in a normal environment, she made much less progress, and she was still considered feeble-minded when she died at the age of ten-and-a-half.

We have no way of knowing just why Anna failed to develop as much as Isabelle. Perhaps Isabelle's close contact with her deaf-mute mother gave her a sense of being loved and secure, and thus a great advantage over Anna in her emotional development, or it may be that she received more expert attention after she was removed from isolation. It is also possible that Isabelle's biological inheritance was greatly superior to that of Anna,

[5] The story of Amala and Kamala is reported by J. A. L. Singh and Robert M. Zingg in *Wolf Children and Feral Man,* New York, Harper & Row, Publishers, 1942.

[6] Bruno Bettelheim, "Feral Children and Autistic Children," *American Journal of Sociology,* March 1959, p. 455. See also in same issue William Fielding Ogburn, "The Wolf Boy of Agra," p. 449.

[7] Kingsley Davis, "Final Note on a Case of Extreme Isolation," *American Journal of Sociology,* March 1947, pp. 432-437.

for it appears to have been established that Anna's mother was mentally subnormal.

Personality as the Product of Both Environment and Heredity. People often ask the question, Which is more important in determining the personality and the success in life of an individual—environment or *heredity?* To this question there is no real answer. It is like asking, Which is more important in making an automobile run—the gasoline or the engine? Quite obviously, if the car is to run at all, both gasoline and an engine must be provided. Similarly, if a baby is to develop normally, it must have both a reasonably adequate biological inheritance and a reasonably adequate social environment.

According to Carlo Valenti, about one in fifty babies is born with some degree of abnormality inherited from its parents; and of the various abnormalities ordered by the genes, which determine the babies' inheritance, more than five hundred are severe enough to be classified as diseases (for example, diabetes).[8] But even normal babies inherit markedly different physical characteristics, and it is reasonable to suppose that they also inherit differences in the brain and nervous system, and that these will result later in mental and emotional differences. Certainly we have no scientific evidence to the contrary.

Environment, especially that part of the social environment we call culture, provides the content of human experience and thus largely determines the specific beliefs, attitudes, and patterns of behavior of every person. But even though this is true, there seems little doubt that if it were possible to expose each of a number of people to identical conditions of environment from birth, they would still show wide differences in personality because of differences in biological inheritance. That they might differ widely in energy, temperament, and intelligence would be denied only by the most extreme environmentalist. They might also show differences in their specific beliefs, attitudes, and ways of behaving.

This last statement should not be viewed as in any way contradicting our earlier insistence that beliefs, attitudes, and patterns of behavior are culturally acquired. We have already pointed out that culturally determined patterns are never completely rigid. Moreover, especially in our type of society, each individual is subjected from birth to varied and often conflicting elements in his social environment. Consciously or unconsciously he makes choices, and it is almost certain that these choices are affected by his heredity. He becomes attracted to and influenced by some elements in his environment more than by others.

Talents and aptitudes represent potentialities, inherited capabilities for doing some things unusually well. However, talents and aptitudes are of no value unless their possessor has opportunities for developing them and putting them to use. But if they are missing to begin with, no amount of education, training, or effort will entirely compensate for their

[8] See Carlo Valenti, M.D., "His Right to Be Normal," *Saturday Review,* December 7, 1968.

absence. To be sure, given the will and the opportunity, we can all raise the level of our knowledge, our understanding, and our achievements, but some of us more than others.

The Well-Adjusted Individual. What do we mean by *good social adjustment?* There are dangers in setting up social adjustment as an ideal to be sought. If an individual were perfectly adjusted to his environment, in the sense of having no problems or tensions and not wishing that anything were different, he would stagnate. On the other hand, if we mean by *a well-adjusted person* one who loves life and finds it interesting and stimulating, he must have dissatisfactions, problems, and goals to be achieved. Good adjustment must be a dynamic concept, and there is no simple formula for it that will apply equally well to everyone. Nevertheless, we will indicate some of the elements that we consider to be important to good adjustment.

A well-adjusted individual is a person who finds living to be an interesting and satisfying experience. He accepts the limitations of his physical and social environment that he cannot control and does not keep himself in a constant state of frustration by rebelling against the inevitable; but neither does he admit too easily that he cannot solve a problem. Within the framework of his environment he finds interests, activities, and relationships with other people that give him pleasure, satisfaction, self-confidence, and a sense of purpose in life. If he sometimes indulges in fantasy or daydreaming, he recognizes it for what it is. His goals are realistic. He does not dwell too much on either his past failures or his past successes. Rather, he lives in the present and plans for the future. He probably has some "philosophy" of life—that is, some beliefs either vague or clear as to the meaning of life and what is important in it. His philosophy of life is not necessarily based on deep religious convictions, but frequently these are one of its foundations.

Psychiatrists and clinical psychologists, who are constantly dealing with seriously maladjusted personalities, believe that maladjustment is frequently the result of deep-seated emotional tensions. Often the patient does not understand these tensions because they result from unfortunate early experiences of which he is no longer conscious. Because the victims of such tensions do not understand their causes, they cannot deal with them effectively. However, the fact that tensions may cause serious maladjustments does not mean that to be well adjusted, one should be free of all emotional tensions and never suffer frustration. A certain amount of tension and strong emotion are necessary for normal living. Behind all motives, ambitions, and purposeful actions are emotional drives. Frustrations are also necessary for the development of a mature personality. Sooner or later everyone must learn from experience that there are limits to his powers, problems he cannot solve, obstacles he cannot overcome.

The truly well-adjusted person has developed a strong and balanced personality that can suffer misfortunes and recover from them. It should be emphasized that disappointment, pain, and grief are common experi-

"Well, son, now that you've found yourself, who are you?" (Courtesy *The National Observer.*)

ences of life that come to all of us from time to time. The well-adjusted person can deal with these without being crushed.

The particular ways in which individuals achieve a satisfactory adjustment to their social environment may vary. A mode of life that one would find very satisfying might to another be unattractive and extremely frustrating. Every person must solve his own life problems in harmony with his own tastes and temperament, or, to put it a little differently, in harmony with what some writers have called "his own life style."

Adjustment and Normality. *Good adjustment* and *normality* do not have precisely the same meaning when applied to personality, but their relationship is very close. In any society a well-adjusted person is likely to be recognized as a normal person. Conversely, a normal person in any society is necessarily a reasonably well-adjusted person. In cultural terms a normal person is one who has acquired the basic attitudes and behavior patterns of his culture sufficiently well to be accepted and approved by the group. He many not in all respects represent the typical person in the group, or the statistical average, but his behavior must not deviate too far from what is acceptable or he will not be regarded as normal. The cultural norms are, of course, determined by the group. Types of behavior that in one culture would be quite normal might in another culture be regarded as wholly abnormal.

Sidney M. Jourard, of the University of Florida, prefers to define normality in terms of the "healthy personality."[9] Other psychologists and

[9] Sidney M. Jourard, *Personal Adjustment, An Approach Through the Study of Healthy Personality,* New York, The Macmillan Company, 1963.

sociologists with much the same idea define it in terms of good mental health. To them the normal person is the person with a healthy mind. Presumably such a person would make a reasonably satisfactory adjustment in almost any social situation in which he might be placed. However, we can judge the mental health of an individual only in terms of the adjustment he has made in his actual environment.

PERSONAL MALADJUSTMENT AND ITS CAUSES

Personal maladjustment is indicated by behavior that departs markedly from well-established social norms. Serious maladjustment is never easy to deal with. First, it is always a matter of degree, and second, it can take many forms. Furthermore, in a complex society different individuals are subjected to social environments that differ greatly. In a society like ours there are many subgroups, and they are not always well adjusted to one another or to the larger group. A person may make a very good social adjustment in his family or his gang; but if the attitudes and patterns of behavior of his family or his gang are not well adjusted to those of the larger group, his total social adjustment may be very poor.

Crime is a form of deviant behavior that violates the standards and expectations of the larger social group. Yet sometimes the criminal is a fairly normal and well-adjusted person in terms of the standards and expectations of the subgroups with whom he is most closely associated. He may have grown up as a member of a slum-neighborhood gang that engaged in theft and other crimes and may have admired the person who showed skill and initiative in such behavior. As an adult he may belong to various underworld groups, and he may have spent years as a member of a prison community made up of criminals like himself. In his own groups he may get along very well; in some cases he may even inspire confidence and loyalty as a leader.

The most common types of personal maladjustment, however, grow out of the inability of an individual to meet adequately the problems of his immediate social environment. This may be due in large part to inherited limitations, or it may be due to an unusually difficult environment or to some injury, disease, or other misfortune.

A person who has once achieved a reasonably good adjustment can withstand a considerable amount of hardship and frustration, but everyone has his limits of toleration. If pushed beyond those limits, he will suffer a mental breakdown. Some of the methods used by the communists to obtain "voluntary" confessions of acts not committed appear to be based on this principle. Moreover, experiments with rats have shown that it is possible to produce in these animals a condition very similar to a mental breakdown in a human being. This is accomplished by first teaching the rats to behave in certain ways in order to obtain food or avoid unpleasant experiences and then repeatedly frustrating the animals by changing the required patterns of behavior.

A marked degree of mental deficiency or feeble-mindedness explains the failure of many individuals to make satisfactory adjustments to their environment. Feeble-mindedness may result from inheritance, from a critically adverse environment, or from disease or injury, possibly before birth. Malnutrition, either before or after birth, can also be a factor. Some medical men believe that a great deficiency of proteins in a mother's diet can prevent the full development of the brain of her unborn child and thus limit its potential for learning and for developing intelligence. Another condition that accounts for many extreme cases of personal maladjustment is dementia, which includes all those mental diseases known as psychoses. A group of nervous and mental disturbances that are less severe in their nature is termed neuroses. Feeble-mindedness, psychoses, and the neuroses represent a great part of the more extreme cases of personal maladjustment.

In the remainder of this chapter we shall consider maladjustment arising from these three sources and shall also consider maladjustment associated with what are often called *character disorders*. People who suffer from serious character deficiencies are technically called *psychopathic personalities*. Some writers, wishing to emphasize the difficulties of such people in making social adjustments, call them *sociopathic personalities*.

MENTAL DEFICIENCY AND PERSONAL ADJUSTMENT

In every human society, individuals have varied in intelligence, and in every society of any size, low intelligence has prevented some people from making an adequate adjustment to their environment. But only in recent decades have systematic efforts been made to define and measure intelligence or other mental qualities.

Mental Tests. Mental tests are intended to discover or to measure the mental characteristics of an individual. One of the earliest mental tests is described in Greek mythology. During the Trojan War, according to the story, a Greek named Ulysses paid no attention to the government's call to arms. The authorities visited him and found him plowing up the beach and sowing salt. Determined to test his sanity, they placed Ulysses' only son in the horse's path as Ulysses kept on plowing. Ulysses quickly turned aside, and the test was deemed conclusive proof that he was sane.

Modern mental tests are based on the assumption that one can predict the reactions of an individual in various situations by giving him specially designed tests in which similar conditions are involved. Furthermore, we assume that by presenting an individual with a large variety of sample situations, we can get an estimate of how his abilities compare to those of other people.

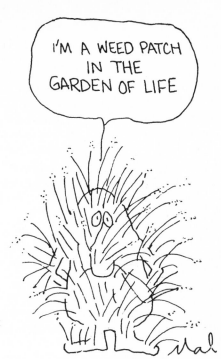

I'M A WEED PATCH IN THE GARDEN OF LIFE

(Courtesy *National Review*, 150 East 35th Street, New York, New York, 10016.)

Psychologists employ various types of tests to determine the character-istics of an individual. One type attempts to measure general intellectual ability. This is known as an *intelligence* test. Another type explores the individual's basic *interests* by presenting him with various hypothetical choices and asking him to express preferences. A third type is intended to measure *aptitudes* for certain kinds of work. A fourth is known as a test of *achievement* and is essentially a test of how well he has learned certain skills or acquired certain kinds of knowledge. A fifth is intended to discover *special abilities or disabilities* and is generally given to handi-capped children or adults. Finally, a sixth type of test used by psychologists tries to determine the personality structure of the individual and his basic emotional needs. This type of test is known as a personality, or *emotional adjustment,* test. All these tests are used by clinical psychologists to diagnose the powers and potentialities of the individual as they exist at any given stage in his development. On the basis of such tests, psycho-logists are able to learn something about the mental difficulties of an individual as a basis for judging the possibilities of helping him to over-come them.

Scientific mental testing began as an attempt to meet the need for identifying mentally deficient persons so that they could be given special training. The pioneer effort in this field is credited to Francis Galton, a cousin of Darwin, who published a scale of mental measurements in 1883. But it was not until 1905 that the first modern psychological test was published. The authors of this test, Binet, a psychologist, and Simon, a physician, had been commissioned by the French government to discover a way to separate the bright, fast learners from the dull, slow learners in the schools of France. The distinctive contribution of this test was that it gave us the concept of *mental age*. If there is such a thing as physical or chronological age, asked Binet and Simon, why not also a mental age?

Many of the early experimenters with mental tests, including Lewis Terman in the United States, believed that they had devised tests that did not rest on acquired knowledge but were essentially a measure of innate or inherited mental ability. Hence, they thought, the scores of individuals on such tests could not be affected by any ordinary differences in environment. However, later experience showed that this thesis was not tenable. Various studies and experiments have demonstrated beyond a reasonable doubt that such factors as differences in family environment and schooling may have a substantial effect on the scores individuals make on standard intelligence tests. For example, when identical twins are separated early and reared in different types of homes, the twin reared by parents of superior social, economic, and educational status almost invariably does better on an intelligence test than the other member of the pair, and sometimes the difference is fairly substantial. Again, studies of children reared in the Kentucky mountains, where economic and social conditions are relatively unfavorable and opportunities for education very limited, show that these children make lower scores, especially as they advance in years, than children in the more favorable environment of the Kentucky blue-grass regions.

The only conclusion that we can draw from such studies is that the scores people make on intelligence tests are a result of their previous experiences as well as of their inherited mental aptitudes. Where conditions of environment have been similar, differences in scores may be a rough indication of differences of innate mental aptitude. However, we must be cautious in assuming that any two given individuals have really had the same, or nearly the same, environment.

Mental Age and the IQ. To estimate mental age, Binet and Simon devised a wide variety of test items, from the very simple to the very complex, and arranged them in order of difficulty. They then tried these items out on a large number of children at various grade levels. On the basis of experience, they assigned a mental-age value to each item. Their procedure in assigning questions or problems to various ages was as follows: If a certain item was responded to correctly by as many as 65 to 75 per cent of the children whose age was, say, eight years, but by a smaller percent of children below that age, it was considered a test of eight-year-old intelligence. They then grouped together several items of appropriate difficulty, usually five, to test children of each age. If a child could answer the questions for all age levels up through those for eight-year-olds, but none of those for the years above that, his mental age was considered to be eight regardless of his actual or chronological age. But he received proportionate credit for any questions actually answered. For example, if he could answer all the questions for eight-year-olds, and three out of five of those for nine-year-olds, his mental age was considered 8.6. If he could also answer two out of five of the questions for age ten, he was assigned a mental age of nine.

Later, other psychologists refined the Binet technique so that each mental year consisted of twelve mental months. For example, each test item might represent two mental months, in which case six items would represent a mental year. Each person tested would then receive two months' credit toward his mental age for each item answered correctly.

Once the concept of mental age was developed, it was but a step to the notion of expressing a ratio between the mental age and the chronological age of an individual. This ratio was called the IQ, or intelligence quotient. The IQ of a person is found by dividing his mental age by his actual age and multiplying the resulting fraction by 100. What multiplying by 100 does is to express the ratio or fraction as a percentage, but it is not customary to write "per cent" after the number expressing an IQ. The formula for finding the IQ may be written as follows:

$$IQ = \frac{\text{Mental Age}}{\text{Chronological Age}} \times 100$$

Let us see how this formula works in practice. A child eight years old having a mental age of eight is an average child. His IQ would be $8/8 \times 100 = 100$. It is apparent, therefore, that an IQ of 100 represents average intelligence. If a child eight years old had a mental age of twelve, as indicated by his score on an intelligence test, he would obviously be extremely bright. This would be indicated by his IQ, which would be $12/8 \times 100 = 150$.

Today the practice is often followed of assigning to an individual a *percentile rank* rather than an IQ when he takes an intelligence test. This percentile rank is based on his total score and shows where his level of development places him with reference to other individuals in a certain group, when they are arranged in order from the most capable to the least capable. The 100th percentile consists of the 1 per cent of the group who have made the highest scores. The first percentile consists of the 1 per cent who have made the lowest scores. Similarly, the 50th and 51st percentiles consist of those who have made average (median) scores.

Tests that give percentile rankings are often used to determine, in part, the admission of students to college. They also give some indication of the kinds and quantity of work that students can carry successfully, and they are therefore useful in counseling. Probably the best known of such tests or groups of tests are the CAT (College Aptitude Test), ETS (Educational Testing Service tests), and the ACT (American College Test Program).

The Problem of Mental Deficiency. In the course of World War II the Army suddenly found itself faced with the problem of what to do with some tens of thousands of soldiers who seemed incapable of learning the tasks of military life. The problem was so serious that by the middle of 1942 the Army found it necessary to organize a corps of military psychologists to sift the inductees and eliminate those who had very little ability to learn.

Mental tests indicate that there are great differences in intelligence in our population. This fact has long been known, but tests have made our knowledge more definite. Though these and other psychological tests are being used more widely than ever before in schools, in government, and in business, they are also being subjected to increasing criticism. Nevertheless, mental tests are probably the best means we have for comparing the mental powers of large numbers of individuals.

However, such tests are likely to be more useful if we recognize their limitations. They tell us something about the probable intelligence of an individual at the time a test is taken, but they do not and cannot "measure" his innate or inherited mental potentialities. A possibly more serious limitation grows out of the difficulty of defining *intelligence* in such a way that all the elements that enter into it can be correctly rated by a test. It is doubtful whether the concept can be defined with much precision and whether the relative intelligence of different individuals, especially at the higher levels, can be determined with much accuracy. Perhaps we can best define *intelligence* as the ability of a person to understand the situations that confront him in his environment, and to make satisfactory adjustments to them insofar as such adjustments depend on learning and thinking. The more intelligent a person is, the better he will be able, among other things, to do the following: (1) to perceive a situation as a whole rather than partially or incompletely; (2) to learn quickly; (3) to concentrate thought and learning in a desired direction; (4) to find satisfactory solutions for his problems, either with or without help from others. High intelligence probably requires considerable imagination and originality, for to solve a difficult problem, one may need to think of and to evaluate a number of novel approaches.

When we assume that a so-called mental test measures intelligence, we are assuming that the mental abilities required for correct answers to its questions are the same as those needed for solving the sometimes complex problems encountered in real life. This is not always true, for mental tests have many limitations. For example, they must be completed within a limited period of time on the theory that this makes the scores of individuals more comparable. But some of the world's greatest achievements have probably been made by people who have acquired the habit of thinking through difficult problems slowly, checking at every step to avoid missing some important consideration. Furthermore, to allow one's mind and imagination to wander with a purpose, to take time to search for the unusual or unlikely aspects of a situation, is one kind of intelligent behavior. It is also an important ingredient in originality or creativeness.

If we do make the assumption that intelligence can be determined by tests, it then becomes possible to rate individuals on a scale that takes age into account. All we need do is to compare their IQ scores. Table 4 shows the terms used by psychologists to describe various levels of mental development and the IQ range that each level represents. The great majority of people, probably more than 80 per cent, have IQ's that range from 80 to 119. As we go down the scale from 80, or up from 119, the numbers represented decline rapidly.

Table 4. *Levels of Mental Development*

IQ Range	Classification of Individuals
0–24	Idiots ⎫
25–49	Imbeciles ⎬ Low grade defectives
50–69	Morons ⎭
70–79	Borderline defectives
80–90	Dull normals
91–110	Average normals
111–119	Bright normals
120–127	Superior individuals
128 and over	Very superior individuals

If *intelligence* means good ability to understand the environment and, therefore, to make satisfactory adjustments to it, *mental deficiency,* or feeble-mindedness, means a very limited ability to understand and to adjust. It may be of interest to note, in Table 5, the grades of mental deficiency that psychologists recognize in adults on the basis of mental age as determined by intelligence tests.

Table 5. *Classification of the Feeble-minded*

Mental Age	Grades of Feeble-mindedness
0 up to 3 years	Idiocy (low, middle, and high)
3 up to 8 years	Imbecility (low, middle, and high)
8 up to 13 years	Moronity (low, middle, and high)

A low-grade adult idiot has a mental age of less than a year and is relatively helpless, although he can usually walk. A middle-grade idiot has a mental age of one year. He feeds himself but eats everything he can place inside his mouth. A high-grade idiot, mental age two years, eats discriminatingly; that is, he can tell food from nonedible objects. A low-grade imbecile, mental age four or five years, does only the simplest tasks. A high-grade imbecile, six or seven years old mentally, does more difficult tasks of short duration, such as washing dishes and running errands. A low-grade moron, aged ten years mentally, makes a good institution helper and can be depended on for many types of routine work. High-grade morons, eleven or twelve years old mentally, are in some respects a greater problem than those of lower intelligence. They can do fairly complicated work with only occasional supervision. They can, for example, use machinery or care for animals on farms. But although they require little supervision while working, they cannot be depended on to plan their work.

Because of arrested mental development, the feeble-minded are unable, in greater or less degree, to deal with many of the ordinary problems of life. But they do have some social intelligence, especially in the case of the morons. Most of them also have vocational possibilities. Those at the higher levels get married and lead quiet family lives. Usually they are not sexually dangerous, even though at one time many people associated the word *moron* with sexual perversion. As a matter of fact, the feeble-minded are often almost inert sexually. It is true that those classified psychologically as morons make up a certain percentage of our delinquents and criminals, but they also make up a part of our law-abiding, unskilled, semiskilled, and to a lesser extent, skilled labor groups.

The Department of Health, Education, and Welfare estimates that about 3 per cent of the population of the United States is mentally retarded. This means more than six million persons. It also estimates that of the more than three million children born each year, about 3 per cent are or will be classified as mentally retarded. The department counts as retarded only the very retarded. On the basis of IQ scores, most of these people would be classified as morons or borderline defectives, with some imbeciles and a relatively small number of idiots. The vast majority of the retarded live in their own homes and communities and are able largely to care for themselves, but in 1966, according to the department, over 250,000 of the most serious cases were patients in public or private institutions. This was substantially more than half the estimated 400,000 persons who were so mentally retarded that they needed custodial care.[10] Presumably, the remainder were cared for by parents or other relatives.

Treatment of the Mentally Deficient. In the long course of history, the feeble-minded have been treated in various ways. They have been abandoned to die, tolerated and allowed to roam about at will, looked upon with superstitious awe, or treated as persons "possessed" by demons. Modern science and humanitarianism have brought better understanding of them and better treatment.

What the treatment of feeble-mindedness should be in a given case depends on (1) what the family of the deficient individual is able or willing to do for him; (2) what the community tolerates or does not tolerate in the way of mental backwardness; (3) the degree of mental deficiency the individual shows on the basis of tests; and (4) his other personality characteristics.

Through testing methods applied by qualified psychologists, it is now

---

[10] U.S. Department of Health, Education, and Welfare, *Public Institutions for the Mentally Retarded,* Washington, D.C., July 1968, p. 8.

possible to diagnose the mentally defective and establish the degree of care they require. Many defectives can be cared for in special classes in regular schools, and most states are appropriating funds for such classes. In these classes, through various special techniques, retarded children can be taught the fundamentals needed for a simple yet not too dependent life. Idiots and imbeciles, of course, need institutional care. Such care is now provided by virtually all states; but often parents refuse for sentimental reasons to release these children to state institutions.

Much progress has been made in the diagnosis and training of mental defectives. The objective of training idiots is to make them easier to care for. There is little hope of teaching them to do useful work. Morons, however, and even imbeciles can be taught to do many things. They can be trained to acquire balance and muscular coordination. They can be taught to pick out colors, to distinguish sounds, and to taste, smell, and touch discriminatingly. Training in speech, personal habits, and the development of useful abilities can also be provided. Some mental defectives do surprisingly well. Some even acquire special talents and give promise of making unusual adjustments along some one certain line. In any case, the provision of living quarters and training facilities for low-grade mental defectives is generally considered a state responsibility.

In a sense, because they require custodial care, idiots and imbeciles are easier to deal with than morons. Morons generally lead their own lives as members of the community, and hence they need special aid in making social adjustment. There is always the danger that they will drift into crime or that unscrupulous people will take advantage of them.

THE PROBLEM OF PSYCHOTIC BEHAVIOR

Amentia means "lack of intelligence," or feeble-mindedness; dementia means "loss of intelligence." Dementia, as has been said, is another name for the mental disorders that psychologists and psychiatrists refer to as psychoses. The term feeble-mindedness is applied to those who have never developed much intelligence; but psychoses, or mental diseases, usually attack those whose previous mental development has been fairly normal. But loss of intelligence is not the major symptom of psychosis. Changes in emotional adjustment are even more prominent. The emotional life of the psychotic is greatly distorted. He shows either too much emotion or an apparent lack of emotion. Other symptoms are delusions and hallucinations.

By delusions we mean beliefs that are out of harmony with reality. Hallucinations are disorders of perception. They arise from within, as it were, and may affect any of the senses: vision, hearing, tactual sensation, taste, or smell. Delusions and hallucinations may be further distinguished. A delusion is a false idea; for instance, believing that one is Napoleon is a delusion. A hallucination, on the other hand, is a false percept, such as seeing pink elephants where there are no elephants at all. In both hallucinations and delusions there is generally a relaxation of attention and of critical ability, a dispersion of thoughts, a lack of interest in or of contact with reality, and a tendency to live in a world of imaginary situations.

Types of Psychotic Behavior. Psychologists and psychiatrists generally recognize two large groups of mental disorders: the *organic* and the *functional*. By organic mental disorders we mean those that result from definite abnormalities in the tissues or the chemistry of the organism. Examples are psychoses connected with syphilis, lead poisoning, changes in the endocrine glands, alcoholism, and changes resulting from the use of morphine. By functional mental disorders we mean those in which there is no known change in the physical constitution of the individual.

We shall make no attempt to name and describe the many forms that organic and functional psychoses can take. Under a few major types, the American Psychiatric Association has listed over seventy kinds. In some types of psychoses the patient is subject to periods of great elation or deep depression, or he swings back and forth between these extremes. In other types there is a slow, progressive deterioration of the entire personality, an increasing apathy, a loss of interest in the world, and a withdrawal from active contact with it. In still other types the patient develops delusions of persecution or of grandeur. Sometimes psychotics engage in meaningless talk or silly behavior, and occasionally they may become violent and dangerous.

It is not surprising to learn that mental abnormalities are often difficult to diagnose. They are also difficult to treat, for many puzzling problems remain to be solved.

The Causes of Psychotic Behavior. As already pointed out, some psychotic disorders are known to be organic and can be explained by known changes in the tissues or the chemistry of the human organism. For other psychoses, we have not been able to find physical explanations, and psychologists and psychiatrists generally regard these as functional. Functional psychoses are presumed to result from unusual stresses and strains to which the individual may have been subjected in early childhood and/or in later years. This trend toward explaining psychoses in terms of the impact of environmental factors on personality was encouraged by the theories of Freud, who, as indicated earlier, believed that most mental and emotional abnormalities were the result of unfortunate experiences of the individual in early childhood.

Today there is a great deal of evidence to show that the experiences of a child in his early years are a major factor in determining his personality and behavior in later life. Nevertheless, a substantial amount of evidence has been accumulated by researchers in the last decade or two that suggests that some mental disorders that have generally been regarded as functional may in fact have organic, or biological, explanations. They may, for example, be caused, not by external stresses and strains, but by the abnormal functioning of certain glands, or by the presence of certain substances in the blood, or the absence of others.

A mental disorder on which much research has been concentrated in recent years is *schizophrenia*. Because of the numbers of its victims, this psychosis presents a major mental health problem. More than 400,000 hospital beds in the United States are occupied by mental patients, and of these almost half are schizophrenics. As a rule this disease first attacks people when they are in the prime of life, between the ages of twenty and forty. It presents a wide variety of symptoms, the most common of which is loss of contact with reality. Other symptoms include hallucinations and either inertness and indifference or extreme anxiety and depression. Sometimes schizophrenics go into a catatonic state in which they become rigid and mute, not even responding to a pinprick. Only a small minority of them recover permanently.

Early in the present century, schizophrenia, along with a number of other psychoses, was generally believed to be hereditary. Later, however, evidence accumulated that seemed to cast doubt on this theory. Then, as the findings and doctrines of Freud spread and became increasingly influential, the pendulum swung the other way, and many psychologists and psychiatrists came to believe that schizophrenia was almost wholly the result of environmental factors. But in the last decade or two, researchers have uncovered new evidence that suggests (1) that inheritance may play a major role in the development of schizophrenia and (2) that the immediate cause of the disease may be the presence or lack in the body of some hormone or chemical.

One study that suggests that inheritance is a major factor in schizophrenia was made some years ago by Franz Kallman, then head of the Medical Genetics Department of the New York State Psychiatric Institute. He collected several hundred cases of schizophrenic twins whose co-twins he was able to find, and he also located all their available brothers and sisters. He found that though the chance of the average person succumbing to schizophrenia is about 1 per cent, this rises to 14 per cent in the case of an ordinary brother or sister of a schizophrenic and to 86.2 per cent in the case of an identical twin. The latter figure is especially significant, because identical twins presumably have identical—or nearly identical—hereditary traits. Though Kallman's methods and interpretations have been widely criticized, his correlations are so high that they are not easily brushed aside.

Another study that suggests that schizophrenia or a high degree of susceptibility to it may be inherited was made more recently by Theophile Raphael at Ypsilanti State Hospital in Michigan. Raphael discovered that the fingerprint patterns of schizophrenics differ distinctly from those of normal people. Schizophrenics often have scrambled or interrupted patterns of a type rarely found in normal people. Since fingerprint patterns are determined before birth, these peculiarities may result from some hereditary insufficiency that also causes schizophrenia. A writer in the *Journal of the American Medical Association* commented that Rafael's study may indicate a "basic or genetic insufficiency" that makes individuals susceptible to the disease.

Other studies give support to the possibility that, whether inherited or not, schizophrenia may result directly from faulty body chemistry. One such study was conducted several years ago by Robert Heath of Tulane University. He found in the blood of schizophrenics a unique protein substance to which he gave the name *taraxein*. When Heath injected taraxein into human volunteers, they developed hallucinations and other symptoms similar to those of schizophrenia. When the substance was injected into monkeys, they went into catatonic stupors. Recent research by Heath has led him to believe that taraxein is an antibody that acts on specific areas of deep brain tissue, and he is attempting to devise a remedy for schizophrenia by finding something that will neutralize taraxein.[11]

It is clear that there are wide gaps in our knowledge of the nature and causes of psychoses and other mental abnormalities. There is still good reason to believe that every person, no matter how "normal," has a limit of endurance and that extreme and prolonged stress and strain, torture, and frustration will ultimately cause any individual to suffer a mental breakdown. On the other hand, it seems increasingly probable that some psychoses that have been attributed to environmental conditions will sooner or later be found to have biological causes.

Extent and Incidence of Psychoses. In the seventy-five years or so preceding 1955, the number of people in mental hospitals in the United States increased several times as fast as the population. This does not necessarily mean that people were becoming more subject to mental disorders than in earlier times. In part it resulted from the more general use of hospitals for the treatment of mental diseases and in part from the increasing proportion of older people, who are more subject to mental disorders. However, after 1955 there was, for the first time, a decline in the number of patients in mental hospitals. In 1955 the number of mental patients in state and county hospitals (about 90 per cent of the total) was nearly 559,000. By 1968 it had fallen to slightly more than 400,000, a decline of over 28 per cent.[12]

Mental disorders were once supposed to be most common among the very young, but statistics show that over the years, until about 1963, there was a steady increase in both the number and the percentage of patients over sixty-five in mental hospitals. Since then there has been a gradual decline in their number, but they still account for about 30 per cent of mental hospital patients. Although psychoses do become more common as people grow older, not all the elderly patients in mental hospitals are

[11] See Arthur J. Snyder in the *Chicago Daily News,* May 4, 1968, p. 20.
[12] National Institute of Mental Health, *Mental Health Statistics, Current Facility Reports,* 344-842/3038, Washington, D.C., U.S. Department of Health, Education, and Welfare, 1969.

really psychotic. Many of them are merely old and feeble, somewhat senile, and difficult to care for. They should be in old people's homes or nursing homes, but these are expensive and often are not available. In many cases, old people have been committed to a public mental institution because this was an easy way for their families to get rid of an unwanted burden. But since the early 1960's, and especially since the advent of the Medicare program, there has been a marked rise in the number and quality of nursing homes. Medicare made it possible financially for more elderly patients to be cared for in these homes, with the result that not as many beds in mental hospitals are being occupied by those who are merely senile.

Certain other aspects of the incidence of psychoses may be noted. First, the inmates of mental hospitals are about equally divided between the sexes, but men somewhat outnumber women. Second, psychosis is somewhat more common among single people than among those who are married. Finally, in large cities studies have shown that psychotic patients, classified by areas of residence, tend to cluster near the center (oldest section) of the city. The highest rate for schizophrenia is found in skid rows, rooming-house areas, and slums, most of which are near the central business district. In general, areas of social disorganization show higher rates than good residential areas.

Treatment of Psychoses. Although the treatment of psychoses presents great difficulties, important advances have been made in recent years. For some psychoses, cures or preventives have been found. The type of mental deterioration called *general paresis* was once supposed to be caused by environmental and emotional factors, but later syphilis was found to be the real cause, and since the discovery that penicillin will cure syphilis, this form of psychosis has become relatively rare. Once many people in the southeastern United States were afflicted by a special type of mental disorder, particularly in the spring; but a cure was easily effected when it was discovered that the cause was a vitamin B deficiency. For other psychoses, especially in the group usually labeled as functional, no easy or dependable cures have been found. However, if some of these eventually prove to have biological origins, the chances of finding effective cures should be good.

Meanwhile, in the absence of real cures, advances have been made in methods of treatment. Even brain surgery has been resorted to and has had increasing success as a treatment for some types of mental disorder. But up to a decade or two ago the chief reliance in treating psychoses was placed on psychoanalysis and other types of *psychotherapy,* in other words on what some psychiatrists call "talking cures." Usually such treatment was individual, but now and then it was tried with large groups. In some cases psychotherapy seemed to give good results, but in others it failed completely, and it did little or nothing to check the steady rise of patients in mental hospitals.

One important advance in treating psychoses was the discovery some years ago that many patients could be helped greatly by *shock therapy.* This consists of subjecting the patient to a series of shocks by administering insulin or metrazol or, more commonly, by using an electric current. Electric shock treatment has proved extremely effective in relieving severe and disabling states of depression, though the resulting relief is not always permanent.

But what many believe to be the greatest advance in the treatment of psychoses has occurred in the last decade or two and consists of the discovery and use of a number of new drugs. These drugs are not cures, but in many cases they control psychotic symptoms to such an extent that the patient can live a fairly normal life at home and even continue to work at his job. According to the National Institute of Mental Health, the drop in resident population in mental hospitals after 1955 was directly attributable to the introduction of large-scale *drug therapy.*[13] The drugs most commonly used are tranquilizers, which control the patient's symptoms by calming him down; but more recently some use has also been made of energizers to overcome inertia and depression. Though as yet no real cure has been found for schizophrenia, many researchers, especially in the field of biochemistry, are convinced that in time one will be discovered.

For many years our facilities in the United States for treating mental disorders have been very inadequate in comparison with those for treating other diseases. However, long agitation by sociologists, psychiatrists, and others interested in the problems of mental health has brought some improvement. Partly because the results from drug therapy are encouraging, greater efforts have been made to treat patients at home and thus avoid committing them to mental hospitals. To encourage this trend, Congress passed in 1963 a measure supported by the late President Kennedy that provides federal aid to community health centers. The hope is that if mental diseases are treated early, the chances of cure will be better. Also it is thought that there are advantages in treating a mental patient in his own home and community environment instead of placing him in the artificial atmosphere of a mental institution.

In spite of progress, there is still need to expand and improve our facilities for treating mental diseases. Almost 366,000 new patients are annually admitted to the mental hospitals of this country for an average stay of two or three years. The number is still rising, but fortunately the number of releases is rising faster. Most mental patients are in state institutions, and many of these, in spite of some improvement in conditions, are still both overcrowded and inadequately staffed. Though in recent years many states have substantially increased their appropriations for the care of the mentally deranged, the average state hospital operates on a budget that allows only about seven or eight dollars a day per patient.

[13] National Institute of Mental Health, *Patients in State and County Mental Hospitals 1967,* Washington, D.C., U.S. Department of Health, Education, and Welfare, 1969, p. 4.

OTHER TYPES OF PERSONAL MALADJUSTMENT

Neurotic Behavior. In recent years the term *neurotic* has achieved considerable popularity. It is often applied loosely to people who are not strikingly abnormal and who have no extreme difficulties in meeting the major problems of life. We call them neurotic because they are a little more eccentric, irritable, or demanding than others, and therefore a little harder to get along with. But most such people are not neurotic in the sense in which psychiatrists and psychologists use the term. To them a neurotic is one who suffers from a definite personality disorder, a disorder belonging to the group known as *neuroses* or *psychoneuroses*. Perhaps the difference is only one of degree, for in many cases it is difficult for even a trained observer to distinguish between the person who is a little strange and the person who has a mild neurosis.

Neuroses are emotional and mental disturbances somewhat less severe than psychoses. They are usually assumed to be functional in nature, though some of them, like some psychoses, may have a biological basis. The maladjustments of a psychotic individual are likely to be extreme. He may have so lost contact with reality that he is unaware of his conflicts, is content with his behavior, does not seek help with his problems, and lacks the ability to concentrate, perceive, judge, and reason adequately. Hence he gets into many difficulties that are obvious to the normal person but beyond his power to perceive and control. A neurotic, on the other hand, is painfully aware of his conflicts, though not of their origin or meaning. He is not content with his adjustment, and he often seeks help with his problems. His mental processes are essentially orderly, since in most respects he is able to perceive, judge, and reason rather correctly.

We shall make no attempt to classify and describe in detail the various types of neuroses. All of them are characterized by mental and emotional conflict resulting from inability or failure to meet certain situations adequately, and all of them involve an element of anxiety. The neurotic individual tends to specialize in some one or two kinds of defensive behavior. This behavior is used in all problem situations, whether it is appropriate or not. It becomes habitual and obstructs intelligent action. The kind of behavior the neurotic exhibits becomes a symptom by which one can recognize the type of neurosis from which he suffers.

Neurotic behavior may take various forms. In some cases, when any problem arises that the neurotic individual is unable or unwilling to meet, he develops symptoms of physical illness—for example, nausea—to excuse him from doing anything about his problem. His illness may be real to him, but it has no organic basis. It is *psychosomatic* in its nature, a habitual physical reaction to his mental and emotional state. In other cases he complains constantly of fatigue; or he suffers from extreme depression; or he is subject to some irresistible compulsion, such as repeatedly washing

"George doesn't have any inner conflicts. He openly hates everything." (Courtesy Richard Decker and *LOOK* Magazine.)

his hands for no apparent reason or repeatedly checking doors to make sure they are locked.

Psychoneuroses are sometimes mild and not completely disabling. In this case, persons suffering from them may live in a normal society and contribute to it without appreciable harm to others. Often much can be done to help the neurotic individual if the real nature of his difficulty can be discovered. Methods that may contribute to this result include the use of psychological tests, psychological counseling, psychoanalysis, and tranquilizing drugs.

Psychopathic Personalities. The term *psychopathic personality,* as usually employed, is difficult to define, because it is little more than a convenient designation for people whose behavior is abnormal in various ways and yet who cannot be classified as mentally deficient, psychotic, or neurotic.

The main difficulty with some psychopaths seems to be an extremely egocentric and hence antisocial philosophy of life. They believe that the world owes them a living and that they have a right to collect by any method whatever. Sometimes they possess a considerable amount of personal charm, and their intelligence as measured by tests may be average or even superior. But they show little or no sense of responsibility toward other people, and in the long run they are unable to make any kind of adequate social adjustment. They are incapable of real love or friendship, and they fail at any kind of work they undertake.

There are other psychopaths who seem merely to lack good social judgment. They get into difficulties that anyone with good sense would avoid, or they even acquire a liking for making trouble for people. Others, from an eccentric impulse within themselves, become fanatic advocates of special causes; still others become pathological liars.

Some writers reserve the term *psychopath* for *moral defectives*. In Freudian terminology such people might be said to have very weak superegos, or superegos that have become isolated from their egos. Psychopaths of this type lack a sense of moral responsibility, and they sometimes commit horrifying crimes with little provocation and without afterward feeling any guilt.

The Many Types of Personal Maladjustment. In discussing maladjustment in this chapter we have concentrated our attention on the problems growing out of certain mental or personality limitations and disorders. In doing this, we have by no means fully covered the subject of personal maladjustment. Even people whose mental and emotional development has been reasonably normal sometimes find themselves badly adjusted to their families, occupations, or business associates. Some of these maladjustments will be discussed in other chapters—for example, in the chapter "The Family." Then there are various groups of people who adjust very poorly to their social environment in special ways or for special reasons. While some of the people in these groups are feeble-minded, psychotic, neurotic, or psychopathic, many—perhaps most—of them are not. The groups we refer to include skid-row bums, alcoholics, juvenile delinquents, and criminals. All these maladjusted groups create social problems of some importance, but lack of space prevents us from dealing with them in this chapter. However, the type of deviant behavior represented by crime and delinquency is such a crucial problem that we shall later devote an entire chapter to it.

A problem to which we should call attention here, though we do not have space to go into all its ramifications, is drug addiction. It is both a personal and a social problem, and it has been with us to some degree for a long time. But in recent years drug addiction has spread rapidly and become increasingly difficult to deal with. In part this results from the revolt of the younger generation against some of the old social values and against many of the restrictions that have traditionally been placed on young people. There is a desire for new experiences, and to find these many have begun to experiment with the use of drugs.

In 1970 a nonprofit research group, Friends of Psychiatric Research, Inc., made a comprehensive study of drug addiction under a contract with the federal Office of Economic Opportunity. Their study included tabulating the experiences of more than 6,500 narcotics addicts in several large cities.[14] They found that most addicts had started their use of drugs with marijuana. (This is a relatively mild drug about whose effects there is much disagreement. Some students of the drug problem consider it rather harm-

[14] See "Friends of Drug Addicts Are Their Worst Enemies," *The National Observer*, November 30, 1970, p. 1.

less.) Later, most of these addicts had proceeded by stages to amphetamines, known as "speed," then to barbiturates or LSD, and finally to heroin. LSD is known to have damaging effects on the health of its users and on their progeny. Heroin is a "hard" drug. Once one has become accustomed to its use, its withdrawal causes extreme distress. Few addicts succeed in overcoming their addiction, and the mental and physical effects are ultimately disastrous.

One finding of this study was that most heroin addicts were introduced to its use by friends and not by pressure from pushers anxious to sell for a profit. But because it is illegal to use or possess any of the drugs that have been mentioned, including marijuana, if they are to be available to users even at high prices, there must be widespread underground traffic in them. Organized criminal groups, and sometimes amateurs seeking quick profits, bring them into the country and distribute them. This involves risk, because most nations make efforts to suppress traffic in drugs and there are international agreements prohibiting their import or export. Some countries deal with violators very harshly, condemning them to long prison terms. As of June 1, 1970, our State Department listed 556 United States citizens who were being held on drug charges in thirty-seven foreign countries.

Efforts to deal with the drug problem include programs for educating the public in the dangers of using drugs, attempts to rehabilitate addicts of heroin and other "hard" drugs through treatment in hospitals or special institutions, and attempts to dry up the supply of drugs by arresting and prosecuting all who sell or possess them. None of these efforts have to date stopped the spread of their use.

IMPROVING PERSONAL ADJUSTMENT

The discussion above should have made it clear to the reader that various types of personal maladjustment create serious social problems. Moreover, these problems are peculiarly hard to deal with because once the personality of an individual has definitely acquired a maladjusted pattern, to change that pattern is very difficult. However, no reasonable effort should be spared to treat and, if possible, cure the maladjusted individual. The greatest hope of increasing the number of well-adjusted people in our society lies in finding and, insofar as possible, removing the causes that lead to maladjustment.

All types of personal maladjustment grow out of the relation between the individual and his environment. In the final result, both biological inheritance and environment play their part. At present we cannot do very much about inheritance, either by selective breeding or by more direct methods for changing the nature of the genes in human chromosomes. As we have said before, this may be just as well. Attempts to improve the human race by breeding would create moral and social problems. Furthermore, if we had wide powers to control human inheritance, there would always be the danger of making unwise changes that would be undesirable or even, in the long run, disastrous. But though heredity plays a part in the development of personality, environment also plays an important part, and perhaps with the majority of people the principal part. This is fortunate, because there are many ways in which it may be possible in the future to improve the environmental conditions under which most children grow up.

Undoubtedly, much personal maladjustment has environmental origins in the early home life of the child. Hence, one of our first objectives should be to improve the early home environment. This is not easy, because maladjusted parents are likely to provide a social environment that will produce maladjusted children. Freud recognized this problem and believed that to improve the personalities of children it would first be necessary to educate parents and teachers in what he conceived of as sound principles of psychology. There are several ways in which progress might be made. If young people could be induced by counseling and education to pick their mates with greater care, there would be more harmony between parents, and this should improve the chances of their children to be normal rather than psychopathic, neurotic, or psychotic. Furthermore, if young people were better trained for parenthood, if they had a better understanding of child psychology and of their own influence on their children, in many cases the children would have a better chance of growing up into well-adjusted adults. It is easy to make such suggestions but not easy to carry them out, because we are all, teachers and pupils alike, products of our past.

Another development that would probably help reduce personal maladjustment in our society is better facilities for the early diagnosis and treatment of real "problem" children. Much might be done for many of these children by special treatment and special schooling. More facilities for research are also needed if we are to deal as effectively as possible with all types of problem children. There is still a great deal that we do not know about human psychology, and it is quite possible some theories that are now popular will be abandoned or greatly modified within a few decades.

Finally, we know that good mental health and the development of a well-adjusted personality depend to an important degree on favorable conditions in the general social environment. This is true for people of all ages, but it is especially true for children and young people. It has long been known that slums breed alcoholism, crime, and other types of maladjusted behavior. If we could eliminate slums and poverty, reduce racial tensions, and provide all of our people with reasonably adequate opportunities for recreation, work, and personal advancement through education, we would without much doubt substantially increase the proportion of normal and socially useful individuals in our society. But to attain these objectives will take much more than wishful thinking. It will require new, imaginative, and realistic approaches in which government must necessarily play an active role.

Terms to Be Understood

socialization	infantile autism	feeble-mindedness
personality	heredity	delusions
instinct	normality	hallucinations
drive	insanity	psychosis
psychoanalysis	sociopathic	functional psychosis
id	personality	organic psychosis
ego	mental tests	schizophrenia
superego	mental age	shock therapy
pleasure principle	IQ	drug therapy
psychic energy	percentile rank	psychotherapy
reality principle	intelligence	neurosis
dynamics of	idiot	psychosomatic
personality	imbecile	psychoneurosis
libido	moron	psychopathic
Oedipus complex	amentia	personality
feral children	dementia	moral defective

Questions for Review and Discussion

1. Does culture control man, or does man control culture? Explain the relationship between the two.
2. The personality of every individual bears the imprint of what four things?
3. What is the basic theory behind the Freudian method of treating mental and emotional disturbances?
4. Why has there been a great deal of opposition to Freud's theories?
5. Explain Freud's theory of the structure and development of personality.
6. Explain the Oedipus complex.
7. Why are the early years of childhood so important in personality development?
8. Explain why two children who grow up in the same family at the same time may have very different social environments.
9. Which is more important in the development of personality, environment or heredity? Explain the relationship between the two, noting what we can learn about it through the study of children who have been kept in extreme isolation.
10. According to Valenti, what proportion of babies inherit some degree of abnormality from their parents?
11. What are some of the most common reasons for the failure of an individual to make a reasonably good adjustment to his social environment?
12. What does it mean to be a "well-adjusted" individual?
13. What is intelligence?

14. Explain what is meant by *mental age,* and tell how it may be determined by the use of mental tests. Discuss the limitations of such tests as measures of intelligence.
15. What is the significance of the IQ of an individual? Give the formula for finding the IQ.
16. Suppose a student applying for admission to a college makes a score on the CAT that places him in the fifth percentile. Explain what this would mean, and why.
17. Name the principal grades of intelligence, from the lowest to the highest, as they are listed in Table 4.
18. Define normalcy, idiocy, imbecility, and moronity in terms of mental age.
19. What can be done to help the mentally deficient?
20. Explain the difference between feeble-mindedness and psychosis.
21. Distinguish between organic and functional psychoses. Discuss the problem of classifying schizophrenia.
22. How extensive are psychoses in the American population, and what groups of people are most affected?
23. To what extent is it possible to cure psychotics?
24. Why have the numbers of mental cases in institutions been decreasing in recent years?
25. What needs must be met if we are to provide adequate treatment for psychotic patients?
26. Explain how neuroses differ from psychoses.
27. What are some of the more common types of neurotic behavior? What can be done to help the neurotic individual?
28. What are common characteristics of psychopathic personalities?
29. How would you explain the recent great increase in experimentation with drugs? And in drug addiction?
30. Why is the drug problem so difficult to deal with?
31. What general suggestions are made at the end of this chapter for increasing the proportion of well-adjusted people in our population? Do you have other suggestions?

For Further Study

Berelson, Bernard, and Gary A. Steiner, *Human Behavior,* shorter edition, New York, Harcourt Brace Jovanovich, Inc., 1967.

Bettelheim, Bruno, *Children of the Dream,* New York, The Macmillan Company, 1969.

Bloom, Benjamin S., *Stability and Change in Human Characteristics,* New York, John Wiley & Sons, Inc., 1964.

Brenner, Charles, *An Elementary Textbook of Psychoanalysis,* paperback, New York, Doubleday & Company, Inc., 1957.

Cohen, Sidney, *The Drug Dilemma,* New York, McGraw-Hill, Inc., 1970.

Dobzhansky, Theodosius, *Heredity and the Nature of Man,* paperback, New York, New American Library, Inc., 1966. Read Chap. 2, "Variety of Human Natures," for an especially good discussion.

Erikson, Erick H., *Childhood and Society,* rev. ed., paperback, New York, W. W. Norton & Company, Inc., 1964.

――――, *Identity: Youth and Crisis,* paperback, New York, W. W. Norton & Company, Inc., 1968.

Eysenck, Hans J., *Biological Basis of Personality,* Springfield, Ill., Charles C Thomas, Publisher, 1967.

―――― (with discussions by others), *The Effects of Psychotherapy,* New York, The International Science Press, Inc., 1966.

Freud, Sigmund, *The Psychopathology of Everyday Life,* edited by James Strachey, paperback, New York, W. W. Norton & Company, Inc., 1966.

Hall, Calvin S., *A Primer of Freudian Psychology,* Mentor paperback, New York, New American Library, Inc., 1954.

Horman, Richard E., and Allan M. Fox, eds., *Drug Awareness,* paperback, New York, Avon Books, 1970.

Lazarus, R. S., *Patterns of Adjustment and Human Effectiveness,* New York, McGraw-Hill, Inc., 1969.

Linton, Ralph, *The Cultural Background of Personality,* New York, Appleton-Century-Crofts, Inc., 1945.

Riesman, David, *The Lonely Crowd,* Anchor paperback, New York, Doubleday & Company, Inc., 1953.

Schuler, Edgar A., et al., *Readings in Sociology,* 3d ed., New York, Thomas Y. Crowell Company, 1960. Part 3, especially the selection by Kingsley Davis, "Final Note on a Case of Extreme Isolation."

Smelser, Neil J., ed., *Personality and Social Systems,* New York, John Wiley & Sons, Inc., 1963.

Chapter 10

The Family

We take the term *family* so for granted that one may question the need for discussing it at any length. But the need for such discussion arises from the fact that the family is the key unit of social organization, the primary group of greatest importance for the individual and for society. It is within the family that we start life and first become oriented to it—become socialized, if you prefer—and it is within the family that we as adults and parents find many of our satisfactions in life and are able to contribute to the perpetuation of our civilization. Likewise, it is within the family that many personal and social problems have their origin.

In the United States we think of the family in terms of what some sociologists call the *nuclear family: father, mother, and one or more dependent children.* However, this concept of the family is by no means acceptable in all parts of the world; neither are some of our other ideas about marriage and the family universally acceptable. In the United States we have come to assume that everyone should have a free choice in selecting a mate, but this is definitely not a universal custom. Likewise, the marriage ceremony to us is the legal, and often religious, contract between one man and one woman under which they are expected to live together and provide a home for their children. But this is not a universal pattern either. Furthermore, we reckon descent on both our mother's and our father's side of the family, but, in many societies, descent is calculated quite differently. Though the peoples of the world are coming into closer contact because of advances in communication, with the result that differences in culture are becoming less marked, there still remains a great diversity of customs related to the family.[1] Only one point of universality can be claimed, but this is important: Throughout history up to the present, among all peoples in the world, the family has been the continuing and basic primary group.

VARIETIES IN THE FAMILY PATTERN

Defining Family. The term *family,* unless otherwise indicated, is used in this chapter to designate the nuclear family described above. However, in common usage the term often has a broader meaning and includes such groups as a childless married couple, a parent living with one or more unmarried children, and also the *extended family,* which consists not only of parents and children, but also of other relatives such as grandparents and aunts and uncles. The Chinese extended family, before the days of communism, and the extended family of feudal Japan are perhaps the most widely publicized examples. The extended family in its most typical form is sometimes called the *patriarchal* family, which consists, if complete, of an older man and his wife (or wives), their married sons with wives and children, and their unmarried children.

Number of Mates. In the Western world the traditional, and in most places the only legal form of the marriage relationship, is *monogamy, meaning one husband and one wife.* This is by far the most widespread form of marriage all over the world, even where other forms are allowed or encouraged. *Polygamy* is the term used for *plural marriage,* but this is divided into two types: *polygyny, meaning one husband and two or more wives;* and *polyandry, meaning one wife and two or more husbands.* A

[1] Williams N. Stephens, *The Family in Cross-Cultural Perspective,* New York, Holt, Rinehart and Winston, Inc., 1963.

polygamous family may be thought of as two or more nuclear families, bound together by the fact that all the children have one parent in common. Some writers also recognize a form of plural marriage called *group marriage, under which several men are married to several women;* but most doubt whether this can be found anywhere as an established form of the marriage relationship.

Where polygyny is sanctioned, it is practiced both for its prestige value and for its economic advantages. Among the Tupis of South America, for instance, as well as in sections of Africa, wealth and distinction are measured in terms of how many wives a man has. Often the wives not only perform domestic services but also work in the fields and thus contribute to the support of the whole family group. Sometimes, as in the Trobriand Islands of Micronesia, the income of a chief will depend on the annual endowments received from the families of his wives. The first wife usually has the responsibility of administering the affairs of the household, but she is not necessarily the favorite wife. In many cases each wife keeps a separate household, and the husband rotates his attention among them.

Polyandry is comparatively rare. It is found mainly in some parts of Tibet and also among some aboriginal tribes of India, where a woman may marry two or more brothers. There are also cases of it among a certain few Eskimo tribes, in the Marquesas Islands, and among the Bahima in Africa, but it is the least common of the three main forms of marriage.

Probably the reasons monogamy has been the most popular type of marriage relationship are these: (1) in most places the ratio of the sexes is almost equal; (2) there are everywhere sets of rules governing division of labor between the sexes, and most men need a wife but cannot afford more than one; (3) no matter what type of mate selection is used, strong feelings of affection and loyalty often develop between one man and one woman, and any other wives are likely to feel unloved and neglected; and (4) in most cases monogamy probably offers the best environment for the rearing of children. But perhaps in making such a judgment we are being too much influenced by ethnocentrism, for in our Western civilization monogamy is the only legal form of marriage and the only one sanctioned by Judeo-Christian teachings.

Selection of Mates. The rules governing the choice of mates are as diverse as the societies in which they have developed. The rules differ not only from one society to another but they also differ between subgroups, such as social classes, within a society. They usually include various limitations on the persons of the other sex who are eligible to marry any given individual.

Let us first consider some of the rules governing eligibility. For instance, in India a person of one caste usually finds it impossible to marry an individual from another; and in a country like South Africa a person of one race is not permitted to marry someone from another race. In some societies one may never marry a blood relative, no matter how distant, and in others one may only marry within the kinship group.[2] The governing factor on the one hand is the fear of incest, or sexual activity among people who are close kinsmen; at the other extreme is the fear of marrying anyone too unlike the social group to which one belongs. In the case of certain small groups this necessarily means marrying a relative. In the majority of modern societies both forces operate, and therefore most people limit their search for acceptable marriage mates to persons not closely related but within the same general social group.

Then there are rules governing the actual choice of a marriage partner. In some societies parents plan marriages, because it is believed that a marriage is as much the concern of the families as of the individuals involved. This was true in feudal Japan, where the prime purpose of marriage was not the happiness of the young couple but the production of children who would be worthy to carry on the family name and honor. Another reason for parents taking the initiative is the belief that young people are too immature, inexperienced, and impulsive to consider properly all the factors necessary to an enduring and successful marriage. Therefore, the parents make the arrangements, either with or without the consent of the couple. Sometimes the parents are concerned with prestige or wealth, or are anxious for other reasons to have their children marry children of their friends; and so, as in parts of India, they arrange the marriage when the children are very young. In some societies the parents of a girl and her suitor agree on a marriage. The agreement may involve wife purchase, dowry, or a period of service by the suitor in the household of the prospective bride. In some primitive societies wives are obtained by kidnapping or by capture, perhaps in a raid on a neighboring tribe. Sometimes the kidnapping is genuine, sometimes it is a ritual that carries out a previous understanding. Where there are many fewer women than men but monogamy is still favored, one finds such solutions to the problem as the automatic inheritance by a younger brother of an older brother's widow. Except for actual kidnapping or capture, all the foregoing are examples of the type of mate selection we may call *marriage arrangement.*

The other principal type of selection we shall call *personal-choice mating.* This is the type we are familiar with in our own society, where we now take for granted the custom of personal freedom in mating, with relatively little interference from others. However, this freedom of choice is not restricted to our own country nor indeed to our own time, although we again emphasize that mating activities must always be carried on within the framework of the prevailing local laws and mores.

The techniques involved in personal-choice mating differ from one society to another, as do also the moral and legal sanctions governing them. For example, among the Polar Eskimos in earlier days there was not

[2] Marriage within the kinship or other social group is known as *endogamy. Exogamy* refers to marriage outside the group.

only complete freedom of choice by mutual agreement in the making of a permanent marriage, but before marriage there was also a sanctioned period of group living, during which experimental mating took place among the youth of the community; and children resulting from this arrangement were not considered illegitimate but belonged to the mother and the man who eventually became her husband. One of the criteria often used by the man in choosing a wife was her demonstrated ability to bear children, just as one of the criteria for the woman in choosing her husband was his demonstrated ability to provide for her and her children. The marriage was usually permanent, although divorce was allowed for certain reasons.

In the United States we have developed, over the years, a technique for mate selection that begins with a period of dating that, if the couple are sufficiently attracted to one another, leads on to engagement and marriage. Though there is as great a freedom of choice here as there was among the Polar Eskimos, the sanctioned rules governing the stages leading to marriage are very different, and even somewhat different from those found today in parts of western Europe. We shall return to a discussion of dating and courtship later.

Family Control. No one type of family control has ever been universal among mankind, but three main patterns have prevailed: *patriarchy,* or father control; *matriarchy,* or mother control; and shared control, or the *equalitarian* family.

In a patriarchal culture, the father is not only the head of the family, but he also considers that the children belong to him and that he has authority over their lives, even, in some cases, giving or selling them in marriage. The patriarchal family was found among the early civilizations around the Mediterranean and has been carried down through Christian civilizations to modern times. Our colonial fathers maintained the patriarchal system, and there are still many families in the United States, as well as in other parts of the world, where the father is the recognized authority in the family, although with some modifications.

Societies in which family control actually rests with the mother are exceptional. In most so-called matriarchal cultures, as among the Zuñi Indians in the Southwestern part of the United States, the mother does not usually have direct control, as one might suppose. More often it is the mother's brother who wields authority and controls the children. But the family takes the mother's name and usually lives with the mother's parents or other relatives. The husband may move in with them, but he is apt to spend more time with his own mother or his sisters' families, helping to control their children. Since with his own children he has no control status, he is actually more of a playmate and friend to them.

Only within the last one hundred years has family control in the United States gradually shifted toward the partnership, or equalitarian form. As women have gained equal educational and political rights and privileges, and tended to assume some of the economic responsibilities for the family as well, the control of the family has more and more come to be shared by both marriage partners.

Reckoning of Descent. In the Western world we use the *bilateral* method of reckoning descent. In other words, we reckon our ancestors on both our father's and our mother's side, which is correct in the sense that our biological inheritance comes from both. However, this is not the universal practice. Many societies use the *unilateral* method, whereby an individual belongs to *either* his father's or his mother's family. That is, his ancestors are reckoned only in the male line of descent, or in the female line, depending on whether the system is *patrilineal* or *matrilineal*. This may not seem logical to us, but it does simplify matters for those who use it and doubtless seems as logical to them as our own system, which is so much more complex. Imagine being asked to name one's ancestors twenty generations back. The African chief, who reckons his ancestry by patrilineal descent, would very likely know the twenty names required. In our society one would have to remember 1,048,576 names! Attention might be called here to the fact that while we acknowledge our descent bilaterally, the name we carry is that of our father, or husband, accenting the patrilineal line of ancestry.

Sometimes one finds—for instance, in Africa—a tendency among certain groups to use both patrilineal and matrilineal reckoning of descent, but with a different connotation. As A. L. Kroeber put it, "There is no conflict, because one descent transmits 'blood,' the other 'soul,' as in the Ashanti. . . . With the Wolof and the Baganda, descent is patrilineal except for the nobility and royalty, who derive from the mother. The Tuareg reverse the procedure: high office comes from the father, descent and inheritance from the mother."[3]

Space does not permit further discussion of variations in the family pattern, but the examples given above will illustrate the many diverse customs that prevail in families throughout the world.

If there is such diversity, are there basic points regarding marriage and the family on which all societies agree? We know that the family as an institution is universal, so there must be some underlying reasons for the survival of this institution through all the changes that have taken place in history. Perhaps the answer can be found in the functions of the family, for although ways of carrying them out differ with each set of circumstances, in every society the basic functions remain, in greater or lesser degree, the force motivating the family as an institution.

FUNCTIONS OF THE FAMILY

The functions of the family can be classified in many ways, but we have chosen to list them under seven headings: (1) biological, (2) physical

---

[3] A. L. Kroeber, *Anthropology*, New York, Harcourt Brace Jovanovich, Inc., 1948, p. 767.

care, (3) economic, (4) psychological, (5) educational, (6) recreational, and (7) social status.

In our Western civilization, rapid technological advances have brought great changes in almost every phase of our family life. Let us consider, then, the functions of the family in a modern industrial society, and especially in our own American society.

Biological Functions. The most important social function of the family is to reproduce the human species under conditions favorable to the children. In modern societies there is no need for producing a larger number of children—the danger is that we shall have too many—but there is need for better quality, for more children who are raised under conditions that will make them useful citizens.

People who marry and have children seldom do so because they feel an obligation to reproduce the race. Rather they are following the culture patterns of their society and are urged on by sex attraction and, often, by romantic love. Having children is one of the great experiences of life to which most look forward and from which they expect to receive great personal satisfaction. In our advanced industrial societies very few married couples voluntarily forego having children, even though their care is a heavy economic burden and a heavy drain on time and energy; but the majority of couples limit the number of their children by practicing some form of birth control.

Reasons for desiring more or fewer children may vary in different societies. In agricultural societies, especially if land is plentiful, people are likely to desire large families, because children tend to be an economic asset. In primitive societies many children may be desired, not only to carry on family lines in spite of a high death rate, but also because they are a source of power and prestige. Furthermore, in some primitive societies reproduction is a religious act, because it is believed that the souls of the dead are transmitted to newborn infants. Again, in many primitive societies a marriage cannot be permanent unless it produces children. Though this is not a recognized condition for permanence of marriage in America, we might in passing observe that divorces are more frequent when marriages are childless.

Under the biological functions of the family, we include the satisfaction of personal sexual impulses. In our society the traditions of the Judeo-Christian teachings, as well as the prevailing social taboos, oppose premarital and extramarital sex relations. The gradual change in attitudes toward sex from World War I to the present, accompanied by increasingly open and unrestricted treatment of the subject, has undoubtedly weakened these taboos but it has by no means destroyed them.

Only gradually do most marriage partners learn to adjust to one another sexually. The initial physical attraction is important, but satisfactory sexual gratification develops from good cultural conditioning toward sex, from an understanding of sex relations, from attitudes of mutual respect and sympathy, and from the wish to please one's mate in *all* interpersonal relations. When based on these foundations, the sexual privilege solidifies the husband-wife relationship. It also plays an important social role in the personality development of the marriage partners by contributing to their sense of security and contentment; this in turn helps to create a climate that is favorable to the rearing of children.

Physical Care Functions. A newborn infant is so helpless that its very life depends on the care given it by other human beings. In the extended family found in some societies, many people cooperate to give the child the physical care necessary. In our American society, according to the customs of the past, it was the mother who gave her baby the necessary physical care, while the father made provision for its economic needs. This pattern prevails in a majority of cases even now; but with the trend toward the equalitarian family, the picture has been changing. No one considers it unusual now for the father to assume some of the physical care of the children, especially if both parents have work outside the home, or if both are attending school. The trend toward urbanization, with the resulting absence of the father during the greater part of the children's waking hours, has led many family counsellors to advocate that he take over part of their physical care when he has a day off, in order to keep in closer contact with them.

Parents must provide some degree of physical care for the normal child until he is grown, which means on an average fifteen to twenty years. Not only food and shelter are required, but also care during illness, although in serious cases children are sent to hospitals. The time and effort parents spend in providing for the physical welfare of their children are often a burden, but they contribute greatly to creating the close personal relationships that are perhaps the chief reward of successful family life.

In the past, once the children were grown, they were expected to take over the physical care of their parents when the latter became ill or incapacitated by age. This is an important family function, which in an agricultural society was usually accepted as a matter of course. But today many families are unable or unwilling to care for aged parents; and sometimes the latter, when they can afford it, prefer to go into hospitals, nursing homes, or homes for the aged. Those with little money face a more difficult problem, but most have been helped by private pension plans or Social Security pensions and by Medicare or Medicaid.

Economic Functions. In every society, we find that by tradition and custom some tasks are recognized as women's work, whereas others are regarded as men's work. In part these distinctions have grown out of physical differences between the sexes, including the greater size and muscularity of men and the fact that women must bear and nurse the children. Though the particular tasks allotted to men or women vary considerably from one social group to another, in every society a husband and wife normally constitute a working team, each performing the functions expected of them by social tradition. Children observe the roles of the parents and grow up identifying themselves with tasks they have come to associate with members of their own sex.

A very important function of the modern family is to provide income and then to spend it to meet family needs. No family in our society can exist without money, and the primary responsibility for acquiring it falls on the father. On the other hand, it is usually the mother who takes the responsibility for cooking the food, doing the daily housework, and making the bulk of the family purchases. All of these are economic functions.

Some sociologists feel that the economic functions have largely been taken away from the family, since the majority of our people receive money for work done away from the family premises. It is true that the family is no longer the type of economic unit found, for instance, in colonial times. At that time most people in this country lived on farms. The parents were actually managers of a diversified factory. Food was produced and preserved, and clothing was made by taking all the steps from raising the sheep to spinning and weaving the wool and sewing the garments. Butter was churned, candles were molded, and in their "spare" time the women and girls knit socks and mittens. The children were taught to be useful almost as soon as they could walk, and by the time they were eight or so, they could perform many tasks that contributed to their own support.

In modern times even the farm family has changed. Farmers tend to specialize more on producing certain crops for the market, and they use machines for doing much of their work. For their own needs they largely depend on manufactured furniture, ready-made clothing, and processed foods. Although farm children are expected, as a rule, to do more chores than city children, it is because there still are more for them to do. Yet they are not as necessary to the family's economic production as in the past for several reasons. Today the farm family often buys food that it formerly produced for itself; also there are fewer routine chores to be performed because horses have been replaced by tractors, and many farms raise no livestock at all; and finally, machines have taken over many tasks that once were performed by people, including the milking of cows on dairy farms. In the large industrial city the family's economic needs are satisfied almost entirely by ready-made goods bought with the father's, and sometimes also with the mother's, wages. The children cannot help much, and therefore they are economic liabilities.

Nevertheless, providing a means of support is still a family function of first importance. The method, to be sure, has changed, at least in the Western world, so that the burden is now carried almost exclusively by the parents. But the *responsibility* for the means of support always rested on one or both of the parents, and this has not changed.

Psychological Functions. Important functions of the family relate to its intangible influences on personality and character. Here we need to remind ourselves, when we say "the family," that we all start our lives in

"Somewhere along the line we've failed as parents, Martha . . . ." (Courtesy William Conlin and *The Saturday Evening Post.*)

one family and, when grown, normally continue in a second family of our own choosing and creating. Personality development receives its greatest stimulus in the early years, but it is not brought to a halt with the arrival of maturity. A certain amount of development takes place throughout life because of the constant adjustments one must make and the responsibilities one must fulfill, especially within the intimacy of the nuclear family.

If family relationships affect the personality development of the husband and wife, they affect that of the child very much more. The family is the child's first social contact. In the first ten years of its life the parents do much to influence the basic attitudes and emotional qualities the child will later show in his adult personality. Both parents share this responsibility, and neither can adequately discharge it alone. Between them, if they are perceptive and have the will, they can give a child that sense of security that most psychologists believe is essential to the development of an emotionally stable and responsive personality. A child must have affection, someone to whom he can turn in time of trouble. In rare cases of extreme rejection by parents, young children may turn inward and become autistic to the extent that they cannot talk or in any way respond to other human beings. But love is not enough. To be secure a child must know what is expected of him; he must be able to trust his parents and he must be disciplined firmly but not harshly when he goes beyond the bounds of acceptable conduct. Increasingly, as he becomes able to meet them, he should be given responsibilities so that he can develop the independence and confidence that will enable him, when he grows up, to assume adult obligations.

Today no function of the family is more important than that of providing its members with a small group in which affection, companionship, and loyalty prevail. Strong family ties help to counterbalance the impersonality of urban life and to give people something to hold on to if they move from one community to another. It is said that children in later life can overcome the effects of extreme poverty more successfully than they can the effects of indifference or rejection, neglect and mistreatment, or overindulgence within the family.

When the child has brothers or sisters, these also play a role in his personality development through the interaction of affection, discipline, work, and play, and by the example of their own attitudes. In no other area does collective responsibility or lack of responsibility play such an influential role as in the psychological one, and probably it is also the area within which the family can be most firmly fused together into a social unit.

All members of the family are influenced by external relationships, often very deeply; however, it must again be stressed that the family is not only the initial social contact, but it is the continuing one and therefore has a proportionately greater influence on personality.

Educational Functions. In any home and in almost any culture, the child is given his most basic education during the first five years, because it is then that his attitudes toward learning are definitely established. If he is satisfied in his quest for knowledge in his early years, he will be stimulated to want to learn more when he reaches the stage of formal education. If, however, he is frustrated, he is apt to develop a feeling of defeatism that will carry over into his schooling.

The parents in a pioneer family, if they themselves were educated and if no schools were available, did not consider it unusual to teach reading, writing, and other subjects to their children at home. Today schools have taken over the function of formal education almost completely. There are good reasons for this, some of which we shall mention later in Chapter 16. At this time we merely point out that one effect of shifting education from home to school has been to give all members of the family greater independence. The children must learn to "stand on their own feet" in their many school relationships; mothers have more time to engage in social activities, pursue hobbies, or work outside the home.

Although the parents have given the responsibility for most of their children's schooling to the educators, they have not necessarily lost interest in the children's educational progress; the activities of the Parent-Teacher associations attest to this. Parents also contribute to the child's education in many other ways. Besides training him in his early years, they supplement his schooling to some degree by aiding and encouraging him and by arousing his interest in music, art, literature, household management, or anything else in which they may be interested.

Moral and religious training was once taken for granted as a family function. The complaint is made that today many parents seem to be indifferent about religious training or seem to believe that it should be left exclusively to the churches and synagogues. However, the child does receive moral training, good or bad, in his own home through the attitudes the parents express every day toward people and events; and even though much religious education has been relegated to the churches, the child's basic ideas of God and moral principles are still received from the family. Such concepts as truth and honor, duty and service, are directly related to the home environment.

Thus we see that although the emphasis has been shifted, the family continues to play a significant role in education.

Recreational Functions. In our modern industrial culture the need for recreation is great. In the first place, much of our work is confining or monotonous, and for many it is carried on only to earn money. At the same time, our machine technology has made possible shorter hours of employment and longer hours of leisure. Whereas two or three generations ago men commonly toiled twelve and fourteen hours a day, six days a week, we now consider the forty-hour week as standard. To be sure, this forty-hour week is to some degree an illusion. Many employees normally work overtime and count on this extra pay as part of their regular income. Others are "moonlighters" and depend on a second job to supplement the wages from their regular one. Still others are business or professional men whose work days have no definite limit. Nevertheless, there are large numbers of workers in routine jobs who do have more spare time than ever before. The questions we are concerned with here are What are these workers doing with all their extra leisure? and Is the family helping to meet their increased needs for recreation?

The provision of recreation has always been a function of the American family. Before the days of the automobile and the shorter work week, outings were few and far between. What recreation people had was centered in the home. This is still true in societies that are not as technologically advanced as ours. But in the United States, as a result of the machine age, a long list of recreational activities has gradually been brought within the reach of almost everyone. However, most of these newer activities are not provided by the family, but by the larger community of which it is a part.

Government at various levels has recognized the need for recreation and has provided an astonishing number of facilities, including playgrounds, public parks, field houses, branch libraries, and swimming pools. Community play programs are common. The churches have instituted many kinds of recreational activities for all ages. The latest improvements in large factories include ambitious recreational facilities for all employees to enjoy during their lunch period or after work. Clubs of one kind or another have sprung up everywhere. Frequently, every member of the family belongs to at least one club or organized group. There are the Scouts, the Rotary clubs, the 4-H clubs, the Y's, the women's clubs, and hosts of others. And last but not least, the commercial entertainment field has grown tremendously. There are movies, theaters, bowling alleys, skating rinks, night clubs, art classes, concerts, and professional ball games—the list is ever expanding.

The very young child still customarily plays at home; but beginning at the age of two or three, efforts are made by most parents to introduce him to outside experiences as a logical step in his social development. If the child has brothers and sisters, the need for this is less urgent; but lacking them, he begins early to play with others outside the home, and he may even be sent to a "head start" or nursery school. As he grows older, his recreational activities increase, and both he and his parents find more and more of their recreational experiences outside the home.

But in spite of the development of outside interests, the family still continues to be the hub for many recreational activities. Recreation rooms have become popular, and almost every home has a radio and a television set. Add to this the reading, hobbies, music, visiting by friends, card games, and general relaxation common to most homes, and it is evident that the family still provides important recreational opportunities for its members. Then consider the family trips during vacations and weekends and the family swims and picnics and outings of all kinds—all of which have been made possible by the automobile. They may not be home centered, but they are family-centered activities and are becoming more popular with each succeeding year.

Because so much emphasis is now being placed on recreation, family life is greatly influenced by the extent to which recreation is related to the home. It is generally agreed that if parents encourage legitimate types of recreation that can be carried out at home, and if they provide leadership for some of the children's activities outside the home, the family is more apt to find stability and happiness. In addition, the parents themselves need to share recreational activities together to add to their own personality development and sense of happiness. The family has not lost the function of providing recreation. It has given much of the responsibility for it to others, necessarily; but there are still many kinds of recreation that can best be enjoyed in the family group.

Social Status Functions. In Chapter 12, attention is directed to the status-conferring function of the family. Many factors combine to give a family status: income, father's occupation, nationality, family background, and education, to mention a few.

Children like the feeling of satisfactory status. They enjoy social approval. We say it gives them moral support to know that their family is admired and respected by the neighbors. They are proud to belong to it, and they develop a certain self-confidence. Opposed to this picture is the one of the socially rejected family, where the children are apt to become either defeatist or belligerent. These are obviously two extremes, and there are many shadings of rank in between. We give them as examples because many teachers and psychologists have noticed how closely related family status is to the kind of adjustment children make in the schoolroom and on the playground. It becomes even more important to the older, teenage child, who begins to realize what prestige or influence can mean in everyday associations.

People who are not satisfied with what Ralph Linton calls their *ascribed,* or inherited, status, will try to win, perhaps through education and occupation, an *achieved* status on a higher level. This status will, in turn, be inherited by their children. Not only do children acquire status on being born into a family, but the parents individually acquire the socially desirable marriage status before the children arrive. Almost all societies give this status a high rating, and likewise, almost every society scorns, to some degree, bachelors and spinsters. This is especially true in primitive or in agricultural societies, where the unmarried individual is likely to be at a great disadvantage in meeting the needs of daily life.

One more thing should be said: It is sometimes possible for a family to change its social status, but such change is the exception rather than the rule. Most families stay at the same general social level into which the parents were born, though in rapidly developing industrial countries like the United States there has been a gradual increase in the proportion of the population that has achieved middle-class status, a trend that will be discussed in Chapter 12.

This summary of the functions of the family should make clear their fundamental importance to human social life. All of the higher animals have a form of family life, but the human family has had to develop much more complex functions, partly because of the prolonged period of dependent childhood characteristic of man. Without families capable of performing these necessary functions, our human societies as we know them could not exist.

THE AMERICAN FAMILY

Though the basic functions performed by the family are similar in all societies, we have seen that the family pattern as we know it in the United States is not a universal one. In this section we shall first describe briefly the distinctive characteristics of the pattern that is familiar to us. Then we shall discuss in more detail the establishment and the development of a typical American family.

Characteristics of the American Family. At the risk of seeming contradictory, the first characteristic of American families to which we call attention is the existence of a great variety in family patterns. With the diversity of our ethnic, racial, and religious backgrounds, it is natural to find variations in attitudes and practices relating to family life. This is why anyone trying to describe a "typical American family" finds it necessary to select rather arbitrarily certain characteristics that, though not always found, seem to be most common. Because ours is so predominantly an urban society, the "typical" pattern we have selected is that of the urban, middle-class family. If a good many of our families have not achieved the characteristics of this typical family, often they are at least striving to do so, for it is constantly held up to them as a model to imitate.

This family is nuclear rather than extended; it is democratic rather than autocratic. Though the father is the titular head, the family tends to be equalitarian rather than father dominated. The union of the parents is voluntary and follows a period of dating and courtship that strongly stresses romantic love. Marriage is monogamous, with taboos against sexual activity with anyone other than one's mate. Children of both sexes are given about equal privileges and responsibilities as well as a great deal of freedom, and often they have a share in the decision making of the family. Frequently both parents work outside the home; and without doubt their average standard of living is higher than anywhere else in the world. Active participation in religious, recreational, and educational activities is encouraged. Sometimes these activities are family centered, but often they are not.

Finally, this typical family is considered the "bulwark of democracy," because it is the social unit where two adult personalities, working and playing together cooperatively, can develop and freely express themselves; and also because it provides the training ground where children first become oriented to the ideals and processes of a democratic society. However, if we are to judge by the divorce rate, the American family of today is less stable than in the past.

Dating as a Preliminary to Mate Selection. In discussing the stages in the development of a family, we have chosen to start with dating. Dating is a modern, and largely an American, social phenomenon. A date is merely a social engagement for a day or an evening involving two people of opposite sex, usually a boy and a girl in their teens or an unmarried man and woman. But a whole group of customs have grown up about dating to give it importance as a prelude to marriage and to the establishment of a family.

Dating, for one thing, serves as a chance for young people to get acquainted with the opposite sex on a more intimate and more mature plane than would be possible in group activities. For another, it gives them an opportunity to evaluate themselves in an interpersonal situation outside the family. For a third, it is a form of recreation. Fourth, it is a way of becoming further socialized by the give-and-take frankness of adolescence. Fifth, it is a way of finding out what qualities in others are compatible with one's own personality. Finally, it carries status or prestige value.

Dating is seldom expected to end in marriage. Usually a young man dates several girls before finding one whom he likes well enough so that he wants to "go steady" with her. Even when he goes steady, he may do so with a succession of girls. This, too, is a modern concept, in that devoting one's date life for a time exclusively to one girl no longer automatically implies courtship. It can simply mean a pleasant and convenient form of date insurance, an arrangement that can easily be terminated by either party when boredom sets in, when there is a change in status, or when a new and, for the time being, more attractive partner becomes available.

An eighth-grade girl explains it thus: "Next year we'll be in high school and then I'll ditch him to date a sophomore. No freshman girl *ever* dates a freshman!" Studies have shown that dating reaches its peak in prestige value in college. Fraternities and sororities have, for instance, been known to value their members by the demand for them as dates and by the prestige this brings to their house.

Choosing a Mate. Eventually, after a period of steady dating during which a pair of young people have become acquainted and very much attracted to one another, they may decide that "this is really love." Although this stage may lead to marriage, it is still not as binding as a formal engagement, nor even as the courtship stage of fifty years ago. However, more seriousness and greater intensity of feeling set this development apart from mere dating.

The word *romance* is a little out of style today, but the kind of love that brings together many modern young couples does not seem to differ greatly from what in a past generation was called romantic love. To be sure, there are always people incapable of forming intense emotional attachments to others and for whom love is apt to be a rather pedestrian experience based largely on liking and practical considerations. Perhaps even romantic love is a little more tempered by "realism" than in the past, but that is not too certain. Clearly one essential ingredient in love between a man and woman, just as in the past, is sexual attraction; but it is very misleading to explain an intense love, or even an infatuation, in purely sexual terms. There are millions of young men and women who are well endowed sexually, but the loved one who counts for everything is always a certain very special person. A strong and developing emotional attraction between a young man and a girl as they exchange and share experi-

"I'm in love, Mother. Please try to understand what that means." (Courtesy Syd Hoff.)

ences and explore each other's personalities always contains an element of romance, even though sexual attraction is a vital factor in rendering it intense and exciting.

Love between a man and woman sometimes, though not always, grows out of a sudden attraction. Such an attraction may be aroused by hair or eyes, by a face or smile, by a spark of recognition. The usual events thereafter are dates, delightful exchanges of confidences and caresses, and perhaps eventually engagement and marriage. Though people differ in their personalities and emotions, more often than not love is a thrilling experience that makes the lover feel as if he (or she) were walking on clouds. He tends to endow the loved one with every charm and virtue, so that she becomes "the one girl in the world." Freud, who was no romantic, called this "the over-estimation of the sexual object." Romantic love that is not balanced by realism may better be called infatuation. Sometimes it develops so quickly that the lovers have had no time to become really acquainted. As a result, each may create a wonderful but unreal image of the other and thus may become victims of what sociologists call the *romantic illusion*. Perhaps they then marry in haste, only to discover later that they have little in common and possibly do not even like one another. Unhappiness follows and probably the divorce court.

Love has strong overtones of romance when it is new, novel, and exciting; but for some people a new partner may be sufficient to rekindle the old feeling a dozen times or more. There is also the kind of love, perhaps commoner between older people, that might be called *companionship love*. This also leads to marriage for many, and occasionally it culminates after marriage in an intense affection that is a form of romantic love.

The sociologists and "realistic" novelists may have made some progress, after years of effort, in disillusioning young people concerning the powers of romantic love; but if so, their success does not seem to have contributed anything toward reducing the divorce rate and increasing the stability of marriage. Actually, romantic love, grounded within a realistic framework, may make a great contribution to the success of a marriage, provided only that the two parties have enough in common to develop it into a deep and permanent attachment. What must not be forgotten is that we can love someone intensely even though we recognize that he or she has faults. This may happen when a person has other qualities that greatly attract us and when strong bonds of sympathy and understanding have been developed.

In our American culture of three or four generations ago, and in some other societies even today, love between a couple considering marriage was often of secondary importance. Economic considerations, or security, or social prestige, or the desire to have children—any one or all four—might have come first. But with the shift in emphasis away from the patriarchal, authoritarian society to a democratic one, and with the trend toward equality of economic opportunities for women, the primary consideration has come to be love, along with much more stress on companionship. In other words, we have moved from emphasis on the practical to emphasis on the personal and psychological. That other factors play an important role in mate selection cannot be denied, but even if all other factors are favorable, to most in our society, especially young people, it is almost unthinkable to marry if one is not also in love.

For love to develop, one must obviously have opportunities to meet and become acquainted with eligible members of the opposite sex. Some sociologists believe that cities offer wider opportunities for social contact than the more rural areas, but others feel that the impersonal nature of urban life actually makes such contacts more difficult. In any case, opportunities to meet members of the other sex come most often in school, church, or business, through mutual friends or through members of one's family.

The comparatively great mobility of our population, as well as our emphasis on individual freedom, makes possible a wider field of eligible marriage partners than in most societies. No one is rigidly limited, unless he so chooses, to his own religious, ethnic, or national group. The few laws relating to the choice of a marriage mate are mainly concerned with prohibiting marriage between close relatives and setting minimum age limits. But though the law may not restrict people very much in their choices, various social pressures do operate, and as a result people tend to marry within their own religious group, racial group, and social class. However, the social pressures that bring this about are not as inflexible in our society as in many others.

Unless love rests on firm foundations, it may fade quickly. Often the engagement period, following a public announcement of intent to marry, is a time of testing, during which both parties have an opportunity to change their minds. Statistics are said to show that engagements of three months or less lead to three times as many divorces as those of two years or more. This is largely because there is less time for a couple to test their love, and for each to evaluate the other's personality, characteristics, cultural backgrounds, family relationships, and attitudes toward common problems. Longer engagements allow time to discover mistakes and to withdraw from the marriage agreement before it is too late.

For a number of decades, gradual changes have been taking place in the United States and other Western countries in social attitudes toward sex. How much effect such changes have had on the process of mate selection is difficult to say. Modern studies, beginning with those of Kinsey more than twenty years ago, indicate that there has been no sudden great change in the patterns of sex behavior, though there seems little doubt that over the years there has been a marked increase in extramarital sex relations among college and high school students. Some explain this by the fact that our attitudes toward sex and sex behavior are now much more open, matter-of-fact, and tolerant than they were at the beginning of this century, or even in the 1920's when this change was already well under way.

This more open attitude toward sex may have been one factor in lowering the average age at first marriage. Young people acquire social and sexual sophistication earlier and begin sooner to consider marriage as a real possibility. Other factors contributing to this result include greater employment opportunities for women and the greater willingness of many parents to give financial aid to married students in college. Whether premarital sex relations bring about earlier marriages, except in some cases of pregnancy, is debatable.

Forecasting Success or Failure in Marriage. Sociologists have devised marriage-prediction tests that attempt to forecast success or failure with a fair degree of dependability. Most writers agree that background factors —especially the early conditioning received through home environment and the parent-child relationship—are particularly influential in determining the ability of each mate to contribute to the success of a marriage. It has often been said that the most important single background factor predictive of marital happiness is the degree of happiness of the respective parents of a married couple. One of the first studies of the influence of early home environment on marital success was made by Lewis M. Terman in the 1930's. He concluded that the ten following background factors contribute most to good marital adjustment.[4]

1. Superior happiness of parents.
2. Childhood happiness.
3. Lack of conflict with mother.
4. Home discipline that was firm, not harsh.
5. Strong attachment to mother.
6. Strong attachment to father.
7. Lack of conflict with father.
8. Parental frankness about matters of sex.
9. Infrequency and mildness of childhood punishment.
10. Premarital attitude toward sex that was free from disgust or aversion.

Since Terman's day sociologists have listed various conditions or qualities that have been found conducive to success in marriage. Those mentioned most frequently include:

1. Love.
2. Compatibility.
3. Emotional maturity, including the ability to assume responsibility.
4. Some common interests outside the home.
5. Adaptability.
6. Moral conservatism.

[4] Lewis M. Terman et al., *Psychological Factors in Marital Happiness,* New York, McGraw-Hill, Inc., 1938, p. 372.

7. A degree of conventionality, as measured by such things as church affiliation, leisure-time activities, and social attitudes.
8. Sociability.
9. Cultural homogeneity, as indicated by similar social backgrounds.
10. Amicable relations between each spouse and his parents.
11. Similar IQ's.
12. Good health, mental and physical.

One could expand the list—for example, to include a sense of humor—but the above items will suffice to show that in the process of mate selection, many considerations should be taken into account. Often people with similar attitudes toward the basic issues of life can adjust rather well in marriage even though their personalities are markedly different. Sometimes differences in personality are complementary and seem to aid in making good adjustment.

Marriage. *Marriage* as a social arrangement is known throughout the world—that is, every society distinguishes between casual unions of the sexes and socially recognized or legal unions. Earlier we defined *marriage* in our society as *a more or less permanent contract between a man and a woman under which they are expected to live together and to provide a home for their children.* The contract has legal, and in many cases religious, sanction.

A couple may be attracted to each other and marry for purely personal reasons, but their marriage creates, from the very first day, many new relationships and responsibilities involving not only themselves but also the two families from which they came and various other social groups. The partners immediately assume new statuses: the husband-wife status, the in-law status, and that of a married couple. Whether the young people before their marriage lived with their own families or apart from them, they now become in some respects an independent unit, customarily establishing their own household and taking responsibility for its maintenance. This independence is a much-coveted goal. Yet they no longer have the same kind of freedom each may have had as a single person, nor the same privacy. Each must immediately begin to share life in the most intimate ways with the other—and only with the other—both in the personal and the practical realms. In all the social groups to which they belong, their status has also changed. They are no longer the eligible man and woman, available for dating. Their roles have changed toward each other, toward their families, and toward outside social groups.

Such a major change of roles, even though desirable and pleasurable, involves a good deal of adjustment. This has not been made easier by the swift pace of social change in America. In a static society the role expected of each spouse is well understood, but in a dynamic society such as ours it is easy to be uncertain as to just what is expected of one. This confusion may be increased in cross-marriages between faiths, nationalities, or races. Even if these hazards are eliminated, our common heritage of diversity is constantly changing the social pattern for everyone. Hence, adaptability has become an important personality characteristic in marital adjustment.

We have mentioned change in status as one factor calling for adaptability in marriage. New roles follow this change, especially for the woman. In our society the girl who has had experience in completely managing a household before marriage is very rare. But this is exactly what she is expected to do as soon as she is married. She may have some help from her husband with certain tasks, but the major responsibility for the physical care of a home is generally hers. If she has been pursuing a career before marriage, she may be frustrated not to continue, or she may be happily relieved, but in either case she must adapt to a new pattern of life. If she continues to work outside her home, the central problem is still there.

There are several areas in which adjustments must be made for successful marriage. These include sex relations, the spending of the family income, social activities, and relations with in-laws and friends. Happiness in marriage is highly correlated with satisfactory adjustments in these areas, and probably readiness to adjust is a strong factor in success. A will to succeed is no less important in marriage than in occupational fields. Further, this will must be maintained throughout the entire period of a marriage, for there never comes a time when some adjustment is not necessary.

Rearing a Family. Arnold M. Rose has given a good description of the impact a child makes on a marriage:

> If marriage requires an important role change, having the first child requires an equally important and difficult one. Assuming the responsibility of a household is not nearly so serious as assuming the responsibility of raising a child. A household can always be broken up, a child cannot be discarded. The relationship of a husband and wife changes when there is a third person in the family with whom they must interact. A child makes strong demands on one's time, freedom, mobility, and sense of privacy and possession. There are countless new techniques and skills one must learn as a new parent, and one cannot avoid the responsibility of learning them and learning them rapidly. A helpless infant, who must make all sorts of demands on his parents in order to survive and to develop physically, emotionally, and socially, probably forces many more changes in the lives of his parents than their marriage does.[5]

In spite of the responsibility and very hard work children bring to a couple, most people feel that the rewards are compensatory. However, the number of children couples are willing to have is smaller than two or three generations ago; and following a temporary rise in the 1940's and the 1950's, the average has been dropping again for at least a decade. The argument over whether it is easier to rear one or several children will never be

---

[5] By permission from Arnold M. Rose, *Sociology: The Study of Human Relations,* New York, Alfred A. Knopf, Inc., 1956, pp. 161–162. © Arnold M. Rose, 1956.

settled. There are advantages in both situations; and studies seem to indicate that, contrary to public opinion, only children are likely to be as well
adjusted and mature as others. Most couples probably want at least two
children, but for many reasons they often have only one and sometimes
none.

Family disorganization and divorce are serious problems, and we shall
deal with them later. However, for many years these problems have received so much attention that the vast number of relatively well-adjusted
families have been almost overlooked. For this reason, it may be well to
call attention to a study that dealt especially with the number and character of successful families.

About a dozen years ago Carle Zimmerman of Harvard University and
Lucius Cervantes of St. Louis University completed a very extensive survey
of family life in the United States. They were concerned, among other
things, with what made a family successful and with the percentage of
such families. They conducted their research on sixty thousand United
States families by asking high school students to answer thirty-four key
questions about their own families and about five closest family friends.
After studying these questionnaires, they set up as a minimum standard
the following three tests: (1) no divorce or desertion; (2) no juvenile arrest;
and (3) no children dropping out of school before completing the senior
year of high school.

The above tests have obvious limitations and are certainly not adequate
to judge the success or failure of every family. Nevertheless, it is interesting to note that, using them, Zimmerman and Cervantes found that 85
per cent of American families were, at that time, successful.[6] After all the
unrest of the 1960's, the results of such a study might now be different.
However, no research project is needed to tell us that, even today, the
typical middle- or working-class American family is far from decadent.
Daily observation and contacts with our acquaintances and friends tell us
unmistakably that most such families are adjusting to the changing scene
of the twentieth century and achieving a fair degree of satisfaction and
happiness.

Later Years. As children grow up and leave home for college, for a job,
or to establish their own households, the family dwindles in size to the
original two. The age at which this occurs is becoming younger than in the
past, because people have been marrying earlier and having their last
children at a younger age.

For many there then follow a number of years, perhaps as many as
fifteen or twenty, before retirement—years in which there is time for more
active participation in social and civic affairs or, for women who have not
had employment outside the home before, for taking a job.

Again adjustment is required. Companionship is now the strong bond

---

[6] Carle C. Zimmerman and Lucius F. Cervantes, *Successful American Families*, New York,
Pageant Press, 1960.

"Remember the night we met and I lost my glass slipper?" (Courtesy Edward
Frascino. Copyright 1969 *Saturday Review, Inc.*)

between the couple. Shared experiences throughout the child-rearing years
cement this bond, but a new and satisfactory pattern of life without the
children at home must be developed if the couple is to remain happy. For
the parents no less than for the children, it is a period of weaning or emancipation. When the children return on visits, their relationship is now on
an adult, companionable basis; and if there are grandchildren, they provide the grandparents with a new interest in life.

When the time finally comes for the husband (and wife, if she is employed) to retire from a regular job, many couples, if in good health, still
have years of activity ahead. This is especially true when workers, as is
often the case, are arbitrarily retired at sixty-five. Opposition is growing
to this practice, because the conditions of life in the United States make
it possible for many people to retain enough youthfulness and vigor to be
productive long after sixty-five. Various occupations do not have definite
age limits, and some that do are gradually modifying their rules.

Surveys have been made that indicate, not surprisingly, that income is
an important factor in a satisfactory adjustment to life after retirement.
A study made several years ago found that most retired couples with an
income of five thousand dollars or more were reasonably happy. An
adequate income not only gives a couple a wider range of choices as to
how and where to live, but it makes travel possible and facilitates the
development of hobbies.

Successful adjustment to retirement also depends on personal temperament. No rules can be laid down that will apply to all. Some individuals welcome the release from routine and/or responsibility; they are flexible enough to have little trouble in finding interesting ways to spend their time; others feel lost when deprived of the work on which they have spent most of their lives. Health, too, is an important factor. The man (or woman) who still has health and energy on retirement is likely to find things that he wants to do. There is always the possibility of taking on a part-time job, especially if he needs more income.

Sometimes a man who has held an important and respected position for much of his life feels discarded on retirement. As Ruth Cavan puts it, he is still motivated by his self-image at his retirement, but he becomes separated from his previous roles and from his evaluative groups, that is, from those with whom he worked and who depended on him or regarded him with respect. He tends to become a social isolate, for he finds distasteful the self-image he now sees reflected in old, and perhaps new, groups.[7] His need is to develop new roles that will be accepted and respected by those he associates with.

But not only a husband who has been the breadwinner must make adjustments. His wife must too. She does not retire but must still manage the household, and her routine is likely to be considerably changed when her husband no longer goes to work every day. She has less freedom, and because he is at home more, he is likely to make greater demands upon her. Unless he finds ways to keep busy, she may resent his leisure while she still has work to do.

Important to the happiness of most retired couples are social contacts. This means not only keeping in contact with old friends but also engaging in activities that enable them to make new friends.

When either member of a marriage partnership dies, problems are created for the survivor, who must then develop a new life pattern. Because, on the average, wives are younger than their husbands and women live longer than men, there are far more widows than widowers. Cavan believes that a widow is often better able to build a satisfactory life for herself and a favorable self-image because she usually retains some of her old group memberships and can attack her problems realistically by increasing her activities in such fields as church work, civic affairs, and voluntary services to schools, hospitals, or charities.

According to the Bureau of the Census, of the 7.4 million widowed persons who in 1968 were over sixty-five years old, about 4.9 million were household heads, the majority of whom lived alone. Of the 2.5 million elderly people who did not maintain their own households, three fourths of the women and more than two thirds of the men were members of families and therefore had at least one relative in the home for com-

---

[7] Ruth S. Cavan, "Self and Role in Adjustment in Old Age," *Human Behavior and Social Processes*, edited by Arnold Rose, Boston, Houghton Mifflin Company, 1962, pp. 526 ff.

panionship.[8] Here again, however, adjustments are necessary within the family group.

FAMILY DISORGANIZATION AND THE BROKEN FAMILY

A disorganized family is one that does not perform its functions well, usually because there is serious discord between the parents or because the family unit is broken by the loss of one parent, either through withdrawal from the family or by death. In this section we are primarily concerned with family disorganization that ends in or results from *divorce, separation,* or *desertion.* We shall give special attention to divorce, but it should not be forgotten that many marriages end, practically speaking, through permanent separation or desertion. Indeed, desertion is so relatively common in the lower classes that it has sometimes been called "the poor man's divorce." Death is in a somewhat different category from the other causes of broken families, but it, too, presents a family with problems that are difficult to solve. Let us consider briefly some of the factors that contribute to family disorganization.

Factors in Family Disorganization. Because no two people have just the same physical and mental characteristics, the same cultural heritage, the same capacities, or the same ideals, some conflict takes place in every marriage. However, it does not become a serious problem unless some vital attitude or resource is lacking in one or both of the marriage partners.

Lack of Love and Affection. The constant adjustments the marriage relationship requires are not likely to be made adequately unless both parties are strongly motivated, and the most effective motivation is a deepseated and mutual feeling of love or affection. Though love and sexual attraction are not the only components needed for a happy marriage, in most cases they are nevertheless vital. To marry solely for a home, or convenience, or money, or social position is to court marital discord and unhappiness.

Differences in Social Background. Incompatibility due to differences in family and cultural backgrounds can be a factor in family disorganization. These differences may involve not only manners, speech, and personal interests but also attitudes toward such vital problems as moral standards, sex, money, the rearing of children, in-laws, and social relationships in general. When the cultural conditioning of the mates is at great variance, the resolution of such problems may be extremely difficult and may require more understanding and character than some people can command.

Money Problems. Another important factor in family disorganization is tension over money. Such tension may result from actual poverty. How-

[8]*Current Population Reports,* Series P-20, No. 187, August 11, 1969.

"I wonder if you'd mind signing this petition asking my husband to take me out to dinner." (Reprinted, courtesy of *The Chicago Tribune*.)

ever, assuming the family has an income above the poverty level, it is usually not the *amount* of money available that causes friction; rather, it is *how* it should be spent. In this connection it is interesting to note that the survey conducted by Zimmerman and Cervantes[9] shows that the children most likely to get into trouble with the police come from the two economic extremes: families with very low incomes or families with exceptionally high incomes. In the former group there is a large percentage of broken homes, working mothers unable to provide supervision for the children, and crowded living conditions. In the latter the trouble stems from too much freedom coupled with too much money.

However, despite the troubles of some children from well-to-do families, it is usually true that the higher the income and occupational status of a group, the lower is its divorce rate. The exception to this rule is that at the bottom of the scale the unskilled are shown to have almost as low a divorce rate as the professional people at the top; but this is thought to be linked to the cost of divorce, for these people also have the highest rates of separation and desertion.

Personality Factors and Sex. The most explosive causes of family disorganization are personality factors. Obviously, alcoholics and sex perverts will disorganize almost any marriage; likewise, psychopaths, psychotics, and confirmed criminals. But much lesser personality difficulties than those of the groups mentioned are often responsible for broken homes. The domineering, the selfish, the oversensitive, the despondent, the antisocial, the irresponsible, the emotionally immature—all these reflect environmental inadequacies, and often hereditary inadequacies as well. Defects of this kind will destroy any marriage unless they can be overcome with the aid of a tolerant, patient, and loving mate.

Even very minor frictions will loom large for the emotionally immature. This is often the case with very young couples, especially those in their teens. Their general inexperience with life and its responsibilities causes

[9] Zimmerman and Cervantes, op. cit.

many of them to give up when confronted by commonplace day-to-day problems that do not fit the rosy picture they had in mind before marriage. They want the happiness they have looked for in marriage, but they are unwilling or unable to accept the responsibilities. At least one third of our teenage marriages end in divorce. Statistics show that women married below the age of eighteen have three times the divorce rate of those who first marry between twenty-two and twenty-four years of age.

Personality factors play an extremely important part in sexual adjustment in marriage. Though sexual problems are frequent causes of marital conflict and divorce, their basis is seldom physiological in nature. Instead, difficulties in sex adjustment usually result either from personality conflicts or from fears, ignorance, or misinformation about sex.

Other Factors in Family Disorganization. Disagreements over how to rear children are another disorganizing factor in marriage. Such disagreements are hard on parents but are most damaging to the children, because they are torn in their loyalties and made to feel insecure by the inconsistent treatment their parents give them.

Difficult problems are created by the illness or bad health of a parent. Often poor health means long separations while the person afflicted is in hospitals or sanitariums. Or it can mean that the breadwinner is no longer able to provide for his family. The death of a parent is almost certain to cause a severe disturbance in the family, not only because of the personal loss but because the way of life of the family is disrupted and their social status changed.

Another situation that appears occasionally is the inability of a couple to make the adjustments necessary for a happy life together after the children are grown. The husband continues in his work and may be even busier than before, but his wife may have lost her chief interest in life with the departure of the children, and so she is left without an emotional outlet. In addition, the couple may have lost their ability to communicate with one another in a satisfying way, so that perhaps the wife begins to wonder if "life is passing her by." Unless she can find other satisfying outlets for her energies and emotions, she may become so unhappy that she will dissolve the marriage.

One frequent cause of family disorganization is the situation that arises when a "triangle" is created—that is, when the affections of either the husband or the wife are transferred to an outsider. Usually this happens only when a marriage has not been very satisfactory, but there are situations in which the advent of a third party can break up a previously successful marriage.

When family strife and disorganization become severe and prolonged, the final stage is likely to be desertion or separation, or ultimately divorce. Because the rising divorce rate of the last sixty or more years is regarded by many as a major social problem, it merits our special attention.

The Divorce Problem. Divorce statistics are often used as a measure of family disorganization, and the present high divorce rate is often cited as proof that the American family is in serious trouble. However, higher divorce rates today than in the past are not entirely the result of more family disorganization. The reader should remember that a generation or two ago many couples were likely to avoid divorce even though their married life was very unhappy. They avoided it because it meant social ostracism; also, in the case of women, because there were few opportunities for them to earn a good living. On the other hand, perhaps many couples worked out their conflicts *because* of these and other restraints, thus eventually achieving a satisfactory marriage. Perhaps also, some couples were more cautious about entering the marriage relationship than they would be today when, because of our changed mores, divorce is easier to consider.

Table 6 shows the approximate ratio of divorces to marriages for certain

Year	Ratio
1890	1 to 18.0
1910	1 to 12.0
1930	1 to 5.8
1945	1 to 3.5
1950	1 to 4.3
1955	1 to 4.0
1960	1 to 3.9
1965	1 to 3.8
1970*	1 to 3.0

Table 6. *Approximate Ratio of Divorces to Marriages, 1890–1970*

* Based on provisional figures.
Source: U.S. Department of Health, Education and Welfare, Public Health Service.

years during the period 1890 to 1970. This ratio reached a high level in 1945, fell rather sharply until 1950, but later rose again to reach an all-time high in 1970.

Though we now have about one divorce for every three marriages, statistics show that at any particular time only a comparatively small portion to total families—about 10 per cent—are headed by divorced, separated, or widowed persons.[10] This is because many persons in these categories do not have children under eighteen living with them and thus cannot be classified statistically as heads of families; also, because divorced and widowed persons are not counted as such by the census if they have remarried.

When we consider, however, the large number of marriages that end in divorce, we must recognize that this constitutes a serious social problem, because the breaking up of a home as the result of discord leaves emotional scars on all its members. For the marriage partners, it means failure in an important area; for the children, if any, it means bewilderment and insecurity. Even the community at large is affected when there is unhappiness and unrest among a considerable number of its members. Such problems as juvenile delinquency, drug addiction, alcoholism, and even ill

[10] *Statistical Abstract of the United States,* Washington, D.C., Bureau of the Census, 1970, p. 38.

health are much more prevalent in broken homes. Although these conditions are sometimes found in well-integrated families, there is a clear relationship between the frequency of such problems and family stability.

Divorce is most frequent in the second or third year of marriage, and according to the latest available statistics, the median period of marriage before divorce is 7.1 years.[11] This would seem to indicate that marriages are often given a very short trial period. Modern couples demand more happiness from marriage than did their grandparents, and they are unwilling to continue it for the sake of convention or convenience if it does not yield the expected satisfactions. Particularly if there are no children, divorce is the easiest way out. However, it does not guarantee happiness. At best it brings relief from one kind of tension, only, in many cases, to create other kinds.

Legal Grounds for Divorce. There are many legal grounds for divorce, and they vary with the laws of each state. Adultery is at present the only ground accepted by all states. Below is a list of the most frequently recognized legal grounds for divorce in this country, arranged in order of the number of states recognizing their validity:[12]

Adultery	Separation
Desertion	Bigamy
Cruelty	Drug addiction
Felony conviction	Pregnancy at marriage (if unknown
Alcoholism	to husband)
Impotence	Fraudulent contract
Insanity	Violence
Neglect to provide	Indignities

Although the legal grounds for divorce are of some interest and significance, they often have little to do with the real reason behind the desire of a couple to end a marriage. Often a husband and wife who wish a divorce cooperate to bring about real or apparent fulfillment of the necessary legal conditions. Either acts are performed that fulfill the requirements for divorce, or facts are misrepresented in court by mutual agreement.

In September, 1969, the California legislature enacted into law a bill that was designed to improve this situation. Instead of the seven grounds for divorce that had previously existed in California, the new law provides only two: "irreconcilable differences" and "incurable insanity." Under the new law a marriage partner need not be declared guilty or at fault as was previously required. The purpose of the law is not to discourage attempts at reconciliation wherever that is possible. Rather, it is designed to make divorce easier for those who have mutually and irrevocably determined

---

[11] Ibid., p. 60.
[12] See *Information Please Almanac* 1971, New York, Dan Golenpaul Associates, p. 660.

that they want it, and at the same time to reduce the emotional and financial strains that often result from a broken marriage.[13] After the passage of this law, divorces rose in California from 121,000 in 1969 to 140,000 in 1970, but some California officials say that much of this rise resulted from Californians' getting divorces at home instead of in neighboring Nevada. The divorce rate in Nevada fell 15 per cent.[14]

DEALING WITH FAMILY DISORGANIZATION

As is the case with many social problems, family disorganization is a problem for which we cannot hope to find a complete solution. There will always be individuals who make mistakes in selecting marriage partners or who are incapable of making the adjustments or meeting the responsibilities any successful marriage requires. Likewise, there will always be families that suffer unavoidable misfortunes. But if we cannot hope to completely eliminate family disorganization, we can strive to reduce it to a minimum.

Most students of the family agree that the most hopeful approach to the problem lies in providing young people with better training and education in the nature and responsibilities of marriage. However, there is also some hope of progress through the improvement of marriage and divorce laws.

Improving Marriage and Divorce Laws. The trend in nearly every state has been toward making divorce, and the remarriage of the divorced, more difficult. However, since every state makes its own laws, we find many differences in them. Some states have laws designed to delay divorce and to encourage couples to reconcile their differences. Increasingly, domestic-relations courts are providing scientific counseling as part of their service. On the other hand, a very few states have laws designed to make divorce easy. The new California law that simplifies divorce procedures is regarded by many as an important reform in divorce legislation, and its supporters hope that other states will adopt similar measures. The National Conference of Commissioners on Uniform State Laws has appointed a commission to draw up a "model" divorce law patterned on the California statute.

One factor that has contributed to the high divorce rate of the last two or three decades is the increase in the number of teenage marriages. Perhaps it would help if some states would raise the legal age of marriage. However, when marriages of the very young break up, each of the partners usually marries again, and frequently a good adjustment is made on the second try. Another factor that contributes to divorce is the number of hasty and ill-considered marriages. Laws that require a certain lapse of time

[13] For the principal provisions of this California statute, see *The National Observer*, September 8, 1969.

[14] *The National Observer*, February 15, 1971, p. 14.

between application for a license and the marriage ceremony prevent at least a few such marriages from taking place.

Education and Marriage. Marriage is a major life undertaking, with the greatest potentials for personal development and happiness; but it is also one for which there is little if any formal training. Unlike education for trades or professions, education for marriage is mostly a matter of "picking it up" from observation and discussion. As Ivo Moscorell wrote in *The Chicago Sunday Tribune:*

> *Almost anyone can get married. No one has to pass an aptitude test or a loyalty quiz to take the vows, so long as he pays the prescribed fee and waits the prescribed number of days. So young people frequently start a home and a family with a preparation so limited that they couldn't last a week in a business office if they had an equivalent amount of training.*

In recent years, however, an increasingly large amount of literature on marriage has been provided in books, magazines, and newspapers. Though not always of high quality, on balance it has probably provided useful information and advice. Even more significant, many high schools and colleges are now giving as electives regular courses on marriage and the family.

In general, the college graduate has the best chance for a durable marriage. It may be that the mere fact of going to college and graduating implies the presence of other favorable characteristics. In any case, the college graduate has the advantage of a certain amount of maturity, and it may even be that some of the courses he takes in college help to educate him for marriage. Also, college graduates can usually command better incomes than others and also positions that confer higher status.

However, the people who have graduated from high school and then held jobs for several years are almost as good a marriage risk as the college graduates, *provided* they have been successful in their work. But the difference in marital success between those who graduate from high school or college, and those who start one or the other but do not finish, is significant.

If it is true that college-educated couples have a greater chance for successful marriage, it then follows that they have the opportunity to pass their formula along to their children. But until the 1940's there had been a tendency for the college-educated couples to have far fewer children, on an average, than the less well educated. During the 1940's this situation changed, and the average number of children for the two groups became more nearly the same. There is some reason to believe that since then the proportion of children born to our better-educated and more successful parents has increased somewhat further.

Meeting Financial Needs. Financial issues are important factors in family disorganization. In our urban civilization, economic security is a necessity. For a family it means not only a decent standard of living but also protection against the hazards of sickness, old age, and unemployment. Circumstances can arise to make it impossible for a family unit to meet its economic needs, and it must then turn to private or government agencies for help. Fortunately, the federal government has become increasingly aware of the importance of family welfare to the nation, and it has taken some measures to help preserve it. For instance, our income tax laws reduce the economic burdens of the family by allowing a tax exemption for each dependent child. Also, the government provides funds for free prenatal clinics, public health services, and nursing services. The Social Security system aids the states in providing payments to mothers with dependent children, and the Federal Housing Administration makes home ownership possible for many by providing long-term loans at low rates of interest. Both state and federal governments provide some public housing for low-income families. These are but examples of a number of programs that indicate growing interest on the part of government in the economic welfare of American families.

Mothers who work to supplement the family income seem not as great a factor in creating family disorganization as was once feared, but this depends largely on whether they can and do arrange for adequate supervision of their children. Since juvenile delinquency often begins with a lack of supervision, it is important for society to meet this problem, perhaps with public day-care centers for younger children and with public-school–sponsored recreational programs after school hours for the school-age children.

THE FUTURE OF THE FAMILY

Some are so alarmed by what they believe to be the deterioration of the family as an effective social institution that they believe we must seek a substitute for it as a means of raising children. But the possibility of our finding any substitute that will perform this function as well as the family seems remote. However, there have been a few experiments in bringing up children in a communal setting. Bruno Bettelheim of the University of Chicago came to some interesting conclusions when he made a recent study of the raising of children in the Israeli agricultural settlements known as kibbutzim (plural of kibbutz). There, children are brought up by the kibbutz while their parents work. They see their parents at certain hours, but they live with their peer group, that is, with those of their own age and status, under the supervision of persons entrusted by the kibbutz with their care, physical welfare, and education.

Bettelheim concluded that in this communal life with little privacy, children become remarkably well adjusted to the expectations of their small peer groups. They have no strong ambitions, no desire to push anyone else down, and few if any of the conflicts often experienced by children who are raised by their parents in a more complex society. In a kibbutz there is no crime, delinquency, or other anti-social behavior, and hence no need for police or jails. But Bettelheim feels that the advantages enjoyed by the children of a kibbutz have a cost. He doubts if they are likely to develop close personal ties or strong individuality or to become innovators, and he therefore doubts if any of them will develop into great artists, writers, or scientists. [15]

In spite of problems, extreme pessimism about the future of the American family seems hardly justified. Today it is being subjected to great pressures from rapidly changing social conditions, but it seems to be making adjustments with reasonable success.

Marriage has never been more popular in the United States than it is today, not only with men and women who have never before been married but also with those who have been divorced. Divorced persons have had the worst possible experience with marriage, and yet statistics indicate that the great majority of them try again. On the basis of marriage figures issued by the Bureau of the Census, out of all adults between the ages of fifty-five and sixty-four, on an average almost nineteen out of twenty are married or have been at one time. [16]

In sum, the family seems likely to survive because it is the institution that can best provide for individuals the stability, security, and satisfactions that make for human happiness in a changing society.

Terms to Be Understood

family	polyandry	matrilineal descent
nuclear family	patriarchy	romantic illusion
extended family	matriarchy	marriage
patriarchal family	equalitarian family	family disorganization
monogamy	bilateral descent	divorce
polygamy	unilateral descent	desertion
polygyny	patrilineal descent	separation

Questions for Review and Discussion

1. Why is the family often regarded as the most important of all social units?
2. Why is monogamy the most widespread form of the marriage relationship?
3. State the principal methods that have been employed, in various societies, for selecting a mate.

[15] See Bruno Bettelheim, *Children of the Dream,* New York, The Macmillan Company, 1969.

[16] *Statistical Abstract of the United States,* Washington, D.C., Bureau of the Census, 1970, p. 32.

4. Why is it much easier to trace one's descent under a unilateral system than under a bilateral system?
5. Name the seven major headings under which family functions are grouped in this chapter.
6. Is the institution of the family really necessary for the propagation of the race and for training children who can carry on and develop the culture of a society? Defend your answer.
7. What changes has the physical-care function of the family undergone in the last few generations? Is it still important?
8. What changes have the economic functions of the family undergone? Are they less important than formerly? Why or why not?
9. Some think the psychological functions of the family are now the most important. Why?
10. In what ways does the modern family contribute to a child's education?
11. During the last few generations what changes have occurred in the role played by the family in providing recreation? What effect have these changes had on family life?
12. Explain the role of the family in providing children with social status.
13. What are the principal characteristics of the typical American family?
14. Describe the custom of dating as practiced in America, and explain the purposes it serves.
15. What are the advantages and disadvantages of basing one's choice of a mate on romantic love?
16. Does "marrying for love" eliminate consideration of compatibility and of economic and social factors?
17. What restrictions does our society place on the choice of a mate?
18. How is the length of the engagement period related to success in marriage? Explain.
19. What factors have contributed to lowering the age of first marriage?
20. List as many as you can of the factors that sociologists believe contribute to a successful marriage.
21. What major adjustments must a newly married couple make in their way of life? What further adjustments are required by the advent of children?
22. To what extent is the average American family "successful"?
23. What are some of the problems that a married couple must meet after the children have left home?
24. When one member of a marriage partnership dies, what problems does the survivor face?
25. Name the principal causes of family disorganization, and explain why each may be crucial.
26. Explain the rise in the divorce rate that has occurred since 1890.
27. It has been said that the legal grounds on which divorces are sought have little to do with the real reasons for which people desire them. Explain.
28. What is the chief provision, and the purpose, of the California divorce law passed in 1969?
29. How can family disorganization be reduced? By better marriage laws? By making divorce more difficult? Or by other methods?
30. Is the family likely to retain its present importance as a social institution? Why or why not? Could a satisfactory substitute be devised?

For Further Study

Berelson, Bernard, *Family Planning Programs: An International Study,* paperback, New York, Basic Books, Inc., 1969.

Bettelheim, Bruno, *Children of the Dream,* New York, The Macmillan Company, 1969.

Cavan, Ruth S., *The American Family,* 4th ed., New York, Thomas Y. Crowell Company, 1969.

Duvall, Evelyn Millis, *Family Development,* 3d ed., Philadelphia, J. B. Lippincott Company, 1967.

Edwards, John N., *Family and Change,* paperback, New York, Alfred A. Knopf, Inc., 1969.

Goode, William J., *Women in Divorce,* paperback, New York, The Free Press, 1965.
——— , ed., *Readings on the Family and Society,* paperback, Englewood Cliffs, N.J., Prentice-Hall, Inc., 1964.

Gordon, Albert I., *Intermarriage: Interfaith, Interracial, Interethnic,* paperback, Boston, Beacon Press, Inc., 1964.

Landis, Judson T., and Mary G. Landis, *Building a Successful Marriage,* 5th ed., Englewood Cliffs, N.J., Prentice-Hall, Inc., 1969.

Mace, David, and Vera Mace, *Marriage: East and West,* Dolphin paperback, New York, Doubleday & Company, Inc., 1959.

Queen, Stuart Alfred, Robert W. Habenstein, and John B. Adams, *The Family in Various Cultures,* 3rd ed., paperback, Philadelphia, J. B. Lippincott Company, 1967.

Rose, Arnold M., and Warren A. Peterson, *Older People and Their Social World,* Philadephia, F. A. Davis Company, 1965.

Rosow, I., *Social Integration of the Aged,* New York, The Free Press, 1967.

Rutledge, Aaron, *Pre-Marital Counseling,* Cambridge, Mass., Schenkman Publishing Company, 1967.

Whiting, Beatrice, ed., *Six Cultures: Studies of Child Rearing,* New York, John Wiley & Sons, Inc., 1963.

Winch, Robert F., and Louis W. Goodman, eds., *Selected Studies in Marriage and the Family,* 3rd ed., paperback, New York, Holt, Rinehart and Winston, Inc., 1968.

Chapter 11

From

a Rural

to an

Urban

Society

there was a time when all the people of the world lived in the country, just as the Australian aborigines or the American Indians do today where they have been little touched by civilization. When the human race supported itself by hunting wild game and by gathering fruits, nuts, and edible plants found in nature, even a large, fertile area could provide subsistence for only a comparatively few people. The introduction of agriculture a few thousand years ago gradually brought great changes. To cultivate the soil, people had to settle down in one place. Some lived in small villages near their land, others in farm cottages scattered over the countryside. Because more food could be raised, populations began to grow; and in time, larger towns developed, some of which eventually grew into cities.

But in every large area, most people still had to live in the country, close to the land, in order to feed the growing population. Not until after the Industrial Revolution, several thousand years later, was there such a revolution in farming methods that one man, working on the land, could feed ten, twenty, thirty, and in time even forty or fifty other people. This, plus a great expansion of trade and industry, brought on the modern phase of urbanization. Today most of the people of industrially advanced countries live in towns or in great cities and their suburbs; and the rural population keeps shrinking both in relative and absolute numbers.

True, we still have in the United States some millions of rural residents, scattered over the country in farming communities and small villages. But because of rapid communication and transportation, the people who live in farming communities are becoming in some respects more and more like those who live in cities; yet rural communities are still important in our society, and life in them still differs from life in urban communities.

COMMUNITIES AND THEIR CHARACTERISTICS

A *community* consists of the people who live in a local area and who therefore have certain interests and problems in common. Because of their very nearness to one another, the members of a community must cooperate and organize. They must find ways of providing themselves with services and facilities of many kinds, including police protection, roads, churches, schools, hospitals, and opportunities for recreation. Once a community becomes established, it tends to develop a common culture. Through social contacts, common interests, and cooperative efforts, its people, within limits, acquire similar beliefs, attitudes, and customs.

Communities and Neighborhoods. Communities vary greatly in character and size. Small rural or village communities are likely to exhibit the greatest degree of unity and the most homogeneous culture patterns. In such communities everyone knows everyone else, and intimate personal contacts are frequent. Large city communities are very different. There, the relations of individuals to one another are mostly indirect, and organization is formal, complex, and highly centralized. People may be served by the same police and fire departments, the same city government, the same school system, the same transportation system, and the same newspapers and television stations, but most of the people never even see one another. When some do come into contact, more often than not their relations are casual and impersonal. In a large city one seldom knows the people one passes on the streets, the taxi driver, the traffic policeman, or the clerks in the stores.

A *neighborhood* differs from a community in that it is smaller and not formally organized. It usually has boundaries that to some degree separate it from other neighborhoods; and those who live in it tend to share a similar culture and economic status and to be more or less acquainted with one another. As a rule a community includes a number of neighborhoods. The community is the major unit of local social organization, and as such it provides most of the services that its inhabitants require in the day-to-day routine of their lives.

Communities as Primary or Secondary Groups. In Chapter 1 there was a brief discussion of the nature of *primary* and *secondary* social groups. Neighborhoods and small rural communities are, like families, primary groups because they are characterized by intimate face-to-face relationships among their members. In small communities, social controls over those who belong are largely informal. People value highly the good opinions of others and they fear disapproval, gossip, and possible ostracism by their fellow citizens.

In a great urban community, we clearly have a secondary group, because individuals have diverse social backgrounds, they seldom know one another, their contacts are mostly indirect, and their direct contacts are to a large extent impersonal. In urban communities, social controls tend to be formal. There, in comparison with the rural community, much more reliance is placed on such agencies as the police and the courts.

Residents of small communities sometimes resent the pressure of informal controls, the fact that "everyone knows everyone else's business." They long for the greater freedom of the city, where few people would know them and where ordinarily little attention would be paid to their behavior. On the other hand, city dwellers are often lonely and long for the intimate contacts and the friendliness likely to be found in small towns. For example, young people living "on their own" in a large city sometimes feel lost, alienated from meaningful social contacts. They suffer from what the great French sociologist Emile Durkheim called *anomie,* a sense of living in a social void in which social norms or values have little meaning.

Communities as Natural Areas. Communities are natural areas in the sense that they do not usually develop because of planning or legislation but, rather, because of certain advantages of location. In most cases they develop around a trading center and become a rural hamlet, a village, or eventually a city. Community centers develop in locations where geographic factors are favorable and especially where there are advantages of transportation. Large urban communities are almost always found where both rail and water transportation give them exceptionally good access to markets and raw materials. Often they serve as points for transferring goods between railroad lines and ships.

Types of Communities. The variety and complexity found in communities often make it difficult to classify them neatly on the basis of common characteristics. This is especially true of our largest cities, which seldom have much cultural or economic homogeneity. In huge urban centers, extreme contrasts exist between slum areas on the one hand and exclusive residential districts on the other; furthermore, their economic life rests on a great number and variety of industries and occupations. Smaller places, however, can often be classified according to the principal economic activity to which they owe their existence. Below is a suggested classification of communities on the basis of this characteristic.

1. *Agricultural communities*—These are farm communities centered about a hamlet or village that provides for their trade and service needs.
2. *Commercial communities*—These are towns or cities of moderate size that serve as major trade centers for smaller communities scattered over a wide area.
3. *Industrial communities*—The basis of the livelihood of these communities is one or more factories.
4. *Transportation centers and railroad towns*—Railroad towns are usually division points where train crews live and where railroad repair shops are located. However, the introduction of diesel engines, other changes in railroad technology, and the increasing use of other forms of transportation has reduced the importance of many of these towns.
5. *Mining centers,* like Butte, Montana.
6. *Political communities,* like Washington, D.C., and numerous state capitals.
7. *College or university towns.*
8. *Health centers,* like Rochester, Minnesota.
9. *Resort communities,* such as Atlantic City, New Jersey, or Miami, Florida.
10. *Communities depending heavily on military or naval establishments,* such as Huntsville, Alabama, where Redstone Arsenal is a major center for missile and space research.

RURAL BACKGROUNDS OF OUR URBAN SOCIETY

We cannot understand American culture and American traditions without some concept of the rural society out of which they developed, and which is still an important segment of American life. For at least the first hundred years of our history as a nation, agriculture and rural life were dominant factors controlling our national development. When the first census was taken in 1790, only 5 per cent of Americans lived in places larger than 2,500, and no city in the country had as many as 50,000 inhabitants. Not until the census of 1820 did the population of our greatest city, New York, pass the 100,000 mark, and not until 1880 did it exceed 1,000,000. Even in 1890, a hundred years after the first census, only 35 per cent of Americans lived in incorporated towns of 2,500 or over. Today, however, the ratio is over 65 per cent.

For many years the Bureau of the Census classified all people living in towns of 2,500 or more as *urban* and all others as *rural*. Such a division point is, of course, arbitrary. In the 1950 census the definition of *urban population* was somewhat extended, principally by adding to the people counted as urban those living in certain densely populated areas just outside the boundaries of cities of 50,000 or more. In the 1960 census, people living in some other densely populated areas were also included. On the basis of present census rulings, more than 72 per cent of all Americans are urban, but some live in areas that are not incorporated.

Figure 8 shows graphically how the United States has changed over the years from a country almost wholly rural to one predominantly urban. If one examines this figure carefully, it also shows the rather startling fact that the farm population of the country declined in the single decade 1950–1960 from about 23 million to considerably less than 14 million, or about 40 per cent. The 1970 census shows a further decline in the farm population to about 10 million, because advances in agricultural technology have continued to reduce the need for manpower. But while the farm

Figure 8. Increasing Urbanization of the United States, 1790–1970. Numbers at left indicate population in millions. (Source of data: U.S. Bureau of the Census.)

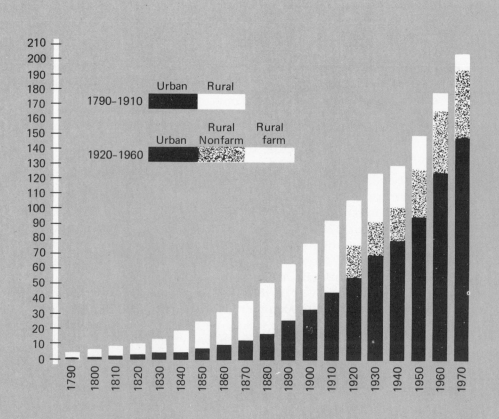

(Courtesy *The Washington Star*.)

population has been declining, in recent years the rural nonfarm population has been rising.

Even though the United States is now a predominantly urban society, we must not underestimate either the past or the present influence of rural culture on American life. Many of the residents of our cities still have a rural background. Birth rates in the country are relatively high; on the other hand, job opportunities are most numerous in the cities. As a result, for many years half or more of the boys and girls raised on farms have moved to towns and cities; this migration is still continuing but is on a smaller scale than in the past because the total farm population is much less. Yet even now some of our more sparsely populated states are predominantly rural, and in the nation as a whole, the political power of the rural population is proportionately greater than its numbers.

Until recently, one reason for the relatively great political power of rural areas was the failure in many states to revise legislative and Congressional districts so as to give the people of cities their proper representation in state legislatures and in the national House of Representatives. This situation has now been changed by a decision of the United States Supreme Court that requires that legislative districts be approximately equal in population. A factor that will continue to weight political power in favor of rural voters is the fact that every state, regardless of population, has two senators in Washington. This gives thinly populated Western states, with largely rural populations, as much voting power in the United States Senate as states like New York and California, which contain great urban centers and many times the number of people.

RURAL COMMUNITIES

The Rural Neighborhood and the Rural Community. The *rural neighborhood* is a limited locality whose few families associate more closely with one another than with outside groups. It may be centered around a church, a school, or a store, but it is not very self-sufficient. The rural neighborhood is a much less important social unit that it once was, not only because of the automobile but also because of the great shrinkage of farm population in recent decades.

A *rural community* is a larger and more fully developed social unit. Its characteristics include (1) a common area, consisting of several neighborhoods grouped about a hamlet or village that serves as a center for trade, professional services, and social life; (2) self-sufficiency in providing for the more common and frequent needs of its people; (3) a feeling on the part of residents that they belong to the area and to the groups within it; (4) to some degree, a common culture; and (5) formal, community-wide social organizations and institutions.

Probably three out of four of the small towns that dot the country grew up as farm trade centers, and many still retain that character. They are residence centers for retired farmers and also for the merchants, professional people, and other service workers who cater to the needs of the surrounding farm families. Other small towns started as mining centers, fishing villages, resort centers, or college communities; still others developed around factories or as suburban residence centers.

But whatever the origin of small towns, as a group they have been able to maintain both population and job opportunities, and many of them have good prospects of future growth. Two trends are working in their favor. One is the widening of suburban areas, not only around large cities but also around cities of moderate size. Today a large portion of the population of many small towns consists of city workers who commute. A second trend is toward decentralizing industry and locating factories in rural villages. With the almost universal availability of electric power, country towns often attract branch plants or small industries because such towns can provide land at low prices and a dependable labor supply at reasonable wages. It is no longer necessary for them to have railroads, because both raw materials and finished products can be transported by truck. This movement of industry to rural areas is already urbanizing in some degree many country towns, and though it results in a greater number and variety of services, occupations, and interests, it also tends to destroy the unity and homogeneity that still characterize a great number of rural communities. In their cultural characteristics, residents of rural villages and towns stand midway between people who live on farms and those who live in cities.

Life on Farms Contrasted with Urban Life. Unlike city people, all farmers depend directly on the land for earning their living. In the city, people earn their living in a great variety of ways, but in a broad sense all farmers are engaged in the same occupation. Because of their occupation, they are extremely dependent on the weather. City people may enjoy good weather and dislike bad weather; to them neither the one nor the other is a matter of great importance. But to the farmer the weather means the difference between success or failure, money in the bank or inability to meet mortgage payments. Consequently, in rural districts the weather is a constant and important topic of conversation.

Though farm people can keep in touch with one another and with the outside world by automobiles, telephones, radios, and television sets, they do not live crowded together with thousands of other people on a few acres of land. Farmers do not have to be at the office or factory right on the hour. They have work to be done, but they also have a certain amount of freedom in deciding how and when to do it. And though they have many contacts away from their farms and their homes, the family group plays a much greater role in their daily lives than it does in those of most city people. As Carl C. Taylor once said:

Farming as a mode of living, a phrase admittedly used vaguely and romantically by many, is conditioned not so much by living on isolated homesteads in the open country as by the close relations of occupational pursuits, business enterprise, and personal and social behavior, all of which are tied intimately to an individual farm. All members of the family spend part of their lives working on the farm or in the farm home; all are constantly aware of the relation of the money-earning power of the farm enterprise to their level and standard of living; and all know that the necessities and conditions of farm work influence what they can and cannot do personally and socially. Thus, a great deal of their participation in all aspects of life is automatically conditioned by the fact that they are farmers.[1]

In spite of many contacts with the outside world and many modern conveniences, farm life is still very unlike city life. For every day that the farmer spends in his market and trade contacts, he may spend ten days working alone or in his family circle. His practice in this respect will vary with the kind of farming he does. Truck and dairy farmers may have more town contacts than average; self-sufficient farmers fewer. But in any case, farming involves a greater degree of isolation than almost any city occupation, and this influences both the personalities of rural people and the character of their social life.

But the fact that rural people differ from city people should not lead us to suppose that all farmers or all rural people are alike. There are great differences between isolated subsistence farmers and suburban farmers, between well-to-do and poor farmers, between owners and tenants, between transient laborers and steady farm workers, and between cotton, grain, and dairy farmers. There are also obvious differences between rural

[1]Carl C. Taylor et al., *Rural Life in the United States,* New York, Alfred A. Knopf, Inc., 1949, p. 8. Copyright 1949 by Alfred A. Knopf, Inc.

people of different national and racial origins. There are differences between people in sparsely settled areas like the Great Plains, with fewer than twenty persons per square mile, and those in thickly settled areas like the Connecticut Valley. Also there are differences between people who live on farms and operate them, people who operate farms but live in town, and people who reside in the country but are not engaged in farming.

Rural Life and Social Change. The great technological advances of the twentieth century have radically changed the character of rural life. The increasing mechanization of farms not only has reduced the need for as many workers but also has made the small farmer almost obsolete. With modern machines a family can cultivate more land than ever before, with fewer people; but because of the heavy investment necessary, it does not pay to operate a small farm, and therefore the total number of farms in the United States is steadily declining as small ones are combined into larger ones. Young people continue to leave the farms because of limited opportunities for employment, but others return to live in rural communities while being employed in nearby cities.

Other technological advances such as good roads and automobiles have brought a constant trend away from strictly local neighborhood relations toward more impersonal or nonlocal contacts. The interests and social activities of farm people are becoming centered to a greater degree in the towns. One-room country schools have practically disappeared in favor of consolidated schools located in the towns. Some country churches have federated, but more have closed as farm people become fewer and as those left increasingly transfer their allegiance to the village or town churches. Because of limited recreational opportunities in rural communities, young people are seeking recreation, often of a commercial type, in nearby towns and cities. Many rural communities are ceasing to be close knit, homogeneous groups. Informal types of social organization, still evident in rural life, are being supplemented or replaced by formal organizations as government and other agencies bring in programs from the outside. Finally, through newspapers, news magazines, radio, and television, farm people are becoming quickly and fully informed about national and world affairs.

CITIES AND THEIR GROWTH

As the United States has become more urban, the role of cities in our culture and the problems of city life have become increasingly important.

What Is a City? We shall define a *city* as *a large number of people, organized into a community and living close together within definite boundaries.* Such a definition does not describe the characteristics and behavior typical of city people, but it does state the basic conditions that give rise to city life. As has already been pointed out, there is no way of determining except on an arbitrary basis just how many people must live close together in order to constitute a city. To the Bureau of the Census, a city is a place of 2,500 people or more. From a legal point of view, the population required to organize a city is determined in each state by the legislature, and in some states a much smaller number of residents can incorporate as a "city." In any case, urbanization is a matter of degree. A town of 10,000 has some of the characteristics of a city, but to the dweller in a great metropolis it is likely to seem rural. Not until we come to cities of 50,000, 100,000, or half a million do we begin to find in some degree the urban characteristics of a modern *metropolitan center.*

What are the "urban characteristics" of such a center? To the late Louis Wirth *heterogeneity* was the outstanding characteristic of city people. According to his widely quoted definition, *a city is a relatively large, dense, and permanent settlement of socially heterogeneous people.* Certainly heterogeneity characterizes a large city, for it contains groups and individuals who vary widely in nationality, race, religion, occupation, economic status, social values, and manner of living. However, even large cities differ greatly in the degree of heterogeneity of their people. In Europe, for example, some have populations that are relatively homogeneous with respect to such matters as nationality, race, and perhaps religion.

Among the characteristics that distinguish urban centers from rural communities and smaller towns, the following should be especially noted: (1) more freedom for the individual and more opportunities for self-expression; (2) the formation of many special-interest groups, including colonies of musicians, artists, and writers; (3) a concentration of museums, universities, and medical facilities; (4) administrative offices of government, corporations, and other institutions; (5) a great variety of occupations; (6) highly specialized services of many types; (7) varied forms of recreation and entertainment; (8) wide social and economic differences; (9) wide differences in social values and manner of living; (10) usually a variety of racial, nationality, and religious groups; and, finally, (11) special problems of government, health, housing, transportation, education, recreation, and crime.

The Role of Cities in Civilization. The growth of cities was essential to the development of what we call *civilization.* All advanced civilizations have an urban base, because it is only in large towns that government, trade, handicrafts, and the arts and sciences can be developed to a high degree. Cities provide the freedom, the contacts, and the opportunities for education and specialization that are needed for the development of the characteristics of culture that distinguish highly civilized societies from their more primitive predecessors.

The first cities arose because new social patterns were slowly developing. City life encouraged the further development of such patterns, and, as a result, society became more dynamic. Tradition grew weaker, nonconformism increased, and legal rules began to replace informal controls. True, many of the characteristics of the older and simpler tribal societies persisted in rural areas for centuries after tribalism had disappeared. Gradually, however, the influence of urban culture expanded and the differences between rural and city people diminished.

Cities in Early Times. The earliest settlements that we would accept as truly urban probably appeared in Egypt, Mesopotamia, and India, in the valleys of the Nile, Tigris, Euphrates, and Indus rivers. Among the factors that contributed to their growth were (1) the development of a settled agriculture, especially the raising of grain; (2) favorable conditions of climate and soil, and the production of more food than was required by those who worked on the land; (3) the development of trade in articles not locally available, and hence a need for central markets; (4) the growth of specialization, including the development of handicraft industries in population centers; (5) the need for political centers from which the king and his officials could carry on government functions; (6) the building of great religious shrines and temples; and, finally, (7) the need for walled places in which people could assemble in time of crisis for the purpose of defense. The people who normally lived in the great towns of the ancient world were government officials, merchants, landowners, craftsmen, soldiers, priests, servants, and slaves. In time some of the early cities of the Middle East became capitals of great empires.

Growth of Cities in the Mediterranean Area. When the first great cities were appearing in Egypt, Babylonia, and India, nearly all Europe was inhabited by backward peoples who lived in tribal groups in small communities. But, beginning with the seaports of Phoenicia, cities grew up one after another around the Aegean Sea and the eastern Mediterranean, and gradually they spread to the western Mediterranean and then northward into Gaul. Some of these ancient Mediterranean cities grew to great size. Carthage at one time may have had a population of 700,000, and Rome may have reached almost a million.

Compared with modern cities most ancient cities were crude agglomerations of people and buildings. They had narrow streets, open sewers or none at all, and accumulations of filth that were never removed. Disease rates and death rates must have been very high as compared with rural areas. A few ancient cities, however, provided certain public utilities not unlike those found in cities today. "In Rome some of the streets were paved; water was brought down from the mountains; sewers emptied into the Tiber; there were public baths; and, in the reign of Augustus, systems of fire and police protection were highly developed."[2]

But in spite of the growth of some great cities, ancient civilizations were predominantly rural. By modern standards, cities of any size were extremely few, and none can be compared to such modern metropolitan centers as New York, London, or Tokyo.

With the coming of the Dark Ages, the cities of classical antiquity de-

[2] Stuart Alfred Queen and David Bailey Carpenter, *The American City*, New York, McGraw-Hill, Inc., 1953, p. 45.

21. Ruins of the Roman Forum. Once the center of the commercial, political, and religious life of the city. (Photo by author.)

clined and in some cases disappeared. By the end of the eighth century, Rome itself had shrunk to a provincial town of fewer than twenty thousand people. This decline was brought about by the breaking up of the Roman Empire, incursions of the German tribes from the north, the decline of law and order, failure to control pirates in the Mediterranean, and the resulting shrinkage or disappearance of industry and commerce. But in the late Middle Ages towns began to grow again, and in the course of time great cities once more came into existence: first Venice, and later places like Paris and London.

The Industrial Revolution and Urbanization. From the late Middle Ages to the present time, the growth of European cities has been stimulated by a succession of developments. The Crusades, the Renaissance, the great discoveries in the New World, the increasing importance of overseas trade, the rise of handicraft industries, the growth of population, and the emergence of nation-states—all these played their part. It was not, however, until about the end of the eighteenth century, when the Industrial Revolution was well under way, that urbanization really hit its stride. At that time Europe contained about 300 towns with 10,000 or more people and 21 cities with over 100,000.[3]

The Industrial Revolution brought the building of factories, with their

[3] Adna F. Weber, *The Growth of Cities in the Nineteenth Century,* New York, Columbia University Press, 1899, pp. 144–145.

need for many workers who had to be provided with homes. Moreover, there was a natural tendency to build factories in groups in locations that had special advantages for transporting coal or other raw materials and for shipping finished goods to markets. As a result, factory towns and cities developed rapidly in a number of areas. In England one of the first great industrial cities to develop was Manchester. In 1750 the population of Manchester was about 17,000; by 1850 it had grown to nearly 400,000.

Other Factors in the Growth of Cities. Advances of industry and transportation have not been the only factors in the growth of modern cities. Advances in methods of governing cities and organizing their activities have also played a part. Even more important have been advances in sanitation, for without modern sanitation life in great cities would be both unpleasant and dangerous to life and health. The development of refrigeration has also been important, for without it the supplying of safe food to the people of great cities would present almost insuperable problems.

One factor in the growth of modern cities that is sometimes overlooked is the part played by agricultural progress. Without the important improvements in agricultural methods that have taken place since 1750, the great shift of population from the country to the cities would have been impossible. In earlier times the vast majority of the labor force of every country had to work on the land in order to provide enough food for the population. But as per capita output has risen in agriculture, more and more workers have been released for employment in the cities. If we assume that all the farm workers reported by the United States Census in 1820 were needed to produce food for the rest of the population, we find that on an average one such worker could provide food for fewer than five people. But today, according to Secretary of Agriculture Clifford M. Hardin,[4] one farm worker can produce enough food and fiber for forty-three people.[5]

The World-Wide Distribution of City Growth. In the last century and a half, cities have grown at a rapid rate in many parts of the world. Even in countries with little industry, such as India, great metropolitan centers have developed in locations especially favorable for carrying on trade. But the largest of these centers are almost as much a product of the Industrial Revolution as are those in industrial countries, because they depend for much of their trade on the manufactured products of other countries, and also on machine-powered facilities such as railroads, ships, trucks, and airplanes.

Though the growth of great cities has been a world-wide phenomenon, it has been most marked in countries that are highly industrialized. Even today it is probable that less than 10 per cent of the people of Asia and Africa live in cities of 100,000 or more, though just recently some cities in the new African countries have started to grow very rapidly. In Europe

---

[4] *National Geographic,* February, 1970, pp. 147–151.

[5] It should be noted, however, that other workers contribute indirectly to farm output, for example, those producing farm machinery and fertilizers.

and North America the proportion in cities over 100,000 is 30 to 40 per cent. Oddly enough, the highest ratio of people living in large cities is found in one of the most recently settled and most sparsely populated countries of the world, namely, Australia. Australia is about the same size as the United States without Alaska, but it has only twelve million inhabitants; and about 60 per cent of them live in its seven largest cities. We are apt to think of Australia as a predominantly agricultural country, but actually only a rather small minority of its people are directly engaged in raising crops and livestock.

Two hundred years ago there was probably not a city in the world with a population close to a million. Today there are about a hundred that exceed this number. However, population figures for the great cities of the world are sometimes misleading and of doubtful value for making comparisons. Censuses are not taken in the same years in all countries, and some of them are thought to be very inaccurate. An even more serious problem

Table 7. *Largest Urban Areas in the World**

Rank	City	Year of Census or Estimate	Population
1	Tokyo	1965 (census)	14,770,727
2	New York	1960 (census)	14,114,927
3	Buenos Aires	1970 (census)	8,408,930
4	Paris	1968 (census)	8,196,746
5	London	1965 (est.)	7,948,270
6	Osaka	1965 (census)	7,781,000
7	Moscow	1970 (census)	7,061,000
8	Shanghai	1958 (est.)	6,977,000
9	Los Angeles	1960 (census)	6,488,791
10	Chicago	1960 (census)	5,959,213
11	São Paulo	1968 (est.)	5,684,706
12	Bombay	1969 (est.)	5,534,358
13	Calcutta	1968 (est.)	5,074,668
14	Mexico City	1960 (census)	4,659,691
15	Essen (Ruhr-Gebiet)	1966 (est.)	4,259,230
16	Cairo	1966 (census)	4,225,700
17	Rio de Janeiro	1968 (est.)	4,207,322
18	Peking	1958 (est.)	4,148,000
19	Leningrad	1970 (census)	3,950,000
20	Victoria, Hong Kong	1968 (census)	3,927,900
21	Seoul	1965 (census)	3,805,261
22	Detroit-Windsor	1960 (U.S. data) 1961 (Canada data)	3,731,074
23	Philadelphia	1960 (census)	3,635,228
24	Delhi	1969 (est.)	3,621,101
25	Tientsin	1958 (est.)	3,278,000

*The "urban areas" on which this table is based include, in some cases, a larger territory than the "standard metropolitan statistical areas" that are used for Table 8.
Source: The 1971 World Almanac, p. 59. Courtesy of 1971 World Almanac and Book of Facts, Copyright Newspaper Enterprise Association, Inc.

is that there is no wholly satisfactory way to determine just what territory should be included in a city. Often large urban sections that are physically, socially, and economically part of a city are not included within its legal boundaries. Table 7 represents an attempt to list in approximate order of size, not the world's largest cities as defined legally, but the world's largest urban areas, each including a central city and all the urbanized territory that adjoins its borders or is close to it and economically dependent on it.

The Great Metropolitan Centers of America. Although over 72 per cent of the residents of the United States are classified as *urban,* this gives us little idea of the extent to which our people are concentrated in or near really great urban centers. We obtain a better idea of this concentration when we note that in 1970 more than one third of our total civilian population lived in our twenty-five largest *standard metropolitan statistical*

Table 8. *The Twenty-five Largest Standard Metropolitan Statistical Areas of the United States in 1970*

Rank	Standard Metropolitan Statistical Area	Population, 1970	Change, 1960 to 1970	
			Number	Percent
1	New York	11,448,500	753,900	+ 7.0
2	Los Angeles–Long Beach	6,974,100	935,300	+ 15.5
3	Chicago	6,892,500	671,600	+ 10.8
4	Philadelphia	4,777,400	434,500	+ 10.0
5	Detroit	4,163,500	401,200	+ 10.7
6	San Francisco–Oakland	3,069,800	421,000	+ 15.9
7	Washington, D.C.–Md.–Va.	2,835,700	759,100	+ 36.6
8	Boston	2,730,200	134,700	+ 5.2
9	Pittsburgh	2,383,800	−21,700	− 0.9
10	St. Louis	2,331,000	226,300	+ 10.8
11	Baltimore	2,045,200	241,500	+ 13.4
12	Cleveland	2,043,400	133,900	+ 7.0
13	Houston	1,958,500	540,200	+ 38.1
14	Newark	1,847,500	158,100	+ 9.4
15	Minneapolis–St. Paul	1,805,000	323,000	+ 21.8
16	Dallas	1,539,400	420,000	+ 37.5
17	Anaheim–Santa Ana–Garden Grove	1,409,300	705,400	+100.2
18	Seattle-Everett	1,404,400	297,200	+ 26.8
19	Milwaukee	1,393,300	114,400	+ 8.9
20	Atlanta	1,373,600	356,400	+ 35.0
21	Cincinnatti, Ohio-Ky.–Ind.	1,373,200	104,700	+ 8.3
22	Paterson–Clifton–Passaic, N.J.	1,369,400	182,500	+ 15.4
23	Buffalo	1,334,500	27,500	+ 2.1
24	San Diego	1,318,000	285,000	+ 27.6
25	Miami	1,259,200	324,100	+ 34.7

Source: U.S. Bureau of the Census, *1970 Census of Population: Preliminary Reports,* PC (P3)-3, November 1970.

areas,[6] each of which contains over a million people. The estimated population of each of these twenty-five metropolitan areas in 1970 is shown in Table 8, which also indicates for each the change by number and percentage since 1960.

Theories of City Growth and Structure. Nearly all modern cities have experienced the greater part of their growth in comparatively recent years. Often what was only a village or a site in the wilderness less than a hundred years ago is now a great metropolis. In this process of development, certain similarities of pattern have become apparent, and in order to explain these, attempts have been made to discover the principles that govern city growth.

The Concentric-Zone Theory. Probably the most widely known theory of city growth is one advanced many years ago by Ernest W. Burgess.[7] Burgess explained the structure of a large modern city in terms of five concentric zones that he believed develop during the growth process. Essentially Burgess' theory was based on the fact that as a city gradually expands, the inner portions, built earliest, tend to deteriorate and become less desirable. Eventually, most of the best residential sections are likely to be found at the far edges of the city or in the suburbs.

Let us note briefly the character of each of Burgess' zones.

Zone 1 is the central business district, where main transportation routes converge and where trade and other business activities are concentrated. Though this zone is not immune to deterioration, Burgess believed that it tends to be maintained or renewed because of the high return from the economic activities carried on within it. In recent years, however, many central business districts have been threatened with deterioration because of competition from huge suburban shopping centers with plenty of space for parking cars.

Zone 2 is the area surrounding the central business district. Burgess called it the *zone of transition,* because certain types of business enterprise overflow into it and speed up its deterioration as a residential area. Here is a concentration of warehouses, wholesale establishments, some factories, slums, and skid rows. Here also are centers of gambling, vice, crime, and juvenile delinquency.

Zone 3 is somewhat further out, and deterioration has not progressed so far. This is an area of workingmen's homes, including second-rate apartment buildings; it also contains some local business districts.

Zone 4, farthest from the center of the city, is the better residential area because it is newest and least crowded. It contains good homes and apart-

---

[6] A standard metropolitan statistical area, as this term is used by the Bureau of the Census, includes a central city (sometimes two or three that are adjacent) with a total population of 50,000 or over, the county in which it lies, and any adjoining counties judged to be urban in character.

[7] Robert E. Park and Ernest W. Burgess, *The City,* Chicago, University of Chicago Press, 1925, pp. 47–62.

ment buildings, residential hotels, and important local business centers. Its inhabitants are chiefly middle-class people with somewhat better-than-average incomes.

Zone 5 is beyond the city limits. It consists of the suburban area from which many people commute daily to the central business district. Zone 5 includes both exclusive suburbs and industrial districts; it also contains country clubs, golf courses, cemeteries, parks, and farms.

Burgess recognized from the beginning that his theory was not a complete explanation of city structure. He knew that, more often than not, no sharp lines could be drawn to separate the zones that he assumed; also, he knew that the growth of every city was affected by special factors, geographical or otherwise.

Figure 9 presents graphically the general pattern of city structure that would result from Burgess' theory if no modifying factors were operating.

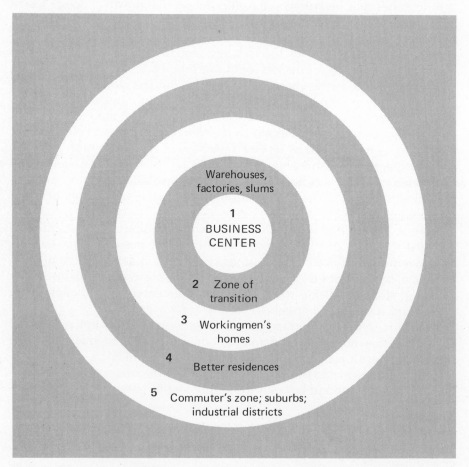

Warehouses, factories, slums

1
BUSINESS CENTER

2   Zone of transition

3   Workingmen's homes

4   Better residences

5   Commuter's zone; suburbs; industrial districts

Figure 9. Concentric-Zone Theory of City Structure. (A simplified diagram representing Burgess's concept.)

The Sector Theory of City Growth. The sector theory of city growth, presented by Homer Hoyt and others, maintains that land use of a certain type, once established in an area near the city center, tends to spread directly outward. For example, a high-grade residential district may extend outward along high ground, along a desirable waterfront, or along a fast transportation line. Meanwhile, less-desirable residential areas may expand outward in directions that offer fewer advantages.

If each is looked upon as a complete explanation of how cities develop, the concentric-zone and the sector theories are obviously in conflict. City patterns, however, are never as simple as either of these theories would imply, and each of them contains an element of truth. There is in fact a tendency for the older and inner areas of cities to deteriorate and for newer and better residential districts to be built in outlying areas. There is also a tendency for certain types of land use and certain groups of people to seek more space by moving outward from the city in directions that offer special advantages. In Chicago, for example, high-grade residential districts extend from near the business center many miles north along the shore of Lake Michigan, almost to Waukegan. To the south, on the other hand, beginning at Seventy-Ninth Street, an industrial district extends along the lake shore all the way to Gary, Indiana. Industries along this route obtain the advantages of lake harbors and of access to several railroads that parallel the lake shore.

The Theory of Development Around Multiple Nuclei. The land-use pattern of cities is influenced not only by the relation of land to the central business district but also by its relation to other centers about which certain types of growth and activity develop. Some of these may have existed from the beginning; others have developed as the city expanded. In addition to a main business district, centers or nuclei about which a city develops may include several important secondary business districts, a harbor and its shipping facilities, a railroad terminus or transfer point, a mine, a group of factories, or a university. Also, it frequently happens that, while a city is relatively small, nearby suburban towns grow to considerable size. Later the city expands and annexes them, but they still retain some of their original character. More-distant suburban towns continue to serve as centers for the development of industry and the growth of population in the metropolitan area.

Figure 10 presents, for purposes of comparison, the concentric-zone theory of city growth, the sector theory, and the multiple-nuclei theory. These theories help us understand the historical development of most great modern cities. But as time passes, other changes occur and the patterns originally established by city growth become increasingly blurred. In very recent times, great changes have been made in many cities by large urban renewal projects and by the construction of wide expressways that cut across built-up sections of a city and that require the demolition and clearance of buildings over large areas.

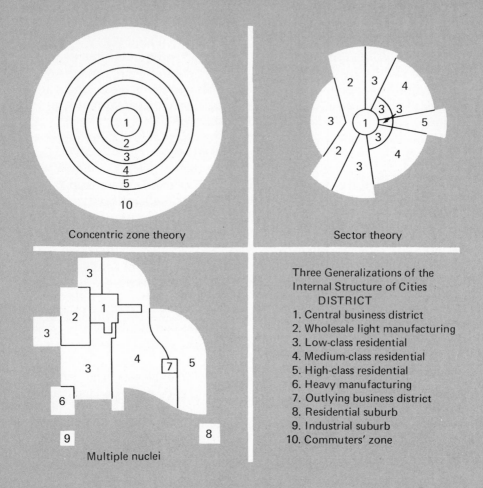

Concentric zone theory

Sector theory

Multiple nuclei

Three Generalizations of the
Internal Structure of Cities
DISTRICT
1. Central business district
2. Wholesale light manufacturing
3. Low-class residential
4. Medium-class residential
5. High-class residential
6. Heavy manufacturing
7. Outlying business district
8. Residential suburb
9. Industrial suburb
10. Commuters' zone

Figure 10. Theories of the Internal Structure of Cities, with Key to the Types of Districts Indicated. (U.S. Federal Housing Administration, *The Structure and Growth of Residential Neighborhoods in American Cities,* Washington, D.C., U.S. Government Printing Office, 1939, p. 13.)

Communities Within the City. A great metropolis is in a sense a community, for its people do have some important interests and problems in common. But it has little homogeneity. Within it are areas and groups that have little contact with one another. Its people do not have the feeling of unity and belonging that can be found in a rural community or even a small city. For some purposes, it is more useful to think of a large city as consisting of a considerable number of communities, each of which has a characteristic culture and economic life of its own, and perhaps a certain amount of community organization. In one study of Chicago, a map was made that outlined seventy-five different "communities" within the political boundaries of the city. But when we attempt to divide a city into a number of constituent communities, we must often be rather arbitrary, and none of them has the unity and self-sufficiency that characterize smaller and more-isolated communities.

In cities we find people segregated to a large degree on the basis of income or social class. One city district or "community" will be inhabited by well-to-do people living in large and attractive houses or in expensive apartments; another will consist of working people living in old houses or perhaps in newly built small ones; still another will be a slum area, inhabited by those who are at the bottom of the economic scale.

Segregation in large cities also takes place on the basis of national, ethnic, and racial groups. As what was originally a good residential neighborhood deteriorates, the original inhabitants are likely to move out, while some less favored group moves in. Two or three generations ago the groups moving in were likely to consist of newly arrived immigrants. People of the same nationality tended to crowd together, so that a whole district might, for example, become German, Polish, or Italian. Later, however, these immigrant groups, or their children, began to move out and to be replaced by new groups. Today the people who move into the deteriorated areas of our cities are likely to be blacks, and occasionally Puerto Ricans, Cubans, or Mexicans.

The Trend to the Suburbs. As our cities have grown larger and larger, living conditions have become very crowded in many areas, and the older parts of our cities have tended to become undesirable places to live because of blight and deterioration. Added to this, most people with children have a longing for things of which the city can provide relatively little—namely, sunlight, clean air, space, and green grass. Hence, with improvements in transportation, there has been an increasing movement of city workers to the suburbs. This has intensified the problems of the central city. Growth often slows up or even stops in the city itself, while the metropolitan area outside still continues to expand rapidly. Often the financial problems of the city are intensified because property values fail to rise in proportion to the increasing costs of government. On an average, the people who move out are likely to have better incomes than those who remain behind.

The trend toward suburban living continued upward during the 1960's. This is reflected in Bureau of the Census estimates of changes in the white population of central cities in metropolitan areas as a whole. For the period 1960–1966 the average annual decline in their white population, largely from a shift to the suburbs, was 141,000, but for the years 1967–1968 the average annual loss had risen to 486,000. In this latter period, central cities suffered an average net annual decline in population of 375,000 because an increase in their black population was much too small to compensate for the loss of whites. Figure 11 shows the distri-

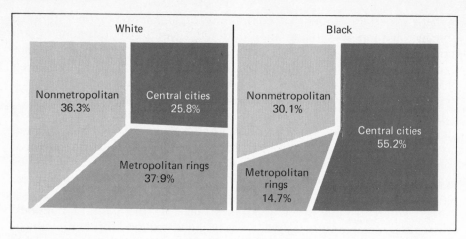

White		Black	
Nonmetropolitan 36.3%	Central cities 25.8%	Nonmetropolitan 30.1%	Central cities 55.2%
	Metropolitan rings 37.9%	Metropolitan rings 14.7%	

Figure 11. Distribution of the White and Negro Populations for the United States by Metropolitan-Nonmetropolitan Residence, 1969. (U.S. Bureau of the Census, *Current Population Reports,* Series P-20, No. 197, March 6, 1970.)

bution, by metropolitan-nonmetropolitan residence, of the black and white populations of the United States in 1969.

Expansion of Urban Population Along Transportation Routes. The increasing use of automobiles has probably been the most important single factor in the spread of urban populations far beyond the boundaries of the central city. The early development of suburbs was principally along rail lines with good commuter service. When the automobile came, it greatly stimulated the growth of many such suburbs by making it possible for people to reach the railroad station quickly from longer distances. Its most striking effect, however, was to bring about a high density of

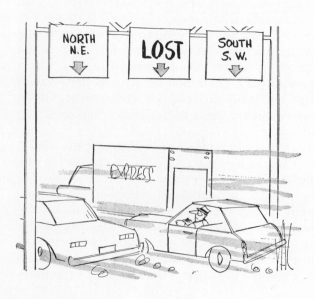

(Courtesy VAL. Copyright 1969 *Saturday Review, Inc.*)

population along many main highways, in areas not readily accessible to rail or other fast public transportation. Some of these areas are incorporated, but many of them are not.

The tendency of population to spread along main transportation routes, especially along main highways and expressways, may in a thickly populated part of the country tend to create a *megalopolis,* that is, a continuous urbanized area linking one city to another for perhaps several hundred miles. In this country the nearest approach to this situation can be found when one travels from Boston to Washington by a route that follows the main concentrations of population.

The growth of suburbs and increasing dependence on the automobile have created great traffic problems in metropolitan areas. In an attempt to solve these, expressways have been built into and through most of our metropolitan centers. Such expressways have complex intersections, designed to permit an uninterrupted flow of traffic. But as automobile ownership keeps rising, even these expressways are becoming overloaded. At best they do nothing to solve the acute parking problems that now plague all large cities and many small ones.

Some Problems of American Cities. We have space to do little more than mention some of the other pressing problems that face the people of every metropolitan center. First, there is the problem of honest and efficient government. Because of the complexity and lack of homogeneity of a modern city, the number of people who live in it, and the impersonal nature of their relations, urban residents are often indifferent to their obligations as voters. Most feel that they can do little to change the political situation, and so they resign themselves to letting someone else control public affairs. Therefore it is often easy for a small group of professional politicians to develop a party machine, or organization, that can control the city government for the benefit of political leaders rather than for the public good. Incompetence and corruption are all too common in American politics and especially in our great cities. Parties are essential in a democracy, and organization is necessary to make them effective, but good government requires that the voting public should take an active part in controlling them.

At best, city governments face difficult problems. City life is expensive compared with that in villages or the open country. When many thousands of people are crowded into small areas, the costs of providing adequate police and fire protection, sanitation, recreation, and transportation are high. In recent years, because of the population explosion, the demand for more services, and the rise in wages and other costs, cities have had special difficulty in levying sufficient taxes. Their chief dependence is on real estate taxes, but it seems to be impractical to increase these beyond a certain point. City governments and other urban agencies also face difficult problems in dealing with such important matters as slums, public health and recreation, education, traffic and transportation, racial tension, and crime and delinquency. Some city problems that once seemed rather minor are now regarded as critical. An example is smoke and smog control, which we discussed in Chapter 4.

The Problem of Governing Metropolitan Areas. When the government of a large city attempts to solve its problems, it is handicapped by the fact that its power is limited to the city proper and ends at the city limits, whereas often the real social and economic unit with which it needs to deal includes a much wider area. Many of the problems of a great urban center can be solved effectively and efficiently only by dealing with the metropolitan area as a whole, yet there is seldom any local government agency whose control extends to the entire area. Sometimes, it is true, such agencies are created for special purposes, as in the case of the Port of New York Authority, but their powers are limited. Only a few cities, among them Toronto, Canada, and Nashville, Tennessee, have succeeded in creating municipal governments with rather adequate powers over the metropolitan area, including the close-in suburbs.

A *metropolitan region* or area includes not only the central city and its residential and industrial suburbs within a radius of ten or twenty miles, but also *satellite cities* that may be thirty to fifty miles away. These satellite cities are too far out for the average commuter to live in them, but their economic life is to a large extent dependent on, or an extension of, the economic life of the central city. Chicago has a typical group of satellite cities, the principal ones being Gary, Joliet, Elgin, Aurora, and Waukegan.

BLIGHTED AREAS AND THE SLUM PROBLEM

How Slums Develop. The growth of our larger American cities has been relatively rapid; as they have expanded outward, whole areas have been built up rather solidly in short periods of time. A newly built and settled area may contain housing units designed for working people or more luxurious units intended for the well-to-do, but in either case it is, while new, a relatively desirable community in which to live.

However, as time passes and the city grows, newer areas are built up farther out, and the older areas begin to deteriorate and to become less desirable. This is especially true where buildings and people are crowded together. Residents who can afford it tend to move out of these older areas, leaving behind only families with less income. Eventually, as suggested earlier, increasing numbers of some low-income group move into the old areas. Meanwhile, as deterioration continues, congestion increases. Buildings are "converted" to provide more and smaller housing units, both to meet the demand of low-income groups for cheap housing and to increase the total rental incomes of owners.

Eventually, deteriorating urban communities become full-fledged slums. Whole families are found living in single rooms. Repairs and maintenance are neglected; toilet facilities are hopelessly inadequate; and plumbing is seldom kept in repair. Porches rot, stairways sag, wallpaper and plaster fall off, and garbage and rubbish are allowed to collect almost anywhere.

Once deterioration is well under way in an urban area, stopping it is extremely difficult. It does not pay individual owners to repair or recondition their buildings, because they cannot find good tenants who will pay enough *additional* rent to justify the high cost. Still less does it pay them to tear down single houses or apartment buildings in such areas and erect new and modern ones, for the people who would be able to rent these new units will not live in areas that are fast becoming slums. Yet the social importance of eliminating slums from our cities can scarcely be overstressed; it has long been recognized that slums breed frustration, vice, crime and delinquency, disease, and moral degradation.

The problem of eliminating slums is twofold. First, some way must be found to rehabilitate existing blighted areas. Second, new blighted areas must be prevented from developing to replace old ones. In a number of cities a beginning has been made toward accomplishing both these objectives, but their final achievement will require both a better understanding of the problem and greater efforts than have yet been in evidence. Some of the basic obstacles to elimination of slums seem scarcely to have been recognized.

Clearance and Reconstruction in Slum Areas. Once an area has deteriorated to the point where it must be classed as a slum, little improvement is likely without organized action on a substantial scale either by government or by some large private agency with government aid. Frequently, such action involves tearing down all or a large portion of the buildings in the slum area, though it is now being recognized that this is often unwise. In many cases, more can be accomplished at less cost and with less disruption of community life if efforts are made to preserve and rehabilitate old but still structurally sound buildings. Sometimes structures in a slum area are completely cleared away in order to provide space for new through highways, parks, civic centers, educational centers, or industrial developments. But usually, if a slum is to be eliminated, the blighted area must somehow be changed into a desirable residential community. This means tearing down and replacing some buildings and repairing and modernizing others. It also requires careful planning for traffic, parks, and all essential community services; and to achieve the desired results such planning must show both imagination and wisdom. Always one great problem is to find the funds with which to finance enough such projects to make a real dent in the slum problem. In many of our cities, slum areas are so large and the costs of clearance and reconstruction so great that the elimination of these areas seems an almost hopeless task.

Another problem that must be dealt with when large slum areas are cleared is the provision of living quarters for the people who are displaced. The law requires, rightly, that other housing must be found for people displaced by urban renewal, but at best this means, for some people, tearing them away from long-familiar surroundings and life-long neighbors. Some of those who must move will always take care of this problem for themselves, but to find suitable housing for the others is usually difficult. To move them into other deteriorated areas is not desirable, and in any case, these are likely to be crowded already. The usual result is long delay plus higher rents or the necessity of moving to locations less satisfactory than those left behind. Ideally, new low-rent housing should be provided in advance for displaced families, but this is seldom practical.

Some aspects of the problem of slum clearance and reconstruction are often overlooked. Many maintain that the great obstacle to quickly eliminating slums is our unwillingness to appropriate enough money. But money is merely a medium of exchange. A more fundamental obstacle to rebuilding our cities at a greatly accelerated rate is limitations on our supplies of needed kinds of skilled labor and of materials. Included in limitations on materials is the power needed for their manufacture and transportation. If we tried to rebuild quickly all the deteriorated areas of our cities by appropriating vastly greater sums of money, the purchasing power of the money would shrink rapidly.

A number of the urban renewal projects carried out in the years following World War II have not been satisfactory because of lack of insight on the part of those who planned them. Not only were sound buildings often torn down needlessly because plans were inflexible but also there was a tendency for much new construction to take the form of monolithic skyscraper or "high-rise" apartments, widely spaced. Often much of the surrounding space was filled with parking lots not skillfully placed and landscaped. Playgrounds, shopping centers, and green areas were also included, but in too many cases the total effect was formal and rather forbidding. The trend was toward grand engineering projects rather than toward giving first consideration to the everyday needs of people. Seldom did urban renewal projects provide interesting and intimate streets, where one could rub elbows with people and drop into small stores, shops, bars, and restaurants. Frequently, also, small service establishments of various types were crowded out.

Public Housing Projects. Plans for the construction of *public housing* had their beginning in the United States in 1933 shortly after Franklin D. Roosevelt became President. In that year, the National Industrial Recovery Act authorized, among other things, "low rent and slum clearance projects," and some of these were soon planned and carried out. The purpose was partly to stimulate employment and partly to provide better housing for low-income groups. Because costs of land and construction were to be partly met out of tax funds, rents could be set at very moderate levels. From time to time, changes have been made in the federal program. Today, except for the Federal Home Loan Bank, all federal agencies concerned with housing and home finance are under the supervision of the Department of Housing and Urban Development, established in 1965. The creation of this department was first suggested by President Kennedy and was later sponsored by President Johnson. Mel Scott believes Johnson was "perhaps more acutely aware than any previous chief executive" of the needs of the cities, and credits his administration with an outstanding achievement "in equipping the nation with the legal tools to renew and develop cities."[8]

Altogether billions of dollars have been spent on public housing projects, but even expenditures on this scale have not been sufficient to reduce appreciably the slum problem. Not only has the public housing program been too limited in scope to contribute much toward eliminating slums, but often projects have been badly planned. Some of the earlier ones are already on the way to becoming new slums. In part this is because many former slum dwellers continue their bad housekeeping practices when they move into new quarters. The new buildings deteriorate fast unless people can be trained to keep them clean and give them proper care.

Private Projects for Rebuilding Blighted Areas. To a limited extent, private builders have undertaken to clear and rebuild blighted areas without any sort of public subsidy. Usually this requires that they be granted the right to buy property by condemnation, for otherwise they would find it impossible to acquire all the land parcels in a given area. But in most cases the costs of slum clearance and rebuilding are too high to attract private capital unless a firm receives some form of subsidy. The most spectacular of the privately financed slum-clearance and redevelopment projects have been carried out with the aid of government subsidies granted under provisions of the Federal Housing Act of 1949. The act provided that if a designated local agency bought land in a slum area and resold it to a private builder at a price lower than cost, the federal government would reimburse the agency for two thirds the difference between the cost of the land and its resale price. The rest of the loss must be borne by the local or state government.

One of the basic obstacles to the rebuilding of our slums and, in general, to the provision of adequate housing for our lower-income groups, is the very high level of building costs. Since World War II, building costs have risen substantially more than the cost of living, and they are especially high in our larger cities. Higher building costs result in part from the constant raising of union wage rates; in part from opposition by unions to the introduction of new construction methods, such as prefabrication, which might reduce jobs for their members; in part from sharply rising costs of building materials; in part from obsolete building codes, which prevent the introduction of some newer and cheaper materials and methods; and in part from high interest rates on the mortgages used to finance building. However, an important underlying cause of rising building costs has been the tremendous demand for new housing since the war. By providing easy credit terms for buyers, especially veterans, the government has greatly

[8] Mel Scott, *American City Planning Since 1890*, Berkely and Los Angeles, University of California Press, 1969, pp. 610, 620, 627.

stimulated building, but in doing this it has also made a substantial contribution to the inflation of costs.

The Prevention of Slums. Rebuilding blighted areas does little to solve the slum problem if new slums are forming faster than the old ones are rebuilt. The situation in Chicago is probably typical of that in most of our larger cities. Some years ago the Interim Commission on Neighborhood Conservation of the City of Chicago stated the problem as follows:

> *While we are laboring to reclaim worn-out areas and return them to economic health, older neighborhoods in all parts of the city are rapidly giving way to the forces that create slums. More than one-fourth of the city—56 square miles—consists of buildings the majority of which were built from 40 to 60 years ago. Much of this property is ripe for physical disintegration. It is the conviction of many close observers that new slums are developing in Chicago faster than we can clear and rebuild the old ones.*
>
> *What are we to do about these older neighborhoods that are in danger of becoming the new blighted areas? The costs of rebuilding . . . are enormous. We simply cannot afford to wait until older areas actually reach the slum state.*

Today *urban renewal* is the popular term both for programs of slum clearance and for plans to reverse the processes of deterioration in older city neighborhoods. So far most plans for reversing deterioration have relied heavily in their initial stages on limited slum clearance through the demolition of substandard buildings in selected small areas and their replacement by new construction. Such programs tend to be restricted by their dependence on government subsidies for acquiring the land and buildings involved.

Rapidly rising costs have been a major factor in discouraging private owners from keeping up or replacing old residential construction. In New York City the problem has been compounded by the continuance of wartime rent controls. Controls tend to keep the income from these buildings low enough so that often it does not pay to meet the inflated costs of maintaining them. Thousands of them have simply been abandoned by their owners.

A rather recent effort of the federal government to help cities eliminate slums is the "model cities" program, started under President Johnson and somewhat modified by President Nixon. Under this program about 150 cities have been receiving substantial grants to aid them in the renewal of selected poverty areas.

Some of the policies that would help prevent the future development of slums are rather clear but not always easy to implement. To begin with, when new areas are first built up, they should be well planned, as insurance against future deterioration. Important considerations are an attractive appearance; avoidance of overcrowding; durable construction of buildings; adequate schools; libraries, churches, parks, and playgrounds; supermarkets and also small shops to provide needed consumer goods and services; properly located traffic and transportation routes; and adequate parking facilities.

In old areas, where deterioration is already under way, only vigorous action can stop it. To take such action requires organization, sufficient power, and willingness to act. Nuisances and eyesores such as dilapidated buildings must be removed. Plans must be made and carried out for desirable new construction. *Zoning ordinances* must be adequate and must be enforced to prevent invasion of the neighborhood by undesirable commercial or industrial activities or undesirable types of buildings. *Building ordinances* must also be enforced to make certain that buildings are kept in safe and sanitary condition. Overcrowding must be prevented, especially the illegal conversion of houses and apartments into extremely small units, with inadequate space, inadequate cooking facilities, and inadequate toilet facilities. Municipal services such as street cleaning, garbage collection, and police protection must be sufficient. Finally, and perhaps most important of all, if any community is for long to avoid progressive deterioration and to remain a desirable residential section, the majority of its property owners must have enough self-respect and community spirit, and also enough money, to maintain their own properties voluntarily at certain minimum standards.

So far, in spite of all efforts, we have not had much success in meeting the slum problem. New slums seem to develop faster than we can eliminate old ones. Many students of the problem believe we would do better if we gave more attention to ways of reducing building costs and less attention to devising crash programs of replacement based on massive government spending. The situation for private builders and home owners would be greatly improved if federal, state, and local governments could devise effective policies and programs for reducing or keeping down building costs by such means as holding interest rates at reasonable levels, encouraging the development of cheaper building materials, stimulating the use of prefabrication and other cost-saving methods of production, and keeping wages of construction workers at reasonable levels in comparison with wages in general. Wages of building trades workers are an especially large element in the upkeep and repair of housing. According to the Bureau of National Affairs, the compensation of construction workers rose much faster than that of factory workers in every year from 1960 to 1970 inclusive. In 1970 the wages of construction workers were increased on the average, in union wage agreements, by about ninety cents an hour, as compared with about twenty-three cents for factory workers. Another helpful approach to stopping the spread of slums would be the wider use by state and local governments of real estate tax laws that would encourage rather than discourage the proper maintenance of older buildings. For example, property improvements might everywhere be made tax-free over a period of several years.

22. "Plug-In" Apartment Building. This model shows that a high-rise apartment building can be created by plugging residential units into a steel frame. Utility lines and elevators run within the permanent core. Hoisting equipment on the roof permits fast initial erection and facilitates subsequent interchangeability of units for remodeling. This model is one of a series of new concepts in mobile homes. (Courtesy Jones & Laughlin Steel Corporation.)

Not long ago Lewis Mumford, an outstanding student of urban problems, remarked before a Senate subcommittee: "Go slow! Experiment with small measures and small units. Whatever you do in extending the policies followed in the past will most surely meet with the same embarrassments and failures. . . . The time for massive action on a large scale has not yet come. But the time for fresh thinking on this whole subject is long overdue."[9]

Perhaps few ideas for planning the rehabilitation and redevelopment of cities are brand new, but in recent years there have been important changes of emphasis in the thinking of city planners. One of the books that gave impetus to such changes was *The Death and Life of Great American Cities* by Jane Jacobs. In this book she denounced the hardships experienced by families displaced by renewal projects; the standardized public housing and redevelopment projects; the destruction of the diversity and the human relationships in older low-income neighborhoods; and the cutting up of cities by express highways.

A trend of recent years that should help in avoiding some of the mistakes made in the past is the movement for giving community leaders, in areas that face urban renewal, a part in the decision-making processes. This greatly increases the chances of getting programs that will conserve any good features of the area, and that will benefit the people who live there instead of just moving them out.

One aspect of the fresh thinking called for by Mumford is the growing emphasis by a few of our outstanding architects and city planners on what some call *environmental design,* which recognizes the importance of creating communities that can meet the human needs of people in everyday living. There is also a growing recognition that we should think several times before we destroy viable neighborhoods where people have their homes, in order to build an expressway or a massive redevelopment project. One of the leaders of the new trends in city planning and designing is Lawrence Halperin, who created the site plan for the Seattle World's Fair. His aim was to provide not only buildings but also an environment that people would find attractive and that could later be used for other purposes. He succeeded so well that the fair site, now Seattle Center Park, is visited by eight million people annually.[10] Another planner who has been attracting wide attention is Constantinos Doxiadis. One of his ideas is that man has never created truly successful human "surroundings" in an area much more than a mile square. He would, so far as possible, divide great cities into a number of smaller communities, in some degree separated from one another physically. Each would be in many respects self-sufficient, and in each it would be easy to walk to parks, schools, factories, stores, and other facilities.

[9] See "Why Experts Are Wrong in Their Prescriptions for Cities," *The National Observer,* May 1, 1967.

[10] See "Planning Space for People, Not Buildings," *The National Observer,* June 23, 1969.

THE FUTURE OF BIG CITIES

Some feel that the future outlook for big cities is dark indeed. They see an unlimited growth of metropolitan areas, with the adjacent suburbs becoming as urbanized as the central cities and with the whole of each area suffering from problems beyond solution: deterioration of large districts; air pollution; increasing difficulties with water pollution and the disposal of waste products; inadequate educational opportunities; poor public transportation; inadequate finances; mounting crime rates; social unrest; riots and turmoil. Such problems, they say, become completely unmanageable if we concentrate too many millions of people within a limited area.

Many of our large cities are already facing very critical problems with the long-run solutions in doubt. New York City is a good example. Some of its problems are more acute than those of most cities because of its great size and diversity. Among the more difficult problems are race relations, labor relations with public employees, education of disadvantaged children, unemployment among minority groups, and huge and ever-mounting welfare costs. Perhaps the most disturbing of all New York City's problems is the difficulties it faces in raising sufficient funds to meet its future needs, even though in 1969 it already had a budget of about $6.2 billion, larger than that of any of the fifty states. One proposal for easing the financial problems of cities is for the federal government to share with states and cities a larger proportion of the federal income tax. Another large city that, though very much smaller than New York, has faced unusual difficulties is Cleveland.

Building New Cities to Relieve Urban Congestion. One proposal for reducing the problems that arise from great concentrations of people in small areas is to build many new cities, limiting the population of each to, say, 200,000 people. The purpose would be to prevent further growth of our largest cities and to divert increases of population to towns and cities of more manageable size. The idea seems to have merit but it would require planning on a national scale, including adequate inducements for people and industry to go to the new cities instead of continuing to concentrate in the old ones. Such a program would have to be spread over time in order to avoid inflation of costs and also to provide the necessary amounts of skilled labor and building materials, not to mention acquisition of land.

There is considerable opposition to the building of new cities from business and political leaders of our present cities. They want to revive their own cities, to make them more attractive, and if possible to bring back to them some of the suburbanites who have left. They fear that new cities would draw away from them more and more people in the middle- and upper-income brackets. President Johnson once suggested a program of new towns "with all the public services, all the industry and commerce needed to provide new jobs, and sufficient housing and cultural and recreational facilities for moderate- and low-income families as well as for the well-to-do." Congress, however, took no action on this proposal.[11]

There are said to be about a hundred new towns that have been planned or are being developed in the United States, but many of them are really new suburbs and most of them are relatively small. Two frequently mentioned examples are Reston, Virginia, and Columbia, Maryland. There the developers have attempted to create communities that by their design and provision of services make positive contributions to the welfare and personal development of their residents.

Some European countries have advanced much further than we in the establishment of new towns and cities. In the last twenty years, the British Ministry of Housing has planned and helped to finance the building of more than twenty new towns in Britain. Eight of these are twenty-five to sixty miles from London and are expected to provide homes and jobs for about 500,000 people who otherwise would live in London or commute to it for work. Larger new cities are now being planned with a population of about 250,000 each. Several of these will be built within sixty to eighty miles of London. At the same time that it is building new towns, the British government is also offering incentives to firms to move their plants and offices out of central London.

London has certain advantages in dealing with its problems that American cities do not have: (1) the National Treasury annually meets about 40 per cent of the city's expenditures; (2) because of national planning programs, effective measures can be taken to reduce pressure on London; (3) the government of London—the Greater London Council— has more power and power over a wider area than do the governments of American cities.[12]

Other western European countries, including the Netherlands, Sweden, and Finland, are also building new towns in order to relieve urban congestion and improve living conditions. In some cases these towns or cities are really suburbs, but they are planned so as to be separated from one another, and sometimes from the central city, by park lands. These both provide recreation and preserve for each town the character of a genuine community of manageable size. This type of planning enables a metropolitan area to expand without becoming a confused, conglomerate mass of urban sprawl. The pattern is something like a flower with petals, between which lie parks and farm lands.

Though the outlook for some of our big cities is not at present very cheering, their problems should not be insoluble. If European cities like London, Rotterdam, and Stockholm have made net progress, as appears to be the case, our own cities should be able to follow suit. But this will take imaginative planning that avoids our many past mistakes. It will also

[11] Scott, op. cit., pp. 603–604.
[12] See "London—One City That Is Solving Its Problems," *U.S. News & World Report,* September 23, 1968.

take more effective cooperation than we have had in the past between our federal, state, and local governments; and it will take money, though if we rely chiefly on money we will almost certainly fail. Finally, because at best rejuvenation of our cities will take time, we cannot afford to delay the implementation of effective policies designed to achieve it.

Terms to Be Understood

community
neighborhood
rural community
city
metropolitan center
heterogeneity
civilization
standard metropolitan
  statistical area

segregation
megalopolis
metropolitan region
concentric-zone
  theory
zone of transition
sector theory
multiple-nuclei theory
anomie

satellite cities
slum
blighted area
public housing
urban renewal
zoning ordinance
building ordinance
environmental design

Questions for Review and Discussion

1. What great technological advance accounted in great part for the original growth of towns and cities? What great change in methods of production largely explains the modern trend toward urbanization?
2. Is an urban community a primary or a secondary group? Explain.
3. List the principal types of communities. Can all communities be classified under one of these types? Why or why not?
4. In what respects can it be said that urban communities in the United States have rural backgrounds?
5. What are the chief characteristics by means of which we can identify a rural community?
6. How do you explain the fact that the rural villages of the United States seem to be holding their own, in spite of a decrease in the farm population?
7. What are the more important differences between rural and urban life?
8. List the more significant changes that are taking place in rural life.
9. List the principal characteristics that distinguish urban centers from rural communities or smaller towns.
10. Explain the role cities have played in the development of civilization.
11. Where and why did cities first develop? Contrast ancient cities with those of today.
12. Explain the influence of the Industrial Revolution on the growth of modern cities. What other factors have also contributed to the world-wide growth of cities?
13. In terms of statistics, to what extent has the United States become an urban nation? Compare the present situation with that of 1790.
14. What are the three principal theories of the development and structure of

modern cities? Explain each with some care, and show how the three are related to one another.

15. What factors, not taken into account by the above theories, tend to change their original patterns?
16. Can a large city be divided into a number of communities? Explain.
17. What city problems are intensified by the migration of people to the suburbs?
18. What are the more common types of residential segregation in large cities?
19. List as many as you can of the social problems that are likely to be more acute in a large city than in rural areas.
20. Why does governing a metropolitan region present special problems?
21. Explain why slums develop in cities.
22. What are the major obstacles to the rehabilitation of slum areas?
23. Describe the role played by each of the following in plans for meeting the slum problem: (a) public housing; (b) private clearance and rebuilding projects; (c) programs for preventing the deterioration of neighborhoods. How much has been achieved, and what is the outlook for the future?
24. What changes have taken place in recent years in our concepts of how to go about urban planning and urban renewal?
25. What are the most difficult problems that our larger cities face?
26. Evaluate the "new cities" idea as a partial solution of our urban problems.

For Further Study

Anderson, Martin, The Federal Bulldozer: A Critical Analysis of Urban Renewal, 1949–1962, New York, McGraw-Hill, Inc., 1967.

Anderson, Nels, The Industrial Urban Community, New York, Random House, Inc., 1968.

Banfield, Edward C., The Unheavenly City: The Nature and Future of Our Urban Crisis, Boston, Little, Brown and Company, 1970. A controversial treatment by a scholar who presents some interesting ideas.

Campbell, Alan K., ed., The States and the Urban Crisis, Englewood Cliffs, N.J., Prentice-Hall, Inc., 1970.

Congressional Quarterly Service, Urban Environment, an Editorial Research Report, Washington, D.C., Congressional Quarterly, Inc., 1969.

Donaldson, Scott, The Suburban Myth, New York, Columbia University Press, 1969.

Doxiadis, C. A., and Truman B. Douglass, New World of Urban Man, paperback, Philadelphia, United Church Press, 1965.

Duhl, Leonard J., M.D., ed., The Urban Condition: People and Policy in the Metropolis, Clarion paperback, New York, Simon and Schuster, Inc., 1969.

Faltermeyer, Edmund K., Redoing America: A Nationwide Report on How to Make Our Cities and Suburbs Livable, Collier paperback, New York, The Macmillan Company, 1969.

Ficker, Herbert, and Victor Graves, Social Science and Urban Crisis, New York, The Macmillan Company, 1971.

Forrester, Jay W., Urban Dynamics, Cambridge, Mass., M.I.T. Press, 1969.

Glaab, Charles, and A. Theodore Brown, *A History of Urban America,* New York, The Macmillan Company, 1967.

Jacobs, Jane, *The Death and Life of Great American Cities,* Modern Library paperback, New York, Random House, Inc., 1969.

———, *The Economy of Cities,* New York, Random House, Inc., 1969.

Knox, Frank, and Jossleyn Hennessy, *Restrictive Practices in the Building Industry,* paperback, Levittown, N.Y., Trans-Atlantic Arts, Inc., 1967.

Lowe, Jeanne R., *Cities in a Race with Time: Progress and Poverty in America's Renewing Cities,* New York, Random House, Inc., 1967.

Mumford, Lewis, *The Urban Prospect,* New York, Harcourt Brace Jovanovich, Inc., 1968.

Redfield, Robert, *The Little Community: Peasant Society and Culture,* Phoenix paperback, Chicago, University of Chicago Press, 1960.

Sjoberg, Gideon, *The Pre-Industrial City,* New York, The Free Press, 1970.

Thomlinson, Ralph, *Urban Structure: The Social and Spatial Character of Cities,* New York, Random House, Inc., 1968.

Wakstein, Allen M., ed., *Urbanization of America, An Historical Anthology,* paperback, Boston, Houghton Mifflin Company, 1970.

Weber, Max, *The City,* New York, The Free Press, 1958.

Wirth, Louis, *On Cities and Social Life: Selected Papers,* edited by Albert J. Reiss, Jr., Chicago, University of Chicago Press, 1964.

Zimmer, Basil G., *Rebuilding Cities: The Effects of Displacement and Relocation on Small Businesses,* Chicago, Quadrangle Books, Inc., 1964. An analysis of an urban renewal program.

Chapter 12

Social

Stratification

he people of every large society can always be divided—sometimes along fairly clear-cut lines, sometimes only roughly—into groups differing in income, occupations, power, privileges, manner of living, and the regard in which they are held by their fellow citizens, This division of people into a hierarchy of superior, intermediate, and inferior groups is the phenomenon called *social stratification*. The unit of stratification is the family, for except in rare cases all members of a family are regarded as belonging to the same stratum, or layer. Ordinarily the top layer is very thin, consisting only of those with the very highest standing. Most people belong to strata further down the social scale.

In some small, primitive societies, social stratification is not found, but in all fairly large and complex societies it appears to be unavoidable. Some activities, some kinds of work, are more important to the society than others, and often they can be carried on only by people of outstanding ability plus special training or experience. Important political offices must be filled, economic activities must be organized, and military forces must be commanded. Those who play important roles in such activities acquire power and prestige. Usually they also acquire larger-than-average incomes and various special privileges. In addition, because they tend to associate principally with one another, they develop common attitudes and modes of living. Sometimes they are able to entrench themselves in their favored position by means of legal and religious sanctions; but even without these, they can, in most cases, pass their own superior status along to their children.

Social stratification, when very firmly established, contributes to social stability. It means general acceptance of the fact that certain groups perform certain functions, and their children after them. Competitiveness is reduced, since almost everyone knows his "place" in society and knows the occupation or occupations he is expected to follow. When social stratification is less rigid and there are more opportunities for an individual to improve his status, dissatisfaction and conflict may be more in evidence.

TYPES OF SOCIAL STRATIFICATION

There are three principal types of social stratification: *estates, castes,* and *social classes.* Our chief interest is in the latter, because they represent the major form of stratification found in modern industrial societies. However, some knowledge of estate and caste systems will contribute to our understanding of the nature of social classes.

Estates. The stratification system that developed in Europe under feudalism is called *estates.* Under this system the estate to which a person belonged and its place in the social hierarchy were determined chiefly by custom, occupation, rights and obligations with respect to land, and other legal sanctions. Estates included such groups as the nobility, the clergy, merchants, craftsmen, and peasants. Each of these large groups, however, was broken down into smaller groups and various grades.

In an estates system, wherever and whenever it may exist, the position of an individual in society is nearly always inherited from his parents, the lines between groups are clearly drawn, and almost everyone knows just where he belongs. He may even be required to dress in a particular way to indicate his station in relation to those above him. Mobility is small, but is entirely possible within the framework of law and custom. A noble may free a serf from his bondage to the land in return for a special service; or the king may grant land to a commoner, knight him, and bestow on him a title of nobility. Military service and the priesthood are also possible avenues of upward mobility in an estates system.

The medieval estates system with its relatively rigid social categories was better suited to a static than a dynamic society. It gradually disintegrated under the impact of such changes as the decline of feudalism, the Industrial Revolution, and the rise of a democratic ideology with its strong emphasis on freedom and equality.

Castes. The caste system is usually associated with India, where it has prevailed for about three thousand years. Under it, just as under an estate system, an individual acquires his social position by birth. However, the great vitality of the caste system seems to arise from the fact that, besides being firmly established by custom, it is an integral part of the Hindu religion. It is based on the doctrines of *karma* and *transmigration. Karma* is the belief that the primary concern of every person should be to fulfill in this life the duties placed upon him, including the ceremonial obligations associated with membership in his caste. The doctrine of transmigration holds that if he fulfills his duties sufficiently well in this life, he will in a future life be reborn into a higher caste. A caste system is even more rigid than an estate system, because in theory there is no way of moving to a higher status except through death and reincarnation. In practice, it is said, a very limited amount of upward shifting does occur.

In a caste system the lines between groups are very clearly drawn. Everyone knows his own place and, at least in the case of small communities, the place of everyone else. As a rule, certain castes engage in certain occupations. In India the Brahman caste provides priests; the Kshatriya, warriors and rulers; the Vaisya, merchants and farmers; the Sudra, artisans and laborers. However, each of these groups contains many separate castes and subcastes, some existing only in certain areas. With rare exceptions, marriage is possible only between persons who belong to the same caste. Moreover, there are elaborate rules governing all contacts between members of different castes. At the bottom of the hierarchy is a group of outcastes, or *untouchables.* Any contact with this group is thought to defile people of higher status.

Mahatma Gandhi deliberately associated with the untouchables in an attempt to break down the caste system, but, in spite of his prestige, he had relatively little success. Given time, however, it seems likely that advancing industrialization and other Western influences will cause the system to disintegrate. Today the Indian government itself is making real efforts to break down caste distinctions. Untouchability is outlawed by the present constitution, and penalties are provided for such acts as refusing to serve an untouchable in a public restaurant or chasing him away from a village well. Recent reports are that untouchability is dying out in the cities, where most people seldom know one another and where they must ride in the same buses and work in the same factories; but in the country districts, where most Hindus still live, it persists in spite of government opposition.

23. Brahman and Untouchable. Here an orthodox Hindu Brahman gives sweets to an untouchable, taking care not to come into contact with the man's cupped hands. Whenever a Brahman dies, his relatives offer sweets and cash to untouchables following the funeral ceremony. (Courtesy United Press International, Inc.)

Social-stratification systems having some of the characteristics of the one in India have been found in other societies. The blacks of the United States, especially in the South, have been called a caste by some writers. To support this usage it was pointed out that they belonged by birth to a socially underprivileged group and that there was ordinarily no possibility of their transferring into the more privileged white group. However, their position differed considerably from that of the members of a low Hindu caste. In the first place, they were subject to no rigid occupational limitations, and some achieved high positions in government, business, and the professions. Even more important, their inferior social position was not based on religious sanctions; rather, it was and is contrary to our religious teachings, as these are understood by most American Christians. It is also contrary to our basic democratic ideals of freedom and equal opportunity for all human beings.

Social Classes. Social classes are the form of stratification that characterizes modern industrial societies. Unlike estates and castes, they are supported by neither legal nor religious sanctions. Furthermore, they are not clear-cut, definitely delimited groups into which every person in the community can be placed without doubt or question. The fact that social classes are not perfectly clear-cut entities seems to be proved by the inability of social scientists to come to any general agreement on just how many of them should be recognized as existing. This is not strange, because in a democratic industrial society *social status is a continuum, with individuals and families scattered all along it from top to bottom.* If we divide people on this *social scale* into two, three, or more "social classes" we must do so rather arbitrarily.

Social scientists also have difficulty in deciding just what criteria should be used in determining social status. Some, following in this respect Karl Marx, would place an individual (or family) in a given class entirely on the basis of economic considerations. Those who take this point of view usually put their chief emphasis on income. Others, probably the great majority, would determine the status and class of an individual by his general social standing—that is, by whether the community, on the basis of various criteria, places him high or low in the social scale. Income might have the major influence on this rating, but it would be only one factor.

Joyce O. Hertzler has the following to say about the difficulties of dividing people into social classes:

There is no general agreement as to the combination of factors or distinguishing characteristics that delineate a social class. . . . An almost unlimited number of distinctions is possible. It is equally difficult to specify the number of classes into which a typical community or society is divided. In fact, there are almost as many schemes of class division as there are social scientists who make them.

The traditional American class division is into upper, lower, and middle classes. Warner and associates, in their study of classes, have fixed upon a refinement of this three-part division and use six: upper upper, lower upper, upper middle, lower middle, upper lower, and lower lower. Hollingshead found five, which he designates merely by Roman numerals (I, II, III, IV, V). Centers, in his rather comprehensive review, posits four main American classes on the basis of self-identification with a class name: upper (3 per cent of the population), middle (43 per cent), working (51 per cent), and lower (1 per cent), with 2 per cent of the population saying "Don't know" or "Don't believe in classes."[1]

Social Class Defined. For our present purposes we shall consider that *a social class consists of those people in a community who are somewhat similar in their economic status, their attitudes and beliefs, their educational attainments, their ways of living, the regard in which others hold them, and their power or lack of power to influence community affairs.* A social class is, in some degree, a *subculture.* People whose social statuses are similar are likely not only to live in the same neighborhoods, associate largely with one another, and marry one another; they are also likely to show similarities of speech, manners, and moral standards as compared with people who are higher or lower in the social scale. It has been ob-

[1] Joyce O. Hertzler, *Society in Action,* New York, The Dryden Press, Inc., 1954, pp. 224–225. Copyright 1954 by The Dryden Press, Inc. Reprinted by special permission.

served, for example, that in some respects lower-class people have a less strict sex code than middle-class people. They also tend to have less formal education, to be less ambitious, and to show some differences in their political and religious affiliations.

Because social classes, like other types of stratification, represent superiority-inferiority relationships, some writers have compared the class structure of society to a layer cake. At the top of the cake is a thin layer consisting of a small group of people who have the highest economic and social status. At the bottom of the cake is another thin layer representing those whose economic and social status is very low and whom the community regards as of little account. Between these two extremes, at various levels, lie thicker layers, which represent the great majority of the population. The chief objection to this analogy is that the divisions between social classes are not as definite as those between the layers of a cake.

Social classes are not organized groups like families or communities. Rather, they are useful concepts. They also are social realities, but only in the sense that the people of any complex society can be divided roughly into a few large groups in such a way that those in each group have about the same general social standing and the other similarities that go with this. However, as has been indicated, the lines of division between classes are both vague and somewhat arbitrary, and many individuals are difficult to place. The more class layers one assumes, the greater is the difficulty of distinguishing them and determining just where individuals should be placed.

Most people do have some idea of the social class to which they belong, though they may not give it the same name as would a sociologist. For example, a family may think of themselves as "good common people" when a sociologist would classify them as belonging to the lower, or perhaps the upper lower class. Members of a social class recognize that they have more in common with others at a similar social level than they do with those above or below them. Also, as we have noted, they are likely to live in those areas and do those kinds of work that bring them into especially close association with members of their own class.

The Family Basis of Social Class. We have said that much the same social status is shared by all members of the immediate family group. As a rule, the most important factors in determining social class are the occupation and the wealth and income of the head of the family. Such occupations as law and medicine, high government positions, and the management of large business enterprises yield considerable prestige, because they require more-than-average ability and training; other occupations, such as keeping small stores or working at skilled trades, are regarded as very respectable; but there are some occupations, especially those that require only unskilled manual labor, that are looked down on by most members of the community. In general, the regard in which an occupation is held is closely correlated with the income it yields, but there are exceptions to this rule. A federal judge, for example, may have more prestige than a business man whose income is several times greater.

Membership in social classes tends to be transmitted in the same family lines from generation to generation because children are likely to acquire much the same attitudes and modes of living as their parents, to receive similar educational advantages, to enter similar occupations, and to inherit whatever wealth their parents may possess. Many families do, of course, move up or down in the social scale, but they are exceptions to the rule.

Mobility in a Class System. Mobility in a class system is much greater than in a caste or estate system. However, it is difficult to measure, and it may vary considerably in different societies. It is often assumed that upward mobility in the United States substantially exceeds that in Europe. However, several studies have been made that cast doubt on this assumption. Perhaps it had more validity in the past; or perhaps the impression that mobility is greater in this country may arise from the fact that incomes are generally higher here, so that the lower or working classes enjoy many conveniences and luxuries that in some European countries would not be

24. Snow-Shovel Salute. A workman pauses from his job to raise his snow shovel in salute as top-hatted members of the Swedish Parliament leave the Great Church of Stockholm after the ceremonial opening of Parliament. (Courtesy Wide World Photos.)

available even to most middle-class people. But income is only one of the criteria of social status, and the fact that working people have relatively high incomes does not necessarily mean that they have moved into the middle class. Net upward social mobility is possible in a society, at least for a time. It is probable that in both this country and western Europe the number of people in the middle class has increased faster than the number in the lower class ever since the Industrial Revolution.

Discussions of class mobility often overlook one simple fact, namely, that room at the top is always limited. Let us make an extreme assumption by supposing that people in the upper class are completely replaced each generation by people from the middle and lower classes. Let us further assume that 5 per cent of the population are always in the upper class. Even on this basis only one person out of nineteen could rise from the lower or middle classes to the top. At the same time all the people in the upper class would have to drop to a lower level. When we talk about social mobility we are apt to think of opportunities to move upward in the social scale, but we must remember that as some people, or their children, move up, others or their children are likely to move down. Assuming no increase in the proportionate size of the upper class, a high degree of mobility means only that it is fairly easy for some citizens who have ambition, energy, and intelligence to move up the social ladder and replace those who are less ambitious or less capable.

What are the conditions that contribute to social mobility? Probably most important of all is social change. In a changing society the old order is always being disturbed, and new ways of achieving wealth or position keep appearing. Industrialization, with its new methods of production and new types of business organization, provided many opportunities for rising on the economic and social ladder. Migration and geographic expansion also provided opportunities. When millions of immigrants were coming to the United States, very few were from the upper classes. As a result, the opportunities for some to rise in the social scale were unusually good. Also, when new areas were settled in our West, there were unusual opportunities for people of initiative and ability to assume leadership in business and community affairs.

In the United States large-scale immigration and, except perhaps for Alaska, the settling of new territories are things of the past. However, other factors continue to promote social mobility. Rapid technological progress keeps creating new occupations and changing the nature and requirements for old ones. Also, the *proportion* of people doing skilled and professional work has risen relative to those engaged in unskilled work or common labor, and this is one reason for some expansion of our middle classes relative to our lower classes. At the same time, we have expanded our educational system. We have made college, technical-school, and university training more easily available than in the past to young people of outstanding talent, even those who come from low-income families; and we are attempting to raise the minimum educational attainment of almost everyone to the high school or even the junior college level. This attempt encounters obstacles and creates frustrations that will be referred to in Chapter 16. In any case, the places at the top of the social ladder are limited, and only the most determined and capable climbers are likely to attain them.

THE WARNER TREATMENT OF SOCIAL CLASSES

Some years ago, when W. Lloyd Warner was at the University of Chicago, he and his associates undertook a series of studies of social class in the United States. These studies attracted wide attention and constitute a landmark of research in the field of social stratification. Nevertheless, a number of sociologists criticized adversely some of Warner's methods and findings. A summary of these studies and some of the chief objections raised to them will give us an insight into the problems that arise when we attempt to analyze the nature and significance of social classes.

Warner, as already noted in a passage quoted from Hertzler, divides the American population into six social classes: upper upper, lower upper, upper middle, lower middle, upper lower, and lower lower. In certain parts of the country, however, he reduces this number to five, because he finds that in areas such as the Midwest it is usually impossible to distinguish a separate upper upper, or "old family" class. Warner seems to feel that his six classes represent rather definite groups, the existence of which is actually recognized in most communities by people who are keen observers, but on this point the majority of sociologists do not agree with him.[2]

Warner uses two methods for determining the social class to which people belong, and he believes that together they provide "accurate procedures for measuring social class and the class position of individuals, for validating results obtained, and for translating social class and socioeconomic status categories into terms which are interchangeable."[3]

Warner calls his first method *Evaluated Participation* (EP). Basically it consists of interviewing selected members of a community and obtaining from them their judgments of the social-class ratings of their fellow citizens. This method assumes "that those who interact in the social system of a community evaluate the participation of those around them" and that they "are explicitly or implicitly aware of the ranking and translate their evaluations of such social participation into social-class ratings that can be communicated to the investigator."[4]

[2] For a critical appraisal of Warner's methods and conclusions, see Ruth Kornhauser, "The Warner Approach to Social Stratification," *Class, Status, and Power,* edited by Reinhard Bendix and Seymour Martin Lipset, New York, The Free Press, 1953, pp. 243–255.

[3] W. Lloyd Warner et al., *Social Class in America,* Torchbook paperback, New York, Harper & Row, Publishers, 1960, p. 35.

[4] Ibid.

Warner's second method of determining social class is to employ an *Index of Status Characteristics* (ISC). This means obtaining ratings for each individual on each of four status characteristics—occupation, source of income, house type, and dwelling area. For each of these characteristics a numerical score is given. Small numbers indicate high social rating; larger numbers indicate low social rating. The numerical evaluations

Table 9. *Warner's Chart for Scoring Individuals on Status Characteristics*

Characteristics	Score
Occupation	
Professionals and proprietors of large businesses (such as doctors or factory owners)	4
Semiprofessionals and small officials of large businesses (such as lab technicians or managers)	8
Clerks and similar workers (secretaries, bookkeepers, etc.)	12
Skilled workers (bakers, carpenters, etc.)	16
Proprietors of small businesses (owners of small groceries, restaurants, etc.)	20
Semiskilled workers (bus drivers, cannery workers, etc.)	24
Unskilled workers (such as warehousemen or ditch diggers)	28
Source of income	
Inherited wealth	3
Earned wealth	6
Profits and fees	9
Salary	12
Wages	15
Private relief	18
Public relief and "nonrespectable" incomes (for example, gambling)	21
House type	
Large houses in good condition	3
Large houses in medium condition; medium-sized houses in good condition	6
Large houses in bad condition	9
Medium-sized houses in medium condition; apartments in regular apartment buildings	12
Small houses in good condition; small houses in medium condition; dwellings over stores	15
Medium-sized houses in bad condition; small houses in bad condition	18
All houses in very bad condition; dwellings in structures not originally intended for homes	21
Area lived in	
Very exclusive; Gold Coast, etc.	2
The better suburbs and apartment-house areas, houses with spacious yards, etc.	4
Above average; areas all residential, larger-than-average space around houses; apartment areas in good condition, etc.	6
Average; residential neighborhoods, no deterioration in the area	8
Below average; area not quite holding its own, beginning to deteriorate, business entering, etc.	10
Low; considerably deteriorated, run-down and semislum	12
Very low; slum	14

Warner uses in measuring status characteristics are given in Table 9. The scores of an individual on all four of the status characteristics are added up to determine where he stands in the social scale. The social-class equivalents for various total ISC scores are indicated in Table 10.

It will be noted in Table 10 that many of the scores fall in the margin that lies between two classes and that they are therefore indeterminate. Warner believes, however, that EP is much more basic than ISC for determining social class. But he finds a high degree of correlation between the two methods, and he regards ISC as a simple and inexpensive way of approximating social class with "a rather-high degree of accuracy."[5]

Table 10. *Social Class as Determined by Scores on Status Characteristics*

Total Score	Social Class
12–17	Upper class
18–22	Upper class probably, with some possibility of upper-middle class
23–24	Indeterminate: either upper or upper-middle class
25–33	Upper-middle class
34–37	Indeterminate: either upper-middle or lower-middle class
38–50	Lower-middle class
51–53	Indeterminate: either lower-middle or upper-lower class
54–62	Upper-lower class
63–66	Indeterminate: either upper-lower or lower-lower class
67–69	Lower-lower class probably, with some possibility of upper-lower class
70–84	Lower-lower class

Source: Table 9 and Table 10 by permission from *What You Should Know About Social Class* by W. Lloyd Warner and Mildred Hall Warner, *Life Adjustment Booklets,* Chicago, Science Research Associates, Inc., 1953, pp. 22 and 25. Copyright 1953 by Science Research Associates, Inc.

Some Limitations of the Warner Studies. Among the adverse criticisms that have been made of the Warner studies by some sociologists are the following:

1. It is said that they exaggerate the rigidity of our social class structure and underestimate the amount of mobility between classes. One reason given for this is that Warner limited his investigations to several relatively small, stagnant communities, presumably not representative of mainstream of present-day American social life. Another reason given is that he took little account of individuals who moved away from these communities, among whom there may have been many most likely to move upward in the social scale.

2. Warner's studies appear to indicate that most people can be placed without much question in one of either five or six (depending on the nature of the community) rather well-defined social classes and that the existence of these classes is clearly recognized by the majority of people in the community who are keen observers. Warner's critics, however,

[5] Ibid., p. 42.

doubt whether it is as easy to place people in definite social classes as he implies. They also doubt whether most "keen observers" are likely, independently, to recognize as clearly distinct entities the five or six social classes that Warner assumes.

3. A third criticism of Warner's studies is that, because they are based on several relatively small and static communities, they cannot at best give a very representative view of social stratification in the United States. Increasingly, Americans are on the move from one community to another and from one part of the country to another; also, they are becoming more and more concentrated in large cities or in the surrounding "metropolitan areas."

The Warner studies were made in three communities: "Yankee City," a New England town of about 17,000 population; "Old City," a Southern town of 10,000; and "Jonesville," a Midwestern town of 6,000. Such communities represent only a minor segment of modern American society. In some very small rural communities the class structure is probably far simpler than that described by Warner, and there is probably less social distance from the top to the bottom of the scale. On the other hand, the class structure of large urban communities is certainly much more complex than that found in the communities studied by Warner.

If one should attempt to fit the population of a great urban center into Warner's five or six social classes, he would surely experience many difficulties. It is doubtful that these classes would have the same meaning in an urban community as in the towns Warner studied. Also, it would be more difficult to rate people socially on the basis of the opinions of others. In a large city, comparatively few individuals know one another, and there is a considerable number of groups that are more or less sharply separated on the basis of religion, nationality, race, and other factors. Furthermore, there is a very great variety of occupations. The usefulness of trying to fit the population of a metropolitan center into a simplified pattern of social classes is at least open to question. Certainly many of the people whom Warner placed in his two upper classes would not be found there if they lived in a great metropolis.

THE AMERICAN CLASS SYSTEM

Any class system is somewhat inconsistent with the democratic ideal of providing all citizens with equal opportunities for life, liberty, and the pursuit of happiness. Certainly, lower-class children do not have the same opportunities as those in the upper classes. However, we have developed in America a remarkably open *class system.* Class lines are not very definite, probably much less so than one might infer from the Warner studies; and for many people the possibilities of moving upward are excellent, while for others the dangers of slipping downward are considerable.

"First you have to bring a note from your board chairman certifying that you're an executive." (Courtesy Donald Reilly. Copyright 1964 *Saturday Review, Inc.*)

Class Consciousness in America. Most Americans are not highly class-conscious. Ambition usually takes the form of a desire for a more satisfying job, more income, or more personal prestige. Any resulting change in social status is usually secondary or wholly incidental. Relatively few Americans have a strong desire to move into a higher social class except insofar as this may help them to achieve other objectives.

Why are Americans so comparatively free of class consciousness? Partly, the reasons are historical. We never did have a hereditary nobility, and, throughout our early history, rapid growth and expansion resulted in considerable social mobility. It is more than a coincidence that, though a number of our Presidents have come from wealthy or aristocratic families, some have had very humble origins. In more recent times other factors have tended to keep class consciousness at a low level. One is the general rise in standards of living. Even though people may not change their position in the social scale, they feel they are making progress when their incomes rise and when they can improve their way of life. Also, in the United States in recent years differences in income between different social classes have somewhat diminished. Another factor that has tended to reduce class consciousness and discontent is *horizontal mobility*. In this country there are many opportunities for moving from one job to another, and often a shift to a better-liked job gives people the feeling of making progress even though the change has little effect on income or social status. Finally, in our society there are many ways of achieving recognition in special groups such as political parties, churches, and fraternal societies, and to many people this is more important than moving into a higher social class.

Class Consciousness and the Labor Movement. One might suppose that the great growth of the American labor movement during the last three or four decades would have increased class consciousness in this country, but there is not much evidence that it has. Undoubtedly, it has increased awareness on the part of workers of their group status and group interests. However, the development of unionism in America has not been a class movement. Rather, it has represented attempts on the part of particular groups of workers to improve their own economic position. There has never developed among working people as a whole any very strong feeling of solidarity. One indication of this is the wide diversity that they often exhibit in their own views on social, economic, and political questions.

Rising Incomes and Class Distinctions. Although, compared with that of the rest of the world, the average American standard of living has been high for a century or more, in the depressed 1930's it was possible to say with much truth that one third of the nation was ill fed, ill housed, and ill clothed. For that matter, many of those somewhat above the lowest third were living in what would seem today a rather meager fashion. In the relatively prosperous 1920's the situation was a little better, but even then the incomes of many were very low compared with the present. However, the continued existence of poor people in this country is indicated by the "war on poverty," instituted by President Johnson in 1964 and continued, with some modification of methods and programs, by President Nixon.

Although neither inequality nor social classes have been eliminated, it remains true that in recent years an increasing proportion of the American people have been able to attain what has traditionally been regarded as the middle-class mode of life. Some of these people doubtless should be regarded as having moved into the middle class, but, in any case, the fact that they have achieved a middle-class standard of living makes them feel that they have moved up in the world. To some degree, class distinctions are blurred by the fact that today many skilled manual workers have such good incomes that they can no longer be identified as members of the lower classes by the houses they live in, the clothes they wear, or the leisure-time activities in which they engage.

In a survey among steelworkers taken in the mid-1950's by the Opinion Research Corporation, it was found that 70 per cent of them owned their own cars, 56 per cent owned their homes, 41 per cent belonged to one or more clubs, and 30 per cent of those with children of college age had one or more of these children in college.[6] Today, nearly all steelworkers have their own cars, and the other percentages have risen substantially.

If we go back to European societies of the seventeenth or eighteenth centuries, social stratification could be reasonably well represented by a pyramid, because most people were near the bottom and because very few were at the top of the social scale. The Industrial Revolution and the resulting advances in technology gradually changed this. There are still not very many people near the top, but there has been a great expansion of the middle classes and a corresponding shrinkage of the lower classes. In the United States today there are far more people in the middle than

[6] *Steelways,* December 1956, pp. 6-7.

near the bottom, and our class structure can no longer be represented as a pyramid.

In characterizing briefly the American social structure, Talcott Parsons says:

One of the most notable features of the American system of stratification is its relative looseness, the absence of a clear-cut hierarchy of prestige except in a very broad sense, the absence of an unequivocal top elite or ruling class, the fluidity of the shadings as well as mobility between groups and, in spite of the prestige-implications of the generalized goal of success, the relative tolerance for many different paths to success. It is by no means a "classless" society, but among class societies it is a distinctive type.[7]

Class Conflict. For anyone who understands the American class system it is easy to see why the kind of class conflict predicted by Karl Marx has never developed here. For that matter, it has never developed anywhere, for even European class systems resemble our own much more than they do the one he described. Marx thought that in industrialized countries the middle class would gradually disappear. There would then remain only two classes with sharply opposed interests, the *capitalists,* or owners of the means of production, and the workers, or *proletariat.* He believed that under capitalistic "exploitation" the condition of the workers would become worse and worse. Eventually they would rise up in revolt, seize the means of production, and establish a socialist state under the "dictatorship of the proletariat." Actually, the standards of living of the working people in most industrial countries, quite contrary to Marx's prediction, have been rising for the last hundred years and more.

In America this rise in the economic status of working people has been more marked than anywhere else in the world. Under the conditions that exist today, taking into account not only economic status but also social attitudes, nothing could seem more unrealistic than the development of class conflict along Marxist lines.

Even the communist revolution in Russia did not follow the pattern outlined by Marx. Instead of a revolt of the proletariat, it represented a seizure of power by a small, determined revolutionary group. This seizure was relatively easy because a corrupt czarist government had been completely demoralized by disasters suffered at the hands of the Germans in World War I, and the Kerensky regime, which first took over the reins of government, was too weak to resist attack. At that time Russia was a peasant country with very few industrial workers.

After the destruction of capitalism, Marx believed that the way would be open for the creation of a "classless society." However, what actually

---

[7] Talcott Parsons, "A Revised Analytical Approach to the Theory of Social Stratification," in *Class, Status, and Power, op. cit.,* p. 122.

happened in Russia was that the old aristocracy was replaced by a new privileged class. This now consists primarily of the members of the Communist bureaucracy, but it also includes those scientists, scholars, engineers, managers of industry, artists, and writers who are willing to adhere to the "party line."

Some Conclusions on the American Class System. In spite of the statement in the Declaration of Independence that "all men are created equal," everyone knows that in many ways men are not equal. They are not born with equal potentialities for learning and achieving, nor are they born into equally favorable social environments. Nevertheless, equality before the law and equality of opportunity are strongly cherished democratic ideals. Over the years we have been striving in America to come closer to these ideals, and since the Declaration of Independence was written, we have made considerable progress toward them.

Probably the two factors that in recent years have contributed most to maintaining or increasing social mobility in this country are the expansion of educational opportunities and the great advances that have been made in technology. The latter have expanded the relative need for educated and specially trained workers and have thus provided new avenues for moving upward on the social scale. Meanwhile, expansion of educational opportunities not only has helped individuals to meet new and more demanding occupational requirements but also has tended to spread middle-class culture and attitudes to a larger proportion of the population. Finally, advances in technology have sharply raised living standards for the vast majority of Americans, and this development, as already pointed out, has tended somewhat to blur the lines of class distinction.

Terms to Be Understood

social stratification	Brahman	Evaluated Participation
social scale	Kshatriya	Index of Status Characteristics
estates	Vaisya	open class system
castes	Sudra	horizontal mobility
social classes	untouchables	class conflict
karma	subculture	capitalists
transmigration	social mobility	proletariat

Questions for Review and Discussion

1. Why is social stratification unavoidable in all large societies?
2. Why may social stratification contribute to social stability?
3. Name the three principal types of social stratification and describe briefly the nature of each.

4. How has the position of blacks in our society resembled, and how has it differed, from the position of a low Hindu caste?
5. What difficulties are encountered when we attempt to divide the people of an industrial society into clear-cut social classes?
6. What is meant when it is said that a social class is in some degree a subculture?
7. Why is social class a family matter rather than an individual matter?
8. Why is upward social mobility necessarily limited in any society?
9. What are some of the principal factors that may contribute to class mobility?
10. Name Warner's six social classes and describe his methods for determining the social class of individuals.
11. Do Warner's six (or five) classes represent social groups that almost anyone can readily recognize and distinguish? Explain.
12. What are some of the major criticisms that have been made of Warner's studies of social class?
13. Why is the problem of classifying people into social classes more difficult in large cities than in smaller communities?
14. Why are Americans not highly class-conscious?
15. What factors have been operating in the United States in recent years to reduce class distinctions? Can you name any factors that, in your opinion, have had the opposite effect?
16. Why has the kind of class conflict Karl Marx predicted never developed anywhere?
17. Characterize the American class system from the standpoint of (a) the sharpness of class distinctions; (b) the degree of class consciousness; (c) the amount of social mobility.
18. Is American society becoming more stratified? Defend your point of view.

For Further Study

Bendix, Reinhard, and Seymour Martin Lipset, eds., *Class, Status, and Power: A Reader in Social Stratification,* rev. ed., New York, The Free Press, 1966. Good reader.

Béteille, Andre, ed., *Social Inequality,* paperback, Baltimore, Penguin Books, Inc., 1970.

Djilas, Milovan, *The New Class: An Analysis of the Communist System,* paperback, New York, Frederick A. Praeger, Inc., 1957.

Hazari, *Untouchable: The Autobiography of an Indian Outcaste,* New York, Frederick A. Praeger, Inc., 1969.

Heller, Celia, *Structured Social Inequality,* New York, The Macmillan Company, 1969.

Isaacs, Harold R., *India's Ex-Untouchables,* New York, The John Day Company, Inc., 1965.

Lipset, Seymour Martin, and Reinhard Bendix, *Social Mobility in Industrial Society,* paperback, Berkeley and Los Angeles, University of California Press, 1964.

Mayer, Kurt B., and Walter Buckley, *Class and Society,* 3rd ed., paperback, New York, Random House, Inc., 1970.

Miller, Seymour M., and Frank Reissman, *Social Class and Social Policy,* New York, Basic Books, Inc., 1968.

Mills, C. Wright, *The Power Elite,* Galaxy paperback, New York, Oxford University Press, 1959.

Reissman, Leonard, *Class in American Society,* New York, The Free Press, 1960.

Sivertsen, Dagfinn, *When Caste Barriers Fall: A Study of Social and Economic Change in a South Indian Village,* New York, Humanities Press, Inc., 1963.

Sorokin, Pitirim A., *Social and Cultural Mobility,* New York, The Free Press, 1959.

Tumin, Melvin M., ed., *Readings in Social Stratification,* paperback, Englewood Cliffs, N.J., Prentice-Hall, Inc., 1970.

Vidich, Arthur, and Joseph Bensman, *Small Town in a Mass Society: Class, Power, and Religion in a Rural Community,* rev. ed., paperback, Princeton, N.J., Princeton University Press, 1968.

Warner, William Lloyd, *Social Class in America,* rev. ed., with two new chapters, paperback, Gloucester, Mass., Peter Smith, Publisher, Inc., n.d.

Chapter 13

Racial

and Cultural

Groups

perhaps never before in the history of our nation has the average man been so keenly aware that intergroup relations are a nation-wide and, indeed, a world-wide problem. Today, almost everywhere in the world, one finds some degree of prejudice, discrimination, and segregation, sometimes between religious groups, sometimes between nationality groups, and sometimes between racial groups. Frequently acute conflict develops. In Cyprus, for example, it has developed between Greeks and Turks, who differ primarily in nationality and religion; in India and Pakistan, between Hindus and Moslems; in Northern Ireland, between Catholics and

Protestants; in the Near East, between Israelis and Arabs; in Guyana, between blacks and East Indians; and in the United States, in some African countries, and even in Great Britain, between blacks and whites.

In this chapter we seek to deal with certain majority-minority situations arising from differences in race or culture, particularly as these are found in the United States. However, before we enter into this discussion we need to define the term *race* and to distinguish between racial and cultural differences.

RACE AND CULTURE

To an anthropologist a *race* is a group of people who have common physical characteristics that are genetically inherited from generation to generation and that distinguish the group from other groups whose physical characteristics are different. In popular usage, however, culture differences are often confused with racial differences. Cultural differences between groups in such matters as nationality, language, and religion are important, but they do not constitute differences in race. It would be incorrect, for example, to speak of the French race or the German race. France and Germany are adjacent countries, and the people who live on one side of the border are physically little different from those who live on the other side. Actually, the border has been changed several times, and in the distant past there have been large migrations across it. It is also misleading to call the Jews a race. They have no physical characteristics by which they can be dependably distinguished from non-Jews in our white population. What holds them together as a group is primarily religion and social tradition.

Racial and cultural differences fall into distinct categories and are largely independent of each other. The frequently made assumption that race determines culture has little scientific or factual basis. Where different racial groups have for some time lived in close association, as in Hawaii, they are likely to have much the same culture; on the other hand, members of the same race living in different parts of the world often exhibit cultural patterns that are radically different. To see the truth of this last statement, we need only compare the culture of Afro-Americans with that of blacks living in the Congo basin of Africa.

The Races of Mankind. Though all men belong to the same species, *Homo sapiens,* they show many physical variations. These include differences in height, weight, skin color, and the shape of the head and face. Any human group that is largely isolated from other groups for a very long period of time will develop some physical characteristics, in its average member, that are different from those of the average member of closely related groups. These differences may be minor and often difficult to identify; but if the characteristics of the group become sufficiently distinctive in comparison with those of other groups, we can call it a race.

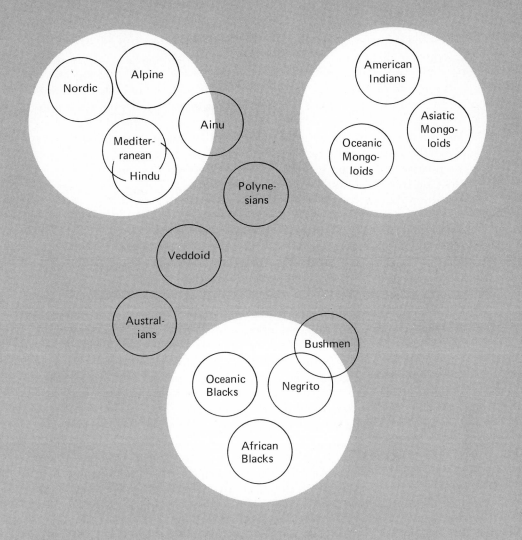

Figure 12. Relationship of Human Races. (From *Anthropology,* by A. L. Kroeber, copyright 1923, 1948 by Harcourt Brace Jovanovich, Inc.)

Yet if we attempt to classify all the peoples of the world by race, we at once encounter difficulties. In the first place, there has been, both in the past and in modern times, much mixing of races through migration and interbreeding. In the second place, even if we limit our classification to peoples whose general physical types have been long established, by searching the world we can find groups who differ from one another only slightly through a continuous series of gradations—for example, from the most dark-skinned black tribes of Africa to the lightest-skinned Caucasian groups in northwest Europe. In spite of such difficulties, many anthropologists attempt to classify the great majority of mankind into a few large racial groups. A widely accepted classification assigns most people to one of three groups, namely, the *Caucasoids,* the *Mongoloids,* and the *Negroids.* However, any such classification is necessarily rather arbitrary. Within each of the three major races, we find important subgroups that differ appreciably from one another and that could themselves be regarded as races. Also, some groups fall between our major groups and are difficult to classify. Figure 12 attempts to indicate the approximate relations of certain subgroups to the three major races.

Most of the Caucasoids, or Caucasians, live in Europe, the Western Hemisphere, North Africa, the Near East, and India. Often we refer to them as "the white race," but, when we do this, we are usually thinking of Europeans or their descendants. Actually, the skin color of Caucasians varies from a light pinkish-white to a very dark olive brown. In India they sometimes have skins as dark as those of African blacks. Caucasians have straight to curly hair that is usually some shade of brown, though it may be black, or very blond, or red. They have rather prominent noses, which as a rule are fairly straight and narrow; little protrusion of the jaws, or *prognathism;* and an appreciable amount of hair on the body. They vary greatly in eye color, body build, and height. Also, they have no characteristic *cephalic index,* the ratio obtained by dividing the maximum breadth of the head by its maximum length and then multiplying the result by 100.[1]

The Mongoloid race is characterized by round heads, dark-brown eyes, and straight, dark-brown or black hair. The skin color varies from light yellow-brown to dark yellow-brown or reddish-brown. The oblique or "Mongolian" eye is peculiar to the Mongoloids of eastern Asia. The American Indians are classified as a Mongoloid subtype, and it is believed that they migrated to the American continent from Asia on a land bridge that may once have existed between Siberia and Alaska. However, they lack the slanted Mongolian eyes, and they also differ in other ways from the Asiatic Mongoloids.

The Negroid race differs more in its physical characteristics from both the Caucasoids and Mongoloids than they do from each other. Negroids typically have black or dark-brown skin, kinky black hair, thick lips, broad noses, long heads, and marked prognathism. Their race includes both the shortest and the tallest of known human groups.

Let us note some of the *subtypes* or *subraces* into which the three major racial groups may be divided. The Caucasians of Europe and of the whole area around the Mediterranean Sea are generally classified into three major types, which are often called races. At one time these may have constituted separate groups living in different areas. However, over the centuries there has been a tremendous amount of migration and mixture, so that

[1] The cephalic index is expressed as a percentage. It indicates a person's head type according to the following scale: over 80, brachycephalic, or round headed; 75 to 80, mesocephalic, or medium headed; below 75, dolichocephalic, or long headed.

25–30. Blackfoot Indian—Tibetan Woman—Mangbetu Woman—Kashmiri Man—Ituri Pygmies—Ainu Man. (Copyright Chicago Natural History Museum; Malvina Hoffman, Sculptress.)

some representatives of all these types are to be found in every European country, sometimes even in the same families. People who belong to the *Nordic* type, which is found in greatest numbers in northwestern Europe, are relatively tall and tend to have blue eyes, blond hair, and long heads. The *Mediterranean* type, which includes most of the people in the area surrounding the sea from which it was named, consists of individuals who also have long heads but who are dark haired, dark eyed, oval faced, and comparatively short in stature. People of the *Alpine* type, most common in central Europe, have wide cheekbones and broad heads. They also tend to have medium stature, dark hair, dark eyes, and fair to medium skin color.

The Caucasoids of India and Pakistan are similar to the Mediterraneans except that their skin color is usually much darker, especially as one goes south in India. This dark color may partly result from climate, but an important contributing factor seems to have been some interbreeding with dark-skinned aborigines who in earlier times inhabited much of India.

The Chinese and Japanese constitute the great majority of the Mongoloid race. The subtypes of this race include several groups on the Asiatic mainland, the Malays, the Eskimos, and the American Indians.

The Negroid race is made up of two main divisions, the African blacks and the Oceanic Melanesians. There is a third distinct subtype, the Negritos or Pygmies, who are few in number but live in scattered areas in New Guinea, the Philippines, the Malay Peninsula, and equatorial Africa, and also in the Andaman Islands in the Indian Ocean. The Australian aborigines have some Negroid characteristics but differ considerably from the Negroes in other respects. For example, their hair ranges from straight to very curly but is not kinky.

Racial Superiority. There are many people in the world who believe that some races are innately superior to others in intelligence and creativeness, and that this largely explains the high degree of civilization certain groups have been able to achieve. This sounds plausible because it is true that the great advances in science and technology, and in economic and political organization, have largely been made by people of certain racial groups. Actually, the majority of such advances in the last several hundred years have been made by white Europeans or by their descendants in other parts of the world.

However, this does not prove that Caucasians have greater innate abilities than the members of other races. For untold thousands of years the people of the whole world lived in primitive tribal societies where change and "progress" were extremely slow. Why civilization should have begun to develop only five or six thousand years ago among certain peoples in certain areas is a great historical mystery. One could argue that it happened because these peoples had gradually developed greater mental capacity than other human groups. More likely it was the result of a fortunate combination of other factors, such as favorable climate and soil, migrations which stimulated change by bringing together peoples with different cultural backgrounds, and the fortuitous making of some important discoveries and inventions. Such advances tended to lead to further advances, a gradual accumulation of technical skills, an increase in food output, a slow growth of population, and the development of towns and cities. Further stimulus may have been given by wars and new migrations.

Over the centuries, the particular groups who have taken the lead in the advances of civilization have changed. First it was the Sumerians and the Egyptians; later the peoples of India and China, the Jews, the Phoenicians, and the Persians; still later the Greeks and Romans; then for a while the

Arabs; and finally the peoples of northern and western Europe. But we need only go back two thousand years or less to find Roman writers who looked upon the then-primitive Britons and Germans as not only crude and uncivilized but also stupid. In other parts of the world well-organized societies developed in the past, but they either disintegrated or were destroyed by invaders. These include the Maya and Inca civilizations in the Americas, and various kingdoms in black Africa south of the Sahara.

There is no convincing scientific evidence to support the contention that some races inherit biologically a greater capacity for development than do others. Every race has its bright and dull individuals, its great intellects and its idiots. On the other hand, it is entirely possible that, on average, there are some inherited mental and psychological differences between racial groups, just as there are physical differences. This is difficult to prove or disprove because we have no way of adequately separating the effects of biology in shaping human personalities from the effects of culture. Even if some inborn mental and psychological differences exist, they do not necessarily mean superiority or inferiority any more than do differences in skin color, hair texture, or head shape. In any case, such differences must be rather minor compared with the great differences that exist between individuals in every race. In a democracy, the important thing is to treat each person as a human being, to judge him on his own merits, and to give him every opportunity to develop and use whatever capabilities he possesses.

Racial Prejudice and Discrimination. Race relations vary greatly in different societies and in different social situations. In some cases there is relatively little friction between members of different races. Prejudice exists, but *ethnic barriers* are not sufficient to prevent considerable social contact and frequent intermarriages. Such seems to be the situation today in Hawaii, where the principal nationality groups are either Mongoloid or Caucasian. Though the various ethnic groups have not yet lost their sense of identity, residentially, economically, and educationally they are very nearly *integrated.*[2] But there are other places in the world where prejudice and discrimination are intense and where racial segregation is the accepted pattern. In the Union of South Africa, for instance, the present government attempts to enforce a policy of *apartheid,* or complete segregation of racial groups except in certain work situations.

What is the explanation for these great variations? Many people feel that prejudice is inevitable, that it is an inherited aversion. But the belief that human beings inherit attitudes has long been discredited by psychologists, and racial prejudice cannot be accounted for by any such simple explanation. Like all aspects of culture, it is something that the individual acquires from his social environment, and its causes are variable and complex.

[2] J. Milton Yinger, "Integration and Pluralism Viewed from Hawaii," *Minorities in a Changing World,* edited by Milton L. Barron, New York, Alfred A. Knopf, Inc., 1967, pp. 125–128.

31. A Hawaiian Family with Ten Children. The father is a Hawaiian-Chinese-Japanese insurance man, the mother a Caucasian New Zealander whom he met during World War II. (Ralph Crane, *Life* Magazine. © Time Inc.)

Racial prejudice has been denounced over and over again as an enemy of society that tends to undermine the whole social fabric; and, unquestionably, it has been the source of many social problems in the United States. The reason for this is that *prejudice, which represents aversion to, or dislike of, people who are strange or different,* leads to *discrimination, which is the active expression of these attitudes.* It cannot be denied that prejudice and discrimination against certain minority groups exist throughout our society despite our professed belief in the American ideals of democracy. To some degree, they appear in nearly all social relations, in schools, churches, offices, factories, and residential areas; and, until recently, discrimination against blacks was still supported in a number of states by law.

The extent of race prejudice in a country like the United States may be partly explained by what Robert E. Park of the University of Chicago many years ago called "an elementary expression of conservatism," or "the resistance of the social order to change." Members of the dominant group do not like to have their way of life disturbed by strange or unlike peoples. They do not understand them very well, they do not feel comfortable in associating with them, and they do not have as much in common with them as with their own kind. But Park concluded after much research that a population consisting of divergent groups will, through successive stages, finally arrive at *assimilation,* or the complete merging of cultures.

The stages he posited in this process of adjustment are (1) contact; (2) competition; (3) *accommodation* or an adjustment by which divergent groups learn to get along with one another but without losing their identity; and (4) assimilation. He believed that, once started, the adjustment process cannot be reversed. More recent studies have led to much the same conclusions, but they have largely been based on our experience with groups of European immigrants. When a minority group differs a great deal from the dominant group, particularly in physical traits that give it what Gunnar Myrdal calls "social visibility," the majority is apt to retard the assimilation process for a very long time by persistent discrimination.[3]

Different writers have suggested various reasons for racial prejudice. Prominent among these are (1) the influence of tradition; (2) the psychological need that individuals feel for "belonging" to a particular, identifiable group; (3) the building up of the ego by cultivating a feeling of superiority; and (4) the usefulness of prejudice as an economic and political weapon.[4] Some even maintain that the chief cause of prejudice is competition for jobs between racial groups.

All the factors just mentioned, and others, doubtless influence the strength of prejudice and the forms that discrimination takes. But the source of racial prejudice probably lies in the aversion that most individuals feel to associating closely with people who are physically, and usually culturally, somewhat strange and different. People feel more comfortable in the company of their own kind. Perhaps esthetic ideals of human beauty, developed in the first years of childhood, are more important than is usually recognized. A child comes to regard as "people," and as more or less beautiful, those with whom he comes into early contact. For instance, such characteristics as "snow-white" skin, rosy cheeks, blue eyes, and golden hair play a role, though not an exclusive one, in Caucasian ideals of beauty. Today American blacks are seeking to boost racial morale and pride through use of the slogan "Black is beautiful." Though there are frequent exceptions, as a rule the child's first close associates are limited to his parents, his relatives, and playmates from his own social and racial group. The result is that people whose physical appearance is very different seem to him homely, or he is afraid of them, or he develops an aversion to them. Such attitudes have an emotional background, and once a child acquires them, it is doubtful that he can ever completely

[3] For references to Park's theories, see Gunnar Myrdal, *An American Dilemma,* New York, Harper & Row, Publishers, 1944, p. 662.

[4] For an analysis of some studies of race prejudice, see George E. Simpson and J. Milton Yinger, *Racial and Cultural Minorities,* 3d ed., New York, Harper & Row, Publishers, 1965.

rid himself of them. This is one argument for integration and desegration, especially in housing and schooling, so that children of all races will adjust early to each other.

UNASSIMILATED MINORITY GROUPS IN THE UNITED STATES

Because of its heterogeneous population and the tendency of immigrant groups ultimately to become assimilated, the United States has often been called "the melting pot." Although the white colonial population was predominantly British, other nationalities were also represented. During the nineteenth century this country received thirty million immigrants, and in the early twentieth century more millions arrived. A few came from almost every section of the world, but the great majority were Caucasians from Europe. The groups whose basic patterns of life were not too unlike those of the early British settlers became assimilated in a relatively short time; others were assimilated more slowly. But there were, from the beginning, non-Caucasian groups whose assimilation seemed impossible, because they differed not only culturally but also racially from the majority of the American people. Today there are still unassimilated groups including the Puerto Ricans and Cubans, who are largely Caucasian but who have come to this country rather recently.

The American Indians. The American Indians were the first settlers of what is now the United States. Anthropologists are generally agreed that they came from Asia, but we do not know when they started to arrive. Formerly, the usual estimate was twelve thousand to fifteen thousand years ago, but some now believe that they came much earlier. According to the Bureau of Indian Affairs, they began migrating from Siberia more than thirty thousand years ago.[5]

After Europeans began to colonize North America, the Indians were slowly outnumbered and eventually conquered by the white settlers and their descendants. Today they are a relatively small minority, and for a long time they were the most isolated of all minority groups and perhaps the most retarded in education; but recently, more successful efforts have been made to bring them into contact with the modern world and to improve their educational and employment opportunities.

The policies of the white man toward the Indian have undergone changes in the past century from (1) enforced isolation and segregation, to (2) forced integration into American society, with almost disastrous results for the Indians culturally, economically, and physically, to (3) a policy of much more gradual assimilation. The present government policy toward them is based on the Indian Reorganization Act of 1934, which

[5] Bureau of Indian Affairs, *Answers to Your Questions About American Indians,* Washington, D.C., U.S. Government Printing Office, 1968, p. 3.

was designed to encourage Indian tribes to revive their own traditions and to manage their own political and economic affairs. This act has been supplemented by various government actions including a Senate Resolution in 1968 that strongly endorsed a policy of giving greater and greater responsibility to the Indians and their tribal governments.

In 1960 the Bureau of the Census reported that there were over 523,000 American Indians, most of whom lived on reservations in the western half of the country. All Indians have the franchise; they are United States citizens and as such are subject to the draft; they pay certain taxes, and they receive Social Security benefits; they may own private property; and they are free to leave the reservation at will and to seek employment anywhere they wish. But off the reservations they encounter prejudice and have difficulty in adjusting to the white man's culture. Also, many of them are greatly handicapped by poor health, by a lack of education and skills, and by the language barrier. Each of the tribes has its own language or dialect, which is usually very difficult for the non-Indian to learn.[6] If in addition the tribe is very isolated, the process of education and assimilation is extremely slow. For instance, it is estimated that more than half of the Navajos in Arizona and New Mexico do not yet speak English.

Though most of our Indians are on reservations, the largest of which are in the West, many are scattered in various communities throughout the country. In a number of cases reservations have been provided by agreements with states and are not under federal jurisdiction. North Carolina has more Indians than any other Eastern state; their number there is now estimated at about fifty thousand.

A small but interesting Indian group is the Seminoles of Florida. At the end of the Seminole Wars in 1858, the United States government attempted to move all the Seminoles to the Indian Territory (Oklahoma), but about 150 succeeded in remaining behind by hiding in inaccessible areas in the Everglades. Today they number more than 1,400. Twenty years ago they were very backward and few could read or write, but in 1957 most of them joined together to adopt a constitution and to incorporate as the Seminole Tribe of Florida. In recent years, they are said to have made notable educational and economic progress. Most of them live in or near three reservations that are under federal jurisdiction. A branch of the Seminole family, the Miccosukees, live along the Tamiami Trail west of Miami. Main sources of Seminole income are renting land to commercial enterprises and raising cattle.

The Navajos are the largest of all our Indian tribes and have the largest reservation, an arid region in the Southwest about the size of West Virginia. In 1967 there were about 110,000 Navajos living in this area, and

[6] According to the federal Bureau of Indian Affairs, there were originally about three hundred different languages spoken by Indians in what is now the United States, and possibly as many as one hundred still survive. Ibid., p. 5.

32. Navajo Indians Sample Modern Life Selectively. A family lives in a hogan without light or water but drives a pickup to the train. Persistent poverty forces many Indians to one-cent used-clothing sales at the Protestant mission. (By Joseph Elkins for *Presbyterian Life 1969.*)

their numbers were rapidly increasing.[7] In the past most of them were seminomadic sheepherders and dry farmers, and many of them still are. Often they live miles from their nearest neighbors. This has made it difficult for the federal Bureau of Indian Affairs to provide schooling for the children or to bring adults together for instruction in health, sanitation, the English language, or vocational training. But conditions are rapidly changing. Only 10 per cent or less of Navajo income now results from sheep raising and farming, whereas more than 70 per cent comes from wages earned both on and off the reservation.

In spite of real progress by the Navajos and other tribes, the majority of American Indians still have lower standards of living, much higher unemployment rates, less education, and poorer health than any other racial or cultural group in our society; also, the majority still live on or near reservations or government-controlled land and are still largely segregated. But they are not a dying race. The Bureau of Indian Affairs estimates that from 1950 to 1960 our Indian population rose about 21 per cent, a greater rate of increase than for the population as a whole. Today our Indian population is close to 800,000, and Indian birth rates are about double those of the United States as a whole.

[7] U.S. Bureau of Indian Affairs, *Indians of Arizona*, Washington, D.C., U.S. Government Printing Office, 1968, p. 2.

In 1962 the median *family* income for reservation Indians was under $1,500, or less than half the poverty threshhold as determined by the Social Security Administration. It was also less than half the median income of black families and only about one fourth that of all American families. Housing on reservations was generally primitive, much of it worse than that found in city slums. Only 10 per cent of reservation housing in the early 1960's met minimum standards. In very recent years, Indian incomes have risen markedly, but, on the average, they are still below those of any other racial group.

Today most Indian children attend school, and the government has made considerable progress with its program for gradually closing segregated Indian schools on reservations and transferring children to public nonsegregated schools. Nevertheless, in 1968 more than 43,000 Indian children were still attending reservation schools operated by the Bureau of Indian Affairs. Adult vocational training is also being provided by the bureau in order to make more Indians employable.

Although the federal Public Health Service has greatly increased its expenditures for providing the Indians with hospitals and medical care, health conditions among them are still poor, sanitation inadequate, and the disease and death rates high. One factor in the high disease rate has probably been superstition. The medicine man has always been an influential force in the Indian culture, and in the past he contributed to the perpetuation of ignorance about the nature of disease. Today, where modern doctors are able to treat Indians in hospitals or clinics, medicine men are sometimes called in to assist because of their psychological value to the patient and his family.

The Bureau of Indian Affairs provides aid, under various programs, to all Indians who wish to leave the reservations to seek better educational and employment opportunities in the outside world. As a result, more than one third of our Indians now live away from the reservations, most of them in large cities. There they lead independent lives and have exactly the same legal privileges and responsibilities as other Americans. But of the Indians who leave the reservations, about one in every three sooner or later returns. Language difficulties, lack of skills, unfamiliar culture patterns, and discrimination prove handicaps too difficult to overcome. Besides, the Indians are generally not anxious to be "integrated." Not only do they find it difficult to make the necessary adjustments, but also, in spite of their poverty and other social handicaps, they take pride in their traditions and their tribal cultures. Hence, efforts at relocation have had only limited success. Now they are being played down, and more emphasis is being placed on creating jobs on the reservations. These attempts are beginning to show real progress. There are at least three reasons for this. First is substantial government aid for the program. Second, the Indians often have available for investment large tribal funds that come from oil, gas, and other mineral rights on tribal lands. Third, it has been found that most Indians, though they may lack the education and training for professional or technical occupations, have an aptitude for manual skills. Hence, once they have adjusted to the requirements of industrial employment, they make excellent workers. Both the tribes themselves and a number of corporations, some well-known, have now built or are planning factories on or near reservations.

The Chicanos. On the basis of a sample survey made late in 1969, the Bureau of the Census found that about 9.2 million people living in our fifty states and the District of Columbia identified themselves as being of "Spanish origin," to use the term employed by the Bureau to include chiefly immigrants from Spanish-speaking countries, or the descendants of immigrants. Of the total number, 55 per cent gave Mexico as their country of origin, about 16 per cent named Puerto Rico, and about 6 per cent named Cuba. The rest indicated various other Spanish-speaking countries. However, of all who considered themselves of "Spanish origin," nearly four out of five were actually born in the United States, or in Puerto Rico, all of whose natives have American citizenship.[8]

The Mexican-Americans, or *Chicanos,* as many now prefer to be called, are the largest of the groups in our country who came, or whose ancestors came, from Spanish-speaking countries. They are of special importance because they are one of the largest of all our minority groups. But they differ from other Americans of "Spanish origin" not only in their national origin but also in their racial background. "To be a Mexican," says Philip D. Ortega, "is to be a member of *la raza,* the race of Montezuma's children. More than two fifths of the Mexican population are pure-blooded Indians, more than half have some Indian blood in them. Yet, despite Indian resilience, the language of the conquerors dominated."[9]

Except for the Indians, Mexicans—or Spaniards from Mexico—were the first settlers of what is now the Southwestern part of the United States. All this area was a part of Mexico before the United States annexed it after the Mexican War. When the first settlers from the United States began moving into the Southwest, Mexicans were thus already there, and many of their descendants can be found there today, especially in Colorado and northern New Mexico, where a few villages are still composed almost entirely of such people. The dominant Anglo-American group calls some of the descendants of the original Mexican settlers, especially the wealthier ones, *Spanish-Americans,* or *Hispanos,* to distinguish them from the great majority of Chicanos who are either immigrants or the children and grandchildren of immigrants.[10]

The modern influx of Mexican immigration came after 1900. It was not affected by the quota restrictions passed by Congress in 1921 and 1924,

[8] U.S. Bureau of the Census, Current Population Reports, Series P-20, No. 213, "Persons of Spanish Origin in the United States; November 1969," Washington, D.C., U.S. Government Printing Office, 1971.

[9] Philip D. Ortega, *The Center Magazine,* "Montezuma's Children," December 1970, p. 23.

[10] Celia S. Heller, *Mexican American Youth,* New York, Random House, Inc., 1966, pp. 10–11.

which greatly reduced the inflow of immigrants from eastern and southern Europe, because these did not apply to the Western Hemisphere. Most Mexicans came as common laborers. Many were employed as seasonal migratory workers in agriculture, while others found jobs on road-building projects or as railroad workers. However, up to 1964 many of our Mexican migratory workers were not citizens or residents of the United States. Rather, they were *braceros,* Mexicans who were allowed to enter this country seasonally as contract workers in agriculture. The law permitting this was allowed to expire in 1964.

Today the Chicanos are one of our most rapidly growing groups, with a rate of increase even greater than that of American blacks. Because of their high birth rate, a large proportion of them are young. More than 85 per cent are native born, and substantially more than half have parents who were born in this country.[11]

Most Chicanos—four out of five—are concentrated in the Southwest. The great majority live in Texas and California, but substantial numbers are found in Arizona, New Mexico, and Colorado. Although some are Caucasian, most are of mixed Caucasian and Indian stock. They tend to live in segregated residential areas, to retain their own customs, and to continue to speak Spanish. This, plus discrimination and lack of education, has slowed their economic and social progress.

Many of us tend to think of them as primarily engaged in agriculture, perhaps because in the not-distant past so many have been migrant farm workers. Chicanos are still found in considerable numbers at harvest time in such areas as New Jersey, the apple country of Washington, and the cherry country of Michigan, or wherever relatively cheap labor is needed temporarily. However, the demand for migrant labor is shrinking, largely because more and more crops are being harvested by machinery; and in some areas migrant Chicanos have been partly replaced by blacks. Today, though many Chicanos are still employed in agriculture and a relatively small number are still migrants, the great majority—close to 85 per cent— live in urban areas. There they do all kinds of work, but relatively few are as yet found in high-ranking occupations. As a group their incomes are much lower than those of native white Americans. But, like the descendants of earlier immigrant groups, some are finding their way up the social and economic ladder.

In the Southwest, the Chicanos are beginning to exert political power. They have produced some leaders, including a few members of Congress. One of their number, Cesar Chavez, has in recent years achieved fame as a labor leader because of his efforts to organize farm workers in the vineyards of California, and especially because of the effective boycott that he organized against California grapes. More recently he has undertaken to organize workers on the California lettuce farms.

Though most Chicanos still live in the Southwest, a considerable number

[11] Heller, op. cit., p. 12.

have found employment in industrial cities in other parts of the country, and in some of these cities they have formed small "colonies."

The Puerto Ricans and Cubans. A new racial-cultural group has now appeared with its own set of problems. This is the large group of Puerto Ricans who have come to the United States in the last twenty or twenty-five years. Though most Puerto Ricans are Caucasians, a substantial proportion of them are of black or mixed ancestry. Small numbers of Puerto Ricans came to the United States in earlier years, but since 1946 it is estimated that they have been arriving in New York at the rate of about forty thousand a year. There are now more than one million Puerto Ricans in New York, and several hundred thousand scattered in other cities.

Because Puerto Ricans are American citizens, they have the same rights as all other citizens, but because of language difficulties, lack of skills, lack of education, and discrimination, those living in the United States usually earn low wages and are forced to live in slum areas where health conditions are poor and crime rates are high. Also, many social difficulties arise because their culture patterns are so different from those they encounter in the United States. Some return home, disappointed. Others "commute," staying only long enough to earn whatever amount of money is needed to carry them for a while. The majority of Spanish-speaking Puerto Ricans are learning English and attempting to become "Americanized," but those who have Negroid characteristics find this especially difficult because of race prejudice.

Since Castro came to power in Cuba, several hundred thousand refugees have come to this country under special Congressional legislation that created a Cuban refugee program. From 1961 to 1969 inclusive, registrations at the Cuban Refugee Center in Miami totaled 356,194. A large portion of the refugees remained in Miami, but about two thirds were resettled in other areas.[12] Many received federal financial assistance.

The Chinese and Japanese. The Chinese first began to reach this country in large numbers when gold was discovered in California. In the single year of 1852 some twenty thousand were admitted. They worked as cooks and launderers and as laborers in the mines. When the gold rush was over, many of them were used in building the western portion of the transcontinental railroad. They also spread out into such occupations as agriculture and fishing. But to the white settlers they were strange and unwelcome. As their numbers grew, antagonism increased, and all types of discrimination were employed against them. There were even riots in which they were chased through the streets and beaten or lynched. Part of this antagonism resulted from competition for jobs. The Chinese were able to live on very little and, if forced to do so, would work for extremely low wages. Finally, in 1882, Congress passed the Chinese Exclusion Act, which virtually suspended all Chinese immigration until 1943.

[12] U.S. Bureau of the Census, *Statistical Abstract of the United States: 1970,* Washington, D.C., 1970, p. 5.

In 1943 Congress put the Chinese under the immigrant quota system. This permitted only a few to enter the country annually, and all Chinese residents became eligible for naturalization, which had formerly been denied them. By 1960 the census showed that more than 237,000 Chinese or persons of Chinese descent were living here. They have spread throughout the whole country, but most live in large cities. Today there is little prejudice against them, partly because their numbers are small and partly because they have proved that they make very good citizens.

After Congress passed the Chinese Exclusion Act, the Japanese began coming to our West Coast in gradually increasing numbers. Most of them settled in California, and before long they too, like the Chinese before them, began to encounter prejudice and discrimination. As with the Chinese, the feeling against them was partly based on conflicting economic interests. Many Japanese became truck gardeners, and because whole families were willing to work hard and live on very little, the native Californian truck gardeners complained that they could not meet Japanese competition. Also it was argued that the strong loyalty of the Japanese to their homeland made assimilation impossible.

Whether these alleged grievances against the Japanese were important causes of anti-Japanese feeling or chiefly rationalizations of strong racial and cultural prejudice, is open to question. In any case, prejudice grew until, under pressure from California, Congress passed a law prohibiting Japanese from becoming naturalized citizens, and California passed laws preventing them from becoming landowners. Finally, in 1907, a "gentleman's agreement" was negotiated with Japan, and this had the effect of stopping further immigration of Japanese laborers. Several years after World War II, federal immigration laws placed the Japanese under the quota system, so that a few were allowed to enter the United States annually. By 1960 the number of Japanese in the country, or persons of Japanese descent, had reached 464,000.

Soon after the United States entered World War II, the government forcibly moved 117,000 people of Japanese birth or ancestry away from the West Coast to Relocation Centers further inland. This was done as a security measure, but it is now generally recognized as an inexcusable injustice, for removal was not based on disloyalty but only on national origin, and it meant gross discrimination against thousands of loyal American citizens. In 1945 the evacuation order was rescinded, but many Japanese did not return to the West Coast, preferring to live in areas where prejudice against them was less marked. In recent years, prejudice against the Japanese has disappeared or greatly diminished, even in California.

The Blacks. Blacks have been in this country since its earliest days, but until World War I, or even later, the great majority were in the South; in some areas of the North they were so few that the average white person scarcely ever saw one. Because they are by far the largest minority racial group in the United States, we shall not discuss them at this point but shall devote the following chapter in its entirety to their background and problems.

NATIONALITY GROUPS AND THE PROBLEM OF AMERICANIZATION

In the early 1900's, when immigration into the United States reached its peak, some one million persons were arriving every year, the great majority from Europe. Nationalities tended to group together and form colonies, sometimes in rural areas, sometimes in the poorer sections of large cities. They became for a while isolated "islands of culture," continuing among themselves to speak their own language and perpetuate their own traditions. At first most immigrants took the unskilled jobs and occupied the lowest place in the class structure, thus pushing into the upper classes a larger proportion of older residents than might otherwise have been found there. These older residents had the advantage of being on the ground earlier, as a result of which they not only knew the language and customs, but in many cases had accumulated property.

In some ways the situation of European immigrants was like that of a minority racial group, but the difference lay in the fact that although most second- and third-generation individuals from racial groups were still set apart and considered unassimilable, no matter how Americanized they became, those from the Caucasian nationality groups had little trouble, in a generation or two, in identifying themselves with the major group.

Restrictions on Immigration. Up to 1890 the majority of immigrants were from northwestern Europe, including Great Britain, Ireland, Germany, the Netherlands, and the Scandinavian countries. Then the immigration from southern and eastern Europe began to exceed that from northern and western Europe, and Mexican immigration also increased. Many "old" Americans, and even some of the earlier immigrants, were strongly prejudiced against southern and eastern Europeans. As a result, demands for restrictive legislation increased rapidly, and various laws were passed limiting immigration in one way or another.

In 1921 the first Immigration Quota Act was passed to reduce immigration to certain annual quotas for each national group. The quota for each country was 3 per cent of the number of people living in the United States in 1910 who were of that national origin. The effect of this legislation was to reduce very sharply immigration from the countries of central, eastern, and southern Europe. Later the quotas were reduced, and in 1924 the maximum total number of immigrants to be admitted annually was cut down to 150,000. The quota laws did not apply to countries in the Western Hemisphere.

During the years following World War II, various immigration acts were passed by Congress to admit considerable numbers of immigrants over and above the quotas. Most of these were Europeans displaced from their homes by World War II or by the Hungarian rebellion, in 1956, against Communist rule and Russian domination. Later, as already mentioned, Cuban refugees were admitted under special legislation.

But in 1965, under pressure from people who considered our immigration laws discriminatory, Congress passed an act that provided for the complete abandonment of national quotas by mid-1968. Under the new act admittance is based, not on national origin, but on the need of this country for the training or skills of a would-be immigrant. However, the number of entrants from any one country is limited to an annual maximum of 20,000. Further, the number from the Western Hemisphere is limited to 120,000 annually, and to 170,000 from the rest of the world. Provision is made for admitting members of the immediate families of residents of this country; other close relatives are given preference but must be included within the total limits on immigration. The act provided that until quotas ended in 1968, any unfilled quotas could be parcelled out among nations with long waiting lists. When the act was passed, the longest lists were in Italy, Greece, Poland, and Portugal.

The Americanization of Immigrants. *Americanization is the name we give to the process by which an alien becomes an integral part of our American society.* An important element in this process is *naturalization, which refers to the legal action necessary to confer American citizenship on an alien.* Although in the United States aliens have most of the rights of citizens, they cannot vote or hold public office, and in some states they are excluded from certain professions.

Much has been written about the contributions the nationality groups have made to our American culture. Not only did their labor help the rapid expansion of agriculture and industry, but many of their traditions and customs have become part of a common American heritage. They have made contributions in many fields, including government, politics, religion, and the arts. Many writers feel that a large part of America's vitality and strength has developed from this fusion of divergent cultures.

OTHER MINORITY GROUPS

There are in this country a number of religious groups whose convictions lead them to follow ways of life somewhat different from the general pattern of American culture. These include such sects as the Mennonites, the Dunkers, the Amish, and the Jehovah's Witnesses. But their total number is small. At one time the Mormons could have been included, but after they abandoned polygamy they became, in their relation to our American culture, not very different from any other Christian sect.

The Jews, however, form an important minority group whose influence on our society is greater than their numbers alone would seem to indicate. They are frequently called a race, but anthropologists remind us that this term is misleading. Originally they belonged to that branch of the Caucasoid race that inhabited the Arabian Peninsula and spread into the "fertile crescent" to the north of it. They once formed a nationality, the ancient Hebrew nation. But later they were dispersed over a wide area, eventually the whole civilized world, and over the centuries they interbred to some extent with the "gentiles" of the countries in which they lived. Also, they converted several non-Jewish peoples to Judaism. The word *Jew* itself comes from *Judaism,* which is their religion. After World War II some of them returned to the ancient homeland and created the new nation of Israel.

The Jews are a unique cultural group in that they have been able to maintain their identity and their religion among alien peoples over many hundreds of years. The Orthodox Jews still cling firmly to their ancient religious and cultural traditions. But the Conservative and the Reform groups now place less emphasis on some of these traditions and, as a result, have had less trouble in fitting into the general pattern of American culture. The Jewish culture, however, reinforced by the prejudice that non-Jews have displayed against the Jews, still maintains them as a definitely identifiable minority group.

To determine the number of Jews in the United States with any great accuracy is impossible. Partly this is because many persons of Jewish ethnic background maintain no affiliation with any temple or other Jewish organization, and partly it is because there has been an appreciable amount of intermarriage between Jews and non-Jews. At present it is estimated that there are more than six million people in this country (and possibly close to seven million) who can be classified as Jews. More than one third of all American Jews live in metropolitan New York, and considerable numbers are concentrated in other large cities, such as Los Angeles, Philadelphia, and Chicago.

Jews are sometimes considered to be primarily a religious group, but in a recent poll taken by *Newsweek* only 43 per cent of American Jews said that they considered themselves religious. According to political scientist Daniel Eleazar of Temple University, only 20 per cent of the Jewish population worships regularly. Of the others, 40 per cent maintain nominal affiliation with a temple, but usually attend services only on Rosh Hashana and Yom Kippur.

On the average, American Jews have markedly higher incomes than the rest of our population, though in the cities some 800,000 of them fall below the family poverty level as set by agencies of the federal government. Jews also, on average, have higher levels of education than other groups and, in proportion to their numbers, are much better represented in business and the professions. [13]

In Europe, prejudice against the Jews, or *anti-Semitism,* has existed for centuries and has been very strong in certain countries. Sometimes it has

[13] *Newsweek,* "The American Jew Today," March 1, 1971, pp. 56–64.

been tied to religion; sometimes it has been justified by dislike on the part of the majority of the population for certain cultural or "racial" characteristics, largely imaginary, attributed to the Jews as a group. In some parts of eastern Europe, anti-Semitism has at times gone to such extremes that thousands of Jews were killed, as in the *pogroms,* or organized massacres, that occurred in czarist Russia. But it was in Nazi Germany that anti-Semitism reached its height, for Jews constituted the great majority of the possibly seven million people who were murdered in Hitler's concentration camps.

In comparison with the situation in some European countries, prejudice against the Jews is mild in the United States. Even so, it is still a real problem in some communities. For many years anti-Semitism in this country slowly diminished, perhaps in part because it was overshadowed by the greater problem of black-white relations. But in recent years some Jews have felt that the level of prejudice was rising. Two factors may have contributed to this.[14] First, when the new nation of Israel was established and conflict with the Arabs began, the majority of Jews were drawn together by a sense of pride, and many gave their full support to Israel. But often their gentile friends did not share their sentiments. Second, as blacks have increased their demands for equality, some of them have tended to identify the Jewish merchant in the ghetto as the symbol of white oppression. In spite of such developments there is no clear evidence that in the country as a whole anti-Semitism is increasing. The long-run trend appears to be in the other direction. Intermarriage seems to be more and more common, and according to polls taken in recent years, Jewish opposition to it has decreased sharply. Whether the Jews in America will, after a few generations, lose their identity as a separate cultural group remains to be seen. But under modern conditions in our society this may happen. At least there are no racial differences of the kind that make the complete assimilation of the blacks relatively difficult.

Terms to Be Understood

race	Alpine	Chicanos
Homo sapiens	prejudice	*la raza*
Caucasoid	discrimination	Hispanos
Mongoloid	ethnic barriers	*braceros*
Negroid	*apartheid*	immigration quotas
prognathism	integration	Americanization
cephalic index	assimilation	naturalization
racial subtypes	accommodation	anti-Semitism
Nordic	"social visibility"	pogrom
Mediterranean		

[14] Ibid.

Questions for Review and Discussion

1. Is there more justification for calling the American Indians a "race" than for applying this terms to the French? Explain.
2. Why are racial and cultural differences largely independent of each other?
3. What three groups are often considered the major races of mankind, and how do they differ from one another?
4. Why is it difficult to classify all the peoples of the world according to race?
5. List the principal subtypes of each of the three major races.
6. Has it been proved that some racial groups are superior to others in their capacity for mental development? Has it been proved that all racial groups are alike in their inborn capacities for mental and emotional development? Explain.
7. How would you explain the existence and the extent of race prejudice in the world?
8. What is the relation of prejudice to discrimination?
9. Give the history, approximate numbers, and present status of each of the following groups in the United States: (a) the American Indians; (b) the Chicanos; (c) the Japanese; (d) the Chinese; (e) the Puerto Ricans; (f) the Cubans.
10. Compare the problem of assimilating European immigrants with that of assimilating minority racial groups.
11. Explain the nature and origin of the quota system for controlling immigration into the United States.
12. Distinguish between Americanization and naturalization.
13. What has been the net effect of immigration on American culture?
14. How do you account for the existence of anti-Semitism in both Europe and the United States?
15. In this country anti-Semitism seems to be diminishing. How do you account for this?

For Further Study

Bettelheim, Bruno, and Morris Janowitz, *Social Change and Prejudice.* New York, The Free Press, 1964.

Clark, Kenneth B., *Prejudice and Your Child,* 2d ed., Gloucester, Mass., Peter Smith, Publisher, 1968.

Coon, Carleton S., and E. Hunt, Jr., *Living Races of Man,* New York, Alfred A. Knopf, Inc., 1965.

Dobzhansky, Theodosius, *Heredity and the Nature of Man,* paperback, New York, New American Library, Inc., 1966. See Chap. 3, "Race," for an excellent discussion.

Driver, Harold E., *Indians of North America,* 2d ed., paperback, Chicago, University of Chicago Press, 1969.

Frazier, E. Franklin, *Race and Culture Contacts in the Modern World,* paperback, Boston, Beacon Press, Inc., 1965.

Garn, Stanley M., *Human Races,* 2d ed., Springfield, Ill., Charles C Thomas, Publisher, 1969.

——— , ed., *Readings on Race,* 2d ed., Springfield, Ill., Charles C Thomas, Publisher, 1968.

Glazer, Nathan, and Daniel P. Moynihan, *Beyond the Melting Pot: The Negroes, Puerto Ricans, Jews, Italians, and Irish of New York City,* Cambridge, Mass., M.I.T. Press, 1970.

Goldsby, Richard, *Race and Races,* paperback, New York, The Macmillan Company, 1971.

Gonzalez, Nancie L., *Spanish-Americans of New Mexico: A Distinctive Heritage,* paperback, Albuquerque, N. Mex., University of New Mexico Press, 1969.

Gordon, Milton M., *Assimilation in American Life: The Role of Race, Religion, and National Origin,* paperback, New York, Oxford University Press, 1964.

Howard, John R., ed. and intro., *Awakening Minorities: American Indians, Mexican-Indians, Mexican-Americans, and Puerto Ricans,* paperback, Chicago, Aldine Publishing Company, 1970.

Josephy, Alvin, *The Indian Heritage of America,* Bantam paperback, New York, Alfred A. Knopf, Inc., 1968.

Kitano, Harry L., *Japanese Americans,* paperback, Englewood Cliffs, N.J., Prentice-Hall, Inc., 1969.

Ling, Andrew W., Hawaii's People, 3d ed., paperback, Honolulu, University of Hawaii Press, 1970.

Lurie, Nancy O., *The American Indian Today,* Deland, Fla., Everett/Edwards, Inc., 1968.

Mason, Philip, *Race Relations,* London, Oxford University Press, 1970.

Park, Robert Ezra, *Race and Culture,* paperback, New York, The Free Press, 1964.

Servin, Manuel, *The Mexican-Americans, An Awakening Minority,* New York, The Free Press, 1970.

Simpson, George E., and J. Milton Yinger, *Racial and Cultural Minorities,* 3d ed., New York, Harper & Row, Publishers, 1965.

Tax, Sol, ed., Acculturation in the Americas, New York, Cooper Square Publishers, Inc., 1967.

Tumin, Melvin M., ed., *Comparative Perspectives on Race Relations,* paperback, Boston, Little, Brown and Company, 1969. A collection of cross-cultural readings.

VanderZanden, James W., *American Minority Relations: The Sociology of Race and Ethnic Groups,* 2d ed., New York, The Ronald Press Company, 1966.

Wagley, Charles, and Marvin Harris, *Minorities in the New World: Six Case Studies,* paperback, New York, Columbia University Press, 1958.

Wallace, Anthony F. C., *The Death and Rebirth of the Seneca,* New York, Alfred A. Knopf, Inc., 1970.

Chapter 14

The

Black

Americans

It is common knowledge that before they were brought to this country as slaves some generations ago, the black ancestors of the black Americans lived in Africa. Africa is a vast continent, larger than North America by more than two million square miles. Its northern edge along the shores of the Mediterranean is inhabited by Caucasoid peoples such as Berbers and Arabs. South of this area lies the great Sahara Desert, extending hundreds of miles from north to south and stretching more than three thousand miles from the Atlantic Ocean to the Red Sea. Travel across the Sahara is difficult, and it was almost impossible before the introduction, early in the Christian era, of camels from Asia.

Black Africa. Black Africa lies below the Sahara. It begins in the Sudan, which is an area stretching clear across the continent just south of the desert. (Only a fraction of it is in the country that, in 1956, took the name Sudan.) The Sudan consists of grasslands and scattered woodlands, and includes some good farmland. Further south it merges into the dense tropical rain forests along the coasts of the Gulf of Guinea and in the basin of the great Congo River. To the east of the Congo basin are mountains and highlands, a series of long lakes, and some plains. To the south are more plains, some highlands, some good agricultural land, and also some very dry areas, including the Kalahari Desert. Most of Black Africa is within twenty degrees of latitude from the equator. Only in the highlands or in the far south can fairly temperate climates be found.

For the greater part of Black Africa our historical knowledge until recent times is very limited because the native peoples developed no system of writing, and most of them in historic times were too isolated from the developing civilizations of Asia and Europe to learn writing by the processes of cultural diffusion. However, in the seventh century A.D., Arabs, who had just been converted to Islam, began to reach the central and western Sudan in increasing numbers. This was part of the great movement of Arab expansion that followed the death of Mohammed in A.D. 632. The Arabs did not conquer the Sudan as they did Spain, North Africa, and most of the Near East, because greater and more accessible prizes were available elsewhere. But adventurers, merchants, and Muslim missionaries penetrated as far as the Atlantic Ocean, and some brought with them Arabian scholarship, including writing and such sciences as mathematics and astronomy. But the scholars, whether Arabs or blacks, did their writing in Arabic, just as European monks in the early Middle Ages had written in Latin and not in the languages spoken by the common people. Many of the native blacks were converted to Islam; in time the Arabs and the blacks whom they had taught established schools and even universities, including the famous one that once flourished in Timbuktu. However, this Arab influence was largely limited to the Sudan and scarcely penetrated the tribal cultures in the rain forests along the Guinean coast to the south.

Because of these contacts with Arab culture, and the resulting written records, we have some knowledge of the history of the Sudan for periods much earlier than for most of Black Africa. We know, for example, about several large kingdoms or empires that were established there, including Ghana and such later states as Mali, Songhay, and Kanem. As to the rest of Black Africa, except for certain areas in the east not too far from the Asiatic mainland, we have few historical records until the Portuguese in the fifteenth century inaugurated the great Age of Discovery and began to visit the more distant parts of the African coast and to establish forts and trading posts. Not until the nineteenth century did the outside world learn much about the interior of Black Africa.

But at the beginning of the modern period of history late in the fifteenth century, Black Africa was far from the most backward of the major continental areas. At that time the Australian aborigines and the American Indians were still in the Stone Age, though a few of the latter were just beginning to learn the use of metals; whereas most Africans were farmers already equipped with tools of iron. As the result of a better food supply, their numbers were much greater. In most cases they were organized into tribes or states powerful enough to discourage outside invaders or settlers until late in the nineteenth century. According to Roland Oliver and John Fage, "It was in large measure the progress already made by the Africans in earlier centuries that enabled them to resist the modern age for so long."[1]

If this was the case, why did the Africans not effectively resist the large-scale exportation of black slaves that began in the sixteenth century? There were several reasons. First, slavery is a very old institution. It has been found in many primitive or archaic tribal cultures, and it existed in most if not all ancient civilizations. In Black Africa it was well established long before contacts were made with Europeans. Second, not only was there local trade in slaves, but some export of black slaves to the Arab countries had been going on for centuries. Third, like most tribal peoples, Africans had little feeling of brotherhood with people of other tribes. Often they regarded them as enemies who, if possible, should be driven away, destroyed, or conquered and enslaved. They were often quite willing to sell Africans of other tribes to European slave dealers.

The African Slave Trade After A.D. 1600. The Portuguese were the first Europeans to explore the more distant coasts of Africa and there to engage in the slave trade. Even in the fifteenth century their ships had brought some black slaves to Portugal and Spain. But the African slave trade did not assume massive proportions until after the discovery of the Americas and the establishment there of plantations. The Portuguese were not able to maintain a monopoly of this trade. Before long, the Dutch were actively engaged in it, and then the French and British. According to one estimate, at least fourteen or fifteen million black slaves were *landed* in the Americas, North and South, from 1600 to the latter part of the nineteenth century.[2] These figures take no account of the millions of Africans who died on slave ships because they were chained under the deck in the narrowest quarters possible during a long sea voyage; nor does it count those who were killed in slave raids by African chiefs, kings, or native slave traders.

The export of black slaves on this scale would not have occurred without the cooperation of Africans. Direct slave raids by Europeans were rare indeed. The difficulties and risks were too great. However, it is said that in Angola the Portuguese sometimes armed and paid gangs of Africans to do slave raiding for them. But on the Guinea coast, according to Oliver and

[1] Roland Oliver and J. D. Fage, *A Short History of Africa,* Baltimore, Penguin Books, Inc., 1966, pp. 13–14.
[2] Ibid., p. 120.

Fage, "Invariably the Europeans bought their slaves from African kings or merchants."[3]

The African Origins of American Blacks. Though the Portuguese obtained some slaves from the Congo for shipment to Brazil, and more from Angola, the main source of slaves was the northern coast of the Gulf of Guinea. The French operated in the west up to and including the Senegal River, but by far the greatest number of slaves was obtained from the part of Guinea that begins with the Gold Coast and extends east beyond the Niger Delta. It was this region, especially the areas behind the coast, that some generations ago was home to most of the black ancestors of the American blacks. This is also the African region in which the bodily and facial characteristics of the people are most strongly Negroid. According to Philip Mason, "'Negro' . . . has two quite distinct meanings, being sometimes confined to the 'true' Negroes of the West Coast of Africa, and sometimes used much more widely to include the Bantu-speaking people of Central and South Africa and Caribbean and American populations whose ancestry includes many who are not African."[4]

Why was the slave trade concentrated on the Guinea coast? First, because the areas just behind the coast were more densely populated than most of Africa. Second, because merchants there had already established trade with the outside world in ivory and gold, and when a demand for slaves developed, they naturally began to provide them also. Third, in the seventeenth and eighteenth centuries several strong kingdoms, especially Ashanti, Dahomey, and Oyo, were established just inland from the coast, and their rulers were anxious to participate in the profits of the slave trade. They expanded southward to the coast to make contact with Europeans, and when they had sold the people who were already slaves (often debtors and convicts), they began to use the firearms they had acquired by trade to make raids further into the interior for the express purpose of capturing slaves for export.

These Guinean states were organized somewhat after the pattern of the great states of the Sudan. Each was created through conquest by some able chief of a strong tribe, and in each the king had absolute power. They represented a considerable achievement in terms of organization and administration, especially when we remember that neither the king, his officials, nor his subjects had any knowledge of writing. But from our modern point of view, these kingdoms were barbaric. Not only did they undertake the wholesale capture of neighboring peoples for sale as slaves, but their religious rituals sometimes required human sacrifices on a large scale. In an account that he wrote some years ago George Murdock, who is a recognized authority on ethnology, describes this unpleasant aspect of Dahomean culture as it once existed.[5] There is evidence that large kingdoms or

[3] Ibid.

[4] Philip Mason, *Race Relations*, London, Oxford University Press, 1970, p. 13.

[5] George Peter Murdock, *Our Primitive Contemporaries*, New York, The Macmillan Company, 1936, pp. 587–589.

empires existed in parts of Black Africa other than the Sudan and Guinea, but because of the lack of written records we know very little about most of them.

Though the inhabitants of Guinea were tribal, nonliterate peoples, they had in some respects a relatively advanced culture by the sixteenth or seventeenth century. Trade and trade routes had developed sufficiently to bring about the growth of a few towns of some size. A Dutch author, writing in 1602, compared Benin in Nigeria rather favorably with the Amsterdam of his day.[6] Besides trading in slaves, the Guinean merchants bought and sold gold, ivory, kola nuts, metal items like cutlasses, copper, cloth, salt, cowrie shells, horses, and cattle. Most of this trade represented items brought in or sent out over long distances, but there was also local trade in which, for example, foodstuffs were exchanged for the handicraft manufactures of a certain area. In some parts of Guinea, especially in the Nigerian region southwest of Lake Chad, the people seem to have been among the leaders of Black Africa in agriculture, metalwork, pottery, and sculpture.[7] Olaudah Equiano, who was a native of Benin, was kidnapped into slavery as a boy sometime in the 1750's. He later traveled widely with his masters, learned to speak and write English, and eventually bought his freedom. In his memoirs he speaks of coming from "a nation of dancers, musicians, and poets."[8] Also, Murdock writes that the Dahomeans were known to display considerable talent in the fine arts. Their wood carvings and sculptured bas-reliefs were notable; also their native musical instruments; but it was in vocal music that they were superior. They were passionately fond of dancing, accompanied either by singing or by instruments.[9]

HISTORICAL BACKGROUND OF BLACKS IN AMERICA

The use of blacks as slaves did not begin in the English colonies of America for more than a century after the Spanish and Portuguese had begun to import slaves in considerable numbers into the West Indies and South America. When the plantation system began to develop in the southern English colonies, plantation owners felt a need for a large dependable work force that they could control. But the free white workers from Europe who had come to America were seeking freedom and independence and were unwilling to work as plantation laborers for any length of time when there were opportunities for them to secure their own land and to be indepen-

[6] Oliver and Fage, op. cit., pp. 106–107.
[7] Ibid., pp. 104, 109–111.
[8] Olaudah Equiano, "The Life of Olaudah Equiano, or Gustavus Vassa, the African, Written by Himself," *Great Slave Narratives*, edited by Arna Bontemps, Boston, Beacon Press, Inc., 1969.
[9] Murdock, op. cit., pp. 577–578.

dent. This created a problem for which the use of black slaves appeared to be a practical solution.

Slavery in Colonial America. [10] Negro slavery in the American colonies may be said to have begun in 1619, when the Dutch brought twenty blacks to Virginia on a man-of-war and sold them to some settlers. Legally, these Africans were supposed to have the same status as white *indentured servants,* but indications are that they were treated differently from the beginning. Later their status as slaves was clearly defined by law. In 1663 Maryland passed a statute making blacks who had been purchased, slaves for life, and their children after them. Before long other colonies enacted similar laws.

The *plantation system* of agriculture encouraged slavery as an institution because, as we have said, plantation owners required a large dependable labor force that they could control; also an economical one in order to make profits. Though black slaves cost more than white indentured servants, the latter had to be released after four years, but blacks and their children were the property of their master for life. This compensated for the problems of training and caring for them and for the difficulties of maintaining the rigid and harsh discipline necessary to force them to work.

Once slavery was established, it continued to expand with the plantation system and became a basic support of the Southern economy. By 1775 there were probably at least half a million slaves in America, most of whom were in the South. Because the plantation system did not exist in the North, slavery on any large scale did not develop there, although well-trained slaves were highly prized as servants.

Blacks played a role in the Revolutionary War that should not be overlooked, especially considering that most of them were illiterate slaves. Crispus Attucks, a runaway slave, is said to have been the first victim of the British in the Boston Massacre of 1770, although General Washington in the early days of the Revolutionary War refused to accept black recruits. Later this policy was changed, partly because the Tory governor of Virginia offered freedom to all slaves who would enlist with the British. By the end of the war it is estimated that about 5,000 blacks had fought for the independence of the United States and had won their freedom if they had been slaves.

Following the Revolutionary War, some of the Northern states provided in their constitutions for the abolishment of the slave system, in most cases by making the children free. Soon after, when the first federal census was taken in 1790, it was found that of the 67,120 blacks in the North, about 40,000 of them were slaves and the remainder were free.

From the Signing of the Constitution to the Civil War. When the Constitution was written, various compromises were made on the status of

[10] Much of the historical material in this section is based on E. Franklin Frazier, *The Negro in the United States,* New York, The Macmillan Company, 1949 and 1957.

slavery, and the hope was that it would gradually disappear. But the reduction in the cost of processing cotton after the appearance of the cotton gin in 1793, and the resulting increase in the demand for it by the textile industry, brought about an increase in the demand for slaves. Though in 1808 the importation of slaves became illegal, for a long time thousands were smuggled into the United States every year.

After the importation of slaves was made illegal, slave trading *within* the country became an increasingly important business. In parts of the Southeastern states, because tobacco plantations were giving way to small farms, the demand for slaves decreased. This was especially true in Virginia. But at the same time, cotton growing in the South expanded westward, and as the new plantations needed more and more slaves to do the hard and unpleasant work, they purchased those who were no longer needed in the East.

The number of free blacks in the United States rose steadily from 1790 to the Civil War. By 1860 they totalled over 430,000, or about 10 per cent of the entire black population at that time. More than half the free blacks were in the South. They kept rising in numbers not only because of natural increase but also because slaves were frequently freed by their owners for one reason or another. Often, white owners who had children by slave mothers set the children free, and it was not uncommon for planters to allow slaves to buy their freedom or that of their children. Though the free blacks were better off than the slaves, their position was not enviable. A few became well educated and managed to prosper, but most of them were held back by prejudice and discrimination. This tended to grow as their numbers increased. Some states took away from them the right to vote, and some even excluded them from public schools when these were made available to all white children.

Not all black people who were slaves accepted their fate. Many ran away and took refuge with free blacks in the North. There were even some insurrections, several of them fairly sizable. The most famous of these was in Southhampton County, Virginia, in 1831, and was led by a slave named Nat Turner. He and his sixty or seventy followers killed fifty-nine white people, slave owners and their families, before they were overtaken by the militia.

With the rise of the *abolition movement* in the North, an organized system was developed for helping runaway slaves to escape to Canada. This became known as the *Underground Railroad*. The Railroad had many "stations" in the homes of its supporters, especially in Ohio. One of these homes was that of the author's maternal grandfather, Asahel Beecher, who lived in Oberlin, a few miles south of Lake Erie. Of all the "conductors" on the Underground Railroad who aided slaves to reach freedom, perhaps the most extraordinary was an ex-slave named Harriet Tubman. After escaping from slavery herself, she returned again and again to the South over a ten-year period, and is credited with aiding more than three hundred slaves to escape.

The Civil War and Emancipation. In the early months of the Civil War the Lincoln administration in Washington made no firm decisions as to how to deal with slavery, but as time passed, sentiment in favor of abolition kept increasing. The power of the Southern aristocracy had as its economic base slavery and the plantation system. Hence, many Northern political leaders believed that, entirely aside from questions of humanitarianism and the rights of man, it was desirable to abolish slavery in order to weaken the military power of the South and thus help preserve the Union. Abraham Lincoln, as indicated by a number of his actions, came gradually to accept this view; finally, on January 1, 1863, he issued the Emancipation Proclamation.

At the end of the Civil War conditions were chaotic in much of the South, and the former slaves were totally unprepared for freedom. Most stayed on with their former masters and worked for them for subsistence or wages. But many thousands became refugees and wanderers, seeking food and shelter wherever they could find it, with no aim but "freedom" and with no doubt that the government would care for them if no one else did. This problem became so acute that Congress, in 1865, set up a *Freedmen's Bureau* to give all possible aid to the refugees in making the adjustment from slavery to freedom. Though the Bureau had only limited success, it did lay the groundwork for future plans for "reconstruction." It also established many schools, including several of our best-known colleges for blacks.

Gradually, the great majority of blacks who had been uprooted either drifted back to work for their former masters or became tenants on small farms elsewhere. For over half a century, nine tenths of our Afro-American population continued to live in the South, principally because that was where they knew how to make a living, even though it was a very poor one.

The Reconstruction Period. The Emancipation Proclamation changed the legal status of the slaves overnight, but the white people of the South could not all accept what this change implied. The general feeling of most Southerners, and even of some people in the North, was that the average black man had a very limited capacity for education and development. They looked on him as an inferior being who might be useful but whom they must look after, and they could not conceive of treating him as an equal. It was not that the majority of Southern whites despised the blacks, but they regarded them as children who did not have the capacity to grow up.

The Reconstruction period after the Civil War was therefore characterized by a struggle between Congress and the Southern whites. Congress tried to give the blacks full rights of citizenship through passage of the Fourteenth and Fifteenth amendments and the Reconstruction acts, and finally through the imposition of military rule on the South. The Southern whites, on the other hand, sought to regain control of their states. During this period, great numbers of blacks were able to vote, and some were even elected to important political offices, including membership in the United States Senate and House of Representatives. The whites, however, made every effort to keep the blacks under their control. Among other methods of doing this they employed the *Ku Klux Klan,* organized shortly after the Civil War. The Klan was a secret organization whose professed purpose was the maintenance of law and order; but a large part of its activities consisted in terrorizing blacks to "keep them in their place." Congress abolished it by law in 1871, but it continued to operate as an underground organization.

It must be recognized that the Southern whites faced a real problem at the end of the war. At the beginning of the war the total population of the eleven states of the Confederacy consisted of about five million whites and four million blacks, and of the latter more than 90 per cent were slaves.[11] After Emancipation the great mass of blacks were illiterate and in no way prepared to assume the responsibilities of citizenship. It could not have been otherwise, because all their lives they had been treated as chattels and subjected to harsh discipline. They had had no experience in managing their own affairs.

However, race relations in the South were in some ways better during Reconstruction and the years immediately following than they were thirty or forty years later. There was, to be sure, no thought of recognizing the blacks as equals, and some types of *segregation,* such as in the armed forces and the schools, were accepted without question even by Northern liberals and the government at Washington. But some Southern whites felt a genuine sense of responsibility toward the blacks and felt a fondness for many of them who had been long-time family servants; and at that time there was no real system of *legal segregation.* Most *Jim Crow laws* were to come later.

All the Southern states were restored to the Union by 1870, and in 1872 Congress terminated the Freedmen's Bureau and passed an amnesty act that pardoned almost everyone who had taken part in the Southern rebellion against the Union. In 1877, when President Hayes withdrew the last of the federal troops that had been occupying the South, the Southern whites were again in full control of their state and local governments.

Changing Status of Blacks Since Reconstruction. When the Southern whites regained full control of their states, there was no sudden change in the status of the blacks. Northern travelers in the South in the 1880's reported that black people were better treated there than in some areas of the North. There was a considerable black vote in parts of the South for years after Reconstruction, and this actually increased in the early 1890's, when the white Southern Populists sought support from the blacks and encouraged them to vote.

Though various types of segregation had long been practiced, syste-

[11] See U.S. Bureau of the Census, *Historical Statistics of the United States, Colonial Times to 1957,* Washington, D.C., 1960, pp. 9, 11–12.

matic *legal* segregation of blacks from whites by means of Jim Crow laws developed very slowly in the Southern states until about 1890. In the following decade such laws spread rapidly, but they did not reach their fullest scope until long after 1900. Though segregation did not originate with Jim Crow laws, these did a great deal to extend and tighten it and to lower further the status of blacks. At their height they required a separation of the races in practically all public meeting places, including restaurants, transportation facilities, schools, and even parks.[12]

Along with the expansion of segregation in the 1890's, there was also a movement to disfranchise blacks. This was backed by an intensive propaganda for "white supremacy." Within a decade or so every state of the old Confederacy had passed laws that, without openly flouting the Fifteenth Amendment, effectively prevented most Afro-Americans from voting.

Disfranchisement and white supremacy propaganda was accompanied by a sharp rise in atrocities against blacks. In the 1890's the reported number of lynchings, nearly all in the South, reached an all-time high average of over one hundred annually. Today, fortunately, public lynchings by mobs are almost unknown in this country. Unfortunately, there are still occasional murders of civil rights workers, both black and white.

In the North there have been no Jim Crow laws in modern times. Nevertheless, there has been a great deal of discrimination. This has tended to vary according to the number of blacks in a given community and according to the distance of the community from the South. The Swedish sociologist Gunnar Myrdal attracted worldwide attention when he made a study in the early 1940's of race relations in our South. In his book reporting this study, which he called *An American Dilemma,* he noted that where there have been comparatively few blacks, they have been accepted more readily, though not actually assimilated. Blacks, like other minorities, have tended to live in groups; but, much more than any other minority, they have been kept within their own groups and have never really been assimilated into the larger American society. Intermarriage of whites and blacks is increasing but is still infrequent, and when it does occur, the children are regarded as blacks. Some light-skinned "blacks" whose ancestry is largely Caucasian successfully "pass" the color line and join the whites, but this has no effect on the status of blacks as a group. In the North, however, there has never been as much discrimination against them in most public places as in the South, and no attempt has been made in modern times to keep them from voting. In the last two or three decades, great progress has been made in reducing some types of discrimination. On the other hand, the great influx of many thousands of blacks into Northern cities within a comparatively short time, and their concentration in "ghettos," has sharpened racial awareness and in many places has increased racial prejudice and conflict.

[12] C. Vann Woodward, *The Strange Career of Jim Crow,* Galaxy paperback, New York, Oxford University Press, 1957. See especially "Foreword to the Galaxy Edition" and also Chaps. 1 and 2.

THE RACE PROBLEM TODAY

The problems of our present-day Afro-Americans differ from those of any other minority group in this country. They are different not only because of the number of blacks in our population but also for other reasons. To begin with, the black man in the United States is so far removed from his African "homeland" that much of his cultural heritage from that region has been lost. He is far removed in point of time or number of generations, and he is far removed in traditions. Though his cultural patterns do differ somewhat from those of other Americans, he is essentially American by culture, including language, customs, education, and religion. But the position of the black minority is still influenced unfavorably by the fact that it is the only minority in this country the bulk of which once served a long period of slavery to the white man. Other minority groups have never experienced the social and psychological upheavals caused by slavery, followed by sudden emancipation and then by a long period of discrimination and segregation, some of it enforced by law. In addition, Afro-Americans, except for some with partly white ancestry, tend to differ from whites in skin color, hair, and features more than do other minority racial groups, and this has contributed·to the strong personal prejudice that sometimes exists between whites and blacks.

American blacks as a group have a considerable amount of white ancestry. Much of this mixing occurred under slavery when slave owners frequently fathered children by black mothers. The great abolitionist leader, Frederick Douglass, was the son of a white father by a slave mother. Just how much white ancestry American blacks have cannot be determined with certainty, but some geneticists have attempted to make an estimate. Most of the ancestors of American blacks came from certain areas in West Africa. By comparing the percentages of the West African natives who carry a certain gene (the rhesus-factor allele $R°$) with the percentages of American blacks and American whites who carry it, the geneticists conclude that, *on the average,* the ancestry of American blacks is probably about 30 per cent white.[13]

Although the status of Afro-Americans has advanced in many ways in recent decades, it cannot be denied that they still suffer from prejudice and discrimination; though perhaps they suffer even more from handicaps that are the legacy of discrimination in the past.

Legal Discrimination and Segregation. We have already described briefly the rise of legal segregation in the South. The constitutionality of the state laws on which it was based was long a matter of dispute because the Fourteenth Amendment to the Constitution of the United States, adopted in 1868, provides that no state may deny any person equal protection by the laws. The question was whether segregation constituted

---

[13] Haig P. Papazian, *Modern Genetics,* Signet paperback, New York, New American Library, Inc., 1968, pp. 266–267.

denial of equal protection. But those who attempted to challenge these laws in the courts had no important success until, in 1954, the United States Supreme Court handed down its momentous decision outlawing segregation in public schools.

This reversed a decision made by the Court in 1896, when in the case of Plessy vs. Ferguson, it had issued a decision approving segregation of blacks and whites by state legislation. The decision in Plessy vs. Ferguson was based on the so-called *separate-but-equal doctrine,* that is, the theory that providing separate educational, recreational, and other public facilities for blacks was not denying equal protection under the laws if these facilities were equal to those for whites. In practice, this equality proved to be a myth.

The decision outlawing school segregation opened the way for challenging other segregation laws, and within a decade or so it became clear that they were all unconstitutional. However, the breaking down of segregation, especially in the case of the schools, proved to be a slow and difficult process, one that has not yet been completed. Some confusion has resulted from disagreement as to whether court decisions, and civil rights acts passed by Congress, merely annul laws or public policies that require or encourage attendance at segregated schools; or whether they also place an obligation on communities and school boards to take positive measures to eliminate *de facto segregation.* Do these decisions and acts make illegal segregation resulting from the fact that some residential areas are wholly black and others wholly white? or make illegal segregation brought about partly because some parents, black as well as white, may prefer to have their children attend segregated schools?

In the deep South the Supreme Court decision met with extreme resistance. In the border states much more progress was made, but it was slow. By the fall of 1964, at the start of the eleventh year after the Court had outlawed segregation, more than 50 per cent of all black pupils in six border states were attending school with whites. In these states the obstacles to integration were not so great, partly because the proportion of blacks in the population was relatively small. But of the 2.9 million black pupils in the eleven states that belonged to the old Confederacy, only about 2 per cent were attending school with whites; the other 98 per cent were still in segregated schools.

The Civil Rights Act of 1964 gave some impetus to desegregation in the deep South because it gives the federal government power to withhold financial assistance from any program that shows racial discrimination. However, in the school year 1968–1969, according to the United States Department of Health, Education, and Welfare, the percentage of black pupils attending integrated schools in the former Confederate states had risen to only 20.3. But this figure counts as integrated only the schools in which a majority of pupils are white. On the basis of this definition complete integration is scarcely possible, as there are districts in the South, including some whole counties, where blacks are in the majority. The number of blacks in integrated schools would have been higher in 1968–1969—possibly 30 to 35 per cent—if all blacks had been counted who were attending schools in which there were some whites. Even this would not have been a very impressive level of integration, because it means that fifteen years after the Supreme Court decision outlawing segregation in public schools, some two thirds of the black pupils in the old South were still attending all-black schools. In the last two or three years increased federal pressure has accelerated integration in the South, but resistance in some areas is still strong.

Though we no longer have, in this country, school segregation by direct legal mandate, there is no doubt that in some areas, in both the North and the South, efforts are still being made to devise public policies that will discourage blacks from going to predominantly white schools, and vice versa. However, in Northern cities, most of the growing de facto segregation in schools does not arise from policies designed to create it. Rather, it results from de facto segregation in housing, and from the increasingly rapid movement of whites to the suburbs while black populations continue to grow in the central cities. An extreme case is Washington, D.C., where well over 90 per cent of all public school children are blacks.

Standards and levels of achievement are likely to be lower in schools attended largely by blacks than in those attended by whites. The exceptions are found mostly in middle- or upper-class black neighborhoods. But it should not be forgotten that white schools in slum areas also tend to be inferior to those in better neighborhoods. What we need to improve is not just the educational level of black children but that of *all* underprivileged children. Racial balance does have advantages if it can be achieved without continuing disorganization and conflict. Also advantageous are good buildings and equipment, reasonably small classes, and well-paid teachers. But the problem of educational standards is not a simple one, and attempts to solve it by achieving racial balance or spending more money on teachers or equipment often give disappointing results. Both black and white leaders need to seek ways to imbue slum children with confidence, to stimulate their interest, and to provide them with educational and vocational goals that seem possible and that they will strive to attain.

One of the great obstacles to the education of underprivileged children seems to be that their family and community backgrounds fail to provide them with incentives for acquiring the kinds of knowledge and skills that schools try to teach. Thousands of children never see books or any other printed matter in their homes; neither are they taught attitudes and habits conducive to learning. This problem will be dealt with in Chapter 16 in connection with Head Start and related programs. It has also been pointed out that many of the children are suffering from malnutrition. To help relieve this problem, many cities, with federal aid, have adopted a program of free lunches and, in some cases, free breakfasts for elementary school children in slum areas.

Economic Opportunities and Professional Training. Though the economic condition of Afro-Americans has, on the average, improved greatly, it has by no means caught up with that of whites. In 1939 four out of five blacks lived in the South. One third of these were still sharecroppers or farm laborers and were earning very low wages. Median wage and salary income of nonwhite families and single individuals (a group of which about 92 per cent were blacks) was only 37 per cent of that of whites.[14] If all types of income, such as rent, interest, and dividends, had been included in these figures, the ratio for nonwhites would have been still lower. But increasing mechanization of agriculture, during and after World War II, reduced the demand for even low-wage farm workers, and hence many of them were forced to seek employment elsewhere. At the same time, the expansion of industry brought a great demand for workers in the cities. As a result, there developed a steady migration of black workers not only to industrial cities in the North and West but also to industrial areas in the South. The median wage and salary income of nonwhites climbed rapidly. In terms of percentages, though not in actual dollars, it rose faster than white income until, in 1947, the second full year after the war, it was 48 per cent of median white income. During the next ten years there was another great increase of income for both groups, but nonwhites made less progress in catching up. Nevertheless, in 1957 nonwhite median income had risen to over 52 per cent of white income; and as we moved into the 1960's, the gains of Afro-Americans, percentage-wise, increased so that by 1969 the median income of black families was 61 per cent of that of white families.[15] However, the percentage of black to white income varied greatly in different parts of the country, from only 54 per cent in the South to 80 per cent in the West.[16] The very low ratio in the South is probably explained in part by extreme poverty and very high unemployment in some rural areas where black labor has been replaced in agriculture by machines.

These advances in income do not mean that Afro-Americans no longer have any cause for grievances. On the other hand, it is doubtful if any other important group in the world has made such great economic advances in the last two or three decades. Today there are probably not half a dozen countries whose citizens have higher average incomes. The trouble is that comparing indexes of income and purchasing power by no means tells us everything about the economic welfare of a group. The very fact that American life is geared to high standards of living, including pleasant and well-equipped homes, cars, television sets, dishwashers, and

[14] U.S. Bureau of the Census, op. cit., p. 167.

[15] U.S. Bureau of the Census, *Current Population Reports,* Series P-20, No. 204, 1970, Washington, D.C., U.S. Government Printing Office, p. 1.

[16] U.S. Bureau of the Census and Bureau of Labor Statistics, *The Social and Economic Status of Negroes in the United States, 1969,* published as BLS Report No. 375; and also as *Current Population Reports,* Series P-23, No. 29, Washington, D.C., U.S. Government Printing Office, 1970, p. 15.

vacation trips, makes life harder for those blacks (and whites) who cannot afford such things.

Naturally, American blacks are more concerned with how their incomes compare with those of other Americans than with how they compare with foreign incomes. Furthermore, not only do our black citizens have relatively low incomes by American standards, but they also have a much higher rate of unemployment than do whites. Though it would be misleading to attribute the poorer jobs (or lack of jobs) and the lower pay of blacks entirely to discrimination on the part of present-day employers, obviously much discrimination still exists. But it must also be recognized that some of the factors that prevent many black Americans from getting good jobs are the result of past rather than present discrimination. Discrimination against blacks in past years robbed many of them of the incentive for acquiring the necessary education and training to fill jobs that require not only willingness to work but also more than average skill, training, and education. They did not believe they would be given such jobs even if they were qualified to fill them. As a result, far too many are scarcely literate and far too few have professional training or readily marketable skills. To make matters worse, in the North a large proportion live in the ghettos of big cities, where crime is rampant and housing substandard; and in 1968, when only 10 per cent of whites fell below the poverty level as set by the Social Security Administration, about 33 per cent of the black population was in that category.[17] Though much of black poverty and unemployment is concentrated in our central cities, the situation is even worse in some parts of the rural South, where relief standards are hopelessly inadequate and where great numbers of unemployed blacks live in dilapidated shacks.

Notwithstanding these problems, the average economic condition of blacks, as we have noted, improved in the 1960's. One indication of this was the movement of many into better jobs, as indicated by the following quote from a Bureau of Labor Statistics report, and as shown in more detail in Table 11, which was taken from the same report: "In the period 1960 to 1969, the per cent of workers of Negro and other races in the highly skilled, well-paying jobs increased much more sharply than the per cent of white workers in these jobs. The percentage decrease in the number of persons employed in laborer and farm occupations was much greater for persons of Negro and other races than for whites."[18]

The major credit for the job advancement of blacks that is noted above should probably go to those individuals among them who have had the ambition and the willingness to work that are necessary for acquiring education and training. But they have been helped by organized efforts to give blacks far greater opportunities than were available to them in the past. These efforts are being made by government agencies, by col-

[17] Ibid., p. 24.
[18] Ibid., p. 41.

Table 11. *Employment by Occupation and Race, 1969; and Net Change, 1960–1969*

| | Numbers Employed, 1969 | | Change, 1960–1969 | | | |
| | | | Numbers | | Percent | |
	Black and Other Races*	White	Black and Other Races	White	Black and Other Races	White
Total	8,369,000	69,452,000	+1,442,000	+10,602,000	+ 21	+18
Professional and technical	692,000	10,031,000	+ 361,000	+ 2,893,000	+109	+41
Managers, officials, and proprietors	254,000	7,721,000	+ 76,000	+ 823,000	+ 43	+12
Clerical	1,078,000	12,282,000	+ 575,000	+ 3,023,000	+114	+33
Sales	163,000	4,488,000	+ 62,000	+ 365,000	+ 61	+ 9
Craftsmen and foremen	704,000	9,485,000	+ 289,000	+ 1,346,000	+ 70	+17
Operatives	1,998,000	12,379,000	+ 584,000	+ 1,843,000	+ 41	+17
Service workers, except private household	1,525,000	6,371,000	+ 311,000	+ 1,535,000	+ 26	+32
Private household workers	712,000	900,000	− 270,000	− 91,000	− 28	− 9
Nonfarm laborers	876,000	2,809,000	+ 75,000	+ 207,000	− 8	+ 8
Farmers and farm workers	366,000	2,986,000	− 475,000	− 1,349,000	− 56	−31

* About 92 per cent black.
Source: U.S. Department of Labor, Bureau of Labor Statistics, *The Social and Economic Status of Negroes in the United States, 1969,* Washington, D.C., U.S. Government Printing Office, 1970.

leges and universities, by corporations, and by various other private groups including some organized by blacks themselves. They range all the way from trying to train the hard-core unemployed for specific jobs to providing qualified blacks with scholarships or fellowships for advanced study.

In the past a significant factor in restricting the economic progress of blacks has been discrimination by labor unions, many of which refused to accept them as members. Some still strongly resist admission of blacks, but their number keeps declining. Building trades unions in large cities have been especially slow in accepting black apprentices except in token numbers, but under pressure they are gradually adopting more liberal policies.

Again, in the past the black business or professional man was pretty much limited to his own community for a market for his services. Today the situation is slowly changing. Many corporations are actively seeking qualified blacks to fill professional or administrative positions. This is not always easy, because there are still relatively few blacks with good college training and even fewer with degrees from graduate or professional schools. But in the future there will be more, because the number of blacks attending college is rapidly rising. In just the short period from 1964 to 1968, it rose 85 per cent.[19] Also, more blacks are doing graduate work and attending professional schools, and as a result, the number of black businessmen, doctors, lawyers, dentists, teachers, and social workers is steadily increasing, and, more slowly, the number of black mathematicians, scientists, and economists. In addition, as black political power has grown and the demands for equality have mounted, more and more professional and administrative jobs have been opened to blacks, especially in the North, in public institutions such as hospitals, schools, and state and local government agencies. The federal government, too, has hired large numbers as clerical workers and an increasing number in administrative and professional capacities. Sometimes employers are even accused of reverse discrimination, that is, of hiring blacks not as well qualified as available whites in order to avoid the appearance of discriminating against the minority group.

A field in which blacks have as yet made very limited progress is business ownership or control. Though corporations are more willing than formerly to hire those who qualify for administrative positions, as yet blacks control comparatively few enterprises of any size. Principal exceptions are some insurance companies, banks, and publishing concerns that chiefly serve the black community. But even the larger black communities, like Harlem, are served for the most part by concerns owned and operated by whites. Why is this so? The author will not attempt to discuss here the obvious problems of discrimination and of access to capital. But one

[19] U.S. Bureau of the Census, *Current Population Reports,* Series P-23, No. 30, Washington, D.C., U.S. Government Printing Office, 1970, p. 2.

reason is that a long history of poverty, discrimination, and denial of opportunity created a widespread feeling among blacks that there was no use in trying to get very far in competition with the white man, who seemed to hold all the aces. In other words, conditions in the black society were not such as to produce a large number of individuals with the self-confidence, ambition, determination, and initiative that are required for outstanding business success.

With the changes that are now taking place in the black society, we can begin to hope for a reversal of this situation. As we have said, some black leaders have made a good start in establishing successful business enterprises. A substantial group of really successful black businessmen, some perhaps of national stature, will create a momentum and will give more and more blacks a greater confidence in themselves and their future. It will also raise the estimation of their race in the eyes of many whites.

Factors that have contributed to such economic advances as blacks have made in the last fifty years include (1) the vigorous growth of American industry; (2) restrictions on immigration that have reduced the inflow of European workers upon whom Northern industries had largely depended for expansion; (3) the great demands for labor brought on by World War II; (4) the efforts of the federal government, begun during World War II and continued with varying degrees of vigor ever since, to eliminate discrimination in hiring government workers or workers in industries producing government goods under contract; (5) the combined impact of Supreme Court rulings, legislation, and pressures of civil rights groups on the business world; (6) the increasing number of blacks whose education qualifies them for higher levels of employment; and (7) effective efforts by black leaders and their organizations to give blacks greater confidence and to provide them with greater economic opportunities.

Other Aspects of Progress Toward Equality. When one considers the extent to which discrimination against blacks prevailed throughout this country from early colonial times to World War II, the progress toward equal treatment since the war has been substantial, even though it has fallen far short of the hopes and expectations of many. Segregation in the armed forces, formerly the unchallenged rule in all branches of the service, was completely abandoned as a policy during the first decade or so after the war. Also since the war, in the North there has been a marked reduction of discrimination against blacks in hotels, motels, restaurants, and other public places, partly because of changes in public attitudes and partly because of laws forbidding it. In the decade following the Supreme Court school decision in 1954, the foundations of Jim Crow laws in the South were destroyed. To be sure, not all the subtler forms of discrimination have disappeared, but at least they are on the defensive.

Another area in which discrimination against blacks has been reduced is in the right to buy property. Formerly, the purchaser of a house might be required to sign a *restrictive covenant* in which he agreed not to rent or sell to members of specified racial or cultural groups. This sometimes made it impossible for many blacks to buy or rent housing except in over-crowded black neighborhoods that were often slums. But in 1948 the Supreme Court ruled that restrictive covenants are contrary to public policy and may not be enforced by the courts. Twenty years later, in 1968, Congress passed an *Open Housing* Act prohibiting racial discrimination in the sale or rental of about 80 per cent of all housing; and in the same year, the Supreme Court interpreted an 1866 federal law as banning racial discrimination in the sale or rental of any housing. Though these actions have not completely eliminated discrimination in the sale of housing, they have made it more difficult, especially for real estate firms; and they explain in part why blacks are now moving to the suburbs in much greater numbers. According to census estimates, in the years 1960 to 1966 the number of blacks living in suburbs increased about 19,000 annually. But for the years 1967 and 1968 the average annual increase was 221,000.

Today Afro-Americans have better protection of their political and civil rights than ever before. Though the Fifteenth Amendment to the Constitution states that the right of a citizen to vote shall not be denied on account of "race, color, or previous condition of servitude," Southern states, as we have already noted, for a long time found ways to prevent most blacks from voting without directly challenging the amendment. A favorite device was the *poll tax,* which had to be paid before a citizen could vote and which most blacks were unable or unwilling to pay. Another method was *literacy tests,* which could be administered by people who saw to it that most blacks failed. If nothing else worked, whites resorted to intimidation and violence to keep blacks from the polls. But in 1965, Congress passed the Voting Rights Act, which suspended literacy tests in states where less than half the voting-age population was registered. It also authorized the Attorney General to send federal examiners to supervise voter registration and to send federal marshalls to protect registrants. Later, in 1966, the Supreme Court ruled poll taxes unconstitutional as a requirement for voting. These developments, combined with registration campaigns by black organizations and their white sympathizers, have brought about a great expansion of the black vote in the South. In the North and West, few attempts have been made in modern times to discourage blacks from voting, and in many cities the black vote has grown to large proportions.

Blacks have often complained of unfair treatment in the courts and frequently of brutal treatment by the police. In many areas these complaints were justified; they still are justified all too often, even though on the whole the situation is better than in the past.

Black-White Social Relations. In *An American Dilemma* Gunnar Myrdal observed that the area of strongest white prejudice against the blacks had to do with intermarriage and other intimate social contacts. This seems still to be true. The great majority of whites believe that blacks should have equality of opportunity in employment, housing, education, health facilities, and legal rights; but most of them are still strongly opposed to intermarriage and do not find it easy to develop other close social contacts.

Even though *social segregation* is much more pronounced in the South than in the North, it is quite general for the country. In the North, many whites in the professions accept individual blacks into their intimate social circles, but they usually recoil from the idea of racial intermarriage. For both groups this is not always a matter of personal prejudice. It is sometimes chiefly a recognition of the fact that in a society where the general level of prejudice is still high, intermarriage creates difficult personal problems both for the individuals directly involved and for their families and their children. Among some groups, in the younger generation, there is a trend toward breaking down the obstacles to social contacts between the races, including those to interracial marriages. A decade ago more than half our states had laws prohibiting marriage between a white person and anyone defined legally as a Negro, but in 1967 the Supreme Court ruled that no state may ban interracial marriages.

THE BLACK REVOLT

What is often called *the black* (or Negro) *revolt*[20] may be said to have begun in 1955 with the bus boycott in Montgomery, Alabama. It was brought on directly by the arrest of Rosa Parks, a black woman who refused to give her seat to a white man when a bus driver ordered her to do so. The black boycott of public buses that followed brought into the limelight the most outstanding leader of the black protest movement, the late Martin Luther King, Jr. He was a prominent clergyman who was elected president of the organization that planned and carried out the boycott. The result was an end to bus segregation in Montgomery. King was a black leader who consistently urged the avoidance of violence in the struggle for civil rights. Because of this, he was awarded the Nobel peace prize in 1964. His tragic assassination in 1968 shocked the whole country.

Though the most firmly established leaders of the Negro revolt urged nonviolence, the revolt was a militant demand by organized black groups for "freedom" and "equality" *now*. They were impatient with gradualism, with what seemed to them the discouraging slowness of black advances; and out of their frustrations grew the conviction that the only way to achieve their goals was by mass, attention-demanding actions. In this they had strong support from a large group of white sympathizers.

Protests and Demonstrations. The successful bus boycotts were followed by other protests and demonstrations against legal segregation in the South. In 1960 some black college students in Greensboro, North Carolina, started a wave of sit-ins in segregated lunch counters, a movement that spread widely. Next, in 1961, came the "freedom riders," groups of blacks and whites who rode buses through the South to test discrimina-

---

[20] See Louis E. Lomax, *The Negro Revolt,* Signet paperback, New York, New American Library, Inc., 1963, especially Part 2.

33. The March on Washington. This historic march was led by the late Martin Luther King, Jr., on August 28, 1963. (Courtesy United Press International, Inc.)

tion in bus terminals used by interstate travelers. This brought an Interstate Commerce Commission order that ended such discrimination late in the same year. Then, in the summer of 1963, came the great March on Washington to dramatize the black demand for new civil rights legislation and for an end to discrimination.

The Civil Rights Act of 1964. One of the major results of the black protests, boycotts, and sit-ins that culminated, in 1963, in the march on Washington, was the civil rights act that Congress passed in 1964. Most important in this act were provisions designed to achieve four results: (1) to implement the Fifteenth Amendment by eliminating practices intended to keep racial minorities from voting; (2) to aid in school integration by providing federal financial and legal assistance to those trying to desegregate schools; (3) to eliminate discrimination in certain places of public accommodation such as hotels, motels, restaurants, and theaters; and (4) to eliminate discrimination in employment because of race, color, religion, national origin, or sex.

Rioting in the Cities. Mass marches and other mass demonstrations have their dangers, even when they are intended to be peaceful, because their leaders may not always be able to control them. Also, opponents of the demonstrations may stir up violence, or the police may overreact to what they see as a potentially dangerous situation. There is no doubt, however, that the demonstrations organized by Martin Luther King at Selma, Alabama, in the spring of 1965 were effective in advertising the fact that some areas in the South still denied blacks the right to register and vote. Partly as a result of them, Congress in 1965 passed a voting rights bill to reinforce the Civil Rights Act of 1964.

Though mass demonstrations brought national attention to the grievances of blacks, they also tended to create unrest, and indirectly they may have contributed to the destructive riots that broke out in the black sections of a number of cities from 1964 to 1968. These were not civil rights demonstrations but were more or less spontaneous outbreaks that reflected the blacks' frustrations over their problems and their unfulfilled expectations.

Early in 1968 the National Advisory Commission on Civil Disorders made its report. The eleven-man commission had been appointed by President Johnson to investigate the causes of city riots in the summer of 1967. Its principal conclusion is expressed in the statement: "White racism is essentially responsible for the explosive mixture which has been accumulating in our cities since the end of World War II." This is probably a correct appraisal if we go back far enough into the history of black-white relations in the United States. Certainly if there had been no racial prejudice against them since World War II (or since the Civil War), blacks would have been much more fully integrated into the mainstream of our society. However, the commission's diagnosis does not tell us very much about the particular developments that, after World War II, led ultimately to the riots of 1967. Perhaps, as we have already noted, racism or race prejudice is a more complex phenomenon than appears on the surface. There is hope that it will eventually disappear, but it cannot be dissipated just by wishes, admonitions, platitudes, or sermons. Sometimes, among other things, it implies contempt or condescension toward the members of another race; sometimes it implies antagonism, jealousy, and hatred; more often it is chiefly a strong preference for people of a person's own kind, people whom he understands and whose behavior and physical characteristics satisfy his culturally acquired tastes.

Some students of the problem have suggested that among the more immediate "causes" of the riots were (1) the progress already made by many blacks that raised unfulfilled hopes of still faster progress; (2) expectations created by politicians seeking votes, expectations that were not met and that in some cases could not have been met; and (3) the continued expansion of big-city ghettos with their high unemployment and other depressing conditions. It has also been suggested that another cause of discontent was the achievement of independence in the early 1960's by the new "nations" of Africa south of the Sahara. Though most of the inhabitants of these nations may have been much poorer and more socially backward

than American blacks, many an Afro-American felt that they had achieved the dignity of controlling their own societies while he remained a "second-class" citizen.

All these things created frustration and anger as well as hardship. Much of the anger was directed against the white community, and justly. But very few whites at the time were really aware of the acuteness of the problem, and still fewer had very sound ideas as to what to do about it. This very unawareness and relative indifference certainly helped to trigger both the black revolt and, later, the riots.

To meet the problem of civil disorders, the President's National Advisory Commission, in its report, urged whites to change their racist attitudes. In addition, it recommended sweeping action in various areas to reverse the trend toward increasing conflict in race relations. Though some types of discrimination had been eliminated and other types greatly reduced, nevertheless, at the end of the 1960's, antagonism between blacks and whites was probably greater in some places than it had been a decade or two earlier. This was especially true in the cities where the black ghettos continued to expand into white communities, and where frustrated blacks became more and more insistent in their demands.

Remedial measures urged by the commission included (1) better government services at the local level; (2) improved relations between police and blacks; (3) tax incentives to create two million jobs; (4) dispersal of six million medium- and low-priced housing units throughout metropolitan areas to break up the ghettos; (5) a large-scale effort to improve ghetto education; and (6) reform of the welfare system and consideration of a national system of income supplementation that would guarantee to everyone a minimum income. All these proposals have worthy objectives, and steps have been taken toward implementing some of them; but all of them face obstacles, and, in some cases, serious ones. One of the most difficult to carry out, except as a long-run project, would be the dispersal of six million medium- and low-priced housing units throughout metropolitan areas. Not only would this cost very many billions of dollars, but an even more serious problem is that it would require a great expansion of our supply of building materials and of certain types of skilled labor. Such an expansion could be brought about only over a fairly extended period of time.

Changes in the Nature of Black Protest. As time passed, some leaders of the blacks grew increasingly militant. In the late 1960's *black power* became the popular slogan of many Afro-Americans, though it meant different things to different groups, all the way from the peaceful use of black political power at the polls to black revolution. Some leaders also began to glorify blackness, to oppose integration, and to advocate black separatism and *black nationalism*. The Black Muslims had already developed doc-

34. Black-American Gothic. Overalled couple take part in the march on Washington. (Paul Schutzer, *Life* Magazine. © Time Inc.)

trines of racism and black ascendancy. Radical militants like H. Rap Brown, Stokely Carmichael, and Eldridge Cleaver maintained that violence is the only way of achieving equality. In a somewhat different category were Roy Innis, known as a "black nationalist," who demanded in 1969 that the nation's banks provide six billion dollars to aid financial institutions in black communities; and James Forman of the Black Economic Development Conference, who in the same year, through the Black Manifesto, demanded that white churches pay three billion dollars in "reparations" for past injuries to blacks.

To the surprise and disappointment of those who had worked for years for integration and who felt that some progress was now being made, in the late 1960's many blacks began to advocate black separatism—in effect, segregation. One example of this was demands by some black student groups in universities and colleges for black dormitories and lounges and for black schools or courses from which whites would be excluded.

Obviously, in a society that is at most 12 per cent black, the blacks who wish to enter the mainstream of American life, with all its economic and social benefits, must work with, compete with, and cooperate with whites. "Black nationalism" is not a realistic solution for their problems. But the black separatist movements probably have had value because they recognize the need for blacks to develop independence and pride and to seek for solutions to their own problems. The ultimate result may be more successful integration. The relatively new interest in black studies by both blacks and whites is also an encouraging development, including the desire of blacks to discover their own past and to find in it cultures, persons, and events in which they can take pride. But to set up, as some black students demand, special schools or departments for blacks only would be doubtful wisdom. White students, too, need to learn more about the past of blacks and their problems. Also, aside from building up pride, it is questionable whether a heavy concentration on black studies would be useful to the average black graduate. Such studies certainly should have a place in the curriculum; but in a centennial speech at Dillard University in 1969, Justice Thurgood Marshall remarked, "Black studies? Sure! African culture? Sure! African culture and black studies only? No!"

THE FUTURE OF BLACK AMERICANS

In the early 1960's, some twenty years after he had completed *An American Dilemma*, Gunnar Myrdal was asked if he foresaw any solution to our race problems. He replied, "Well, you can find solutions to technical problems; but in social problems—particularly those that are so intrinsically difficult and mixed up as the Negro problem—there is no solution in an absolute sense."

In his study Myrdal called the race problem in America a white problem because the whites are the great majority and hold the bulk of wealth

and power. He saw that progress by blacks is dependent on white cooperation, on a lifting of the bars of discrimination. But it is clear that even
if all whites (and blacks) could quickly and completely rid themselves of
race prejudice, it would still take time for the blacks as a group to completely overcome all the effects of generations of slavery followed by
decades of extreme discrimination.

No group can "give" equality to another group except in the sense of
treating it fairly and sympathetically and helping to provide it with opportunities. But opportunities will not be realized unless those to whom
they are open, whether black or white, have an incentive and a determination to take advantage of them. Education, for example, cannot be poured
into people even by the best schools and teachers. These can help, but unless pupils can somehow be imbued with a positive desire to learn, not
much will be accomplished. Neither disadvantaged blacks nor disadvantaged whites will achieve equality with the average citizen merely by being
given jobs for which they are not qualified or by being admitted to colleges whose academic standards they cannot meet. They can, however, be
offered opportunities for job training and, if they have the will and ability,
chances to make up academic deficiencies.

Taking the long-run viewpoint, one of the encouraging aspects of the
race problem today is the improved breadth and quality of top black leadership and of black organizations. This in itself has been made possible by
a very slow loosening of some of the bars of discrimination and by the
opening of greater opportunities to at least a portion of the black community. One of the oldest and perhaps the most effective of the organizations that have worked to secure the civil rights of the blacks is the National Association for the Advancement of Colored People (NAACP), established in 1910. In the same year, the Urban League was founded to help
rural black families adjust to city life. For many years these two organizations carried the major part of the burden of striving for the rights and advancement of blacks. But within a few years of the Montgomery bus strike,
several newer organizations came into national prominence. These included the Southern Christian Leadership Council (SCLC), which was
headed by the late Martin Luther King, Jr.; the Congress of Racial Equality
(CORE); and the Student Nonviolent Coordinating Committee (SNCC).

The Problem of Continuing Discrimination. It is doubtful whether racial
prejudice and discrimination can be completely eliminated as long as
blacks and whites constitute rather distinct racial and social groups in our
society. Discrimination is inherent to some degree in most social relationships all over the world. It occurs in the contacts of individuals, between
individuals and groups, and between groups of many types, including
families. But to deny to an entire racial or cultural group equal civil rights
and equal educational, political, and economic opportunities is a type
of discrimination that all who really believe in justice and democracy
should not tolerate.

If *racial* prejudice and discrimination in this country *completely* disappeared in all human relationships, in a few generations blacks would disappear as a separate group. They would be biologically absorbed into the general population and in the process would somewhat change the average physical characteristics of what is now the great white majority. In the very long run this is likely to happen, but few objective students of the race problem believe that such an outcome can be expected for a very long time. Conceivably the black revolt could develop separatist characteristics strong enough to slow up the long-run process of assimilation by making both blacks and whites more group conscious.

Black Progress, Past, Present, and Future. Today many blacks underestimate the progress that they have made as a group since the days of slavery because they are frustrated by the discrimination and the many handicaps that remain and by the wide gap that still exists between the economic position of the average black and the average white. They suffer from "relative deprivation," and any black who does not demand that they be given complete economic, political, and social equality *now* is apt to be labeled an "Uncle Tom." But the progress of blacks as a group has been great and very real even though it has until recently been slow. Large numbers have achieved education, confidence, success, and leadership and have given incentive to others in many fields of endeavor. Blacks are having outstanding success in sports, entertainment, writing, the professions, government service, and politics. They have notably increased their political power, partly because of their influx into Northern cities, partly through better leadership, and partly as a result of court decisions and federal laws protecting their voting rights. Some of the gains made by them in the 1950's and 1960's are notable not only because of the immediate benefits gained but also because they have laid a firm foundation for future progress. These gains include (1) the outlawing of legal segregation; (2) the widening of educational opportunities, especially in colleges and universities; and (3) the gradual opening to blacks of many jobs from which they were formerly excluded, including professional and administrative positions.

Having said all this, it remains true that the struggle for full equality is far from won. Prejudice persists and an unduly large proportion of blacks remain in poverty at the bottom of the economic and social scale. But no one with any sense of realism believes that there is any magic formula for quickly eliminating all ghettos (or other slums) or for suddenly raising to a high level the average educational and social attainments of ghetto children. Meeting such problems will require not only good will but also research and unremitting efforts.

Though all race prejudice and discrimination will not suddenly disappear, the hope is that within a reasonable time discrimination against the black minority can be so reduced that individual blacks will feel that they have the same privileges and opportunities as whites of equal character, education, and abilities. For this to happen, friendly relations between the races are very important. As the distinguished black Senator from Massachusetts, Edward W. Brooke, said several years ago, "The Negro, to win his battle for equality and justice, has to win allies rather than conquer enemies. There is a great wealth of non-Negro people who are sympathetic."

Today, the great majority of whites, though by no means free of all race prejudice, recognize more and more that blacks have been badly treated, and they approve efforts to give them a fair deal. They are even tolerant, up to a point, of what they consider unreasonable demands by black militants. But such demands can be dangerous to all if they result in violent confrontations. Nothing could be more harmful to the country, especially to the minority groups, than a great escalation of racial ill feeling and conflict.

The progress of blacks depends heavily on the orderly processes of democratic government. Such advances as they have made in this country they owe in great part to the United States Constitution, to interpretations of it by the courts, and to acts of Congress and many state legislatures. The few black leaders who advocate overthrow of the United States government by revolution as the only means of gaining black equality forget that under any kind of dictatorship minority groups are likely to suffer most. Certainly that was their experience in Germany and Russia. What we need is not a new kind of government. Rather, it is a change in our attitudes and priorities that will result in determined, patient, and intelligent efforts to remold our political, social, and economic system—"the establishment" —so that it will better serve the interests of all.

Terms to Be Understood

indentured servants
plantation system
abolition movement
Underground Railroad
Freedmen's Bureau
Ku Klux Klan
segregation
Jim Crow

legal segregation
separate-but-equal
  doctrine
de facto segregation
reverse
  discrimination
restrictive covenants
open housing

poll tax
literacy test
social segregation
the black revolt
black power
black nationalism
NAACP
SCLC

Questions for Review and Discussion

1. What is the area that is sometimes called Black Africa?
2. Why do we know more about the history of the Sudan from the seventh century to the time of the great explorations than we do about the rest of Black Africa?
3. How extensive was the African slave trade from 1600 to about 1860? What factors made it possible?
4. What were the physical and cultural characteristics of the people of Guinea?

5. What role did the major Guinean kingdoms play in the slave trade?
6. What brought an end to the West African slave trade?
7. Give a brief summary of the history of blacks in the United States from Colonial times to the present. Note (a) why blacks came to be treated differently from indentured white servants; (b) why the number of slaves grew rapidly in the South and not elsewhere; (c) the position of the free blacks; (d) the abolitionist movement and the activities of the Underground Railroad; (e) the early adjustments of the blacks to Emancipation: (f) their position during the Reconstruction Period; (g) "white-supremacy," the Ku Klux Klan, and the rise of Jim Crow legislation.
8. Why is the position of the black minority different from that of any other minority group?
9. What caused the influx of blacks into Northern cities? What effect has it had on race relations?
10. What effect have Supreme Court decisions had on legal segregation?
11. What are the obstacles to the elimination of de facto school segregation?
12. How does the economic position of blacks compare with that of whites? List the major factors that have brought economic gains to blacks.
13. What advances have been made in protecting the civil and political rights of American blacks? Which do you think have been most significant? Discuss what still needs to be accomplished.
14. Beginning with the bus boycott in Montgomery, review briefly the history of the black revolt.
15. How can the race riots of the 1960's be explained? Do you think we are likely to have more large-scale riots of this type? Why or why not?
16. Are blacks continuing to improve their social, political, and economic position? Defend your point of view.
17. Do you believe the interests of blacks would be best served if they could set up their own independent society, separate from white society? Why or why not?
18. What problems would disadvantaged blacks (and whites) still face if all race (and class) prejudice should disappear?
19. What does Myrdal mean when he says that no social problem as complex as the American race problem is ever solved in an "absolute" sense?
20. Why are friendly relations between the races important to both the majority and the minority groups?

For Further Study

Adams, Russell L., *Great Negroes, Past and Present,* 3d ed., Chicago, Afro-American Publishing Company, 1969.

Aptheker, Herbert, ed., *And Why Not Every Man: A Documentary Study of the Fight Against Slavery in the United States,* paperback, New York, International Publishers Co., Inc., 1969.

Billingsley, Andrew, *Black Families in White America,* paperback, Englewood Cliffs, N.J., Prentice-Hall, Inc., 1968.

Bloch, Herman D., *Circle of Discrimination: An Economic and Social Study of the Black Man in New York,* New York, New York University Press, 1969.

Chambers, Bradford, *Chronicles of Black Protest,* paperback, New York, New American Library, Inc., 1968.

Chapman, Abraham, ed., *Black Voices, An Anthology of Afro-American Literature,* paperback, New York, New American Library, Inc., 1968.

Franklin, John Hope, *From Slavery to Freedom: A History of American Negroes,* 3d ed., Vintage paperback, New York, Random House, Inc., 1969.

Frazier, E. Franklin, *The Negro Family in the United States,* abr. ed., Phoenix paperback, Chicago, University of Chicago Press, 1966.

Genovese, Eugene D., ed., *Slavery in the New World: A Reader in Comparative History,* paperback, Englewood Cliffs, N.J., Prentice-Hall, Inc., 1969.

Ginzberg, Eli, *Business Leadership and the Negro Crisis,* New York, McGraw-Hill, Inc., 1968.

——— , *The Middle-Class Negro in the White Man's World,* paperback, New York, Columbia University Press, 1967.

Goldston, Robert, *The Negro Revolution,* New York, The Macmillan Company, 1968.

Holland, Jerome H., *Black Opportunity,* New York, Weybright & Talley, Inc., 1970.

King, Martin Luther, Jr., *Where Do We Go from Here?* paperback, New York, Bantam Books, Inc., 1968.

——— , *Why We Can't Wait,* New York, Harper & Row, Publishers, 1964.

Lomax, Louis E., *The Negro Revolt,* Signet paperback, New York, New American Library, Inc., 1963.

Middleton, John, ed., *Black Africa, Its People and Their Culture Today,* paperback, New York, The Macmillan Company, 1970.

Murdock, George Peter, *Africa: Its People and Their Culture History,* New York, Mc-Graw-Hill, Inc., 1959.

Myrdal, Gunnar, *An American Dilemma,* paperback in 2 vols., New York, McGraw-Hill, Inc., 1964.

Osofsky, Gilbert, ed., *Puttin' on Ole Massa: The Slave Narratives of Henry Bibb, William Wells Brown, and Solomon Northrup,* New York, Harper & Row, Publishers, 1969.

Owens, Jesse, with Paul G. Neimark, *Blackthink,* New York, William Morrow & Company, Inc., 1970.

Quarles, Benjamin, *Black Abolitionists,* New York, Oxford University Press, 1969.

——— , *The Negro in the Making of America,* Collier paperback, New York, The Macmillan Company, 1964.

Whitten, Norman E., Jr., and John F. Szed, eds., *Afro-American Anthropology,* paperback, New York, The Free Press, 1970.

Woodward, C. Vann, *The Strange Career of Jim Crow,* paperback, New York, Oxford University Press, 1957.

Chapter 15

Crime

and

Delinquency

C rime is a serious problem in most modern societies. The United States, far from being an exception to the rule, has a higher crime rate than most other Western countries. And not only is our crime rate high, but most of the available evidence indicates that it is increasing alarmingly.

The Meaning of Crime. In the broadest sense a crime is any act that a social group strongly condemns as injurious to the welfare and safety of the group or its members. But whether or not a given act is regarded as a crime depends on the culture patterns and the social values of the particular group. Because group standards differ widely, an act that is regarded as criminal in one society may not be so regarded in another.

In its more usual and limited sense, crime is a legal concept; and *legally a crime is an act the law forbids and for the commission of which it provides punishment.* In common usage, however, the word *crime* tends to be reserved for serious infractions of the law. Minor crimes, punishable only by small fines or short jail sentences, are generally referred to as *misdemeanors.*

Every society must determine what acts it considers so contrary to its mores and its welfare as to require legal prohibition. If, in time, changes occur in the basic social attitudes and values of its people, this will bring changes in its laws and in the kinds of behavior that are defined as criminal. Often, however, changes in laws lag behind changes in attitudes and values.

Criminals and Juvenile Delinquents. By and large, our laws, police, and judges define crime in terms of the nature of the act and not in terms of the nature of the individual who commits it. However, there are exceptions to this rule. For example, acts committed by the insane are not treated in the same way as acts committed by people who are regarded as sane and therefore responsible for their behavior. But the most important exception has to do with the age of the offender. The very young offender is called a *juvenile delinquent,* or often just a *delinquent,* rather than a criminal; the law makes provisions for treating him differently from adult offenders; and the younger he is, the more inclined judges are to take him into custody for his own benefit as well as for the good of society. The young offender is regarded as not yet fully responsible for his acts.

The Extent and Cost of Crime and Delinquency. Everyone is interested in how much crime there is in his country and community and whether it is increasing or decreasing. In many cases he is concerned about his personal safety and that of his family. Unfortunately, we have no very accurate statistics; but such evidence as we have indicates that the crime rate of the United States has risen greatly in recent years. Observation seems to support this conclusion, and today there is wide recognition of the fact that crime has become a critical social problem in this country. To make matters worse, there is very little agreement as to how this problem can be met. Social scientists have theories but have only limited evidence to support them and do not have much power to implement the kinds of experiments that would test them.

Our best available statistics of crime in the United States are compiled by the Federal Bureau of Investigation on the basis of reports sent in voluntarily by local police. From city police departments these take the form of reports on the number of certain major crimes known to the police, the number of arrests for these, and the number of convictions. Cities also report on total arrests for all law violations. From rural areas, information is received only on the number of major crimes. Because all the reports are voluntary, they do not cover the whole population. They do, however, enable the FBI to estimate the number of more serious crimes for the entire country. A summary of this information, under the

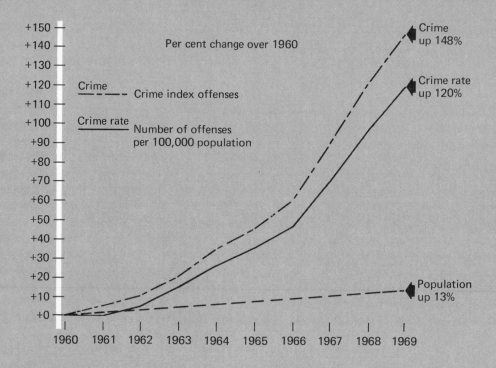

Figure 13. Crime and Population, 1960–1969. (Reproduced by permission from *Uniform Crime Reports—1969,* p. 2, Federal Bureau of Investigation, U.S. Department of Justice, Washington, D.C.)

heading "Uniform Crime Reports," is published annually by the FBI in a booklet called *Crime in the United States.*

In measuring the trend of crime in this country, the FBI employs a "crime index" that is based on the total number of serious crimes reported in the following seven categories: murder, forcible rape, robbery, aggravated assault, burglary, larceny of fifty dollars or more, and auto theft. Figure 13 shows the percentage increase in the total number of index offenses from 1960 to 1969 and also shows the percentage increase in the *crime rate,* or the number of such offenses per 100,000 of the population. Because the population has grown, the percentage increase in the total number of offenses is greater than that in the crime rate. We note in Figure 13 that the total number of serious crimes increased from the year 1960 to the year 1969 by almost 150 per cent, a truly disturbing figure. At the same time, the crime *rate* increased 120 per cent, which means that the average citizen's chances of being the victim of a serious crime were more than twice as great in 1969 as in 1960. Figure 14, "Crime Clocks," shows how often, on the average, each of the more serious crimes occurs somewhere in the United States.

According to President Nixon, juvenile arrests involving the use of drugs rose by almost 800 per cent from 1960 to 1967. The FBI reported in *Uniform Crime Reports—1970* that arrests for narcotic drug law violations in 1969 were up 45 per cent over 1968. Fifty-five per cent of those arrested were under twenty-one. The FBI considers addiction to habit-forming drugs

Figure 14. Crime Clocks, 1969. (Reproduced by permission from *Uniform Crime Reports—1969*, p. 29, Federal Bureau of Investigation, U.S. Department of Justice, Washington, D.C.)

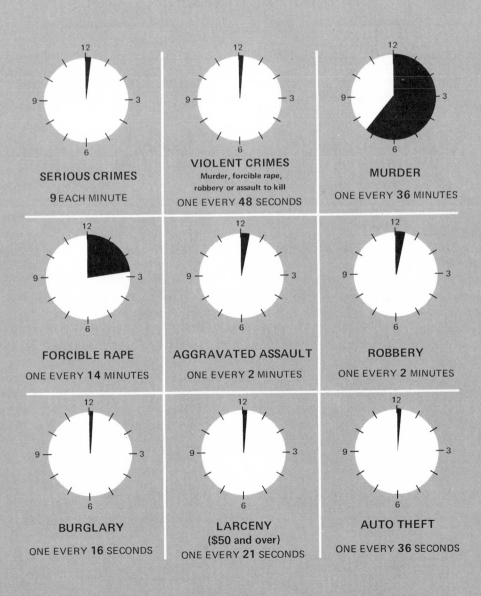

like heroin a primary cause of the great increase of street crimes in the last decade. Some addicts will commit practically any offense in order to obtain the drugs they crave.

FBI statistics also indicate that, though by far the highest crime rates are found in large cities, in recent years rates have increased rapidly in suburban and rural areas. The FBI does not claim its figures are precisely accurate. As has been pointed out, they do not cover the entire country. Furthermore, an apparent increase might not be real. It might mean merely that the police had become more vigorous in enforcing the laws or that they had kept better records. However, such factors probably do not account for very much of the indicated increase in crime.

Juvenile Delinquency. An important source of statistics on juvenile delinquency is the Children's Bureau of the Department of Health, Education, and Welfare (HEW). The statistics this agency collects are based on reports from the juvenile courts concerning the number of delinquency cases. The bureau estimated that in 1968, excluding traffic offenses, about 811,000 delinquency cases were handled by the juvenile courts of the United States. Because some children were referred to the courts more than once, the number of *different* children was about 699,000. These represented 2.3 per cent of all children in the country aged ten through seventeen. The increase in delinquency cases in 1967 over 1966 was 8.9 per cent, though the child population aged ten through seventeen increased only 2.2 per cent. Thus, as in most years since 1950, the increase in delinquency greatly exceeded the increase in the number of children. Delinquency rates are almost three times as high in urban areas as in rural areas. If traffic offenses are included, the total number of juvenile court cases in 1968 was 1,360,000.

When interpreting the delinquency statistics of the Children's Bureau, the reader should remember, as the bureau itself is careful to point out, that the number of cases handled by juvenile courts is not necessarily a very good measure of the total amount of delinquency. The kinds of cases over which these courts have jurisdiction vary from state to state and sometimes within the same state. Even when jurisdiction is the same, the portion of cases actually brought to the courts varies greatly between communities. In some communities, many cases are dealt with informally by other agencies. However, for the country as a whole there is probably a significant correlation between changes in the total amount of delinquency and changes in the number of cases handled by the courts.

What are the principal offenses committed by juveniles? Juvenile court records show that most of the boys get into trouble for stealing or malicious mischief, whereas most of the girls are brought in for being ungovernable, running away, or committing a sex offense. But juveniles are also responsible for considerable numbers of rapes, homicides, and assaults.

One of the frequently mentioned aspects of crime and delinquency is their economic cost to the nation. There can be no doubt that the total

"How do you figure it—we had less juvenile delinquency when we didn't understand child psychology." (Reprinted, courtesy *The Chicago Tribune.*)

annual crime bill of the United States is huge. Some thirty years ago it was estimated by the Chicago Crime Commission at $15 billion. A 1970 estimate by *U. S. News & World Report* placed the total cost of crime to the country at over $51 billion. Such figures are impressive, but they have no very clear meaning, because there is really no satisfactory way of estimating all the direct and indirect costs of crime.

FACTORS INFLUENCING CRIME

It is of some importance to recognize to what extent crime is influenced by such factors as age, sex, heredity, economic status, type of community, association of individuals with antisocial groups, family relationships, psychological attitudes, and the development of organized criminal syndicates. These factors will be discussed in the order listed.

Age and Sex. Reports of the FBI and the Children's Bureau call attention to the high rate of crime by juveniles and youths and to the apparent increase in such crime. Its extent is further borne out by the fact that in many of our penitentiaries a large portion of all prisoners committed for a first offense are under twenty-one.

The Children's Bureau statistics indicate that boys outnumber girls almost four to one in cases brought before the juvenile courts. The FBI reports that in 1969 the total of all male arrests outnumbered female arrests by six to one. In prisons and reformatories, males outnumber females about twenty to one. But percentage-wise, in the period 1960–1969, arrests of females under eighteen rose 176 per cent against 93 per cent for males under eighteen. *Total* female arrests in the same period rose by 56 per cent, and total male arrests by 20 per cent. Divorced and separated women commit more crimes, by sizable margins, than do unmarried women; and married people of both sexes are less frequently involved in crime than are unmarried people.

The distribution of crimes as outlined above suggests that where there are serious problems of adjustment, along with physical vigor, criminality is greatest. This theory would account for the fact that criminality is highest between the ages of fifteen and thirty. The same factors may largely account for the distribution of criminality by sex and marital status. In our culture, men engage in a wider range of competitive activities than women. Partly because men are more actively involved in the struggle for achievement, they are more often found among criminals. Though women, on the average, have a much lower crime rate, as we have noted, the rate rises sharply for the groups of women (such as divorced and separated women) who have more problems, both psychological and economic.

Hereditary Factors in Criminal Behavior. Is heredity a cause of criminality? Are criminals "born that way"? Writing in the late nineteenth century, a noted Italian criminologist, Cesare Lombroso, maintained that they are. He measured the physical dimensions of many criminals and studied their reactions. He claimed that criminals are both less sensitive to pain and more subject to epilepsy than normal individuals. He found them to have heads higher at the rear than at the forehead, longer lower jaws, flattened noses, scanty beards, long ears, and other physical peculiarities. He explained these peculiarities as atavistic reversions to the characteristics of early savage ancestors.

Later studies have discredited Lombroso's theory that there is a definite and recognizable criminal type, but they have not convinced all investigators that there is no relation whatever between crime and inheritance or between crime and the physical characteristics that are a part of every person's inheritance.

More than thirty years ago, William H. Sheldon and his associates at Harvard began to make studies that attempted to correlate certain types of personality with certain types of body build.[1] They sought to show that behavior is related to bodily form and that it can to some extent be predicted on the basis of careful physical measurements.

Sheldon, who holds both an M.D. degree and a Ph.D. in psychology, assumed that there are three basic body types and that every human being will combine in various degrees the characteristics of these types. *Endomorphy* means a tendency to soft roundness throughout the body. *Mesomorphy* means predominance of muscle, bone, and connective tissue; mesomorphs are athletic in build. *Ectomorphy* means predominance of skin and nerves; hence ectomorphs tend to be thin, fragile people. In a study of two hundred problem boys in a Boston institution, Sheldon found that as a group they were predominantly mesomorphic.

Later, extended research on delinquent youth by Sheldon Glueck and Eleanor Glueck, both of Harvard Law School, gave qualified support to

[1] See William H. Sheldon et al., *Varieties of Human Physique,* New York, Harper & Row, Publishers, 1940.

Sheldon's findings. [2] In a large group of delinquents whom they studied intensively, they found that more than 60 per cent were predominantly mesomorphic, whereas in a nondelinquent group of similar size and with similar social and ethnic backgrounds, the proportion was only half as great. The Gluecks suggest that the predominance of mesomorphs among delinquents may be explained by the fact that this physical type "is more highly characterized by traits particularly suitable to the commission of acts of aggression (physical strength, energy, insensitivity, the tendency to express tensions and frustrations in action), together with a relative freedom from such inhibitions to antisocial adventures as feelings of inadequacy, marked submissiveness to authority, emotional instability, and the like." [3] It might be well to note at this point that some of the qualities that the Gluecks believe lead many mesomorphs into crime may enable others, who have had a more favorable social environment, to become effective leaders in politics, legitimate business, or the professions.

However, the Gluecks made it clear that they are not reviving the Lombrosian theory that criminals are a distinct hereditary type with atavistic or degenerative characteristics. [4] They regard mesomorphy as only one of the many factors that may contribute to criminal behavior. Their general point of view is well expressed in the following quotation:

The emphasis in American criminology and in psychoanalysis since the turn of the century regarding the formation of personality and character has been on the "conditioned," the acquired. The stress placed on the construction of the ego and superego through the emotion-laden experiences of the growing child in relation to the adults close to him during his earliest formative years, and on regional cultural influences in later years, has tended to obscure the fact that there are also differences in original nature. The processes of ego and superego differentiation and crystallization and the sociocultural stresses of the disorganized family and community have varying original constitutional materials to work upon. It has been established, for example, that the predominantly mesomorphic constitution has greater strength and a different rhythm of energy discharge and control of impulse than the obese endomorphic or the fragile ectomorphic types. It has also been shown that the delinquency of ectomorphs would seem to stem largely from their over-sensitiveness and over-responsiveness to the unwholesome influences of home and family life. Consequently, though an essentially genetic explanation of varying behavioral inclinations may be criticized as onesided, essentially psychoanalytic or socio-cultural explanations are open to like criticism. [5]

[2] In 1958 Harvard University awarded honorary D.Sc. degrees to both of the Gluecks for their research in criminology and juvenile delinquency.

[3] Sheldon and Eleanor Glueck, *Physique and Delinquency*, New York, Harper & Row, Publishers, 1956, p. 226.

[4] Ibid., p. 2.

[5] Ibid., p. 272.

Economic Factors in Criminal Behavior. Do economic factors enter into crime? Obviously they do, for some of the commonest crimes have as their objective obtaining the money or property of other people. These include pocket picking, larceny, burglary, auto theft, robbery, and embezzlement. But if we ask, Is substandard income, lack of income, or poverty a major cause of crime? the answer is not so clear. There is no doubt that people who have no money at times risk reputation, liberty, and life to acquire necessities, and sometimes luxuries, through criminal action. A famous example from fiction is that of Jean Valjean in *Les Miserables,* whose troubles started with the theft of a loaf of bread. But economic hardship does not always lead to crime, and, perhaps more significant, the rate of property crimes sometimes increases in societies where standards of living are rising and the number of people in poverty is diminishing. This seems in fact to have been the case in the United States for more than a decade.

Many years ago E. R. Mowrer of Northwestern University made a study of the influence of the depression of the 1930's on delinquency in Chicago. Except for burglary, he reported no significantly larger percentage of criminal offenses. This was true not only for the city as a whole but also for the areas hardest hit by the depression. One explanation may be that in the 1930's the government for the first time provided relief on a large scale and also opportunities for employment on government projects. This made it unnecessary for great numbers of people, who might otherwise have been desperate, to resort to crime. Today some crimes are undoubtedly fewer than they would be if we did not have public aid to dependent children, unemployment insurance, and Social Security pensions.

But though poverty sometimes leads people to crime, we must not suppose that only poor people commit crimes for economic motives. Statistics on teenage delinquents who commit crimes against property show that many of them come from homes with adequate or above-average incomes. Furthermore, even wealthy people commit crimes, and sometimes their motive is the economic desire to become still richer. Many examples could be cited, including corporation officials, bankers, and even a former president of the New York Stock Exchange.

Blighted Areas and Criminal Behavior. A landmark study in juvenile delinquency was made years ago by the late Clifford Shaw, a sociologist for the Illinois Institute for Juvenile Research. In his well-known book *Delinquency Areas,* Shaw showed that there is a direct relation between types of city communities and their delinquency rates. He found that the highest delinquency rates are in the slum areas close to the central business district or near major industrial developments. Such blighted areas are characterized by marked distintegration of both traditional institutions and neighborhood organization, which normally function as agencies of social control. Most significant of all, Shaw found that though the nationality composition of these areas over a period of two decades had changed almost completely, the delinquency rates had remained constant. Furthermore, he noted that as the older nationality groups moved out, their rates of delinquency showed a consistent decrease. Other studies have shown that the same nationality groups who show a high rate of criminality in slum areas often show a remarkably low rate when found in normal, well-organized communities. Today many of these slum areas are occupied by blacks, and they in their turn show a high rate of crime.

It appears that blighted areas possess characteristics that contribute directly to the delinquent habits and attitudes of their residents and especially to those of the children. These habits and attitudes are merely a response to the expectations of the criminal gangs or other antisocial groups with whom children are likely to associate in such a neighborhood.

Influence of Association with Antisocial Groups. The intimate groups with which an individual has close associations do much to shape his personality and his behavior. When such groups are antisocial, in the sense of upholding values and approving patterns of action contrary to the standards of the larger community, the people who belong to them are very likely to drift into crime. The family is the intimate group that normally has the most influence on a child, and sometimes the family itself is an antisocial influence. More often the trouble is, especially in slum communities, that family control breaks down and that the child seeks elsewhere for satisfaction of his social needs, including his desire for status. Often the group that becomes the dominant force in his life is the neighborhood gang. But the typical gang in a slum neighborhood, instead of condemning delinquent behavior, is likely to admire it. As a result, its members gain admiration and status by pilfering in stores, burglarizing apartments, and committing other crimes; and thus they early establish patterns of criminal behavior. They may be well adjusted within their own small groups, but they are not equipped for living useful and satisfactory lives in the larger community. Today the problem of gangs, including gang murders, has assumed major proportions in some of our black ghettos. There it is especially difficult to deal with because it is complicated by the problems of racial discrimination and conflict.

Although antisocial groups are most common in slums, they are by no means limited to such areas, and children may fall into bad company in almost any community.

Family Influences on Criminal Behavior. To what extent are family conditions instrumental in promoting crime? Cases in which parents have actually induced their children to engage in crime are unusual, but they do exist. Sometimes, also, older brothers and sisters teach younger children to pilfer from stores or steal from apartments. But even when members of the family do not directly lead a child into crime, unfortunate home conditions are a major factor in contributing to delinquency. For example, it is well known that broken families have a significant relation to criminality. Various studies indicate that a much larger proportion of children from such homes become delinquent than from normal homes. Other studies show that the proportion of delinquents is also abnormally high among children whose families receive public relief or private charity. Many such families live in blighted areas, where, as noted earlier, family influences are sometimes unfavorable and where family control often breaks down. Whenever home conditions are such as to create tensions and unhappiness for children, there delinquency rates are likely to be high.

Psychological Factors in Criminal Behavior. To what extent do psychological factors enter into the causation of crime? The first of these factors we might consider is intelligence. Are criminals more or less intelligent than people in the general population? A partial answer is that there undoubtedly are dull criminals, and many of them have been apprehended both because they are dull and because they are criminal. But the frequent assumption that low intelligence is a chief cause of crime is open to question. Most studies of prison inmates indicate that their IQ's are not very different from those of the population at large.

Among psychological factors that seem to contribute to crime are mental and emotional conflicts. Several sources of such conflicts may be noted: (1) revolt against father's authority, where the father is an especially forbidding, unsympathetic parent; (2) envy of brother or sister, where one gets the feeling that the brother or sister has privileges one cannot secure; (3) a deep-seated attitude of inferiority, induced by ridicule and discouragement, and the wish to overcome it by attracting attention.

These conflicts, arising in the family environment, may of course remain in it, but often they are shifted outward and are the basis of criminal action in the larger community. Mental conflicts become especially acute when the individual is faced with new responsibilities. Adolescence is often a difficult period; and so is early adulthood, when an individual must make his own decisions and seek a vocation and when he often feels lost and alienated in our urban society unless he can find a satisfactory marriage mate. In general, periods of transition from one social role to another are difficult, as in the case of a woman who has been separated or divorced.

Organized Crime. One of the most serious problems that we face in this country today is how to deal with large-scale *organized crime*. Organized crime, an inheritance from prohibition days, is carried on by groups of criminals who establish enterprises that operate somewhat like legitimate business. However, the chief purpose of these enterprises is to make money by carrying on illegal activities.

Because organized criminals act in defiance of the law instead of under its protection, they must themselves provide the means of protecting and expanding their operations. They do this in two ways. First, they seek to control law-enforcement officials, legislators, and judges by bribery or intimidation or even by attempting to influence the election of candidates to public office. Second, they resort to terrorism, violence, and murder to control their own organizations and eliminate competitors; and they give "protection" in order to collect tribute from various individuals and groups whom they force to deal with them. The methods they have developed for employing violence make detection and prosecution of its perpetrators very difficult. The men who really control organized crime keep under cover as much as possible and act through agents. Often if a beating or murder is ordered, hoodlums will be brought in from a distant city to carry it out.

In recent years the greatest profits of organized crime, according to FBI director J. Edgar Hoover, have come from gambling and loan sharking; but in testimony before the House Subcommittee on Appropriations, he noted that another very profitable activity is major thefts, primarily because of the manpower, weapons, transportation, storage facilities, and "fencing" specialists available to the hoodlum leaders. These thefts include truck hijacking and wholesale pilferage at airports and docks. More recently, the organized *crime syndicates* have been stealing securities and have been distributing and using stolen or counterfeit credit cards. Other activities include the distribution of narcotics and also union takeovers for the purpose of looting union funds and making profitable arrangements with employers. In the long run, perhaps the most dangerous aspect of organized crime to the community is the success that it has had in taking over some legitimate business enterprises by fraud and intimidation or by simple purchase.

For several years, the FBI has been sharply increasing its efforts against organized crime, especially against the major group of crime syndicates called the *Mafia* or, alternatively, *Cosa Nostra*. In his testimony before the House Subcommittee on Appropriations, on April 17, 1969, Hoover described as follows the results of these FBI efforts:

FBI investigations of organized crime led to an all-time high of 281 convictions during the fiscal year 1968. Included among those convicted were some of the most influential decision-makers of organized crime operations in this country. The total represents an increase of 84 over the previous year's high of 197 and was accompanied by a corresponding increase in the number of hoodlum, gambling, and vice figures who had been arrested or indicted and were awaiting trial—from 330 at the end of fiscal 1967 to 831 as of April 1, 1969.

The FBI has been unrelenting in its drive to penetrate the forces of organized crime despite the heavy requirements for our resources in other investigative areas. At the end of the fiscal year 1968 we were conducting investigations of 6,070 racketeers, hoodlums, and others having substantial underworld interests. In contrast, the number of investigations pending at the end of the previous fiscal year totaled 5,740.

Our investigations reflect that in the Cosa Nostra there are 26 separate "families" with membership approximating 3,000. These 3,000 in turn control the criminal activities of many times their own number.

Though all these efforts of the FBI are commendable, it remains to be seen how much effect they will have in breaking up criminal syndicates.

So far, attempts to suppress organized crime have not been very success-ful. However, in recent years Congress has passed several measures intended to aid law-enforcement officials in their efforts. In 1961 it pro-hibited (1) interstate travel for the purpose of aiding racketeering enter-prises; (2) interstate use of wire communications for betting; and (3) interstate transportation of betting equipment. Another aid in the war on organized crime is a provision in the Truth in Lending Act of 1968 that prohibits extortionate extensions of credit if they involve the use of threats, violence, or other criminal acts to harm the borrower, his property, or his family. Two more weapons are provided by the Omnibus Crime Control and Safe Streets Act of 1968. One provision permits giving immunity from prosecution to witnesses who testify concerning a wide range of specified offenses, offenses that include many of the activities of orga-nized crime. A second provision permits law-enforcement agencies, after seeking and obtaining a court order, to use electronic surveillance (including wire tapping) in the investigation of certain offenses, among them kidnapping, extortion, and various federal gambling and racketeer-ing violations.

The greatest obstacle to the elimination of organized crime is undoubt-edly the control that the syndicates exercise over many corrupt and fearful state and local politicians, judges, and law-enforcement officers.

THEORIES AND METHODS OF DEALING WITH CRIMINALS

Every large and well-established society has ways of dealing with per-sons convicted of criminal behavior, and nearly all the methods employed constitute punishment, whether or not that is their primary purpose. However, the punishment employed and the theories behind their appli-cation may vary widely.

Theories of Punishment. There are four principal theories behind the punishments meted out to criminals. The first is *retribution,* or the belief that justice requires that a person who has injured others should have an equal injury meted out to himself. What good this will do is open to question. Apparently, the chief benefit will be the satisfaction that injured parties and other members of the community may feel because "justice" has been done. The second theory of punishment is *deterrence,* or prevention. According to this concept, we should punish an offender more or less severely not only because it will deter him from criminal acts in the future but even more because it will deter other would-be criminals. If people know that criminal acts are punished, it is believed that they will refrain from committing crimes and that the community will thus be protected. The third theory of punishment is *disablement.* This view emphasizes the primary importance of protecting society but holds that the best way to protect society is to execute the criminal or imprison him for life so that he will be unable to perpetrate further crimes. Fourth and last, we have the theory of *reformation,* which demands that our primary concern in dealing with criminals should be to re-educate and rehabilitate them so that, when released, they will become good citizens.

The last three of the above theories all have the merit of seeking to protect society by reducing crime. Unfortunately, none of them is a panacea.

There can be no doubt that fear of punishment deters many people from committing crimes, and yet high crime rates have persisted in various societies in spite of the harshest forms of punishment. Sometimes there seems to be little relationship between the number of crimes committed and the severity of the punishment. For example, in those of our states that do not have the death penalty, murders are said to be no more common than in those that do. Many criminologists believe that as a deterrent to crime, *certainty* of punishment is more important than extreme severity.

If punishment of criminals is not too effective in deterring others from committing crimes, perhaps we can employ it to disable criminals so that they cannot further injure society. However, it is not very effective for this purpose either. Life imprisonment and execution are unreasonably severe punishments except for the most extreme offenses. In modern civilized countries the public would not tolerate them for the majority of crimes. Hence, most criminals are eventually released and can, if they choose, commit new crimes.

This leaves reformation, which many insist should be our only objective in dealing with criminals. The weakness of this theory is that many criminals seem quite immune to even the most enlightened attempts to reform them. Yet it remains true that a great deal could be done to re-educate and rehabilitate delinquents and criminals if our police, courts, reformatories, and prisons had greater resources and more competent personnel and employed methods really designed to aid in rehabilitating offenders.

Crime Detection: The First Step in Dealing with Criminals. In spite of the efforts of the police, the perpetrators of many crimes are never discovered. Figure 15 shows that though most major crimes against the person are "cleared by arrest," in the case of crimes against property, those who commit them avoid discovery more often than not. But even when an arrest is made, a crime is not necessarily solved, for often evidence is insufficient to obtain an indictment and a conviction.

Another problem is to prevent innocent persons from being convicted of crime. All too frequently, new evidence comes to light long after a trial and shows that some person who has spent years in prison was convicted erroneously. To imprison a person not guilty of crime is the height of social injustice, yet such imprisonment cannot be blamed entirely on the activities of the police. Prosecutors, judges, and other public officials all share the responsibility. The police have often been charged with indifference to their work. They have also been charged with corruption and arrogance. But attempts to build cases against innocent people are seldom due to negligence, corruption, or arrogance. More often they result from the eagerness of the police to prove their worth and to allay what is sometimes unfair criticism.

Unfortunately, the determination of the police to solve cases sometimes has tempted them to resort to brutal "third-degree" measures. Such brutality rightly elicits violent protests from the defenders of civil liberties and in the past has given some American metropolitan police a very bad reputation. Part of the trouble was that many of our policemen had little basic education and little training in crime detection or other aspects of police work. Today the situation, though far from perfect, is greatly improved.

Introducing and using scientific methods of crime detection tends to decrease police dependence on third-degree methods. At the same time it enables them to get better results in finding criminals and building up evidence. The use of scientific methods requires training in such fields as ballistics, chemistry, microscopy, microphotography, fingerprinting, and lie detection. Now computer and communications technologies are being increasingly applied to police problems and are playing a major role in improving law enforcement. The FBI has an electronic "master brain" in Washington that can aid police throughout the country in apprehending criminals by providing them quickly with a great variety of needed information. The men employed by the Federal Bureau of Investigation are often regarded as models of what good police officers and good detectives should be. They are college bred, grounded in accounting and law, and intelligent. As police forces improve their methods of garnering evidence and become better educated and better trained, we should have more efficient crime detection, less mistreatment of suspects, and fewer innocent victims of the law.

Figure 15. Crimes Cleared by Arrest, 1969. (Reproduced by permission from *Uniform Crime Reports—1969*, p. 30, Federal Bureau of Investigation, U.S. Department of Justice, Washington, D.C.)

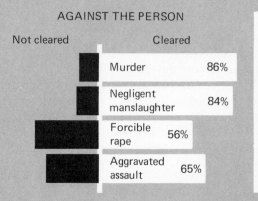

AGAINST THE PERSON

Not cleared — Cleared

Murder	86%
Negligent manslaughter	84%
Forcible rape	56%
Aggravated assault	65%

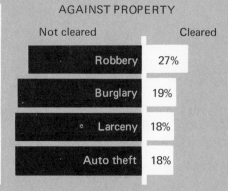

AGAINST PROPERTY

Not cleared — Cleared

Robbery	27%
Burglary	19%
Larceny	18%
Auto theft	18%

"My client claims police brutality! In receiving the parking ticket, his windshield wiper was bent!" (Reprinted, courtesy of *The Chicago Tribune*.)

Indictment, Trial, and Conviction. When an accused person is brought to trial, the state is taking the second step in dealing with him. But whether the evidence against him will be correctly interpreted depends on the competence and honesty of lawyers, prosecutors, judges, and jurors.

Juries present special problems. A *grand jury* has the function of determining whether the evidence against various accused persons is sufficient to justify indicting them. An *indictment* has the effect of holding for trial an individual suspected of a crime. Often when a grand jury investigates crimes in an attempt to find independent evidence, it is hampered in its work by its dependence on the office of the state's attorney or by the fact that its term may come to an end after a limited period, such as a month. *Petit* or *trial juries* also present problems. They consist of twelve citizens brought together to determine guilt or innocence in individual cases. Though an accused person may elect to be tried by a judge, he has the right to demand trial by jury. Unfortunately, the members of trial juries are not inevitably intelligent and responsible citizens, and at best they are handicapped by their lack of knowledge of legal procedures. Sometimes they are reached by outside influences, even including bribery. In theory, a trial jury is protection for the innocent, because an accused person cannot be convicted unless every juror agrees to the verdict. But sometimes the decisions of juries appear to be travesties of justice, with the result that many thoughtful observers believe that we should either reform the jury system or seek a better substitute.

Probation and the Suspended Sentence. Once a person accused of crime has been convicted, there are several ways of disposing of his case. One possibility is the *suspended sentence*. This means that the accused is granted his freedom, subject to good behavior for a period of time and to his reappearance in court at a later date. It differs from a *probationary sentence* in that it carries no supervision with it, whereas probation means release under surveillance. In either case, if the offender misbehaves, he may be required to serve his sentence. The first probation law was enacted in 1901, and probation is still considered the most hopeful form of treatment, especially for first offenders whose crimes are not too serious. It gives the offender not merely a change to resume normal life, but when properly administered it also affords him the aid of a person specially trained to help him make new social and economic adjustments. In many cases social workers assist probation officers, especially in the treatment of juvenile delinquents. Probation officers themselves, in the more progressive urban centers, tend to be college-trained individuals with broad experience in social work.

Some criminologists maintain that we could to advantage make far greater use of probation than we do. This would cost something, because it would require that our probation systems be much better organized and manned than is now the case. But the advocates of expanding the use of probation feel that in the long run such a policy would be cheaper than maintaining so many prisons and that it would also be more effective in reducing crime. The question is not one for which there is any simple answer. A "soft" policy toward first offenders who commit serious crimes, even if these offenders are juveniles, brings the law-enforcement agencies into disrespect. On the other hand, for many young offenders, jails or prisons are merely training schools in crime.

According to Time, the California Youth Authority recently made an experiment in which convicted juvenile delinquents were immediately returned to their homes where probation officers grouped them on the basis of their special characteristics and then provided intensive supervision and aid. After five years only 28 per cent of the experimental group had their probations revoked. On the other hand, 52 per cent of a similar group that had been locked up and later put on parole had their paroles revoked. By putting six hundred delinquents on probation in this way, the State of California saved the seven million dollar cost of building a new reformatory.[6]

Paroles, Commutations, and Pardons. Suspended sentences and probation do not involve terms in prison, but paroles always follow such terms. A parole is really a continuation of an individual's sentence outside of prison. When a prisoner is paroled, he is granted his freedom, but subject to good behavior and to making regular reports to a parole officer for a period of time. Paroles are usually granted by a state parole board on the basis of good behavior of the applicant while in prison.

Pardons differ from paroles in several ways. They are acts of executive clemency by a mayor, governor, or president, and they release a convicted person without any reservations. They may be granted immediately after a sentence is passed or at some later time. Their object is not only to save the individual from going to prison but also to remove the stigma of guilt from his record when it appears that he was unjustly convicted.

[6] Time magazine, March 28, 1968, p. 22.

Commutations shorten a sentence, part of which has been served, but, unlike pardons, they do not remove the implication of guilt. Commutations are usually approved by a parole board, and in most cases a released prisoner is placed on parole.

The institution of parole is found in most states and is considered by many criminologists to be one of the greatest achievements in the treatment of offenders. Yet it has frequently been opposed by those who refuse to admit that most prisoners will eventually return to society and that it is in the interests of society that they be helped to make a good adjustment. The nature and length of a sentence may be fixed by the legislature (through law) or by a judge. But when legislation provides for indeterminate sentences, judges do not fix their length with precision. They merely set the minimum and/or the maximum, leaving it to the parole board to decide how long the prisoner is to remain confined.

Parole Prediction. For many years sociologists have entertained the hope that a scientifically valid *parole-prediction scale* could be devised. Such a scale, if accurate enough, might be used, they thought, to predict whether a certain prisoner, when paroled, would live up to the conditions of his release and make an adequate adjustment outside. Ernest W. Burgess, of the University of Chicago, made the first attempt to devise a parole-prediction scale for prisoners. His original scale was prepared in 1929 but was revised by Burgess frequently. Based on a searching analysis of available material on parole violation, it attempted to give a prisoner a *rehabilitation quotient* that would indicate the chances of his becoming a law-abiding citizen on his release. This quotient was based on evaluating and averaging twenty or more factors relating to the personality, social background, and criminal history of the prisoner. At one time, several states were using Burgess's prediction scale, but they found it of limited value. Other researchers have since devised similar scales but with no striking success.

One problem with parole-prediction scales is that some of the factors on which they are based are difficult to evaluate. Another is that the factors seem to change in importance so that a table that at one time gives fairly good results may be much less useful a few years later. In a review of the history of parole-prediction methods, Karl Schuessler concluded that they have been disappointing in that they have not greatly reduced the uncertainty attached to forecasting individual behavior on parole.[7]

Prisons and Their Limitations. In modern civilized countries, imprisonment is the chief method of dealing with convicted criminals. Mutilation, the torture chamber, and the stocks were given up long ago, and whipping has almost disappeared. However, in more backward parts of the world,

---

[7] Karl Schuessler, "History of Parole Prediction," *Sourcebook on Probation, Parole, and Pardons,* edited by Charles L. Newman, Springfield, Ill., Charles C. Thomas, Publisher, 1958.

35. Interview Through Bars. (Photograph by David Gahr.)

many of these early forms of punishment still survive, and even in many of the more-advanced countries death is still the penalty for a few crimes, especially murder.

Because imprisonment is our chief method of dealing with criminals, we can appropriately ask, What purposes are served by sending criminals to prison? First, many people are deterred from committing crimes by the knowledge that if caught and convicted they might go to prison. But just how effective the deterrent effect is we do not know. We do know that many criminals after their release from prison commit new crimes. Second, and most obvious, imprisonment prevents criminals during their incarceration from carrying on their antisocial activities. Ideally they should also be re-educated—reformed—while serving their terms, so that on release they will fit into society as good citizens instead of reverting to criminal careers. But as institutions of reform most of our prisons are dismal failures.

What proportion of criminals could, if intelligently dealt with, return to society and make good adjustments we do not know. But there is reason to believe that the number would be much greater than it actually is if our prisons were better financed and better managed. In the long run the cost to the taxpayers might be less. Among the most serious faults still to be found in many prisons are: (1) inefficient administration; (2) the employment of incompetent personnel; (3) inflexible routine; (4) lack of useful employment; (5) abominable and sometimes unsanitary living conditions; (6) poor and inadequate food; (7) mistreatment; (8) overcrowding; and (9) "postgraduate" instruction from fellow inmates in vice and crime at the expense of the taxpayers maintaining these institutions. These dangerous and demoralizing conditions call for continuing efforts toward prison reform. The price of better prisons, like the price of liberty, is eternal vigilance on the part of the public. But such vigilance is difficult to achieve because the general public has little contact with prison life.

Reform of Prisons. The history of penal reform is long and venerable. The names of great men and women have gone into the records of our nation and of foreign nations because they tried to take a rational point of view on the matter of penal treatment. But each age has its own ideas of how prisoners should be treated and hence has its own concept of prison problems.

One of the reforms needed in our prisons is better classification. Some prisons still do not classify their inmates in any way. On the basis of a well–thought-out classification, however, different groups of prisoners can be treated differently to best meet their own needs and the needs of society. Those who are obviously feeble-minded or suffering from serious mental diseases should be removed to hospitals, where they belong. The others should, to begin with, receive all available medical aid for curing remediable physical illnesses and for removing or relieving handicaps. Psychopathic conditions should receive psychiatric and psychological assistance in the hope of establishing new social attitudes.

The next problem is social re-education. No realist believes that practical methods can be devised that will make it possible to reform all criminals so that they will be good citizens when they return to society. However, many prisoners do make good citizens after their release; and if our prisons were better equipped, better manned, and more intelligently directed, the number would be much larger. It may not be desirable to make prisons pleasant places in which to live, but it is very desirable that life in them should be tolerable and that opportunities should be provided for prisoners who hope, on their release, to lead normal lives and not to revert to crime. In some prisons efforts have been made to give prisoners an opportunity to participate in community life in preparation for their later freedom. Whether the outside world recognizes it or not, a prison is in fact a community. Perhaps the most important thing a prison can do for its inmates is to provide opportunities for education and for training in trades and professions, so that when a prisoner is released, he can earn an adequate living. Many if not most prisons provide such opportunities, but they are often very limited and sometimes they train people in skills that are no longer employed in industry.

A few experiments are now being conducted in this country that permit jail prisoners who are considered reliable to work at outside jobs during the day and return to their cells at night. Finland is experimenting with a plan under which convicted prisoners work on government construction jobs such as road-building during the day and then go home for the night.

There is much to be said for separating first offenders in prisons from inmates who are more experienced in crime. But prisons, by their nature, are places in which criminals are brought together, and there is no simple way to prevent them from being, for some prisoners, a kind of training school for crime. This is one argument for putting first offenders on probation for crimes that are not too serious. Still, having noted the limitations of prisons and the vast possibilities for improving them, we should also recognize that some progress has been made. Most modern prisons are much better equipped to care for their inmates than were the prisons of fifty years ago, and, on the average, those who run them treat inmates more intelligently. Unfortunately, there are still extreme exceptions.

Institutions for Delinquent Children. According to the Children's Bureau of the Department of Health, Education, and Welfare, every year more than a hundred thousand boys and girls are committed to public institutions for delinquents. These vary greatly in quality, but few of them are equipped and organized so as to prepare their inmates to make a better social adjustment in the outside world. Most of them are too large, or crowded, and inadequately staffed. Some engage in the worst practices of adult prisons and are little more than schools for crime.

THE PREVENTION OF CRIME AND DELINQUENCY

There is no social problem more difficult to deal with than that of crime, whether its perpetrators are adults or juveniles. Although criminologists can agree in a general way on many of the factors contributing to crime, they seldom agree on the relative importance of these factors or on just what should be done to improve the situation. Moreover, many of the remedies suggested are very difficult, if not impossible, to apply. We have already referred to one remedy that has possibilities, namely, the improvement of prison administration and practices in order to reduce the number of inmates who revert to crime when released.

Upon one point there is rather general agreement—namely, that honest and efficient judges, prosecutors, and police officials can do a great deal to keep down the crime rate in any community. Many potential lawbreakers will hesitate to operate in areas where it is known that the police departments give their members thorough training in law-enforcement methods and strive to introduce new and more efficient techniques. A fairly recent technique that has spread widely is the use of trained police dogs. These dogs greatly increase the effectiveness of officers on patrol duty, especially at night.

Two Basic Aspects of the Crime Problem. There are two basic ways of attacking the problem of controlling crime. They are not mutually exclusive, and each should receive attention; but some individuals and groups tend to emphasize one, some the other. The first is to organize more effectively the means the government employs to discourage and suppress crime, including police, public prosecutors, courts, and the laws that give them the authority to arrest, try, and punish criminals. The second way of attacking the crime problem is to determine and remedy the conditions that lead some persons into careers of crime although the great majority of the population remain relatively law-abiding. Neither of these ways of attacking the problem is easy, but the second is probably more difficult than the first, because the conditions that lead individuals into crime are often complex and difficult to discover. Some of them are also very hard to change.

Today there are many leading Americans who believe that the rising crime rate in this country reflects, first of all, a partial breakdown in law enforcement. Some, including lawyers, police officials, and even a number of judges, place much of the blame on the courts, especially the United States Supreme Court. They believe that the courts, in their zeal to protect the civil rights of individuals accused of crime, have given too little consideration to the rights of the law-abiding public and that the courts have often gone so far as to paralyze police action in situations involving serious crimes. The argument is that the police have been deprived of reasonable discretion in dealing with persons suspected of crime and also that the rules of evidence have been so narrowed that more and more criminals are being released by the courts on technicalities even when there is clear evidence of their guilt.

One of the great weaknesses of the American system for dealing with crime is the long delays that often occur before an accused person is brought to trial or before his case is finally disposed of. Even if he is convicted, he may be allowed a number of appeals, and even if they are unsuccessful, it may be years before his sentence is finally carried out. Such delays tend to weaken respect for law and to give criminals hope, sometimes justified, that they can avoid punishment. The courts of Great Britain and of most countries in western Europe deal out justice more promptly and firmly. In a recent interview in *Life* magazine, Chief Justice Warren Burger called attention to the advantages of the justice system in such countries as Holland, Denmark, Norway, and Sweden, where criminal trials are held before three professional judges with no jury.[8] There, guilt or innocence is determined swiftly, and convictions are followed by humane and compassionate treatment of offenders. He believes our system, on the one hand, permits too much contention, and on the other, has too little concern for the accused once he is convicted. He also ex-

[8]*Life* magazine, August 7, 1970.

pressed the opinion that in this country, in recent years, elaboration of defendants' rights by Supreme Court decisions has contributed to the log jam in the courts and has created a system in which it is difficult to convict even those who are plainly guilty.

Recently there seems to have developed a greater recognition of the problems of the police. An earlier decision of the Supreme Court had been interpreted as forbidding police to search people unless there was probable cause for an arrest, but in a decision rendered in June, 1968, the Court upheld the right of policemen to stop suspicious-looking persons and frisk them for weapons. A little later Congress passed the Omnibus Crime Control Act, already mentioned, which contains a provision that suspects can be held and questioned for as long as six hours. Other problems of the police, according to the FBI, include "the sharp increases of police work-loads in criminal and noncriminal matters, riots, disturbances, marches, etc.; the almost static ratio of police strength to population, which is not commensurate with the sharp increase in crime; and the increasing mobility of those who commit crimes."[9]

Although we must not underrate the importance of developing better laws and more-efficient agencies for repressing crime, it would clearly be even more desirable to eliminate, so far as possible, the psychological and social conditions that lead individuals to commit crimes. As idealists we would like to sweep aside these conditions. As realists we know that a better world can be achieved only a little at a time by patient, persistent, and dedicated efforts. One thing that is certain is that a great deal of adult crime is merely a continuation of delinquency patterns established during childhood and adolescence. Even when that is not the case, it often results from personality traits that developed in early childhood. Perhaps if we could identify potential delinquents in childhood, we could help them develop into normal, nondelinquent adults.

The Gluecks' Attempt to Understand and Predict Delinquency. One of the most thoroughgoing attempts to understand the factors that contribute to delinquency was begun at Harvard by the Gluecks in the 1940's and has been continued up to the present time. As the basis for their major study, they selected five hundred persistent delinquents from the boys in two Massachusetts juvenile institutions and also, for purposes of comparison, five hundred proven nondelinquents from the public schools of Boston. Efforts were made to see that both groups came from similar ethnic and social backgrounds. With the aid of a group of cooperating specialists of different types, they rated each boy on the basis of over four hundred personality traits and social-background factors that might contribute to delinquent behavior. They then compared the ratings of the delinquent and nondelinquent boys in order to discover the factors that were significantly different between the two groups. Their hope was that if boys likely

---

[9] Federal Bureau of Investigation, *Uniform Crime Reports, 1969,* Washington, D.C., U.S. Department of Justice, 1970, p. 31.

to become delinquent could be discovered at an early age, remedial action might be effective.[10]

On the basis of their findings the Gluecks constructed a rather simple *delinquency-prediction table* but one that, in their judgment, has demonstrated a high degree of reliability. With this table they believe it is possible to select from a first-grade school population the boys who will probably become persistent delinquents unless preventive measures are taken. The table is based on five personal relationships within the family, each of which is scored on the basis of its adequacy or inadequacy. The five factors on which the table is based are as follows:

1. Supervision of boy by mother.
2. Discipline of boy by father.
3. Affection of mother for boy.
4. Affection of father for boy.
5. Cohesiveness of the family.

In 1952 the New York City Youth Board began a study in delinquency prediction based on the Glueck table. The boys studied were six-year-olds entering school for the first time. Originally they included 130 white, 131 black, and 42 Puerto Rican youngsters from two schools in a neighborhood with a high delinquency record. However, in this study the items used for prediction were reduced to three, namely, items 1, 3, and 5 in the table above. The two items dealing with father-son relationships were discarded because so many of the boys came from families where there was no father. In applying this delinquency-prediction test it was necessary, of course, to employ well-trained workers who could correctly evaluate the three items used.

Apparently, the table predicted delinquency with remarkable success. In 1962, ten years after the beginning of the experiment, of the boys for whom delinquency had been predicted, 85 per cent met this expectation; of those for whom nondelinquency was forecast, 95 per cent maintained a record of good behavior. These results were published in 1964 in a manual intended for the use of workers administering the Glueck prediction table.

Meanwhile the Gluecks continued to trace, so far as possible, the later life experience of the 500 delinquent and 500 nondelinquent boys whose backgrounds they had first studied in the 1940's. Of the 442 law-abiding boys whom they were able to trace to the age of 31, about 85 per cent stayed out of trouble as adults and most of the others were arrested for only minor offenses. But of the 438 delinquents whose lives they could follow, only about 19 per cent avoided arrest between the ages of seventeen and twenty-five. An additional 12 per cent were arrested only once,

---

[10] Sheldon and Eleanor Glueck, *Unravelling Juvenile Delinquency*, New York, The Commonwealth Fund, 1950.

and all the others, almost 69 per cent, were multiple offenders. The record of the group as adults showed a marked increase over their record as juveniles in homicide, forcible or pathological sex crimes, and robbery. This suggests that the upsurge in juvenile delinquency in the last decade is likely to be followed by a further increase of adult crime.

Between the ages of twenty-five and thirty-one the record of the former delinquents was better. Almost 40 per cent avoided arrest and almost 20 per cent were arrested only once.[11]

The Basis of a Program for Reducing Delinquency. Any program for the prevention or control of delinquency must be based on one or more of three types of activity: (1) organizing the constructive forces of the community to improve the general social environment and to support organizations and activities, including the schools, that may guide children into desirable patterns of behavior; (2) discovering potentially delinquent children and referring them to individuals or agencies competent to give them help; and (3) wise handling of children's cases by the police, the courts, and correctional institutions.

We have noted that both hereditary and environmental factors may contribute to criminal behavior on the part of an individual. At present not much can be done about hereditary factors. Fortunately, however, we have reason to believe that a really favorable environment would prevent all but a very few individuals from becoming criminals. We shall therefore note briefly some possible ways of reducing crime by making changes in the human environment.

Poverty, Slums, and Leisure-Time Activities. The reduction of extreme poverty in the United States in recent years, and the general rise of incomes, has reduced the pressure on many people to commit some kinds of crime against property—and yet the crime rate has continued to rise. Nevertheless, many criminologists still believe that elimination of the extreme poverty now found in city slums, for instance, would make a significant contribution to the lowering of crime rates. The present high level of production in our economy makes it possible to attack the slum and poverty problems with some chance of success. But as noted in Chapter 11, the elimination of slums will not be an overnight achievement, because the obstacles to be overcome are too great.

From the standpoint of controlling crime, an especially difficult problem is the criminal youth gangs that are found in ghettos, and their practice of recruiting members by force and threats, and even by murders to lend credence to their threats. In the short run this is a problem of more effective control of gangs by the police and courts, but such control is difficult to achieve unless leaders of the communities affected will cooperate.

A need that should be met, especially in the crowded areas of our cities, is the provision of more adequate opportunities to engage in desirable

---

[11] Sheldon and Eleanor Glueck, *Delinquents and Non-Delinquents in Perspective,* Cambridge, Mass., Harvard University Press, 1968.

36. Alley "Playground" in Slums. (Courtesy Wide World Photos.)

leisure-time activities. Status-giving activities are especially important. A boy who has status in legitimate group activities, like those of the Boy Scouts, or Little League baseball, is less likely to seek status in criminal gangs. Activities that help to develop legitimate talents are also important. A boy who has his talents recognized and who can hope for their utilization in the future is not likely to rob or kill for distinction or even for profit.

Improving Family Life. Family factors loom large in the causes of crime. Broken homes, mismanaged homes, or homes torn by conflict should be curable to an extent. Parental education demands new approaches that will give greater insight into family relations and the problems of children. All true, but such prescriptions are rather glib and not easy to apply. Could we induce most parents or prospective parents to seek seriously education in family relations, household and money management, child care, and child training? And if they should seek such education, could we find enough competent teachers or counselors who could give them the kind of information and advice they really need? We might require all high school students to take a course in marriage and the family. Increasingly, high school curricula are including such studies, but to make them effective requires teachers with unusual knowledge, insight, and skill. It also requires students who really want to learn.

Dealing with Psychological Factors. Finally, we come back to the psychological causes of crime. The suggestions along this line can be stated rather briefly. Mental conflicts should be detected at an early age, and some attempt should be made to relieve them. We must recognize the need for early psychological, psychiatric, and sociological diagnosis of every child who shows signs of serious maladjustment. Such children can often be helped by giving their lives direction through vocational guidance at the beginning of adolescence or even in the preadolescent period. Nothing so stabilizes a young person as confidence that he will have a place in the social structure, a role that will bring him security, recognition, and other benefits. Much of the youthful unrest of today is among young people who feel lost or else who have vague and sometimes grandiose ideas about their future. What they need most is to settle down to the hard task of preparing for a vocation that will bring them benefits and satisfactions and that will also contribute something to the social welfare.

The suggestions made above barely scratch the surface of the problem. Although we know a great deal about the causes of crime, we still have much to learn; we have even more to learn concerning the development of practical methods for substantially reducing crime. Often, policies that criminologists believe would be effective are not supported by adequate scientific evidence; or they do not have public acceptance; or they require huge amounts of money, labor, and materials and at best can be carried out only over a long period of time. An example in point is the elimination of blighted areas, slums, and ghettos.

Terms to be Understood

crime

misdemeanor

crime rate

juvenile delinquency

endomorphy

mesomorphy

ectomorphy

delinquency areas

organized crime

crime syndicate

Mafia

Cosa Nostra

retribution

deterrence

disablement

reformation

grand jury

indictment

petit jury

suspended sentence

probation

parole

pardon

commutation

parole-prediction scale

rehabilitation quotient

delinquency-prediction table

Questions for Review and Discussion

1. Why may an act be a crime in one society but not in another?
2. What is the crime situation in the United States today? Where are crime rates highest? Where are they rising fastest?
3. How do you explain the fact that in 1969 male arrests outnumbered female arrests by six to one? But arrests of females under eighteen rose 176 per cent against only 93 per cent for males under eighteen. Why?
4. The Gluecks believe there is a relationship between delinquency and inherited characteristics. What is their theory and how does it differ from that of Lombroso?
5. To what extent do economic factors determine criminal behavior? Defend your answer.
6. What objective evidence do we have that living in blighted areas makes criminal behavior much more likely?
7. Would it be possible for an individual to be well adjusted to his intimate social group and still engage in crime? Explain.
8. Explain the relation of criminal behavior to (a) family conditions, (b) intelligence, (c) emotional conflicts.
9. What makes possible the operation of large-scale criminal syndicates?
10. List five or six major sources of income for organized crime.
11. Review recent efforts of the FBI, and of Congress through legislation, to control organized crime.
12. Which one of the "theories of punishment" should we accept? Or should we combine several? Defend your answer.
13. What can be done to improve crime detection and the apprehension of criminals?
14. What are some of the weaknesses of the jury system?
15. Do you approve granting paroles to prisoners on the basis of good behavior? Defend your answer.
16. Explain the nature of parole-prediction scales. Why have they not been too successful?
17. What are the chief objections to our modern system of punishing criminals by imprisonment?

18. Outline what you would consider an effective program for making our prisons socially more useful.
19. What changes are needed in our institutions for delinquents?
20. List some of the major problems of the police in dealing with crime.
21. What aspects of our court system increase the difficulties of dealing out justice promptly and fairly?
22. Describe the method employed by the Gluecks in their attempts to discover the causes of delinquent behavior.
23. Describe the New York experiment with the Glueck delinquency-prediction table.
24. What did the Gluecks discover had happened in the 1960's to the same groups of delinquents and non-delinquents they had studied in the 1940's?
25. Of the methods that it would be reasonably practical to apply to the reduction of crime and delinquency, which ones do you believe would be rather effective? Why?

For Further Study

Amos, William E., and Charles F. Welford, eds., *Delinquency Prevention: Theory and Practice,* Englewood Cliffs, N.J., Prentice-Hall, Inc., 1967.

Bennett, James V., *I Chose Prison,* New York, Alfred A. Knopf, Inc., 1969. An autobiography of the man who was Director of the Federal Bureau of Prisons for twenty-seven years.

Bersani, Carl A., ed., *Crime and Delinquency: A Reader,* paperback, New York, The Macmillan Company, 1970.

Cavan, Ruth S., ed., *Readings in Juvenile Delinquency,* 2d ed., Philadelphia, J. B. Lippincott Company, 1969.

Clinard, Marshall B., *Sociology of Deviant Behavior,* 3d ed., New York, Holt, Rinehart and Winston, Inc., 1969.

Cressey, Donald R., *Theft of the Nation: The Structure and Operations of Organized Crime in America,* paperback, Harper & Row, Publishers, 1969.

Dressler, David, *Practice and Theory of Probation and Parole,* rev. ed., New York, Columbia University Press, 1970.

———, *Readings in Criminology and Penology,* New York, Columbia University Press, 1964.

Federal Bureau of Investigation, *Crime in the United States: Uniform Crime Reports,* Washington, D.C., U.S. Department of Justice. See latest annual issue.

Fyvel, T. R., *Troublemakers,* New York, Schocken Books, Inc., 1964. Comparative studies of juvenile delinquency in England, western Europe, the U.S.A., and Russia.

Glaser, Daniel, ed., *Crime in the City,* paperback, New York, Harper & Row, Publishers, 1969.

———, *Effectiveness of a Prison and Parole System,* paperback, Indianapolis, The Bobbs-Merrill Company, Inc., 1969. A study of one of the largest and most-advanced correctional systems.

Glueck, Sheldon, and Eleanor Glueck, *Family Environment and Delinquency,* London, Routledge & Kegan Paul, Ltd., 1962.

————, *Delinquents and Non-Delinquents in Perspective,* Cambridge, Mass., Harvard University Press, 1968.

Hazelrigg, Lawrence, ed., *Prison Within Society: A Reader in Penology,* paperback, New York, Doubleday & Company, Inc., 1969.

Hewitt, John P., *Social Stratification and Deviant Behavior,* paperback, New York, Random House, Inc., 1970.

Johnston, Norman, et al., eds., *Sociology of Punishment and Correction,* 2d ed., paperback, New York, John Wiley & Sons, Inc., 1970.

Juvenile Court Statistics, Washington, D.C., Children's Bureau, U.S. Department of Health, Education, and Welfare. See latest annual bulletin.

Maas, Peter, *The Valachi Papers,* New York, G. P. Putnam's Sons, 1968. About organized crime.

Newman, Charles L., ed., *Sourcebook on Probation, Parole, and Pardons,* 3d ed., Springfield, Ill., Charles C Thomas, Publisher, 1968.

Quinney, Richard, *The Problem of Crime,* paperback, New York, Dodd, Mead, & Company, Inc., 1970.

Reid, Ed, *The Grim Reapers: The Anatomy of Organized Crime in America,* Chicago, Henry Regnery Company, 1969.

Salerno, Ralph, and John S. Tompkins, *The Crime Confederation,* New York, Doubleday & Company, Inc., 1969. A study of the Cosa Nostra.

Sellin, Thorsten, and Marvin E. Wolfgang, eds., *Delinquency: Selected Studies,* New York, John Wiley & Sons, Inc., 1969.

Stratton, John R., and Robert M. Terry, eds., *Prevention of Delinquency: Problems and Programs,* New York, The Macmillan Company, 1968.

Volz, Joseph, and Peter Bridge, eds. and comps., *Mafia Talks,* paperback, New York, Fawcett World Library, 1969. Mafia conversations secretly recorded by the FBI.

Wolfgang, Marvin E., et al., eds., *Sociology of Crime and Delinquency,* 2d ed., paperback, New York, John Wiley & Sons, Inc., 1970.

Chapter 16

Education

Sometimes education is thought of as including everything that helps to shape the human personality. In this sense it is equivalent to socialization, or the whole process through which an individual acquires the culture of his society and reacts to it. In common usage, however, *education* has a more limited meaning. *It refers especially to successful efforts, usually by the more-mature members of a society, to teach each new generation the beliefs, the way of life, and some portion of the knowledge and skills of the group; it also refers to successful efforts to learn, on the part of those who are the objects of teaching.* In this sense, education is always an active process on the part of both teacher and learner.

Informal Versus Formal Education. In nonliterate tribal societies, education of the young is a somewhat simpler process than in modern industrial societies, partly because some of the subjects or skills that we regard as the basic essentials of an education—such as reading and writing—are wholly unknown. In these nonliterate societies, education is largely *informal* in the sense that it is not, for the most part, carried on by means of special institutionalized arrangements such as schools. Rather, it takes place in the family and in other social groups of which the child is normally a member. Yet even in primitive societies a certain amount of *formal* education, corresponding to what we would call "schooling," is often found. For example, at an appropriate stage in their development, adolescent youths may be required to gather together for the special purpose of receiving a course of instruction from their elders in the traditions, religious rites, and magical practices of the tribe.

In modern societies, informal education through family and community contacts is still very important, but it has a more limited role. Many aspects of modern culture are so complex, or difficult, or extensive, that they can be effectively transmitted to the next generation only through special arrangements created for that purpose. For instance, until schools were made available to the masses, only a tiny proportion of the people of Western countries ever learned to read and write. Today, by means of schools, we are able to give the great majority of each new generation some competence in such fundamentals of our culture as reading, writing, and arithmetic.

But in an industrial society the accumulation of knowledge and skills is so great that any one person can acquire, at best, only a very small part of the total. To transmit to each new generation the entire cultural heritage, it is necessary for many individuals to specialize in particular fields of knowledge. Furthermore, in many fields, such as medicine, engineering, or economics, the knowledge and skills required have multiplied until they not only take years to learn but also require highly specialized educational arrangements in colleges, universities, and research institutions. Thus, as our modern industrial society increases in complexity, it becomes more and more dependent on formal education—that is, on a system of schooling—both for transmitting and for developing its cultural heritage.

In the United States we have created a school system that provides more opportunities for more people than any the world has ever known. In the school year 1969–1970 we spent altogether, according to the United States Office of Education, about $62 billion to meet the needs of over 58 million students at all levels of the educational ladder. Between the years of 1947 and 1969 total expenditures on education rose from less than 3 per cent of the gross national product to almost 7 per cent.

Although an educational system such as ours provides great opportunities, it also creates many problems. In recent years there has been much controversy as to whether fundamental changes are needed to make it serve more adequately the needs of the country. This controversy began before the launching by Russia of Sputnik I, but the latter event greatly intensified it by leading great numbers of Americans to believe that Russia was outstripping us in scientific and technical education, including mathematics. More recently, student protests and disorders have raised questions as to the quality of education, its relevance to student needs, and who should control it.

In the late 1960's the word *relevant* began to be very popular with both student protesters and writers on education, but some of those who used it most freely did not take the trouble to spell out very clearly what they thought education should be relevant to or just how their ideas of relevance were to be achieved. There are certain basics, like the three R's, a reasonable mastery of which will contribute to the future success and usefulness of almost any student; and if a student has definite vocational aims, it is usually easy to determine some of the other subjects he should master. Beyond that, it is often difficult for, say, a high school or college student, or even his elders, to determine just what kind of education will be most relevant to the future satisfactions he hopes to gain from life. Sometimes he must experiment, studying a variety of courses before he finds the field that evokes his greatest interest; or he must work at some job and wait for greater maturity in order to see his future needs more clearly.

Schools as an Agency of Social Control. Because the primary purpose of education is to transmit to individuals the knowledge, ideals, and way of life of the group, education is an important agency of social control; that is, it is a principal means by which the group influences the individual to behave according to socially approved patterns.

Today two chief types of government are found in the world, democracy and dictatorship, and each has far-reaching effects on all aspects of social life. In Chapter 25 we shall discuss more fully both of these types of political organization, but at present we are concerned only with their relationship to certain aspects of education.

Both modern democracies and totalitarian dictatorships put emphasis on universal education, and both attempt to indoctrinate students with the basic principles of their societies. But democracies, especially as students advance in their education, tend to encourage some degree of independent thinking and also a certain amount of criticism of the social order. This is considered important because in democratic societies the citizens themselves ultimately choose their own leaders and determine the general policies of government by voting in free elections. Dictatorships, on the other hand, tend to inculcate strict adherence to the political philosophy and the policies of those in power—in other words, to the "party line." Loyalty and obedience are expected of the majority of citizens, but not independence. They are not permitted to take a direct part in selecting their leaders or in determining public policy.

In democracies, the patterns of education are likely to be less stereotyped than in dictatorships. One reason is that teachers and school administrators have somewhat greater *academic freedom,* that is, freedom to teach the truth as they themselves see it. Another is that democracies often encourage the operation of private as well as public schools, especially at the higher levels, and these private schools are permitted to develop their own educational concepts and practices. Many of the private schools are operated by religious bodies. In the United States the most extensive private system consists of the parochial schools of the Catholic church. In 1970 almost 12 per cent of all students at the elementary and secondary levels attended private schools, and about 28.5 per cent of those at the college and university level. In the United States there is still another reason for variations in the educational pattern, namely, that control of our public school system is decentralized. Each state sets up its own school system, and often each community or school district is given a considerable amount of independence in school matters.

Contributions of Education to American Democracy. Education, especially free public education, has made great contributions to the growth of American democracy. First, by teaching the masses of our citizens to read and write, public education makes it possible for them to communicate with one another more effectively beyond the local community and to learn something of politics and public policy by reading newspapers, magazines, and books. Even modern radio and television are a poor substitute for reading. They seldom cover topics with the breadth and depth required for real understanding, and they often give misleading impressions. The reader can more easily find needed information and varied points of view. Though the ability to read does not solve all the problems of democratic government, it has enabled our people to vote more intelligently and to choose leaders more wisely than would otherwise have been possible. Second, the public schools teach children to get along with different kinds of people. In many areas the children who attend these schools come from widely varied social, economic, national, and racial backgrounds. Though going to school together will not necessarily make all children love one another, if outright antagonism and conflict can be avoided, it does tend to create better understanding and to give all groups a keener sense of their common American heritage. Third, our system of public support for education reduces inequalities of opportunity at all educational levels. The masses of our people, even at the lower-income levels, are now receiving a grade-school education, and increasingly they are going on through high school. Larger numbers than ever before are also going on to college, partly because they can attend publicly supported schools that charge little or no tuition.

Finally, and by no means least important, our public school system has enabled us as a nation to make much more effective use of our human resources. In the public schools we discover, even from unfavorable social backgrounds, many children who have unusual ability. Most such children would never be brought to light if it were not for free public schools. Once discovered, they can often be encouraged and helped to develop their

37. Potential Friends: First Day at School. (Steve Schapiro—*Life* Magazine.
© Time Inc.)

capacities to the maximum. Thus, not only do they themselves lead fuller lives, but as scholars, scientists, or leaders in other fields, they make a much greater contribution to the welfare of the nation than would otherwise be possible. Our public school system is by no means a perfect instrument, either for achieving complete equality of educational opportunity or for enabling us to make maximum use of our human resources, but it has helped us to take great strides toward both of these objectives.

THE DEVELOPMENT OF AMERICAN EDUCATION

American interest in education goes back to earliest colonial times, but the Puritan colonies of New England were especially notable for their efforts, at that time unique, to provide all children with at least the rudiments of an elementary education.

Education in the Early New England Colonies. Within about fifty years of the first settlement at Plymouth, all the New England colonies except Rhode Island had passed legislation making it mandatory for parents and the masters of apprentices to see to it that their charges learned a trade and also learned the elements of reading, writing, and religion. Before long, laws were passed making it compulsory for the towns to establish elementary schools. Enforcement of these laws was by no means adequate, but many schools were actually set up under them. However, few of the schools were free. They received some public support, but they also charged tuition.

To provide secondary education for the social and economic elite, there were also established in the New England colonies *Latin grammar schools*. These were closely modeled on the English *secondary schools* of the time and taught principally Latin, some Greek, and religion. They were regarded as providing training for the ministry and the learned professions and as preparatory schools for Harvard College, which was established in 1636. Until the founding of Yale in 1701, it was the only college in New England.

The early New England schools were not the immediate forerunners of our present system of free public education in America. In the course of time, interest in popular education waned, and the principle of compulsory education was abandoned. Nevertheless, throughout our history, New Englanders have continued to provide educational leadership, though today they share it with other regions.

American Education Before the Civil War. In spite of early beginnings in New England, the idea that all citizens of a democracy should at least be taught reading, writing, and arithmetic was slow in taking hold in this country. The founders of our republic were not thoroughly *democratic* in the modern sense of the word. In spite of the pronouncement in the Declaration of Independence that all men are created equal, most of our early leaders had limited faith in the ability of the common man either to vote wisely or to profit from education. Everywhere the right to vote was restricted to the few by property and other qualifications, and, except perhaps in New England, only a small minority of the people even learned to read and write. This situation did not change radically until well into the nineteenth century. At this time a new spirit of democracy began to be felt. It permeated the whole country, but it was especially strong in the recently settled regions west of the Alleghenies and along the rapidly advancing Western frontier.

This new surge of democratic sentiment brought about the election of Andrew Jackson to the presidency in 1828. Jackson himself was a product of the frontier, a man of the people, and he represented the new democracy of the expanding West. In the period from Jackson's election to the Civil War, public elementary education became firmly established in this country. By 1860, tax-supported elementary schools had been established in many of the states. During these years some publicly-supported high schools were also established, but for the most part secondary education continued to be provided by the private *academies* that had succeeded the early colonial Latin grammar schools. These academies increased rapidly in number, but not until some time after the Civil War did the idea of publicly supported high schools begin to gain wide acceptance.

The development of education in the United States before the Civil War included not only the spread of elementary and secondary education but also a great expansion of higher education. During the whole colonial period only 10 colleges had been founded, and between 1780 and 1830 only 50 more were added. But in the next thirty years approximately 170 colleges or universities were established, or nearly three times as many as in the preceding two centuries. Though the vast majority of these were private institutions, deriving their income entirely from gifts and tuition, at the outbreak of the Civil War there were already 17 state-supported institutions of higher learning.

American Education Since the Civil War. During the last hundred years there has been a phenomenal expansion of education in this country. In 1870, five years after the end of the Civil War, the number of children attending elementary schools was less than seven million, while enrollment in public high schools was only eighty thousand.[1] Some children were also attending private grade schools and academies. By 1970, total enrollment in nursery schools, kindergartens, and elementary schools, public and private, had risen to over 36 million. Meanwhile, enrollment in all secondary schools had risen to more than 14 million. In 1870, less than half the children five to seventeen years old were attending school, and the average number of days attended by each child was only fifty. By 1970 more than 85 per cent of the children from the ages of five to seventeen were in school, and on the average, each child attended for more than 165 days of the year.

The most phenomenal expansion of education in the twentieth century has been in the colleges and universities. In 1920 there were less than 600,000 students enrolled in all our institutions of higher learning. Enrollment in colleges and universities was less than 25 per cent of high school enrollment. By 1970 the number of students in colleges and universities had increased more than twelve times, to about 7.5 million, and total enrollment in such institutions was more than half of that in the high schools.

Attendance at publicly supported institutions of higher learning has increased faster than at those under private control, but more than one fourth the total number of students is still in private schools. A number of leading state and municipal institutions of higher learning now have enrollments running into many thousands. Some of the privately endowed schools have also become very large. New York University, a private school, recently reported a total enrollment of nearly 32,000.

Table 12 shows for certain years the number of students enrolled in

[1] Newton Edwards and Herman G. Rickey, *The School in the American Social Order*, Boston, Houghton Mifflin Company, 1947, p. 675.

elementary schools, secondary schools, and institutions of higher learning from the school year 1899–1900 to the school year 1977–1978. Figures for 1974–1975 and 1977–1978 are projections of current trends. The table covers students in parochial and most other privately controlled schools as well as in public schools.

Table 12. *Enrollment in Educational Institutions of the United States, 1899–1900 to 1977–1978**

Year	Elementary Education†	Secondary Education†	Higher Education	Total
1899–1900	16,262,000	699,000	238,000	17,199,000
1919–1920	20,964,000	2,500,000	598,000	24,062,000
1939–1940	21,127,000	7,130,000	1,494,000	29,751,000
1949–1950	22,207,000	6,453,000	2,659,000	31,319,000
1959–1960	31,511,000	9,271,000	3,572,000	44,354,000
1964–1965	35,025,000	12,691,000	5,280,000	52,996,000
1969–1970	36,600,000	14,500,000	7,541,000	58,641,000
1974–1975‡	35,500,000	16,200,000	9,550,000	61,250,000
1977–1978‡	35,300,000	16,600,000	10,668,000	62,568,000

*Numbers are rounded to the nearest 1,000.
†Includes regular public and private schools but not all special schools.
‡Projected estimates.
Source: U.S. Office of Education, Washington, D.C.

Child-Labor Laws and School-Attendance Laws. Two factors that have contributed over the years to increased school attendance at the primary and secondary levels are child-labor laws and compulsory school-attendance laws. With the coming of industrialization, employment of children in factories became increasingly common in many areas. As the evils of this situation were recognized, more and more states passed laws designed to prevent the employment of children, especially young children, in industry. Eventually, state child-labor legislation, much of it inadequate and poorly enforced, was supplemented by federal legislation. The first federal child-labor law, passed in 1916, was declared unconstitutional in 1918, but child-labor provisions were later included in the Wages and Hours Act of 1938, and these were upheld by the courts.

Besides passing child-labor laws, the states also passed compulsory school-attendance laws. These also were often inadequate and poorly enforced, but they tended to support the child-labor laws and to increase school attendance. Between 1852 and 1918 all the states enacted some kind of compulsory-attendance legislation. In recent years the tendency has been to extend the years of required schooling at both ends, going as far down as age six and as far up as age eighteen. However, some educators and social scientists question whether the compulsory principle should apply beyond the ages of fifteen or sixteen. They maintain that many older children who cannot adjust to school would be better off, and that the schools would be better off, if they withdrew and went to work. This might well be true for some if they could find jobs.

Democratic Structure of the American School System. The school structure of the United States is basically quite different from that which is traditional in Europe. Before World War I nearly all European countries had what is called a *dual school system,* and in spite of some changes since, European schools, including those of Russia, still retain much of this dual character. A dual system separates, at an early age, the children who expect to go on to a college or a university from those who do not, and provides a different type of education for each group. In imperial Germany, children destined for university training had to be placed in a "secondary" or university preparatory school at about the age of nine. Because the preparatory schools charged tuition fees, few except the children of the middle and upper classes were able to enroll in them. All others attended the "people's school" and normally completed their education on finishing the eighth year. A school system of this type served well to perpetuate the sharp class distinctions that prevailed in Germany under the kaisers. Today most European children who are not headed for the university go to some type of vocational, agricultural, or technical school after completing their elementary education.

In the United States we developed in the late nineteenth century a so-called *unitary system.* Under this plan most children (insofar as they did not drop out along the way) attended the same school, and all followed a course of study that eventually led to graduation from high school after twelve years. They were then ready, supposedly, to go on to a college or a university. The door to further education was, so far as possible, kept open all along the line. This type of school system seemed especially suited to the needs of a democracy, where the ideal is to provide equal educational opportunities for all citizens. But up to 1900 or later, few children actually entered high school, and fewer still attended a college or university.

Today, however, the situation has changed. As larger numbers of students enter high school, many are not suited for or do not desire the traditional academic courses. Though students of all types still (with some exceptions in our larger cities) go to the same high schools, not all take courses that prepare them to enter a college or a university. Even so, our school system is still fairly successful in keeping open the doors to further educational advancement, because the student who has not taken a college preparatory course can often qualify for some type of college training by merely making up a few required admission units. Also, many colleges have become more flexible in their entrance requirements for students who give evidence, by test scores or otherwise, that they have the ability to do good work in college.

The Progressive Education Movement. Modern *progressive education,* in the broad sense, had its beginning more than two centuries ago, and its development is associated with such great names in education as Rousseau, Pestalozzi, Froebel, and, more recently, Montessori. However, what is commonly thought of as the progressive education movement in the United States is largely a product of the period since 1900 and is usually associated with the name of John Dewey. At about the turn of the century, Dewey established the Laboratory Schools of the University of Chicago. Later, for many years, he taught philosophy at Columbia University.

Supporters of the progressive education movement, as it developed in this country in the first half of the twentieth century, believed that schools should be "child centered" and should encourage the free and natural development of children according to their needs. They were much more concerned with meeting the current needs of the child, as they understood these, than they were with the mastery of any particular subject matter. One of their favorite slogans was "We are teaching children, not subjects." Dewey himself put great stress on the importance of "learning by doing"; also on the need for preparing children to live in a rapidly changing society.

As the influence of progressive education spread in the public school system, its disciples often summed up their aims in the expression *education for life adjustment.* They urged that the schools should accept responsibility for the total development of the child: mental, moral, emotional, and social. They also urged that schools should become "community centered," and some even went so far as to maintain that they should accept a large degree of responsibility for the reconstruction of society.

The progressive education movement was in part responsible for the introduction into the schools of many new subjects, both practical and cultural. It also contributed to a declining emphasis in the high schools and colleges on such "intellectual" subjects as the sciences, mathematics, and foreign languages. Mastery of such subjects requires sustained, disciplined effort, and many progressive educators felt that most students had little need for them.

Though without doubt the progressive movement made some valuable contributions to educational progress in this country, efforts to apply its theories did not always have happy results. In the period following World War II, many educators became increasingly critical of the movement. They believed that by attempting to assume too many responsibilities, schools frequently failed to perform well even their most essential functions, namely, to provide children with the basic knowledge and skills needed in a modern industrial society. They also felt that in attempting to meet the currently felt needs of children and young people, schools often failed to meet adequately their future needs and those of the nation.

PROBLEMS OF AMERICAN EDUCATION

One of the outstanding characteristics of the American educational system is the great variety to be found within it. We have schools administered by state authorities, schools administered by local authorities under the provisions of state law, and a great variety of private schools. There is no overall authority, as is the case in most European countries, to determine what shall be taught or to set up uniform standards of achievement. Though it is true that standards for accrediting a school are set by the various states and by certain voluntary associations of secondary schools and colleges, these standards vary and are often quite flexible.

The wide variations to be found among American schools at supposedly the same educational level is often confusing to Europeans. In the field of higher education, for example, they find that along with institutions equal to the best universities of Europe, we have others whose standards scarcely match those of a good secondary school.

This great diversity in our educational institutions and standards makes generalizations about the American school system difficult. It is something that must be kept in mind in any discussion of our educational problems.

Inequalities of Educational Opportunity. Although the American educational system provides greater opportunities for the masses of the people than that of any other country, there are still inequalities that are difficult to justify. The most striking of these is found in comparing the situation of blacks with that of whites. However, because we have already dealt with this problem in an earlier chapter, at this point we shall limit our discussion to certain other inequalities in educational opportunities.

Geographic Differences in Educational Opportunity. Variations of taxable wealth in different regions and localities are also a significant cause of variations in educational opportunities. Per capita wealth and income differ greatly among the states. For example, per capita income in New York and California is nearly twice that in Mississippi, Arkansas, or Alabama. Furthermore, in almost every state there are poor and thinly populated rural areas that find it impossible to provide adequate school facilities for their children. Often the areas with the smallest economic resources are those that have the largest proportion of children in their populations.

The problem of meeting the needs of the poorer rural areas has been partly solved in two ways. First, the consolidation of small rural districts into larger districts and the transportation of children by bus has made it possible to provide better schools. Second, the financial difficulties of poor school districts have been partially relieved by state distributive funds, taken from general state revenues or raised by special taxes. Such funds are divided among the school districts of the state on the basis of school enrollment and in some cases also on the basis of financial need.

Federal Aid to Education. For some years before 1965, the federal government, under various special programs, had contributed about two billion dollars annually to the support of the nation's schools. Federal aid to education goes back many years. An early and notable example was the Morrill Act of 1862. Under this legislation a large amount of federal land was given to each state for the support of a college of "agriculture and mechanical arts." At least sixty-five *land grant colleges* were established in the United States under the provisions of this legislation. Another source of federal aid is the Smith-Hughes Act of 1917. Under this law, grants are made to the public schools for the support of vocational education. Still another important contribution of the federal government to education was the G.I. Bill of Rights, which provided educational allotments to the veterans of World War II, and as later amended, to nearly all veterans who have served in the armed forces since then.

For a number of years, however, there had been agitation for greatly expanding federal aid to the schools and for putting it on a broader basis. But until 1965 all attempts at expanding school aid on a broad basis failed. Aside from the always-present problem of money, three obstacles prevented the needed legislation: (1) some opposition from the more-prosperous states to paying part of the school bills of those less prosperous; (2) strong disagreement among educators, politicians, and the public as to whether parochial schools should participate in federal aid; and (3) the fear of many people that federal aid would ultimately bring the school system under the control of the federal government.

In spite of these obstacles, Congress, in 1965, passed legislation greatly expanding federal aid to the schools at all levels. A large part of this aid was to go toward improving the educational opportunities of underprivileged children, both in city slums and in poverty-stricken rural areas. Some aid was also provided for parochial schools, especially in the form of services and *shared time.* This latter expression refers to arrangements by which parochial school pupils are permitted to attend some public school classes or to use the facilities of public schools at certain periods of the day or week. According to the Office of Education, total federal aid to educational activities was about $3.9 billion in 1965, and rose to $9.2 billion in 1969.

Family Income and Educational Opportunity. Various studies have shown that there is a close correlation between the amount of schooling received by children and the income status of their families. The higher the family income, the greater the likelihood that a child will finish high school or go to college. However, it would be a mistake to assume that financial obstacles are the only reason that children from low-income families receive less education than their more-fortunate school mates. Differences in their social and family backgrounds are often an important factor. Parents in low-income families often have little education and few intellectual interests, and they therefore fail to develop intellectual interests in their children. In many cases they encourage their children to find jobs and earn a living as soon as possible, even when this is not absolutely necessary.

Today the student who needs funds has better chances of obtaining aid than ever before, either from endowed scholarship funds, university loan funds, or state and federal aid programs. On the other hand, aid is more necessary than ever before. Since 1900, the cost of living in the United States has risen to more than four times its level in that year; meanwhile, the cost, including all items, of attending one of our leading colleges or universities has increased by ten or twelve times. In 1900 the *minimum* average cost of going to such a school was about $300 per year; by 1970 it was well over $3,000. True, by going to a publicly supported school a student who must get help and/or earn part of his expenses can avoid heavy tuition charges, but he still must pay his living expenses, and these are a large part of the cost of a college education.

We have mentioned the educational allotments that the government has provided for veterans ever since World War II. From time to time these have been increased by acts of Congress. For full-time students they were raised in 1970 to $175 a month for unmarried veterans and to $205 for married veterans without children, with additional allowances for those having children. Congress has also provided aid for nonveteran students in several ways. Of special importance is the provision in the National Defense Act of 1958 that permits a college student to borrow up to a total of $5,000. Students in graduate and professional schools may borrow as much as $2,500 a year, up to a combined total of $10,000 for undergraduate and graduate study. No interest is charged until repayment begins after graduation. Repayment may be spread over ten years with 3 per cent interest on the unpaid balance.

Adult Education. In recent years the need for providing educational opportunities for adults has been increasingly recognized, and many agencies have made efforts to meet this problem. Public schools, universities, business concerns, and various other organizations now offer a wide variety of classes, mostly in the evening, for millions of older students. Some of these classes carry credit, some do not. They give many people the educational opportunities that were missing in their early youth and thus enable them to develop wider interests and prepare themselves for better jobs.

If we take into account all types of adult education programs, the number of persons affected runs into the millions. It includes those who seek further education through public school programs, regular college or university classes, special evening classes, correspondence courses, extension courses offered on radio or television, on-the-job training programs, and individual instruction or self-directed study. Such programs are supported by colleges and universities; federal, state, and local agencies; labor and farm organizations; public libraries; churches; the YMCA; and other agencies.

Financing American Education. In the years immediately after World War II, American education was faced with difficult financial problems. Building of school facilities had lagged during the war, and price inflation had meanwhile greatly increased construction costs. Moreover, teacher shortages made it imperative to raise teachers' salaries at least in proportion to increases of income in other occupations. To make matters worse, elementary school enrollments began to rise rapidly after 1948 because of the higher birth rate. As a result, some areas experienced critical shortages of teachers and classrooms for the next ten or fifteen years.

Though the financing of education in the United States is still a great problem, we have been phenomenally successful since World War II in raising more funds. Estimates by the federal Office of Education indicate that from the school year 1945–1946 to the school year 1969–1970 annual expenditures on schools at all levels, public and private, increased more than fifteen times, from about $4 billion to over $62 billion. Sharply higher costs, including teachers' salaries, plus a doubling of enrollments, have made this increase necessary. Various circumstances have helped provide the additional money. Higher rentals and land values have made it possible to raise real estate taxes. Other taxes have also been increased, and new taxes have been devised. State and federal aid to local school systems has been greatly expanded. All this has been possible largely because rising money incomes and a generally high level of prosperity have raised the tax-paying capacity of the public. However, the rise in taxes has been so great that they are meeting more resistance. In the years ahead, the problem may be eased a little as school enrollments increase more slowly, or possibly even decline, because of the present lower birth rate. But now teachers are forming unions, and their salaries are still rising rapidly.

Financial Problems of the Private Colleges and Universities. Our colleges and universities that depend entirely on endowments, other gifts, and tuition payments have been hard hit by inflation ever since World War II. Their costs have generally risen faster than their income from endowments. One reason for this is higher salaries for college teachers. As college enrollments have risen, there has been keen competition for competent teachers, especially from the rapidly expanding state-supported schools. Aside from obtaining larger gifts, the only way in which private schools can meet higher costs is to raise tuition. Most of them have raised it sharply, but unless a school has great prestige, increases must be kept within limits to avoid losing too many students.

The only acceptable solution for the financial problems of the endowed colleges seems to be more generous support from private sources. To some extent, such support has materialized. One reason is an increased awareness on the part of the public of the important role that privately controlled colleges and universities play in our educational system. Another reason is to found in the tax situation. High inheritance taxes tend to cut down large estates very sharply, but these taxes do not apply to gifts for religious, charitable, or educational purposes. Similarly, high-income surtaxes greatly reduce the disposable incomes of many of the wealthy, but gifts to charitable, religious, or educational organizations, up to 50 per cent of income, are generally exempt from the tax. Hence, if a person's income is high enough to, say, put him in the 70 per cent tax bracket, every hundred dollars he gives to a college actually costs him only thirty dollars.

Because bequests for charitable purposes are not subject to the federal inheritance tax nor to most state inheritance taxes, many wealthy persons have created charitable foundations to which they have willed large portions of their estates. These foundations have been an important source of funds to many private educational institutions. Some of them, like those established by the Fords and Rockefellers, are familiar to almost everyone. Business corporations have been another source of gifts to private education, and some schools have also benefited from carrying on research projects for the government under contract.

In spite of the success of our endowed institutions of higher learning in obtaining more funds, including gifts from alumni, many have found it necessary to limit their enrollments in order to maintain the quality of the education they offer. Tuition charges, even though they have been raised, almost never cover more than part of the cost of educating a student. The tax-supported schools have been able to expand more rapidly, and as a result the proportion of students attending private institutions has fallen. The Office of Education predicts that from 1970 to 1977 total enrollment in all institutions of higher learning will increase by 2.8 million.[2] If this proves to be correct, a great deal more money will have to be spent by schools of all types to provide education at this level.

The Supply of Teachers. For some years after World War II, educators complained that there was a great shortage of qualified teachers in our elementary and secondary schools. In the school year 1958–1959, the United States Office of Education estimated that the nation needed 132,000 more "fully qualified" teachers than were actually available. *Fully qualified teachers* refers to those whose training meets the certification standards set by state departments of education or by school accrediting agencies.

Today the teacher shortage is being replaced by a surplus. There is now a shortage only for school systems that pay relatively low salaries or have special problems that make them unattractive to many teachers. In recent years, for example, the author has noticed that many young teachers avoid our larger cities, even at a sacrifice in pay, because they are apprehensive of crowded classes, regimentation, or other unfavorable working condi-

[2] U.S. Office of Education, *Projections of Educational Statistics to 1977–78,* Washington, D.C., Government Printing Office, 1968, p. 9.

tions. They are especially reluctant to teach in ghettos, where they fear unusual disciplinary problems or even violence.

Higher salaries have been an important factor in relieving the teacher shortage. From 1950 to 1970 the average salaries of public school teachers increased more than two-and-a-half times and the average salaries of college and university teachers more than doubled. Factors other than salary have also contributed to drawing more and better students into the teaching profession. These include a widespread public interest in the problems of education; new ideas about how and what to teach; an upgrading of teacher-training courses; and special aid by various agencies, including the federal government, to students in teacher-training programs.

Problems of Teacher Training. A century or more ago there were almost no standards of training for teachers, particularly at the elementary level. Except in the colleges and some of the academies, teaching was seldom regarded as a profession or even a permanent occupation. Salaries were low, teachers had little prestige, and even in the most advanced states, like Massachusetts, the average district school kept open for only three or four months in the year. Often teachers had only an elementary education themselves. At best, teaching was regarded as a steppingstone to more-respected positions, a stopgap between schooling and marriage, a type of seasonal employment, or, in some cases, a missionary enterprise. At worst it was a refuge for incompetents.[3]

As the public school system expanded and as school terms were lengthened, efforts were made to improve teacher training. By 1860 twelve *normal schools,* supported by state funds, had been established. For many years, however, chief dependence was placed on the colleges and universities for teachers in academies and high schools, and on the latter institutions for elementary teachers. However, partly because teaching was unattractive, the supply of teachers with secondary-school training was never adequate. The early normal schools were unpretentious institutions. They admitted almost anyone, and though they usually offered courses that were one or two years in length, most students attended only a few months.

Gradually, the normal schools increased in number, raised their admission standards, expanded their programs, and improved the quality of their instruction. In time, pedagogy, or education, developed as a special field of study, and normal schools began to put increasing emphasis on theories and methods of teaching. Beginning about 1880, the universities began to establish special professorships or departments of education. Meanwhile, the normal schools continued to expand, and in recent decades most of them have been transformed into teachers' colleges or even universities. As teachers' colleges they have achieved full collegiate standing, offer four-year courses leading to degrees, and in most cases even offer graduate work.

[3] See Edwards and Rickey, *op. cit.,* pp. 762–763.

The development of teachers' colleges and university departments of education eventually created a vigorous controversy in educational circles over whether teacher training should put major emphasis on knowledge of subjects to be taught or on an understanding of the theory and methods of teaching. Teachers' colleges varied considerably in their programs, but their critics alleged that in many cases they devoted so large a portion of their curriculums to educational theory and methods that the training they offered in such *content subjects* as history, mathematics, science, and languages was rather skimpy. A few decades ago, a careful examination of catalogues would have been sufficient to show that most teachers' colleges put more emphasis on specialized teacher training and less on "content" courses than did most university teacher-training programs. But in recent years the trend everywhere has been toward greater emphasis on knowledge of the subjects to be taught and also on an upgrading of courses in educational theory and methods.

In the early years of the twentieth century, nearly all of our primary school teachers, and most of our high school teachers, were women. Employment opportunities for women were still limited, and the expanding school system, particularly the high schools, attracted to the teaching profession some of the ablest women graduates of our colleges. This was true in spite of the relatively low level of salaries. But after World War II it became clear that teacher-training programs were attracting neither the number nor the quality of students needed for teachers in our expanding public school system. Many people became concerned about the quality of our prospective teachers. When the Selective Service Qualification Test was given in 1951–1952 to more than 400,000 college undergraduates to determine whether they should be drafted or allowed to continue their studies, students of education made much the poorest showing of all major groups.[4] When this test was given again somewhat later, 53 per cent of students in all fields passed, but only 27 per cent of those majoring in education.

Among the factors that at the time tended to repel able students from the teaching profession were the already-mentioned low salaries, plus lack of prestige, difficult working conditions in some school systems, and often lack of freedom in the personal lives of teachers. Many were also repelled by the general character of some teacher-training programs, with their emphasis on wordy and repetitious courses in education.

But changes were already in the making. Early in the 1950's a number of colleges and universities cooperated in organizing a program to improve the training and quality of our teachers. The principal objectives were to emphasize mastery of the intellectual disciplines ("subject matter" courses) and to attract abler students. Under the leadership of Harvard, twenty-nine Eastern colleges adopted a plan for giving selected holders of B.A. degrees a higher degree in teaching after a fifth year of study; this

[4] "A Dent in the Teacher Shortage," *Life* magazine, August 3, 1953, p. 28.

fifth year included a practical internship in the public schools. The programs of all the colleges subscribing to this plan had the backing of the Ford Foundation.

We have mentioned that the launching of Sputnik I brought greater emphasis on the teaching of mathematics, science, and engineering. It also brought about greater emphasis on all the basic school subjects, including reading, geography, history, English, and foreign languages.

The Problem of Educational Leadership. In the last 150 years great progress has been made in our knowledge of the learning process and in the development of more effective methods of teaching. Many people of great ability, both in the United States and abroad, have contributed to this progress by intensive study of the educative process and by carrying on various types of experiments. The development of educational psychology, in particular, has made important contributions to the effectiveness of modern teaching.

We have noted that about the year 1880 the universities began to establish professorships of education. The first was established in 1879 at the University of Michigan; and by 1900, departments or schools of education had been established at a number of universities. Before the end of the second decade of the twentieth century, a theory and doctrine of education had been well established. Increasingly, university departments or schools of education began to carry on research, to promote graduate study, and to grant higher degrees.

By the beginning of World War I, educational leadership, at least so far as the public schools were concerned, had already fallen largely into the hands of those who were the products of the university graduate schools of education. This is the group who are now often called *educationists,* to distinguish them from other teachers, especially at the college and university level, all of whom may properly be called *educators.* On the face of it, this assumption of leadership in the schools by "experts" trained in the theory and practice of education would seem to have been a most fortunate development. However, there were some who did not agree. In the years following World War II, there was a rising tide of criticism of the theories and practices of the educationists and of certain changes that they had introduced into our schools. Arthur E. Bestor, a history teacher at the University of Illinois, became one of the most effective of the postwar critics of American education and one of the first to gain wide public attention.

The more-extreme critics of the educationists charged that schools of education were attracting few first-rate scholars to their faculties; that many students drifted into graduate schools of education because they found other academic fields too difficult; that courses in education were usually thin, trivial, repetitious, and badly taught; that the textbooks were often amazingly poor; and that professors of education commonly failed to keep in close touch with the actual teaching of content subjects and hence failed to grapple effectively with the real problems of the classroom teacher. These real problems, it was maintained, have to do with transmitting to students specific kinds of skill and knowledge. The critics further charged that most educationists, in attempting to develop educational theories, relied heavily on a rather vague social philosophy, on empty generalizations, on well-worn aphorisms, on slogans, and on the invention of new names for old ideas.

To what extent such charges were justified is difficult to say, but they were supported by numerous teachers who had taken their quota of education courses in their student days. Certainly, if applied as a blanket indictment, they did a great injustice to many able scholars in the field of education. Nevertheless, after allowing for exaggeration, there was a measure of truth in the charges of the critics.

Despite all the criticism, the educationists have by no means completely abdicated from their position of leadership in American education. They too are gradually changing their theories and methods with the times. However, to a greater extent than in the past they are now sharing leadership with other groups.

Structural Changes in the School System. The structure of our school system has frequently been the subject of adverse criticism. The early elementary schools in the United States were ungraded district schools, and the early academies and high schools offered programs of study that typically varied in length from two to four years. But by 1880 the structure of the American schools had definitely evolved into the familiar 8–4-4 system—a graded eight-year elementary school, a four-year high school, and a four-year college. In most American communities a year of kindergarten was later added at the bottom of the scale, preceding the first grade. Later still, private nursery schools became common for very young children, and in much more recent years Head Start programs have been introduced for young children from disadvantaged backgrounds. Long before these developments, education had been extended at the upper levels, so that by one year of study beyond college an able student could obtain an M.A. degree, or by three years of such study he could, with industry and good fortune, obtain a Ph.D.

The 8-4-4 system was scarcely well established before it began to receive criticism. The principal charge against it was that eight years were not necessary for an elementary education. It was maintained that secondary education should begin sooner, either to provide more time for college preparation or to enable pupils to finish high school earlier. Some educators also felt that the first two years of college or university work were really secondary education and should be moved down to the secondary level.

Though we have never reduced the standard number of years required from kindergarten to graduation from college, increasing criticism of the 8-4-4 system began to have results after World War I. One effect was the establishment of *junior high schools* in many communities. These took over the seventh and eighth years of schooling from the grades and took the first year from the senior high school. The junior high school made it possible to begin secondary education earlier and facilitated the introduction of new types of courses. Another development after World War I was the establishment of an increasing number of *junior colleges,* both private and public, that provided the first two years of college training.

The junior college movement developed slowly at first. In the early 1920's there were only a few throughout the country. The first public junior colleges were usually established by school districts as a kind of extension of the high schools. Often they were begun in high school buildings and their classes were taught by high school teachers, preferably those with some graduate-school training; and just as some educators had argued earlier that the first two years of college should be moved down to the secondary level, some now regarded the junior college as an extension of secondary education. In fact, however, most of the early junior colleges followed rather closely the curriculums of the first two years of the four-year colleges and the universities, and they were chiefly concerned with preparing their students to enter such institutions in their junior year. By the end of the 1930's the number of junior colleges had substantially increased, and since most of them were established in communities where college education had not earlier been available, they gave many young people a better opportunity for getting at least some college training.

After World War II, responding to the increased demand for higher education, the number of junior colleges rose rapidly. By 1968 there were more than eight hundred in the United States, with a total enrollment of about 1.3 million students.

Gradually, as junior colleges multiplied and as more and more students crowded into them, the concept of their function changed. They were no longer regarded primarily as institutions for preparing students for entering four-year colleges, though they still do this, but they began to be thought of as *community* colleges, designed to serve the diverse needs in each community of students who could benefit from some extension of their high school education, and not just to serve the needs of those planning to go on to a four-year institution. Various types of vocational training were introduced, some of it technical. Courses were offered to train auto mechanics, beauty-shop operators, salesmen, medical and dental assistants, laboratory technicians, and various other types of workers. The community college has become an institution that is seeking not only to give training that will make better citizens but also to meet the needs of our economy for a greater number of trained workers and the needs of young people for jobs that will yield both satisfaction and a reasonable level of income.

Curriculum Problems. During the past hundred years great changes have taken place in the *curriculums* of our schools. Most of these changes represent additions. In the elementary schools, to the basic subjects of reading, writing, spelling, grammar, and arithmetic have been added such subjects as geography, history, social studies, natural science, domestic arts, manual training, music, art, and physical education. Some of these are now taught in most schools, others only in certain schools or to certain groups of pupils. High school curriculums have undergone similar changes, with some further additions, such as commercial subjects. High school curriculums have also suffered some losses. The classical languages have completely disappeared from most of them. Furthermore, under the present elective system, it is usually not necessary for a student to study any foreign language, or even mathematics, in order to receive a diploma; though under the impact of the postwar wave of change, there was some revival of emphasis on foreign languages, mathematics, and science.

For many years there has been a slow expansion of vocational training in our school system. More recently the trend has accelerated. Vocational training in some form is not new, for preparing people to earn a living has always been a function of schools. The New England Latin grammar schools and the early academies were primarily designed to prepare students for training in the professions. However, it was some years before schools were established to train people for other kinds of work. The establishment of the agricultural land grant colleges marked an important step in the development of vocational education, but not until after 1900 was any great progress made in the development of vocational education at the high school level. Gradually, however, commercial subjects such as typing and bookkeeping began to be introduced into high school programs for those who chose to take them; and in 1917 a considerable stimulus was given to vocational education through the passage by Congress of the Smith-Hughes Act. This law made federal funds available to the states for promoting the teaching of agriculture, trades, home economics, and industrial subjects.

Aside from those of a vocational nature, most of the subjects added to the curriculums of grade schools and high schools over the years have been intended to "enrich" their educational programs. To some degree this purpose has been achieved, for most of the newer subjects have a certain amount of intellectual, cultural, or practical value for the average child. Too often, however, there has been a tendency to overload the curriculum with subjects and activities. Teachers and pupils are sometimes so burdened with classes, special programs, assemblies, excursions, and other activities that their efforts are scattered and relatively little is accomplished. Though few of us would advocate eliminating from curriculums all the newer subjects and all extracurricular activities, it seems clear that in many schools pupils would be better off with simpler programs, a calmer atmosphere, fewer demands on their attention, and the opportunity to concentrate on a smaller number of studies and activities.

Many students of child development and education feel that in our modern society we tend to overorganize the lives of children, not only in school but through activities sponsored by such groups as the Boy and Girl scouts, churches, and YMCA's. Partly the idea has been to keep them out of mischief, and partly to provide them with maximum opportunities for development. But if children are to make the most of their own special interests and abilities, they need free time, not all of which is spent in watching television. This may be especially true of children with above-average ability. Bruno Bettelheim, head of the Orthogenic School at the University of Chicago and professor of psychology and psychiatry, once suggested that parents who suspect that their child is gifted should let him have leisure time to develop his mind and his interests. "If he is bored," said Bettelheim, "he is not gifted. One of the characteristics of giftedness is that you can occupy your mind."

The College Curriculum. Until the middle of the nineteenth century the content of higher education consisted chiefly of the ancient languages, mathematics, philosophy, and theology. Some attention was also given to modern foreign languages and the social sciences, but these held a place of less importance. However, after the Civil War the curriculum began to show the effects of new developments in science, technology, and other fields of knowledge. As enrollments increased and the interests of students became more and more diverse, scientific, technical, and vocational training was increasingly introduced at the college level. Subjects and courses of study multiplied until it became impossible for any student to take more than a very small part of the total offerings. To meet this problem, the *elective system* was adopted. This permitted students, with some restrictions, to determine their own courses of study. But the results were not always satisfactory, for often students chose a hodgepodge of unrelated subjects, and at the same time they frequently missed entirely any acquaintance with some of the basic fields of human knowledge.

The shortcomings of the elective system led to two developments. First, colleges began to require students to major in some one field of knowledge, by taking a substantial proportion of their work in this field. Second, they began to require students to spread some of their courses in such a way that they became acquainted with at least several of the basic fields of knowledge. The expression *liberal education* came to be associated especially with the attempt to give students breadth of understanding.

Courses Covering Broad Fields of Knowledge. Efforts to give students greater breadth of understanding led to the rapid spread in the 1930's of *survey courses* covering broad fields of knowledge such as physical science, biological science, social science, and the humanities. Sometimes all students were required in their freshman and sophomore years to take a *core curriculum* consisting of several of these survey courses. After World War II, courses of this type continued to spread, but it was increasingly recognized that they should be designed to introduce the student to a field of knowledge rather than to attempt a complete survey of it. As a result, some changes were made in the nature of these courses, and they came to be called *general courses* rather than *survey courses*. However, this expression is not wholly fortunate, for the word *general* suggests a certain vagueness and lack of purpose.

The author would prefer to apply the term *basic* to courses that deal with broad fields of knowledge. He believes that in the field of social science the primary objectives of such a course should be to give students a clear understanding of the nature of human societies, their origin, development, institutions, differences, and some of their more important problems. Though such a course can only introduce students to the study of social science, if its objectives are achieved, it should be of great value either as a terminal course or as the foundation for more-advanced study.

This textbook was written for a course of this type. Actually, as the reader has problably noted, it is chiefly concerned with the characteristics of our modern American society, but it attempts to make these more understandable by showing how they are related to other cultures and societies and to Western and world civilization.

Today the term *general education* is often applied to college programs that are intended to broaden the intellectual horizon of students. Sometimes it is used merely as a substitute for the older term *liberal education.* Both expressions refer to a type of training designed to go much beyond narrowly practical or vocational objectives. But while liberal education emphasizes the desirability of learning something about a variety of subjects, general education puts more stress on the importance of not missing completely any of the major fields of human knowledge.

How Good Are Our Schools? To the question How good are our schools? there is no simple answer and certainly no answer to which everyone will agree. Some of them are very good indeed; others are very poor. There are critics who allege that in the last generation or two there has been a marked decline in the effectiveness with which our grade schools teach

"I have deep perceptive thoughts, but I can't get them into sentences."
(Courtesy Robert Censoni. Copyright 1969 *Saturday Review, Inc.*)

the fundamentals of reading, writing, spelling, and arithmetic. Whether this is true is hard to tell. It seems probable that our best schools are teaching these fundamentals more effectively than ever. But one thing of a disturbing nature does appear to be true, namely, that some of our grade schools and even our high schools are producing large numbers of scarcely literate graduates, people who cannot read ordinary English prose with much understanding or write a clear and properly constructed sentence. Thirty or forty years ago most such students would have received failing grades somewhere along the line and would eventually have dropped out of school. Today many of them are receiving diplomas. This problem of schools that fail to educate is especially acute in the slums and ghettos of our central cities, but it is not limited to them.

Some Reasons for Low Academic Standards. For several decades a number of factors have tended to lower *academic standards* in many of our public schools. We have already mentioned the crowding of students' programs with extra subjects and numerous extracurricular activities. This often means that a student finds little time to study his basic academic courses.

Another development that has tended to lower standards is the trend toward carrying a larger and larger proportion of children through grade school and high school. Today most children complete the eighth grade, the great majority go on to high school, and a large proportion are graduated. But many of these children have little interest in and little ability to master traditional academic subjects. Teachers are then under pressure to lower standards. It seems unreasonable to give failing grades to, say, 50 per cent of a class, no matter how poor it is; naturally many principals and parents would blame the teacher. Besides, teenagers with little schooling now have trouble getting jobs. If they leave school, they may just wander in the streets and get into trouble. So in many schools most of them are "passed" regardless of their lack of achievement.

The tendency to pass students from grade to grade on the basis of little or no achievement is strengthened in some schools by the policy of *social promotion.* This means promoting children along with their classmates regardless of whether they reach a minimum standard of achievement in their studies. The theory is that it is better for social reasons to keep them with their own age group, whether they learn anything or not, and at all costs to avoid putting on them the stigma of failure. However, promotion on this basis does not help matters much. The pupil who has not learned elementary mathematics in the lower grades becomes completely frustrated or indifferent if he must attend math classes in the upper grades. His "education" consists only in going through the motions of attending classes. Not only does he become a problem to the teacher and prevent the other students from learning much, but he often feels his own inadequacy more keenly than if he had been held back. Whether under these conditions he gains anything by remaining in his own age group or by staying in school at all is open to question. If this problem can, for many

"He took a speed-reading course. Now he finishes the Sunday 'Times' in thirty minutes and has nothing to do the rest of the day." (Courtesy Bob Schochet. Copyright 1969 *Saturday Review, Inc.*)

children, be solved, we probably must attack it early in a child's life. Later we shall call attention to some attempts that are being made to do this.

Another factor that contributes to low achievement by many children is the use—or misuse—of new and inadequately weighed and tested methods of teaching. A case in point is rapid reading. Some years ago studies of the reading habits of children and adults showed that many people read very slowly, even when they read silently, partly because they make unconscious lip or throat movements to enunciate each word. With proper training they can learn to read much more rapidly, and with many types of material they can do this without any loss of comprehension. As a result of this discovery, many educators began to put great emphasis on the teaching of rapid reading in elementary schools. In many schools the teaching of phonetics was abandoned, and every effort was made to eliminate oral reading or reduce it to a minimum, for fear that enunciating words would interfere with rapid reading.

But the results of overemphasis on silent reading and speed were often disastrous. Some children were blocked in their attempts to learn, because the mysteries of letters, phonetics, words, and meanings were not adequately unravelled. Others succeeded in reading fast, but no sufficient check was made on whether they could pronounce words or even understand them. As a result they acquired the habit of guessing at meanings or ignoring what they did not understand, and so became incapable of reading the most ordinary prose with real comprehension. Though there are advantages in being able to read rapidly, a student must walk before he runs. Oral reading and phonetics must be given their due share of attention. Furthermore, children should understand that some kinds of materials must be read slowly and thoughtfully if they are really to be understood at all.

The advantages of reading habitually at great speed are usually exaggerated and its drawbacks overlooked. Much of the material that can be read very rapidly without loss of comprehension is not worth reading at all. It can be scanned and discarded, or parts worth reading can be found and read at a leisurely pace. Reading important material fast often means failure to catch fine distinctions or to follow completely complex thought processes that an author has taken great pains to express. Furthermore, it is a mistake to assume that the whole purpose of reading is to acquire the information and ideas expressed in a passage. Those who put extreme emphasis on speed assume that reading is just a process of absorption; but it should be an experience in which the reader is constantly reacting to the writer. It is likely to be much more rewarding when one takes time, as he goes along, to criticize and to test what is said against his own knowledge and thought. Reading—if not done too fast—is also useful for giving the reader a sense for good style in writing and a feeling for good sentence structure. The teaching of rapid reading in the schools may be one of the reasons "Why Nobody Can't Write Good."[5] Reading at a more moderate rate, and especially oral reading, also helps us to appreciate the cadences of language, including the sounds, rhythms, rhymes, and repetitions that, in addition to imagery, are so essential to the quality of good verse. Fortunately, some of the mistakes made when rapid reading first became popular in the schools are now being corrected.

Raising the Level of Student Achievement. In the final analysis, the quality of any educational system is measured by what it teaches and by the level of student achievement: in knowledge and in understanding; in learning how to apply his knowledge in his personal life and in fulfilling his obligations as a citizen; and in acquiring learning habits that will enable him to continue to educate himself throughout life. Among the things that can raise the level of achievement are better teachers, better-equipped school buildings, and better teaching aids; vocational training and work-study programs to meet the needs of some students; special classes or programs for superior students to help them utilize their abilities to the utmost; and the money needed to pay all the costs.

Recently increased attention has been given to programs of job training, especially those designed to help young people who have dropped out of school, who have no special skills, and whose prospects for earning a living are poor. But preparing school failures for good jobs presents many problems. Inability to read and write reasonably well is a handicap in most occupations, and more often than not students who do poor work in academic subjects also do poor work in vocational courses.

Another and quite different idea for raising the achievement of school

[5] See article by John Fischer, *Harper's Magazine,* February 1964, p. 18.

children has also been receiving attention. It has long been observed that, as a group, children from poor homes do poorly in school, especially children who come from slum areas. Sometimes they are dull simply because they do not get enough food or the right kinds of food. But many psychologists and educators believe that one reason for their backwardness is the poverty of their social and cultural experiences in their early years. Efforts are now being made to find ways to overcome this handicap. The idea is to place these *culturally deprived* children, in their preschool years, in special *Head Start* groups designed to give them some of the needed experiences they would otherwise miss and the lack of which might greatly slow their further progress.

This ties in with the belief of some leading educators that we have been badly neglecting the great potential for learning that children have in their preschool years. George W. Beadle, Nobel prize–winning geneticist and former president of the University of Chicago, expressed this viewpoint in a speech made several years ago at a convocation: "We are missing the boat in our educational systems, for they largely ignore the most sensitive and receptive period of development." The present emphasis on the importance of the preschool years accounts largely for a revival in this country of *Montessori-method* nursery schools and kindergartens. Maria Montessori was a famous Italian educator of the early twentieth century who believed firmly that children between the ages of eighteen months and five years have a greater capacity for some kinds of learning than they will ever have in later years.

However, attempts to raise the level of achievement of disadvantaged children by beginning to teach them in their preschool years have yielded mixed results. Studies have indicated that children from the Head Start program showed improved performance but that this did not last very long after they had entered an ordinary school. Some explain this on the theory that a child who has participated in Head Start must not be left to shift for himself as soon as he enters regular school. Experiments have been made with a program that continues for several more years and that gives the child special help in adjusting to school. The results appear to have been very beneficial. Another theory offered to explain the limited success of many Head Start programs is that they come too late. The programs usually take children three to five years old, and many students of child development maintain that the critical years for learning some things and for developing basic human relationships are the first three years of life. Proposals are being made for day-care centers to be established by the federal government for preschool children of working mothers. If these could be competently run, with enough trained help and good equipment, it would almost certainly give children—especially those in poorer areas—a better chance to succeed in school.

Other efforts to raise student achievement include promising new approaches to subject matter and to the problems of teaching. Many teachers and their students find *"the new math"* exciting and stimulating.

This is essentially a new way of organizing and presenting subject matter. Another new method of teaching and learning that some educators believe will have a tremendous impact on our schools is *programmed instruction.* Programmed instruction makes it possible for students to learn many things much more easily than before. It provides printed forms, or electronic devices, by means of which the learner can, independently, go through a whole series of simple steps, or "frames." Each step has been carefully planned, and the answer to each can be immediately checked by the learner.

Besides movies, phonographs, tape recorders, and television, a great variety of mechanical devices are being employed as aids to teaching and learning. Many of these are very helpful. However, the result is not always pure gain. Often, some of the contact between the mind of the teacher and that of the student is lost. A good illustration is excessive dependence on objective tests graded by machines. Many students complain that our large universities are now carrying on mass education and that it is becoming mechanized and impersonal. This was certainly one factor that contributed to the student unrest, demonstrations, and even violence that became a problem on many college and university campuses in the late 1960's.

Recognizing that many children, especially in poor families, watch television a great deal, some educators have made interesting experiments in developing programs that would both entertain children and teach them. In 1970 one of the most successful of these, "Sesame Street," was already appearing on a large number of educational TV stations throughout the country. By watching this program regularly, a child could, among other things, make a good start at learning how to read. Another program that has attracted favorable attention began earlier and operates on a different basis. In "Misterogers Neighborhood" a low-key, friendly approach is used in presenting both fact and fancy.

The Needs of Individual Students. All learning is by individuals, and the ultimate value of anything learned depends directly or indirectly on whether it enables individuals to live more interesting and satisfying lives and to make greater contributions to the social welfare, that is, to the welfare of all.

To provide each child, so far as possible, with the right curriculum is only one aspect of meeting the educational needs of the individual. Another aspect of this problem is to discover the study and learning difficulties of each pupil and to help him solve them. But much of the modern theorizing about treating every child as an individual is idle talk, because in great numbers of schools conditions are allowed to develop that make it impossible for children to get as much personal attention as they usually did a generation or two ago. Small classes, an uncrowded schedule, and a minimum of record-keeping give an intelligent teacher the peace of mind and the time to observe the progress and discover the difficulties of each pupil. She can then give help where needed, remove stumbling blocks, and see to it that each child keeps going forward. Crowded teaching schedules, too many outside activities, large classes, disciplinary problems, and the strain and confusion growing out of these make it impossible for the teacher to discover the difficulties of individual children or to give them much help. Even a requirement that teachers keep individual record cards on the behavior, characteristics, and problems of each child may defeat its avowed purpose, because it may rob the teacher of time that could be better spent in personal contact with the children.

To raise student achievement some schools are experimenting with the *ungraded* system, under which each child is allowed to advance at his own pace. This worked well in many of the old one-room country schools when the teacher was capable and the pupils were few. In some modern ungraded schools, teachers of different subjects work together under a plan called *team teaching*. This appears to have given good results in some schools where the pupil-teacher ratio was not too high. But it is clearly impossible for a teacher, whether working with a team or not, to give effective individual direction to a large number of children when each child may be doing something different. Team teaching is also being experimented with in some graded schools and is thought to be working out well, but the experiments are still too few and too recent to evaluate the desirability of applying this technique to schools everywhere.

How Much Education Should the Average Citizen Receive? How far should the formal education of the average citizen be carried? Should he finish grade school, or high school, or junior college? This is a basic question that must be answered as our school system changes and develops, but there is no simple answer. For every person there is certainly a limit to the time that it is desirable to spend in acquiring a formal education. Where this limit is depends on the temperament, abilities, interests, and purposes of the individual; on the kinds of education available to him; and on the costs that must be met by him, his parents, and the community.

Today few people would question that a grade school education is desirable and is worth the cost for almost everyone. Also, there is rather general agreement in this country that a high school education is desirable and worth the cost for the majority of young people, though perhaps for many of them we are not providing the most helpful kind of curriculum. The situation with respect to higher education is somewhat different, and we may well question whether it is desirable for the great majority of young people to go through a college or university. Many people believe that we should set admission standards that would limit enrollments in four-year colleges and universities. But there seems to be increasing support for the point of view that eventually most young people should have at least the equivalent of a two-year junior college course.

With junior colleges and community colleges becoming more adaptive to the needs of the times, high school graduates can today more easily find the kind of further education that suits their abilities and needs. For those who have no liking for it, there is no magic in the indefinite extension of formal academic education. But it is increasingly difficult for adolescents without training to find jobs. This largely explains the increasing emphasis on providing more vocational schools and also more vocational courses in community colleges.

But what of individuals who are not interested in further schooling and who in some cases may have little ability to benefit from a high level of vocational training? There is still a great deal of relatively unskilled work that needs to be done and for which people would pay if willing workers could be found at reasonable wages. One difficulty is that we have been downgrading the dignity of commonplace work, of jobs that are useful but that provide only small or moderate pay and offer no glamorous future. In doing this we have robbed many young people of limited ability of the chance to learn how to work and, by gaining confidence and experience, to find eventually a useful and independent place in life. Other factors contributing to their problems of finding employment include automation, legal restrictions on the employment of young people, compulsory school-attendance laws, minimum-wage laws, and union rules that limit apprenticeship opportunities.

NEW PROBLEMS COME TO THE FORE

Except perhaps for race conflict, crime, and Vietnam, no problem received more publicity in our news media in the late 1960's than student unrest and the demonstrations and rebellions to which it gave rise in many colleges and universities.

That students had some legitimate grievances is clear. In the first place there was, after World War II and the Korean War, a tremendous expansion of our population of school age and also a great increase in the percentage attending school, especially at the higher levels. Table 12 on page 415 shows that from 1950 to 1970 the number of students in colleges and universities rose from about 2.7 million to 7.5 million. The increase in numbers was too great to be absorbed easily. There was a trend toward mass education. In spite of the establishment of new institutions, many state universities expanded to mammoth size and became "multiversities." There were shortages of money and of competent instructors. Increasing dependence was placed on graduate students for teaching classes and on using professors to lecture to very large groups. Grades were given on the basis of objective tests scored by machines. Education tended to become impersonal with a minimum of human contacts between students and their teachers, with the result that many students felt disappointed, discouraged, and lost. The system had become more or less rigid, and administrators and faculty were so engrossed in their own problems that they failed to pay very serious attention to student problems and complaints.

Some, like Bruno Bettelheim, believe that another reason for student

(Reprinted, courtesy of *The Chicago Tribune*.)

dissatisfaction was that as social pressures and higher family incomes induced a larger and larger proportion of young people to attend a college or a university, their numbers included a great many who had little interest in or aptitude for intellectual pursuits. Bettelheim points out that in earlier societies the great majority of young people did not spend years in the state that we call adolescence. Shortly after puberty they began taking on adult responsibilities. They went to work, married, and began raising families. What makes for adolescent revolt, Bettelheim thinks, is that our society keeps the next generation too long dependent, waiting with angry impatience for the "real" life to come.

Bettelheim believes that universities should be only for those who really seek intellectual adventure, and whose home and school experiences have prepared them for the necessary years of "waiting." The others, he thinks, would be better off with a high level vocational education, closely linked to a work program that would give scope to their needs for physical activity and visible, tangible achievement.

In its 1969 report to the Department of Health, Education, and Welfare, the National Advisory Council on Vocational Education stressed somewhat different aspects of the education problem, but its conclusions lent support to Bettelheim's belief that for the average child we are overemphasizing the desirability of university education. The following quotation is from the report:

Racial unrest, violence, and the unemployment of youth have their roots in inadequate education. . . . At the very heart of the problem is a national attitude that says that vocational education is for somebody else's children. This attitude is shared by businessmen, labor leaders, administrators, teachers, parents, students. . . . We have promoted the *idea that the only good education is an education capped by four years of college. This idea, transmitted by our values, our aspirations and our silent support, is snobbish, undemocratic, and a revelation of why schools fail so many students. The attitude infects the Federal Government, which invests $14 in the nation's universities for every $1 it invests in the nation's vocational-education programs.* [It also, the report notes, affects other levels of government.] *It infects students, who make inappropriate choices because they are victims of the national yearning for educational prestige.*

The attitude must change. The number of jobs which the unskilled can fill is declining rapidly. The number requiring a liberal-arts education, while growing, is increasing far less rapidly than the number demanding a technical skill. In the 1980's it will still be true that fewer than 20 per cent of our job opportunities will require a four-year college degree.

Another factor, emphasized by many in explaining student unrest, is the permissive attitudes toward raising children that became popular with parents a generation or two ago, especially in upper–middle-class circles. Now some of the undisciplined children are in colleges and universities, and many of the permissive parents are presidents, deans, or faculty members. Some critics of higher education think that the coercive and violent aspects of the student revolt would have been brought quickly under control if administrators and faculties had been less permissive and had taken prompt disciplinary measures, with the aid of the police and the courts when necessary, against the perpetrators of such illegal and disruptive activities as seizures of university buildings. They believe that if prompt measures had been taken before success caused these actions to spread, the problem would have been minor.

Other factors also contributed to student unrest. There was the civil rights movement, including the demand by black students for greater and more relevant educational opportunities. There was the Vietnam War and the draft, and the groups who maintained that both were unjust and immoral and who therefore demonstrated against campus ROTC units and university research projects sponsored by the armed forces. Then there were the hard-core leftist activists, a small group chiefly interested in destroying the universities or in using them as instruments to destroy our whole social structure. Another thing must also be kept in mind. While young people strive to grow up and become independent of their elders, they are very sensitive to social pressures from their peer group. Hence, with out modern media of communication, new fashions in dress, speech, ideas, and behavior can spread very fast among them.

Though coercion and violence in colleges and universities can do serious damage to them and to our whole society, student rebellion has had the good result of calling attention to real grievances and to the desirability of listening to students and paying attention to their problems. As a result, many colleges have provided more-effective arrangements for conferences between students and administrators or faculty, and some have accepted

"Actually, I'm a right-of-center business-management major—but haircuts now cost $2.50; dungarees are 6 per cent less than slacks; what I save on shaving-gear gives me a ten-year subscription to 'U.S. News & World Report'—and I pay my broker's commissions by getting suits and jackets at Salvation Army stores." (Courtesy John A. Ruge. Copyright 1969 *Saturday Review, Inc.*)

one or more student representatives as members of their policy-making and executive boards or committees.

Daniel P. Moynihan, President Nixon's former Assistant for Urban Affairs, warned against allowing either the new left or the new right (if we should have one) to impose its particular moral demands upon the processes of our democracy. "Without exception these movements are repressive, and almost without exception they are elitist. Their purpose is to impose the superior values of a minority on the inferior lives of the mass."[6]

THE PROGRESS OF AMERICAN EDUCATION

Not all the developments in American education in recent years have been on the plus side. Education, to be most effective, requires academic freedom, that is, freedom of both faculty and students to express ideas and to discuss and argue them. It also requires order so that intellectual pursuits can be carried on systematically without interruption. When some minority group tries to *force* its ideas and demands upon the major-

[6] See *The American Scholar,* Autumn 1969, pp. 580–581.

ity, both academic freedom and order are endangered. There is no doubt that in many schools and areas the cause of education in this country has been hurt, at least temporarily, by various disruptions, including student sit-ins and boycotts, struggles over integration, and even teacher strikes. And one very serious educational problem that we have not made much progress in solving is what to do about the great number of children, especially in our slums and ghettos, who seem to learn relatively little by attending school. Nevertheless, if we look back over the past hundred, or even the past fifty years, the record of educational progress in this country is impressive. Let us list briefly some of the advances that have taken place:

1. The great majority of teachers have far more education and training than ever before.
2. The quality and variety of textbooks and other teaching materials have, on the average, increased greatly. Also, teaching materials now include motion pictures, recordings, radio, television, and a variety of specialized teaching machines.
3. The findings of educational psychology plus research and experimentation have enabled us to develop some improvements in teaching methods, though at times we seem to have introduced methods that failed, either through lack of adequate research and testing or of proper implementation.
4. We have found new and better ways of organizing and presenting some types of subject matter, for example, mathematics.
5. Our schools meet a wider range of individual needs than in the past. We have a great variety of vocational schools, business schools, schools for the handicapped, technical schools, and professional schools, not to mention correspondence schools and programs of adult education.
6. Even after allowing for inflation, our expenditure per pupil for schools is many times greater than it was in 1900. In 1969 the average expenditure was over $1,000.
7. We have almost completely replaced the typical one-room, ungraded district school with centralized schools that are larger and better equipped.
8. Instead of attending school for only a few weeks or months a year, as was usual a hundred years ago, pupils now go to school eight to ten months a year.
9. Instead of only a small percentage of the population receiving more than three or four years of schooling, now most children complete grade school and more than half of them are graduated from high school.
10. There has been a tremendous expansion of higher education and of college and university enrollments in liberal arts, technical, and professional courses.
11. Finally, within the last decade or two, we have made some prog-

ress toward providing more adequate educational opportunities for students of unusual ability; and we have begun seriously to attack the more difficult problem of finding ways to raise the educational level of the great number of children in our schools who seem unable to learn to read well or to perform elementary mathematical computations.

Terms to Be Understood

education
formal education
informal education
academic freedom
Latin grammar school
academy
secondary school
dual school system
unitary system
progressive education
education for life
  adjustment
land grant college
shared time

general course
fully qualified
  teacher
normal school
content subjects
educationist
8-4-4 system
junior high school
junior college
community college
curriculum
elective system
liberal education
survey course

basic course
core curriculum
general education
academic standards
social promotion
culturally deprived
  children
Head Start program
Montessori-method
  schools
"the new math"
programmed instruction
ungraded school
team teaching

Questions for Review and Discussion

1. Explain the difference between education and socialization.
2. Contrast the functions of education in a democracy and a dictatorship. Is the difference relative or absolute?
3. In what ways has education contributed to the better functioning of our democratic society?
4. Trace briefly the development in the Colonies and later in the United States of the following: (a) elementary education; (b) academies and high schools; (c) colleges and universities.
5. Is a unitary school system more democratic than a dual system? Defend your answer.
6. What were the principal characteristics of the progressive education movement in the United States?
7. Explain the reasons and suggest remedies for geographic differences in educational opportunity.
8. Describe the nature and extent of federal aid to education.
9. What has been done to aid students from low-income families to meet college expenses?
10. What explains the acute financial problems of American public school systems?

11. How are private colleges and universities trying to meet their financial problems?
12. What has happened to the teacher shortage? Why?
13. What was formerly the most common criticism of the curriculums of teachers' colleges? Is this criticism still justified?
14. What charges have been levied against educationists and schools of education by their more-extreme critics? To what extent are these charges now justified?
15. What do you believe could still be done to improve the training of American teachers?
16. What is the traditional structure of the American school system, and why has this structure been criticized? What changes have been made?
17. State and explain the changes that have taken place in the last century in the curricula of our (a) grade schools; (b) high schools; (c) colleges.
18. Why do most colleges require students to elect a "major" field of study? Why have many colleges also introduced "general" courses and core curriculums?
19. Do you think academic standards in our schools are now declining? Why or why not?
20. Why are many high school graduates unable to read or write reasonably well?
21. What were the reasons for the wide introduction of Head Start programs? What are possible reasons for children from these programs losing some of their gains after entering regular schools?
22. Why is it difficult for our public schools to deal effectively with the problems of individual students?
23. Suggest ways for raising the general level of student achievement in our schools.
24. What do you think should be the goals of our primary and secondary schools? of our colleges and universities?
25. Do you think it should be our aim to provide at least two years of college education for most Americans? Discuss both the advantages and drawbacks of this idea.
26. Why is there increasing emphasis on vocational education?
27. Do you agree with the list of factors given in the text as causes of the student unrest of the 1960's? What other causes would you give?
28. List the principal advances in American education over the past hundred years.

For Further Study

Binder, Frederick M., ed., *Education in the History of Western Civilization: Selected Readings,* New York, The Macmillan Company, 1970.

Birch, Herbert G., M. D., and Joan Dye Gussow, *Disadvantaged Children,* New York, Harcourt Brace Jovanovich, Inc., 1970.

Campbell, Roald F., Lucy Ann Marx, and Raphael O. Nystrand, eds., *Education and Urban Renaissance,* New York, John Wiley & Sons, Inc., 1969.

Chall, Jeanne S., *Learning to Read: The Great Debate,* New York, McGraw-Hill, Inc., 1967.

Dewey, John, *The Child and the Curriculum* and *The School and Society,* Phoenix paperback, Chicago, University of Chicago Press, 1956.

DeYoung, Chris A., and D. R. Wynn, *American Education,* 6th ed., New York, McGraw-Hill, Inc., 1968.

Frankel, Charles, *Education and the Barricades,* New York, W. W. Norton & Company, Inc., 1969.

Fuchs, Estelle, *Teachers Talk: Views from Inside City Schools,* New York, Doubleday & Company, Inc., 1969.

Holt, John, *How Children Fail,* paperback, New York, Dell Publishing Company, Inc., 1964.

Hook, Sidney, *Academic Freedom and Academic Anarchy,* New York, Cowles Book Company, Inc., 1970.

Kay, Harry, et al., *Teaching Machines and Programmed Instruction,* paperback, Baltimore, Penguin Books, Inc., 1968.

Kelman, Steven, *Push Comes to Shove: An Escalation of Student Protest,* Boston, Houghton Mifflin Company, 1970.

Keniston, Kenneth, *Young Radicals: Notes on Committed Youth,* New York, Harcourt Brace Jovanovich, Inc., 1968.

Kennan, George F., *Democracy and the Student Left,* paperback, New York, Bantam Books, Inc., 1968.

Leonard, George B., *Education and Ecstasy,* New York, Dell Publishing Company, Inc., 1969.

Margolis, John D., ed., *The Campus in the Modern World,* New York, The Macmillan Company, 1969.

Schwab, Joseph J., *College Curriculum and Student Protest,* Chicago, University of Chicago Press, 1969.

Silberman, Charles E., *Crisis in the Classroom,* New York, Random House, Inc., 1971.

Standing, E. M., *Maria Montessori, Her Life and Work,* Mentor paperback, New York, New American Library, Inc., 1962.

Swomley, John W., Jr., *Religion, the State, and the Schools,* New York, Pegasus, 1969.

Taylor, Harold, *Students Without Teachers: The Crisis in the University,* New York, McGraw-Hill, Inc., 1969.

Umans, Shelley, *The Management of Education: A Systematic Design for Educational Revolution,* New York, Doubleday & Company, Inc., 1969.

Woodring, Paul, *Higher Learning in America: A Reassessment,* paperback, New York, McGraw-Hill, Inc., 1968.

Part Three

Economic
Organization
and
Social
Problems

Chapter 17

The

Organization

of Economic

Activities

conomic wants and economic activities loom large in the lives of the people of every social group. This is necessarily so, because if any group is to survive, it must have certain kinds of goods that are relatively scarce, that is, goods that cannot be had for the asking but whose acquisition or production requires someone to carry on the type of economic activity we usually call labor. The most universal economic want of human beings, one that cannot be denied, is that for food; ever since man first appeared upon the earth, it is pretty certain that most people have spent the greater part of their waking hours in efforts to provide themselves with enough to eat. Only in modern industrial countries has food become relatively plentiful and easy to obtain, so that people have been able to spend a large part of their time and effort in producing other kinds of scarce goods.

As stated in Chapter 2, *economics* is the social science that concerns itself with the ways in which men earn a living. Defined somewhat more precisely *it is the study of the social organization by means of which the people of a society satisfy their wants for scarce goods, including services.* It is not concerned primarily with the activities of individuals but rather with their relations to one another and with the social institutions they have created to facilitate the production, distribution, and consumption of goods. Because earning a living is a very urgent and time-consuming activity in all human societies, economic considerations permeate the whole of human life and have had an incalculably great influence in shaping human cultures and human societies.

Economic Wants and Economic Goods. *Economic wants* are desires for things that can be obtained by labor or through exchange and upon which, in a modern society, a money value can be placed. Not all wants are economic. People want love and affection, respect, health, happiness, and many other things that cannot be measured in money. These things may be affected by the economic circumstances of the individual, but they are not primarily economic. A certain amount of money and the things that money can buy are necessary to sustain life and to make it worth living, but beyond that the relationship is not so clear. Indeed, some observers have asserted that the rate of suicide among millionaires is greater than for the population at large.

The things that money can buy and that are the objects of our economic wants we call *economic goods.* If we possess such goods, we can obtain money or other valuable things in exchange for them. If we wish to acquire them, all that we need do is to offer money, provided we have enough to pay the price demanded. In some cases we can produce them for ourselves if we are willing to apply the necessary labor.

Economic goods have money value because they are desirable and because they are scarce. Because the whole supply is owned or controlled by people, if we want more of such goods than we already have we must either produce them for ourselves or offer something valuable in exchange in order to induce others to part with them.

Economic goods are not necessarily material. They may consist of services like those of a housekeeper or a doctor. Anything the benefits of which can be enjoyed in exchange for a definite sum of money is an economic good. Economic goods in the form of services can be obtained from things as well as from people. If a person wishes to enjoy the benefit of a house, he usually has a choice: he may buy the services of one by the month in return for a payment called rent; or he may buy one outright, thereby obtaining all the benefits it is capable of yielding until it wears out or falls down. But when we wish to enjoy the benefits of a housekeeper or a doctor, we do not have this choice. Because slavery is illegal, we have to be content with buying their services.

Material economic goods—the kind we can see, feel, and accumulate—are called *wealth*. All economic goods take the form of either wealth or services.

The Economic Aspects of Culture. Many of the economic aspects of culture have already been emphasized, especially in the chapters dealing with the natural environment and technology. Man's problems in adjusting himself to his physical environment are largely economic. Their solution requires producing the kinds of goods that the environment demands; for example, in a cold climate, such things as warm clothing, fuel, and well-insulated houses. Technological progress is also largely motivated by man's attempts to improve his economic situation, for it consists principally of two things: first, of finding easier or better methods of producing economic goods; and, second, of devising new kinds of economic goods.

Economic factors also play an important role in shaping the mores and the institutions of every society. Many of our most firmly held beliefs of what is right and wrong have to do with property and property rights, as illustrated by our strong condemnation of theft, robbery, swindling, and embezzlement. Most of our social institutions, even those that are not usually regarded as primarily economic, have economic aspects of major importance. The family is an excellent example of this. When a man and woman marry, they not only signify their intention of living together and establishing a family, but they also undertake important economic obligations. The man, for instance, acquires a legal obligation to support his wife, and both acquire the obligation to support to the best of their ability any children they may have.

Though all social institutions are likely to have their economic aspects, in the modern world many institutions have been developed primarily to serve economic needs. These include credit unions, farmer's cooperatives, insurance companies, manufacturing enterprises, mail-order houses, banks, and many others.

The Nature of an Economy. In modern industrial societies, economic relationships are very complex. Scarcely anything can be produced and made available to the final buyer without the help of a variety of economic institutions and the conscious or unconscious cooperation of great numbers of workers. This is true of almost every commodity, whether it be a shirt, a pair of shoes, a fountain pen, or an automobile. Our ability to satisfy our daily economic wants depends on the existence of many highly systematized social arrangements. Without these our economic efforts would be largely futile, and most of us, especially in the cities, would soon starve to death.

Taken together, all the complex social arrangements by means of which we satisfy economic wants constitute an economic system, or an *economy*. An economy may be defined as *the social organization by means of which the people of a given society produce and distribute economic goods*.

An economy must perform at least four basic functions, and ideally it should perform them in such a way as to confer maximum benefits on the community. It must determine (1) the kinds of goods to be produced, (2) the amount of each good to be produced, (3) the resources that are to be allocated to its output, and (4) the ultimate division of the goods among those who are to enjoy them. In addition, it is very desirable that an economy should provide a favorable environment for economic progress.

The Great Economic Problem. To produce economic goods to satisfy human wants requires resources. These resources, sometimes called *factors of production,* are of three principal types: first, *labor,* or the efforts of human beings; second, *natural resources,* which are the basis of all the material products that man makes; and, third, *capital,* or productive equipment, which includes tools, machines, factory buildings, and all the things that man has made to help him produce more easily and efficiently the kinds of goods he ultimately requires to satisfy his own personal wants. Goods in the form of capital do not *directly* satisfy human wants. Their importance is that they ultimately enable man to produce a much greater quantity and variety of consumer goods than would otherwise be possible, and often goods of a more-desirable kind or quality.

However, all productive resources—labor, natural resources, and capital—are limited in quantity, whereas in modern societies, human wants seem to be practically unlimited. Our own society may be affluent in comparison with others, and a very small minority of its members may have few wants of consequence that remain unsatisfied, but the vast majority find it difficult to stretch their incomes enough to provide all the things they very much desire. *The great economic problem that faces every modern society is to make the scarce resources available satisfy as fully as possible the ever-expanding wants of its members.* But, as has been noted in earlier chapters, we cannot continue indefinitely to satisfy greater and greater economic wants for an ever-increasing population without encountering shortages of resources and more and more pollution of the environment. However, at any given time, we should make the best possible use of the resources that we do employ. This is one aspect of what is called *economizing.*

Economic progress means, more than anything else, increasing the productive power of resources by making advances in technology. As long as technological progress continues in America at the present rate, we should be able, year after year, to satisfy our economic wants more or less adequately provided we can control population and pollution. But there is little reason to suppose that we shall ever be able to achieve an "economy of abundance" if we mean by that expression a society in which all goods are so plentiful that everyone can have everything he wants. For as long a time as we can look into the future, we will need to economize both in our use of resources and in our personal consumption of goods if we wish to maximize our satisfactions by improving the overall quality of life.

THE INCREASING COMPLEXITY OF ECONOMIC RELATIONSHIPS

Though the people of every human society must organize their economic activities to some degree, the forms that economic organization takes vary greatly from one society to another.

The Economic Organization of Primitive Societies. The economies of primitive or, as many anthropologists prefer to call them, nonliterate societies, are not only different from those of modern industrial societies, but they are also much simpler. In primitive groups the family or household is generally the principal economic unit, and the chief division of labor is between the sexes. Certain kinds of work are traditionally done by men, other kinds by women. Except for this, each member of the household usually learns to perform all the various tasks that are necessary to get a living. Because goods are relatively few, this is possible, although it may involve acquiring a considerable variety of skills. When all economic goods are produced by the family group to satisfy its own wants, the need for economic organization is reduced to a minimum. The household is a self-sufficient unit, and there is no need for carrying on trade or other economic relations with the world outside.

Often, however, the economic life of primitive peoples is not quite so simple as the picture painted above would indicate. In many nonliterate societies much work, including agriculture and the building of shelters, is done cooperatively by large groups who come together for the purpose. Also, among some nonliterate peoples certain members of the tribe specialize exclusively in making certain products. A good example of this is the ironworkers' guilds found among some tribes in Africa. Furthermore, there are likely to be a few highly desired commodities, such as salt or iron, that a tribe cannot produce in its own territory, and hence it may be obliged to carry on some trade with the outside world. Nevertheless, the general picture of the economic life of nonliterate peoples includes a relatively small variety of goods, a rather high degree of self-sufficiency of the household and of the tribe, a very limited amount of specialization and trade, and hence a rather simple type of economic organization.

Not only do primitive peoples have fewer goods and simpler types of economic organization than are found in a modern society, but also they are likely to have a very different attitude toward the accumulation of wealth. In most cases private ownership of land is not recognized. This limits the forms in which wealth can be accumulated to personal property of various sorts, sometimes including herds of cattle or sheep. Among some peoples possessions give prestige, and this becomes a major reason for desiring them; but among others prestige seems to be acquired chiefly in other ways, as by courage and skill in hunting. Where the latter is the case, after immediate wants for food, clothing, and shelter have been satisfied, people may have little incentive for making further economic efforts. They know nothing about the comforts, the luxuries, and the fascinating mechanical gadgets available in a modern industrial society. However, once they become familiar with such things, they soon develop a desire to have them.

The difficulty of fully satisfying people's economic wants in a modern industrial society arises in large part from the great variety of goods available and the high cost of many of them. Adequate food, clothing, and shelter are not enough; people are constantly attracted by innumerable comforts and luxuries. Moreover, in an industrial society wealth is always a major source of prestige, especially such forms of wealth as land, fine houses, industrial plants, expensive cars, and large bank accounts. Hence, people seem constantly to be seeking larger incomes and to be competing with one another for the acquisition of wealth.

The Growth of Specialization and Its Economic Effects. Early in human history, populations began to grow in certain parts of the world. In time, cities became established, and tribal organization gave way to larger political units. One result of these developments was a gradual increase of *economic specialization.* Though the majority of people still tended herds or tilled the soil, others in ever greater numbers became government functionaries, professional soldiers, or well-to-do landowners. Still others, especially in the towns and cities, began to concentrate on making certain products, like shoes or clothing, for those people in the population who were no longer economically self-sufficient.

This growth of specialization meant a corresponding growth of trade. Obviously, specialization and trade go together, for people who produce only one or two products are obliged to go into the market and buy everything else they need. Either they must offer their own products directly in exchange for those of others, or they must offer money obtained from the sale of their products.

Trade and the Use of Money. A limited amount of trade can be carried on by *barter,* or *the direct exchange of goods for goods,* but as soon as people begin to depend heavily on trade for satisfying their daily needs, barter becomes impractical. It is too difficult to keep on hand at all times goods that will be acceptable in exchange for the things one wants and whose values will just match the values of the things one wishes to purchase. Storage and transportation present almost insuperable problems. Often, too, it is difficult to estimate the relative values of goods if one has no scale of money prices on the basis of which to make comparisons. A modern economy, in which almost everything is produced for sale, would break down completely if an attempt were made to carry on all trade by barter.

So when specialization and trade develop to any extent, people soon discover that it is convenient to keep on hand some commodity with characteristics that make it readily acceptable in trade. Such a commodity should be more or less durable, easily divided into convenient quantities, fairly valuable, and in general demand. In the early stages of the growth of trade, tobacco might be a good choice. Gradually everyone would become willing to take tobacco in exchange whenever he had anything to sell. He might not want to use it himself, but he would know that he could always pass it on in trade to someone else. As people acquired the custom of making all payments with tobacco, they would also acquire the habit of estimating the values of other goods in terms of pounds or ounces of the same commodity. When this stage was reached, tobacco would be performing the essential functions of money.

Money may be defined as anything that, in a given society, is the common medium of exchange and the common measure, or standard, of value. By the *common medium of exchange* we mean anything that, in a given society, is customarily offered when goods are purchased, or accepted when they are sold. By the *common standard of value* we mean anything that is customarily employed for estimating the exchange values of different kinds of goods and for comparing these values. Earlier societies employed such things as tobacco, beads, and scarce seashells as crude forms of money. The use of such mediums of exchange was a great improvement over direct barter; but in economies where trade assumes really large proportions, people are more likely to use as money gold and silver coins and paper currency. Ultimately, they are also likely to use demand bank deposits that can be transferred by check.

The Growth of Regional Specialization. In very early times, as specialization developed, there appeared a trend toward regional specialization. Among nonliterate peoples some tribes could produce such commodities as iron, salt, or ivory because they lived in areas where these were available, and they might carry such commodities for considerable distances for use in trading with tribes that could not produce them. At least as long ago as the Middle Ages, and perhaps much earlier, spices were grown in the East Indies and transported to the Middle East and even to Europe. But in former times, regional specialization was kept within very narrow limits because of the difficulties, dangers, and high costs of transportation and communication. Only expensive luxury products, or products like salt and iron, small quantities of which might be very necessary to a people, could profitably be transported for any distance.

But as time went on and transportation and communication improved, regional specialization increased. With the discovery of the New World and with improvements in sailing ships, first England and later other countries of Western Europe began to import raw materials from the undeveloped areas of the world; they also began to expend a part of their own energies on the production and export of manufactured goods.

Specialization and Interdependence. Specialization develops because it is profitable to those who engage in it. Some regions can produce goods that others cannot, or can produce them more easily and cheaply. Some individuals, by concentrating on the production of one thing, can acquire such skill and speed that they can turn out a better and cheaper product than would be possible without specialization. But when regions or individuals specialize, they become dependent on others for buying their

38. An Example of Economic Interdependence. Norwegian freighter unloading American truck for British Lumber Company in Darvel Bay, North Borneo. (Photo by author.)

products to give them income, and they become dependent on others for producing the goods they themselves consume. Increasing specialization brings increasing interdependence, along with a greater and greater complexity of economic relationships. As a result, if the economy is to run smoothly, increasingly difficult problems of economic organization must be solved.

Industrialization and Some of Its Major Effects. *Industrialization* of an economy through the introduction of power machines and the factory system increases the complexity of economic relationships in many ways. For one thing, it causes specialization to be carried much further than it otherwise would be. In most cases, machines themselves are highly specialized, because to be efficient they must be designed for particular and limited uses. If one equips a factory to produce shoes, he cannot use it to weave textiles. When the processes of production are highly mechanized, a given plant can seldom produce more than a single product, or at most several closely related products. Using machines also increases specialization in other ways. In an industrial economy there must always be men who specialize in the operation of different types of machines, in the designing of machines, in building and repairing machines, in keeping accounts, in industrial management, and in many other types of work.

Industrialization also greatly increases the quantity and the relative importance of wealth in the form of capital goods—that is, machines and other types of durable productive equipment. It tends to shift the balance of economic power into the hands of the owners of industry and away from those with whom it formerly resided, the owners of land. In an industrial economy, the production of capital goods is an important source of employment and income, but also, unfortunately, an important source of economic instability. This is because in periods of business optimism corporations will buy new plant and equipment on a large scale and thus create work, but in periods of pessimism the demand for such goods may almost completely disappear, with the result that millions of workers lose their jobs.

Industrialization has increased the complexity and the problems of our economy in other ways. It has created very large-scale enterprises in many industries, and this has raised new problems with respect to the organization of enterprises and has greatly increased the importance of efficient business management. It has also created a need for a legal form of business organization that can bring together large amounts of capital and that is relatively permanent, a need that has been met by the development of the modern business corporation.

With the rise of the factory system, large-scale enterprise, and the corporation there developed a relatively small group—some would say a "class" —of capitalists and managers, the people who largely own and control industry. At the same time there developed a large group of industrial workers who soon began to organize unions to strengthen their position in dealing with their employers, and who thus eventually created powerful labor movements.

When an industrial economy operates smoothly and efficiently, it is highly productive. But to keep such an economy operating steadily in high gear presents problems of the greatest difficulty. A modern economy like that of the United States is not only very complex, but it is sensitive to many types of disturbance. Unless the government is always ready and able to take effective countermeasures, it can suffer very severe partial breakdowns. It was such a breakdown that brought on the great depression of the 1930's.

MODERN ECONOMIC SYSTEMS

Though a modern industrial economy is very complex and must be well organized if it is to function properly, that does not necessarily mean that it has to be planned and directly operated by some central authority. There are two principal ways of organizing and operating an industrial economy. The first is to give individuals freedom to own and operate productive enterprises, to depend on their initiative for producing economic goods, to allow them to develop specialized institutions like banks and insurance companies as the need arises, and to rely largely on the impersonal forces of market competition to regulate the economy as a whole. The second is to give some central governmental authority the power to plan, own, and operate directly all productive activities. The first method results in the type of economy called *free enterprise* (also called *private enterprise* or *capitalism*); the second creates the kind of economy called *socialism*.

An economic system based on free enterprise is sometimes called an *unplanned economy* to contrast it with a socialized or *planned economy*. But this is somewhat misleading, because there is always a great deal of planning in a free-enterprise economy. There is planning on the part of private business enterprises, and there is also planning on the part of government to provide conditions that will aid private business, protect the public, and make the whole system work better. But in a free-enterprise economy there is, as already noted, no central planning of all economic activity and no direct central control of the production and distribution of most kinds of goods.

Free Enterprise. Free enterprise, or capitalism, is an economic system that relies on the initiative of private citizens for the production of economic goods. In such a system those who organize and control production must have incentives, and under free enterprise the chief incentive is the possibility of making profits. With some restrictions, anyone who chooses is free to undertake the establishment of almost any kind of business enterprise. He can choose both the products to be produced and the methods to be employed in their production. He can buy materials, labor, and managerial services, and he can sell his products wherever people will buy them and at any price they are willing to pay. His chief problem in getting started is likely to be finding sufficient capital. If the new business is to be small, his own capital plus his personal credit or borrowing power may be sufficient. But if the business is to be larger, his only chance will be to interest other people and induce them to contribute capital as partners or, if a corporation is formed, as stockholders.

There is no such thing as a "pure" or absolute free-enterprise economy, because freedom itself is always relative. When we describe our own economy as a free-enterprise system, we do not mean that anybody can establish just any kind of business without meeting obstacles. We mean that in most cases it is quite feasible for people who can obtain capital, and who have the necessary personal qualities, to organize and operate new business enterprises, and that they have a wide range of freedom in making the decisions involved. But in some industries there are obstacles that would be difficult to overcome. In the automobile industry, for example, the capital required to establish a new company would be huge, and the risk of failure great; and in the public utility industries local monopolies are usually supported by law because this is believed to be in the public interest. Free enterprise, however, means more than the right to start a business. Fully as important is the right of those who already own business enterprises to operate and control them—to determine policies—subject only to necessary and reasonable restrictions.

The difficulty of approaching "purity" in an economic system is probably even greater for free enterprise or capitalism than for socialism. A socialized economy can operate with some degree of success—as in Russia —even when government control has been pushed to extreme limits in practically all fields of production; but the successful operation of a free economy could never be achieved if it were really free of all government control. The government must provide the legal and economic framework and the general rules within which private enterprises operate. Although government participation in economic affairs may be great or small, no government has ever followed a complete policy of *laissez faire,* or "let alone," with respect to the economic activities of private individuals.

The Role of Markets and Prices. In a free-enterprise system, markets and prices play a dominant role in organizing and controlling economic activities. Any commodity that cannot be sold in the market at a profitable price will not be produced, at least not for long, whereas any commodity that can be sold at a profit is pretty certain to be produced by someone sooner or later.

When prices are not regulated and when markets are highly competitive, price changes keep adjusting production to consumption, and consumption to production. For simplicity, let us assume that by a competitive market we mean one in which there are many small independent sellers of the same product and many independent buyers.[1] Under these conditions, if people wish to increase their purchases of a commodity, the resulting increase of demand will cause the price to rise, with the effect that production will be stimulated. However, the rise in price will restrict the increase of market demand. On the other hand, if people decide to decrease their purchases, the price will fall, and this will discourage production; but the lower price will tend to limit the decline of sales and consumption. If more of the commodity is still being produced and offered for sale than people are willing to buy, the price will drop even further. In very competitive markets, the price always tends to rise or fall until the amount of a commodity that is being produced and offered for sale is just equal, at the market price, to the amount that consumers are willing to buy.

Figure 16 is far too simple to take account of all the conditions in a real market, but it does illustrate the tendency under competition for the price of a commodity to rise or fall until *market demand* (the amount of a product that people are willing to buy at a given price and time) equals *market supply* (the amount that others are willing to sell). The vertical Y-axis measures the price of potatoes per bushel; the horizontal X-axis measures bushels. The *demand curve, DD,* shows the number of bushels buyers would be willing to purchase at different prices in the market, say a town, on a certain day. The *supply curve, SS,* shows the number of bushels sellers would be willing to offer at different prices on the same day. The point of intersection, *P,* shows that under the assumptions made in constructing these curves, the *market* price would tend to be two dollars. The price

---

[1] This situation approximates what economists sometimes call *pure* or *perfect* competition. But competition exists in various degrees and different forms. Even a monopolist is likely to be subject to *vertical* competition. This will be discussed in Chapter 18.

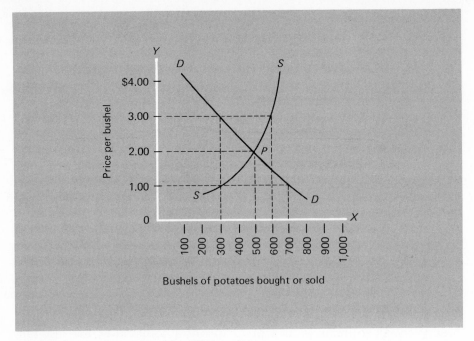

Figure 16. Determination of Equilibrium Price.

could not, for example, stay at three dollars, for then buyers would only take three hundred bushels whereas sellers would offer six hundred bushels. Because there are many competing sellers, some would soon reduce their prices as they saw that sales were lagging. Likewise, the price could not stay at one dollar, for in that case buyers would want seven hundred bushels, but sellers would offer only three hundred. As soon as buyers sensed that there were not enough potatoes to go around, some would raise their offers. Only at the *equilibrium price* of two dollars would the forces of supply and demand be in balance, for at that price buyers would be willing to take five hundred bushels, just the amount that sellers would offer.

The Role of Government Under Free Enterprise. In a society like that of the United States, where most people believe strongly in the free-enterprise principle, governments at all levels—local, state, and national—usually avoid carrying on productive activities that could just as well be undertaken by private business. But even in a free-enterprise economy, the government must, as already noted, provide the legal and economic framework within which businesses operate. One very important function is to establish and maintain a sound monetary system. Other government activities that are essential or helpful include maintaining law and order, protecting property rights, enforcing contracts, granting patents, protecting the rights of workers and consumers, and providing statistics and other types of information for the aid of businessmen and of citizens generally.

Most economists believe that government should also, except in special cases, assume responsibility for maintaining free and competitive markets, and that it should use its taxing, spending, and monetary powers to maintain a reasonably stable price level and a satisfactory rate of production and employment.

Government units at all levels provide, without any direct charge, various essential public services of the kind not practical or desirable to sell on a commercial basis. Examples are the building and maintenance of roads, parks, and public schools, and the improvement and development of harbors and navigable rivers. In certain cases where the public interest is very directly involved, government units also produce services for sale. In the United States the Post Office and the Tennessee Valley Authority (TVA) are notable examples.

Though governments under free enterprise produce relatively few goods or services for sale, they regulate private business in many ways, and the extent of government regulation of business tends to increase as the economy becomes more complex and as business units become larger.

The expansion of the economic activities of government is not necessarily either good or bad. Some of it is very necessary and desirable. Sometimes, however, government economic controls benefit favored groups at the expense of the public; and sometimes, when they are based on a misunderstanding of how the economy operates, they injure in the long run almost everyone by creating effects entirely different from those intended.

The Relation of Free Enterprise to Personal Freedom. Freedom, as we have said, is a matter of degree, and it is quite conceivable that some personal freedoms could be preserved in a society with a completely socialized economy. Those who favor socialism even advance the doubtful proposition that many new freedoms would be created. But to abolish free enterprise would certainly destroy or restrict some important personal freedoms. The effects of such action would not be limited to taking away from the man of wealth and influence his freedom to organize and operate a large business. It would also take away from the substantial and ambitious middle-class citizen his right to establish a restaurant, a filling station, or a garage; and it would take from the farmer what freedom he still has to choose the crops he plants and to sell them where he pleases, for his own profit. It would greatly reduce the consumer's freedom of choice. Under capitalism he can choose from a great number and variety of commodities, produced and offered for sale by innumerable private business enterprises, each of which tries to outdo the others for the consumer's favor. In a fully socialized economy the consumer's only choices would be among goods that the government might decide to have produced.

Even in the special case of products whose manufacture, in a free-enterprise economy, is concentrated in the hands of a few firms, it seems quite unlikely that consumers would have the degree of choice under socialism that they enjoy under capitalism. Take passenger automobiles as an illustration. Though the number of legally and financially independent

American producers can be counted on the fingers of one hand, each keeps striving to gain a larger share of the market by offering consumers a variety of models and by frequently changing these in the hope of making a stronger appeal to consumer desires. Moreover, in recent years our domestic automobile producers have had to meet important competition from foreign imports. But in a fully socialized economy all automobiles would be produced by the government, and, as a complete monopolist, the pressures upon it to cater to the tastes of the public would not be nearly as great as those now felt by private producers. If the government chose, it could completely forbid the importation of foreign cars. The government might avoid "built-in obsolescence" resulting from needless changes in styling, but as a complete monopolist it would be under little pressure to raise quality or to introduce other desirable improvements.

Socialism. An economic system under which society as a whole takes the primary responsibility for producing economic goods is called *socialism*. This is defining socialism as equivalent to direct public control of production. As will be noted later, the term often has a more restricted meaning. Under socialism the agency directly responsible for production would be the government, because in an industrial society government is the only organization that represents the entire social group. In a fully socialized economy there would be no private business enterprises, because all means of production would be owned and operated by the government through government employees. An individual might still be allowed to own personal possessions, even his house; he might also be allowed to leave his job without special permission and to seek employment in any of the various productive establishments operated by the government. Whether he would be allowed these privileges would depend on the policies of the socialist government. Under socialism, wages would not necessarily be equal. Most socialists advocate paying workers wages that reflect in some degree the importance of their services, making due allowance for training, skill, ability, and experience.

Though complete socialization would eliminate all private business, there are many socialists who advocate only partial socialization. Under their plan, the government would take over only the major basic industries, such as banking, coal, steel, the railroads, and other public utilities. The great majority of industries would continue to be privately operated.

Communism. As we shall see later, *communism* is very different from socialism as the latter expression is understood by the socialist parties of the Western world; but communism is a form of socialism if we use the latter term in its narrow economic sense to apply to any social system in which the means of production are socially controlled and operated. In modern Russia, which calls itself the Union of Soviet Socialist Republics, the economy is almost completely socialized. Nevertheless, Russia does not operate according to communist ideals as these are described by communist writers. We call the Russians communists because in theory they are trying to establish a communist society, but the Russian leaders themselves make no claims of having, as yet, achieved this goal.

In the early nineteenth century, a number of small, experimental communities were established on communist principles both in the United States and abroad, but none of them have survived. Those with a religious background—like the Shaker colony at Oneida, New York—were the most successful.

In a society actually operating on communist principles all means of production would be completely socialized; but it is not entirely clear whether that would mean that all productive undertakings would be owned and operated by the state. Communist ideology assumes that ultimately the state will "wither away."[2] Presumably after the state had withered away, production would be carried on by cooperative groups of workers in complete harmony and without any need for coercion.

In the ideal society envisioned by the communist theorists the citizen would be completely free of coercion by the state, and he would be so happy about his position that he would voluntarily accept all his social responsibilities. Social classes would disappear. Everyone would work, the entire product of the economy would go to labor, and all workers would have equal rights to share it. They would share, however, not equally but according to need. If money was used as a medium of exchange, presumably wages would be paid to workers according to their needs. In any case, certain basic essential goods would be provided free to all citizens.

Quite obviously, this ideal communist society bears little resemblance to modern Russia. We shall explain later the relation between the two.

Origins of Socialist and Communist Ideology. Early in the nineteenth century there developed in England a movement that came to be called *utopian communism,* or sometimes *utopian socialism.* Robert Owen was one of the leaders of this movement. The concept of the ideal society held by the utopian communists was in some respects similar to that held by modern Russian theorists. Their method for attaining such a society was, however, very different. They believed that communism could be brought about by education and by the voluntary acceptance and spread of communistic ideals and practices. The setting up of small groups who would follow and exemplify communist principles was to be the beginning of this movement. The Russian communists, however, believe that communism can be brought about only by overturning capitalist governments, and they are quite willing to use force if necessary.

Many, though not all, of the theories and policies of the Russian communists are explained by the fact that they are followers of Karl Marx. Marx, a brilliant German economist and revolutionist, worked out a sys-

---

[2] This may be interpreted to mean not the complete disappearance of government as an administrative mechanism but the complete disappearance of any need for controlling people by force.

tematic theory of the development of society and in particular of the "inevitable" downfall of capitalism. He was a firm believer in the doctrine of the economic determination of history, or the theory that the whole course of human events is shaped by economic forces. This is a very plausible theory, but most modern thinkers are convinced that it is false. Though economic factors have played a very important role in human history, other factors have also had a major influence.

Greatly simplified, Marx's theory of the downfall of capitalism ran somewhat as follows: Because of the advantages of large-scale production, big business would ultimately eliminate the small businessman and hence the middle class. There would be left in society only, on the one hand, a small group of *capitalists* controlling the means of production and, on the other hand, a large group of wage earners—the *proletariat*. The capitalists would then increasingly exploit the workers so that their position would become progressively worse. Finally, a struggle would develop between the classes, and the proletariat, becoming conscious of its power, would revolt, seize the government by force, dispossess the capitalists, and take over and operate industry for the workers. At first the new government would be a "dictatorship of the proletariat," but eventually, through a process of education and adjustment, the ideal communist society would emerge. Marx soon began to attract small groups of followers in various European countries.

The democratic socialist movements of England and western Europe have accepted some of Marx's ideas, but, unlike the communists of Russia, they have rejected the use of force. Though they do not believe, as did some of the utopian communists, that socialism can be achieved by establishing small voluntary communities, they do believe that it can be brought about at the polls through democratic political action. They are democrats first and socialists second.

The Russian communists are not willing to wait for victory at the polls; for that matter, they are not even willing, as was Marx, to wait for the proletariat to revolt. Their method is to develop a small elite group of revolutionists, "the party," inculcate in them iron discipline and unquestioning obedience to their leaders, and then seize power. Because this seizure of power is presumably for the ultimate purpose of creating the ideal communist society, the end is held to justify any means whatever, including treachery, deceit, treaties they have no intention of honoring, torture, and murder.

After the Russian revolution of 1918, the international communist movement came under the control of Moscow. Since then communism has applied "Trojan horse" tactics by seeking to establish communist groups in all capitalist countries. The expectation is that when the time is ripe, these groups will seize power and establish communist dictatorships, as, for example, they did in Cuba. Though the long-range communist aims have changed very little since the Russian revolution, in recent years serious dissension and enmity have arisen within the communist ranks, notably

"And what did Karl Marx have to say about a tired, run-down feeling?" (Drawing by Muccio. © 1964 *The New Yorker Magazine, Inc.*)

between the Russian and Chinese communist leaders. This dissension seems chiefly to concern the policies to be employed in achieving the communist objective of bringing the whole world under communism.

Mixed Economies. We can set up ideal concepts of free enterprise, socialism, or communism, but no real society would closely fit any one of them. Every economy is likely to contain at least some of the characteristics of each of these systems. It is also likely to have some unique institutions that distinguish it from other economies that, in their basic nature, may be rather similar.

When an economy contains, as it usually does, significant elements of more than one economic system, it may be called a *mixed economy.* As a rule, however, we classify economies on the basis of the system that seems to be dominant.

The Economic System of the United States. The United States is usually regarded not only as an example of free enterprise or capitalism but as the outstanding example. This is a reasonable point of view, because the predominant characteristics of our American economy are definitely those of free enterprise. To some degree, however, we actually have a *mixed* economy, because our American system not only contains elements of socialism but even, if one searches for them, elements that can be regarded as communistic.

Though private business predominates in the United States, as already noted, many enterprises are publicly owned, and they very definitely constitute a step in the direction of socialism. They account, to be sure, for a small fraction of our national output, but their total number is considerable.

Government regulation of business is another step that the United States has taken in the direction of socialism. Free enterprise means more than nominal ownership of business; it means also control of enterprises by their owners. In the United States private owners of business firms still have wide powers of control. Nevertheless, there has been a significant restriction of these powers in recent years, especially in the public utility industries. For business in general, restrictions have taken such forms as safety and health regulation, minimum wage legislation, controls over collective bargaining, social security requirements, and sometimes regulation of prices and of the use of raw materials.

Elements in our economy which might be regarded as communistic include the sharing of goods on the basis of need within the family group, and the provision by government, without charge, of such services as fire protection, the use of parks, and public education.

The British Economy. We have used the word *socialism* to refer broadly to any economy in which the government owns and controls the means of production. However, most of the groups who today call themselves socialists use the term in a much narrower sense. To them socialism usually means an economic and social system similar to that developed in Great Britain by the Labour Party after World War II.

The program of the British Labour, or socialist, Party calls for only partial socialization of the economy. Though several basic industries were taken over by the government while the party was in power, the great majority of business enterprises remained in private hands. What this policy actually created was a mixed economy, but one in which free enterprise was still dominant. Socialization probably affected directly less than 20 per cent of British output.

While they were in power after World War II the British socialists tried to carry out three major policies. First, certain basic industries were nationalized. Second, certain important welfare services were provided for the people by the government, notably free medical and hospital service. Third, democratic institutions, including free elections, were scrupulously preserved and in so far as possible strengthened.

The British socialists believe firmly in overall economic planning. They maintain that if the government owns and operates basic industries, it can guide the economic activity of the whole country in such a way as to raise output and standards of living. This would be accomplished by such methods as eliminating needless duplication of plants or products and spreading production out evenly over time. Unfortunately, we can draw no very definite conclusions about the economic effects of socialism by studying conditions in postwar Britain, because many of the difficulties experienced by the country were the aftermath of World War II. But it is interesting to note that the results actually achieved in the nationalized industries of Britain did not lend impressive support to the claims that socialism can increase production. For example, in the coal industry under nationalization, absenteeism of workers rose to a level more than twice as high as that under private ownership; and in spite of an increase in the needs of British industry for coal in the early postwar years, as late as 1953, production was still below the rate of output in 1937. Today coal-production figures are not very significant because in recent years Britain and western Europe have shifted increasingly to the use of imported oil, natural gas, and atomic reactors.

On the return of the Conservatives to power in 1951, the socialization program was halted and to a limited extent reversed. The steel industry was returned to private ownership; some of the commodity exchanges were reopened in order to re-establish private trading at competitive prices; and finally, in 1954, the last price and rationing controls were removed from consumer goods. Perhaps this last action would have been taken even if the Labour Party had remained in power, but of that there is some doubt. However, many of the economic changes made by the Labour government were retained. In late 1964 the Labour Party returned to power under Prime Minister Harold Wilson and, after some delay, redeemed its pledge to renationalize the steel industry. But in 1970 the Conservatives again regained power under Prime Minister Edward Heath; however, there is as yet no evidence that they plan any major changes in the organization of the British economy.

During the last fifteen years Britain has participated in the unparalleled prosperity of western Europe, but it has not experienced an economic expansion comparable to that of West Germany. Some observers believe that the German expansion has been greater because of the willingness of the German government to go further in reducing business burdens and restrictions and in encouraging private enterprise. The Germans actually transferred some government industries, among them Volkswagen, to private ownership.

Prosperity and rising standards of living under capitalism have changed the policies of the socialist parties of western Europe. In some countries, while still advocating the expansion of welfare policies, they are no longer urging the nationalization of industry.

The Russian Economy. We have used *communism* to refer to the ideal society of the communist theorists, but the word is more often used simply to designate the social system and the political and economic policies of present-day Russia or China. The social system and the policies of both countries are basically similar, but there are important differences that result from differences in leadership and in the stage of economic development.

Looked at from an economic point of view, modern Russia represents almost complete socialization. Factories, stores, and other capital goods are owned by the state, and nearly all productive activities, even farming, are carried on under state control. Very few vestiges of private enterprise remain. Perhaps peasant families are allowed small plots of land on which to raise crops for their own consumption, with the privilege of selling anything they do not use themselves; but beyond that, little remains of private business enterprise.

The effect of communism on Russian living standards is difficult to determine. These have always been low compared with western Europe, though they appear to have risen somewhat since czarist times. The rate of improvement appeared to accelerate in the 1950's but how much it accelerated is uncertain. About a decade ago, based on figures issued by the Russian government, American statisticians estimated that the output of the Soviet economy had increased at an average rate of 8 per cent annually during the 1950's. This was more than twice our own rate of expansion for the same period. Later, however, considerable doubt was cast on the reliability of the Russian statistics. In 1962 an exhaustive study of Soviet industrial expansion was made in this country by the National Bureau of Economic Research. As a result, G. Warren Nutter, who headed the project, estimated that Soviet industrial production in 1961 was less than 30 per cent as great as ours, instead of the more than 60 per cent claimed by Russian economists. Since then, whatever the statistics, it has become clear that the Russians have encountered many problems and that output has not risen according to plans.

Though the overall output of the Russian economy is still low compared with that of the United States, no one doubts that it can produce scientific and technical products of a very high quality when those who control it direct their best industrial, technical, and scientific talent in a given direction. This has long been known and is evidenced by their space program and the quality of their military weapons. Nevertheless, most foreign observers of Russian production report that there appears to be widespread inefficiency in the use of labor. In many cases this amounts to "concealed unemployment," in that workers are kept on a job when there is no apparent need for them. The most striking contrast between the Russian economy and ours is in the efficiency of farm labor. In the United States we employ less than 10 per cent of our labor force on our farms, and with this we produce enough food not only to maintain a high average level of nutrition for our population but also to provide substantial food surpluses. Russia, on the other hand, employs over 40 per cent of its labor force on the land and, in spite of this great use of manpower, is frequently plagued by shortages and is able to provide her people with a much less varied diet than our own.

In a country where all productive activities are directly controlled by the government, the economic system is little more than an extension of the political system. Politically, modern Russia is a police state, a dictatorship and a despotism. As compared with the Western democracies, personal liberties are few. Restrictions are still put on travel and changing jobs. Freedom of speech is very limited, and anyone suspected of opposing the regime is likely to be seized by the secret police and held without trial. When Nikita Khrushchev succeeded Josef Stalin, there was a relaxation of control by terror, but the basic system remained the same and the terror could readily be revived. Khrushchev's successor as secretary of the Communist Party, Leonid Brezhnev, seems to have partly reversed Khrushchev's more liberal policies.

Though the Russian communist state has employed some of the language and forms of democratic government, these have little meaning. This is well illustrated by the holding of elections. Only the Communist Party is allowed to present a candidate for each office; thus, all that the voters can do is to rubber-stamp the choice of the regime in power.

ECONOMIC SYSTEMS OF THE FUTURE

It is always intriguing to try to look into the future, but it is also somewhat baffling, because we know that most long-range prophecies turn out to be wrong. During the present century, even if we overlook the communist countries, there has been a strong trend toward socialization in the industrially advanced countries of the world. It has been least noticeable in the United States and Canada, much more marked in western Europe. Is this trend a result of underlying factors that eventually will bring the downfall of free enterprise everywhere?

Some observers believe it is just that. They see socialism as a "wave of the future" that cannot be resisted. Perhaps in the United States it will come slowly as *creeping socialism* and not as any definite decision to make a changeover; but they believe that enterprises will keep growing larger and economic interdependence will keep increasing, until the forces of the market will no longer be able to bring about the adjustments that are required in a private-enterprise economy if it is to function reasonably well. This, they think, will mean increasing government intervention. As government intervention increases and free markets tend to disappear, capitalism will work more and more badly, because it can operate efficiently only in reasonably free markets. The end result, they say, will be complete socialization. Some see "liberalism" as a major force contributing to this result. American liberals, in their view, are committed to a policy of trying to cure all social ills by expanding the controls of the federal government over all phases of social life.

On the other hand, it is obvious that our present American economy, with free enterprise as its most outstanding characteristic, has achieved remarkable advances in productivity and has given us a standard of living that can be matched nowhere else in the world. It is also apparent that most Americans want to maintain our present system. Of course they want to improve it, because progress is part of the American credo of social values. But the idea that the government should produce everything and employ everyone does not appeal to them.

Many economists do not believe that there is any inevitability about socialism in this country, at least not so far as the foreseeable future is concerned. They believe that if we choose, we can retain free enterprise indefinitely, remedy weaknesses that we find in it, and make it work even better than in the past. Much depends on our political decisions in the next fifty years. Today, it seems fair to say, the Democratic Party tends to push toward socialization, whereas the Republican Party tends to hold back. Both parties, however, respond in varying degree to whatever are the dominant social and political pressures at any given time, and both contain strongly liberal and strongly conservative elements.

If America's free enterprise survives, it will not, of course, be "pure" free enterprise; but that is something it never has been. New kinds of economic controls may be necessary; however, if they are of the right kind, so the argument goes, they need not seriously restrict the freedom and progress of private business. Further attention will be given in Chapters 18 and 19 to the economic controls required even in a free-enterprise economy.

Terms to Be Understood

economics
economic wants
economic goods
wealth
an economy
factors of production
labor
capital
economizing
economic
  specialization
barter

money
common medium
  of exchange
common standard
  of value
industrialization
an unplanned economy
a planned economy
free enterprise
capitalism
laissez faire
market demand

market supply
demand curve
supply curve
equilibrium price
socialism
communism
utopian
  communism
capitalists
proletariat
mixed economy
creeping socialism

Questions for Review and Discussion

1. Give examples of wants that are economic and of wants that are not.
2. What are some of the more important ways in which economic factors have influenced the development of human culture?
3. What four important functions must every economy perform?
4. What is "the great economic problem"? Can we ever solve it completely? Explain.
5. Describe the general character of economic organization among nonliterate tribal peoples.
6. Why do the attitudes of primitive peoples toward the acquisition of wealth often differ from those found in a modern society?
7. Explain the relationship of specialization to trade, to economic interdependence, and to productive efficiency.
8. Why did the use of money replace barter as a means of carrying on trade?
9. List and explain the more important economic effects of industrialization.

10. Why is there no such thing as a "pure" free-enterprise economy?
11. Explain how price adjustments tend to equalize production and consumption in a free-enterprise economy.
12. Describe the role of government in a free-enterprise economy.
13. Explain the relationship of communism to socialism.
14. Would there be less personal freedom under socialism than under capitalism? Defend your answer.
15. Contrast the ideal communist society with modern Russia.
16. Summarize the social doctrines of Karl Marx.
17. Contrast the doctrines of the English socialists with those of the Russian communists.
18. Does the United States have a free-enterprise economy or a mixed economy? Explain.
19. Compare the economic and political systems of the United States with (a) those of England; (b) those of Russia and China.
20. Do you favor socializing all major industries in the United States? Why or why not?
21. Do you believe that socialism is inevitable in this country whether we want it or not? Give reasons for your answer.

For Further Study

Firth, Raymond, and B. S. Yamey, eds., *Capital, Saving, and Credit in Peasant Societies,* Chicago, Aldine Publishing Company, 1964. Studies by direct observation in communities in Asia, Oceania, the Caribbean, and Middle America.

Hayek, Friedrich A., *Collectivist Economic Planning,* New York, Augustus M. Kelley, Publishers, 1967.

Hazlitt, Henry, *Economics in One Lesson,* paperback, New York, Macfadden-Bartell Corp., 1962.

Heilbroner, Robert, *Making of Economic Society,* 2d ed., paperback, Englewood Cliffs, N.J., Prentice-Hall, Inc., 1968.

————, *The Worldly Philosophers,* rev. ed., paperback, New York, Simon and Schuster, Inc., 1967.

Hunt, Elgin F., and Jules Karlin, eds., *Society Today and Tomorrow,* paperback, New York, The Macmillan Company, 1967. See therein "Economic Organization and Free Enterprise" by Paul A. Samuelson.

Hunt, R. Carew, *The Theory and Practice of Communism,* Pelican paperback, Baltimore, Penguin Books, Inc., 1963.

Richards, Aubrey L., *Hunger and Work in a Savage Tribe,* Meridian paperback, Cleveland, World Publishing Company, 1964.

Turgeon, Lynn, *Contrasting Economies: A Study of Modern Economic Systems,* 2d ed., paperback, Boston, Allyn & Bacon, Inc., 1963.

Umbreit, Myron H., Elgin F. Hunt, and Charles V. Kinter, *Fundamentals of Economics,* 3d ed., New York, McGraw-Hill, Inc., 1957. See therein Chaps. 1 and 2.

Wilcox, Clair, et al., *Economies of the World Today,* 2d ed., paperback, New York, Harcourt Brace Jovanovich, Inc., 1967.

Wilczynski, J., *The Economics of Socialism,* Chicago, Aldine-Atherton, 1971.

Wright, David M., *Capitalism,* paperback, Chicago, Henry Regnery Company, 1962.

Chapter 18

The

American

Economy

most of us know that the United States is the wealthiest and most productive country in the world, but probably few realize how great is our advantage over the rest of mankind. We may therefore find it interesting to compare per capita income in other countries, expressed in our own dollars, with per capita income in the United States. In the year 1968, average per capita personal income in this country was over $3,578. Next, but trailing well behind, were Sweden, $2,905; Switzerland, $2,294; Canada, $2,247; Denmark, $1,960; West Germany, $1,928; France, $1,927; and Australia, $1,807. Trailing somewhat was Great Britain (once near the top of European countries in average personal income) with $1,451. Russia, there is reason to believe, was somewhat further down the scale, though no dependable recent estimate seems to be available. But as we go to other parts of the world, the drop becomes rapid: Japan, $1,122; Venezuela, $803; Bolivia, $147; Kenya, $107; India, $77; and Malawi, $52.[1]

Money income is not, to be sure, the only factor that enters into the relative welfare of different national groups; furthermore, some of the above estimates of per capita income may not be very accurate. Nevertheless, they serve to dramatize the fact that extreme differences in income and economic well-being exist among the nations of the world, and they suggest that the writer who said that one half of the human race goes to bed hungry every night may not have been far from the truth. Today the United States, with about 6 per cent of the people of the world, has about one third of world income. Probably this relative advantage will diminish somewhat as industrialism progresses in other countries. However, that depends on developments of which we cannot be certain. A decade or more ago, economic expansion seemed to be lagging in this country, but later it returned to a high level. In 1970 it slowed again because of efforts by the government to control inflation.

The Rising Productivity of the American Economy. In the chapter on technology we called attention to the extraordinary growth of the American economy in the last 150 years or more. We noted not only the phenomenal increase of population and total output but also the tremendous rise in *productivity,* or output per man-hour. Actually, average output per man-hour for the whole economy is difficult to measure in a meaningful way, and if we go back more than sixty or seventy years, data become so scanty that estimates of productivity are only educated guesses. A fairly safe guess is that productivity in the United States has increased more than fifteen times since, let us say, the War of 1812; but the United States Department of Commerce, in *Historical Statistics of the United States, Colonial Times to 1957,* carries its index of productivity for the whole economy back only to 1889. Even since that year, output per man-hour has increased about six times.

Expansion of the American economy during its long period of growth has not been steady and uninterrupted. Occasionally there have been setbacks. The worst of these was the great depression that was ushered in by the stock market crash of 1929. But sooner or later, after each setback, total production, per capita income, and employment have risen to higher levels than ever before.

During the long depression of the 1930's, most Americans looked back on 1929 as a year of unprecedented prosperity, the like of which might never return. Yet today the output of our economy makes that of 1929

[1] Data from *United Nations Statistical Yearbook,* New York, Publishing Services of the United Nations, 1969.

look meager in comparison. By 1970, production and income were so great that, in spite of a population increase of nearly 85 million and a much higher level of taxes, the purchasing power of the average American was about double that of 1929.

Purchasing Power in the United States and Russia. Because so much has been said in recent years about the efforts of the Soviet Union to catch up with the United States in production, it is interesting to compare the purchase cost of consumer items in the two countries as measured in hours of labor. In any country the standard of living of the people depends largely on what they can buy with their labor.

Figure 17 is based on a study made by Keith Bush, an economic analyst for Radio Liberty. The situation that he found in 1969 is very similar to that revealed by a study made by the United States Department of Labor in 1962. The Figure shows the time that a Moscow worker must spend on

TO BUY BREAD - AND LUXURIES.....	A RUSSIAN WORKS	AN AMERICAN WORKS
A loaf of bread (1 pound)	12 minutes	6 minutes
A TV set (23-inch screen)	695 hours	57 hours
A month's rent for modest apartment (3 bedrooms, unfurnished)	11 hours	38 hours
A small car (including taxes)	5,716 hours	720 hours
A sirloin steak (1 pound)	132 minutes	24 minutes
A pound of butter	161 minutes	20 minutes
A local phone call	2 minutes	2 minutes
A pack of cigarettes (20)	15 minutes	9 minutes
A bar of soap (small)	25 minutes	2 minutes
A man's haircut	39 minutes	46 minutes
A subway fare	5 minutes	5 minutes
A washing machine (automatic)	204 hours	53 hours
A refrigerator (small)	343 hours	32 hours
A man's business suit	197 hours	13⅓ hours
A man's cotton shirt	11½ hours	1 hour
A man's pair of shoes (black)	49 hours	4½ hours
A pound of new potatoes	9 minutes	2 minutes

Comparisons based on average monthly take-home pay in April, 1969, after deductions for income tax and social security of $119.28 for Russian worker and $460.09 for American worker. Prices: Moscow and New York, April, 1969.

Figure 17. To Buy Bread and Luxuries . . . . (Reprinted from *U.S. News & World Report.* Copyright 1969 U.S. News & World Report, Inc.)

the job, in comparison with a New York worker, in order to purchase a given amount of certain standard and representative consumer items. It will be seen that to purchase most items required from two to twelve times as many hours' work in Moscow as in New York.

It is true that the Russian worker is provided with free medical care, education, and pensions and also with very low-cost housing. However, the housing shortage is so great that the majority of Moscow families still live in one or two rooms and share bathroom and kitchen facilities with other families.

WHY OUR ECONOMY IS SO PRODUCTIVE AND PROGRESSIVE

We have pointed out that the economy of the United States is unique in that it produces more goods and provides more income per capita than any other economy in the history of the world. Does this give us a perfect society? Far from it. But it does give us a greater potential power than poorer societies to eliminate extreme poverty and to ameliorate many social ills. Yet even we must avoid waste if we are to maximize social progress, and we must set priorities for the use of our resources. We are not so affluent that we can satisfy all the personal desires and social needs that work, goods, and an advanced technology can help to meet.

Because a high rate of production can contribute so much to personal and social welfare, it is important that we should understand why we have been able to raise our economic output to its present high level. Otherwise there is always danger of drifting into policies that are well intentioned but that in the long run tend to stop progress and bring about retrogression.

Individual Initiative and the Profit Motive. No one who has studied American history can doubt the role that individual initiative has played in the growth of our economy from pioneer days to the present. Individual initiative, it is true, has also played a major role in the development of other capitalist economies. But in the New World the opportunities for bettering one's economic position have been greater than in the countries of western Europe. Educational opportunities have been less restricted, social classes have been less rigid, fewer restraints have been placed on business enterprise, and, finally, a large supply of natural resources has been available to those who have had the foresight and the energy to utilize them. Slowly, however, we have learned that these resources are not unlimited.

Today our economy is complex and highly industrialized, yet there are probably as many opportunities as ever for men with energy, ideas, and ambition to organize business enterprises and make profits; and in spite of high taxes, profits can still be very substantial for the successful. To be sure, some opportunities, such as settling on free land, are gone; and in a number of industries, the need for producing on a very large scale makes entry of newcomers almost impossible. But even our mass-production industries, like steel and automobiles, create many opportunities for the successful operation of small enterprises. The automobile industry is a good example. Not only do the large automobile manufacturers buy parts and materials from thousands of small suppliers, but the cars they produce also provide innumerable opportunities for the establishment of dealerships, repair shops, gas stations, and similar enterprises. Opportunities to go into business are numerous in other fields. In retailing and in the service industries many thousands of new concerns are established every year, most of them with a relatively small amount of capital. Though a large proportion of these do not survive, others grow and become highly successful.

But if it is still relatively easy to start a new business in this country and to carry it on successfully, it is only easy for those people who have special qualifications. The necessary qualifications include initiative, intelligence, imagination, the willingness to take risks, and the willingness to work. Also very important is the ability to win the respect and confidence of other people, for the man who organizes a new business of any size is likely to have to obtain most of the needed capital by inducing others to invest in his enterprise. Business opportunities are, of course, not limited to the possibilities of starting new concerns. In old, established enterprises, including the industrial giants themselves, there are many opportunities for men of initiative and ability. It is from such men that big business must draw its future leadership if it is to continue to be efficient and progressive.

Economic Significance of Our Millions of Independent Enterprises. Much of the productivity and progressiveness of our American economy is a result of the sheer numbers of our independent business enterprises. These millions of enterprises, large and small, represent millions of potential sources of ideas. The businessmen who control each concern (sometimes one man, sometimes a small group) are in a position to experiment, at their own risk, with new methods and new products. Though not all of those who control business enterprises carry on progressive experimentation, many thousands of them do, so that for the economy as a whole there is constant improvement in products and methods of production and a constant increase in the average output per hour of labor.

The large number of *independent* sources of ideas and experiments to be found in a free-enterprise economy probably constitutes the greatest single advantage of free enterprise over socialism. Under socialism there is only one really independent or final source of authority, the government. All those who directly operate productive undertakings are merely employees, government appointees. Not only are their activities restricted by the orders and policies of those above them, but they are not likely to have the enthusiasm of the independent businessman for trying out new methods of production and new products. In the first place, they are more likely to have been chosen primarily because of loyalty to the party in power rather than for having demonstrated unusual skill in organizing and carrying on a business enterprise. In the second place, they lack the profit motive. They will share little if at all in any monetary gains resulting from improved products or lower costs. To be sure, the men who control large corporations sometimes own a relatively small part of a company's total stock. However, they usually have stock holdings that are important to them, and often they hold options to buy more stock at a fixed price. If the company is successful and the stock rises in value, these options may become very valuable. Another incentive to good performance by the managers of a large corporation is the fact that their performance is being constantly checked by institutional investors and security analysts, all seeking to serve the interests of portions of the investing public.

Competition, Horizontal and Vertical. Another factor that has stimulated productivity and progress in the American economy is the vigor of business competition. In spite of much talk about the growth of monopoly, there is no clear evidence that, in the economy as a whole, competition is diminishing in importance. Outside of the public utilities, which are government regulated, there are few if any important industries in which complete monopoly prevails, for *monopoly,* in the economic sense, means a single producer or seller. True, there are some industries, like steel and automobiles, where production is carried on by only a few large producers. But even in these industries competition is very active, though it seldom takes the form of aggressive price-cutting. Each company is constantly striving to increase its share of the market through sales efforts and through making its product more attractive to buyers. Also, in the long run, domestic producers must take into consideration imports from abroad. The fact that we do not find in our economy much competition that closely resembles what economists call *pure* or *perfect competition* should not be taken to mean that competition is disappearing. Even in times past there was probably not nearly so much pure competition as many writers assume. [2]

When estimating the importance of competition in the economy, we must remember that competition is *vertical* as well as *horizontal.* Horizontal competition takes place between like products; vertical competition occurs between products that are unlike but that can to some degree be substituted for each other. Even monopolies face vertical competition, and often such competition is very effective. A company might, let us say, have a monopoly of aluminum, but for many uses its product would face stiff competition from copper, magnesium alloys, other metals, and even plastics. A familiar case of very active vertical competition is that which takes place among transportation agencies—railroads, water carriers, pipe lines, trucks, and airplanes.

Natural Resources, Machines, and Power. In an industrial economy, productivity depends first of all on adequate natural resources and an

[2] See footnote on page 457.

advanced technology. We have pointed out in previous chapters that the United States is more fortunate than any other area of similar size in the quantity and variety of its natural resources; also, that it has been a world leader in scientific research, in the development of machine technology, and in the use of power. The productivity of labor has kept rising in this country, because year after year we have applied science to production and have provided workers with more and better power machines. This is reflected in the amount of natural power we generate. Per capita consumption of power in the United States exceeds by a wide margin that of any other country.

The Size of Our Domestic Market. Another factor that makes a significant contribution to the productivity of our economy is the size of our domestic market. Within the confines of the United States, unobstructed by tariffs or other serious trade barriers, is a market whose total purchasing power is about one third as great as that of all the rest of the world. This huge market, well serviced with communication and transportation facilities, permits mass-production techniques to be employed to their fullest advantage.

The automobile industry illustrates this well, just as it does many other aspects of large-scale production. The United States market can absorb the domestic automotive output of three industrial giants, plus that of one large "independent." No country in Europe has a market that would be sufficient to absorb more than a minor fraction of this output. A country with a domestic market too small to permit the full development of mass-production techniques can gain their advantages only through developing a large export trade. But this is seldom a satisfactory solution, because as soon as trade crosses international boundaries, it encounters tariffs, currency restrictions, and other obstacles. However, some countries of western Europe have made progress toward solving this problem; for example, we now find German Volkswagens almost everywhere in the world. Japan, too, has become a large exporter of various products.

The Efficiency of Our Transportation System. With little more than one third the area, the United States has four times as much railroad mileage as the Soviet Union; and no other country in the world even approaches the Soviet Union in this respect. We also produce annually in this country several times as many trucks as the Russians, and our road system, though seriously deficient by our own standards, is magnificent in comparison with theirs, because only a few of the main highways of Russia are paved.

Our great rail and road transportation system is effectively supplemented by an important network of pipelines and by water and air transport. The net result is the most efficient system in the world for transporting food, raw materials, and manufactured goods over considerable distances at relatively low cost.

Education and Industrial Research. Stress has been laid in earlier chapters on both the extent of educational opportunities in this country and the extent to which we have developed industrial research. Both of these factors have made great contributions to our productive efficiency. Education has contributed both indirectly and directly, the most direct contributions being those of our vocational and technical schools. Industrial research has contributed by assuring constant improvement of products and of methods of production.

Other factors could also be mentioned that have helped to develop the American economy, but those already cited are among the most important. Fortunately, the United States has had a substantial advantage over the rest of the world with respect to a number of the conditions that tend to expand production.

FORMS OF BUSINESS ORGANIZATION

As an economy becomes more complex, and especially as the size of the typical business enterprise increases, business organization assumes greater and greater importance. A business operated by one man with two or three employees presents very simple problems of organization; but when a business employs 50,000 men and manufactures a complicated product, problems of organization become difficult, and their satisfactory solution becomes absolutely essential to carrying on production. Large numbers of men and quantities of machines and materials will produce nothing unless they are organized; and whether they will produce a small output at high cost, or a large output at low cost, will depend for the most part on how efficiently they are organized.

When a new business is to be started, one of the first decisions that must be made is whether to operate it as a *single proprietorship,* a *partnership,* or a *corporation.* These are the three principal legal forms of business organization, and each has advantages and disadvantages. The form of organization that is finally chosen will depend on various factors, among them the nature of the commodities to be produced, the way in which capital is to be raised, and, most important of all, the probable size of the new enterprise.

The Single Proprietorship. There are still more single proprietorships in our economy than any other form of business organization, but corporations, because they include almost all large businesses, account for the major part of production and employment. Single enterprises are likely to be rather small. They include almost all farms along with many such establishments as repair shops, gas stations, and retail stores. Most businesses, in fact, start as single enterprises.

The single enterprise has several distinct advantages: (1) It is easy to start it or to liquidate it, without consulting anyone else. Usually there are few legal barriers, and these can readily be dealt with by anyone who has the qualities of a good businessman. (2) The amount of capital required is likely to be comparatively small. (3) The single proprietor is free to make all decisions, without the need for consulting anyone else.

This provides flexibility and makes it possible to meet new situations promptly. (4) The single proprietor also has a very strong incentive to put his best efforts into the business, because he receives all profits and must bear any losses.

But the single proprietorship has definite disadvantages: (1) As the business grows, it may not be possible to secure sufficient new capital for expansion. High taxes may make it difficult to accumulate substantial amounts out of profits, even if these might otherwise be satisfactory. (2) The owner of a single enterprise assumes full liability for all its debts. This means that if the business fails, he may lose not only what he has put into it but also any other property he possesses. (3) The single enterpriser must assume the management of the entire business, even though he may not be at all expert in some phases of its operations. He can hire assistants, but he has no one with whom to share ultimate responsibility. (4) The whole life of the business is likely to depend on the owner. If he must relinquish it because of illness or death, there is often no one who can step in and take his place. As a result, a successful business may have to be terminated and liquidated, usually with heavy loss to the owner or his heirs.

The Partnership. A second common form of business organization is the partnership. When a single enterpriser is confronted with such problems as the need for more capital, expert management in areas with which he is not familiar, or a desire for someone with whom to share his responsibilities, he naturally begins looking around for a partner with capital and business experience.

A partnership comes into existence when two or more individuals agree to organize a business and operate it jointly. Usually all of them contribute both capital and their services. The legal basis of a partnership is a contract, usually written, that specifies the rights and obligations of various partners. Frequently states provide by law for special types of partnerships that vary somewhat from the common pattern.

Important advantages of the partnership include the following: (1) Other things being equal, it can provide more capital than the single enterprise. (2) Frequently it brings together several men each of whom has expert knowledge of some important phase of the operations of the business. (3) From a legal point of view a partnership is almost as easy to form as a single enterprise. (4) If the partners can work in harmony, they may be able to make decisions and adjust policies almost as easily as a single proprietor.

But a partnership does have disadvantages, and these must be taken into account: (1) If the partners cannot agree, there is likely to be no hope of carrying on the business successfully. (2) A partner, like a single enterpriser, is liable for all the debts of the business. To be sure, losses will ordinarily be shared; but if one partner has property and the others do not, he must bear the whole burden. (3) This liability for debts, along with the need for close cooperation, usually limits the practical size of a partnership to three or four persons. One can risk going into partnership only with individuals whom one knows well and trusts. (4) The partnership is not very permanent. If a partner dies, the business may have to be liquidated in order to pay off his heirs. The other partners may be able to avoid this only by buying out his share or by finding someone else who is able and willing to do so and who is acceptable to them as a new partner.

The Corporation. Because of the disadvantages of both the single proprietorship and the partnership, most businesses of any considerable size are organized as corporations. A corporation is created by a legal document, called a *charter,* which is issued by the state. A charter is granted at the request of a group of individuals who wish to organize and operate a business as a corporation and who meet certain legal requirements. The people who own and control a corporation are known as *stockholders.* However, the stockholders as a body do not directly control most aspects of corporation management; instead, they elect for this task a group called a *board of directors,* and this group in turn elects a president and other officers to carry on the routine business of the company.[3]

A corporation charter states the name of the corporation, the objects for which it was formed, its place of business, the number and kinds of shares of *stock* it is authorized to issue, the names of the original directors, and other pertinent information. While it is generally true that corporations are organized for rather specific business projects, often their charters are so broad as to permit them to undertake almost anything.

Once a corporation is organized, it becomes an entity in its own right, an artificial legal "person" that is in some respects separate from and independent of the individuals who own it. When we say that a corporation is legally a person, we mean that it has certain characteristics recognized by law that ordinarily pertain only to real people. It may sue and be sued, make contracts, own property, and be required to pay taxes.

Origins and Development of the Corporation. The origins of the corporation can be traced back to the ancient world, but the business corporation is a development of modern times. Forerunners of the business corporation of today may be found in some of the early land and trading companies of the seventeenth and eighteenth centuries. The Plymouth Company, which established the first colony in New England, was originally financed by London merchants for profit, though later their interest was purchased by the colonists themselves. Among the more important early trading companies organized to develop overseas trade and territories were the East India Company and the Hudson's Bay Company.

The modern business corporation began to come into use in the United States not long after 1800. With the growth of public utility enterprises,

---

[3] If a corporation has several classes of stockholders, usually only those who hold what is known as common stock have the right to vote on company affairs. This will be explained later.

manufacturing, and banking in the period following the War of 1812, the single enterprise and the partnership could no longer meet the needs of some of the larger enterprises. But not until after the Civil War did the corporation achieve its full importance and development in this country; ever since that time it has played a major role in our economic development. Without this flexible form of business organization the exploitation of our natural resources, the populating of the West, and the growth of industry and technology could scarcely have taken place as rapidly as they did.

Originally, corporation charters were granted by special acts of the king, parliament, or legislature. This frequently led to favoritism, bribery, and other evils. To correct this situation, *general incorporation acts* were passed that set up standard requirements, procedures, and fees for establishing any corporation. In this country the states began passing such acts before the Civil War, and in a few decades they became practically universal.

The policies followed in granting charters differ somewhat from state to state. Certain states have purposely placed few restrictions on corporations and have made charters especially easy to obtain. By inducing enterprises to incorporate under its laws, a state gains some advantages. These include the collection of charter fees and certain taxes and also the right to require newly organized corporations to set up their home offices within the state boundaries. Delaware early acquired a reputation for giving corporations very liberal treatment. In recent years some writers have urged that the chartering of business corporations should be shifted from the states to the national government. This would insure uniform requirements for obtaining a corporation charter and would also facilitate Congressional regulation and control of business. But whether this latter effect would be desirable depends on one's point of view.

In this chapter our main interest is in the business corporation organized for profit, and this is the kind of corporation we have described. But it should be pointed out that there are other kinds of corporations, public and private. For the most part these are not organized for profit and do not have stockholders. They include local municipal governments and various government agencies; also educational and religious bodies and charitable and research foundations of various kinds.

Advantages of the Corporation as a Form of Business Organization. From the standpoint of those who own and operate a profit-making business enterprise, the first and greatest advantage of the corporation arises from the principle of limited liability. In an ordinary business corporation, each shareholder, if he has paid the full par value of his stock, is liable only to the extent of his investment. If the corporation fails, he can lose this investment, but no matter how great the debts of the corporation, its creditors have no claim on any other property he owns.

A second great advantage of the corporation is the relative ease with which it can bring together large amounts of capital. This is not to say

39. Busy Day at the New York Stock Exchange. This was the scene on the floor of the Exchange November 20, 1967, during trading in the first session following devaluation of the British pound on November 18. (Courtesy Wide World Photos.)

that just any corporation can collect large amounts of capital. But if the public has confidence in the prospects of a business and in the men who control it, the corporate form of organization enables large numbers of people to invest with comparative ease and safety. More than anything else, it is the limited-liability feature that makes it possible for a corporation to obtain large amounts of capital. Without this feature, it would be folly for the ordinary investor to buy stock in a corporation; for no matter how small his investment, in case of failure he might lose all his property.

The extent and growth of stock ownership in the United States is indicated in estimates made by the New York Stock Exchange. According to these, the number of individuals owning corporation stocks rose from 6.5 million in 1952 to about 31 million in 1970. More than 20 per cent of all stock now listed on the New York Stock Exchange is owned by banks, insurance companies, investment trusts, and other institutions.

A third advantage of the corporation is its permanence. Both the single enterprise and the partnership are dependent for their existence on the lives and participation of the individuals who constitute them, but the corporation has a legal existence that is independent of its owners or stockholders. If a stockholder withdraws by selling his shares, his place is automatically taken by the person or persons who buy them; if he dies, his place is taken by his heirs. Corporation charters are usually granted for an indefinite period of time, subject to termination only by failure, by voluntary action of the stockholders, or by action of the state. A number of successful corporations in this country have been in business for more than a hundred years.

A fourth advantage of the corporation is the ease with which one can acquire an interest in a business or transfer this interest to someone else. Anyone who wants to purchase stock has only to pay the price that is asked by the owners; further, because the stock of most of our larger corporations is constantly being bought and sold, he is usually able to buy as many shares as he can pay for at close to the current market price. Similarly, anyone who owns stock can always sell it if he is willing to take the price offered in the market.

Other advantages of the corporation are often listed. Most of them, however, are merely advantages of size. Though not all corporations are large, a really successful one usually has little trouble in expanding its capital. Hence, in comparison with other business enterprises corporations are in a favorable position to take advantage of any gains that may be had from large-scale production.

Possible Disadvantages of the Corporation. For most business enterprises of any size, the advantages of the corporation heavily outweigh its disadvantages, but, for some very small enterprises, the corporate form of organization might be needlessly unwieldy and expensive. Also, corporations are subject to somewhat more government regulation than are single enterprises and partnerships. As to taxes, there are cases in which the corporation has advantages and others in which it does not.

Perhaps the most commonly cited disadvantage of the corporation is that it can often be controlled by a small group of "insiders" who have very little invested in it. Though theoretically one must hold over 50 per cent of the voting stock to be assured of control, in the case of large corporations with many stockholders, effective control can often be secured and retained by those who hold only a minor fraction of the total stock.

Sometimes minority control is exercised by one or several individuals who are large stockholders. Often the group that exercises control is the "management"—in other words, the board of directors. In most large companies the members of the board own a very small proportion of the total stock outstanding, though their holdings may be enough to be important to them as individuals. In any case, they are in a position to circularize the stockholders, and they can almost always obtain enough *proxies*[4] to keep themselves in office and to assure adoption of the policies they advocate. Most stockholders know little about the affairs of a company. Hence, when issues arise, they either fail to vote or, by sending in proxies, they allow the management to vote for them. In a situation like this, the great majority of the stockholders, who are the real owners of the business,

---

[4] A proxy is a statement that a stockholder signs authorizing someone else to vote his stock.

become dependent on a board of directors who conceivably may not operate the corporation for their benefit. If the members of the board are unscrupulous, they may be able to line their own pockets at the expense of the stockholders without even breaking any law. One of the simplest methods is to elect some of their members as officers and then to vote to pay excessive salaries, bonuses, and retirement benefits. On the other hand, corporations must report such payments to stockholders, and, as we have said, corporations of any importance are watched closely by security analysts and federal regulatory agencies.

Corporation Securities. As corporations have increased over the years in number and size, corporation securities have taken on greater and greater importance. To regulate properly both their issuance and their purchase and sale, Congress in 1934 created the *Securities and Exchange Commission.* Long before that a number of *stock exchanges* had been established to provide convenient centers for trading in securities. The first and largest of these, the New York Stock Exchange, was established in 1817. At this exchange, on a typical business day, twelve million to more than twenty million shares are now traded.

Every business corporation must issue *stock,* for stock is the device by which the ownership of a corporation is divided up among those who have invested in it. If only one kind of stock is issued, it is what we usually call *common stock.* The holder of a share of stock in a corporation is a part owner. If the corporation has issued and sold 1,000 shares, the holder of one share has a 1/1,000 interest in the company and in any profits it may make. Each holder of common stock has the privilege of voting on matters affecting the corporation, but he votes not as an individual but as a stockholder, and he has as many votes as he owns shares. That is why, as already noted, anyone who owns more than 50 per cent of the voting stock can always carry a corporate election no matter how many other stockholders vote against him. When a corporation makes profits, it usually sets aside a portion of them as reserves and as surplus for expansion. The remainder

"If I buy a stock, do I get a ten day free trial?" (Courtesy *The Chicago Tribune.* Drawing by Henry.)

is paid out to the stockholders as *dividends* in proportion to the number of shares each owns.

Every business corporation issues common stock (or in rare cases its equivalent under some other name), and many also issue one or more classes of *preferred stock.* Preferred stock gets its name from the fact that its owners usually have preference over the holders of common stock in case the company should be liquidated, and they also have preference in the receipt of dividends. But as a rule they can never receive more than a fixed dividend—say four dollars a share—annually, whereas the dividends of the holders of common stock are limited only by the profits of the company. The company, however, cannot pay dividends on the common stock unless it also pays the agreed amount on the preferred. Frequently, preferred stock is *cumulative.* This means that if dividends on it are not paid in certain years, they accumulate and must be paid off in full before the holders of common stock can receive anything. In most cases, holders of preferred stock do not have the right to vote.

In addition to obtaining capital by issuing stock, corporations also acquire funds through the sale of *bonds.* A bond is a long-term promissory note. It is the promise of a corporation to pay back in the future—perhaps ten, twenty, or thirty years hence—the face value of the bond and, in the meantime, to pay interest at regular intervals. A bond represents a debt of the corporation, and the bondholder is a creditor. Bondholders have no control over the affairs of a corporation unless it defaults on its obligations to them.

Whether a corporation that needs additional capital raises it by selling common stock, preferred stock, or bonds depends on many circumstances. These all relate to two general considerations. First, in the current state of the market, which type of security will be most salable? Second, which type of security, on other grounds, will be best for the corporation and its present stockholders? As to the first consideration, when business is good and the stock market is rising, it may be easy to sell new issues of stock at good prices. On the other hand, in a period of depression, the market may be better for bonds, because buyers regard these as safer. As to the effect of new securities on the corporation and its stockholders, it is safer for the corporation to sell stock than to sell bonds. Bondholders must be paid their interest and eventually their principal, even though the corporation fails to make profits. Stockholders, on the other hand, never have to be paid unless the company has substantial earnings. However, if a company is very prosperous, the present stockholders will not wish to divide their high dividends with newcomers. They will not want the company to issue more common stock, at least not to outsiders, but they may be willing that it should sell preferred stock, which receives a limited dividend, or bonds, which receive a fixed rate of interest.

Today, if interest rates are not extremely high, there is a great tax advantage to a company in raising funds by the sale of bonds rather than preferred stock. Any money a corporation pays out to bondholders for inter-

"One tries to break out of corporate anonymity by his mid-forties or one doesn't do it at all." (Courtesy of *The Rotarian*. Drawing by Herb Brammeier, Jr.)

est can be deducted from profits as a cost, and hence is not subject to the federal corporation income tax. However, dividends paid to stockholders cannot be so deducted. They must be included in corporation profits and are therefore subject to the tax.

The Corporation in American Life. In spite of the great importance of corporations in our economic life, numerically they represent only a small fraction of all business concerns. Today the vast majority of our 2.9 million farms are still operated as single enterprises, and in 1967, if we include agriculture, only about one eighth of all firms were corporations. Approximately four fifths were individually owned, and about one twelfth were partnerships.[5]

But the importance of corporations in our economy arises not from their numbers but from the fact that they include all really large business enterprises. As a result, excluding agriculture and the professions, they account for about three fourths of the total output of all private business. Though nearly all large businesses are corporations, it does not follow that all corporations are large. Actually, most of them are rather small; more than half have fewer than twenty employees each. Nevertheless, the outstanding contribution of the corporation to our economy has been to permit private financing and private control of large-scale enterprises. Without the corporate device or some substitute for it, private groups could seldom have brought together sufficient capital to finance our great public utilities and our major mass-production enterprises. Either large-scale production with its benefits would never have developed, or else it would

[5] U.S. Bureau of the Census, *Statistical Abstract of the United States: 1970,* 91st ed., Washington, D. C., Government Printing Office, p. 468.

have been undertaken almost entirely by government so that by now our economy would be largely socialized.

The Extent of Industrial Concentration. Though everyone admits that large-scale production is now essential to efficiency in a number of important industries, there are many who feel that "big business" will ultimately destroy both competition and free enterprise. They believe that small business is being gradually destroyed and that all productive activities are slowly falling into the hands of a relatively few giant corporations and of a small group of business and financial leaders who control them. Ultimately, they fear, this will lead us to an economic oligarchy controlled by big business or, as the only alternative, to government socialism.

However, we should note that some recent studies have cast doubt on the thesis that there is a strong tendency for American business to become increasingly concentrated in the hands of a few large corporations. Though our greatest corporations are far larger than ever before, so is our whole economy. Actually, in a number of important industries concentration is less than it was sixty or seventy years ago. Oil and steel are good examples. In the oil industry, at the turn of the century the Standard Oil trust controlled the great bulk of production and consumption; now production and marketing are shared by a considerable number of legally independent companies. In the steel industry, when the United States Steel Corporation was first organized in 1901, it produced about two thirds of the nation's steel; but in 1965 its proportion had fallen to less than 25 per cent. This does not mean that there is perfect competition in either the oil or steel industries, but it does mean that no company can set prices unless the others will go along; and if the prices set are too high in relation to demand, some companies are likely to openly reduce them or else make private discount deals with customers. Furthermore, if it can be proved that companies have agreed to fix prices, they can be prosecuted under the antitrust laws. In addition, they have the problem, today a serious one, of foreign competition.

We should also point out that if the small independent business is slowly being crowded out by the expansion of big corporations, we should expect a gradual decrease in the total number of business enterprises in relation to our population. Over the years there seems to have been no trend in this direction. From 1945 to 1967 the population of this country increased about 40 per cent while the number of business enterprises increased about 70 per cent.[6]

Government Enterprises and Cooperatives. Though most productive enterprises in this country are conducted under one of the three forms of organization already described, there are some exceptions. For example, a number of enterprises, especially in the utility field, are owned and operated by governments. Sometimes they are carried on by public corporations or special government agencies created for the purpose by legisla-

[6] Ibid.

tion; sometimes they are operated directly by the federal government or by a state or municipal government. They include the United States Post Office, the Tennessee Valley Authority, most local water systems, and numerous bus lines and electric power plants.

When such undertakings are operated by a government instead of by private owners, it is usually the theory that this is in the public interest. However, there are many persons who argue that privately owned utilities, under government regulation, are likely to give better service at lower cost. It is not safe to generalize too much on this point, for the performance records of government-operated utilities vary widely. But some studies indicate that, if full account is taken of freedom from taxes and the frequent privilege of borrowing government funds at below-market rates of interest, most of them have rather high costs. Strictly speaking, a government undertaking is not a *business enterprise,* because *the latter is usually defined as a private organization created for the purpose of making profits.*

For many years, the United States Post Office was regarded as an outstanding example of a government-owned and -operated service enterprise, but for some years it has been operating at a deficit and giving poorer and poorer service. President Johnson had earlier recommended postal reforms, and in 1970, at President Nixon's urging, Congress passed an act that was intended to take the postal service out of politics, increase its efficiency, and make it financially self-sustaining. The new United States Postal Service is now an independent establishment within the executive branch of the government.

Another form of organization for production is the *cooperative.* Though cooperatives account for a very small part of American business, they have attracted a good deal of attention. Cooperatives are modified corporations that have some of the characteristics of the partnership and some of those of the corporation. They are of two principal types: consumer cooperatives and producer cooperatives. In either case their purpose is to serve certain needs of their own members. The most common type of consumer cooperative is a retail grocery owned by its customers. The most common type of producer cooperative consists of a group of farmers banded together for the purpose of processing or marketing their own products in order to increase their profits. They may, for example, operate a creamery or a grain elevator.

Further attention will be given to the nature and activities of cooperatives when we come to the chapter that deals with the consumer.

GOVERNMENT REGULATION OF BUSINESS

We referred in Chapter 17 to the doctrine of *laissez faire,* the theory that government should interfere with business as little as possible, except for maintaining law and order and enforcing property rights. After the Industrial Revolution, laissez faire became the dominant theory of the proper relationship between government and business. But the abler advocates of laissez faire never maintained that it was either possible or desirable to dispense *completely* with government controls, and today, as a result of the great economic changes of the last century, all competent observers recognize the need for a very considerable amount of government regulation of business. However, there are still wide differences of opinion as to both *how much* and *what kind* of regulation is desirable. It is clear that many government controls have served the public interest; but to economists it seems equally clear that some that were intended to do so have not.

As the American economy has become increasingly complex, government has necessarily played a more and more direct and positive role in economic life; and in the chapters that follow, attention will be called to some of the various forms government controls have taken. But in this chapter we shall concentrate our attention on two types of government regulation of business that have been of special importance. These are (1) controls designed to maintain competition and free markets by preventing the growth of monopoly and (2) federal and state provisions for regulating public utility enterprises. Both these types of regulation have had an important effect on the structure and functioning of our economy and both have been closely associated with the growth of corporate enterprise and large-scale production.

Big Business and the Trend Toward Monopoly. It was in the period from the Civil War to about 1900 that there first developed in this country those very large enterprises that today we often refer to as "big business." This was also the period in which, as noted earlier, the corporation was becoming increasingly popular as a form of business organization. Some of the great enterprises formed at this time were railroad systems and others were industrial corporations, but both types showed a strong tendency toward the development of *monopoly.* As used by economists, *monopoly* means that in a given market there is only one producer or seller of a certain product. In the case of railroads, the trend toward monopoly was inevitable. Railroads are public utilities, and, as will be explained later, public utilities can seldom be operated on any other basis.

However, in the case of industrial enterprises there is seldom any necessity for monopoly. Ordinarily there is nothing to prevent a number of producers of manufactured or processed products from competing with one another. But late in the nineteenth century, certain conditions prevailed in this country that made it possible to create nationwide monopolies in some industries. For one thing, there were certain industries in which the advantages of large-scale production were rapidly increasing. This resulted not only from technical advances in manufacturing processes but also from the development of national advertising and a national transportation system. In industries where size brought substantially lower costs of production, large firms tended to keep growing larger and to drive the small firms out of business. Once this process had gone so far in an industry that only a few firms remained, the survivors could often be induced to combine in order to gain the advantages of monopoly. If some firms refused to join the monopolistic combination, the size of the latter sometimes enabled it to drive them out of business. Frequently it employed extremely unfair if not high-handed methods of competition to achieve this result.

Because the first great industrial combinations were created by a legal device known as a trust agreement, very soon all such combinations were popularly referred to as *trusts,* and once the combination or trust movement had started, it developed rapidly. First came the Standard Oil Trust, created in 1879. This was followed rapidly, within a ten-year period, by the "Whiskey Trust," the "Sugar Trust," the "Tobacco Trust," and several others.

Although the trust agreement was soon declared illegal as a means for creating industrial combinations, other methods were available for achieving much the same results. Temporary combinations could be achieved by merely making agreements. However, these were easily dissolved or broken. A simple way of achieving permanent combination was to merge or consolidate several corporations into one. Another method that became rather popular was to create a *holding company.* A holding company is a corporation organized for the purpose of acquiring a controlling stock interest in other corporations, thus bringing them under unified management. The companies controlled by a holding company are called *subsidiaries.*

The Sherman Antitrust Act. Though there appears not to have been, at the time, any great tide of public protest against the trusts, by 1890 they were unpopular enough to enable Congress to pass the Sherman Antitrust Act. The legal basis for this legislation is the powers the Constitution grants to Congress to regulate interstate and foreign commerce. The principal provision of the act is found in the first sentence of Section 1: "Every contract, combination in the form of trust or otherwise, or conspiracy, in restraint of trade or commerce among the several states, or with foreign nations, is hereby declared to be illegal." Section 1 also states that any person who shall make such a contract or engage in such a combination or conspiracy shall be fined not over $5,000, or imprisoned not over one year. Section 2 provides the same penalty for anyone who shall "monopolize" trade; and Section 7 says that anyone injured by anything forbidden in the act may sue for triple damages.

Many people felt that the Sherman Act was a loosely drawn and rather ineffective piece of legislation. Its terms are somewhat vague, for it does not define either monopoly or a combination in restraint of trade. That is left entirely to the courts. Seldom have attempts been made to enforce its criminal provisions. Furthermore, it did not, at least for some time, even check the growing combination movement; for in the years from 1897 to 1903 more trusts were formed than in any other similar period in our history. Therefore, we must conclude that in its early years the act had little influence on economic developments. To some extent its ineffectiveness was the result of the failure of the administrations in power at Washington to make any serious effort to enforce it.

But later the situation changed. Under the administrations of Theodore Roosevelt (1901–1909) and William Howard Taft (1909–1913) attempts at enforcement were more vigorous, and in 1911 the Supreme Court handed down a decision ordering the dissolution of the great Standard Oil Company of New Jersey. On the surface, this appeared to be a great victory for the antitrust forces. To careful observers, however, this was not at all clear. At the time, Standard of New Jersey was the agency through which the Rockefeller interests exercised almost complete dominance over the oil industry of the entire country. It was a holding company, and its chief function was to control thirty-three subsidiaries through ownership of their stock. But under the dissolution order of the Supreme Court every stockholder of the New Jersey company received his pro rata share of the stock of each subsidiary. This meant that the same group of stockholders who owned the New Jersey company now owned directly all the subsidiaries, with the result that control was just about as concentrated as it had been before. Apparently, therefore, the dissolution was more or less meaningless; that was the opinion of most observers at the time.

In the long run, however, dissolution of the old Standard Oil Company of New Jersey did contribute substantially to breaking up the Standard Oil monopoly. As stock of the various subsidiaries changed hands through death of owners and through sales, gradually the companies of the old combination came under the control of different groups, and they became more and more independent of one another. Breakdown of the monopoly was further aided by a rapid growth of the entire oil industry and the establishment of a number of large and new independent companies.

The Clayton Act and the Federal Trade Commission Act. When President Woodrow Wilson took office in 1913, there was a strong demand for "putting more teeth" into the Sherman Antitrust law. Also, there was a strong demand from labor for changes in the act to exempt unions from its provisions; for though the Sherman Act was aimed primarily at industrial combinations, in a number of cases it had been successfully invoked against organized labor. The most famous case was that of the Danbury Hatters.[7]

In 1914, to meet both these demands, two important measures were passed, the Clayton Act and the Federal Trade Commission Act. The Clayton Act was intended to do two things: (1) strengthen the Sherman Act, especially by forbidding a number of specific practices tending to lessen

---

[7] The Danbury Hatters case first came to the U.S. Supreme Court in 1908. After declaring that acts of labor unions were covered by the Sherman law, the Supreme Court remanded the case to a lower court. In a final decision in 1915, the Supreme Court held that, under the Sherman Act, a boycott sponsored by the United Hatters' Union was a conspiracy in restraint of trade. It approved a lower-court judgment of more than $250,000 against the officers and members of the union.

competition or create monopoly, and (2) exempt labor from the provisions of the Sherman Act. To some extent, the first aim was achieved; but the second was not, because the courts interpreted the law in a way unfavorable to labor. The Federal Trade Commission Act was intended to provide a better administrative procedure for enforcing the antitrust laws, especially in respect to the control of unfair trade practices. It created the Federal Trade Commission and defined its powers. The Commission had the function of investigating alleged violations of the antitrust laws and the power to issue "cease and desist" orders against any illegal practices it might discover. If its orders were not obeyed, it might apply to the federal courts for enforcement.

Effects of Antitrust Legislation. Since the passage of the Clayton Act and the Federal Trade Commission Act, the vigor with which the antitrust laws have been enforced has had many ups and downs. During wars, enforcement has been largely neglected. Also, the importance placed on efforts to prevent excessive industrial concentration has varied from administration to administration. Some legislation has even been passed that has tended to weaken the antitrust laws. Notable in this respect are the Webb-Pomerene Act of 1918 and the National Industrial Recovery Act of 1933 (later declared unconstitutional). The former law exempted from the antitrust laws combinations for carrying on export trade; the latter law tended to encourage monopolistic agreements by permitting each industry to establish a "code" and set "fair" prices that were to be binding on all firms. On the other hand, there have been times when antitrust prosecutions have been carried on with unusual vigor.

There is no way of estimating with any accuracy the total influence of the antitrust laws on the American economy, because there is no way of knowing just what the situation would have been without them. But in spite of all the changes that have taken place since the Sherman Act was passed in 1890, the antitrust laws have gradually been accepted by the public and the great majority of business men as a basic and desirable feature of our American system of government and business. Forty or fifty years ago many—perhaps most—writers were convinced that they had been a complete failure. Few combinations had been dissolved, and few if any monopolies broken up as the direct result of court action. But since World War II, the climate of opinion seems to have changed. Most observers now appear to be in agreement that the antitrust laws have, over the years, had very important effects on the development of our American economy.

The antitrust laws have not prevented the growth of very large business enterprises—that would be impossible and undesirable in an age of mass-production techniques. Neither have they prevented a great many industrial combinations from taking place. But they do not pretend to forbid all combinations—only monopolies, and combinations "in restraint of trade." Obviously this last expression is very vague. As a result, the courts have made little attempt to enforce it, except when they have held that there has been "unreasonable" restraint of trade, such restraint usually involving monopoly. The term *monopoly* itself is, in legal usage, vague, and the courts have had to interpret it as best they could.

Yet with all their weaknesses, it is pretty clear that the antitrust laws have, over the last seventy-five years, done much to restrain monopoly. They were a warning that if public opinion was sufficiently aroused, stronger measures would follow. Moreover, they have enough teeth in them so that there is always the fear of successful prosecution. Without them, monopolistic combination would probably have gone much further in this country than it has. It is quite possible that a number of important industries—perhaps including steel and automobiles—would have fallen completely into the hands either of a single producer or of a tightly organized legal combination of producers similar to the European cartels. A *cartel* is a group of companies who have some type of pooling agreement. Such agreements are legal in many countries. The companies may, for example, agree to divide market territories among themselves in a certain way, or they may allot to each company a production or sales quota. If such monopolies had been permitted in this country, it would probably have been difficult to resist demands for more government control of industry or even for government ownership.

For most of our industries, there is little indication that the *proportion* of total output controlled by two or three giant corporations has increased in the last fifty or sixty years. In automobiles it has, partly because of the great advantages of production on a very large scale. Steel and oil, however, are examples of industries in which there has been a great decrease in concentration along with an increase in competition. Competition takes

(Courtesy of Joseph G. Farris.)

various forms, and a dozen independent companies in an industry provide much more of it than would only two or three.

But we should note that in very recent years there has been a trend toward *conglomerates,* huge companies producing a variety of quite different products. This is a development that if continued could ultimately have the undesirable effect of greatly restricting competition. Whether our present antitrust laws can deal with it adequately remains to be seen.

REGULATION OF PUBLIC UTILITIES

The *public utility* industries are somewhat difficult to classify, and in the final analysis the placing of an industry in this category depends on court decisions. However, the principal industries in the group are those concerned with transportation, communication, and the production and transmission of power. Railroads, bus lines, telephone and telegraph systems, radio and television companies, and electric power companies are all public utilities. To these we can add airlines, ferries, ship lines, gas companies, pipe lines, and others. Obviously, public utilities provide services which are indispensable to the operation of our economy and to the daily activities of great numbers of people.

We have already noted, in connection with railroads, that an outstanding characteristic of most public utilities is their tendency to become monopolies. This tendency results from certain conditions under which they operate and has been a major factor in bringing about demands for their regulation. First of all, utilities usually serve limited areas, and in those areas they generally require expensive installations that spread over the landscape in the form of tracks, wires, cables, or pipes. To build competing systems to serve the same territory would be so expensive and wasteful as to be quite out of the question. Moreover, it would be highly objectionable to clutter the public view with duplicate sets of tracks, poles, or wires. Second, for public utilities to build the installations they require, they are obliged, as a rule, to obtain *franchises,* or grants from local governments, which permit them to use public property for their installations. Usually such franchises are granted on an exclusive basis. Even if a utility buys its own right of way, to do so successfully it must obtain from the government the privilege of exercising the right of *eminent domain,* so that where necessary it may buy property through condemnation proceedings; today a government would never grant this right of eminent domain to more than one public utility of a given kind in a given area. Utilities like airlines, radio, and television do not need rights of way, and hence more competition is possible. However, they must have government permission to use air routes or broadcasting bands. These must be controlled to assure orderly and efficient use for the public benefit.

The Development of Public Utility Regulation. The first of our great modern public utilities was the railroads. As early as 1860 there was already an extensive rail system in the developed areas of the United States. As a natural consequence, it was in connection with the railroads that the problem of utility regulation first came into prominence. Scarcely was the Civil War over before agitation began for the regulation of railroad rates. Two or three years after the war, agricultural prices began a sharp decline, and this made the farmers very resentful of what they considered unreasonable and discriminatory freight rates. Soon they organized the Grange movement and began to put pressure on state legislatures to pass laws limiting railroad rates and prohibiting certain unfair railroad practices. The Illinois legislature was the first to take action. In 1869 it passed a statute requiring that railroads should charge "just, reasonable, and uniform" rates. Other states soon followed, especially after the panic of 1873; and in 1887, federal regulation of railroads was begun with the creation of the Interstate Commerce Commission.

When electric power companies, gas companies, and street railway companies began to be important, regulation was applied to them also. Sometimes their rates were regulated by the terms of their franchises or by legislation, but as time went on, the states placed this function in the hands of *public utilities commissions*. These were similar to commissions already established for the regulation of railroad rates.

Problems of Public Utility Regulation. Public utility regulation goes much further than the regulation of rates. It also involves control over the quality and the kinds of service rendered to the public and over the methods by which the utilities conduct their business. The railroads, for example, must follow uniform accounting practices as prescribed by the Interstate Commerce Commission, and they cannot drop a scheduled train, nor add one, nor abandon an unprofitable line, without first obtaining permission. Nevertheless, except for radio and television broadcasters, for whose services listeners and viewers seldom make a payment, the great problem in regulating utilities has been to set fair and reasonable rates.

When utility commissions set rates, their usual objective is to make them as fair as possible both to the public and to those who have invested their capital in utility properties. This is not as simple as it might seem. The first problem is to determine the real value of the investment in a utility. The next problem is to decide upon a fair rate of return to the investors. Of these two problems, determining the value of the investment is the more difficult. Usually utility commissions attempt to solve it by estimating the original cost of the property of the company and then making allowances for depreciation, improvements, and additions. In setting a fair rate of return, utility commissions take into account the rate of earnings in other industries and also current rates of interest. But in practice they are greatly influenced by their own decisions in the past and by the decisions of other utility commissions.

Once the value of the investment in a utility has been determined and also a fair rate of return to investors, it still remains to translate these decisions into rates to be charged to customers. This may involve serious problems for two reasons. First, it may be difficult to estimate how much money a given rate will bring in. Second, it may be difficult to decide the rates that should be charged to different classes of customers. For example, an electric power company may find that it pays to charge especially low rates to those who use current in off-peak hours, that is, when little current is being used by the majority of customers.

Federal Public Utility Commissions. The first federal commission for the control of utilities was the Interstate Commerce Commission (ICC); but for many years after its establishment, the federal government left the regulation of other types of utilities largely to the states. In 1920 the Federal Power Commission was created to supervise power developments on streams under federal jurisdiction, but not until 1935 was it given regulatory authority over companies transporting power across state lines, and not until 1938 was its authority extended to cover interstate movements of natural gas.

In 1934 the Federal Communications Commission (FCC) was established, with authority to regulate interstate telephone, telegraph, radio, and—later —television communications. This commission has become extremely important, mainly because it has the power to allocate radio and television wave bands and to license radio and television stations; also to make various rules concerning the operation of these stations.

In 1940 Congress took another important step in utility regulation by placing motor and water carriers under the jurisdiction of the ICC, thus subjecting them to the same type of regulation under which the railroads had long been operating.

Has Utility Regulation Been Successful? It is fair to say that utility regulation in this country has been moderately successful in achieving its objectives. It has protected the public against unnecessarily high prices and at the same time has permitted most utilities to provide satisfactory service at a reasonable profit. However, regulation has often been rigid and has prevented utilities from making adjustments desirable from the standpoint of both their own long-run interests and those of the public. Some railroad executives have argued that the Interstate Commerce Commission should control only the general level of rates. They believe that the railroads themselves should be allowed to determine the rates on particular commodities so as to meet special circumstances, including the competition of other types of carriers. Frequently, utilities complain that they are not allowed to charge rates adequate to maintain their properties and still leave a reasonable profit. The railroads in particular have often made this complaint. Many students of the problem believe that the recent financial troubles of the Penn-Central Railroad were a result of unwise regulatory policies in the past. Many students of transportation also believe that regulatory policies contributed to the decline of passenger trains. We shall now see whether the government can revive passenger service by directly operating the AMTRAK system.

Undoubtedly, utility regulation is not always in the public interest. A highly controversial case is that of pay-television. Although the Federal Communications Commission has allowed some small experiments with this system, it has thrown obstacles in the way of those who have sought to establish it on a scale large enough to test fully its merits.

Pay-television might greatly benefit the United States. First, if it succeeded financially, more stations would be established, and competition in the television industry would be substantially increased. Because all new TV sets are now being equipped for UHF, many new stations are possible. Today television is dominated by three monolithic networks. In an industry that controls an important medium of communication, more competition is highly desirable. Second, many people who now seldom watch television, because of what they consider the generally poor quality of the programs and also because of their constant interruption by commercials, might be enabled to enjoy its potential benefits. It seems highly probable that out of our more than 200 million people there are several million who would be willing to pay for good programs, especially if they were not interrupted by commercials. If some group were allowed to risk its own capital by making such programs widely available, we would find out.

Naturally, the present networks and the theater owners have done their best to block pay-TV because, like most businessmen, they do not want more competition. They have tried hard to convince the public of the highly doubtful proposition that pay-TV would take all the good programs from "free" TV. They do not point out that programs are now free only to people who like commercials (as some doubtless do) or who put a low value on their time.

Already for more than fifteen years the FCC has prevented any widespread use of pay-TV. Though this system may not be the answer to all our television problems, there seems to be no really good reason for not allowing it to be tried out on a large scale as soon as possible. The prospects now look brighter, but it is best to keep one's fingers crossed. The author still has in his files an article that he found in *Barron's* for May 2, 1955. It is entitled "Pay-as-You-See TV? The Fight over Its Adoption Is Nearing A Climax."

The term *pay-TV* has usually been applied to a system under which a TV station provides special programs that can be viewed (for a fee) only by its subscribers. On the sets of other people the picture is scrambled, but subscribers are provided with a device that, attached to their sets, enables them to bring it in clearly. *Cable-TV* is a different type of pay-TV. Originally, cable-TV companies built high towers to bring in stations that otherwise were too far away for reception, or for good reception. Then they ran cables to the TV sets of those willing to pay monthly fees for the service. Today, by use of long-distance cables or even satellites, it is technically possible for cable-TV companies to relay programs over great distances and thus offer subscribers a greater variety of programs. Usually, however, such programs still include commercials. Cable-TV systems have spread widely over the years in regions where TV reception was otherwise difficult or unsatisfactory. However, they have been placed under many restrictions by the FCC. Only recently have they been allowed to operate in our larger cities under franchises granted by local authorities.

The blocking of pay-TV is only one example of the tendency of government regulation to obstruct or slow down the introduction of new products, methods, and services. Earlier we noted the tendency of obsolete building codes to prevent the introduction of better and cheaper methods of construction; and even excessively stringent regulation of the introduction of new drugs could needlessly prevent the use of some that might save the lives of many people.

Special Significance of the Antitrust Laws and Utility Regulation. We have already observed that when a private monopoly has effective control of goods or services essential to the general welfare, it cannot be allowed to deal with the public just as it pleases. Sooner or later the government must act to protect the interests of the people. In taking such action it has three possible choices: (1) it may attempt to break up the monopoly and restore competition; (2) it may regulate the prices and the products of the monopoly; (3) it may take over the monopoly and operate it as a public enterprise.

In meeting the monopoly problem, in the United States we have usually chosen policies designed to maintain as much economic freedom and as much private enterprise as is consistent with protecting the public interest. First, where that seems possible, we try to preserve (through the antitrust laws) enough competition to make direct government regulation of business enterprises unnecessary. Second, where effective competition cannot be maintained (as in the public utilities), in most cases we choose government regulation rather than government ownership, in order to keep the responsibility of government at a minimum and to allow as much freedom as possible for the exercise of private initiative.

But in most western European countries, at least until very recently, the policies followed were quite different. Most of them made little attempt to preserve competition by preventing monopolistic combinations, and producers could form cartels without encountering any legal obstacles. Furthermore, much greater reliance was placed both on direct government controls and on public ownership. In a sense, our antitrust laws and our policy of permitting private ownership of public utilities, subject to regulation, are substitutes for socialism, or at least for the type of partial socialization now found in Great Britain and to a degree in some countries on the Continent.

Though our economy is far from perfect, it serves the economic needs of the great majority of citizens better than any other economic system ever developed. Our problem is to preserve the characteristics that account for its productivity and growth and to be alert to developments that could stifle it. At the same time, we must seek to extend some of its benefits to those of our citizens who are still impoverished; and we must devote a larger portion of our economic efforts to programs designed to preserve and improve the environment.

Terms to Be Understood

productivity
horizontal competition
vertical competition
pure or
  perfect competition
single proprietorship
partnership
corporation
charter
stockholders
board of directors
general incorporation
  acts

proxy
stock
stock exchange
common stock
preferred stock
cumulative preferred
  stock
dividend
bond
industrial concentration
business enterprise
cooperatives
laissez faire

monopoly
trust
holding company
subsidiary
cartel
conglomerate
public utility
franchise
eminent domain
public utility
  commission
cable-TV
pay-TV

Questions for Review and Discussion

1. How do incomes in the United States compare with those of other countries? What change has taken place in per capita purchasing power in this country since 1929?

2. Show how each of the following helps explain the high productivity of the American economy: (a) individual initiative and the profit motive; (b) the existence of millions of independent enterprises; (c) competition, both vertical and horizontal; (d) natural resources; (e) machines and power; (f) the size of our domestic market; (g) our transportation system; (h) education and industrial research.

3. In what ways can a high rate of productivity contribute to social welfare? Can it solve all our social problems? Why or why not?

4. What do you think would have been the effect on our economic development if the Constitution, which went into effect in 1789, had provided for the nationalization of all means of production, including farms? Defend your answer.

5. Is competition disappearing from the American economy? Defend your answer.

6. Explain the principal advantages and disadvantages of the single proprietorship as a form of business organization.

7. Explain the nature and the advantages and disadvantages of the partnership.

8. What is a corporation? Explain the roles played by the charter, the stockholders, and the board of directors.

9. What are the four great advantages of the corporation as a form of business organization?

10. Explain how the control of a corporation can become separated from its ownership.

11. Explain carefully the nature of common stock, preferred stock, and bonds and tell the principal privileges that go with ownership of each of these types of security.

12. Compare the advantages of stocks versus bonds as a means of raising additional corporation capital.

13. Excluding agriculture, only about one business enterprise in eight is a corporation. Why, then, is it often said that corporations dominate American business?

14. What is the outstanding contribution that the corporation has made to the development of our modern free-enterprise economy?

15. Are the giant corporations gradually crowding small businesses out of the economic picture? Defend your answer.

16. Why is there more need today for government regulation of business than there was a century ago?

17. Explain why a number of great industrial combinations came into existence in the United States between the late 1870's and about 1905.

18. Why was the Sherman Antitrust Act passed? What were its chief provisions? Did it break up industrial monopolies?

19. Why was dissolution of the Standard Oil Company of New Jersey ineffective at the time in destroying its monopoly? Why did this monopoly eventually break down?

20. What were the chief purposes of the Clayton Act? the Federal Trade Commission Act? the Federal Trade Commission?

21. Evaluate the long-run effects of the antitrust laws on the American economy.

22. Why must government regulate public utilities?

23. Should the FCC both permit and encourage the rapid expansion of pay-TV? Why or why not?

24. Explain why the determination of fair public utility rates is a difficult problem.

25. What in your opinion are the chief weaknesses of public utility regulation as practiced in this country?

26. Explain the significance of the role the antitrust laws and utility regulation have played in the American economy.

For Further Study

Barber, Richard J., *The American Corporation,* New York, E. P. Dutton & Company, Inc., 1970.

Berle, Adolf A., and Gardiner C. Means, *The Modern Corporation and Private Property,* rev. ed., paperback, New York, Harcourt Brace Jovanovich, Inc., 1969.

Edwards, Edgar O., ed., *The Nation's Economic Objectives,* Phoenix paperback, Chicago, University of Chicago Press, 1964.

Galbraith, John K., *The Affluent Society,* 2d ed., Boston, Houghton Mifflin Company, 1969.

———, *The New Industrial State,* Boston, Houghton Mifflin Company, 1967. Analysis includes the federal government plus the great corporations.

Hunt, Elgin F., and Jules Karlin, eds., *Society Today and Tomorrow,* paperback, New York, The Macmillan Company, 1967. "Competition, Concentration, and Government Policy" by George Stigler.

Kaplan, A. D. H., *Big Enterprise in a Competitive System,* rev. ed., Washington, D.C., The Brookings Institution, 1964.

Letwin, William, ed., *A Documentary History of American Economic Policy Since 1789,* Chicago, Aldine Publishing Company, n.d.

McAvoy, Paul W., ed., *Crisis of the Regulatory Commissions,* paperback, New York, W. W. Norton & Company, Inc., 1970.

Mark, Shelley M., and Daniel M. Slate, eds., *Economics in Action: Readings in Current Economic Issues,* 4th ed., paperback, Belmont, Cal., Wadsworth Publishing Company, 1969.

Samuelson, Paul A., *Economics,* 7th ed., New York, McGraw-Hill, Inc., 1967. See therein Chaps. 5 and 8.

Servan-Schreiber, J. J., *The American Challenge,* translated by Ronald Steel, New York, Atheneum Publishers, 1968.

Wilcox, Clair, *Public Policies Toward Business,* 3d ed., Homewood, Ill., Richard D. Irwin, Inc., 1966.

Woytinsky, Emma S., *Profile of the U.S. Economy: A Survey of Growth and Change,* New York, Frederick A. Praeger, Inc., 1967.

Chapter 19

Stability,

Growth,

and

Employment

though economic forces are by no means the sole determinants of culture and the course of human history, every culture must have an economic base. Likewise, for satisfactory participation in the life of his society, every individual must have some way of getting a living, and a living that is reasonably adequate according to the standards of the group.

In a modern industrial society, getting an adequate living generally means finding a job that pays an acceptable wage or salary. Hence, if a modern economy is to function smoothly and meet the basic needs of its members, it must always be able to provide employment for at least the great majority of those who are willing and able to work.

When jobs are available for *all* who will accept them at current wage rates—when no one able to work is *involuntarily* idle—we say that a condition of *full employment* prevails. Obviously, full employment is a very desirable condition in any industrial society; but, as we shall see later, it is not a condition that is easy to achieve and maintain. Moreover, *full employment does not mean that at any given time all workers actually have jobs.* For various reasons, there will always be people out of work temporarily, perhaps because they want a vacation or perhaps because they want to take a little time to find the best job available.

In America we are fortunate in having an economy that can outproduce any other in the world and that in "good times" can provide jobs for the great majority of those who are willing and able to work. In the past, however, our economy has had one great weakness: A period of rapid progress, high production, and high employment has always been followed, sooner or later, by a period of falling output and falling employment; this in turn has merged into a more or less protracted period of low production and high unemployment. Such a period we call a *depression.* In this chapter one of our tasks is to explain the causes of economic fluctuations, including depressions, and to seek ways of stabilizing the economy. Another of our tasks is to seek ways of encouraging economic growth. Without this it would be difficult to maintain satisfactory levels of production and employment if our population and labor force continue to expand.

Prosperity and Depression. Forty years or more have now elapsed since the onset of the great depression of the 1930's, but it is still fresh in the memories of many of our older citizens. Likewise, it still remains the outstanding example of the tragic effects that can follow a severe and prolonged reduction of output and employment.

Most Americans, judged by today's standards of income and consumption, were relatively poor in the middle and late 1920's; but we must be cautious in judging the past by the present, for in comparison with anything they had known before, they were enjoying a period of unprecedented prosperity. True, some groups, including the farmers, did not share in this prosperity; but most people had achieved higher incomes than ever before. Furthermore, a great speculative rise in the prices of real estate and stocks had helped to create a general feeling of optimism. This feeling was soon dissipated by rude shocks. In October, 1929, there was a spectacular break in the stock market, and this was only the first of a series of developments that, by 1932, brought the country to the greatest depths of depression in its entire history. From 1929 to 1932 industrial production and national income dropped by about half, and unemployment rose from about three million to between twelve million and fifteen million, or about a quarter of the nation's labor force. These developments brought losses, discouragement, and great hardship to millions of people.

To explain just why this vast shrinkage of income, production, and jobs took place is not simple. It was not the result of a decline in our physical capacity to produce, because we had more factories and a larger and more efficient labor force than ever before. The trouble was that we did not understand our economy well enough to be able to control economic activity in such a way as to keep our labor and equipment busy producing the goods people needed. The great contraction of business in the years following 1929 was merely a phase of that curious phenomenon of modern life, the *business cycle*.

Types of Business Fluctuations. Changes in the general level of business activity are of three principal types: *seasonal, secular,* and *cyclical.*

Seasonal fluctuations result not only from seasonal changes in consumer needs and the fact that crops must be planted and harvested at certain times of the year but also from certain social conventions, like the custom of giving gifts at Christmas or wearing new clothes at Easter. Partly because summer vacations are over and partly because most crops have just been harvested, general business activity tends to reach a high level in the fall. Many businesses are then expanding their output, the crops are being shipped and stored, and the farmers have more money to spend. On the other hand, partly because of the Christmas and Easter holidays, retail trade reaches its highest levels in December and in the spring.

By *secular* movements of business we mean those upward or downward trends in activity that cover long periods of years and result from changes in population, wealth, and technology. Ever since the arrival of the first settlers from Europe, the secular trend in America has been

"What goes up . . . ." (Courtesy Ellinwood and Tuscon Daily Star.)

upward, because our population has been growing, because we have been accumulating wealth, and because our technology has been advancing. This long-time expansion of total output and output per capita is what we have in mind when we talk about *economic growth.*

By *cyclical* fluctuations we mean those rather marked upward and downward movements of business that in the past have required from two or three years up to as many as ten or twelve years from one peak of prosperity to the next. Such movements are a striking characteristic of an industrial free-enterprise economy. In many respects, however, they are highly irregular, and sometimes minor cycles occur within major cycles. Because of their irregularity, business cycles cannot be used as the basis for making accurate predictions about the future.

A *major business cycle* consists of a complete upward and a complete downward swing in business activity, the one succeeding the other. However, to determine with any certainty the direction and extent of the cyclical movement of business at a given time, we must first make allowance for seasonal changes and the secular trend. If there is normally a seasonal decline of business in January, but in a certain January it is much less than usual, that is an indication that the cyclical movement is upward. Again, if there is reason to believe that the secular trend is upward, but in a certain year no rise in business activity occurs, that may indicate that the cyclical movement is downward.

The Four Phases of a Major Business Cycle. Though a major business cycle consists of a complete upward and a complete downward swing, which of these movements should be considered to come first is a matter of choice or opinion. In this chapter we shall assume, for convenience, that a cycle begins with the upward movement. We can then think of a business cycle as having four successive phases. Starting at the close of a period of very restricted activity, the following rise is called *recovery.* This merges into a period of high activity called *prosperity;* and this, in turn, is followed by a period of decline called *recession.* Finally, the cycle is completed by a return to that low level of activity known as *depression.* Figure 18 is a diagram representing a typical business cycle.

If business cycles covered definite periods of time and attained uniform intensities, we could easily foretell their course. Actually, however, they have followed such irregular patterns that attempts to forecast them have met with limited success. In the past, major cycles have covered anywhere from six to twelve years, and both the upward and the downward swings have often been interrupted by minor movements in the contrary direction. The extent of such minor movements and the time required by them have varied so greatly that their significance could only be determined afterwards. Even today, when business starts to decline, we cannot be sure whether we are witnessing a minor interruption of an upward trend or the beginning of a continuing period of recession.

The Problem of Business Cycles and Mass Unemployment. If government is unable to devise effective measures for stabilizing it, a free-

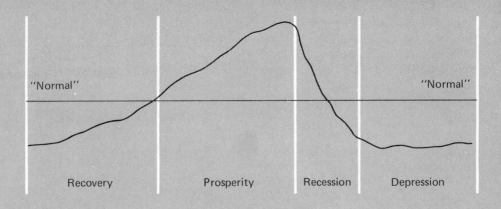

"Normal"   "Normal"

Recovery   Prosperity   Recession   Depression

Figure 18. A "Typical" Business Cycle.

enterprise economy seems by its very nature to be subject to alternating periods of expansion and contraction. Once expansion gets well under way, it causes further expansion or becomes cumulative; but finally it generates the very forces that stop and then reverse it. Then, when contraction gets under way, it too becomes cumulative and in turn generates forces that ultimately stop it and that later set in motion a new upward movement.

The worst aspect of a major business cycle is, of course, the mass unemployment that accompanies the depression phase. Surprisingly, up to the great depression of the 1930's, economists had no very clear understanding of the causes of business cycles or of the policies by which a government might effectively control them or at least minimize them. Developments after World War I, especially the great depression, led to more intensive study of the cycle problem and to a better understanding of its nature.

Since World War II, business cycles have been much less severe than in earlier times. In part, at least, this is because we know more about them and about the policies that can be applied to smooth them out. But it would be far too optimistic to say that we have learned how to "fine tune" the economy and thus to eliminate cycles completely. The control of business cycles still presents difficult problems. Some of these are political, some have to do with the structure of our economy, and some grow out of the difficulty of knowing in advance how the public will react to certain economic situations. However, most economists agree that today the government can and would prevent a recurrence of a depression comparable in severity to what occurred in the 1930's.

The social damage resulting from a severe and prolonged depression can be so extreme as to approach a national catastrophe. In the great business contraction from 1929 to 1933, the purchasing power of the people of the United States fell 40 per cent. This would have been bad enough if the loss had been spread evenly over the whole population, but actually the greater part of it fell on the unemployed. At the bottom of the depression as many as 25 per cent of all workers, most of them with families, had their wage or salary incomes completely cut off. The only thing that prevented starvation for many—or, possibly, revolution —was the granting of relief payments by the federal government. The relief burden was far too great to have been carried by private charities, especially at a time when even the well-to-do were suffering heavy financial losses.

Figure 19 shows unemployment as a percentage of the labor force in each year from 1900 through 1968. By the *labor force* we mean *the number of persons over fourteen who are able to work and who either have jobs or are seeking employment.*

Measuring Fluctuations of Business. If we are to understand business cycles and attempt to control them, we must have statistical information that indicates the changes that take place in the general level of business activity. In the last half century we have made great progress in developing the needed statistical measures. Not only do we have reasonably dependable figures on production, employment, sales, and other relevant factors for a large number of industries, but we also have indexes that

Figure 19. Unemployed as a Percentage of the Labor Force. (Adapted from *Economic Growth in the United States,* New York, The Committee for Economic Development, February, 1958, p. 35. Years 1957–1964 and 1965–1970 based on figures in *Federal Reserve Bulletins,* October, 1965, p. 1326, and August, 1970, p. A 64.)

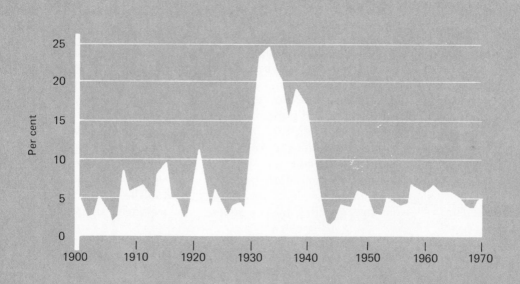

bring some of this data together to give us a picture of the level of economic activity as a whole.

Various statistical series have been found useful in the past for indicating and interpreting changes in the general level of business activity. Among the oldest of these are changes in the output of iron and steel, and fluctuations in the total of railway car-loadings. An index much in use today, because it covers a wide range of output, is the Federal Reserve index of the physical volume of industrial production. Other useful business indicators include bank clearings and debits;[1] bank loans, deposits, and reserves; employment and payrolls; sales at wholesale and retail; building contracts let; and prices.

Today, probably the most widely used indicators of general business activity are the national product and income estimates of the Department of Commerce. One of these estimates, *gross national product,* is especially useful because it attempts to measure the total output of the economy. *Gross national product* may be defined as *the money value of all goods, including personal services, produced in a given year.* Considerable use is also made, in analyzing business trends, of the estimates that the Department of Commerce makes of personal income, disposable personal income,[2] and personal consumption expenditures.

Figure 20 shows variations of industrial production from the long-run trend for the period from 1931 to 1969. The long-run trend has been steadily upward, but it is represented here as a horizontal line. The figure shows that, since World War II, fluctuations in economic activity have been smaller than before the war and depressions less severe. Partly this can be explained by changes in the structure of the economy, to which we shall refer later. But partly, as already noted, it has resulted from a better understanding of the cycle and a greater willingness on the part of government to take remedial action if unemployment approaches an abnormally high level.

WHY WE HAVE BUSINESS CYCLES

Business cycles of the modern type are a relatively recent phenomenon. So-called trade cycles doubtless existed in the seventeenth century or

---

[1] Bank debits are the total charges made against demand and time deposits at commercial banks. For the most part, they represent checks charged against customers' accounts. Because every check is ultimately charged to the maker, bank debits are a measure of the total volume of payments made by check. And because most payments in this country are so made, changes in bank debits are an indicator of changes in the volume of all payments. Complete figures on bank debits are not available, but since 1919 the Federal Reserve authorities have collected debit statistics from reporting banks in a number of important cities.

[2] Disposable personal income is the income of all individuals after payment of personal taxes, the major element in which is the federal income tax.

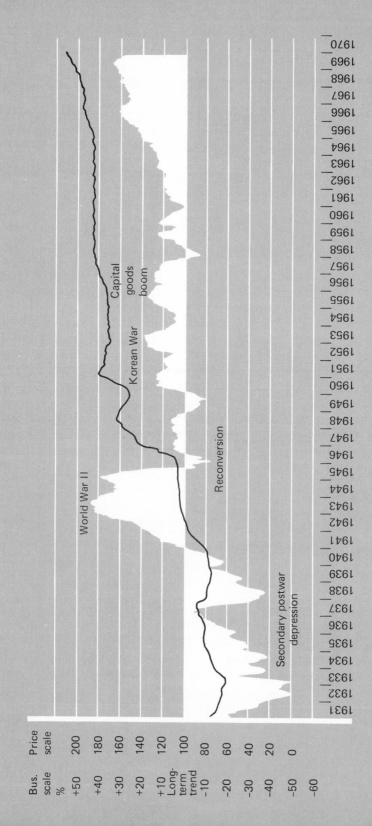

Figure 20. American Business Activity, 1931–1969. The black line represents wholesale prices. (The Cleveland Trust Company, Cleveland, Ohio.)

earlier, but the cycle did not begin to take on its present character and importance until the Industrial Revolution was well under way.

The Role of Specialization and Trade in Business Fluctuations. Fundamentally, the business cycle is a by-product of specialization, trade, and the use of money. It could not exist in a self-sufficient economy where each family satisfied all, or nearly all, its wants by applying its own labor to materials of its own gathering. In such an economy trade and fluctuations in trade would be relatively unimportant. A man would never be unemployed, for he would always have the job of working for himself and his family. Any falling off in production would be the result of misfortunes such as epidemics or drought or war, and would have no tendency to be cumulative. But in the modern world we are not self-sufficient. If we are farmers, we may concentrate on two or three crops; if we are manual workers, we perform some particular service in a factory. We produce scarcely any of the things we need in everyday life. Instead, we obtain them through trade. To get the money to buy the things we need, we must sell such material goods as we ourselves produce or else we must sell our own labor. But if the public reduces its total purchases, we cannot sell as much as before, and with less money we cannot buy as much.

But why does the public sometimes reduce its purchases? Perhaps it has been buying new houses and automobiles at an unusually high rate, so that for the time being most people who can afford them already have them; or perhaps the public has developed a fear of recession and unemployment, and so people in self-protection begin to hoard their money. But whatever the cause may be, an important drop in *total spending* will bring on depression because it means less sales, less income, less production, and less employment. Let us consider, for example, how the workers for an automobile manufacturing company will be affected. If sales fall off, new cars will begin to accumulate in the storage yards of the company, and the money it spends in producing them will no longer keep flowing back to it from buyers. It must then, in order to protect its working capital, cut production and lay off men; as a result, many workers will lose their incomes.

Why Business Fluctuations Are Cyclical. Up to a point, either expansion or contraction of business activity tends to be cumulative. This results from certain fairly simple relationships that exist in an economy where people produce goods and services for the market and not for their own use. An increase in demand for one or more important products, no matter what the reasons, brings an increase in sales. An increase in sales induces producers to expand output. To expand output they must employ more workers, and this results in greater total wage payments. Increased wage income, in turn, enables workers to increase their demands for all types of consumer goods, thus bringing additional increases in sales, production, and wage payments. As business optimism rises producers, in order to expand their output, begin to buy more capital goods in the form of new factories and machines, and the construction of these raises employment and wage income to still higher levels. By this time a process of cumulative business expansion is well under way. It may continue for some time, but eventually it will taper off and be followed by a period of cumulative contraction.

Various factors contribute toward starting business contraction in the later stages of a period of prosperity. For one thing, many industries approach capacity production and find further increases in output both difficult and expensive. Sooner or later, interest rates on bank loans are likely to rise, and even more serious, labor shortages develop and wage costs go up. As business costs increase, profit margins tend to decline, and the building of new factories and the purchase of new machines become less attractive. Consumer prices may also rise, so that even with more money income, consumers cannot much increase their purchases. Eventually, total expenditures on capital goods and consumer goods begin to fall. Then the whole process is reversed, and a cumulative contraction gets under way.

But sooner or later this contraction is checked and reversed. For one thing, as incomes shrink, people are under greater and greater pressure to spend all their remaining income on living expenses and even to spend savings and borrowed money. Also, business spending on inventories shrinks, until these reach the point where further reduction is difficult. When total spending finally stops contracting, sales, production, employment, and income also stop contracting; and, eventually, spending begins to rise again. Some individuals and business enterprises always have substantial cash balances, and when they see that the worst is over, they start spending these more freely on both consumer goods and capital goods.

The above explanation is greatly oversimplified, especially as applied to the relatively mild business cycles that have been characteristic of the period since World War II. Nevertheless, it gives some idea of the nature of the forces that, in an uncontrolled free-enterprise economy, tend to bring about business expansion or contraction and then reverse it.

Stable Spending as the Key to Stable Production and Employment. In any attempt to analyze the nature and causes of economic fluctuations, it is very important to understand that *the level of income, production, and employment is directly controlled by total spending.* In a specialized industrial economy, people produce goods, not for their own use, but for sale. As long as goods can be sold at satisfactory prices, it will pay to make them because their sale will provide incomes for producers; as long as people will keep spending sufficient money for goods, they can be sold; and as long as they can be produced and sold to advantage, and in sufficient quantities, employers will be willing and even anxious to hire all the workers who are available. If we assume stable prices, *once a high level of income, production, and employment is achieved, the whole secret of maintaining prosperity is to find ways of preventing any* *contraction of total spending.* If spending can be kept at a high enough level, there will always be full employment. However, changes in the price level are likely to create problems, and these we shall discuss later.

In studying the problem of economic stability, it is very helpful to keep in mind that the direct source of nearly all money income is money expenditure.[3] Money received by one person is money that was paid out by someone else. Likewise, it is helpful to remember that the source of most (though not all) expenditure is current income.[4] Money is constantly being spent, thus creating income, and then being respent to create income again. This is the process we refer to when we talk about *the circulation of money.* Any reduction in the total amount of money spent must necessarily reduce the total amount of income received. This loss of income will be felt by the public in the form of lower wages, lower receipts of rent and interest, smaller profits, lower dividends, and loss of wages from unemployment.

Keynes and the "New Economics." By far the most influential economist of the first half of the twentieth century was John Maynard Keynes.[5] His major work, published in 1936, is a book entitled *The General Theory of Employment, Interest, and Money.* This volume largely reflects Keynes' reactions to the problems of the great depression of the 1930's. Its principal emphasis is on economic fluctuations and the policies needed to maintain a high level of production and employment. It is a book that is difficult to understand, and, as a result, it became the basis of much argument, discussion, and interpretation among economists. Not all Keynes' conclusions have been supported by experience or by later economic studies. Nevertheless, he developed a technique of analysis that has proved invaluable to economists interested in the problems of stabilizing or expanding production and employment. It was chiefly his genius that created what later became known as the *New Economics.* The use of this expression to refer to Keynes' theories spread rapidly among economists after World War II, but it probably did not become known to the average reader of the business pages of the newspapers until after the election of John F. Kennedy to the Presidency in 1960. Kennedy attempted, with some success, to apply the principles of the New Economics in order to expand production and employment.

We shall make no attempt here to give a full explanation of Keynes' economic theories. To do that would require a book rather than a few paragraphs. We shall, however, call attention to certain aspects of his approach to the problems of economic stability and employment.

---

[3] Minor sources of money income are money losses (of others), thefts, and gifts.

[4] Sometimes important sources of expenditure in a given period are cash balances accumulated in the past, or money borrowed from banks.

[5] Keynes was an Englishman who had an extraordinary career. In addition to being an outstanding academic economist, he was a mathematician, an editor, a successful businessman, a patron of the arts, and an advisor to the British government. Incidentally, he was the husband of a well-known Russian ballet dancer.

Keynes saw that production and employment, within the limits of available resources, are determined directly by the total amount of money spent for goods. This spending he called *aggregate demand,* but in our discussion we shall use the more self-explanatory expression *total spending.* Keynes included in *total spending* not only the total amount of money spent on consumption goods but also the amount spent by businessmen on investment or capital goods such as new factories and machines. He thus divided total spending into consumption spending and investment spending, which he called, for short, *consumption* and *investment.* [6] A marked decline in either consumption spending or investment spending will reduce total sales, production, and employment and thus bring on depression. However, Keynes believed that investment spending is more unstable than consumption spending and more subject to extreme contractions. Hence, if we wish to stabilize economic activity, or increase it, we must find ways of stabilizing or increasing investment spending.

Keynes also pointed out that, in a period of declining business, any attempt by people to protect themselves by saving and hoarding more money in their pockets or in the bank would only make matters worse. In trying to build up their cash balances they would decrease their purchases, further decreasing total spending; and this would bring an additional decline in production, employment, and income. The only way to offset a business recession is to increase spending, not reduce it.

However, an increase in saving does not *necessarily* mean a decrease in spending. If people save more by spending less on *consumption goods,* and then use the extra saving to buy more *investment goods,* there is no decrease in total spending. As long as people are willing to spend on investment goods as much as they are willing to save, total spending will be maintained, and likewise employment and income. Nevertheless, there is still an increase in saving, because to Keynes *saving* is any income not spent on *consumption* goods. The trouble comes when people try to hoard their savings by building up their idle cash balances. Actually the public *as a whole* cannot build up its cash balances by merely trying to save *and keep* more money. At any given time, there is only so much money in currency and bank deposits in an economy; hence, if some individuals are able to increase their cash balances, it will be at the expense of others whose cash balances are reduced. If everybody should try hard to accumulate more cash, everybody would spend less and the principal result would be to bring on a depression.

Keynes and his followers also pointed out that large-scale unemployment represented not only hardship for the unemployed but also the loss to the community of huge amounts of goods. These could easily be produced if only some way could be found to put the unemployed to work.

[6] It should be noted that Keynes gave to *investment* and *consumption* meanings different from those usually assigned them.

One of his proposals for doing this was large-scale government spending on needed public works.

Because the key to stable production, employment, and income is stable spending, we will now examine briefly some special factors that cause spending to fluctuate.

SOME REASONS FOR FLUCTUATIONS IN TOTAL SPENDING

We noted that Keynes divides total spending, or aggregate demand, into consumption and investment spending. For some purposes it is more useful to divide it into three parts, as follows: (1) private consumption spending, (2) private investment spending, and (3) government spending. Of these three types of spending, private consumption spending is the largest, and it is likely to be relatively stable as long as consumers' incomes do not change greatly. In the United States, consumers in normal years consistently spend well over 90 per cent of their total disposable incomes. They become accustomed to certain standards of living and as a group will reduce their spending very little unless they are forced to do so because their incomes decline. Total consumer income and spending tend to rise gradually because of increases in population, employment, production, and spending by business and government; also because the banks and the government gradually increase the money supply. Government spending is, as a rule, relatively stable in the short run under normal peacetime conditions, though for many years its long-run rate of increase has been much more rapid than that of population or national income. But, to meet national emergencies, it can undergo great changes in short periods of time. When war breaks out, government spending rises rapidly, falling again on the return of peace, though usually not to its original level. The type of spending that in time of peace is most subject to wide fluctuation is private investment.

Why Investment Spending Fluctuates. The instability of investment grows out of the fact that most investment expenditures are made by business enterprises not to meet pressing current needs but in the hope of future profits. Most investment goods are *durable,* like railroad lines, rolling stock, heavy machines, factory buildings, hotels, and office buildings. Frequently it takes several years to plan them and produce them. When business sentiment is optimistic with regard to demand and profits over the next few years, many firms will undertake large programs of plant expansion, and their expenditures for labor and materials create jobs and incomes for millions of men. But if something happens to undermine seriously the confidence of businessmen in the future—if they think there will be no markets for the output of additional plants—then investment spending may fall to very low levels, with the result that millions of men are directly thrown out of work. The great depression that began in 1929 was the direct result of a shrinkage of investment. In part, this shrinkage was brought about by the pessimism generated by the stock-market crash in the fall of that year. When the bottom of the depression was reached, *net* investment had completely disappeared. That is, expenditures for plant and equipment were no longer sufficient to offset depreciation on the stock of capital goods already on hand.

The Unstable Demand for All Durable Goods. The wide fluctuations that take place in production and employment in an industrial economy are explained in part by the fact that a large portion of the goods produced in such an economy are durable. Not only are most investment goods durable, but also many consumer goods, such as refrigerators and automobiles. The industries producing durable goods are the most affected by optimistic or pessimistic future expectations. Though consumer spending as a whole is more stable than investment spending, in the case of durable goods, consumers can often delay their purchases for a long time; and if prices are dropping or people are afraid of losing their jobs, the demand for such goods may fall sharply. Then, when confidence returns, and large numbers of people who have deferred their purchases reenter the market, demand may rise to a level so high that it cannot possibly be maintained for any great length of time.

Unlike the demand for durable goods, the demand for perishable goods is relatively stable. We must consume a certain amount of food every day,

"What's hurting the nation's economy are people who refuse to live beyond their means." (Courtesy George Borg—*Chicago Tribune Magazine*.)

and because we are unable to keep large supplies on hand, we cannot long put off our buying. But if we are thinking of buying a new automobile, we can probably put off action two or three years and meanwhile continue to drive the old one. If we plan to purchase a new house, we can probably wait even longer; indeed, unless the time comes when we have confidence in the future, we are not likely to buy it at all.

The Multiplier. As we have stated before, a given increase of total spending in the economy will directly create an equal increase in income, because any money spent by one person is sooner or later received as income by someone else in such forms as wages, rent, interest, direct profits, or dividends. But ultimately it is likely to create an amount of income several times as great, for the reason that the people who receive the initial increase will spend at least part of it and thus will create additional income for still other people. They, in turn, will create more income by spending part of what they receive, and so on, ad infinitum. This tendency of a given *initial* increase of spending to increase income by a total several times greater was called by Keynes the *multiplier.* It refers to the same phenomenon that earlier, in connection with the effects of an increase in government spending, had often been called "pump-priming." Keynes was chiefly concerned with the multiplier effect of increases of investment spending. He argued that because of this effect, a moderate rise in the rate of investment would eventually result in a relatively large rise not only of income but also of production and employment.

The multiplier effect operates equally well in reverse. If the rate of total spending is reduced by even a moderate amount, some businessmen and workers find their incomes decreased or cut off, the workers perhaps through losing their jobs. This forces them to reduce their spending, which in turn cuts down the incomes and spending of other people, and so the process continues.

The multiplier effect contributes substantially to the instability of an industrial economy. It is one way of explaining the cumulative character of economic expansion and contraction, already described briefly in an earlier paragraph.

The Acceleration Principle. A factor that undoubtedly contributes to cyclical fluctuations of total spending is the somewhat peculiar relationship between changes in the demand for finished goods and changes in the demand for the equipment used to produce them. *A small percentage change in expenditures for finished goods may cause a much greater percentage change in expenditures for productive equipment.* This relationship is called the *acceleration principle.*

To illustrate the operation of the acceleration principle, let us take the automobile industry. Suppose that at the beginning of a cyclical upswing of business, only half the families of the country have automobiles. No new automobile factories are being built except as old ones wear out, because for some time the demand for automobiles has been on a replacement level, and the factories already in existence have been just sufficient to meet this demand. The production of machines for making automobiles has also been on a replacement level.

Now let us suppose that a general increase in prosperity causes automobile sales to rise 10 per cent a year for a period of several years. We will further assume that, before this rise started, new plant and equipment was being produced (for replacement purposes) at an annual rate equal to 10 per cent of the amount already in existence. Now, however, an additional 10 per cent will have to be produced in order to take care of the increase in automobile sales. In other words, the amount of *new* plant and equipment produced annually will double, or increase 100 per cent. This new rate of output is likely to be *maintained* as long as automobile sales continue to rise at the rate of about 10 per cent annually.

But suppose that at the end of five years most of the families that want cars have them and that therefore the demand for automobiles ceases to expand further. Even though the demand should not contract, the mere fact that it has *stopped expanding* means that there will no longer be a need for adding to total plant capacity. The demand for new factories and their equipment will again drop back to a replacement level; and annual production of new plant and equipment may drop from 20 per cent of the existing amount back to 10 per cent, a reduction by half, or 50 percent. This will bring acute depression to those producing automobile-making equipment. Many men will lose their jobs, and total consumer purchasing power will be reduced.

If contraction of the kind just described should occur in only one or two industries producing capital goods, it might be offset by expansion elsewhere. However, if a similar situation should develop at about the same time in a number of industries producing such goods, it is almost certain that a downswing of the business cycle would be precipitated. The acceleration principle is one factor contributing to the wide fluctuations of investment spending and hence of total spending.

The Effects of Speculation. Because of the frequent tendency of the business community as a whole either to overestimate or underestimate the future, *speculation* plays an extremely important role in cyclical fluctuations of total spending.

Speculation, as we are using the term, means buying or selling goods in order to take advantage of price changes expected in the future. Most commonly we think of it in connection with buying commodities, securities, or real estate in the present with the hope of selling them at a higher price later; but the manufacturer who accumulates unusually large inventories of raw materials in the hope of avoiding higher prices is also speculating; and in some cases speculation involves selling things in the hope of buying them back later at a lower price.[7] Speculation not only contributes to the

---

[7] Selling a stock short is a good illustration of selling to make a profit by buying back at a lower price.

cumulative character of recovery or recession but also helps to explain the reversal in trend that takes place at the bottom and at the top of a business cycle.

Suppose we start at the bottom of a period of depression. Contraction has stopped, but pessimism is widespread and there are few indications of recovery. Prices are low. When this situation has continued with little change for a period of time, some people, judging by their past experience, will become convinced that the worst is over and that improvement is only a matter of time. For example, some manufacturers will begin spending to build up their stocks of raw materials, in the belief that prices can go no lower and are very likely to rise. This increased demand for materials will eventually bring a rise in prices and will also increase production, employment, and payrolls in the industries directly affected. As recovery gets under way, it will be stimulated to an increasing degree by speculation. Rising prices will encourage manufacturers, merchants, consumers, and outright speculators to buy more and more goods, not for current use, but in order to avoid paying higher prices later or in order to sell later at a profit. But buying goods ahead has limits. Funds and storage space run low. In time more and more people begin to recognize that some prices are reaching a level that is not likely to be maintained.

When the price rise slows down, some of those who are holding goods in the hope of selling at a profit decide the time has come to unload. Soon others rush to sell, with the result that prices drop rapidly. When this happens, businessmen who have built up inventories are likely to stop all buying until inventories are reduced. The demand for goods falls off sharply while the speculative stocks are being used up. Falling prices lead people to expect a further fall in prices. In time, however, the downward movement loses momentum. Ultimately, stocks of goods are reduced to the point where buying must begin again. As a result, the fall in prices is checked, and before long the stage is set for a new rise.

Although speculation based on price changes is by no means the only factor contributing to the instability of our economy, it is at times a powerful force, capable in itself of causing very noticeable cyclical fluctuations of total spending and hence of production, income, and employment.

INFLATION AND THE PROBLEM OF FULL EMPLOYMENT

We have emphasized that to prevent depressions and to provide full employment at all times it is only necessary to raise total spending (aggregate demand) to a sufficiently high level and then to keep it there. But unfortunately there is always the problem of raising it just enough and not too much; for if total spending *exceeds* the amount of spending necessary to maintain a reasonably high level of employment, the result will be *inflation*.

Inflation and Total Spending. We might define *inflation* as simply a rise of the general price level regardless of its extent or duration. In actual usage, however, *inflation means a fairly rapid rise in the price level, and one that continues for some length of time.* Any significant increase of total spending will somewhat raise prices, even if it begins in a period of depression when many factories and workers are idle. But in a depression period the chief effect of more spending is to raise production, and any increase of prices is a secondary matter. Producers are glad to put idle factories and idle men to work as soon as there is a prospect of selling their product; as a result, supply does not fall very far behind demand. Prices may rise moderately, but as a rule we do not think of this as inflation. The direct cause of an inflationary price rise is usually an increase of total spending and money incomes at a time when the economy is already producing goods at a rate close to capacity. If people keep receiving and spending more money when the output of goods can be increased very little, there will not be enough goods to go around at the current price level. Demand, in other words, will outrun supply, and the only possible result in free markets will be a rise in prices. Only through such a rise can the goods available for sale be equated to the amounts of money that people are able and willing to spend.

Business Spending, Bank Credit, and Inflation. In times of peace and in periods of prosperity a limited amount of inflation may result from a rapid expansion of business spending for new plant, equipment, and inventories. But where do business enterprises get the funds for such an increase of spending? Largely they come from three sources: (1) idle cash balances that investors use to buy corporate securities like stocks and bonds, (2) idle cash balances held by business firms themselves, and (3) funds borrowed from *commercial banks.* Commercial banks are the ordinary banks that carry checking accounts and make loans and investments.

Whenever there is an inflationary expansion of business spending, the commercial banks always play a significant role in making it possible by expanding credit to businessmen in the form of loans. But when the banks increase their *total* loans, what they are really doing is creating new money and making it available to business enterprises for spending.[8] The process by which the banks create this new money is fundamentally a simple one, and yet it completely mystifies a great many people. One reason for this is that people have difficulty in grasping the idea that *demand bank deposits,* or checking accounts, are in themselves a form of money and that they do not really represent currency and coin held by the banks. Actually, the total amount of currency and coin in the vaults of the ordinary commercial banks is less than 3 per cent of their demand deposits.

Commercial banks do, it is true, have additional funds in the form of deposits in other banks. If they are members of the *Federal Reserve System,*

---

[8] In the past, banks lent very little to consumers, but today consumer loans are assuming increasing importance.

40. Money-Counting Machine in a Federal Reserve Bank. (Courtesy Wide World Photos.)

the bulk of their *legal reserves* must be kept as deposits with a *Federal Reserve bank*. But even these Reserve deposits of the member banks amount to less than 20 per cent of the demand deposits that they hold for the public.

The Federal Reserve System. The Federal Reserve System consists principally of twelve *Federal Reserve banks;* a government agency called the *Board of Governors,* which controls many of their policies; and the ordinary or *member banks,* which belong to the system. Each Federal Reserve bank has its own district, and together they cover the country. Ordinarily Reserve banks do not deal with the general public, but they make loans to and receive deposits from member banks and also regulate them in various ways. In addition, they act as bankers and financial agents for the federal government and sometimes for foreign governments or central banks.

Bank Deposits as Money. In recent years it has become increasingly clear to students of money and banking not only that bank deposits are money but also that in some respects they are the most important kind of money now in use. Legally, it is true, a checking account is merely the right to receive from a bank on demand a certain amount of currency or coin. But to spend a bank deposit, it is not necessary to draw out paper money or coin. All that the depositor need do is to write out a check, thus transferring his claim against the bank—or some part of it—to someone else. If we include in the *money supply* of the country, paper money, coin, and demand deposits, we find that demand deposits constitute almost four fifths of the total money purchasing power that the American people hold at any given time.[9] Obviously, if most depositors tried at any given time to draw out all their money in the form of currency and coin, the banks would be unable to meet their demands.

To a bank, deposits of its customers are merely debts. They represent obligations to pay to depositors or to their order certain sums of money, either in currency and coin or in some other form that the depositors will accept. Because a deposit is merely a bank debt, to create a deposit for a customer, a bank does not have to receive any kind of money from him. All it needs to do is to agree to honor his checks up to a certain amount.

When a businessman borrows from a bank, the normal procedure is for the bank to credit his checking account with the amount of the loan. Let us suppose that Mr. Smith borrows $50,000. His bank credits his account with this amount, and he can then use this *bank credit* to buy anything he chooses by writing checks. But where did the $50,000 come from? From the bank's cash or from someone's deposits? No, it is *new* money. To be sure, in order to provide Mr. Smith with this deposit credit, the bank must have had some "excess" reserve in currency or on deposit in a Federal Reserve bank, that is, reserve over and above the minimum percentage it is required by law to carry against its total deposits. Nevertheless, the $50,000 borrowed by Mr. Smith is a net addition to the total amount of money—cash balances—held by the American public.

Even if Mr. Smith should draw out the whole $50,000 in paper money and pay his bills with currency, this currency would soon get into the hands of merchants or other businessmen who would deposit it in their own banks. As a result, the total amount of bank deposits held by the public would still be $50,000 greater than before Mr. Smith borrowed from his bank. The point to fix in mind is this: *When the banks expand their total loans by a given amount, other things being equal, the total cash balances held by the public are increased by an equal amount.*

If tens of thousands of businessmen in a period of prosperity keep borrowing larger and larger amounts from the banks, the total volume of deposits held by the public may rise by billions of dollars; when this money is spent by the original borrowers, total spending rises by a similar amount; and when the multiplier effect begins to operate, it rises even more. *But if the production of goods was already at a high level and cannot be much increased, the principal effect of the increase in total spending will be an inflationary rise of the price level.*

Government Spending and Inflation. Although some inflation can result from an increase of business spending alone, in modern times the primary source of major inflations has been government spending. Whenever a government spends more money than it collects in taxes, and borrows a major portion of the extra money from banks, it keeps adding to both

---

[9] Some writers also count savings deposits as money. Legally, a bank may demand thirty days' notice before paying savings deposits, but in practice they are usually paid on demand. They cannot, however, be transferred by check.

the money supply and total spending, and if in percentage terms it spends a great deal more than it takes in, inflation is inevitable. Even in times of peace politically and economically unstable countries have often experienced uncontrolled inflation. For example, at the end of the period 1948–1963 the price level in Brazil was more than fifteen times higher than at the beginning; in Argentina more than twenty times; and in Chile about thirty times. Prosperous and well-governed countries are not apt to experience inflation on this scale, and certainly not in time of peace; but in wartime it is very difficult for any country to avoid a substantial amount of inflation.

When a country becomes involved in a major war, it is forced to expand its armed forces as much and as quickly as possible. This means a rapid rise of government spending, and hence of total spending. Employment and wages also rise rapidly, thus giving consumers much more money to spend. But there is little increase in the output of consumer goods, and there may be a decrease, because a large part of the resources of the country is now devoted to producing war goods. Hence there will be a rapid rise in the price level as consumer spending increases with no corresponding increase in the supply of goods. Price controls and rationing may temporarily slow down this inflation, but such measures create difficulties of their own. If continued after the war is over, they can be a greater evil than moderate inflation, because they depress production and economic growth and because their administration consumes vast amounts of time and effort.

The inflation resulting from a war would not occur, or at least it would be very much less, if all the extra money the government spends were raised by increasing taxes or by borrowing from the general public rather than from banks. In that case, the increased spending by government would be largely offset by decreased spending of consumers, because the latter would have less to spend. But there are a number of reasons, political, economic, and psychological, that make it impractical for a government to obtain from these two sources all the funds needed to fight a major war. Taxes will, to be sure, be increased, and also more money will be borrowed from the public; but a large part of the funds required for the war will be borrowed by selling government securities to banks.

Government securities are simply the government's promises to pay, and when it uses them to borrow from banks the effect on bank deposits is precisely the same as when businessmen borrow from the banks. In World War II, when the banks bought government bonds, they paid for them by merely crediting on their books the account of the federal Treasury. These credits represented new money, and when the Treasury paid its bills, this money was transferred by government checks to the general public. This explains why total demand deposits rose during the period of World War II (figures are for December, 1941, to December, 1945) from about $39 billion to nearly $76 billion.

It should be noted that when bank deposits increase and prices rise, people require more paper money and coin to transact their daily business. They obtain it by drawing out part of their bank deposits in this form. Because the ordinary banks hold only enough currency and coin for their daily business, when withdrawals are persistent they have to get more from the Federal Reserve banks. Even the Federal Reserve banks do not have great quantities of it, but they can always get more paper money by issuing additional *Federal Reserve notes,* [10] and they can obtain more coins by buying them from the United States mints.

There is no *close* relation between the *money supply* (the total amount of currency, coin, and demand deposits that people hold) and total spending. The amount of money spent in a given period of time can rise without any change in the quantity of money. All that is necessary is that people should spend their money faster, and thus increase the velocity with which it circulates. However, to increase beyond a certain point the speed with which money is spent creates problems. Some money must always be kept on hand if the needs of daily life are to be met conveniently. As a result, if people still have confidence in their money, increases in velocity eventually encounter strong resistance. Hence no *large* and *long-continued* rise in total expenditures will take place unless there is a large increase in the money supply to support it.

Inflation and the Public Debt. A rapid rise of the public debt is likely to be inflationary for the simple reason that the debt rises rapidly only when the government is increasing total spending by using large amounts of borrowed money, much of which comes from banks. Because of the multiplier effect, total spending will ultimately rise much more than the amount by which government spending is increased. Oddly enough, however, inflation makes it easier for the country to support a national debt of any given size in terms of dollars. This is because a rise in prices means a rise in the money value of property and a rise in money incomes, and therefore a rise in tax receipts. Interest on the public debt is easier to pay, and the principal represents a smaller part of the national wealth. Today, the United States government debt is about $360 billion. But this is less of a burden on the country than a debt of $100 billion would have been in 1940, because since 1940 the national income, measured in money, has increased more than nine times. Though a good deal of this increase reflects our larger population and our larger output of goods, much more than half of it can be accounted for by inflation.

Summary of Factors Affecting Inflation. For a clear understanding of the process of inflation, the reader should fix in mind the following relation-

[10] Federal Reserve banks can issue more paper money in the form of Federal Reserve notes whenever such notes are needed, provided they can deposit with the Federal Reserve Agent, who represents the government, adequate collateral. Formerly, they had to give the Reserve Agent gold certificates equal to 25 per cent of the notes issued, plus enough government securities and commercial paper to cover the balance. The actual gold was held by the Treasury. But in 1968 Congress removed the requirement for holding actual gold, and the Treasury gave the Federal Reserve banks "gold certificate credits" which they can substitute for gold certificates.

ships: (1) a rise of total spending will not cause inflation as long as the production of goods increases proportionately; (2) if total spending rises faster than production, some degree of inflation must result; (3) an important rise of total spending is almost always initiated by a rise of business or government spending, though higher consumer spending may also be a factor; (4) a rapid rise in government debt is inflationary because it means a rapid rise in government spending of borrowed funds; (5) because of the multiplier effect, the total increase in spending will exceed the initial increase in business and government spending; (6) any large and long-continued increase in total spending must be supported by an increase in the money supply, though in the short run the rate of total spending can vary a good deal without corresponding changes in the money supply; and (7) in our kind of economy any important increase of the money supply begins with the expansion of bank deposits that results when banks increase their total loans to business and/or government.

The Evils of Inflation. The evils of inflation are very real, but just how serious they are depends on the degree of inflation. When inflation is rapid and goes to great extremes, as in the classic example of Germany after World War I, it can completely disorganize the economic life of a nation and in the process impoverish millions of citizens. In 1923, toward the end of the German inflation, people would spend money for almost anything because they feared that the next week, or even the next day, it would buy less. Prices rose so fast that, before very long, savings accounts, bonds, pensions, and all other forms of property representing fixed sums of money became completely worthless. Originally, a mark was equivalent to about twenty-four cents, but before the inflation ended, a million marks or more were needed to buy such a small item as a loaf of bread or a pound

"Sure I know the value of a dollar. That's the reason I asked for two." (Courtesy Leo Garel and *The Saturday Evening Post*.)

of sugar. Under these conditions it hardly seemed worthwhile to work for wages or salaries. About the only chance of getting ahead was to speculate in the stock market or in land, commodities, and foreign currency.

The situation is quite different when inflation is relatively moderate and limited. In the United States we had enough inflation between 1941 and 1971 to raise the level of consumer prices by more than 150 per cent; and though it had some very undesirable effects, no one can reasonably say that it was a national disaster; but it could become one if we allow the rate of inflation to keep accelerating. Up to now, total output of goods, per capita output of goods, and average standards of living have all risen, so that most people are better off than ever before in spite of higher prices. Nevertheless, great numbers of people living on relatively fixed incomes have suffered undeserved hardships. The group that has suffered most consists of elderly retired people who had planned to spend their old age comfortably on savings or pensions. High prices have forced many in this group to live in extreme poverty or else to depend on relatives and public aid.

Is Inflation Necessary for Full Employment? Though we rightly regard inflation as an evil, it may not always be an unmitigated evil. Some economists believe that a moderate amount of inflation helps to keep production and employment at high levels. The constant expansion of total spending provides markets for increasing amounts of goods (if they can be produced) at rising prices. Many believe that inflation made a substantial contribution to the rising level of production and employment that was maintained in the United States in the years following World War II.

But inflation, if it is very great, discourages saving by casting doubt on the future value of dollars. Also, as we have noted, it causes unfair losses and hardships to many people. On the issue of whether it is really necessary for the maintenance of full employment, there is no complete agreement. Though probably no economist of repute would argue that very much inflation is desirable, some believe that a slowly rising price level is an essential condition for maintaining full employment. They think that many prices will be forced up anyway by government controls or the wage demands of labor unions, and they fear that full employment cannot be maintained unless income and spending increase enough to take such goods off the market at these higher prices.

Other economists, however, are opposed to the idea of a constantly rising price level. They would prefer to increase total spending only enough to take off the market increases in output resulting from growth of the labor force and technological progress, without allowing for any increase in prices. They think that this would maintain a reasonably high level of employment, and they feel that a constantly rising price level, even if the rise were slow, would be objectionable because over a period of years it would greatly reduce the value of money savings. They also feel that if we fully accepted inflation as a policy, slow inflation would before long degenerate into very rapid inflation. We would then find it necessary, in order to save the economy from complete disorganization, to take measures that would bring on a depression. Today there is a tendency in this country to ignore slow changes in the price level. Many writers talk as if prices were stable in the early 1960's. Relative to other recent periods they were. The wholesale price level changed very little from 1959 to 1964, and the consumer price level rose only about 6 per cent altogether in the same five-year period, or a little more than 1 per cent a year.

During the Johnson administration, tax reduction plus liberal monetary and credit policies plus a great escalation of deficit spending (only partly accounted for by the Vietnam War) brought employment and production to a high level; but before President Johnson left office, they had also brought about a sharp rise in the rate of inflation. In the last year of his administration, January, 1968, to January, 1969, the consumer price level rose 5.5 per cent. To check this inflation, he proposed not only to reduce

It's a long way to the ground on either side of the wire. (Courtesy *Detroit News.* Drawing by Poinier.)

government spending but also to levy an income surtax of 10 per cent, which was duly enacted into law by Congress.

However, once inflationary pressures have been built up and the public has come to expect more inflation, it is difficult to reverse the trend. When President Nixon assumed office in January, 1969, the rate of inflation was still rising. In the first six months of that year consumer prices rose at an annual rate of about 6 per cent. To meet this problem, the President undertook to check the rise of total spending in three ways: (1) by extending the income surtax that had been put in force the previous year; (2) by avoiding any substantial increase in government spending; and (3) by encouraging the monetary and banking authorities to restrict the money supply by restricting bank reserves and bank lending, and permitting high interest rates. Inflation can be checked by such measures if they are maintained for a period of time, but not without the risk of creating an unacceptable level of unemployment along with a business recession. At the end of the first two years of the Nixon administration, it was clear that the results of the policies adopted had been disappointing. Acceleration in the rate of inflation had been stopped, but the actual rate had been reduced little if at all. Part of the trouble was that Congress in some cases made larger appropriations than the President asked. Even so, the restrictions actually applied resulted in a considerable increase in the level of unemployment. Later Nixon reversed some of his policies in an attempt to stimulate the economy. Also, in 1971, he imposed temporary wage and price ceilings to reduce inflation.

If inflation is to be stopped, income in general *must not expand at an appreciably faster rate than the production of goods.* But when workers have become used to inflation, they tend to demand and receive wage and salary increases greater than increases in productivity in order to protect themselves from higher prices in the future. The resulting rise in spending brings on the expected higher prices. The government itself shares the blame. Congress not very long ago set what some consider to be a very bad example, not only by increasing rather liberally the wages and salaries of most government employees and officials, including the President, but also by approving large increases in the compensation of its own members.

One way of attacking the problem of inflation would be to devise and enforce some policy for limiting income increases for a relatively long period. However, such a policy would not be easy to either devise or administer; in some ways it would reduce the flexibility and efficiency of the economy; and it would also encounter powerful opposition from a number of groups. The New Economics tells us that we can pull an economy out of a depression by increasing the rate of total spending. But, unfortunately, the New Economics does not seem to offer any very satisfactory way to keep employment at as high a level as we would like and at the same time to prevent an unacceptable acceleration in the rate of inflation.

THE PROBLEM OF ECONOMIC GROWTH

In the long run, just to stabilize production and employment is clearly not enough. If population and the labor force grow, we must gradually increase output to provide goods for more consumers and jobs for more workers, including those who are displaced from some industries by automation and other technological advances. As we have already said, increases in total output are what we mean by *economic growth*. In most countries, production must increase substantially faster than population for the rate of economic growth to be considered satisfactory.

Requirements for Sustained Economic Growth. It is relatively easy for the government to follow policies that increase spending, but this will not necessarily bring the desired growth. Once production begins to approach existing capacity, unless there is a corresponding expansion of plant and equipment, the result of a continued rise in spending will be chiefly inflation rather than more production and jobs. A number of requirements must be met if an expansion of spending is to be accompanied by a roughly corresponding expansion of plant, production, and employment.

Conditions that will help bring about a sustained increase in production and employment include (1) technological advances; (2) availability of the needed raw materials and labor; (3) an educated and trainable labor force; (4) reasonably stable wage rates with increases that do not much exceed increases in productivity; (5) able and imaginative businessmen; (6) freedom of business enterprises from unnecessary controls and restrictions; (7) adequate incentives for businessmen and investors, especially a real possibility of making attractive profits to offset the high risks of loss; and (8) a high level of investment spending. Investment must be sufficient not only for the constant replacement of old and obsolete capital goods with new and more efficient types but also for expanding our total supply of factories and equipment in order to increase production and provide new jobs. It has been estimated that the average investment of American industry in plant and equipment, per production worker, is over twenty thousand dollars. In some industries it is much greater.

Probably nothing contributes more to the economic growth of a nation than to have a substantial number of businessmen who are free to act and who have a good share of initiative and imagination. They need an insight into economic trends and the ability to gauge the unsatisfied wants of consumers. It is pretty clear, at least in the world's more prosperous countries, that people do not want more wheat and more potatoes. But they do want more of many other things. These include better houses and furnishings; more attractive streets and parks; more and better education for their children; more and better opportunities for recreation; more summer cottages; more travel; and more services of various kinds. If we can succeed in directing our idle capital and labor into producing things that will meet unsatisfied wants, we shall have solved the most difficult part of the problem of raising standards of living and maintaining a high level of employment. But one very tough aspect of this problem is to find ways of providing the hard-core unemployed, who have no skills, with incentives, training, and jobs.

Obstacles to Sustained Growth. Unfortunately many obstacles are likely to prevent us from expanding output to the maximum. For example, excessive taxes may discourage investment in plant and equipment, and may make many potentially productive enterprises so unattractive that they are not even undertaken. Excessive union wage rates, or union rules that require the hiring of unneeded workers, or payment for work not actually done, may have similar effects. Again, government restrictions on farm output directly reduce production of farm products, and government support of farm prices reduces public purchasing power by raising both taxes and the cost of food. Even such well-intentioned measures as minimum-wage laws probably reduce employment and output somewhat by pricing out of the labor market handicapped, untrained, or young and inexperienced workers. Such workers could produce something, but employers cannot afford to pay them a relatively high wage. It might be much better in the long run to let such people work for whatever wage they could earn and thus let them acquire work habits and experience that might eventually enable them to earn more. Those whose wages would be extremely low could be given small supplementary income payments or the benefits of a negative income tax, a device that will be explained in the next chapter. Meanwhile, instead of being a dead weight on the rest of the community, they would have the satisfaction of doing useful work and they would be contributing something to their own support and to the total supply of goods available for consumption.

An excessive build-up of government reports and controls can also restrict the output of goods and services. In the *Wall Street Journal* several years ago an editorial writer described the case of an upstate New York nursing home that had been cited by state officials as "a shining example" of what such an establishment ought to be. However, not long afterward, the owner of this home, a Mrs. Gudrun, closed it down with the following explanation: "It was just impossible. There were 18 state and federal agencies putting forms, questions, and statistical requests across my desk. Medical reports . . . census figures . . . Social Security . . . unemployment insurance . . . workmen's compensation . . . withholding taxes . . . daily time sheets . . . work plans. . . . It was just one thing after another." According to Mrs. Gudrun, she sometimes spent eighteen hours a day just handling the government paperwork required for only twenty patients and fourteen employees.

The Need for New Jobs. From 1950 to 1960 the number of employed workers increased from nearly 59 million to about 66 million. By the summer of 1970 it had risen to over 80 million, an increase of more than 14 million in ten years. But if we are to avoid rising unemployment, the increase must be even greater in the 1970's, because in that period the large

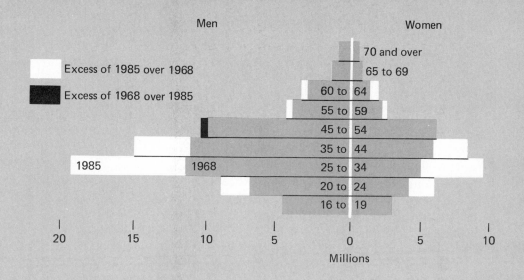

Figure 21. Age-Sex Profile of the Total Labor Force (actual 1968 and projected 1985). (*Monthly Labor Review, May 1970,* p. 9. U.S. Department of Labor, Bureau of Labor Statistics.)

numbers of babies born in the 1950's will be reaching maturity and joining the work force.

However, the chances seem reasonably good that the economy will be able to meet this challenge. Contrary to the belief of many, jobs and employment have increased faster in recent years than the population of labor-force age. This is true whether one measures rates of increase from the business peak of 1955 or from that of 1960. The fact that a troublesome amount of unemployment persisted into the mid-1960's resulted in part from a constant increase in the number and proportion of women entering the labor force. From 1950 to 1968 the total of women holding jobs rose from 17.3 million to 27.8 million, an increase of 60 per cent. During the same period the number of men employed rose from 41.6 million to 48.1 million, or only 16 per cent.

Figure 21 shows the age and sex composition of the labor force in 1968 and its projected composition up to and including 1985. The movement of women into the labor force includes wives and mothers, and it is likely to continue unless we have a substantial business recession that makes jobs, especially part-time jobs, harder to find. According to one estimate, in early 1969 well over one third of all women living with their husbands held jobs.[11]

[11] *U.S. News & World Report,* November 17, 1969, p. 95.

RESPONSIBILITY OF GOVERNMENT FOR STABILIZATION AND GROWTH

It should now be clear to the reader that in an economy like ours, total spending, if left uncontrolled, is likely to fluctuate greatly and, in doing so, is likely to cause wide fluctuations in production, employment, and income. Because the social cost of such fluctuations is high, it is essential to seek ways of controlling them.

Why Businessmen Cannot Prevent Depressions. Even our biggest business corporations represent, individually, a very small fraction of the entire economy; and the decision of any one of them to increase or reduce its expenditures for plant and equipment would have very little effect on the size of total demand for the nation. It is true, to be sure, that the action of one company may at critical times influence others, but there is seldom any certainty that this will be the case.

Of course, if most of our large corporations got together and decided to follow similar policies, they could very much influence the total money spent for goods and hence general business conditions. But, in the first place, it is not very likely that they could agree on what ought to be done. In the second place, if they could agree to follow common policies, to allow them to do so would be to put a dangerous amount of power into the hands of private business. In the third place, agreements among large corporations, no matter what their original purpose, would tend to reduce competition and greatly increase the monopolistic elements in our economy. At present our antitrust laws set rather narrow limits to legal cooperation between large corporations, and we are probably fortunate to have these laws.

The Role of Government in Stabilization and Growth. Because individuals and private business enterprises can do little to control total spending, and hence little to prevent depressions, the primary responsibility for economic stabilization must fall on government, and especially on the national government. The national government is the only agency that represents all the American people and the only agency that can implement its policies on a scale large enough to influence significantly the total money demand for goods. Most of the time, fortunately, a free-enterprise economy works reasonably well if dependence for its smooth operation is placed on the "automatic" forces of the market. Its greatest weakness is that from time to time it is subject to serious contractions of total spending; and it is then that the government must be ready to step in with effective measures to prevent depression.

The responsibility of the federal government for both stabilization and economic growth was officially recognized by Congress in the Employment Act of 1946. Although the act does not specify the means to be used in achieving its objectives, it places general responsibility on the President and Congress for maintaining conditions that will provide "useful employment, including self-employment, for those able, willing, and seeking to work" and that will "promote maximum employment, production, and purchasing power." The Employment Act also created the President's Council of Economic Advisers. Their duty is to report economic trends to the President, who in turn reports to Congress.

Monetary and Credit Policy. We have already explained the role of the banks in creating deposit money, and how this money, when spent by businessmen, increases total spending. The expression *monetary and credit policy* refers principally to *policies of the banking authorities designed to regulate the volume of loans extended by the banks,* and hence the volume of money held by the public in the form of bank deposits. In this country, monetary and credit policy is largely controlled by a government agency already mentioned, the Board of Governors of the Federal Reserve System. If the board feels that inflation is threatening the country, it takes measures designed to make it more difficult for banks to lend to businessmen or else it takes measures that raise interest rates and thus discourage businessmen from borrowing. Such measures are sometimes referred to as a *hard money* policy because they are designed to prevent a fall in the value of money and hence to keep it "as good as gold." On the other hand, if the board feels that depression is threatening, it does everything it can to make lending easy for the banks and to encourage businessmen to borrow. The objective is to induce businessmen to spend borrowed funds and thus help to maintain total spending, production, and employment.[12]

Fiscal Policy. *Fiscal policy refers to efforts to use the taxing, borrowing, and spending powers of the federal government for the purpose of achieving economic stability or growth.*

Public Works. One way of applying fiscal policy to offset a recession is to set up and carry out a *public works program.* If, when private spending declines, the government steps into the gap by spending large amounts on public works, this may be sufficient to bring employment and income back to their former levels. The multiplier effect will contribute toward the desired result. But to achieve this result, the government will have to go into debt, because if it raised the funds needed by increasing taxes, the greater amount of spending by government would be largely offset by decreased spending on the part of the public.

For a public works program to lift the country out of a major depression, government spending might have to be very large. The program undertaken in the 1930's by the New Deal administration of President Roosevelt was on far too small a scale to be very effective. It was fairly successful as a relief measure but not as a recovery measure. Those who instituted it counted too heavily on the multiplier effect, which at that time was re-

---

[12] Students who wish to study further the nature and operations of the Federal Reserve System may obtain free of charge an excellent little book issued by the System entitled *The Federal Reserve System: Purposes and Functions.* Write for latest edition to Publication Services, Division of Administration Services, Board of Governors of the Federal Reserve System, Washington, D.C. 20551.

ferred to as "pump-priming." But there is no question that government spending, if large enough, can overcome any depression. In World War II, expenditures were so huge that they not only completed the process of pulling us out of depression, but they also caused a considerable degree of inflation. However, spending on that scale should not be necessary to prevent depression. A comparatively modest program of public works spending might be effective if planned ahead of time, put into effect with reasonable promptness, and combined with other desirable measures.

Subsidies. Another method that could be employed to increase total spending would be to subsidize private undertakings on a large scale. Little use has been made of *subsidies* as an antidepression measure, but they have possibilities. One of their incidental advantages is that they would leave the actual selection and direction of specific projects in private hands. Because private funds would also be involved, this might result in a better choice of projects and in greater productive efficiency. It would certainly be more in accord with our American free-enterprise philosophy.

An even more obvious advantage of subsidies is that to increase investment by a given amount the government would only have to spend part of the required funds instead of all of them. For example, suppose it appeared that an expenditure of five billion dollars on new hydroelectric plants would be a useful antidepression measure. If by subsidizing the construction of such plants to the extent of 20 per cent of the cost, the government could induce private companies to undertake them, the government would be required to pay out only one billion dollars, instead of the five billion dollars necessary if they were undertaken as public projects.

A field in which government subsidies might effectively stimulate investment is residential building. If the government put up as much as one fourth or one third of the cost, a great many people might decide to build. However, some would object strongly to such a plan for fear that a large amount of subsidy-induced new building would depress the value of existing properties. A more general objection to subsidy programs is that, once instituted in a depression, they might not be dropped on the return of prosperity. A very serious objection is that their greatest benefits would go to limited groups of individuals and private companies.

Another possible way of stimulating total spending and employment would be for the government to offer loans for the carrying out of private projects, on favorable terms and at low rates of interest. This method has actually been employed, but to a very limited extent as a strictly antidepression measure.

Compensatory Spending. For a number of years some economists have been advocating that the government should attempt to keep business at all times at a relatively high and stable level by means of a policy of *compensatory spending.* Under such a policy the government would behave as follows: first, it would make every attempt to forestall the development of a serious recession by the use of monetary and credit policies. But if these proved inadequate, and it was obliged to resort to increased government spending, it would spend on a sufficient scale to bring about economic recovery. To do this would, of course, mean large-scale borrowing and a substantial increase in the national debt. But as prosperity returned and private spending rose, and as more taxes began to flow into the treasury, the government would taper off its spending and begin to accumulate a budgetary surplus. This surplus would then be used to reduce the debt accumulated while the economy was operating at a subnormal level. Thus, in theory, the economy could be kept rather stable without any long-term increase in the national debt.

But a policy of compensatory spending is very difficult to apply in practice, because the public always wants lower taxes, whereas some powerful pressure groups with special interests always want more government spending. If surpluses begin to appear in periods of recovery and prosperity, they are usually absorbed by tax cuts or by still more spending. In the long run the government debt seems always to rise.

But is there any great harm in adding constantly to the public debt? That is a question economists have long debated. Much depends on how fast the debt rises. One thing is certain. If the public debt is large and if it rises rapidly and persistently, inflation is sure to follow, because, as we have said, a rapid rise in debt means that the government is constantly increasing total demand by spending large sums of borrowed money. A growing debt also means that it must pay out larger and larger sums of money for interest. But what do we mean by a "rapid" increase in the public debt? A rise of seven billion dollars in our present debt would be an increase of only about 2 per cent; and it would represent less than 1 per cent of our gross national product. If production and the labor force were growing rapidly, annual increases of this magnitude might not be inflationary. In part, that would depend on the nature of other policies followed by government, business, and labor.

Tax Policy. In recent years politicians and businessmen have given increased attention to changes in tax rates as a means of either stimulating the economy or checking inflation. Tax reduction can be used independently as a means of stimulating the economy, or it can be used to reinforce the effects of a liberal monetary policy or increased government spending. A sharp tax reduction increases total spending by leaving more income in the hands of the general public. Though it is not likely that all this extra income will be spent at once, most of it will be eventually. When taxes take a substantial part of the national income, as is true in the United States today, reducing them sharply is bound to stimulate spending. However, if the government reduces taxes, it is likely to go further into debt in order to meet its own bills. So far as the effect on the public debt is concerned, there is little choice between reducing taxes to stimulate business and spending money on public works to achieve the same purpose.

The great advantage of tax reduction as a method of stimulating spending and employment is that it does not require setting up in advance a ponderous program of public works, many of which may not be needed. Instead, it permits individuals to spend more money rather promptly on the things they want. A tax reduction, especially if applied to the corporation income tax, also stimulates investment spending. By raising corporation profits, it gives businessmen both more incentive for investing and more funds to invest.

The first President to propose a substantial tax reduction with the object of stimulating the economy was John F. Kennedy. However, when he made his proposal in 1963, the country was not in a depression. Though a moderately high level of unemployment was a troublesome problem, business was rather good and was improving. President Kennedy wanted the tax cut in order to stimulate economic growth. The bill putting the cut into force was not actually passed until early in 1964 under President Johnson, who estimated that it reduced personal and corporate income taxes by about $11 billion. This tax reduction undoubtedly contributed to the vigorous expansion of the American economy in the several years that followed; but, as already noted, expansionary policies were pushed too far, and by the end of the decade they had brought about what most economists considered an unacceptable level of inflation.

Automatic or "Built-in" Stabilizers. It is generally believed that our economy is no longer vulnerable to such severe depressions as those that occurred between the two world wars. Not only is the government more able and willing to take action to reverse any serious recession, but largely as a result of the great depression of the 1930's, government programs and policies have been adopted that tend automatically to reduce the shrinkage of income and total spending in a period of business recession. Nearly all these programs involve either changes in government spending or changes in tax receipts.

One automatic stabilizer is the progressive income tax. Because large incomes pay higher tax *rates* than small incomes, as average incomes shrink, average tax rates fall by a greater percentage, and so the *proportion* of income that must be paid out for taxes also falls. This slows down the decline in the amount of income left for spending. Another stabilizing factor is unemployment benefits under the Social Security program. Today, when a worker loses his job, instead of having his income cut off completely, he receives unemployment payments for a considerable period of time. Other stabilizing factors include old-age pensions and veterans' benefits, which continue to be received and spent regardless of business conditions; and they also include farm price supports, which prevent farm prices and farmers' incomes from dropping anywhere near as sharply as they otherwise might.

Perhaps the most important automatic stabilizer in our economy is the large portion of total spending that is done by the federal government. In 1929, federal expenditures were less than 4 per cent of the gross national product; in 1969 they had risen to about 20 per cent. Because there is, practically speaking, no possibility of reducing federal spending greatly, most of this contribution to total spending is assured. Actually, federal spending would rise sharply in case of a severe depression, because today it would be politically impossible for the government to avoid undertaking a considerable amount of antidepression spending.

Stability, Growth, Employment, and Free Enterprise. If we believe, as many of us do, that free enterprise can provide more freedom, greater production, more resources for meeting social problems, and higher standards of living than would be possible under socialism, then we have a special interest in finding ways to increase stability, growth, and employment within the framework of our present system. It seems probable that one or two periods of severe and prolonged depression would raise irresistible demands for the government to take over the major industries of the country. One or two depressions of that character would be regarded as demonstrating the inability of a free economy to cope with the economic conditions of the modern world, though much of the trouble might really be attributable to unwise government interference with the operation of free markets. Fortunately, in monetary, credit, and fiscal policies, we have the means, if we will fully employ them when they are really needed, to prevent severe depressions without destroying the essential character of a free economy. It cannot be stressed enough that the most important characteristic of such an economy is the freedom of businessmen and business enterprises to seek profits and to make their own decisions on policy—subject, of course, to the general "rules of the game" as established by law and custom for the protection of everyone.

The advantages of monetary, credit, and fiscal policies for regulating a free-enterprise economy grow largely out of the fact that they are *indirect* controls. They can be used to maintain total spending without the necessity for direct interference with the organization and management of individual business enterprises. By intelligent use of these indirect controls, we should be able to make our economy operate at more stable levels than in the past without putting it in a straitjacket that might greatly reduce its flexibility, its productive efficiency, its power to grow, and the opportunities that it offers for the exercise of individual initiative.

In the coming decade our greatest economic problem is apt to be, not to prevent severe depressions, but to keep inflation under control while at the same time maintaining a rate of economic growth sufficient to provide jobs for our rapidly expanding labor force.

Terms to Be Understood

full employment	economic growth	recession
business cycle	minor business cycle	depression
seasonal fluctuations	major business cycle	gross national product
secular fluctuations	recovery	disposable personal
cyclical fluctuations	prosperity	income

labor force
the circulation of
  money
the New Economics
aggregate demand
total spending
consumption
  spending
investment spending
durable goods
multiplier effect
acceleration
  principle

speculation
inflation
commercial bank
bank credit
demand bank deposit
Federal Reserve
  System
Federal Reserve bank
Board of Governors
member bank
the money supply
Federal Reserve
  notes

monetary and credit
  policy
"hard money" policy
fiscal policy
public works
  program
subsidy
compensatory
  spending
tax policy
automatic stabilizers
indirect economic
  controls

Questions for Review and Discussion

1. What are business cycles? Why do we have them?
2. List five or six indexes of economic activity and tell why each is a fairly good indicator of the general level of business activity.
3. Would a society in which each family produced all the goods it used have business cycles? Why or why not?
4. Why does industrialization increase economic fluctuations?
5. Why do business movements of either expansion or contraction tend to be cumulative, and why are they eventually reversed?
6. Explain some of the ways in which Keynes contributed to an understanding of business cycles.
7. Explain why the level of income, production, and employment is directly dependent on total spending.
8. When will an increase in saving by the public tend to depress production and employment and when will it not have this effect? Explain.
9. Why is it impossible for the people of a country to increase their total holdings of money simply by trying harder to save?
10. If the total amount that the public saves is just equal to the amount it spends on investment goods, what is the effect on the economy?
11. Explain why each of the following contributes to fluctuations of total spending: (a) the fact that many goods are durable; (b) the multiplier principle; (c) the acceleration principle; (d) speculation.
12. Explain inflation in terms of the relation of total spending to production.
13. What are the principal sources of funds that make possible an increase in total spending?
14. Why are bank deposits considered money?
15. Explain why the banking system is actually creating new money when it increases its total loans to businessmen.
16. Explain why wars cause inflation.
17. Can the level of spending increase without an increase in the money supply? Explain.

18. Why would a rise of 100 per cent in the public debt in five years result in substantial inflation?
19. Compare the evils and the benefits that accompany inflation. What, in your opinion, should be our attitude toward inflation? Defend your answer.
20. Does a long-run increase of total spending necessarily cause inflation? Why or why not?
21. Is increased spending by government, business, or consumers a sure way to achieve and maintain as high a level of employment as we might wish? Is it likely that just by spending more we would reduce unemployment to less than 1 per cent of the labor force and keep it at that level? Why or why not?
22. What factors contributed to the rapid price inflation of the years 1968–1971?
23. Make a list of major factors likely to aid in sustaining economic growth.
24. The text mentions certain factors as likely to restrict economic growth. Do you agree in all cases? If not, explain why.
25. Since 1948, jobs have increased faster than the population of working-force age, yet we still have a troublesome unemployment problem. Explain.
26. Why are businessmen unable to prevent depressions?
27. Explain the theory of controlling the business cycle (1) by means of monetary and credit policy; (2) by means of government spending; (3) by means of tax policies.
28. Explain why each of the following is sometimes regarded as a "built-in" stabilizer of the economy: (1) the progressive income tax; (2) unemployment insurance; (3) old-age pensions and veterans' benefits; (4) farm price supports; (5) all federal expenditures.
29. Explain the theory and the limitations of compensatory spending.
30. Why is a fair degree of economic stability essential to the preservation of a free-enterprise economy?
31. What is the great advantage, in a free-enterprise economy, of using indirect rather than direct economic controls whenever possible?
32. Why is control of inflation apt to be our greatest economic problem during the next ten years or more?

For Further Study

Burns, Arthur F., *The Business Cycle in a Changing World,* New York, National Bureau of Economic Research, 1969.

Gordon, Robert A., *Goal of Full Employment,* New York, John Wiley & Sons, Inc., 1967.

Hunt, Elgin F., and Jules Karlin, eds., *Society Today and Tomorrow,* paperback, New York, The Macmillan Company, 1967. See therein "Can we Cure Depressions?" by Abba P. Lerner.

Kuznets, Simon, *Postwar Economic Growth,* Cambridge, Mass., Harvard University Press, 1964.

Lebergott, Stanley, ed., *Men Without Work: The Economics of Unemployment,* paperback, Englewood Cliffs, N.J., Prentice-Hall, Inc., 1965.

Lerner, Abba P., *Economics of Control,* reprinted, New York, Augustus M. Kelley, Publishers, 1969.

Morgan, Theodore, and George W. Betz, eds., *Economic Development: Readings in Theory and Practice,* paperback, Belmont, Cal., Wadsworth Publishing Company, 1969.

Roll, Eric, *The World After Keynes: An Examination of the Economic Order,* New York, Frederick A. Praeger, Inc., 1968.

Rostow, W. W., *Process of Economic Growth,* rev. ed., New York, W. W. Norton & Company, Inc., 1962.

Samuelson, Paul A., *Economics,* 7th ed., New York, McGraw-Hill, Inc., 1967. See therein Part 2.

Survey of Current Business, Washington, D.C., Department of Commerce. See recent issues for comment and statistics.

Umbreit, Myron H., Elgin F. Hunt, and Charles V. Kinter, *Fundamentals of Economics,* 3d ed., New York, McGraw-Hill, Inc., 1957. See therein Chaps. 7–9 and 12–14, dealing with income, aggregate demand, and employment.

Chapter 20

Inequality, Poverty, and Social Security

two major objectives of economic activity are *income* and *security*. Among very primitive peoples, income is likely to take form of actual goods—food, clothing, and shelter—produced by the individuals or families who consume them. It is seldom possible for the people in such societies to attain any great degree of economic security. However, a certain amount of security against future hunger can sometimes be achieved by storing food. For example, some American Indians were able to keep deer or buffalo meat for considerable periods by making it into pemmican; this involved cutting it into strips, drying it in the sun, pounding it into a powder, mixing it with fat, and then storing it in bags of buffalo hide. Sometimes, also, a degree of security is attained by primitive peoples through customs that require sharing among the members of the tribe in times of scarcity.

In the modern world *income* means to most of us the receipt of money; but what is ultimately important is not the money we receive but the goods we can buy with it. It is this *real income* in goods that determines our economic welfare or our *standard of living*. The object of all economic activity is to satisfy wants, and, to satisfy wants, we must have income. But it is not enough for us to be able to satisfy our wants today. It is equally important that we have some security for the future—some assurance that our income will continue so that we can satisfy our wants tomorrow, next year, and in all the years to come.

In all modern societies, we find marked inequalities of income between individuals or families. Some people are notably more successful than others in their efforts to acquire money and goods, and hence they can satisfy their wants much more adequately. Differences in economic security are more difficult to measure than differences in income, but in most groups it is obvious that they exist. Moreover, security is always a matter of degree, and in no society does anyone have *complete* security of income.

In the world in which we live, risks of one kind or another cannot be avoided. Every day we risk accident, illness, and death; also the loss of friends, the loss of our jobs, and the loss of our property. But though we cannot eliminate such risks completely, fortunately we can often find ways to reduce them.

At times efforts to increase income and efforts to achieve economic security support each other, but often they come into conflict. Other things being equal, it is probably true that the larger one's income, the more secure he is from real want. On the other hand, the search for security may tend to limit income for the individual and even for the whole economy.

For individuals, this is illustrated by the man who takes a civil service job at moderate pay because it gives him rights of tenure and a pension; yet he may have qualities that would enable him, if he were more adventurous, to make a good deal more money in private industry, perhaps even in a business of his own.

Illustrations of how the search for security may limit the income of society by limiting production can be found in the policies of certain labor groups. For example, in many cities organized labor in the building trades makes every effort to prevent the construction of low-cost prefabricated houses, the purpose being to protect the jobs and incomes of skilled workers who produce houses by traditional but less-efficient methods. But workers using the old methods produce less, and people buying the houses pay more and have less money to spend on other goods.

In this chapter we have two principal tasks. The first is to analyze economic inequality: its causes, its results, and what if anything should be done about it. In connection with our discussion of inequality, we shall give attention to the related problem of poverty. Our second principal task is to examine the problem of personal and family economic insecurity and to point out what has been done and what might be done to minimize it, with special attention to the federal Social Security program.

ECONOMIC INEQUALITY AND POVERTY

Economic inequality has two aspects that, though closely related, should be clearly distinguished. The first is differences in income; the second is differences in wealth. Our knowledge of income differences in fairly adequate, but our statistical information concerning the extent of differences in wealth is very limited and unsatisfactory. Nevertheless, we know enough about the distribution of wealth to be sure that it is much more unequal than the distribution of income; for though at one extreme a relatively few people own fabulous amounts of wealth, at the other extreme many millions have practically none. On the other hand, almost anyone who is able and willing to work can, except in periods of depression, receive a certain amount of income by selling his labor in the market for what it will bring. In recent years about 75 per cent of all personal income in the United States has been received by employees as compensation for their services.

Although the ownership of wealth often gives social prestige and a certain amount of economic and political power, its chief advantages to those who hold it are, first, greater security, and second, the receipt of income. It is income that largely determines the manner in which a person can live, and in our discussion of economic inequality, we shall be primarily concerned with the way in which income is distributed among individuals and families.

Why Incomes Differ. Differences in income arise directly from two sources—namely, variations in earnings from personal services and variations in the amounts of property owned. Earnings from personal services take such forms as wages, salaries, commissions, and fees. Differences in the earnings of individuals are based partly on occupation and partly on the personal qualities of those engaged in each occupation. The most basic of the factors that determine income variations between occupational groups is demand and supply. In general, occupations that are not easy to enter because they require special aptitudes and long training are highly paid, because the supply of workers is small relative to the demand. On the other hand, occupations classified as "common labor," which anyone can enter with relatively little ability or training, tend to be poorly paid. But within each occupational group there are often great differences in individual earning power, especially at the higher professional and managerial levels. Some doctors, lawyers, engineers, and busi-

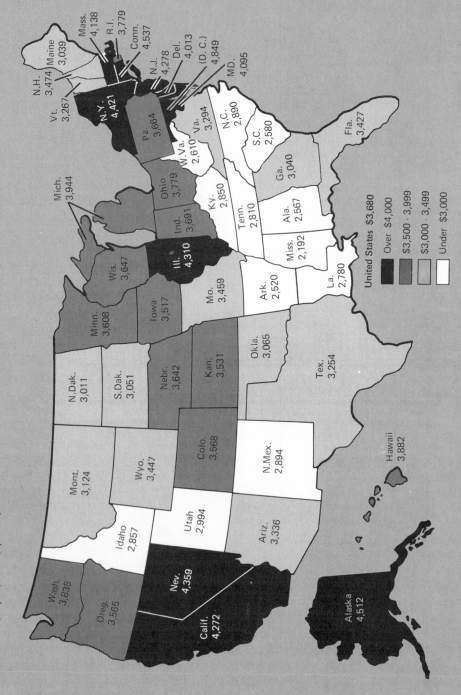

Figure 22. Average Per Capita Income in the United States, 1969. (Source of data: *Survey of Current Business*, U.S. Department of Commerce, Office of Business Economics, April, 1970, p. 14.)

ness executives make very much larger incomes than others, usually because they have reputations for competence that create special demands for their services as individuals. Because of this they can demand higher prices for their work, and in addition they often put in longer hours than other workers.

Differences in wealth are also important in explaining differences in income. Property brings income to its owners in such forms as interest, rent, dividends, royalties, and direct business profits; as a rule, the very largest incomes have as their chief source ownership of property.

To explain fully why some people hold large amounts of wealth and others little is not a simple matter. An adequate understanding of the present distribution of wealth in the United States would require a thorough study, to begin with, of what is sometimes called *the institution of private property*. In a society like that of Soviet Russia, which does not recognize private property in "the means of production," differences of wealth (though not necessarily of income) would be much less than in our society. To understand the institution of private property as it prevails in this country would mean delving into the laws and customs that regulate and limit the acquisition, transfer, and ownership of property; and it would also mean an examination of the effects of our tax laws on the accumulation of wealth. Because such a study is beyond the scope of this chapter, for present purposes it will suffice to say that some wealth is acquired by saving out of normal sources of income; some as the result of unusual business or speculative profits; some through theft, fraud, or other illegal activities; and some by inheritance.

Inequalities of Income in the United States. Though our chief interest is in the unequal distribution of income among individuals and families, we should not overlook the fact that there is also considerable inequality between workers in different industries and between geographic regions. For example, in January, 1970, average hourly earnings in the primary metals industries were $3.86, whereas in the textile mills they were only $2.47. Comparing regions, the far West and the northern part of the country east of the Mississippi have long been high-income areas; the Southeast has been an area of low incomes. In recent years, however, regional differences of income have been gradually narrowing. The map in Figure 22 shows average per capita income by states in 1969.

Probably the most important aspect of inequality is the unequal distribution of income among families and individuals. Table 13 shows, for the years 1950, 1960, 1965, and 1969, the percentage of all the families in the United States that fell into the income groups indicated, and it also shows the great inequalities that existed. For example, in 1969, at the lower end of the scale, 9.3 per cent of all families received annual incomes of less than $3,000, whereas at the upper end 3.6 per cent of all families received over $25,000. Actually, the range at the top was much greater than the table shows, for a few of the high-income families received more than $1,000,000 a year. The great increases in money incomes since 1950 should be noted. For example, in 1969 the proportion of families receiving over $25,000 was greater than the proportion receiving over $10,000 in 1950.

Table 13. *Distribution of Family Income in the United States, 1950–1969*

| | Percent of Families in Each Group | | | |
	1969	1965	1960	1950
Under $1,000	1.6	2.9	5.0	11.5
$1,000 to $1,999	3.1	6.0	8.0	13.2
$2,000 to $2,999	4.6	7.2	8.7	17.8
$3,000 to $3,999	5.3	7.7	9.8	20.7
$4,000 to $4,999	5.4	7.9	10.5	13.6
$5,000 to $5,999	5.9	9.3	12.9	9.0
$6,000 to $6,999	6.4	9.5	10.8	5.2
$7,000 to $7,999	7.3	9.7	8.7⎫	5.8*
$8,000 to $9,999	14.4	14.5	11.3⎭	
$10,000 to $14,999	26.7	17.7	10.6⎫	
$15,000 to $24,999	15.6	6.2	2.6⎬	3.3*
$25,000 and over	3.6	1.4	0.9⎭	
Median income	$9,433	$6,957	$5,620	$3,319
Total families (thousands):	51,237	48,279	45,456	39,929

*For 1950, all families with incomes from $7,000 to $9,999 were put in one group, and likewise all those above $10,000.
Source: U.S. Bureau of the Census, *Current Population Reports,* Series P-60, No. 70, July 16, 1970, p. 3.

However, not all the income referred to above is spendable. Though people in the lower-income groups may pay little or no federal income tax, this tax sometimes takes more than half the income of those in the higher groups. But this does not mean that people in the low-income groups escape taxation, because when they spend their money they usually pay heavy sales taxes and because the rents they pay include real estate taxes.

Income and Standards of Living. As already implied, a person's real income in goods and his standard of living are essentially the same thing. His standard of living is simply a rough measure of the degree to which he satisfies his economic wants. For any two persons at a given time and place, their relative standards of living are likely to be measured fairly well by their relative money incomes. But exceptions occur, because some consumers use much greater judgment and skill than others in spending their money and thus obtain more satisfaction from it. This explains why one person may live considerably better than another, even though the two have the same amount of money income. Sometimes, however, what appear to be differences in standards of living are merely differences of taste. For example, one man may dress poorly and another man well; but this may mean only that the first prefers to spend his money on books and the opera and that the second prefers to spend it on clothes.

When we speak of the standard of living of a particular social group, we refer to a level of consumption based on the kinds and quantities of goods to which typical members of the group have become accustomed.[1] Many writers like to classify standards of living on some such basis as the poverty standard, the minimum-subsistence standard, the minimum standard for health and decency, and the comfort standard. Such a classification may be useful for some purposes, but it is necessarily somewhat arbitrary. A generation or two ago the income judged necessary for a minimum standard of health and decency was sometimes set so high by sociologists and economists that a very large proportion of families fell below it. But over the years the purchasing power of the typical American family has risen so much that the great majority now have incomes that, by any reasonable standard, must be rated as above the minimum for health and decency.

However, in all modern societies most people wish to live at least as well as their neighbors, the Joneses. Though they may be glad to see that the Joneses are prosperous, they would like to share in such prosperity and not feel poor by comparison. Since there are Joneses in every neighborhood whose way of life is a notch or two above that of the average family, when standards of living in a society rise, the amount of income people feel they must have to live "decently" also rises. Who today would deny the right of the worker not only to adequate food, clothing, shelter, and medical care but also to a good car and a color TV set? In any case, he is apt to buy the car and the TV set even if he must skimp a bit on the other items in order to do so.

But people in the lowest-income groups are obliged to spend a very high proportion of their incomes on the basic necessities of life, especially on food. As incomes rise, though food expenditures increase, the *proportion* of income spent on food falls. This relationship was observed a hundred years ago by a German named Ernst Engel and is called *Engel's Law*. It applies between income groups not only within a country but also between countries. In extremely poor countries, like India and China, the percentage of personal income spent on food is much higher than in western Europe or the United States. In this country, according to the United States Department of Commerce, less than 20 per cent of total disposable personal income is spent on food. This does not include expenditures on alcoholic beverages and tobacco, which frequently are grouped with food expenditures.

Inequality, Waste, and Social Stratification. It is sometimes maintained that one of the great evils of economic inequality is social waste. Wealthy people, it is said, spend large amounts of money on things that have relatively little importance for them, merely because to them dollars are cheap and abundant. Spectacular examples include lavish parties costing

[1] A few writers refer to this as the *plane of living*. They used *standard of living* to refer to the kinds and amounts of goods people think they should be able to consume to live a satisfactory life.

$100,000 and even more. Through purchasing unimportant luxuries at high prices, the wealthy, according to this theory, divert substantial amounts of labor and materials that might much better be spent in producing the many kinds of goods that are urgently needed by poor people.

In the view of some writers, most money spent by the wealthy represents *conspicuous consumption.* This is the epithet that Thorstein Veblen long ago coined for expenditures designed principally to enhance the prestige of the spender by impressing others with his wealth and importance.[2]

Economic inequality is the chief bulwark of social stratification. Though a high standard of living may not automatically put an individual or a family in one of the upper classes, if maintained over a generation or two it will usually enable the members of a family to acquire the other characteristics necessary for upper-class status. On the other hand, if an upper-class family is reduced to a low standard of living it is not likely to be able to maintain any semblance of upper-class standing over more than one or two generations.

The Problem of Poverty. In this country it is certainly true, *other things remaining the same,* that if we abolished the unequal distribution of income we would abolish poverty. By dividing total personal income received in the United States in 1969 by the population in that year, we find that average per capita income was about $3,680; and even if, before dividing, we subtract federal income taxes from personal income to obtain *disposable personal income,* the average is still about $3,100. Thus if personal disposable income had been divided equally, each family of four people would have had $12,400.

How much poverty do we have in the United States today? That depends largely on how the word is defined. In terms of what poverty means in India or China, or even in terms of what it meant in this country or Europe a hundred years ago, we have very little. Almost no one literally dies of starvation or sleeps in the streets for lack of shelter as tens of thousands do in the cities of India. On the other hand, there are large numbers of people who must depend on welfare payments to live; and there are also many who do not receive such payments but whose incomes are so small that they must live in depressing surroundings, wear shabby clothes, and buy cheap foods. They cannot afford to spend money for travel, entertainment, or education; and if they are out of work or if an emergency like serious illness arises, their only recourse is charity or public aid. Many of these poverty-stricken Americans may be better provided with goods than are primitive peoples who do not feel poor, and better provided with them than the masses in India and China; but in their own society they are near the bottom of the scale. They are deprived of many things that the vast majority of Americans take for granted; and though they seldom starve, they are often malnourished, sometimes not so much from lack of income

---

[2] See Thorstein Veblen, *The Theory of the Leisure Class,* Mentor paperback, New York, New American Library, Inc., 1954.

as from lack of knowledge of how to prepare adequate meals on a very limited budget.

How can we determine the number of Americans who live in a state of poverty? Actually we cannot, except on the basis of some partly arbitrary definition. When President Johnson announced his "war on poverty" in 1964, he implied that all families with money incomes under three thousand dollars should be included in this group. At the time that meant putting into the poverty classification more than one in six of all American families. However, many examples could be found of elderly couples, or even younger ones, who lived very modestly but quite comfortably on incomes of less than three thousand dollars. This was especially true of those who owned homes, or who lived in the country or in small towns. In large cities it is more difficult to live pleasantly on very small ncomes.

Aside from special legislation for the depressed Appalachian region, most of President Johnson's 1964 proposals for attacking poverty were embodied in the Economic Opportunity Act passed by Congress later in the same year. This act was especially designed to aid young people. It set up (1) a *Job Corps* to give work, remedial education, and fifty dollars a month in pay to as many as 100,000 unemployed youths; (2) a work-training program to give part-time employment to young people to train them for jobs and to help them stay in school; and (3) a work-study program to help needy college students earn part of their expenses by getting work on or off the campus. It also provided limited aid for adult education, farm families, migrant workers, small businesses, and the unemployed; and it set up *VISTA* (Volunteers in Service to America), which, it was hoped, would become a kind of domestic Peace Corps.

The reader should keep in mind that President Johnson's proposals for alleviating poverty were by no means the first efforts made toward that objective. Already federal, state, and local governments were spending about forty billion dollars annually to raise or supplement individual incomes. This spending supported such programs as public assistance, food stamps and surplus-food allotments, subsidized school lunches, medical care and pensions for veterans, grants to depressed areas to create jobs, housing subsidies, training programs for the disabled, aid to handicapped children, low-cost loans to college students, vocational training programs, help for Indians, and Social Security pension payments.

Undoubtedly, President Johnson's antipoverty program was a sincere attempt to help many persons whom earlier programs had not reached, but it was not on a scale great enough to notably reduce the total amount of poverty. Also, many difficulties were encountered in organizing the various agencies needed to carry it out, and the ultimate costs proved high in relation to the number of people benefited.

Measuring Poverty. In order to measure the amount of *poverty* in a country, we must define the term in such a way that we can determine which individuals and families have standards of living so low that they should be classified as poverty-stricken and which have standards of living

41. Black Leaders Conferring with President Johnson on His Poverty Program.
From left are Roy Wilkins, Executive Director of NAACP; James Farmer, National
Director of CORE; the late Martin Luther King, Jr., head of SCLC; the late
Whitney Young of the Urban League; and the President. (Courtesy United Press
International, Inc.)

that are above the poverty line. The Social Security Administration and
the Bureau of the Census attempt to do this by determining the minimum
amount of income needed to maintain a living standard above the poverty
level. This amount of income is called the *poverty threshold*. Obviously,
the poverty threshold will be lower for an individual than for a family,
and it will differ for families of different size. It will also change with
fluctuations in the cost of living.

The poverty statistics now published by the Bureau of the Census are
calculated by using the Consumer Price Index to represent the cost of living. To be above the poverty level, an individual or family must have
enough income to obtain food, clothing, and shelter that will maintain
health, plus some margin for other very necessary expenditures. Just what
minimum income is essential at any given time and place cannot be determined with any great precision, and hence any specific poverty threshold
is to some degree arbitrary. However, if it is determined, after a careful
and objective weighing of the facts, it can have enough meaning to be useful. Each year, the Bureau of the Census publishes poverty thresholds for
single ("unrelated") individuals and for families of various sizes. In 1969
the poverty level was set at $3,743 for the average nonfarm family of four,

and $3,182 for the average four-member farm family. It was assumed that a farm family can usually get along as well as a nonfarm family on a somewhat smaller money income, partly because it produces more food and services for its own needs. In any case, as consumer prices rise, more income is required to provide a given standard of living for any family, and hence the poverty threshold also rises.

In recent years, however, incomes have, on the average, usually risen faster than prices. As a result, even though the poverty threshold has been raised by inflation, the number of Americans in poverty has declined. According to the Bureau of the Census, from 1959 to 1969 the total number of Americans below the poverty level, counting single individuals and the members of families, fell by 38 per cent.

The decline of poverty in the 1960's was unusually great; moreover, poverty had been falling in this country, with minor interruptions, ever since the days of the great depression in the 1930's. Why then did it suddenly become such a major social and political issue in the mid-1960's? Possibly because it then contrasted more sharply than ever with the relatively great prosperity that the majority of Americans were enjoying; and for the first time people began to feel that, if we chose, we could eliminate it. Perhaps also because it tied in with the race problem, since the percentage of blacks in poverty was and still is much greater than the percentage of whites. Also President Johnson's antipoverty program brought the issue to public attention in a rather dramatic fashion.

Figure 23 shows that, according to census estimates, the total number of Americans in poverty in 1959 was about 39.5 million and that by 1969 it had dropped to 24.3 million. The figure also shows the decline in poverty, in millions, for blacks and other nonwhites and for whites.

Though the chart indicates that in 1969 24.3 million Americans were in poverty, such a figure should be accepted with some reservations. Undoubtedly, many of those included had incomes that were only temporarily extremely low, or had savings with which to supplement current income, or owned homes and lived in communities where they could get along reasonably well on a small income, or were young people getting help from parents. However, after all such allowances are made, it is clear that at the beginning of the 1970's there was still a substantial amount of extreme poverty in this country. Much though not all of this poverty was concentrated in certain areas. These included the black ghettos of central cities where unemployment was high and also the hill country of the Adirondack region, which is largely populated by whites but where the land is poor and nonfarm jobs have been scarce. But undoubtedly the greatest concentration of extreme poverty was to be found in certain areas of the deep South, such as the delta counties of Mississippi, where large numbers of unemployed blacks lived in dilapidated shacks and received relief payments that were wholly inadequate.

Hunger and Malnutrition. In 1968 the Citizens' Board of Inquiry into Hunger and Malnutrition in the United States, a private group consisting

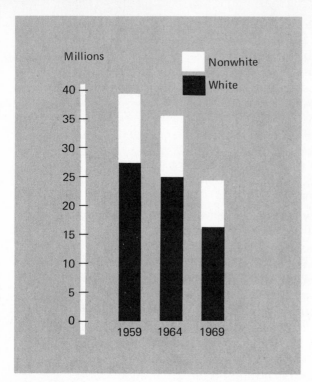

Figure 23. Americans Below Poverty Level, 1959–1969. (Based on statistics from U.S. Bureau of the Census, *Current Population Reports,* Series P-20, No. 204, July 13, 1970, p. 6.)

of doctors, clergymen, labor leaders and others especially concerned with the effects of poverty on nutrition, issued a report intended to alert the country to the seriousness of the problem of malnutrition.[3] According to the board, a "conservative estimate is that 10 million Americans are chronically hungry." Actually, however, the Board of Inquiry had no facilities for making a thorough and objective study, and many students of the problem, including some government officials, believe that such an estimate for hunger or serious cases of malnutrition is far too high. Though malnutrition is most common among the very poor, it often results not from lack of enough food but from choosing and eating the wrong kinds of food. It may also be caused by internal parasites, such as roundworms or whipworms, which take nourishment that should go to the human body and which afflict many people where standards of cleanliness are low. The chief contribution of the report on hunger was to make the public and government officials more keenly aware that widespread and serious malnutrition among the very poor really existed and that measures for combatting it were urgently needed.

Can Poverty Be Eliminated? The practical elimination of poverty in this country should be possible if what we mean by eliminating poverty is just providing everyone with enough income for physical comfort and security.

[3] *Hunger, U.S.A.: A Report by the Citizens' Board of Inquiry into Hunger and Malnutrition in the United States,* Boston, Beacon Press, Inc., 1968.

But if we define poverty in relative terms, as many sociologists will, then to some degree the problem will always be with us. No matter how much incomes rise, if we assume the continuance of substantial inequalities, people with relatively low incomes will continue to be deprived of various things that the rest can enjoy.

Poverty of the more extreme type results directly from little or no earning power, the reasons for which are various. They include limited opportunities for employment in some areas, physical or mental handicaps, lack of education and training, illness, accident, and old age. But a country with an overall level of production as high as ours should be able to make reasonable provisions for those who desire to earn a living but find it impossible to do so. It is, however, important to develop ways of alleviating poverty that do not destroy work incentives for people who could earn all or even a part of their own keep.

One difficulty with our present relief program is that in most cases a relief recipient who accepts employment must give up almost a dollar of relief benefits for every dollar earned. Until 1968, *Aid to Dependent Children* (ADC) payments were reduced dollar for dollar by any earnings made by a mother receiving such aid for her children. But in that year Congress passed legislation reducing payments by only 70 per cent of earnings instead of 100 per cent. Another objection to the current relief program is that benefits under the ADC program cannot be received by a family if the father is present in the household. This is believed to have induced many fathers to desert their families because they cannot earn as much as the ADC payments would amount to or because they are glad to escape the burden of supporting a family when they know that the government will take over if they just disappear. A large portion of these fatherless families are found in the black ghettos of our central cities.

President Nixon has advocated an entirely new welfare plan, designed to encourage those on relief to seek employment. This plan would, for the first time, make the "working poor" eligible for some federal welfare benefits. Families in which no member is employed would receive five hundred dollars each for the first two members and three hundred dollars for each additional member. These payments would be supplemented by a state welfare payment and also by a greatly expanded *food-stamp plan*. These stamps could be bought by the poor at very low cost and then exchanged at stores for food of much greater value. But to receive these benefits the father (if present) and the mother (unless she has pre-school children) would have to register for employment and accept a suitable job or else job training. If a man with a wife and two children was on welfare and got a job, he would be allowed to keep the first $60 of his monthly pay, or $720 a year, without any reduction in his minimum federal benefit. He could also keep half of anything he earned over $60, but as his earnings increased, his federal benefits would gradually decrease until, when his earnings reached $4,000 per year, they would stop. To further in-

42. Surplus Commodity Supper for Family in Appalachia. (John Dominis, *Life* Magazine. © Time Inc.)

duce people on relief to seek employment, there would be an expanded job training program and a system of day-care centers for children.

Sweden is widely credited with having eliminated the traditional type of poverty through a highly developed social security or welfare system. This has been possible, at a high cost in taxes, because the country has some unusual advantages. It is a rather large area, well endowed with natural resources, and has a rather small population. Its people are relatively homogeneous, well educated, and well trained. It is technically and scientifically advanced and has enjoyed 150 years of peace. As a result it has one of the most productive economies in the world and a high average standard of living. In some respects the problem of eliminating extreme poverty in this country is more difficult than it was in Sweden. We have a vastly larger and much more heterogeneous population. On the other hand, our average per capita wealth and productivity are substantially greater.

Income and Social Justice. As already suggested, eliminating the traditional type of poverty does not solve all the problems that grow out of inequality. As long as there continue to be wide differences of wealth and income, these are likely to create some social unrest. Many of those with small incomes are dissatisfied because they feel a deep sense of injustice when comparing their situation with that of their more fortunate fellow citizens. This sense of injustice is likely to be particularly strong when workers on modest wages compare their position with that of people who receive incomes from inherited fortunes and who are therefore able to live in luxury without making any personal efforts. But the ordinary wage earner is less likely to resent larger incomes received by others if he feels these large incomes are deserved. He seldom objects to paying a substantial salary to his union president if he feels that this officer is working effectively to protect the interests of union members; and he is often willing to vote for some extremely wealthy politicians such as Herbert Hoover, Nelson Rockefeller, or John F. Kennedy if he feels that they will best serve the interests of the whole country, including the common people.

Economic inequality creates unjust differences in opportunity between the rich and poor, and especially between their children; in practice it also results in unjust differences in other areas of life—for example, in the treatment of citizens by the courts. Though theoretically all citizens have equal rights before the law, it takes money to hire good lawyers. Consequently, a poor man accused of a crime is more likely to be convicted than a rich man similarly charged.

Yet if we try to find any simple objective standard for the "just" distribution of income, our search is fruitless. Justice is a cultural concept, a social value, and it means different things to different people. Some people (a very few) would see justice in an equal distribution of income; some in a distribution based on need; some in one based on labor or effort; and some in one based on productivity. But, except for equal distribution, we could not apply any of these standards except in the loosest fashion, because we have no very adequate ways of measuring either need, labor, effort, or productivity for any given individual.

The Social Advantages of Economic Inequality. One of the most firmly entrenched ideals in our American culture is equality. We feel most strongly that all citizens should have equal opportunities and be equal before the law, and we tend to apply this ideal of equality to various other aspects of social life. For example, we may feel that a true democratic society is impossible unless inequalities of income are eliminated or reduced to an absolute minimum, whatever that may mean. We are realistic enough to know that complete social equality is impossible, because individuals differ in their native abilities and hence in their powers for leadership and achievement. Yet we often have an uncomfortable feeling that people ought to be equal. We do not like social classes, and we do not like economic inequalities—not, at least, unless we are near the top of the ladder and derive satisfaction from a feeling of superiority. Yet inequalities of one kind or another are unavoidable in any complex society, for some must always organize, lead, and exert power, whereas others must do the routine work of the day; and economic inequality, like other forms of inequality, has social advantages as well as disadvantages.

It is doubtful whether modern civilization as we know it could ever have developed had there not been economic inequalities in the past. Inequalities of wealth and income have played an important role in enabling people with special abilities to use their talents to the best advantage, not only for themselves but for society. Throughout the ages the great writers, musicians, artists, and scientists have been able to do their special kinds of work and make their special contributions to our culture, either because they had wealth and perhaps even slaves, or because wealthy patrons who recognized their abilities were willing to support them.

Even in the modern world, economic inequality has its advantages for the group. It is true that if all personal income now received in the United States were divided equally, we could all live relatively well; but unless the equality was temporary, it might soon result in a great shrinkage of the total income to be divided. The existence of incomes and accumulations of wealth that are considerably above the average does have some real social advantages.

In the first place, men who hold important positions and carry great responsibilities need larger-than-average incomes in order to do their work well. The President of the United States, an ambassador, the president of a great corporation, and to a lesser extent many other men in key positions require relatively large incomes. Their work is very important to society, and to do it most effectively, they need to be freed from frittering away their time on buying the groceries or taking their clothes to the cleaners. They need servants and assistants, and that means they need more income than other people. Frequently they must also travel widely and meet a great variety of social responsibilities.

Another advantage of large incomes is as a source of savings for the investment capital required by modern industry. Because people with average or small incomes save relatively little, the bulk of personal saving must come from the well-to-do. Though it is true that banks, savings and loan companies, and insurance companies collect considerable amounts of investment capital by combining the funds of many small savers, aside from the reinvested earnings of corporations our chief reliance for new capital must still be individuals with better-than-average incomes. Savings from this source play an especially important role in furnishing investment funds for new enterprises that involve risk; and the constant organization of such enterprises is an important factor in raising production and creating new jobs in our economy.

Extremely large incomes and fortunes are probably on balance socially undesirable. Yet even these have often been employed to provide important social benefits. They have been used to endow many useful institutions, including private colleges and universities, special funds for the advancement of education, charitable organizations, hospitals, and foundations devoted to scientific research. Though many of the functions of such organizations could be carried on by the government, there is no assurance that government agencies could adequately replace our free, privately endowed institutions. Because of their relative freedom, these institutions provide opportunities for experiment, for the application of new ideas, and in various ways for the exercise of individual initiative. They are especially well suited for meeting many of the needs of a democratic society.

Income and Wealth as Economic Incentives. Perhaps the strongest argument for accepting a substantial degree of economic inequality in our society is the social need for employing economic incentives as a stimulus to production.

For an industrial economy to operate efficiently, it must have great numbers of well-trained workers in both the skilled trades and the professions. To a large degree, the hope of receiving higher-than-average incomes is what induces people to undergo the long, expensive, and arduous training that is often required. Likewise, for an industrial economy like ours to be highly productive, there must always be capable individuals—businessmen—who are able and willing to keep established businesses operating efficiently, and there must be others who will take the troubles and risks involved in organizing and expanding new enterprises. Here again it is the hope of receiving large incomes that, in the judgment of most economists, provides them with their chief incentive. Profits are both the substance and the symbol of business success. The businessman who continues to suffer losses fails and is forced to give up the struggle.

But are income and wealth necessary incentives for inducing people to make their greatest contributions to production? Could not other incentives easily be substituted, such as various forms of public recognition for tasks well done? Some argue that they could be. Socialists often maintain that business profits, in particular, are not needed as an incentive to obtain efficient operation or productive undertakings; but even they seldom argue that all workers should receive equal pay regardless of ability or training. Moreover, it is not just a matter of incentives. Some men lack the ability to operate a business efficiently no matter how hard they try. In a profit-and-loss system, incapable businessmen are eliminated by failure. On the other hand, if a socialized enterprise loses money because the political appointees who run it are poor managers, it may go on operating indefinitely at the expense of the taxpayers and to the detriment of the economy.

Though we may readily grant that income and wealth are not the only considerations that induce people to work and to do their work well, in our own society any careful observer of his fellow citizens should soon become convinced that most of them do their daily work principally in order to making a living, and as good a living as possible. In primitive societies the situation if often different. There the group is usually small, everyone is known to everyone else, and most people produce goods for their own use. Opportunities to accumulate wealth are limited, and frequently there is little desire to receive either wealth or income beyond that required to meet daily needs. But in an industrial society, goods are sold for money in an impersonal market, and money becomes a symbol of great importance; the chief incentive of those who produce goods tends to be the income they receive in the form of paychecks, fees, commissions, or profits. In a society like ours it seems quite unrealistic to suppose that without substantial economic incentives, and the degree of economic inequality necessary to permit them, we could maintain our present high and rising level of productivity. Even Soviet Russia, it should be noted, has made no attempt to eliminate economic inequalities. Instead, it has made systematic use of high wages, high salaries, and other economic benefits as incentives for the capable and the ambitious who are regarded as loyal to the regime in power.

ECONOMIC INEQUALITY AS A SOCIAL PROBLEM

Because few people would favor a completely equal distribution of wealth and income, and because neither justice nor expediency would seem to be favored by such a policy, any practical program for meeting the problems of economic inequality must represent a compromise among several objectives. Such a program should take into account (1) the social importance of raising the standards of living of the people who are at the bottom of the income scale; (2) the desirability of an income distribution that the public can accept as more or less just; (3) the importance of providing all children with adequate educational and economic opportunities, regardless of their parents' incomes; (4) the need for private savings as a source of capital for industry; and (5) the need for adequate incentives to stimulate efficient production and economic progress.

If we can eliminate real poverty without creating a class of people who depend permanently on a dole, we will have cured one of the worst evils of an unequal distribution of income. If we can solve the problem of providing all children with educational and economic opportunities that match their potentials, we will have solved another. Perhaps we should also seek ways to prevent an excessive concentration of wealth and economic power in the hands of a relatively small number of individuals and families. We already have taken steps in this direction through heavy income surtaxes and estate taxes. We could make these taxes both higher and more difficult to evade. The danger is that this might seriously reduce both economic incentives and the flow of capital to industry for expanding production and employment. As it is, huge fortunes tend ultimately to be dissipated, but it is sometimes a very slow process.

THE PROBLEM OF ECONOMIC SECURITY

Security, like freedom, is relative. Even in a highly productive country like the United States, for most people the fear of poverty and want lies just around the corner. With good luck all goes well, but the possibilities of disaster are always present in such forms as accident, illness, death of a breadwinner, loss of property, and periods of mass unemployment. Because of this fear of economic disaster, people have tried to build defenses against it, but not always successfully.

The traditional defenses against economic insecurity are insurance and savings. These are strong defenses, but they are inadequate in many situations. The federal government has therefore sponsored a *social security* program, which is really a program designed to give a minimum of economic security. It provides limited amounts of income as protection against loss of earning power from old age, unemployment, and certain other contingencies.

Nature and Limitations of the Traditional Defenses Against Insecurity. Probably the most widely used method by which individuals try to protect themselves against a great variety of economic risks is *saving;* and saving is a very effective road to security, *provided one can save enough.* But the average worker on a modest wage finds it very difficult to save sufficient money to carry him for any length of time if he suffers illness, accident, or unemployment.

Insurance is a highly developed defense against some aspects of economic insecurity. Many large and successful corporations have been organized for the express purpose of providing this kind of protection.

The most familiar types of insurance today are automobile, fire, accident and health, and life insurance. Automobile insurance is a combination of several types of protection. It usually covers direct loss of property (the car) through fire, theft, or collision, and also legal liabilities to others that may result from accidents involving either property damage or personal injury. Life insurance has played an important role in this country in providing families with support after the death of the breadwinner. By 1972 the total amount of life insurance in force in the United States is likely to be $1.5 trillion or more, a sum four or five times as great as the national debt; and yet few men can afford to buy enough life insurance to give their families really adequate protection.

All insurance operates on the principle of dividing among a large number of people losses that are actually suffered by only a few. When people take out insurance and make periodic payments called *insurance premiums,* they are buying protection for themselves, but they are also helping to pay the bills for those who actually suffer misfortune. In addition, their premiums pay the operating costs of the insurance companies.

Though insurance is an effective protection against some types of loss, against others it gives only partial protection, and against still others it cannot be applied at all. For example, the owners of a business cannot insure against the loss that would result if the business failed.

Contributions of Industry to Worker Security. Industry contributions to the economic security of workers have a long history, but in recent years they have increased greatly in importance. Group life insurance plans sponsored and often paid for by business firms are very popular, and provisions for medical and hospital care of workers are also common. Today pension plans are commonly provided by large corporations, and in recent years there has been a great increase in their number. Some companies attempt to protect their workers against layoffs by "guaranteed annual wage" plans. A few of these plans, like that of Proctor and Gamble, were established a great many years ago. To meet demands of the United Auto Workers, the automobile companies made a start in this direction in 1955 and have since then increased the benefits substantially.

THE AMERICAN SOCIAL SECURITY SYSTEM

The first comprehensive government-administered social insurance system in the world was established in imperial Germany more than eighty years ago. It was sponsored by Bismarck, who apparently conceived of it as a plan for allaying social unrest. In the years from 1883 to 1889 legislation was passed providing workers with sickness insurance, accident insurance, and retirement pensions in old age. More than twenty years later somewhat similar legislation was enacted in Britain and France, and in time most other European countries followed suit.

Today one of the most extensive of all social insurance systems is that of Great Britain. It includes weekly payments to mothers for each child until the child is fifteen; unemployment compensation; sickness and accident benefits; old-age pensions; and, in addition, complete medical and hospital care.

In this country there was no broad program of social insurance until after passage of the Social Security Act in 1935, although before that time both the states and federal government had passed various laws that contributed to the security of workers. Among the benefits thus provided were compensation of workmen for industrial accidents, pension programs for public employees, and pensions for all railroad workers. Railroad pensions were first provided for in the Railroad Retirement Act of 1934. However, the Supreme Court declared this legislation unconstitutional, and the present act, a modified version, was not passed until a year later.

The Need for Social Security Legislation. We have already called attention to the difficulty that most people experience in providing themselves with enough savings or insurance to meet adequately the economic contingencies of life. But today output and purchasing power per capita are much greater than in the past, and we might suppose that people would find it easier to provide themselves with future security. In some ways, however, the problem of achieving security becomes more difficult as a society reaches a higher degree of industrialization. When our economy was largely agricultural, the problem of security in old age was likely to be less acute. Family solidarity was greater in rural regions, and as the operation of a farm was gradually taken over by a son and his family, the old people often stayed on. Moreover, on a farm there are always jobs that older people can do as long as they are not completely incapacitated.

In an industrial society, on the other hand, family ties are likely to be weaker. Each worker and his immediate family often live in a rented house or apartment, and in any case he is chiefly dependent on wages or salary from a job. When a man loses his job, or when he reaches retirement age and his job stops, his connection with it is likely to be broken off both abruptly and completely. Today even if a worker has savings that he once thought would be sufficient for retirement, their value is likely to be greatly reduced by inflation. If a retired worker does not have an adequate source of income, his position is unenviable. He and his wife may go to live with one of their children, but often the children do not have room for them and feel that their care is a burden.

In 1935 it was clearer than ever before that various groups of people were in great need of economic aid. We were still in the midst of the worst depression in history. Millions were unemployed and had little to live on except relief payments. Other millions, including great numbers of retired people, had lost their savings in closed banks, defaulted real estate bonds, or other investments whose value had contracted or disappeared.

Organization of the Social Security System. Though the original Social Security Act, which was passed by Congress in 1935, did little or nothing to meet the immediate needs of people in the depression, it was a major step toward providing greater future security for the majority of American workers. Over the years it has been amended a number of times, and, in the process, benefits have been greatly increased, new programs have been added, and changes have been made in its administration.

Today there are four major Social Security programs set up by federal legislation. First and most familiar is the *old-age and survivors insurance* (OASI), which is entirely controlled by the federal government. Second is *medicare,* also controlled from Washington, and designed to cover most of the cost of hospital and medical care for the great majority of citizens over sixty-five. Third are the various *unemployment insurance* plans set up by the different states with federal aid. Fourth and last are the *public assistance* programs, under which public funds are used to aid certain types of needy persons, including dependent children, who are not protected by old-age or unemployment insurance. These programs are also set up and administered by the states but are partly financed by the central government. In addition to these major programs, the Washington government contributes in other ways to the social security of various groups of citizens. For example, it has set up retirement pension systems for railroad workers and federal employees, and it provides special benefits for veterans, and various welfare services for children.

Responsibility for OASI and medicare rests on the Social Security Administration, an agency in the Department of Health, Education, and Welfare. Another agency in this department, the Social and Rehabilitation Service, is responsible for the federal aspects of public assistance and, through its Children's Bureau, for certain child-welfare services. But the Bureau of Employment Security in the Department of Labor represents the federal government in approving and aiding state unemployment insurance programs.

Because old-age and survivors insurance, unemployment insurance, public assistance, and medicare are of outstanding importance in the federal Social Security system, we shall describe each of these programs briefly, with special emphasis on the old-age and survivors insurance plan.

Old-Age and Survivors Insurance. OASI was originally restricted to wage earners in industry. It provided workers who were covered for a long enough period, and who retired at sixty-five or older, with pensions that ranged from ten dollars to eighty-five dollars per month. In 1939 the Social Security Act was amended to provide benefits for wives and children, and in 1950 further substantial changes were made. Not only were benefits greatly increased, but as of January 1, 1951, coverage was extended to regularly employed domestic workers, to some agricultural workers, and, under certain conditions, to government employees and employees of nonprofit institutions such as colleges or hospitals. Coverage was also extended to include the self-employed, except for farm operators and professional workers like doctors, lawyers, accountants, and engineers; but later acts extended coverage to include farm operators and employees and most professional people.

Today the great majority of American workers are covered by OASI. The several million who still remain outside the system include most federal employees, a large proportion of public school teachers, and many state and local government employees. However, the greater part of the workers not under OASI are protected by other retirement systems, most of which are operated by federal, state, or local governments. Many workers who are covered by OASI are also entitled to benefits under other pension plans. Examples are the steel, coal, and automobile workers, who, on retirement, not only receive Social Security payments but also pensions under plans established by the companies for which they work.

Some other significant changes have been made in OASI. In the Social Security Act of 1956, Congress for the first time provided that covered workers who became totally and permanently disabled might receive indemnities after reaching the age of fifty. Also, women were granted the right to receive pensions after reaching sixty-two instead of waiting to attain sixty-five. In the case of covered workers, women who elect to retire and take their pensions before sixty-five receive smaller payments. However, widows of covered workers may receive at sixty-two the same pension to which they would be entitled at sixty-five, and under the Act of 1965 they may receive a reduced pension at sixty. The Act of 1960 permitted totally disabled workers under fifty to receive benefits, and

"Easy, Agnes. You don't want to make us ineligible for our social security benefits." (Copyright 1969 *Saturday Review, Inc.* Drawing by Barney Tobey.)

that of 1961 extended to men the privilege of retiring at sixty-two with a reduced pension.

Other changes made over the years include (1) substantially liberalizing the amount of income that a "retired" worker can earn without losing his Social Security benefits; (2) raising the amount of earnings that can be credited toward Social Security benefits and that are subject to the Social Security tax; (3) increasing monthly benefits; and (4) raising Social Security tax rates. Almost every major revision of the Social Security Act has increased the number of workers in *covered employment* and has raised both benefits and taxes. Social Security taxes, it should be noted, are increased not only by raising the basic rates but also by raising the amounts of income on which they are levied.

As OASI now operates, a covered worker receives regular monthly benefits when he retires, provided he has reached at least the age of sixty-two and provided his earnings after "retirement" do not exceed certain limits. Beyond the age of seventy-two he receives his full pension benefits no matter how much he earns. Under some conditions a worker may be entitled to additional benefits for his wife and certain other dependents.

If a worker dies, benefits are available to his dependents regardless of his age at death, provided they can meet certain conditions specified by law. For example, children cannot receive payments after they are eighteen unless they are disabled or unless they are not yet twenty-two, are unmarried, and are enrolled as full-time students. A widow, unless she has children under eighteen or is disabled, cannot receive a pension until she is sixty. All benefits are paid from a trust fund that is built up from

Social Security taxes on employers, employees, and the self-employed and that, except for a working cash balance, is invested in government securities.

Under the Social Security Act, as amended in 1969, each wage earner in a covered job paid a *Social Security tax* of 4.8 per cent on any wages received up to $7,800. This included both OASI and hospital insurance. The tax was scheduled by law to rise by stages to 5.9 per cent in 1987, so that a worker earning $7,800 or more would then pay a total tax of $460.20. But in 1971 Congress enacted legislation that raised to $9,000, beginning in January, 1972, the maximum amount of income on which Social Security taxes must be paid. The new act also stepped up the schedule of future increases in the tax *rate,* so that, under the present law, a worker earning as much as $9,000 a year must, in 1987, pay a Social Security tax of 6.05 per cent on that amount, or a total of $544.50. A worker's Social Security tax is deducted from the worker's pay by his employer, who must contribute an equal amount and then pay the total to the government.

Obviously, the tax on a self-employed person must be handled differently. To receive Social Security credits, such a person must be in a covered occupation and must receive from it at least $400 annually. In 1970, if he met these requirements, he paid a tax of 6.9 per cent on any income received up to $7,800. This tax was also scheduled to rise, by stages, to a high point in 1987. But the act passed by Congress in 1971 raised to $9,000, effective in January, 1972, the amount of self-employment income subject to the Social Security tax, and it also stepped up the schedule of rate increases. Under present legislation the Social Security tax on self-employed persons will be 7.5 per cent in 1987, and the total amount payable by a person earning $9,000 or more will be $711. But on the basis of past experience, and especially if inflation continues to be a problem, further changes in Social Security taxes and benefits are likely to be made long before 1987.

The benefits a worker receives on retirement are based primarily on his average monthly earnings in covered employment. The minimum time for which he must be covered to receive any benefits, and which applies only to workers who retired in 1957 or earlier, is six quarters, or one-and-a-half years. This rises to ten years for workers who retire in 1991 or later. For a quarter to count, wages earned during it must amount to fifty dollars or more.

Special payments of forty-six dollars a month (sixty-nine dollars for a couple) can be made to certain people who have reached the age of seventy-two or over and who have not qualified for Social Security benefits; but all who became seventy-two, in 1968 or later, need some work credits under Social Security in order to receive such payments.

For a self-employed person to be insured under OASI, the requirements are the same as for a wage earner, except that a self-employed person must be credited with at least one hundred dollars of earnings in a quarter to have it count; but credits are actually based on yearly earnings. To illustrate, a self-employed person who earns only two hundred dollars in a year is credited with only two quarters of covered employment; if he earns four hundred dollars or more, he is credited with four quarters. Wages and self-employment income up to a total of $9,000 a year may be combined to receive quarters of coverage or earnings credits.

Table 14 gives examples of present monthly benefit payments to various types of Social Security beneficiaries. Maximum retirement benefits (for workers with higher incomes) will not be payable to anyone for some years to come because earnings of more than $4,200 cannot be credited for any year before 1959; more than $4,800 before 1966; more than $6,600 before 1968; and more than $7,800 before 1972.

Table 14. *Examples of Monthly Social Security Benefit Payments, 1971*

	Average Yearly Earnings After 1950			
	$923 or Less	**$3,000**	**$5,400**	**$7,800**
Retired worker, 65 or older; disabled worker, under 65	70.40	145.60	208.80	275.80
Wife, 65 or older	35.20	72.80	104.40	137.90
Retired worker at 62	56.30	116.50	167.10	220.70
Wife at 62, no child	26.40	54.70	78.30	103.50
Widow at 62 or older	70.40	120.10	172.30	227.60
Widow at 60, no child	61.10	104.20	149.40	197.30
Disabled widow at 50, no child	42.80	72.90	104.50	138.10
Wife under 65 and one child	35.20	77.20	181.10	202.20
Widow under 62 and one child	105.60	218.50	313.30	413.80
Widow under 62 and two children	105.60	222.60	389.80	477.80
One child of retired or disabled worker	35.20	72.80	104.40	137.90
One surviving child	70.40	109.20	156.60	206.90
Maximum family payment	105.60	222.60	389.80	477.80

Source: Your Social Security, Social Security Administration, Washington, D.C., February 1970. Because Congress, in 1971, raised all Social Security Benefits 10 per cent, this amount, rounded to the nearest ten cents, has been added to the 1970 figures to give those for 1971.

Though the actual figures in Table 14 may be outdated before long, we insert the table because it presents to the reader at a glance certain characteristics of the OASI benefit system. If and when benefit payments are changed in the future, the new schedules will presumably be printed in the current issue of the booklet *Your Social Security,* published by the Social Security Administration and available at any Social Security office.

Unemployment Insurance. The unemployment insurance programs set up under the Social Security Act are state-organized and state-administered. As a result they vary greatly, even though they must meet certain minimum requirements of the act. To induce all the states to establish unemployment insurance plans, the act originally levied a 3 per cent tax on the payrolls of all employers having eight or more workers, but it also provided that if a state passed a satisfactory unemployment law, nine tenths of this tax on firms within its borders would be remitted by the federal government and could be levied by the state to build a special trust fund for the payment of unemployment benefits. Later, the federal tax was raised to 3.1 per cent and was applied to all employers with four or more workers. Some states tax employers with fewer workers.

All states, as well as the District of Columbia and Puerto Rico, now have unemployment insurance plans. Originally all the states levied on payrolls a tax at least equal to the amount remitted from the federal tax, but now, in all states, employers who seldom or never lay off workers are excused from paying part or all of this tax.

Benefits vary greatly under state unemployment laws. In 1969 maximum benefits for total unemployment ranged from thirty-six dollars a week in Puerto Rico and thirty-eight dollars in Oklahoma to seventy-six dollars in Connecticut, and the maximum period of coverage in a fifty-two week period ranged from twelve weeks in Puerto Rico to thirty-nine in Oklahoma.[4]

Public Assistance. The use of public funds to aid those who cannot support themselves is an old practice in the United States. In earlier times the whole burden was carried by towns or counties, and the aid provided was often very meager. The Social Security Act of 1935 enabled the federal government to help the states provide monthly cash payments to certain types of needy persons not covered by old-age or unemployment insurance. Such persons now include the needy aged, the blind, the permanently disabled, and children deprived of support because of the death, disability, absence, or unemployment of a parent. Public assistance is not insurance, and its benefits are granted solely on the basis of need.

Each state initiates and administers its own public assistance program, but, if it is to obtain federal aid, this program must meet certain requirements of the Social Security Act. In spite of the great expansion of OASI, the number of people receiving public assistance and the total costs of the program have risen sharply over the years.

Under public assistance programs it is necessary to determine what is a reasonable minimum standard of living. This, along with an individual's resources, is the basis for determining his need. Most programs recognize that a person receiving assistance should be allowed to keep a modest home and small reserves for such expenses as illness and burial. Though a substantial portion of public assistance expenditures goes to needy children, an important purpose of the program is to aid old people to maintain themselves in health and in reasonable comfort. In some cases, people receiving OASI payments are also given public assistance, either to meet special medical and hospital costs or because the OASI benefits are very inadequate.

[4] *Monthly Labor Review,* January 1970, pp. 63–66.

Medicare. For many years one of the great differences between social security in the United States and in countries like Great Britain or Sweden was that our program made no provision for medical or hospital care. It still makes no provision for such coverage for active workers, but under the *medicare* program adopted in 1965 Social Security was extended to cover, under a compulsory plan, most of the hospital costs of citizens sixty-five or older. Under a voluntary plan, available to those who agree to pay a small monthly premium, it also provides for the greater part of their medical expenses. Under both plans, the beneficiary is free to choose his own doctor. The benefits of medicare are available not only to retired people who are covered by OASI but also to most other citizens who are over sixty-five.

The basic or compulsory medicare program meets most hospital expenses of a beneficiary for a limited period of time. For each single illness, it pays for up to sixty days of hospital care, except for a relatively small fixed sum that must be paid by the patient. If an additional thirty days is needed, medicare meets the bill except for a minor portion of the daily charge. Each insured person also has a "lifetime reserve" of sixty additional hospital days for which his insurance pays all covered costs except for a somewhat larger portion of the daily charge. After a patient leaves the hospital he may, if necessary, spend as much as twenty days in a nursing home free, and up to eighty days additional by paying only a small sum daily. When he returns home from the hospital or nursing home, he is

". . . In sickness and in health, with or without medicare . . ." (Courtesy Sidney Harris.)

entitled during a single illness to receive free, if his doctor orders it, up to a hundred visits by nurses and other health workers.

The voluntary medicare plan is designed to cover most of the fees of physicians and surgeons. If an older citizen wishes to join this plan, he can do so if he enrolls within certain specified periods. For his insurance to begin promptly at age sixty-five, he should enroll during the three-month period before the month he reaches sixty-five. After his insurance is in force, he must pay a modest monthly premium, which the government matches dollar for dollar. This premium can be increased as the cost of medical services rises.

Under the voluntary plan the government will not only pay the greater part of a beneficiary's medical and surgical bills, but it will also provide for him a long list of diagnostic, therapeutic, and nursing services that are additional to those provided in the compulsory program.

Obviously, medicare is not a complete program of compulsory health insurance. Active workers are still unprotected unless they belong to private hospital and medical plans. Opposition to a program that would cover almost everybody is still strong, though not as adamant as it once was. Those who oppose such a program maintain that private plans can effectively meet the needs of the great majority of workers, and they insist that the costs of a comprehensive government program would greatly exceed the usual estimates. They also maintain that such a program would overburden doctors, tend to destroy the personal relationship between doctor and patient, and ultimately lead to government control of medicine. The problems of the medical profession in Great Britain give substance to some of these fears. There, it is said, doctors are overburdened, their incomes relative to other groups have fallen, many are leaving the country, and the medical profession no longer has the appeal that it once did to able young students when they choose their careers. Nevertheless, in the years to come, the chances seem good that there will be strong pressures on Congress to expand medicare to cover, in some form, most or all of our population.

SOME PROBLEMS OF THE SOCIAL SECURITY PROGRAM

Provision of a broader program of hospital and medical benefits is only one of a number of problems that are involved in developing the Social Security System of the United States. Some of these problems grow out of the failure of the present program to meet certain important needs; others relate to its organization, administration, or financing. We have already called attention to President Nixon's proposals for replacing our present relief program with a radically different system of payments that would give greater help to the poor and at the same time, hopefully, encourage them to accept work training and jobs and eventually become self-supporting.

Problems of the OASI Reserve Fund. When OASI was set up, it was supposed that workers and employers would contribute to the *OASI reserve fund* through taxes sufficient money to cover the actuarial cost of the old-age pensions and other benefits that would later be paid. In fact, however, the taxes levied have not been sufficient to meet this cost. There are at least two reasons for this. One is that many older people were admitted to the OASI system by amendments to the Social Security Act in 1950 and later years and were allowed to receive substantial benefits after paying Social Security taxes for a relatively short time. Another reason is that inflation of prices has several times induced Congress to increase benefits to people already retired and no longer paying Social Security taxes. The result is that the pensions of retired people are now being paid partly from current taxes on younger people who are still working. When these younger workers retire, their benefits will probably be met in part by taxes on the following generation. Though the reserve fund is substantial, it is nowhere near large enough, by private insurance standards, to meet the accumulated obligations of OASI. The chief purpose that the reserve fund serves is to make certain that OASI can always meet its obligations in the short run. But a persistent decline in the fund would sooner or later have to be met by increasing Social Security taxes.

Receipts from taxes are still exceeding benefits paid only because the number of active workers paying taxes is so very much greater than the number of retired people receiving benefits and also because Congress has kept raising both Social Security tax rates and the amount of income on which such taxes must be paid. At present, the government spends the difference for its ordinary expenses, replacing this money in the Social Security fund with its own promises to pay in the future—in other words, with government securities.

There are now three smaller trust funds within the Social Security System, namely (1) the Federal Disability Insurance Trust Fund; (2) the Federal Hospital Insurance Trust Fund; and (3) the Federal Supplementary Medical Insurance Trust Fund.

How Large Should OASI Benefits Be? There are wide differences of opinion as to the social function that old-age pensions should serve. The prevailing view seems to be that they should roughly provide a minimum subsistence standard of living, thus preventing extreme want but at the same time encouraging people who desire something better to plan and save on their own initiative. Some, however, feel that the government should guarantee to all retired workers enough income to enable them to live in comfort. On the one side of this difference of opinion are those who wish to preserve the principle of individual responsibility; on the other are those who feel that the government should take a paternal attitude in looking after the needs of its citizens.

One objection to making old-age pensions really liberal is that this would put a heavy burden on that part of the population actually doing the work. The goods consumed by any economy are the goods that it currently produces. If old people are able to consume a disproportionately large share of such goods, there will be that much less available for the younger people of working age. If old-age pensions are high, it is these younger people who will really bear the burden. The cost will fall on them either through direct taxation or else through the higher prices that would result from greater competition for a limited supply of goods.[5]

Should Old-Age Pensions Be Universal? There are some who argue that instead of going through all the motions that are involved under OASI in relating old-age benefits to employment, we should automatically grant to every citizen who attains the age of sixty-five a pension sufficient for subsistence. Such a pension would, presumably, be paid out of general tax funds. Those who advocate such a policy maintain not only that it would better serve the ends of justice and humanity, but also that old people must be taken care of anyway, and that this plan would make charity or other types of special assistance entirely unnecessary except in unusual situations. It would also prevent some cases of gross injustice that may arise when pensions are based solely on earnings. There are many people who have earned little or no money during their adult years and who yet deserve pensions as much as others. As an illustration, take a woman who has spent most of her life in caring for invalid parents.

A plan like that just suggested would result in another important gain. It would eliminate a large part of the complex, cumbersome, and very costly record keeping that the present system entails. The costs to both business and government of keeping detailed records of the tax obligations and work credits of millions of employees are very considerable.

However, from the standpoint of our American system of values, the present program does have one great advantage. This is that it makes both the receipt of a pension and its size bear some relation to the contributions to production of each individual. Today the retired worker who receives an old-age pension is likely to feel that it is a just reward for years of work and also a return on the money he himself has paid in as Social Security taxes. In the minds of many people, this feature of the present OASI program outweighs the objections to it.

Terms to Be Understood

income	conspicuous	Job Corps
real income	consumption	VISTA
standard of living	disposable personal	poverty threshhold
Engel's law	income	ADC

---

[5] In other words, if the money incomes of old people are substantially increased without reducing by taxation the money incomes of workers, total spending will rise, and this will cause inflation. In practice, however, workers seem to have greater success in raising their incomes to meet inflation than do retired people, and this can result in even more inflation.

food-stamp plan   OASI   unemployment
social security   public assistance   insurance
  insurance   Social Security tax   medicare
  insurance premiums   covered employment   OASI reserve fund

Questions for Review and Discussion

1. Give examples to show that the search for income and the search for security sometimes reinforce one another and sometimes come into conflict.
2. Differences in income arise directly from what two sources? Explain why these differences exist.
3. Why does Table 13 (page 544) somewhat exaggerate the degree of economic inequality in this country?
4. Why may two individuals with the same money incomes have different standards of living?
5. How can it be determined whether an individual or a family is living in poverty?
6. List major features in President Johnson's "war on poverty." What problems arose under the program?
7. Explain how the Social Security Administration attempts to measure the amount of poverty in the United States.
8. The number of Americans classified as poverty-stricken has declined sharply in recent years. Why?
9. Do you believe that all of the 24.3 million people whom the Bureau of the Census classified as suffering from poverty in 1969 considered themselves to be impoverished? Why or why not?
10. Why is it difficult to measure the amount of hunger and malnutrition in the country?
11. Why is it necessary to qualify any answer to the question Can poverty be eliminated?
12. What are the most serious objections to the present (1971) welfare programs? Do you think President Nixon's proposals, if implemented, would improve the situation? Why or why not?
13. Would it be just to divide the national disposable income equally among all the people? Defend your answer.
14. List possible social benefits from the existence of economic inequalities.
15. In order to maintain a high level of output and a high rate of progress in an economy, is it necessary to offer people substantial economic incentives? Is it desirable to eliminate somewhat ruthlessly the businessmen who keep losing money no matter how hard they try? Discuss.
16. How, in your judgment, should we deal with the problem of economic inequality? Defend your proposals.
17. Point out the limitations of both savings and insurance as protections against economic insecurity.
18. State briefly the history of social insurance legislation up to 1935.
19. State the nature of each of the four major parts of the Social Security System that was set up by the Social Security Act of 1935.
20. Outline the OASI plan, explaining briefly (a) who are eligible for coverage; (b) the payment of Social Security taxes; (c) the reserve fund; and (d) the principal benefits.

21. Describe the unemployment insurance program.
22. Who are benefited under the public assistance program?
23. What major benefits are provided by (a) the basic or compulsory medicare program? (b) the voluntary program? How is each financed?
24. Do you favor a broad program of compulsory health insurance for all workers covered by Social Security? Defend your answer.
25. From the standpoint of our system of social values, what great advantage does our present Social Security System have?

For Further Study

Birch, Herbert G., M. D., and Joan Dye Gussow, *Disadvantaged Children,* New York, Harcourt Brace Jovanovich, Inc., 1970.

Coates, Ken, and Richard Silburn, *Poverty: The Forgotten Englishmen,* paperback, Baltimore, Penguin Books, Inc., 1970.

Hamilton, David, *Primer on the Economics of Poverty,* paperback, New York, Random House, Inc., 1968.

Hansen, Niles, *Rural Poverty and the Urban Crisis: A Strategy for Regional Development,* paperback, Bloomington, Indiana University Press, 1970.

Harrington, Michael, *The Other America,* paperback, Baltimore, Penguin Books, Inc., 1963. One of the books credited with starting the crusade against poverty.

Hazlitt, Henry, *Man vs. the Welfare State,* New Rochelle, N.Y., Arlington House Publishers, 1969.

Krinsky, Fred, and Joseph Boskin, *The Welfare State,* paperback, New York, The Free Press, 1968.

McGuire, Joseph W., and Joseph A. Pichler, *Inequality, the Poor and the Rich in America,* paperback, Belmont, Cal., Wadsworth Publishing Company, 1969.

Moynihan, Daniel P., ed., *On Understanding Poverty,* New York, Basic Books, Inc., 1969.

Myrdal, Gunnar, *Asian Drama: An Inquiry into the Poverty of Nations,* Pantheon paperback, New York, Random House, Inc., 1968.

Ornati, Oscar, *Poverty Amid Affluence,* paperback, New York, Twentieth Century Fund, Inc., 1966.

Pechman, Joseph A., Henry J. Aaron, and Michael K. Taussig, *Social Security: Perspectives for Reform,* Washington, D.C., The Brookings Institution, 1968.

Ross, Arthur M., and Herbert Hill, eds., *Employment, Race, and Poverty,* paperback, New York, Harcourt Brace Jovanovich, Inc., 1967.

Social Security Bulletin, Washington, D.C., Social Security Administration of the U.S. Department of Health, Education, and Welfare. See current issues; also see other publications of the Social Security Administration.

Turnbull, J. G., et al., *Economic and Social Security,* 3d ed., New York, The Ronald Press Company, 1968.

Wilcox, Clair, *Toward Social Welfare: An Analysis of Programs and Proposals Attacking Poverty, Insecurity, and Inequality of Opportunity,* Homewood, Ill., Richard D. Irwin, Inc., 1969.

Chapter 21

Labor Relations and the Public Welfare

an important by-product of the Industrial Revolution has been the rise and growth of the labor movement. With the coming of the factory system, the typical town worker, instead of being an independent handicraft tradesman, became a wage-earning employee. Moreover, because most factories hired a large number of workers, the individual employee was usually of little importance to his employer, and hence he frequently received small consideration. If he complained about bad treatment or bad working conditions or asked for a raise, he was likely to be dropped from the payroll and told to look for another job. Other jobs might or might not be available, but even if they were, to change his work often put an employee to a good deal of personal inconvenience and in some cases even forced him to move to a different community. In time, because of their precarious situation and their inability to protect their interests individually, industrial workers began to organize into labor unions in order to present a united front in dealing with employers.

As labor unions have become larger, more numerous, and more powerful, the problem of maintaining good relations between unions and employers has assumed greater and greater importance. In many fields, especially in the skilled trades, the public utilities, mining, and the mass-production manufacturing industries, a very large proportion of all workers are organized into unions. Recently, public employees, including teachers and policemen, have been forming more and more unions, and increasingly they have been engaging in strikes, even when these are forbidden by law. In 1970 for the first time there was a strike by postal workers, and though only a minority joined the walkout, mail service was seriously disrupted. All this means that adequate methods for settling disputes between organized labor and its employers are very essential if we are to avoid recurring work stoppages in important industries or essential public services.

At best, such stoppages are costly and disrupting; at worst, as in the case of a general railroad or truckers' strike, they can paralyze the entire economy. In many labor disputes the public has as much or more at stake than workers and employers, but often its interests receive little consideration.

THE DEVELOPMENT OF LABOR ORGANIZATION IN AMERICA

Early History of Labor Unions in the United States. In certain of the skilled trades the labor movement in the United States goes back to the eighteenth century, but most of the early labor unions were local, and sometimes they were temporary in nature. For many years the growth of the labor movement was slow and sporadic, so much so that it was not until the decade just preceding the Civil War that the first permanent trade unions were organized on a national scale.

But attempts to organize the labor movement as a whole on a nationwide basis had little success until some years after the Civil War. In 1869 the tailors of Philadelphia created an unusual type of labor organization, which they called the Knights of Labor. This group attempted to bring together all types of unions and all types of workers. It included not only craft unions of skilled workers but also general labor unions, which admitted to membership any worker regardless of his occupation or skill. At first the Knights of Labor grew rather slowly, but in the early 1880's it began to expand rapidly, achieving in 1886 a total membership of over 700,000. For a time its prestige and power were so great that it played an important part in national politics, but after 1886 it experienced a quick decline. Apparently, its greatest weakness was in attempting to bring together a miscellaneous group of workers who had few interests in common. Its political activities may also have contributed to its downfall.

The AFL and the CIO. The Knights of Labor was succeeded on the national scene by the American Federation of Labor (AFL). This group, organized in 1886 as an association of *craft,* or *trade,* unions, gradually increased in importance and influence. For many years after the decline of the Knights it remained our one great national labor federation.

It was not until the depression years of the 1930's that a second national federation came into being. When the AFL met for its national convention in 1935, there was a widespread feeling that the time had come to attempt to organize workers in the mass-production industries. Very soon, however, a bitter dispute developed among the delegates as to how this should be accomplished. One group, headed by John L. Lewis of the United Mine Workers, felt that the only way to organize these industries successfully was to bring all the workers in each of them into a single union. A union of this kind is called an *industrial union*. It differs in principle from a *craft union,* because the latter is open only to workers in a certain trade, like the plumbers or the machinists. But the AFL consisted primarily of unions organized on the craft principle, and most of these were strongly opposed to any plan for organizing industrial unions in the mass-production industries. They were determined, if possible, to bring the skilled workers in such industries into their own ranks.

After a long controversy, the final result was that representatives of an important group of national unions, acting independently of the AFL convention, formed the Committee for Industrial Organization. Later this group, under the leadership of John L. Lewis, broke off all relations with the AFL and changed its name to the Congress of Industrial Organizations, which became commonly known as the CIO. In its early stages the CIO grew very rapidly, in great part because of its extraordinary success in organizing industrial unions among the steel and automobile workers.

For many years there was a good deal of ill feeling between the two major labor organizations. Gradually, however, this diminished. By 1955 the CIO had attained a membership of perhaps five million and the AFL claimed more than ten million. In that year, following long negotiations, the two organizations were merged to create the new American Federation of Labor and Congress of Industrial Organizations under the presidency of George Meany. This new federation includes the great majority of all labor unions in the country. Nevertheless, we still have a number of independent unions, among them such important organizations as the Teamsters, the United Mine Workers, and the Automobile Workers. The last two groups belonged at one time to the AFL-CIO.

The Structure of Organized Labor. Though unions vary a good deal in their structure, the majority have certain features in common. The basic unit is the *local.* When a community is small, the local may include all the workers in a given craft or industry. But in a large city, where workers are many and widely scattered, such an organization would be unwieldy. There it may be necessary to form locals in different sections of the city or in each of a number of separate plants. Where a union has several locals in the same general area, they usually join together to form a *district council*.

Though the basic unit of organized labor is the local, power over policies is usually centered in the *national union*. In most cases national unions started out as loose federations, but in order to secure united action the locals gradually put more and more power into the hands of the central organizations. Finally the point was reached where the national unions were allowed to make the rules that the locals had to follow. Much of the power of the national unions results from the fact that they generally control strike, disability, pension, and other benefit funds. If a local refuses to submit to the authority of the national union, it may run the risk of having benefits withheld from its members.

A *general federation* is a voluntary association of different unions for the purpose of advancing their common interests. When a federation is local, it is often called a *city central*. Federations are also found at the state, regional, and national levels. Because federations are voluntary associations, they have little if any control over their member unions. They cannot, for example, call strikes. Their influence and prestige rest almost entirely on the voluntary support they receive. If at any time a member union should choose to withdraw, it is free to do so.

Strength of the Labor Movement in America. Until the New Deal administration of President Franklin D. Roosevelt came into power, organized labor represented a very small fraction of all American workers, and its only real strength was among those who were highly skilled. In 1900 total union membership was less than one million. By 1920, under the stimulus of World War I, it had risen to over five million, but in the next few years it dropped back to less than four million. However, after passage of the National Labor Relations Act in 1935, an act highly favorable to organized labor, union membership rose rapidly. By 1955 it had reached seventeen million, but since then it has risen rather slowly. In 1968 it had increased, according to the Bureau of Labor Statistics, by only three million to a total of about twenty million. One reason for this slow growth was that after 1955 the number of production, or blue-collar, workers, instead of increasing, declined appreciably. But from 1955 to 1968 the labor force as a whole expanded by more than sixteen million. Most of the increase, however, was in technical and white-collar workers, who are difficult to organize.

In spite of the great power of organized labor, only about one worker in every four in our labor force belongs to a union. This is partly because of apathy on the part of many workers, partly because of employer opposition, and partly because in some areas of the country public opinion is not well disposed toward organized labor. But a more important explanation probably lies in the fact that many types of workers would be very difficult to organize effectively. Outstanding examples are domestic help and farm labor. In such industries as manufacturing, railroads and trucking, construction, mining, and public utilities, labor unions are very strong. In textiles and the service industries they have made progress; also, as we have noted, they have recently succeeded in organizing many government employees. But they are generally weak to very weak in the clerical occupations, retail and wholesale trade, and agriculture.

The power of American labor unions results not so much from the total number of union members as from the fact that certain unions control the labor supply in strategic industries. This is often true locally in the building industry. Then there are national labor unions, like the Teamsters, the Steel Workers and the Mine Workers, who can, by striking, paralyze some basic industries throughout the nation. It was a series of nationwide strikes, following World War II, that helped to pave the way for passage of the Taft-Hartley Act in 1947.

COLLECTIVE BARGAINING AND THE LABOR CONTRACT

One way of explaining the need for workers to organize in defense of their interests is to say that the individual worker has practically no *bargaining power* in relation to his employer. This is true in the sense that, so far as the jobs in a particular plant are concerned, the employer is a monopolist (the sole buyer of labor);[1] whereas the workers, if they are not organized, must constantly compete with one another to obtain and hold their jobs. But if workers can organize effectively and prevent nonunion men from working in the plant, they also put themselves in a monopoly position, because the union becomes the sole provider of labor to the plant in question. Unfortunately, bargaining between two monopolists presents difficulties, and this is one reason that labor relations often fail to run smoothly.

The Nature of Collective Bargaining. In theory, *collective bargaining is bargaining between an employer or his agents and the freely chosen representatives of his organized workers.* It is carried on between two parties, each of whom has some monopoly power. When neither side in a labor dispute will concede enough to make an agreement possible, there is a stalemate, and perhaps a protracted strike on the part of the workers. However, both sides lose heavily from a long work stoppage, and hence each side has an incentive for making concessions.

The Bargaining Process. Before collective bargaining can take place, a meeting must be arranged between the representatives of the employer and the union. Such a meeting is not likely unless the employer is willing to *recognize* the union or else is required to do so by law. Some years

---

[1] Today economists usually employ the term *monopsonist* to indicate a sole buyer, reserving *monopolist* for the situation in which there is only one seller.

ago unions often found it impossible to gain recognition from an employer, but since 1935 the right of workers to organize and to bargain collectively with their employer has been recognized by law. This privilege is one of the provisions of the National Labor Relations Act. However, to gain the right to bargain with an employer, a union must demonstrate that it represents his workers.

If an employer refuses to recognize a union, the latter may go to the National Labor Relations Board and demand that it hold an election to determine whether the majority of the workers want the union to represent them. If the union receives a majority vote from the workers, it is then certified as their bargaining agency, and the employer must recognize it as such and must agree to meet its representatives for the purpose of bargaining.

The Labor Agreement or Contract. Usually collective bargaining involves, first, the negotiation of a general agreement respecting terms and conditions of employment. Such an agreement, sometimes called a *labor contract,* is put in writing and is often quite detailed. It runs for a certain period of time, usually about two years. However, once it is accepted, there still remain the problems of interpreting it and carrying it out, and these require arrangements for continuous contact between the employer and the union. One such arrangement is the setting up of a *grievance committee,* which contains representatives of both parties and is designed to deal with minor grievances or disputes that may arise from time to time. Although a labor agreement has some of the characteristics of a contract, there is often doubt concerning the authority of the courts to enforce its provisions.

Wages and Hours. Though unions over the years have shown an increasing interest in other matters, wages are still the major item in most labor agreements. Rates of pay for different kinds of work, for different classes of workers, and for beginners and the more skilled and experienced are specified in detail. In mass-production industries these wage schedules are often very complex, as they must take into account not only a great variety of workers but also special rates for overtime and for work done on Saturdays, Sundays, and legal holidays. Generally employees receive time-and-a-half for Saturday work and double pay for Sundays and holidays. These higher rates are justified by union leaders on the ground that overtime is a hardship for workers and also on the theory that if overtime is kept within limits, more new jobs will be created.

Labor agreements usually set a standard work day of eight hours and a work week of five days. Though the matter of scheduling is likely to depend on the nature of the industry, or to fit into a community pattern, provisions concerning work schedules, and changes in them, are commonly found in labor contracts. These schedules deal with such matters as split shifts, lunch time, rest periods, holidays, time for putting away tools, and the like.

Over the years average weekly working hours in industry in the United

States have declined greatly, and organized labor has had a share in bringing this about. Since 1881 the average work week has declined from sixty-three hours to about forty hours. In spite of this reduction, technological progress has brought about a sharp rise in output per worker.

Working Conditions. Perhaps next in importance to wages and hours in the labor agreement comes the matter of agreeing on the general conditions under which work is to be performed. The expression *working conditions* is often used broadly. It can cover a great variety of items, among them ventilation and sunlight, safety precautions, water fountains, rest rooms, dressing rooms and showers, and eating places and coffee breaks. It may also cover such matters as limitations on shifting workers from one job to another, the definition of *seniority* and its privileges, and protection of the dignity of workers.

Seniority rules are today a matter of great importance to workers and are certain to be included in a labor agreement. Though *seniority rules* vary greatly, their general purpose is to give workers with many years on the job certain advantages over those who have been employed for shorter periods. Perhaps the most important advantage that seniority rules give such workers is a certain amount of job protection. They are likely to require that if workers must be shifted from one job to another, the newer workers should be shifted first; also, if men must be laid off, those with the longest service records have the right to be laid off last. Long-service men also have other privileges. For example, when vacations are being scheduled, they may be permitted to choose the periods they prefer; also, they may have the right to demand transfer to a better job if it becomes available.

However, seniority rules are usually applied in limited areas and are subject to some qualifications. They create difficult problems if they apply, for example, to such a matter as promotion. If promotion is based only on seniority, the result may be to put unqualified men into positions that should be filled by those of special competence. Sometimes seniority rules require that a worker who is promoted under them meet some minimum standard of performance during a trial period.

Union Security. Very important to a union are the provisions in a labor agreement that tend to protect the union itself as an organization by aiding it in maintaining its membership, keeping the loyalty of its members, collecting dues, and enforcing its rules and regulations.

Formerly, most unions sought, if possible, to make a *closed shop* agreement with an employer. Under this arrangement all workers in a plant had to belong to the union, and usually new workers were provided for the employer by the union. This assured to the union 100 per cent membership of the workers. It compelled the employer to rely on the union for new workers, and it meant that the workers owed their jobs to the union rather than to the employer.

The closed shop was made illegal by the Taft-Hartley Act, but a modification of it, the *union shop,* is permitted in states that do not have so-called right-to-work laws. Under the union shop all workers must join the union after a specified period, but a new worker need not belong at the time he is hired. This arrangement enables the employer to select new workers, though there may be an agreement that experienced union men will be hired as long as they are available.

Though most unions would rather have a closed shop than a union shop, they greatly prefer the latter to the *open shop*. Where an open shop exists, workers may join the union or not, at their own choice.

The *checkoff* is an arrangement that most unions value highly because it makes the position of the union more secure by helping it to maintain both its income and its membership. When this provision is in a labor contract, the employer deducts union dues and assessments from the workers' pay and transfers the funds to the union. The checkoff may be a source of some small expense to an employer, but it may also promote better labor-management relations, because its acceptance by the employer indicates his willingness to give full recognition to the union.

Effect of Right-to-Work Laws. Labor leaders usually argue that the welfare of workers has been increased chiefly by organization, and hence they believe that no worker has a right to enjoy these benefits without belonging to a union and doing his share to maintain and extend them. It is on this ground that they justify their demands for the closed shop or, since that cannot be obtained, for the union shop. On the other hand, many people maintain that every man has a right to seek employment wherever there may be an opening for him and that he should not be forced to join a labor organization in order to get a job. As a result of this latter point of view, Congress included in the Taft-Hartley Act a provision permitting the states to pass *right-to-work* laws that made the union shop illegal. According to George Meany, the late Senator Taft himself was opposed to this provision. In theory, right-to-work laws are intended to protect the freedom of the individual worker, but most of the states that have them are largely agricultural; a number are in the South and represent relatively low-income and low-wage areas where there is also a good deal of antiunion sentiment.

Fringe Benefits. The importance of *fringe benefits* is suggested by the fact that their total cost to employers now greatly exceeds the sum total of corporation profits after payment of the corporation income tax. Today many unions and their members seem to be just as much interested in pensions, insurance, unemployment benefits, vacations, and medical care as in higher wages. In 1968 fringe benefits in all industries (not including agriculture) were estimated to constitute over 20 per cent of all labor costs. Their average annual amount per worker is now substantially more than one thousand dollars. These benefits include the company share of Social Security taxes; payments to company or union pension funds, to insurance companies, and to medical care plans; paid rest periods, lunch periods, and vacations; payments for other time periods in which work is not actually done; and also profit-sharing and bonus payments. Not all these payments for fringe benefits are covered in labor agreements, but most of them are.

Though labor agreements usually run for about two years, provisions are often made that enable either party, under certain conditions, to re-open negotiations sooner. How well a labor agreement actually works depends in large part, as we have indicated earlier, on how it is interpreted and carried out. There must be permanent arrangements for clarifying its provisions and for handling the disputes that are sure to develop.

The Settlement of Labor Disputes. When reasonably good relations between a union and a company have been established, minor grievances of workers can usually be settled in a routine fashion through a grievance committee or other special arrangements, or through informal consultation between union representatives and the company's supervisory staff. When serious disputes arise, especially in connection with negotiating a new labor contract, reaching an agreement is more difficult.

There are several methods that may be used to iron out differences between an employer and a union. The simplest is for the representatives of management to meet directly with the representatives of the union in an attempt to decide the points at issue. But when there are wide differences of viewpoint with perhaps a certain amount of distrust or ill feeling on both sides, such an attempt may fail. However, it may still be possible to resort to conciliation, mediation, or arbitration.

Conciliation, Mediation, and Arbitration. At times the terms *conciliation* and *mediation* are used interchangeably; but some writers consider that a conciliator merely attempts to bring about a better understanding between the parties to a dispute by acting as a go-between, whereas a mediator makes definite proposals for settlement. Both conciliation and mediation involve bringing in a disinterested third party who listens to both sides and tries to identify the exact source of disagreement. The parties to a dispute usually know that there will be a compromise eventually, but often an outsider can help them to reach it sooner and to accept it more gracefully. Both the federal government and many of the states have conciliation services that can be called on when labor negotiations become deadlocked.

Another method that may be resorted to for settling a dispute is *arbitration.* In this case both sides agree upon an arbitrator, and both agree to submit their dispute to him and abide by his decision. Sometimes, instead of a single arbitrator, they employ an arbitration board. Often each side selects one member, and the two so chosen agree on a third member who is presumed to be impartial.

If all efforts to reach agreement fail, the result is likely to be labor warfare. Each side resorts to the weapons at its disposal, provided it believes that it may safely employ them.

The Weapons of Organized Labor. The principal weapon of a union is the *strike,* which simply means ordering all workers to leave their jobs in order to shut down the business. The effectiveness of a strike depends,

43. Picket Line. (Courtesy Wide World Photos.)

first, on whether the majority of the workers are union members and sufficiently under union discipline to be willing to leave their jobs on orders from the union. Second, the success of a strike depends on the ability of the union to induce or prevent other workers (strikebreakers or *scabs,* as they are sometimes called) from taking the places of the strikers if the employer tries to keep his plant in operation. The most common method for discouraging nonstriking workers from entering a struck plant is to set up a picket line.

Picketing is legal only when it is peaceful. In theory, the legitimate use of pickets is to advertise the fact that a strike is in progress and to induce possible strikebreakers to stay away voluntarily, by presenting to them the workers' side of the controversy. Also members of nonstriking unions providing services to the plant are likely to honor a picket line by refusing to cross it. In practice, picketing sometimes results in the use of force. In *mass picketing,* so many strikers gather around the gates of a plant that no one can get through. Even when picketing is peaceful and within the law, it is often fear of force that makes it effective in keeping possible strikebreakers away. When a strike is in progress, law enforcement should, of course, be impartial, but too frequently the officers of the law are actually in the camp of either the strikers or the employer.

In order to win their demands, striking workers are likely to employ any method they regard as legitimate. They may, for example, declare *boycotts* against firms that trade with their employer. However, it is very important for them to avoid antagonizing the public and, if possible, to win public support. If a union and its members succeed in bringing the public to their side, and if they can hold out for some time, they have a good chance of winning their dispute; for few employers are able or willing, especially in the face of adverse public opinion, to stand heavy losses for any length of time. Whether the concessions that may be won by a strike are worth the hardships and losses that it imposes on workers will depend on the circumstances of each particular situation.

The Weapons of Employers. The first line of defense of employers against organized labor is to attempt to prevent the establishment of effective unions in their plants. Under present laws this is more difficult than it was in the past, but it is still possible if the workers are not very much interested in organizing. Today employers fighting organized labor by traditional methods are likely to find themselves subject to prosecution under the National Labor Relations Act or state labor laws. These traditional methods include (1) attempts to keep union organizers out of a plant; (2) discharge on some pretext of any worker suspected of union activities; (3) placing spies among their workers to discover early any attempts to unionize; and (4) circulation among employers of a *blacklist* containing the names of former employees who are regarded as labor "agitators."

Once a labor controversy actually breaks out between an employer and an established union, if the parties to the dispute have trouble in reaching an agreement, the employer may try to exert pressure on the union by declaring a *shutout.* In other words, he shuts the plant down and turns the workers away without waiting for a strike. Shutouts are today very uncommon, and when they occur they are apt to be camouflaged by giving some other reason for closing down than that of putting pressure on a union.

Unfortunately, physical violence has been all too common in labor disputes. In years long past, employers frequently hired professional strike-breakers and large contingents of company "police" in order to harass and intimidate striking workers. Today they are unlikely to resort to such tactics, first because they are much more sensitive to public opinion, and second because unions have better legal protection and more political influence. Union-encouraged violence still occurs but is also less common than in the past. In any strike situation, both unions and employers are likely to make strenuous efforts to win the public and the law-enforcement agencies over to their side while bargaining between the contesting parties continues.

ESTABLISHING THE RIGHT TO BARGAIN COLLECTIVELY

Recognition of the right of labor to bargain collectively is a rather modern development. Under the English common law, labor unions were regarded as criminal conspiracies, and because our legal system was brought over from England, our American courts adopted the same point of view. However, during the nineteenth century this doctrine was abandoned both in England and the United States.

Abandonment by the courts of the doctrine of conspiracy as applied to labor cases was a very gradual process. In a famous case in 1842, Chief Justice Shaw of Massachusetts stated this doctrine as follows: "Conspiracy is a combination of two or more persons, by some concerted action, to accomplish some purpose not in itself criminal or unlawful, by criminal or unlawful means."[2] However, in the same decision Justice Shaw stated that in his opinion combinations of workers in support of their legitimate interests were legal. Nevertheless, many years were to pass before most courts were willing to recognize the legality of joint action by workers to disrupt the business of an employer in order to gain higher wages or shorter hours.

The Antitrust Laws. The most important element in the antitrust legislation of the United States is still the Sherman Antitrust Act, passed in 1890. This act was not intended to be directed against labor unions, but rather against industrial monopolies. However, it stated in very general terms that "every contract, combination in the form of trust, or otherwise, or conspiracy in restraint of trade . . . is hereby declared to be illegal." As a result, the courts applied it in a number of labor cases. An 1895 decision held that the Pullman strike was a conspiracy by labor in restraint of trade, and hence a violation of the Sherman Act.[3] Again, in the once famous Danbury Hatters' case of 1908, the Supreme Court held that the union, through attempting to boycott the product of an employer, was guilty under the Sherman Act of an unlawful conspiracy in restraint of trade.[4] These and other similar cases convinced organized labor that the Sherman Act was a danger to the labor movement and an obstacle to its growth.

Actually, both labor and business were dissatisfied with some of the provisions of the Sherman Act. As a result, Congress passed the Clayton Act in 1914. This act contained several provisions dealing with labor. It stated that "nothing contained in the Anti-Trust laws shall be construed to forbid the operation of labor unions." It further declared that nothing in the Clayton Act was to be construed as restraining members of unions from seeking to achieve legitimate objectives. In addition, the act appeared to put limits on the use of court injunctions. Many labor leaders believed that the Clayton Act was a great victory for labor, but it actually did little more than to state that labor had the right to organize and to carry on lawful activities.

Injunctions and the Norris-LaGuardia Act. In the early part of the present century the legal device that employers found to be most effective in curbing labor union activities was the *injunction*. An injunction is a court order forbidding some action that might otherwise be legal. The

[2] *Commonwealth* v. *Hunt,* Metcalf Reports III, Mass., 1842.
[3] *In re* Debs, 158 U.S. 564, 1895.
[4] *Loewe* v. *Lawlor,* 208 U.S. 274, 1908.

proper use of the injunction is to protect persons or property from serious injury. Any person who feels that he has good reason to fear injury from someone else's action may request a court to issue an injunction. However, labor leaders came to feel that though the courts seldom refused the request of an employer for an injunction against the activities of a labor union, they were much less likely to accede to the request of a union for an injunction against an employer. In some cases, the courts granted injunctions against unions without even making an investigation, and at times the terms of an injunction were so broad that the union was not permitted to do much of anything to further the interests of its members.

In the 1920's, labor leaders were again seeking legislation to limit the use of injunctions. Finally, in 1932, Congress passed the Norris-LaGuardia Act. This act restricted the power of the federal courts to issue injunctions against labor unions by defining the circumstances under which they could be issued. The act declared that certain normal and peaceful activities of unions in connection with industrial disputes were legal, and it forbade the federal courts to issue injunctions against such activities. Further, it reaffirmed the right of workers to organize and to bargain collectively through representatives of their own choosing. Unlike the Clayton Act, the Norris-LaGuardia Act proved to be fairly effective in strengthening the legal position of labor, though it did not, as is sometimes supposed, completely outlaw the use of injunctions in labor disputes.

LABOR AND THE NEW DEAL

The passage of the Norris-LaGuardia Act in 1932 may be said to have marked a turning point in public acceptance of labor unions and their objectives. However, under the New Deal administration of President Franklin D. Roosevelt, who assumed office in March of 1933, organized labor made its greatest and most rapid gains.

The National Labor Relations Act. In 1935, the third year of President Roosevelt's first term in office, Congress passed the National Industrial Relations Act, a measure intended to strengthen the legal position of unions in relation to employers. Its most important feature was a section that forbade employers to engage in certain labor practices designated as unfair. In particular, they were prohibited from doing the following: (1) interfering with the rights of their employees to organize and to bargain collectively through agents of their own choosing; (2) discriminating in hiring or discharging employees for the purpose of encouraging or discouraging membership in a labor organization; (3) discharging or otherwise discriminating against any employee who might file charges or testify under the act; (4) refusing to bargain collectively with representatives of employees chosen according to the provisions of the act. In addition, the government was made responsible for holding elections to determine, in case of doubt, which union should have the right to represent the employees of a plant when bargaining took place. The National Labor Relations Act, sometimes called the Wagner Act, has been modified by later legislation, but it is still the basic law controlling labor relations in the United States.

Those who supported this legislation believed that the welfare of workers could best be advanced through organization. They also believed that the obstacles to effective organization were great and hence that workers needed special protection and encouragement from government in their attempts to form unions and bargain collectively. Some also believed that the chances for industrial peace would be greater if employers recognized that unions were necessary and that they must be dealt with in good faith.

The National Labor Relations Act greatly strengthened the position of organized labor, but many felt that it went too far and that it often put employers at an unfair disadvantage in dealing with strong unions. In any case, the belief of some that strengthening the bargaining power of labor would bring industrial peace was not borne out, for in the years following passage of the National Labor Relations Act there were a number of costly nationwide strikes.

The National Labor Relations Board. In 1934 Congress had passed a resolution empowering the President to appoint a National Labor Relations Board. It was this board that undertook the difficult task of carrying out the provisions of the National Labor Relations Act. Among its important duties it had the task of deciding, if necessary by holding elections, which unions were entitled to represent the workers at various plants. It also had to deal with many disputes between unions and employers and to handle great numbers of complaints of unfair labor practices by employers.

THE TAFT-HARTLEY ACT

Background of the Act. In the period just after World War II a public reaction against organized labor set in. Under the New Deal and during the war, labor unions had steadily increased their membership and power; but finally many people began to feel that they were gaining too much power and that some of their leaders were becoming arrogant and disregarding the public interest. Also, there was some resentment against organized labor because of the numerous strikes that had occurred during the war. The result was a widespread feeling that new legislation was needed.

The death of President Roosevelt in 1945 and the election in 1946 of a Congress in which both houses were controlled by the Republicans smoothed the way for the introduction of a labor bill to amend the National Labor Relations Act. The bill that finally emerged gave scant consideration to the views of union leaders; nevertheless, it was passed by overwhelming Congressional majorities and came to be known as the Taft-Hartley Act. When the bill was first passed, in 1947, President Truman vetoed it; but his veto was promptly overridden by Congress. Sentiment in favor of the measure was so strong that not only did most of the Republican members support it, but also more than half the Democrats. No sooner, however, was it on the statute books than the majority of labor leaders began to condemn it in the most bitter terms. They called it a slave-labor law and maintained that it was intended to undermine the very foundations of labor.

However, those who had helped to draw up the act and who had piloted it through Congress conceived of it quite differently. To quote the late Senator Robert A. Taft:

> One of the motivating causes for amending the Wagner Act was to restore some balance of power at the bargaining table. The scales had been weighted by eleven years of experience under an act which placed duties and obligations upon employers but none whatsoever upon labor organizations. . . . Many provisions of the law, however, have nothing to do with redressing discrimination against management. For the first time, protections have been extended to the public and to individual workers against abuses of power by labor organizations. These are the reforms which have drawn the heaviest fire of the union officials.[5]

The reader should keep in mind that the authority of Congress to pass such legislation as the Taft-Hartley Act, as well as its predecessor, the National Labor Relations Act, derives from the clause in the Constitution that gives the federal government power to regulate interstate trade. Therefore the act applies only to workers for employers who, as interpreted by the courts, are engaged in interstate trade. Relations between other workers and their employers are controlled by state law.

Provisions of the Taft-Hartley Act. No attempt will be made here to give a complete analysis of the Taft-Hartley Act, but in order that the reader may have some idea of its character, attention will be called to its more important provisions, including some that became the source of considerable controversy.

Certifying a Union as a Bargaining Agent. The Taft-Hartley Act reaffirms the right of workers, as established by the Wagner Act, to bargain collectively through representatives of their own choosing. A union may apply to the National Labor Relations Board to be certified as *the bargaining agent* for the workers in a certain plant. If, at an election supervised by the board, over half of the workers in the plant vote for the union, it becomes the legal bargaining agent for dealing with the employer.

Unfair Practices of Unions. To balance the unfair labor practices forbidden to employers in the Wagner Act, the Taft-Hartley Act forbids certain unfair practices of unions. One of these is charging excessive initiation fees. Another is the requirement that an employer pay for certain types of work not needed or not done, an example of which was a requirement of

---

[5] Robert A. Taft, "The Taft-Hartley Act: A Favorable View," *The Annals of the American Academy of Political and Social Science,* March 1951, p. 195.

the musicians' union that a qualified musician be present during the playing of records at a radio station.

Two common union practices that the act forbade were the *secondary boycott* and the *jurisdictional strike*. A *boycott* is a concerted action by an organized group to keep its members, and if possible other people, from dealing with a certain business. A *primary boycott,* which is legal under most circumstances, is an attempt by a union to induce its own members and the general public to have no dealings with a company against which the union is striking. A *secondary boycott,* of the kind outlawed by the Taft-Hartley Act, is an attempt by the union to prevent people from doing business with any firm that deals with the struck company. The purpose of a secondary boycott is to put pressure on such a firm to boycott the company the union is striking against. A *jurisdictional strike* is one that grows out of a dispute between two unions over the rights of their members to do certain kinds of work. In this situation one union may strike in order to force an employer to transfer work from the other union to its own members. The employer is then caught in the middle through no fault of his own.

The Closed Shop, the Union Shop, and the Checkoff. The closed shop had long been a matter of controversy between labor and management in a number of industries. The Taft-Hartley Act makes it illegal, but does permit the union shop. There are, however, exceptions. As already noted, under the terms of the act the union shop is not legal where state laws forbid it.

Though the union shop assures almost 100 per cent membership among the employees of a plant, it takes away union control over hiring. Hence abolition of the closed shop was strongly resented by some of the older unions, which had operated under this arrangement for years.

The checkoff of union dues is still permitted, but each employee must now give written permission for this deduction.

Rights of Employers. One of the avowed objectives of the Taft-Hartley Act was to protect the rights of management as well as employees. One right of employers that is specifically affirmed is the right of free speech. Before the Taft-Hartley Act was passed, the National Labor Relations Board had held that for employers to express their opinions to workers on labor matters was illegal interference with the right of workers to bargain collectively. The Taft-Hartley Act provides that they may express themselves provided they make no threats or promises of reward for action favorable to the employer. It also affirms the right of employers to sue unions in the federal courts for damages that may result from illegal strikes or other illegal union activities.

Rights of Individual Workers. Certain rights of the individual worker are also specifically affirmed. A worker may not be coerced by either management or labor to join or not join a union, except under the terms of a union-shop agreement. Also, an employee who has a grievance is not obliged to present it through his union representative. He may, if he chooses, go directly to his employer.

The Use of Court Injunctions. The Taft-Hartley Act in effect somewhat modifies the Norris-LaGuardia Act. It provides that when illegal boycotts or strikes occur, the NLRB may, and in some cases must, seek injunctions against unions in the courts. However, individual employers may not do so.

National Emergencies. Special provision is made for the situation where a strike or threatened strike affects an entire basic industry and thus creates a national emergency. If the President determines that this is the case, he may set up a special Board of Inquiry, and on the basis of its report he may ask the Attorney General to seek an injunction against the strike. But if no settlement is reached within eighty days, the injunction must be withdrawn, the union can order its men out on strike again, and if necessary the President can then seek aid from Congress.

Political Contributions, Union Finances, and Welfare Funds. The Taft-Hartley Act prohibits unions from making expenditures in connection with a federal election. This provision, however, has been circumvented by labor through setting up independent organizations to carry on political action. The act also requires unions to make regular reports to their members concerning their finances and internal organization and to file a copy with the Department of Labor. If the union has a welfare fund, an employer may contribute to it only if it meets certain standards and if the employer participates in its administration.

An Evaluation of the Taft-Hartley Act. The Taft-Hartley Act has now been on the statute books more than twenty years, and so far as could be expected of a complex piece of legislation dealing with only certain aspects of labor-management relations, it seems to have stood the test of time fairly well. We have noted that, when it was first passed, some labor leaders claimed that it was designed to destroy the labor movement. Organized labor, however, continues to thrive. That the act does not wholly satisfy either labor or management is to be expected, and even the impartial observer would not maintain that it is an ideal law. In any case the major provisions of the National Labor Relations Act still stand, and largely as a result of these, the power of organized labor is vastly greater than it was before the days of the New Deal.

Proposals for repealing the Taft-Hartley Act or for weakening it by amendments were turned down by a succession of Congresses, regardless of the party in power. However, in 1957 the Senate Committee on Improper Activities in the Labor or Management Field began investigating the affairs of several important unions. As a result, a demand developed in the nation and in Congress for labor-reform legislation, including amendments to the Taft-Hartley Act, principally for the purpose of clarifying or strengthening some of its provisions.

The committee referred to, under the chairmanship of Senator McClellan, uncovered some cases of large-scale corruption, embezzlement, and labor-management collusion against the interests of employees. One type of such collusion is what is sometimes called a *"sweetheart" contract*. This is a contract that favors the employer and that he bribes union officials to sponsor. The findings of the McClellan Committee led to the introduction in Congress of bills designed to eliminate the practices referred to. Though such practices were not widespread among unions, enough cases were found to be disturbing. Some of the most flagrant examples were brought to light in an investigation of the International Brotherhood of Teamsters, then headed by Dave Beck and later by James R. Hoffa. In December, 1957, Beck was sentenced in Seattle to a three-year prison term for embezzling union funds. In 1964 Hoffa was convicted of tampering with a federal jury and was sentenced to eight years in prison.

THE LABOR REFORM ACT OF 1959

The Labor Reform Act of 1959, sometimes known as the Landrum-Griffin Act, grew out of the investigations of the McClellan Committee. It is regarded as a relatively "strong" labor law, and it contains a wide range of provisions intended to correct various abuses in unions and in union-management relations.

Union Democracy, Financial Reports, and Anticorruption Provisions. In a number of ways the 1959 law protects the personal rights of individual union members under a "Bill of Rights" section. It also attempts to protect their right to vote for union officers and to participate in union meetings. It requires local unions to elect officers by secret ballot at least once every three years. National unions must elect officers once every five years, either by secret ballot or by the votes of delegates elected by secret ballot.

Unions are now required to file financial reports annually with the Secretary of Labor, and these reports must show the financial condition of the union and list all payments and receipts of any considerable size; it is made a crime not to file a report. The act states that union officers hold positions of trust, and it makes the misappropriation of funds a crime.

Taft-Hartley Revisions. The Labor Reform Act includes the first major amendments of the Taft-Hartley Act after its passage in 1947. These amendments relate chiefly to (1) "no man's land" labor cases; (2) secondary boycotts; (3) "hot cargo" contracts; and (4) organizational picketing.

"No Man's Land" Labor Cases. Under the National Labor Relations Act, Congress gave the National Labor Relations Board the power to regulate labor-management disputes in industries engaged in interstate commerce. If an employer or a union has occasion to complain of labor practices that are forbidden by law as "unfair," the complaining party can appeal to the National Labor Relations Board for redress. The board, if necessary, can appeal to the federal courts for injunctions to enforce its orders.

However, the NLRB had refused to handle many of the labor cases over which it has legal jurisdiction. For the most part these involved relatively few workers, and the board maintained that it was not justified in incurring the expense that would have been involved in dealing with them. Also, the board's facilities were limited, and it felt that it could not handle all the cases brought to it. Because the board would not accept many small cases, employers and unions began to take them to the state courts and to state labor relations agencies. But in 1957 the United States Supreme Court ruled that the states had no jurisdiction over these cases, because they were covered by legislation passed by Congress. The result was that many businesses and unions had no recourse to either a state or a federal agency against illegal labor practices—in other words, they were left in a jurisdictional "no man's land."

The Labor Reform Act of 1959 remedied this situation by permitting state agencies to deal with labor-relations cases that the NLRB refuses to handle.

Secondary Boycotts. From the beginning organized labor was strongly opposed to the provisions against *secondary boycotts* contained in the Taft-Hartley Act. Employers, on the other hand, wanted these provisions strengthened by closing several loopholes that sometimes enabled unions to evade the antiboycott clauses.

The clauses in the Labor Reform Act that deal with secondary boycotts are somewhat technical, and we shall not attempt to explain them all here. However, several of the loopholes referred to above were closed. One provision of the new act that contributed to this result should be mentioned. The Taft-Hartley Act did not apply at all to agricultural workers, local government employees, or workers controlled by the Railway Labor Act; but all these groups were brought under the antiboycott and the picketing provisions of the Labor Reform Act.

"Hot Cargo" Contracts. A *"hot cargo"* contract is an agreement between a union and an employer under which the employer agrees not to require his workers to handle "unfair" goods—that is, goods going to or coming from a sweatshop, a nonunion shop, or a firm where a strike is in progress. The 1959 act outlaws hot cargo contracts, but it permits certain exceptions in the case of clothing makers and construction firms.

Organizational and Recognition Picketing. Under the Taft-Hartley Act it was generally legal for a union to picket a plant peacefully to induce workers to join the union or to induce employers to recognize it. Such an action was illegal only if another union had been recognized as bargaining agent for the workers after winning an NLRB election. This situation resulted in some abuses. A union could continue picketing indefinitely even if the workers in the factory did not want to join the union or have it represent them, and this picketing might seriously injure an employer's business. The workers might even have rejected the picketing union at an NLRB election, or they might already belong to another union.

The new act prohibits *organizational* or *recognition picketing* if there has been any NLRB election at a plant within a year, if another union has won an NLRB election, or if the employer has recognized another union voluntarily. In any case, a union is prohibited from carrying on picketing for more than thirty days if by the end of that time it has not asked for an NLRB election to determine its status as bargaining agent. The act also prohibits the picketing of stores to prevent them from handling goods produced by firms where a strike is in progress.

On the whole, businessmen approved of the Labor Reform Act, though many would have liked to have it go further in the regulation of union activities. On the other hand, the reaction of labor leaders was generally adverse. They felt that the law retarded expansion of the labor movement (1) by giving state courts with broad injunction powers control over more labor cases, (2) by permitting transactions with struck firms because "hot cargo" agreements were outlawed, and (3) by limiting organizational and recognition picketing.

SOME QUESTIONS AND PROBLEMS

Unions and Democracy. One of the great difficulties that arise in a voluntary organization, especially if it attains considerable size and power, is to maintain democratic control. In large unions, labor leaders have to be politicians in order to obtain and keep their jobs, and in some cases they become firmly entrenched political bosses. This may result in the individual union member being given little consideration. He is treated as one to take orders instead of as an independent worker with a right to express his opinion and to vote freely on matters of union policy.

The situation becomes especially serious when the men who get in control of a union are, as has occasionally happened, either communists who use the union to serve the ends of "the party," or racketeers who use it soley for their own personal gain.

Union Policies and the Public Interest. Powerful and well-entrenched unions have sometimes been guilty of following policies contrary to the public interest in shortsighted attempts to protect the immediate interests of their own workers. This often explains jurisdictional strikes, featherbedding rules requiring employers to pay for work not actually done, excessive initiation fees, and efforts to prevent the introduction of new materials and new ways of doing work. When workers are under economic pressure, it is difficult for union leaders to resist such policies if they have the power to carry them out successfully.

Today many union leaders feel that labor ought to have a share in the management of the businesses it works for. This seems to them only a reasonable application of democratic principles to industry. Because workers take risks in production and contribute to the final result as well as employers, it is argued that they should share the responsibilities of control. Employers, however, are adamant in their opposition to this idea.

They feel, first, that control is and should be inseparable from ownership and, second, that the diffusion of authority involved in such a scheme would hurt everyone, including workers, by destroying the efficiency and the high productivity of our economy.

Wage increases themselves, which traditionally are the primary objective of organized labor, are not always in the public interest or even in the interest of all members of a union. They may force an employer to raise prices to the public, and this may reduce both demand and employment; they may force him to give up a program of expansion that would have increased output and jobs; or they may put pressure on him to attempt a more rapid replacement of men by machines, a replacement that might be uneconomic if wages remained at a lower level.

Unions, Wage Rates, Inflation, and Employment. Many economists believe that unions, by constantly pressing for higher wages, put upward pressure on prices and that this has often been an important factor contributing to inflation. It has certainly not been the only reason for inflation, yet there seems little doubt that a wave of large wage increases can affect the price level and increase the difficulty of stabilizing prices by means of monetary and fiscal policies. Payments to workers, including wages, salaries, and fringe benefits, are the major item in the overall cost of producing goods. Several studies have indicated that they probably account for at least 75 per cent of all costs. In the private sector of the economy the total compensation paid to employees each year is likely to be eight or ten times the total of the profits left to corporations after they have paid the federal income tax.[6] An employer must not only pay his own workers directly, but indirectly he must pay the workers who built his factory and all those who contribute in any way to the production of his finished product. Such workers include, of course, those who produce the materials or parts he buys, because the cost of their labor is covered by the prices he pays. Hence, if wages in the whole economy persistently increase more rapidly than output per man-hour, with a resulting rise in unit costs of product, an employer must soon demand higher prices. He must do this not only to maintain his profit margin but, in the long run, in order to stay in business.

If employers have to raise prices and the public is unwilling or unable to expand total spending proportionately, sales will fall off, production will lag, and unemployment will increase. Business failures will also become more numerous, and the rate of investment will decline because firms with losses or narrow profit margins will have little incentive for expansion and would also have difficulty in obtaining money for new plant. Hence, there will be an especially marked contraction of production and

[6] In any issue of the *Survey of Current Business* or the *Federal Reserve Bulletin,* find the national income estimates of the Department of Commerce and compare the data on compensation of employees with that on corporation profits before and after payment of taxes. Not all of the employees in the private sector of the economy work for corporations, but the great majority do.

"I forget . . . . Is it the company's turn to go for a price increase, or is it our turn to try for a raise?" (Courtesy Al Kaufman. Copyright 1969 *Saturday Review, Inc.*)

employment in industries that, like steel, produce construction materials and heavy industrial equipment.

When President Kennedy took office in 1961, he not only recognized the importance of maintaining a stable price level; he also saw that businessmen needed a satisfactory level of profits if investment was to reach and maintain a level that would stimulate economic growth and provide more employment. Any economy will languish unless investment can be maintained at a reasonably high level. He therefore suggested that wage increases should be kept within *guidelines* that would prevent them from becoming inflationary or from unduly squeezing profits. The limit he and his advisors suggested for the total of wage and fringe increases per year was 3.2 per cent, on the assumption that this represented the average annual increase in output per man-hour that could reasonably be expected in the economy. Unfortunately, this guideline was disregarded, as was probably to be expected in view of the many pressures to which union leaders and corporation executives are subjected. It was exceeded substantially in a number of wage settlements made both before and after President Kennedy's death. Whether guidelines without legal sanctions to enforce them can be effective in keeping wage increases from contributing to inflation is questionable, but as a temporary expedient they may help. Up to the time of this writing, they have not been employed by the Nixon administration.

One common fallacy about wage increases is that they are always a net addition to the total purchasing power in the economy. That is not true. If unions win wage increases that total a billion dollars annually, their members can spend a billion dollars more each year (less income taxes), but employers have that much less to spend on replacement of machines or on new plant. To be sure, the employers, if corporations, may be able to get this money back by reducing dividends, but then dividend receivers have less to spend. Or they may get it back by raising prices to consumers, but in that case the purchasing power of the general public is reduced by a billion dollars.

Organized Labor, Productivity, and Real Wages. Spokesmen for organized labor often maintain that the labor movement has been chiefly responsible, over the last hundred years, for the great increase in the *real wages,* or purchasing power, of the average American worker. It cannot be denied that strong unions have often obtained substantially higher wages for their own members than the latter would otherwise have received. But in some cases this has been at the expense of unorganized workers, whose wages did not rise, or did not rise as fast, and whose purchasing power was held down by the high prices they were forced to pay for goods or services provided by union workers. For example, many workers whose incomes are low or moderate and who own homes are unable to keep their properties in good repair partly because of the present high level of wages in the building trades.

As we explained in Chapter 19, in the long run the people of a nation cannot consume more goods than they produce, and the only possible source of any great rise in the average level of real wages for workers at all levels is greater average output per man. Greater output per man results principally from (1) improvements in technology; (2) the production and use of great quantities of capital goods; (3) improvements in the health, training, and skill of the labor force; and (4) improvements in business organization and methods of management.

But it is interesting to note that since 1950 there has been a marked in-

Figure 24. Distribution of National Income, 1950 and 1969. (Based on data from *Federal Reserve Bulletin,* February, 1970, p. A 68.)

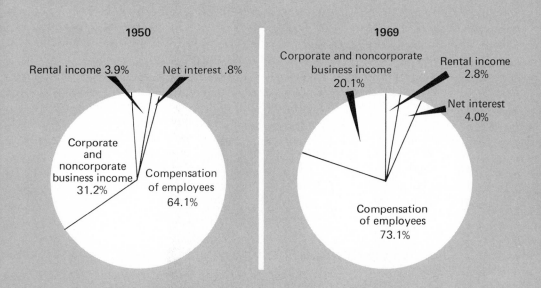

crease in the *proportion* of national income that represents compensation of *employees,* and union activities have probably helped to bring this about. Figure 24 shows the increase that took place from 1950 to 1969.

On balance, it appears that unions have contributed to raising the general level of employees' purchasing power. In any case, it cannot be doubted that they have done much, as was said earlier, to improve working conditions, to give employees greater self-respect and security, and to support the passage of legislation that has provided various kinds of benefits for workers, including a greatly expanded public school system.

Labor Disputes and the Public Interest. The prompt settlement of labor disputes on any terms that are reasonably fair not only to labor and management but also to the public, is of great importance to all concerned. The losses to the workers and employers directly involved in a major strike are huge, but the total losses to the public through disruption of the economy are sometimes even greater. Moreover, constantly repeated major strikes create pressures for more and more government interference in economic activities, and such pressures could ultimately lead to socialism. But an employer is not always serving the public interest when he makes an overgenerous settlement in order to end a strike. Employers are most likely to make such settlements at times when they think it will be easy to pass them on to consumers in higher prices. In the long run the public bears most wage increases, not the corporations that originally grant them. Also, as we have noted, excessive wage increases can both restrict employment and contribute to inflation.

The federal government and the states try to preserve industrial peace by providing conciliation services. Also, the Taft-Hartley Act provides that sixty days' notice must be given by either side when an employer or a union decides to terminate a labor contract. It further provides that if an agreement has not been achieved after thirty days of negotiation, the federal or state conciliation services must be called on for aid.

The Role of Government in Industrial Relations. The primary role of government in industrial relations is to provide a legislative framework, and also certain services, with the aid of which these relations can be carried on as smoothly as possible. The settlement of industrial disputes might proceed more smoothly, at least on the surface, if the great preponderance of power were placed in the hands of either the employers or the unions, or if the government, through some system of compulsory arbitration, dictated the terms of all labor contracts whenever the parties directly involved could not come to quick agreement. But if real collective bargaining is to be an integral part of our democratic, free-enterprise society, we must maintain some sort of balance of power between labor and management, and also, insofar as possible, we must protect the rights and freedom of all those involved in the bargaining process. This means protecting the unions, the individual workers, the employers, and, last but not least, the general public. This is what the Taft-Hartley Act, in the view of proponents such as the late Senator Taft, attempted to do, and it was also the major purpose of the Labor Reform Act of 1959.

But if real collective bargaining is to be maintained, the government must make every effort to avoid stepping in and making the decisions. If the parties to an industrial dispute know that the government will decide it in case they fail to do so, *and if one side believes that it will be favored by the government,* there is no longer much likelihood of reaching a truly voluntary agreement. The development of national unions in basic industries like coal, steel, and the railroads has led to nationwide strikes. Because such strikes constitute national emergencies that must be ended, they make it peculiarly difficult for the government to avoid dictating the terms of settlement.

Some writers have suggested that a solution for this problem would be to outlaw nationwide collective bargaining. Bargaining would be allowed only between a company and a union (or local of a union) representing its own employees. Perhaps national labor unions would be outlawed completely, as constituting monopolies of a type contrary to the public interest. The theory behind such a proposal is that in most cases a strike against any one company would not create an emergency that would force the government to intervene.

At present there seems little possibility that Congress could be induced to pass legislation outlawing either national unions or nationwide collective bargaining. Labor would be violently opposed to such action, and even many impartial students would question its wisdom. It scarcely needs to be said that such legislation, if ever passed, should prohibit employers as well as unions from combining with one another for the purpose of carrying on collective bargaining.

The long steel strike of 1959 raised in the minds of many people the question of whether it is wise public policy to allow either unions or employers to stop production in a basic industry throughout the entire nation. Not only does a long strike in a major industry greatly damage the whole economy, but if the two sides simply cannot get together, the government is ultimately forced to step in and bring about a settlement; this means the breakdown of genuine collective bargaining. On the other hand, if strikes were limited to one company and its own workers, and there were no prospect of government intervention, both sides would be under strong pressure to reach an agreement. The employer could not afford indefinite heavy losses of money, and of business to his competitors, and the workers could not afford indefinitely to be out of jobs. However, most labor leaders would maintain that in such a situation a great advantage would usually be held by the employer.

Even under nationwide collective bargaining there are, fortunately, pressures that in most cases are likely to bring agreement before a strike is called. For the most part neither employers nor unions want government intervention. They would rather be free to bargain independently, and they hesitate to risk having their activities placed under rigid regulation.

But in the final analysis the vital interests of the public must come first. In industries like the railroads and the truck lines, it is well understood that the government would be forced to act fast to stop any nationwide strike, and in no basic industry could such a strike be permitted to continue indefinitely. When no other solution can be found, the government must intervene and apply whatever coercion is necessary to reach a settlement. One way of attacking the problem would be to outlaw strikes and require labor and management to submit unresolved disputes to a board of arbitration and then abide by its decision. Compulsory arbitration is not very popular in this country, but in Australia it seems to have worked fairly well for many years. There, special labor courts make final and binding decisions when employers and workers cannot agree. Permanent courts have some advantages over arbitration boards that are set up to meet each individual situation.

A problem that increasingly is facing governments at all levels in this country is strikes by unionized public employees, including teachers, police, firemen, postmen, and others. Sometimes these strikes are illegal, but they occur anyway, and frequently if legal action is taken against them it is very ineffective, either because public officials are sympathetic, or because they are fearful of losing votes, or because the penalties provided by law are inadequate to make legal action effective. There are strong arguments on the ground of public safety against permitting policemen and firemen to strike; and whether it is justifiable to permit any group to disrupt an essential public service as a means of enforcing its economic demands is a much debated question. A nationwide strike of postal workers, such as the one that started to develop in the spring of 1970, could, if permitted to continue for any length of time, bring immeasurable inconvenience and loss to the whole country.

The labor movement has undoubtedly created social and economic problems, for some of which we have as yet no generally acceptable solutions. On the other hand, it has, over the years, made contributions of incalculable value to the welfare of workers and to the development in America of an increasingly democratic society.

Terms to Be Understood

craft union	labor contract	fringe benefits
trade union	grievance committee	conciliation
industrial union	seniority rules	mediation
a local	union security	arbitration
district council	closed shop	strike
national union	union shop	scabs
general federation	open shop	picketing
city central	checkoff	mass picketing
collective bargaining	right-to-work laws	boycott

blacklist
shutout
injunction
bargaining agent
primary boycott

secondary boycott
jurisdictional strike
"sweetheart" contract
"no man's land"
  cases

"hot cargo" contracts
organizational
  picketing
recognition picketing
guidelines

Questions for Review and Discussion

1. Why is the labor movement a by-product of the Industrial Revolution?
2. Review briefly the history of the labor movement in the United States, noting especially the roles of the Knights of Labor, the AFL, the CIO, and the merging of the latter two groups.
3. Evaluate the importance of the American labor movement in terms of its numbers and its influence.
4. Describe the collective bargaining process. In what sense do both unions and employers have some monopoly power?
5. List as many as you can of the subjects likely to be covered by a labor contract.
6. Why do unions strongly desire (a) the closed shop or the union shop; (b) the checkoff?
7. What are the various methods that can be employed to settle labor disputes?
8. By what methods do unions attempt to enforce their demands on employers? What methods may employers use in resisting these demands?
9. Summarize the historical development in this country of the right of labor to bargain collectively, noting the significance of the Sherman Act, the Clayton Act, and the Norris-LaGuardia Anti-Injunction Act.
10. What was the relation of the National Industrial Recovery Act to the National Labor Relations Act? State the general purposes and the principal provisions of the latter act.
11. What are the principal functions of the National Labor Relations Board?
12. Why did Congress pass the Taft-Hartley Act? What are its main provisions?
13. On the whole, do you approve or disapprove of the Taft-Hartley Act? Defend your point of view.
14. What are the chief provisions of the Labor Reform Act of 1959?
15. Why is it sometimes difficult for the rank-and-file members of a union to control its policies?
16. To what extent have the policies of organized labor resulted in higher real wages for workers in general? increased output per worker? In each case defend your answer.
17. When unions win wage increases, do these raise total purchasing power in the economy by an equal amount? Why or why not?
18. List the important contributions that, directly and indirectly, the labor movement has made to worker welfare.
19. What policies would you suggest as a means of reducing the number of strikes?
20. In the long run who is likely to pay most of any persistent wage increases that exceed increases in productivity? Why?
21. Could such wage increases result in unemployment? Why or why not?
22. What role should government play in the collective bargaining process? Defend your point of view.

23. What difficult problem is created by the existence of national unions and nationwide collective bargaining?
24. How are labor disputes settled in Australia when employers and unions cannot agree?
25. Should public employees be allowed to strike? Defend your answer.

For Further Study

Bloom, Gordon F., and Herbert R. Northrup, *Economics of Labor Relations,* 6th ed., Homewood, Ill., Richard D. Irwin, Inc., 1969.

Blum, Albert A., ed., *Teachers Unions and Associations: A Comparative Study,* Urbana, University of Illinois Press, 1969.

Dulles, Foster Rhea, *Labor in America: A History,* 3d ed., paperback, New York, Thomas Y. Crowell Company, 1967.

Greenstone, J. David, *Labor in American Politics,* New York, Alfred A. Knopf, Inc., 1969.

James, Ralph C., and Estelle D. James, *Hoffa and the Teamsters: A Study of Union Power,* Princeton, N.J., D. Van Nostrand Company, Inc., 1965.

Kassalow, Everett M., *Trade Unions and Industrial Relations: An International Comparison,* New York, Random House, Inc., 1969.

Lister, Richard A., ed., *Labor: Readings on Major Issues,* paperback, New York, Random House, Inc., 1965.

———, *Manpower Planning in a Free Society,* Princeton, N.J., Princeton University Press, 1966.

Marx, Herbert L., Jr., ed., *Collective Bargaining for Public Employees,* New York, H. W. Wilson Company, 1969.

Matthews, P. W. D., and G. W. Ford, eds., *Australian Trade Unions: Their Development, Structure, and Horizons,* Melbourne, Australia, Sun Books Pty, Ltd., 1968.

Monthly Labor Review, Washington, D.C., Bureau of Labor Statistics. Current issues.

Pelling, Henry, *American Labor,* edited by Daniel J. Boorstin, Phoenix paperback, Chicago, University of Chicago Press, 1960. Shows how working conditions and labor organization have been shaped by circumstances peculiar to New World history.

Phelps, Orme W., *Introduction to Labor Economics,* 4th ed., New York, McGraw-Hill, Inc., 1967.

Reynolds, Lloyd G., *Labor Economics and Labor Relations,* 4th ed., Englewood Cliffs, N.J., Prentice-Hall, Inc., 1964.

Ross, Philip, *Government as a Source of Union Power: The Role of Public Policy in Collective Bargaining,* Providence, R.I., Brown University Press, 1965.

Rowan, Richard L., and Herbert R. Northrup, eds., *Readings in Labor Economics and Labor Relations,* Homewood, Ill., Richard D. Irwin, Inc., 1968.

Chapter 22

Agriculture
and the
Farm
Income
Problem

robably no area in the world of similar size is so well endowed with good farm land as is the United States. Some writers estimate that our potential capacity for producing crops is at least as great as that of Russia, even though the latter has far more than twice our land area. If this is true, one reason is that a much larger proportion of our land has soil, rainfall, and climate favorable for the production of a great variety of crops. Excluding Alaska, more than 60 per cent of the land area of the United States is included in the nation's farms.

However, the fact that the United States is well provided with good land has not prevented our farmers from having to face many difficult problems. Indeed, one of their most difficult problems has been the low prices that have often resulted from a too rapid expansion of farm output. But before we discuss some of the problems of the farmer, let us consider briefly the history and development of American agriculture.

Colonial Farming. From the time of the earliest settlements until long after the Revolutionary War the overwhelming majority of the American people lived and worked on the land. Throughout the colonial period agricultural methods, by modern standards, were extremely crude. Implements and tools were primitive. Plows and harrows were of wood, drawn by horses or, more often, by oxen. Seed was scattered by hand, reaping was done with scythes, and grain was threshed by beating it with a jointed stick called a flail. Crop rotation and breeding for the improvement of livestock were almost unknown, though in England these methods made a good deal of progress during the eighteenth century. Among the reasons for this backwardness were the isolation of most farm communities and the seemingly limitless supply of fertile virgin land.

As a rule, early American farms were largely self-sufficient. The aim was, so far as possible, to produce everything that a family needed, including food, clothing, and shelter. Partly this was necessitated by the absence of cities or towns of any size, the poor transportation facilities in most areas, and hence the lack of markets. Limited opportunities to sell farm products meant that farmers had little money with which to buy goods from the outside. This was especially true in the newly settled regions along the frontier.

To this general pattern of *subsistence farming* there were important exceptions near the larger towns and where water transportation was available along the seaboard and the navigable rivers. In the middle colonies some export trade developed in wheat, flour, and smoked or salted meat; in Virginia large plantations were established for the primary purpose of producing tobacco for export; and in the Carolinas rice and indigo were raised on plantations for shipment abroad. In the beginning much of the work on Southern plantations was carried on by indentured servants, but before long these were completely replaced by black slaves.

Agriculture from the American Revolution to the Civil War. Though the Revolutionary War brought no sudden transformation of American agriculture, it did usher in a period of more rapid change. Even in colonial times, farmers who lived near commercial centers were able to sell food, firewood, horses, and other products to those who did not grow their own; and as the urban population grew in the period following the American Revolution, many local agricultural markets expanded greatly. At the same time, transportation facilities kept improving so that products could be shipped over much longer distances. One of the great forward strides in the history of American transportation was the completion in 1825 of the Erie Canal, connecting the Hudson River with Lake Erie. This made water transportation to the seaboard available to the whole region surrounding the Great Lakes.

With improvements in transportation, the development of the West, and a rapid growth of population, agricultural production was greatly stimulated. Increasingly, farmers turned from subsistence farming to *commercial farming* as good markets developed for certain kinds of farm products. In the Southeast there was a phenomenal expansion of cotton growing after the invention of the cotton gin by Eli Whitney in 1793, and, by the time of the Civil War, cotton culture had spread as far west as Texas. In Virginia the growing of tobacco was greatly expanded, and it spread into North Carolina and westward into Kentucky. In the states of the old Northwest Territory, in the areas having access to the Great Lakes and the Erie Canal, wheat growing increased rapidly, and later so did the production of corn, pork, and beef.

After 1830, railroads became an increasingly important factor in transportation. This brought about a further great expansion of farm markets. One result was that, long before the Civil War, Eastern farmers had largely given up the production of wheat and pork for market, because these could be produced so much more cheaply in the newly opened areas of the Mid-west. Another result was a constantly increasing flow of American farm products to European markets. A third result was a great stimulus to settlement of the West. By the time of the Civil War, the railroads were carrying two thirds of the nation's internal trade.

The Civil War was disastrous for Southern agriculture, especially for cotton, because the foreign markets for this product were largely cut off by the federal blockade of Southern ports. Recovery in the period after the war was relatively slow, partly because of difficult adjustments made necessary by the freeing of the slaves. However, the war seems to have stimulated agriculture in the North. Throughout the conflict production increased, not only because large armies had to be fed but also because of a rise in foreign demand, especially for wheat. Apparently, the war had little effect in slowing up the settlement of the West. In the period from 1860 to 1870, aided by passage of the Homestead Act in 1862, more than 600,000 new farms were established, raising the total for the nation to 2,660,000.

Technological Progress in Agriculture. For hundreds of years agricultural technology changed very slowly, so much so that in many respects it was not very different in A.D. 1800 from what it had been in the time of Christ. Since 1800, however, there has been a revolution in agricultural methods that is no less significant than that which has taken place in industry. In fact, advances in agricultural technology have been one of the essential foundations of our modern industrial and urban civilization. At one time the average per capita output of farm workers was so low that 90 per cent of our entire working force had to be employed on the land in order to feed the population. A farmer and his family could produce little more than enough to satisfy their own needs. Today, in contrast, only about 4 per cent of our working force is employed on the land, and this small group produces food and fibers for all the rest of our population, plus some for storage or export. But we should not attribute farm output exclusively to those who work on the land. A very important contribution is also made by workers who produce farm machinery, fertilizers, electric power, and other things needed for the efficient operation of farms.

The fifty years from 1830 to 1880 were significant because they brought a tremendous change in some types of farm work, with an extensive substitution of animal power for manpower. Among the devices that came into widespread use during this period were the all-steel plow; the reaper; the harvester, which included a device for binding sheaves of grain with twine; and the combine, which threshed grain at the same time it was harvested. Perhaps the greatest saving of manpower was in the wheat fields. According to one estimate, the man-hours of work required to plant and harvest an acre of wheat fell from seventy-five in 1830 to thirteen in 1880.[1]

Another revolutionary change in farming began about 1910, when machines began to replace animal power. In that year there were not more than 1,000 tractors on American farms. By 1920 the number had risen to 246,000, by 1940 to 1,567,000, and by 1968 to about 4,800,000. From 1940 to 1968, grain combines increased from fewer than 200,000 to more than 1,000,000. Later, as farms became larger but fewer and as combines became more efficient, this trend was reversed, and the number of combines declined moderately. Farmers also depended more and more on automobiles and trucks for transportation. Meanwhile, the number of mules and horses on farms contracted from over 23 million in 1910 to about 3 million in 1960. Since then the government has discontinued making estimates. Other farm machines that came into widespread use included milking machines, corn huskers, corn pickers, and cotton pickers.

However, in giving so much attention to the increasing use of power and machines, we run the risk of overlooking other advances in agricultural technology that have been equally important. These include increasing knowledge of soil chemistry, improved fertilizers, soil conservation, the control of injurious insects, the control of plant and animal diseases, the introduction of new crops, and the breeding of improved varieties of animals and plants. A striking example of the importance of this last factor is the great increases in production that have resulted from the development of hybrid varieties of corn.

Prosperity and Depression in Agriculture. In colonial and pioneer days, price changes were not very important to the subsistence farmer, because he was not much concerned with buying and selling. But as farming became more and more a business that produced goods for the market, the welfare of farmers came increasingly to depend on demand and prices. During the Civil War, high prices for farm products brought prosperity to Northern farmers. High prices, however, also stimulated the settlement of new lands and the introduction of machinery; and the resulting increase

---

[1] George Soule, *Economic Forces in American History,* New York, William Sloane Associates, Inc., 1952, p. 77.

44. Rice Harvesting in a Peoples' Commune in Red China. (Courtesy Rapho Guillumette Pictures. Photograph by Caio Carubba.)

45. Harvesting in the United States. A modern combine operated by one man can harvest and thresh more than 3,000 bushels of grain in a ten-hour day. Earlier combines handled as much grain, but they required four men for their operation. (Courtesy *Deere and Company*.)

in production brought a sharp decline of prices soon after the end of the war. From 1867 to 1868 the price of wheat dropped from $1.45 to $0.78 a bushel, and corn fell from 57 cents to 32 cents.

Some agricultural prices recovered a little in the next few years, but from the early 1870's the general trend was downward until about 1897. Many farmers could not pay their mortgages, and the whole period was one of agrarian protest. Nevertheless, the majority of farmers must have done fairly well, for though farm prices fell, output per worker rose sufficiently to bring about a rise in farm income per capita. Also, land values were rather well maintained; and total farm output increased enormously. "Evidently," says George Soule, "commercial farming as a whole was in no such straits as were its more unfortunate fringes; it was gaining with the growth of the country."[2]

From about 1897 to the outbreak of World War I, the American farmer experienced a long period of relative prosperity. When war actually began in Europe in 1914, this prosperity was soon transformed into a boom that lasted until after the end of the war and that carried farm prices and output to new high levels. However, when the collapse of wartime prices finally came in 1920, farmers generally were worse off than they had been before the war. This was because the decline in agricultural prices was much greater than the fall in the general price level and also because during the war many farmers had incurred heavy mortgage debts in order to buy land.

During the middle and late 1920's, when most industries were more prosperous than ever before, the farmers continued to have economic difficulties; and with the coming of the great depression in the 1930's, their position inevitably became much worse. Some, unable to meet mortgage payments, lost everything they had. Many others were forced, as the result of low prices for farm products, to reduce their standards of living to a poverty level. Relatively few, however, actually accepted government relief payments. Unlike city workers, most of them had a place to live and could raise much of their own food; also, they could usually make some sales even though prices were very low. In addition, they had a strong sense of pride in their independence and were unwilling to apply for aid except as a last resort.

THE PROBLEM OF FARM PRICES

Agriculture as a whole is still by far our largest industry; it gives employment directly to three or four million workers, and indirectly to many more. This explains in part why its problems have attracted so much attention from politicians and the general public.

[2] Ibid., p. 81.

The Instability of Farm Prices. The prices of the things the farmer sells create serious problems for him principally for two reasons: (1) the prices are often too low to give him a good living and (2) they often undergo wide and unpredictable fluctuations, so that he can never be at all certain of what his economic position will be from one year to the next.

The very efficiency of our agriculture has been the chief source of the difficulties of small farmers, who still constitute the great majority of all our farmers. For over a hundred years we have, in this country, reversed the predictions of Malthus. Instead of population tending to outrun the food supply, the food supply has tended to outrun population. This has meant an almost chronic condition of prices too low for the majority of farmers to make a good living. For the most part, they have experienced real prosperity only in periods when conditions resulting from war have temporarily brought sharp increases in demand and prices.

Wide fluctuations in farm prices result, first of all, from the uncertainty of the seasons. In a year when growing conditions are good, crops will be large and prices low; but the very next year conditions may be bad, crops small, and prices high. Moreover, relatively moderate changes in the output of an agricultural product may cause wide changes in price. Take potatoes by way of illustration. The demand for potatoes is said to be *inelastic*. This means that most people eat about so many potatoes and that they tend to maintain their usual rate of consumption regardless of price. Even if the price goes very low, they will not eat very many more. So if in some year the potato crop is 25 per cent larger than usual, it will be very hard to sell the extra output. When the entire crop is thrown on the market, the price is likely to drop so low that all potato growers lose money. But if the crop is a little smaller than usual, the situation is reversed. Consumers will try to obtain the quantity they are accustomed to eating, and because of this competition of buyers for the limited supply, potato prices will rise to a high level, and the growers will experience a year of prosperity. *Because the demands for most staple farm products are inelastic, relatively small changes in output are likely to cause relatively large changes in price.* Furthermore, changes in farm prices caused by seasonal variations are often accentuated by cyclical fluctuations of business or by the outbreak or ending of a war.

Many people are disturbed by the fact that, on the average, what the farmer receives for his products is only a fraction of the price paid by the ultimate consumer. Figure 25 shows that in 1968 about a third of what housewives spent for food went to the farmer. This low proportion often leads to the assumption that middlemen are receiving excessive profits. In fact, however, that is rarely the case. Studies of wholesaling and retailing indicate that people in these industries seldom make unusually large profits on their investment. The real explanation of the gap between what the consumer pays and what the farmer receives lies in the costs involved in the marketing of goods. To get products from the farmer to the urban

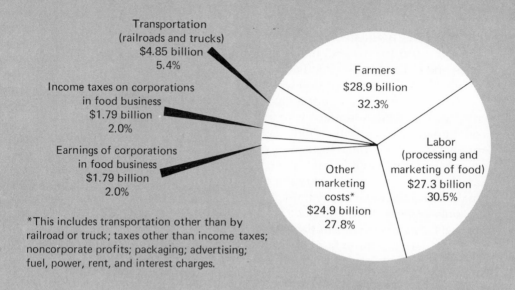

Figure 25. Where the Food Dollars Go. (Based on U.S. Department of Agriculture data for 1968.)

consumer requires huge investments in railroads, trucks, warehouses, stores, and other types of capital goods. It also requires the services of great numbers of people who operate railroads, trucks, and warehouses, and of others who work in wholesale and retail establishments, restaurants, and processing plants like flour mills. In many cases there seems little doubt that the total amount of work required to bring a food product to the final consumer at the right time and place is greater than the work required to produce it on the farm. Also, many of the workers engaged in food distribution belong to strong unions and are able to command relatively high wages. For example, though delivering milk requires no great skill, in many cities the drivers of milk delivery trucks are highly paid workers. Often they make better incomes than the average dairy farmer.

Preliminary estimates by the Department of Agriculture indicate that, in 1969, civilian expenditures for farm food were about $96 billion. Of this, marketing costs took some $64 billion and the farmers received about $32 billion.

Though there is no way of eliminating the costs of marketing, anything that increases the efficiency of our marketing organization is likely to benefit both farmers and consumers. In some cases, farmers have reduced the costs of marketing their products by organizing farmers' cooperatives to handle sales.

As a general rule, when farm prices are rising rapidly, the farmer's share of the consumer's dollar increases, because the costs of marketing do not rise as fast. Later, his share is likely to fall again as these costs catch up. When farm prices decline, the share going to the farmer also declines, because the costs of distribution fall slowly if at all, and sometimes continue to rise even though farm prices are going down.

Are Farm Prices Too Low? Ever since the decline that followed World War I, most people have assumed that farm prices have been too low, except, of course, for the period of high prices during and just after World War II. The assumption that prices ought to be higher is based on the fact that most of the time the average small farmer has been unable to make a good living. In the depression years of the 1930's the situation of many became desperate; and even today the average (mean) income of a farm family is only about 60 per cent as great as that of a nonfarm family. Even if we take into account the fact that a farm family can raise part of its food and that some other costs of living are less than in a city, most farm incomes are still low.

Does this mean that farm prices are too low? That depends on the basis one employs in judging them. Undoubtedly they are too low to give a very good living to the majority of farmers, who by modern standards have small farms that produce relatively little. At the same time, they may be entirely sufficient to give a good living to that substantial and growing minority who have large and efficient farms. Today it is these farms that are producing most of our agricultural output. The constant increase in numbers and output of such farms keeps prices down to a level at which the small farmer cannot make a decent living unless he receives substantial aid. On a small farm it does not pay to invest in the most modern machines and equipment.

Surplus Farmers. The basic problem afflicting farmers and farm workers is that there are too many of them. As noted earlier, in 1800 a farmer and his family had about all they could do to raise enough food and fibers for their own use. There was some surplus, but it was not great. Since then agricultural technology has advanced at a rising tempo, until now one American farmer can on the average produce enough food and fibers for perhaps fifty other people.

Today the small farmer who depends on his land for a living is fast becoming an anachronism. What he produces, we do not need; yet the government, at heavy cost to the public as taxpayers and consumers, attempts to raise the prices of farm products so that all farmers can make a living from the land. But in spite of the money and effort put into the federal program, it has, as we shall explain later, had very limited success in providing small farmers and farm laborers with adequate incomes. As a result, small farmers and farm hands have been steadily leaving farm work and seeking employment in the towns and cities. Since 1950 the number of workers in agriculture has dropped by over half, but there are still more farmers and farm workers than are needed to fill all our requirements for

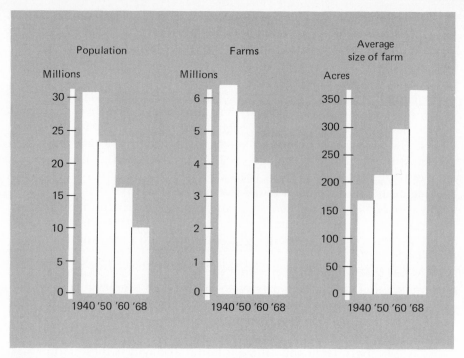

Figure 26. Farm Population, Number of Farms, and Farm Size, 1940–1968. (U.S. Bureau of the Census, *Statistical Abstract of the United States: 1969,* Washington, D.C., 1969, p. 586.)

farm products. Because of the relatively low level of prices and the over-supply of labor, the hourly wage of a hired farm worker who does not re-ceive board and room is about half that of the average industrial worker.[3]

Farms that will produce enough to induce somebody to cultivate them but not enough to provide an acceptable living are called *marginal.* Either they are too small or the land is too poor. If the land is good, they can be combined into larger farms, but that eliminates workers, who must then find jobs somewhere else in the economy. However, a man who owns even a small farm has, *if it is good land,* an asset that will bring a high price and aid him in making a new economic adjustment. On the other hand, if he is only a tenant, his problem is much more difficult. Sometimes the marginal farmer who owns his land and wishes to remain on the farm can solve his economic problems by getting a job in a nearby factory. Occa-sionally, if his land is valuable, he can even raise enough capital to go into some business such as the operation of a motel or gas station. Farming then becomes a side line, or he gives it up and rents or sells his farm land to a neighbor.

[3] *Survey of Current Business,* U.S. Department of Commerce, February 1970, PS-15.

Figure 26 shows graphically that, since 1940, farm population has declined by more than two thirds and the number of farms by more than half. Meanwhile, the average size of a farm has more than doubled.

Migratory Farm Workers and Their Problems. In spite of the general oversupply of farmers and farm workers, there is always need for more labor when certain crops are being harvested, especially the fruit crops. It is then that our migratory farm workers enter the picture. Formerly, the need for additional help at harvest time was much greater than it is today. But machines have been perfected to harvest wheat, pick corn and cotton, and dig various root crops with relatively little human labor. Efforts are even being made, and with some success, to develop and perfect machines to pick various types of fruit. However, we still need several hundred thousand extra workers at harvest time to gather crops that cannot yet be handled by machines.

As we noted in an earlier chapter, many of the migrant workers were, in the past, Mexicans who came to this country just for the harvest season. They were either wetbacks who entered illegally or *braceros* who came in on temporary permits; but since 1964 this supply of migrants has been rather effectively cut off by legislation and by tightened border controls. However, many of our migrant workers are now Chicanos, or Americans of Mexican descent, most of whom live in our Southwest. Others are blacks, and still others have various backgrounds. The Immigration and Nationality Act permits the importation of foreign workers if like workers are not available in this country, and under its provisions some forty thousand workers were admitted in 1969. These included about seventeen thousand from the United States Virgin Islands.[4]

Though migrant workers are now better paid than formerly, their wages are still relatively low, and, by the nature of the work they do, their employment is irregular and uncertain. Often they travel by families in old cars or trucks and bring along small children, and in most cases the places where they must live while they do their work are shacks with wholly inadequate furnishings and sanitary facilities. Efforts are now being made to set up and enforce adequate minimum housing standards for these workers and to provide them with medical and health services. The greatest number of migrant workers in season is found in such states as Florida, Texas, New Jersey, and California, but some are employed in widely scattered areas, including the cherry-raising country in Michigan and the apple country of Washington.

In a previous chapter we mentioned Cesar Chavez, his efforts to unionize field workers in the California vineyards, and the successful consumer boycott that he organized against California grapes. In 1970, as head of the AFL-CIO's United Farm Workers Organizing Committee, he succeeded, after five years of struggle, in signing labor contracts with grape growers

[4]U.S. Bureau of the Census, *Statistical Abstract of the United States: 1970* (91st edition), Washington, D.C., Government Printing Office, 1970, p. 95.

representing three fourths of California's production. Not all the workers covered by these contracts are migratory, but a large portion of them are, and their unionization will undoubtedly result in higher wages and improved working conditions.

The Future of the Family Farm. Though the size of the average farm is now approaching four hundred acres, in most cases it is still a family-operated enterprise. With modern machines and equipment, a family can cultivate more land than ever before and with less hired help. This is especially true on the farms, now numerous, that have no domestic animals. But seasonal help is still needed by farmers who raise crops, including most kinds of fruit, for which satisfactory harvesting machines have not yet been developed. Though the family farm is still the rule, there is some corporate farming, and this may increase slowly.

One interesting modern development is the growth of commuting by farmers. In the early 1960's, Calvin Beale, farm-population specialist in the United States Department of Agriculture, reported in the *Wall Street Journal* that about 300,000 full-time farmers were living in town and commuting to work. They represented about 10 per cent of all full-time farmers. In part, commuting is made possible because machines reduce the time needed for many tasks. It may also require other changes in the nature and organization of farm work. It may, for example, mean giving up the raising of chickens and other livestock; or, if these are important, it may require a further expansion of mechanization through the purchase of automatic feeding equipment.

46. Automated Egg Factory. Caged hens are moved past conveyor-fed food and water troughs in climate-controlled building. (Photo by Carl Iwasaki.)

GOVERNMENT SUPPORT OF FARM PRICES AND INCOMES

Demands by farm organizations that the government do something to improve farm prices and incomes date back at least as far as the latter part of the nineteenth century. At that time, many farm spokesmen favored the issue of more greenbacks and the free coinage of silver, not only in the hope of making it easier for farmers to obtain credit but also because they thought these policies would help to raise agricultural prices. After 1897, as farm prosperity gradually increased, demands on the government to do something to raise farm prices were largely forgotten. But not long after World War I, when farm prices again dropped to low levels, they were renewed with vigor.

Price-Support Efforts in the 1920's and 1930's. In the 1920's several plans for supporting agricultural prices were given serious consideration by farm organizations and by Congress. One of these was embodied in the McNary-Haugen bill, which was passed by Congress in 1927 and again in 1928, but both times promptly vetoed by President Coolidge. Then, in 1929, early in President Herbert Hoover's administration, Congress passed the Agricultural Marketing Act. This created the Federal Farm Board and a *revolving fund*[5] of $500 million to be used for price stabilization. The board was to make loans to farmers' cooperatives, which would then take surpluses off the market to prevent an unreasonable decline in prices. The assumption was that farm production was temporarily high because of stimulation by World War I, and hence that prices were abnormally low. But a more permanent force was at work to increase farm output and decrease farm prices, namely, rapid technological progress. In any case, with the coming of the great depression the plan broke down completely and was abandoned in 1933, after more than half of the revolving fund had been lost.

In the 1930's, after Franklin D. Roosevelt became President, Congress passed several acts intended to limit farm production and raise farm prices. The first one, the Agricultural Adjustment Act of 1933, was soon declared unconstitutional by the Supreme Court, but one of the concepts that it introduced, that of *parity prices,* became a major element in later legislation.

The parity-price concept is based on the theory that if farmers are to have an adequate standard of living, there must be a certain minimum ratio between the prices of the things they produce and sell and the prices of the industrial goods, like clothing, farm machinery, and processed foods, that they are obliged to buy. Because in the period just before World War I the farmers had been relatively prosperous, the Agricultural Adjustment Act accepted as normal, or parity, the average relation of farm prices to industrial prices for the years 1909 to 1914 inclusive. Furthermore, it stated that Congress sought to "re-establish prices to farmers at a level

---

[5] A revolving fund is a loan fund that, as loans are repaid, can be used over and over again.

that would give agricultural commodities a purchasing power with respect to articles that farmers buy, equivalent to the purchasing power of agricultural commodities in the base period."

To clarify the meaning of *parity,* let us consider a single commodity, such as wheat. Suppose that the average price of wheat from 1909 to 1914 was $1.00 per bushel. Then suppose that in following years the general price level rose, so that in some later year the prices of goods purchased by farmers averaged twice as high as in the base period, 1909 to 1914. If the price of wheat was also twice as high, or $2.00, wheat would have maintained parity. But if the price of wheat was less than $2.00, say $1.50, wheat would have fallen below parity. In this case its price would be only 75 per cent of parity, and it would purchase for the farmer only 75 per cent as much as it did in the base period.

In 1936, in an attempt to find some way of limiting production that would be constitutional, Congress passed the Soil Conservation and Domestic Allotment Act. This provided, among other things, for payments to farmers who withdrew land from cultivation in order to conserve and increase its fertility. Though this act may have improved land use, it was not effective in limiting production.

The most important farm measure passed by Congress in the 1930's was the Agricultural Adjustment Act of 1938. Like the preceding acts, its main purpose was to reduce the output and marketing of agricultural products in order to raise farm prices to parity; but some of its methods were different. Its most important provisions were as follows:

1. The soil conservation program was continued and extended.
2. In case of overproduction of cotton, wheat, corn, tobacco, or rice, *marketing quotas* were to be established for producers of these products in order to limit sales. Penalties were provided for sales in excess of the quotas.
3. *Acreage allotments* were provided for on a voluntary basis. As an inducement to cooperate, payments were made to farmers whose acreage for each crop did not exceed the allotment.
4. An attempt was made to establish an *"ever-normal granary"* plan.

To achieve this last objective, the act provided, first, that a farmer who wished to hold commodities off the market because of overproduction and low prices could offer them as security and could borrow from the Commodity Credit Corporation (CCC), the agency that administered the program, from 52 to 75 per cent of the parity price. The idea was not only to support prices at a reasonable level and to assure that farmers could obtain a certain amount of cash, but also to create and hold in storage a reserve of commodities. Farmers who chose not to repay their loans could settle them by surrendering to the government the products they had offered as security. The act further provided that supplies withheld from sale because of marketing quotas might be released in time of shortage.

But aside from the possibility of war, any expectation of serious shortages seems to have been wholly unrealistic.

The Agricultural Adjustment Act of 1938 was not much more successful than earlier acts in limiting production and thus raising prices. Farmers who reduced their acreage tended to keep their best land under cultivation and to farm it more intensively. Even if they reduced their production of some crops, they were likely to offset this by increasing their output of others. As a result, stored surpluses of grain, pledged against government loans, began to accumulate.

Price Support in Wartime. The outbreak of World War II in 1939 soon brought a radical change in the American farm outlook. Within a few months the demand for our agricultural products began to rise rapidly both for export and domestic consumption; and after we entered the war, the great problem was not to raise farm prices but to keep them at reasonable levels for the protection of consumers. One might suppose that the price-support program would have been abandoned for the time being. But, instead, Congress increased to 90 per cent of parity the amounts the CCC would lend farmers on their crops. *Price supports* were also extended to many more commodities on the theory that this would encourage maximum production by protecting producers against any conceivable loss.

Shortly after the German surrender in 1945, the War Food Administration announced that our farms had produced 50 per cent more food annually in World War II than in World War I, and with 10 per cent fewer farm workers.

Price Support After the War. For several years after World War II, no changes were made in agricultural legislation. The recovery of farm production in Europe took time; and as long as demand for our output remained high, American farmers had few problems. But by 1948 some farm prices had fallen sharply; and because of the legislation making it mandatory for the Secretary of Agriculture to maintain the prices of many products at 90 per cent of parity, the government now entered the market as a buyer whenever they fell to the support level. As a result, large surpluses began to accumulate in storage.

The Agricultural Act of 1949 was an attempt to remedy the situation by providing that the percentage of parity at which the Secretary of Agriculture must maintain prices should gradually drop, beginning in 1951. But the outbreak of the Korean War in 1950 brought higher prices for some farm products and checked the accumulation of surpluses; and, as a result, Congress kept deferring the date for reducing support levels. However, in 1954, after the Korean War, when prices fell and surpluses again began to accumulate, legislation was finally passed that permitted the Secretary of Agriculture to reduce price supports at his discretion, but only by a very limited amount.

From 1955 to the mid-1960's, the value of stored farm products owned by the federal government or held as security for loans remained very high. In 1963 and 1964, for example, it amounted to more than seven billion dollars.

Efforts to Reduce Stored Surpluses. Because it seemed politically impractical to abandon price supports or to lower them enough to stop the accumulation of stored surpluses, much less to reduce them, other methods were sought for achieving this result. Under an act passed in 1954, Congress authorized the sale of surplus commodities abroad on special terms, and in exchange for local currencies that were not to be converted into dollars. It also authorized barter of such commodities in exchange for strategic and other materials of value to the United States; and, in case of famine or other urgent needs for relief, it authorized donations to friendly peoples. Use of agricultural surpluses to aid other nations is now called the *"food or peace"* program. Whether the plan helps to preserve the peace is debatable, but it does help to meet some acute human needs.

Under later acts and administrative decisions, the whole program for disposing of surpluses was further expanded. Because the domestic price of such commodities as wheat and cotton was for a time supported in this country at a level higher than the world price, the government paid exporters a subsidy to make up the difference. Otherwise, no wheat or cotton would have been sold to foreign buyers. When later the support price was lowered to less than the world price, such subsidies became unnecessary. Another method of disposing of farm surpluses was mentioned in Chapter 20. This is to distribute them to people on relief, either directly or in exchange for stamps that they can purchase at low prices and redeem at stores for food of much greater value. Surplus food is also used to help provide subsidized lunches to a large portion of the school children of the nation, especially those who live in low-income areas.

Some of the methods employed to distribute inventories of surplus farm products obviously involve heavy cost to the taxpayers. However, if we are not willing to accept any other solution, to give away these surpluses is better than to store them indefinitely. Not only do they provide some help to the needy, but if the government continued to hold them in warehouses, in only a few years the costs of handling and storage, plus administrative costs, insurance, and loss of interest on the investment represented, would exceed the value of the commodities stored. Over the years, the Commodity Credit Corporation has paid out several billion dollars in handling and storage charges alone.[6]

In the 1950's and early 1960's, new attempts were made by legislation to reduce farm output and raise prices by paying farmers to withdraw land from production, but these attempts had little more success than earlier efforts of the same kind. Part of the trouble was that as long as price supports were high, farmers would manage to increase output on their remaining acres. However, in 1964 and 1965 Congress passed legisla-

[6] *Agricultural Stabilization and Conservation Service Background Information,* BI No. I, April 1966, p. 13.

tion that provided for attacking the problem a little differently. As a result, the farm *income support* programs of the later 1960's and of 1970 and 1971 set the price support levels at which farmers could borrow from the CCC at considerably lower rates on some basic commodities.[7] But to compensate for this, the farmers who cooperated by keeping within their acreage allotments for each crop and, where these applied, within their marketing quotas, were given per-bushel or per-pound subsidies on a certain portion of their output. These subsidies took the form of *marketing certificates* that were credited to a farmer on the basis of the amount of his production that qualified for a subsidy. Ordinarily the farmer did not actually receive the certificates, but instead was given *market certificate payments*. The per-bushel or per-pound price for the certificates was set each year by the Department of Agriculture on the basis of crop and marketing conditions and parity price. The government then reimbursed itself from food processors, who were required by law to buy at the price already fixed enough certificates to cover their purchases. For example, under the wheat program, flour mills had to buy a corresponding number of certificates whenever they purchased wheat, and the cost was passed on to bakers and other buyers in higher prices for flour.

Under the 1970 wheat program, price-support loans were available to farmers on the entire production from their acreage allotments. The amounts of money they could borrow varied a little from county to county, but the national average was about $1.25 per bushel. In addition, they received marketing certificates on 48 per cent of the projected output of their full acreage allotments. The per-bushel value of the certificates was equal to the parity price of wheat less the loan level of $1.25. This assured farmers of receiving parity for nearly half the output of their acreage allotment. It was expected that when the parity price for 1970 was finally determined, the certificates would be worth more than $1.50 per bushel. Farmers could also receive *diversion payments* if they chose to divert part of their allotted wheat acreage to other approved uses. These payments were equal to 50 per cent of the loan rate on the output projected for the diverted land before its withdrawal from wheat production.

Besides providing for land withdrawal in annual crop programs, the Food and Agriculture Act of 1965 set up a *"cropland adjustment"* program that was designed further to limit agricultural output by removing land from wheat cultivation for longer periods. This program was basically similar to land withdrawal plans set up from time to time by earlier acts. Under it the Secretary of Agriculture was "authorized to enter into 5- to 10-year contracts with farmers calling for conversion of cropland to practices or uses that will conserve water, soil, wildlife, or forest resources, or establish or protect or conserve open spaces, national beauty, wildlife, or recreational resources, or prevent air or water pollution. Payments are to be not

---

[7] The so-called basic crops in the price-support program are wheat, corn, cotton, rice, peanuts, and tobacco. Corn is now included in the feed-grains program, which also covers oats, rye, barley, and grain sorghum.

more than 40 percent of the value of the crop that would have been produced on the land."[8]

The agricultural programs of the late 1960's and of 1970 were no more successful in reducing output than were earlier ones, but they probably slowed down the increases in total output that population growth and continuing technological advances were bringing about. In any case, there was, in the late 1960's, a marked reduction in the stored surpluses of farm commodities owned by the CCC or held as security for loans. The value of these, as of June 30, dropped from over $7 billion in 1964 to about $4.7 billion in 1969.[9] But this decline was probably largely accounted for by two factors other than withdrawing land from cultivation. The first was an increase in efforts to give away surpluses to the needy and unfortunate or to dispose of them abroad even at a loss. The second was that support prices were set at a lower percentage of parity than they had been in the 1950's or the early 1960's. This resulted in market prices more frequently rising above the support level (the amount farmers could borrow from the CCC) and sometimes made it advantageous for them to sell in the market rather than use their products as security for a CCC loan. It also gave the CCC more opportunities to sell some of its holdings in the market without forcing prices below the support level.

QUESTIONS RAISED BY THE SUPPORT OF FARM PRICES AND INCOMES

Though the agricultural policies followed in the late 1960's reduced the stored surpluses of the CCC, they did little to reduce the costs of the farm income-support program. Price supports were reduced, but land diversion payments were maintained and direct crop subsidies were established or increased. In 1970 the Bureau of the Budget estimated that federal outlays on agriculture for the fiscal year (ending June 30) would exceed six billion dollars, and undoubtedly the greater part of this sum was accounted for by programs related to the support of farm prices and incomes. By any standard, six billion dollars is a large amount to spend for the benefit of any single industry or special economic group. It amounted to some thirty dollars for every man, woman, and child in the country and two thousand dollars for every farm. The latter figure was equal to about 40 per cent of the net income from the average farm, though of course this would vary somewhat from year to year. Incidentally, in June, 1969, the Department of Agriculture had one employee for approximately every twenty-four farms. The number of farms has kept going down, but the number of employees of the department has kept going up.

[8] Wayne D. Rasmussen and Gladys L. Baker, "A Short History of Price Support and Adjustment Legislation and Programs for Agriculture, 1933–65," *Agricultural Economics Research,* July 1966, p. 78.
[9] U.S. Bureau of the Census, op. cit., p. 596.

Though agriculture is not the only industry the federal government has subsidized, it is a special case for two reasons. First, the cost of farm income support is many times greater than that of any other subsidy. Second, because of its cost, it has an appreciable effect on the tax burden and the cost of living that must be met by every citizen. It is true that, in recent years, food expenditures have been a diminishing percentage of total consumer expenditures. But it is also true that technological advances in agriculture and increases in productivity per man-hour have been much greater than in most other industries. As a result it is probable that outlays for food should represent an even smaller proportion of consumer expenditures than they now do. There is little doubt that government policies intended to restrict farm output and maintain farm prices have had an appreciable effect, though one difficult to measure, in keeping food prices higher than they would otherwise be.

Should the Public Subsidize the Farmer? Though special benefits that farmers receive under the income-support program may not be a major portion of the average citizen's food and tax bills, their impact is not negligible. Whether it is justifiable, year after year, to tax the general public both directly and in higher food prices for the special benefit of farmers is questionable. Few would object to aiding them if they were temporarily in a desperate situation. In the great depression of the 1930's, many farmers were in just such a situation, and there was great need for giving them some form of relief. Unfortunately, the price-support program did not aid them much in the short run, when their need was greatest; but once it was established, dropping it became politically impossible. We have noted that even in World War II, when farm prices were rising to high levels because of high demand, supports were retained and even raised on the doubtful theory that they were needed to stimulate maximum production.

Even when government price supports plus direct subsidy payments do raise the farmer's receipts per bushel or pound, this is not all pure gain. The farmer may receive more for each unit of product, but he receives it on smaller sales or output if his sales have been restricted by quotas or his output by acreage limitations. Also, reduced output means higher cost per unit because his overhead or fixed cost will be spread over a smaller amount of product. However, a high return per unit may induce him to go on producing a crop for which demand is shrinking, instead of shifting to one for which it is increasing. Conceivably, the income-support program might cut down his sales and raise his unit costs so much that his income would be less than without such a program. But it is true that if a depression should come along, price supports and/or subsidies might be his salvation. If they are set at moderate levels, the best argument for them is that they help both to prevent a depression and to give the individual farmer some protection if one develops.

However, what is not generally realized is that most of the benefits of the farm program go to a relatively small proportion of all farmers, namely, the prosperous ones whose farms are large and well managed. In a Twentieth Century Fund Report made a decade ago, Edward Higbee estimated that though small and marginal farmers were far more than half of the total, they received only about 7 per cent of the benefits from the federal farm program. From time to time, economists and journalists call attention to the fact that some farms receive subsidy payments of over a million dollars. In 1966 five such farms, four in California and one in Hawaii, received a total of nearly nine million dollars.[10] In an interview in 1969, former Secretary of Agriculture Orville Freeman noted that twenty farms were receiving payments of $500,000 or more.[11] Payments of $50,000 up to $500,000 are numerous, yet when Congress took action in 1969 to extend the farm program, the Senate voted down a House-sponsored proposal to put a ceiling of $20,000 on benefit payments to any one farmer. However, in the Agricultural Act of 1970, designed to apply to farm policies through 1973, a provision was included limiting to $55,000 the amount of subsidy a farmer can receive under any one crop program. This still permits rather large payments, for if a farmer raises three different subsidized crops, he can conceivably collect from the government as much as $165,000. Also, there are loopholes. If he has enough land, it may pay him to give some of it to members of his family or to lease part of it. Then each owner or lessee could also receive up to $55,000 under each crop program.

But could the present farm program be better justified if it were effectively modified so as to channel most of its benefits to the small, low-income farmer? In that case, it would clearly be a make-work relief program. It might help many small farmers to stay on the farm, but, as we have said, most if not all of their output is entirely unneeded. All the farm products that the nation will need for years to come can be produced by fewer men on larger farms at lower costs and prices.

Some Economic and Social Effects of Price Supports. The agricultural surpluses that the government has held or disposed of at a loss were created by price supports and crop subsidies. If prices had always been allowed to seek their market level and farmers had not received subsidies, in some years prices and farm incomes might have been very low, but most products offered for sale would have been sold and any significant surpluses would have been temporary. Farmers over the years would have shifted even more rapidly from agriculture to industry, to the service occupations, and to professional and semiprofessional work. If this had happened, agriculture would be much less of a problem than it now is because there would be fewer small and inefficient farms. Price supports and crop subsidies have tended to create surpluses by slowing down the movement of workers away from the farms, by stimulating production, and by reducing sales, especially in export markets.

Presumably, price supports would not create continuing surpluses if they were set well below the normal market level and thus came into

[10] *The National Observer,* February 5, 1968, p. 12.
[11] *U.S. News & World Report,* January 13, 1969, p. 79.

operation only when the farmer was threatened with disastrously low prices in the very worst years. But farm price supports inevitably become a matter of politics, and inevitably some farm organizations put pressure on Congress to support prices by law at higher levels than are likely to be justified by market conditions. As a result, the government is forced to become a buyer to prevent further declines.

Another problem that supports create is the disruption of normal price relationships among agricultural commodities. Because of this disruption, some farmers are benefited at the expense of others. It is difficult, for example, to find an acceptable formula for supporting the prices of hogs and cattle; but if the prices of livestock are allowed to fall to a low level, whereas the prices of corn and other feed grains are supported, producers of livestock are worse off than they would have been if there had been no price supports at all.

We have noted that high price supports can destroy foreign markets. The world prices of most commodities depend on conditions of supply and demand that cannot be controlled by any one country. If the price of, let us say, American cotton is kept above the world level by price supports plus tariffs or quotas on imports, foreigners will naturally not buy any of our cotton in the normal course of trade.

One great objection to agricultural price supports, especially if they are kept at high levels, is that they are almost certain to bring about increasing regimentation of farmers. Adverse reactions from taxpayers set a limit on the amount of commodities that the government can buy up and store. If surpluses continue to accumulate rapidly, as is likely to be the case under a system of high and rigid price supports, the only remedy (short of reducing or abandoning the supports) is increasingly rigid restrictions on production. A farmer may avoid the effects of some restriction on acreage planted by cultivating the rest of his land more intensively, but he cannot do much about the matter if absolute limits are placed on his production or sales of all crops, and are enforced. If such restrictions spread, he begins to find himself in a straitjacket, with less and less freedom to use his own good judgment in planting crops and managing his land. He no longer has a chance to raise his income by increasing output. The result is likely to be not only a loss of freedom but also a less efficient use of land, less technological progress, and higher unit costs.

Already we have had crop programs that went far toward regimenting the farmer and creating a bureaucracy to enforce this regimentation. Some years ago, Stanley Yankus operated a farm on which he produced chickens and eggs near Dowagiac, Michigan. Under the program for controlling wheat production that was then in force, Yankus was allotted fourteen acres for growing wheat. However, because he needed more wheat to feed his chickens, he exceeded his allotment. As a result, after a six-year court battle, he had to pay more than five thousand dollars in federal fines—this in spite of the fact that all the wheat he raised went to feed his own chickens. Other farmers have had their land seized and sold at auction to meet similar penalties. Yankus and his difficulties received national publicity chiefly because, in disgust, he decided to move with his family to Australia. If we should keep multiplying regulations of this kind, America would not for very long remain the land of free enterprise—and the extent to which other personal freedoms would be able to survive is open to question. In one respect our more recent wheat and feed grain programs have been more liberal than some of the earlier ones. Most of them have been voluntary in the sense that they have permitted a farmer to produce legally as much as his land would permit, but only if he has been willing to forgo all special government benefits.

These recent wheat and feed grain programs have set price supports at a relatively low level. This can reduce or prevent the accumulation of stored surpluses, but it does not necessarily reduce the cost of the farm income-support program to the public if subsidies on the farmer's crops are substituted for high price supports as a means of raising his total returns to a level near parity. If these subsidies are paid for by selling marketing certificates, they raise the price of food to the consumer.

The Income-Support Program and Politics. Traditionally, American farmers have been individualists. When the price- and income-support program was first introduced, most of them were probably opposed to it except, perhaps, as a temporary depression measure. But once the farmers had become accustomed to the system, some began to feel that whenever prices rose, the supports were responsible; now many fear that the removal of price supports and subsidies would leave them without protection against the recurrent declines to which agricultural prices have in the past been subject. Though people living on farms are now only about 5 per cent of our total population, their interests are closely allied to those of other rural residents whose number is much larger. The political power of rural people is still great. In some of the less-populous states they control elections, and in other states they constitute an influential minority.

However, a very substantial proportion of farmers are strongly opposed to the government farm program, at least in its present form. This opposition has been spearheaded by the American Farm Bureau Federation, the largest of all our farm organizations. Its membership consists of farm families, and in 1970 it claimed 1.86 million such families, or substantially more than half of the total. For many years it was under the leadership of its recently retired president, Charles B. Shuman, and it has consistently opposed all income-support plans that would give farmers crop payments or impose marketing and acreage restrictions. Perhaps this attitude was partly explained by the fact that the bureau, reputedly, represents our larger and more prosperous farmers, many of whom believe they could do better in a free market with no restrictions placed on their production or sales. Two other farm organizations of some importance are the National Grange and the Farmers' Union.

The Farm Bureau has objected to current agricultural programs on various grounds, and in 1970 it advocated the following changes:

1. A gradual shift to a market-oriented program. Under a bill introduced unsuccessfully in Congress in 1969, and supported by the Farm Bureau, crop payments would have been reduced annually by 20 per cent of their present level, which would have brought them to an end after five years.
2. The continuation of price-support loans, but they would be related to recent market prices, not to "parity" as now defined by law. The bill just referred to would set loan rates at 85 per cent of average market prices for the previous three years.
3. Avoidance by the government of sales that would undermine current market prices. The government would be prohibited from selling its stocks of feed grains, cotton, wheat, and soy beans except at prices set substantially above the current loan rate.
4. The retirement of at least fifty million acres of cropland from cultivation under five- to ten-year contracts, with grazing prohibited. The bureau favors the withdrawal of whole farms. (Presumably, the government would make these contracts with farmers and pay them compensation for withdrawing their land.)
5. The establishment of a special transitional program for low-income farmers. This would include retraining and adjustment assistance to aid them in shifting to other occupations.[12]

The above program would not mean a complete abandonment of government support of farm incomes, and probably few economists would approve the recommendation that the government pay farmers to withdraw fifty million acres of cropland from production for five or ten years. The cost would run into billions of dollars, and, because of its scale, the program would, if successful, almost certainly have some effect in raising food prices. But some of the other proposals seem to many students of farm problems to represent steps in the right direction. What restrictions should be put on the sale of government-owned farm surpluses is debatable, but certainly they should be disposed of gradually over a period of several years.

If so large and influential a group of farmers as that represented by the Farm Bureau is opposed to the present farm income-support program, why has so little progress been made in modifying it? The reasons are (1) partly that some other farm organizations, such as the Farmers' Union, sincerely believe that the survival of their members depends on the continuance of production and marketing controls along with government subsidies; (2) partly that many other Americans have come to assume that our farmers simply could not get along without these controls and subsidies; and (3) partly that, once a government program has been established and a bureaucracy built up to administer it, to get rid of either the

[12] Farm Bureau Leaflet, *A Farm Program for the 1970's,* Chicago, American Farm Bureau Federation, April 1, 1970.

program or the bureaucracy is almost impossible. Though innumerable politicians give lip service to free enterprise, free markets, and government economy, very few are willing to take a clear-cut stand against the continuance of the present farm income-support program. Today, however, there does seem to be some hope that it can eventually be modified to serve better the long-run interests of both the farmers and the nation as a whole.

Possible Effects of Abandoning Price and Income Supports. Do farmers really need a government program to support prices and farm income? A case can be made for moderate price supports to protect them against the hardship that would result from an extreme drop in prices. But many economists feel that the farm program as actually operated has contributed very little over the years to the welfare of farmers and has been very costly to the public. To be sure, if it were *suddenly* abandoned, unwarranted hardship would be imposed on many people because agriculture has become adjusted to the controls and benefit payments. If these are ever completely abandoned, the change should be gradual over a period of several years, certainly not less than five.

Opinions differ widely as to the effects of a gradual phasing out of the farm control program. Former Secretary of Agriculture Freeman takes a dim view of the proposal. In an interview published some years ago, he was quoted as saying: "In the absence of any kind of government programs to work with and supplement a normal farm distribution, it is estimated that, in five to six years, prices would drop in the neighborhood of 30 to 50 percent. Now, I think this would mean economic catastrophe."[13] However, most economists who favor a gradual removal of agricultural controls (except, perhaps, for price supports based on an average of market prices in recent years and set appreciably below them) would not expect this to bring a sharp drop in prices. Though some prices might decline, such declines would probably be gradual and moderate. For one thing, as prices fell, sales should increase, especially in world markets. Also, lower prices for feed grains would reduce costs of production and prices, and hence would increase sales, of some commodities with relatively elastic demands. These include dairy products, meat, poultry, and eggs. Increased consumption of such foods would increase the demand for feed grains and cushion the fall in prices. It is also probable that the domestic consumption of cotton would rise somewhat with a decline in price. At least there should be a slowing down in the rate at which cotton is being replaced by synthetics.

Other effects of a gradual removal of subsidies, quotas, acreage controls, and high loan-support levels would include (1) the elimination of large stored surpluses; (2) some desirable shifts in production from one crop to another; (3) the more rapid movement of unneeded farm workers into other occupations, possibly with government aid to reduce hardship;

[13] *U.S. News & World Report,* July 31, 1962, p. 50.

(4) a further reduction of farm costs because farmers would be free to use their best judgment in planting crops and managing their land, and also because many would find it easier to consolidate small, inefficient farms into large, mechanized units; (5) somewhat lower taxes and living costs for the public and hence a greater demand for industrial goods and services and more employment in businesses producing them; and (6) an overall increase in the rate of economic growth because labor and other resources would no longer be wasted in agriculture.

In the long run all of us, including the farmer, might be better off if the government gradually abandoned all attempts to support farm income except in real emergencies. However, there is little prospect that such attempts will be given up in the near future. For more than forty years our political leaders have been searching unsuccessfully for ways to solve "the farm problem," and there is no certainty that they will not continue this search for some years to come. However, the shrinkage of the farm population, a growing recognition of the costs and wastes inherent in the present farm program, and the opposition to certain aspects of it by a large proportion of farmers, may in the fairly near future bring some desirable changes.

A solution of the farm problem that would please *everyone* is not to be found. Such a solution would (1) assure all farmers of a satisfactory income; (2) protect farmers against losses in bad years or depressions; (3) aid in shifting marginal farmers and farm workers into other occupations; (4) give farmers complete freedom in managing their farms; (5) keep consumer prices at a minimum; and (6) cost the taxpayers little or nothing.

Terms to Be Understood

subsistence farming	revolving fund	"food for peace" program
commercial farming	parity prices	income supports
inelastic demand	marketing quotas	marketing certificates
surplus farmers	acreage allotments	diversion payments
marginal farms	"ever-normal	"cropland adjustment"
price supports	granary" plan	program

Questions for Review and Discussion

1. What was the general status of agriculture and the farmer in colonial America?
2. Trace the development of American agriculture from the Revolutionary War to the Civil War.
3. How did the Civil War affect northern agriculture? Why? Southern agriculture? Why?
4. What major changes have taken place in farm technology since 1800?
5. What was the situation of the American farmer from shortly after the Civil

War to 1897? from 1897 to 1920? from 1920 to the outbreak of World War II? from World War II to the present?

6. Why have farm prices often been so low that many farmers have not made a good living?

7. Why do farm prices show wider fluctuations than most prices?

8. Why does the farmer receive less than half the retail price that the consumer pays for food products?

9. Why have farmers and farm workers been steadily leaving the farms and seeking employment elsewhere?

10. Is the family farm disappearing? Explain.

11. What was the plan for stabilizing farm prices under the Agricultural Marketing Act of 1929? Why did the act fail to achieve its purpose?

12. Explain the meaning of *parity prices* and tell how they were originally determined.

13. What were the major purposes of the Agricultural Adjustment Act of 1938? State four important provisions it contained. Why did it have little effect in reducing production?

14. Describe agricultural developments during World War II. What was the chief argument that was advanced for raising price supports during World War II?

15. List the various methods the government has employed in its attempts to dispose of farm surpluses.

16. Why were the agricultural policies followed by the government in the 1960's and in 1970 more successful than earlier policies in reducing surpluses held by the CCC?

17. Describe the "cropland adjustment" program that was part of the Food and Agriculture Act of 1965.

18. What effect do high agricultural price supports tend to have on (a) the social usefulness of the individual farmer; (b) the national rate of economic growth; (c) foreign markets; and (d) the ability of farmers to use their own judgment in operating their farms. In each case explain why.

19. Have government farm income-support policies kept food prices higher than they would otherwise be? Why or why not?

20. Should the public be taxed, either directly or through high prices, in order to subsidize the farmer? Defend your answer.

21. When price-support policies bring higher prices, why is the farmer not always benefited?

22. Would all reasonable objections to the federal farm program be removed if the benefits went only to small farmers? Why or why not?

23. Why may price supports benefit some farmers at the expense of others?

24. Why do farm price supports disrupt foreign markets?

25. Why do price-support policies tend to regiment farmers?

26. The Farm Bureau Federation is opposed to some government price-support policies. What kind of supports does it favor?

27. Is it likely that a gradual abandonment of the whole government program for supporting farm prices and incomes would be a disaster for our farmers? Why or why not?

28. What benefits might accrue to the public from a gradual abandonment of the farm program? What problems might be created?

For Further Study

Benson, Ezra Taft, *Freedom to Farm,* New York, Doubleday & Company, Inc., 1960.

Duscha, Julius, *Taxpayers' Hayride: The Farm Problem from the New Deal to the Billie Sol Estes Case,* Boston, Little, Brown and Company, 1964.

Hathaway, Dale E., *Problems of Progress in the Agricultural Economy,* Glenview, Ill., Scott, Foresman and Company, 1964.

Higbee, Edward, *Farms and Farmers in an Urban Age,* paperback, New York, Twentieth Century Fund, Inc., 1963.

Mellor, John W., *Economics of Agricultural Development,* paperback, Ithaca, N.Y., Cornell University Press, 1969.

Metcalf, D., *Economics of Agriculture,* paperback, Baltimore, Penguin Books, Inc., 1969.

Ruttan, V. W., et al., eds., *Agricultural Policy in an Affluent Society: An Introduction to a Current Issue of Public Policy,* paperback, New York, W. W. Norton & Company, Inc., 1969.

Schultz, Theodore, *Economic Growth and Agriculture,* New York, McGraw-Hill, Inc., 1968.

——, *Transforming Traditional Agriculture,* paperback, New Haven, Conn., Yale University Press, 1964.

Snodgrass, Milton M., and Luther T. Wallace, *Agriculture, Economics, and Growth,* New York, Appleton-Century-Crofts, Inc., 1964.

Soth, L., *Agriculture in an Industrial Society,* paperback, New York, Holt, Rinehart and Winston, Inc., 1966.

Chapter 23

The

Consumer

many of us are so much concerned with the problems of obtaining the money needed to buy goods that we give far too little attention to the problems related to their purchase and use. Yet, as the Better Business Bureau reminds us, "To be able to make money is a valuable skill. But it is an equally valuable skill, if less readily recognized, to be able to spend it properly. Many a dollar you worked hard to earn can be lost through uninformed or careless buying."[1]

[1] Better Business Bureau, *Consumer's Buying Guide,* New York, Award Books, Universal Publishing and Distributing Company, 1969, p. 3.

If we speak in the broadest terms, the great problem of the consumer is to satisfy his wants as fully as possible with a limited amount of money. But to do this he must deal successfully with several secondary problems: (1) he must decide what kinds of goods (including services) he should buy, and in what proportions; (2) he must decide which of the various varieties or brands of each commodity are best in quality; (3) where goods of better quality cost more money than others, he must decide whether they are worth to him the difference in price; and finally (4) when he has purchased goods, he must use them wisely and not wastefully, in order to obtain the maximum amount of use and satisfaction from them.

Consumption is an exceedingly important economic activity because, as Adam Smith[2] once said, it is the sole end and purpose of all production; also because it involves the consumer, who is an important fellow because he is everybody.

THE ECONOMIC STATUS OF THE CONSUMER

People who have a special concern about consumer problems often complain that it is difficult to get consumers to organize to protect their common interests. Undoubtedly this is true, and one reason is that, because consumers include everybody, they are not really a special-interest group. The welfare of consumers is only one aspect of the general welfare of society, and, as is so often the case, what is everybody's business tends to be nobody's business.

The average consumer is likely to take for granted the general conditions under which he purchases goods. If at times he is dissatisfied with these conditions, he feels that there is not much that he can do about it. He knows that individually he cannot raise the general quality or reduce the price level of goods on the market, and he has little confidence that he can achieve these objectives by joining with others. Even if he could achieve them in some degree, he is not sure it would be worth the necessary time and effort.

The Dual Role of the Consumer. The typical adult in his active years plays a dual role: He is both a consumer and a producer. In his role as consumer he spends money and uses goods; in his role as producer he earns money to buy the goods. However, he is likely to be much more concerned about earning money than spending it. Earning is often difficult but spending seems easy. Hence, when the average consumer thinks about improving his standard of living, he is likely to concentrate on the problem of increasing his money income rather than spending wisely what he already has. Whether or not he ever realizes them, there seem to be a great many ways by which he might make more money, but the possibili-

---

[2] Adam Smith was a Scottish philosopher who is often regarded as the father of modern economics. His great treatise, *The Wealth of Nations,* was published in 1776.

ties of living better on the income he already has seem very limited. In any case, he is not much interested. He would rather, in his role as producer, concentrate on closing some profitable business deals, getting a better job, or organizing a union to bargain with his employer for better wages. Yet in many cases he would probably be better off if he devoted more of his time and attention to the problem of wise buying.

The Household as the Chief Consumer Unit. We have been talking about the consumer as if he were a more or less independent and isolated individual. Actually, the chief consumer unit is the family or household. A large portion of the purchases of a family is for the joint use and satisfaction of all its members. Even when clothing and other personal goods are purchased for the exclusive use of an individual, the needs of the household and of other members of the family must be kept in mind so that available funds can be employed equitably and to the greatest advantage of all.

Every family must find some acceptable way of controlling its spending. In some families, close control is kept by the husband; in others, it is the wife who largely regulates the use of family funds; in still others, there is a division of responsibility. Probably in the majority of households the wife controls routine spending for food and other household needs, though she may make her purchases out of an allowance granted by the husband or determined by mutual agreement between them. Sometimes the making of larger purchases, such as a house or car, is left to the husband, though it is probably more common for the wife and husband together to make such decisions, and in many families the children are allowed to participate.

The household is not only the chief consumer unit, it is also the chief income-receiving unit. Traditionally the provision of income is the husband's responsibility, but today more and more wives are finding jobs and earning part of the family income. Furthermore, in working-class families, older children often contribute to the family income, though this is not so common today as in the past.

Consumer Influence on Production and Prices. Though as individuals or families consumers have little influence on the kinds and qualities of goods in the market or on their prices, as a group their influence is very great. In our kind of economy, goods are produced to sell, and the only goods that can be sold are those that consumers want. Also, the more consumers want a good, the more they will, if necessary, be willing to pay for it. The businessman who hopes to succeed must anticipate consumer wants and must produce the kinds of goods that will best satisfy them. If he produces things for which consumer demand is increasing, he will be able to make profits by selling his products at prices above his costs; but if he persists in producing goods for which consumer demand is rapidly declining, he may have to accept such low prices and heavy losses that he will soon be out of business.

Though it is true that businessmen can continue to produce and sell only the goods that consumers want, such a statement requires some qualification. For example, most automobile buyers, if they thought about it and had a choice, would not want a car with bumpers that are not adequate to protect it against expensive damage from low-speed front or rear impacts with other cars; yet most cars in 1970 had such bumpers, perhaps because current body styles demanded them and consumers, when they buy a car, are usually not thinking about the likelihood (and costs) of minor accidents. In any case, their choice is limited because there are only three major domestic producers of automobiles and each of them may decide that styling is more important in attracting sales than is protection against small accidents. Another and related problem is the fact that car bodies are usually constructed in such a way that even small damage is difficult and hence expensive to get at and repair. These two defects of the modern automobile have the unfortunate effect, among others, of appreciably raising the cost of automobile insurance. What is the remedy for this situation? Do we need new laws to regulate automobile construction or will a little publicity bring the needed changes?

An even greater problem, because it may result in major accidents, is the defects usually found in new cars. In 1969 Consumers Union bought and tested a large number of such cars and found an average of thirty-six defects, both minor and serious, per vehicle. Defects of consequence should be very rare in new cars, and it is hard to understand why companies who value their reputation allow great numbers of defective cars to leave the factory. Are workers on the assembly lines careless because they feel that their jobs are secure? Or are they under so much pressure that they cannot avoid making numerous mistakes? Certainly inspection procedures on cars must be very inadequate. Possibly the production of near-perfect cars would be more costly and mean higher prices, but besides increasing safety it would probably save car owners money in the long run.

Consumer Ignorance and the Variety of Goods. We have noted that the standard of living of a consumer depends not only on his income but also on how he uses it. The wise consumer tries to get the most satisfaction for the money he spends, but this is not always easy. He is faced with a vast variety of goods, and in many cases he has no possible way of judging their quality accurately or of determining just how well they will fit his particular needs.

Never before in the history of the world have consumers been confronted by so many choices. Today a large city department store, such as Marshall Field and Company in Chicago or Macy's in New York, carries in stock many thousands of different items. Most commodities in common use are manufactured by a number of producers under different brand names. Very seldom can the consumer judge accurately, at the time of purchase, the quality of the things he buys. This is certainly true of mechanical goods, of many foods, and of most drugs.

A good illustration is the situation of a consumer who is installing a new furnace in his house. He may have a choice between six or a dozen makes, and any of them may keep his house reasonably warm. But some are almost certainly considerably better than others in efficiency and durability. Moreover, they may vary in price by several hundred dollars, and there is no likelihood that there is any close correlation between price and quality. If he makes the right choice, he may get the best furnace and also save a good deal of money on the purchase price and in operating expenses, but he seldom has any way of really knowing what the right choice is.

It is obviously impossible, in a single short chapter, to deal adequately with all the problems the consumer meets. We can, however, call attention to the nature of his major problems, to some general principles and practices that may help him to meet them, and to some of the sources to which he can turn for aid and information.

FACTORS AFFECTING CONSUMER BUYING

Rational Choices, Foresight, and Saving. Whether man is or is not a rational creature or to what extent he is a rational creature has often been debated, usually without throwing much light on the question. Anyone who has carefully observed human behavior knows that it contains both rational and irrational—or perhaps we should say nonrational—elements. Rationality may have little to do with determining an individual's ultimate goals in life—his basic personal and social values—but once he knows his goals, a good deal of his behavior takes on a definitely rational character. He weighs possible lines of action and chooses the one he thinks most likely to achieve a desired result. He does not, to be sure, always do this, for often he acts in anger or on impulse, or else he is too tired, lazy, or indifferent to think through his problems. But the more important the decision facing him, the more likely he is to weigh alternatives carefully and to choose the one that he believes will give him the most satisfaction.

A consumer often pays little attention to what seem minor expenditures. He buys various small items day after day from habit without realizing, therefore, that he could get more satisfaction from buying something else. Also, if he is a careless person, he buys many things that appeal to him at the moment and realizes only afterward that he does not much want them. But in the case of a large expenditure, he will think twice before making it.

Rational spending involves the exercise of foresight. When the wise consumer disposes of his income, he must consider not only his needs for today and for the current year but also his possible requirements in the more distant future. For example, he must keep in mind the necessity of replacing his car after several years, and he must weigh the importance of saving something to provide for misfortunes or to give him an income in his old age. If he has dependents, he will almost certainly decide to spend something on life insurance, and he may decide to buy a house on a long-term payment plan.

Budgeting. A *budget* is a plan for spending. Without a budget, the ordinary consumer finds it difficult to keep in mind his whole financial situation, and especially all the various demands that will be made upon his income during the course of a year. Consequently, he may spend money on things he could dispense with, only to find later that he has nothing with which to buy necessities or to buy things that, if not necessities, are very important to him. Budgeting is not a method for getting everything one wants. If it is to be of any value, it will result in the consumer sacrificing some things he wants in favor of others that he wants more.

Budgeting involves two processes. First, the consumer must estimate how much he thinks he must or should spend for various purposes during the coming year and also how much he should be able to save. Second, he must keep a careful record of his actual expenditures. Later, when he compares his budgeted or estimated expenditures with his actual spending, he is likely to find that he has spent more on some things than his budget called for, and less on others. His problem then becomes to modify his next budget and his future expenditures to make them more fully satisfy his basic wants.

Though keeping a careful budget is often a useful procedure, it involves a good deal of time and effort, and for many people it may not be worth the trouble. This depends in part on the size of the consumer's income and in part on the kind of person he is. Many people succeed in controlling and allotting their expenditures in a satisfactory way without a formal budget; for others, this seems to be impossible. Some people find it useful to keep account of expenditures occasionally—say for three months every two or three years—as a check on what is really happening to their money. However, because some expenditures are seasonal or perhaps come only once a year, the consumer can gain a more accurate picture of his expenditures by recording them for a whole year.

Persons who are interested in setting up a budget can find at any good stationery store various types of account books to aid them. Also, they will

"We've liked living on our weekly budget so much that we've been living on it every three days." (Courtesy *The Chicago Tribune*. Drawing by Salo.)

find discussions of budgeting in any good textbook on consumer economics.

Though every individual or family that keeps a budget will have its own special problems, it may be interesting to note in Table 15 how Americans as a group divide their consumption expenditures among the major types of goods and services they buy.

Table 15. *Percentage Distribution of Consumption Expenditures in 1963 and 1968 by Type of Product*

Type of Product	Per cent		Per cent Change
	1963	1968	
Food, beverages, and tobacco	25.4	23.2	—2.2
Clothing, accessories, and jewelry	9.9	10.3	+0.4
Personal care	1.7	1.7	0.0
Housing	13.1	14.4	+1.3
Household operations, furnishings, etc.	14.0	14.1	+0.1
Medical care and death expenses	6.8	7.2	+0.4
Personal business	6.6	5.5	—1.1
Transportation, including automobile outlays	12.6	13.5	+0.9
Recreation	6.1	6.3	+0.2
Private education	1.5	1.6	+0.1
Religious and welfare activities	1.4	1.5	+0.1
Foreign travel and payments abroad, net	0.9	0.7	—0.2
Total consumption spending	100.0	100.0	

Source: United States Department of Commerce.

Custom and Fashion. Probably no factor is more significant than *custom* in determining the particular kinds of goods consumers desire. Physical needs, it is true, are an important factor in guiding our purchases. We must have food to keep us from starving and have clothing plus a house or an apartment to protect us from the weather. But the particular kinds of food, clothing, and houses that we want are determined by the customs of the society in which we live, in other words, by our culture. Not only the kinds but also the quantities are largely a matter of custom. This may not be true for food, but it certainly is for clothing and housing. Were it not for the custom of wearing different clothes on different days and for different occasions, and clothes coming up to a certain standard of appearance, we could greatly reduce our purchases without suffering any physical discomfort. Likewise, if it were not customary to have separate kitchens, dining rooms, living rooms, and bedrooms, and to fill them up with certain kinds of furniture, we could live quite comfortably, as the Eskimos and other primitive peoples do, in much smaller and simpler houses.

A *custom* is sometimes defined as a *group habit.* It is a way of behaving that is so firmly established in a group that it is relatively permanent. A *fashion,* on the other hand, is temporary. It is a type of behavior, or clothing, or furniture that becomes popular for a time because people like variety and change as well as sameness. To be among the first to adopt a new fashion is a way of getting ahead of other people, of being different, and of attracting attention. But as soon as a new style becomes widely adopted, it no longer serves these purposes, and so it fades more or less rapidly. Those who first took it up seek for a new fashion to keep them ahead of the crowd and to maintain their reputation as style leaders. Changes in fashions are often rather superficial. They tend to take place within limits set by the firmly established customs of a society.

Fashion, nevertheless, has a powerful effect on many consumer choices. Its power is perhaps most evident in the purchase of clothing, but it is a strong influence on the buying of many other things, including furniture, jewelry, houses, and automobiles. Producers often cater to and encourage fashion changes in order to increase sales. They believe—and rightly—that many people will discard their old clothing, houses, or automobiles, and buy new ones, not because the old ones are in any sense worn out, but just because they have become unfashionable. Fashion also determines styles in hair, beards, and speech, and it even to a considerable extent determines ideas, beliefs, and behavior.

Keeping Up with the Joneses. Closely related to the influence of custom and fashion on consumer purchases is the strong desire most people have to live as well as other people. If a family occupies a house that is small and shabby compared with others in the block, or if it wears clothes that are old or dowdy compared with those of its neighbors, its members are ashamed and unhappy. To be comfortable and happy, people must feel that they belong to the group and that they are like other people. Perhaps they do not really want to be like everyone else, but if they are different, it must be in ways that attract favorable attention so that they can feel a sense of pride. To most people a "decent" standard of living means one that at least closely approaches the standard customary in the group or class to which they belong, or wish to belong.

When people have much more income than others, they are sometimes tempted to buy many goods largely for the purpose of advertising their wealth. Through the possession of mink coats, custom-built foreign cars, showy mansions, and other things that only the very wealthy can afford, they gain a sense of superiority and satisfaction. As we noted earlier, Thorstein Veblen, in his famous essay "The Theory of the Leisure Class" applied the term *conspicuous consumption* to this kind of spending.

Advertising and Salesmanship. Advertising in the United States is a huge business. For some years, at least since 1955, advertising expenditures have been equal to about 3.5 per cent of total consumer spending. In 1969 they were about $20.1 billion, which was still very close to this percentage. Many people have questioned whether outlays on this scale are justified. They feel that much advertising is unproductive and serves no socially use ful purpose. On the other hand, its more enthusiastic defenders are inclined to credit it with a large part of the economic progress that has taken place in the last hundred years.

From a social viewpoint, the most useful function of advertising is spreading information among consumers and making them aware of the various kinds and qualities of goods available in the market and the prices at which they sell. Some advertising is highly informative—for example, the catalogues of the mail-order houses or the advertisements of merchants in the daily newspapers. Newspaper advertisements are often very valuable to their readers in telling them where different kinds of goods can be found, what their prices are, and when special sales are being carried on. But a great deal of advertising, such as that of the cigarette companies, has almost no informational value. Its chief purpose is to create a favorable impression on the consumer by means of suggestion, in order to shift his demand from other brands of cigarettes to the one being advertised.

In recent years much cigarette advertising has been concentrated on the merits of filter tips, which remove some of the nicotine and tars from the smoke. This approach is a result of the steadily accumulating evidence relating cigarette smoking to lung cancer and to diseases of the heart and arteries. The implication is that filter tips somewhat reduce these dangers. The dangers, of course, are not admitted or even mentioned. In 1970, federal legislation was passed to ban cigarette advertising on TV programs and it took effect in January, 1971.

Various claims are made about the social benefits of advertising, but many of them are questionable or not very important. At times there may be some truth in the contention that advertising improves the quality of goods. Certainly a company that has spent millions of dollars building up the reputation of a commodity should be unwilling to destroy that reputation by putting out an obviously inferior product. Advertising is also said to benefit the public by bearing the cost of radio and television entertainment and a good part of the cost of newspapers and magazines. However, the quality of much of this entertainment and reading is not very high, and the public might be better off if some way could be found for it to bear the whole cost directly and in return get more of what it really wants.

Aside from calling attention to its usefulness in spreading information, perhaps the best defense that can be made of advertising is to point out that it is a more or less indispensable feature of our competitive free-enterprise economy. It is hard to see how competition could operate very effectively under modern conditions if a firm did not have the privilege of calling attention to itself and its products by advertising of one kind or another. Advertising appears to be especially important for new and growing business enterprises.

Unfortunately, advertising at times plays on the fears, ignorance, and gullibility of some consumers. It can be full of misleading suggestions, various degrees of misrepresentation, and sometimes outright lies. As a result of action by government and by business organizations, the situation is better than in former years, but there is still room for improvement. Fortunately, most consumers are well insulated against the exaggerations of advertisers and view them with a mixture of annoyance, tolerance, and amusement. Apparently, advertising has its greatest effect through simply keeping before the public, by constant repetition, the names of certain companies and products.

A charge that is often made against advertising is that, because it raises the costs of doing business, it increases the prices consumers must pay for goods. Firms substitute advertising for price competition. If they did not advertise, so it is said, they would be able to compete by selling at lower prices, and this would increase the purchasing power and the standards of living of consumers. However, it should be pointed out that, where there are a number of competing firms, there are almost sure to be some who will do a minimum of advertising and depend largely on low prices for getting business. As a result, the consumer who is willing to buy a little-advertised product can often do so at a lower price.

Salesmanship is another important factor that influences many consumer choices, especially of such things as clothing, automobiles, houses, and life insurance. Salesmen are often very helpful to consumers, but we are all familiar with the "high pressure" type of salesman who uses every possible method of inducing the customer to buy something that he does not need or want. The wise consumer regards with reservations the claims of both salesmen and advertisers, because he knows that the primary interest of both is in selling their products and that the needs of the consumer are a secondary consideration. However, firms that expect to stay in business often insist on honesty in advertisements and salesmanship as a means of building consumer confidence.

Products That Save Consumers Time and Trouble. During the last fifty years great changes have taken place in the methods employed in preparing goods for the market. These changes have been especially notable in the case of foods.

One of the earlier developments was packaging. At the beginning of the present century, some packaged foods were already available, including, for example, certain breakfast foods. However, such staple products as sugar, molasses, and flour were still measured out by the grocer from barrels. Gradually, the use of packages increased, until today almost nothing can be purchased from a grocery store in bulk. In many cases, even fresh fruits, vegetables, and precut meats are packaged in cellophane. Packaging is a great convenience to the buyer. It is also a selling device, and every effort is made by producers to design packages that will appeal to the consumer.

It is often assumed that packaging is a luxury or convenience that adds to the cost of goods. This assumption is almost certainly incorrect. Though packaging does cost money, it protects foods from contamination and at the same time it saves many outlays for labor by simplifying the handling of goods and by making possible modern self-service stores, including supermarkets. Packaging does have the drawback of adding to the solid wastes that we must dispose of, but for most products it would be both difficult and expensive to dispense with its benefits.

In the last two decades there has been a great development of specially prepared foods designed to appeal to consumers. Quick freezing has been employed to provide a wide variety of foods that retain their freshness and flavor to a high degree. Also, specially prepared food products have been developed for the purpose of saving the housekeeper time and labor. These include a variety of soups, precooked meats, biscuit and cake mixes, frozen pies ready for baking, frozen dinners, and instant coffees. Such labor-saving products are a great help to the increasing number of employed housewives, and often they cost no more or even less than similar foods completely prepared at home.

Money-Saving Opportunities for Consumers. Alert consumers are greatly influenced in their buying by the many money-saving opportunities available to those who look for them and who plan ahead of time the making of important purchases. On many kinds of goods large savings can be made with no reduction in choice or quality by watching for special sales and by taking advantage of regular seasonal sales. Often, too, money can be saved by purchasing through mail-order houses or chain stores. Frequently these organizations sell products, under their own brands, that are equal or superior to similar nationally advertised products that command substantially higher prices. Then there are the *discount houses*. In every city of any size, a number of these establishments can usually be found, and they sell a great variety of standard products at discounts of anywhere from 15 to 40 per cent from the retail price suggested by the manufacturer. The claim is often made by "legitimate" merchants, and by manufacturers who wish to protect their system of high price markups, that it is not safe to deal with discount houses; but the experience of many people attests to the fact that some of these firms are highly reliable and give excellent service. Consumers should, of course, avoid dealing with firms that have a poor reputation for fair treatment of customers.

In the last few years the success of discount houses has been so great that many other merchants, in order to compete, have felt compelled to reduce their own prices. Many states, it is true, have so-called *fair-trade* laws. These permit manufacturers to set the retail prices of their products, and they prohibit retailers from selling for less; but, fortunately for consumers, fair-trade laws have been very difficult to enforce. Today many manufacturers have abandoned the attempt to control the retail prices of their products. In many cities, the discount price has now become the regular price at most stores. The result has been to benefit consumers by narrowing the margin between factory and retail price.

Changing Consumption Patterns. Over the years marked changes have taken place in the consumption patterns of the American people. Partly these changes have resulted from the introduction of new products. Auto-

"It's simple . . . if we skip two payments on the washer and one on the car, we'll have the down payment on a color TV." (Copyright 1969 by The Kiplinger Washington Editors, Inc.)

mobiles and their operation have long taken a substantial fraction of the incomes of most consumers. Many other products introduced in recent decades also demand a share of income, including automatic washing machines, freezers, air-conditioning equipment, stereophonic record players, and television sets. Changes in consumption patterns have resulted partly from a great increase in per capita and family purchasing power. Larger incomes have enabled consumers not only to spend more money on new products but also to increase greatly their spending on such things as vacation trips, education, personal services, and medical care. They are also saving more money and making greater contributions to religious and charitable organizations.

CONSUMER CREDIT

Consumer credit in one form or another undoubtedly goes back for several thousand years. Even buying on the installment plan, which is often supposed to be of recent origin, has a fairly long history; it is said to have been first introduced in this country in 1807 in connection with the sale of high-grade furniture to people with relatively large incomes. Although the volume of consumer debt outstanding has undergone wide fluctuations, the general trend over the years has been upward. At the end of February, 1970, the total exceeded $120 billion, an amount equal to about 18 per cent of annual disposable personal income.[3] These figures include only short-term and intermediate-term debts, and not long-term debts such as those represented by mortgages on homes. The largest item in consumer

[3] *Federal Reserve Bulletin,* April 1970, pp. A54, A59.

credit is *installment credit,* which in February, 1970, totalled about $97 billion. It includes both the outstanding balances on installment purchases of goods and the outstanding amounts of money loans that are liquidated by small regular payments. The *Federal Reserve Bulletin* also includes in installment credit the outstanding amounts owed for purchases on bank credit cards.

Many people look upon consumer credit as a danger spot in our economy. Some sellers feel that consumers abuse credit privileges, and some consumers feel that their financial difficulties are a result of buying too many things on the installment plan, either under the influence of high pressure salesmanship or as a result of their own failure to weigh carefully the demands upon their resources. Also, many economists and businessmen fear that a high volume of consumer credit greatly increases the danger that any slackening of business will develop into a major recession. The reason for these fears is that consumer credit ties up future income. If a period of reduced employment comes, some consumers will have difficulty in meeting their outstanding credit obligations and will have to reduce new purchases. Moreover, confidence will be shaken, so that both buyers and sellers will adopt a cautious attitude. This is likely to contract sales and production and thus intensify unemployment. That there is basis for such fears cannot be doubted. Some economists, however, believe that if consumer credit is granted on a conservative basis, the economic dangers it presents are not great.

Consumer credit is of four principal types: (1) store charge accounts; (2) credit cards; (3) installment purchase agreements; and (4) cash loans from lending agencies. Let us consider each type briefly.

Charge Accounts. *Charge accounts* are carried widely by many types of stores, though discount houses and chain stores (especially those handling groceries and variety goods) usually sell strictly for cash. But most chain department stores do carry charge accounts.

Many consumers consider charge accounts of the traditional type a great convenience. Because bills are generally mailed at the end of a monthly billing period and are then payable within fifteen days, they do not provide credit for any length of time. On the other hand, no charge is made to the customer for carrying such accounts, and they make it unnecessary for him to use much cash or to keep writing checks. Also, they may make it easier for him to keep a record of his expenditures.

However, many department stores and mail-order houses now employ *revolving-credit* charge accounts. These do not have to be paid in full shortly after the end of the month, but a customer is expected to make a certain minimum payment each month on his debt. Then, as it is reduced, he can make new purchases. But this kind of credit is expensive. The customer usually pays a monthly charge of 1.5 per cent on any balance that is carried over. Because this is an annual interest rate of 18 per cent, if his debt for a year averages $1,000 he will pay $180 in interest charges. Some stores carry *option accounts.* At the end of each month the customer has the choice of either paying his entire bill and thereby avoiding a service charge, or of meeting only a part of it and then paying interest on the remainder on a revolving-credit basis.

Credit Cards. *Credit cards,* except those issued by stores to identify the holders of charge accounts, are a relatively recent development. They are intended to enable the holder to obtain goods or services from a wide range of stores and other establishments without paying cash. The seller of the goods or services sends the bill to the issuer of the credit card and receives payment less a discount of from 1 to 6.5 per cent. The holder of the card is then billed periodically for the full amount of his accumulated transactions. Today there are three well-known issuers of what are sometimes called *"travel and entertainment"* cards: American Express, Diners' Club, and Carte Blanche. These cards give a certain amount of prestige because there is an annual fee of $15 and they are seldom issued to anyone with an income of less than $7,500. In addition, a number of big oil companies also issue credit cards, primarily for use in purchasing gasoline and other products handled by service stations. Also there are "convenience cards" issued by car rental companies or airlines. But the most recent and dramatic expansion of credit cards has been in those issued by banks. Originally, many of these *bank credit cards* were mailed to depositors who had not requested them and who were not even aware that they were being sent.

"The plan to use only credit cards and create a cashless society seems to be working quite well with us. We're stone broke." (Courtesy of Publishers-Hall Syndicate.)

The great majority of the banks now in the credit card business use one of two national licensing systems: BankAmericard, developed by California's Bank of America, and the Master Charge card, introduced in 1967 by competing San Francisco banks. In May, 1970, the BankAmericard system claimed over 3,300 member banks, 31 million cardholders, and annual billings of over two billion dollars. About the same time, the Interbank Card Association, which issues the Master Charge card, claimed over 4,400 member banks and 35 million cardholders. But Federal Reserve economists estimated that only about half the people who held bank cards were actually using them.

Whether credit cards are a boon to the economy and to consumers is debatable. To the author, they seem to complicate more than to simplify the problem of making payments, but obviously there are millions who do not agree. Certainly, the expense of operating a credit card system is considerable, and someone must pay it. Initially this cost is met by those who sell to credit card holders because their bills are discounted; but, in the long run, consumers are almost certain to bear the cost by paying higher prices. Besides accepting payment at a discount, the seller must do a little extra bookkeeping for every transaction. Because of the trouble and expense, the use of credit cards for many very small purchases is quite impractical. Even for larger purchases there are still department stores, restaurants, and other establishments that will not honor them; and though they reduce the amount of money (or traveler's checks) that must be carried by a person, their theft or loss may be a serious matter for the holder, especially if he is not aware of it at the time. He can, for a price, protect himself against such losses by taking out insurance. In the case of a bank card, the holder is not liable for purchases that someone else makes with his card, *provided* he has notified his bank of its loss within twenty-four hours. Bank cards can prove expensive if used as a source of credit for any length of time. The holder who goes into debt to his bank and who does not pay his bill within twenty-five days is usually charged interest at the rate of 1.5 per cent a month, or 18 per cent a year.[4]

Installment Purchases. *Installment buying* has greatly expanded in the years since World War II. From only $2.5 billion in 1945 it had risen to $98.2 billion by the end of 1969, when it accounted for four fifths of all short- and intermediate-term consumer credit. Most installment credit is not actually carried by the seller of a commodity but by a bank or finance company that takes over the seller's contracts with buyers.

From the standpoint of the businessman, installment selling is a sales device, though in some cases it is also a means of increasing his profit on sales. Whether installment selling increases the total sales of all goods is more than doubtful, but it probably substantially increases sales of durable goods that are relatively high priced. If so, *it does this at the expense of reducing sales of perishable goods and services.* For example, the man with limited income may find it almost impossible to save enough money to buy a new automobile outright. He constantly succumbs to the temptation to "fritter away" his income as he receives it on entertainment, clothing he could dispense with, and various odds and ends. But he can buy an automobile on the installment plan, because if he is under pressure to

[4] For a good discussion of bank credit cards, see Paul O'Neil, "A Little Gift from Your Friendly Banker," *Life* magazine, March 27, 1970, pp. 48–58.

"Well, we've reached the halfway point. We've paid $25,000 on our $25,000 house!" (CITIZEN SMITH, by Dave Gerard, reproduced by permission of The Register and Tribune Syndicate.)

meet monthly payments, he will cut down on his expenditures for other types of goods. Thus, to the purchaser, the great advantage of installment buying is that it enables him to obtain some kinds of goods sooner than he otherwise could.

But buying on the installment plan is likely to reduce a consumer's ultimate total purchasing power, because interest and other carrying charges make goods bought in this way cost more than goods purchased for cash. The buyer will discover, if he takes the trouble to read his contract, that he is almost invariably paying from 10 to 50 per cent interest on any unpaid balance, and sometimes other charges as well. Frequently he thinks he is paying 6 per cent or less. Also, if he reads the fine print in his contract, he is likely to find that the seller has a right to repossess the commodity whenever the buyer fails to meet a payment and that the seller, if necessary, can enter the buyer's house in order to get it. Moreover, the payments already made will be completely lost. Some states, however, have passed legislation giving the installment buyer a certain amount of protection, and most well-established business houses tend to be fair in dealing with installment buyers for the sake of protecting their own reputations.

Small Cash Loans. The consumer who has good collateral in the form of securities or a savings account can get the cheapest and most convenient form of credit by borrowing directly from his bank. In normal times (when the country is not experiencing rapid inflation), he is not likely to pay an interest rate of more than 5 to 7 per cent a year. If he does not have such collateral, he may still be able to borrow, but probably at considerably higher cost.

Today, licensed *small-loan companies* operate in most of the states, and their maximum legal charges range from 2 to 3.5 per cent a month on the unpaid balance of a loan, or, in other words, from 24 to 42 per cent a year. The reason for permitting such high rates of interest is that the risks involved in the kinds of loans that they make are high, as are also the costs of collection. Small-loan companies specialize in making loans of up to five hundred dollars—and often much larger ones—to people who do not have collateral of the type that would be acceptable to a bank but who are otherwise relatively good credit risks. If a borrower has an assured job, they may lend simply on his signature, but usually they will want it reinforced with a friend's signature or by a *chattel mortgage*[5] on furniture or a car. Obviously, this is an expensive form of credit, and it is more likely to be used for meeting personal emergencies or past debts than for buying goods. It does fill a need for those unable to take advantage of less-expensive forms of credit.

However, many consumers who lack collateral are able to borrow on more-favorable terms from *credit unions.* There were in 1970 about 25,000 credit unions in the United States with more than twenty million members. Credit unions are cooperative lending agencies, most commonly organized among the employees of a given plant or company. Credit unions generally charge their members 1 per cent a month on the unpaid balance of a loan, an annual rate of 12 per cent. But to borrow on this basis and pay cash is usually cheaper than to buy goods on the installment plan. Also, many banks have now gone into the business of making small loans to people who do not have the usual types of acceptable collateral, provided they are otherwise good credit risks. On such loans, banks usually charge interest rates comparable to those of credit unions.

GETTING THE MOST FOR YOUR MONEY

Space does not permit the presentation here of a course in consumer economics, but we will suggest a few general principles and practices that, as a consumer, you should always keep in mind.

1. *Learn as much as you can about products that you purchase frequently or that represent a relatively large outlay.* Try different brands, including the private ones of department stores and food chains. Make use of government grades when possible and of labels showing the ingredients in a product. In the case of mechanical goods, buy only the products of well-known manufacturers and be sure that adequate repair services are available.
2. *Compare prices of different sellers for the same goods or goods of the same type and similar quality.*
3. *Buy only from reputable dealers.* This applies especially to goods that you cannot readily identify or judge as to quality. "Reputable dealers" will include some discount houses.
4. *Check prices against the relative contents of large and small containers.* Large containers are sometimes a bargain, but sometimes, in proportion to price, they give the buyer no more, or even less, than small containers.

[5] A mortgage on movable property.

5. *Plan ahead.* Keep looking for what you want at a good price. Take advantage of genuine sales and other special opportunities.
6. *Pay cash if you possibly can, or else use a monthly account on which there is no interest charge.*
7. *If you must have credit for a fairly long period, use the cheapest available form.* Be sure that you understand the cost and conditions of your loan or purchase and that you fully understand any papers you sign when reasonably possible.
8. *Know what you are getting for your money when you buy insurance.* Seek disinterested sources of information. An insurance agent is often more interested in his commission than in giving you what you need at lowest cost. A useful source of consumer information about life insurance and life insurance companies is *Life Insurance from the Buyer's Point of View,* listed in the bibliography at the end of this chapter.
9. *Make every effort to save at least a small amount of money regularly.* This encourages wise spending, contributes to a better economic future, and gives a sense of self-respect and security. Small savings should be put into insured bank savings accounts, insured savings and loan company accounts, sound credit unions, or government bonds.

But when one's assets become sizable, the wisdom of keeping too much of them in the above forms is doubtful. Banks and government bonds will keep your dollars safe, but in the long run these dollars will probably lose much of their value through inflation. The experiences of other countries, the constant trend toward higher taxes, the persistence of deficit spending by our federal government, the constant tendency of wage increases to outrun productivity, and political pressures to increase the money supply to reduce unemployment—all these factors point toward more inflation. In the long run, good real estate, such as a well-located home or stock in a good investment trust may be safer investments than savings accounts or government bonds. This is because in a period of inflation their money value is ultimately likely to rise. High-grade corporate bonds also become attractive when interest rates on them rise to 8 or 9 per cent, as they did in 1970; but even such a return can be disappointing if inflation persists at a rapid rate. Unfortunately, many investment problems are difficult and complex and hence beyond the scope of a short chapter on consumer problems.

THE CONSUMER MOVEMENT

We have already noted some of the obstacles to organizing consumers for the protection of their common interests. Nevertheless, there has developed in the United States in the last several decades what may fairly be called a *consumer movement.* Various organizations have been created for the specific purpose of dealing with consumer problems, and other groups have taken an interest in them and have contributed toward their solution by such methods as encouraging consumer education and supporting consumer legislation.

Consumer Education. Consumer education as such is a comparatively recent development in our schools and colleges, but a great deal of it has been carried on for years in home-economics courses. Today, courses in consumer problems are often found in high schools, and very frequently such subjects as advertising, consumer cooperatives, home ownership, life insurance, and budgeting are introduced into other courses. In addition, many of our colleges and universities have for some years offered courses in consumer economics. But much of the most effective consumer education is carried on outside the classroom, by women's clubs, professional groups, cooperatives, certain independent consumer services, business groups, and government.

Independent Consumer Services. The two outstanding consumer services in this country are Consumers Research and Consumers Union.[6] Consumers Research was organized in 1929, Consumers Union a few years later by a group who withdrew from the older organization because they were dissatisfied with some of its policies. Today Consumers Union, much the larger of the two, has a membership of about two million.

Both Consumers Research and Consumers Union are nonprofit organizations whose principal activities consist in testing as wide a variety of important consumer goods as their funds will permit and then reporting to their members. The former reports its findings in a monthly magazine called *Consumer Bulletin;* the latter employs a similar magazine called *Consumer Reports.* Neither publication carries advertising. Products are listed by their brand names and described under such headings as "Best Buys," "Acceptable," and "Not Acceptable," or "Recommended," "Not Recommended," and "Intermediate."

The value of these services grows out of the fact that they are headed by people of independence and ability who are loyal to the interests of consumers and who have no connection with any commercial enterprise. Insofar as that is possible, their testing and reports appear to be objective and impartial. Occasionally, a consumer may not agree with their findings, or the particular article he buys may not behave in accordance with the tests, but he can learn enough from such services to help him make better choices in purchasing many commodities.

A monthly magazine that is helpful to consumers is *Changing Times.*[7] It does not provide a product-rating service, as do *Consumers Union* and *Consumers Research,* but it publishes a variety of information that is useful

[6] Consumers Research is located at Washington, New Jersey. Consumers Union has its offices at Mount Vernon, New York.

[7] *Changing Times* is published by The Kiplinger Washington Editors, Inc., Editors Park, Maryland.

to consumers when they invest or spend their money and when they make plans for everyday living. Though *Changing Times* is not a nonprofit enterprise, it accepts no advertising.

There are also consumer services that undertake to furnish their subscribers with lists of dealers from whom automobiles and standard brands of many types of merchandise can be purchased at substantial discounts. How useful such arrangements are to the average consumer is open to some doubt. Dealers listed may not be readily accessible; there are questions of service; and often the consumer can probably do just as well with less trouble by going to ordinary discount houses or waiting for sales.

Consumer Aids Provided by Business. In spite of the fact that the chief interest of businessmen in the consumer is to sell him something, or perhaps because of this, business enterprises have aided him in a number of ways. Perhaps it is not necessary to mention the more obvious contributions of business to consumer welfare, and yet it is well to keep them in mind. First of all, business provides most consumers with employment and income, and, second, it provides all consumers with the quantities and varieties of goods that make possible the American standard of living. But, beyond this, business has provided many aids for consumers primarily because its own existence and success depend in the long run on holding a large measure of consumer confidence. This is true not only of business as a whole but also of individual enterprises. The firm that desires to maintain sales and profits must retain the confidence of the public.

We could give many illustrations of business aid to consumers. Most newspapers, and magazines, to protect their own reputations and earning power, will carry no advertising that they suspect is fraudulent. That is one reason that so little patent-medicine advertising is found in print today in comparison with former times. There is still exaggeration in describing the merits of many trademarked drug preparations, but bald falsehoods are no longer common. Another type of business aid to consumers is provided by brands and trademarks. To be sure, a producer creates and advertises a brand or trademark chiefly to increase his own profits. But it will not be effective in doing this unless it gains and holds consumer confidence. Some producers make a great effort to keep trademarked goods up to a standard, so that the consumer can buy with confidence.

Perhaps the most effective effort of the nation's substantial businessmen to protect consumers is to be found in the Better Business bureaus. There are more than 140 of these in cities throughout the country. They are supported by the local business community and their services are free. The businessmen who maintain them are attempting to protect the consumer against misleading or fraudulent advertising and selling practices, partly because they wish to maintain the faith of the public in the great majority of business firms whose practices are ethical.

Among the things that Better Business bureaus do to aid consumers are the following:

1. Provide needed information as to the reliability of a firm. The best time for a prospective customer to get in touch with his local bureau is before doing business with an unknown firm.
2. Handle justified complaints, or tell the consumer how he should deal with them.
3. Develop and attempt to maintain honest and ethical standards in advertising and selling.
4. Check on questionable advertising claims, not only to protect consumers but also to protect other businessmen.[8]

Consumer Legislation. Two very important pieces of legislation by the federal government are the Pure Food and Drug Act of 1906 and its successor, the Food, Drug, and Cosmetics Act of 1938. This latter act bars from interstate trade any adulterated or misbranded food or drug, any food injurious to health, and any poisonous cosmetics. It is enforced by the United States Food and Drug Administration, which is a division of the Department of Health, Education, and Welfare.

A 1958 amendment to the Food, Drug, and Cosmetics Act banned the use of food and drugs containing any substance found harmful if used in significant amounts in the diet of animals. The chief purpose was to apply stricter regulations to *food additives*. Most of these additives are substances put in food to keep it from spoiling, to color it, or to improve its flavor. Today more than seven hundred chemicals are being used for this purpose. Formerly, the government had to prove that a chemical would have a harmful effect before it could be barred from use. Under the new law responsibility is placed on the manufacturers to prove that an additive is not harmful.

Rarely do activities of the FDA attract much public attention. However, a decade or more ago Francis Kelsey of the Food and Drug Administration prevented the sale in the United States of a sleep-inducing drug called Thalidomide because she was not convinced of its safety. When later the drug caused thousands of deformed births in Europe, she gained national fame and approval. Another action that attracted wide attention and some disagreement was the order, in 1969, forbidding the continued use of cyclamates in food products as a substitute for sugar. Experiments had shown that, given in large doses to mice, cyclamates tended to produce cancer.

Other federal legislation for the benefit of consumers includes the Clayton Act, one provision of which forbids false advertising; the Wheeler-Lea Act, which deals with both unfair advertising and unfair trade practices; the Meat Inspection Act, which requires that meat entering into interstate commerce be inspected to insure that it is fit for human consumption; the Poultry Inspection Act; and the Wool Products Labelling Act. This last act requires that all wool products bear a label telling the per-

[8] *Better Business Bureau Consumer's Buying Guide,* New York, Award Books, Universal Publishing and Distributing Corporation, 1969. See especially Chap. 1.

"For what we are about to receive . . . additives and antibiotics notwithstanding . . ." (Courtesy *National Review,* 150 East 35th Street, New York, New York 10016.)

centage of wool they contain and whether it is new wool, reprocessed wool, or reused wool (shoddy). In 1958, Congress passed legislation requiring that a label be attached to all new automobiles showing the manufacturer's suggested retail price for the car and for each major accessory.

Under some of the acts mentioned above and under other legislation, the federal government provides various services for consumers. The National Bureau of Standards sets and maintains standard weights and measures; and various departments of the government have bureaus that provvide consumer information. Also, for a small fee, the Department of Agriculture will grade meats for packers who desire this service, and on a similar basis it will grade canned fruits and vegetables.

The most significant consumer legislation passed by Congress in the last decade consists of the Fair Packaging and Labelling Act of 1966 and the Truth in Lending Act of 1968. The original bills on which these acts are based were first considered by Congress in the very early 1960's, but several years elapsed and some compromises were made before Congress was willing to pass them.

The Fair Packaging Act was intended to enable shoppers to compare readily the quantities of a product in different packages so that they can more easily compare prices per ounce, pound, or pint. The act requires that statements of net quantity, in reasonably large type, be placed on the front of every package entering into interstate trade. Quantities must be expressed in standard measures and in specified ways that make direct comparisons possible. Producers were allowed considerable time to adjust their packages to the requirements of the act, but by the end of 1969 most of its provisions had come into force. The act appears to have given shoppers some help in determining differences in cost per unit of the contents of different packages, but these still come in so many odd sizes that the average person has difficulty in making the necessary calculations quickly. It would be more helpful to the shopper if the price per ounce, pound, or pint were printed on a package.[9] But this would involve some difficulties. A manufacturer, for example, might put suggested retail prices on his packages and indicate the resulting price per ounce, dozen or pint but these prices might not be those at which retailers would actually sell the products. To be sure, each retail outlet can be required to mark its own price per unit on all its packaged goods, but this is expensive in labor cost, and the cost is almost certain to be passed on to consumers. This problem was solved for a cooperative supermarket in Chicago by a volunteer group of members who affixed price-per-ounce labels to the shelves, just below each product.

The Truth in Lending Act covers nearly all consumer credit. It is intended to protect a borrower by requiring the lender to state in full in the loan or installment purchase contract the borrower's obligations and privileges. All finance and interest charges must be clearly revealed, and their total must be stated in both dollars and as an annual percentage rate on the amounts borrowed.[10] The act does not limit finance or interest charges. It merely requires full disclosure in terms that should enable the borrower to compare the relative cost of loans from different types of lenders so that he can choose the most advantageous of the borrowing options open to him. He may even decide that a loan is too expensive and that he can avoid it by deferring a planned vacation trip or the purchase of a car.

The Government and "Consumerism." Interest in consumer problems is not new in this country, but discussion of them in the 1960's was stimulated by certain actions of the government, by publicity concerning possible dangers from drugs and from residues of insecticides in foods, and by such "crusades" as those for greater automobile safety and for the reduction of pollution. To cover this new interest in consumer problems, someone coined the term *consumerism*. Ralph Nader, who might be called an "activist" writer and investigator, is one of a number of people who have contributed to bringing consumerism into the limelight.

The role of government as a friend of the consumer is an ambiguous one. We have pointed out some of the activities of government that aid consumers. On the other hand, when there is a conflict between the interest of consumers (the general public) and some well-organized special-interest group, government is apt to give in to the political pressures of the organized groups. For example, by setting up tariffs or quotas on imports, instituted or maintained to meet demands of the steel industry, the oil industry, the sugar producers, and others, government has supported high prices, or brought price increases in various products. By acceding to the demands of some farm groups to pay farmers for keeping land out of production,

[9] See "What's Happened to Truth-in-Packaging?" *Consumer Reports,* January 1969, pp. 40 ff.

[10] See "Truth in Lending," *Federal Reserve Bulletin,* February 1969, pp. 98–102.

"The additive that bothers me the most is the price." (Courtesy of Publishers-Hall Syndicate.)

while also paying them subsidies on their actual production, it has helped to raise both the prices and the taxes paid by consumers. Also, it has been unwilling or politically unable to deal firmly with the problem posed by unions that are in a strategic position to demand and obtain inflationary wage increases because if their demands are not met they can paralyze essential public services. Perhaps the greatest injury to vast numbers of consumers as a result of federal government actions was in the middle and late 1960's, when the government followed monetary and fiscal policies that brought about a rapid inflation of almost all prices.

But it is always good politics to show an interest in consumers. Early in 1962, President Kennedy directed his Council of Economic Advisers to set up a Consumer Advisory Council. In January, 1964, President Johnson created the office of Special Assistant to the President on Consumer Affairs and appointed Esther Peterson, Assistant Secretary of Labor, to fill the post (on a part-time basis). She was succeeded by Betty Furness, well known to television viewers; and she, in turn, under President Nixon, was succeeded by Virginia Knauer, who for about a year had headed Pennsylvania's Bureau of Consumer Protection. It is not clear that either the Advisory Council or the various special assistants to the President have done a great deal to advance the welfare of consumers, but a beginning has been made that may bring greater progress in the future. One of the problems has been that they have had a small budget and little power. Some members of Congress are now advocating a special consumers' agency in the government with adequate powers and financing, or even a department for consumer affairs, whose head would be a member of the President's cabinet.

There are some rather simple things that the government could do to aid consumers, but as yet has not done. One would be to release to the public the results of government tests conducted on a great range of consumer products by such agencies as the Food and Drugs Administration and the Agriculture and Defense Departments. Failure in the past to release such information has probably been due in part to opposition by some business groups.

CONSUMER COOPERATIVES

Consumer cooperatives are merchandising establishments organized by groups of consumers for the purpose of meeting their own needs for goods. The typical consumer cooperative is a local grocery store. But when cooperatives become fairly numerous in a country, they usually organize on a regional and national basis for the purpose of carrying on the wholesale as well as the retail distribution of goods. Sometimes, as in Great Britain and Sweden, they even acquire factories and other producing facilities in order to serve the needs of their members. Consumer cooperatives do not always limit themselves to handling groceries. Frequently they carry on such enterprises as nursery schools, housing developments, gas stations, milk routes, and even department stores. Credit unions, mentioned earlier, are a special type of consumer cooperative. Another special type is the farmers' cooperatives organized under the Rural Electrification Administration for the local distribution of electric power.

From the standpoint of organization, consumer cooperatives are a modified type of business corporation. As in most other corporations, the owners, or members, hold stock; but control is democratic, because each member has only one vote regardless of how much stock he may own. Moreover, on his stock he receives either no dividends or a limited dividend equivalent to the usual rate of interest. Beyond this, any "earnings" of the cooperative that can be spared are refunded to members in proportion to their purchases and are known as patronage dividends. In theory they represent not profits, but the savings of members on purchases. Cooperatives do not sell goods at cost, but, for several reasons, they sell them at usual market prices. In the first place they do not wish to incur the ill feeling of the owners of other businesses; and even more important, they need funds for working capital, as reserves, for educational activities, and for expansion.

Most of the characteristics of modern consumer cooperatives go back to the early history of the movement. The original cooperative was a grocery store in Rochdale, England, established by a group of weavers in 1844. The principles on which this first group operated are still rather closely followed by modern cooperators. Important among these *Rochdale principles* are the following: (1) membership is open to all; (2) control is democratic; (3) sales are for cash at prevailing prices, and "profits" are refunded to members in proportion to purchases; (4) strict neutrality is maintained on religious and political issues; and (5) returns are allowed on capital, represented by either stock in or loans to the cooperative, but at no more than the legal or current interest rate.

The basic purpose of consumer cooperatives is to reduce the cost of goods to their members by enabling them to keep for themselves the money that would otherwise go as profits to the owners of an ordinary business. In some countries, among them Great Britain and the Scandinavian nations, cooperatives have been very successful and have expanded to the point where they account for a large proportion of all retail trade. In the United States, consumer cooperatives are fairly common, and they have increased greatly in numbers in recent years. Nevertheless, they still do a very small fraction of the total retail business. Possibly the principal reason for this is that the distribution system we already have in this country is highly efficient. Our chain stores make good profits because of low costs and a huge volume of sales, but their profit margins are extremely small, sometimes less than 1 per cent of gross sales. Actually, most cooperatives can really save very little for their members. Such success as they have had in this country is probably based more on the ideological appeal that they have for many people than on any substantial economic benefits to be derived from them. In many cases, also, they serve as centers of social life and recreation.

It should, however, be emphasized that there is nothing communistic nor even, strictly speaking, socialistic about consumer cooperatives. They are private businesses operated for the benefit of their owners just as much as is any other private business. The fact that their ownership is spread among a number of people makes this no less true. Many of our ordinary business corporations have tens of thousands of stockholders, and often no single stockholder owns as much as 1 per cent of the total stock outstanding. Incidentally, cooperatives that become large organizations are likely to have one problem in common with many ordinary business corporations—namely, that it is difficult to prevent real control from slipping away from the rank and file of members or stockholders and falling into the hands of a self-perpetuating "management" group. But insofar as cooperatives can satisfy consumer wants more effectively than other types of business, their growth should strengthen and not weaken our free-enterprise economy. In some cases, cooperatives have developed efficient supermarkets that give their members excellent service.

Consumer cooperatives are not the only type of cooperative enterprise. In this country the most important group of cooperatives consists of those organized by farmers for the purpose of marketing their own products at lower cost. Although *farm cooperatives* have in their organization some similarities to consumer cooperatives, their basic purpose is usually to increase the profits of producers and not to benefit the ultimate purchaser. In some cases, however, they play a dual role and serve the needs of their members not only as producers but also as consumers.

CONSUMER NEEDS AND THE GENERAL WELFARE

Despite the undoubted need for a broader and more effective program of general consumer education, we must recognize that the average individual has many interests and many obligations and that it is neither possible nor worth his while to learn everything about all the goods that at times he considers purchasing. Everyone, to be sure, should try to master some of the rudimentary principles of good buying; but in many cases consumers are best served by having readily available and dependable sources of information. Services such as Consumers Union and Consumers Research help to meet this need. Consumers would also be benefited if goods more commonly carried dependable grades and descriptive labels, and this is a need that could be met to some extent by carefully drawn-up legislation.

Because the consumer is everybody, his economic welfare and that of the whole country are identical, and the only real test of economic progress is a rising consumer standard of living. All attempts to benefit special groups by limiting production and/or maintaining prices are likely to be contrary to the public interest in the long run, because whatever their claims, they are nearly always paid for by the consumer. This applies equally to protective tariffs, high monopoly prices, farm price supports, fair-trade laws, featherbedding practices, and union restrictions on output or the use of materials. If restrictions of this kind were pushed far enough — if *every* group of producers were in a position to restrict output and raise prices for its own benefit — it is obvious that these practices would defeat their own purpose. The net result would be *to raise the prices and restrict the output of everything.* If this should happen, we could not even maintain our present standards of living. Any possibility of raising them would be definitely ended.

Yet policies of this kind have a tendency to keep spreading. The cost to the individual consumer of each action that restricts output or raises price is usually so minor that he does not bother to try to protect his interest. But the benefit to some special group may be great. The benefited group will then fight to put the measure into operation, whereas the public, which pays the cost, remains indifferent. This illustrates again what was said earlier in this chapter — namely, that what is everybody's business tends to be nobody's business.

Fortunately, the productivity of the American economy has risen so rapidly, in spite of obstacles, that consumer purchasing power has also kept rising. It could, however, rise faster if we developed a really powerful consumer movement to protect the public against exploitation by special-interest groups. In spite of our supposed affluence, we still do not have the resources to maintain satisfactory levels of family purchasing power and at the same time to undertake all the slum clearance, pollution control, and other projects that would be socially very desirable.

Terms to Be Understood

budgeting
custom
fashion
conspicuous
  consumption
discount house
fair-trade laws
consumer credit
installment credit

charge account
revolving credit
option account
credit card
"travel and
  entertainment" cards
bank credit cards
installment buying
small-loan company

credit union
the consumer
  movement
food additives
consumerism
consumer
  cooperatives
Rochdale principles
farm cooperatives

Questions for Review and Discussion

1. What four things must the consumer do to get the most for his money?
2. Why is it difficult to organize consumers effectively for the protection of their interests?
3. What is the chief consumer unit? Why?
4. How much control do consumers have over production and prices? Explain.
5. Why was it difficult in 1970 for consumers to get autos with adequate bumpers?
6. What basic difficulties face the consumer in choosing the goods that will best satisfy his wants?
7. Do consumers behave rationally in disposing of their incomes? Explain.
8. Explain the possible gains from budgeting, its limitations, and why some may not think it worthwhile.
9. Show that custom and fashion largely determine not only the kinds but also the quantities of goods that people buy.
10. If you buy a new dress or a new car because your old one is shabby or out of style, is that an example of conspicuous consumption? Why or why not?
11. Is advertising worth its cost to the country? Why or why not? If you think not, what would you suggest doing to improve the situation?
12. What are the principal types of products introduced in recent years to save consumers time and trouble? Do these products raise the cost of living? Why or why not?
13. Would food products be cheaper if they were not packaged? Defend your answer.
14. List as many as you can of the real money-saving opportunities that are available to alert consumers.
15. What important changes have taken place in recent decades in our patterns of consumption?
16. Why do some economists regard consumer credit as a danger spot in our economy?
17. List the principal forms of consumer credit and explain the nature of each.
18. Explain the advantages of bank credit cards; also their dangers, limitations, and costs.
19. If one has the choice, when will it be better to purchase a commodity by bor-

rowing cash, and when will it be better to buy on the installment plan or to use a revolving-credit charge account? Explain fully.

20. List as many practices as you can that aid consumers in getting more for their money.
21. What is meant by the *consumer movement?*
22. Explain the nature of Consumers Research and Consumers Union, and describe the services they provide.
23. In what ways do business enterprises aid consumers in buying wisely?
24. What are Better Business bureaus, and how do they aid consumers?
25. Tell how each of the following protects consumers: (a) the Food, Drug, and Cosmetics Act; (b) the 1958 amendment to this act; (c) the United States Food and Drug Administration; (d) the Federal Trade Commission Act; (e) the Clayton Act; (f) the Meat Inspection Act; (g) the Wool Products Labelling Act; (h) the 1958 legislation concerning prices for automobiles; (i) the Fair Packaging and Labelling Act of 1966; and (j) the Truth in Lending Act of 1968.
26. What officer is the official representative of the consumer in the executive branch of the federal government?
27. Why is the role of government in consumer protection an ambiguous one?
28. Explain the organization, purposes, and policies of consumer cooperatives.
29. How do farm cooperatives differ from consumer cooperatives?
30. Why are policies that benefit special groups at the expense of consumers allowed to continue and even to spread?

For Further Study

American Institute for Economic Research, *Life Insurance and Annuities from the Buyer's Point of View,* Great Barrington, Mass. 01230. Write for latest edition.

Better Business Bureau, *Consumer's Buying Guide,* paperback, New York, Universal Publishing and Distributing Corporation, 1969.

Better Homes & Gardens, ed., *Money Management for Your Family,* paperback, Des Moines, Iowa, Better Homes & Gardens Press, n.d.

Caplowitz, D., *The Poor Pay More: Practices of Low Income Families,* New York, Free Press Paperbacks, 1963.

Consumer Reports Buying Guide, paperback, New York, Doubleday & Company, Inc. Issued annually for Consumers Union.

Consumer Reports Editors, *Consumers Union Report on Life Insurance: A Guide to Planning and Buying the Protection You Need,* paperback, New York, Harper & Row, Publishers, 1968.

Editors of *Changing Times, 99 New Ideas on Your Money, Job, and Living,* paperback, Editors Park, Md., Kiplinger Washington Editors, Inc. Latest edition.

Gordon, Leland, and Stewart M. Lee, *Economics for Consumers,* 5th ed., Princeton, N.J., D. Van Nostrand Company, Inc., 1967.

How to Avoid Financial Tangles, Great Barrington, Mass. 01230, American Institute for Economic Research, 1969, or later edition.

Kohlmeier, Louis M., Jr., *The Regulators: Watchdog Agencies and the Public Interest,* New York, Harper & Row, Publishers, 1969.

Magnuson, Warren J., and Jean Carper, *The Dark Side of the Marketplace,* Englewood Cliffs, N.J., Prentice-Hall, Inc., 1968.

Margolis, Sidney, *How to Make the Most of Your Money,* paperback, Des Moines, Iowa, Meredith Press, 1969.

―――― , *Innocent Consumer vs. the Exploiters,* Pocket Book paperback, New York, Simon and Schuster, Inc., 1968.

Marshall, Robert A., *Before You Buy a House,* paperback, Maplewood, N.J., Hammond, Incorporated, n.d.

Money Management Institute Booklets, covering all important areas of personal and family finances. Are available individually or in a set of twelve. Write to Household Finance Corporation, Prudential Plaza, Chicago, Ill. 60601.

Nader, Ralph, *Unsafe at Any Speed,* Essandess paperback, New York, Simon and Schuster, Inc., 1965.

―――― , Lowell Dodge, and Ralf Hotchkiss, *What to Do with Your Bad Car,* New York, Grossman Publications, 1971.

Smith, Carlton, and Richard Putnam Pratt, *The Time-Life Book of Family Finance,* New York, Time-Life Books, 1969.

Springer, John L., *Consumer Swindlers . . . and How to Avoid Them,* Chicago, Henry Regnery Company, 1970.

Sullivan, George, *The Dollar Squeeze and How to Beat It,* New York, The Macmillan Company, 1970.

Troelstrup, Arch W., *Consumer Problems and Personal Finance,* 3d ed., New York, McGraw-Hill, Inc., 1965.

Veblen, Thorstein, *The Theory of the Leisure Class,* Minerva paperback, New York, Funk & Wagnalls Company, 1967.

Young, James Harvey, *The Medical Messiahs: A Social History of Health Quackery in Twentieth-Century America,* Princeton, N.J., Princeton University Press, 1967. Paperbound copies available from Consumers Union, Mt. Vernon, N.Y., at $2.

Part Four

Political

Organization

and

Social

Problems

Chapter 24

The

Role of

Government

people often disagree violently over the role that *government* should play in society, and this disagreement accounts for many of the political conflicts within a nation and for much of the antagonism between those who support such different ideologies as democracy, fascism, and communism. There are, however, certain basic functions that government must perform in any modern society, and in this chapter we shall be primarily concerned with those functions that are common to all countries. Nevertheless, we cannot entirely ignore either conflicting theories of government or changes that appear to be taking place in the role of government.

CONTRASTING VIEWS OF THE NATURE OF GOVERNMENT

There is an immense area of study, called *political theory,* that deals with controversial opinions on politics and government, and a good deal of it is concerned with the nature of government. Our purpose here is not so much to discuss political theory as to examine the ways and means by which government actually influences human behavior. However, it is helpful to understand at the outset three possible ways of viewing the nature of government: (1) *it is a necessary evil;* (2) *it is a positive good;* (3) *it is an unnecessary evil.*

Government as a Necessary Evil. Nothing is surer than death and taxes, and government imposes the taxes. Moreover, government prohibits us from burying our dead until it issues a burial permit. We cannot be born legitimately unless our parents have paid a government fee and have been married by a person licensed by the government. We may be delivered at birth only by a person who is government approved. Before we are old enough to cross the street alone, government compels us to attend school. Government follows us all through life telling us what we can and cannot do. If we want to drive a car, we must first pass a government examination and buy a government license; then government forbids us to park in convenient places and fines us for exceeding the speed limit. It forces us to stay in school when we want to go to work. (We are told that we are too young to work.) Two or three years later it may take us out of school (when we want to remain) and compel us to enter military service. We cannot buy a package of cigarettes or attend a movie without paying a tax. Before we can become a lawyer, doctor, butcher, baker, or candlestick maker, we must first secure a license from the government. If we earn any substantial amount of money, we must give government a generous share. If we are fortunate enough during our lifetime to accumulate wealth to give to our children, government steps in with an inheritance tax and other rules regarding the settlement of estates. Such activities as these make government the object of complaint and abuse and cause many people to feel that, at best, government is only a necessary evil.

This picture of government is, of course, biased, but it does portray the very essence of government, which is to prohibit, to restrain, to regulate, to compel, and to coerce. Government possesses the authority to pass laws and possesses the power to enforce them with physical violence if necessary. Parents, priests, and employers may cajole and condemn, but only government can legally imprison and put to death. Government is a compelling organization from which there is no escape. It has the power to hurl millions to their death in defense of the homeland or in pursuit of empire. It has power to utilize for its purposes the products of farm and factory. It regulates the affairs of family, church, and economic enterprise in accordance with its conception of public security, morality, and welfare. Of all institutions of social control, government is the most inclusive and the most powerful. Here, indeed, is a power so great that no man can safely ignore it, refuse to understand it, or fail to make efforts to control it.

Government as a Positive Good. Another picture of government can also be painted. Many years ago Supreme Court Justice Oliver Wendell Holmes was asked by a young law clerk: "Don't you hate to pay taxes?" Mr. Holmes is reported to have answered: "No, young man, I like to pay taxes. With taxes I buy civilization."

Some years later, when taxes were much higher, Supreme Court Justice William O. Douglas wrote:

Government is the most advanced art of human relations. It dispenses the various services that the complexities of civilization require or make desirable. It is designed to keep in balance the various competing forces present in any society and to satisfy the dominant, contemporary demands upon it. As a result it serves a high purpose; it is the cohesive quality in civilization.[1]

Former President Franklin D. Roosevelt stated in his Second Inaugural address:

We dedicated ourselves to the fulfillment of a vision—to speed the time when there would be for all the people the security and peace essential to the pursuit of happiness. Instinctively we recognized a . . . need to find through government the instrument of our united purpose to solve for the individual the ever rising problems of a complex civilization. Repeated attempts at their solution without the aid of government had left us baffled and bewildered. . . . We of the Republic sensed the truth that democratic government has innate capacity to protect its people against disasters once considered inevitable, to solve problems once considered unsolvable . . ., to master economic epidemics just as, after centuries of fatalistic suffering, we had found a way to master epidemics of disease. We refused to leave the problems of our common welfare to be solved by the winds of chance, the hurricanes of disaster. . . . The people . . . will insist that every agency of popular government use effective instruments to carry out their will.

Men such as those we have quoted think of government as a *positive good.* They realize there is some truth in Thomas Paine's contention that government is necessary "to supply the defect of moral virtue," to force us to do right when our moral weakness would lead us to injure one another. They do not, however, consider government a "necessary evil," produced by "our wickedness," promoting "our happiness . . . *negatively* by restraining our vices."[2] For them government is more than a "punisher";

---

[1] William O. Douglas, *Being an American,* New York, The John Day Company, 1948, p. 51.
[2] These quotations give the essence of Paine's conception of government as set forth in his famous *Common Sense.*

it is a *promoter of the common good.* It is the proper social instrument for positive action to bring the essentials of the good life to all the people. Government is a positive good, because it does "for the community of people," in the words of Abraham Lincoln, "whatever they need to have done, but cannot do so well for themselves in their separate and individual capacities." It not only restrains the evil in man; it organizes his good will. It not only reduces conflict; it increases cooperation.

Government as an Unnecessary Evil. Another picture of government is given by writers of communist "scripture." Lenin[3] and Stalin,[4] for example, have portrayed government as an *instrument of oppression,* "special machinery for the suppression of one class by another." All capitalist governments, so the argument runs, are tools of the rich used to enforce the exploitation of the poor. Capitalist democracy allows the people "once every few years, to decide which particular representatives of the oppressing class should be in parliament to represent and oppress them!" The task of communists is to seize the government of the state and establish a dictatorship of the proletariat. According to Stalin, "the proletarian state is a machine for the suppression of the bourgeoisie, . . . the dictatorship of the exploited majority over the exploiting minority." Machinery for suppression will be necessary only until the internal and external enemies of communism are converted or destroyed. In general, communist theory pictures government, or at least the coercive powers of government, as an unnecessary evil of our day, to be abolished as soon as possible.[5]

In this respect, communist theory resembles that of the anarchists. They have always considered government to be an unnecessary evil and have advocated the abolition of political authority and all instruments of coercion.

There are elements of truth in all these views of the role government plays in society. Differences of opinion arise in part from differences in governments and in part from the different functions that every government performs. Governments have been oppressive and have exploited the masses; they have at times been almost exclusively concerned with restraining the unruly elements in human society; they have also been used by society to promote by positive means the common good. A rational evaluation of government must be based upon many considerations, and important among these is an examination of the primary functions of government common to all modern societies. But before we discuss these functions, let us try to explain the deep distrust with which many people view all governments.

Distrust of Government. Distrust of government is widespread today, but it was even greater in the past. The American Founding Fathers feared

---

[3] V. I. Lenin, *State and Revolution.* A good edition in English is the revised edition, New York, International Publishers Co., Inc., 1932.

[4] Joseph Stalin, *Foundations of Leninism,* New York, International Publishers Co., Inc., 1939.

[5] See the brief discussion of communism and socialism in Chap. 17.

government, for they believed they had suffered unjustly because of it. History reveals the extent to which governments have been used to perpetuate slavery and serfdom and to promote the interests of a chosen few. Recent history is filled with examples of governments that have enslaved the people, provoked needless wars, and even engaged in wholesale murder. The distrust of government is the result of experience. People fear government for the same reason that they fear the power of nature—it has harmed man. Government in the hands of power-mad men has destroyed freedom and has forced the masses to serve the interests of an absolute monarch, a hereditary aristocracy, a self-chosen elite, a totalitarian dictator, or the supposed rather than the real interests of the "mother" country. Government has been corrupt; it has failed to perform necessary functions; it has wasted the taxpayers' money.

To the extent that democracy has been realized, the fear of government has become less, because in a real democracy the government is the servant of the people or at least of the great majority. Distrust of government has certainly decreased in the democracies, and the tendency for some years has been to increase the powers and functions of government. A proper understanding of the social role of government and the indispensable functions it performs provides an explanation of why even bad government has usually been tolerated and why large numbers of people regard government as the chief instrument for promoting the social welfare.

THE PRIMARY FUNCTIONS OF GOVERNMENT

In every society of any size some form of organized government develops because of the need for an agency capable of exercising overall social control. The role of government can be better understood if attention is given to the specific functions it performs. The average American taxpayer might find his tax load less onerous if he were to make a detailed list of the specific services rendered by his local, state, and national governments. A study of the administrative departments, bureaus, and commissions on each level of government should convince him that he is buying a great deal with his tax dollar.[6]

Government levies taxes, prohibits, regulates, protects, and provides services in order to benefit individuals, groups, and the whole of society. Whether he thinks about it or not, every person every day is affected by the demands of government and by the benefits that it provides. Whenever a citizen leaves home in a car, he drives on streets and roads provided by government; he can enjoy parks set aside by government; he can send his children to government-supported schools at no charge; he can travel abroad on a government-issued passport, and in case of trouble can go

[6] See chart on the government of the United States, p. 709.

"When we overthrow the government, what happens to my compensation check?" (Courtesy George Borg—*Chicago Tribune Magazine*.)

to the consular or diplomatic agents of his government for aid; he can receive help from the government when he is unemployed or disabled; if his house catches fire, he can get help from government-paid firemen; and if he is accused of breaking a law, he can be heard in a court established by government. These are only a few of the ways in which individuals are taxed, controlled, or benefited by government, all for the purpose of promoting the general welfare.

Maintaining Internal Order and External Security. Though the functions of government are many and varied, its basic function is, and always has been, to protect the social order against internal and external enemies. The highest value in every political society—in our age this means every nation—is self-preservation, and the government is the one agency that is equipped to protect a nation against internal disorder and foreign attacks. It alone possesses the power to enforce obedience to the rules of life that the society has established, and it alone has at its disposal all the military might that the nation can provide to repel aggression.

Government, as the guardian of internal social order, employs police, prisons, and courts in its attempts to protect persons, property, rights, and whatever society designates as worthy of preservation. None of our other social institutions could exist without the "domestic tranquillity," the peace and safety, that government provides. Wherever law and order break down, the government is unable to perform its other functions; the people become fearful, and all aspects of society begin to disintegrate. Anarchy is a condition so injurious to society, so detestable to human beings, that, after a period of social confusion, people often welcome as a blessing an absolute monarch or a modern dictator who can restore peace and order. Recognition of this fact led Thomas Hobbes, the seventeenth-century English philosopher, to conclude that government results from a contract among free men desirous of preserving life and of increasing its contentment, "that is to say, of getting themselves out from that miserable condition of war" that necessarily results from the absence of effective government.[7] Most modern nations have eliminated internal warfare and reduced internal violence to such a low level that nearly all the conflicts that arise among their citizens are settled in an orderly and peaceful manner.

A disturbing aspect of American life in recent years has been a rise in the level of internal violence, as evidenced by the increase in violent crimes and by student rebellions and racial riots. The reasons for this violence are complex and are discussed in other chapters. But part of the responsibility must be placed on government, first for its failure to restrain those who take the law into their own hands without regard for the rights of others; and, even more important, for its failure to prevent the development of conditions that give rise to violence.

Protection from external enemies is the most expensive function of government. It also constitutes the greatest unsolved problem of modern political societies. If we include interest payments and veteran's benefits resulting from past wars, expenditures growing out of efforts to provide for the common defense constituted about 60 per cent of all the money spent by our federal government in 1965. In the estimated budget for the fiscal year 1971, the percentage had fallen to 49, but this did not mean that defense expenditures were less; actually, they had risen rather sharply because of the Vietnam War and inflation. Instead, it meant that other types of government spending had risen even faster. Some other nations, including Russia, also spend a large proportion of their tax funds on defense. Yet these huge expenditures give only limited protection against the possibility of becoming involved in a vastly destructive nuclear war. This is a problem that will be discussed in Chapter 32.

Ensuring Justice. The belief in *justice* appears to be universal, and every modern government professes devotion to it. Justice is a concept that involves the relationships of individuals (and groups) both to society and to one another. All governments based on popular support strive to convince the people that they are being treated justly. In fact, justices of the peace, sheriffs, judges, and courts exist in some form almost everywhere, and their main function is to administer justice. *Justice* means different things to different people. No definition has been agreed upon that describes its content, but every society considers it to mean "to every man his due." People the world over have confidence in their government to the extent that it metes out rewards and punishment in accordance with the popular conception of justice. People willingly submit their private disputes for public settlement when they have faith that justice will be done. When government fails to perform this function adequately, and to enforce its decisions, lawlessness begins to spread, and even revolution may result.

[7] Thomas Hobbes, *Leviathan,* New York, E. P. Dutton & Co., Inc., 1950 (Everyman's Library). See Part 2, Chap. 17.

Safeguarding Individual Freedoms. Without government in some sense, there can be no organized, stable society; and without a stable society there can be little real freedom for individuals. The strong would always be exploiting the weak and then struggling with one another. Consequently, even in a dictatorship, government safeguards certain freedoms by maintaining law and order. However, democratic governments have come to accept the defense of individual freedoms as a primary function. The American Declaration of Independence and the French Declaration of the Rights of Man declare "liberty" to be a legitimate object of government. The Constitution of the United States declares that a fundamental purpose of the Union is to "secure the Blessings of Liberty to ourselves and our Posterity." In Britain, after centuries of struggle, the importance of personal freedoms is also fully recognized by government.

But in past times, when modern democracies were in the very early stages of their development, government was often considered to be the enemy of freedom. Faith in government as the defender of individual freedoms has developed slowly over the years, until now in modern democracies there is an increasing trend to look toward government for their protection. Our federal government, for example, has taken action against monopolies, vigilante groups, corrupt political practices, and discrimination against blacks. There are, to be sure, two sides to this picture. Sometimes government regulations unjustly or needlessly restrict personal freedom, and there is always the danger that government may fall under the influence of special interests and fail to reflect the will of the majority. It must not be forgotten that individual freedoms can be safe only when large numbers of individuals, and also organized groups, are dedicated to their defense.

The Regulatory Function of Government. In the growth of modern societies, many institutions and groups have developed to perform various functions. Some of these institutions and groups provide important social services, but often they also have selfish interests that are contrary to the welfare of society. Where this is true, government may find it necessary to regulate their activities. Our great public utility enterprises illustrate this well. Because of the nature of their business, they tend to be monopolies, and, in the past, when they were left to themselves, they often charged excessive prices and gave poor service. Therefore, to protect the public, the government established procedures for controlling them.

Promoting the General Welfare. Government as the agency for overall social control cannot escape the task of promoting the general welfare in a variety of ways that go beyond the functions we have discussed above. The general-welfare activities of government have multiplied many times in recent decades, but governments have always in some degree undertaken by positive means to promote the material well-being of their citizens. Even the governments of antiquity carried on some welfare activities; at times they gave aid to farmers, subsidized other private enterprises, and even controlled prices. The Bible tells how Joseph in Egypt supervised an extensive government program of buying and storing surplus grain to provide food in times of famine. The modern state simply extends and intensifies an ancient function of government.

Welfare activities of government include health services, education, provision of recreational facilities, flood control, social security systems, and various other benefits. Governments furnish these to meet public demands and to increase their own strength. Even oligarchies and dictatorships find it in their interest to provide workers with vacations and recreation, and also with pensions on retirement. People who are deprived of their liberties are less likely to revolt against a government that appears to show consideration for their welfare. In the democracies, where the political system makes public policy more directly responsive to public opinion, government in recent decades has greatly broadened its welfare activities in response to the wishes of an enlarged electorate.

For centuries students of politics have believed that if the masses were given the right to vote they would demand a redistribution of wealth and privileges. In modern democracies this has in fact happened in varying degrees. Wealth and income have been redistributed by such means as progressive income taxes, inheritance taxes, social security benefits, welfare payments, and public housing projects. Just as important, total output and income have been increased by giving individuals freedom and incentives. Greater income has meant more privileges for the common man, and his privileges have been further increased by the welfare activities of government.

SOCIETY, THE STATE, AND GOVERNMENT

Who performs these "primary functions of government" that we have been discussing? Can we distinguish that portion of society we call government from the remainder of society? These questions are not easily answered; moreover, those who have tried to answer them have often disagreed. Because much of the controversy over the proper role of government in society arises from different conceptions of the relationships between society, the state, and government, a rational discussion of political and governmental questions requires some common agreement on the meaning of these terms.

Society. A *society*, it will be recalled, is a group of people who are organized and bound together by established relationships. The word *society* implies all the human relationships that exist within any organized group anywhere in the world. The people of the United States and the entire network of their social relationships constitute our national society. Similarly, the people within each city, and their relationships with one another, constitute an urban society. Each society has a government, but *society* is the all-inclusive term because it includes the government. Government is only one of the primary social institutions. A common government, like common economic, religious, and family institutions, helps to bind a group of people together into a community or society.

The State. A *state* may be legally described as a group of people, living in a definite territory, under a common government, and recognized by other states as possessing *sovereignty*. To be sovereign, a political entity must possess a government with power to rule its people effectively and to fulfill the international obligations of a state. It must possess supreme authority over its citizens and be subordinate to no other government. In this sense the United States is a state but Texas is not, because the latter is not sovereign. However, Norway and Luxembourg possess the legal characteristics of states. There are about 160 sovereign states in the world today that are nominally equal in their legal rights and status. But some states that are nominally sovereign (like Czechoslovakia, the other Russian satellites, and certain very small states) are not really independent.

If the sovereign state possesses supreme authority over all its citizens, who has authority over whom? Do all the people have supreme authority over the state, and hence over themselves? Devotees of democracy want to believe that they do. To be realistic, however, we must admit that the state is always an abstract concept, because it cannot be found in any concrete form other than when it expresses itself through government.

In practice the state is what the society makes it. States vary in character under different social and governmental systems, and certainly communist Russia is not the same kind of state as is the United States. However, all states have this element in common: The people are highly organized for political purposes. In every state there will be found complex political relationships; but because these relationships differ, states likewise differ. Proponents of democracy like to think of the state as merely an agency for carrying out the will of society, or at least the will of a majority of those who compose it. This conception of the state (which is almost identical with the democratic conception of government) makes society superior to the state and thus superior to the government that acts for it. The totalitarian dictator, on the other hand, tends to equate society with the state, the state with the government, and the government with himself; he then proceeds to speak authoritatively for all of society in all of its aspects—religious, economic, and social, as well as political. This produces the totalitarian state, which grants no freedoms to either individuals or institutions if these might interfere with absolute rule.

Government. As we have indicated, the state expresses itself only through government. Government, however, existed long before the sovereign state. In the sense of some institutional arrangement for exercising authority over the whole social group, government is an essential element in all community life. Nomadic tribes had government, though sometimes it may have been rather informal. There was government in the manorial villages of the Middle Ages. The North American Indians had government. Government existed among the natives of inner Africa long before its exploration by the white man. However, the word *government* is not always used with precisely the same meaning.

Government as Social Control. Government is sometimes equated with *social control.* It is said to exist in all social institutions, because they all regulate human behavior. Sometimes this control is exercised by custom and the pressure of public opinion. At other times it is vested in a father, an employer, a Pope, or a board of directors, because orderly group behavior often requires that some should exercise *authority* over others. If government is equated broadly with social control, it becomes necessary to distinguish between *private* and *public government—private government* referring to the controls exercised by all social institutions other than the state, and *public government* referring to the activities of the state.

Public Government. Ordinarily, we reserve the term *government* for *public government. Used thus, it refers to political authority that is exercised on the entire public, whether tribe, city, or nation, through designated channels, such as a tribal chief, a king, or a parliament.* Even used in this sense, *government* may still have different meanings. Sometimes we employ it to refer to the institutional framework within which controls operate. Sometimes we use it to refer collectively to those who occupy public office, such as executives, legislators, judges, police, administrators, and all other bureaucrats. This usage is convenient, for these are the people who exercise governmental authority and perform the "primary functions of government." Sometimes we employ *government* in a narrower sense to refer to the legislators and government officials who represent the party in power. Thus we speak of the English Conservative government or of the Republican or Democratic government.

Various theories have been presented as to the origins of government and the state. In the seventeenth and eighteenth centuries a very influential one was the *social-contract theory,* associated with the names of the English philosophers Thomas Hobbes and John Locke. This theory held that originally people lived in a "state of nature" free from restrictions. However, as society developed, in order to protect the interests of all, it became necessary for people by deliberate agreement to create a government and select a ruler, who thus became a party to the contract. The social-contract theory seems to have been an imaginative attempt, with little basis in fact, to rationalize the existence of government. Viewed more realistically, government and the state seem to have developed gradually out of the need for introducing order into the relationships of human beings living in groups, especially when these groups attained considerable size.

The Relationship of Government to Other Social Institutions. Even in the democracies, where the belief prevails that government authority should be limited, the government of the state is by far the most powerful of all social institutions. It possesses a monopoly of extreme physical coercion, and it has taken over countless functions and responsibilities that once resided in the family, the church, or business enterprises. But though government today is in a position to regulate and control all other social institutions, it is in turn "controlled" by them. The beliefs and attitudes of people, and the ways they behave in the family, the church, and business enterprises will determine the kind of government they develop; and often the expansion of government functions results from the failure of other institutions to meet social needs.

POLITICS, POLITICAL POWER, AND THE POLITICIAN

Government is people, and the people in government are *politicians.* Government represents *political power,* and the officials who carry on government or the party leaders to whom they are loyal possess most of the political power in society. He who desires to understand the role of government in society must understand *politics,* political power, and the politician.

In its broadest meaning, *politics* is the science or art of government, *but in a narrower and more common sense it refers to the activities involved in organizing, supporting, or controlling political parties; in attempting to win elections; and in seeking by various means to influence governmental policies.* The study of politics is almost exclusively concerned with the study of power and the powerful. This is illustrated daily in the newspaper or news broadcast where, in a few words, the reporter explains who got what and when and how, or who wants what and how he intends to get it. This is the interesting game of politics, often played for high stakes and played by people whose motives are not necessarily selfish but whose determination to "win the fight" is pronounced.

Political power, the basic concept in the study of politics, is one form of social power. Physical power is energy or the capacity to do work. Social power is influence or the capacity to control the behavior of others. A movie star often possesses social power, which is manifested by the number of people who copy her hairdo or dress style. The religious leader often demonstrates his social power by recruiting followers and securing desired behavior. All forms of social power may be directed into political channels for political ends. *Political power is social power used for political purposes—that is, power used to influence the selection of public officials or public policies.* When the Pope asked the Italian electorate not to vote for communist candidates, he was attempting to exercise political power. The movie stars who campaign for political candidates are trying to convert their social power into political power. But political power is so closely related to other forms of social power that a clear line of demarcation is hard to draw.

Political power, like other forms of social power, expresses relationships between people. There are always the influential and the influenced. A power wielder, such as the late President Kennedy, can express his views

47. Televised News-Conference. President Nixon recognizes one of four reporters seeking to ask questions. (Courtesy Wide World Photos.)

on a proposed law, and millions of people will be ready to support him. The political boss of a large city may hold no public office, but his decree concerning the official attitude toward burlesque shows or gambling is usually followed by police and other public officials. But such power wielders as these cannot ignore the wishes of their followers. The current of influence flows in both directions. A relationship exists that is considered beneficial to both leader and followers. In this relationship, consent and coercion are usually blended in varying amounts.

Political power is possessed by groups as well as by individuals. The ability of labor to influence legislation has increased many times as a result of the organization of labor unions. All the so-called pressure groups are power groups; they can exert pressure in proportion to their power. Nations themselves illustrate this very well. The United States and the Soviet Union are giant *powers;* they are causal agents in world politics; they cause things to happen. Most of the other nations are the followers. Yet here, too, influence works in both directions, for neither the United States nor Russia can entirely disregard the desires of the nations from whom they hope to receive support. In international relations, political power depends a great deal on military power or supposed military power; the ability to coerce plays a large role.

Political leaders within a nation acquire their power through personality, political skill, organization, hard work, and success in acquiring other forms of social power. Political skill includes the capacity to understand what the people want and the ability to convince them that a certain political leader can obtain it for them if they will elect him and follow his policies. The successful politician almost invariably has the capacity to compromise conflicting interests; he knows how to work with others; he is a master salesman and an able diplomat. He keeps in touch with public opinion, seeking both to understand it and to influence it. One of the methods that recent Presidents have used both to sound out public opinion and to influence it are periodic news conferences with leading newsmen in which the newsmen ask questions and the President answers them. Recently, these conferences have been televised so that people all over the world can watch them and listen in.

The particular qualifications required of a politician for his success also depend a great deal on existing economic and social conditions. For instance, if conditions in 1932 had been the same as in 1928, Herbert Hoover would probably have won the election over Franklin D. Roosevelt. In any case, political power is seldom acquired without much hard work and the determination to win, because political success depends considerably on gaining the confidence of others and their willing and loyal support.

The politician is indispensable to government. His job is not easy, and only the strong can bear the abuse he receives. He is, however, the compromiser, whose work enables conflicting interest groups to dwell together in reasonable harmony and safety. Moreover, he provides us with the emotional satisfaction of a fierce battle without bullets and with a scapegoat to blame for our misfortunes. In victory and in defeat the politican performs an important service. It is appropriate that we should attempt to improve the service he renders and to reduce its cost. We should recognize that one thing the country needs is more and better politicians, more citizens of ability who are dedicated to the public welfare and who take an active part in politics. Let us also recognize that although some of our present politicians may be clever, self-seeking scoundrels, many of them are able, patriotic public servants. If that were not true, American democracy would long ago have been replaced by some other political system.

Lord James Bryce, the great English political scientist, asserted that all goverments are by the few, regardless of whether they claim to rule in the name of one, the few, or the many. Though it must be qualified, this assertion contains much truth. The *political elite* in every nation constitute only a small fraction of the population. The political social pyramid is steep, and it has room for very few at the top. Whether we look at democratic America or dictatorial Russia, those with great political power are comparatively few in number. Democratic theory tends to obscure this concentration of power in the hands of the political elite by its insistence that political power belongs to the people. The fact is sometimes overlooked that this power is delegated to, and exercised by, a very few who occupy key public positions.

There is, however, a vast difference between the nature of political power in a dictatorship like Russia or Red China and in a democracy like the United States. In Russia, once the political elite or its top members have achieved power, they are self-perpetuating. They may, at times, have power struggles within their own group, but they do not need to submit their leadership to the test of free elections. They must, to be sure, have loyal support, but such support from a small and well-organized minority may be quite sufficient to keep them in power. In a democracy, however, the political leaders in power always have competition from the political leaders of opposition parties, and the voters in recurrent elections decide by majority vote which group is to control the government. In that sense, as long as elections are really free, government in a democracy is government of the people and not of the few. The goal in a democracy is to keep those who govern responsible to the governed and sensitive to their needs and wishes.

Terms to Be Understood

government	state	social-contract theory
political theory	sovereignty	politics
authority	private government	political power
social control	public	politician
justice	government	political elite

Questions for Review and Discussion

1. What three different attitudes toward government are described in the text? Which do you accept? Why?
2. Why did the American Founding Fathers distrust the power of government?
3. Explain the relation of private government and public government to government as social control.
4. State five primary functions of government. Are these all interrelated? Do they overlap one another? Explain.
5. Why can taxes sometimes be the wisest means of purchasing services?
6. What is the relationship between society, the state, and the government?
7. How are political institutions related to other social institutions?
8. List the qualifications you believe a politician should have.
9. Justify the statement What America needs is 150 million politicians.

For Further Study

Almond, Gabriel A., *Perspectives on Political Development,* Boston, Little, Brown and Company, 1970.

Barker, Ernest, *Reflections on Government,* Galaxy paperback, New York, Oxford University Press, 1967.

Bell, David B. J., Karl W. Deutsch, and Seymour Lipset, *Issues in Politics and Government,* paperback, Boston, Houghton Mifflin Company, 1970.

Dragnich, Alex N., et al., *Government and Politics,* New York, Random House, Inc., 1966.

Ebenstein, William, *Modern Political Thought: The Great Issues,* New York, McGraw-Hill, Inc., 1960.

Friedrich, Carl, *Introduction to Political Theory,* New York, Harper & Row, Publishers, 1967.

Hayek, Friedrich A., *The Constitution of Liberty,* Chicago, University of Chicago Press, 1960.

——, *The Road to Serfdom,* Phoenix paperback, Chicago, University of Chicago Press, 1955.

Hobbes, Thomas, *Leviathan,* paperback, Baltimore, Penguin Books, Inc., 1969.

Locke, John, *Of Civil Government, Second Essay,* paperback, Chicago, Henry Regnery Company, 1960.

——, *Two Treatises on Government,* edited by Peter Laslett, paperback, New York, Cambridge University Press, 1960.

Merriam, Charles E., *Political Power,* Collier paperback, New York, The Macmillan Company, 1964.

Paine, Thomas, *Common Sense, and Other Political Writings,* paperback, Indianapolis, Ind., Bobbs-Merrill Company, Inc., 1953.

Ranney, Austin, *The Governing of Men: An Introduction to Political Science,* rev. ed., New York, Holt, Rinehart and Winston, Inc., 1966.

Chapter 25

Democracies

and

Dictatorships

perhaps the problem that most concerns people today is that of maintaining peace without sacrificing freedom. The causes of World War I were many and complex, but in the democracies chief blame was placed on the autocratic empire builders who dominated the government of imperial Germany. After World War I it was the developing fascist dictatorships that posed the great threat to peace; and since the defeat of the major fascist powers in World War II, they have been replaced as a threat to peace by the communist dictatorships, in particular Soviet Russia and Red China.

Former President Woodrow Wilson once

declared that American participation in World War I was for the purpose of making the world "safe for democracy." World War II was described by Franklin Roosevelt and Winston Churchill as a life-and-death struggle between democracy and despotism, and an Allied victory was sought as a guarantee of the Four Freedoms to all peoples. But after both wars, new threats to freedom and democracy developed. Following their victory in World War II, the democracies almost immediately became involved in a *cold war* with communism, as represented chiefly by their former ally, Russia. This cold war still continues and from time to time has been considerably enlivened by "hot" wars of limited scope in such countries or areas as China, Korea, India, Malaysia, the Congo, Vietnam, and the Near East. In all these struggles, the democracies have been combating the threat to the Free World posed by communist dictatorships and their professed goal of world revolution.

Democracy Versus Dictatorship. Perhaps the most significant classification of governments today is into *democracies* and *dictatorships*. However, in our present discussion, we shall not be especially interested in temporary military dictatorships of the type designed only to carry a country over a period of disorder and confusion. The dictatorships with which we are primarily concerned are those that are based on an ideology, such as communism or fascism, that is designed to perpetuate their existence. When a country "chooses" between dictatorship and democracy, it is deciding a very fundamental issue: Shall government be despotic, autocratic, dictatorial, totalitarian, arbitrary, without adhering to clearly defined principles of law? Or shall government be popular, democratic, free, limited, constitutional, and subject to law? Shall the great political decisions be made by a few men behind closed doors? Or shall important public policies be determined by public opinion formed through the free play of competing ideas freely expressed? Shall individuals exist for the sake of the state? Or shall the state exist to serve the needs of individuals? Shall the government be the servant or the master of men? *Dictatorship* as a principle of government is in many important respects diametrically opposed to democracy.

The purpose of this chapter is to compare and contrast democracies and dictatorships, but a word of caution is appropriate at the outset. No government or society is perfect. Democracies are not completely democratic, and dictatorships are not always completely dictatorial. Though we tend to speak in absolute terms, we would be wise to remember that differences are often a matter of degree. Most of the nations of the world are neither perfect democracies nor absolute dictatorships, but fall somewhere between these two extremes.

Different Concepts of "Democracy." *Democracy* is a word that means different things to different people. To Plato it meant mob rule, or anarchy. To some people today it means capitalism; to others it means socialism; to still others it means the Russian brand of communism. Before the nineteenth century there were few people in the world who considered democracy desirable. But today comparatively few people will admit opposition to democracy. Now almost every important nation, including communist Russia, claims to be democratic. In Russian terminology, communism is the only true form of democracy. Even the Red Chinese, who have some sharp disagreements with the Russians, call their state the People's Republic of China; but to most Americans a *republic* is a representative democracy whose officers are chosen by the people in free elections. According to the communists, all capitalist nations are *oligarchies*—that is to say, *states ruled by aristocratic or wealthy minorities.* On the other hand, most people in the Western democracies are quite certain that the communist states are dictatorships. Some people in the West even go so far as to maintain that democracy and any form of extensive governmental interference in the economy are, in the long run, incompatible—that we can have one or the other, but not both. On the other hand, numerous adherents of democracy believe that its professed ideals can be realized only through more governmental regulation designed to effect greater economic and social equality.

The above facts indicate that scarcely any word in current usage has more shades of meaning than are at times ascribed to the word *democracy.* As one writer suggests, the word "has undergone a kind of political beatification, in the sense that just about everyone in the modern world apparently believes that democracy is noble and good and that its enemies are ignoble and bad."[1]

Obviously, *democracy* cannot be defined in any precise way that will satisfy everyone. However, we can clarify some of the concepts and opinions involved. For instance, we can distinguish between democracy as a form of government and *democracy as a theory of economic and social relationships.* We can describe the characteristics that the West considers to be included under the term *democracy;* and, having done this, we can distinguish between profession and practice and between democratic ideals and democratic realities.

ESSENTIALS OF POLITICAL DEMOCRACY

Though in modern usage we apply the terms *democratic* or *undemocratic* to a wide range of social relationships, in this chapter we are primarily concerned with democracy as a political concept, and especially as a form of government. Communists are likely to call a government *democratic* if it supposedly governs for the good of the people, even though they do not control it. To communists, *democracy* appears to mean government *for* the people. In the West, however, it means government both *for* and *by* the people. It is a form of government in which the su-

---

[1]Austin Ranney, *The Governing of Men,* New York, Holt, Rinehart and Winston, Inc., 1958, p. 171.

preme power is vested in the people and exercised by them or their elected representatives under a system of free elections.

Popular Sovereignty. In the strict meaning of the word, democracy as a *form* of government denotes government by the many, as opposed to government by *one* or the *few*. But in deciding whether a government is really democratic, we must consider whether *popular sovereignty* prevails in fact or only in form. Although 99 per cent of the eligible voters in Russia may go to the polls and vote "yes" for public officials, the Soviet Union is not democratic. The only candidate for office to appear on a ballot is the one already selected by the elite of the Communist Party. Thus, universal manhood or adult suffrage is not sufficient to make a political system democratic if the voters have no real choice between candidates.

The essential requisite for political democracy is that the people (not a king, an elite, or a class) are ultimately sovereign. As James Madison said in *The Federalist,* a democracy "is a government which derives all its power directly or indirectly from the great body of the people" and is administered by persons subject to popular control. Not only are the people the source of all political power; they are the master of any government they establish to serve their interests. The "consent of the governed" means more than passive acquiescence; it means the power to control. In order for the people to control the government, there must be (1) freedom of speech, (2) effective legislative organs to represent the people, and (3) free elections by means of which the people may change the government by legal and hence peaceful methods. If we are to protect freedom of speech and free elections, some things must not be tolerated. These include attempts to *coerce* individuals by threats, by violence, or by other methods that interfere illegally with the normal and proper activities of people. Democracy can operate successfully only when order and law are reasonably well maintained in order to protect human rights.

Modern democrats consider freedom or liberty to be an essential element in democracy. But popular sovereignty means, in effect, majority rule, and there is always some tension or conflict between this and the ideal of individual liberty. There is no way of completely resolving this conflict, but if the ruling majority are reasonably tolerant, they will attempt to limit personal freedom only in situations where such freedom would seriously interfere with the freedom and rights of others.

Liberty, Constitutional Government, and Democracy. Historically, *liberalism,* with its emphasis on personal freedoms, preceded modern democracy. In Britain, liberal government may be said to have had its beginnings with the Magna Charta and its great development in the seventeenth, eighteenth, and nineteenth centuries. The American Constitution of 1789 provided for liberal government, but it did not provide for universal suffrage. Liberalism in politics and economics slowly emerged with the rise of the industrial aristocracy and the middle class. Constitutional government was established, and a wide range of individual liberties was guaranteed. Considerable emphasis was placed upon property rights and upon freedom from governmental interference in economic activities.

Liberal government means *constitutional government;* the rulers are limited by a basic law of the land. Liberal government guarantees basic individual rights and freedoms, such as habeas corpus, jury trial, freedom of speech, religion, and assembly, and freedom to form a political opposition. British and American governments in the late eighteenth and early nineteenth centuries were liberal, but they were not democratic in the modern meaning of the term. They were governments controlled by a privileged minority. Universal adult male suffrage was not attained in Britain until the 1880's; America achieved it for white males in the 1840's, but not for females until 1920. Blacks were guaranteed the right to vote by the Fourteenth Amendment to the Constitution of the United States, adopted in 1868, but many years passed before most were actually allowed to exercise this right in the South. Even today, with the aid of recent federal legislation, it is doubtful whether the struggle to give all Southern blacks the privilege of voting has been completely won.

Thus we see that a government may be liberal without being democratic in the modern sense. However, the liberal tradition in economics and politics was certainly an important force in the rise of democracy. Constitutional monarchies and liberal aristocracies (both republican and monarchical) "grew" into the democracies of the nineteenth and twentieth centuries; and the liberal tradition—the concept of constitutional government and extensive individual freedoms—is considered an essential part of Western democracy.

Government by the People and for the People. Political democracy today means, above all, that government must be by the people and for the people and that the whole political process must be permeated with the spirit of freedom. If the government is *by* the people, then the people must control it; if it is *for* the people, it must serve *their* interests. The nature of the participation must be characterized by freedom. The people must be free to hold opinions, to express opinions, to organize into interest groups, to propagandize for objectives. In short, they must be free to decide what their interests are. They do not want a Hitler or a Mao Tsetung, a Politburo, or a political boss to decide what is good for them and to give it to them whether they like it or not. Believers in democracy will not object if an Indira Gandhi, a Richard Nixon, or a Georges Pompidou expresses an opinion as to what will promote the general welfare, but they insist on the freedom to oppose the policies that may be recommended. They believe communist Russia is a dictatorship even if the people approve of the government policies, because the people are not free to originate the ideas, to work for their adoption, or to oppose them. Those who support democracy insist that there are two sides to almost every question, and they demand that the press, the church, and the various interest groups be free to present both sides. They believe, in the words of

48. Man in Motion. President Nixon and Housing and Urban Development Secretary George Romney in Washington, D.C., ghetto area. (*Newsweek* photo by Wally McNamee. Copyright Newsweek 1970.)

Justice Holmes, that "the best test of truth is the power of thought to get itself accepted in the competition of the market." The logical corollary of this was stated by Thomas Jefferson when he said, "Error of opinion may be tolerated where reason is left free to combat it."

Government *for* the people implies that government should serve the common interests of the people, of *all* the people, and that the benefits of government should not be restricted to any one class or group. Today governments universally—fascist, communist, and democratic alike—profess to serve the common interests of all. No longer is it considered proper to operate government in the interest primarily of royalty or of a landed or financial aristocracy.

A strong appeal of communism is its insistence that government should serve the masses. To the communists, however, this means everybody, because theoretically under communism no privileged class is permitted to exist. But the individual must subordinate his personal interests to the common good, which is presumed to reside in the theories and programs of the communist party. Modern democrats do not insist on removing all class distinctions, because in large human societies that is not possible; but they do maintain that government should serve equally the interests of all groups—the wealthy and the poor, the rural and the urban dweller, the employer and the employee. The distinguishing characteristic of democracy in this connection is its increasing insistence that various interest groups should be free to express their desires and to attempt to achieve them by political means. Liberal democracy manifests a high degree of realism in recognizing that society contains conflicting interest groups and that the so-called common interest is most likely to be arrived at by discussion and compromise.

Other Characteristics of Liberal Democracy. Perhaps the greatest distinction between liberal democracy and dictatorship lies in the emphasis of democracy upon individual and private liberty for all the people. Modern democracy is *limited government*. As individuals and in private associations (labor unions, churches, political parties, and the like), the people have liberties that in theory may not be taken away. Among these liberties are such essential characteristics of political democracy as, (1) the right periodically to elect or reject the government; (2) the right to mobilize public opinion against the government; and (3) the right to demand that government operate within the law rather than above it. Care is taken to surround the rights of the individual with special safeguards (such as *due process of law*), and efforts are made to limit the power of the government and to keep it fully responsible to the people.

The methods of liberal democracy are as follows: (1) Conflicting opinions on public policy are presented to the electorate by discussion, debate, and exhortation. Freedom of expression gives an opportunity for all significant opinions to reach the potential voter. (2) Following the presentation of arguments, public policy is determined by the peaceful and orderly process of voting. (3) Once public policy has been determined by majority support, the minority in opposition abide by the decision. If sufficient concessions have been made to minority opinion, the issue may never be raised again. It is not uncommon, however, for yesterday's minority to begin today to agitate by peaceful means for a change in the newly established policy. Tomorrow they may be the majority; by this process, labor laws have been changed, constitutional amendments have been made and cancelled (for example, the Prohibition Amendment in America), Supreme Court decisions have been reversed, and one political party has followed another into office.

Key words that indicate important aspects of the democratic method are *free discussion, accommodation* or *compromise, moderation, tolerance* and *reconciliation*. If these characteristics are assumed to exist to a sufficient degree, the definition of *democracy* as *majority rule* is perhaps acceptable. But democracy really means more than majority rule, for in the absence of these characteristics a majority can be just as tyrannical as any absolute monarch or modern dictator. Democracy denies that the end justifies the means. *It holds that no goal, however desirable, is worth the price of sacrificing democratic methods.*

DEMOCRATIC CONCEPT OF THE INDIVIDUAL

Every philosophical, social, and political system is based upon certain assumptions concerning the nature of man, and no political system can be understood without a knowledge of its conception of man and of his relationship to society and government. Democratic assumptions concerning the nature of man are worlds apart from those made by dictatorships.

They cannot all be scientifically demonstrated, but they are part of the democratic faith and the democratic ideal. In the absence of these assumptions, democracy could not operate successfully, for no other system of government puts so much faith in the average man or depends so much on him for its success. Democracy demands that the common people exercise sovereign authority over themselves, maintain freedom, and employ the judgment needed to secure the blessings of good government.

Rationality and the Democratic Way of Life. Democratic theory assumes that man is capable of developing a culture in which individuals will have learned to listen to discussion and argument, and in which they will try to discover the truth by a rational weighing of the evidence. It assumes that a human society is possible in which the common man will realize that no one can get all he wants from government, and that it is therefore in his interest to make compromises. In a successful democracy every important group must be willing to make such concessions to the interests of others as are necessary. As Carl Becker has said, democracy has faith in the capacity of man "to achieve the good life by rational and humane means."

Equality. Democratic theory holds that all men should be regarded as equal, not in ability or in achievement, but in legal status and in their right to seek the good life. It does not insist that people are equal in beauty, brawn, and brains, in money and morals, or in power and prestige; but it does assert that all men are equal in the sight of God and before the law. It may even be said that the basic assumption underlying democratic government is that all—or at least most—citizens are potentially capable of reaching wise political decisions. It follows, therefore, that all men should be given equal opportunities to participate in the political process: to vote, to hold office, to have opinions, and to strive to make their opinions prevail. No individual group is regarded as having a monopoly of political wisdom. Equality implies that public laws shall apply equally to all and that they shall be impartially administered.

A sharp difference of opinion has prevailed for some time as to whether *democratic equality* means merely *legal and political equality* or whether it necessarily implies *social and economic equality.* In practice, the debate has been partially resolved by compromising on the ideal of *equality of opportunity,* because there seems to be an inherent contradiction between *individual freedom* and *perfect equality.* Any attempt to achieve a flat level of economic, social, and intellectual equality would not only fail but would destroy fundamental freedoms. On the other hand, there has been an increasing awareness of the limits placed on freedom by great inequalities in social and economic status. The result has been a tendency to strive for greater equality of opportunity through free public education, a greater voice for labor in economic decisions, and the elimination of racial, religious, and ethnic discrimination. The democratic goal is to reduce social barriers to a minimum so that the individual may be free to realize his potentialities to the fullest, regardless of the circumstances of his birth. However, it must not be forgotten that freedom is always relative, never complete or absolute; and that it is no more possible to remove all social restrictions on human behavior than it is to remove all physical limitations.

The democratic ideal of equality has developed considerably since the Declaration of Independence and has played an important role in eliminating slavery, in expanding educational opportunities, and in stimulating efforts to eliminate extreme poverty. Its work is still unfinished and necessarily always will be, but the widespread sharing of respect and power that democracy implies depends on a wide distribution of economic goods and the means of intellectual enlightenment. A closer approach to equality of opportunity will bring closer to full realization the ideal of popular control of government and should improve the quality of popular political decisions. As the middle class expands, the chances for effective democratic government increase.

Primacy of the Individual. Democratic philosophy and democratic government put primary emphasis upon the dignity and worth of the individual. Government and society are considered to exist for the individual. The best organization of society—the best form of government—is regarded as the one that enhances the dignity of the individual and provides for the fullest and richest development of his personality. The individual is considered to be the primary unit, whose interests should be served by all social institutions. Individuals are not to be considered as *means;* they are *the ends,* for which all else exists.

The primary values of liberal democracy are freedom for and respect for the individual personality, and it is these that provide the basis for resolving the apparent contradictions between other democratic values. [2] For example, freedom and equality are permitted and promoted insofar as they create the best environment for the development of individual personality. Freedom that disrupts social order is prohibited, because order in society is necessary for the fullest exercise of the kind of freedom that promotes the development of wholesome personality. Freedoms for individuals or groups that seriously limit the freedom of the majority are curtailed, because the goal is as much freedom as possible for all, in order that all may lead full and satisfying lives. A dead level of social equality is not enforced, because such enforcement would destroy the individual freedom required for personality development.

Democracies may at times have exaggerated the value of *individualism* and failed to give full recognition to the value of *social cooperation* for the common good. But the world of today appears to be in no danger of exaggerating the importance of individualism. The doctrine of laissez faire, which opposed almost all government regulation of business, is dead; and in all democracies the general welfare functions of government

---

[2] Cf. James A. Corry, *Elements of Democratic Government,* New York, Oxford University Press, 1951, Chap. 2, especially pp. 22–27.

have substantially increased. In a world in which many nations are glorifying the state and tending to completely subordinate the individual, the democratic emphasis upon the value, freedom, and dignity of the individual personality serves as a powerful bulwark to protect the social progress made by Western man through centuries of struggle.

FORMS OF DEMOCRACY

The fundamental requirements of democracy are not to be confused with any precise type of governmental organization. There is common agreement among students of government that political democracy exists in many forms. It may be *direct* (as in a New England town meeting, which every citizen can attend) or *representative* (as it must be in all units with large populations). It may be *presidential* (as in the United States) or *parliamentary* (as in Britain, Canada, and Italy). It may be *unitary* (as in Britain and France) or *federal* (as in Canada and the United States). It may exist where there is either a *written* or an *unwritten constitution;* but there must in some sense be a constitution or fundamental law that the government respects. It may exist in a *republic* (as in the United States and France) or in a *constitutional monarchy* (as in Sweden and Britain). [3]

Democracy Under Capitalism and Under Socialism. There is widespread disagreement as to whether democracy is possible in both *capitalist* and *socialist* societies. The socialists in Western countries believe that democracy, to be fully successful, must be more than a political system. It must also result in the reduction if not the abolition of special privileges and of inequalities of wealth and income; and they believe that this can best be accomplished through socialization of a large part of the means of production. On the other hand, the modern supporters of capitalism think that the general welfare can best be promoted by a system of free enterprise. They believe that such a system is more productive than a socialized economy would be and that under it not only will average standards of living be higher but also there will be a greater economic margin for meeting the problems of poverty and for improving education and other essential public services. They also believe that socialism is "undemocratic" because it greatly restricts individual freedom in the economic sphere. Furthermore, most defenders of capitalism believe or fear that socialism is not compatible with political democracy. They think that a government completely responsible for both the basic industries and the political activities of a country would become so unwieldy that it would be unable to solve its problems by democratic processes. Sooner or later some political leader would seize dictatorial powers either for his personal glory or in an attempt to restore order and efficiency.

[3] See Chapter 26 for an explanation of the terms used in this paragraph.

The disagreement between capitalists and socialists arises in part from the fact that the former tend to emphasize freedom while the latter tend to be more concerned with equality.

TYPES OF DICTATORSHIPS

Dictatorships, like democracies, come in many varieties. Antiquity had authoritarian rulers in the clan, tribe, city-state, and empire. The names of some of the great Roman dictators are well known: Julius Caesar, Augustus, and Marcus Aurelius. The short-lived and very limited democracy in the Greek city-states was replaced by dictatorships under men like Pisistratus, the Athenian tyrant. The medieval kings and emperors were not really dictators, because they shared so much of their power with the feudal lords and the Catholic Church; however, they were not responsible to the people, though they were regarded as bound by custom and feudal law. The absolute monarchies that emerged from the disintegration of feudalism in the Middle Ages constituted the modern type of authoritarian rule before the emergence in the twentieth century of fascism and communism. Like the twentieth-century dictatorships, these absolute monarchies were marked by arbitrary rule, which at times tended to become irresponsible. Nevertheless, many of their rulers provided "popular" or "benevolent" government. Unlike most contemporary dictatorships, the absolute monarchies were fairly stable, because usually one hereditary ruler followed another without incident and without introducing any very basic changes in society.

In the twentieth century various types of dictatorships have developed in accordance with different conditions in different countries. The two basic types are the *totalitarian* and the *nontotalitarian.* Of these, the totalitarian dictatorships are much the more important. They have been generally classified as either *communist* or *fascist;* But this is somewhat misleading because communism and fascism are not really different types of government. Rather, they are different systems of social, economic, and political theory that have produced totalitarian governments of a very similar character. The differences are largely matters of detail and of ideology, but the ideological differences are of some importance, as shown by the fact that fascism was originally established to combat communism. They are not, however, as great as appears on the surface. Both communism and fascism claim to be seeking the greatest good of a nation and its people. But both put all power in the hands of a dictator and a ruling elite, both greatly restrict personal liberty, and both are willing to resort to force, if needed, to achieve their ends.

Fascism and Nazism. *Nazism* is a variant of *fascism,* and, as movements of the extreme "right," they are so similar as to merit being grouped together under the common label of *fascism.* The ideologies of both, as typified by Nazi Germany and Fascist Italy in the 1930's, were *totalitarian* in that they emphasized the supreme value of the state and the complete subordination of individuals and other social institutions to the supposed welfare of the state. Both denied the traditional democratic values of popular sovereignty, equality, freedom, individualism, and constitutionalism; and both emphasized obedience, discipline, and the unquestioned authority of a ruling hierarchy. Both advocated the preservation of private property, and both regulated private property and the whole economy to promote the power and prestige of the state. Nazi Germany, however, was more totalitarian than Fascist Italy. Nazi ideology emphasized the superiority of the "Nordic race," and this *racism* with its violent anti-semitism was not characteristic of Mussolini's regime in Italy. Hitler resurrected the old German tribal gods as a substitute for Christianity, whereas Mussolini accepted the Catholic Church as one of the traditional props for his new Italy. Of the two, Nazism was more strongly emotional, antirational, antiliberal, fanatical, ruthless, and barbaric.

Communism. Communist ideology, as interpreted by Russian and Chinese leaders of today, claims to accept the fundamental democratic values of liberty and equality but maintains that they do not exist in capitalist countries and that they can never be realized except in a classless society. *Communism,* they hold, must forcibly destroy economic inequality in order to produce the *classless society.* In the classless society, men will live in complete harmony. The state—or at least its coercive functions —will eventually "wither away," and all men will then enjoy perfect liberty and equality. Such is the professed faith of communism. The present antagonism between Russia and China stems partly from historic conflicts of national interests, including conflicting territorial claims, and also from the fact that the Chinese profess to adhere to the true doctrines of communism and accuse the Russians not only of adopting some capitalist practices but also of making concessions to the capitalist nations and even of conspiring with the United States against the interests of China.

In practice, however, the communist state exhibits many of the characteristics of the ruthless fascist dictatorships. The elite at the top of the hierarchy enjoy all the privileges of the wealthy in capitalist countries, and the state shows no signs of withering away. With all the emotional fervor of a newly founded religion, the communists have attempted to destroy the "bourgeois heretics" who believe in Buddhism, Christianity, capitalism, democratic socialism, or anything else that the communist heirarchy places on the "subversive" list. In practice, the average citizen has little protection against seizure by the secret police or against arbitrary punishment on unfounded charges.

Nontotalitarian Dictatorships. Different social and cultural traditions largely determine the different patterns that dictatorships reveal in various countries. Thus the Japanese totalitarian military dictatorship that planned and fought World War II differed considerably in its ideology and organization from the dictatorships in Germany and Italy. The present dictatorships of Marcelo Caetano in Portugal and Francisco Franco in Spain still retain fascist characteristics, but it is doubtful if today they should be classed as *totalitarian*. They do not emphasize fascist ideology as did Hitler and Mussolini nor do they impose such tight controls over business and citizens. Franco has even officially announced the restoration of the monarchy after his retirement or death and has designated Prince Juan Carlos to become the future king. But before World War II, Franco's dictatorship was definitely fascist and totalitarian.

A general type of dictatorship, of which there are many variants, developed in the nineteenth century in the Latin American presidential-type republics. It has been called *Caesarism, military dictatorship,* and *caudillo,* or *chieftain dictatorship.* It is autocratic and dictatorial, and it tolerates no opposition from press or party. However, it does not attempt to control the total life of the citizens, and it seldom employs systematic propaganda to secure the support of the masses; in fact, it has no ideology to propagate. It is in large part the product of a society in which the masses are ignorant and inarticulate, so that the struggle for power goes on among a small elite. The military play the dominant role in politics, because a new "president" can usually be put in power by the use of force.

Communists have been attempting for many years to build up their power in Latin America. Their first notable success came when they seized leadership of the leftist government of Guatemala in the early 1950's. However, in 1954 an armed force of returning exiles, under Colonel Armas, succeeded in overturning this government. Later, in Cuba, the communists did better; there they achieved their greatest success in Latin America up to the present, namely, the seizure of power by Fidel Castro in 1959.

In Argentina, the Peron regime, before its overthrow in 1955, had many of the characteristics of fascism. In most of Latin America, stable, democratic governments have been difficult to maintain, though a few countries, including Chile, Costa Rica, Mexico, and Venezuela, have had them for a number of years. In recent years one of the great trouble centers has been Brazil, a country whose territory covers one half of South America.

Military dictatorships continue to exist in Latin America. Usually they are conservative or rightest and represent upper-class groups. In 1966 a military junta took over in Argentina and placed Lieutenant General Juan Carlos Ongania in the presidency. In 1968 military leaders in Peru ousted the elected president and replaced him with General Juan Velasco Alvarado. Frequently, military leaders justify such seizures of power by claims (sometimes correct) that the elected governments have grossly mismanaged the finances and the economy of a country.

THE TOTALITARIAN DICTATORSHIPS

An adequate understanding of the differences between democracies and dictatorships requires considerable knowledge of the basic characteristics of the Russian, German, and Italian dictatorships. The following pages are therefore primarily concerned with a fuller description and analysis of these characteristics.

Totalitarianism. *Totalitarianism* has become almost synonymous with *dictatorship* in popular speech, and it is no exaggeration to say that the outstanding characteristic of the leading dictatorships that came into power after World War I was their policy of controlling the *total* life of individuals and private groups. With some justification all the attributes of these dictatorships could be considered merely different aspects of totalitarianism, for all the devices employed by them were designed to make possible the effective control by the state of all social activity. The sphere of private freedom, which democracy attempts to maximize, is narrowly restricted by totalitarianism. *Total* government attempts to regulate all of life for state ends. Capital and labor, press and religion, family and fraternal organizations, work and play, individuals and society—all are subject to strict controls designed to promote the general welfare and to enhance the power and prestige of the state.

Totalitarianism in greater or less degree distinguished the regimes of Fascist Italy, Nazi Germany, the Japan of World War II, and Communist Russia from earlier dictatorships. Today it characterizes Russia and her

49. Mussolini at Bengazi in 1937. With hands on hips and chest thrown out in the best tradition of dictators, he received the cheers of some of his Libyan subjects. (Courtesy Wide World Photos.)

satellites, and also Red China, North Korea, North Vietnam, and several other communist countries.

Loyalty to the Party and the State. Totalitarian regimes demand complete loyalty and obedience to the party and the state. Fascist theory glorified and exalted the state.[4] Communism exalts the social revolution, and requires of the individual complete dedication to the objectives of the communist party. But under both systems the party and the state are for most purposes identical. The communist state, for example, is little more than the instrument for carrying out the policies of the communist party. Both fascism and communism demand that the individual, where there is any conflict, completely subordinate his own interests to those of the party and the state. Actually, communist regimes have expanded government functions even more than did Hitler or Mussolini because they have siezed private property and given agencies of the state complete responsibility for the production of all economic goods.

Autocracy and Irresponsibility. *Dictatorship* obviously means rule by one or a few. An *autocracy* is a government that exists independently of, beyond, or in spite of the will of its citizens. Dictatorship is autocratic. It may or may not act in contradiction to the wishes of those it governs. It is important to note that a *dictatorship is irresponsible;* that is, it rules in spite of the will of the people, and they have no way of calling it to account. Its right to rule does not depend on majority support. The right to rule derives from the assumption that the self-chosen elite possess the "best brains," the "best blood," the "highest political insight," the "capacity to rule."[5] The dictator does not expect the people to know what is good for them, so he tells the people and hopes they will believe; if they do not believe, he will do what is "good" for them anyway.

Arbitrary Rule. Democracy emphasizes constitutionalism and rule by law; a dictatorship is characterized by the *arbitrary rule* of men. Even the absolute monarchs of the past were theoretically restrained by the basic law of the land, but contemporary dictatorships, though they usually adorn their regimes with a constitution, are *not limited* by any basic law. Unrestrained rule is almost inevitably arbitrary rule, subject to the whims of those in power. Due process of law is abandoned or is hypocritically retained as an empty promise. The rules of the political game may be

---

[4] Mussolini wrote: "For Fascism the State is an absolute before which individuals and groups are relative. . . . When one says Liberalism, one says the individual; when one says Fascism, one says the State. . . . The Liberal State does not direct the interplay and the material and spiritual development of the groups, but limits itself to registering the results; the Fascist state has a consciousness of its own, a will of its own." "The Doctrine of Fascism" quoted in William Ebenstein, *Great Political Thinkers: Plato to the Present,* New York, Holt, Rinehart and Winston, Inc., 1951, pp. 597, 598.

[5] Hitler said: "A philosophy of life which, by rejecting the democratic concept of the mass-man, endeavors to give this earth to the best nation, the highest type of human beings, must in turn, logically, obey the same aristocratic principle within that nation and must secure leadership and greatest influence for the best brains. It rests on the basis of personality, not on that of majority." Translated from *Mein Kampf,* Munich, 1938, p. 493 (earlier editions in 1925 and 1927).

changed arbitrarily to meet the purposes of the moment; no law or established procedure is permitted to interfere with the continued existence and absolute rule of the power holders. Under such circumstances life, liberty, and property are insecure, for a person may be found guilty on false charges without any genuine trial. Arbitrary rule is an aid in inspiring terror and discouraging disobedience.

The Ideologies of Dictatorships. One of the most striking characteristics of the totalitarian regimes that arose after World War I was the impressive *ideologies* they developed. They made deliberate attempts to formulate social and political ideals that would justify their policies and win public support.

In the broadly literate world of today, ideologies or "isms" are characteristic of *all* dynamic societies. Each well-developed ideology represents a system of principles and practices that its supporters believe would lead to the ideal society and the ideal "way of life." Each ideology has its own version of the ideal relationship between the individual and society, of the best government, of the proper balance between individual liberty and the general welfare, and of all the evils and dangers in opposing ideologies. Because of the imposing ideologies developed by the dictatorships, the democracies were forced in self-defense to reaffirm their own beliefs and to make them more specific.

Each totalitarian dictatorship developed an ideology that had to be accepted on faith and was not subject to discussion; it was a creed, a dogma, which all must learn. It had to be learned because it was the key that unlocked all truth; in addition, it prescribed specific ways of thinking and acting, departures from which would be severely punished. The Nazi-Fascists frankly spoke of their ideology as a creed or myth;[6] the communists maintain that theirs is a science. Both, however, are a mixture of fact and fiction, truth and falsehood; both are secular "religions," and definitely unscientific, because they are presented as articles of faith, as final, indisputable, irrefutable "truth." He who disagrees with the dogma is guilty of more than dissent; he is guilty of heresy and treason. The purpose of these ideologies is to provide a moral background for dictatorship, to provide a justification for exterminating Jews or the bourgeoisie, for unifying the nation, and most of all for perpetuating the political power of a self-appointed elite over the masses of men.

Propaganda Machines and Intellectual Conformity. Totalitarian dictatorship invariably employs an elaborate propaganda machine designed to secure mass support through intellectual conformity and emotional fervor. No opposition is tolerated, and brutal methods are used to eliminate all forms of dissent. The ruthless suppression of dissent is carried

---

[6] The Nazi-Fascist ideology was frankly acknowledged as antirational. See Alfred Rosenberg, *Der Mythus des 20. Jahrhunderts* (Munich, 1939). Mussolini said in 1922: "We have created our myth. The myth is a faith. It is passion. It is not necessary that it shall be a reality. . . . Our myth is the nation, our myth is the greatness of the nation." See Herman Finer, *Mussolini's Italy*, New York, Holt, Rinehart and Winston, Inc., 1935.

out through a highly disciplined state political party, a secret police, and perhaps the army. All discussion and debate over basic political issues are forbidden. Freedom of religion, speech, press, assembly, and political opposition are denied. Every channel of communication is censored. The people are denied the privilege of hearing the "other side" of any issue. He who persists in exercising traditional democratic freedoms is exterminated or sent to prison or a slave-labor camp.

The totalitarian dictator, however, does not abolish the schools, the associations, and the mass media of communication; he uses them as parts of his propaganda machine. Every possible device is used to indoctrinate the people with the official dogma. From the cradle to the grave they are instructed in what to believe, whom to love and hate, and what to do to promote the "cause." With monotonous regularity they are bombarded with the same slogans, shibboleths, and symbols. The dictator or his propaganda minister decides what the "party line" is to be on any new issue or development, and then this new "truth" is rapidly passed down to the masses so that they may be "enlightened" and conform. Thus through physical and intellectual coercion, through negative and positive means, the will of the dictator is enforced.

One-Party Monopoly. The totalitarian dictatorship desires a monopoly of control; it tolerates no organized opposition; but it makes use of a political party. The one highly disciplined party that exists may have begun as a traditional political group struggling for parliamentary control. Once in power, however, it loses its private character and becomes an official control agency of the state. The purposes it serves are very different from those served by parties in a democracy. It offers the people no alternatives, and it gives them no opportunity to participate in the formulation of public policy. Its purpose is to serve the organizational needs of the dictator and his followers. It provides for close contact between the rulers and the people, for the dissemination of the party line, and for the control and regimentation of the people in the interest of the rulers. It may, as in Russia and Red China, possess a legal monopoly of the power to nominate candidates. Regardless of its legal position, the state party carries out the will of the dictator and prevents the people from forming a legal opposition party to challenge the present rulers. Thus the party becomes in practice synonymous with the state; its personnel, policies, and programs become those of the state.

The Secret Political Police. The most typical symbol of dictatorship is the *secret political police*. All of the totalitarian dictatorships have their dreaded secret political police, which, as agencies of coercion, are "as quietly efficient as the swoop of an owl on an unsuspecting rodent."[7] Millions have lived in terror of the Russian Cheka, OGPU, NKVD, or MVD, and of the infamous German Gestapo. Such agencies of coercion recog-

[7] Robert Rienow, *Introduction to Government*, New York, Alfred A. Knopf, Inc., 1952, p. 129.

nize few legal restraints upon their actions. Their objective is to discover and destroy all those who oppose the regime; and all methods, however cruel, that help to achieve this goal are considered legitimate. The secret police spy on everyone and, of course, on each other. No one is above suspicion or immune from seizure by night, a secret trial, and a hasty departure from this earth or to a slave-labor camp. Lavrenti Beria, once the Number Two man in Russia, received in 1953 exactly the kind of treatment he had given many others. Due process of law and all the procedural safeguards guaranteed to an accused person in the democracies are denied. A respected citizen is arrested in the middle of the night, and the public and his family may hear nothing of him until they read of his execution in the newspaper.

In dictatorships, the police have the power to do what in democracies can be done only by the highest courts through trial by jury. Such a system is the price that must be paid for outlawing political opposition. A one-party monopoly forces those who wish to express their disagreement with the regime to commit treason, and treason cannot be tolerated by any people.

Pseudo-Democracy. Totalitarian dictatorships have made great efforts to show that they possess all the good qualities of democracies, that they serve the interests of the people, and that they are popularly supported.[8] Much of the "machinery" of democracy is retained or created, such as legislative bodies, constitutions, and elections. The communists boast that in election after election 99 per cent of the votes are cast for the communist party candidates. The 1936 edition of the Russian constitution is in form very democratic, guaranteeing all the traditional civil rights plus the right to steady employment, leisure, and wholesome recreation. But the falseness of this democracy—if we accept any meaning the word *democracy* has in the English language—is revealed by the fact that the constitution does not restrain the rulers, the legislature does not make laws but merely rubber-stamps them, and the elections have little meaning, because there is only one slate of candidates, that of the Communist Party. If this is what *democracy* means in Russian, then we should find some other word for it when we translate it into English.

Socialization. All of the totalitarian dictatorships have advocated and practiced some form of state ownership, operation, or control of the means of production. However, dictatorships do not have a monopoly on the idea of socialization. The democratic socialists also advocate it, and in some democratic countries, among them Great Britain, socialization of production has been fairly extensive. Communists undertake to achieve

---

[8] The communists profess to have the highest type of democracy. Joseph Stalin, in a speech on the Draft Constitution of 1936, compared "bourgeois" democracy with communist democracy: "They talk of democracy. But what is democracy? Democracy in capitalist countries, where there are antagonistic classes, is, in the last analysis, democracy for the propertied minority. In the U.S.S.R., on the contrary, democracy is democracy for the working people, i.e., democracy for all." Joseph Stalin, *Leninism,* London, Universal Distributors Co., 1946, p. 579.

complete state control of the means of production by simply expropriating all business property. The fascist states did not go quite so far. Hitler and Mussolini were content to take over control of the great industrial corporations without formally expropriating them from their owners. But all totalitarian dictatorships have found in some type of socialization an important means for increasing the power and prestige of the state.

Imperialism. Democracies have sometimes been imperialistic, and dictatorships have sometimes found it inexpedient to expand, but the degree to which twentieth-century dictatorships have adopted aggressive foreign policies has led many to conclude that, in the present-day world, dictatorships are especially prone to imperialism. Communism makes a show of advocating peace and international cooperation, and the Soviet Union was in fact not aggressive during the first twenty years of communist rule. However, the great aggressors of the mid-twentieth century have been Communist Russia and Red China; and it was the dictatorships in Japan, Germany, and Italy that precipitated World War II by their policies of imperialism. After the war Red China became a leader in applying policies of aggressive imperialism, most notably in Korea, Tibet, and India.

The communist plan for world domination, unlike that of Hitler, does not foresee war as inevitable. The communists expect "degenerate capitalism" to collapse primarily because of its own defects; however, they intend to do all they can to hasten the downfall of the capitalist societies, which "carry within themselves the seeds of their own destruction." If war is necessary for communist advancement and security, it will be accepted, just as starvation of peasants, concentration camps, and bloody purges have been. The Soviet Union maintains mighty military forces, including nuclear weapons that, if we may believe Secretary of Defense Melvin Laird, are likely soon to equal or exceed in power those of the United States; but it prefers if possible to use them only for prestige or intimidation, and for strengthening propaganda. The Soviets believe that the democracies will be too cautious and timid or too trusting and inert to offer effective resistance to persistent pressures. The hope for the future is that Soviet Russia will ultimately give up its dreams of world domination and be willing to make agreements that genuinely limit its military power.

CONDITIONS PRODUCING DICTATORSHIPS

Whether certain conditions must necessarily produce dictatorship is not known. It is clear, however, that dictatorships do not arise simply because a Hitler, a Mussolini, a Lenin, or a Mao Tse-tung happens along. Certain economic, political, and social conditions must exist before a dynamic personality can bring about dictatorship. Perhaps both the conditions and the personality are necessary; but in any case the student who would understand why dictatorships arise must become acquainted with the social soil from which they grow.

The Tradition of Autocracy. It is not surprising that the peoples who have never known political freedom tend to accept as "natural" an autocratic government. This historical fact accounts in large part for most of the autocracies that man has known. Dictatorship in some form is very likely to continue where there have been centuries of experience under autocracy and where the mores, and sometimes religion, sanction an authoritarian regime. Such a situation goes far to explain the communist dictatorship in Russia and the dictatorships in Germany, Latin America, Eastern Europe, and Asia. In some cases dictatorship was also made easier by the poverty and ignorance of the masses.

Failure to Make Democracy Work. Regardless of our devotion to democracy, we must recognize that it has not worked satisfactorily everywhere. Democracy, like dictatorship, is the result of historical developments. In large societies it is a more recent type of government than dictatorship or some form of autocracy; and unless the necessary foundations have been well laid, it is a more difficult form of government to operate with reasonable success. A democratic government may be brought into power by a revolution, but for it to have a good chance of survival, the people of a country must previously have developed a sense of responsible citizenship and a faith in democratic principles. Where these are lacking, democracy is likely to fail. Many Italians prior to Mussolini's rise to power were sick of parliamentary bickering, governmental inefficiency and weakness, and the resulting social chaos. Many Germans became frightened at the inability of the Weimar Republic to cope with the economic and social problems that were giving the communists an opportunity to flourish; the fear of communism existed in pre-Fascist Italy also. Between the two world wars dissatisfaction with democracy was extensive in Greece, Poland, Roumania, Portugal, Spain, and elsewhere, and in these countries some type of authoritarian regime emerged. Where attempts to maintain democracy result in extreme confusion, corruption, and disorder, dictatorships are likely to take over, especially where the tradition of autocracy is still recent.

The present democratic governments of Japan, Italy, and West Germany have had their problems, but they appear to be gaining, gradually, in strength and stability. Many people feared that Charles de Gaulle would become a dictator in France, and some assert that while in office he was one. But in spite of his power, he was not a dictator in the sense in which we are using the word in this chapter. France has an elected parliament that enacts legislation, opposition parties may place candidates on the ballot, and the president himself, now Pompidou, must be elected at least every seven years by an electoral college that consists of some thousands of national and local elected officials.

Dictatorship is encouraged if numerous political parties are widely divided on basic issues and cannot form a stable government, if the people's desire for order and security is unfulfilled, and if the masses are willing to sacrifice individual freedom for the promise of prosperity, security, and national power. The unprecedented prosperity that much of western Europe has enjoyed in recent years has helped to strengthen the position of democratic government, especially in West Germany and Italy.

War. War and the conditions to which war gives rise have certainly played an important role in producing dictatorships. Practically all of the major twentieth-century dictatorships can be traced directly to war, defeat in war, and postwar crises. Today the conduct of a major war requires great centralization of power in the executive, the curtailment of traditional freedoms, extensive governmental regulation of production and consumption, and unquestioning obedience from the whole population. Thus war experience, even in the democracies, tends to habituate the people to authoritarian government; but in stable democracies, such as the United States and Great Britain, neither World War I nor World War II brought about dictatorship, and in the postwar period government controls were relaxed. Nevertheless, in both countries the two world wars seem to have brought some permanent expansion of government functions and powers.

The emotional stress of exaltation that war creates may breed revolution, and revolution (especially of the communist type) breeds dictatorship. Defeat in a major war is likely to bring either very high taxation or runaway inflation, economic and political disorganization, and general hardship. The middle class (the bulwark of democracy) often suffers most, and disillusionment leads to despair. Defeat in war tends to shatter the traditional props of society, so that not only traditional political institutions but also religion and morality suffer some degree of disintegration. Defeat in war may make it easy for a small, well-organized group to seize the government, as the communists did in Russia after the Russian defeat in World War I; or defeat may enable a foreign power to impose dictatorial regimes, as Russia did on the satellite countries after World War II. Communist theory emphasizes the role that war can play in producing the conditions favorable to revolution and the dictatorship of the proletariat.

On the other hand, defeat in a war led by a dictatorship may disillusion people as to the advantages of this type of government and so aid in the restoration of democracy. This was true after World War II in both Italy and West Germany. In both cases aid from the United States was a significant factor in making possible the re-establishment of democratic government.

Economic and Social Crises. Periods of social unrest and disorganization are always favorable to revolutionary movements, whether these result in democracy or dictatorship. Hence it is not strange that the major twentieth-century dictatorships have been created in periods of extreme economic and social crisis. This fact is amply illustrated in the history of the rise to power of Lenin, Hitler, and Mussolini. Russia in 1917 experienced defeat by Germany, the abdication of the czar, the revolt of the peasants and urban workers, economic chaos, and general disorder.[9] The Germany that gave rise to Hitler had experienced crushing defeat in World War I, the abdication of the kaiser, the restrictions of the Versailles Treaty, the complete debasement of money through inflation in the early 1920's, and, after the onset of depression in the early 1930's, the rapid rise of unemployment and communism. Many Germans felt the humiliation of defeat and had a strong desire for revenge. Following World War I, Italians felt widespread disappointment over the Italian failure to acquire territory that her allies had promised. In addition, they were faced with such difficult problems as chronic unemployment, strikes and lockouts, a weak and inefficient democratic government, lawlessness marked by the rise of robber bands that jeopardized life and property, and the rapid spread of communism and the spirit of revolt.

When such conditions exist, a savior with a plan of salvation will find many listeners. Dictators may seize power by armed revolution (Lenin in Russia) or by *coup d'état;* but they may also take over through legal elections or by appointment. Both Hitler and Mussolini were installed in office through lawful procedures, although Nazi terror tactics during the German election "encouraged" people to vote for Hitler's party, and Mussolini's private army practically dictated his appointment as prime minister by the king. Once in power, the dictator and his followers proceeded as quickly as possible (and as ruthlessly as necessary) to destroy all opposition. Nations have discovered to their sorrow that dictators are easy to "hire" but very difficult to "fire." In many cases a dictatorial government can be terminated only by revolution or defeat in war.

THE CHANGING PICTURE SINCE WORLD WAR II

From shortly after World War I to the end of World War II fascism played a major and rather frightening role in world history. But with the defeat of the major fascist powers it has faded rapidly as a social and political force. As already noted, the surviving dictatorial regimes associated with fascism, those of Caetano in Portugal and Franco in Spain, are no longer aggressively following totalitarian policies. Communist dictatorships, on the other hand, continue to spread. After Red China came North Korea, North Vietnam, and Cuba. Furthermore, regimes in other countries, including several in Africa, show strong communist influence, and some of these nations may become full-fledged members of the communist group. Also, of course, there is still the problem of South Vietnam, and the question as to whether the military and diplomatic efforts of the United States, aided by those of the South Vietnamese themselves, can prevent

[9] Remember, however, that the communist dictatorship in Russia merely replaced another form of autocracy.

that country, and with it others such as Laos and Cambodia, from being taken over by communist regimes.

Meanwhile, communism itself, at least in Russia, has been undergoing slow changes. Its fundamental doctrines and objectives may be the same, but in Russia it is more than fifty years old, and the new generation does not have quite the faith and fervor that was possessed by those who actually carried out the revolution. When Khrushchev assumed power he rejected Stalinism, with its heavy reliance on terror, concentration camps, and murder to repress any possible opposition to the regime. Though controls over freedom of speech and opposition to government policies were not removed, they were relaxed; and for a while Russians enjoyed more freedom and security than they had had for many years. However, under Khrushchev's successor, Leonid I. Brezhnev, restrictions on freedom were gradually tightened; and the military invasion of Czechoslovakia in 1968 convinced some doubters in the West that the Russian leaders were as ready as ever to use force, if necessary, to maintain control of the satellite nations.

Communist control of all China was established several years after World War II, and the methods used in seizing and consolidating power were as ruthless as those of Stalin. The first decade of communist rule was devoted to liquidating the old order, building an administrative system, and establishing order throughout the country. But by the early 1960's party chairman Mao Tse-tung began to experience difficulties and failures in carrying out programs designed to lead China toward a more rigorous communal and egalitarian communism. Blaming conservative or revisionary elements within the party, he and his close associates organized a purge, which they called the Great Proletarian Cultural Revolution. The Red Guards, consisting mostly of millions of loyal young students, were the chief instrument of the purge. However, as they roamed over China, spreading "Mao's thought" and removing from office or liquidating "unworthy" officials, they got out of hand and not only fought with reactionary forces but also among themselves. The result was two or three years of disorder and confusion throughout much of China and a disruption of the economy and of various government programs, including the production of nuclear weapons. But by late 1968, when the government seemed to have the situation under control, it held in Peking a mass celebration of the victory of the Cultural Revolution. Through all this Red China continued to maintain its hostile attitude toward both Russia and the Western democracies.

Communism still poses two great threats to democracy and the Free World. The one is the threat of direct military aggression; the other is that of the constant expansion of communism through subversion and revolution, supported by money and arms from Russia or China. The latter threat is now a very real one in some countries of Africa and Latin America.

Terms to Be Understood

cold war
democracy
dictatorship
republic
oligarchy
democracy as a
  theory of economic
  and social relationships
political democracy
popular sovereignty
liberalism

constitutional
  government
limited government
democratic equality
direct democracy
representative
  democracy
totalitarianism
fascism
Nazism
racism

communism
Caesarism
statism
autocracy
irresponsible
  government
arbitrary rule
ideologies
political police
pseudodemocracy
imperialism

Questions for Review and Discussion

1. Why is *democracy* difficult to define?
2. What has been the chief threat to the survival of political democracy since World War II?
3. List the essential characteristics of political democracy.
4. According to the theories of political democracy what should be the position of the individual in society?
5. Name and describe the several different forms that political democracy can take.
6. Is a constitutional government necessarily democratic? Why or why not?
7. Defend the statement Although 99 per cent of the eligible voters in Russia go to the polls to vote for candidates for public office, the Soviet Union is not democratic.
8. How would you differentiate totalitarian from nontotalitarian dictatorships?
9. List as many as you can of the common characteristics of totalitarian dictatorships.
10. What were the chief differences between fascist and communist dictatorships?
11. Under what social conditions is democratic government most likely (a) to succeed? (b) to fail?
12. What conditions tend to produce and maintain dictatorships?
13. How would you classify the type of dictatorship traditional in South America when democratic government breaks down?
14. Show how democracies and totalitarian dictatorships differ in their conceptions of the proper relationship between the following: (a) ends and means, (b) liberty and authority, (c) the individual and the state, (d) society and the state, (e) political parties and the government, and (f) the executive and the legislature.
15. How has the status of the totalitarian regimes and their relation to the democracies changed since World War II?

For Further Study

Almond, Gabriel A., and Sidney Verba, *Civic Culture: Political Attitudes and Democracy in Five Nations,* paperback, Boston, Little, Brown and Company, 1965.

Beer, Samuel H., et al., *Patterns of Government: The Major Political Systems of Europe,* rev. ed., New York, Random House, Inc., 1962.

Cohen, Carl, ed., *Communism, Fascism, and Democracy: The Theoretical Foundations,* paperback, New York, Random House, Inc., 1962.

Ebenstein, William, *Today's Isms: Communism, Fascism, Socialism, Capitalism,* 6th ed., paperback, Englewood Cliffs, N.J., Prentice-Hall, Inc., 1970.

——, *Two Ways of Life: The Communist Challenge to Democracy,* New York, Holt, Rinehart and Winston, Inc., 1966.

Hill, Norman L., *International Politics,* New York, Harper & Row, Publishers, 1963. See therein Chap. 6.

Hitler, Adolf, *Mein Kampf,* paperback, Boston, Houghton Mifflin Company, 1962.

Lipson, Leslie, *The Democratic Civilization,* paperback, New York, Oxford University Press, 1969. See therein Chaps. 1–4.

Mill, John Stuart, *Considerations on Representative Government,* Gateway paperback, Chicago, Henry Regnery Company, 1962.

——, *On Liberty,* Gateway paperback, Chicago, Henry Regnery Company, 1959.

Nolte, Ernst, *Three Faces of Fascism,* paperback, New York, New American Library, Inc., 1969.

Rostow, W. W., *The Dynamics of Soviet Society,* rev. ed., paperback, New York, W. W. Norton & Company, Inc., 1967.

Rubinstein, Alvin Z., *Communist Political Systems,* Englewood Cliffs, N.J., Prentice-Hall, Inc., 1966.

——, ed., *Foreign Policy of the Soviet Union,* 2d ed., paperback, New York, Random House, Inc., 1966.

Schuman, Frederick L., *Government in the Soviet Union,* 2d ed., paperback, New York, Thomas Y. Crowell Company, 1967.

Shapiro, L., *The Government and Politics of the Soviet Union,* rev. ed., paperback, New York, Random House, Inc., 1967.

Sherover, Charles M., ed., *The Development of the Democratic Idea: Readings from Pericles to the Present,* paperback, New York, Washington Square Press, 1966.

Stalin, Josef, *Foundations of Leninism,* paperback, New York, International Publishers Co., Inc., n.d.

Woolf, S. J., ed., *European Fascism,* paperback, New York, Random House, Inc., 1969.

Chapter 26

Democratic

Government

in America

in this chapter we shall set forth some of the most important features and characteristics of American democratic government. But it should be kept in mind that government is only one aspect of American democracy, the broad structure of which has been built on the hopes, dreams, and achievements of many generations.

The study of American democracy is more than the study of a government; it is the study of a developing culture. The character of the nation's economy, its labor force, its population; the concepts that constitute its social creed; the mass of its past thought and the nature of its changing historical objectives—all these are a proper and necessary part of the subject matter of the American democratic system.[1]

Throughout the years, America has increasingly become not only a political democracy but also in some degree a social democracy, a racial democracy, a religious democracy, and an economic democracy. All these different phases of American democracy are very closely interrelated, and each influences the others. From this rich body of social experience, some of the outstanding aspects of our political democracy are selected for discussion in this chapter.

HISTORICAL DEVELOPMENT OF AMERICAN GOVERNMENT

With due respect to the Founding Fathers, the American system of government was not wholly the creation of a convention that met in Philadelphia during the hot summer of 1787. Governmental systems grow slowly, and the American system had been developing over a long period. The beginnings go back at least as far as ancient Greece and Rome; but the most obvious antecedents of our government are found in seventeenth- and eighteenth-century England. For 168 years England ruled the American colonies, and during this time English political ideas and institutions were adapted to conditions in America.

Our British Heritage and Its Influence. Cultural borrowing is a common phenomenon, and America borrowed much from the mother country. Because the great majority of colonists came from England, it was natural that they should put into effect many of the ideas and institutions familiar to them. All of the following, and many more, were direct transfers from England to America: representative government, "no taxation without representation," personal rights, the common law, *habeas corpus,* trial by jury, sheriffs, coroners, and justices of the peace. By far the most important influence on the Founding Fathers was the cultural heritage from England.

Experience in *adapting* the British heritage to government and politics in the colonies was the next greatest influence at the Constitutional Convention. For instance, most of the colonies had a *royal* or *proprietary* governor, who was an agent of the crown and came to be a symbol of oppression; only in two *charter* colonies was the governor elected by the lower house of the legislature, and the political privileges of these colonies came to be envied and desired by the others. Again, although suffrage was severely limited in all colonies by property qualifications, and in some by religious requirements, the beginnings of government by popular consent were made. With two exceptions the colonies had *bicameral legislatures*—that is, legislatures similar to the British parliament in that they

---

[1] John M. Swarthout and Ernest R. Bartley, *Materials on American National Government,* New York, Oxford University Press, 1952, p. ix.

consisted of two houses. Usually the upper house was a council that, with the governor, was appointed by the king. Representatives in the lower house were elected by all qualified voters. The power of these representatives was considerable, because only the lower house could originate tax laws or bills appropriating money.

At this point we should note briefly the influence of the colonial governments on the state governments that succeeded them just after the Declaration of Independence. Each new state produced its own constitution embodying its own ideas of "free" government; however, these constitutions were significantly similar. All of them provided for *limited government* and *popular sovereignty*. Fear of oppressive government and of the executive power of the governor was widespread. Hence, elaborate and liberal bills of rights were produced to protect the individual citizen. Also, there was a tendency to limit the powers of the governor and to increase those of the popularly elected legislature. The governor was chosen by the legislature in eight states and elected by the voters in the others; usually his term of office was only one year. Most of the legislatures were bicameral, and the courts and the local governments remained practically the same as they had been in the colonial days.

Background of the American Revolution. In 1754 there began a long struggle between the French and British in North America, and in 1756 the British issued a formal declaration of war. This conflict, known in the colonies as the *French and Indian War,* was a part of what in Europe was called the *Seven Years' War.* After many changes in fortune, the British finally achieved victory in America by capturing Quebec in 1760. In 1763 the war was formally ended by the Treaty of Paris, in which the French relinquished all their claims to Canada and the American Midwest.

When the English first began to settle along the Atlantic seaboard, the different colonies had little contact with one another. They were small and widely scattered, and each had difficult problems of its own. However, by the time of the French and Indian War, there was a colonial population of some size. The war confronted the colonies with a mutual danger, forced on them a certain amount of cooperation, and brought to them the realization that they had important interests in common. Much of the fighting during the French and Indian War was carried on by colonial militiamen, and some of the colonial legislatures voted substantial sums of money to support the struggle.

When the war was over, the British government was free to give colonial affairs more attention. In an attempt to force the colonies to deal only with the mother country, it began to tighten up its controls over colonial trade. It also began to levy taxes on the colonists without obtaining the consent of their legislatures, thus raising the issue of "taxation without representation." These policies brought economic losses to the colonists and hence became a source of rapidly increasing irritation. Four actions on the part of the British government were especially resented: (1) the attempt to stop colonial trade with the French and Spanish West Indies;

(2) an attempt to place upon the colonists the burden of supporting British troops in the colonies, presumably for their defense; (3) the *Stamp Act,* which for a time placed heavy taxes on legal documents; and (4) the levy of import duties, including a special tax on tea.

The Continental Congresses and the Declaration of Independence. In 1774, for the first time, the American colonies took common action in their relations with the mother country. In that year the First Continental Congress met and unsuccessfully petitioned the English government for relief from what it regarded as oppression. When the Second Continental Congress met in 1776, feeling among the delegates was running high against England, with the result that on July 4, 1776, the congress issued the famous Declaration of Independence and resolved to draw up a Constitution for the United States of America. This was probably the most significant and dramatic action ever taken in the history of American democracy.

The Declaration of Independence, a truly revolutionary document, declared that (1) the people have the right to revolt against oppressive government; (2) legitimate government must be based on the consent of the governed; (3) both the ruler and the ruled are obligated to preserve a government that pursues legitimate purposes; (4) all men are created equal; and (5) all men are endowed with certain inalienable rights, including those to life, liberty, and the pursuit of happiness. The Declaration also contained a long list of unredressed wrongs of which the English rulers were deemed guilty.

The Confederation. The plan for a union government that was drawn up was called the *Articles of Confederation.* It was submitted to the states for ratification in 1777 and became effective in 1781. It provided for a confederation in which the states retained their sovereignty and the right to withdraw from the Union. The states, not the people of the nation as a whole, granted the confederation the power to conduct foreign relations, declare war, and coin and borrow money. But it was denied the power to tax, to regulate interstate commerce, and to enforce its decisions through the courts or by any other means. It had no judiciary and no real executive. The only organ of government created was a unicameral congress in which each state had from two to seven delegates but only one vote. This congress could not make adequate laws, the laws made could not be adequately administered by congressional committees, and the only agencies to enforce laws upon individuals were those of the separate states. The fundamental weakness of any confederation is that each member state retains its full sovereignty—in other words, its right to do just as it pleases about any issue that may arise.

It is little wonder that the countries of Europe held the American "nation" in contempt. The threat of foreign intervention was generally recognized. The Confederation could not pay its foreign debts and gave no evidence of being able to meet its other international obligations. It could not govern at home. By the use of tariffs and other means, the states interfered with interstate commerce. Both commerce and business became stagnant. In several states there was talk of secession from the Union, and in some, of reunion with England. Border clashes between the states became frequent and alarming. The high hopes of 1776 were rapidly giving way to disillusionment and despair. But, fortunately, some great leaders existed who possessed the will and the ability to call a convention of the states, to draw up a constitution, to get agreement on it, and to secure its ratification, thus establishing "a more perfect union."

The Constitutional Convention at Philadelphia. In an attempt to settle the problem of interstate commercial rivalries that were bringing economic disaster, the Virginia legislature invited all the states to send representatives to a conference. Five states responded, and their delegates met at Annapolis in 1786. This group decided little could be accomplished without cooperation from the other states, and consequently they adopted a resolution requesting Congress to call a convention of all the states for the purpose of amending the Articles of Confederation so as to give the central government powers "adequate to the exigencies of government and the preservation of the Union." A desperate Congress issued the call for a convention to meet at Philadelphia in May, 1787, "for the sole and express purpose of revising the Articles." Amendments could be made only with the approval of Congress, and they required ratification by all of the thirteen states.

All the states except Rhode Island accepted the invitation; seventy-three delegates were chosen, fifty-three attended, and forty-four remained until the close of the convention; but only thirty-nine attached their signatures to the Constitution. The Convention was composed largely of conservatives. Only eight of the signers of the Declaration of Independence were present, and among those absent were Samuel and John Adams, Patrick Henry, Thomas Jefferson, and Thomas Paine. The "common people" of town and farm were unrepresented. The men who dominated the Convention were Alexander Hamilton, the greatest advocate of a strong central government; George Washington, the convention chairman and the delegate with the most prestige; James Madison, who realized the weakness of confederations through his studies of Greek and Italian governments; Gouverneur Morris, an eloquent aristocrat; Edmund Randolph, the youthful and erratic governor of Virginia; Benjamin Franklin, the diplomatic octogenarian; James Wilson, a brilliant Scottish lawyer whose talents were at the service of the advocates of a strong national government; and Luther Martin, John Dickinson, and William Patterson, able defenders of the interests of the small states.

The two most important decisions made early in the convention were (1) to hold all meetings in secret and to prohibit all delegates from disclosing the proceedings and (2) to exceed their legal powers and proceed to draft a constitution for a new government rather than limit themselves to proposing amendments to the Articles. Secrecy made possible bargaining and compromises and permitted the delegates to pursue their revolutionary goal of planning a new government without interference from their state governments. The second decision was a masterpiece of courageous statecraft.

Compromises at Philadelphia. Great political talent, as well as a determination to form a workable government, was necessary to reach acceptable compromises on crucial issues. The following decisions of the convention were of special importance in making possible the eventual ratification of the Constitution by all of the states: (1) The greatest compromise, and the greatest American contribution to the art and science of government, was the decision to establish a federal system. *Federalism* is a compromise between confederation and a unitary, or completely centralized, government. (2) The Connecticut Compromise resolved the conflict between the large and small states over representation in Congress by giving all states equal representation in the Senate and proportional representation in the House. (3) The Three-Fifths Compromise, also dealing with representation, provided that for purposes of apportioning representation and direct taxes a slave should count as three fifths of a free person. (4) Fear in the South of adverse treatment of Southern agricultural exports led to the provision that ratification of treaties should require a two-thirds majority in the Senate; it also gave rise to the prohibition of any taxation on exports. (5) A provision for establishing an *Electoral College* to choose the President compromised the controversy over whether the President should be elected directly by the people, by Congress, or by the state legislatures. In the Electoral College each state was allowed to have as many electors as it had representatives and senators in Congress, and each state legislature was to determine the method of choosing its electors. (6) Disagreement over whether Congressmen should be selected by the legislatures or by the people was compromised by providing for legislative selection of Senators, and for election of members of the House of Representatives by the qualified voters of each state. (7) Disagreement over qualifications for voting was compromised by leaving this important issue to the separate states. In addition to those just mentioned, compromises on many other issues were necessary, because there was very extensive conflict of interests and opinions.[2]

Ratification of the Constitution. The Constitution was signed on September 17, 1787, and forwarded to Congress with the recommendation that it be submitted to state conventions for ratification and that it become effective as soon as accepted by nine states. An unhappy Congress followed the suggestion. There then ensued the Great Debate on whether to adopt or not to adopt. Those who supported adoption became known as *Federalists,* and several of their leaders contributed the greatest com-

[2] For entertaining and informational reading on this subject, see Max Farrand, ed., *The Records of the Federal Convention of 1787,* New Haven, Conn., Yale University Press, 1911. Also Catherine Drinker Bowen, *Miracle at Philadelphia: The Story of the Constitutional Convention, May to September 1787,* Boston, Atlantic Monthly Press, 1966.

mentary on American government ever written. The *Federalist Papers*[3] constitute one of the great classics in political literature. The Anti-Federalists, led by the fiery Patrick Henry, condemned the secrecy of the convention and also condemned the delegates for exceeding their instructions in presenting a plan for an "all-powerful" national government. The small farmers, who constituted a majority of all citizens, were suspicious of a plan drawn up by "lawyers, financiers, and aristocrats." The struggle for ratification was long and hard, and victory was obtained by slim margins in several of the most important states. New York and Virginia failed to ratify until after the required minimum number of ratifications had already been obtained. North Carolina and Rhode Island delayed until after the new government had begun to function.[4]

The Bill of Rights. Many of the states ratified the Constitution on the condition that amendments protecting private rights be adopted as soon as the new government was formed. The first ten amendments, adopted in 1791, accomplished this *insofar as the national government was concerned.* This so-called *Bill of Rights* forbade the national government to invade basic private rights. But not until 1868, by the Fourteenth Amendment (and the later broad interpretation of it by the Supreme Court), were these rights given some protection against invasion by the states.

THE FUNDAMENTAL CHARACTERISTICS OF AMERICAN GOVERNMENT

Certain fundamental characteristics can be selected from the multitude of political and structural principles, from political practices, processes, and problems, and from the details of governmental organization that characterize government in America. These fundamental characteristics will be explained briefly in the following paragraphs.

Government on Three Levels. As a result of the *federal nature of our government,* government in the United States operates on three levels: (1) national, (2) state, and (3) local. It is customary to study our system under these three headings, and every college library contains several texts on each, though state and local government are often combined. In recent years most attention has been given to our national government, but only a few decades ago courses in the geography, history, and government of the state were a customary requirement in elementary schools and high schools. The growth of nationalism has tended to minimize in the opinion of the public the importance of state and local governments. Nationalism has been strengthened in part by wars, in part by advances in

---

[3] *The Federalist,* written by Alexander Hamilton, John Jay, and James Madison under the pen name of Publius was printed in New York newspapers. Paperback editions include Anchor, Mentor, and Modern Library.

[4] An interesting account of this dramatic page in American history is recorded by Carl Van Doren in *The Great Rehearsal,* New York, The Viking Press, Inc., 1948.

communication and transportation, and in part by the increasing complexity and nationwide scope of social problems. Nevertheless, state and local governments are still of great importance both to the individual and to our whole society.

Each of the fifty states, with its independent constitution and its own governmental agencies, exercises jurisdiction over most personal relationships, such as those of husband and wife, parent and child, and employer and employee, and also over property and business matters, including contracts, deeds, wills, corporations, and partnerships. Each state regulates commerce within its borders; establishes and controls local governments; protects health, safety, and morals; conducts elections; and provides education.

Local governments are subdivisions of the state, are incorporated by the state, and possess varying degrees of autonomy. They include the county, city, town, township, village, borough, and school district and also include special agencies such as park districts and sanitary districts. Local governments are close to the individual, and he can hardly escape noticing the services they provide. The sidewalks, lights, schools, public health service, police and fire protection, parks, beaches, and libraries are largely provided by local governments.

Structure of the National Government. The national government of the United States as established by the Constitution is divided into three branches, each performing different functions.

First, there is the *executive branch,* headed by the President. Under the President and directly responsible to him are the members of his cabinet—that is, the heads of the twelve major administrative departments of the government. These cabinet members, or "secretaries," are appointed by the President, subject to approval by the Senate. Within the executive department there are also a number of "independent" offices and commissions. The extent to which these are responsible to the President is determined by law. The executive branch of the government is primarily concerned with enforcing the laws and with carrying on daily the many activities in which a modern government must engage. However, the President also plays a very important role in determing governmental policies.

Second, there is the *legislative branch,* which consists essentially of the two houses of Congress to which reference has already been made. The legislative branch is chiefly the policy-making agency of government. It determines government policies by passing laws, or *statutes.*

Finally, there is the *judicial branch* of government. In the case of our national government it consists of the Supreme Court and of the various lower and special federal courts. The function of the judicial branch is to interpret the laws as they apply to particular cases that may arise. Once the meaning of a law has been decided in its application to a case, a *precedent* is said to have been established, and similar cases are likely to be decided in the same way. The federal courts interpret not only the laws passed by Congress but also the Constitution itself. For legal purposes, the Constitution of the United States means whatever the Supreme Court says that it means. If the Court should obviously and persistently misinterpret the Constitution, the only possible redress would be for the House of Representatives to impeach the justices responsible. Then the Senate would try them and, if they were convicted, remove them from office.

Figure 27 is worth careful study. It provides a simple outline of the structure of our national government.

Four Basic Characteristics of Our National Government. If a short answer is desired to the question, What kind of national government do we have? it would contain as few as four words: *democratic, republican, federal,* and *presidential.* Our national government is *democratic* rather than *dictatorial* or *oligarchic;* it is *republican* rather than *monarchical;* it is *federal,* in contrast to most of the governments of the world, which are *unitary;* and it is *presidential* rather than *parliamentary.* Incidentally, it should be noted that the governments of all the fifty states have the same basic characteristics as the national government except that they are unitary rather than federal.

Why Our Government Is Both Democratic and Republican. There is an old but fruitless argument as to whether the United States is a democracy or a republic. Actually, it has the essential characteristics of each of these forms, and therefore it may be described as both *democratic* and *republican.* The United States is a *republic,* in the strict meaning of the word, because the head of the state, the President, does not inherit his office but is elected by those citizens who are qualified to vote. Furthermore, other policy-determining officials are also elected, including the members of Congress. Our Supreme Court has expressed the American concept of a republic as follows: "The distinguishing feature of the republican form of government is the right of the people to choose its own officers." This makes *republic* synonymous with *representative democracy,* which is the kind of government we have. In a representative democracy the people make most governmental decisions not directly but through elected representatives. However, the United States is not a *pure democracy,* because that means a system under which all citizens vote directly on every piece of legislation. Pure democracy is possible only in relatively small communities.

The Meaning of Federalism. No one doubts that our government is federal, but differences of opinion have existed as to just what federalism implies, and whether it is good or bad, permanent or likely in time to become obsolete and disappear. *Today it is generally agreed that a federal government is a political arrangement under which the people delegate a portion of their sovereignty to a state, province, or canton, and a portion to a central government,* and this division of power cannot be changed by either government acting alone. *In a unitary government all the power is centralized in the national government,* and this central government may grant or withdraw power from geographical subdivisions (such as counties

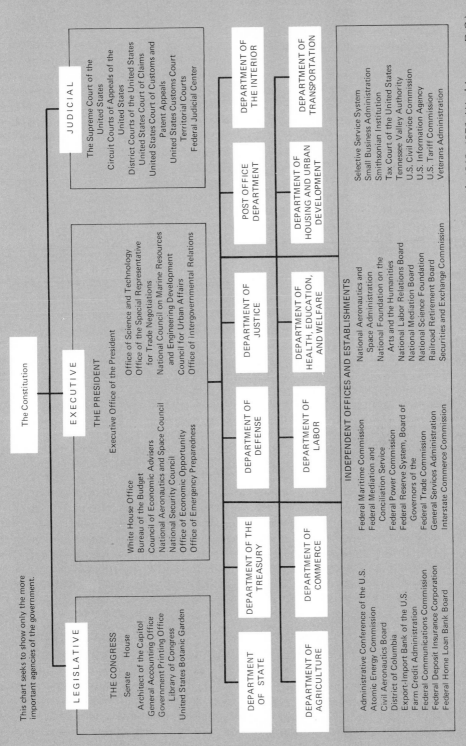

This chart seeks to show only the more important agencies of the government.

The Constitution

LEGISLATIVE

THE CONGRESS
Senate   House
Architect of the Capitol
General Accounting Office
Government Printing Office
Library of Congress
United States Botanic Garden

EXECUTIVE

THE PRESIDENT

Executive Office of the President

White House Office
Bureau of the Budget
Council of Economic Advisers
National Aeronautics and Space Council
National Security Council
Office of Economic Opportunity
Office of Emergency Preparedness
Office of Science and Technology
Office of the Special Representative for Trade Negotiations
National Council on Marine Resources and Engineering Development
Council for Urban Affairs
Office of Intergovernmental Relations

JUDICIAL

The Supreme Court of the United States
Circuit Courts of Appeals of the United States
District Courts of the United States
United States Court of Claims
United States Court of Customs and Patent Appeals
United States Customs Court
Territorial Courts
Federal Judicial Center

DEPARTMENT OF STATE

DEPARTMENT OF THE TREASURY

DEPARTMENT OF DEFENSE

DEPARTMENT OF JUSTICE

POST OFFICE DEPARTMENT

DEPARTMENT OF THE INTERIOR

DEPARTMENT OF AGRICULTURE

DEPARTMENT OF COMMERCE

DEPARTMENT OF LABOR

DEPARTMENT OF HEALTH, EDUCATION, AND WELFARE

DEPARTMENT OF HOUSING AND URBAN DEVELOPMENT

DEPARTMENT OF TRANSPORTATION

INDEPENDENT OFFICES AND ESTABLISHMENTS

Administrative Conference of the U.S.
Atomic Energy Commission
Civil Aeronautics Board
District of Columbia
Export-Import Bank of the U.S.
Farm Credit Administration
Federal Communications Commission
Federal Deposit Insurance Corporation
Federal Home Loan Bank Board

Federal Maritime Commission
Federal Mediation and Conciliation Service
Federal Power Commission
Federal Reserve System, Board of Governors of the
Federal Trade Commission
General Services Administration
Interstate Commerce Commission

National Aeronautics and Space Administration
National Foundation on the Arts and the Humanities
National Labor Relations Board
National Mediation Board
National Science Foundation
Railroad Retirement Board
Securities and Exchange Commission

Selective Service System
Small Business Administration
Smithsonian Institution
Tax Court of the United States
Tennessee Valley Authority
U.S. Civil Service Commission
U.S. Information Agency
U.S. Tariff Commission
Veterans Administration

Figure 27. Structure of the National Government. (*United States Government Organization Manual, 1969–1970,* Washington, D.C.)

and cities) as it sees fit. Also, the central government is absolutely supreme over all other governments within the nation. A *confederation* differs from either a federal government or a unitary government, because in it the governments of the major subdivisions, such as states or provinces, possess all the power, and they are free to grant it to the central government or withdraw it as they see fit. The central government, if it can be called a government, is completely subordinate to the sovereign state governments. A confederation is likely to be unstable, but it may be a stage in the development of federalism. In a federal system, certain powers are allotted to each of the two levels of government; each is supreme in its own sphere; and, unlike the situation in a confederation, the central government can levy its own taxes and act directly upon the people through its own agencies. For financial support and the enforcement of its laws, it need not depend on the states.

Federalism was an absolute necessity in America after the Revolutionary War. Nationalism was too weak to overcome state patriotism completely, and federalism provided the desired "unity in diversity." It still serves this purpose, although now it is praised by some and lamented by others.

The Meaning of Presidential Government. We have noted that the American national government is *presidential*. In this form of government the chief executive (usually called the president) is elected for a definite period of years independently of the legislative or lawmaking body, and he has certain powers that he derives directly from the constitution. In contrast, under the *parliamentary* form of government the executive branch is a committee, or cabinet, that represents the majority party in the legislative body and holds office only as long as it can command a majority in this body. Great Britain is a good example of parliamentary government. There the cabinet and its chief, the prime minister, are responsible to Parliament; and they can hold office only as long as Parliament supports their policies. This makes for close coordination of the executive and legislative departments. Under the presidential system, as exemplified in the United States, it is possible for the President and the majority in Congress to represent different parties and therefore to fail to cooperate. On most issues, however, party lines are not sharply drawn. In practice, the President usually takes the leadership in developing a legislative program, and insofar as he succeeds in doing this effectively, our system of government operates somewhat like the parliamentary system.

The President has two major functions. One is to take the lead in formulating policies and proposing legislation to Congress. Unfortunately, there are times when he and the majority in Congress may clash on major issues and not be able to resolve their differences. This may make it difficult for the President to take decisive and effective action to meet problems as they arise both at home and abroad. The second major function of the President is the administrative one of keeping the vast and unwieldly government organization operating smoothly and efficiently to perform its various normal functions. This includes many important responsibilities, among which is that of acting as commander of the nation's armed forces.

In the summer of 1970, President Nixon created two new agencies to help the Chief Executive in exercising effectively his two major functions. The first is the *Domestic Council,* established to coordinate and formulate domestic *policies,* insofar as the President can control or influence these. The council consists of the President, Vice-President, and the cabinet secretaries primarily concerned with domestic affairs. The second new agency is the *Office of Management and Budget.* This will be the President's principal means for *implementing* the Domestic Council's policies. It will direct and coordinate the activities of all the various agencies and departments that come under the President's jurisdiction.

Distribution of Powers by the Constitution. A broad view of the national Constitution as originally devised, and as it stands today, reveals a wide distribution of political power. The Founding Fathers, though desiring a central government strong enough to govern, feared too great a concentration of power and attempted to devise means for preventing the abuse of power. Broadly speaking, power is distributed in accordance with three constitutional principles as follows: (1) *federalism,* by which power is divided between the national government and the separate states; (2) *separation of powers,* by which legislative, judicial, and executive powers are divided among three separate branches of the national government; and (3) *limited government,* by which power is divided between the people and the government. This third principle includes the democratic doctrines of popular sovereignity, the inviolability of personal rights, and constitutionalism. The casual reader will not find these principles explicitly stated in the Constitution, but the careful student will discover that they permeate our entire constitutional system.

Division of Powers Between the Nation and the States. One of the great problems under federalism is how to divide powers between the central government and the states. In America the national government theoretically possesses only powers *delegated* to it and all others belong to the states. Powers delegated to our federal government are of two kinds, *enumerated* and *implied.* The enumerated powers are those expressly delegated by the Constitution, which include the grant of legislative powers to Congress (Article I, Sections 1 and 8), executive powers to the president (Article II), and judicial powers to the Supreme Court and other federal courts (Article III). In general, the enumerated powers delegated to the national government are those dealing with all international affairs and those domestic affairs of a national, rather than merely state, concern. The implied powers, however, have provided the flexibility necessary for the national government to meet the new problems arising from economic and social change. They have also, as some critics of expanding federal powers put it, enabled the central government to encroach greatly on the rights and functions of the states. The implied powers are based upon the so-called *elastic clause* (Article I, Section 8), which gives Congress the power "to make all laws which shall be necessary and proper for carrying into execution the foregoing powers, and all other powers vested by this Constitution in the government of the United States, or in any department or officer thereof."

The constitutional provisions for the division of powers also distinguish, though not very clearly, between *exclusive* and *concurrent* powers. Exclusive powers are those belonging only to the national government or only to the states. Concurrent powers are those belonging to both, such as the power to tax, borrow, and spend. Many governmental powers were not mentioned in the original Constitution, and the general understanding was that these belonged to the separate states. The Tenth Amendment made it plain that these *reserved* or *residual* powers "are reserved to the States respectively, or to the people."[5]

In the final analysis, however, it is clearly evident that in spite of a careful attempt to separate powers, *national supremacy* has become a principle of the American constitutional system. This principle grows out of the *supreme-law-of-the-land clause,* which states that the Constitution, laws of Congress in pursuance thereof, and treaties are the supreme law of the land, despite anything to the contrary in state constitutions and laws. In case of conflict, the states must make the necessary changes to conform to national law. Moreover, a branch of the national government, the Supreme Court, decides the issue when a conflict exists, so that in effect the national government judges its own case. *The national government is obviously, and fortunately, supreme.*

Separation of Powers of the Branches of Government. As an additional safeguard against "tyranny," the Founding Fathers divided governmental powers on a functional basis in accordance with the principal of separation of powers. James Madison wrote:

> *No political truth is certainly of greater intrinsic value, or is stamped with the authority of more enlightened patrons of liberty, than that . . . the accumulation of all powers, legislative, executive, and judiciary, in the same hands . . . may justly be pronounced the very definition of tyranny.*[6]

American political experience and the writings of Locke and Montesquieu influenced the decision to place legislative, executive, and judicial powers in three different branches, each independent of the others. The overconcentration of power in the colonial royal governors and the exalted position of the legislatures in the state governments of the Revolutionary war era had both proved unsatisfactory. The Founding Fathers feared tyranny by a majority of the electorate as well as by a strong executive. Most of the Fathers were conservatives who wanted, among other things, to safeguard property against the "ill-humor" of popular majorities.

---

[5] In some federal systems (Canada, for example) the reserved powers belong to the national government.

[6] *The Federalist, op. cit.,* No. 47.

Each of the three branches of government was designed to be not only independent of the others but also directly dependent on different sources for office. The President was to be chosen by electors, for four years; senators by state legislatures, for six years; representatives directly by the people, for two years; and judges by the President and Senate, for life. As a consequence, it would be difficult for even the majority of citizens to "seize" complete control of the government and "tyrannize" over the minority, even though these constitutional mechanisms might not frustrate the will of the majority forever.

However, where the powers of the branches of government are separated, it is not easy in every case to draw lines between legislative, executive, and judicial powers or to prevent one branch from encroaching on the others. Problems of this kind do not arise in a *parliamentary* form of government. There the ultimate powers of government all rest in the legislature. The executive branch is a part of the legislature and is responsible to it. Also, the courts are created by the legislature and in the final analysis are under its control. As a result, no occasion can arise for one department of government to encroach on the powers of another. But in our presidential system there may be attempts at such encroachment, especially if one political party controls the executive and another the legislature. Advocates of the parliamentary system deplore the deadlocks that they consider characteristic of presidential government and that from time to time frustrate the majority. On the other hand, majorities shift, and there are advantages in preventing small and temporary majorities from making radical changes in the laws of the nation.

Checks and Balances. Supplementing and modifying the principle of separation of powers is that of *checks and balances.* Because of the latter principle there has never been in practice a *complete* separation of executive, legislative, and judicial powers. Broadly speaking, the separation of powers is part of the checks-and-balances system, for it fulfills Madison's dictum: "Ambition must be made to counteract ambition." Strictly speaking, however, the checks and balances involved refer to *restraints* placed on each branch by requiring it to divide some of its powers with the others so that it cannot exercise independently the major functions allotted to it. Despite some popular opinion to the contrary, the authors of the Constitution never intended the three branches to be completely independent of each other. What they wanted to prevent was *all* legislative powers and *all* executive powers from falling into the same hands.

The Constitution clearly provides for interdependence between the three branches, which Madison also said was essential to free government.[7] Each branch of the government has some responsibility and power to influence the functions of the other two. Congress enacts laws, but they

[7] In *The Federalist, op. cit.,* No. 48, he stated that ". . . unless these departments be so far connected and blended as to give to each a constitutional control over the others, the degree of separation which the maxim requires, as essential to free government, can never in practice be duly maintained."

are subject to the President's veto, and his veto can be overridden by a two-thirds majority in each House. The Supreme Court can declare acts of Congress void, but Congress determines the appellate jurisdiction of the Court, and the President and the Senate appoint the judges. The President can make treaties, but only with the advice and consent of the Senate, and his appointments to government offices must receive Senate confirmation. The President and two thirds of the Senate can make a treaty, but the House of Representatives must approve if any money is involved. The President administers the laws, but Congress must establish the departments and agencies and provide for their support. Many of the regulatory commissions (which are administrative agencies) created by Congress actually exercise executive, legislative, and judicial powers. Congress, by investigative committees and other means, attempts to secure the faithful administration of the laws. In a very real sense, all three branches participate in the making and the administration of public policy.

Limited Government. Our national government under the Constitution has limited power. First, it shares power with the states. Second, at fairly frequent intervals, the voters, at free elections, may reject those in office or extend their tenure. Third, at all times certain powers are considered to reside in "the people" and to be forbidden the government. For example, citizens have certain rights and privileges that the government may not deny them. These include freedom of speech, assembly, and religion, and they also include the right not to be tried, convicted, and punished for crime without *due process of law*—that is, without being given the benefit of certain procedures and privileges that the law provides for an accused person to assure him of a fair trial.

An Independent Judiciary and Judicial Review. American tradition places great faith in an independent judiciary, one free of all pressure and all fear of political reprisal. Democratic theory has not demanded that the courts be directly subject to popular control. The American Constitution provides for a Supreme Court relatively free of the executive and legislative branches, for once the judges are appointed, they can be removed only by impeachment. This applies not only to Supreme Court justices but also to judges in nearly all the lower federal courts, principally courts of appeal, circuit courts, and district courts. The higher courts in all the fifty states are equally independent of the other branches of government, though in some states their members are elected for limited terms of office. The function of the courts is to interpret the law and apply it in individual cases, and for this task independence is desirable. All federal judges are appointed for life, and one of the most advocated reforms of government in America is to abolish the frequent practice of electing state judges for short terms, and instead, as in the case of federal judges, to have them appointed for life. Actually, it might be wise to set an upper age limit to the tenure of all judges, perhaps seventy or seventy-five years.

Judicial review is exercised by the supreme courts, both national and state, when they pass judgment upon the constitutionality of a legislative or executive act. This is the greatest power exercised by any court. The national Constitution does not expressly grant or deny the Supreme Court the power of judicial review, but the Court has exercised it since 1803, when Chief Justice John Marshall concluded in the case of *Marbury* v. *Madison* that the Court must do so to fulfill its expressed duty of exercising jurisdiction over all cases arising under the Constitution. Whether the Founding Fathers intended it to be so is uncertain, but our system of government required that this function be performed by some agency, and the Court was the logical choice. Marshall's opinion may have been partially political, but it was essentially logical and has proved expedient. His basic assumption, which democratic theory endorses, is that the Constitution is superior to ordinary law.

The necessity for judicial review arises from federalism, the separation of powers, and the inviolability of private rights. The Court decides whether the national government has encroached upon the powers reserved to the states; whether the states have exceeded their constitutional powers; whether the President or Congress has encroached upon the rightful sphere of the other; and whether the national or state governments have violated constitutionally guaranteed private rights. This, of course, provides no safeguards against encroachment by the Court upon the allotted spheres of the other agencies, including the states.

The aspect of judicial review that has provoked the greatest opposition is the voiding of acts of Congress. To nullify acts of Congress is to frustrate the will of the people expressed by democratically elected representatives, so the critics have argued. There is truth in this accusation, but most Americans prefer having the majority will occasionally frustrated to having a system of government in which the majority is free of constitutional restraints. If a measure really has powerful public support, the people can always resort to a constitutional amendment to "reverse" a Supreme Court decision.

Over the years the Supreme Court has gained great prestige by the manner in which it has protected the constitutional rights of national and state governments, Congress, the President, and individuals. However, its prestige has fluctuated greatly from time to time, and its decisions have never, of course, pleased everyone. During the early years of Franklin D. Roosevelt's administration, the President and the Court came into conflict. Roosevelt accused it of being reactionary when it found much of his New Deal legislation unconstitutional. However, public respect for the Court was so great that when the President attempted to obtain legislation permitting him to "pack" it with new justices sympathetic to his policies, he met firm opposition in Congress even from his own party. But within a few years, the President did succeed in somewhat changing the character of the Court through the appointment of new justices to replace those who retired or died. Since then, the Court, reflecting changes in the political climate, has become increasingly "liberal," that is, more willing to find legal justification for giving the federal government greater power to deal with national problems, to expand its real or alleged welfare activities, and to protect individual rights when the states fail to do so.

Even federal judges do not sit in an ivory tower rendering their decisions completely apart from public opinion. When the Court reverses a previous decision, this almost invariably reflects a basic change in public opinion. In 1954 the Supreme Court rendered a long-awaited decision on the constitutionality of "separate but equal" public school facilities. It reversed a fifty-year-old decision and found segregation in public schools to be a denial of "equal protection of the laws." Some people of the South accused the Court of "playing politics," but, in this case the learned judges were making a reasonable interpretation of the Constitution that agreed with majority opinion in America.

Two characteristics of American government, both of which are closely related to the subject of judicial review, require special comment at this point. One is the recognition by our laws and Constitution that every citizen has certain *inalienable rights*. The second is the fact that, though our federal Constitution is difficult to amend, the meanings ascribed to many of its clauses change gradually, as new situations arise, through the process of reinterpretation by the courts. For this reason it has sometimes been called a *living constitution*.

Our Inalienable Rights. Under any government there are always pressures that tend to override the *civil rights* of individuals, and nothing is more characteristic of America than the constant attempts to protect and extend freedom. Many of the early settlers came in search of greater religious freedom. The Revolutionary War was a struggle for political freedom from English rule. The Civil War was precipitated in part by the opposition of the North to slavery. The chief American slogan of World War I was "Make the world safe for democracy." President Roosevelt declared that the purpose of the Allied struggle in World War II was to secure, for all the people of all nations, the Four Freedoms. To him these were freedom of worship, freedom of speech, freedom from want, and freedom from fear. The Statue of Liberty in New York is a symbol of our devotion as a nation to the ideal of freedom.

The Preamble of our Constitution contains the declaration that one of the great purposes of government is "to secure the blessings of liberty to ourselves and our posterity." The American concept of limited, constitutional government is based on the proposition that the people reserve to themselves certain areas of freedom that government may not invade, that people have *inherent* rights that no political authority may either give or take away. Democratic government assumes that the majority will rule, but also that the minority has the right to dissent. In America, as in any democracy, the majority rules legitimately only so long as it respects minority rights.

The Founding Fathers considered government to be largely an enemy of freedom rather than a friend. As stated above, the original Constitu-

50. Symbol of Their Dream. Abraham Lincoln, the President who freed the slaves, is present symbolically as participants in the March on Washington are massed at the Lincoln Memorial to hear the late Rev. Martin Luther King, Jr. (Courtesy United Press International, Inc.)

tion and its Bill of Rights provided safeguards *against* the national government, and the Fourteenth Amendment extended most of these to the states.[8] We have learned through experience that government can be both the enemy and the friend of freedom. We do not regret that our government was forbidden the right to invade a wide sphere of private rights, though we may no longer believe that government is a necessary evil. We

[8] Every responsible American citizen would do well to acquaint himself with these rights and their significance for his welfare. They include (1) *Substantive Rights,* such as freedom of religion, of the person, of speech and the press, and of peaceable assembly; (2) *Procedural Rights,* such as due process of law, just compensation for property taken for public use, specific warrant for arrest or search, writ of *habeas corpus,* speedy and fair trial by jury, and freedom from excessive bail, unusual punishment, bills of attainder, double jeopardy, compulsory self-incrimination, and ex *post facto* laws.

know that liberty and security are inseparable and that without the security provided by stable, effective government, there would be few freedoms to enjoy. Thus, the trend for the last century has been toward *popular dependence on government to promote basic human rights.*

In spite of the emphasis on freedom and equality in the Declaration of Independence and in the Constitution with its Bill of Rights, curiously the majority of white Americans in the early days of the nation did not see any great inconsistency in their failure to extend freedom and equality to the blacks. Many felt that the blacks were a strange and inferior people, perhaps a different species of the human race, fit only to perform heavy tasks under the direction of others. The long struggle of the blacks, aided by their many white allies, to achieve "first-class" citizenship has been told in Chapter 14. Their hopes and aspirations were well stated by Martin Luther King, Jr., the modern hero of their struggle for equality, when he delivered his famous "I have a dream" speech from the Lincoln Memorial in 1963. In this speech he said:

I say to you today, even though we face the difficulties of today and tomorrow, I still have a dream. It is a dream that is deeply rooted in the American dream. I have a dream that one day this nation will rise up, live out the true meaning of its creed: "We hold these truths to be self-evident, that all men are created equal."[9]

Rights Versus Duties. Rights are never absolute. Furthermore, rights involve duties. The right to freedoms involves the duty of respecting the freedoms of others, whether these concern their choice of religion, political party, economic philosophy, or place of residence. Our freedoms are guaranteed only so long as we exercise them responsibly and refrain from using them as a cloak for indecency, slander and libel, polygamy, murder, public nuisances, incitement to riot and insurrection, and other unlawful acts. It is always the duty of the courts to draw a line between the legitimate and the illegitimate exercise of freedom, between controls essential for the welfare and safety of society and controls that unnecessarily invade the area of protected personal freedoms. No duty of government is more important or more difficult than this one.

There is no simple way of drawing a hard and fast line between the "inalienable" rights and freedoms of the individual, and the controls that are required to protect the rights and freedoms of others. Many people, including a number of respected lawyers and judges, feel that in recent years the Supreme Court, in its efforts to guard the civil rights of individuals, has gone too far in reversing convictions for crime on legal technicalities. Some critics assert that it has shown more concern for the rights of those accused of crime than for the rights of their alleged victims. Other critics, equally respected, defend the Court's decisions on the ground that

---

[9] Coretta King, "Tragedy in Memphis," *Life* magazine, September 12, 1969, p. 62.

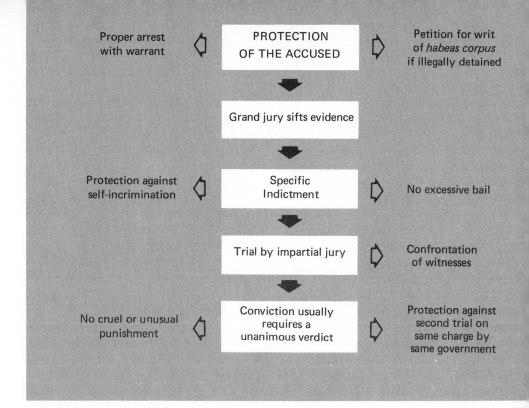

Figure 28. Civil Liberties: An American Heritage.

protection of accused persons who may be innocent requires strict adherence to correct legal procedures.

Figure 28 shows the basic rights that, under our American system of government, are designed to protect an accused person against an unfair trial. One great protection is the right to trial by jury. In criminal cases conviction requires a unanimous decision. (Some states do not require unanimity for deciding civil cases.)

Growth of the Living Constitution. American government is constitutional government, and we are proud of our written Constitution. In Great Britain, democratic government and the fundamental principles on which it is based developed slowly, so that no need was felt for a formal written document expressing these principles. But in America, a new nation had to be suddenly created out of thirteen independent colonies or states, and the only solution for this problem was to draw up in writing a formal agreement describing the structure and powers of the new government and also expressing the principles upon which it was based. Because of our long and successful experience with this written Constitution, we have perhaps come to feel that fundamental political principles cannot be trusted to provide a framework for government unless they have been formally agreed upon and duly recorded.

A written constitution is, however, *rigid* in the sense that it cannot be easily amended.[10] As time goes on, there is danger that it will more and more represent the dead hand of the past. Few attempts have been made to amend the Constitution; of these only sixteen have succeeded since the original Bill of Rights, and of these sixteen only a very few have altered the structure of the government. But the American people have been progressive, optimistic, and realistic; they have believed in growth and in desirable changes. Hence, in spite of the difficulty of bringing about amendments, they have found ways to make the Constitution into a flexible instrument for meeting new situations. As we have already noted, it has changed, not so much through amendment as through reinterpretation by the courts to meet new practices and new situations that those who drew up the Constitution could not have foreseen. It thus became a *"living Constitution"* in the sense that it was able to adjust in many ways to the changing beliefs and needs of the people.

Through custom, the undemocratic elements of the Electoral College were largely eliminated. Originally the plan was that the people should elect leading citizens to the college and that these should then select the President. But the practice soon grew for candidates to the Electoral College to pledge themselves to a Presidential candidate in advance, so that for all practical purposes when a citizen voted for an elector, he was voting directly for a certain man for President. The rise of national political parties has brought considerable unity to our national government in spite of the separation of powers provided for in the Constitution. Also, the growth of nationalism, the need for giving the executive great powers in times of crisis, and other influences have resulted in the emergence of the President as a strong unifying element in government. The people now look to him for leadership, and, as head of his party, he is in a strategic position to influence Congress, though his position may be difficult if the opposing party has a majority in the House, or Senate, or both.

Much expansion of government functions has also been made possible by new interpretations of the Constitution. When the people wanted the government to play a more vigorous role in the regulation of business activity, they and their Supreme Court found the necessary authority *implied* in the enumerated powers of the Constitution. When new social problems arose and the people demanded more government services, the needed authority was again found to exist, *by implication,* in the original document.

If the reader will look at Figure 29 and note the major agencies of the

[10] The amendment procedure stated in Article V of the national Constitution provides for two methods of proposing and two methods of ratifying amendments. They may be proposed by two thirds of both houses of Congress (the only method ever used) or by a constitutional convention called upon the petition of two thirds of the states. They may be ratified by legislatures in three fourths of the states (the method used all but once) or by conventions in three fourths of the states (the method used to ratify the Twenty-first Amendment). Many of the state constitutions, such as those of Illinois and Indiana, are even more difficult to amend than the national Constitution.

executive branch of the federal government as they are shown there, he will have some idea of the vast expansion in government functions that has taken place over the years.

Whenever new conditions arise, in spite of the seeming rigidity of our Constitution and our form of government, ways are found to meet them. When world conditions thrust upon the United States the leadership of the Free World, the capacity of our nation to play this role under strong executive guidance was not seriously impaired by our check-and-balance system. Furthermore, under the Constitution our government has become not only "big government," but also "big business" (the biggest in the land), and "welfare government."

However, a word of caution is in order at this point. Although liberal interpretation of the Constitution has helped us to meet many difficult national problems, there are dangers in carrying such interpretation so far that we can read into the Constitution almost any meaning we desire. This would in time rob it of its power to give our government stability, to maintain our system of checks and balances, and to protect the rights of states and political minorities. A provision in the Constitution that has been much used to expand the powers of the federal government is the clause that gives Congress the right to regulate interstate commerce. In the opinion of many, including former Supreme Court Justice Charles E. Whittaker, who retired in 1962 because of ill health, the Court has interpreted this clause so broadly as to subject to federal control many activities that the writers of the Constitution certainly meant to be left to the jurisdiction of the states.[11]

In recent years many critics of the Court have accused it of frequently *making* law rather than sticking to its proper function of *interpreting* it. The line between these two courses of action is often difficult to draw, and, as a result, there is a continuing controversy between those who believe that the Constitution should be interpreted rather freely and those who favor a more strict construction. But to decide how the Constitution applies to the various cases that come before the Court is often difficult. The justices themselves frequently disagree, as is demonstrated by the fact that in recent years many decisions have been made by the narrow majority of 5 to 4. Those who think that the Constitution should be interpreted more strictly than has been the case in recent years believe that the newest members of the Court, Chief Justice Warren E. Burger (appointed in 1969) and Justice Harry A. Blackmun (appointed in 1970) lean toward their views.

If the price of liberty is eternal vigilance, clearly one form of vigilance that the citizens of a democracy should never fail to exercise is watchfulness over the policies and actions of government. But having said this, we should not fail to note that our own government has been remarkably stable and that it has made great contributions to our national welfare.

[11] See "When a Former Justice Speaks Out Against the Supreme Court," *U. S. News & World Report,* November 9, 1964, p. 21.

**THE
PRESIDENT**
OF THE
UNITED STATES

EXECUTIVE OFFICE OF THE PRESIDENT

THE WHITE HOUSE OFFICE
BUREAU OF THE BUDGET
COUNCIL OF ECONOMIC ADVISERS
COUNCIL FOR RURAL AFFAIRS
COUNCIL FOR URBAN AFFAIRS
ENVIRONMENTAL QUALITY COUNCIL
NATIONAL AERONAUTICS AND SPACE COUNCIL
NATIONAL COUNCIL ON MARINE RESOURCES
    AND ENGINEERING DEVELOPMENT

NATIONAL SECURITY COUNCIL
OFFICE OF ECONOMIC OPPORTUNITY
OFFICE OF EMERGENCY PREPAREDNESS
OFFICE OF INTERGOVERNMENTAL RELATIONS
OFFICE OF SCIENCE AND TECHNOLOGY
SPECIAL REPRESENTATIVE FOR TRADE
    NEGOTIATIONS

DEPARTMENTS

Secretary	Secretary	Secretary	Attorney General	Postmaster General	Secretary
DEPT. OF STATE	DEPT. OF THE TREASURY	DEPT. OF DEFENSE	DEPT. OF JUSTICE	POST OFFICE DEPT.	DEPT. OF THE INTERIOR

AGENCIES, BOARDS, AND COMMISSIONS

11 Member Council	26 Members	11 Commissioners	2 Co-Chairmen	5 Commissioners
ADMIN-ISTRATIVE CONFERENCE OF THE UNITED STATES	ADVISORY COMMISSION ON INTERGOV-ERNMENTAL RELATIONS	AMERICAN BATTLE MONUMENTS COMMISSION	APPALACHIAN REGIONAL COMMISSION	ATOMIC ENERGY COMMISSION

Commissioner	5 Members	5 Directors	13 Members	3 Members
DISTRICT OF COLUMBIA	EQUAL EMPLOYMENT OPPORTUNITY COMMISSION	EXPORT-IMPORT BANK OF THE UNITED STATES	FARM CREDIT ADMINIS-TRATION	FEDERAL COAL MINE SAFETY BOARD OF REVIEW

5 Commissioners	7 Members	5 Commissioners	3 Members	Administrator
FEDERAL POWER COMMISSION	BOARD OF GOVERNORS OF THE FED. RESERVE SYSTEM	FEDERAL TRADE COMMISSION	FOREIGN CLAIMS SETTLEMENT COMMISSION	GENERAL SERVICES ADMINIS-TRATION

	5 Members	3 Members	25 Members	9-13 Directors
NATIONAL FOUNDATION ON THE ARTS AND HUMANITIES	NATIONAL LABOR RELATIONS BOARD	NATIONAL MEDIATION BOARD	NATIONAL SCIENCE FOUNDATION	PANAMA CANAL COMPANY

14 Regents	5 Members	16 Judges	3 Directors	Director
SMITHSONIAN INSTITUTION	SUBVERSIVE ACTIVITIES CONTROL BOARD	TAX COURT OF THE UNITED STATES	TENNESSEE VALLEY AUTHORITY	U.S. ARMS CONTROL AND DIS-ARMAMENT AGENCY

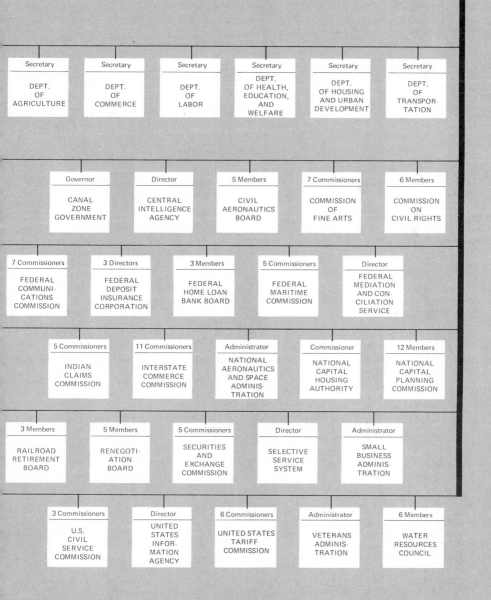

Figure 29. Executive Branch of the Government, 1970. (Executive Office of the President, Bureau of the Budget.)

Notwithstanding today's widespread social unrest, most Americans have confidence in it, though many will disagree, some violently, with certain policies of any given administration. In spite of its size, complexity, and power and in spite of controversies and sometimes mistakes, most people believe that on balance our government is and will continue to be a government of the people, by the people, and for the people.

Terms to Be Understood

bicameral legislature
limited government
popular sovereignty
Stamp Act
confederation
federalism
Electoral College
Bill of Rights
executive branch
legislative branch
judicial branch
democratic
  government
representative
  democracy

pure democracy
republican government
federal government
oligarchy
unitary government
presidential
  government
Domestic Council
Office of Management
  and Budget
parliamentary
  government
separation of powers
delegated powers
enumerated powers

implied powers
elastic clause
exclusive powers
concurrent powers
reserved powers
supreme law of the
  land
national supremacy
checks and
  balances
due process of law
judicial review
inalienable rights
civil rights
living constitution

Questions for Review and Discussion

1. Is America a democratic society? Explain your answer.
2. In what positive and negative ways did English politics and government influence the American Constitution?
3. How did the French and Indian War help prepare the way for American independence?
4. What serious problems arose under the Confederation?
5. How did experience with colonial and early state governments influence the American Constitution?
6. What two very important decisions were made early by the Constitutional Convention?
7. What major compromises were made at the Philadelphia Convention?
8. What are the three levels of government in the United States and how are they related to one another?
9. What are the three branches of our national government, and what is the function of each?
10. What are the four basic characteristics of the American system of government?
11. Why is America both a democracy and a republic?
12. Compare federal government with unitary government.

13. Compare presidential government with parliamentary government.
14. What are the two major functions of the President? What new agencies did President Nixon establish in 1970 to aid him in performing these functions more effectively?
15. In what ways does the Constitution distribute power?
16. How does the principle of checks and balances modify that of separation of powers?
17. How have political practices modified the separation of powers?
18. What is the meaning and significance of *judicial review*?
19. How has the people's attitude toward the national government changed since the Constitution was written? What have been the results of this change in public opinion?
20. Why did the Founding Fathers not extend to blacks the freedom and equality emphasized in the Declaration of Independence and the Constitution?
21. How is the "living Constitution" related to the written one, and how does it keep pace with changing conditions and new problems?
22. In recent years, many Americans, including lawyers, judges, and even present or former members of the Supreme Court itself, have criticized adversely a number of its decisions. Why?

For Further Study

Becker, Carl L., *The Declaration of Independence: A Study in the History of Political Ideas,* Vintage paperback, New York, Random House, Inc., n.d.

Burkhart, James, et al., eds., *American Government: The Clash of Issues,* 3d ed., Englewood Cliffs, N.J., Prentice-Hall, Inc., 1968.

Burns, James M., and Jack W. Peltason, *Government by the People: Dynamics of American Government,* 7th ed., Englewood Cliffs, N.J., Prentice-Hall, Inc., 1969.

Carr, Robert K., et al., *American Democracy in Theory and Practice,* 5th ed., New York, Holt, Rinehart and Winston, Inc., 1968. Vol. 1: "National Government"; Vol. 2: "National, State, and Local Government."

De Toqueville, Alexis, *Democracy in America,* edited and abridged by Richard D. Heffner, Mentor paperback, New York, New American Library, Inc., 1956.

Dewey, Robert, and James A. Gould, eds., paperback, *Freedom: Its History, Nature and Varieties,* New York, The Macmillan Company, 1970.

Dumbauld, Edward, *The Bill of Rights and What It Means Today,* Norman, University of Oklahoma Press, 1957. Reprinted 1968.

Fraenkel, Osmond K., *Our Civil Liberties,* Port Washington, N.Y., Kennikat Press, Inc., 1969.

Griffith, Ernest S., *Congress: Its Contemporary Role,* 4th ed., paperback, New York, New York University Press, 1967.

Levine, Erwin L., and Elmer E. Cornwell, Jr., *An Introduction to American Government,* paperback, New York, The Macmillan Company, 1968.

Lockard, Duane, *The Politics of State and Local Government,* New York, The Macmillan Company, 1969.

Mason, Alpheus T., *States Rights Debate: Antifederalism and the Constitution,* paperback, Englewood Cliffs, N.J., Prentice-Hall, Inc., 1964.

———— , and William M. Beaney, *The Supreme Court in a Free Society,* paperback, New York, W. W. Norton & Company, Inc., 1968.

Padover, Saul K., *The Living United States Constitution,* rev. ed., Mentor paperback, New York, New American Library, Inc., 1968.

Pierson, George Wilson, *De Toqueville in America,* Gloucester, Mass., Peter Smith, Publisher, Inc., 1960.

Rossiter, Clinton, *The American Presidency,* rev. ed., Harvest paperback, New York, Harcourt Brace Jovanovich, Inc., 1960.

United States Government Organization Manual, Office of the Federal Register, National Archives and Records Service, Washington, D.C., Government Printing Office. Issued annually.

Chapter 27

Political

Parties

and

Elections

both political parties and free elections are essentials of democratic government in large and populous areas. In a democracy the power the rulers exercise is granted provisionally by the electorate, and periodically this power must be redelegated in the secrecy of the voting booth. The people's right to rule is meaningless unless they are free to organize for political action, to express their choice of policies and personnel at fairly frequent elections, and to secure an honest count of their votes.

The Political Process. For some purposes it is convenient to divide both government and political science into three areas: (1) *politics,* or policy formation; (2) *judicial interpretation* of policies, as they are expressed in established legal doctrines, in court decisions, and in legislation; and (3) *administration,* or the implementation of policies. Though this division is useful, we should recognize that it is somewhat arbitrary and that the three areas listed tend to overlap. For example, in interpreting the law, judges often have or take a certain amount of leeway, and thus, by their decisions, influence policies; and administrators affect policies by the way they carry them out or by failing to carry them out.

In this chapter we are primarily concerned with politics, with special emphasis on political parties and elections. The ways in which government policies are developed may be called the *political process.* In a democracy the main factors in policy formation, as classified by political scientists, are public opinion and propaganda, pressure groups, political parties, nominations and elections, and, finally, legislation.

PUBLIC OPINION AND PRESSURE GROUPS

Democratic government is government in accordance with the will of the people, freely formed and freely expressed; it is government in accordance with *public opinion* or, more precisely, in accordance with the majority opinion. Politics deals largely with controversial matters, and hence there will be at least two sides to most questions. In other words, there will be a minority opinion in opposition to any decision made by the majority.

Because democratic government is responsive to public opinion, all who desire to influence the personnel or the policies of government are concerned with influencing public opinion. In order to do this they employ various agencies and techniques. *Political parties* and organized *pressure groups* are two of the important agencies, and the techniques include the use of *propaganda.* There are continuous attempts to influence public opinion in order to control the outcome of elections and to secure the passage of bills in the legislature. These efforts are made by groups of all kinds—religious, economic, social, and governmental—who try to influence not only the public but also the leaders of political parties and the officials of government at all levels. They even try to influence one another. In short, people of similar opinions (in government as well as out) unite to defend and to promote their interests by constant efforts to influence all those individuals and groups who are capable of helping or hindering them.

Public Opinion Polls. For many years such attempts to measure public opinion as the Gallup and Harris polls have attracted wide attention. These polls and others try to determine the beliefs of the public on many topics. They do this by sending out trained workers to question what the poll organization has determined to be a representative sample of the public. The results are not always very enlightening, because the questions asked are not really understood by many who answer them, because the ques-

"Put me in with the majority!"
(CITIZEN SMITH, by Dave
Gerard, reproduced by permission of The Register and
Tribune Syndicate.)

tions are difficult to answer simply, because they suggest answers, or because they concern matters about which many people have not made up their minds. Nevertheless, public opinion polls are the best means we have of trying to measure public attitudes toward many issues. At times they have certainly influenced the actions of public officials.

Probably the public has the greatest interest in public opinion polls when these polls attempt to forecast the outcome of elections. The polls usually succeed in predicting how people will vote with an error not greater than 3 or 4 per cent, but since elections are often close, the polls frequently fail to pick the winning party or candidates. Some observers believe that opinion polls significantly influence the outcome of elections; but, on the basis of the record, this seems doubtful. One reason that even the most carefully planned survey of public opinion may fail to predict correctly election returns is that many independent voters, when questioned, do not know or will not tell how they will cast their ballots. Another problem is that some people will change their minds after a poll is taken and before they vote.

The Role of Pressure Groups. *Pressure groups* fill the gap in a two-party system, enabling people with common interests to petition government for redress of grievances and to make their will known on many specific issues. By the use of lobbyists they keep national and state legislators and executives informed as to what the people they represent really want from government. Business groups, with small membership but much money, have always exercised this function; at present their best-known organizations are the United States Chamber of Commerce and the National Association of Manufacturers. In addition, several thousand trade associations guard the interests of their respective industries. The influence of the farm element in politics is largely the result of agrarian organizations such as the American Farm Bureau Federation, the National Grange, and the Farmers' Union; the political effectiveness of these organizations is attested to by much of the farm legislation of recent decades. Industrial workers constitute another important pressure group. Powerful unions, with large memberships and many votes, have increased the political power of labor to the point where domination of government by "big labor" may be more probable than domination by "big business." Professional people have also been able to exert political pressure through organizations like the American Medical Association. Other groups that often try to influence the actions of government include those seeking political reforms or seeking to promote the general welfare by urging adoption of measures to conserve natural resources and protect the environment.

One influential type of pressure group that is sometimes overlooked is the departments and other agencies of the federal government itself. Men who have spent years carrying on certain activities are likely, rightly or wrongly, to regard these as very essential. They usually feel that their agencies should have more money in order to do their work better, and they exert whatever influence they can on Congressmen to increase appropriations for them. If any attempt is made to abolish their agencies or to reorganize them radically, they are likely to resist it bitterly, because this would change or endanger the jobs of many of them. Such large organizations as the Department of State and the Department of Agriculture are often accused of being extremely conservative and resistant to change.

But the largest department of all in terms of personnel and expenditures is that of Defense. It includes all the generals, admirals, and others who direct the vast activities that are controlled from the Pentagon, and it is capable of exerting powerful political pressures. In recent years the term *military-industrial complex* has come into wide use to refer to the Department of Defense and the major corporations that supply military goods. However, the term means somewhat different things to different people.

To some, it implies little more than the great complex of industrial and military arrangements necessary to maintain our armed forces. People who regard it in this way may feel that we are fortunate to have been able to build up a military-industrial complex capable of meeting our needs for defense. However, they are usually aware that generals, because of their training and occupation, tend to see great deficiencies in our military forces and urge Congress to make larger appropriations for them. They are also aware that corporations that are large suppliers of military goods, for example manufacturers of airplanes, frequently use political pressure, often with the support of their employees and local politicians, in favor of programs that will give them business. Obviously, in such cases, the generals and the companies have a common interest and are capable of exerting great pressures. Their demands should be viewed critically by the public, Congress, and the President and should be met only if the demands seem justified.

Many people, however, view the military-industrial complex as a more ominous phenomenon. They look upon it as a tight alliance between the

Pentagon and the major corporations supplying military goods, an alliance so powerful that it not only spends unneeded billions of dollars on the armed forces but also threatens to turn the United States into a militarist society. Some go even farther. They regard the Pentagon and its allies as a kind of second government in the United States, one that controls the armed forces and dominates foreign policy. They think "Pentagonism" needs war in order to survive, that it threatens to dominate civilian power, that it threatens other nations, and that it may in the end arouse the wrath of the whole world.[1]

Obviously, in a modern democracy, pressure groups play an important part in the formation of public policy, and it is clear that there are inherent dangers in their growth. Certain special interests may become so powerful that, unless the public is very alert, they frustrate the will of the majority and thus obstruct government by and for the many. The general welfare may be sacrificed to those special interests that are best organized, that have the most financial backing, and that can deliver the most votes. Fortunately, one powerful interest group (such as organized labor) is often balanced by another powerful interest group (such as business). However, there are certain interest groups that lack effective organization, such as hired farm labor and consumers, and these groups tend to suffer from pressure-group government. But to say that consumers are likely to suffer from the activities of pressure groups is only one way of saying that the public interest is likely to suffer, for, as was pointed out in an earlier chapter, consumers include everybody. Some of the objectionable practices of pressure groups have been corrected through the Legislative Reorganization Act of 1946. Under Title III of this act, anyone hired to influence bills in Congress must register, indicate the name of his employer, and tell how much he is paid. Another corrective measure taken by the national government is the Corrupt Practices Act of 1925 along with the Hatch Acts of 1939–1940, which amended it. These limit the amount of money that can be contributed by an individual or organization to campaign funds, and they also limit the amount that can be spent by a candidate for Congress.

Some writers maintain that the most effective defense against special-interest pressure groups is the organization of still other groups to check and balance those that now exist. The weakness of this theory is that great numbers of people cannot, for one reason or another, organize effectively to protect their interests; and in the scramble of special-interest groups to protect themselves, the general interests of the public—which in total may constitute the most vital interests of every group—are often neglected. Maybe we need to make more general use of *ombudsmen* who, in Scandinavian countries, are government officials who investigate complaints of citizens against the government.

[1] See Juan Bosch, *Pentagonism: A Substitute for Imperialism,* New York, Grove Press, Inc., 1968.

FUNCTIONS OF POLITICAL PARTIES

Though *political parties* in the modern sense did not begin to develop until the middle or latter part of the eighteenth century, today they are universal in the democracies. Whether the one party in a fascist or communist state should be called a *political* party is debatable.

George Washington advised the new American nation to avoid dividing into parties, and they are not mentioned in the United States Constitution. But as democratic government developed, they came into existence because they met an important need. They are not the result of theory, but of practical experience; and they are necessities in representative democracies. Because their functions are of special concern to all American citizens, let us note and discuss briefly those that are most important.

Selecting Candidates and Appointive Officials. Most candidates for political office are selected by the parties. In large communities it would scarcely be practical for the voters to select them directly, and the only alternative is to have them chosen by organized groups. Occasionally, an independent candidate can get his name on the ballot if his supporters can organize and obtain enough signatures of registered voters to fulfill the requirements of the law, but rarely does such a candidate win an election. Parties do not necessarily select the best candidates. Nevertheless, when there are two or more candidates, people do have some choice; and each party tries to influence their choice by publicizing the claimed virtues of its own candidate and the alleged limitations of his opponents. Parties are organized primarily to win elections, but by announcing their policies and choosing candidates pledged to action, they also provide people with an opportunity to vote on issues. There are in the United States well over half a million elective officials, all but a few thousand of whom are at the local level.

In addition to all these elective officials, there are great numbers of appointive officials. For example, the President must appoint more than two hundred federal judges, plus federal marshals and hundreds of other officials. The President, governors, and mayors could not be expected to select all the many appointive officials without guidance. The political party performs the function of suggesting individuals for office.

Today the general rule is to make only the more important officials appointive, especially those who have policy-making functions. At one time, however, all government employees except those elected were chosen by some higher official. When the party in power changed, the common practice was to apply the principle "To the victor belong the spoils." In other words, the newly elected officials would dismiss most government employees hired by their predecessors and give the vacated jobs to their own supporters, whether qualified or not, as compensation for help in winning the election. This is known as the *spoils system.* Its evils, however, have been greatly reduced through the widespread introduction of *classified civil service systems.* Under these, most government employees are chosen on the basis of an examination, and they acquire permanent tenure after a specified period of satisfactory service. Many civil service systems work rather well, but, at the local level, politicians sometimes find ways of controlling or circumventing them.

Molding Public Opinion. The average person is busy with his private affairs, and, without the stimulating effect of political campaigns and partisan politics, the public would probably fail to form opinions on many important issues. Government, however, can be truly democratic only if it expresses public opinion. Political parties are largely responsible for stimulating the people to form opinions on issues relating to public policy. Parties usually present a biased view of these issues, but even so they aid in educating the electorate on important matters and thus help to make possible "government by the people." Competing candidates for office make use of pamphlet, pulpit, newspaper, magazine, radio, television, automobile, and airplane to bring to the people the issues of the day. Good government is possible only if a large portion of the people possess the education and good sense to sift the partisan propaganda; but the political parties at least give them something to sift.

However, one of the unfortunate aspects of campaigning for an important political office is that the publicity required to win costs a great

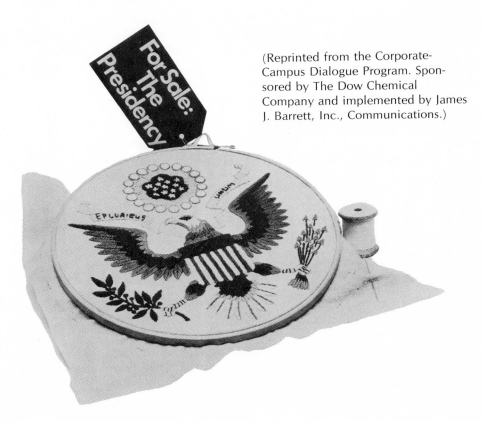

(Reprinted from the Corporate-Campus Dialogue Program. Sponsored by The Dow Chemical Company and implemented by James J. Barrett, Inc., Communications.)

deal of money, sometimes millions of dollars. The parties solicit campaign funds, but because these frequently fall short of meeting all the expenses, people complain that the only men who can afford to enter such a contest are either those who are very wealthy or those who can win the approval and financial support of wealthy men.

Stimulating Voting. By arousing interest in political issues, political parties encourage people to vote. Party loyalty also draws them to the polls to "keep the party of prosperity in office" or to throw out the "radicals," "reactionaries," or "crooks." The effort expended by party workers to get people to the polls on election day is also important. The telephone is used to remind people to vote, and frequently baby sitters and transportation are provided free. But one unfortunate result that occasionally accompanies party efforts to win elections in certain areas is fraudulent voting or the intentional miscounting of votes.

Assuming Responsibility for Government. When a party wins a national election in a country with a two party system and a parliamentary form of government, as in Great Britain, it clearly assumes responsibility for national policy. Under the American system of checks and balances, responsibility is not always so definitely fixed, especially when the President's party differs from that of the majority in Congress. Nevertheless, even in America, the President's party usually takes the credit and receives most of the blame for the policies and programs that are put into effect. When a party is in power, it attempts to direct the government in such a manner as to please the majority of the electorate; it *never* forgets the next election. In one way or another, every presidential candidate calls attention to the claimed merits of his own past accomplishments and those of his party, and attacks the alleged failures of his opponents.

Acting as the Loyal Opposition. The party that loses an election becomes a watchdog for the people, keeping on the alert to find fault with the party in power. Because the opposition party naturally desires to unseat the ruling party at the next election, it searches diligently for acts of corruption, extravagances with public money, and failure to fulfill campaign promises; at the same time, it tries to improve its own program and its public image so that it will be in a position to receive majority approval at the next election. The unattractive side of this function is the tendency of the opposition to exaggerate the faults of the party in power, and sometimes to "help" it to fail by refusing to cooperate on programs that would benefit the public.

Unifying Government. The political party performs a valuable service in the presidential type of government by bringing some unity into the actions of the separate branches of the government. Unified action is often possible despite the principle of separation of powers, because the political party assumes responsibility for the policies of the entire government. Friction and deadlocks between the executive and the legislature are likely to be eliminated or greatly decreased when both branches are controlled by the same party. If the political party in power supports a definite program, then the people can hold it responsible for government policy. Party activity may also bring some unity in policy and program among the separate jurisdictions of national, state, and city governments where the same party is in power at all levels. In many cases, however, local issues and national issues have little or nothing in common.

Compromising Conflicting Interests. In a dynamic society many conflicting interest groups compete for control of the government and for favorable legislation. The majority of these sincerely believe that their programs represent justice, progress, and morality, but they cannot all have their way. No government can provide at the same time for prohibition and the right to manufacture, sell, and consume intoxicating beverages; for outlawing strikes and the freedom to strike; for no racial discrimination and restrictive covenants; for the complete separation of church and state and publicly supported church schools. If all the conflicting groups that arise from differences in race, nationality, social class, creed, economic interest, and geographic location refused to accept any compromises, a unified national policy would be impossible. In countries with two-party systems most of the necessary compromises are brought about within each political party. In countries with a multiplicity of parties the problem, as we shall note a little later, is more difficult.

The political party, especially in the two-party system, acts as mediator and cushion between, on the one hand, the individuals and groups that belong to it and, on the other hand, the government. Individuals and interest groups can bring pressure to bear on the party to adopt policies they favor. The organized party then seeks to reach compromise agreements and to convert them into legislation. It thus acts as a buffer, absorbing many of the strains to which government would be subjected if each conflicting interest group were represented directly by a certain group of legislators. The party serves also as the great discipliner, for in it we are taught to compromise on smaller things in order to achieve the larger aims of the party. By being obliged to compromise many conflicting interests within the party, we are better prepared to make those final compromises on national policy that patriotism requires.

When a Republican has come to terms with all who pass as Republicans —it is a motley gang . . . —he will not find it too hard to stomach Democrats. Equally, when a Democrat has come to terms with all that squeeze into his party—it is a motley gang . . . —he will not find it too hard in a congressional pinch to stomach Republicans.[2]

[2] T. V. Smith, "In Praise of the Legislative Way," *Antioch Review,* March 1949, pp. 46–59. This article by the philosopher-politician Smith, once a democratic member of the House of Representatives, is an excellent description and analysis of the "compromising" function of parties. Much of the discussion in this section is based on Smith's article.

Patriotism demands that we subordinate our differences to the larger good of the nation; the political party trains us for this act of sportsmanship and good citizenship.

TYPES OF PARTIES

Despite their similarities, parties may be classified in various ways, and each classification will reveal something about the different ways that people organize for political action. One classification designates three types of parties: (1) personality parties, (2) program or principle parties, and (3) parties of power.

Personality Parties. The *personality party* is one that centers around a dynamic leader. It is generally small, and it is likely to die with the leader, for it is not based on an ideology or program. It is most often found in backward countries where the masses are poorly educated and where representative government is little known. In the past, personality parties were common in China, Japan, and the Balkans. The French party called Union for the Fifth Republic was originally organized to support Charles de Gaulle. Today personality parties can be found in some African and Latin American states.

Principle or Program Parties. The party based on a *specific principle or program* tends to be larger, better organized, and more permanent than the personality party. This type of party has a definite ideology, such as prohibition, populism, monarchism, republicanism, agrarianism, anticlericalism, communism, or socialism. Principle or program parties are likely to be prevalent where the social struggle has been especially bitter, so that groups cling tenaciously to their own narrow view of what is "right" and are unwilling to compromise for the common good. France has several such parties, and they are characteristic of southern Europe. They were found in pre-Nazi Germany and in most of the countries of prewar eastern Europe. The student of history will observe that parties of this type often become personality parties and sometimes pave the way for dictatorship.

Parties of Power. *Parties of power* often have dynamic leadership, and they also adopt a program, but the are especially characterized by their willingness to compromise on issues in order to secure control of the government. The Republican and Democratic parties in the United States illustrate this type. The two American parties, despite their efforts to find "issues," seldom show sharp and clearcut differences in program or principle, and often differences that appear to exist before an election tend to disappear once a party gets into power.[3] It would be a mistake, however,

[3] During the infancy of our nation the Federalists and the Jeffersonian Democrats were theoretically divided on principle, with the Democrats pledged to a strict interpretation of the Constitution that would limit the power of the national government and foster that of the states. As President, however, Jefferson made more extensive use of the central government, as in the purchase of Louisiana, than his Federalist predecessors. Andrew Jackson, who had opposed centralization, became perhaps the greatest nationalist of all our Presidents.

"I think I prefer the Republicans for clichés, but the Democrats for platitudes." (Courtesy Leonard Spencer and *The Saturday Evening Post.* © 1964 by the Curtis Publishing Company.)

to insist that the two parties are just alike, for at times they do show significant differences. In recent years, for example, the Democrats (except for those in the South) have been more strongly oriented than the Republicans toward the special interests of labor and of minority groups; and they have also been more willing to expand social reforms, real or alleged, by raising taxes and by expanding the powers and the expenditures of the federal government.

In Britain, where a similar two-party system exists, the Labour and Conservative parties differ more sharply in their programs and principles than do the American parties, but even so they attempt to attract a majority of the voters by compromising on most of the issues that divide them. The Conservatives regained power in 1951 by promising that they would not turn the "socialist" clock back very far. In 1964 the Labour Party again won control of parliament, but by a very narrow and tenuous margin. In the campaign the Labour Party played up scandals in the Conservative government and urged that it was "time for a change." The most clear-cut issue was nationalization of the steel industry, favored by the Labourites and opposed by the Conservatives. In the late 1960's, to the surprise of many, the Labour government set limits on wage increases. This was not popular with some of the unions, but was regarded by Harold Wilson, who was then prime minister, as necessary to fight inflation and to prevent an unfavorable balance of payments that would endanger the foreign-exchange value of the pound. In the election of 1970, the Conservatives were again returned to power, partly as a result of dissatisfaction with British economic conditions and with some of the policies by which the Labour government attempted to deal with them.

Parties of power are found in most of the British dominions and wherever an effective two-party system exists. Though these countries also on occasion produce both personality and principle parties, such parties are usually short-lived or small and unimportant. Often they tend to serve more as pressure groups that, from time to time, supply the two major parties with additional planks for their platforms.

Rightist and Leftist Parties. Politically speaking, a party may be said to be "on the right" or "on the left" depending on whether its policies are, on the one hand, basically reactionary or conservative, or, on the other hand, basically liberal or radical. Putting the matter another way, parties of the right believe that social and political changes should be slow and gradual; parties of the left believe that great and rapid social change is needed in order to raise the status of the masses of the people. But such terms as *reactionary, conservative, liberal,* and *radical* not only mean different things to different people but also different things at different times. One reason is that as times change some policies that were once regarded as radical, that is, as involving great changes that might endanger the whole social system, later become generally accepted and hence are looked upon as conservative.

In Europe the political left has traditionally included the various socialist parties in each country, along with the communists; the right has included the more conservative parties. In the United States, however, we seldom use the terms *right* and *left* when discussing our own politics. It is clear, nevertheless, that the Democratic Party is somewhat to the left of the Republican Party on a number of issues.

PARTY SYSTEMS

There are three important types of party systems: the one-party, the biparty, and the multiparty.

The One-Party System. The *one-party system* is characteristic of contemporary dictatorships and especially of the totalitarian regimes. Strictly speaking, the single parties under this system are not parties at all, if a *political party* is defined as an organization representing the political views of a certain group of citizens and devoted to the purpose of maintaining or securing control of the government by obtaining the most votes in free elections. They achieve control by whatever means is expedient, including force. Once in power, they become only an agency—and the most important agency—of the state. They cannot be displaced by the political process, because other parties are not permitted. In present-day Russia about 13 million Communist Party members, out of a total population of some 250 million, have a complete monopoly of political power and of all the means whereby political power can be created and organized. The members of either communist or fascist parties are highly disciplined political "soldiers," who are pledged to carry out the will of the party leadership. If they falter in zeal, they are expelled and punished. They attempt to secure mass support for the regime by monopolizing all political power, by ruthlessly destroying all actual or potential opposition, and by propaganda and sometimes terror. They also act as publicity agents for the dictatorship and enforce many of its policies.

The Biparty System. The *biparty system* is found almost exclusively in the United States, Britain, and some of the British commonwealths.

"... And if I am re-elected Senator I solemnly promise to keep all those promises I made six years ago." (Courtesy A. S. Habbick. Copyright 1969 *The Saturday Review, Inc.*)

We have already identified this type with parties of power, and its merits have been set forth in our discussion of the functions of political parties. The two-party system has proved the most satisfactory for effective representative democracy. The most valid criticism of it is that it often fails to provide the electorate with a clear choice on issues at election time, because, in attempting to attract people from all interest groups, the two parties tend to promise everything to everybody. The voter who wants to throw his weight in favor of some particular policy (such as extension of civil liberties, more public housing, gradual elimination of farm price supports, or a planned reduction of foreign aid) feels frustrated. However, in a nation as large and diverse as the United States, unity is essential, and each of our major parties performs the valuable function of bringing together under one umbrella a number of groups whose interests vary considerably. This makes possible government by a strong and responsible majority, and also provides a strong opposition party to keep watch on the party in power. Minority interests, whether based on race, religion, class, or occupation, are still better protected by a biparty system than they would be by proportional representation or a multitude of program parties.

The Multiparty System. The *multiparty system* under a parliamentary type of government has been characteristic of continental Europe, but it has often proved unsatisfactory as a means of providing stable and effective democratic government. Many parties of the program and personality type give the voter an opportunity to express himself on issues; but, in the absence of a unified majority, weak coalition governments are a frequent result. Moreover, there are times when even a weak coalition government cannot promptly be formed, and the nation is left for a time without a premier or other responsible executive. In periods of domestic or international crisis this can be serious. Both Hitler and Mussolini came to power under these conditions. Before the return of de Gaulle to power in 1958, and the adoption in 1969 of the new constitution that he proposed, France in the twentieth century had frequently presented the sorry spectacle of not being able to plan a necessary international conference, because either there was no government or it was feared there would be none by the scheduled date. The new constitution greatly increased the powers of the president in relation to those of the National Assembly and the Senate and lengthened his term to seven years. Since 1969, first under the presidency of de Gaulle and later under that of Pompidou, the French government has shown greater stability. But it is no longer a strictly parliamentary government, because the president is elected by popular vote, and he, not the legislative body, chooses the premier.

PARTY ORGANIZATION IN THE UNITED STATES

In this country, as we have already said, major political parties are held together by both ideology and organization. Of the two, organization is often of greater importance, though it tends to be a loose kind of organization. The role of ideology should not be minimized, however, because most people do have political beliefs and, further, they desire a justification or reasonable explanation for their choice of party. Actually, in the United States great numbers of people choose political parties primarily because of family tradition, sectional tradition, religion, special interests, or the personal appeal to them of some political leader. But even when this is true, the ideology of the party (its professed principles and aims) is likely to provide them with values, opinions, and a "yardstick" for criticizing the other party. No major party could be created or long endure without ideological weapons of offense and defense.

Organization, on the other hand, is the cohesive agency that makes possible the creation and perpetuation of the ideology and furnishes the opportunity for status and rewards for the party workers. Moreover, party organization at all levels brings "government" or political activity within reach of all. Any person can, if he chooses, find work to do in a party organization and can share in the excitement of competition and the joy of achievement.

Though party organization is very necessary, it has, unfortunately, objectionable features that sometimes prevent government from making its maximum contribution to the social welfare. These are revealed by such familiar terms as *political boss, political machine, invisible government,* and *spoils system*. No one acquainted with parties in America will deny the existence of political bosses who, through control of political machines (strong party organizations), have sometimes controlled cities and even states in ways contrary to the public interest; of small, closely-knit groups that have perpetuated themselves in power by "honest" graft; of some leaders who have made secret political decisions of an unsavory nature in "smoke-filled rooms"; and of the practice of rewarding faithful party workers, without too much regard for their other qualifications, with government appointments, jobs, and contracts.

It is probably true, however, that parties are becoming increasingly democratic. The extent to which they are democratically controlled is largely determined by the percentage of the voters who are alert, informed, and politically active. A former "boss" of the Bronx, Edward J. Flynn, who was also head of his party, explained why he entitled his autobiography *You're the Boss.*[4]

> *It came to me then that there are really eighty million political bosses in America. And I determined to try to tell them how, through misguided zeal, misspent energy, and just plain laziness, most of them had been shirking their duty as soldiers of democracy. So this book is respectfully addressed to you, the reader, because you're the boss.*

The democratic principle of popular sovereignty gives to each member of the electorate the right to be his own political boss; but leadership in political parties is necessary for organized, cooperative efforts. An alert and informed citizenry will keep political leadership responsible to the people.

Though it is well to remember that many variations are found as one goes from country to country, party organization in the United States illustrates the general nature of party organization in the democracies. All party organizations are *pyramidal*—that is, leadership at the top tends to initiate and direct policy, at least on a national level.

In the United States, however, *parties are decentralized to a great extent* because of both *regionalism* and *federalism*. Regionalism means that people who support the same national party may, in different sections of the country, differ substantially in their views on some questions and, as a result, may support very different policies. For example, Democrats in New York State are likely to oppose school segregation, whereas those in Mississippi are likely to favor it. Federalism encourages decentralization of parties because it leaves the states with considerable autonomy, especially in regard to qualifications for voting, the election system, the nominating process, and laws regarding party organization.[5] The party

[4] New York, The Viking Press, Inc., 1947.

[5] As a consequence, details of party organization may vary from state to state, although political customs for over a century have tended to produce considerable similarity. Within any particular state the organization of the two major parties is almost identical.

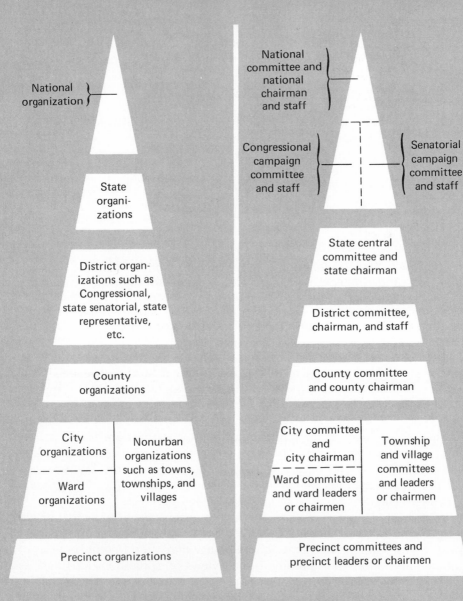

Figure 30. Units of United States Party Organization. (From R. Wallace Brewster, *Government in Modern Society,* 2d ed., p. 186. Reproduced by courtesy of Houghton Mifflin Company, Boston. © 1963.)

Figure 31. Party Officers and Personnel at Various Unit Levels in the United States. (From R. Wallace Brewster, *Government in Modern Society,* 2d ed., p. 186. Reproduced by courtesy of Houghton Mifflin Company, Boston. © 1963.)

organization within each state is far more centralized than the national organization. Usually county, city, ward, and precinct organizations are subordinate divisions of the state organization, although in the large cities considerable independence is often found. Within each state political power tends to be concentrated in the state central committee; locally it is likely to gravitate to a city or county committee.

It should be emphasized that even though party organization is pyramidal, in democratic countries a political party is not a disciplined organization like an army. Leaders at the top seldom have the power to give orders to those next below them, and this holds true all down the line, even to the rank-and-file party members. Party organizations at various levels often have a good deal of autonomy and independence, and the lines of power or influence are as likely to run upward as downward. A possible exception to this is a city, county, or state where a *political boss* has succeeded in building up a *political machine* that is firmly under his control. But the old-fashioned boss who personally dictates policies and chooses candidates is becoming rare.

Figure 30 gives a simplified picture of how, in the United States, the units of party organization are related to one another at various levels. Figure 31 shows the party officers and personnel at different levels.

Local and District Party Organization. At the base of our American party system are the precinct organizations. In most states *precincts* are not separate units of government. They are merely a device for dividing voters, geographically, into groups of convenient size in order to simplify the administration of elections. It has been estimated that there are in the United States more than 150,000 precincts. Their size varies from two hundred or fewer voters in thinly populated areas to two thousand or more in large cities; the average is in the neighborhood of four hundred. Because it is in the precincts that voting actually takes place, it is to the advantage of a political party to be organized in as many precincts as possible. There are, however, a great number of precincts, especially in sparsely populated areas, that contain no party organizations. There are many others in which only one party is organized. In the Deep South, for example, there are still some areas that have no Republican precinct organizations.

In each precinct party organization there is a precinct leader. Sometimes he is called a *precinct committeeman,* more often a *precinct captain.* He is a key figure in local politics. Formerly he was usually appointed by some higher party official, but today nearly all state laws require that he be chosen in the primary election, usually for a two-year term. In some precincts the leader is assisted by a *precinct committee,* which consists of several active party workers.

The chief responsibility of a precinct leader or captain is to deliver votes for his party candidates. To do this he must serve the interests of the people for whom he is the political leader. As a dispenser of good will and as a mediator between the individual and the government, he personalizes government. Nearly everywhere the seeker after party patronage uses him as a go-between. In the larger cities he has ample opportunity to serve the people by helping them to get such things as better street cleaning, better garbage collection, needed jobs, or welfare payments. He may even go so far as to provide bail for persons under arrest, adjust tax problems, stay eviction proceedings, secure temporary housing for those whose homes have burned, and intercede for anyone in difficulty with the government. His success often depends upon his ability to secure additional party workers on election day. These ring doorbells, distribute literature, transport voters to the polls, serve as baby sitters, and do the many things necessary to "deliver" the precinct. A party that is well organized at the "grass roots," or precinct level, usually wins elections.

After the precinct the next larger units of political organization, in urban areas, are first the ward and then the city. In nonurban areas the roughly corresponding units are the town (in New England), township, or village. The county organization covers a still wider territory and is usually very important. Members of a *city or county party committee* are in most cases also members of a precinct, ward, village, or township committee. In either a city or county organization a *committee chairman* serves as the nominal party leader for managing campaigns and distributing patronage. Sometimes he is really the boss, the man who makes the final decisions on most matters of importance. If he is the boss, he will be consulted by elective officials of his party before large government contracts are granted, before Congressmen whose districts are in his territory recommend candidates for federal appointments, or before the party supports any important legislation affecting leading members of his organization or voters in the area where he has political control.

Today nearly all city and county chairmen are elected. However, the real head of a political party is not necessarily the chairman of the party's committee. Indeed, he may hold no elective or appointive office whatever and yet may exert more influence than a mayor or governor because the elected officers of government may depend on him for retaining their positions.

Between them the two major parties have a total of over five thousand county committees in the more than three thousand counties of the country. Because the electorate tends to ignore county government, these committees are often self-perpetuating and become very powerful political agencies. In addition to the county patronage they control, they have general jurisdiction over the precinct organizations within the county and are therefore in a position to influence patronage in villages and towns, influence state and national appointments in their respective areas, and influence the votes of delegates to the state and national conventions. Those eager to increase popular control of government might well concern themselves with the democratization of county committees.

The districts that elect members of the state legislature or the United States House of Representatives seldom correspond to the boundaries of cities or counties. Hence, in addition to the types of organization already mentioned, political parties usually create special *campaign committees* to function in such districts during the period before an election. These committees are likely to consist of ward, city, and county leaders, and their purpose is to raise money and carry out campaign strategy for the benefit of party candidates.

State Party Organization. In every state each major party has a *state central committee,* which is the real center of political power in party organization.[6] It consists of the main political leaders from the precincts, wards, cities, and counties.

At one time the state party convention exercised supreme authority in party affairs, but the state committee has now, almost everywhere, taken over the greater part of its functions. Today the nomination of party candidates for office, once a function of the convention, is carried on through direct primaries, but the candidates whose names appear on the primary ballot are selected by the committee. The only important business left to the convention is the preparation of a state party platform.

In practice, the chairman of a state committee often exercises most of its functions and thus becomes one of the most powerful figures in American politics. The duties of the committee include (1) arranging for the state convention, (2) directing statewide party campaigns, (3) providing literature and speakers for local organizations, (4) supplying suitable candidates for party slates, and (5) dispensing party patronage. Presumably, it acts as an agent of the national committee in presidential elections, but in some states sectional interests occasionally dictate a policy of nonsupport for national candidates. More often than not, it is the national organization that comes begging for the support of the state committees, for it has no power to command their support.

National Organization. The national organization is a very loose confederation of state organizations. Although it performs dramatically in the presidential nominations and campaigns, it does little else. At the top of the party pyramid is a *national committee,* with a chairman and over 100 members. Every four years it plans a *national convention,* which nominates candidates for President and Vice-President and draws up and adopts a party platform. The national committee consists of one man and one woman from each state and territory and from the District of Columbia. Members are selected in different ways, by the different states. The four methods in use are (1) election by state delegates to the national convention; (2) election by the state convention; (3) appointment by the state central committee; and (4) election in a direct primary. At each convention the national committee goes through the formality of electing members of the new national committee, who have in fact already been chosen

---

[6] Members of such a committee are usually selected by direct primary, although it is not uncommon for them to be chosen by party convention or caucus. State central committees range in membership from a score or less to several hundred.

51. Hubert Humphrey Campaigning for the Presidency. Humphrey acknowledges cheers after making a speech at the United Steelworkers convention, 1968. (Courtesy United Press International, Inc.)

by the methods indicated, and of electing a new *national chairman*. Actually, the new chairman is selected by the presidential candidate. Because the national committee seldom meets, the chairman assumes most of its duties, though an executive subcommittee meeting frequently may assist him.

The national chairman, aided by a research, publicity, and public relations staff, directs the presidential campaign. His political wisdom may be an important factor in determining the success of his party in plucking the biggest of political plums—the Presidency of the United States. Traditionally, if his party was victorious, he was offered the position of Post-

52. Richard Nixon Campaigning for the Presidency. Nixon responds to crowd in New Orleans French Quarter, 1968. (Courtesy Wide World Photos.)

master General, an office that controlled considerable patronage.[7] However, in 1970, legislation was enacted to change the Post Office from a government department to a government corporation, and, as a result, post office jobs are not likely to be a source of patronage in the future.

The Congressional and Senatorial Campaign Committees. Though the national committee does little except during presidential-election years, each major party has two other committees that now function continually on a national scale and reach the peak of activity during the midterm election years. They are the Congressional Campaign Committee, composed of several party members from the House of Representatives, and a similar Senatorial Campaign Committee, composed of party members from the Senate. These committees attempt to maintain or increase party membership in Congress. Each committee maintains a permanent staff in Washington to plan Congressional campaigns, and during Congressional election years these committees work very closely with state committees in an attempt to secure the election of their party's candidates for Congress.

THE SUFFRAGE

Democratic government implies the wide extension of the franchise—the right to vote. Citizens of modern dictatorships also enjoy this privilege, though for them it is a privilege stripped of power. The right to elect government officials and to vote on public policies has been achieved by centuries of effort. We have already noted how suffrage was restricted in early America by rigid property and religious qualifications. In 1790, because of such requirements, only about 15 per cent of adult white males could vote. Since then the gradual trend throughout the world has been in the direction of extending the franchise and making it universal for all responsible adult citizens. The latest movement has been to reduce the voting age from twenty-one to eighteen. This movement reached it climax in the early summer of 1971. At that time the necessary thirty-eight state legislatures had ratified the twenty-sixth amendment to the Constitution, which gives eighteen-year-olds the right to vote in all elections. One argument for reducing the voting age was that this would give young people, at earlier ages, a greater interest in politics as well as some political experience. But the argument that was probably most effective was that it is the eighteen- to twenty-one-year-old group that fights the wars.

Obstacles to Effective Popular Control. The right to vote is not equivalent to the power to control the government. "We the people" in many lands have had our ballot power weakened in many ways: (1) by overburdening the voter with a long ballot, (2) by permitting him to participate

---

[7] President Harry S. Truman broke this tradition in 1947 by appointing as Postmaster General Jesse M. Donaldson, a career man in the department.

only in indirect elections, (3) by forcing him to declare publicly his choices, (4) by inadequate voting facilities, (5) by nominations controlled by the privileged few, (6) by limitations on who can hold office, (7) by corrupt administration of elections, (8) by denying elected officials the right to rule, and (9) in communist countries, by placing on the ballot only candidates sponsored by the official government party. Some of these limitations have existed and still exist in America and other democracies.

The Nonvoter. In America perhaps 65 to 70 per cent of the civilian population of voting age exercise their franchise in presidential elections; in the off-year congressional elections only about 55 per cent participate; and in local elections a mere 15 per cent is not uncommon. In Britain and the other democracies the percentage is considerably higher. Why do Americans fail to vote? There are many reasons; for example, the long ballot, qualification laws, and lack of interest.

The Long Ballot. It has not been unknown for the American voter to be faced with a ten-foot ballot, containing nominations for half a hundred public offices, a dozen or two city measures, and a few constitutional amendments. The ballot in Omaha, Nebraska, in 1946 was over thirteen feet long. Such cases are extreme, but ballots too long to make possible intelligent voting are still not uncommon. To escape frustration many voters fail to complete their ballots, or they decide to stay away from the polls and "let George do it."

The *long ballot* also encourages straight-ticket voting, because the citizen's inability to vote intelligently on all the candidates leads him to mark an X in the party square and hope that "the party" has put the right men on the ballot. An alternative to straight-ticket voting is the use of a trusted newspaper's selections. In either case the sovereign voter is exercising control in a very general way.

Qualifications for Voting. Under our federal system the separate states, subject to certain restrictions, determine who can vote, and therefore the election laws are not uniform. All of them, however, require citizenship, residence, and registration. The *residence laws* were designed to insure that the voter was acquainted with local problems, but they formerly disqualified many from voting in national elections. Some required two years in the state, one year in the county, and thirty days in the election district. The wisdom of these residence requirements in a highly industrialized mobile society was frequently questioned. Under the Voting Rights Act passed by Congress in 1970, the residence requirements for voting in *presidential* elections are reduced to a maximum of thirty days. This provision has been declared constitutional by a Supreme Court decision. The *registration requirement* for voting is designed to reduce illegal voting, but where repeated registrations are necessary—some states now provide for permanent registration—this requirement can become burdensome. Also, especially in the deep South, blacks have frequently been kept from voting by preventing them from registering. As noted in an earlier chapter, a number of states formerly required would-be registrants to pass literacy tests. But under the Voting Rights Act of 1970 all use of literacy tests as a qualification for voting is forbidden. We have already mentioned that as a result of a recent amendment to the Constitution all persons eighteen years old or over, who are otherwise qualified, must now be allowed to vote.

Not so long ago, some states required citizens to pay poll taxes in order to vote. These taxes were very small, but they probably discouraged some poor people, including most blacks, from voting. Early in 1964 the needed number of state legislatures ratified the Twenty-fourth Amendment to the federal Constitution. This prohibits a poll tax as a requirement for voting in a *national* election. Later the Supreme Court declared poll taxes unconstitutional as a requirement for voting in *any* election, on the ground that they violate the Fifteenth Amendment.

Lack of Interest and Lack of Knowledge. Many people fail to vote because of indifference produced by lack of political education and experience. They are not conscious of the burdens of the long ballot or of voting qualifications; they simply feel no compulsion to participate in the electoral process. Many of them come from homes with a long tradition of nonparticipation in political affairs. They are often considered selfish and unpatriotic, but in many cases ignorance of issues and candidates is the main reason for not voting.

Compulsory Voting and Citizenship Training. Nonvoting could be greatly reduced through compulsory voting. It has worked satisfactorily in Australia, Belgium, and other democracies; but its existence in Soviet Russia has led some Americans to regard it as undemocratic. Some students of government feel that it is just as well that the disinterested and ignorant should not vote. Others, however, have long felt that voting is a duty as well as a privilege. As yet the emphasis on the duty to vote has not reached the stage where Americans are willing to fine the person who fails to perform this duty. We are more inclined to trust to informal methods of inducing people to go to the polls. Perhaps more citizenship education and training in the school and community will increase participation in the electoral process and strengthen social disapproval of the nonvoter. Unfortunately, effective citizenship training is difficult to provide, and much that passes under that name in our schools is of little value. But if intelligent voting is desired, and it is certainly desirable, citizenship training of the right kind is more likely to produce it than legal compulsion.

The Short Ballot. The short ballot should also aid in reducing the number of nonvoters. Terms of office can be lengthened; elected offices can be limited to those that deal with policy formation; and routine administrative measures, as well as most political measures, can be left off the ballot. The national government has pointed the way in the use and value of the short ballot; the voter is asked to vote for no more than four offices: President, Vice-President, Senator, and Representative. Anyone reasonably responsible can vote intelligently for these offices, and democratic government is not impaired by the fact that secondary administrative officers and judges are appointed. Probably 75 per cent of the elective offices on the long ballot could be filled to advantage by executive appointment or through the state and city civil service systems. Good government is not promoted by asking the voters to elect coroners, dog catchers, meat inspectors, municipal court clerks—or even judges. The people are entitled to choose the representatives who will determine public policy; but other officials should be appointed, because the voters are also entitled to a ballot short enough to enable them to exercise the franchise easily and intelligently.

NOMINATIONS

In the United States there are more than half a million elective offices, and competing political parties select their candidates for these through the process of *nomination*.

The Caucus. Nominations were first made by *self-announcement*, or self-nomination, and the *parlor caucus*. The parlor caucus was a private meeting of persons interested in controlling public affairs. In selecting candidates for state and national offices, these methods were soon replaced by the *legislative caucus*, composed of party members in the legislative bodies of nation or state. But this method was criticized for being unrepresentative and soon gave way to the *delegate convention*, which was first used in the presidential election of 1832 and has been employed ever since for selecting candidates for the Presidency.

The National Convention. The national conventions of the two major parties, which meet in the summer of each presidential-election year, now usually in July or August, are big shows at which excitement often reaches a high pitch. However, if the President of the United States belongs to the party holding the convention, and if he is eligible for another term,[8] it is usually a foregone conclusion that he will be the nominee. This circumstance robs a convention of much of its drama.

A national convention often looks like a circus, but this is a surface characteristic, especially if it must really choose a candidate for the highest office in the land. In this case the stakes are high, and most of the serious business of the convention is carried on in meetings of committees or prominent political leaders where bargaining is carried on and compromises are reached with little fanfare.

In about two thirds of the states the national delegates are chosen by state and district conventions or party committees; in other states they are chosen in presidential primaries. In the latter case the voter may or may not have an opportunity to indicate his choice of a presidential can-

---

[8] Under the Twenty-second Amendment to the Constitution no one can be elected to the Presidency more than twice, and no one who has held the office of President for more than two years while completing someone else's term can be elected more than once.

53. Democratic National Convention, 1968. Delegates group their standards
in front of the speaker's platform and cheer the men they chose as their
presidential standard-bearers. (Courtesy Wide World Photos.)

didate. Even if he is permitted to express a choice, he still may be given
no opportunity to vote for a slate of delegates actually committed to the
candidate whom he prefers. Presidential primaries are not as popular now
as they were in the 1920's, largely because the main presidential aspirants,
the party hierarchy, and the majority of voters recognize that they seldom
determine who the candidate will be.

The Direct Primary. With some exceptions, the most notable being the
President and Vice-President of the United States, the *direct primary* has
practically supplanted the convention as a nominating device at all levels
of government. It is a method whereby the voters of a given party choose
their party's candidates in a party election. It is held at public expense
and in accordance with state law. The primary candidate is not running for
office. He is merely seeking the privilege of later facing in an *election*
the victorious candidates of the other parties.

Closed and Open Primaries. Primary elections in most states are *closed,*
and this limits the primary ballot of a party to those who can prove that
they belong. The voter must show in some way his party affiliation. In
many states he indicates it on his registration card, and this card is then
used by the election officials to determine which party ballot he will be
given in the primary. The biggest criticism of the *closed primary* is that it
infringes upon the individual's right to exercise the franchise in the secrecy
of the voting booth.

A few states have an *open* primary, in which one may vote in the party of his choice without disclosing which one he chooses. The voter is not required to register his party affiliation, and he need have none. Independent voters naturally prefer this type, for they are disfranchised in the closed primaries. They are often numerous enough so that, if allowed to vote, they could determine the selection of candidates. The chief objection to an open primary is that political machines can use its freedom to "raid" the other party. *Raiding* is the practice of sending machine members to vote for the weakest candidate of the opposition party, so as to weaken it at the general election.

Washington State has adopted an open primary that employs a ballot of the *office-block* type. Candidates of all parties for nomination for a particular political office are listed, together with their party affiliations after their names. This kind of ballot makes it possible to vote a split ticket even in a primary election. The person of each party receiving the highest vote for each office is nominated.

Evaluating the Primary. The direct primary originated as a reform movement, and its advocates maintained that it would replace boss rule. It has tended to weaken the control of political machines, but it has not replaced boss rule. Any party member can usually get his name on the ballot by paying a small fee and securing a relatively small number of signatures on a petition. [9] Critics of the primary maintain that it (1) weakens party responsibility, (2) enables the rich to win nominations by underwriting heavy campaign expenditures, and (3) is an extravagent waste of public money. These criticisms are half-truths; but the high hopes of the early advocates of the primary have not been realized. The "people" have not responded to the opportunity to participate in nominations by selecting as candidates the most honest and capable citizens. The quality of the candidates has been little changed. One reason for this is that the party leaders frequently hold a preprimary convention at which they choose an *organization slate,* which is usually approved by the voters in the primary. In most cases the number of citizens who vote in a primary is small. But the primary does give the people the power to vote against a bad organization slate, and occasionally they use that power to promote good government.

THE VOTING PROCESS

In a democracy the voters determine the winners on election day. After the pressure groups, the political parties, the press, and all interested persons have campaigned for their favorites, the day of decision arrives. A fair and honest count of legitimate votes cast in secrecy has become the democratic ideal for elections, and in spite of serious problems in certain

[9] In 1954 the Republican primary ballot in Illinois contained nine candidates for the Senate nomination.

areas, the United States has made considerable progress toward realizing this ideal.

The government administers elections and pays all the expenses. Police protection is furnished in abundance, and the parties provide their own poll watchers to guard against ballot frauds and other illegal behavior. Much care is taken to provide voting secrecy, which is made possible by the use of the Australian ballot.

The Australian Ballot System. Secrecy in voting was not provided until late in the nineteenth century, with the introduction of the *Australian ballot*. The essentials of this system are as follows: the only ballots used are those provided by the state at state expense; they are all uniform; they contain the names of all the candidates; and they are on good paper (to prevent party workers from seeing the marks through thin paper). Public officials deliver the ballots at official polling places on election day and account for every ballot used. The ballots are marked in secret and immediately deposited in the ballot box. After the polls close, the ballots are carefully counted under the watchful eye of representatives of two or more parties. As an additional precaution all ballots, valid and invalid, are put under lock and key so that they may be referred to and checked if the election is contested.

This system provided a reform that was needed to safeguard the right of the citizen to cast his ballot freely at elections. However, it has not entirely eliminated fraudulent practices. The "cemetery vote," "ballot stuffing," "chain voting," destruction of ballots, and dishonest counts are practices that still appear on the American political scene; but they are certainly less common than they were formerly.

Types of Ballots. There are two general types of secret ballots used in America in regular elections: (1) the office-block, used in some states, and (2) the party-column. The *office-block type,* which we have already mentioned in connection with state of Washington primaries, is sometimes called the *Massachusetts ballot*. It is divided into blocks, one for each office, with the candidates of all parties listed under the office with their party designations. The voter must mark the name of the candidate he chooses for each office. Because this type of ballot makes voting a straight ticket as difficult as voting a split ticket, it is believed to encourage intelligent voting. It certainly discourages straight party voting; but it is also time consuming, and when the voter is allowed only a limited time, it may prevent him from completing his ballot.

The *party-column type* (*Indiana ballot*), used in most states, lists all candidates of one party in a single column. To vote a straight ticket the voter makes only a single mark at the top of the ballot. Party officials prefer this type because it discourages independent, split-ticket voting.

The *voting machine* is a mechanical adaptation of the secret ballot, and it can be used for either type of ballot described above. It tabulates the votes automatically and thus provides for a speedy and accurate count. However, until voters become familiar with the machines, they often find them difficult to operate, especially if they vote a split ticket. On the other hand, voting machines make impossible some kinds of vote frauds that can be practiced with paper ballots. Today machines are common in large cities, and, despite their high original price, they probably reduce election costs over a period of years.

EVALUATION OF THE DEMOCRATIC POLITICAL PROCESS

The political process in America and the other democracies is complex and confusing but nevertheless challenging. To win election to a major office takes time, work, money, and patience; from an idea to the enactment of a law is often a long journey. To reach such goals mountains of obstacles must be scaled and arid deserts of electoral inertia must be crossed. Compromises are necessary, and concessions must be made to many conflicting interest groups, each of which has a somewhat different destination in mind. Ignorance and other human limitations must be taken into account all along the route. Fraud and favoritism are constant dangers. But democracy offers the common man the challenge of the opportunity to rule himself. To the extent that he accepts the challenge, his self-respect is enhanced. His burden is not light, and he may be unwilling to accept it; or having attempted to carry it, he may become discouraged and finally indifferent. He may even turn to a dictator to solve his problems for him, now and for the indefinite future.

But in America, as in some other Western countries, democracy has been long established and has had a long period of growth. The democratic way of life has become so firmly embedded in our culture and has brought us so many personal and social advantages that few of us can really conceive, for ourselves, of living under any other social system. No other system can give us an equal degree of personal liberty, nor so well protect our individual rights. If at times we complain about the faults of democracy and its failure to achieve perfection and to bring us Utopia, we are only being human. When we consider the alternatives, most of us believe that our American brand of democracy is providing us with benefits that can be matched in few other countries; and we believe that, if we meet our responsibilities, it will provide these benefits in greater measure in the future.

Terms to Be Understood

politics	spoils system	parties of power
political process	classified civil	rightist
political party	service systems	leftist
pressure group	personality party	one-party system
military-industrial	principle or	biparty system
complex	program party	multiparty system

political boss
political machine
invisible
  government
pyramidal party
  organization
decentralized parties
precinct
  committeeman
precinct captain
precinct committee

city committee
county committee
state central
  committee
national committee
national convention
national chairman
party convention
campaign
  committees
nomination

election
long ballot
short ballot
caucus
direct primary
closed primary
open primary
Australian ballot
  system
office-block ballot
party-column ballot

Questions for Review and Discussion

1. As listed in the text, what are the main factors in the political process?
2. How is public opinion related to politics and government in a democracy?
3. What useful purposes, if any, do pressure groups serve? Are their activities ever undesirable? Discuss.
4. How great a danger is the military-industrial complex to our democratic society? Defend your point of view. Can we dispense with this complex? Why or why not?
5. Are political parties necessary in a democracy with a large population? Why or why not?
6. How do public opinion polls attempt to measure opinion? Why do they frequently fail to pick the winners in an election?
7. Make a list of the major functions performed by political parties in the United States.
8. Do honestly administered civil service systems have any drawbacks? If so, what are they?
9. Describe the different types of political parties.
10. What are the advantages of a two-party system in a democracy?
11. Distinguish between rightist and leftist parties.
12. How does the organization of an American political party differ from that of an army or a corporation?
13. Describe the organization of the national political parties of the United States.
14. What is the role of the Congressional and Senatorial Campaign committees?
15. Explain the importance of compromise in a two-party system.
16. Is it unfortunate that our two major parties seldom differ sharply in their behavior toward major issues? Why or why not?
17. Trace the "democratization" in America of the right to vote.
18. The right to vote is not always the power to control. Why?
19. Should all citizens be required to vote, and subjected to a fine for noncompliance, or is it better to leave voting to those willing to take the trouble? Defend your answer.
20. Point out the advantages and disadvantages of each of the different methods of nominating candidates for office.
21. Compare open and closed primaries, pointing out the advantages and disadvantages of each types.

22. Compare the *office-block* and the *party-column* ballots, and indicate how each affects voting behavior.
23. Since in every national election in the United States there undoubtedly is some fraudulent voting and fraudulent counting of ballots, can we say that our elections express the will of the people? Discuss.

For Further Study

Banfield, Edward C., and James Q. Wilson, *City Politics,* Cambridge, Mass., Harvard University Press, 1963.

Berelson, Bernard, and M. Janowitz, eds., *Reader in Public Opinion and Communication,* 2d ed., New York, The Free Press, 1966.

Burns, James M., and Jack W. Peltason, *Government by the People,* 7th ed., Englewood Cliffs, N.J., Prentice-Hall, Inc., 1969.

Campbell, Angus, *Elections and the Political Order,* New York, John Wiley & Sons, Inc., 1966.

Deutsch, Karl W., *Politics and Government: How People Decide Their Fate,* paperback, Boston, Houghton Mifflin Company, 1970.

Ferguson, John H., and Dean E. McHenry, *The American Federal Government,* 9th ed., New York, McGraw-Hill, Inc., 1967.

Hunt, Elgin F., and Jules Karlin, eds., *Society Today and Tomorrow,* 2d ed., paperback, New York, The Macmillan Company, 1967. See therein "Government by Concurrent Majorities" by John Fischer.

James, Judson, *Parties on Trial,* paperback, New York, Western Publishing Company, Inc., 1969.

Jennings, M. Kent, and Harmon Zeigler, eds., *The Electoral Process,* Englewood Cliffs, N.J., Prentice-Hall, Inc., 1966.

Lane, Robert, and David Sears, *Public Opinion,* Englewood Cliffs, N.J., Prentice-Hall, Inc., 1964.

Lang, Robert, and Gladys Engel Lang, *Politics and Television,* Chicago, Quadrangle Books, Inc., 1968.

Lipson, Leslie, *The Great Issues of Politics,* 3d ed., Englewood Cliffs, N.J., Prentice-Hall, Inc., 1965.

McGinnis, Joe, *Selling of the President 1968,* paperback, New York, Pocket Books, Inc., 1970.

Nimmo, Dan, *The Political Persuaders: Techniques of Modern Election Campaigns,* Spectrum paperback, Englewood Cliffs, N.J., Prentice-Hall, Inc., 1970.

Peirce, Neal R., *The People's President: The Electoral College in American History and the Direct-Vote Alternative,* New York, Simon and Schuster, Inc., 1968.

Pomper, Gerald M., *Nominating the President: The Politics of Convention Choice,* paperback, New York, W. W. Norton & Company, Inc., 1966.

Rossiter, Clinton, *Parties and Politics in America,* Signet paperback, New York, New American Library, Inc., 1964.

Rourke, Francis, *Bureaucracy, Politics, and Public Policy,* paperback, Boston, Little, Brown and Company, 1969.

Sorauf, Frank J., *Party Politics in America,* Boston, Little, Brown and Company, 1968.

Whale, John, *The Half-Shut Eye: Television and Politics in Britain and America,* New York, St. Martin's Press, Inc., 1969.

White, Theodore H., *The Making of the President 1968,* paperback, New York, Pocket Books, Inc., 1970.

Chapter 28

Government Finance and the Social Welfare

Some small, archaic, and relatively isolated societies needed no formally organized system of government. Informal social controls were sufficient to meet the needs of such groups fairly well. But over the centuries many societies have grown phenomenally in size and complexity. Along with this growth has come a vast increase in the importance of government and in the variety of the functions it has undertaken to perform. Even some pre-literate societies, that is, societies that have no form of writing, have developed relatively complex systems of government.

As government has increased in importance and in the scope of its activities, its financial needs have also increased, not just in proportion to increases in population and output of goods, but at a much more rapid rate. Today, in most advanced industrial countries, the tax burden for the maintenance of government activities absorbs from 25 to 40 per cent of the entire national income.

What We Get for Our Taxes. When taxes take such a large proportion of the income of a nation, we naturally wonder whether government and its services are worth their cost. Would it not be better if people were allowed to keep this money and spend it for themselves? The general answer is that no modern society could operate successfully for a week without government. Government, if the choice is between having it or not having it, is worth almost anything it may cost. It performs innumerable indispensable services from which we all benefit. On the other hand, it is quite probable that some of the activities carried on by government are not worth a fraction of their cost in taxes. Also, it is possible for graft, inefficiency, and waste to develop on a large scale in the operations of a government. Taxes are never too high when they are spent by government to provide the people with greater benefits than they would receive if they kept the tax money and spent it themselves. Taxes are always too high if they are wasted or are spent on activities that benefit favored groups at the expense of the general public.

Other things being equal, the amount of money a government requires depends on the number and character of its functions. There are some government services that most of us regard as indispensable, such as protecting the nation against foreign enemies and maintaining law and order at home. In addition, there are many government services that are desirable and important and that could not as a rule be performed by private enterprise, or could not be performed as well. These include public health services, welfare services, most road building, airport construction, harbor dredging, conservation of natural resources, maintaining free schools, and providing police protection and a system of courts. But all government services cost money, and no matter how desirable they may seem, their benefits should always be weighed against their costs. In the final analysis these costs are always paid by the public, and the higher the level of taxes, the less money people have to meet their own personal needs.

THE HIGH COST OF GOVERNMENT

The Rise in Government Expenditures. In all industrial countries the costs of government have been rising for many decades, whether expressed in monetary units or as a percentage of national income. At the end of a war there is a temporary decline, but the long-run trend seems always to be upward. In the United States this rising trend has been especially sharp since the outbreak of World War I in 1914.

Table 16 shows the increase in government expenditures in this country for selected years from 1890 to 1968. It shows total expenditures per capita and then breaks the totals down into dollar and percentage expenditures at the federal, state, and local levels. During this period of almost eighty years, the total of government expenditures per capita, measured in dollars, increased more than a hundred times, whereas personal income per capita was increasing, on the basis of the best estimates available, not more than twenty times. In other words, government spending rose five times as fast as incomes. It should be noted that though federal spending from 1890 to 1913 was only about one third of the total, in 1968 it was almost twice state and local spending combined. Taken alone, federal spending per capita increased about 190 times.

Table 16. *Government Expenditures, Federal, State, and Local: Per Capita and Percentage Distribution, Selected Fiscal Years 1890–1968*

| | Dollars Per Capita | | | | Percentage Distribution | | |
Year	Total	Federal	State	Local	Federal	State	Local
1890	$14	$5	$1	$8	35.7	7.1	57.1
1902	21	7	2	12	34.5	10.8	54.8
1913	33	10	4	19	30.2	11.6	58.3
1922	85	34	12	39	40.5	13.6	46.0
1932	100	34	21	45	34.3	20.6	45.1
1940	155	77	35	44	49.3	22.3	28.5
1944	821	751	30	40	91.4	3.7	4.9
1948	380	246	66	69	64.6	17.3	18.1
1953	697	507	89	101	72.7	12.8	14.5
1958	781	498	135	148	63.8	17.3	18.9
1962	955	614	158	182	64.4	16.6	19.1
1964	1,033	662	176	195	64.1	17.0	18.9
1966	1,153	734	201	219	63.6	17.4	19.0
1968	$1,444	$947	$247	$250	65.6	17.1	17.3

Source: Facts and Figures on Government Finance, 1958–1959, p. 19, and 1969, p. 18. Copyright 1958 and 1969 by the Tax Foundation, Inc., New York.

Why Government Costs Have Risen. The extraordinary rise of government spending that is shown in Table 16 has resulted from three factors. First, there has been a great increase of government outlays for an ever widening variety of public services. Second, in the period covered, the United States was engaged in two world wars and three important "secondary" wars: the Spanish War in 1898 and the much more recent ones in Korea and Vietnam. These wars were not only tremendously expensive in themselves, but they have been followed by conditions that require us to maintain, in time of peace, vastly larger armed forces than formerly. Also, they have resulted in our paying out very large sums annually for veterans' benefits of various kinds, besides interest on a huge public debt, and billions of dollars in aid to foreign countries. Third, and largely as the result of war, there has been a great inflation of the price level, so that by 1970 the money prices of goods and services were more than three-and-a-half times as high as in 1914 and about five times as high as in 1890.

Obstacles to Reducing the Cost of Government. Rising costs of government and high taxes create urgent demands that something be done to correct the situation, but in spite of President Nixon's efforts to reduce federal spending, it rose during his first two years in office. Part of the trouble was "built-in" increases resulting from programs established in the past. In fiscal year 1970 the government paid out about eighteen billion dollars just for interest on the public debt. Part of the trouble was inflation of prices and costs, likewise a result of past federal policies.

State and local spending have also risen rapidly and will probably continue to do so. Inflation and a fast-growing population have put our local governments under constant pressure to find more funds for important services for which they are largely responsible. These include better street maintenance, the provision of parking facilities and expressways to relieve traffic congestion, better garbage collection, better police protection, slum clearance, the provision of more parks, the improvement and expansion of education, and more-adequate welfare payments. Many of our larger cities face very difficult financial problems. Those of New York City seem almost insoluble, but except in degree they are similar to those of other cities. New York's projected budget for fiscal year 1971 calls for welfare expenditures alone of over $1.1 billion, and total expenditures for the fiscal year of about $8.6 billion. The latter amount represents an increase of 90 per cent just since 1966. It is more money than was spent by our federal government in any single peace-time year before 1939, except for 1919, the year just after the end of World War I. The state governments are likewise under pressure for more funds, partly in order to aid local governments and partly to meet needs of their own. State needs include funds for the expansion and improvement of highway systems, prisons, mental hospitals, and state colleges and universities, and also for the abatement of pollution.

In the case of the federal government, the prospect of holding costs in line is not very encouraging either. New expenditures are constantly being incurred, such as those for higher Social Security benefits, the whole anti-poverty program, more aid to the states, and substantial salary increases for federal employees, including large ones for Congressmen and the President. Interest payments on the public debt and veterans' benefits also keep rising; and in the long run there is not much prospect of holding down military spending, which is the largest item of all. Some expenditures could be cut without loss to the national welfare, but politics or just lack of understanding makes this exceedingly difficult. Many believe that much of the money spent on both the farm program and foreign aid is really wasted, but at present the outlook for permanently reducing such spending is uncertain. Many others believe we should increase, not decrease, our contributions to less-developed nations.

Inefficiency, Waste, and the Problem of Big Government. Most students of the problem would agree that there is a great deal of waste and inefficiency in the performance of government functions, though there is no way of measuring such waste very accurately. At the local and even the state level, waste and inefficiency are sometimes obvious in such cases as when temporary employees, appointed in payment for political services, do little or no work, or when important public services are inadequately planned and supervised. Such problems may possibly be more common in state or local governments than at the federal level; but the efficient operation of the federal government poses other problems that are not met in like degree by governments at lower levels.

In the first place our federal government is so huge and complex an organization that no one person can completely grasp the whole picture of its operations. This one fact greatly increases the difficulty of planning and coordinating its activities so as to achieve a high degree of efficiency. Most of its administrative departments, commissions, and agencies were not planned as part of a coordinated whole but were created one by one to meet various social and economic situations as they arose. As a result, functions are sometimes duplicated by different agencies, much work of doubtful value is performed, and as red tape proliferates, office staffs grow larger and larger. Moreover, each established government agency and its friends are likely to resist vigorously any attempt to abolish it or even to reduce its functions or personnel. Also it should be noted that there is no individual or board, as there would be in a business corporation, that has the power to reorganize or control all the parts and operations of the federal government. Efforts to reduce waste are made from time to time by

54. Storage Problem for Red Tape. Records for the federal government require storage space estimated by second Hoover commission as equal to seven Pentagons. (Courtesy *U.S. News & World Report.*)

Congress, the President, or department heads, but the difficulties encountered are great. An unusual achievement in the field of government economy was the elimination a few years ago, by Secretary of Defense Robert McNamara, of a number of unneeded military establishments such as certain army training camps, shipyards, and Air Force bases. But even McNamara did not succeed in eliminating all the waste that undoubtedly occurs in the operations of our vast military establishment.

One of the obstacles to efficient operation of the federal government is the difficulty of controlling the buying of government supplies. Adequate procedures for approving and recording government purchases are necessary, or else the way would be open for all sorts of misuse of funds. But these procedures can easily develop into such complex red tape that its cost is all out of proportion to the value of the goods bought. For example, a House of Representatives committee once found that it cost the government $37.15 to buy $10 worth of lumber. The extra $27.15 was the cost of the various kinds of paper work involved.

The extent of waste in the federal government was brought out clearly some years ago by two successive presidential commissions, appointed to study the organization of the government for the purpose of recommending reforms. Both commissions were under the chairmanship of former President Herbert Hoover. The first Hoover commission did its work in the period 1947–1949 under President Harry S. Truman, who deserves considerable credit for recognizing both the need for reform and the fact that Hoover was especially well qualified for the task delegated to him; the second commission operated in the period 1953–1955 under President Dwight D. Eisenhower. Largely as a result of the reports of these two commissions, plus enabling legislation passed by Congress, some important reforms in government organization were instituted. In a pamphlet issued in 1958 by the National Citizens Committee for the Hoover Report, former President Hoover is quoted as follows: "Economies totaling $7 billion can be traced to the First Commission's Report. And we are on our way to savings of upwards of $3 billion a year as a result of the Second Commission's recommendations."

There is, however, no complete solution for the problem of eliminating waste and inefficiency from the operations of our national government. This is one of the penalties that we pay for "big government," and it is a very good reason for not further extending the powers and functions of the federal government unless there is clearly no acceptable alternative. Few people fully realize the vast size of our government. In comparison, our "big business" corporations, like General Motors or American Telephone and Telegraph Company, are of moderate size and are certainly much more manageable.

Public Apathy and the Pressure of Special Interests. Big government is not the only explanation of inefficiency and waste—and, it must be added, graft—in public affairs. Much of this is found in governments at all levels, and graft is probably a more serious problem in city government than in the national government. Reform is difficult because of relative public indifference. It is true that the public pays the bill, but often the individual is not really aware that he has a personal part in meeting it; at most, the cost to him of any one government expenditure is likely to be negligible. It is another case where what should be everybody's business becomes nobody's business.

A further obstacle to reducing government expenditures is the pressure of special interests. The farmers want price supports; the shipping companies want subsidies; and almost every city or region wants a new post office, a dam, an airfield, a shipyard, or some other government enterprise that would bring it direct benefits. Still another obstacle is all the social ills for which we seek remedies that require more spending.

GOVERNMENT REVENUES AND TAXATION

Sources of Government Funds. Governments occasionally obtain their revenues from unusual sources. For example, the governments of Saudi Arabia and several other Arab states receive their chief income from royalties on petroleum, which they allow foreign corporations to extract and export. Ordinarily, however, there are only three sources of funds open to a government: (1) the sale of services and commodities, (2) taxes, and (3) borrowing.

The sale of services and commodities is usually a negligible source of government income, though here and there one finds local communities in the United States that sell a utility service such as electric power to the public at a profit. Selling a service of this kind at a high enough price to yield profits is a kind of taxation and is a partial substitute for taxes of the usual type. Our federal government likewise sells goods and services, notable examples being postal service and the electric power services of the TVA. Also, we must not forget public lands, and surplus equipment of the armed forces. On balance, however, it is very doubtful whether the federal government has made any net profit over the years on sales of this kind.

For most governments, the major source of revenue is taxes. Next in importance to these as a source of funds is borrowing. However, funds obtained by borrowing are not revenue, for they must ultimately be repaid, and in the meantime they necessitate the payment of interest. To pay interest, more taxes must be levied, and likewise to repay the principal, unless old debts are continually paid off by creating new ones.

Because taxes are the chief source of government revenue and because today their total amount is more than 35 per cent of the national income, it is important to understand the nature of taxation and the problems to which it gives rise.

The Nature of Taxes. *Taxes are compulsory payments made by an individual or an organization for the support of public services,* but ordinarily there is little relation between the amount of taxes paid by individuals and the benefits received. Taxes are levied either on the basis of some status the taxpayer enjoys, such as being an owner of property or a receiver of income, or else on the basis of some activity in which he engages, such as buying goods, selling goods, or making gifts.

Taxes are sometimes distinguished from the *fees* that are required by law for the services of government officials or for the exercise of certain legal privileges. When a fee represents a payment to a government officer for some special service, and when it no more than covers the cost of the service, perhaps it should not be regarded as a tax. But many fees are simply payments that must be made for the privilege of doing something that would otherwise be illegal, such as getting married, owning and driving a car, or operating a tavern. As a rule the funds received are used for public purposes and not for the special benefit of the fee payer. Such fees should probably be regarded as taxes.

A *special assessment* is another type of payment. It is a tax because it is compulsory and its proceeds are used for public purposes. But it is levied on a property owner because he is presumed to receive some direct benefit from a certain public improvement, such as the paving of a street in front of his house.

Characteristics of a Good Tax System. There are certain general characteristics that a good tax system should have in as large measure as possible. First, it should be capable of meeting necessary public expenditures. Also, it should be simple, so that the taxes levied under it are easy to understand, easy to pay, and easy to collect. The tax laws should be clear and definite, in order that everyone may readily determine, with no uncertainty, just how much he must pay. In addition—and this is likely to follow from the other conditions just mentioned—a good tax system should be inexpensive to administer, for obviously it is undesirable that the proceeds of taxes should be consumed by the costs of collecting them.

There are two further characteristics of a good tax system that require our special attention. One is that it should, in the judgment of the community, distribute the tax burden fairly. The other is that it should impair economic incentives and opportunities as little as possible.

Fairness in Taxation. We are all agreed that people should be treated "fairly." But there is no complete agreement as to just what is fair or unfair, and so, in attempting to achieve fairness in taxation, the best we can do is to follow the rough consensus of the community. Practically everyone would agree that a man with an income of a hundred thousand dollars should pay more taxes than one with an income of ten thousand dollars. But precisely how much more?

Today the generally accepted basis for distributing the tax burden is *ability to pay.* On first thought, it might seem that taxes ought to be distributed on the basis of *benefits received.* This, however, would present two great difficulties. First, the money value of benefits received from government can seldom if ever be measured even roughly; and second, if it could be measured, many people might be unable to pay for their share of the total. As a guide for apportioning taxes, the ability-to-pay principle is not only more practical, but it is really fairer. Granted that there is no way of measuring or pricing all the benefits that we receive from the government, we are all members of the community, and in a sense we depend on it for everything that we have. Hence, we should, it is said, be willing to support it according to our ability.

But acceptance of the ability-to-pay principle does not go very far in enabling us to set up a fair tax system. Various questions at once arise. Should we tax people in direct proportion to their incomes (or wealth), or should we levy taxes at a higher percentage on people with large incomes? Should we, in addition, take into account a man's dependents, debts, or other special obligations? In our modern income tax, to which reference will be made later, allowance is made for some of these factors.

Maintaining Economic Incentives. It is very desirable that taxes should impair economic incentives as little as possible. Taxes on corporations and other business enterprises should not be so high as to discourage them from trying to expand in order to increase their earnings, nor so high as to make it excessively difficult for new and small enterprises to get started and to accumulate capital out of earnings. Neither should taxes on large incomes be so high that it is not worthwhile for people to try to earn such incomes or to invest their capital in productive enterprises that involve substantial risk but which, if successful, will provide employment and income for many people.

Regressive, Proportional, and Progressive Taxes. A tax is technically *regressive* if the *rate* falls as the value of the thing taxed rises. To illustrate, if the real estate tax were levied on this basis (which it is not), a man with a $10,000 house might pay a tax equal to 3 per cent of its value, whereas the man with a $25,000 house might be taxed at a rate of only 2 per cent. Certainly no modern government would consider levying a tax that was regressive in this sense. But sometimes taxes that are levied on a proportional basis are *regressive* in the sense in which we commonly use the term, that is, they take a larger *proportion* of income from the poor than from the well-to-do. This is true of a general sales tax, because poor people spend a larger proportion of their incomes in stores than do rich people. The latter save relatively more and also spend relatively more in ways that are not usually subject to the sales tax, for example, on hiring servants.

A tax is *proportional* if the *rate* remains the same regardless of the value of what is taxed. This is the basis on which the real estate tax is actually levied. If the rate is 2 per cent, it applies equally to a piece of property with an assessed value of a thousand dollars or to one valued at ten million dollars.

A tax is *progressive* when the *rate* rises as the value of the thing taxed increases. Modern personal income taxes illustrate the progressive principle. Unless legal *loopholes* are available for avoiding the higher rates on larger incomes, these taxes take substantially higher proportions of income from the well-to-do than from the poor. This fits in with the ability-to-pay

"The propulsion for this new ICBM will be the usual type—middle-class taxpayer." (Courtesy Don Wilder. Copyright 1970 *The Saturday Review, Inc.*)

principle, on the theory that the more income a man has, the larger the proportion of it he can pay in taxes without suffering any great hardship. However, extremely high tax rates on large incomes are not only likely to discourage people from making the efforts or taking the risks required to obtain such incomes; they are also apt to make tax evasion irresistibly attractive.

Just what proportion of income is taken by taxes from people in different income groups is not easy to say. A few years ago, with the top income surtax above 90 per cent, many people had the idea that our tax laws were designed to "soak the rich." But today it appears that, taking all taxes into account, the highest *proportionate* burden falls on the lower-income groups. Though the federal income tax is progressive, other taxes that are not and that fall heavily on people with relatively small incomes have risen greatly, including sales taxes, Social Security taxes, and real estate taxes. Even the higher excise and income taxes paid by corporations tend to be passed on to the general public in higher prices. Two or three years ago, the Economic Unit of *U. S. News & World Report* made a study that indicated that taxes absorbed about 34 per cent of incomes under $3,000 annually but only 28 per cent of those above $15,000.[1]

Shifting the Burden of a Tax. One of the difficulties encountered by a government when it attempts to distribute taxes equitably is that the people from whom a tax is collected do not necessarily bear its burden. Often they are able to shift it to someone else, at least in part. This is not the place to go into a detailed discussion of the economic theory of the shift-

[1] *U. S. News & World Report,* December 9, 1968, pp. 66-67.

ing and incidence of taxes, but it may safely be said that as a rule the major part of any tax placed on commodities that enter into trade is borne by the ultimate buyer in higher prices. A good example of this is the federal excise tax on cigarettes. The final buyer bears most of such a tax because the producer cannot, in the long run, stay in business unless he can sell at a price that will cover all costs, including taxes. However, when a tax is imposed on a commodity, the producer may find that if he raises his price by the full amount of the tax, his sales, and therefore his profits, will decline very sharply. He may be better off to raise his price by less than the amount of the tax. In this case he bears part of the tax and receives smaller profits; but, provided he is not forced to operate at a loss, he can still stay in business.

It seems probable that most taxes on business, whether levied directly on commodities or not, are largely borne by consumers, because, in the long run, businessmen will not keep producing goods unless they can cover taxes and all other costs and at the same time make a normal profit for themselves.[2] Personal income taxes, on the other hand, must usually be borne by those who pay them. There is seldom any very effective way of shifting them to other people.

KINDS OF TAXES

Aside from fees and special assessments, the nature of which has already been explained, the principal kinds of taxes levied in the United States are the general property tax (which includes taxes on personal property and real estate), sales taxes, excise taxes, import duties, income taxes, inheritance and gift taxes, Social Security taxes on both individuals and employers, and payroll taxes on employers only, to support unemployment insurance.

The General Property Tax. *The general property tax* is a tax levied at a uniform rate on all real and personal property. If we go back sixty years or more, it was the only important source of revenue for state and local governments in the United States. But as the financial needs of governments rose over the years, it became increasingly difficult to raise tax rates on property sufficiently to obtain the amount of funds required.

One reason for the inadequacy of the property tax was that a large amount of personal property—especially so-called intangibles like stocks, bonds, and bank accounts—escaped taxation entirely. Ownership of such property could often be concealed, and to discourage this it became customary in many localities for the tax authorities not to try to collect on it in full. As a result, the property tax fell largely, sometimes almost entirely, on real estate.

[2] This *normal profit* is itself a cost, in the economic sense that it is necessary if production of any commodity is to continue indefinitely.

For some years the trend has been to abandon the general property tax and to retain from it only the tax on real estate. Where the general property tax has been kept in effect, often little effort is made to collect on personal property except from people whose holdings are relatively large. In addition to the fact that it is hard to collect, a strong argument for abandoning the *personal property tax* is that people who hold large amounts of intangibles are already taxed heavily on the income received from them because they must pay the federal income tax and sometimes a state income tax as well.

The difficulty of raising sufficient funds by means of property taxes led the states many years ago to begin searching for other sources of revenue. By 1915 they were receiving only about half their incomes from property taxes, and by 1929 less than 20 per cent. Today such taxes account for a very small proportion of state revenues. They still, however, provide more than 35 per cent of the total revenues of local government units such as counties, villages, and cities.

Sales Taxes, Excise Taxes, and Import Duties. There is no very clear distinction between *sales taxes* and *excise taxes,* the two terms sometimes being more or less interchangeable. But in this country the expression *excise tax* is commonly employed in referring to special taxes levied by the federal government on particular goods and services. Sometimes these taxes are levied on the producer, sometimes on the retailer, but in either case they are largely passed on to the consumer. Frequently they are specifically added to the price he pays. We are all familiar with excise taxes on telephone messages, tobacco products, alcoholic beverages, and other items.

The term *sales tax* is more often applied, not to taxes on particular commodities, but to state taxes that cover all or most retail sales. However, some state sales taxes cover other transactions, such as the purchase of services. Use of sales taxes was begun in the depression years of the 1930's. They are now found in the great majority of states and have become a major source of state revenue. The most common type is the retail sales tax, and the most common rates are from 3 to 5 per cent of the price of goods purchased.

Many people object strongly to state sales taxes because they believe that taxes of this kind tend to fall most heavily on the lower-income groups. But this objection is weakened by the existence of the federal income tax, which places very high rates on people with large incomes. Sales taxes have the advantage of raising substantial amounts of revenue and of being relatively easy to collect. Also, some studies suggest that they do not depress the incentives for earning income as much as do income taxes.

Import duties or tariffs are taxes on goods brought into this country from abroad, and at one time they were the principal source of income for our national government. They are now only a minor source of revenue, but because they still have an impact on our foreign relations, they will be discussed in Chapter 30 in connection with international trade.

Income Taxes. A federal income tax was first levied by Congress in 1863, and it continued in force until 1873; but when Congress in later years passed income tax laws, they were declared unconstitutional by the Supreme Court. However, in 1913 the Constitution of the United States was amended in such a way as to permit this type of taxation, and later in the same year Congress passed a new income tax law. Today the income tax is the principal source of revenue of the national government, and it applies to both individual and corporation incomes, with a flat rate for corporations (beyond an income of $25,000) and steeply progressive rates for individuals. Most states also receive an important amount of revenue from state income taxes. However, the federal tax is so high that the rates the states can charge are limited. Otherwise the burden on many taxpayers would be intolerable.

The Personal Income Tax. The Tax Reform Act of 1969 made a number of changes in the income tax as it applies to individuals and brought about a moderate reduction in the tax burden, especially for the lower-bracket income groups. As a reform measure, its success is debatable. Not much progress, if any, was made toward what many consider the most needed reform, namely, to make the tax laws simpler and the tax forms easier to fill out.

For twenty-two years the federal income tax, as applied to individuals, had exempted the first $600 of income plus $600 for each dependent. Additional $600 exemptions were given to certain classes of individuals, such as to the blind and to persons over sixty-five. The act passed in 1969 provided for a gradual increase in personal exemptions up to $750 in 1973. Over the years, the value of the personal exemption had declined greatly because of inflation, and raising its amount in money to $750 will only partially compensate for this. Other significant changes made by the act included (1) complete elimination after June, 1970, of the 10 per cent tax surcharge that had been imposed in 1968 as an anti-inflation measure; (2) lower rates for single individuals and heads of households, beginning in 1971, to put them at less of a disadvantage as compared with married couples filing joint returns; (3) a reduced maximum rate on earned income from 70 to 60 per cent in 1971 and 50 per cent thereafter; and (4) a three-stage rise in the standard deduction from 10 to 15 per cent of income, but not more than $2,000, by 1973 and thereafter. The *standard deduction* is the amount of income that can be excluded from taxation to allow, without listing them, for such items as gifts to charity, contributions to religious or educational institutions, and dues to unions or professional associations.

As the tax laws now stand, after making allowable deductions, the rates for individuals on any remaining income range from 14 per cent on the first $500 to 70 per cent on any income over $200,000 (unless it is earned income). Taxes above the 14 per cent basic or minimum rate are called

"I'm going to be a tax loophole specialist when I grow up." (Courtesy Cartoon Features Syndicate.)

surtaxes. Married couples are still given special treatment by the tax laws. If they file a joint return, they can make appreciable savings. A minor but interesting aspect of income taxes is that they also apply to money or the money value of merchandise won in contests.

Though most people approved many of the changes that the Tax Reform Act of 1969 made in the federal income tax laws, the act did not, as we have noted, do much to simplify them. For many people who have varied sources of income, the tax laws are still so complex and difficult to interpret that making out returns is a real hardship. Over the years so many special provisions and exemptions have been added to the law, and so many special rulings have been made by the Internal Revenue Service, that often taxpayers cannot prepare a return with any certainty that it will be accepted as correct. Another problem created by exemptions and special provisions is that of so-called *tax loopholes.* Though the act of 1969 eliminated or reduced several of these, some taxpayers who pay for competent advice can still find legal ways to reduce greatly their income tax payments, whereas others, with about the same income but from different sources, must pay the standard rates. Elimination of most exemptions and other special provisions would not only simplify making out tax returns but would also make possible a reduction in rates. But it appears to be difficult to draw up a simplified income tax program that Congress would be willing to enact into law.

Those who favor income taxes as the chief source of government revenue assert that income, taken in conjunction with the number of a person's dependents, is the most reasonable basis for apportioning tax burdens among individuals. They point out that income taxes are direct, so that everyone knows just what he is paying, and that it is seldom possible to shift their burden to someone else by raising the price of a service or a commodity. Also, in relation to the amount of revenue realized, the cost of collection is not great; and though making out his tax return is a nuisance and sometimes a real burden for the individual citizen, in most cases he need concern himself with it only once a year. But a large number of taxpayers, mostly in the middle-income and higher-income groups, must also fill out and send to the Internal Revenue Service an estimate of their tax obligation for the coming year; and unless nearly all of his tax is covered by current deductions from wages or salary, each of these taxpayers must pay his estimated tax in quarterly installments during the year. In addition to the trouble and inconvenience placed on taxpayers, a weakness of the federal income tax is the ease with which some kinds of income can be concealed or greatly underestimated. Though penalties for tax evasion are severe, it remains a serious problem for the Internal Revenue Service; but the IRS hopes to make it more difficult by an extensive use of computers in processing tax returns.

The Corporation Income Tax. The *corporation income tax* is now 22 per cent on any net income (profits) up to $25,000, and a flat 48 per cent on anything over that amount. At first thought one might wonder why the progressive principle is not applied (beyond $25,000) to the corporation income tax as well as to the personal income tax. One reason is that there is no necessary relation between the size of a corporation and the incomes of individual stockholders. A relatively small corporation with moderate profits might be wholly owned by several wealthy men, whereas a very large corporation with large profits might be largely owned by thousands of stockholders, most of them with very modest incomes. In this case it would obviously be unfair to tax the small corporation at a low rate and the large one at a high rate. On the other hand, the lower tax on the first $25,000 of corporation income may be justifiable on the ground that small enterprises often have special handicaps, especially in their early stages.

Unlike the personal income tax, which is usually borne by those on whom it is levied, there is no certainty as to who bears the corporation income tax. In all probability the greater part of it is not, in the long run, borne by the corporations and their stockholders, but is passed on to the general public in higher prices. Insofar as this is true, the corporation income tax bears heavily on people with low incomes just as does the sales tax. There is, however, no way of determining with any certainty the extent to which this tax is shifted, because the profits of corporations from year to year are affected by a wide variety of factors. Insofar as the tax is actually borne by the corporations and their stockholders, it represents double taxation, in the sense that when profits, after having been taxed once, are paid out in dividends, they are then taxed again as personal income. Whether such double taxation of corporation profits is fair is a question on which opinions differ. Our income tax laws make a small concession to stockholders by permitting them to exclude one hundred dollars of dividends from their taxable income.

Inheritance, Gift, Social Security, and Payroll Taxes. The federal government and all the states except Nevada have either *inheritance* or *estate taxes*. The first is levied on the amount received by each heir or legatee of a decedent, whereas the latter applies to the estate taken as a whole.

About three fourths of the states have inheritance taxes, but the federal tax is levied against estates. Under the federal tax, after allowing for certain deductions, $60,000 worth of property is exempt. Beyond that amount the tax ranges from 3 per cent on the first $5,000 to 77 per cent on anything over $10 million. However, in computing the federal tax, any amount up to 80 per cent of it may be deducted to offset taxes that are paid to a state.

The federal government also levies *a tax on total gifts* made to any one individual during the lifetime of a giver. However, the rates are lower than those of the estate tax, and there are important exemptions. Hence a wealthy man can considerably reduce the tax burden on his estate by giving much of his property to his family during his lifetime. This is especially true if he spreads his gifts among several persons.

Attention was called to *Social Security* and *payroll taxes* in Chapter 20 in connection with the discussion of Social Security. It should be recalled that Social Security taxes are levied by the federal government on both workers and employers to support OASI. Payroll taxes to support unemployment insurance are levied only on employers by the federal government and sometimes also by the states.

BALANCING EXPENDITURES AND REVENUES

The Nature of a Budget. Planning public finances involves budgeting. A *government budget is a statement of its expected revenues and expenditures over a period of time,* and the main purpose of a budget is to aid in organizing and controlling financial policy. In the United States, budget making is a comparatively new development. In the earlier days of our history, public functions and public expenditures were relatively few, so that little need was felt for formal planning. Today the drawing up of government budgets receives a great deal of attention, and they are debated by legislators, administrators, newspapers, and the public.

A budget may be drawn up by a committee of the legislative body of a government unit after it receives from various administrative departments estimates of their needs; or it may be drawn up by the chief executive officer, such as the mayor, governor, or President, and then presented to the legislative body for approval. The former is called a *legislative budget,* the latter an *executive budget.*

The executive budget is now by far the most popular type and is the one employed by the federal government. Under this plan the chief executive officer receives estimates of needs from his department heads, usually through an officer with some such title as director of the budget. This officer consults with the chief executive. With the aid of a staff of experts he studies the estimates, consolidates them into a unified whole, balances expected revenues against anticipated needs, suggests to the spending agencies possible reductions, if necessary suggesting additional taxes, and finally presents to the chief executive a budget plan for the coming fiscal period.

Once a budget has been accepted by the chief executive, it must be presented to the city council, the legislature, or Congress—as the case may be—for consideration and for possible changes. Eventually, it is approved, and the necessary tax and appropriation measures are passed to put it into effect. Under both the state and federal constitutions public funds can be spent only in accordance with appropriations made by law.

The Supervision of Expenditures and the Custody of Funds. The funds provided for under a budget are actually spent by the various administrative agencies to which they are allotted. Certain of these agencies are directly under the control of the chief executive, but others are independent. This fact often creates problems with respect to the proper control and coordination of public spending. There are great advantages in some degree of centralization of fiscal control, perhaps in a special administrative agency, and in the standardization of such matters as salaries and purchasing procedures.

Provision must also be made for the safekeeping, investment, and general supervision of public funds, from the time they are collected until they are paid out according to law. This function is usually performed by an officer with the title of treasurer. Usually, also, an independent auditing service is created to check on whether the spending agencies of government are making proper uses of the money allotted them. For our federal government this function is assigned to the General Accounting Office under the supervision of the Comptroller General of the United States. The GAO has frequently exposed needless waste by government agencies. One of its duties is to report to Congress any irregularity or violation of law in connection with government contracts or expenditures.

The Federal Budget. In the federal government the Office of Management and Budget, created by President Richard Nixon in 1970, is the agency now directly responsible, under the general supervision of the President, for preparing the budget. It is also responsible for supervision of the items in it after they have been approved by Congress. The Office of Management and Budget replaced the old Bureau of the Budget, but it has much broader functions and powers. As mentioned in Chapter 26, its chief purpose is to see that the policies of the Domestic Council, headed by the President, are carried out effectively. Its director has wide powers to demand cooperation from the various government departments and agencies that are responsible to the President.

Up to 1968, budget estimates for the following fiscal year were prepared by the Bureau of the Budget in a form called the *administrative budget,* but in March of 1967 President Lyndon Johnson appointed a presidential commission to examine budgeting concepts and practices and to make suggestions for presenting the budget in a form that would better show total government receipts and outlays. As a result, the federal budget estimates for fiscal year 1969 were based on the *unified-budget* concept, as recommended by the commission. All budgets prepared since then have taken this form. The most important difference between the unified budget and the previously used administrative budget is that the unified budget includes in federal receipts and outlays the transactions of the government trust funds, such as those for Social Security and unemployment compensation. By far the largest of the trust funds is that for Social Security.[3]

Because a large fraction of all government receipts and expenditures is accounted for by the trust funds, their total as reported in the unified budget is much larger than it would be if the administrative budget were employed. At the same time the surplus is greater or the deficit smaller because in recent years the receipts of the trust funds have substantially exceeded their expenditures. For example, the taxes from which the Social Security fund derives its revenues have been enough not only to meet current disbursements but also to provide a reserve sufficient to cover a part of the obligations that are being incurred for the future.

Figure 32, showing where the government dollar comes from and where it goes, is based on the unified budget. In the representation of the dollar labeled "Where it goes," the expression "Human resources" includes not only payments made under a great variety of welfare programs but also pension payments to retired workers who are covered by the Social Security system.

Near the beginning of each calendar year the federal budget for the following *fiscal year* is presented in a long and complex document that contains several hundred pages. A fiscal year, which runs from July 1 to the following June 30, is always named after the calendar year in which it ends. Unified-budget estimates for the fiscal year 1971, as made by the old Bureau of the Budget and presented to Congress by President Nixon early in 1970, called for outlays of $200.8 billion and receipts of $202.1 billion. But early in 1971 it was already clear that receipts had been overestimated and expenditures underestimated and that fiscal 1971 would show a substantial federal deficit.

To analyze in detail so complex a document as the federal budget would be almost impossible. However, it is very easy to obtain a rough idea of the principal sources of revenue and of the general purposes for which funds are spent. Figure 32, to which we have already referred, shows this in a simplified way. One striking fact about federal spending is the large proportion that is accounted for by obligations from past wars and by military spending to build up and maintain our present armed forces.

---

[3] For purposes of calculating the federal deficit or surplus, the unified budget also includes the net increase or decrease in outstanding federal loans. This item is included because a net increase of loans must be financed from current Treasury funds or by borrowing, while a decrease releases funds for other purposes or reduces the need to borrow.

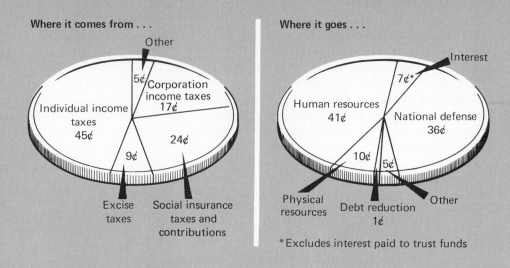

Figure 32. The Government Dollar, Estimate for Fiscal Year 1971. (Executive Office of the President, Bureau of the Budget.)

Federal Spending and Inflation. From 1964 to the end of 1968, total spending in our economy rose faster than production and brought about a sharp increase in the rate of price inflation. The rise in total spending resulted largely from the combined effects of two factors, namely, liberal monetary policies on the part of the Federal Reserve authorities, and a 50 per cent increase in government spending without a corresponding increase in tax receipts. Instead of raising taxes, the government met its additional outlays in large part with new money obtained by selling government securities to the Federal Reserve banks. As a result, the rise in consumer prices accelerated until, in 1969, they were increasing at an annual rate of nearly 6 per cent.[4] Part of the increase in government spending during the middle and late 1960's was a result of the war in Vietnam, but, contrary to a widespread popular impression, the greater part of it was for domestic programs. During the four-year period 1964–1968 the federal government accumulated deficits totalling $39 billion.

Much of our trouble in dealing with problems of government finance is that most of us are subject to the *money illusion*. We keep all our accounts, personal and public, in terms of money, and we forget that the real limit on the nation's power to meet its needs is what it can produce. By using government securities to borrow from the Federal Reserve banks, the federal government can obtain unlimited amounts of money. (If the

[4] *The Budget in Brief* for fiscal year 1971, Washington, D.C., Executive Office of the President, Bureau of the Budget, 1970, p. 8.

law limits such borrowing, the law can be changed.) But this is new money, created by crediting the government's bank accounts.

When the government spends this money, buying labor (services) and goods, it goes to the public which then has, in total, that much more money to spend. This, as was noted in Chapter 19, is sometimes called *priming the pump,* or *pumping money into the economy,* and it is a useful device in times of depression when it can create jobs for large numbers of unemployed. But, in times of relative prosperity, it upsets the law of supply and demand. There are only X number of people and a limited amount of plant and equipment available for producing X number of goods and services. If the government buys more of these, the public will have to compete for what is left, and prices will go up. When money incomes rise, prices can remain stable only if the total production of goods can somehow be raised in proportion to the increase in incomes. Perhaps we could check inflation by price controls, but to make these effective for any length of time we would have to ration goods. The nation cannot have more food, clothing, new houses, expressways, automobiles, and all the rest than it can produce with available human and material resources.

During the last year or two of his administration, President Johnson recognized the dangers from inflation and made a belated effort to control it by checking the expansion of federal spending and obtaining from Congress legislation placing a 10 per cent surtax on incomes. President Nixon continued this effort with even greater determination; but at the end of two years, though a further rise in the rate of inflation had been checked, he had had little success in reducing the rate already established. Once inflation has become rapid, to stop it is difficult and costly. One of the greatest obstacles is likely to be a lack of effective measures for preventing inflationary wage increases, that is, wage increases substantially in excess of increases in the productivity of labor. When workers have come to expect rising prices, they try to protect themselves by demanding substantially higher wage settlements, and such settlements tend to raise prices still higher by further raising business costs. Monetary and fiscal measures can slow inflation in time, but if employed alone they also slow the rate of economic growth and create unemployment; and if continued too long they may bring on a serious recession.

In any case, to reduce federal spending greatly in any one year is almost impossible because many expenditures are relatively uncontrollable in the short run. Among the reasons for this are the following: (1) Congress often appropriates money that is to be spent over a period of several years. (2) Some spending, such as veterans' pensions, represents commitments that the government is morally obligated to meet. (3) Projects that have been started must be completed unless the money already invested in them is to be accepted as a loss. (4) Some government activities are so essential to the public welfare that they cannot be dispensed with or very much reduced. (5) Some expenditures increase automatically from year to year. For example, as our population grows (and grows older) an increasing number of workers retire annually on Social Security pensions. (6) When government securities such as bonds fall due, higher interest rates may have to be paid for the money needed to redeem them. (7) Finally, it must be recognized that any large and *rapid* drop in government outlays would have serious economic (and political) repercussions. It might put thousands of people out of work, including both government employees and the employees of firms from which the government makes large purchases.

The Rising Government Debt. In the discussion of economic stabilization in Chapter 19, attention was called to the size of our federal debt. The *gross* federal debt on which the government pays interest is approaching $400 billion. In the proposed budget for fiscal year 1971, interest payments alone were, as we have said, estimated at almost $18 billion. But much of the gross federal debt is held by government agencies, especially the trust funds, and in paying interest to these agencies the government is really paying money to itself. However, such payments as those to the trust funds represent long-run obligations to the public, including a portion of future payments to those who retire on Social Security pensions. Congress sets a *statutory debt limit* which, from time to time, it has to raise in order to enable the government to meet expenditures that exceed receipts. Obviously, the gross federal debt is a huge sum, but it does not seem quite so formidable if we note that it is less than half the gross national product for a single year.

Only *changes* in *the federal debt held by the public* (for example, in bonds) directly affect the annual government surplus or deficit as reported in the unified budget. On June 30, 1969, this type of debt amounted to $279.5 billion. Debt held by the public is owned by individuals and by a variety of organizations such as state and local governments, industrial corporations, insurance companies, savings and loan associations, and banks, including the Federal Reserve banks.[5] The latter usually hold very large amounts of government securities.

In addition to actual debts, the federal government and its agencies have also acquired *contingent liabilities* that now substantially exceed a trillion dollars. These consist chiefly of liabilities for guaranteed loans, pension payments, and insurance. The largest insurance liabilities are those that protect deposits in banks and savings and loan associations and that cover atomic power plants.[6]

SOME PROBLEMS OF GOVERNMENT FINANCE

Meeting the Needs of Local Governments. Attention has been called to the increasing needs of local governments, especially cities, for funds

[5] Ibid., pp. 15–16.
[6] *U. S. News & World Report,* July 29, 1968, pp. 54–55.

to provide important public services. The pressure on them has been especially great ever since World War II because of such factors as inflation, increasingly acute traffic problems, the rising rate of crime, the rapidly growing school population, and the need for upgrading the schooling and training of young people seeking jobs. Their chief source of revenue, the property tax, has proved wholly inadequate.

The search for additional funds has not been easy, but under the pressure of necessity large sums have been raised. Most states, for example, have greatly increased their *grants-in-aid* to local government units, not only for operating schools but also for such purposes as improving arterial highways and meeting welfare expenditures. In addition, many states have been induced to share with local governments certain state-collected taxes, especially the gasoline tax and the general sales tax. Cities have obtained some additional revenue by increasing license fees, especially those for taverns, night clubs, and other places of entertainment. Various special taxes have been resorted to, such as auto fees and cigarette taxes, and some cities have established municipal sales taxes or municipal income taxes. Parking meters are another new source of income for many municipalities; and finally, some of them have obtained temporary relief by inducing state legislatures to raise the limits of their legal borrowing power. But, even so, the financial problems of cities have, as already noted, become acute, and the means of solving them uncertain.

Financial Problems of the States. We have already called attention to the pressure on the states for better highways, for dealing with pollution, and for more-adequate prisons, mental hospitals, and universities, as well as for giving more aid to local government units. On the whole, the efforts of the states to find new sources of revenue have been much more successful than those of local taxing bodies, and it is this fact that has enabled them not only to relinquish most of the proceeds of the property tax but also to provide substantial aid to the schools and other activities of local units. Today about one third of the total expenditures of the states represents such aid.

The states themselves receive important aid from the federal government, aid that now totals about one quarter of their revenues. This aid has been expanded over the years to meet various needs, including road building, urban renewal, pollution control, and the administration of unemployment insurance plans. The source of most state income is, of course, taxes. Most important, in the order named, are general sales taxes, income taxes on both individuals and corporations, and gasoline taxes. Other major sources of revenue include unemployment compensation taxes, motor vehicle license fees, and taxes on alcoholic drinks and tobacco. But, as stated in Parkinson's second law, "Expenditures always rise to meet income," and in spite of these various sources of revenue most of the states still feel a great need for more funds.

Government Finance and the Public Welfare. We have noted the great difficulty of operating efficiently so huge an organization as our federal government. During the depression of the 1930's and the war years, the activities and costs of government increased so rapidly that efficiency and economy tended to receive little attention. Since then, real attempts have been made to improve this situation because it is more and more being recognized that, great as are the resources of the United States, they are limited. If we are to meet our most pressing needs at all adequately, we must make all reasonable efforts to conserve our resources and to use them efficiently. We have mentioned that some years ago the two Hoover commissions made a significant contribution toward increasing the economy and effectiveness with which the federal bureaucracy operates, and today there is hope that President Nixon's new Office of Management and Budget will ultimately bring further gains.

The sharp rise in federal nonmilitary expenditures in the late 1960's went to meet urgent needs for urban renewal, the expansion and upgrading of education, and the alleviation of poverty; but it also, as has been pointed out, helped to bring on an unacceptable rate of price inflation. If Congress, to alleviate social ills, were to appropriate on "crash" programs all the money demanded by various groups, the action would be self-defeating. True, the federal government by borrowing from the Reserve banks can create unlimited amounts of money. But since our physical resources and manpower are limited, a vast expansion in the money supply could result only in runaway inflation, disorganization of our economy, a reduction in its power to produce goods, impoverishment of some groups, and generally lower standards of living.

If government is to make its greatest contribution to the national welfare, the American people and their leaders must do three things. First, they must decide what our most-urgent problems are. Second, those primarily responsible for implementing public policies must decide, on the basis of knowledge rather than wishful thinking, what can really be done to meet these problems. Third, priorities must be set. The money that a government can raise and spend *without creating a damaging rate of inflation* is largely limited by the taxes people can and will pay without offering extreme resistance. This money should be spent in ways that will most benefit the whole nation.

Already, as we have mentioned, more than 35 per cent of our national income is absorbed by taxes. Unless we elect Congresses and Presidents who use care in spending tax money and who resist spending proposals of doubtful value, the portion of our national income going to taxes could easily rise to a crippling 50 per cent.

Inflation is likely to be one of our major economic problems in the years to come (1) because the tendency of government spending to rise faster than revenue will probably continue, (2) because of the power of many unions to obtain successive wage increases that exceed increases in the productivity of labor, and (3) because in periods of recession or depression "easy" money policies and increased government spending increase production and employment, and there is a temptation to continue such policies even after prosperity has been restored, with the result that inflation becomes rapid and difficult to control. Inflation has one interesting characteristic. If a nation regards it as a great evil, and so makes effective efforts to hold it within narrow limits, the harm it does may be minor. But if resistance weakens, and people begin to accept it as a simple solution for government financial problems or as an easy road to perpetual prosperity, the past record in many countries shows that slow inflation soon becomes uncontrolled inflation, with resulting incalculable damage to the whole economy. Among the nations that have gone through such an experience in peacetime are our Latin American neighbors Chile, Argentina, and Brazil.

No subject is more closely related to the public welfare than government finance. Its management largely determines the amount of income we can keep for our own uses; the amount and quality of government services available to us; the stability and the rate of growth of both the economy and our standards of living; our success in controlling and reducing pollution; and, finally, whether prices remain reasonably stable or are inflated at a rate that rapidly reduces the purchasing power of the dollar.

The fact that over 35 per cent of the national income goes to taxes is not necessarily bad. Most of the services provided by government are vitally essential to all of us. What is really bad, in view of our many needs, is to allow large sums of public money to be lost through graft, wasted by gross inefficiency, or spent on programs that add little or nothing to the nation's welfare. We should never forget that what the government spends comes ultimately from the general public, that is to say, from you and me.

Terms to Be Understood

tax	personal property	inheritance tax
fee	tax	estate tax
special assessment	sales tax	gift tax
ability-to-pay	excise tax	legislative budget
principle	import duties	executive budget
benefits-received	personal income	administrative
principle	tax	budget
regressive tax	standard deduction	unified budget
proportional tax	surtax	fiscal year
progressive tax	tax loophole	the money illusion
general property	corporation income	statutory debt limit
tax	tax	contingent liabilities

Questions for Review and Discussion

1. Does government cost too much? Defend your answer.
2. Account for the great rise in government spending since 1890. Why has federal

spending risen much more rapidly than that of the state and local governments?

3. Are we likely to have much success in reducing government spending? Why or why not?
4. What special problems make it difficult to hold down the costs of the federal government?
5. What three sources of funds are usually open to a government? Which is most important?
6. Are fees and special assessments a type of tax? Discuss.
7. What are the principal characteristics of a good tax system?
8. What are the principal difficulties involved when an attempt is made to establish criteria on the basis of which to apportion taxes fairly?
9. What do we mean when we say that a sales tax is regressive?
10. How can taxes sometimes be shifted in whole or part to people other than those who pay them directly?
11. Why has the general property tax proved inadequate as a source of state and local revenue?
12. As sources of government revenue, compare the advantages and disadvantages of income taxes and sales taxes.
13. State the principal objections that might reasonably be raised against (a) high taxes on corporation profits; (b) progressive tax rates on corporation profits; (c) taxation of personal income from dividends.
14. List five significant changes that the Tax Reform Act of 1969 made in the federal personal income tax.
15. Would it be possible to draw up a simplified income tax plan that would be about as fair to everyone as the present income tax laws? Why or why not?
16. What are the functions of the Comptroller General of the United States and the General Accounting Office?
17. What agency prepares the federal budget? What does the budget show?
18. How does the unified budget, now employed by the federal government, differ from the administrative budget, which was formerly used?
19. What are the principal sources of federal revenue and the principal purposes for which funds are spent?
20. Why is government spending of borrowed money, especially of money borrowed from the Federal Reserve banks, inflationary?
21. List at least seven obstacles to a rapid reduction in federal spending.
22. The total contingent liabilities of the federal government are several times greater than the national debt. What do they largely consist of?
23. Summarize recent trends in (a) local government finances; (b) state government finances.
24. Why is inflation likely to be a continuing problem in the years to come?
25. Why is good management of government finances vitally important to the public welfare?

For Further Study

Bennis, Warren G., ed. and intro., *American Bureaucracy*, paperback, Chicago, Aldine Publishing Company, 1970.

Buchanan, James M., *Public Finance in the Democratic Process,* Chapel Hill, N.C., University of North Carolina Press, 1967.

Davis, James W., ed., *Politics, Programs, and Budgets: A Reader in Government Budgeting,* paperback, Englewood Cliffs, N.J., Prentice-Hall, Inc., 1969.

Due, John Fitzgerald, *Government Finance: Economics of the Public Sector,* 4th ed., Homewood, Ill., Richard D. Irwin, Inc., 1968.

Eckstein, Otto, *Public Finance,* 2d ed., paperback, Englewood Cliffs, N.J., Prentice-Hall, Inc., 1967.

Goode, Richard, *The Individual Income Tax,* Washington, D.C., The Brookings Institution, 1964.

Heilbroner, Robert L., and Peter L. Bernstein, *Primer on Government Spending,* 2d ed., paperback, New York, Random House, Inc., 1970.

Mosher, Frederick C., and Orville F. Poland, *The Costs of American Government: Facts, Trends, Myths,* paperback, New York, Dodd, Mead & Company, Inc., 1964.

Office of Management and Budget, *The Federal Budget in Brief,* Washington, D.C., U.S. Government Printing Office. Published annually.

Parkinson, C. Northcote, *Parkinson's Law and Other Stories in Administration,* paperback, New York, Ballantine Books, Inc., 1968. A humorous but all too realistic account of how administration works, including what happens to taxes.

Phelps, Edmund S., ed., *Private Wants and Public Needs: Issues Surrounding the Size and Scope of Government Expenditures,* rev. ed., New York, W. W. Norton & Company, Inc., 1965.

Pryor, Frederic L., *Public Expenditures in Communist and Capitalist Nations,* Homewood, Ill., Richard D. Irwin, Inc., 1968.

Schultze, Charles L., *The Politics and Economics of Public Spending,* paperback, Washington, D.C., The Brookings Institution, 1969.

Stein, Herbert, *The Fiscal Revolution in America,* Chicago, University of Chicago Press, 1969.

The Tax Foundation, *Facts and Figures on Government Finance,* Englewood Cliffs, N.J., Prentice-Hall, Inc. Published every odd-numbered year.

Part Five

International Relations

Chapter 29

The

World

Community of

Nation-states

Shortly after his defeat when he was the Republican candidate for President in 1940, Wendell Willkie traveled around the world in 160 hours of air time, visiting enroute with all types of people. Air travel was then in its infancy, and on his return he wrote a book that he called *One World,* a term epitomizing the most pronounced impression that he had gained from his tour. The term caught the public attention, because never before had most people realized how small the world really is and how closely all its peoples are being drawn together by rapid transportation and communication. With the same conception of the world in mind, the International Law Commission of the United Nations opened its Draft Declaration on the Rights and Duties of States (1950) with an assertion that the states of the world "form a community."

To understand this "community," with its component states and their objectives, its problems and their possible solutions, its history, its economy, its wars, and its processes of order and stability—all this is the task of those who would understand contemporary international relations. Real as this world community is, the reader should be warned that it differs greatly from communities of individual persons, because its units—states—are so different from the men and women who inhabit towns, cities, and nations.

THE STATES OF THE WORLD COMMUNITY

The term *state* has different meanings. In this country it is most commonly used to refer to any one of the fifty members of our national union. But as the word is used in discussing international relations, and as we are using it in this chapter, *a state is an independent political unit that can carry on negotiations or make agreements with other such units*. In this sense the United States qualifies as a state, but such political entities as Alabama, California, and Michigan do not.

If a person were to sit down with an up-to-date map of the world in front of him, he could count a total of about 160 states that carry on relationships among themselves and have the power to make and implement agreements. However, not all of these states are fully sovereign or independent in all respects; and the map reader would be impressed, were he to pursue his investigations, with the extreme variations among them in physical characteristics and in such matters as religion, education, ethnic background, industry, standards of living, and government. For instance, in area they range from the Soviet Union, with 8,650,000 square miles, down to Monaco, with less than 1 square mile, and tiny Vatican city, with a mere 106 acres of land; only eight states possess more than 1 million square miles of territory. In population the largest states are China (perhaps 750 million people) and India (525 million); the smallest are Andorra (14,000) and Vatican City (1,000); twelve states can boast of a population of 50 million or more. Some states are overwhelmingly Roman Catholic in faith (such as Spain and France); some are almost entirely Protestant (Denmark and Sweden); others are both Catholic and Protestant (the United States and Germany). There are also states in which other religions prevail, including Mohammedanism, Buddhism, Judaism, and Hinduism. Average per capita incomes in 1969 ranged all the way from over $3,800 in the United States to estimates of less than $100 in some countries in Africa and eastern Asia. The United States and Canada, most of the western European nations, and some others are democracies; Russia, continental China, and about a dozen more are under communist dictators; Spain and

Portugal are governed by dictatorships that have some fascist character-istics; and some countries that are normally or nominally democracies, including several in Latin America, are ruled by military dictatorships. These and many other differences within the community of states account in part for the problems and misunderstandings that so often mar inter-national relationships.

The Nation-state. In this chapter we are using the terms *state* and *nation* more or less as synonyms. Strictly, however, they carry different meanings, and in the precise language of international law and diplomacy only *state* is employed; this is true, for instance, in the Charter of the United Nations, in the Statute of the International Court of Justice, and in treaties generally. The characteristics of a state, according to the Charter of the Organization of American States (1948) are (1) a permanent population; (2) a fixed ter-ritory; (3) a government; and (4) a capacity for international relations. It is this last qualification that, as already noted, eliminates Alabama, California, or Michigan from the category of true (independent) states. The term *nation* was originally applied to groups of people with the same ethnic background, such as the Germans or the French, both of whom can point to a common language and a common cultural heritage.

The explanation of the modern popular practice of using *state* and *na-tion* as synonyms lies in the fact that for some centuries now the political state has tended to include substantially the same people as the ethnic nation; in effect, therefore, we have *nation-states* today. The French state, for instance, is for the most part made up of a French-speaking people with a common historical and cultural background. True, there are rela-tively small numbers of minority peoples living in France—some Germans, Italians, and others—and there are a small number of Frenchmen living in other states, but these exceptions are not sufficiently consequential to upset the general rule. There are some nation-states, however, including Switzerland, India, and Canada, that do not have a common language. In cases such as these, there are other unifying factors. Sometimes the mere fact that people have lived under the same government over a long period tends to give them common interests and loyalties, and hence a sense of national unity. But differences in language, usually combined with other differences in culture, can cause problems, as we have seen in recent years in Canada. Some of the new African states, including Nigeria, have been handicapped in achieving unity by tribal and language dif-ferences. But it is said that in many cases the growing cities, by bringing together people from different tribes, are tending to promote a sense of national loyalty.

Origins of the Nation-state. The present system of *nation-states* stands out in sharp contrast with the political structure of society in the ancient world and in medieval Europe. The Sumerians in the Tigris-Euphrates valley lived in *city-states* about 5000 B.C. The city-states of the ancient Hellenic peoples—Sparta, Athens, Thebes, and others—developed one of the finest civilizations recorded in man's long history. City-states flourished in parts of medieval Europe, notably in northern Italy, and some, among them Venice and Florence, became rich and powerful. The principal alternative to the city-state until a few centuries ago was the empire; ancient China, India, Persia, Egypt, and Rome built and maintained large empires of subject peoples.

The modern nation-state was constructed upon the ruins of feudalism in western Europe. In the conflict of feudal lords with each other, a certain lord within an area would emerge as victor, and eventually large areas where the people spoke similar dialects were brought together under a ruler who called himself king. England was one of the first nation-states, and by the latter part of the twelfth century the authority of the king, then Henry II, extended over almost all of the country, as well as over parts of what is now France. Most of France was unified a little later, and by the middle of the fifteenth century, English authority had been forced off the continent; by the end of the reign of Louis XI (1461–1483), France could claim to be a new nation-state. Other nation-states gradually emerged, so that in time the map of Europe showed a substantial group of them — England, France, Spain, Denmark, Hungary, Russia, Poland, Norway, Sweden. The Treaty of Westphalia (1648) put its stamp of approval upon the new system by recognizing that the authority of the Pope and of the old Holy Roman Empire was dead. The nation-state had come into its own.

The Establishment of New Nation-states and the Disappearance of Old Ones. Since 1648 many new nation-states have sprung into being, and from time to time old ones have died out. During the nineteenth century, Turkish authority was expelled from most of Europe, and new states took its place on the Balkan Peninsula: Greece, Bulgaria, Serbia, Romania, Albania, and Montenegro (later included with Serbia in Yugoslavia). Twenty new states were formed from the old holdings of Spain and Portugal in the New World. About the middle of the nineteenth century, China and Japan, ancient countries of the Far East, opened their doors to Western trade. They, too, were admitted into the community of nation-states, in 1842 and 1854 respectively.

World War I tore down the old multinational state of Austria-Hungary and built up several new states: Poland, Czechoslovakia, Austria, Hungary, Latvia, Lithuania, and Estonia. It also added to the territory of already-existing states such as Serbia and Romania. World War II snuffed out Latvia, Lithuania, and Estonia, but it led directly to the revival of Ethiopia and the division of Korea into two new political units. Within a few years, many other new states were created, most of them directly or indirectly as a result of the war. In Chapter 31 we shall give special attention to this development, including the great surge of *nationalism* that took place in the colonial areas of Africa in the 1960's. In the world as a whole, more than sixty-five new and nominally independent nation-states have been formed since World War II. A number of them were formerly parts of the British or French empires, and some of them are very small.

The Sovereign State. In Chapter 24 we defined *sovereignty* as the power of a state to rule its people effectively and to fulfill its international obligations. A sovereign state is legally subordinate to no other state but in theory may negotiate with and make agreements with other states as an equal. This is the basic concept of *sovereignty,* but in practice the independence of a state is limited. If others will not accede to its demands or respect its independence, it may resort to war, but many nominally sovereign states have very little power, and must, unless they have strong allies, bow to the dictates of powerful neighbors.

Though the legal meaning of *sovereignty* is fairly clear, in popular usage it is often a vague concept. To many people it means, if anything, the right of their government to follow whatever foreign policy it pleases. Some might qualify this by saying that its policies must be compatible with international law and also with the Charter of the United Nations, which contains limitations imposed on themselves by the member states; but others would contend that national sovereignty relegates international law and the Charter to the status of mere ethics. In any case, sovereignty is still regarded by many as a prime essential of national welfare, to be preserved at any cost.

Influence of the Sovereignty Concept on International Affairs. Whether the state is really sovereign in its external relations is much less decisive in its policy making than the fact that most people think it possesses that quality. In other words, the vitality of sovereignty as a force in international affairs rests more on popular beliefs about it than upon its actual or theoretical validity. These popular beliefs about it have sometimes been an obstacle to international cooperation. This is indicated by the effectiveness of the arguments advanced by opponents of the League of Nations in 1919–1920. At that time many Americans were greatly impressed by the assertion that their country would lose its sovereignty should it join that organization, and that this would be a national disaster. Much later, in 1948, the Soviet Union appealed to the popular emotions still attached to sovereignty when its spokesmen argued that any state that accepted the Marshall Plan would surrender its sovereignty to the United States. But today faith in the virtues of sovereignty is not as strong as it once was. There is a growing recognition that international amity and cooperation require some limitations on sovereignty. Nevertheless, most states are still unwilling to relinquish very much of their assumed right to make completely independent decisions.

When states operate on the assumption that they are free to do whatever they please in their foreign relations, even if this means overriding international law and the Charter of the United Nations, they inevitably inject into world politics an atmosphere of cutthroat competition and a degree of anarchy. They adopt economic policies harmful to others, they refuse to make enforceable agreements for stopping armaments races, and they take advantage of smaller states by making them satellites or by exacting from them special privileges. The friction that is ever present in international relations should not, however, be ascribed to sovereignty alone, for there are many other forces behind foreign policies. Indeed, sovereignty is itself not so much a force as it is a justification or a rationalization of state conduct. It furnishes the facade behind which a state gives free play to a multitude of forces that actually shape policies, such as the ambition for power and security, the desire to expand, and the drive for economic advantages.

POWER IN THE WORLD COMMUNITY

Nothing is more basic to an understanding of international relations than an appreciation of the role of power. Current expressions such as "power politics," the "great powers," the "small powers," and the "balance of power" all attest the importance of that role. There are authorities who see in international relations nothing but power politics; the whole thing, so they believe, is a scramble on the part of states for the utmost power, plus a willingness to use that power for the support of their policies. Some analysts go so far as to say that without power a nation can have no foreign policy worthy of the name. That power is extremely important in world affairs, that it is even the most important single factor, is not difficult to admit. However, the extremists who see nothing in the policies of states but power motives open themselves to the charge of being off-balance, for all conduct, whether of individuals or of states, is inevitably too complicated to be reduced to any one simple explanation.

The Nature and Sources of National Power. In the final analysis, the power of a state consists of the means it possesses for promoting its vital interests by influencing or controlling the behavior of other states. Though military force is the most obvious type of power, it is not the only one. The principal forms of pressure available to states in their dealings with each other are military power, power over opinion at home and abroad, and economic power.

By its actual employment or by threat of employment, the military power of a nation can be decisive if it is great enough. But since World War II the development and improvement of intercontinental missiles and nuclear bombs, and of defense systems against them, have greatly changed the nature of military power. One result has been to place the greatest part of it in the hands of two superpowers, the United States and Russia, because so far they are the only two nations possessing both the resources and the technology for producing long-range nuclear missiles on a large scale. A second result has been to create powerful inhibitions against employing this ultimate form of military power. Up to now neither the United States nor Russia has been willing to use nuclear weapons or to permit their use by allies, for fear of starting a full-scale nuclear war that would be vastly destructive of life and property in both countries, if not in the whole world. The result has been a *nuclear standoff*.

But while this standoff has been in effect, a number of relatively small, "limited," and undeclared wars have been fought with nonnuclear weapons. This means that the ability of a country to employ such weapons effectively or to furnish them to its allies and protégés is still an element in a nation's total military power. More about this in Chapter 32.

The effectiveness of military power in supporting foreign policies of a nation-state depends not only on the size and training of its armed forces and the extent to which they are provided with the most modern and effective weapons. It also depends on good judgment by political leaders in deciding whether or when to use such power, and on the judgment and skills of its military commanders. Furthermore, the ability of a nation to achieve its goals because of its military power also depends, especially in a democracy, on the willingness of the vast majority of its people to support government policies. If a large minority of citizens is strongly pacifist and ready to resist the use of armed forces at critical junctures, that in itself can greatly reduce the effectiveness of military power. The nation's commitments are likely to lose credibility. Its allies begin to doubt that they could count on its aid in a real crisis. They wonder whether, even as a last resort, it would be willing to use nuclear power to preserve their freedom or even to preserve its own freedom. What may be even more dangerous, its enemies gain confidence that they can safely override its interests.

After a major war, not many years need pass for many people to forget or greatly discount its lessons and to develop a false sense of security. Each new generation is apt to repeat the mistakes of the past because for it even the fairly recent past is only history and not something actually experienced. When Adolf Hitler rose to power in the 1930's, he soon began, in violation of the Treaty of Versailles, to rebuild the German army. But inertia and a false sense of security—an unwillingness to believe that Hitler would really attack his neighbors—kept France and England from taking military measures to stop Hitler, even though he broke treaties, before it was too late to avoid a desperate, prolonged, and destructive war.

Public opinion, at home and abroad, is a major factor in determining both the foreign policies of a government and its power to implement them. The government of a democracy is likely to reflect public beliefs and attitudes whether these are realistic or not. But even if the leaders directly responsible for formulating policies believe that the public, as represented by the majority, is wrong, they cannot ignore public opinion and stay in office, nor can they completely ignore the beliefs of important minorities. They may try to change public opinion, but this is not easy in a democracy where other points of view can be freely expressed. Totalitarian governments are much less dependent on public opinion. In the first place, they can largely shape it through tight control of the media of communication. In the second place, if in spite of such control, dissent develops, they can use the secret police to ferret out and "liquidate" or imprison its leaders, if necessary by the hundreds or thousands.

Though the government of a totalitarian state may be able to shape public opinion at home, it has no direct control over foreign opinion. In their attempts to influence opinion abroad, both totalitarian and democratic governments are likely to resort to propaganda; and though there are no very dependable ways of measuring its results, it is safe to assume that the large-scale propaganda campaigns conducted by all strong nations would not be undertaken unless they were thought to be effective, either in strengthening home morale and winning support abroad or else in undermining the morale of potential enemies.

Besides using propaganda, a nation may influence world opinion by its conduct. A record of reasonableness and fair dealing, and of honoring commitments, is likely to give a nation a good reputation and to win friends and potential allies. The policies of the United States during much of our history have been such that we have enjoyed the confidence of most other nations. However, to behave so as to win such confidence is not as simple as it might seem. This is illustrated by the wide differences of opinion as to the wisdom and justice of our giving military support to the government of South Vietnam against the communist Viet Cong rebels and their North Vietnam allies.

If some nations tend to have less confidence in the United States today than at times in the past, it is partly because we now have great power and because there is a tendency to fear and distrust the motives of the powerful; it is also partly because dissension at home has raised doubts abroad as to the ability of our government to follow consistent and firm foreign policies; and finally it is partly because the governments of certain communist countries have conducted systematic propaganda campaigns to discredit us.

The utility of economic power in international relations has been demonstrated often. During the struggle against Napoleon Bonaparte it enabled Great Britain not only to expand its own military forces but also to provide money and supplies for its allies. More than a century later, it enabled the United States to do likewise in both world wars; and after World War II it enabled us to make an important contribution to rebuilding the economies and the military forces of the countries of western Europe that had been overrun by the Nazis and that later felt threatened by the vastly expanded military power of Soviet Russia.

Though the sources of a nation's power are varied, some of them are more basic than others. Today, for a state to generate great national strength, it must first of all be large, both in area and population. Size is an advantage possessed by both Soviet Russia and the United States; it is also possessed by China and India, but they have not yet developed to a comparable degree some of the other sources of power. Industrial might is another vital source of power, for in its factories a country must produce the equipment for modern warfare, including tanks, ships, planes, missiles, and nuclear bombs. The high industrial output of the United

States is a great asset in the power game, and this is one reason for Russia's intense efforts to catch up with us by means of her successive five-year plans. A third major source of power is dependable access to adequate supplies of raw materials, because without these no nation can develop and maintain a large and efficient industrial complex. A fourth condition that is still a factor in national power is geographic location. This can, among other things, affect both access to raw materials and the degree to which a nation is vulnerable to a military attack. Geographic location is one element of American strength. We are separated by oceans from any other major power, and though these can be crossed in a few minutes by missiles bearing nuclear bombs, there are, as has been pointed out, strong deterrents to the use of such weapons. Meanwhile, the oceans still protect us against attack by great armies using conventional weapons.

However, given size, a well-developed industry, and dependable access to adequate raw materials, perhaps the most important source of a nation's power is the characteristics of its people. Among the people there should be a substantial number of able scientists, educators, businessmen, military leaders, and politicians; also a great many highly skilled workers of all types. But in a democracy perhaps the characteristic of a people that, if they have it, contributes most to the power of the nation in dealing with others is a strong sense of patriotism and loyalty that makes them willing to support their government in any policy that they consider reasonable. But in dealing with foreign countries the governments of democracies often face difficult problems at home. Negotiations cannot be carried on by all the people; they must be conducted by those who represent them in government. This creates no great problem if those who represent the country are following policies with which the vast majority of the people agree. Frequently, however, there are large dissenting minorities; or there may even be an almost equal division of public opinion as to the wisdom of government policies. When such differences of opinion concern questions about which people have strong emotions, the power of a government to formulate clear foreign policies and to make satisfactory agreements with other countries is likely to be greatly impaired.

The Balance of Power. In a world community of sovereign nation-states, there are several ways in which a given state could conceivably attempt to achieve security from attack without war and at the same time could gain some of its other international objectives.

If it is a very large state, like the United States or Russia, with adequate resources and industrial development, it might attempt independently or *unilaterally* to build up its military power to the point where no other state or probable combination of states would dare to challenge it. In the world of today this would be a difficult achievement for any nation. First, it would mean diverting to military uses vast amounts of resources badly needed to improve the living conditions of its people and also needed to meet various other social problems. Second, other nations, fearful for their safety and their power to control their own affairs, would tend to form alliances against it.

Another conceivable approach to the problem of security, one that a group of cooperating states could attempt to implement, would be to organize the states of the world into a system of *collective security*. To have much chance of success, such a system or organization would have to include most of the states of the world, especially the more powerful ones. It would have to be a kind of federation or superstate, with courts for settling disputes between nations and with a military establishment capable of forcing a recalcitrant nation to accept court decisions. The chances of establishing such a system in the presently foreseeable future are probably small, because most power is in the hands of several very large countries, some of whose interests appear to be in diametric opposition. Furthermore, as has been noted, few nations seem willing to give up much of their sovereignty, or their right to adopt any foreign policies they please. The United Nations, which we will discuss in Chapter 32, may be regarded as a first step toward a system of collective security, but actually it has very little power to protect its members or to prevent war. It does, however, perform many useful international services.

At present, as for a long time past, the most hopeful way of preventing or at least indefinitely delaying a disastrous war between the world's most powerful nations is to develop and, if possible, maintain a stable *balance of power*. The term *balance of power* is sometimes used with other meanings, but to students of foreign relations, who are attempting to view the world situation with some objectivity, it means an equilibrium or adjustment of power that for the time being no nation is willing to disturb. During the century that followed the Congress of Vienna (1815), a fairly effective power balance was maintained; for though that era did witness some adjustments of power and even several sizeable wars, no state attempted to challenge radically the existing balance. Today the nuclear standoff between the United States and Russia, each with its allies or satellites, is the modern version of the balance of power. This, too, will be discussed in Chapter 32.

FOREIGN POLICIES

Relationships between states that affect the national security or general welfare of each are the core of international relations. The *foreign policies* of a nation are the objectives that it attempts to achieve through its dealings with other nations. As a rule the nation's primary purposes are to increase its own security and its own general economic welfare. Sometimes, however, a foreign policy may further the interests of some politically powerful pressure group rather than those of the nation as a whole. When this is so, those who support it usually attempt to convince the majority that it benefits the entire nation.

Generally speaking, the foreign policies of a state are designed to serve the national interests as these are conceived by the public and/or by those in direct control. Security and prosperity are always major objectives; other objectives may include the spread of an ideology such as communism or the expansion of national power and prestige. Debate over policies occurs when there are divergent points of view as to their importance and how they can best be advanced. Those who shape policy sometimes make serious mistakes, even fatal ones, in the methods they employ to achieve national goals. The Nazis did this when, embarking on a course of conquest, they greatly underestimated the obstacles in the way. There is no formula that will guarantee that the right foreign policy decisions will always be made. But in a democracy, *when there are wide divergencies of opinion,* someone must make the decisions; and the president or premier and his advisers or cabinet are likely to be in a better position to make wise decisions than most other people. They usually have access to information not available to the general public; and because the responsibility for making decisions is largely theirs, they are forced to study any given situation intensively.[1]

Geography and Foreign Policy. Conspicuous among the facts and forces that act as determinants of foreign policy is, as we have pointed out, the geographic position of a nation. For the promotion of the country's security and prosperity, policy makers must give heed to such matters as (1) the defensibility of the nation's boundaries, (2) the effects of distance on its powers of offense and defense by means of nuclear missiles, (3) the availability of ports for useful trade and for naval bases, (4) the attitudes of neighboring states and their size and power, and (5) the nation's own size and natural resources. If a state is satisfied with its geographic lot in life, it can direct its efforts toward protecting what it has; if it is dissatisfied, it will, if possible, maneuver its policies toward the elimination of its alleged handicaps, asserting itself dynamically, perhaps even aggressively, in order to get from others what it believes it needs.

The term *geopolitics* has been used for many years to refer to the relation between geography and security that foreign policy makers attempt to take into account. According to Nicholas Spykman, geopolitics is "the planning of the security policy of a country in terms of its geographic factors." No nation has pursued the subject so seriously as did prewar Germany, which under the Nazis embraced the theories of earlier geopoliticians, and through General Karl Haushofer worked out a "scientific" policy of expansion, calculated to secure Germany's position as a master power for an indefinite future, all at the expense of the "decadent" neighbors.

[1] See Chapter 9, "Presidential Leadership," in Norman L. Hill, *The New Democracy,* Lincoln, Nebr., University of Nebraska Press, 1970.

Without constructing a complicated theory of geopolitics comparable to that of the Nazis, most nations, nevertheless, have exhibited in their foreign policies their geographic aspirations. Russia for centuries has sought good warm-water ports; she has wanted control over the Dardanelles; and she has tried to get buffer territory on her western frontier to make up for her lack of defensible boundaries there. Her present support of the Arab states in the Middle East can well be regarded as a continuation of her traditional policies of expansion. France long felt that her geographic position required her to seek a frontier on the Rhine and to undermine the strength of her dangerous neighbor, Germany, which had several times invaded her territory. In the Far East, Japan attempted before World War II to add to the security of her position by absorbing Korea, Manchuria, Formosa, and many islands of the Pacific.

For various reasons, geography still plays a major role in determining national policies, but in the nuclear age such factors as natural frontier barriers, fortifications, oceans, and great distances no longer provide as much protection against military attack as they once did.

Ideologies and Foreign Policy. Since World War I, foreign policies have been strongly impregnated with ideologies. This has resulted from the contest of various social doctrines, especially fascism, communism, and democracy, for the control of men's minds and for dominance in world affairs. In the 1930's, fascism played the role of aggressor, with democracy on the defensive; but as we noted earlier, the defeat of Germany and Italy in World War II destroyed the leaders of that ideological setup, and now the aggressive nations are the communist bloc of Soviet Russia and her satellites, plus Red China and such states as North Korea and North Vietnam. The smoldering fires of fascism, surviving now chiefly in Spain and Portugal, have been sufficiently cooled to cause little alarm.

To what extent communist ideology accounts for the aggressive nature of Russia's foreign policy is difficult to say. The communist doctrine that only by world revolution can the economic system of Marx and Engels be made universal is undoubtedly a spur to Russia's expansionist policies, to her propaganda activities abroad, and to her generally obstructionist conduct in diplomacy. The difficulty of estimating the importance of this factor in Russian policy is that ideologies are not only ends in themselves to be promoted by foreign policy, but they are also means for the advancement of other ends. Except for brief periods Russia has always shown an expansionist tendency and has long been a threat to her neighbors. Is Russia using communism to get the support that she needs at home and abroad to expand and improve her power position in world politics? Or is she concerned with communism chiefly as an end in itself? Although one hesitates to hazard a definite answer, it seems probable that communist ideology is both a means and an end in Russian policy. Many suspect, and with some reason, that the most important objective of the Soviet rulers and those closely allied with them is to maintain and expand their own power.

Technology and Foreign Policy. International relations have not escaped the influence of cultural changes, especially in the realm of technology. Most obvious is the manner in which the Industrial Revolution of the last two centuries has drawn nations closely together into a system of mutual interdependence. The complicated products of modern industry contain trade items assembled from many parts of the world: the automobile made in Detroit displays chrome from Turkey, nickel from Canada, rubber from Indonesia, and other products from various areas. Communication has become almost instantaneous, and the rapid transportation facilities of today enable millions of people to travel abroad every year either for pleasure or for business.

Some of the wonders of modern science challenge the restrictions placed upon their usefulness by the nation-state. The airplane, by way of illustration, is handicapped in its commercial activities by the boundaries of those nations that deny it entrance; without permission, given ordinarily by treaty or executive agreement, frontiers are understood to be closed. The radio has exposed the artificiality of these sovereign boundary lines by dispatching its messages across them everywhere, sometimes hostile messages intended to affect internal political developments. Russia has tried to prevent her people from receiving unwanted messages by jamming tactics. Facts of this nature provide one of the arguments of the world federalist to the effect that technology has outmoded the nation-state and that our planet should be a single political unit.

Perhaps most important of all, science and the new technology have become a vital adjunct of national power, enabling a nation with knowhow to devise weapons of war that will keep it in the front ranks of the great nations. This fact alone threatens to outmode all past concepts of international power relations and of war.

DIPLOMACY

Diplomacy is the means by which states carry on official relationships with one another. Through its facilities, states endeavor to advance and to justify their foreign policies. Because a nation's welfare, even its ability to avoid war, is so closely tied to the successes and failures of its diplomats, every state maintains a highly organized system of diplomacy and tries to keep that system at top efficiency. At the center of the system is invariably a foreign office, called in the United States the Department of State, and this office is responsible for the nation's conduct in diplomacy. In the United States, the Secretary of State is appointed by the President, with the consent of the Senate, and is accountable to the President, who, under our Constitution, is the official spokesman of the country in its foreign relations.

Bilateral Diplomacy. Today each state maintains *bilateral diplomatic relations* with every other state that it recognizes, sending to and receiving from every such state permanent *diplomatic missions.* This system was taken over by the modern nation-states from the practice of the city-states of northern Italy in the fifteenth century. Among those city-states, Genoa in 1455 was the first to send permanent instead of temporary diplomatic missions to its neighbors, and Venice, by sending one to London in 1496, was the first to dispatch a permanent mission outside Italy. The new practice of maintaining permanent missions gained general approval, and soon all the new nation-states of Europe had fallen in line. Since that time every national capital has housed missions from all parts of the world.

The Diplomatic and Consular Services. According to international law, there are four ranks to be assigned to the heads of diplomatic missions: highest is the *ambassador* (and the papal legate); second, the *minister plenipotentiary;* third, *the minister resident;* and, fourth, the *chargé d'affaires* (accredited to ministers of foreign affairs rather than to heads of state). Nowadays the rank of ambassador is the most commonly used of all, and in American practice the great majority of the chiefs of mission hold that rank, partly because sending a chief of lesser status to a small nation might be regarded as an affront to its dignity. International

55. The United States Embassy in Manila, Philippines. (Photo by author.)

law leaves states free to devise their own methods of selecting diplomats, except for the requirement that they must be acceptable to the receiving states.

In addition to the chiefs of missions, the foreign service of a nation includes a number of subordinate officials, both diplomatic and consular, ranging from a score or so for some small countries to a thousand or more for the larger states. In the embassies and legations of the United States abroad, there are, in addition to the heads of missions, foreign-service officers of six different classifications, foreign-service reserve officers, foreign-service staff officers, and a group of native employees. The embassy in London, for instance, now employs several hundred Americans and native Britons. *Consular officials,* also designated by the United States since 1924 as *foreign-service officers,* are located in specified cities of the country to which they are sent as well as in the capital. Although consular officials are occasionally called upon to perform diplomatic functions, for the most part their work centers about the promotion of trade. They also aid American citizens when emergencies arise, and they issue *visas* to foreigners who plan to go to the United States. A *visa* is an endorsement on a passport. It permits the bearer to enter the country that gives it.

Prominent among the many duties of the diplomat is that of reporting back to his foreign office the developments he has been able to observe and thus keeping his country informed of economic, political, and social trends within the nation to which he is accredited. In this capacity he is "the eyes and ears" of his country. In a way he is also "the mouth" of his government abroad, for he must try to make known to the government and the people of the country to which he is accredited the purposes and hopes and desires of his native land. The diplomat also speaks for his government when, in the process of negotiating, he tries to find solutions to problems and embody those solutions in treaties and agreements. Not least among his duties is that of protecting the interests of his nation and its citizens abroad; because of tourist travel and of large-scale investments in other countries, this duty today takes on substantial proportions.

Raising the Quality of Our Foreign Service. During this last half-century the United States has been endeavoring to improve the quality of its foreign service by making of it an attractive career that will induce able young men to enter it and to stay with it throughout their active lives. Today ambassadors and ministers are frequently chosen from the permanent foreign-service personnel, whereas formerly they were almost always leading businessmen or politicians. To become a foreign-service officer, a candidate now must take examinations (written, oral, and physical); and during their periods of service close records are kept of the work of all foreign-service officers in order to make promotions whenever deserved. Officers are given leaves of absence, and they are provided with pensions on retirement. The Foreign Service Act of 1946 introduced several new features: (1) foreign-service officers may become heads of diplomatic missions without any loss of pension credits or other service advantages that they may have accumulated (the majority of the heads of missions now are career men); (2) foreign-service staff officers are provided to handle the clerical side of the work; and (3) foreign-service reserve officers are also available to serve as experts on technical subjects coming within the purview of diplomacy. Gradually the United States has strengthened its foreign service to the point that it now compares favorably with the services of other nations.

Multilateral Diplomacy. As new subjects of diplomacy such as health, labor conditions, drug control, road signs and signals, education, food production, conservation and pollution have pressed into the foreground and taken on importance, the necessity of getting a large number of states together in the negotiating process has brought forth new methods of procedure. Multilateral diplomacy, the answer to the problem, originally took the form of occasional international conferences. The first conferences to deal with peacetime subjects, as distinguished from the problem of peacemaking after war, occurred early in the nineteenth century. Among them were the meetings of the Quadruple Alliance between 1815 and 1822 and the Panama Conference of 1826. They increased in number as the century drew to an end. In those days it was necessary for every conference to be called and prepared by some interested state, for there was no international organization available to which the work could be assigned. After World War I the conference idea was rapidly extended, and in the 1920's and 1930's a long list of meetings occurred, some organized by the League of Nations and others by individual states as before. These meetings included the Washington Disarmament Conference (1921–1922), the London Economic Conference (1933), the Geneva Disarmament Conference (1932–1934), the Munich Conference (1938), and many other important gatherings.

Today multilateral diplomacy has reached a high point of development. There are still independent conferences, such as the San Francisco Conference of 1951 to sign the treaty of peace with Japan, but the majority are now called by some permanent organization. The United Nations and its specialized agencies arrange scores of conferences every year, in addition to the hundreds of meetings of the Security Council, the General Assembly, the Trusteeship Council, the Economic and Social Council, and the subordinate committees and commissions of those groups. The Organization of American States also arranges conferences and meetings of many kinds. Still other permanent organizations, such as the Council of Europe and the North Atlantic Treaty Organization, add further to the multilateral side of diplomatic activities.

Secret and Open Diplomacy. Traditionally there has been a great deal of secrecy surrounding the activities of diplomats. During World War I President Woodrow Wilson assailed this practice and advocated "open covenants openly arrived at." Not much objection has been raised to his plea for "open covenants"; the present procedure of registering and publishing treaties, begun by the League of Nations and now continued by the

United Nations, increases the probability that most covenants will be open. The extent to which covenants can be "openly arrived at" is much more debatable. To open the processes of diplomacy to public view is an invitation to deadlock, for the compromises so essential to successful negotiations meet with little or no approval on the part of the average newspaper reader or radio listener; compromises, to most people, suggest weakness, even chicanery.

Dag Hammarskjold, former Secretary-General of the United Nations, expressed the danger of *open diplomacy* when he said that it is likely to be "frozen diplomacy." Although it may be maintained that the people are affected by what goes on in diplomacy, the usual conclusion that "therefore they are entitled in the interests of democracy to be kept informed on the details of the negotiating" does not necessarily follow. A democratic people should be expected to have confidence in negotiators appointed by the government they have elected; their job is to judge the results achieved by their government, a duty great enough to absorb all the interest and energy they can give.

During the past thirty years the processes of diplomacy have been opened to public view more than every before, and the results have not been reassuring. After the Paris Peace Conference of 1946, General Jan Smuts, a delegate from the Union of South Africa, explained to an audience of Scottish businessmen that the failures of the Conference had been caused in large part by its openness. The organs of the United Nations have operated in the open almost constantly, and they have thus provided the Soviet delegates an excellent opportunity for propaganda. Most of the sessions of the Berlin Conference (1954) of the foreign ministers of the United States, Soviet Russia, the United Kingdom, and France were open, and again there was voluminous propaganda and little in the way of agreement. True, during recent years the East-West split might have prevented compromises in diplomacy even had it been closed, for the will to agree is always an essential element of successful negotiations. That too much openness has accentuated the problems of contemporary diplomats is, however, a point of view widely supported by critical observers.

THE UNITED STATES IN THE WORLD COMMUNITY

The separation-of-powers doctrine, modified by a system of checks and balances, was embodied in the American Constitution of 1787 in order to prevent tyranny, and it applies within the field of foreign affairs as well as in domestic politics. Although the judiciary has no hand in policy-making and is confined in its work to the interpretation and application of treaties and statutes, the other two branches of the government—the President and Congress (especially the Senate)—are both equipped with far-reaching authority to determine foreign policies.

The President and Foreign Policy. The President derives great power in foreign affairs from his right to appoint (with the consent of the Senate) diplomats and to receive the diplomats of other countries. As the Supreme Court stated in *United States* v. *the Curtis-Wright Export Co.* (1936), ". . . the President alone has the power to speak or listen as a representative of the nation."[2] This means that he has ultimate responsibility for the diplomatic messages our government transmits abroad and for the operations of the Department of State generally. His control of diplomacy gives him a strong initiative in foreign affairs, for diplomatic correspondence can be a vehicle of policy, as in 1899 when Secretary of State John Hay originated the Open Door Policy in China by messages to selected governments. The President's prerogative in diplomacy confers on him, too, the right to deny or to extend recognition to a new government or state, for it is usually by establishing diplomatic relationships that recognition is accorded. Because many agreements between the responsible agents of governments are in the form of exchanges of notes, the President's position in diplomacy enables him to conclude such informal arrangements as those made by President Franklin Roosevelt during World War II at Yalta (1945).

The President has the initiative in treaty making, too, but here his actions require the approval of two thirds of the Senators present when a vote is taken. This arrangement, indeed, is a good example of the system of checks and balances that pervades the whole field of government in the United States. Vital foreign policies are embodied in such treaties as the North Atlantic Treaty (1949), the Charter of the United Nations (1945), the Japanese Treaty of Peace (1951), and the Nuclear Test Ban Treaty (1963). Much criticism has been aimed at the Senate for its obstructive tactics in its consideration of treaties, notably the Treaty of Versailles (1919), and several proposals have been submitted to amend the Constitution to substitute a majority of both houses of Congress in place of two thirds of the Senate in treaty making, but such proposals have never had much support.

The President's authority in foreign affairs is augmented by some of his more general powers. As commander-in-chief of the armed forces he can dispatch the Army, Navy, or Air Force to any part of the world to carry out a policy, and he can conclude executive agreements by which bases abroad are placed at the disposal of the services; for instance, in 1950 he moved the armed forces into Korea to prevent communist expansion, and in 1958 he sent American troops into Lebanon at the request of the Lebanese government to meet what appeared to be a threat to Lebanon's independence. Beginning in the late 1950's he sent increasing numbers of men from our armed forces into South Vietnam, first as military "advisers" and later as active participants in the actual fighting against the communist Viet Cong rebels and their North Vietnam allies. Late in 1969 President Nixon announced that American troops would gradually be withdrawn

[2] 299 U.S. 304.

and the defense of South Vietnam turned over to its own forces, but he set no definite schedule and no date for their final complete withdrawal.

The President can also initiate policies by his messages to Congress and his speeches to the general public. The Monroe Doctrine, an American policy of basic significance designed to prevent the European powers from taking over parts of this hemisphere, was proclaimed to the world by President James Monroe in 1823 as a message to Congress. In 1947 President Harry S. Truman declared to Congress that it was the policy of this nation to come to the assistance of countries trying to protect themselves against communist aggression. Greece and Turkey were directly threatened at the time.

Congress and Foreign Policy. Though the President has great power in the field of foreign affairs, he is dependent on Congress in many ways. In addition to the fact that the Senate must approve his appointments to diplomatic posts and consent to the treaties he negotiates, Congress as a whole is in a position to exercise a great deal of authority through the general power of legislation. The Marshall Plan of economic assistance to the nations of Europe, for instance, would have died at birth had not Congress made it a law and appropriated the money required. Among the many measures passed by Congress that have embodied foreign policies, special mention may be made of (1) the International Development Act (1950), extending technical assistance to underdeveloped countries; (2) the Mutual Security Appropriation Act (1951), making more than seven billion dollars available for military and economic aid to friendly nations; (3) the Trade Expansion Act of 1962, which gave the President unprecedented power to cut tariffs through agreements with other nations; and (4) the appropriation of funds in 1969 to start construction of an anti-ballistic missile system (ABM).

So divided between the President and Congress are the powers by which foreign policies are made that only by cooperation can the two branches of the government avoid paralyzing deadlocks. On occasion, cooperation has not been forthcoming, and the nation has found itself seriously embarrassed. The President has signed treaties that the Senate would not approve (such as the Treaty of Versailles, 1919–1920); the President has dispatched troops overseas and then taken a broadside of criticism from Congress; the President has publicly announced a policy only to be contradicted in an address by the Chairman of the Senate Foreign Relations Committee advocating another course of action (for example, President Franklin Roosevelt and Senator Burton Wheeler in 1939–1941). By the nature of the American constitutional system, a President has much less control over the actions of Congress than the prime minister of Great Britain has over the House of Commons. Clement Attlee, former Labour Prime Minister of Great Britian, once pointed out this fact and complained that the separation-of-powers system in the United States leaves other nations quite uncertain of what American foreign policy really is at any given time.

American Foreign Policies. Nothing is more significant in modern international relations than the changed position of the United States in the community of nations. Throughout the nineteenth century this nation was deeply committed to a policy of *isolation,* according to which it made no alliances abroad and kept as free as possible from the political embroilments of Europe. Even after the Spanish-American War (1898), the nation remained aloof, though the acquisition of scattered dependencies as a result of the war had widened American interests a great deal. *Isolationism* broke down when the United States in 1917 became a belligerent in World War I, but it was revived in 1919–1920, when membership in the new League of Nations was rejected by the Senate. Although under attack in the 1920's and 1930's, isolationism continued to have strong support, as shown by American neutrality legislation (1935 and later) and by the efforts in 1939–1941 to keep the United States from becoming involved in World War II.

But Pearl Harbor changed all this. The United States quickly became enmeshed in world politics, and has continued to be deeply involved ever since. In the present-day world, we probably have no alternative if we hope to maintain peace and our national security. After World War II we made or affirmed a number of alliances, maintained troops or military outposts in various parts of the world, especially in Europe and the Far East, and became an active member of the United Nations and a major source of financial support for many of its activities. We have played a role in almost every power situation that has arisen in the world and have committed large military forces to the fighting of two local undeclared wars, namely those in Korea and Vietnam. Although many factors have contributed to the radical change of our position in world affairs, undoubtedly the most important of these was the threat of Russian expansion that developed after World War II and that was greatly intensified by the development of intercontinental nuclear missiles of ever-increasing power and accuracy.

Much of our foreign policy since World War II has been designed to implement a doctrine that President Truman set forth in 1947. Essentially the Truman Doctrine was that if any country threatened by communist aggression was willing to resist that threat, and asked for help, the United States would come to its aid. This was often called a policy of *containing* communism. If the United States had not taken the lead in resisting the aggressive moves of the U.S.S.R. and the other communist nations supported by it, there would probably have been no very effective opposition.

As a part of our effort to protect nations against communist aggression, we have helped to organize alliances among the nations of the Free World. In the North Atlantic Treaty Organization (NATO), formed early in 1949, we eventually lined up fourteen nations besides ourselves. All are pledged to resist attack upon any one of the members. NATO has had its problems. Two of its members, Greece and Turkey, had difficulties over Cyprus; and in 1967 President Charles de Gaulle withdrew France from the military alliance of NATO, though he continued a political affiliation. To counter NATO, in 1955 Russia organized the Warsaw Pact, but this includes only the Soviet and its satellites, namely, Bulgaria, Czechoslovakia, East Germany, Hungary, Poland, and Romania. Figure 33 indicates the members of NATO; also the Warsaw Pack countries, plus Lithuania, Latvia, and Estonia, which Russia had annexed in 1940.

Figure 33. Europe and System of Military Alliances. (Reprinted, courtesy of *The Chicago Tribune.*)

Another defensive alliance that the United States has joined is the Southeast Asia Treaty Organization (SEATO). We also have defensive alliances with most of the countries in the Western Hemisphere under the Inter-American Treaty of Reciprocal Assistance which was drawn up in Rio de Janeiro in 1947. In addition, we have defensive alliances with Australia, New Zealand, the Philippines, Japan, and South Korea. But social developments in the United States, including vocal and sometimes violent opposition to the Vietnam War, the draft, the military establishment, and military spending, have raised some doubts in other countries as to how far the United States would be willing and able to go, in some future crisis, in order to support its commitments.

In a report to Congress on February 18, 1970, President Nixon propounded a new doctrine that can be regarded as a modification of the Truman Doctrine and that is designed to somewhat reduce the global commitments of the United States. The President described the Nixon Doctrine as follows:

Its central thesis is that the United States will participate in the defense and development of allies and friends, but America cannot—and will not—conceive all the plans, design all the programs, execute all the decisions, and undertake all the defense of the free nations of the world. We will help where it makes a real difference and is considered in our interest.

This new doctrine does not, of course, release the United States from specific commitments that it has made to other nations by treaty, but it does indicate that we will not attempt unilaterally to police the world.

The general nature of the foreign policy of the United States is well summed up by Irving Kristol in an article in Foreign Affairs:

Though there is much fancy rhetoric, pro and con, about the purpose of American foreign policy, there is really nothing esoteric about this purpose. The United States wishes to establish and sustain a world order that (a) ensures its national security against other great powers, (b) encourages other nations, especially the smaller ones, to mold their own social, political, and economic institutions along lines that are at least not repugnant to (if not actually congruent with) American values, and (c) minimizes the possibility of naked armed conflict.[3]

Terms to Be Understood

state	city-state	collective security
nation	sovereignty	geopolitics
nation-state	national power	foreign policy
nationalism	balance of power	diplomacy

[3] Foreign Affairs, July 7, 1967, p. 609.

bilateral diplomacy
diplomatic mission
consular officials
ambassador

minister
chargé d'affaires
visa
multilateral diplomacy

open diplomacy
isolationism
NATO
SEATO

Questions for Review and Discussion

1. In what sense do the nation-states of the world form a community?
2. As the term is used in this chapter, which of the following are states? Alaska, Luxembourg, Scotland, Bavaria, Australia, Michigan, Abyssinia, Hong Kong. On what basis did you make your selection?
3. Of certain states it is sometimes said that they are not really nations. What is meant?
4. List the more important differences that exist between nation-states.
5. Explain the origin of the modern nation-state.
6. Has the nation-state outlived its usefulness? Why or why not?
7. What problems does the sovereignty concept create in international relations?
8. The effectiveness of a nation's military power in supporting its foreign policies depends on what factors in addition to the size, training, and equipment of its armed forces?
9. Why are democratic governments more restricted in their actions by public opinion than are totalitarian governments?
10. What basic conditions must exist in some degree if a nation is to develop great power, including military power?
11. What are three possible approaches to the problem of achieving some degree of national security? Explain each.
12. Do you believe that the President of the United States should have more power or less power to determine and carry out foreign policies? Defend your answer.
13. How may foreign policies be influenced by (a) geography? (b) an ideology? (c) modern technology?
14. What are the advantages of multilateral diplomacy? Can it be employed in all situations? Why or why not?
15. Secret diplomacy has been assailed by many, including President Wilson. What are the drawbacks of open diplomacy?
16. What powers does the President of the United States have in foreign affairs? What powers are held by Congress? Point out the advantages and disadvantages of this division of responsibility.
17. What is the nature of the international obligations that the United States has assumed since World War II?
18. Explain the shift of American foreign policy away from an attitude of aloofness to one of active participation in world affairs.
19. What are the primary objectives today of American foreign policy?

For Further Study

Bailey, Thomas A., *The Art of Diplomacy: The American Experience,* New York, Appleton-Century-Crofts, Inc., 1968.

——, *A Diplomatic History of the American People,* 8th ed., New York, Appleton-Century-Crofts, 1969.

Beilenson, Laurence W., *The Treaty Trap,* Washington, D.C., Public Affairs Press, 1969.

Crabb, Cecil V., Jr., *Nations in a Multipolar World,* New York, Harper & Row, Publishers, 1968.

Deutsch, Karl W., and William J. Foltz, eds., *Nation-Building,* enlarged ed., New York, Atherton Press, 1966.

Draper, Theodore, *Abuse of Power,* paperback, New York, The Viking Press, Inc., 1967.

Gurtov, Melvin, *Southeast Asia Tomorrow: Problems and Prospects for U.S. Policy,* paperback, Baltimore, Johns Hopkins Press, 1970.

Hartmann, Frederick H., *The Relations of Nations,* 3d ed., New York, The Macmillan Company, 1967.

Hill, Norman L., *International Politics,* New York, Harper & Row, Publishers, 1963. See especially Part 1.

——, *Mister Secretary of State,* paperback, New York, Random House, Inc., 1963.

——, *The New Democracy in Foreign Policy Making,* Lincoln, Nebr., University of Nebraska Press, 1970. Deals with what the author believes should be the role of the President.

Kennan, George F., *On Dealing with the Communist World,* New York, Harper & Row, Publishers, 1964.

Lerche, Charles O., *America in World Affairs,* 2d ed., New York, McGraw-Hill, Inc., 1967.

Morgenthau, Hans J., *A New Foreign Policy for the United States,* New York, Frederick A. Praeger, Inc., 1969.

——, *Politics Among Nations,* 4th ed., New York, Alfred A. Knopf, Inc., 1967.

Osgood, Robert E., *Alliances and American Foreign Policy,* Baltimore, Johns Hopkins Press, 1968.

Pounds, Norman, *Political Geography,* New York, McGraw-Hill, Inc., 1963.

Rodee, Carlton C., et al., *Introduction to Political Science,* 2d ed., New York, McGraw-Hill, Inc., 1967.

Rostow, W. W., *The Diffusion of Power,* New York, The Macmillan Company, 1970.

Schuman, Frederick L., *International Politics,* 7th ed., New York, McGraw-Hill, Inc., 1969.

Ulam, Adam B., *Expansion and Coexistence: The History of Soviet Foreign Policy, 1917–67,* New York, Frederick A. Praeger, Inc., 1968.

Chapter 30

International

Economic

Relations

he conflicts of interest that arise between nations more often than not have their economic aspects. Hence our understanding of these conflicts is certain to be inadequate unless we know something about the economic relationships of nations, including international trade, foreign exchange, foreign investment, and foreign aid. All are important, but because the source of most international economic relationships is trade, its study becomes our first concern. The volume of international trade has now reached such huge proportions that the economic welfare of many nations is largely dependent on it.

INTERNATIONAL TRADE

There was a time in the history of every region when trade was either nonexistent or was local and relatively unimportant. But as specialization developed and as transportation was improved and trade routes became safer, commerce was carried on in ever-increasing volume. Goods began to cross seas and alien territories and to travel ever greater distances, until today a large part of the commodities common to everyday living comes from places scattered all over the world. As the volume of trade grew, economic relationships developed among nations and constantly increased in variety and importance.

The Advantages of International Trade. Trade is the lifeblood of a modern economy, and the benefits of international trade are so great that it is inconceivable that a modern nation should adopt a policy of complete economic isolation. The full utilization of power machinery, with its attendant specialization, requires mass production, and mass production calls for extensive trade in very wide markets. To limit the market of an industry to one country would often mean reduced efficiency and higher costs. Also, modern peoples require for consumption and as raw materials for their industries a great variety of goods: tea, coffee, cotton, rubber, petroleum, iron, manganese, aluminum, nickel, coal—a complete list would be long indeed. No country has or can produce all these products. The missing ones can be obtained only through trade. When trade flows freely between countries, the world tends to become more prosperous. When trade languishes, production lags, unemployment increases, and the world's income shrinks.

The primary advantages of international trade are three. The *first* advantage is that it enables a country to obtain products that cannot be produced at home at all or that cannot be produced in adequate quantities and at acceptable costs. Sometimes the inability of a country to produce certain things is a matter of climate, as with tea and coffee in the United States. In other cases it is a lack of certain natural resources. Italy, for example, has no good coal deposits, and Britain does not have enough good farm land to meet its demands for food.

The *second* advantage of international trade is that it often enables a country to get a better product than can be produced at home. This may be due to differences in climate and soil or to differences in natural resources. Sometimes, however, it is owing to the fact that the people of some foreign country have, over a long period of time, acquired certain techniques that are not easily transferred. English factories for years produced finer woolens than most American factories, because they had specialized in fine woolens for generations.

A *third* advantage of international trade is that it often makes products available at a lower price than would be possible if they were produced at home. This raises standards of living by increasing consumer purchas-

56. Broomstraw from Argentina Being Unloaded in Venezuela from a Norwegian Freighter. Cartons in ship's hold contain television parts made in Sao Paulo, Brazil, for shipment to Mexico. (Photo by author.)

ing power. Consider a country that, like Great Britain, produces only about half of its food supply. Conceivably, Britain might be able to raise enough food within its own borders to feed its people after a fashion. However, any attempt to do this would mean inadequate amounts of many foods and the almost complete absence of such commodities as oranges, tea, and coffee. It would also mean high prices for the foods that could be produced. Britain has a large population relative to the amount of land available for cultivation. To raise all its food it would have to cultivate its good land more intensively, in spite of the tendency toward diminishing returns; it would also have to resort to inferior land not really suitable for agriculture. Both methods are expensive and result in high prices. In the long run, it can provide its people with better standards of living by selling industrial goods and buying abroad a substantial portion of its food supply.

It is sometimes maintained that, though foreign trade may be vital to some countries, it is not of much importance to the United States. It can be pointed out, for example, that while in 1968, a fairly typical year, our exports of merchandise were over $34 billion and our imports over $33 billion, our gross national product in that year was about twenty-five times either of these amounts. It is therefore apparent that only a very small part of our national income was a direct result of foreign trade transactions.

But the argument that foreign trade is not important to the United States has several weaknesses. For one thing, it fails to take account of the fact that, once export industries become established, people employed in them furnish a part of the market for industries producing for domestic consumption. Hence, if exports should decline, production and employment would, in accordance with the multiplier principle, also fall off in other industries. Another thing it fails to recognize is that a number of our imports are necessary or desirable commodities that we cannot produce ourselves, such as coffee, natural rubber, nickel, and tin.

The Interdependence of Exports and Imports. In the United States, as in most countries, there is a tendency to encourage exports and discourage imports. Just as it seems plain that selling goods abroad gives profits and wages to American producers, so it seems equally plain that buying goods abroad robs American producers of the profits and wages that they might have received had these goods been purchased at home.

However, the notion that American producers as a group are injured by foreign purchases is, in fact, a fallacy. As we shall show shortly, if trade is on a business basis, in the long run the United States can sell goods to other countries only if it also buys goods from them. If we reduce our imports, we reduce our exports. Though we may gain home markets for the products of some American workers, we do this only at the expense of losing foreign markets for the products of other American workers. For the whole country this cancels out, and the net result is that American consumers pay higher prices or receive inferior goods.

On the other hand, if we increase our imports, in the long run our exports will also increase. Any decline in the home market for American goods will be offset by an increase in the foreign market. If we buy English textiles because they are cheaper or better than domestic textiles, and if the English buy American electric refrigerators because they are cheaper or better than those made in England, the consumers of both countries gain. Further, there is no loss in employment. In America the smaller demand for labor in the textile industry is offset by the larger demand for labor in the refrigerator industry. In England the smaller proportion of refrigerator workers is offset by the larger proportion of textile workers.

Why Exports Depend on Imports. Why is it that we can sell goods to other countries only if we also buy goods from them? Briefly, the reason is that, in the long run, foreign countries can pay for what they buy only with the goods they sell. Let us explain as simply as possible how imports pay for exports, and vice versa. For simplicity, we will first assume that trade takes place only between England and the United States.

Suppose that at a certain time an English importer wishes to buy a million dollars' worth of American machinery. The American firms that have this machinery for sale are unlikely to want English money, or pounds sterling. Rather, they will want dollars. Therefore, in order to buy the machinery, the English importer must find some way to change his English money into dollars. He must be able to find someone who has dollars and who is willing to sell them in exchange for pounds.

Who are the people who will have dollars and be willing to exchange them for pounds? For the most part they can be found in two groups: (1) Americans who wish pounds in order to buy goods or services from Englishmen and (2) English exporters who have accepted checks or drafts in dollars for English goods that they have sold to Americans. In either case, the source of the dollars available to Englishmen to buy American goods is the payments Americans have made, or plan to make, for English goods.

If for any reason American imports of English goods should decline, then the English would be forced to curtail their purchases of American goods because they could no longer obtain sufficient dollars to buy in the previous volume.

For the sake of simplicity, the above explanation disregards certain complicating factors. Actually, English importers do not go directly to English exporters to obtain American money. The banks act as middlemen. If an English exporter accepts, in payment, dollar checks drawn on an American bank, he does so because he can take them to his bank and there exchange them for pounds sterling that he can deposit to his own account. His bank can then deposit these checks in a New York bank and sell dollar drafts to English importers who need them in order to pay for American goods.

Another factor that our explanation disregards is that trade does not take place just between England and the United States. Other countries come into the picture. For example, English exporters might receive dollars for textiles sold in the United States, and English importers might in turn use these dollars to buy beef in Argentina. The dollars would then be available to Argentine importers to buy machinery in the United States. In this case, the dollars we spent for British textiles made it possible for Argentines to buy our machinery.

In the long run, if we expect foreigners to pay for the goods they receive from us, foreign purchases of American goods cannot greatly exceed our purchases of foreign goods. In the short run, however, this statement must be qualified. Over considerable periods of time foreigners may be able to buy from us substantially more than they sell to us. This can happen for two reasons: (1) they may have stocks of gold that they are willing to send us in payment for their purchases, and (2) we may be willing to sell them goods on credit. However, the gold reserves of foreign countries are limited, and credits, if good, must some day be repaid.

There is only one method by which we could continue indefinitely to sell to foreigners substantially more than we buy from them. That method is to *give* to foreign countries the dollars with which they buy our goods. We did this under lend-lease, we did it under the Marshall Plan, and we are still doing it on a considerable scale in order to help friendly nations maintain their armed forces or to give economic aid to certain less developed nations. Whether we shall be willing to continue such giving indefinitely remains to be seen. For our government to keep giving money to foreigners, *just to create a market for our goods,* would be silly. We could achieve this result equally well by reducing income taxes in this country or by distributing the money to our own poor.

Visible and Invisible Trade. Many people, when they think of imports and exports, have in mind only material goods such as wheat, pianos, or machinery. Such things constitute the *visible* items of trade; but to think of foreign trade as consisting of them alone is very misleading, because the so-called *invisible* items may be just as important.

Invisible items of trade consist of services of all sorts for which the people of one country pay those of another. For example, in normal years we pay Englishmen and other foreigners large amounts in freight charges for carrying American goods on their ships. Likewise, American tourists pay Englishmen, Frenchmen, Italians, and others large sums to buy hotel accommodations and railroad transportation in their countries. Such items represent purchases abroad just as truly as do imports of coffee or shoes. Another important invisible item of trade is interest received by Americans from foreign investments. This is payment for permitting foreigners to use our capital, something that is just as truly a service as their permitting us to use their hotel rooms.

So far as the visible items of trade are concerned, before World War II we normally exported much more than we imported. But in respect to the invisible items, the reverse was true. Hence, for the most part, imports equalled exports, so that our money payments to other countries were offset by their payments to us. However, this balance was upset by World War II. Ever since its outbreak, our government has been making large gifts (and also loans) to other countries with the result that total exports, visible and invisible, have substantially exceeded imports. This has been possible only because a part of our exports have been given away; that is, they have been paid for by money given by our government to other countries as aid.

The Balance of Trade and the Balance of Payments. The term *balance of trade* should logically refer to the relation of our total exports to our total imports. Traditionally, however, it has referred only to physical exports and imports. When commodity exports exceeded commodity imports, the balance was said to be *favorable*. If the reverse was true, it was said to be *unfavorable*. The only reason for this usage was the mistaken belief that it is always advantageous for a country to export more physical goods than it imports.

The term *balance of payments* refers to the relation of *total* payments made abroad to *total* payments received from abroad. Normally most of these payments are made for goods and services. However, even before the war, a minor part of our payments to foreigners represented gifts, principally the remittances of immigrants to their relatives in the old country. Another part represented the making of loans and investments in foreign countries.

Whatever may be the purpose of payments, actual transfers of wealth from one country to another can usually be made only in the form of goods or gold.[1] If for any reason a country cannot export enough goods to pay for its imports, it must settle the balance by shipping gold or by borrowing abroad. The only other possibility, except for default, is to receive foreign gifts. Before World War II, gifts were seldom available in peacetime on a large scale, but since the war many countries have received very large gifts from the United States for relief, reconstruction, military aid, or economic development. In recent years some economically backward countries have also received gifts from other prosperous countries in the Free World, and also from Soviet Russia.

In the years just after World War II even massive aid from the United States was not sufficient to satisfy the needs of the devastated countries of western Europe. These needs were so great, and their own productive power so low, that they spent for our goods not only the money we lent or gave them, plus the money received from their exports to us, but also a large part of their limited gold reserves. As a result, up to about 1950 the gold holdings of the United States continued to grow.

After 1950 the situation gradually changed. The ability of Europe to produce and export goods increased, and the urgency of its needs for imports declined. This brought about a decline in the excess of our exports over imports, and eventually our receipts from exports for which foreigners paid us with their own money (and not our gift money) became inadequate to meet our foreign obligations. We then began to experience outflows of gold, which in time became very large. In ordinary business transactions our exports still exceeded imports, but besides paying for the imports we spent, as noted, large sums on foreign aid and our military forces abroad. In 1971 President Nixon took drastic measures intended to check inflation and improve the business outlook. Included were a temporary wage-price freeze, the imposition of a 10 per cent surtax on most imports, and stopping redemption in gold of dollars held abroad. This last action brought a moderate decline in the exchange value of the dollar in most foreign currencies.

In recent years two factors helped to cut down somewhat our loss of gold and to delay a forced devaluation of the dollar in terms of gold and foreign currencies. First, many dollar payments made to foreigners were invested in the United States instead of being exchanged by them for foreign currencies or gold. Much of this investment was in the form of buying stocks in American companies. But when the stock market fell sharply in 1969 and 1970, and interest rates rose, foreign investment tended to shift to the making of high-interest commercial loans or to the purchase of high-grade bonds yielding returns of from 8 per cent to more than 9 per cent. A second factor tending to reduce the drain on our

[1] Strictly speaking, gold is a commodity, and it could, therefore, be included in the category of goods. It should also be noted that there are times when some currency with high prestige may to some degree be accepted internationally as a substitute for gold. This was especially true of dollars for a long time after World War II, and to a lesser degree it is still true.

gold supply was the frequent willingness of foreigners, instead of exchanging dollars for their own currencies or gold, to keep them in foreign banks or the foreign branches of American banks in the form of deposits payable in dollars. They were willing to do this because in recent years such deposits had paid very high rates of interest. These dollars deposited abroad are called *Eurodollars*. Their importance in international finance is indicated by the fact that total bank loans in Eurodollars at the end of 1969, less redeposits by borrowers, were estimated to exceed $37 billion.[2]

But there was always a possibility that conditions would change and that foreigners might sell their American investments on a large scale and try to exchange their Eurodollars for gold. Such action would create an acute balance-of-payments crisis for the United States, forcing us to devalue the dollar officially or to stop redeeming it for gold.

If we had succeeded in doing two things, we could probably have brought our balance of payments into fairly stable equilibrium without devaluing the dollar or stopping gold payments. First, if we had controlled inflation effectively, American prices would have been lower in relation to foreign prices, our exports (and receipts from them) would have been greater, and our imports (and payments for them to other countries) less. Second, we could have reduced foreign payments substantially by sharply curtailing foreign aid and our military commitments abroad. When Nixon finally stopped the redemption in gold of dollars held abroad, the action was probably wise, but it was also a step toward removing the last vestiges of the restraints that the old gold standard once exercised over inflation. For the time being it left the foreign exchange value of the dollar to be determined by supply and demand, as influenced by the monetary policies of various countries.

FOREIGN EXCHANGE

The Meaning of Foreign Exchange. *Foreign exchange* refers to the process of exchanging the money of one country for that of another. Goods are generally paid for in terms of money, but in international trade the buyer uses one kind of money and the seller another, so that the price that one pays and the other receives depends in part on the rate at which their two currencies exchange. For example, in the summer of 1949, when the official price of the British pound was still $4.03, a set of chinaware selling for £ 10 in London would have cost an American tourist $40.30. Late in September of the same year, after the British government had devalued the pound to $2.80, the same set of chinaware would have cost an American tourist only $28.00.

In studying foreign exchange, we are concerned first of all with *exchange*

[2] *Monthly Economic Letter,* First National City Bank, July 1970, p. 79.

rates and how they are determined. It is desirable for exchange rates between two countries to be at a level that will encourage trade. They should also be reasonably stable. Erratic fluctuations in exchange rates are a handicap to trade, because they increase the uncertainty and risk involved in transactions that require time for their completion.

Foreign Exchange Under the Gold Standard. For many years before World War I the principal trading countries of the world maintained monetary systems based on the *gold standard.* During the war this standard broke down in most countries, and though it was revived for a time after the war, it suffered a second general breakdown with the coming of the great depression in the early 1930's.

When two or more countries are on the gold standard, one of its great advantages is that only very small fluctuations can take place in the exchange rates between their currencies. Under the traditional gold standard, each country will exchange its paper money freely for a fixed amount of gold, and vice versa. When paper money and gold are freely interchangeable in each of two countries, the relative values of their currencies will depend almost entirely on the relative amounts of gold they represent.

For example, let us suppose that the French franc once represented four grains of gold and the American dollar twenty grains of gold. [3] Then a dollar would always exchange for approximately five francs. Slight variations in the exchange rate could still occur because of the cost of shipping gold. For example, though under the gold standard an American could always exchange his dollars in this country for a fixed amount of gold, in order to use this gold to obtain francs in Paris he would first have to pay the cost of shipping it to France.

The weakness of the gold standard was that, in order to maintain it, a government had to keep on hand enough gold to meet all demands for redeeming its currency. The advantage of this standard was that, *as long as there was a determination to maintain it,* it was an effective check on inflation. It forced a government to limit the expansion of bank deposits and the issue of paper money. Otherwise, demands for conversion of paper into gold would soon reach such a level that the government would be forced to stop redemption, thus automatically placing its money on a paper or *fiat* standard.

Paper Standards and the Gold Exchange Standard. Under a paper standard, the basic monetary unit of a country is represented by engraved pieces of irredeemable paper. These have value only because they are somewhat limited in quantity and, in the country of issue, are legal tender and acceptable in trade. But unless controls of some sort are set up, when a currency ceases to be redeemable in gold, its value is likely to fluctuate widely in terms of the currencies of other countries.

During the depression of the 1930's and the period of World War II, the

[3] Under the gold standard as it existed before World War I, American gold coins actually contained 23.22 grains of pure gold per dollar, and French gold coins slightly less than one fifth of this amount per franc.

countries of the world generally abandoned the gold standard, and exchange rates were at times very unstable. Even the United States, as early as 1933, stopped redeeming its currency in gold if the gold was to be kept within this country, and it also called in all gold coins. The Treasury continued, however, to provide gold for meeting foreign obligations, though only at the rate of slightly over 13.7 grains of pure gold per dollar (one troy ounce for thirty-five dollars) instead of 23.22 grains as formerly.

After World War II, attempts were made, with the aid of the International Monetary Fund, to introduce order into foreign exchange markets and rates. Today most nations of the Free World are on what is sometimes called the *gold exchange standard.* Under this arrangement they do not ordinarily redeem their paper money in gold or keep gold coins in circulation, as would be the case under the traditional gold standard; but they do undertake to provide gold, or some foreign currency that is readily convertible into gold, for making payments to foreign creditors. Of course, to do this they must have reserves of gold or of convertible foreign currencies, or they must in some way be able to obtain these.

Exchange Rates and the Balance of Payments. Whether a country increases its reserves of gold and foreign currency, just maintains them, or keeps losing them depends largely on the exchange rates between its monetary unit and the units of other countries. In 1949, when the British pound exchanged for $4.03 in American money, Britain was losing gold reserves because it was paying more money to foreign countries for imports (and to meet other obligations) than it was receiving from them for its exports of goods and services. After the value of the pound was reduced to only $2.80 in American money (and correspondingly in the money of many other countries), the gold drain was reduced. British exports increased greatly because British goods became much cheaper to foreigners. At the same time, imports decreased, because foreign goods became much more expensive in Britain. British receipts from abroad rose as expenditures declined, and this soon brought about a better balance of payments. In later years, further inflation of wages and prices in Britain created another dangerous deficit in the balance of payments and forced the government, in 1967, to again devalue the pound, this time to a price of $2.40 in American money.

The International Monetary Fund. *The International Monetary Fund* (IMF) was set up, just after World War II, both to aid in the adjustment and stabilization of exchange rates and to bring about the development of free exchange markets. Its membership consists of more than 110 nations, and they supply its subscribed capital of over twenty billion dollars.[4] The IMF is in a position to help its members meet temporary exchange difficulties by lending them limited amounts of gold or redeemable foreign currency. Members may also raise or lower the values of their currencies in foreign money. However, any change in excess of 10 per cent of the

---

[4] *New York Times Encyclopedic Almanac,* New York, World Publishing Co., 1970, p. 698.

originally agreed-upon par value of a currency must have the approval of the IMF.

Though the IMF did not entirely live up to the hopes of its founders, it has undoubtedly helped to stabilize foreign exchange markets. In recent years it has been greatly aided in its efforts by the return of prosperity to the industrial countries of the free world. However, threats to the stability of exchange rates continue, especially in countries where inflation is a great problem. We know now that even the dollar cannot maintain its value in other currencies in the face of large and persistent deficits in the balance of payments. Some economists think we should always allow currencies to "float," so that demand and supply determine their exchange values.

Although gold and currencies redeemable in gold, especially the dollar and the pound, have been the principal forms of money widely accepted as payment in international transactions, a plan to supplement these with *paper gold,* or Special Drawing Rights on the International Monetary Fund, was recently ratified by enough nations to bring it into operation. These Special Drawing Rights can now be used, within limits, for meeting international obligations, and they can be lent by the IMF to countries whose gold or other reserves are being rapidly reduced by an adverse balance of payments.

The chief objection to this paper gold is that in the long run it is likely to be inflationary. If a country can borrow more freely to replace losses of its monetary reserves, it is more likely to delay taking effective measures to check inflation in order to stop such losses.

RESTRICTIONS ON INTERNATIONAL TRADE

In most cases nations would derive the greatest economic advantage from international trade if they allowed it to follow its natural paths. This, however, is not the usual practice; instead, numerous controls are applied. These controls include subsidies on exports, tariffs, quotas, exchange controls, and bilateral barter agreements. In the past tariffs have been the principal device for regulating trade, but in recent years other methods of control, especially quotas, have assumed greatly increased importance.

Tariffs on Imports. A *tariff is a tax, or duty, usually on an imported commodity.* Tariffs may also be levied on exports, but this is much less common, and in the United States is prohibited by the federal Constitution. When tariff duties are levied as a fixed charge per pound or yard, they are said to be *specific;* when they are levied as a percentage of the value of a commodity, they are said to be *ad valorem.*

Tariffs for Revenue and Tariffs for Protection. A tariff generally has one of two purposes—to raise revenue or to protect the market of a domestic industry by keeping out the products of foreign competitors. To a degree these two purposes are incompatible, because a tariff that would keep the foreign product out entirely would raise no revenue at all. In practice, however, *protective tariffs* are seldom high enough to exclude imports completely and hence do raise some revenue. But if the chief purpose of a tariff is to raise revenue, it should not be high enough to discourage imports. Further, instead of being levied on a commodity produced both at home and abroad, it should, if possible, be levied on one that cannot be produced at home. This eliminates the possibility that imports and revenues may fall off because buyers turn to home producers.

Though *tariffs for revenue* interfere with trade to some extent, that is not their purpose, and such interference is usually kept at a minimum. Their discreet use is in no sense incompatible with a policy of free trade. Whether they represent a desirable kind of tax is another question; and we might point out that, unless they are levied chiefly on luxuries, they have the same drawback as the sales tax—namely, that their burden falls more heavily upon people of low income than upon the well-to-do. On the other hand, the only justification for a protective tariff is a belief that it is in the public interest to keep people from buying goods abroad and to force them to buy at home.

Most economists oppose the levying of protective tariffs and the setting up of other trade barriers designed to limit competition and maintain or raise prices. Studies of Congressional hearings and debates indicate that protective tariffs are nearly always enacted as a result of political pressure from business and labor groups interested in the production of a certain product, and who expect to benefit from a reduction of foreign competition.

The Case Against Protective Tariffs. The basic argument against protective tariffs is that, by restricting international trade, they rob us of part of its benefits. As we have already mentioned, through international trade we are able (1) to obtain goods abroad that cannot be produced at home, (2) to obtain goods of better quality than those produced at home, and (3) to obtain goods at lower prices than would have to be paid for home products. Further, it should be emphasized again that free admission of imports is one of the most effective ways of expanding the foreign markets of home industries, because it is payments for our imports that furnish foreigners with most of the funds with which to buy our exports.

The Arguments in Favor of Protection. The advocates of protection support their point of view with a number of plausible arguments: the home-market argument, the high-wages argument, the infant-industry argument, and the self-sufficiency argument.

Home-Market Argument. One of the most effective of the claims made by the protectionists is the *home-market* argument. According to this reasoning, a tariff that keeps out foreign goods increases the market for American goods and thereby increases home profits and employment. Undoubtedly there is some truth in this contention if we consider only short periods of time; but, as has already been pointed out, the final result is that a home market is created for some goods at the expense of losing a foreign market for others. This loss of the foreign market comes all the faster because, when we raise our tariffs on their goods, other countries retaliate by raising their tariffs on our goods. Meanwhile, as we have seen, American consumers pay higher prices or receive inferior products.

High-Wages Argument. A second claim that protectionists make is expressed by the *high-wages* argument. They assert that the tariff maintains the American wage level and the American standard of living by protecting our workers from having to compete with cheap foreign labor. This argument is also plausible, but a little analysis and observation robs it of most of its force. In the first place, if a tariff makes possible higher wages, it does so only by enabling a producer to sell his product at a higher price. This may benefit one group of employers and workers, but it reduces the purchasing power and standard of living of all others who must buy the product. If this kind of price raising were applied to a great many products, the general reduction in standards of living might be very serious.

Furthermore, there is not much evidence that tariffs actually do raise wages in protected industries. If this were the case, one would expect to find high wages in such industries and low wages in others. Often the contrary is true. The textile industry was highly protected for many years, yet, during most of this time, textile workers were rather poorly paid. On the other hand, the automobile industry has been able from the beginning to pay relatively high wages with little protection. The truth seems to be that our high standard of living has been achieved in spite of, rather than because of, the tariff. It results chiefly from the quality and quantity of our natural resources and the efficiency of our business organization, labor, and machines.

Infant-Industry Argument. A third defense of the protective tariff is the *infant-industry* argument. Those who advance it often disclaim any wish to give *permanent* tariff protection to an industry not able to survive without it. But, they say, a small new industry in the United States cannot hope to produce at so low a cost as an old established industry abroad. Let us give it protection until it can get established and grow. Eventually it may become more efficient than its foreign competitors. If so, it can provide consumers with goods at reduced prices, and it will no longer need tariff protection.

The infant-industry argument has been advanced in America at one time or another in support of tariffs to protect various industries, including steel and dyes. In theory it is sound, but it is difficult to find any clear case where it has been successfully applied—that is, where an industry has been established as a result of tariff protection and then has continued successfully without such protection.

Self-Sufficiency Argument. A final argument for protective tariffs is that they make a country more self-sufficient and thus less dependent on foreign countries for essential commodities in time of war. This argument is sound in theory, but the situations to which it can usefully be applied in practice are probably rather limited. Though our experience in World War II emphasized the importance of having dependable supplies of vital raw materials, to keep such products out of the country by tariffs would not always result in building up home production. Moreover, many products once deemed essential are less so today because of greatly improved substitutes. Familiar examples are wool, tin, and natural rubber.

Where there is real danger of a shortage of strategic materials in time of war, the best solution is probably to build up stockpiles. The United States government has followed this policy with a number of minerals; but many students of the problem believe that much of this stockpiling has been unjustified and is just a waste of the taxpayer's money.

Import Quotas. Another device for protecting home industries is the *import quota*. A quota limits the quantity or the value of a commodity that can be brought into a country in a given period of time. For example, the government may decide to limit sugar imports to two million tons a year, and it may decide to assign definite parts of this quota to specified foreign countries. Usually, import quotas, like protective tariffs, are imposed to keep out foreign goods for the benefit of domestic producers, but sometimes they are imposed chiefly to limit payments to foreign countries in order to conserve limited supplies of gold and foreign currency.

Quotas are an old device. They were widely employed when mercantilist doctrines prevailed in the seventeenth and eighteenth centuries, but they were largely abandoned in the nineteenth century. However, the economic dislocations resulting from World War I brought about their revival. The United States has made relatively limited use of quotas, but it has applied them to some products, including sugar and low grades of fuel oil, and an effort is now being made to apply them to textiles.

Quotas on fuel oil keep its price in this country above the world level and thus increase the profits of domestic oil companies. However, the companies argue that this higher price is very much in the public interest because it makes possible expensive drilling to find the new petroleum reserves necessary to keep the United States independent of foreign supplies in an emergency. This is an argument of doubtful validity, all the more so because several of our states limit the production of petroleum to less than the full capacity of existing wells and because large new reserves have been found in Canada and Alaska.

Our sugar quotas are of a special type. Before Fidel Castro came to power, a large but limited amount of Cuban sugar was admitted to this country annually at a reduced rate of duty. When this privilege was withdrawn from Cuba, smaller quotas of this kind were assigned to certain other sugar-producing countries. Because import duties and quota restrictions keep the price of sugar in the United States above the world level, these special tariff reductions are in effect a gift or subsidy to foreign producers. American consumers would be better off if both import duties and quotas on sugar had been completely removed. However, this would have been strongly opposed by our own sugar producers because they are subsidized by the American consumer in the form of high prices made possible by import restrictions.

Many advocates of freer trade consider quotas more objectionable than tariffs. For one thing, though quotas restrict trade, they bring no revenue to the government of the importing country as would a tariff. But for those who wish to restrict imports, quotas have certain advantages over tariffs. Often they do not require special legislation but may be imposed or changed by administrative decrees. Moreover, a quota can be fixed to admit a definite amount of a commodity, whereas if a protective tariff is levied, there is no way of knowing just how much of it will enter.

FOREIGN INVESTMENT

Foreign investment is largely dependent on trade. If a country is to continue to make substantial foreign loans and investments, it must keep selling to foreigners more goods and services than it buys. Its citizens and/or its government will then have an excess of foreign receipts over payments. This excess they can leave abroad to use for making loans to foreigners or for buying foreign securities, real estate, or factories.

But if a country makes large foreign loans and investments over a long period of years, the day may come when interest, dividends, and repayments of principal will exceed new investment. Therefore, any country that expects to get its foreign investments back, or to receive a steady flow of interest, dividends, and other direct profits from them, should be willing ultimately to import more than it exports. If it is not willing to do this but instead sets up tariffs and other barriers to keep foreign products out, it is unwittingly doing its best to prevent repayment and to force its foreign debtors to default.

Types of Foreign Investment. Foreign investments are of many kinds. Broadly speaking, private foreign investments may be divided into three classes: (1) properties abroad to which Americans hold title, (2) shares of stock held by Americans in foreign corporations, and (3) claims of Americans as creditors against foreign individuals, corporations, and governments. The first class is called *direct investments,* and it includes foreign plants owned by American corporations. The third class includes not only such securities as government and corporate bonds, but also direct loans of money and the credits that exporters extend to foreign buyers.

Foreign investments may also be classified on the basis of the period of time for which they are made. First, there are the *short-term credits* that generally run for a year or less. Such credits may be extended by banks in the form of loans to foreign banks or business houses, or they may be extended by exporters to foreign importers. In most cases banks and business houses cooperate in granting or obtaining them. Second, there are long-term foreign commitments, *investments* in the narrow sense of the word. These include stocks, corporation and government bonds, and property directly owned by American citizens or corporations.

No discussion of foreign investment would be complete without some mention of loans by one government to another. Such intergovernmental loans are usually extended for long periods of time and are made, not for monetary profit, but for reasons of national policy. Even before World War I certain European governments had long followed the practice of extending credits abroad, sometimes to increase trade but more often for frankly political reasons. During and after both World War I and World War II the United States made huge loans to its allies. These loans we shall discuss a little later.

Debtor and Creditor Relationships Between Countries. In advanced industrial countries, with high production and standards of living, savings tend to be relatively large. Demand for capital may also be strong, but often there are greater opportunities for making profitable investments in countries that are in the early stages of industrial expansion. Hence, if investors are confident that their property rights will be respected (and this is often the crucial question), there tends to be a constant flow of funds from the more developed countries to those still in the early stages of expansion, a flow that is reflected in an excess of exports for the former and of imports for the latter. However, such a situation is only temporary. In time, a country absorbing loans and investments on a large scale will have to make greater and greater payments to *creditor countries* in such forms as interest and dividends; as its needs for foreign capital decline, it may even begin to repay former loans. Eventually, an inflow of funds is likely to be reversed, with the result that an excess of imports is replaced by an excess of exports.

Many historical examples can be cited of the effect of foreign investing and lending on trade. Even before World War I, Canada was absorbing large amounts of foreign capital, and hence it developed a very substantial excess of imports over exports. Canada is still absorbing large amounts of foreign capital and therefore still tends to have an excess of imports. Britain, before her great losses in two world wars, represented a very different situation. For generations her people had invested so heavily abroad that at last the payments received for interest and profits exceeded the outflow of new investments. The result was that up to World War II, on ordinary trade items, Britain normally had an excess of imports over exports. That is, it could not only buy foreign goods with the proceeds of the goods that it exported, but it could also buy them with the money it received from foreign investments.

World War I was a heavy drain on Britain, and by the end of World War II it had largely exhausted its foreign resources. This left it in a very difficult position. The British no longer had available sufficient foreign funds to buy the food and raw materials on which their economy had come to depend. At first they were helped to meet this problem by American aid; later they were able to greatly expand their exports.

The United States as a Creditor Country. For many years the United States has been a creditor country, but up to World War I it was a *debtor country.* All through the nineteenth century we had need of capital to develop our great natural resources. This resulted in many profitable investment opportunities that induced Europeans to make large commitments here. By the end of the century we had begun to export capital, but our foreign obligations were still greatly in excess of our credits. World War I, however, rapidly changed us from a debtor nation to an important creditor nation. Many Europeans were obliged to sell their American investments to our own citizens; and not only our government but also our citizens lent vast sums to our allies.

In 1919, after the war had ended, the Department of Commerce estimated that private American investors held a net credit position of about $3.7 billion as against the rest of the world. That is to say, private investments of Americans abroad exceeded private investments of foreigners in this country by that amount. During the prosperous period of the 1920's, American individuals, industrial corporations, and banks continued to lend or invest in Europe at the rate of one billion dollars or so a year. By 1930 the net credit balance of private American investors had risen to about nine billion dollars. Unfortunately, however, this credit position was built up at a time when economic and political conditions throughout the world were very unstable. During the depression years that followed 1930, American capital ceased to flow abroad, and a great part of the foreign investments made in the 1920's was lost. In addition, considerable foreign capital was transferred to this country for safety as soon as it became evident that another war was in the making in Europe. As a result, by 1939 the net creditor position of American investors had declined to less than two billion dollars.

But after World War II both private American loans and investments abroad, and government credits, began to rise rather rapidly, so that by 1969 the *total* net creditor position of the United States, as calculated by the Department of Commerce, was more than $67 billion.[5]

FOREIGN AID

Though the granting of economic aid by one nation to another for military or political purposes has a long history, in the present century such aid has assumed much greater proportions than ever before. In both world wars the United States extended economic aid to its allies on a vast scale; and since World War II we have, for reasons political, military, and humanitarian, continued to make large loans and gifts to foreign nations. Moreover, some of the other more prosperous industrial countries of the world are also extending substantial foreign aid, largely to help poor and underdeveloped countries in their efforts to raise output and standards of living.

Wartime Aid to Our Allies. During and shortly after World War I the United States government loaned approximately thirteen billion dollars

[5] *Survey of Current Business,* U.S. Department of Commerce, October 1970, p. 21.

to the nations of Europe. Most of this sum went to our wartime allies, and almost none of it was ever repaid. The original idea was that the debtor nations would obtain most of the funds for repayment from German reparations. But the Germans were unwilling, and perhaps unable, to pay the huge reparations demanded from them. In addition, we ourselves made it almost impossible for our allies to pay us, because we raised tariff barriers so high that they could not obtain the necessary dollars by selling goods in our markets. Eventually it came to be generally recognized that, for the most part, the World War I debts never would be paid. Meanwhile, for some twenty years, they were a great source of international friction.

Soon after the outbreak in Europe of World War II, our government began to support the Western allies in various ways. Before long, this support developed into the policy of giving all possible aid, short of war. Months before our active entry into the war, Congress, in March, 1941, passed the famous Lend-Lease Act. Under this act the President was empowered to sell, exchange, lease, or lend any defense article to any country whose defense he deemed vital to the defense of the United States.

To avoid the difficulties that arose in connection with repayment of World War I loans, it was provided that the debtor nations should repay us only in goods. Later, when the United States had entered the war, special agreements were made that released the countries receiving *lend-lease* from any obligation to replace materials actually expended in the war effort.

The economic aid we gave to our allies under the Lend-Lease Act ultimately reached huge proportions. By July 31, 1946, Congress had appropriated more than fifty billion dollars to carry out the purposes of this act, a sum that represented a far greater drain on our economy than would a hundred billion dollars today.

Postwar Relief and Reconstruction. At the end of World War II, western Europe was in a state of economic exhaustion. This was true not only in the former enemy countries but also in those allied or neutral countries that had been occupied by the Germans. Even Great Britain found its position extremely difficult.

Long before the end of the war, plans were made to meet the various problems, political and economic, that were sure to arise once the war was over. The chief instrument created to carry out these plans was the United Nations. Although many supporters of the United Nations hoped, and some believed, that it could keep the future peace of the world, the conviction was widely held that peace could be kept only if some very troublesome political, economic, and social problems could be solved. To meet some of these problems, various agencies were set up or planned —some within the framework of the United Nations, some on a more or less independent basis. Among these agencies were the International Labor Organization, the International Food and Raw Materials Organization, the United Nations Relief and Rehabilitation Administration, the

International Bank for Reconstruction and Development, and the International Monetary Fund.

The most urgent economic need when the war ended was to provide sufficient food to combat widespread malnutrition in western Europe. Next came the restoration and development of production. In modern times western Europe has never been economically self-sufficient. It has always had to import large amounts of food and raw materials, and it has paid for these largely by exporting a great variety of finished goods. At the end of the war, much of the industry of the European countries had been destroyed or damaged, and, as was noted earlier, they were unable to export sufficient goods to pay for the imports they desperately needed.

Though a number of international agencies were set up to deal with postwar economic problems, the United States was in fact the only country able to extend help to others on a large scale, so a great part of the funds of these various international agencies was provided by our government. The United States also extended large amounts of aid directly to relieve distress abroad. Most of this aid, whether direct or indirect, went to Europe, but a considerable amount also went to countries in other parts of the world. Some of the postwar aid extended by the United States took the form of credits, but much of it consisted of outright gifts. From July 1, 1945, to December 31, 1948, total foreign aid made available by our government was over $26 billion.

The Marshall Plan. By 1947 many Americans were convinced that, to protect our own interests, we would have to continue giving aid to other countries, especially in western Europe, for some time. This belief was greatly strengthened by the wide rift that had already developed between Russia and the nations of the Free World.

The *Marshall Plan* was an attempt to place our aid to western Europe on a systematic basis over a period of several years. Officially known as the European Recovery Program (ERP), it was first outlined by Secretary of State George C. Marshall in June, 1947, and was enacted into law by Congress early in 1948. At the same time, Congress created the Economic Cooperation Administration (ECA) to carry out the program that was outlined. In 1949 a group of European countries founded the Organization for European Economic Cooperation (OEEC) to help in allocating Marshall Plan aid and to work for postwar recovery. By the end of 1949, total aid had exceeded seven billion dollars. In 1961 OEEC was replaced by the Organization for Economic Cooperation and Development (OECD). However, its membership and economic objectives are broader. In addition to eighteen European countries, it includes the United States, Canada, and Japan. Jugoslavia and Australia also take part in some OECD activities.

Foreign Aid as a Continuing Program. After 1950, improvement of conditions in Europe made possible a great reduction in our *economic* aid. However, the widening rift with Russia, and the Korean War, had created strong sentiment in Congress in favor of increasing our *military* aid

Agonizing Reappraisal! (Justus in *The Minneapolis Star.*)

to friendly nations, especially to those of western Europe; so as economic aid declined, military aid rose, until during the 1950's it became greater than economic aid. Later it declined, but present conditions in the Middle East and the Far East, including South Vietnam, may bring a new increase. Meanwhile, as economic prosperity reached a high level in western Europe in the late 1950's, most of our economic aid was transferred to the less developed countries in other parts of the world.

From July 1, 1945, to the end of December, 1969, total foreign aid extended by the United States was more than $121 billion.[6] This included not only direct gifts and loans but also contributions to various agencies of the United Nations. Total aid during this period greatly exceeded the aid given to our allies during World War II under the Lend-Lease Act.

There is little question that United States loans and gifts to our allies helped to win World War II. There is also little doubt that postwar aid made an important contribution to European economic recovery after the war, a recovery that was essential for checking communist expansion and for in-

[6] U.S. Bureau of the Census, *Statistical Abstract of the United States, 1970,* Washington, D.C., Government Printing Office, 1970, p. 769.

creasing the security of the United States. To what extent foreign aid has contributed to the welfare of this country in more-recent years is not so certain. Some of it has clearly been worth the cost, but there appear to have been numerous cases of mismanagement, waste, and corruption. Some of that is probably inevitable in any program so vast in scale. What is perhaps even more serious, there have been cases in which the wisdom of giving aid seemed very doubtful on policy grounds. For example, aid was continued to Indonesia in 1964 even after its president, Achmed Sukarno, had expressed sympathy for Red China and had actually undertaken guerrilla warfare against Malaysia, a well-governed nation belonging to the British Commonwealth.

As has been noted before, once a bureaucracy develops to administer a government program, it has a vested interest, and both the program and the bureaucracy become difficult to get rid of, or even much reduce. At best foreign aid projects are difficult to choose wisely and to administer in such a way as to benefit both the United States and the nations receiving aid. Critics of foreign aid point out that if money is transferred directly to foreign governments, it can easily be diverted from its intended uses. There is also danger of granting funds for the wrong kind of projects, and danger that the receiving nations will become permanently dependent on aid instead of using it to increase production and pave the way to self-sufficiency.

Point Four and the Peace Corps. A foreign aid program of special interest was initiated by President Harry S. Truman in *Point Four* of his inaugural address of 1949. Under this program American agricultural and industrial experts have been sent to various countries, and in some cases foreign groups have been brought here to learn our technology. The purpose is to raise standards of living in less developed countries by exporting American know-how.

The *Peace Corps* was first established by an executive order of President John F. Kennedy in May, 1961. It is an organization composed of selected volunteers who agree to serve in foreign countries for a period of two years. They are sent only to friendly nations that request their services, and before leaving on an assignment they are given a brief period of special training by the government. They do not receive compensation on the job, but their expenses are paid, and at the end of their service they receive the modest termination pay of seventy-five dollars for each month worked. The purpose of the Peace Corps is to provide personnel to help the less developed countries to carry out various needed projects. Teachers, people with agricultural training, engineers, and nurses are much in demand. A further purpose of both the Point Four program and the Peace Corps is to create good will toward the United States. Both are relatively inexpensive aid programs, and they seem to be well worth their cost.

The Peace Corps, in particular, has received wide public approval and support. Its members vary greatly in age, training, and social background, but they tend to be people who combine in various degrees idealism, enthusiasm, and a spirit of adventure. Because they are selected from a large number of applicants, they also tend to be people with special qualifications of one kind or another. Their average age is about twenty-five, though a handful are sixty or more and a few are teenagers of eighteen or nineteen. Included in their number are many college students and several hundred married couples. On the average, the educational level of volunteers is high; and some are well-trained technical and professional experts. When they go to their assignments in some of the less developed countries of the world they find social conditions that are unfamiliar and living conditions that are often difficult. Nevertheless, only a very small proportion—about 2 per cent—have given up and left the Peace Corps before the end of their term of service. Perhaps one reason they stay is that they have usually been given a friendly welcome by the people of the countries in which they work.

In 1969 the Peace Corps included over eleven thousand volunteers and trainees. Projects were being carried on in fifty-nine countries in four major areas as follows: Latin America, Africa, the Near East and South Asia, and the Far East and Oceania. Projects included programs for raising the level of education, developing rural communities, building roads, renewing slum areas in cities, improving health conditions, and raising the level of agricultural output.

The Road to Economic Growth. It is not easy for an underdeveloped country to achieve what W. W. Rostow calls a "take-off" into economic growth. Rostow, though recognizing the importance of other factors, puts special stress on the need for raising the level of investment to a certain minimum proportion of the national income. Other economists believe that what is most essential, and what must develop along with any substantial increase of savings and investment, is an understanding on the part of the people of how a successful industrial society operates. They must then be able and willing to develop the attitudes, the patterns of behavior, and the initiative that are essential to vigorous economic growth. Just to pour in foreign capital is not enough.

Sometimes, because of lack of understanding or to satisfy the pride of politicians, countries striving for economic growth spend their available capital on the wrong things. They may, for example, produce such impressive government projects as steel mills or power dams, when what would help most, *initially,* might be greater production of food. Economic growth will proceed faster if it is balanced, if a foundation is gradually laid for a broad expansion of output. Before too many steel mills or power plants are built, increased provision should be made for certain types of education and training; transportation, communication, and banking facilities should be provided; and efforts should be made to gradually raise standards of living in order to increase both the welfare and productivity of workers and also to make possible a significant amount of saving and investment.

THE PROBLEM OF EXPANDING FOREIGN TRADE

If trade could flow *freely* and *securely* throughout the world, economists believe that there would be a great expansion of its total volume and that in the long run all nations would be more prosperous. There would be less talk of have-not countries and less need for foreign aid, because every country would have free access to the markets and raw materials of the world. The average price of consumer goods would be lower everywhere. There is, of course, no prospect of the early attainment of such an ideal situation. Nevertheless, it is worthwhile to ask, What changes are needed to free the flow of world trade and to increase its volume?

The Problem of Trade Restrictions. Nothing would contribute more to the expansion of world trade than removal of the great mass of restrictions that have been placed upon it by government action. These restrictions include tariffs, quotas, exchange controls, and license requirements for imports and exports.

One of the most stubborn obstacles to the free flow of trade is the fact that the world is divided into communist and noncommunist countries. In communist countries, trade is a government monopoly, and there is a tendency to keep trade with the Free World at a minimum. It is often impossible for private traders in noncommunist countries to make satis-factory trade arrangements with the agencies of communist governments. In addition, some Western nations, especially the United States, are unwilling to permit unrestricted trading with communist countries, in particular when this involves exporting to them strategic materials that might be used to strengthen their military forces.

Within the Free World, restrictions on the import of foreign goods seem to result chiefly from two factors: (1) the belief that certain home indus-tries should be protected so that in time of war supplies of their products will be available and (2) pressure from certain industry groups whose products are subject to foreign competition. In the long run this second factor is probably the most difficult obstacle to the removal of foreign-trade barriers. In the last generation or two, economists have succeeded in convincing a great many people that in the long run there is no net economic gain for the whole nation, but rather a loss, in keeping foreign goods out of the country to protect home industries. At any given time, however, there will always be some industries that face difficult problems because of foreign competition. The problem is how to aid such industries to make adjustments without sacrificing the interests of the nation as a whole by maintaining or even building up trade barriers.

The tariff is probably less important, as a protection to American business and workers, than most people suppose. In 1954 the President's Commission on Foreign Economic Policy (the Randall Commission) estimated that only 200,000 workers would lose their jobs if all our tariff duties were removed. Such loss of jobs would be temporary, because any increase in American imports would tend to stimulate exports, and any increase of exports would, of course, create new jobs.

Fortunately the United States has succeeded, in the last forty years, in greatly reducing its tariff barriers. The Reciprocal Trade Agreements Act of 1934 empowered the President to make reciprocal trade agreements and to reduce tariff duties by as much as 50 per cent in return for trade concessions by other countries. Though the original authority was granted for only three years, the act was extended and amended from time to time. Finally, the Trade Expansion Act of 1962 was passed by Congress, giving the President even greater powers to reduce tariffs. What is frequently called the Kennedy Round of international tariff negotiations was opened formally in May, 1964, and ended in May, 1967. As a result, almost fifty countries, accounting for about 80 per cent of world trade, made an average cut in their tariffs of about one third. At the time the *reciprocal trade program* was inaugurated in 1934, our tariffs amounted to about 50 per cent of the value of all dutiable imports; in 1969 they amounted to only 11 per cent.[7]

Regional Agreements to Reduce Trade Restrictions. Since World War II, a number of efforts have been made in the direction of expanding world trade. One of the most significant of these was the creation in 1948 of the Benelux *Customs Union,* which was expanded to the Benelux *Economic Union* in 1958. This Union consists of three small but commercially important countries: Belgium, the Netherlands, and Luxembourg; its purpose was to remove gradually economic barriers between these countries. The idea of removing trade barriers within a group of countries was carried even further when, by a treaty signed in Rome in 1957, the *European Common Market* (ECM) was created. This consists of the Benelux countries plus France, West Germany, and Italy. The importance of the Common Market can be appreciated when we note that it accounts for a substantially larger portion of world trade than does the United States.

The main objective of the European Common Market is to remove gradually all barriers to the movements of goods, people, capital, and business within its area. Originally it was hoped that this goal would be achieved in twelve to fifteen years. Actually by the middle of 1968 all internal tariffs had been eliminated after a gradual reduction, and, at the same time, common external tariffs had been established. Also, great progress had been made in establishing freedom of movement of workers, and common agricultural policies.

The six Common Market countries sometimes refer to their group as the *European Community,* an organization that includes not only the Common Market but also the European Community for Coal and Steel and the European Atomic Energy Community (Euratom). The purpose of the coal and steel organization is to expand markets and output for coal and steel, and to this end the organization has removed such barriers

[7] Ibid., p. 787.

to trade among the member countries as customs duties, quantitative restrictions, double pricing, discriminatory freight rates, and currency restrictions. The purpose of Euratom is the cooperative development of atomic energy to meet a portion of Europe's future needs for power.

A number of nations that are not full members of the Common Market are associated with it through special arrangements, and some of them may become full members. They include Greece, Turkey, and a number of African countries. The United Kingdom and six[8] other nations that do not belong to the Common Market agreed at Stockholm in 1959 to set up a new organization to be called the *European Free Trade Association* (EFTA). However, the EFTA is a looser combination and has not attempted to achieve very much economic integration. Figure 34 shows the original six Common Market countries and the seven members of the EFTA.

In 1961 the United Kingdom actually applied for membership in the Common Market, as did several other EFTA countries a little later. But negotiations broke down, partly because the United Kingdom had special trade arrangements with the dominions that would have interfered with joining the Common Market on the same basis as its original members. Later President Charles de Gaulle of France indicated opposition to admitting Britain. But now that de Gaulle is out of the picture and since close relations with their European neighbors seem increasingly important to the British, the prospects seem fairly good that the United Kingdom and several other EFTA nations will soon become full members of the Common Market. Prime Minister Edward Heath strongly favors British membership, if satisfactory terms can be negotiated, but many Britons oppose it, partly because they fear it will damage the relationships of the United Kingdom with the nations of the British Commonwealth.

Controls of Agricultural Products and Raw Materials. Countries that are primarily producers and exporters of basic agricultural crops or of any type of raw materials are especially vulnerable to the effects of cyclical fluctuations of business. In periods of depression the demand for their products falls off sharply, and prices may drop to a very low level. As a result, producers suffer heavy losses and turn to the government for aid.

In some cases a country has a monopoly or a near-monopoly of an important product. Where this is true, the government may be able, at least for a time, to maintain the world price at an artificially high level by restricting supply. It may accomplish this restriction by limiting exports, by limiting production, or by storing or destroying a part of the annual output. Before World War II the British and Dutch cooperated to limit exports of rubber from the principal producing areas in the East Indies and Malaya. For many years the Brazilian government has supported coffee prices in various ways, sometimes in cooperation with other countries. At times it has bought up huge surpluses, and in one year these were so great that it resorted to burning them or dumping them into the sea.

[8] Austria, Denmark, Norway, Portugal, Sweden, and Switzerland.

Figure 34. "The Six" and "The Seven." (Reprinted by permission from *The New York Times.* Adjusted population estimates are for 1968.)

When exporting countries use their monopoly power to maintain excessively high prices for important foods or raw materials, they restrict trade and impose a burden on importing countries. Conceivably, this might create an intolerable situation. Fortunately, however, such controls have seldom been very successful in the long run, even when supported by international agreements. Sooner or later some of the parties to such arrangements become dissatisfied. Meanwhile, higher prices stimulate output in old producing areas or new ones and encourage the development of substitute and synthetic products.

THE PROBLEM OF EXPANDING FOREIGN INVESTMENT

As explained earlier, foreign investment is closely tied to foreign trade. If we could bring about a sound and steady growth of foreign trade by freeing it from hampering restrictions, this would do much to encourage expansion of foreign investment. Free foreign-exchange markets also directly facilitate the expansion of foreign investment. This is true because if large investments are to be made abroad, it must be easy to buy foreign funds. It must also be easy to exchange foreign money for domestic money, so that an investor can receive in his own currency interest and dividend payments, as well as principal payments when they fall due.

In the final analysis the basic requirements for a great expansion of private foreign investment are confidence and stability. Before they will send their funds abroad, potential investors must believe that foreigners will deal with them in good faith and that foreign governments will protect their property rights. They must also believe that foreigners will be able to meet any financial obligations assumed. This means that world economic and political conditions must be reasonably stable. Peace must be established on a basis that is believed reasonably secure. If investors believe that in a certain country there is danger of a communist revolution and the seizure of private property, they naturally will hesitate to risk their funds there.

Actually, in recent years there has been a very substantial expansion of private foreign investment. In the postwar period United States business firms have greatly increased their foreign commitments by building factories in other countries. For several years the annual total of new private foreign investments by Americans has been about four or five billion dollars. Most of these funds have gone to Canada, Europe, Latin America, and the Near East. From time to time, however, something occurs to give investor confidence a setback. An example of this was the seizures of land and business enterprises by the Cuban communist government in 1959 and 1960. A more recent example was the expropriation by Peru in 1969 of the American-owned International Petroleum Company.

The World Bank Group. *The World Bank Group* includes three international institutions affiliated with the United Nations and having the

57. An Example of Help Given by the World Bank. A convoy of lumber trucks is shown traveling along a new road in Gabon, Africa. A $12 million World Bank loan has helped to construct vital highways to open up new forest regions to commercial logging operations. (Photo by Alain Prott/CIRIC for World Bank, 1967. Courtesy International Bank for Reconstruction and Development, Washington, D.C.)

common goal of helping their member countries develop their economies. It plays a role of special importance in aiding some of the less developed countries.

The principal member of the group, the World Bank, is officially known as the International Bank for Reconstruction and Development. It was established, first, to meet some of the most urgent capital needs for reconstruction in countries damaged by World War II, and second, to provide funds badly needed in other countries for the development of natural resources and the raising of standards of living. The bank is a lending institution to whose capital, in 1969, some 110 nations had subscribed. Its total assets exceed ten billion dollars.[9] The second member of the group, the International Development Association (IDA) is owned by 102 member countries. Its activities are similar to those of the bank, but it makes loans on highly favorable terms to countries that cannot afford to borrow on normal terms. The third member is the International Finance Corporation (IFC). It is owned by ninety-one countries and, unlike the World Bank and IDA, which lend only to governments or to organizations whose loans are secured by a government guarantee, it invests in private enterprises without any government guarantee. As a rule, it combines loans with stock purchases.[10]

ECONOMIC RELATIONS AND WAR

During the period from World War I to the outbreak of World War II there was much discussion about the need of the have-not countries, especially Germany, Italy, and Japan, for raw materials. Compared with the other great powers, all three of these countries were poor in natural resources under their political control. Frequently it was argued that if they were not allowed to acquire their share of colonies by peaceful means, they would have to fight for them to avoid economic strangulation. This was a useful argument for the imperialists of each nation, because it seemed to put economic necessity on their side. But the argument was weak, because these have-not nations had access to the raw materials of the world through the same means available to most other nations— namely, trade.

The German Nazis sometimes advanced economic arguments, among others, to justify their action in starting World War II. Yet practically all their economic worries, including those over raw materials, arose from their determination to make an all-out preparation for war. They could have bought plenty of food for their people and plenty of raw materials for their peacetime industries if only they had not sacrificed such imports in favor of purchasing supplies for making armaments. To get wheat from Poland, Romania, or the Ukraine, they did not need political control of those countries in time of peace. They needed only to offer money for the things they required, money which they could obtain in exchange for their industrial products, just as West Germany, for example, does today. But when a nation decides to embark on a career of conquest, it must have as complete control as possible of all the essential food supplies and raw materials necessary for waging a successful war.

The causes of war are many, and they will be discussed more fully in Chapter 32. They include the desires of the people of a nation for power,

[9] *Annual Report,* Washington, D.C., World Bank, 1969, p. 64.
[10] *World Bank Group,* June 1969. (A brochure distributed by World Bank Group, 1818 H Street, N.W., Washington, D.C., 20433.)

for security, and for national glory; the ambitions of political leaders; and fanatical devotion to revolutionary ideologies. Economic conflicts and rivalries may be sources of ill feeling and may thus contribute to bringing on wars. However, no nation whose leaders were in the least rational would ever as a "business" venture start a war with another country of anywhere near the same size and military power. That the costs of modern war are many times greater than any possible economic gains to the victor has been demonstrated overwhelmingly by both World War I and World War II.

Terms to Be Understood

visible items of trade
invisible items of trade
balance of trade
balance of payments
favorable balance of trade
Eurodollars
foreign exchange
exchange rate
gold standard
paper standard
gold exchange standard
exchange stabilization
International Monetary Fund

paper gold
specific duty
ad valorem duty
tariff
protective tariff
tariff for revenue
home-market argument
high-wages argument
infant-industry argument
self-sufficiency argument
import quota
direct investments
short-term credits
debtor country

creditor country
lend-lease aid
Marshall Plan
Point Four program
Peace Corps
reciprocal trade program
customs union
European Common Market
European Free Trade Association
World Bank Group

Questions for Review and Discussion

1. What are the three main advantages of international trade?
2. Exports depend on imports, and vice versa. Why is this true?
3. Is it more desirable for a country to build up its visible or its invisible trade? Explain.
4. Is a favorable balance of trade possible? Is it desirable? Explain.
5. In what ways can a country meet an excess of foreign payments over foreign receipts? Can it meet such an excess indefinitely? Explain.
6. What two factors in recent years have tended to reduce the drain on our gold reserves, even though the payments we make to foreigners substantially exceed our receipts from them?
7. What possible developments would be more dependable (see question 6) in checking or reversing the drain on our gold reserves?

8. Why were foreign-exchange rates stable under the gold standard?
9. Explain how a change in exchange rates can change the balance of trade and the balance of payments.
10. What is the purpose of the International Monetary Fund? What is the chief objection to allowing it to issue paper gold?
11. State and evaluate the principal arguments for protective tariffs.
12. Recently, the use of quotas to limit imports has been spreading. Are import quotas less damaging to consumers than tariffs? Why or why not?
13. What are the principal types of foreign investment?
14. Explain the ways in which foreign investment depends on and influences foreign trade.
15. Review briefly the history of the United States as a debtor or creditor nation: (a) up to World War I; (b) between world wars; (c) from World War II to the present.
16. Could the debts of our allies, incurred in World War I, have been repaid? If not, why not? If so, what method of repayment would you have suggested?
17. Most of the lend-lease aid extended by the United States was later made a gift. Do you think this was wise or unwise? Explain.
18. In the period after World War II the United States government made very large loans and gifts to aid in European reconstruction and recovery. What were our purposes in extending such aid?
19. If it served no other purpose, could foreign aid be justified just on the ground that it creates a foreign market for American goods? Explain.
20. Do you believe that the Peace Corps has been successful? Why or why not? Do you believe it helped to keep peace in the world? Why or why not?
21. What conditions are necessary to start a static or a slowly developing economy on the road to vigorous economic growth?
22. Do you believe that it is possible to expand the volume of foreign trade very much? If not, why not? If so, what measures would you employ?
23. Why do most countries set import quotas on many products, and/or levy duties?
24. Is the United States now a high-tariff country? Why or why not?
25. What is the nature and purpose of each of the following? (a) the Benelux Economic Union; (b) the European Common Market; (c) the European Community; (d) the European Free Trade Association.
26. What are the principal obstacles to expanding the volume of private foreign investment?
27. Explain the nature and purposes of each of the three institutions in the World Bank Group.
28. Are economic rivalries or ambitions, of individuals or nations, the major causes of war? Why or why not?

For Further Study

Aubrey, Henry G., *Atlantic Economic Cooperation: The Case of the OECD*, published for the Council on Foreign Relations, New York, Frederick A. Praeger, Inc., 1967.

Cooper, Richard N., *The Economics of Interdependence*, New York, McGraw-Hill, Inc., 1968.

————, ed., *International Finance,* paperback, Baltimore, Penguin Books, Inc., 1969. Book of readings.

Galbraith, John Kenneth, *Economic Development,* Cambridge, Mass., Harvard University Press, 1967.

Gardner, Richard N., and Max F. Millikan, eds., *The Global Partnership: International Agencies and Economic Development,* New York, Frederick A. Praeger, Inc., 1968.

Goldman, Marshall I., *Soviet Foreign Aid,* New York, Frederick A. Praeger, Inc., 1967.

Hagen, Everett E., *On the Theory of Social Change: How Economic Growth Begins,* Homewood, Ill., Richard D. Irwin, Inc., 1962.

International Bank, annual reports, Washington, D.C.

Kamarck, Andrew M., *The Economics of African Development,* New York, Frederick A. Praeger, Inc., 1967.

Kaplan, Jacob J., *The Challenge of Foreign Aid: Practice, Problems, and Opportunities,* New York, Frederick A. Praeger, Inc., 1967.

Kindleberger, Charles P., *International Economics,* 4th ed., Homewood, Ill., Richard D. Irwin, Inc., 1968.

Levinson, Jerome, and Juan de Onis, *Alliance for Progress: A Reappraisal,* paperback, New York, Twentieth Century Fund, Inc., 1969.

Myrdal, Gunnar, *Asian Drama: An Inquiry into the Poverty of Nations,* Pantheon paperback, New York, Random House, Inc., 1968.

————, *International Economy: Problems and Prospects,* Torchbook paperback, New York, Harper & Row, Publishers, 1969.

Paddock, William, and Paul Paddock, *Famine Nineteen Seventy-Five: American Decision, Who Will Survive?* Boston, Little, Brown and Company, 1968.

Perloff, Harvey S., *Alliance for Progress: A Social Invention in the Making,* published for Resources for the Future, Inc., Baltimore, Johns Hopkins Press, 1970.

Rostow, W. W., *The Evolution of the World Economy,* New York, The Macmillan Company, 1970.

Sullivan, George, *The Story of the Peace Corps,* rev. ed., New York, Fleet Publishing Corporation, n.d.

United Nations: Various agencies of the UN from time to time publish reports and statistics on world economic conditions in particular nations. Write to United Nations Office of Public Information, New York, N.Y.

Ward, Barbara, and P. T. Bauer, *Two Views on Aid to Underdeveloped Countries,* paperback, New York, Transatlantic Arts, Inc., 1967.

Chapter 31

Nationalism,

Imperialism,

and Communist

Expansion

dean Acheson, when he was Secretary of State under President Harry S. Truman, remarked that two major facts had dominated postwar international politics: (1) the rebellion of the nationalist-inspired peoples of Asia and Africa against the old imperialism of Europe and (2) the imperialistic ambitions of Soviet Russia. To these we might now add the growing power and ambitions of Red China and the antagonism of the Arab nations toward Israel. Certainly a large percentage of the events that make up the record of world affairs during the last twenty-five years tie into one or another of these forces. This is apparent from an enumeration of a few of the international problems that have arisen since World War II: the Indonesian rebellion against the Netherlands (1947–1949); the communist threat to Greece (1946–1951); the communist *coup d'état* in Czechoslovakia (1948); the Russian blockade of Berlin (1948); the invasion of Korea (1950–1953); the surrender of North Vietnam by France to the communist rebels (1954); the Suez crisis (1956); the emergence from colonial status of over thirty new countries in Africa south of the Sahara (1957–1968); suppression by Red China of the revolt in Tibet (1959); invasion of Indian territory by Chinese border troops (1959 and 1962); support by Red China, Russia, and North Vietnam of the communist Viet Cong guerrillas in South Vietnam (1959–1971, and probably longer); the Israeli invasion of Egypt in 1965; the Six-Day War between the Arab nations and Israel in 1967; the Russian invasion of Czechoslovakia in 1968; and the rapid expansion of Russian military aid to the Arab countries in 1970. This central position of nationalism and imperialism (both the old and the communist new style) in contemporary world affairs justifies an analysis of them.

NATIONALISM

The Nature of Nationalism. *Nationalism* in its extreme form might be defined as a firm belief that one's own nation is superior to all others, plus a conviction that loyalty to the nation should take precedence over all other loyalties. Though nationalism may not as a rule go to such extremes, its essence is an attitude of loyalty to one's own nation-state. It is the sentimental attachment of a Frenchman to his native France or of a Turk to his Turkish homeland. Like all strong emotions, it is sometimes capable of dominating the behavior of men, even to the exclusion of rational considerations.

Patriotism is a broader term than nationalism, because it covers more situations; but the two words have much in common. A person may feel patriotic to any kind of group or state, whether it be a city-state, a nation-state, or an empire. The Greeks of antiquity were patriotic to Athens, Sparta, Thebes, or whatever city they inhabited, but they had very little feeling for the Greeks as an *ethnic group* or nation. In the Middle Ages, people were loyal mainly to feudal lords of their local districts, with slight consciousness of the ethnic units we now call nations. Their loyalty was therefore a manifestation of patriotism but not of nationalism. Patriotism becomes nationalism only when the object of devotion is either a nation-state or a national group ("nationality") that, lacking statehood, is struggling to attain it. As the French may be loyal to the nation-state they constitute, so the people of Lithuania (now a part of Russia) may be loyal to the ideal of statehood that they cherish for themselves.

Because of the hold that nationalism can have over the lives of men, some have compared it to religion.[1] The god of nationalism is said to be the fatherland; its ritual centers about the flag; its theology derives from the doings and exhortations of the early fathers (for instance, George Washington or Frederick the Great of Prussia); and its heretics are the traitors who give aid and comfort to the nation's enemies. Like religion, nationalism may be alive and vigorous or faltering and ineffectual. Being an emotional phenomenon, it calls forth varying degrees of fervor in different people or even in the same people at different times. A national crisis, in particular a major war that threatens the nation's existence, is likely to raise national feeling to a high level of intensity. There are nationalist fanatics as there are religious fanatics. In the years before and during World War II, the Nazis of Germany, the Italian Fascists, and the Japanese militarists were conspicuous examples.

The Growth of Nationalism. Nationalism originated in Europe. Its beginnings go back even to the late Middle Ages, when some semblance of national consciousness first became evident. Though it continued to make slow headway, it did not become a great political force until the time of the French Revolution. In Revolutionary France, as Norman D. Palmer and Howard C. Perkins have said, "The Jacobins formulated a kind of secular religion and applied it to national ends."[2] This nationalism of the Revolution was closely related to the new democratic theories of the period; and it was stimulated by the idea of national conscription, by patriotic societies, by a new system of education, and by the fear of foreign enemies.

By his conquests, Napoleon carried the new feeling of nationalism to other parts of Europe, for wherever he took his armies, the native people resented the presence of foreign troops and tended to unite against French occupation. This was especially noticeable in the German states, where the nationalistic foundations of the new Germany were laid. Even in faraway Russia the people rose up to repel the foreign invader.

The nineteenth century was a period of rapidly spreading nationalism. Men like Herder, Fichte, and Mazzini wrote and talked about its virtues, and statesmen like Bismarck, Cavour, and Garibaldi used this popular zeal to build new nations. The German states were united with the aid of several wars, and finally the new Germany was born (1871). In the same year, Italy completed its unification by annexing Rome and the Papal States, and set forth on its career as a new nation-state. In the Balkans, the Empire of Turkey was gradually rooted out, and from the nationalism of the peoples living there new nation-states were fashioned—Greece, Bulgaria, Romania, Serbia (later Yugoslavia), and Albania. By the end of the century, all Europe had fallen under the spell of nationalism.

[1] See Frederick L. Schuman, "The Making of Nations," in *Society Today and Tomorrow*, 2d ed., edited by Elgin F. Hunt and Jules Karlin, New York, The Macmillan Company, 1967.
[2] Norman D. Palmer and Howard C. Perkins, *International Relations*, Boston, Houghton Mifflin Company, 1953, p. 45.

Never have the claims of nationalism been recognized more than in the peace settlement that followed World War I. President Woodrow Wilson and other Allied leaders had advocated during the war the principle of self-determination for national groups then living as subject minorities in other states, so that when the terms of the peace were written, some degree of adherence to those pretensions became necessary. In the name of national self-determination the old multinational state of Austria-Hungary was liquidated, and out of its holdings several new states were set up—Austria, Hungary, Czechoslovakia, Poland (with some land from Germany and Russia)—and territory was added to Serbia (to make Yugoslavia) and to Romania. Boundaries were shifted about, many of them to conform more closely to the ethnic contour, and in a number of places where the national preferences of the people were uncertain, local plebiscites were held.

Europe continues to be a continent of nationalisms. In the 1930's the extreme form of nationalism sponsored by the Nazis in Germany and the Fascists in Italy combined with militarism and expansionism to produce a series of diplomatic crises that culminated in World War II. Today one of the most striking facts in Europe is the increased hold of nationalism on the Russian people, despite the professed antipathy of communism to nationalistic sentiments. During World War II appeals to the loyalty of the Russian people were based upon their nationalism rather than on their communism.

Most significant among recent developments is the extension of nationalism to all parts of the world; it is no longer a monopoly of Europe. It reached the Western Hemisphere with the American Revolution. In the Far East, nationalism came to Japan first; by the turn of the century it was beginning to make itself felt in China and the Philippines; by the 1930's it was rampant everywhere. In the Middle East, its aspirations and demands were strongly in evidence for the first time during and after World War I. At about the same time, the people of North Africa attracted world attention with their nationalism, and in the last few years nationalism has spread rapidly far south of the Sahara desert.

Nationalism as a Source of International Problems. In recent years some students of human affairs have treated nationalism as if it were essentially an evil, but this is far from true. Nationalism has made indispensable contributions to modern civilization and to human welfare. It has made possible the organization of large human populations into societies within which law and order can be maintained, and the arts, sciences, and industry effectively developed. Without nationalism we could hardly have had the great progress in human welfare that has taken place in the more-advanced parts of the world. Furthermore, we have as yet no real substitute for it. *If the people of this country should completely lose the faith and loyalty we call patriotism, the United States would cease to be an effective unit for aiding its own people and influencing world affairs.* A dedication to the United Nations or the human race would not be an adequate substitute, because it will be a long, long time before we have a world government that can adequately perform the functions of our present nation-states. What we need now is a more rational nationalism that recognizes that nations must cooperate to promote the needs and interests of all.

But, for two reasons nationalism is difficult to keep within reasonable bounds. In the first place, like all mass emotions, once on the loose it has a tendency to run wild. As it is hard to hate just a little and is easy to let hatred become a consuming passion, so is it difficult to prevent a mild nationalism from degenerating into an extreme or a fanatic one. In the second place, governments are aware that the loyalty of nationalism is a reservoir of national power, that an intensely loyal people will get behind governmental policies, sacrifice for them, and even die in battle for them if called upon to do so. Always anxious to enhance national power, governments are prone to promote a dynamic nationalism among their respective peoples. So obvious has been this desire of governments for a strong, unwavering loyalty that someone has aptly remarked that today "the state makes nationalism fully as much as nationalism makes the state." The close tie between nationalism and power means, in effect, that restraints upon the former are as difficult as they have generally been upon the latter.

Among the various tensions that nationalism causes in international relations is that arising from *minorities*. Many countries, especially in Europe, contain ethnic minorities: in Romania, for instance, there are 1,500,000 Magyars and about 350,000 Germans; and in Bulgaria there are more than 1,100,000 minority people—Gypsies, Jews, Romanians, and Macedonians. When minorities are persecuted, the home state, if there is one and if it is powerful, is likely to come to the rescue. An international crisis with dangerous emotional ingredients then ensues, as was the case when Germany in 1938 made an issue out of the alleged (but not substantiated) persecutions of Germans in Czechoslovakia. More recently, in the nominally independent state of Cyprus, struggles between the Greek majority and the Turkish minority threatened to involve Greece and Turkey in war. Even when there is no home state to intervene, mistreatment of minorities, as in the case of Jews in Nazi Germany, is likely to inflame public opinion in other countries. No adequate solution of the minority problem on a world-wide scale has been found to date. Should the United Nations succeed in concluding a human rights covenant of general application, then, in international law, though not necessarily in fact, minorities would have a guaranteed position.

Minorities complicate international relations, too, by adding to the problem of boundaries between states. So haphazard is the geographical distribution of ethnic groups—especially in Europe—that no boundary lines could possibly be found that would separate those groups exactly. Consequently, there are many areas of conflicting claims, some of which have become known everywhere just from the bitterness engendered by the struggle to possess them. They include Alsace-Lorraine (between

Germany and France), Trieste (Italy and Yugoslavia), and Kashmir (India and Pakistan).

In recent years one of nationalism's corollaries, *self-determination,* has been at the bottom of a great many international problems. According to this corollary, an ethnic group should have an opportunity to determine its own destiny, and, if it wishes to be free and independent, it should have the chance to form a state of its own. The idea is one that President Wilson did a great deal to promulgate; in a message to Congress on February 11, 1918, he declared that self-determination is "an imperative principle of action, which statesmen will henceforth ignore at their peril." Whether they are justified or not, every subject people smitten by the virus of nationalism cries out for an opportunity to set up a nation-state.

When President Wilson preached the doctrine of self-determination, he was thinking primarily of the subject peoples in Europe, particularly of those in Austria-Hungary; it is doubtful whether he gave much thought to its applicability to the colonial peoples of the European empires in Asia and Africa. Since World War II, however, these are the people who have been claiming self-determination, and with such success that, as already noted, most of the former colonial areas are now free.

IMPERIALISM

The Nature of Imperialism. Although the word *imperialism* is admitted by all who use it thoughtfully to be a difficult one to define with precision, most people would agree that its essence is "the political domination of a state over an alien people, usually for an indefinite period of time but conceivably with a promise of eventual independence."[3] The term *imperialistic* is properly applied to a national foreign policy designed to eventuate in or to continue such domination.

The domination that is characteristic of imperialism may be exercised in varying degrees, depending on the exact form of the legal relationship set up between the ruling state and the *dependency* in question. There is no cut and dried pattern. Working out whatever legal relationship it wishes with its dependencies, a ruling state may control a great many political activities or only a few; it may allow native self-government on a small or on a large scale; it may or may not set up a native legislature with substantial authority; and it will use its discretion about admitting natives into the civil service or into the courts as judges. When old-style imperialism was still vigorous, the *metropolitan state* (the ruling state) was usually most anxious of all to have charge over the foreign affairs, the defense, and the police system of a dependency in order to be reasonably able to perpetuate its superior position.

A dependency was often given an improved status with the passing of

[3] Norman L. Hill, *International Politics,* New York, Harper & Row, Publishers, 1963, p. 52.

time, obtaining more and more self-government until it reached virtual or even absolute independence. In the British Empire, Canada and some of the other dependencies of the nineteenth century gained more and more self-government until they were recognized after World War I as *dominions*. Now, as self-governing parts of the British Commonwealth of Nations, they are as independent as Great Britain herself.

Under the constitution of the Fifth Republic, sponsored by General de Gaulle and adopted in 1958, the former French Empire became the French Community. Overseas French territories were given an opportunity to choose their status. All except Guinea in Africa, which chose complete independence, voted to remain French or to retain some degree of association with France. Of the other African territories, several voted to become members of the Community, the remainder to become *associates* by preserving certain cultural and economic ties.

The United States has never been a great imperial power, but after the Spanish-American War it annexed the Philippines and Puerto Rico. The Philippines were given complete independence in 1946. Puerto Rico, on the other hand, has gradually been elevated from the status of a colony to that of a territory that is largely self-governing and whose inhabitants have been granted United States citizenship.

In some instances the control of a nation over a dependency was indirect. Oldest among arrangements of this kind was the *protectorate*. Under this plan the native government was usually left intact, but its authority was limited to purely domestic matters. Later the most common type of indirect control was through *puppet* regimes, which appeared on the surface to be completely free and independent but actually were controlled in some way by strings pulled by the ruling state. Japan in 1931–1932 created the new state of Manchukuo out of Manchuria and equipped it with all the appurtenances of a sovereign state. But by means of advisers attached to all the important departments of government, she dominated its affairs about as effectively as though she had annexed the area. The *satellite* regimes of the U.S.S.R. are modern puppets. They are effectively controlled from Moscow through the Communist Party organization plus an underlying threat of force. That the threat is not an idle one is indicated by the experiences of Hungary (1956) and Czechoslovakia (1968) when they tried to assert a degree of independence.

The Empires. The records of history reveal the rise and fall of many *empires:* the Assyrian, the Persian, the Roman, the Holy Roman, the British, and many others. The modern empires, being possessions of nation-states, had their origins during the sixteenth and seventeenth centuries when those states were still in their infancy. By the beginning of the American Revolution in 1776, Great Britain, France, Portugal, the Netherlands, and Spain had staked out for themselves fair-sized overseas holdings, and the late decades of the nineteenth century saw Africa divided in a new era of empire building. As a result, imperialism was at its zenith when World War I broke out, even though the Spanish Empire had been virtually dissolved by the revolt of the Latin American peoples in the early 1800's and by the cession of the major island possessions of Spain to the United States in 1899. Since 1914 the empires of Germany, Italy, and Japan have been destroyed by war, and those of the United Kingdom, the Netherlands, and France have shrunk to small proportions.

Today the British Empire, if it still included the completely free dominions, would have an area considerably larger than all of Soviet Russia, including Siberia, and a population three or four times as great. But colonial territory legally under some degree of British control has now shrunk to a number of relatively small, widely scattered areas, with a total population of about six million, two thirds of which lives in Hong Kong. The French Empire has similarly shrunk to a number of minor scattered dependencies. The Belgian Empire disappeared with the freeing of the Congo, Rwanda, and Urundi. The Netherlands now holds only Dutch Guiana and some Caribbean islands. Portugal still has the large areas of Angola and Mozambique in southern Africa and a few small dependencies in other parts of the world; Spain has the Spanish Sahara in northwest Africa and some small islands; and Denmark possesses Greenland. The dependencies of the United States include Wake, Samoa (part only), Guam, the Panama Canal Zone (leasehold), Puerto Rico (largely self-governing), the Virgin Islands, and some small islands in the Pacific, most of which are in trust areas. The empire of the U.S.S.R. is composed of the six East European satellite countries, the Kurile Islands, Sakhalin Island, Estonia, Latvia, Lithuania, and large areas in Europe and Siberia inhabited by non-Russian peoples. The empire of Red China includes Tibet. The precise relation of China to North Korea and North Vietnam is today somewhat ambiguous.

International Problems of Imperialism. Empire building and empire keeping are both processes that involve the interests and well-being of many states and peoples, and consequently they bring nations into close contacts in numerous ways. More often than not, their contacts produce friction, and more than once imperialism has figured prominently among the causes of war.

Making an empire will almost invariably require fighting, either against the natives to be subdued or against outside nations that see in the program a threat to their own interests and ambitions. Italy was obliged to fight the Ethiopians in 1935 in order to bring them into Benito Mussolini's empire, and the enterprise was so obnoxious to other nations that the League of Nations was induced to apply its economic sanctions against the aggressors. Again, in the early 1950's Red China siezed control of Tibet, but in 1959 it had to suppress a revolt.

Often, when an empire is liquidated, serious international repercussions follow. Someone has said that World War I resulted from the demise of the Turkish Empire in the Balkans, that World War II began in central Europe where the Austro-Hungarian Empire had been demolished in 1919, that the Korean struggle was brought on by the destruction of the Japanese Empire, and that the Vietnam War in which we are still involved was a result of the disintegration of the French Empire. To simplify the causes of any war is always a mistake, and clearly empire liquidation was not alone responsible for these conflicts. To explain each of them, many events and forces must be fitted together to get a total picture of the situation; but it is obvious that empire liquidation preceded all of them. What happened in each case was that a long-established power had been defeated and obliged to move out, thereby creating something of a vacuum, which competing states, for one reason or another, were anxious to fill. Rather than as a cause of war in itself, therefore, the exodus of imperial authority may be properly looked upon as an unusually favorable occasion for the operation of the other forces that tend to bring on war.

The Balance Sheet of Imperialism. The builders of empires always hope to derive special advantages from the dependencies they amass, and invariably they argue that they are intent upon improving the lot of native peoples. Among the motives frequently ascribed to the builders of national empires are the following: (1) to strengthen the nation's power position, (2) to gain prestige for themselves and their nation, (3) to carry the benefits of civilization to undeveloped peoples, (4) to find relief from population pressure, and (5) to obtain wealth. Whether any or all those purposes can or will be attained depends on conditions that are so uncertain that analysts have raised serious doubts as to whether imperialism has, in modern times, been a paying proposition. Shortly before World War II, Lord Halifax, British Foreign Secretary, spoke deprecatingly of dependencies as "burdens." In a study by the Royal Institute of International Affairs, published in 1937, the disadvantages, perils, and costs of empires were so clearly brought out that the conclusion seemed inevitable that most dependencies were creating more problems and expenses than they were worth.

When an augmentation of national power was sought from a dependency, the mother country usually hoped that it would provide one or more of the following: (1) bases for military operations, (2) an army of colonial troops, (3) strategic raw materials, or (4) a *buffer territory* to hold off a threatening enemy. The study made by the Royal Institute pointed out that such advantages were not always forthcoming and that most of them could not be realized unless the country involved could control the ocean lanes in time of war in order to utilize bases, transport troops, or import raw materials. A state already powerful, the United States for example, would be strong enough to claim such advantages, whereas a weak state, such as the Netherlands, would only spread its meager power and resources out thin if it tried to hold and protect an empire. Another obstacle to the attainment of military objectives might be the unfriendliness of the natives, their hostility to alien bases, or their reluctance to serve in an army.

The motive of prestige or glory is often not admitted by empire builders, but it has undoubtedly been an important objective in acquiring colonies, and it has often helped win public support for such a policy. In the not very distant past, many an Englishman felt a thrill of pride in his nationality when he thought of the far-flung British Empire.

The humanitarian motive in imperialism, the *white man's burden* as Rudyard Kipling called it, has been mentioned frequently. Though it has often been the butt of criticism, many people in imperialist states took it seriously. Altruistic people, missionary groups in particular, often made great efforts to improve the condition of subject peoples. Activities of home governments for the improvement of their "backward" peoples by means of schools, hospitals, road building, housing, and industrialization were always given wide publicity, but in most cases the results were not too impressive. The Dutch were in the East Indies for about three and a half centuries, and, when they turned over their authority to the natives in 1949, the great masses were still illiterate. We must, however, remember that the Netherlands is a small nation and that even in most European countries mass education is not much more than a hundred years old.

As population outlets, dependencies were definitely disappointing. Italy for years complained that she had more people on her land than she could care for, yet for many years before World War II she had held several good-sized *colonies* in Africa. Nathaniel Peffer pointed out in 1936 that more Italian emigrants were living in New York City alone than in all the Italian colonies.[4] Japan, another nation with a large and growing population crowded together in a small area, succeeded in getting only a few hundred thousand people to migrate to Korea, Formosa, and Manchuria when those territories were under her control. The fact is that in modern times few emigrants have cared to go to relatively undeveloped areas where life may be difficult, where employment is limited, and where the chances for making a good living are uncertain.

Whether imperialism really brought wealth to the mother country is highly questionable, but a widespread belief that it did helped to encourage colonial expansion. Much of the talk about the economic benefits of colonies has been misleading. Often, writers speak as if a country, by annexing a colony, had enriched itself to the full extent of the colony's wealth, in spite of the fact that everyone knows that the same groups who owned the wealth of a colony before annexation owned it afterwards unless it was purchased from them.[5] Again, some writers imply that the total money value of colonial trade was a net addition to the wealth of a nation and, further, that this addition resulted from the possession of the colonies. The obvious truth is that trade, however essential, is merely an exchange of wealth and that trade with territories not under national control may be just as profitable as trade with one's own colonies.

[4] Nathaniel Peffer, "The Fallacy of Conquest," *International Conciliation*, March 1936, p. 121.
[5] Note, however, that the Nazis developed special techniques for "buying" property in occupied territories at no cost to themselves. They simply printed special issues of paper money for an invaded country, made it legal tender, and used it for their purchases. This was, of course, only confiscation streamlined. Communist countries are also quite willing to confiscate private property, and they seldom bother to disguise the process.

Contrary to much public opinion and even to statements in some history books, most colonies were probably an economic burden rather than an asset. Colonies may have brought real profits to small but politically influential groups in the mother country, and this may sometimes have accounted for their establishment; but any increase in income resulting from them was usually, for the nation, more than offset by higher taxes to cover the costs of administration and defense. And though the colonial relationship favored trade with the mother country, it is interesting to note that no nation in modern times has ever carried on the greater part of its trade with its colonies.[6] The popular belief that a country with a colonial empire could grow rich by "exploiting" subject peoples appears to be little more than a plausible myth. To be sure, wage rates and living conditions were usually low in primitive colonial areas, but so was the productivity of labor.

In the years just after World War II various writers suggested that the relatively impoverished condition of Great Britain was partly a result of the loss of India and Burma. But in fact it was the war that impoverished Britain, and as a result of her impoverishment, she could no longer afford the luxury of keeping these great colonies and meeting the problems and costs involved.

There is no doubt that Great Britain benefited economically from the relative peace and security that prevailed in the world during the century preceding World War I. This peace contributed to the expansion of production, trade, and investment, and it was maintained to a large extent by British colonial forces and the British Navy. However, other nations, among them the United States, Germany, and Japan, also received the economic benefits of this British peace, and they did so without paying the bills.

We might note that Switzerland, completely lacking colonies, had for decades the highest per capita purchasing power of any country in Europe. Today this position is held by Sweden, which likewise has no colonies. Further, in spite of a widespread belief that the wealth of the Netherlands was somehow based on exploiting the 70 million people who lived in its former colonies in the East Indies, since losing those colonies it has attained the highest level of prosperity in its entire history. Today these former colonies (now the new nation of Indonesia) have a population of about 120 million.

Though imperialism was probably not a paying proposition for the "mother" countries, until the establishment of the League of Nations it was the only means available for opening up to the world large sections

[6] In the case of the Netherlands, a small country that before World War II had large and prosperous colonies, only about one eighth of its trade was with its colonies in the period 1938–1939. In 1958, Great Britain carried on less than half its trade with areas in the "Empire," even if we include not only true colonies but also India and all the other free dominions. These rough approximations are based on trade figures in the *Statesman's Year Book*, 1941 and 1959.

of Asia and Africa. To have left those areas isolated and closed until the establishment of the League in 1920 would probably have been contrary to the long-run interests of all the peoples concerned. The League of Nations first, and later the United Nations, provided ways of making the development of "backward" areas a joint project of the community of nations. Consequently, there is now a substitute for old-time imperialism. Under its trusteeship system, the United Nations assumed responsibility for a number of *trust areas,* which were formerly parts of the old empires of Germany, Italy, and Japan. Under the authority of the United Nations, strong and well-developed nations were given the task of governing those areas, subject to an obligation to account for their actions to the Trusteeship Council.

Some of the trust territories have become independent states since World War II, but the United States is still the *administering authority* of the United Nations for the Marianas, Marshall, and Caroline Islands, all located in the Pacific Ocean. These islands were all former *mandates* of Japan under the League of Nations, and, still earlier, they were parts of the old German Empire. As the administering authority, we submit to the Trusteeship Council annual reports on our activities and policies, and we receive from the Council criticisms and recommendations.

IMPERIALISM VERSUS COLONIAL INDEPENDENCE

The old *colonialism* had shown some signs of decline even before World War II. After the war it disintegrated rapidly, as colony after colony demanded independence. In a few cases it has been superseded by the trusteeship system of the United Nations, but in the more important colonial areas it has been replaced by independence and statehood. Of the nations of the West that held important dependencies, only Portugal still resists this trend. Russia and Red China, of course, have no intention of freeing conquered territories.

Traditional colonialism bore within itself the seeds of its own destruction. It was a product of European nationalism, but as the concept of nationalism spread to the far corners of the globe, colonial peoples were inspired to develop their own brands of nationalism and to demand independence and statehood. Many of the peoples of Europe achieved national unity and independence long ago. Now most of the former colonial peoples of Asia and Africa are also independent, but they have achieved this independence only recently, and some of them have not attained full national unity and stability. Memories of colonialism tend to give their nationalism an anti-Western bias, but this has been modified by the willingness of the former imperial powers to help them solve their many difficult social and economic problems.

To support the cause of colonial nationalism, some of the ex-colonial states, with the help of a few others, have been sponsoring in the United

Nations the doctrine that there is a *right* of *self-determination*. They were able to incorporate into the Draft Covenant on Civil and Political Rights (1952), as formulated by the Commission on Human Rights, a statement that "All peoples and all nations have the right of self-determination, namely, the right freely to determine their political, economic, social, and cultural status." The Covenant was given final form in 1966, but by 1968 it had been ratified by only thirty-eight nations. However, the statement on self-determination does seem to embody the beliefs of the Asian and African nations; and the United States has generally taken the position that people who are prepared for self-government should be permitted to have it and to choose the form it should take.

Successes of the New Nationalisms. Since World War II a large number of new states have been forged out of the old empires of the West in Asia and Africa. First to be noted are those in the Middle East, which prior to World War I had been a part of the Turkish Empire.

The Arab States and Israel. With the collapse of Turkish power in 1914–1918, the Arab community in the Middle East entered a new era in which parts of it became mandates under the League of Nations (Palestine, Iraq, Transjordan, Syria, and Lebanon), whereas others were soon recognized as independent without having had an earlier status as mandates (Saudi Arabia in 1932 and Yemen in 1934). Great Britain recognized Iraq as a kingdom in 1922; in 1932 the mandate over the kingdom was terminated, and it was admitted into the League of Nations as a sovereign state. After World War II the mandates in Transjordan, Syria, and Lebanon were ended, and thus three more states sprang into being. The British mandate in Palestine at this time came up for reconsideration, but disorders there had reached serious proportions. They involved the British authorities, the Jewish majority who sought independence, and the Arab minority who opposed Jewish domination. Early in 1948, in the hope that a solution could be found, the British government turned the problem over to the United Nations. While the British were evacuating Palestine, the Jews declared their independence, established the state of Israel, and were immediately recognized by the United States.

Which of the new Arab states that have come into existence out of the old Turkish Empire are, or will become, true nation-states is still a question. All of them—Transjordan, Yemen, Saudi Arabia, Iraq, Syria, and Lebanon—are Arab in language and culture. It is conceivable, though perhaps not likely, that eventually they will combine into a single nation-state, which might also include Egypt and some other Arab states in North Africa and the Arabian Peninsula. In 1945 the six states first mentioned, along with Egypt, formed the Arab League, a loose system of voluntary cooperation and mutual assistance. Later the League was joined by Libya, the Sudan, Tunisia, Morocco, Kuwait, and Algeria. However, various antagonisms between Arab states have reduced the value of the League as a unifying force. In 1958, for example, Egypt and Syria united to form the United Arab Republic, but in 1961 friction arose and Syria withdrew; later Egypt supported the rebel government in Yemen while Saudi Arabia supported the forces that had rallied around the son of the assassinated king. Today the strongest bond between the Arab nations seems to be their common hatred of Israel.

The Republic of the Philippines. The new Republic of the Philippines started its career on July 4, 1946. The Islands had come under the authority of the United States in 1899, when Spain, after a defeat in war, ceded them to the United States. At that time the Filipinos, led by Emilio Aguinaldo, declared their independence and fought for it by guerrilla tactics until 1902, when American rule was made effective. Throughout the period of American control over the Islands the demand of the natives for independence was often asserted; finally, in 1934 Congress passed the Tydings-McDuffie Act, which immediately gave them additional self-government as a "commonwealth" and further provided for complete independence in 1946.

Indonesia. As we have already indicated, Indonesia is another new state created by a persistent nationalism opposing an old imperialism. Local nationalism began to assert itself early in the twentieth century —especially on Java, the most populous island—and it succeeded to the extent of winning occasional political and economic reforms. As has so often been the case in the colonial areas, the leaders of the new nationalism were young natives who had studied in Europe and who brought home those Western ideas that so easily stimulate the sentiment of nationalism. During World War II, Japanese occupation of the islands strengthened the new nationalism to such an extent that a stubborn opposition arose to the return of Dutch authority. After the Japanese left, hostilities between the Dutch and the natives ensued, and an alarming international situation developed that held the attention of the Security Council of the United Nations for more than two years. Hostilities ceased on January 1, 1949, and later in the same year arrangements were concluded for the exodus of Dutch authority. There followed, however, unsuccessful revolts in some of the outer islands, whose people oppose domination by the Javanese.

India, Pakistan, Burma, and Ceylon. Nationalism in India first became a force to be reckoned with in the 1880's, when the Hindu National Congress was formed. By the end of World War I it was so widespread that the British made substantial concessions to it in governmental matters. Throughout the 1920's and 1930's it continued to thrive under the astute leadership of Mahatma Gandhi, whose tactics of nonviolent revolt against the British proved to be extremely effective. As the result of World War II, Great Britain was so weakened that she was in no mood to combat nationalist opposition any longer, and in 1947 Parliament enacted a law by which the British Empire in India passed out of existence. In this case, instead of the emergence of one new state, two were set up: India itself, a Hindu state, and Pakistan, composed of Moslems who were determined not to be included in a Hindu-dominated nation.

Both are today independent units in the British Commonwealth of Nations. In the same year, 1947, Burma and Ceylon also received their independence and became members of the Commonwealth.

Indo-China. After World War II the Japanese invaders withdrew from Indo-China, and the French returned to take over its administration. Very soon, however, hostilities developed between the French and various insurgent groups. When hostilities were ended in 1954 and the French agreed to withdraw, Indo-China was in effect divided into four independent states: North Vietnam (under communist control), South Vietnam, Laos, and Cambodia. But the freeing of Indo-China solved few problems, for ever since then the communists of North Vietnam have been attempting to gain control of Laos and South Vietnam by sending supplies, and later troops, to support communist guerrillas in those countries. Red China and Russia have contributed large amounts of arms and munitions.

Nationalism in Africa. In Africa the nationalist movement has made spectacular headway since World War II. In North Africa it is not a new development; Egyptian nationalists as early as 1922 obtained from Great Britain acknowledgement of the independence of their country. After World War II the independence of Egypt became firmly established and the country finally succeeded, in 1956 under Gamal Abdel Nasser, in gaining complete control of the Suez Canal. This was possible, however, only because the United States and the United Nations intervened to

58. Chanting Nationalist Demonstrators Yell "Free-DOM!" in Ghana, 1959.
(Courtesy LOOK Magazine. Copyright © 1959.)

prevent Britain, France, and Israel from taking military action to prevent it.

When the French relinquished their control of Tunisia and Morocco in 1956, all the countries of North Africa had achieved independence except Algeria. The French had no intention of giving up their hold on that country, because it contained an important minority of French settlers. But in 1954 a nationalist rebellion broke out, and after years of indeterminate and very costly warfare, the de Gaulle government, against the opposition of powerful elements in the French army, granted Algeria independence. This became effective in January, 1962.

From 1957 to 1968, inclusive, there was a phenomenal spread of nationalism south of the Sahara. In this region new states were established one after another. First came Ghana (1957) and Guinea (1958); but the great year for African independence was 1960. Before the year ended, sixteen new states had been created south of the Sahara, including such important ones as Nigeria and the former Belgian Congo. In addition, Somalia gained its freedom in East Africa; and in the Indian Ocean off the coast of Africa the island of Madagascar became the Malagasy Republic. From 1961 to early in 1965, nine more independent states were created in Africa south of the Sahara. Late in 1965 Rhodesia declared its independence, but without the consent of the home country, Britain. Then came Botswana and Lesotho in 1966, and Swaziland and Equatorial Guinea in 1968.

Figure 35 is a map of Africa showing the states that were independent before 1950, those that have gained independence since, and the areas that are still colonies or protectorates. Note that today the only major dependent areas are in the far south. They are the two important Portuguese colonies of Angola and Mozambique, and Southwest Africa, which is a trust territory of the Republic of South Africa.

Whether the new nation-states of Africa were ready, in the best interests of their own people, to assume the responsibilities of self-government is questioned by many observers. To give weight to their doubts they point, for example, to the disorders and massacres that soon followed independence in the former Belgian Congo, to the recent civil war in Nigeria, and to cases where democracy has broken down and a "strong man" has seized the reins of government. The critics also point out that there is still much illiteracy and that tribal loyalties often cause friction.

But considering the short period of their existence, the progress that some of these states have made in establishing order, in developing their economies, and in approaching nationhood is rather astonishing. Their cities are growing very rapidly, and in them, as we noted earlier, it is said that tribal loyalties tend to break down and be replaced by national loyalty. These new states still face many difficulties, but it appears to be true that the art of self-government can be mastered only through experience.

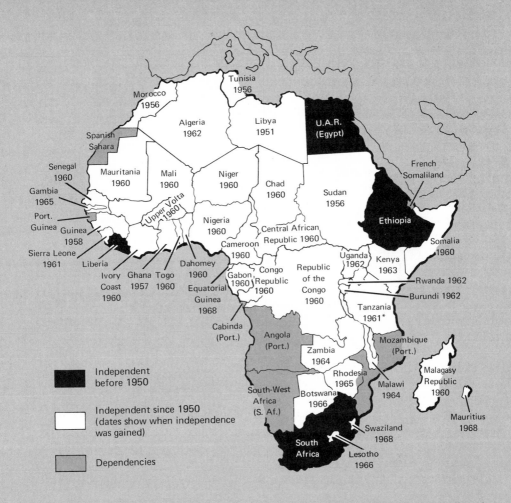

Figure 35. Political Map of Africa, 1970.

Map labels:
Tunisia 1956
Morocco 1956
Algeria 1962
Libya 1951
U.A.R. (Egypt)
Spanish Sahara
Senegal 1960
Mauritania 1960
Mali 1960
Niger 1960
Chad 1960
Sudan 1956
French Somaliland
Gambia 1965
Port. Guinea
Guinea 1958
Sierra Leone 1961
Liberia
Ivory Coast 1960
Ghana 1957
Togo 1960
Upper Volta 1960
Nigeria 1960
Dahomey 1960
Cameroon 1960
Central African Republic 1960
Ethiopia
Somalia 1960
Gabon 1960
Equatorial Guinea 1968
Congo Republic 1960
Republic of the Congo 1960
Uganda 1962
Kenya 1963
Rwanda 1962
Burundi 1962
Tanzania 1961*
Cabinda (Port.)
Angola (Port.)
Zambia 1964
Mozambique (Port.)
Malawi 1964
Malagasy Republic 1960
Rhodesia 1965
South-West Africa (S. Af.)
Botswana 1966
Swaziland 1968
Mauritius 1968
South Africa
Lesotho 1966

Legend:
Independent before 1950
Independent since 1950 (dates show when independence was gained)
Dependencies

*Tanganyika became free in 1961, the island of Zanzibar in 1963; on joining in 1963 they took the name Tanzania.

COMMUNIST IMPERIALISM

While the old empires of western Europe have been shrinking in the face of the new nationalisms in Asia and Africa, the revived imperialisms of Russia and Red China have been prospering.

Russian Imperialism Before the Communist Revolution. The expansion of Russia has a history that goes back several hundred years. Under

Peter the Great (1682–1725) and Catherine the Great (1762–1796) important additions were made to her territory, so that she entered the nineteenth century with promising prospects of future greatness. The new century witnessed even larger territorial acquisitions, most notably the vast area of Siberia, which stretches across northern and central Asia all the way to the Pacific. Most of this region was taken over during the reign of Alexander II from 1855 to 1881.

In spite of these great acquisitions, the czars failed to achieve all of their ambitions for expansion. Their desire to dominate the Slavic peoples of the Balkans was thwarted by the great powers of Europe, and so, too, were their recurring efforts to take over the Straits area between the Aegean Sea and the Black Sea. Great Britain prevented the absorption of Persia in the Middle East, and in the Far East Japan rolled back the Russian advances in Manchuria.

For the first two decades and more of communist rule in Russia, expansionism was out of the question. When Stalin came into full power (1927), he advocated emphasis upon internal development, and this precluded external ventures of any consequence. Then, after the rise of Hitler, German power on the west and Japanese power on the east were strong obstacles to aggressive Soviet expansion.

Russian Expansion During and After World War II. The first chance for renewed expansion came at the beginning of World War II. In accordance with the Soviet-German Nonaggression Pact of August 24, 1939, Russia promptly seized a large strip of territory from Poland. After a war with Finland in 1939 and 1940, Petsamo and part of Karelia were annexed. In the summer of 1940, with Germany busy occupying France and other countries in western Europe, and no one on hand to prevent it, Bessarabia and northern Bukovina were detached from Romania, and the independent states of Estonia, Latvia, and Lithuania along the Baltic were absorbed.

At the end of World War II, with the destruction of German and Japanese power and the weakening of Great Britain and France, the way seemed open for expansion on a grandiose scale. Only the United States was in a position to offer opposition, and it seemed far enough away and sufficiently anxious for peace to warrant an effort by the Kremlin to bring more neighboring peoples under its domination. Soon after the Japanese surrender, Russian troops took over the Kurile Islands and the southern part of Sakhalin Island, both of which had belonged to Japan. Russian troops remained in Manchuria long enough to ensure that the Chinese Communists, then carrying on a civil war with Nationalist China, would be in a position to take over the territory. Russian help to the Chinese Communists was one factor in the victory that they finally achieved over the Nationalists in 1949, a victory that foreshadowed the probability that China would come under some degree of Soviet influence or control, although exactly how large a degree no one could foretell.

In eastern Europe, Soviet imperialism continued after World War II by turning one after another of the states there into *satellites,* or *puppet regimes.* This was accomplished without the direct use of military force, through the machinations of the communist parties within those states. Better organized than the democratic parties and supported by Russian intrigue and power, the communists were able to insinuate themselves into the governments and eventually to take over completely. For instance, in Czechoslovakia the Communists in 1946 went into a coalition government with three other parties, and used the advantages gained thereby to stage, in February, 1948, a *coup d'etat,* that is, an illegal seizure of power by force and surprise.

The Satellites as New-Style Colonies. The satellites are dominated by the U.S.S.R. about as much as though they were old-style colonies, as a representative of Yugoslavia asserted before the Trusteeship Council of the United Nations as early as 1952. This follows principally from the fact that the communist parties that govern them are largely controlled by the Communist Party of the U.S.S.R. When the satellites fail to satisfy the U.S.S.R., dissidents can be purged by the party. One of the main devices used by Russia to exert her influence over the economic life of the satellites is the *joint company,* whose stock is owned in part by the Soviet Union and in part by the native government. But if in spite of these methods of control, a satellite government becomes recalcitrant, the Soviet Union is always prepared to use naked force, as it did in Hungary in 1956 and in Czechoslovakia in 1968.

59. Defying the Invasion. A Czechoslovak student waves the national flag while standing on a Soviet tank in Prague shortly after the invasion on August 22, 1968. (Courtesy Wide World Photos.)

Behind the imperialism of the U.S.S.R. are, no doubt, most of the factors that motivated the expansionist policies of the czars: the search for warm-water ports; the desire to dominate the Balkan Slavs; and the quest for security on the open frontier to the west through the possession of buffer territory. In addition, there is now the ideological motive of extending the area in which communism holds sway, in accordance with the communist doctrine of the necessity for a world revolution. According to communist theory, world peace, prosperity, and welfare can be assured only after capitalism and the capitalist democracies have everywhere been destroyed. The latest major move of the Soviet Union has been to obtain a foothold in the eastern Mediterranean by supporting Egypt and the Arab countries against Israel.

Chinese Imperialism. In China the development of communism and nationalism have gone together. The Chinese Communists did not gain full control of the mainland until 1950. Thereafter they cooperated with Russia in policies designed to expand communist control. In the summer of 1950 they aided and encouraged communist North Korea to invade South Korea, and when the invaders faced defeat, they sent Chinese troops to their aid. Later, with the Russians, they gave help to the communist rebels in Vietnam and thus contributed to the establishment in 1954 of the communist state of North Vietnam. In 1950 the Chinese

60. Refugee Housing in Hong Kong. One of a large complex of buildings built by the government to house some of the great numbers of people who have fled Red China. Each nine-by-twelve room houses a whole family. Ground floor is used for small shops. (Photo by author.)

Communists also invaded Tibet, which, though nominally a dependency of China, had long been practically independent. Gradually they tightened their hold on the country, but in 1959, as already noted, they had to suppress a revolt. After that, they took over full control, and the head of the Tibetan state, the Dalai Lama, fled to India. The Panchen Lama, chosen by Peking, was then installed as a puppet ruler. Later he was deposed, and in 1965 Tibet was incorporated into the People's Republic of China. In 1959 the Chinese claimed that the correct boundaries of Tibet extended beyond the established border with India, and without previous negotiation or warning they sent patrols into India to seize certain border territories. In 1962 they made even greater incursions into Indian territory. Later India and China agreed to enter into peace negotiations under a plan drawn up at Colombo, Ceylon, at a conference of several "nonaligned" nations.

The takeover of mainland China by the communists created an acute problem for the small British colony of Hong Kong on the China coast. At the time of World War II, Hong Kong had a population of about a million. Since then its population has increased to about four million, largely because of the influx of refugees from the communist mainland.

Reaction of the West to Communist Expansion. Alarmed by the extension of the empire of the U.S.S.R. during and after World War II, the West felt itself obliged to set up barriers against further conquests. This explains the fact that contemporary international politics revolve so often about the East-West issue. Under the leadership of the United States, various policies were evolved to protect the Free World against communist aggression. The Truman Doctrine, under which the United States undertook to assist nations striving to avoid absorption by the U.S.S.R., was announced in 1947; the Marshall Plan for economic aid to European nations was set in motion in 1948; the North Atlantic Treaty system for common action against aggression was established in 1949; and the rearmament of the West was pushed forward. Proof that the West was in earnest in its opposition to further communist expansion was given in 1950, when the troops of Soviet-dominated North Korea invaded South Korea and were met by the armed forces of the United Nations. These forces were largely American, but there were also units from a number of other nations. By this time it seemed clear that the peace of the world and the continued independence of free nations required a containment of the imperialistic designs of the U.S.S.R.

In the years since the Korean War, the Soviet Union and, to a lesser extent, Red China have kept expanding their influence and power at every opportunity, as indicated by their activities in Cuba, Africa, Vietnam, and the Near East. They have not engaged in any major warfare, which at this stage would be very costly and probably disastrous, but they have done their best to advance their interests by infiltration, subversion, and aid to communist rebellions in other countries. Meanwhile, they have not neglected military research and the strengthening of their armed forces. Today Russia has built up its nuclear missile striking force until many students of armament believe this force will soon be equal or superior to that of the United States. Russia has also for the first time created a powerful navy, including nuclear submarines of the latest design armed with long-range nuclear missiles. Even Red China now has operational intercontinental ballistic missiles and is on the way to producing them in quantity.

Meanwhile, the war in Vietnam has been a frustrating experience for the American public. One of its effects has been to encourage the development of *neo-isolationism,* a desire on the part of many for the United States to withdraw from any major role of leadership and responsibility for aiding the Free World, which includes ourselves, to resist communist aggression. This could be a dangerous development unless we can safely assume that the communist leaders have given up their imperialistic ambitions for ultimate domination of the world. At present there appears to be little basis for such an assumption, except for the fear that all nations have of an atomic war. It is true, however, that the Soviet Union has generally been cautious in its foreign policies, perhaps more so than this country. Whenever possible, it has avoided using its own military forces to carry out its policies. With rare exceptions, it has done so only when, as in Hungary and Czechoslovakia, it could act quickly with irresistible force and feel certain that no major power, in particular the United States, would intervene.

Terms to Be Understood

nationalism	puppet regime	mandate
patriotism	satellite regime	colony
ethnic group	empire	colonialism
imperialism	buffer territory	self-determination
dependency	white man's burden	*coup d'état*
metropolitan state	trust area	joint company
dominions	administering	new-style colony
protectorate	authority	neo-isolationism

Questions for Review and Discussion

1. Was ancient Greece a nation? Why or why not? Did it have any of the qualities of a modern nation?
2. Explain why the French Revolution started a rapid expansion of nationalism in Europe.
3. Many people hold nationalism responsible for a great part of the ills of the world. Do you believe that on balance it has aided or held back social progress? Defend your answer.

4. Is nationalism outmoded? Why or why not? Is it growing or declining? Explain.
5. Is the right to self-determination a sound doctrine? Why or why not?
6. What were the two great periods of modern empire building?
7. Does the disintegration of empires promote or hinder world peace? Explain.
8. What advantages does a nation hope to gain by building an empire?
9. Does the acquisition of dependencies add to the power of a nation? Discuss.
10. How much truth is there in the popular belief that certain nations in Europe grew rich by "exploiting" the people of their colonies? Defend your answer.
11. What nation-states have succeeded in significantly reducing population pressures at home by sending people to their colonies? Can you give examples?
12. Why did traditional colonialism bear within itself the seeds of its own destruction?
13. On balance, has imperialism benefited or injured the peoples of the world? Defend your answer.
14. Make as long a list as you can of new states that have sprung into existence since World War II.
15. What serious obstacles are there to a union of all the Arab states into a single nation-state?
16. In what sense, and why, are the boundaries of the African states south of the Sahara mostly arbitrary?
17. Which of the important characteristics of nationhood are not yet fully developed in some of the new African states?
18. What factors are contributing to breaking down tribalism and building up a sense of national loyalty in some of these states?
19. What seem to be the present objectives of Russian imperialism?
20. In the communist countries, to what extent has communism replaced nationalism?
21. Is the danger of a third world war less today than it was at the time of the Korean War? Why or why not?

For Further Study

Deutsch, Karl W., *Nationalism and Its Alternatives,* New York, Alfred A. Knopf, Inc., 1969.

Ebenstein, William, *Today's Isms,* 6th ed., paperback, Englewood Cliffs, N.J., Prentice-Hall, Inc., 1970.

Greene, Fred, *Dynamics of International Relations: Power, Security, and Order,* Holt, Rinehart and Winston, Inc., 1964. See therein Part 5, "Nationalism and Imperialism."

Hallowell, J., ed., *Soviet Satellite Nations: A Study of the New Imperialism,* paperback, Gainesville, Fla., Kallman Publishing Company, 1958.

Hill, Norman L., *International Politics,* New York, Harper & Row, Publishers, 1963. See therein Chap. 10, "World Forces and Movements."

Hunt, Elgin F., and Jules Karlin, eds., *Society Today and Tomorrow,* 2d ed., New York, The Macmillan Company, 1967. See therein "A New Look at Nationalism" by Hans Kohn.

Kedourie, Elie, *Nationalism in Asia and Africa,* paperback, Cleveland, World Publishing Company, 1969.

Kohn, Hans, *The Age of Nationalism: The First Era of Global History,* Torchbook paperback, New York, Harper & Row, Publishers, 1968.

Millikan, Max F., and Donald L. M. Blackmer, eds., *The Emerging Nations: Their Growth and United State Policy,* Boston, Little, Brown and Company, 1961.

Schuman, Frederick L., *International Politics,* 7th ed., New York, McGraw-Hill, Inc., 1969.

Schwartz, Benjamin I., *Communism and China: Ideology in Flux,* Cambridge, Mass., Harvard University Press, 1968.

Ward, Barbara, *Lopsided World,* paperback, New York, W. W. Norton & Company, Inc., 1968.

————, *Nationalism and Ideology,* paperback, New York, W. W. Norton & Company, Inc., 1966.

Chapter 32

The

Search for

Peace

War has always been regarded by many as evil, but never has its prevention seemed so urgent as now. Even in the past, war, though some once called it the "sport of kings," was brutal and destructive. Usually, however, it was on a limited scale, and often it had little effect on the ordinary citizen who did not happen to be in the battle zone. But modern war is a phenomenon that can reach into the life of every individual, spell doom even to the "victor," despoil a civilization, and perhaps annihilate whole nations. The new technology with its devastating weapons has forced mankind into an unprecedented dread of war. The submarines, tanks, machine guns, and vast armies of World War I served to stimulate much sober thinking in the 1920's and 1930's toward averting future conflict. Still more thought provoking were the weapons and slaughter of World War II, particularly the atomic bomb. Now atomic and thermonuclear weapons are many times more lethal than the bomb dropped on Hiroshima on August 6, 1945. What is even more disturbing, they can be attached to intercontinental ballistic missiles and carried to almost any part of the world in a few minutes; and today one missile can carry a number of independently targeted bombs.

THE PROBLEM OF WAR

War in History. War has had a prominent role in every period of history. A monumental study of war made at the University of Chicago some years ago brings out its central place in the development of the nation-state.[1] Twenty wars are listed from 1750 to 1800; forty-one from 1800 to 1850; forty-seven from 1850 to 1900; and twenty-four from 1900 to 1941. From 1850 to 1941, Great Britain was in thirteen wars, France nine, and the United States six.

The total costs of war cannot be measured. Some of the direct costs, such as those in casualties and government spending, can be estimated with a fair degree of accuracy. In the nineteenth century in France thirty deaths out of a thousand were caused by war, and in the twentieth century (up to 1941) there were sixty-three out of a thousand. American casualties in the nineteen months of World War I were 333,132 men; in the forty-four months of participation in World War II, they were 1,049,741; and in the thirty-seven months of the Korean War they were 157,530. Our casualties in the Vietnam War have already exceeded those in Korea. World War I cost the United States approximately $25 billion, and World War II cost $326 billion. Though the Vietnam War is on a much smaller scale than World War I, we are spending on it *annually* about as much money as we spent *altogether* on World War I. According to Deputy Secretary of Defense David Packard, we spent on this conflict about $29 billion in fiscal 1969 and about $23 billion in fiscal 1970.[2] However, this increase in the money costs of war is less remarkable if we remember that in the period from World War I to 1970 inflation had greatly reduced the value of the dollar.

The indirect effects of war may be quite as important as the direct losses it causes. World War I paved the way for communism in Russia; it helped to bring on the great depression of the 1930's; and it unleashed forces that produced Fascism in Italy and National Socialism in Germany. World War II gave communism an opportunity for further expansion. These

[1] Quincy Wright, *A Study of War,* 2 vols., Chicago, University of Chicago Press, 1942.
[2] *U.S. News & World Report,* August 3, 1970, p. 46.

results of war, and others like them, are rarely anticipated when hostilities are in progress.

The Causes of War. Modern war is a complex product of a complex society. Simple explanations of its recurrence are never convincing, for invariably they exaggerate some one or two causes and ignore many others. During and after World War I, secret diplomacy was in disrepute, as though war were to be attributed mainly to the designs of evil-minded diplomats; today, in contrast, the feeling is widespread that extreme openness in the negotiating phases of diplomacy can produce more friction than harmony. The communists reduce the causes of war to the machinations of capitalism, quite indifferent to the prevalence of conflict in precapitalist centuries and to the threatening international crises brought on in recent years by their own machinations. Free traders, as for example Richard Cobden, have seen little or nothing besides trade barriers in the hostilities of nations. Exponents of disarmament have often argued as though the only reason nations fight is that they possess guns, failing to look into the question as to what causes nations to arm themselves.

This flair for oversimplification has been extended to analyses of the causes of particular wars as well as of war in general. It is easy to think of World War I as the result of the assassination of the Archduke of Austria-Hungary or perhaps as the work of a few madmen in Germany, but in fact it was the product of many forces. To explain World War II we must do more than point to the evil actions of Hitler; answers must be found to many questions: why the Nazis came into power in Germany; why they wanted to expand; why the U.S.S.R. was willing to conclude the Nonaggression Pact of August 24, 1939; why France and Great Britain decided to call a halt to Nazi expansion to the east; and how it happened that the United States in the 1930's was so wedded to the idea of neutrality. The motives behind national action are seldom readily discernible, and therefore answers to such queries are often no more than opinions.

Analyzing the causes of war is not a subject on which a person can afford to be dogmatic. He can point to many forces that he can see at work, and he can reason as to how they work; but he cannot with exactitude draft any formula that will fully explain, evaluate, and relate the many pressures, conditions, emotions, ambitions, and practices that he may believe he can identify behind international discord. Generally speaking, to identify forces that tend to bring about war is easier than to explain or evaluate them. As noted in an earlier chapter, factors that may contribute to bringing on war include the desires of a nation for power and for prestige or glory, economic rivalries, social unrest, the ambitions of political and military leaders, fanatical devotion to revolutionary ideologies, and even the search for security.

Characteristics of Nation-states That Tend to Involve Them in War. Basically, it seems fair to assume that there is something in the nature of states that accounts for their tendency to make war. One's attention is immediately focused on their right to possess and to use power, for, after all, war is but an explosion of this element of statehood. States are in the habit of relying on their power to promote their interests, and when thwarted, they are able to fight. Because all states possess fighting capacity in some degree, there is a marked tendency for each to suspect and fear the others, and therefore all are constantly beset by a security problem; the situation resembles that faced by the carnivorous denizens of the jungle. Seeking security, states easily transgress the rights and interests of others, particularly by (1) huge armaments that threaten some or all members of the world community and (2) imperialistic expansion to gain territory useful for military bases or as buffer territories to protect them against powerful neighbors. An aggressive search for security is always a temptation, especially for large nations, and the measures that seem to provide security for one nation may easily bring insecurity to others.

War as a means of seeking security for the group seems to have a longer history than the nation-state. According to Ralph Linton, the late well-known anthropologist, the great League of the Iroquois Indians began as a defensive alliance against the Algonquins. But as soon as it had put an end to the menace, it embarked on an amazing career of conquest. This was rationalized, in modern fashion, as "a war to end war," for obviously the League could be sure of peace only after all its enemies had been destroyed.[3]

The nationalism on which the state is based is another characteristic that makes it bellicose. The nation-state, as represented by public opinion and by its leaders, may be sensitive, quick to take offense and to retaliate. It can be arrogant and selfish to a high degree, as witness Nazi Germany when it fostered the doctrine of racial superiority, spurned those groups it considered inferior or decadent, and ignored their rights. The nation-state easily hates, and it easily maintains feuds with its neighbors, such as the one that existed for many years between France and Germany.

To strengthen its authority and to provide a theoretical basis for whatever action it may wish to take in its relations with others, the state calls itself *sovereign*. Being sovereign, it holds that its freedom of action cannot be limited without its consent. It is then free to adopt whatever trade, immigration, armament, and expansionist policies it pleases, no matter how much its action may harm or offend others.

Because states are the work of men, inquiry as to the causes of war goes back to the nature of human beings. Although psychologists and biologists admit that war may seem to reflect the impulses and emotions of men—anger, hatred, fear, suspicion, frustration—the opinion is general that man is not so made that he requires war for the satisfaction of his basic drives. Man's part in war making is believed to depend more on acquired attitudes, beliefs, and points of view than on his inherent nature. His cultural patterns are now such that he maintains the nation-state with its sover-

[3] Ralph Linton, *The Study of Man*, New York, Appleton-Century-Crofts, 1936, p. 241.

eignty, nationalism, and power. Earlier his culture was such that he maintained a system of feudalism, which also provided fighting communities. At a still earlier period he was organized into tribes. But even then warfare was a common, though perhaps not universal, phenomenon. Can he, sometime in the future, develop a type of culture and social organization that will eliminate war? We cannot be sure, but it seems quite possible.

Within states as we know them or within the community of states as a whole, conditions often exist that add to the chances of war at any given time. As former Secretary of State Cordell Hull often pointed out, poverty in a nation may produce a restlessness that breeds civil strife, and this in turn may result in international war or lead to dictatorships that foster warlike "isms." Dissension or economic depression within a state may cause governments to welcome war in order to establish national unity or to create a diversion from internal problems incapable of solution. When a spirit of militarism has been developed within a nation, as in the Germany of the 1930's, touching off a war is relatively simple.

Among conditions in the international community that are conducive to war is a sharp ideological split like the present one between democracy and communism. A rift of this nature is particularly dangerous when one side is communist or fascist and hence supports an ideology frankly aggressive in its aims and methods. The existence of a power vacuum of sizable proportions is another hazardous condition in the world community and, as explained in the preceding chapter, one frequently to be found when an empire has just been demolished.

APPROACHES TO THE PROBLEM OF WAR

Throughout history most people have probably desired peace, though in some tribal societies war, in combination with customs like war dances, head hunting, and scalp collection, had become an integral part of the group culture. It helped to give life meaning by providing danger, excitement, and opportunities for winning prestige. Nevertheless, the quest for peace goes back at least to the prophet Isaiah's long look ahead to the time when "nation shall not lift up sword against nation, neither shall they learn war any more." Ever since nation-states began to develop in the late Middle Ages, various poets, philosophers, and statesmen have presented plans for maintaining peace. They include Dante, King Henry IV of France, William Penn, and Immanuel Kant. But none of these plans were practical, nor did they reach the masses or receive serious consideration from governments.

Diplomacy for the Prevention of War. The most available means to peace in the community of nation-states has always been diplomacy. The problems of states are first of all handled by the diplomats, usually with success. Occasionally, however, diplomacy fails, and then a dispute has arisen whose settlement may be a matter of moment not only to the countries involved but to the entire world. Because a serious dispute, once out of hand, can eventuate in war, states that are genuinely anxious to stay at peace will keep their diplomats at work as long as there is any hope of solution. Throughout the history of the nation-state, diplomacy has done much to avoid war.

The contributions of diplomacy to peace include the efforts of third states as well as the parties to disputes. By its *good offices* a disinterested state may try to get disputants together for further negotiations when they for some reason reach a deadlock and when unfortunate developments appear imminent; or, injecting itself a little further into a controversy, a third state may attempt *mediation,* a procedure that calls upon the mediating government to make suggestions for solutions, thus concerning itself with the merits of the issues involved. Good offices and mediation may be used to terminate a war as well as to prevent one; President Theodore Roosevelt mediated to end the Russo-Japanese War in 1905. In order to encourage third states to offer their good offices or their mediation, the Hague Conference of 1899 drew up a convention defining these terms and prescribing conditions for their application. This convention is still in effect.

International Law and International Courts. For centuries the ideal of a world ordered by a system of law has persisted. The ancient Greek city-states applied among themselves an elemental body of rules relating to such matters as diplomacy, treaties, and war. In Rome there was a *jus gentium* to regulate the relations of the diverse peoples within the empire. As soon as the system of nation-states got under way centuries ago, it began constructing for itself a body of law. Hugo Grotius, a Dutchman, is usually referred to as the founder of modern *international law* because of his systematic organization and discussion of the law of his day in his famous book entitled *The Law of War and Peace* (1625). Following Grotius, other eminent writers, such as S. Pufendorf in *The Law of Nature and of Nations* (1688) and E. de Vattel in *The Law of Nations* (1758), continued to add to its clarity and to promote its development. Often, however, emphasis was put on what nations ought to do rather than on their customary behavior. But by the nineteenth century the actual practices of states in their relations to one another began to be stressed more and more in discussions of international law, and less attention was paid to what they ought to do from the point of view of abstract justice. Today established procedures in the form of custom, treaties, and conventions are the chief basis of international law. Its subject matter is extensive, embracing such items as the recognition of new states and governments, diplomatic privileges and immunities, the acquisition of territory, nationality, extradition, the treatment of aliens, treaties, the jurisdiction of states, the responsibility of states, the beginning of war, the conduct of war, and the effect of war upon treaties.

The Limitations and the Usefulness of International Law. The utility of international law in the maintenance of order and peace among nations has always been limited. No system of criminal law and prosecution has been established to date, though the war crimes trials of Nazi leaders at Nuremberg after World War II were a step in that direction, and later the International Law Commission of the United Nations has considered the project of an international criminal court. Without criminal processes and courts, the community of nations lacks an important instrumentality of order. Then, too, the community has no real legislature, and consequently the making of new law must be through the media of treaties or by the slow development of fixed custom. In these processes of lawmaking, no sovereign state can be bound by a new rule without signifying its assent in one way or another; consequently, lawmaking is now slow, and the confusing situation may arise that what is law for one state may be quite different from that applying to another. Furthermore, there are no effective means available to the community of states for the enforcement of the law. A violator may be threatened by the injured party, it may be the object of retaliatory measures, and in the last analysis it may be challenged in war, but these are not orderly procedures comparable to the methods possessed by a state for enforcing laws internally.

Despite these deficiencies of the community of states, the utility of its international law should not be underestimated. Nations may be able to violate the law and get away with it, but they much prefer not to do so, for they do not like to be regarded as lawbreakers. A bad reputation can be harmful to a state, even to its power position. The fact that nations constantly appeal to the standard of the law in their communications and negotiations with each other, both in claiming rights and in meeting their duties, is evidence that they at least like to appear law-abiding. John Bassett Moore, an authority on international law, once expressed the opinion that violations of such law by states are no more frequent in proportion to the number of occasions when it is applicable than are violations of national law within a state. Let it be remembered, too, that most charges of violations are never substantiated and that many of them are made for propaganda purposes.

Arbitration of Disputes, and Adjudication by Courts. The utility of international law is increased considerably by the fact that *international courts* are available and can be used, if the parties so desire, to determine and apply the law in specific controversies. The Jay Treaty of 1794 between the United States and Great Britain began the modern period of arbitration, a procedure that had been employed in ancient times and in the Middle Ages but thereafter had fallen into a long period of disuse. Throughout the nineteenth century the practice of nations engaged in arbitration was to set up temporary, or *ad hoc,* courts. In management-labor disputes, these would be called *arbitration boards.* Many disputes during the nineteenth century were turned over to such tribunals for decision, including a considerable number in which the United States was a party, such as the Alabama claims case (1872), the Bering Sea dispute (1893), and our boundary disputes with Canada. In 1899 a Permanent Court of Arbitration was created with headquarters at The Hague in the Netherlands. It is still in existence, although it has not been used since 1928.

The main criticism of the process of arbitration has been that the judges who constitute a tribunal are selected by the disputants. Ordinarily, each party appoints one or two judges from its own citizens or from those of friendly states, and one more is selected from an impartial state as a kind of umpire. This means that the award is usually made by the umpire. Furthermore, a different group of judges is selected for each case; this has even been true in the Permanent Court of Arbitration, for its only element of permanence is a long list of names from which judges are taken for specific cases. Arbitration is therefore criticized on the ground that it is not a judicial process in the proper sense. Early in the present century a strong movement developed for the creation of a real court of justice. In 1907 the Central American nations did set up for themselves a Central American Court of Justice, which during the decade of its existence adjudicated several disputes.

After World War I the Permanent Court of International Justice—a bona fide court of justice—was established and, though it was not an official organ of the League of Nations, it was nevertheless closely affiliated with the Geneva organization; it was known popularly as the *World Court*. This Court was active from 1922 to 1940, when the German invasion of the Netherlands (where it was housed) closed its doors. After World War II the present International Court of Justice replaced the old Permanent Court of International Justice, at least in a technical sense; for all practical purposes, however, the present tribunal is a continuation of the older one under a new name and a new constitution (or *Statute,* as it is officially known), which differs from the old Statute only in minor details. The present International Court of Justice, like its predecessor, sits at The Hague. It is an official organ of the United Nations. The bench of the Court includes fifteen judges selected by the General Assembly and the Security Council. The Court has given out several fairly important judgments, including the Corfu Channel case (1949) between Great Britain and Albania and the Anglo-Norwegian Fisheries case (1951).

Although international courts have been a great boon to international law, both in its application and in its development, their usefulness has been restricted by the limitations of their jurisdiction. Generally speaking, a sovereign state may not be brought before any court without its consent. Offers of arbitration or adjudication have often been rejected by a disputant that prefers not to submit to such procedures.

States that are members of the present International Court of Justice (like members of the old Permanent Court of International Justice) may, if they wish, accept the jurisdiction of that tribunal as compulsory in legal disputes, with or without reservations. More than forty of the Court's members have done so. Moreover, some treaties stipulate that disputes regarding their application shall come within the *compulsory jurisdiction* of the Court. The Court, therefore, possesses a considerable area of jurisdiction that is compulsory in the sense that many states have agreed in advance to accept the Court's authority with respect to disputes of certain types. Often, therefore, one state may bring a case against another without getting the other's consent in the individual instance. However, the procedure of starting a case by allowing one state to sue another is limited to the kinds of cases that both parties have previously agreed to place under the jurisdiction of the Court. The general rule that a sovereign state may not be sued without its consent remains inviolate.

In addition to binding decisions, under Article 96 of the Charter of the United Nations the Court may give advisory opinions on any legal question when requested to do so by the General Assembly or the Security Council. Other organs or agencies of the United Nations may also ask for advisory opinions when authorized to do so by the General Assembly.

The League of Nations. The first large-scale approach by the community of states to the problem of war was embodied in the Covenant of the League of Nations. This Covenant was drafted at the Paris Peace Conference (1919), right after World War I, in answer to President Woodrow Wilson's announcement in his famous Fourteen Points that "A general association of nations must be formed under specific covenants for the purpose of affording mutual guarantees of political independence and territorial integrity to great and small nations alike." Sixty-two states became members of the organization at one time or another, but only for about a year were there as many as fifty-eight at the same time (1937–1938). The United States never joined, but after the first five years of the League's history, our government cooperated more and more with the Geneva organization.

Organization of the League. There were three main organs of the League: the Assembly, the Council, and the Secretariat. Each member state was entitled to representation in the Assembly, and each had one vote regardless of its size. The Assembly met annually, and sometimes in special sessions; it dealt with the budget, the election of new members, and international problems generally, but it had nothing at all in the way of legislative power. The Council was composed of two types of delegates: (1) those from designated large states that were entitled to permanent representation and (2) those elected for terms of three years by the Assembly from among the remaining members of the League. The number of states with permanent representation in the Council varied from two (at the end of 1939) to six (1934–1935), depending on which of the great powers were in the League at a given time; the nonpermanent membership also varied, starting out with only four but after 1936 containing eleven. The Council had a variety of duties, most important of which was that of dealing with international disputes. The Secretariat of the League, containing an international civil service of about six-hundred officials, carried on such activities as research, the publication of information and documents, preparing meetings, taking the minutes of meetings, keeping custody over records, and the registration and publication of treaties.

Constructive Accomplishments of the League. During its lifetime of about two decades, the League of Nations was intensely busy trying to promote international cooperation and peace. With the aid of auxiliary agencies of a technical nature—the Economic and Financial Organization, the Communications and Transit Organization, the Health Organization, and a group of permanent advisory committees—cooperation in nonpolitical matters was carried to such a high point of usefulness that the United States, a nonmember, was prompted to take an active part in it. A great deal of constructive work, often through the conclusion of treaties, was accomplished relating to cooperation among scientists and other scholars, slavery, the opium traffic, the protection of children, health, minorities, ports of international concern, customs formalities, and a host of other subjects.

Failure of the League to Settle Major Disputes. In the political sphere, the League was equipped with several procedures designed to preserve the peace: (1) the formulation of plans for the reduction of national armaments, (2) the settlement of disputes between nations, and (3) the protection of the member states against external aggression by means of military and economic sanctions against aggressors. Efforts to promote armament reduction culminated in the famous Geneva Disarmament Conference (1932–1934), where the problem was taken up from every conceivable angle, but without success. Throughout the history of the League, disputes were treated in the Council, and occasionally they were placed before the Assembly; but, though the results in minor cases were often auspicious, in the major controversies discussion always ended in failure. The League failed particularly in its efforts to deal with (1) the Japanese invasion of Manchuria (1931–1932), (2) the Italian conquest of Ethiopia (1935), and (3) the Japanese attack on China (1937).

The history of the League of Nations may be divided into three periods. The first stage (1920–1927), one of beginnings and gradual growth, was marked by optimism, some of it rather naive. The second period (1927–1932) was characterized by uncertainty. It opened with the conclusion of the Pact of Paris (1928), which renounced war as an instrument of national policy; but skepticism developed when the League failed to stop Japanese aggression in Manchuria (1931–1932), a feeling that deepened under the pressures of the world economic depression. The third period (1932–1939) was one of decline and collapse, marked by (1) the League's inability to stop Italian aggression in Ethiopia, (2) German rearmament and occupation of the Rhineland in violation of existing treaties, (3) the angry withdrawal of several states from the organization, and (4) the League's paralysis at the time of the Spanish Civil War (1936–1939) and during the Japanese invasion of China (1937), the German seizure of the Sudentenland (1938), and the Nazi occupation of all of Czechoslovakia (1939).

Why the League Failed. There were various reasons for the failure of the League of Nations to live up to the high hopes that had been held for it. According to the report by the International Consultative Group of Geneva, the principal causes of failure were the following:

1. The peace settlement after World War I had produced a great deal of dissatisfaction and restlessness, especially in Germany and Italy, so that the international atmosphere became one of growing tension.
2. The United States did not join the League, but reverted to its isolationist tendencies.
3. There was a lack of adequate leadership in many, if not most, of the nations.
4. A feeling of national insecurity was prevalent.
5. Social and economic discontent was general.
6. The development of a "new spirit" of internationalism, essential to a proper functioning of the Covenant, had proved impossible.[4]

In truth, the League had provided machinery and processes with which the nations could cooperate for peace as much or as little as they pleased. Apparently they were not ready politically or morally to measure up to the opportunities that the League offered. Deep in the rut of power politics, nations found it impossible to advance along the road to peace charted by the Covenant. Also, the League had little or no power, except as the member states were willing to carry out its policies.

ORIGIN OF THE UNITED NATIONS

A new surge of enthusiasm for a world organization able to keep the peace took form after the vicissitudes of World War II. On August 14, 1941, Prime Minister Winston Churchill and President Franklin Roosevelt announced in the famous Atlantic Charter the need for a "permanent system of general security." On January 1, 1942, soon after the United States became a belligerent, a United Nations Declaration was signed confirming the objectives of the Atlantic Charter. Having thus attained an official status, the term *United Nations* was readily available for the postwar organization that was to come.

As early as 1941 the Department of State began a study of postwar problems, and a little later it brought the question of a new international organization under its purview. In Great Britain the subject was explored by a Post-Hostilities Planning Committee. By 1944 the United States had ready for discussion the draft of a charter for the new organization, and from August 21 to October 7, 1944, this was the subject of official con-

---

[4] International Consultative Group of Geneva, "Causes of the Peace Failure, 1919–1939," *International Conciliation,* No. 363, October 1940, pp. 335–342, 346–348.

versations held at Dumbarton Oaks in Washington, D.C., at which representatives of the United States, the United Kingdom, the Soviet Union, and China took part. The revised draft of the Charter that emerged was given wide publicity in order to stimulate public interest and criticism. One problem not solved at Dumbarton Oaks—namely, the voting methods of the Security Council—was taken up at the Yalta Conference early in 1945. At that time a provision that is still in force was adopted, namely, that *any one of the five great powers may veto a decision of the Council.*

In accordance with another agreement made at Yalta, the San Francisco Conference met on April 25, 1945, to put the United Nations Charter into its final form. The fifty national delegations in attendance began their deliberations in a spirit of high optimism, but as the conference wore on, baffling problems produced heated differences of opinion, especially on the issue of the veto in the Security Council. By June 26, however, the debate came to an end and the Charter was signed. It came into force on October 24, 1945, by which time it had the required number of ratifications, including that of the United States.

STRUCTURE OF THE UNITED NATIONS

The structure of the United Nations consists chiefly of six principal organs through which it performs its major functions: (1) the General Assembly, (2) the Security Council, (3) the Secretariat, (4) the Economic and Social Council, (5) the Trusteeship Council, and (6) the International Court of Justice. We shall describe briefly each of these organs and the way in which it operates.

The General Assembly. First among the six principal organs of the United Nations, as named in the Charter, is the General Assembly. Like the Assembly of the old League of Nations, it includes the representatives of all the states that are members of the organization. It meets annually, with occasional special sessions when needed. Like all deliberative bodies, the General Assembly maintains a group of committees, among which these six committees are the most important: (1) Political and Security Committee; (2) Economic and Financial Committee; (3) Social, Humanitarian and Cultural Committee; (4) Trusteeship Committee; (5) Administrative and Budgetary Committee; and (6) Legal Committee. All members are entitled to representation on each committee. At the suggestion of the United States, the General Assembly in 1947 created an *Interim Committee,* popularly known as the Little Assembly, to handle preliminary and unfinished work between sessions. Though it was at first on a temporary basis, the Interim Committee has since been given a permanent status. The General Assembly elects a new president and seven vice-presidents at each session. The staff of interpreters and others needed to facilitate the work of the Assembly is provided by the Secretariat.

The General Assembly may concern itself "with any questions or matters within the scope of the present Charter or relating to the powers and functions of any organs provided for in the present Charter. . . ." It has no legislative power, but it may and does discuss international problems of many types. Usually when a decision of some kind is taken, it is in the form of a recommendation either to states or to other organs. Its wide range of subject matter and its freedom of debate led the late Senator Arthur Vandenberg to call it the "town meeting of the world."

61. Headquarters of the United Nations. A general view of the permanent headquarters in New York. The buildings are the thirty-nine-story Secretariat, the General Assembly (center), and the Library (foreground). In the background are the new Alcoa buildings, where the UN Development Program and the UN Children's Fund now maintain their offices. (Courtesy United Nations.)

Among the subjects of deliberation in the General Assembly is the work of other United Nations organs, most of which report to it. At times the Assembly initiates studies of existing problems, or it considers matters relating to "general principles of cooperation in the maintenance of international peace and security," as the Charter puts it. Also among its duties are the adoption of a budget, the election of new members of the United Nations (on the recommendation of the Security Council), the election of nonpermanent members of the Security Council, the election of a Secretary-General (on the recommendation of the Security Council), and the election, in conjunction with the Security Council, of judges for the International Court of Justice.

The General Assembly has dealt with a number of international disputes, and indeed, its work in this field has often overshadowed that of the Security Council. All told, the work of the General Assembly is so extensive that the length of its agenda has been a cause of concern. Its decisions are taken "on important questions" by a two-thirds vote of the members present and voting, and "on other questions" by a single majority of those present and voting.

The Security Council. The Security Council, another of the principal organs of the United Nations, is composed of fifteen states, of which five— Nationalist China, France, the Soviet Union, the United Kingdom, and the United States—were made permanent members. At that time, these five were considered the great powers. Later, the Nationalist Chinese were driven out of mainland China by the communists and forced to take refuge on the relatively small island of Formosa. But the United Nations refused to admit Red China to membership, and so Nationalist China still retains its permanent seat in the Security Council. The other ten members, the nonpermanent ones, are elected by the General Assembly for terms of two years, with the elections staggered so that five new ones come into office each year.

The Security Council has, according to the Charter, "primary responsibility for the maintenance of international peace and security." To meet this responsibility, the Council deals with international disputes and decides when aggression is taking place or when there is a threat to the peace and what measures members of the United Nations shall be called upon to apply on each occasion. The Council also has other duties to perform, including the recommendation to the General Assembly of new members of the United Nations and of a Secretary-General, and the election (with the General Assembly) of judges for the International Court of Justice.

Decisions taken by the Security Council must have the affirmative vote of nine of its members; when an issue is procedural in nature, any nine suffice, but in all other cases the nine affirmative votes must include those of all the five permanent members of the Council. On major questions that involve policies or action, each of the five permanent members has, therefore, a *veto*, as it is popularly called. In practice the veto has been used a great deal, particularly by the Soviet Union, which often finds itself a minority of one. It has been used not only in votes on disputes before the Council but also in votes on the admission of new members to the United Nations. Much anxiety has been expressed over the fact that a large number of states that have applied for membership have been turned down, either by the veto or by lack of the affirmative vote of as many as nine members of the Council. Projects for a modification of the veto have been seriously discussed by the General Assembly, but with little success.

The Secretariat. The Secretariat, the third principal organ of the United Nations, is headed by a Secretary-General. The first man to hold the office was Trygve Lie, a Norwegian. He was succeeded in 1953 by Dag Hammarskjold of Sweden, who was killed in 1961 in a plane crash while he was on a mission in the Congo to get a cease-fire between United Nations forces and the troops of secessionist Katanga Province. U Thant of Burma was then appointed by the General Assembly and still holds the office. Under the Secretary-General there is a staff of several thousand employees, selected from many states, including a few nonmember states. In the performance of their duties the Secretary-General and his staff are required by the Charter not to "seek or receive instructions from any government or from any other authority external to the organization." The secretariat is subdivided into departments, such as the Department of Security Council Affairs, the Department of Economic Affairs, the Department of Social Affairs, the Legal Department, and others.

The activities of the Secretariat include: (1) research; (2) preparing meetings and conferences; (3) taking records of meetings and conferences; (4) custody over documents; (5) publication of documents; (6) providing interpreters and translators; (7) communication with states and organizations; and (8) registering and publishing treaties made by members. In addition, many special duties are assigned to it by other organs, especially by the General Assembly. The Secretary-General has come in the course of time to have a political role of some consequence by reason of his influence on matters of policy with the organs of the United Nations or with governments. A good idea of the work of the Secretary-General and his staff may be gleaned from the annual reports he is required to make to the General Assembly. The Assembly debates these reports and often makes them the basis of recommendations for a modification of a practice or activity within the Secretariat or elsewhere.

The Economic and Social Council. The Economic and Social Council, the fourth principal organ, is composed of twenty-seven states, of whom nine are elected every year by the General Assembly to serve three-year terms. As a matter of practice, the five permanent members of the Security Council are always re-elected. Subsidiary to the Economic and Social Council are a group of commissions, each of which operates in an assigned field: Transport and Communication Commission; Fiscal Commission; Statistical Commission; Population Commission; Social Commission; Commission on Narcotic Drugs; Commission on Human Rights; Commission on the Status of Women; and three regional economic commissions. The *specialized agencies* of the United Nations relate themselves to the Economic and Social Council (ESC) by means of agreements with it, and the ESC in turn has the duty of coordinating their activities. Most prominent among the specialized agencies are the following: the United Nations Educational, Scientific and Cultural Organization (UNESCO); the World Health Organization (WHO); the International Labor Organization (ILO); the Food and Agriculture Organization (FAO); the Universal Postal Union (UPU); the International Monetary Fund (IMF); and the International Bank.

A somewhat later addition to the specialized agencies is the International Atomic Energy Agency, established in July, 1957. Its primary purpose is to assist in speeding and enlarging the contribution of atomic energy to peace, health, and prosperity throughout the world.

The Trusteeship Council and the International Court of Justice. The other two principal organs of the United Nations—the Trusteeship Council and the International Court of Justice—have been slightly less conspicuous than the four that have just been described. The main duty of the Trusteeship Council is to have general charge over the supervision of the administration of trust areas by the states to which they are assigned. These areas are mainly the former mandates of the League of Nations in Africa and in the Pacific Ocean. The competence of the International Court of Justice, as brought out earlier in this chapter, extends to disputes of a legal nature between states, and to the issuance of advisory opinions on legal questions brought to it by authorized organs of the United Nations.

Membership in the United Nations. Today more than 125 nation-states belong to the United Nations, and a large portion of these have been admitted since the organization was first created. For a state to be admitted to membership it must be recommended by nine or more members of the Security Council, *including all the permanent members.* It must then receive a two-thirds vote in the General Assembly. As noted earlier, the requirement of a recommendation by all five of the permanent members of the Security Council in effect puts a veto in the hands of each. This has contributed to preventing certain nations, such as East and West Germany, North and South Korea, North and South Vietnam, and Red China, from joining the United Nations.

THE UNITED NATIONS AS AN AGENCY FOR PEACE

First among the purposes of the United Nations named in Article 1 of the Charter is that of maintaining "international peace and security." This in fact was the motive that in World War II dominated the minds of statesmen and laymen alike in their demand for a new organization to replace the League of Nations. The difficulty encountered by the makers of the Charter at San Francisco was that they were obliged to provide a mechanism of peace that would leave the sovereign state essentially intact. Given this limitation, the Charter makers had to rely primarily on international co-operation of a voluntary nature as the means to peace. Coercive authority over the sovereign state in vital matters was out of the question.

Attempts to Lay the Social Foundations of Peace. Several approaches to the problem of peace are embodied in the operations of the United Nations. There is first the long-range approach carried on by the Economic and Social Council and the specialized agencies. The theory here is that maintaining peace entails more in the way of activities than preventing disputes and crises from deteriorating into war. Peace, so the argument runs, requires a reasonable assurance that human beings everywhere can live contentedly with a decent standard of living, satisfactory working conditions, reasonably good health, and a chance for an education. This doctrine—that the material, moral, and intellectual well-being of mankind is a cornerstone on which the structure of a lasting peace must be founded —has furnished the impetus for widespread efforts to improve living conditions in many parts of the world. However, though such improvement is much to be desired, the notion that more education and higher standards of living necessarily contribute to perpetuating peace is not a self-evident truth, and it should not be accepted uncritically. There is little evidence that literate and prosperous nations are less likely to engage in war than illiterate and poor nations. A little education and prosperity give a nation more power and may make it more aggressive.

The International Labor Organization illustrates the efforts of the United Nations to achieve social progress. For years it has tried to improve the conditions under which men labor. Established in 1919 as an adjunct of the League of Nations, it was converted in 1946 into one of the specialized agencies of the United Nations. During its lifetime it has undertaken thousands of studies of labor problems, held hundreds of conferences, and sent to various nations by request many hundreds of experts to give technical advice and assistance. International agreements and recommendations negotiated at its conferences have dealt with such subjects as the eight-hour day, holidays with pay, working conditions on ships, the right of workers to organize, old-age insurance, the employment of children, and forced labor.

The World Health Organization, to mention one more specialized agency, has expanded the work of international cooperation in health matters to the highest point yet attained. The Constitution of the WHO was drafted in 1946, and, following the organizational pattern of most of the specialized agencies, it has an annual conference or "assembly" of all its members, an executive board, and a secretariat. During its short career, it has fought against malaria, set up tuberculosis centers in dozens of places, checked the spread of cholera wherever asked to do so, and maintained a constant warfare on diseases of all kinds. It has advanced the work of standardizing biological products, improved health statistics, revised international agreements or conventions, sent health experts to national health services, and engaged in other activities too numerous to mention.

Of special interest among the economic and social activities of the United Nations are those embodied in its *technical assistance program*. In substance, this program is the United Nations' version of the American policy called Point Four, which aims, as President Truman explained in his inaugural address of January 20, 1949, at "making the benefits of our scientific advances and industrial progress available for the improvement and growth of underdeveloped areas." Fewer than 1 billion of the more than 3.5 billion people of the world live in countries that have the advantages of a modern industrialized society. In the less developed countries both standards of living and life expectancy are very low.

Almost from the beginning the United Nations has been active in giving poor countries aid for industrialization and social improvement. In 1957 the General Assembly established a special fund, to be supported by the contributions of members. By means of this fund more than a hundred million dollars has been made available annually for technical assistance and economic development. Usually aid takes the form of technical advisory services, demonstration projects, the training of natives, and pilot plants. Today the technical assistance program has become in large part a plan for mutual sharing among nations of technical knowledge and skills. Several *regional commissions* have been set up to aid nations in various parts of the world to solve their common economic problems. One of these is the African Commission, established in 1958.

The International Bank (World Bank), one of the specialized agencies of the United Nations, has provided very substantial assistance to many countries in need of development. By June 30, 1969, it had made more than six hundred loans in eighty-six countries, to a total value of over $12.6 billion. These loans were made for desirable projects capable of repaying their cost.

The Settlement of Disputes. A second major approach of the United Nations to the problem of peace is found in its attempts to solve international disputes. Here, as in many other areas of activity, it has drawn heavily on the experiences of the League of Nations.

Disputes may be brought either to the Security Council or to the General Assembly under conditions specified in some detail by Chapter VI of the Charter, but when the former is dealing with a controversy, the latter is not allowed to make any recommendation regarding it unless requested by the Council to do so. Neither body has the authority to make a decision that binds the disputants, as a court of law might do; both are limited to recommending procedures of settlement and, under certain circumstances, terms of settlement. In order to know the facts of a dispute and thus proceed more intelligently in their deliberations, the Council and General Assembly may dispatch *commissions of inquiry* to the appropriate place or places, whose job it will be to investigate and report. On occasions they send *mediators* or *conciliation commissions* abroad to endeavor to get the parties together on a method of settlement. If the issue is legal in nature, a recommendation is in order for the disputants to take their case to the International Court of Justice, or, as an alternative, the Council or Assembly might ask the Court for an advisory opinion on the questions involved. One of the most extreme forms of action taken by either body is the issuance of a *cease-fire* order, asking the parties to stop fighting and to withdraw their respective forces behind designated lines.

A good many disputes have been placed before the Security Council, and quite a number have been before the General Assembly; the latter organ has been more active in the treatment of disputes than was expected, probably because it has the advantage of operating without a veto.

One of the most important conflicts dealt with by the United Nations was that involving the Suez Canal in 1956. Late that year the Israelis attacked Egypt's Gaza strip and the Sinai Desert territory in an attempt to settle various disputes with Egypt. Egyptian troops offered no effective resistance and were rapidly driven back or captured. Almost immediately the British and French attacked the Suez Canal area, ostensibly to prevent hostilities between Israel and Egypt from interfering with the movement of shipping through the Canal.

In an attempt to meet this critical situation, the United Nations General Assembly was called together for an emergency session; it at once adopted a resolution demanding that all parties involved in the hostilities should agree to an immediate cease-fire. In a short time a cease-fire was negotiated, and later the attacking countries agreed to withdraw their forces from Egyptian territory. As the invading troops withdrew, a United Nations Emergency Force moved in to keep the peace. This force had been brought together quickly and consisted of small contingents of troops contributed by several member nations. It became the first uniformed peace-preserving unit of the United Nations.

Most observers would agree that the United Nations has helped to settle justly some international disputes, though in other cases the wisdom and value of its actions have been questioned. Its processes are always available, and if disputants are in a mood to reach agreement, the facilities to do so are at hand. But if the disputants are not looking for peaceful solutions and are not responsive to world opinion, there is little that the United Nations can do unless the member states are willing to apply sanctions.

The Sanctions. A third means available to the United Nations for the maintenance of peace is *sanctions,* or methods of exerting pressure on a recalcitrant state. In the event that there is a "threat to the peace, breach of the peace, or act of aggression," the Security Council may invoke sanctions against the state that is to blame. Three types of coercive measures are listed in the Charter: (1) *severance of diplomatic relations;* (2) *the complete or partial interruption of economic relations with the guilty state;* and (3) *the use of armed forces.* The amount of pressure that the *diplomatic sanctions* can be made to produce would ordinarily be very limited; for several years heads of diplomatic missions to Spain were withdrawn following a recommendation by the General Assembly in 1946, but there is no evidence that the fascist regime, against which the action was aimed, suffered appreciably. The economic sanction has not been attempted by the United Nations, though some African states are urging that it be applied against South Africa to force that state to change its *apartheid* policies.

The military sanction is supposed to be the final recourse of the United Nations in its peace-making efforts. To make the system function more smoothly, the Charter imposes on each member of the organization the duty of making agreements with the Security Council defining its contribution to the joint effort should an occasion for military sanctions arise. A Military Staff Committee was created to have "strategic direction" of whatever military forces might be placed at the disposal of the Security Council.

Impressive as the Charter provisions regarding military sanctions may appear at first glance, in fact they have been of little value. When the North Korean communist army attacked South Korea on June 25, 1950, the Security Council had no force on which it could draw, because the agreements that members were expected to make defining their respective obligations had not been concluded. The failure to make those agreements had resulted from the inability of the Military Staff Committee to specify the general principles that such agreements should embody; no nation had yet undertaken a definite obligation with respect to any joint military action that might be undertaken.

When the report came that South Korea had been invaded, a meeting of the Security Council was immediately called to deal with the problem. The Council urgently asked for a cessation of hostilities and a withdrawal of the invading troops behind the thirty-eighth parallel. Because, two days later, the cease-fire order had not been respected, the Security Council set to work to apply military sanctions against North Korea. It improvised a United Nations army under General Douglas MacArthur to stop the aggressor. This action would undoubtedly have been vetoed by the Soviet Union had its delegates been present, but months earlier they had withdrawn from United Nations meetings in anger because Red China had not been given the Chinese seat in the organization.

An army of several hundred thousand men, nominally under the United Nations, fought against the North Koreans, and later against the Chinese Communists when the latter joined the conflict. The struggle continued more than three years, until the final conclusion of a truce on July 27, 1953. Though the UN army that fought in Korea contained small and valiant units from other countries, it was overwhelmingly American and South Korean, and it was President Truman's decision to commit American forces that made resistance to the communists possible. During the three years of hostilities, the fortunes of the opposing forces changed several times, but on the date of the truce, they were facing each other near the thirty-eighth parallel, from which the invasion had been started in 1950. This undeclared war had been expensive both in men and in money, but it had at least pushed the aggressor back and deprived him of the fruits of victory.

On September 20, 1950, not long after military action had been started against North Korea, Secretary of State Dean Acheson made a proposal that was intended to strengthen the power of the United Nations to apply military sanctions. He suggested to the General Assembly a plan known as "The Uniting for Peace Resolution"; it was adopted by the Assembly on November 3. In essence, it enables the Assembly to recommend to United Nations members, joint military action against an aggressor when the Security Council is blocked by a veto. Presumably, the Assembly would be able to act in most cases, because its decisions are taken by a two-thirds vote, with no veto applicable.

A fundamental obstacle present in all systems of international sanctions is the sovereign state. Hiding behind the doctrine of sovereignty, the state opposes any effective system of coercion of which it might be made the victim. Neither does it want a system in which it is legally obligated to act against an aggressor; it does not object to being requested to participate in sanctions against another, but it has no use for any system that would impose a legal obligation to act.

Other United Nations Approaches. The approaches of the United Nations to the problems of peace are many. In addition to those that have been described, the following have been attempted: (1) the registration of treaties in order to avoid obstructive secret treaties; (2) the further development of international law; (3) the promotion of education through the programs of UNESCO; (4) the encouragement of *regional arrangements* devoted to the preservation of peace; (5) the international control of atomic energy; and (6) the regulation of national armaments, including missiles and nuclear bombs.

The practice of having treaties registered and published by the Secretariat has become firmly established, and, though it does not guarantee that secret agreements will be eliminated, it does reduce the chances of their existence. An International Law Commission has been trying to promote the progressive development of international law, and it has been making headway slowly. The programs of UNESCO have aimed at the furtherance of fundamental education, technical and vocational education, the exchange between nations of books, the exchange of students, and many other objectives, all designed to produce a better international outlook on the part of people everywhere. However, these methods for advancing the cause of peace are necessarily slow, and their results somewhat uncertain.

Regional arrangements, made in accordance with Chapter VIII of the Charter, have a more immediate and direct relationship to the problem of peace. Members of the United Nations are encouraged under the Charter to handle international disputes, where possible, within regional organizations. In enforcement action against an aggressor, the Security Council is authorized to utilize regional agencies, but ordinarily a regional organization may not itself engage in enforcement procedures without the authorization of the Security Council. The Organization of American States is conceded to be a regional arrangement of the type envisaged by the Charter; it has established means for the peaceful settlement of disputes among the twenty-four American republics that constitute its membership, and by a treaty of 1947 it maintains a system of collective security. The Arab League, created in 1945, is commonly regarded as another regional arrangement under the Charter. Others include the Southeast Asia Treaty Organization (SEATO, 1954) and the Central Treaty Organization (CENTO, 1958). A later addition to this group was the Organization of African Unity (OAU, 1963) which in 1970 had forty-one member states.

Efforts by the United Nations to establish international control of atomic energy and national armaments have yielded no great results, partly because of the insecurity felt by nations and partly because of the unwillingness of Russia to give up its basic aim of world domination. For some years Russia and the United States made occasional attempts to agree on limiting the testing or production of nuclear bombs. The stumbling block was always the Russian unwillingness to permit adequate inspection, as a guarantee that any agreement made would be carried out. However, in 1963, under the urging of President Kennedy, the United States, the United Kingdom, and the Soviet Union did sign an agreement banning nuclear tests in the atmosphere, or any tests that could spread radioactive wastes to areas outside the nation conducting them. Nations are still permitted to carry on underground testing. As long as this treaty is observed, there will be less pollution of the atmosphere, but it is not clear that there will be much less danger of war. The treaty is open for the signatures of all states, and more than one hundred have now signed it. However, France and Red China, both of which have already made some nuclear bombs, have not done so.

Some Problems of the United Nations. In view of the difficulties encountered, the widespread efforts of the United Nations to establish an enduring peace have been impressive. That it has some constructive accomplishments to its credit is generally recognized. That it has accomplished much less than was originally expected of it is also a widely held opinion. Certainly it has not healed the deep affliction suffered by the world as a result of communist violence and infiltration, nor has it by any means attained such a position of authority and prestige that its members feel able to place much reliance upon it for their security. It operates under at least two basic handicaps: (1) its member states retain their sovereignty, and (2) most of the power of the world is concentrated in two great states, the United States and Russia, and the interests of these two states are sometimes in sharp conflict.

At present the United Nations serves, to some extent, as a forum for bringing conflicts of interest into the open so that the pressure of world opinion can be brought to bear on them. As a security agency it is primarily useful as a mediator between opposing points of view. But it is not a *super-state*. It has not been too successful in stopping even small wars, and it is certainly not capable of coercing the largest and most powerful members of the international community.

Loyal supporters of the United Nations still hope that in time it will develop into an organization capable of maintaining international law, order, and justice. As the world grows smaller and smaller and as the range and deadliness of weapons keeps increasing, the need for such an organization becomes ever greater. But, unfortunately, new conditions and problems keep adding to the difficulties that it faces.

Perhaps no "peace-keeping" action of the United Nations raised more controversy than its handling of the Congo situation from 1961 to 1963. Many thoughtful people in the Free World were strongly opposed to its use of military power to prevent Katanga Province from seceding from the Republic of the Congo, the new state formed from what was formerly known as the Belgian Congo. At the time many felt that the Congo was not yet truly a nation but, rather, a large area that had been brought together by the processes and politics of European colonial expansion. It contained a number of different tribes, often hostile to one another and speaking a variety of languages. In the period following Congo independence, the province of Katanga was one of the few areas in the new state that was able to maintain a reasonable degree of law and order. Those who opposed intervention believed that it was a tragic mistake for the United Nations to fight a minor war in order to force Katanga to submit to the authority of the Congo, when such smaller and less-developed areas as Rwanda and Burundi were allowed to become independent states.

But other persons who studied the rapidly changing African situation, including those who controlled the policies of our own government at the time, believed that it was in the long-run interests of the people of the Congo to preserve it as a unit; and they believed that the resources of Katanga, which include important copper mines, would aid in the Congo's future development. In any case, recent reports seem to indicate that the Congo, which still includes Katanga, has made great progress in the last few years toward establishing order and some degree of prosperity.

Many fear that the growing power of Red China will further endanger world peace and pose additional problems for the United Nations; but whether this will in fact be the case remains to be seen. Though a few years ago Red China appeared to be adopting a policy of imperial expansion by seizing Tibet and some border areas in India, its leaders apparently believed that these were territories that had been taken from China in the past. Some observers question whether the Red Chinese are determined to make further territorial acquisitions beyond, if possible, regaining the Nationalist stronghold of Formosa. In any case, a recurring question for the United Nations (and for the United States) is whether Red China should be offered membership.

A circumstance that tends to create problems in the United Nations is the admission in recent years of many small, new states formed in the economically less developed areas of the world. Most of these states have little wealth, territory, population, or power, yet the vote of each counts as much in the General Assembly as the vote of the United States or Russia.

THE OUTLOOK FOR PEACE

Because the states of the world are unwilling or unable to give the United Nations the authority needed to assure world peace, the outlook for the future is uncertain. The armed peace, or *cold war,* that now prevails between major nations is based on a balance of power just as has been the case with periods of peace in the past. On the one side of the balance is most of the communist world under the leadership of Russia; on the other side are the democratic Western nations, led by the United States. Neither side is a closely unified group. Not all of the so-called democratic nations can be counted on to support the United States in a major crisis, nor can all of the communist nations be counted on by Russia. But most of the strategic military power is concentrated in the two superpowers, and on each side the armed strength is so great that for the time being neither is willing to risk a war that at best would be vastly destructive to both. For some years the quarrel between the Russian and Chinese communists has redounded to the advantage of the West, and at present it probably makes a major war less likely. But in spite of its more than 700 million people, Red China does not yet have the capacity to carry on a full-scale war with either the United States or Russia. Gradually Red China's power will increase, and the long-run effects of this are very uncertain. The two major communist countries may patch up their quarrel, especially after the death of Party Chairman Mao Tse-tung. A few writers have suggested that Russia might even engage in a "preventive" nuclear war with Red China before the latter's atomic power becomes too great to be quickly destroyed.

The Communist Threat. After the death of Josef Stalin and during the period when Nikita Khrushchev was head of state, some changes took place in Russia. How fundamental these were is a matter of disagreement in the Free World, but in the long run they may well prove to have been important. They included some relaxation of police controls over the lives of individuals, a little more consideration for the welfare of the masses of workers, and some lowering of the barriers against contacts with the West. One result was an interchange of visits between leading statesmen of Russia and the Free World, including Khrushchev's visit to the United States. Another was a more liberal policy toward foreigners who wished to visit Russia and who were willing to make tours under the control of Intourist, the Russian state travel agency. But all this did not mean that

Russia had given up its program of expanding its power base wherever possible; one evidence of this was its attempt to set up missile bases in Cuba, an attempt that was thwarted by President Kennedy.

Many students of Soviet policies believe that since the ouster of Khrushchev in 1964, the Russian hierarchy has somewhat tightened internal controls and checked the movement toward increased contacts with the West. Though there has certainly been no reversion to the reign of terror and the wholesale bloody purges that characterized the Stalin era, it remains true, as pointed out by Robert Conquest in *Foreign Affairs,* that Leonid Brezhnev, Alexei Kosygin, and other present-day party leaders are products of the political machine created by Stalin. They took the first big steps in their careers during the purges of the 1930's, when only the most ruthless officials advanced or even survived; though they have not indulged in some of Stalin's excesses, they have reaffirmed the principle of strife against all noncommunist regimes; and under them the Soviet Union has been steadily building up its navy and its strategic nuclear power. Their strategy has been interpreted by many observers as one of preparing and waiting, of holding satellite countries firmly in line, if necessary by force (Czechoslovakia), and of making advances against the West whenever there is an opportunity to do so at not too great risk or cost as, for example, in Vietnam and the Near East.

In a speech to the Moscow City Party Conference in 1968, Party Chairman Brezhnev said: "Our Party has always warned that in the ideological field there can be no peaceful coexistence, just as there can be no class peace between the proletariat and the bourgeoisie." Neither can there be, he added, "political indifference and passivity or neutralism."[5]

Democracies are often at a disadvantage in a contest with communist (or fascist) dictatorships. Their leaders must give greater weight to public opinion than must a dictator, and they have less control over it. The great majority of the citizens of almost any country want peace, not war. Any illusions they may have had that war was easy, glorious, and profitable have been rather effectively dispelled by the experiences of this century. When a national crisis arises that cannot be dodged and that means war, they may meet the situation with courage and determination, but in between such crises they are chiefly concerned with their private affairs, and they would rather make almost any concession to an aggressor rather than face up to the possibility of war, and especially of nuclear war. But a dictatorial regime is subject to less restraint by this public aversion to war. It does not have to submit its actions to the public for approval or even have to let the public know what it is doing and planning. It exerts more control over public opinion and is freer to play the game of making threats or carrying out aggressions whenever there is an opportunity. The

[5] See Robert Conquest, "The Limits of Detente," *Foreign Affairs,* July 1968, especially pp. 741–742.

government of a democracy, however, must have the support of public opinion for its major policies, and it has relatively little power to control that opinion.

The result is that democracies, in the face of aggression by dictatorships, are likely to resort to *appeasement,* that is, to accept a series of relatively minor aggressions and to justify this by arguing that the most important thing is to avoid war. Actually, such action may make war inevitable when it might have been avoided if earlier aggressions had been resisted. The most famous and unfortunate example of justifying appeasement as a means of avoiding war was provided by British Prime Minister Neville Chamberlain in 1938. After his return to England from the Munich Conference, where he had agreed to the annexation by Germany of the Czechoslovakian Sudetenland, he announced to a cheering crowd that he believed the concessions made to Hitler at the conference would insure "peace in our time." The next year Hitler started World War II by marching into Poland.

Since World War II the United States has made many contributions to "containing communism" and at the same time preventing a major conflict. These include (1) an active part, begun during the war, in creating the United Nations; (2) building up and maintaining a powerful military force; (3) taking a major part, through foreign aid, in rebuilding the economies of the nations of western Europe; (4) preventing the communists from overrunning South Korea; and (5) taking the lead in creating and arming the North Atlantic Treaty Organization (NATO).

On the other hand, many students of world affairs feel that the United States, since World War II, has allowed to slip away many of the gains that might have been realized from the sacrifices of war. It has often followed a "soft" foreign policy, one sometimes suggesting appeasement and sometimes suggesting indecision or the lack of a firm and clear-cut purpose. That some of our mistakes have not led to disaster can probably be attributed to our great economic and military power. Meanwhile, the communists keep advancing, little by little, wherever opportunity offers: in Laos, in Cambodia, in Vietnam, in Africa, in Latin America, and in the Middle East.

The Vietnam War. The war in Vietnam, in spite of the numbers of men involved, must be classed as a secondary or limited war that, at least in the short run, is not likely to upset the world balance of power. Our participation in it grew out of the policy of the United States, expressed in the Truman Doctrine, of aiding noncommunist countries to resist communist aggression. This policy was in direct conflict with the determination of North Vietnam to gain (with the aid of the Viet Cong, Red China, and Russia) control of South Vietnam. As early as 1955 we were giving economic aid to South Vietnam and sending advisers to help train its army; in 1965 we began aiding them in combat with our own air, naval, and ground forces; and by early 1969 we had nearly 550,000 troops in Vietnam.

By late 1969 our casualties there had exceeded 300,000, including more than 40,000 who were killed in action or who later died from their wounds.

There are still wide differences of opinion in this country as to the justification of our intervening in any way in Vietnam. Some maintain that the Viet Cong guerillas represent a people's revolt against a corrupt and tyrannical government at Saigon. It is worth noting, however, that three successive American Presidents, Eisenhower, Kennedy, and Johnson, believed that the struggle in Vietnam represented an attempted communist takeover and that we had an obligation in our own interests to aid the South Vietnamese to resist this. These three Presidents were different in many ways, but they had some things in common. They were all able men who had achieved positions of leadership, and they were all patriotic Americans in the best sense of that expression.

In the earlier stages of our aid to South Vietnam, when it consisted wholly or largely of money, munitions, and military advisers, there was relatively little public concern or opposition in this country. But in the later 1960's, as participation by our own military forces rose to a high level and resulted in heavy casualties, opposition of the American public to the war rose rapidly. Partly, at least, because of this rising tide of opposition, President Johnson in 1968 unilaterally reduced and limited the bombing of North Vietnam and succeeded in inducing the North Vietnamese to begin negotiations at Paris. They apparently, however, had no intention of making concessions, for up to the summer of 1971 there had been no tangible results from the Paris talks.

When President Nixon assumed office in 1969 he felt the need for finding some formula for withdrawing from the war. He was unwilling to withdraw our forces immediately and unconditionally for fear that this would leave the South Vietnamese at the mercy of the enemy and be interpreted widely as an indication of weakness and undependability on the part of the United States. He therefore announced his policy of *Vietnamization of the war,* that is, of preparing the South Vietnamese to take over their own defense completely while the United States gradually withdrew its own forces. He did not, however, set a definite schedule for final withdrawal. Many Americans agreed with him that it would have been unwise to tell the enemy just when we were going to leave. Many others, however, criticized him strongly for not announcing a schedule. Still others believed he should have withdrawn all American forces as fast as possible, if necessary without setting any conditions. By early 1971 not far from half the American combat forces in Vietnam had been withdrawn, but the date of final complete withdrawal was still uncertain. Whether it would have been possible to withdraw troops faster, without ultimately sacrificing more lives than those saved, is debatable.

Norman Hill observes in the preface of his latest book: "Democratic processes lend themselves awkwardly to the conduct of foreign relations. . . . American blundering in Vietnam is a sobering example of demo-

Quite a Posture! (Justus in *The Minneapolis Star*.)

cratic policy at its worst, as both doves and hawks would admit, albeit for different reasons."[6] Whether we should have employed our own forces in Vietnam at all is highly questionable; in any case, nearly all Americans would probably agree today that we should have heeded the advice General MacArthur once gave against engaging in a land war in Asia. It is clear that our policy makers in Washington and their Pentagon advisers greatly underestimated the power that the enemy, with Russian and Red Chinese arms and munitions, could exert in the swamps and jungles of Vietnam. Apparently they also failed to take into account the skill and tough determination that the enemy had already demonstrated against the French.

At the present time it is not possible to determine the ultimate effect of either the American military action in Cambodia or the South Vietnamese operations in that country and in Laos. Likewise, and more impor-

[6] Norman L. Hill, *The New Democracy in Foreign Policy Making,* Lincoln, Nebr., University of Nebraska Press, 1970, p. vii.

tant, we have no way of being certain whether the South Vietnamese, once American forces are completely withdrawn, will be able to defend themselves successfully against their enemies.

The Nuclear Balance of Power. Back in 1964 our then Secretary of Defense Robert S. McNamara asserted that our military strength far exceeded that of any other nation and would continue to do so for the foreseeable future. True, he remarked, Russia might kill a hundred million Americans in the first hour of nuclear war; but we could kill even more Russians.[7] At that time some students of military technology felt that he was too complacent about our nuclear superiority. They maintained that the foreseeable future is never very long and that the technical revolution in weapons and systems of defense was by no means over.[8] They insisted that we needed to increase greatly the amount of effort and funds devoted to the kind of research needed to bring new breakthroughs.

By 1970 it seemed clear to most informed observers that the Soviet Union had made great strides toward catching up with the United States in strategic military power. Some maintained that Russia had achieved full equality and was well on the way to superiority. It had greatly increased both the number and power of its missiles and nuclear bombs, and it had built a modern and efficient navy, including nuclear submarines armed with long-range missiles.

In recent years two major developments have taken place that introduce new elements of uncertainty into the arms race and into the relative status of the two major powers. One is the development of the *multiple individually targeted re-entry vehicle* (MIRV), which enables a missile to deliver separate nuclear bombs to several widely dispersed targets. The other, once thought to be quite impractical, is the development of *anti-ballistic missile* (ABM) *systems* that give promise of providing a substantial degree of defense against attacks by *intercontinental ballistic missiles* (ICBM's).

But even if ABM systems were fully developed and installed, the probability is that during an enemy attack some ICBM's would get through. Many people believe that the very destructiveness of such missiles is now our best guarantee against a war between the chief nuclear powers. They think fear of retaliation and vast destruction of life and property will deter both the East and West from starting a major war. We can hope that they will prove right, but when we remember the frailties of the human personality, the mistakes in judgment that leaders of nations have made in the past, and the fact that communism is a movement with ambitions for world domination, fear of mutual destruction seems a rather weak support on which to rest our hopes for a lasting peace. Especially is this true when

[7] Robert S. McNamara, "Strongest Peace Force in the World," *The Reader's Digest,* February, 1965.
[8] See Hanson W. Baldwin, "Slow-Down in the Pentagon," *Foreign Affairs,* January, 1965, pp. 262–280.

"The war can't start for another five hours. Our missiles are caught in a holding pattern over Kennedy International." (Courtesy Roland Michaud. Copyright 1970 *Saturday Review, Inc.*)

some nations are controlled by dictators, so that the mistaken judgment or irresponsible act of only one man might sometime start a nuclear war.

The Problem of Arms Limitation. One of the great obstacles that faces both the United States and Russia in attempting to maintain a balance of strategic nuclear power is that each would prefer a superiority. This leads to an arms race with huge and ever-rising costs. Even so, neither nation is quite sure that its armament is sufficient to survive a surprise attack or sufficient to convince the enemy that it could do so, and thus deter him, for fear of reprisal, from making such an attack. If an effective arms-limitation agreement could be achieved, it would release large resources in both countries for reducing taxes, raising standards of living, and providing needed social services. It might also produce a degree of *detente,* that is, of relaxation of international tension, and thus increase the chances of peace.[9]

The difficulties of making an agreement to limit strategic armaments, an agreement such that neither party to it can take advantage of the other, are great. The firm opposition of the Russians to direct inspection of their armaments increases these difficulties. Today, however, much can be learned at a distance about another country's armaments by various monitoring devices, including "spy" satellites. In the hope of reaching a workable agreement, the United States and Russia began *strategic arms limita-*

[9] Conquest, op. cit., pp. 733–742.

62. Nuclear Missile: Threat or Protection? (Courtesy *Fortune* Magazine. Photo by Marvin Koner.)

63. Report on the Strategic Arms Limitation Talks (SALT). President Nixon conferring in December, 1969, with four members of the U.S. delegation to talks with the Russians in Helsinki. (Courtesy Wide World Photos.)

tion talks (SALT) at Helsinki in the fall of 1969. Since then they have been continued alternately at Vienna and Helsinki. President Nixon appears to believe that his plan for constructing an ABM system, approved by Congress in 1969, provides the United States with a bargaining position that may make it possible to obtain a meaningful arms-limitation agreement. The chief argument for an ABM system (which Russia already has in the Moscow area) is that it would prevent Russia from destroying most of our missile sites in a first strike. Thus an effective ABM system, by preserving our power to retaliate, would deter such a strike. However, some scientists have doubts as to whether we could construct an ABM system that would really be effective. But if we ever allowed our nuclear power to deteriorate in relation to Russia's until it became clear that we could not strike back, we would be open to nuclear blackmail, that is, to being forced to accede to any demands that the Soviet might make.

Some writers are skeptical about the success of the SALT meetings. One suggests that if they fail the United States should depend increasingly on missiles carried by submarines as a means of retaining its power to retaliate against an attack. He maintains that antisubmarine warfare has made little progress in locating and destroying the modern, quiet, deep-diving ships that can carry missiles of great range.[10]

Roads to Peace. Despite assertions that a nuclear war is "unthinkable," it is at best doubtful that peace can be maintained indefinitely among the

[10] See Jeremy J. Stone, "When and How to Use SALT," *Foreign Affairs,* January 1970, pp. 268–269.

major powers of the world as long as they remain sovereign nation-states. Too many things can happen as governments change, as nations stagnate or develop, and as power is gradually redistributed.

However, there are at least two conceivable roads to the ultimate establishment of a lasting peace. One would be the creation of an effective *world federation of nations.* This would require the relinquishment of complete sovereignty by individual states and the establishment of a central world government with enough power to maintain international order. Ideally, each member state would control its internal affairs but all international disputes would be adjudicated by the courts of the World Federation. A second road to peace would be through the creation of a *world empire,* as a result of the success of some powerful nation-state in extending its rule over the entire globe.

Neither of these solutions is likely in the foreseeable future, though the author's guess is that, unfortunately, the chances during the next fifty or one hundred years are better for a world empire than for a world federation. The obstacles to an effective federation are great. Differences in language, customs, ways of thinking, religion, race, and economic status all make more difficult the problem of bringing the peoples of the world together in complete amity and peace. Differences in ideology between capitalist or socialist democracies and totalitarian communist states also complicate greatly the problem of forming a viable world federation. Nationalism is another serious obstacle. Would people ever transfer their loyalties from their nation-state to a world federation? Loyalty to one's nation is encouraged by the element of struggle or competition with other nations. It is a little like loyalty to a school or a football team. But a world federation would have no competitors. Also, in a federation there might be revolts or civil wars unless the central government had firm control of overwhelming military power, including a monopoly of nuclear power.

Even if a stable world federation could be established, only a naive utopian could view the prospect without some misgivings. Perhaps the world government would gradually expand its authority and ultimately take over many of the powers of the member states to manage their internal affairs, much as the federal government of the United States has slowly but rather steadily expanded its powers at the expense of the powers of our states. The final result might be that human freedoms would shrink and that civilization would be smothered by bureaucracy and red tape, by rules and regimentation on a scale that up to now we have not even imagined.

The ultimate establishment of a world empire is by no means inconceivable, but, to the democracies, that would mean loss of most of the freedoms for which they have struggled over the centuries. At present the most likely candidate for the ruling state in such an empire is Soviet Russia. It is large enough and has enough industry to create a powerful military establishment; it is ruled by a dictator or an inner circle of party leaders who can control public opinion; and it has an ideology that calls for the overthrow of capitalist democracies and the establishment of communism throughout the world. The chief obstacle in its way is the United States. Today we probably have at least an equally powerful military establishment; but we are a democracy, and from time to time the public is likely to be lulled by a false sense of security into demanding that our expenditures on guns (and missiles) should lapse in favor of greater spending on various urgent social needs. As has been emphasized in this text, some of our social needs are indeed urgent. Nevertheless, we still live in a dangerous world, and if we wish to preserve our freedom we cannot neglect our defenses.

Perhaps the reader will have a better understanding of the defense problems of the United States if we pause here to list our eight formal treaties of alliance, some of which include a number of countries. In addition, we have military agreements with various countries not covered by treaty. The treaties obligate us to take action if any of the countries included are attacked. These are commitments that we cannot just renounce offhand without in the long run greatly endangering our own security. The eight treaty agreements are (1) the Rio Treaty (1947) with the OAS nations; (2) the NATO Treaty (1949) which includes most nations of western Europe, plus Canada, Turkey, and Greece; (3) the Philippine Treaty (1951); (4) the Tripartite (ANZUS) Treaty with Australia and New Zealand (1951); (5) the South Korea Treaty (1953); (6) the Republic of China (Taiwan) Treaty (1954); (7) the SEATO Treaty (1954); and (8) the Japanese Treaty (1960).

The slowly growing power of Red China will introduce new complications into the world balance of power. Some students of international affairs maintain that, in its actual behavior, as opposed to its sometimes bellicose pronouncements, Red China has been less aggressive than the Soviet Union. They believe the United States has made a mistake in treating Red China as an outcast while making every effort to placate Russia in spite of the Berlin crises, the Cuban missile episode, Soviet meddling in the Congo, and the military "crack-downs" on Hungary and Czechoslovakia. There is, of course, the problem of Formosa between the United States and Red China; also, it is Russia with which we must negotiate first if we hope to limit the arms race. Nevertheless, many believe that much would be gained and little lost by giving Red China treatment at least equal to the treatment we accord the Soviet Union.

Clearly the problem of finding a formula for keeping the peace, without sacrificing hard-won freedoms, is still with us, and it is probably the greatest single problem facing the human race.

The present situation is rather well summed up by George W. Ball, who is a former Under Secretary of State and who was in 1968 the Permanent Representative of the United States to the United Nations. His statement follows:

I come back, finally, to the theme that this is still a polarized world and that the best hope for peace continues to depend on the ultimate broadening of common interests between the superpowers. Meanwhile, the world as I see it is likely to be a far more hazardous place if the United States either fails to maintain an effective power balance with the Soviet Union or ceases its efforts to resolve local quarrels when they arise in strategic areas of the world. And since we cannot wait to perfect the institutions that will satisfy the purists—we may all be blown up before then—we must settle for the possible. . . . Meanwhile, we should get on with the bitterly hard task of trying to stabilize the military balance between ourselves and the Soviet Union, something that cannot be done in a climate of self-induced fright but only by avoiding hyperbole and getting on in a practical mood with the grubby but essential business of diplomatic haggling. This is a high endeavor in the mutually reward-ing purpose of world survival.[11]

Terms to Be Understood

good offices
mediation
jus gentium
international law
international courts
ad hoc courts
compulsory
   jurisdiction
veto (in Security
   Council)
Interim Committee

specialized agencies
   of the UN
technical assistance
   program
regional commissions
commission of inquiry
conciliation
   commissions
cease-fire order
sanctions
regional arrangements

superstate
cold war
appeasement
Vietnamization
MIRV
ABM
detente
SALT
world federation of
   nations
world empire

Questions for Review and Discussion

1. How do you explain the prevalence of wars throughout human history?
2. Were the indirect effects of World War I and World War II a more serious setback for the Western World than the direct losses? Defend your answer.
3. What is there about the nation-state that often gives it a warlike character? Why are some nation-states more bellicose than others?
4. List what seem to you the principal factors in bringing on wars.
5. Under what conditions can diplomacy be successful in settling international disputes?
6. In what way, if at all, would the world be worse off without international law?
7. What forms of compulsory jurisdiction does the International Court of Jus-

---

[11] George W. Ball, "Slogans and Realities," *Foreign Affairs,* July 1969, pp. 639–641.

tice now have? Why are nations often reluctant to give a court compulsory jurisdiction in all disputes of a legal nature?

8. What constructive accomplishments can be credited to the League of Nations?
9. Why did the League of Nations ultimately fail?
10. What was the official name applied to the constitution of the League of Nations? to the constitution of the United Nations?
11. Explain the origin of the United Nations.
12. Name the six principal organs of the United Nations.
13. Describe the composition of the General Assembly and the Security Council. How do they differ in their functions and powers?
14. Criticize the veto power of the permanent members of the Security Council.
15. What are the functions of each of the following? the Secretariat; the Economic and Social Council; the Trusteeship Council; the International Court of Justice.
16. What has prevented certain nations, like North and South Korea, from joining the United Nations?
17. How does the United Nations attempt to lay the social foundations for peace?
18. What methods do the Security Council and the General Assembly use in dealing with international disputes? Can either of these organs make a decision in a dispute as a court of law may do?
19. How did the United Nations deal with the British-French-Israeli attack on Egypt in 1956?
20. To what extent did the Korean "police action" demonstrate the effectiveness of the United Nations in dealing with aggression?
21. Do you think President Truman used good judgment in refusing to attack by air Chinese bases in Manchuria? Why or why not?
22. What are the two greatest handicaps of the United Nations in its attempts to gain authority and power in order to preserve world peace?
23. Whether the United Nations was justified in using force to keep Katanga in the Republic of the Congo depends on the assumptions one makes. Explain.
24. Of what value for maintaining peace are efforts of the United Nations to (a) have all treaties registered with it? (b) encourage regional arrangements intended to preserve peace? (c) induce nations to agree to limit armaments?
25. Evaluate the utility of (a) the diplomatic sanction of the United Nations; (b) the economic sanction.
26. What was the purpose of the Uniting for Peace Resolution of the General Assembly?
27. What are the "regional arrangements" provided for by the United Nations Charter? Name several.
28. To what extent has Russian policy changed since Stalin's time (a) internally? (b) in foreign relations?
29. Why are democracies often at a disadvantage in dealing with totalitarian dictatorships?
30. Why did Presidents Eisenhower, Kennedy, and Johnson all favor aiding the South Vietnamese in their struggle against the Viet Cong and North Vietnam?
31. Do you approve President Nixon's policy of Vietnamization of the war, and the gradual withdrawal of American troops? Why or why not?
32. What two developments of recent years have introduced new uncertainties into the arms race?

33. What are the chief arguments for building an ABM system now? What are the arguments against it?
34. Do the SALT meetings have a chance of success? Why or why not?
35. Do you believe World War III can be postponed indefinitely or forever? If so, how?
36. Is an arms-limitation agreement between the United States and Russia the best hope for peace? Why or why not?

For Further Study

Clark, Grenville, and Louis B. Sohn, *World Peace Through World Law: Two Alternative Plans*, 3d ed., Cambridge, Mass., Harvard University Press, 1966.

Collins, J. Lawton, *War in Peacetime: The History and Lessons of Korea*, Boston, Houghton Mifflin Company, 1969.

Commission to Study the Organization of Peace, *The United Nations: The Next Twenty-five Years*, the 20th report of the Commission, paperback, New York, United Nations Publishing Service, 1969.

Conquest, Robert, *The Great Terror*, New York, The Macmillan Company, 1969. A study of Stalin's Great Purge and its effect on Russia today.

Coyle, David Cushman, *United Nations and How It Works*, rev. ed., Mentor paperback, New York, New American Library, Inc., 1969.

Crabb, Cecil V., Jr., *American Foreign Policy in the Nuclear Age*, 2d ed., New York, Harper & Row, Publishers, 1965.

Divine, Robert A., ed., *Causes and Consequences of World War Two*, paperback, Chicago, Quadrangle Books, Inc., 1969.

Dougherty, James E., and John F. Lehman, Jr., eds., *Arms Control for the Late Sixties*, paperback, Princeton, N.J., D. Van Nostrand Company, Inc., 1967.

Draper, Theodore, *Israel and World Politics: Roots of the Third Arab-Israeli War*, New York, The Viking Press, Inc., 1968.

Etzioni, Amitai, and Martin Wenglinsky, eds., *War and Its Prevention*, New York, Harper & Row, Publishers, 1970.

Fine, Sidney, ed., *Recent America*, 2d ed., paperback, New York, The Macmillan Company, 1967. See therein "The Lessons of Korea," pp. 363–379.

Hill, Norman L., *International Politics*, New York, Harper & Row, Publishers, 1963. See therein Chaps. 7–8, 13–20.

Kahn, Herman, *On Thermonuclear War*, 2d ed., New York, The Free Press, 1969.

Munves, James, *A Day in the Life of the UN*, paperback, New York, Washington Square Press, 1970.

Reed, Edward, ed., *Coexistence: The Requirements of Peace*, paperback, New York, Grossman Publishers, Inc., 1968.

Reischauer, Edwin O., *Beyond Vietnam: The United States and Asia*, New York, Alfred A. Knopf, Inc., 1968.

Rostow, Eugene V., *Law, Power, and the Pursuit of Peace*, paperback, New York, Harper & Row, Publishers, 1968.

Rostow, W. W., *The United States in the World Arena*, Clarion paperback, New York, Simon and Schuster, Inc., 1969.

Schuman, Frederick L., *The Cold War: Retrospect and Prospect*, 2d ed., Baton Rouge, La., Louisiana State University Press, 1967.

Townley, Ralph, *The United Nations: A View from Within*, paperback, New York, Charles Scribner's Sons, 1968.

Index

Banks (*cont.*)
commercial,
defined, 518
legal reserves of, 518–19
member, of Federal Reserve System,
518–19
Bargaining agent, labor union as, 585
Barter, 452
Beadle, George W., 434
Beale, Calvin, 610
Becker, Carl, 682
Benelux Customs Union, 834
Benelux Economic Union, 834
Beria, Lavrenti, 692
Berlin Conference, 803
Bestor, Arthur E., 425
Bettelheim, Dr. Bruno, 211, 429, 437, 438
on raising children in kibbutzim,
268–69
Better Business Bureau, 626, 645
Bible, the, 666
Old and New Testaments in, 115–17
Bicameral legislature, 701–702
Bilateral descent, 242
Bill of Rights, 706, 707, 718
Binet, Alfred, 218, 219
Birth control, 175–76
Birth rate,
American Indian, 336
Chicano, 339
defined, 166
failure to marry and, 175
influence of social and economic factors
on, 176–78
inverse relation of, to education, 178
late marriage and, 175
new decline of, 181–82
prosperity and, 180–81
reasons for long decline in, 174–76
rise of, after 1930's, 178–81
social position of women and, 177–78
standards of living and, 176–77
urbanization and, 177
war and the, 180–81
Bismarck, 558, 845
Black Americans,
African ancestry of, 351–52
the ballot and, 355, 356, 357, 366
black power and, 371
the black revolt and, 367–72
black studies and, 372
in business and professions, 361–65
as a caste, 310
changing status of, after Reconstruction,
356–57
civil rights of, 359, 365–66, 368, 369
Civil Rights Act and, 359
demonstrations by, 367–71
desegregation of,
in armed forces, 365
in education, 359–60

in housing, 365–66
early legal status of, 353
economic advances of, 361–65
free, numbers and status of,
in Colonial times, 353
after the Revolution, 353–54
future of, 372–75
historical background of, in U.S., 352–57
intermarriage and, 357, 366–67
Jim Crow laws and, 356, 357, 365
labor unions and, 364
lynching and, 357
numbers of, 169–70
in politics after Emancipation, 355–56
prejudice against, after Emancipation,
355–57
problems of, after Emancipation, 355
progress of, 361–66, 374–75
role of, in Revolutionary War, 353
in skilled occupations, 362–65
slavery and, 352–54
white ancestry of, 358
See also Discrimination, Prejudice
Black Economic Development Conference,
372
Black Manifesto, 372
Black Muslims, 371
Black nationalism, 371
Blacklist, 581
Blackmun, Harry A., 721
Blighted areas, 294–301
Bloom, Benjamin S., 208
Board of directors, of corporation, 479
Bodhisattvas, 110
Bonds, corporation, 484
Boulding, Kenneth E., 142
Boycotts, 580–81
defined, 586
Boyle's law, 30
Braceros, 339
Brahman caste, 309
Brain, of man and apes, 12
Breeder reactors, 160
Brezhnev, Leonid I., 467, 697, 891
British Ministry of Housing, 303
Brooke, Edward W., 375
Brown, H. Rap, 372
Bryce, Lord James, 672
Buddha, 109–10
Buddhism, original, 102
Budgets,
consumer, 631–32
government, 773–75
Buffer territory, 851
Building ordinance, 299
Bureau of the Budget, 774, 775
Bureau of Indian Affairs, 334, 336, 337
Bureau of National Affairs, 299
Burger, Warren E., 399, 721
Burgess, Ernest W., 287, 288, 395
Bush, Keith, 472

Business,
   big, and monopoly, 486, 488–89
   government regulation of, 463–64, 487–93
Business cycles, 504–505
   reasons for, 507–13
   specialization, trade, and, 509
   unemployment and, 505–506
Business enterprise, defined, 487
Business enterprises,
   government-owned, 486–87
   number of, in relation to population, 486
   numbers of, as source of progress, 474–75
Business fluctuations,
   acceleration principle and, 515–16
   cumulative character of, 509–10
   durable goods and, 514–15
   effect of speculation on, 516–17
   farm and raw materials prices and, 835
   measurement of, 506–507
   multiplier effect and, 515
   reasons for, 503–504, 509–10
   types of, 503–504
Business organization, forms of, 477–87

Cable-TV, 496
Caesar, Augustus, 685
Caesar, Julius, 685
Caesarism, 687
Caetano, Marcelo, 687, 696
California Youth Authority, and
      delinquency, 394
Caliph, 112
Calvin, John, 119
Capital, as factor of production, 450
Capital goods, 454–55
Capitalism, 456
   democracy and, 684–85
   personal freedom under, 459
   the Protestant ethic and, 121
Capitalists, 321, 462, 684
Carlos, Prince Juan, 687
Carmichael, Stokely, 372
Carson, Rachel, 71
Cartel, 492
Castes,
   doctrine of Karma and, 109
   social status and, 109
Castro, Fidel, 340, 687, 824
Catherine the Great, 860
Catholic Church,
   Roman,
      number of members in U.S., 123
      problems of, 129–33
      schisms in, 118–19
Caucasoid race, 328–30
Caucus, legislative and parlor, 750
Cavan, Ruth, 260
Cavour, 845
Census, defined, 166
Central American Court of Justice, 874

CENTO (Central Treaty Organization), 888
Cephalic index, 328, 328 n.
Cervantes, Dr. Lucius, 258, 262
Chamberlain, Neville, 892
Changing Times, 644, 645
Charge accounts, 638–39
Chargé d'affaires, 800
Charter, corporation, 479
   policies followed in granting, 480, 481–82
Chattel mortgage, 642, 642 n.
Chavez, Cesar, 339, 609
Checkoff, 578, 586
Chicago Crime Commission, 383
Chicanos,
   as migrant workers, 339, 609
   as minority group, 338–40
Chinese, as minority group in U.S., 340–41
Chinese Exclusion Act, 340
Christian missions, opposition to, in non-
      Christian lands, 131
Christianity,
   early, 117–18
   during Middle Ages, 118–19
   missionary movement in, 119, 130–32
   the Orthodox Church and, 118
   problems of modern, 126–132
   the Reformation, 119
Christians, American, number of, 123
Churches,
   membership in, in U.S., 127
   problems of modern, 126–32
Churchill, Winston, 676, 877
Cities,
   ancient, 282–83
   building new,
      in Europe, 303
      in U.S., 302–304
   characteristics of, 280–81
   communities within, 290–91
   defined, 280, 281
   expansion of suburbs of, 303
   factors in growth of, 278, 283–84
   future of, 302–304
   planning rehabilitation of, 301
   populations of 25 largest U.S., 286 t.
   problems of, 293–94
   public housing in, 296–97
   role of, in civilization, 281–82
   satellite, 294
   segregation in, 291
   slums in, 294–301
   theories of growth and structure of, 287–90
   the trend to suburbs, 291–93
   urban renewal in, 295–96, 298–301
   world-wide distribution of, 284–85
   world-wide growth of modern, 283–86
   world's largest urban areas, 286 t.
Citizens' Board of Inquiry into Hunger and
      Malnutrition in the United States,
      549, 550

child-labor laws and, 415–16
colleges and universities,
   community colleges, 427
   cost of attending, 420
   enrollments in, 414–15, 422
   establishment of first, 414
   financial problems of private, 421–22
   junior colleges, 427
   land grant colleges, 419
   teacher training in, 423–26
compulsory education laws, 415–16
cost of total program of, 421
culturally deprived children and, 434
demands for change and, 409–10
development of, 412–17
federal aid to, 419
how much, for average citizen? 436–37
integration and, 359–60
job training and, 363–64
for life adjustment, 417
meeting individual needs, 435–36
new approaches to teaching and, 434–36
in New England colonies, 412–13
opportunities for, 409, 412
   family income and, 419–20
   geographic differences and, 418–20
pedagogy as a field of study and, 423
problem of mass, 435, 437
problems of,
   educational leadership, 425–26
   educational standards in slum schools,
     360
   elimination of segregation, 359–60
   financial, 421–22
   low academic standards, 431–33
   raising achievement levels, 433–35
   supply of teachers, 422–23
   teacher training, and methods v. con-
     tent controversy, 423–26
programmed instruction and, 435
progress in, 425, 440–42
rapid reading and, 432–33
taxes and, 421–22
veterans' allotments and, 420
vocational, 428, 437, 438–39
ETS (Educational Testing Service tests), 219
Educationists, criticism of, 425–26
Educators, 425
Ego, 205–206, 231
Eisenhower, Dwight D., 763, 893
Eleazar, Daniel, 344
Elective system, in schools, 429
Electoral College, 705, 720
Electron microscope, 157
Electronic computers, 155–56
Electronics, 152
Emancipation Proclamation, 355
Eminent domain, the right of, 493
Empires,
   communist, 843, 850, 859–64
   extent of today's, 850

liquidation of, and war, 850–51
past and present, 790, 849–50
Employment,
   control of, by spending, 510
   increase of, 1950–1970, 528–29
   inflation and, 524–26, 528
   machines and, 149–51
   why many young people cannot find, 437
Employment Act of 1946, 530, 531
Endomorphy, 384
Engel, Ernst, 545
Engels, Friedrich, 798
Engel's law, 545
Environment,
   cultural, influence of, 57–58
   v. heredity, 212–15, 218
   influence of, on individual, 209–10, 212–
     15, 218
   man-made geographic patterns in, 56, 58
   natural,
     defined, 56
     influence of, on culture, 58–70
   social,
     defined, 56
     personal adjustment to, 212–15
     significance of differences in, 209–10,
     218
Environmental design, 301
Environmental ethic, need for new, 76
EPA (Environmental Protection Agency),
   76, 79
Equiano, Olaudah, 352
Equilibrium price, 458
Equipment, of social institutions, 46
Ethnic barriers, 331
Ethnic groups, 844, 846; as minority
   groups, 847
Ethnocentrism, 51–53
Eugenics, 194–96
   negative, 196
Euhemerus, 107
Eurodollars, importance of, 818
Euratom (European Atomic Energy
   Community), 834–35
ECM (European Common Market), 834–35
European Community for Coal and Steel,
   834–35
EFTA (European Free Trade Association),
   835
European Recovery Program. See Marshall
   Plan
Evaluated Participation, 315
"Ever-normal granary" plan, 612
Evolution,
   defined, 7
   of man, 10–16
   social, defined, 86
   of species, 6–10
Exchange rate, 818–19
Exchange stabilization, 819–20
   and IMF, 820–21

Experimental method, 31–32

Factors of production, 450
Fage, John, 350
Fair Packaging and Labelling Act, 647
Fair-trade laws, 636, 652
Family,
  character training and, 245–48
  crime and, 387, 404
  defined, 238
  disorganized, 261–68
  equalitarian, 241–42
  extended, 238
  farm, 245, 278–80
  functions of, 242–50
  influence of, on juvenile delinquency,
    387–88
  influence of, on personality, 208–209,
    245–49
  modern American,
    characteristics of, 250–51
    dealing with disorganization of, 266–68
    divorce and, 263–66
    federal aid for, 268
    later years in, 258–61, 263
    mate selection in, 252–55
    money problems in, 261–62, 267–68
    rearing children in, 257–58
    successful, 258
  nuclear, 238
  patriarchal, 238
  reckoning of descent in, 242
  social stratification and, 249–50
  types of control in, 241–42
  universality of, 238
  varied patterns in, 238–42
  working mothers and child supervision
    in, 268
Farm cooperatives, 650, 651
Farm income-support program, 614–23
  cost of, to public, 616–18
  effects of abandoning, 622–23
  payments for withdrawing land from
    production and, 612–16, 621
  politics and, 620–22
  questions raised by, 616–23
  regimentation of farmers and, 619–20
  subsidies through marketing certificates
    and, 615
  why most benefits go to large-scale
    farmer, 617–18
  See also Farm price supports
Farm price supports,
  depression and, 617
  economic and social effects of, 618–20
  foreign markets and, 618, 619
  history of, 611–16
  opposition to, 620–21
  parity and, 611–12
  problem of surpluses and, 614–16
  subsidizing exports and, 614, 618, 619

  as subsidy, 617–18
  during World War II, 613
Farm prices,
  are they too low? 607
  farmer's share of consumer's dollar and,
    615–17
  government support of, 611–16
  inelastic demands and, 605
  instability of, 605–607
  problem of, 604–610
  seasonal changes and, 605
Farm surpluses,
  beginning of, 612–13
  cost of storing, 614
  "cropland adjustment" program and,
    615–16
  efforts to reduce, 614–16
  "food for peace" program and, 614
  value of, 1955–1964, 613–14
  value of, in 1969, 616
Farm workers,
  increased output of, 284, 601–602
  migratory, 609–10
  surplus, 280, 607–609
Farmer as commuter, 610
Farmers' Union, 620, 621, 729
Farming, as mode of life, 278–80
Farms in U.S.,
  area included in, 599
  change in size and number of, 280,
    608–609, 610
  commercial, 601
  future of, 610
  marginal, 608
  subsistence, 600
Fascism, 868
  as extreme form of nationalism, 845, 846
  ideology of, 685–86
Fashion, and influence of on consumer,
    632–33
Fecundity, defined, 175 n.
Federal aid to education, 419
FBI (Federal Bureau of Investigation),
    379 ff.
FCC (Federal Communications Commis-
    sion), 495, 496, 497
Federal Disability Insurance Trust Fund,
    567
Federal Farm Board, 611
Federal Hospital Insurance Trust Fund, 567
Federal Housing Act of 1949, and slum
    clearance, 297
FHA (Federal Housing Administration), 268
Federal Power Commission, 495
Federal Reserve banks,
  government securities held by, 778
  member banks, 518–19
  as source of currency and coin, 520, 522
Federal Reserve Bulletin, 638
Federal Reserve economists, and bank
    credit cards, 640

Galton, Francis, 8, 217
Gandhi, Indira, 679
Gandhi, Mahatma, 309, 856
Garibaldi, 845
Garst, Russell, 161
GAO (General Accounting Office), 774
General education, 429–30
General incorporation acts, 480
General Motors, 763
Genes, 8–10
Genetics, 7–10
Geneva Disarmament Conference, 802, 876
Geopolitics, 797
Gestapo, 691
Ghettos,
  blacks in, 357, 369
  Jewish, 112
G.I. Bill of Rights, 419
Gilfillan, S. C., 143, 144, 152
Glueck, Sheldon and Eleanor, 384, 385,
    400, 401
Gold exchange standard, 819–20
Gold reserves, fluctuations in, 817, 820
Gold standard, 819–20
Good offices, in international disputes, 872
Goodall, Jane Van Lawick-, 6 n.
Government,
  as agency of social control, 660–61,
    663, 664, 666, 669
  by and for the people, 673, 679–80, 724
  coalition, 740
  as common need, 48
  communist view of, 662, 680, 688, 689,
    692
  constitutional, 678–79
  contrasting views of, 660–63
  democratic, meaning of, 708
  distrust of, 662–63
  essence of, 660
  federal, 684, 705, 706
    meaning of, 708–710, 711
  functions of,
    ensuring justice, 665
    maintaining internal order and
      external security, 664–65
    promotion of general welfare, 663–64,
      666–67
    regulatory, 660–61, 666
    safeguarding freedoms, 666
  interaction of, with social institutions,
    669–70
  invisible, 740
  liberal, characteristics of, 678–79, 681
  limited, 681, 702
  by military dictatorships in Latin
    America, 687
  parliamentary, 684, 715
    meaning of, 710
  political power and, 670–72
  as predecessor of state, 668–69
  presidential, 684, 708

  meaning of, 710–11
  private and public, 669
  recreational facilities and, 248
  relation of, to society, 667–70
  republican, meaning of, 708
  role of, under free enterprise, 458–60
  as social control, 669
  the state as expression of, 668
  totalitarian types of, 686–89
  unitary, 684
    meaning of, 708–710
Government debt,
  contingent liabilities and, 778
  inflation and, 522, 523, 526
  interest on, in 1970, 761
  problem of, 532–33, 761, 777–78
  size of, 522, 778
Government expenditures,
  balancing, with revenues, 773–78
  difficulty of reducing, 761–74, 777–78
  effect of inefficiency and waste on, 762–
    64
  inflation and, 520–22, 776–78
  rapid rise in, 759–61
Government finance,
  budgeting and, 773–75
  the money illusion and, 776–77
  problems of, at city and state levels, 761,
    778–79
  the public welfare and, 779–81
  spending for welfare and, 761
Government revenue,
  sources of, 764
  taxation and, 764–73
Government of U.S.,
  characteristics of, 706–724
  checks and balances in, 713–14
  civil rights under, 716-18
  conflicting pressures on, by consumers
    and special interest groups, 648–50
  economic services provided by, 458–59
  economic stabilization and, 513, 520–26,
    530–35
  executive branch of, 707
  foreign policy determination in, 803–808
  four basic characteristics of, 708–711
  function of President in, 710–11
  growth of nationalism in, 706–707
  historical development of, 701–706
  individual freedoms and, 716–18
  influence of British heritage on, 701–702
  judicial branch of, 707, 713, 714–16
  judicial review under, 714–16
  legislative branch of, 707
  as limited government, 702, 714
  national, state, and local units of, 706–
    707
  pollution control and, 79
  popular sovereignty in early, 702
  powers of, under the Constitution,
    civil rights and, 716–19

Nirvana, 102, 110
Nixon, Richard M., 487, 526, 649, 679,
    761, 775, 777
  ABM system sponsored by, 898
  creation of Office of Management and
    Budget by, 711, 774
  import surtax and, 817, 818
  "model cities" program and, 298
  Nixon Doctrine, 808
  proposed welfare plan of, 551, 566
  SALT and, 898
  stopping of gold redemption of dollar
    by, 817, 818
  Vietnam War policies of, 804–805, 893
  wage-price freeze by, 817
Nixon Doctrine, 808
"No man's land" labor cases, 589
Nomination of political candidates, 750–52
Nordic subtype, 329
Normal school, 423
Normality,
  mental health and, 214–15
  social adjustment and, 214–15
Norris-LaGuardia Act, 587
  and labor injunctions, 582–83
North Atlantic Treaty, 804, 900
NATO (North Atlantic Treaty Organiza-
    tion), 802, 806, 807, 863, 892
Nuclear fission, 157
Nuclear power, 792
Nuclear standoff, 792–93
  as version of balance of power, 796
Nuclear Test Ban Treaty, 804
Nutter, Warren G., 466

Oakley, Kenneth, 16
Oedipus complex, 206–207
Office of Management and Budget, 780
  creation and functions of, 711
  federal budget and, 774
Ogburn, William F., 137
OASI (Old-Age and Survivors Insurance),
  case for covering all citizens, 568
  changes in, 560–61
  covered employment under, 560, 561
  how large should benefits be? 567–68
  merits of present system, 568
  present benefits under, 561, 562–63
  requirements for being fully insured, 561,
    562–63
  reserve fund for, 561–62, 567
  self-employed persons and, 562
  social security taxes and, 562
Oligarchy, 659
Oliver, Roland, 350
Ombudsmen, 731
Omnibus Crime Control and Safe Streets
    Act of 1968, 390, 400
One World, 787
Ongania, Juan Carlos, 687
Open class system, 318

Open Door Policy, 804
Open Housing Act, 366
Opinion Research Corporation, 320
Option account, 638–39
Organization, as element in social institu-
    tions, 46
OAU (Organization of African Unity), 888
OAS (Organization of American States),
  definition of state in Charter of, 789
  as regional arrangement under UN
    Charter, 888
  Rio Treaty with, 900
OECD (Organization for Economic Cooper-
    ation and Development), 829
OEEC (Organization for European
    Economic Cooperation), 829
Organized crime, 388–90
Ortega, Philip D., 338
Orthogenic School of University of
    Chicago, 429
Owen, Robert, 461

Packard, David, 868
Pact of Paris, 876
Paine, Thomas, 661, 704
Palmer, Norman D., 845
Panama Conference of 1826, 802
Pangenesis hypothesis, 8
Pantheon of gods, 105
Paper gold, 821
Paper standard, 819
Pardon, of criminals, 394
Paris Peace Conference, of 1919, 875
  of 1946, 803
Paris talks with N. Vietnamese, 893
Parity prices, 611–12
Park, Robert E., 332, 333
Parkinson's second law, 779
Parks, Rosa, 367
Parole, 394–95
Parole-prediction scale, 395
Parsons, Talcott, 321
Partnership, 478–79
Patent system, 142–43
  origin in Venice, 142
Patents, 142
  number of, 143
Patriarchal culture, 241
Patriarchy, 241
Patrilineal descent, 242
Patriotism, nature of, 844
Patterson, William, 704
Pay-TV, 496–97
Peace,
  cold war and, 890–92
  diplomacy and, 871–72, 901
  effect of economic and social conditions
    on, 883–84
  as greatest social problem, 900
  nuclear balance of power and, 895–97
  outlook for, 890–901

problem of arms limitation, 897–98
problem of Vietnam War and, 892–95
threat to, from communism, 890–92
two roads to, 898–900
UN as agency for, 882–90
Peace Corps, 831–32
Peffer, Nathaniel, 852
Penn, William, 122, 871
Penn-Central Railroad, 495
Pentagon, as pressure group, 730–31
Percentile rank, in intelligence tests, 219
Perkins, Howard C., 845
Permanent Court of Arbitration, 873–74
Permanent Court of International Justice, 874
Peron regime, 687
Personality,
  biological basis of, 203–204
  defined, 203
  development of, 203–207
  dynamics of, 206
  effect of isolation on, 210–12
  Freudian concept of, 204–206
  influence of family on, 208–209, 245–47
  maladjusted, 213, 215–16, 231–32
  as product of environment and heredity, 209–10, 212–13
  shaped by four factors, 203
  well-adjusted, 213–15
Personnel, as element of social institutions, 46
Pestalozzi, 417
Peter the Great, 860
Peterson, Esther, 649
Petit jury, 393
Pfeiffer, John E., 14, 15, 16
Philippine Treaty, 900
Picketing,
  mass, 580
  organizational, 589–90
  recognition, 589–90
Pilate, 117
Pisistratus, 685
Pithecanthropus erectus, 14
Plantation system, and slaves, 353–54
Plato, and democracy, 676
Pleasure principle, 205
Plessy v. Ferguson, 359
Plymouth Company, 479
Pogrom, 345
Point Four Program, 140, 831, 884
Politburo, 679
Political boss, 671, 740 ff.
Political elite, 672
Political machine, 740–43
Political parties,
  the Constitution and, 732
  decentralization of, 741–43
  functions of, 732–36
  importance of ideologies of, 740
  molding public opinion, 728, 733–34

organization of, in U.S.,
  campaign committees, 747
  city and county committees, 743–45
  effect of federalism on, 741–42
  effect of regionalism on, 741
  local and district, 743–45
  national, 745–47
  national chairman in, 745, 746–47
  national committee in, 745, 746
  national convention in, 745
  nature of, 740–43
  precincts and wards, 743–45
  state, 745
as political machines, 740–43
Republican v. Democratic, 735, 736–37, 738
rightist or leftist, 737–38
systems of, 738–40
totalitarian dictatorships and, 691
types of, 736–37
use of propaganda by, 728
Political police, secret, 691–92
Political power,
  in dictatorships and democracies, 671, 672–73
  nature and sources of, 670–71
Political process,
  defined, 728
  democratic, 727–28
  evaluation of, 754
Political science, 27–28
  areas of, 727–28
Political theory, 660
  Politician, role and importance, 670–72
Politics,
  defined and explained, 670, 727–28
  as study of power, 670–71
Poll-tax, 366
Pollution,
  anti-pollution movement, 70–71
  cost of controlling, 79
  government efforts to control, 79
  of natural resources, 69–80
  need for research on, 76–79
  problems of, 70–80
    air, 72
    land, by pesticides, 74–75
    land, by solid wastes, 73–74
    noise, 75
    power generation, 77–78
    water, 72
  UN efforts to control, 79
Polyandry, 238, 239
Polygamy, 238
Polygyny, 238, 239
Polytheism, 103–107
Pompidou, Georges, 679, 694, 740
Pope, the, 669, 670, 790
  becomes head of Christian church, 117
Pope John XXIII, 128
Pope Paul VI, 130, 132

Population,
American Indian, 335, 336
biological quality of, 193–96
composition of in U.S. by age and sex, 189–91
defined, 165
expansion of urban, 283–87
in U.S., 286–87, 292–93
food supply and, 166–67
future trends, 173–83
geometric ratio of increase in, 183
growth,
and birth control, 175–76
of blacks relative to whites, 169–70
changing trends in, 173–83
decline of birth rate and, 174–75
decline of death rate and, 174
effect of, on schools, 415, 437
effect of sanitation and medicine on, 171
in Europe, 168
immigration and, 170–71
influence of Industrial Revolution on, 171–72
pollution problems and, 69, 75–76, 78
positive and preventive checks on, 184
problem of, in less developed countries, 171–72, 173
rate of, by social classes, 194
in U.S., 168–69; as problem, 187–88
in world, 166–68, 171–73
means of subsistence and, 183–85
metropolitan-nonmetropolitan distribution of blacks and whites, 291–92
migration of, to U.S., to our West and to cities, 191–93
natural resources and, 69, 185–88
optimum, 186–87
percentage of,
in cities, 286 t.
on farms, 620
quality of, and eugenics, 194–96
Population explosion, 167
Positive checks, on population growth, 184
Post-Hostilities Planning Committee, 877
Poultry Inspection Act, 646
Poverty,
as contributing to crime, 402–404
extent of and problem of, 546–52
programs for alleviating, 547, 551
progress in reducing, 549
reasons for, 551
statistics, 548–49
War on, 547
Poverty threshold, how determined, 548–49
Power politics, in international relations, 792, 877
Precinct, 743–44
Prejudice,
causes, variations, and extent of, 331–33
discrimination and, 331–34

ethnic, 342 ff.
meaning of, 332
racial, 330–34
racial superiority and, 330–31
as socially acquired, 331–34
See also Black Americans, Discrimination, Minority groups
President of the U.S.,
as commander-in-chief, 804
foreign policy and, 803–805
President's Commission on Foreign Economic Policy, 833
President's Council of Economic Advisers, 531
Pressure groups, 729
as obstacle to technological progress, 161
Preventive checks, on population, growth, 184
Prices, farm, 603–604
instability of, 605–607
Primary elections, 751–52
See also Voting
Primary groups, defined, 21
Primates, 7–12
Primitive societies, economic organization of, 451–52
Prisons, faults of and reforms in, 397–98
Probation, 393–94
Proctor and Gamble, guaranteed wage, 558
Production, control of, by total spending, 510–13
Productivity of labor, defined, 149, 471
Prognathism, 328
Programmed instruction, 435
Progress, defined, 86
Progressive education, 416–17
Proletariat, 321, 462
Propaganda,
under dictatorships, 793
in international relations, 793–94
in political campaigns, 733
Prosperity,
contrasted with depression, 502–503
as phase of business cycle, 504
relation of total spending to, 510–11
Protectorate, 849
Protestant ethic, and capitalism, 121
Proxy, 482 n.
Psychic energy, 205–206
Psychoanalysis, 204
Psychology, nature of, 28
Psychopathic personality, 216, 230–31
Psychoses,
as cause of maladjustment, 216
causes of, environmental and hereditary, 224–26
extent and incidence of, 226–28
nature of, 223–24
organic and functional, 224
treatment of, 227–28
types of, 224, 225, 227
Psychosomatic illness, 229

Psychotherapy, 227
Public assistance, 559, 564
Public opinion,
    influence of, on foreign policies, 793
    measuring, by polls, 728–29
    molded by political parties, 728, 733–34
    pressure groups and, 728, 729–31
    totalitarianism and, 793–94
Public utilities,
    franchises for, 493
    as monopolies, 475, 493
    nature of, 493
    use of public property by, 493
Public utility commissions, 494–95
Public utility regulation, 493–97
    development of, 493–94
    v. government ownership, 486–87
    problems of, 494–95
    successes and failures of, 495–97
Public works to combat depression, 512–13,
        531–32
Pufendorf, S., and *The Law of Nature and
        of Nations*, 872
Puppet regimes, 849, 861
Purchasing power,
    of U.S. market v. rest of world, 476
    of U.S. workers v. Russian, 472–73
Pure, or perfect, competition, 457 *n.*, 475
Pure Food and Drug Act of 1906, 646

Race,
    belief in racial superiority, 330–31
    major races, 328–30
    meaning of, 326
    racial subtypes, 328–30
Racial v. cultural differences, 326–30
Racism, white, 369
Radar telescope, 156
Radio, control of, 145, 493, 495
Radio Liberty, 472
Railroad Retirement Act of 1934, 558
Railway Labor Act, 589
Ramapithecus, 14–15
Randolph, Edmund, 704
Raphael, Dr. Theophile, 225, 226
Recession, as phase of business cycle, 504
Reciprocal Trade Agreements Act, 834
Reciprocal trade program, 834
Recovery, as phase of business cycle, 504
Recycling, of solid wastes, 74
Redfield, Robert, 52
Reflexes, human, 17
Reformation, the, 119
Reformation of criminals, 391
Regional specialization, 67
Rehabilitation quotient of criminals, 395
Religion,
    in ancient Egypt, 105–106
    the arts and, 122
    denominationalism in, 127–29
    early Christian, 117–18

of early Greeks, 106–107
the ecumenical movement in, 127–29
education and, 122
future of, 132–33
literature and, 122
need of early man for, 101–102
origins of, 101, 102–103
of primitives, 103
of Romans, 107
the social gospel and, 129
social role of,
    in primitive societies, 119
    in Western culture, 106, 120–22
as source of moral values, 120–21
as source of social conflict, 120
the spread of secularism and, 123–26
of Teutons, 107
in the U.S., 122–26
Religions, modern,
    Buddhism, 109–111
    Christianity, 115–19
    Confucianism, 108
    Hinduism, 108–109
    impact of science on, 124–26
    Islam, or Mohammedanism, 112–15
    Judaism, 111–12
    materialistic philosophies and, 124–26
    missions and, 130–33
    Shintoism, 108
Religious liberalism, 126
Religious underground movement, 133
Renaissance, the, 118–19
Republic, a, 677
Republic of China (Taiwan) Treaty, 900
Restrictive covenants, 365–66
Retribution, 390
Reverse discrimination, 364
Revolving credit, 638
Revolving fund, 611, 611 *n.*
Right-to-work laws, 577–78
Rightist, in politics, 737–38
Rio Treaty, 900
Ritual, as element of social institutions, 46
Rockefeller, Nelson, 553
Rockefeller Foundation, gifts of, to
        education, 422, 425
Role, defined, 46
Roles, changed,
    by children, 257–58
    in later years, 258–61
    on marriage, 256–57
    by status changes, 46
Roman Empire, 117
Romantic illusion, 253
Roosevelt, Franklin D., 531, 583, 584, 611,
        661, 672, 676, 804, 805, 877
    Four Freedoms of, 716
    public housing and, 296
    Supreme Court and, 715–16
Roosevelt, Theodore, 490, 872
Rose, Arnold M., 257

Rostow, W. W., 832
Royal Institute of International Affairs, 851
Ruckelshaus, William D., 76
Rural Electrification Administration, 650
Rural life v. urban life, 278–80
Russian Cheka, 691

St. Patrick, 130
St. Paul, 130
San Francisco Conference, 802
Sanctions, in UN Charter, 885–87
Sanskrit, 108–109
Satellite nations, maintaining control of, 697
Satellite regimes, 849, 861
Satellites, spy, 897
    development of, 158
Saving, by hoarding v. investing, 512
Savonarola, 118
Scabs, 580
Scarce goods, defined, 68
Schizophrenia, 225–26
Schoeps, Hans-Joachim, 102, 117
School systems,
    dual, 416
    8-4-4, 426
    public, importance of, 409, 411–12
    unitary, 416
Schools, as agencies of social control, 410
Schools in U.S.,
    academic standards of, 431–33
    attendance at various levels, 414–15
    contributions of, to democracy, and vice
        versa, 411–12
    control of, 410–11, 418
    curriculums of,
        basic courses, 419–30
        core, 429
        elective system, 428, 429
        overcrowding, 427–28
        vocational training, 428, 437, 438–39
    democratic structure of, 416
    development of public, 412–15
    diversity in, 418
    junior high schools, 426–27
    nonacademic subjects and activities,
        428–29
    normal, 423
    private,
        enrollment in, 411
        financial problems of, 419, 421–22
        parochial, 411; and "shared time," 419
    segregation in, 359; black separatism as,
        372
    social promotion in, 431–32
    statistics on, 409
    structural changes in, 426–27
    student unrest in, 437–40
    supply of teachers in,
        and certification requirements, 422
        and salaries, 422–23
    team teaching in, 436

ungraded, 426, 436
use of mechanical teaching aids, 435
Schuessler, Karl, 395
Scientific inquiry, conditions favorable to,
    28–29
Scientific law, 30
Scientific method, major steps of, 29–30
Scientific theory, 30
Scopes, John, 29 n.
Scott, David, 154
Scott, Mel, 296
Seaborg, Glenn T., 160
Seasonal business fluctuations, 503
Secondary groups, defined, 21
Secondary school, 413, 414
Sector theory of city growth, 289
Sects, defined, 119
Secular business fluctuations, 503–504
Secularism, 123–24
Securities and Exchange Commission, 483
Security,
    collective, among nations, 796
    contributions of industry to worker, 557–
        58
    income and, 539–40
    problem of economic, 539–40, 556–58
    search for, and war, 869–70
Segregation,
    legal, of black Americans, 356
    in public schools, Supreme Court ruling
        outlawing, 716
    social, 367
    of social groups in cities, 291
Selective Service Qualification Test, 424
Self-determination of peoples, 846
    meaning of, 848, 855
    right of, 855
    after World War I, 846
    after World War II, 848
Self-sufficiency argument, 823–24
Seminole Tribe of Florida, 335
Senate Committee on Improper Activities
        in the Labor and Management
        Field, 587
Senatorial Campaign Committee, 747
Separate-but-equal doctrine, 359
Separation, to terminate marriage, 261, 265
Separation of powers,
    foreign policy of U.S. and, 803–805
    in U.S. government, 711, 712–14
"Sesame Street," 435
Sex relations,
    adjustment to, in marriage, 243–44, 263
    birth control and, 243
    changing attitudes toward, 243, 254–55
"Shared time" in schools, 419
Shaw, Chief Justice, 582
Shaw, Clifford, 386
Sheldon, William H., 384
Sherman Antitrust Act, 489–90, 491
    and labor, 582

Shock therapy, 228
Short-term credits, as foreign investments, 825
Shuman, Charles B., 620
Shutout, 581
Siddharta, Prince Gautama, 109
Simon, Dr. Thomas, 218
Simpson, George Gaylord, 10
Single proprietorship, 477–78
Slave trade, African, 350–51, 353
Slavery, Negro, 350–54
Slichter, Sumner, 149
Slums,
    development of, 294–95
    prevention of, 298–301
    reconstruction and renewal of, 295 ff.
Small-loan companies, 641
Smith, Adam, 627
Smith, Joseph, 122
Smith, T. V., 735 n.
Smith-Hughes Act of 1917, 419
Smuts, Jan, 803
Social adjustment,
    contribution of public schools to, 411
    of well-adjusted individual, 213–15
Social change,
    cycle theory of, 87
    factors contributing to rising rate of, 84–85
    factors controlling, 87–93
    golden age theory of, 86
    inevitable progress theory, 86
    influence of geography and climate on, 91
    planned, 90–91
    in relation to evolution and progress, 86
    resistance to, 92–93
    social mobility and, 314
    social problems and, 93–99
    v. social stability, 93
    technological progress and, 137, 139–42, 144–52, 161–62
Social class,
    American system of, 318–22
    consciousness of, in U.S., 319
    defined, 311–12
    family and, 312–13
    income as criteria of, 311 ff.
    occupation and, 312–13
    open system of, 318
    rising incomes and, 320–21
    Warner treatment of, 315–18
Social classes,
    conflict among, 321–22
    dividing people into, 310–11
    horizontal mobility in, 319
    in industrial societies, 313–14
    mobility between, 313–15
    nature of, 310–11
    as subcultures, 311
Social conscience, 98
Social contract theory, 669

Social control,
    defined, 38
    role of government in, 660–61, 663, 664, 666, 669
    schools as agencies of, 410
    social science and, 37–39
Social controls, formal v. informal, 21–22
Social experiments, obstacles to control of, 31–32
Social gospel, 129
    and missionary movement, 131
Social institution,
    defined, 44–45
    language as a, 45
Social institutions,
    organization of, 46
    stability of, 92–93
Social mobility,
    conditions contributing to, 313–15
    in U.S. v. Europe, 313–14
Social problem, defined, 94
Social problems,
    culture lag and, 95–97
    difficulty of dealing with, 93–95
    relation of, to social values, 97–99
    social change and, 93–99
Social promotion, 431
Social psychology, nature of, 28
Social scale, 307, 311
Social science,
    defined, 4
    as field of knowledge, 25–28
    methods of, 32–37
        case method, 34–35
        comparative method, 35
        cross-cultural method, 35
        historical method, 34
        interdisciplinary approach, 37
        use of statistics and surveys in, 36–37
Social sciences, specialized, 26–28
Social scientist,
    functions of, 39
    interests of, 4
Social security, 557
Social Security Acts,
    of 1935, 558, 564
    of 1939, 1956, 1960, 1965, 560
    of 1950, 560, 567
    of 1961, 561
    of 1969, 562
    of 1971, 162–63
Social Security Administration, 337, 548, 559
Social Security pensions, 244, 778
Social security program, meaning of, 557
Social Security System of U.S., 189
    four major programs in, 559–66
    history of, 559, 560–61
    medicare, 565–66
    need for, 558–59
    problems of, 566–68

Taxes (*cont.*)
  state, 770
  what they buy, 759
Taylor, Carl C., 279
Team teaching, 436
Teamsters, International Brotherhood of,
    573
Technological progress,
  in agriculture, 158
  attitudes toward security and, 161–62
  effect of pressure groups on, 161
  factors that check it, 161–62
  the future of, 159–62
    and ecology, 160
    nonmaterial aspects of culture and, 96–
      97
  recent, 152–58
  requirements for, 161–62
Technology,
  defined, 95, 136
  effect on tempo of human life, 148
  government and, 151–52
  importance of, to productivity, 475–76
  inventions and, 88
  machine,
    defined, 137
    self-expanding character of, 137–38
  the material basis of culture and, 137–45
  nature of, 136
  progress of, 152–59
  social effects of, 147–52
  social problems created by, 147–48
  standardization and, 146
  standards of living and, 148–49
Television,
  cable, 496
  control of, 145, 493, 495, 496–97
  pay-TV and the FCC, 496–97
  use of, in education, 435
TVA (Tennessee Valley Authority), 459,
    487, 764
Terman, Lewis M., 218, 255
Thant, U, 881
Theodosius, 117
Theory of the Leisure Class, The, 633
Thompson, Warren S., 169, 176, 179, 194,
    195
Three-Fifths Compromise, 705
Tools, human *v.* animal use of, 6
Topography, and population, 60
Torah, the, 111
Total spending,
  contribution of government to, 534
  as controlling production and employ-
    ment, 510–11
  income and, 510–11
  inflation and, 517–18
  investment expenditure and, 512, 513–14
  meaning of, 512, 513
  relation of, to money supply, 522
  why it fluctuates, 513–17

Totalitarianism,
  imperialism and, 693
  nature of, 685–86, 688–89
  one-party monopoly under, 691, 692
  propaganda and, 690–91
  pseudo-democracy and, 692
  secret political police and, 691–92
  socialism and, 692–93
  suppression of dissent under, 690–91
Toynbee, Arnold, 87
Trade,
  economic specialization and, 452
  international,
    advantages of, 812–14
    balance of, and balance of payments,
      816–18
    communist policies as obstacle to, 833
    exchange controls and, 818–20
    import quotas and, 824–25
    import surtax and, 817
    importance of, to U.S., 813–14
    importance of Eurodollars in, 818
    interdependence of exports and im-
      ports in, 814–16
    maintaining prices of raw materials in,
      835–37
    problem of expanding, 833–37
    reducing restrictions on, 833–35
    regional agreements in, 834–35
    relation of, to foreign investment,
      825–27
    restrictions on, 821–25
    tariffs and, 821–24
    visible and invisible items of, 816
  limited, with colonies, 853, 853 *n.*
  role of, in business fluctuations, 509
  use of money and, 452–53
Trade Expansion Act, 805, 834
Transistor, 153
Transmigration, doctrine of, 309
Transportation,
  influence of, on agriculture, 600–601
  natural environment and, 67
  regional specialization and, 67, 453
"Travel and entertainment" cards, 639
Treaty of Paris, 702
Treaty of Versailles, 696, 793, 804, 805
Trinity, doctrine of the, 118
Tripartite (ANZUS) Treaty, 900
Truman, Harry S., 584, 747 *n.,* 763, 843
  Korean War and, 886
  Point Four program of, 831, 884
Truman Doctrine, 863, 892
  announcement of, 805
  explanation of, 806
  Nixon Doctrine, as modification of, 808
Trust areas, 854
Trusts, 489
Truth in Lending Act, 390, 647, 648
Tubman, Harriet, 354
Turner, Nat, 354